A
CONTEMPORARY
WESLEYAN
THEOLOGY

Francis Asbury Publishing Company was founded in 1980 by several members of the Asbury community in Wilmore, Kentucky. Its aim was to meet the spiritual needs of that segment of the evangelical Christian public that is Wesleyan in outlook and to communicate the Wesleyan message to the larger Christian community.

In 1983 Francis Asbury Publishing Company became a part of Zondervan Publishing House. Its aim remains the spread of the Wesleyan message through the publication of popular, practical, and scholarly books for all Wesleyan denominations.

FRANCIS ASBURY PRESS
Box 7
Wilmore, Kentucky 40390

VOLUME ONE

A CONTEMPORARY WESLEYAN THEOLOGY

Biblical, Systematic, and Practical

Charles W. Carter
General Editor

R. Duane Thompson
Charles R. Wilson
Associate Editors

A CONTEMPORARY WESLEYAN THEOLOGY—VOL. 1
Copyright © 1983 by The Zondervan Corporation
Grand Rapids, Michigan

FRANCIS ASBURY PRESS is an imprint of Zondervan
Publishing House, 1415 Lake Drive, S.E.,
Grand Rapids, Michigan 49506

Library of Congress Cataloging in Publication Data
A Contemporary Wesleyan theology.

   Includes bibliographies and index.
   1. Wesley, John, 1703-1791—Addresses, essays, lectures. 2. Theology, Doctrinal—Addresses, essays, lectures. I. Carter, Charles W. (Charles Webb), 1905-   . II. Thompson, R. Duane. III. Wilson, Charles R., 1918-
BX8495.W5C76 1983   230'.7   83-5957
ISBN 0-310-45650-9

All rights reserved. No part of this publication may be reproduced, stored in a retrieval system, or transmitted in any form or by any means—electronic, mechanical, photocopy, recording, or any other—except for brief quotations in printed reviews, without the prior permission of the publisher.

Edited by Gerard Terpstra
Designed by Louise Bauer

Printed in the United States of America

Unless otherwise indicated, Scripture quotations are from the New American Standard Bible © The Lockman Foundation, 1960, 1962, 1963, 1968, 1971, 1972, 1973, 1975, 1977. Used by permission.

84 85 86 87 88 / 10 9 8 7 6 5 4 3 2

ADVISORY COMMITTEE

Agnew, Colonel Milton S., Salvation Army

Ballantyne, V. A., President, Evangelical Church of North America

Cho, John Chongnahm, President, Seoul Theological Seminary, Evangelical Church of Korea

Duewel, Wesley, Former President, OMS International, Free Methodist

Earle, Ralph, Professor of New Testament, Nazarene Theological Seminary, Church of the Nazarene

Geiger, Kenneth E., President, The Missionary Church

Hermiz, Thomas H., President, World Gospel Mission, Church of Christ in Christian Union

Kinlaw, Dennis F., Former President, Asbury College, United Methodist Church

Kuhn, Harold B., Professor of Philosophy of Religion, Asbury Theological Seminary, Friends Church

McIntyre, Robert W., General Superintendent, The Wesleyan Church

Parsons, Elmer E., Bishop, The Free Methodist Church

Phillips, Harold L., Professor of New Testament, Anderson School of Theology, Anderson Church of God

Salter, Darius, Executive Director, Christian Holiness Association, Friends Church

Wood, A. Skevington, Principal, Cliff College, Calver via Sheffield, England, Methodist Church of England

CONTENTS

PREFACE	11
1. FRONTIERS IN CONTEMPORARY THEOLOGY	
GILBERT W. STAFFORD	19
2. HISTORICAL AND MODERN SIGNIFICANCE OF WESLEYAN THEOLOGY	
RICHARD S. TAYLOR	55
3. A HISTORICAL AND CONTEMPORARY APPRAISAL OF WESLEYAN THEOLOGY	
TIMOTHY L. SMITH	77
4. THEISM	
THE ETERNAL, PERSONAL, CREATIVE GOD	
ALBERT TRUESDALE	107
5. COSMOLOGY	
THE HANDIWORK OF GOD IN CREATION	
EUGENE E. CARPENTER	149
6. ANTHROPOLOGY	
MAN, THE CROWN OF DIVINE CREATION	
CHARLES W. CARTER	195
7. HAMARTIOLOGY	
EVIL, THE MARRER OF GOD'S CREATIVE PURPOSE AND WORK	
CHARLES W. CARTER	237
8. REVELATION AND INSPIRATION	
THE SPOKEN WORD OF GOD	
RALPH EARLE	287
9. CHRISTOLOGY	
THE INCARNATE WORD OF GOD	
CHARLES R. WILSON	331
10. THE HOLY TRINITY	
THE TRIUNE GOD	
J. KENNETH GRIDER	375
11. PNEUMATOLOGY	
THE DOCTRINE OF THE HOLY SPIRIT	
MILTON S. AGNEW	415

12. **INITIAL SALVATION**
    THE REDEMPTIVE GRACE OF GOD IN CHRIST
    R. LARRY SHELTON   473

13. **ENTIRE SANCTIFICATION**
    THE DIVINE PURIFICATION AND PERFECTION OF MAN
    WILBER T. DAYTON   521

PREFACE

The inevitable question arises as to the reason for another Christian theology. That question deserves an answer.

First, that there has been a revival of vital interest in Wesley and his theological thought in recent times is generally recognized in the area of scholarship. That interest demands a contemporary investigation and reevaluation of the thought and work of this eighteenth-century scholar and evangelist whose work changed the course of human history, not only for England and the British Isles but in large measure for the modern Western world, and also made its impact on the modern missionary movement throughout the entire globe during the past two centuries.

Second, deviation from the sound principles of Wesley's teachings, even among many who profess to be in the Wesleyan tradition, demands a restatement and reemphasis of those teachings today.

Third, in a news release the Zondervan Corporation stated:

A two-volume textbook on Wesleyan theology has not been published in over forty years. The Zondervan Publishing House will break this pattern in 1983 with the publication of *A Contemporary Wesleyan Theology,* under the general editorship of Charles W. Carter, M.A., Th.M., D.D., of Marion College, Marion, Indiana. Associate editors are R. Duane Thompson, Ph.D., of Marion College, and Charles R. Wilson, Ph.D., of Taylor University.

In publishing this major work, Zondervan is responding to repeated requests for such a work to meet the needs of Wesleyan collegians, seminarians, and clergy today. The text is designed to uphold the sound biblical teachings of the eighteenth-century Wesleyan Movement by covering the full range of theological topics, plus a number of chapters on current topics that have not yet been included in such a theological work. This biblio-systematic textbook brings Wesleyan theological scholarship up to date by including such contemporary themes as: Frontiers in Contemporary Theology; Historical and Modern Significance of Wesleyan Theology; Theological Anthropology; Evangelism and Missiology; Social Involvement; Incarnational Preaching of God's Word; Instructional Theology; Theology of the Human Psyche; Hymnology—The Theology of the Wesleyan Hymns; Angelology and Demonology, and various other new approaches to contemporary theology.

This *Contemporary Wesleyan Theology* is designed for a two-semester Christian college and seminary text as well as for the minister's study and for the interested Christian layman.

A CONTEMPORARY WESLEYAN THEOLOGY

In the spring of 1978 Pat Zondervan, chairman of the board of the Zondervan Corporation, visited Marion College where he delivered some lectures to the faculty. During that time he expressed the Zondervan Corporation's vital interest in publishing a contemporary Wesleyan theology for which his company was receiving repeated requests. This remark appeared providential, as there had been a revival of interest on the part of certain Wesleyan scholars in the production of such a work. Thus negotiations began with the Zondervan Corporation with a view to the production of the present two-volume *Contemporary Wesleyan Theology*.

An extensive survey of the potential market was made by Zondervan to ascertain the extent of interest in such a work. The results of this survey proved highly favorable. Consequently, the Zondervan Corporation requested the present writer to serve as general editor, select a team of associate editors, formulate a plan for the commentary, and present it for approval by the publishers.

Accordingly, Drs. R. Duane Thompson of Marion College and Charles R. Wilson of Taylor University were named associate editors. An advisory committee from fourteen different Wesleyan-orientated denominations was selected, and more than twenty seasoned and experienced writers were chosen from seven different denominations, each of whom was assigned a chapter of approximately thirty thousand words in the area of his specialization and expertise.

This twenty-four–chapter, two-volume work is distinctly and unapologetically a contemporary Wesleyan theology that is "biblio-systematic" in design and execution. Thus it is neither strictly systematic nor biblical per se, but a work that mediates between the traditional systematic schematic and the more radical contemporary biblical methodology of recent times. It is topical, biblical, exegetical, expositional, contextual, dynamic, positive, relevant, and nonpolemical. While the contributors all hold a high view of the Judeo-Christian Scriptures, they strive to be progressively evangelical rather than traditionally conservative. The authors view the Bible holistically and regard the divine revelation as a continuum from the creation account in Genesis to the close of the apocalypse of John in the Book of Revelation. They purposely avoid involvement in any of the extreme or controversial theological issues of the day, as far as possible.

The authors frankly recognize that while the divine revelation in the Judeo-Christian Scriptures is the plenary-dynamic, inspired, authoritative record of God's nature and will for mankind, and thus is absolute and infallible in itself, theology is man's rational understanding and interpretation of that absolute revelation and is thus necessarily relative to time and human culture. While man's understanding of God's revelation is progressive, that revelation per se is final and complete in the person of Jesus Christ. The Bible is regarded as Christocentric. While Christ as Messiah is implicit throughout the Old Testament, in the New Testament He is explicitly revealed as the only begotten Son of God and the one and only Mediator between God and man who offers Himself as the Savior to all mankind. Through the unique incarnation of God in human form Jesus Christ came to be perfect God and perfect Man in one Person.

While this two-volume *Contemporary Wesleyan Theology* purposes to perpetuate the spiritual insights and sound biblical scholarship of the eighteenth-century evangelical Wesleyan movement, it aims to express these values in the context of contemporary thought and life. Although the authors are basically Wesleyan orientated in their theological persuasions, they are not narrow or constricted in their religious views or interpretations. They do not hesitate to investigate and appropriate the best from all theological scholarship that serves to illuminate and enforce the truth of God's divinely revealed Word. Nor are the authors bound to absolute or uncritical agreement with the theological positions expressed by John Wesley or the Wesleyan theologians of his day or subsequent times. That Wesley was progressive in his understanding and interpretation of the Bible as new light dawned on him is generally recognized. If subsequent scholarship should improve on his understanding, Wesley would without doubt be the first to commend that improvement. Theology, whether Wesleyan or otherwise, must never be static, as it is the expression of finite man's progressive understanding of the revelation of the infinite mind and being of God as revealed in Christ and the Judeo-Christian Scriptures.

The general editor expresses his indebtedness and sincere appreciation for the invaluable service and encouragement of the associate editors, Drs. R. Duane Thompson and Charles R. Wilson; for the faithful and efficient work of his secretaries, Cindy (Black) Trammell, Teri Witmer, and Lori Freelan; and for the extremely valuable advice, direction, and cooperation of the Zondervan editors, Dr. Stanley N. Gundry and Gerard Terpstra, without whose assistance this task would have been impossible. Likewise, sincere appreciation is expressed to the members of the advisory committee representing the fourteen different denominations.

May the God who sent His Son to be the Savior of all mankind be pleased to bless and use these labors of love to the salvation of mankind and the upbuilding of His kingdom in the present and future generations.

The basic Bible text used in this work is the New American Standard Bible. All other Bible versions quoted or cited by the authors are identified by their proper symbols. Quotations and citations by the writers from various authors and copyrighted works are duly acknowledged in the end notes or documentations at the conclusion of each chapter.

This work is sent forth with the earnest prayer that it may prove a blessing to many throughout the years to come.

Charles W. Carter
General Editor

CHAPTER 1

FRONTIERS IN CONTEMPORARY THEOLOGY

Gilbert W. Stafford

Gilbert W. Stafford is Associate Dean, Associate Professor, Christian Theology, Anderson School of Theology, Anderson, Indiana. He received his M.Div. degree from Andover Newton Theological College, Newton Centre, Massachusetts, and his Th.D. degree from Boston University School of Theology. From 1962 to 1976, with the exception of one year, he served as a pastor in Massachusetts and in Michigan. In 1976 he accepted his present position.

Dr. Stafford is the author of two books: Living as a Redeemed People *and* The Life of Salvation. *He is a member of the Wesleyan Theological Society, the Liturgical Conference, Indiana Academy of Religion, and the North American Conference of Ecumenists.*

CONTENTS

INTRODUCTION / 19

I. DYNAMIC FRONTIERS / 20
    A. The Relationship Between Past, Present, and Future / 20
        1. Restorationism / 20
        2. Existentialism / 21
        3. The Theology of Hope / 22
    B. The Relationship Between Process and Fixity / 23
    C. The Relationship Between Secularization and Sacredness / 25

II. ECCLESIAL FRONTIERS / 28
    A. The Relationship Between the Subjectification of the Gospel and Its Objectification / 28
    B. The Relationship Between Ecclesial Apartness and Ecclesial Togetherness / 30
    C. The Relationship Between Heterodoxy and Orthodoxy / 32

III. FORMAL FRONTIERS / 34
    A. The Relationship Between Biblical Theology and Theologies in the Bible / 35
    B. The Relationship Between a Natural/Philosophical/Social Orientation to Systematic Theology and a Biblical/Confessional Orientation / 37

NOTES / 41

GLOSSARY OF SPECIAL TERMS / 46

DISCUSSION QUESTIONS / 46

RECOMMENDATIONS FOR FURTHER READING / 47

BIBLIOGRAPHY / 48

Frontiers in Contemporary Theology

INTRODUCTION

What is meant by a frontier in theology? The word *frontier* as it is being used here refers to an incompletely developed relationship between two or more interfacing perspectives in theological discourse. Some of these interfacing perspectives have to do with differing dimensions of the same reality, such as the past, present, and future dimensions of time, so that we can say, for instance, that one of the frontiers in contemporary theology has to do with the relationship between pastness, presentness, and futurity.

Other interfacing perspectives on the contemporary scene have to do with differing emphases of concern regarding the Christian life, such as the modern charismatic emphasis on personal experience vis-à-vis the emphasis of *Verdict*, a contemporary theological journal, which stresses the objective work of God in Christ.[1]

Besides differing dimensions of reality and differing emphases of concern, there are also differing basic starting points that inevitably predetermine ultimate conclusions, as, for instance, a fundamentally humanistic starting point as over against an approach that begins with God as Revealer.[2] Also, there are differing schools of interpretation that, even though they may share common commitments to the God of biblical revelation, nevertheless see the same data from divergent points of view. For example, are those, on the one hand, who view the whole biblical canon as setting forth one singular theology, and those, on the other hand, who see the canon as a collection of divergent theologies.

Within the scope of this chapter, eight major frontiers understood as interfacing dimensions, emphases, starting points, and interpretations are identified as special challenges for careful address at this particular juncture in theological history. The interface between the differing perspectives just mentioned may result either in exclusive demarcation, in complementation, or in integration. The challenge of working in the frontiers of contemporary theology is to determine which interfacing perspectives call for exclusive demarcation, which call for complementation, and which call for integration.

In the case of exclusive demarcation, it must be determined when two perspectives are so completely incompatible that any interconnectedness whatsoever would rob both of them of their genuineness and result in a *tertium quid*. When it comes to complementation, however, the challenge is to deal with two perspectives what while different are nevertheless interdependent, and to deal with them in such a way that both their respective uniqueness is in no way destroyed and their interdependency is coherently maintained. The third kind of interface is characterized by integration, an integration correcting the distortion caused by the breaking apart of that which inherently belongs together.

As we survey the following frontiers, our goal is not that of exegeting the writings of each of the principals involved, but rather to develop a view of the frontier as a whole.

I. DYNAMIC FRONTIERS

These frontiers are characterized by the vigorous interplay between basic components of thought such as pastness, presentness, and futurity; process and fixity; secularity and sacredness.

A. The Relationship Between Past, Present, and Future

On the contemporary scene a confrontational state of affairs exists between those whose focus is primarily on the past, the restorationists; those whose focus is primarily on the present, the existentialists; and those whose focus is primarily on the future, the theologians of hope.

1. Restorationism Classical Protestantism has always had a restorationistic strain, whether of the Lutheran type regarding the restoration of the apostolic doctrine of salvation, of the Reformed type regarding the restoration of New Testament ecclesiological patterns, or of the Anabaptist type regarding the restoration of Christian lifestyle to biblical norms. The plethora of denominations in Protestantism is in no small measure due to the earnest desire to restore the Christianity of the past, which, it is held, was Christianity in its unadulterated form. The restorationists' glorification of the past so completely turns them toward it that it might be fair to say that they back into the future.

In the United States, restorationism is in a state of robust health, whether viewed ecclesiastically, popularly, or literarily. For instance, the restorationist churches in the tradition of the nineteenth-century American movement led by Barton W. Stone, Thomas and Alexander Campbell, and Walter Scott make up a major segment of American Protestantism, with over 3,885,000 members in the three contemporary church groupings that are in historical continuity with the movement.[3] The group among them that gives greatest emphasis to its restorationism, the Churches of Christ (noninstrumentalists), is the largest of the three.

Restorationism also thrives in the form of religious television programs that capitalize on a return to the past. Jerry Falwell, pastor of the Thomas Road Baptist Church in Lynchburg, Virginia, has struck a responsive chord among many Christians with his Old Time Gospel Hour telecast.

The search for roots is earnestly pursued not only in the Christian community but in society in general. The popular response to the 1977 television presentation of Alex Haley's *Roots*[4] indicates the great popular interest Americans have in the past and in their own personal rootage. The quest not only for their forebears but also for their God, their values, and their religion is one highly visible dimension both of America as a whole and of American church life in particular.

The epitome of restorationism is set forth in the rationale for the publication of *Verdict,* a transdenominational, international theological journal published in English, Dutch, German, and Spanish. The statement reads as follows:

> *Verdict* is . . . dedicated to the restoration of New Testament Christianity and committed to upholding the great Reformation principles. . . . Our vision is a new Refor-

mation that will recover what the Reformers bequeathed us and complete the restoration they so nobly began.⁵

2. Existentialism Existentialism⁶ begins not with the records, authorities, and reported experiences of the past, but with the human condition as it is lived out in the present. Its primary goal is to get in touch with the nature of human beingness and to discover in the process of plumbing the depths of our experience that which is authentic for us. The emphasis is on participation in the depths of life in place of disengaged observation of objectified reality. Existentialist thinkers stress the native freedom inherent to human life, the consequent personal responsibility for ourselves that that freedom implies, and the decision-making nature of human existence.

The person considered to be the father of modern existentialism is Søren Kierkegaard⁷ (1813–55), who as a student at the University of Copenhagen studied the intensely rationalistic philosophy of Georg W. F. Hegel (1770–1831). According to Hegel, God is the Absolute Idea encompassing the whole of reality on which His ideas are written. Consequently, the only way we can know about God is to read the whole of reality rationally. Since our thinking processes are an integral part of the whole of reality, it is inherently possible for us to read the thoughts of God. Hegel's system was a thoroughly rational approach to God and to the world. In this view, existence is a systematized whole of which we are neatly fitting parts.

Against this sophisticated abstraction of God, the world, and the self, Kierkegaard reacted by positing the infinite qualitative distinction between God and us. He holds that it is absurd to think that we can study God with such rationalistic exactitude that we can thereby write systematic treatises about Him. God is in heaven and we are on earth, and between us there is an infinite qualitative difference that makes our objective systematization of Him invalid. Kierkegaard scathingly critiques the superficiality, compromise, and secularism of the Christendom of his day that he felt had trivialized God by institutionalizing Him and reducing Him to a mere item of belief. According to Kierkegaard, God is the Wholly Other who is known only in His divine self-giving, and not by our ingeniously rational powers for building systems of thought about Him.

The major philosopher developing existentialist themes has been Martin Heidegger (1889–1976), the philosophical mentor to Rudolf Bultmann (1884–1976), the existentialist New Testament scholar. Heidegger's *Being and Time* is generally considered the most comprehensive analysis of matters pertaining to human existence and the most authoritative in existentialist thinking.⁸

The weight of existentialism has been felt most directly in the field of biblical studies, particularly in connection with hermeneutical methods for discovering the meaning of the New Testament message. There is perhaps no clearer example of the mutual influence between biblical studies and theological studies than the work of Bultmann. Not only did he himself overtly affirm the philosophical/theological presuppositions of existentialism for New Testament studies, but he has also led the whole contemporary theological community into a reconsideration of hermeneutical method in the light of existentialist questions. In order to appreciate many of the issues raised in seminary classrooms today, one must know something about Bultmann's widely promulgated perspective.

He contends that critical research into the past is unable to recover the actual historical events of Jesus' life. Not only is such knowledge nonessential for the experience of faith, it is actually motivated by that which is a threat to faith, in that it seeks legitimation, any form of which is a denial of the essential nature of faith. As he says in *Jesus Christ and Mythology:* "There is no difference between security based on good works and security built on objectifying knowledge."⁹ Faith is the self-authenticating experience of God and needs no external verification in order for it to be legitimate. Faith, in his view, is not centered in the historical figure of Jesus who lived in the past but in the presently proclaimed Christly message. Even the New Testament records give evidence that there were many who, even though they knew the historical Jesus, nevertheless did not have faith in the kerygmatic Christ. The kerygma does not stand or fall on the adequacy or inadequacy of historical research but depends ultimately on its power to call forth existential faith.

The word most often associated with Bultmann is *demythologizing*. Simply put, Bultmann held that myth is that which gives worldly objectivity to that which is unworldly.[10] In his concern to release the kerygmatic Christ from any and all historical, cultural, and cosmological limitations, which he designates as myths, he sets out to demythologize the New Testament Christ figure.

In the Epilogue to his *New Testament Theology,* Bultmann maintains that the kerygmatic Christ opens up a new "believing self-understanding" not only of oneself but also of oneself in relation to God and to the world. He does not mean "'understanding' as in a scientific anthropology which objectifies man into a phenomenon of the world, but . . . an existential understanding of myself which is at one with and inseparable from my understanding of God and the world."[11] This new existential self-understanding is Bultmann's conception of what it means to come to faith. That which we have faith in is not a past event but a present happening. Faith, he explains, "is man's response to God's word which encounters him in the proclamation of Jesus Christ. It is faith in the kerygma. . . ."[12]

There may be sufficient data for saying that whereas the restorationist backs into the future as he rejoices in the past, the existentialist lets the future approach as he experiences faith in the present.[13] For the restorationist the past is primary, the present secondary, and the future tertiary. For the existentialist the present is primary, the future secondary, and the past tertiary.[14] For the futurist, the future is primary, the present secondary, and the past tertiary. We now turn to a consideration of the futurist position.

3. The Theology of Hope Many of the books by Jürgen Moltmann, professor of systematic theology at the University of Tübingen in Germany and the leader in the theology of hope, have been translated into English, among which are such illuminating titles as *The Experiment Hope; Hope and Planning; The Gospel of Liberation; Religion, Revolution, and the Future;* and *Theology of Hope: On the Ground and Implications of a Christian Eschatology,* his foremost statement of futuristic thought.[15]

Perhaps the best way to come to a concise understanding of the theology of hope is to indicate what it is not so that the statement of what it is may be understood by contrast. The theology of hope does not propose that society is inevitably getting better and that theologians have the responsibility to identify positive, hopeful events that can serve as an encouragement to people. Neither is the theology of hope based on an evangelical offer that if persons will invite Jesus Christ into their hearts, life will become excitingly hopeful. Nor does the theology of hope hold that because humankind is incurably hopeful, we always manage out of our own resources to rise above life's experiences of despair. The first view might be called the societal view of hope, the second, the personalistic view, and the third, the heroic view. None of these is reflective of the theology of hope, especially as it is developed by Moltmann. In his view, humankind is plagued with the experience of despair, which arises out of the contradictions between the way we actually find human existence to be, on the one hand, and the expectations we have for human existence, on the other. In the midst of this despair, God speaks a word of promise that gives rise to hope. In fact, it is in the form of promise itself that God reveals Himself. God is not to be understood as one who has at some time in the past revealed Himself, and who now gives us a promise, but rather He is the God whose revelation takes place in the promise itself and in no sense apart from it. Since God's revelation is in the form of promise, and promise has to do with future fulfillment, the revelation of God always has an eschatological character to it. "God is not 'beyond us' or 'in us,' but ahead of us in the horizons of the future opened to us in His promises. Thus the 'future' must be considered as mode of God's being."[16]

According to Moltmann, the Bible is to be understood as the Word-history of promise. It is neither merely the divine Word apart from human history nor merely the history of Israel. The Word is mediated in the history, and the history is understood as the experience of the Word of promise. The biblical Word of God does not have an informational structure, as though it were a catalog of facts about God, but rather a promise structure that reveals God in the message of promise-hope-eschatological fulfillment. In the midst of our experience of godforsakenness, we come to know the promises of the God who has always been faithful in the fulfillment of His promises. In a very real sense, our experience of despair is an integral part of the revelation of God in that apart from despair, promise would be irrelevant.

In his critical analysis of all the major influences on Moltmann's thought, M. Douglas Meeks in *Origins of the Theology of Hope* gives major attention to the work of Ernst Bloch, the Marxist revisionist philosopher. Although an atheist, Bloch has great fascination for the practical function that promise, hope, and ultimate goals play in the Bible. As a Marxist philosopher he is concerned with the revolutionary transformation of society. He maintains, however, that this will not take place without practical devotion to a utopian goal, from which goal we discover who we really are. We know who we are only in light of some reality that transcends out present human condition. This anticipatory relationship to the future not only gives meaning to our present lives but also becomes the basis for the political desire to change the present so that it might more nearly conform to the transcendent goal.[17]

For Bloch, of course, the transcendent goal arises out of the material world, while for Moltmann it is created out of the faithfulness of God. But as with Bloch, even so with Moltmann: the eschatological goal not only tells us who we are but also politicizes us so that we develop practical ways of bringing about change in the present. The theology of hope is very sensitive to matters of pain, suffering, and injustice, but instead of seeking a philosophical solution to these matters, it calls for a practical approach for the alleviation of pain and suffering, and for the restoration of justice.

This, then, is one of the frontiers in contemporary theology: the challenge of determining whether the interfacing perspectives of restorationism, existentialism, and the theology of hope call for exclusive demarcation, complementation, or integration.

B. The Relationship Between Process and Fixity

Process thought[18] is both a reaction against the concept that some reality is fixed, changeless, static, finished and an affirmation that the only unchanging reality is the fact of a world that is, throughout its whole structure, in process of becoming.

Alfred North Whitehead (1861–1947), the fountainhead of process philosophy, wrote his *magnum opus, Process and Reality,* in 1929, at age sixty-eight, some five years after his move from England to Harvard University, where he had begun teaching philosophy in 1924.

Henry Nelson Wieman, who had studied under Whitehead while working on his doctorate at Harvard, brought process thought to the University of Chicago when he began teaching there in 1927. Even though Wieman later abandoned Whitehead's metaphysical superstructure, Chicago became the major center for process studies primarily through the leadership of Charles Hartshorne, who further developed Whitehead's doctrine of God.[19] Two other outstanding persons in process theology, Schubert M. Ogden and John B. Cobb, Jr., also studied at the University of Chicago.[20]

Three of the foundational themes that one finds running throughout the writings of all process thinkers are the following:

1. It is held that a dynamic concept of reality must be developed to replace the old static concepts of unchanging substances, both in relation to the material world and in relation to God. The idea that God is a transcendent, changeless being who exists outside of the created order is rejected. Rather than understanding God as a fixed eternal substance, God should be viewed as an eternally becoming reality. In Whitehead's words, "He is the unlimited conceptual realization of the absolute wealth of potentiality."[21] This is what Whitehead calls the primordial nature of God, but there is also the consequent nature of God that, in short, is His concrete relationship to the world, a world that affects God. God's nature in this second sense is "consequent upon the creative advance of the world."[22] His succinct summary of this "dipolar" character of God is as follows: "The primordial nature is conceptual, the consequent nature is the weaving of God's physical feelings upon his primordial concepts."[23] While it is incorrect to assume that all process thinkers adopt, without revision, Whitehead's dipolar concept of God, it is correct to say that his basic concept of a God who is both in process and affected by the world is a persistent theme among all process theologians.

But it is not only God who is dynamic; the basic unit of all physical reality is what Cobb discusses in *God and the World* as "energy-events," "successions of events," or "happenings." These are the "building blocks of the universe."[24]

It is on the basis of this dynamic, processive view of God and of the world that process thought conceives of physical reality being spiritual, and spiritual reality being physical. There is no cleavage between the two since the building blocks of the physical world are themselves spiritual, i.e., energy-events. To conceive of God as a spiritual reality apart from another reality known as the physical world, or to conceive of the physical world as being nonspiritual is to betray a basic misunderstanding of both the nature of God and the nature of the world. God, in process thought, is intimately involved in and affected by the world, and the world's process is inextricably bound up in the process of God's own becoming.

2. Another important theme has to do with the genuine choices that human beings are called on to make. We do not have the mere illusion of being free to make genuine decisions; we actually are free to make both good and evil decisions. God deals with the givenness of our choices by creatively using each and every one of them for the realization of the divine purpose. Lewis S. Ford in his treatment of the biblical background for process theism argues that "it is not so much that a being is first created and then acts, as that its responsive activity in actualizing its own potentiality is part of the creative process itself."[25] God divinely persuades us to achieve the very best that is within us. This divine persuasion "maximizes creaturely freedom by respecting the creature's own integrity in the very act of guiding its development toward greater freedom."[26] God as the ultimate power of the future, rescues us from "degeneration into chaos by the relentless provision of ever-new creative possibilities."[27] The genuine freedom of choice that is ours is the necessary context for the fulfilling freedom to realize our optimum divine potential. God

makes use of every exercise of the freedom of choice, as well as all consequences of that exercise, with the intention of leading us to the freedom of divine fulfillment. John Cobb discusses this whole issue in terms of "the experienced power of Christ as creative transformation."[28] Christ is the image of hope, the symbol of divine transformation from self-destruction to human fulfillment.

3. Process thought is understandably inclusive of all philosophical, theological, and religious viewpoints. Since reality is a unitary process, each of the individual parts has a role to play in the cosmic, creative movement of God and the world. Just as each and every "energy-event" is creatively "lured"[29] by God, even so we should give ourselves to the creative understanding of the contribution each and every dimension of human culture has for us. Indeed, we find Cobb talking about a "Christianized Buddhism and a Buddhized Christianity."[30] For him, the creative transformation mentioned earlier has to do with the remaking of antagonistic pluralism into harmonious pluralism.

But where is the cosmic process going? On the one hand, the Whiteheadian answer is one of uncertainty. There is no single climax toward which we move. In fact, he conjectures that ours is only one cosmic epoch among many, and that our own epoch contains within itself incompatible characteristics from other epochs. This interpenetration of epochs seems chaotic, but this seeming "vast confusion" is "mitigated by the few, faint elements of order contained in its own defining characteristic of 'extensive connection.' "[31]

On the other hand, Teilhard de Chardin (1881–1955)—Jesuit priest, paleontologist, philosopher, and theologian—holds that the cosmic process does indeed have a unitary goal, that is, Christ, the Omega Point.[32] The evolutionary development of the whole universe moves in harmony with Christ, and toward the personal Christ. He writes in *The Phenomenon of Man* that "the Universal and Personal . . . grow in the same direction and culminate simultaneously in each other," and he concludes that "the Future Universal could not be anything else but the Hyper-Personal—at the Omega Point."[33]

Is process thought compatible with biblical thought? Is God in process of becoming? Does process theology uncover a lost dimension of biblical theology? These are some of the questions to be answered in this frontier of contemporary theology.

C. The Relationship Between Secularization and Sacredness

Secularization, as the word is being used here, is that process whereby human life is viewed increasingly from a perspective that is informed primarily by cultural experience in general and decreasingly from a special perspective understood by those adhering to it as being divine. As Harvey Cox puts it in *The Secular City,* "Secularization occurs when man turns his attention away from the worlds beyond and toward this world and this time."[34]

The twentieth century has witnessed major struggles centering around secularization. In 1918 Karl Barth's first edition of *The Epistle to the Romans* was published, followed by five subsequent editions in 1921, 1922, 1924, 1926, and 1928. His major concern was with a Christendom characterized by a secularized religion more desirous of being relevant to the contemporary culture than it was of proclaiming the biblical Word of God irrespective of the human measuring sticks of relevancy. Barth felt that there had been something of a marriage between contemporary culture and the church so that the prophetic function of the biblical message was replaced by an overly optimistic and overly idealistic view of social change. The outlook was that with enough time and patience church and society could, by working together, bring into being a more socially advanced and pleasantly equitable human community. Rather than dealing with the transcendence of God, the church stressed His immanence; instead of divine judgment, divine love; instead of personal faith, social change; instead of universal evangelization, universal culture; instead of an emphasis on the other world, this world was emphasized. Barth held that the secularized religion of early-twentieth-century Europe was not gospel-centered but self-centered; not focused on the divine Word of God in Christ, but on the religious experience of secular society.

And so, the proclamation of the divine Word, the Word that judges the values of both secularized culture in general and secularized religion in particular, became the badge of what we know as neo-orthodoxy.[35]

In the United States, another kind of secularization battle took place during the early part of the twentieth century, in what we know as the Fundamentalist-Modernist controversy. It was felt by many that Protestantism had been unduly influenced by facts of modern life considered alien to biblical Christianity, facts such as the following: the ultimate authority of science; the historical-critical approach to biblical studies; the view that the Judeo-Christian faith had borrowed from other religions and cultures what had always been viewed as specially revealed truth; and the naturalistic and cultural concept of progress and development, with its consequent appreciation of societal, ethnic, and religious divergencies.

Fundamentalism emerged as a protest against what it considered to be secularized religion, i.e., modernism.[36] The Fundamentalist war against modernism was evidenced in the publication of the Scofield Reference Bible in 1909; the spread of Bible conferences inspired by the model of the Niagara Bible Conferences held during the last quarter of the nineteenth century; the publication of a twelve-volume series entitled *The Fundamentals,* 1910–15; the perpetuation of the Fundamentalist strain no longer comfortable in Princeton Seminary, through the establishment of Westminster and Faith seminaries; church struggles especially among Presbyterians and Baptists in the North; and the John T. Scopes evolution trial in Dayton, Tennessee, in 1925.[37]

Those church leaders perceived as secularists, both those addressed by Barth's *Romans* and those fought by American Fundamentalism—although being addressed from very different cultural, religious, and theological vantage points—were nevertheless in the position of having to defend themselves against the charge that they did not take seriously the divine Word of God (Barth) or that they did not conform to the teachings of Scripture (Fundamentalism). Such church leaders were pressured into becoming defenders of their position.

However, with the arrival of the sixties a major change took place. Instead of the approach of the earlier era characterized by a positive, careful, sophisticated, church-related defense of the more liberal position, the sixties witnessed a vigorous, shock-oriented, offensive call for overt secularization in theology. According to Cox in his widely read *Secular City,* first published in 1965 and revised in 1966, the church should have no fear of secularization, but rather should understand it, affirm it, and assume the human responsibility that it implies. In fact, in his view, the Bible is the history of secularization beginning with the story of the creation of the world by God, the result of which was the human "disenchantment with nature" as being alive with either "friendly or fiendish demons."[38] The biblical sources of secularization also include the "desacralization of politics" of which Exodus is the focal point. By this Cox means that the idea that kings rule by divine right is challenged by the new idea that leaders rule by virtue of their capacity to act in the best interest of their respective societies.[39] Finally, he discusses the Sinai Covenant as the "deconsecration of values," by which he means that societal rules are relativized. The Decalogue is seen as Israel's values, relative to Israel's needs, but not incumbent on the whole of humanity.[40]

The 1960 theologians of vigorous secularization found profound inspiration in Dietrich Bonhoeffer (1906-1945), a leader in the anti-Nazi Confessing Church of Germany, who was hanged for his involvement in the resistance movement against Hitler. In *The Seduction of the Spirit* (1973), Cox discusses the great influence that Bonhoeffer's theology had on his writing of *The Secular City*.[41] Such statements as the following from the writings of Bonhoeffer encouraged the theologians of secularization: "Man has learned to cope with all questions of importance without recourse to God as a working hypothesis. . . . It is becoming evident that everything gets along without 'God,' and just as well as before."[42] The theologians of secularization held that the world "come of age," devoid of its continuing need for the tutelage of God, is becoming more and more responsible for itself. Whether Bonhoeffer would have agreed with the implications the theologians of the sixties read into his statements on secularization is certainly an open question. Nevertheless, the fact remains that in Bonhoeffer, they had not only a mentor but also a widely respected martyr.

Fervent theologizing about secularization penetrated the consciousness of the public in general with the publications of the so-called death-of-God theologians Thomas J. J. Altizer,[43] William Hamilton,[44] Gabriel Vahanian,[45] and Paul Van Buren.[46] While there are certainly differences among these men, the commonality of their approach includes the conviction that the modern world is characterized not by the absence of the experience of God (which implies that He might be there even though we do not experience Him), but the experience of the actual absence of God. However, Hamilton's approach to this reality does leave the door open for the possibility of some future experience of the presense of God.[47] Nevertheless, all of the death-of-God theologians agree that the idea of a transcendent God exterior to the world who has responsibility for human life is no longer tenable either philosophically, theologically, or experientially. The position set forth by Altizer is very specific about this matter, holding that the Incarnation was the occasion when God divested Himself of transcendence, once and for all time, and moved into the temporal order, so that the idea itself of a transcendent God is completely contrary to the new ontological reality ushered into history at the time of the Incarnation.[48]

The secular world is all there is, according to these theologians. Consequently, human responsibility for our —not God's—world is the major task of human beings. Life by being desacralized becomes truly and fully humanized. The humanization of our consciousness, of our approach to life, of our values, of our hopes, of our work, should be the goal of all our endeavors.[49]

A decade or so after this new secularized theology came on the scene, two differing approaches, both grounded in the basic assumptions of the theology of secularization, had developed. One was a theology concerned basically with emotional matters whereas the other was concerned basically with conceptual issues. The first approach stresses getting in touch with oneself, enjoying life with its full range of emotions, sensitizing oneself to the rhythm of life, developing stories about existence that are meaningful to us, affirming the fleshliness of existence, and discovering purpose from the feeling level of life. Theology is viewed as being fundamentally an imaginative response to the emotional nature of life. The titles of some of the books expressive of this approach give evidence of its fleshliness: *The Feast of Fools: A Theological Essay on Festivity and Fantasy* and *The Seduction of the Spirit: The Use and Misuse of People's Religion,* both by Harvey Cox;[50] *Ascent of the Mountain, Flight of the Dove,* by Michael Novak;[51] and *To a Dancing God,* by Sam Keen, the final chapter of which is entitled "The Importance of Being Carnal—Notes for a Visceral Theology."[52] In his critique of what he calls "Cultural or Story Theology," Stanley

Sutphin laments that "despite their years of mastering the formal disciplines . . . [cultural and story theologians] are more interested in writing a 'best seller' than in working out a reasonably defensible theological position."[53]

There is another approach, however, that has produced the carefully developed theological positions called for by Sutphin. These theologians, of whom Gordon D. Kaufman of Harvard Divinity School and David Tracy of the University of Chicago Divinity School are examples, hold that even though their theology cannot begin with the assumption that there is a transcendent God who is ontologically exterior to the world, a case may be made for functional transcendence, that is, for a God concept that is originated by us for the purpose of the conceptual integration of life.

Tracy in his "revisionist model for Christian theology" maintains that the goal of Christian theology is "best understood as philosophical reflection on the meanings present in common human experience and the meanings present in the Christian tradition."[54] The "truth" of the reflective statements resulting from this philosophical endeavor is dependent on whether these statements show their "'adequacy to experience' by explicating how a particular concept (e.g., . . . God) functions as a fundamental 'belief' or 'condition of possibility' of all our experience."[55]

Those who agree with Francis Schaeffer's book title about God, *He Is There and He Is Not Silent*[56]—that is to say, the God who is eternally transcendent to the world, nevertheless communicates with us—find themselves confronted not only with the theology of secularization but also with the secularization of theology, as well as with the attempt to completely secularize the God concept itself. They are faced with a theological method that leads one theologian to say that "the criteria for assessing theological claims turn out in the last analysis . . . to be pragmatic and humanistic."[57] This is perhaps the most critical of all frontiers in contemporary theology.

II. ECCLESIAL FRONTIERS

The structure of the church's life is at issue whenever we consider such matters as the subjectification of the gospel and/or its objectification; the balance between togetherness (unity) and apartness (separation); and the relationship between heterodoxy and orthodoxy.

A. The Relationship Between the Subjectification of the Gospel and Its Objectification

Much of the church's history can be understood as an ongoing process of shifting back and forth between subjectification and objectification. The rise of Lutheran Pietism in the seventeenth century was a shift away from the rigid objectification of the gospel espoused by scholastic Lutheranism, to the warm, heartfelt experientially oriented subjectification of the gospel. Such Lutheran theologians as Martin Chemnitz (1522-1586) and Johann Gerhard (1582-1637) had produced theological systems that appealed to those concerned with doctrinal details, but in so doing the personalized, devotional experience of the gospel suffered. This shift toward subjectification is identifiable with such leading figures as Philipp Jacob Spener (1635-1705), August Hermann Francke (1663-1727), and Count Nicholaus L. von Zinzendorf (1700-1760).

My purpose here is not to attempt even a thumbnail sketch of the shifts between subjectification and objectification, but rather to indicate that this continues to be one of the ecclesial frontiers in present-day theology.[58]

The objectification of the gospel has to do with its out-there-ness. The gaze of the believer is turned toward what God did once and for all in Jesus Christ instead of toward what happens in the believer's own life. As Robert D. Brinsmead puts it, "The Christian faith consists primarily in rehearsing God's great deed in Jesus Christ."[59] In response to theologians of subjectification who criticize those who stress the gospel's out-there, once-and-for-all character and its declarative, legal categories as being cold and lifeless, Brinsmead writes, "The moment the subjective element of the believer's transformation is allowed to intrude into the process of justification, he is robbed of the objective ground of acceptance because he confuses spiritual acceptance with spiritual attainments."[60]

The subjectification of the gospel, on the other hand, has to do with its in-here-ness. The major attention is focused on what God is doing to, in, and through us. The literature of revivalist and charismatic renewals is replete with testimonies like the following, which reflect the subjectification of the gospel:

> The tall man came down from the platform and placed his hand on my forehead; and then it happened—Jesus Christ came into my life! I felt myself being turned inside out. All the black, evil, sin-stained life was stripped away and I was reborn, a child of God![61]

The degree to which the gospel is objectified or subjectified is observable in the worship life of the church. Hymns of praise to God for His work in creation and Christ, strictly exegetical and expository biblical preaching, a sacramental understanding of baptism and the eucharist, and absolute adherence to either the cruciality of the Word being preached in every service of worship or the cruciality of proper liturgical procedure in every service—these are some of the indicators of an objectification theology. The implication of the foregoing list is not that all of these indicators will be found together as a unit, but rather that any one of them is in and of itself expressive of the objectification of the gospel.

On the other end of the spectrum, the worship indicators of the subjectification of the gospel are: songs of personal rejoicing and introspection; preaching that deals mainly with the personal experience of salvation, evidences of righteousness and holiness, helps for living the Christian life, and moral and ethical matters; an ordinance view of baptism and the eucharist; a relaxed view toward the necessity of the preaching of the Word in every service, thus allowing for its replacement by such modes as personal testimonies, the experientially centered singing of special groups, and festivals of favorite songs; and, most importantly, strict adherence to the cruciality of an altar call in every service of worship. Here again, it is not to be implied that all of these indicators are inevitably found together, but rather that whenever one is found, it shows some degree of the theology of subjectification.

During the two decades 1960–1980, while academic theology was being greatly influenced by secularization with its high view of the importance of human responsibility, the theology of the people in the church pews was being greatly influenced by subjectification with its high view of the importance of the human experience of God. Both, though vastly different in religious orientation, actually had a basic commonality insofar as both had a high estimate of human experience. The theologians of secularization looked to humanity in general, with little or no use for the God of ontological transcendence; the theologians of subjectification looked to born-again, Spirit-filled humanity as the confirmation through divine immanence, that the God of ontological transcendence does indeed exist.

In 1977 mainline evangelical theologians, such as Donald G. Bloesch of Dubuque Seminary and Roger Nicole of Gordon-Conwell Seminary, to mention only two out of forty-three from other evangelical institutions, issued "The Chicago Call: An Appeal to Evangelicals." This call seeks to strike a balance between objectification and subjectification with neither negating the other. However, it is evident that the signers of the call were convinced that the major threat at the present time lies in subjectification. For instance, it urges Evangelicals to seek a recovery of historic Christian roots, warns about undercutting the "objective character of biblical truth," deplores a "creedless church that languishes in a doctrinal vacuum," and stresses the need for a new appreciation of the sacramental nature of baptism and the eucharist. In the section entitled "A Call to Holistic Salvation" there is a good example of the attempt to state a concern in such a way that both the objective and the subjective dimensions of salvation are affirmed in holistic fashion. In their words, they "deplore the tendency of evangelicals to understand salvation solely as an individual, spiritual, and other-worldly matter to the neglect of the corporate, physical and this-worldly implication of God's saving activity."[62] The position assumed is that salvation is both other-worldly and this-worldly. It is rooted in "the atoning work of Christ on the cross," which indeed produces personal salvation, the healing of physical and emotional ills, societal orientation, and ecological sensitivity. Salvation has to do with what God did in Christ, exterior to us, as an objective reality, as well as with what God through that objective reality does to, in, and through us.

There seems to be sufficient historical evidence to say that whenever the objectification of the gospel is allowed to deemphasize its subjectification, creedalism, dogmatism, and liturgicalism abound; and whenever subjectification is allowed to deemphasize objectification, experientialism, individualism, and emotionalism abound. Contemporary evangelical theologians are seeking to avoid both pitfalls. One hears Donald Bloesch warning against not only the dangers of religious enthusiasm and perfectionism—as one would expect a Reformed theologian to do—but also the dangers of sacramentalism and predestinarianism.[63] One senses an urgency in the *Christianity Today* editorial that declares that "the church needs both true biblical doctrine and deep spiritual fervor."[64]

Is there among those churches with a basically objectification theology, (i.e., Lutheran, Reformed, and Baptist) a new appreciation of the emphasis on subjectification in the Wesleyan, Holiness, Pentecostal, and Charismatic churches?[65]

Furthermore, is there among those churches with a basically subjectification theology, a new appreciation of the emphasis on objectification in the Lutheran, Reformed, and Baptist churches?

B. The Relationship Between Ecclesial Apartness and Ecclesial Togetherness

The twentieth century may be quite appropriately designated the century of struggle over the degree and nature of togetherness that the church should have. Is it the will of God that some apartness be maintained in order for the divine economy to function, or is it His will that togetherness be pursued even when it means sacrificing theological commitments to biblical truth not universally affirmed? What kind of apartness among believers makes their witness to the gospel ineffective? What kind of togetherness compromises too many convictional and doctrinal matters? Every age of the church's history has had those forces concerned chiefly with togetherness for the sake of peace, as well as those forces concerned primarily with apartness for the sake of purity. During the present century, however, the former type of forces have been welded into a sociologically definable entity known as the ecumenical movement.[66]

Ecumenicity among Protestant churches is highlighted by such dates as the 1910 World Missionary Conference held in Edinburgh, Scotland; the 1925 Universal Christian Conference on Life and Work held in Stockholm, Sweden; the 1927

World Conference on Faith and Order held in Lausanne, Switzerland; the 1948 First Assembly of the World Council of Churches held in Amsterdam, the Netherlands; and the subsequent dates of the WCC Assemblies: 1954 in Evanston, Illinois; 1961 in New Delhi, India; 1968 in Uppsala, Sweden; and 1975 in Nairobi, Kenya.[67]

Among Roman Catholics, the Second Vatican Council (1962–65) dramatized the twentieth-century spirit of ecumenicity. Indeed, virtually no major segment of the Christian world has been left unaffected if not by direct involvement in interconfessional relationships, at least by the development of intraconfessional fellowships around the world, such as the Lambeth Conference of the Anglican Communion, the World Alliance of Reformed Churches, the Lutheran World Federation, the Baptist World Alliance, the Pentecostal World Conference, and the Methodist World Conference. Interdenominational endeavors such as the National Association of Evangelicals and the Christian Holiness Association, both North American organizations, are further evidences of the twentieth-century spirit of ecumenicity. Indeed, virtually no major segment of is the additional phenomenon of denominational mergers (with, of course, the inevitable result that minority segments in each church resist merger and in some cases form new denominations). Twentieth-century mergers have taken place across a wide spectrum of the Protestant church scene: The Church of South India in 1947 (between Methodists and Anglicans), the United Church of Christ in 1957 (between the Evangelical and Reformed Church and the Congregational Christian Churches), the United Methodist Church in 1968 (between the Methodist Church and the Evangelical United Brethren), and the Wesleyan Church that same year (between the Pilgrim Holiness Church and the Wesleyan Methodist Church). The most ambitious attempt at merger in the United States is the Consultation on Church Union first proposed by Eugene Carson Blake in 1960 and presently including ten denominations, four of them Methodist, one Anglican, two Presbyterian, and three Congregationally oriented,[68] with a total membership of over 22,500,000.[69]

On a more personal and intimate level of ecclesial life, the drive toward togetherness has been very influential through the popular appeal of the theology of relationships, set forth by such Protestant writers as Keith Miller and Bruce Larson[70] and by such Roman Catholics as Henri J. M. Nouwen[71] and Rosemary Haughton.[72]

But the contemporary church knows not only the drive toward togetherness but also the drive toward apartness. The appearance of Harold Lindsell's *Battle for the Bible* in 1976 questioned the theological integrity of denominational leaders and seminary faculties, by using the singular issue of the textual inerrancy of the original scriptural autographs as the *sine qua non* of evangelical orthodoxy. Lindsell holds that in the original autographs there is a total lack of error "in matters of fact, science, history, and chronology, as well as in matters having to do with salvation."[73]

In both his first volume and his subsequent one, *The Bible in the Balance* (1979), Lindsell sets forth a massive collection of material indicating that many denominations and seminary faculties do not agree with his position regarding inerrancy and should therefore be viewed with alarm.[74] The widespread response to Lindsell's battle cry may be due to a felt need among many American church members to have a rallying point for the expression of their displeasure over what they consider to be theologically weak ecumenicity. At any rate, the movement toward apartness for the sake of purity is a lively contemporary concomitant to the movement toward togetherness for the sake of peace. Contemporary ecclesial apartness is evidenced in the burgeoning of what is commonly called the electronic church, which for the most part centers on television personalities who function independent of ecclesiastical structures. The teaching responsibility exercised on such programs is assumed primarily by the television personalities themselves rather than by a historical ecclesial community. It is the personal theology of the television preacher/teacher that is espoused rather than the communal theology of an organized church.

In February 1981 the National Council of Churches Communication Commission sponsored a consultation on the electronic church, which included such TV personalities as Pat Robertson and Robert Schuler. In the *NCCC Chronicles* report of the consultation, Father Richard P. McBrien, professor of theology at Boston College (Roman Catholic), is quoted as saying, "The evangelical wing of the electronic church may be the unwitting catalyst for renewing some of the sharpest Reformation conflicts: Scripture versus tradition, grace versus works, authority versus private interpretation. . . ."[75]

The conflicts mentioned by McBrien do indeed suggest historic issues having to do with the relationship between ecclesial apartness on the one hand (i.e., devotion to the truth of Scripture even when the historic community of faith issues condemnation; commitment to holy living even at the expense of separation from fellow believers whose style of life is viewed as bringing reproach on the cause of Christ; and faithfulness to one's personal conscience as it is informed by Scripture and illumined by the Spirit, regardless of ecclesiastical pronouncements), and ecclesial togetherness on the other hand (i.e., adherence to the traditional ecclesiastical interpretation of the biblical message, emphasis on the universality of grace for all believers, and the maintenance of good order in both faith and practice through the ecclesiastically approved teaching ministry of the church).

The cruciality of these matters has given rise to much serious theological thought about the nature of the church, from many different perspectives, as for instance, Wesleyan/Holiness theologian Howard A. Snyder (*The Community of the King*),[76] Roman Catholic Karl Rahner (*The Shape of the Church to Come*),[77] Reformed theologian G. C. Berkouwer (*The Church*),[78] Pentecostal Melvin L. Hodges (*A Theology of the Church and Its Mission: A Pentecostal Perspective*),[79] and Reformed theologian of hope, Jürgen Moltmann (*The Church in the Power of the Spirit*).[80]

The question that calls for creative address at the present time is whether the corporate nature of the church is enhanced or endangered by a togetherness that negates all ecclesial apartness. On the one hand, do we know the difference between an apartness that is essentially together and an apartness that is devotedly separatistic? On the other hand, do we know the difference between a togetherness that appreciates certain kinds of apartness and a togetherness that compromises conscience? Do we know the difference between appreciation for the whole with all of its parts and the inflated view of the part as though it were the whole?[81]

C. The Relationship Between Heterodoxy and Orthodoxy

Orthodoxy means right doctrine; heterodoxy means doctrine different from that which is approved. The consideration here has to do with the relationship between orthodoxy and heterodoxy, not as it pertains to one particular, narrowly conceived tradition of Christianity but as it pertains to Christianity broadly conceived. There is a generally agreed upon doctrinal perspective held in common by the Roman Catholic church, the Orthodox churches, and the churches of classical Protestantism.[82] Even though there are many historical, cultural, doctrinal, and ecclesiastical differences among these churches, there is general agreement on the following matters: that God is eternal Trinity; that the nature of the Incarnate Second Person of the Trinity was fully human and fully divine, yet one person; that God is the creator of the universe; that sin is a universal affliction; that Jesus Christ is the only eternal Savior; that salvation is by the grace of God; and that the apostolic tradition inscripturated is fundamental for Christian thought. There are, of course, variations of understanding among the churches regarding these matters, as for instance, the Roman Catholic view that both Scripture and tradition are authoritative, as over against the conservative Protestant view of *sola Scriptura*. Nevertheless both, different as they are, agree that Scripture is fundamental for Christian thought. Christian orthodoxy is ecclesiastically committed to these broadly conceived doctrinal agreements, whereas heterodoxy as used in this context, takes positions that differ substantially from these universally held orthodox ones.

Some outstanding examples of organized heterodoxy are the Jehovah's Witnesses with their rejection of both the trinitarian God and the coeternity of the Son with the Father; the Mormons with their rejection of trinitarian monotheism and their acceptance of postbiblical special revelation; the Unification Church of Sun Myung Moon with its view that another Messiah, the Lord of the Second Advent, is needed to complete the salvific work of Christ. The heterodoxy of the type just illustrated is not a matter of some casual departure from orthodoxy, resulting from ignorance, but a systematic development of belief that is in self-conscious opposition to the teachings of orthodoxy and is devotedly promulgated. Heresy is the time-honored word used to describe this kind of willful heterodoxy. The organized religious opposition to Christian orthodoxy is increasingly considered to be a—some would say *the*—major frontier in contemporary theology. While exact statistics are unavailable, it has been estimated that there may be between two and three million people in the United States involved in groups actively opposed to the Judeo-Christian tradition in general.[83] A large segment of these are, to be sure, opposed particularly to Christian orthodoxy. Some churches are so concerned about the phenomenon that they are making use of special consultants as they attempt to address the issues, both emotional and doctrinal, raised by heretical groups. Joel McCollam, serving the Episcopal Church in this capacity, has written *Carnival of Souls*;[84] Herbert F. Beck, serving the Lutheran Church–Missouri Synod, has written *How to Respond to the Cults*.[85] Other writers in this field include such widely known specialists as Walter Martin, author of *The Kingdom of the Cults*, which has gone through multiple printings since being first published in 1965, and others, as for example, Ronald Enroth, James W. Sire, and Jack Sparks, who are newer to the field.[86]

However, this particular frontier in contemporary theology has to do with heterodoxy not only outside of orthodoxy, but inside as well. Within the Roman Catholic church, bastion of christological conservatism, the pontificate of Pope John Paul II has witnessed the investigation of leading theologians including Hans Küng of the University of Tübingen in West Germany and Edward Schillebeeckx of Nijmegen University in the Netherlands.[87] While there are several reasons for the Vatican's displeasure with them, it centers primarily on their christology. Inquiries have been made as to whether they do indeed teach the orthodox doctrine that Jesus Christ was fully God, the coeternal Second Person of the Trinity, incarnated; for example, Schillebeeckx questions the validity of the interpretation that holds that the Chalcedonian Symbol (451) teaches that the man Jesus was an eternally divine Person who in the Incarnation had both a human and a divine nature.[88] If that be the case, Schillebeeckx reasons, Jesus was not completely authentic as a human being. Such a viewpoint "overexposes" His "being coessential with" the Father and "underexposes" his genuine humanity.[89]

Likewise, Küng expresses concerns about the metaphysical assumption on which the Chalcedonian formula is based, namely, the eternal nature of the Second Person of the Trinity. According to Küng, the speculative assumptions regarding the eternal nature of the Second Person is that which informed the Chalcedonian declaration that He was truly God and truly man. It was His preincarnational Godhood that determined the Chalcedonian christology (in that sense, it is a christology from above), and not the actual, historical life of Jesus. In Küng's "up-to-date positive paraphrase of the ancient formula, 'truly God and truly man,'" he stresses that "for believers, God himself as man's friend was present . . . in this Jesus who came among men as God's advocate and deputy, representative and delegate. . . ." He goes on to say that terms such as divine sonship, preexistence, and incarnation are merely the symbolic means by which substantiation takes place for "the uniqueness, underivability and unsurpassability of the call, offer and claim made known in and with Jesus."[90]

In his discussion of the "truly man" terminology, he says that "all tendencies to deify Jesus" must be resisted and that stress must be placed on the fact that He was thoroughly human, with all that that involves, including the "possibility of error." But, Küng says, He was not "merely man, but true man," by which he means that He was "a model of what it is to be human."[91]

Karl Rahner in his *Theological Investigations* develops a terminology for the two basic types of christology under discussion, one being the christology of saving history, which begins with the historical life and ministry of Jesus of Nazareth; and the other being metaphysical christology, which begins with a concept of divinity. He refers to the latter as a descending christology.[92] While Rahner, though clearly committed to a christology of saving history, has maintained an essentially orthodox position, others such as Piet Schoonenberg of the Netherlands, Jacques Pohier of France, and Jon Sobrino of El Salvador have not been able to avoid the charge of heterodoxy.

Among those Roman Catholic theologians staunchly defending orthodox christology is Walter Kasper of West Germany, who in his *Jesus the Christ* declares that "a Christology purely 'from below' is . . . condemned to failure. Jesus himself understands himself 'from above' in his whole human existence."[93]

The challenge of this orthodoxy-heterodoxy frontier gets to the very heart of the belief life of the church. The approach made to the nature of orthodoxy and the degree of tolerance or intolerance of heterodoxy will, to a great extent, determine the effectiveness of the church's ministry both to those within her fold and to the world in general. Some questions that need to be considered are these: Is that which appears at first sight to be heterodoxy, actually a corrective for distorted orthodoxy? When does concern for orthodoxy degenerate into what we might call in the light of the 1979 Islamic revolution in Iran, Khomeini-ism, a rigid anti-pluralism that is suspicious of the slightest linguistic deviation from the orthodox position and intolerant of any dialogical thought? On the other hand, are we sufficiently appreciative of the full doctrinal ramifications of orthodoxy so that we are sensitive to heterodoxical positions that seriously compromise the essence of Christian thought?

III. FORMAL FRONTIERS

On the contemporary scene there are major questions about the function of the historical disciplines—such as New Testament studies, Old Testament studies, systematic theology, biblical theology, dogmatics, and historical theology—in their relationship to each other. It is not altogether clear whether the various disciplines are to be thought of as competitive or as compatible, as compartments or as complements.

A. The Relationship Between Biblical Theology and Theologies in the Bible

That there is theological diversity within the Bible as a whole is the methodological presupposition on which works like the *Wesleyan Theological Perspectives* series, written and edited by Wesleyan scholars, are based.[94] In the first volume, *An Inquiry into Soteriology from a Biblical Theological Perspective,* the theme of salvation is studied according to the divisions of the canon; first, the Old Testament, followed by chapters on soteriology in the Synoptics, the Gospel of John, Paul's writings, Hebrews, the General Epistles, and the Apocalypse. The assumption made is that the soteriological theme in Scripture is developed diversely enough to call for this kind of segmented treatment.

The question presently at issue is one having to do with the extent to which one goes either in the direction of emphasizing diversity or in the direction of emphasizing unity. In an earlier era, the impulse to stress the unity of the whole of Scripture almost obliterated the diversity, whereas during the twentieth century, the impulse has been to stress the diversity so greatly that the idea of canonical unity has at times been considered at least problematical, if not antiquated. Joseph Blenkinsopp, professor of theology at the University of Notre Dame, in his *Prophecy and Canon,* a study of the Old Testament corpus, observes that "the unity and authority of the Bible can no longer be taken for granted as central theological data."[95] The problem is obvious: if the Bible is a collection of diverse theologies with no overarching, inherent, and/or underlying unity, the question arises as to what criteria are to be used for deciding the authoritative value of the various theologies. Of course, what is in view here has to do not only with the diversity among the books of the Bible but also the diversity within the canonical books themselves, resulting from accretions, changes, expansions, interpretations, and attempts at validation that have taken place in the course of both oral and written transmission. Biblical criticism as the systematic analysis of Scripture is commonly divided into two general categories: textual criticism (also called lower criticism), which seeks to determine the best renderings of the original scriptural writings, and so-called higher criticism.[96] There are several approaches in this second category, including literary criticism, which analyzes the overall nature and internal characteristics of the writings themselves; historical criticism, which is concerned with dating, authorship, the historicity of events reported, and the relationship of the piece of literature under consideration to other pieces both inside and outside the canon; form criticism, which analyzes the oral and written history of the canonical end product;[97] and redaction criticism, which concentrates on an analysis of the theological intention of the writers, who, according to the basic assumption of this approach, are to be considered more as theologians writing about the significance and meanings of persons and events rather than as historians reporting the bare facts about those persons and events.[98]

The contemporary thinker, then, is faced with the question about the unity and/or diversity not only among the different books of the Bible but also among the different sources, redactors, and interpreters within the books themselves. One approach to the diversity issue is to call into question the type of biblical criticism that has denigrated the unity of the whole of Scripture.[99] Another approach is to rethink the whole concept of canonical unity within the context of canonical diversity, without sacrificing allegiance to the historical-critical method. Blenkinsopp is one who has taken the second approach. He maintains that "if biblical theology means a theology of the Bible it must take account of the Bible in its final form and what that form means for theology."[100] His own particular conclusion, for example, is that the biblical canon, as a unit, shows us the constant tension between law (the "rational order") and prophecy (the "unpredictable and disruptive") and is necessary as an ongoing reminder of this "unresolved tension," this "unstable equilibrium."[101]

In their preface to *Canon and Authority*, the editors, George W. Coats and Burke O. Long, link the decline of biblical authority to the "overwhelming and undeniable sense of the diversity" within the canon that has resulted from the "undoubtedly productive methods of biblical study" of the last hundred years.[102] This concern for the recovery of unity within the canon is illustrated by Bernhard W. Anderson's "Stylistic Study of the Priestly Creation Story" in *Canon and Authority*. For instance, he concludes that the story "is a unified and symmetrical whole," that "the theological meaning of the story is also disclosed by considering its *function* in the larger narrative whole,"[103] and that the "widely accepted hypothesis that the present shape of the text is the end-result of literary or traditio-historical stages in which *Tatbericht* [emphasizing creation by making] and *Wortbericht* [emphasizing creation by fiat] were conflated and harmonized" proves to be unsatisfactory.[104]

In an even more recent expression of concern about historical criticism, Anderson maintains that it "tends to take us away from the text in its final form and fails to deal with the Word of God as Scripture, as literature."[105]

David Kelsey in *The Uses of Scripture in Recent Theology* deals with the concept of canon by analyzing the underlying assumptions implicit in the idea that the Bible is the literary canon of the Christian faith. In doing so, he distinguishes between the canon as having a unity and the canon as having the character of wholeness. His position is that it is not necessary to prove a unity among all the parts in order for its wholeness to be maintained. He writes:

> To call them "canon" is to say that the writings taken together, no matter what their diversity from one another, function *ensemble* when used in the common life of the church and serve as the sufficient occasion for that presence of God that preserves the church's identity as a singular, integral, living reality. No matter how great its inner diversity, this set of writings is to be taken as mirroring in a wholeness of its own the unity of the church's own identity.[106]

Just as an unbalanced emphasis on canonical unity may evoke in those with a conservative bent a protective effort at ingenious harmonization and in those with a liberal bent a daring effort at exposing the great diversity in Scripture, even so an unbalanced emphasis on canonical diversity may evoke in those with little patience an "overwhelming sense of diversity"[107] and in those with great patience the desire to rediscover the Bible's unity and wholeness. Contemporary theology is alive with thinkers at all of these pressure points: there are those desiring to prove unity through harmonization;[108] there are those who earnestly call into question the validity of the harmonization approach by stressing evidences of diversity;[109] there are those who no longer take the biblical text seriously;[110] and there are those who concentrate on the nature, function, and importance of the biblical canon.[111] As James D. Smart observes,

> One healthful sign in American scholarship recently has been the attention that has been given to the importance of the canon of Scripture in setting the stage for interpretation. [Karl] Barth, and then [Hermann] Diem and [Friedrick] Mildenberger, emphasized the serious theological consequences in interpretation when, as so often happened in historical criticism, the church's canon was ignored.[112]

One who exemplifies this "healthful sign" is Brevard S. Childs in his *Introduction to the Old Testament as Scripture*, in which he deals with the canonical nature of Scripture as a matter of first-order importance. After his comprehensive discussion of the canon, he proceeds to consider each book of the Old Testament by dealing first of all with critical problems, then with "the canonical shape" of the book, and finally with theological and hermeneutical implications. His canonical approach is, in his own words, "an attempt to hear the biblical text in the terms compatible with the collection and transmission of the literature as scripture."[113]

B. The Relationship Between a Natural/Philosophical/Social Orientation to Systematic Theology and a Biblical/Confessional Orientation

In light of the discussion throughout this chapter, perhaps we are in a position to look comprehensively at the entire theological enterprise. First of all, what can be said about theology that is inclusive enough to take into account all that we by common consensus call theology?

Even though the word *theology*, rooted in two Greek words, *theos* ("God") and *logos* ("discourse") literally means discourse about God, historically it refers to more than just casual talk about Him. The discipline called theology is the contemplative, analytical, and holistic study of the God concept. It contemplates either the concept itself (e.g., Paul Tillich's concept of God as being itself),[114] data that lead one to a concept (e.g., Gordon Kaufman's emphasis on "phenomenological description" as the first moment in theological construction),[115] or the experience of the personal God whose revelation has to do with conceptualizations (e.g., the observation of Purkiser, Taylor, and Taylor that "the opening chapters of Genesis assume that the knowledge of God comes through an encounter with God").[116] Furthermore, theology seeks to analyze logically, consistently, and coherently either the concept itself, the data informing the concept, or the revelatory data assumed to have been given by God Himself, and it attempts to do so holistically by insisting that the internal logic of the analysis be consistent with the external phenomena of that which is being analyzed and that the system set forth be coherently related to the whole field of general human discourse.

There are obviously many types of theology, some classical categories of which are natural or philosophical theology, biblical theology, dogmatic or confessional theology, historical theology, spiritual or devotional theology, systematic theology, and applied theology. Our purpose here is not to consider each and every one of these but to identify what appears on the contemporary scene to be the major frontier pertaining to these categories. The discussion in this chapter leads one to the conclusion that the major frontier has to do with whether systematic theology is to be fundamentally oriented (even though perhaps not exclusively) in the direction of a natural/philosophical/social mode of thought or in the direction of a biblical/confessional mode.

The difference between the two orientations is first and foremost a difference of focus. For instance, whereas the former is centered on either the God concept itself or the data leading one to the concept, the latter is centered on the revelatory data assumed to have been given by God Himself in Scripture and confessed by the continuing community of biblical faith. Whereas the former begins with natural, conceptual, and social data not necessarily controlled by Scripture, the latter begins with the data contained in Scripture itself and confessed by the church.[117]

Two contemporary theologians who epitomize the basic differences between these two orientations are Gordon Kaufman and Carl F. H. Henry. Whereas Henry begins with the God who reveals, Kaufman begins with phenomenological description.

In his book *God, Revelation and Authority,* Henry writes:

> Divine revelation is the source of all truth, the truth of Christianity included; reason is the instrument for recognizing it; Scripture is its verifying principle; logical consistency is a negative test for truth and coherence a subordinate test. The task of Christian theology is to exhibit the content of biblical revelation as an orderly whole.[118]

Henry goes on to discuss the dependent role of theology by saying that "the knowledge of God is both as limited and as vast a topic as God himself is in his revelation; only on the basis of God's self-disclosure is man able to make any legitimate statements whatever about him."[119]

Taking a completely different approach, Kaufman develops the idea of what he calls first-, second-, and third-order theologies. First-order theology works on the assumption that God is really out there over against us, revealing Himself to us. Therefore, the task of theology is simply to describe that revelation. Second-order theology takes into serious consideration that there are other claims to revelation, thus raising the question regarding the whole process of the human evaluation about the adequacy/inadequacy and superiority/inferiority of various claims. The crucial point in second-order theology is that the theological enterprise is conceived as a distinctively human endeavor using human criteria. Third-order theology assumes that the theological enterprise begins with us and not with a God who is out there revealing Himself. According to Kaufman, this kind of theology "must now take control (so far as possible) of our theological activity and attempt deliberately to construct our concepts and images of God and the world; and then we must seek to see human existence in terms of these symbolical constructions."[120]

Theology, then, in Kaufman's view should be thought of as being essentially "a construct of the imagination which helps to tie together, unify and interpret the totality of experience."[121]

If the positions of these two theologians are considered as the two ends of a continuum, along the line between these two points one finds other theologians who do not feel comfortable at either end but nevertheless have a kinship to both.

David Tracy, for example, in his "revisionist model" for systematic theology, attempts to revise the articulation of that which is perceived to be the best about the past and to do so in such a way that it is both relevant to and coherent with contemporary understandings. He cautions against trying to return to either a biblical past, a theological past, or a cultural past (for instance, historical liberalism). Theology, in his view, has the task of dealing with both the general human consciousness and the Christian faith. Each, however, has to be continually reinterpreted in the light of ongoing human experience. He sees "the central task of contemporary Christian theology" as being "the dramatic confrontation, the mutual illuminations and corrections, the possible basic reconciliation between the principal values, cognitive claims, and existential faiths of both a reinterpreted post-modern consciousness and a reinterpreted Christianity."[122]

This call for reinterpretation is joined by another contemporary theologian, Langdon Gilkey, who in his *Message and Existence: An Introduction to Christian Theology* appears to be particularly sensitive to the charge that reinterpretation signals "a simple 'capitulation' to modern culture."[123] He insists that reinterpretation "cuts both ways": not only are the "Christian symbols" to be reinterpreted in light of contemporary understandings, but contemporary understandings are also to be reinterpreted by the traditional Christian symbols, such as "creation or providence, incarnation and redemption."[124]

He presses his contention that reinterpretation is not capitulation by pointing out that "the view of reality is *not* naturalistic but theistic, dominated by the transcendent figure of God," and that "the view of human nature is not humanistic but classically Christian." Furthermore, "the view of redemption is Christological and not immanentist," and "the view of history is theonomous and eschatological, not autonomous and progressivist." His goal is a "*Christian* interpretation of *modern* experience" and he views Scripture and the Christian tradition as the "sources" for this work, and "various aspects of present experience" as the "resources" for this work. In other words, theologians make use of contemporary understandings for the purpose of relating the classical Christian symbols to those same understandings, as symbols of judgment, healing, and meaning.[125]

The theologian who serves as an excellent example of one who does not fit neatly into either of the two orientations being considered here, is Wolfhart Pannenberg, who while giving much evidence of being biblically oriented is at the same time oriented toward the general phenomena of history as being God's revelatory data, of which, of course, biblical history and more particularly the historical data regarding Jesus Christ are a part.[126] Pannenberg rejects three common approaches to the validation of faith: first, the biblicist approach, which claims that whatever the Bible says is true, simply because it is in the Bible; second, the special redemptive history approach, which claims that in Israel's history God revealed Himself somewhat in discontinuity from universal history; and third, the existentialist approach, which rests its assurance of faith on subjective experience. In his view the biblical data must be dealt with by the same historical method that all other historical data are. There must be no special categories for studying that which the Bible records.

It is within this frame of reference that Pannenberg studies the resurrection of Jesus, concluding that it is indeed historically substantiated in the biblical documents. The truthfulness, though, of the resurrection is fully dependent on historical investigation and is dependent neither on the fact that the Bible says it nor on personally confirming subjective experiences. Theology, then, in Pannenberg's view, is very much related to historical studies. E. Frank Tupper, a major systematizer of Pannenberg's thought, comments on the important function of research for the purpose of substantiating and validating faith. He writes as follows:

> Since the Enlightenment critique of the authority of traditions greatly intensifies the problem of religious belief, theology must strive to justify the trustworthiness of the claims of the Christian kerygma whereupon faith lives. Hence, theological knowledge, the goal of theological research, makes its contribution to faith when it convincingly provides reasons for the decision of faith.[127]

Pannenberg belongs at neither end of the continuum mentioned above. While his theological method takes the biblical record with all historical seriousness, he does not view it as the self-authenticating Word of God. Furthermore, while his approach to the theological task places an extremely high premium on human cognition regarding the analysis of and research into the stuff of human life, he nevertheless maintains that the God thus revealed is transcendently there, instead of being a mere human construct of thought. It is obvious that he fits the theological company of neither Henry nor Kaufman, but neither does he fit the company of Tracy and Gilkey in their revisionist (Tracy) and reinterpretive (Gilkey) endeavors. Pannenberg does not attempt to bring about an interpenetration of contemporary understandings with the biblical message. His aim is not to make the old message new and relevant. Rather, the task as he sees it is to validate the object of faith by the historical evidences. One might say that he collapses the continuum by placing the biblical/confessional end of it within the context of the natural/philosophical/social end and names all of it history; and then within that framework he views faith as being historically rooted and the transcendent object of faith as being a proper subject for human validation.

While for Pannenberg, theology takes place within the arena of historiography, for other contemporary theologians, the so-called political theologians, it takes place within the arena of contemporary historical action.[128] For Pannenberg, God reveals Himself in His action in history; for the political theologians, history is the place where we reveal God through our historical action.

The rise of political theology is a major development of the twentieth century, given impetus by (1) the increasing dialogue between Marxists and Christians, especially in Eastern Europe where the church has settled in to the new historical reality of living under Marxist governments;[129] (2) new sensitivity to "Christianized" forms of oppression and injustice;[130] (3) a growing dissatisfaction with that form of theological conceptualization that is unrelated to political, social, and economic realities;[131] (4) the wave of antiestablishment, antiecclesiastical, anti-Western, anticolonial, and anticapitalist sentiment;[132] (5) the new call for power among minorities, the disenfranchised, third-world peoples, and all who feel oppressed;[133] and (6) widespread frustration over the tenacity of the establishment in its pursuit of causes not generally understood and supported by the public—for instance, the Viet Nam War.[134]

Political theology is an umbrella term for all those theologies that have as their ultimate goal right action rather than merely the right conceptualization of doctrines. Political theologies understand the major motif of Scripture as being that of the liberation of the oppressed from their oppressors and the concomitant radical change of the social order for the purpose of establishing justice, equality, and the opportunity for optimum development. Furthermore, they stress the cruciality of human responsibility for helping to bring this about. Salvation, in this framework, is viewed as the reordering of social structures for the benefit of individuals and the complete obliteration of those structures that do violence to persons.

Political theologies include the theology of hope already discussed in this chapter, Jürgen Moltmann being the major representative; the theology of revolution,[135] and the theology of liberation led primarily by Roman Catholic thinkers in Latin America, and preeminently by Gustavo Gutiérrez (*A Theology of Liberation*), Hugo Assmann (*Theology for a Nomad Church*), Julio de Santa Ana (*Good News to the Poor*), Leonardo Boff (*Liberating Grace*), Juan Luis Segundo (*The Liberation of Theology*), and Paulo Freire (*Pedagogy of the Oppressed*).[136]

Included in the general category of political theologies are black theology, with thinkers like James Cone and J. Deotis Roberts,[137] and feminist theology, with leaders such as Rosemary Ruether, Virginia Mollenkott, and Rachel Conrad Wahlberg.[138]

Having surveyed the various frontiers in contemporary theology, we should ask, What *modus operandi* is compatible with the perspective with which theologians holding Wesleyan convictions work as they participate in the multifaceted theological endeavor of the universal church? I offer the following ten challenges: Those directly involved in Wesleyan theology should (1) unequivocally reaffirm its commitment to both the hearing and the living out of the whole biblical counsel of God; (2) bravely measure its own distinctive emphases according to the severe judgment of the canon of Scripture; (3) strongly resist the temptation to manipulate Scripture in order to support its own traditions; (4) critically analyze its own theological heritage in light of the understandings of the entire fellowship of the faithful; (5) creatively enunciate those biblical themes that may be missing in other Christian communities; (6) graciously understand the theological perspectives of other Christly believers; (7) consciously sensitize itself to the secular order so that it may speak forth the biblical message with even more directness; (8) humbly pursue a practical theology of loving holiness and of holy living; (9) increasingly discover and model holy ecumenicity and ecumenical holiness; and (10) earnestly devote itself both to rigorous scholarship that is baptized in disciplined spirituality and to disciplined spirituality that praises God with its rigorous scholarship.

NOTES

[1]*Verdict* (formerly *Present Truth*), ed. Robert D. Brinsmead (Fallbrook, Calif.: Verdict Publications).

[2]Cf. Helmut Thielicke, *The Evangelical Faith*, trans. and ed. Geoffrey W. Bromiley, 2 vols. (Grand Rapids: Eerdmans, 1974), vol. 1, part 1 develops two basically different approaches to doing theology: the Cartesian (Theology A), which begins with the human creature as thinker, and the Non-Cartesian (Theology B), which begins with the Divine Creator as Revealer.

[3]The three contemporary groupings of the Restoration Movement are The Christian Church (Disciples of Christ) with 1,231,061 members, Christian Churches and Churches of Christ with 1,054,266 members, and Churches of Christ with 1,600,000 members. Statistics taken from Constant H. Jacquet, Jr., ed., *Yearbook of American and Canadian Churches, 1981* (Nashville: Abingdon, 1981), pp. 226-27.

[4]Alex Haley, *Roots* (Garden Grove: Doubleday, 1976).

[5]*Verdict*, inside front page of all issues through June 1981.

[6]For introductory works on existentialism, see Wesley Barnes, *The Philosophy and Literature of Existentialism* (Woodbury, N.Y.: Barron's Educational Series, 1968); Will Herberg, *Four Existentialist Theologians: A Reader from the Work of Jacques Maritain, Nicholas Berdyaev, Martin Buber, and Paul Tillich* (Garden Grove: Doubleday, 1958); Nino Langiulli, *The Existentialist Tradition* (Garden Grove: Doubleday, 1971); John Macquarrie, *Existentialism* (Philadelphia: Westminster, 1972); J. Rodman Williams, *Contemporary Existentialism and Christian Faith* (Englewood Cliffs: Prentice-Hall, 1965).

[7]The English titles of Kierkegaard's writings are as follows: *Attack Upon Christendom; The Concept of Dread; Concluding Unscientific Postscript; Either/Or: A Fragment of Life; Fear and Trembling; For Self-Examination; Journals; Judge for Yourselves; On Authority and Revelation; Philosophical Fragments; Repetition; The Sickness Unto Death; Stages on Life's Way; Training in Christianity;* and *The Works of Love.*

[8]Martin Heidegger, *Being and Time*, trans. John Macquarrie and E. S. Robinson (New York: Harper and Row, 1962).

[9]Rudolf Bultmann, *Jesus Christ and Mythology* (New York: Scribner, 1958), p. 84.

[10]Ibid., p. 19.

[11]Rudolf Bultmann, *Theology of the New Testament*, trans. Kendrick Grobel, 2 vols. (New York: Scribner, 1951, 1955), 2:239.

[12]Ibid.

[13]Cf. Gerhard Ebeling, *The Nature of Faith*, trans. onald Gregor Smith (Philadelphia: Fortress, 1961), chapter 15, "The Future of Faith."

[14]Two excellent treatments of existentialist theology are found in the following: John Macquarrie, *Existentialism* (Philadelphia: Westminster, 1972), pp. 215-18; and Stanley T. Sutphin, *Options in Contemporary Theology* (Washington: University Press of America, 1979), chapter 4.

[15]Other English titles of Moltmann's translated works are *The Crucified God, Man,* and *The Theology of Play.*

[16]Jürgen Moltmann, "Theology as Eschatology" in Frederick Herzog, ed., *The Future of Hope* (New York: Herder and Herder, 1970), p. 10. Also see Jürgen Moltmann, *Theology of Hope*, trans. James W. Leitch (London: SCM, 1967), p. 42.

[17]Cf. M. Douglas Meeks, *Origins of the Theology of Hope* (Philadelphia: Fortress, 1974), pp. 16-19.

[18]Comprehensive treatments of process theology are found in Delwin Brown, Ralph E. James, Jr., and Gene Reeves, eds., *Process Philosophy and Christian Thought* (Indianapolis: Bobbs-Merrill, 1971); John B. Cobb, Jr., and David Ray Griffin, *Process Theology: An Introductory Exposition* (Philadelphia: Westminster, 1976); Ewert H. Cousins, ed., *Process Theology* (New York: Newman, 1971); Robert B. Mellert, *What Is Process Theology?* (New York: Paulist, 1975); and Eugene H. Peters, *The Creative Advance* (St. Louis: Bethany, 1966).

For a critique of process thought, see Robert C. Neville, *Creativity and God: A Challenge to Process Theology* (New York: Seabury, 1980). For a Wesleyan evaluation, see John Culp, "A Dialog with the Process Theology of John B. Cobb, Jr.," *Wesleyan Theological Journal*, vol. 15, no. 2 (Fall 1980): 33-44. Also Michael L. Peterson, "Orthodox Christianity, Wesleyanism, and Process Theology," *Wesleyan Theological Journal*, vol. 15, no. 2 (Fall 1980): 45-58.

[19]For further discussion of the Chicago School, see Cobb and Griffin, *Process Theology*, pp. 176-80.

[20]Major works of this Chicago foursome are:
John B. Cobb, Jr., *A Christian Natural Theology* (Philadelphia: Westminster, 1965); *Christ in a Pluralistic Society* (Philadelphia: Westminster, 1975); *God and the World* (Philadelphia: Westminster, 1969); and *The Structure of Christian Existence* (Philadelphia: Westminster, 1967).

Charles Hartshorne, *The Divine Relativity* (New Haven: Yale, 1948); *The Logic of Perfection and Other Essays in Neoclassical Metaphysics* (LaSalle, Ill.: Open Court, 1962); and *A Natural Theology for Our Time* (LaSalle, Ill.: Open Court, 1967).

Schubert M. Ogden, *Christ Without Myth* (New York: Harper and Row, 1961); and *The Reality of God* (New York: Harper and Row, 1966).

[20] Henry Nelson Wieman, *Religious Experience and Scientific Method* (New York: Macmillan, 1926); and *The Source of Human Good* (Chicago: University of Chicago Press, 1946; Carbondale: Southern Illinois University Press, 1964).

[21] Alfred North Whitehead, *Process and Reality* (New York: Macmillan, 1929), p. 521.

[22] Ibid., p. 524.

[23] Ibid.

[24] Cobb, *God and the World*, pp. 67–86.

[25] Lewis S. Ford, *The Lure of God: A Biblical Background for Process Theism* (Philadelphia: Fortress, 1978), p. 20.

[26] Ibid., p. 21.

[27] Ibid., p. 36.

[28] Cobb, *Christ in a Pluralistic Society*, p. 186.

[29] *Lure* is a word used not only in Ford's *Lure of God*, but also in Norman Pittenger, *The Lure of Divine Love: Human Experience and Christian Faith in a Process Perspective* (New York: Pilgrim, 1979).

[30] Cobb, *Christ in a Pluralistic Society*, p. 209.

[31] Whitehead, *Process and Reality*, p. 148. Also see p. 171.

[32] As Sutphin, *Options in Contemporary Theology*, p. 74, points out, Teilhard de Chardin was primarily influenced not by Whitehead but by Darwinianism and by the French philosopher Henri Bergson and his concept of process as the essential nature of man.

[33] Pierre Teilhard de Chardin, *The Phenomenon of Man* (New York: Harper Torchbooks, 1965), p. 260. Other English titles by Teilhard include *The Appearance of Man*, *The Divine Milieu*, *The Future of Man*, and *Hymn of the Universe*.

[34] Harvey Cox, *The Secular City*, 2d. ed. rev. (New York: Macmillan, 1966), p. 2.

[35] Other leading theologians associated with neoorthodoxy include Emil Brunner, Josef L. Hromádka, Reinhold Niebuhr, and T. F. Torrance.

[36] Henry P. Van Dusen in *The Vindication of Liberal Theology* (New York: Scribner, 1963) argues that liberalism should be sharply distinguished from modernism, since the former is informed by both modern thought and Christian faith and judges both by "the faith of Jesus of Nazareth" (p. 24), while the latter is a capitulation to modernity as ultimate authority (p. 23).

[37] See James Barr, *Fundamentalism* (Philadelphia: Westminster, 1978); Stewart G. Cole, *The History of Fundamentalism* (Hamden, Conn.: Archon, 1963); Norman F. Furniss, *The Fundamentalist Controversy, 1918-1931* (Hamden, Conn.: Archon, 1963); and Louis Gasper, *The Fundamentalist Movement* (The Hague: Mouton, 1963).

[38] Cox, *Secular City*, 2d. ed. rev., pp. 19–21.

[39] Ibid., pp. 22–26.

[40] Ibid., pp. 26–32.

[41] Harvey Cox, *The Seduction of the Spirit* (New York: Simon and Schuster, 1973), pp. 123–32.

[42] Dietrich Bonhoeffer, letter of June 8, 1944, *Letters and Papers from Prison*, ed. Eberhard Bethge (London: SCM, Fontana, 1963), pp. 106–7.

[43] See Thomas J. J. Altizer, *The Gospel of Christian Atheism* (Philadelphia: Westminster, 1966).

[44] See Thomas J. J. Altizer and William Hamilton, *Radical Theology and the Death of God* (New York: Bobbs-Merrill, 1966).

[45] See Gabriel Vahanian, *The Death of God* (New York: Braziller, 1961); idem, *No Other God* (New York: Braziller, 1966).

[46] See Paul M. Van Buren, *The Secular Meaning of the Gospel* (New York: Macmillan, 1963). It is, of course, not to be implied that these theologians continue to hold to all positions set forth during the sixties; for example, see Paul M. Van Buren, "Probing the Jewish-Christian Reality," *The Christian Century*, vol. 98, no. 21 (June 17–24, 1981): 665–68.

[47] Hamilton, *Radical Theology*, p. 40.

[48] Altizer, *The Gospel of Christian Atheism*, pp. 43ff.

[49] For a theological and historical analysis of death-of-God theology, see Thielicke, *Evangelical Faith*, 1:221–336.

[50] Harvey Cox, *Feast of Fools* (Cambridge: Harvard University Press, 1969); idem, *The Seduction of the Spirit* (New York: Simon and Schuster, 1973).

[51] Michael Novak, *Ascent of the Mountain* (New York: Harper and Row, 1971).

[52] Sam Keen, *To a Dancing God* (New York: Harper and Row, 1970).

[53] Sutphin, *Options in Contemporary Theology*, p. 10.

[54] David Tracy, *Blessed Rage for Order: The New Pluralism in Theology* (New York: Seabury, 1975), p. 34.

[55] Ibid., p. 71. (See also p. 148: "For the Christian religion at least, the word 'God' has a primary use or function to refer to the objective ground in reality itself for those limit-experiences of a final confidence and trust disclosed in Christian God-language.")

[56] Francis Schaeffer, *He Is There and He Is Not Silent* (Wheaton: Tyndale, 1972).

[57] Gordon D. Kaufman, *An Essay on Theological Method*, 2nd ed., rev. (Missoula, Mont.: Scholars, 1976), p. 76.

[58] For a discussion of this contemporary frontier, from an evangelical perspective, see Robert K. Johnston, "Of Tidy Doctrine and Truncated Experience," *Christianity Today*, vol. 21, no. 10 (February 18, 1977): 10 [550]–14 [554].

[59] Robert D. Brinsmead, "Christ, the Meaning of All Scripture, Life and History (Part 3)," *Verdict*, vol. 2, no. 3 (May 1979): 9.

[60] Ibid., p. 15.

[61] Robert Ashkettle's personal testimony quoted in William J. Samarin, *Tongues of Men and Angels* (New York: Macmillan, 1972), pp. 249–50.

[62] "The Chicago Call: An Approach to Evangelicals," *Christianity Today*, vol. 21, no. 18 (June 17, 1977): 28[1036]–[1037]29.

[63] Donald G. Bloesch, *Essentials of Evangelical Theology*, 2 vols. (New York: Harper and Row, 1978, 1979), 2:19.

[64] Editorial, "When Piety Prevails," *Christianity Today*, vol. 21, (July 29, 1977): 22[1122].

[65] Clark Pinnock, a Baptist, writes: "If theological rationalizing is one obstacle to realizing the blessings God has for us, another is our fear and suspicion about the Pentecostal movement. . . ." See his article "Opening the Church to the Charismatic Dimension," *Christianity Today*, vol. 25, no. 11 (June 12, 1981), 16[785].

[66] For a definitive treatment, see *A History of the Ecumenical Movement*, eds. of vol. 1 (1517–1948) Ruth Rouse and Stephen Charles Neil; ed. of vol. 2 (1948–1968) Harold E. Fey (Philadelphia: Westminster, 1967, 1970).

[67] From its inception, churches of ancient orthodoxy have been involved in the World Council of Churches.

[68] The ten cooperating denominations are African Methodist Episcopal Church, African Methodist Episcopal Zion Church, Christian Church (Disciples of Christ), Christian Methodist Episcopal Church, Episcopal Church, National Council of Community Churches, Presbyterian Church in the U. S., United Church of Christ, United Methodist Church, and United Presbyterian Church in the U.S.A.

[69] Jacquet, ed., *Yearbook of American and Canadian Churches, 1981*, p. 237.

[70] For example, see their book *The Passionate People* (Waco: Word, 1979). The nature of the togetherness they espouse is indicated by their common commitment to tell "about a compassionate God who is calling together a band, a family, of passionate people to find out how to live together and to love a world and a church which is terrified of pain, difficulty, and rejection," p. 233.

[71] Titles of his books include *Intimacy, With Open Hands, The Wounded Healer, Aging,* and *Reaching Out*. In the latter (Garden City: Doubleday, 1975) he develops three human movements: from loneliness to solitude, from hostility to hospitality, from illusion to prayer.

[72] See her *Transformation of Man* (Paramus, N.J.: Paulist Press, Deus Books, 1967).

[73] Harold Lindsell, *The Battle for the Bible* (Grand Rapids: Zondervan, 1976), p. 107.

[74] Fuller Theological Seminary has been a major object of Lindsell's criticism. For the Fuller response, see the seminary's publication, *Theology, News and Notes*, Special Issue (1976).

[75] "Christians Debate Response to Electronic Church," *NCCC Chronicles*, vol. 80, no. 1 (Spring Issue): 4.

[76] Howard A. Snyder, *The Community of the King* (Downers Grove: InterVarsity, 1978).

[77] Karl Rahner, *The Shape of the Church to Come* (New York: Seabury, 1974).

[78] G. C. Berkouwer, *The Church*, trans. James E. Davison (Grand Rapids: Eerdmans, 1976).

[79] Melvin L. Hodges, *A Theology of the Church and Its Mission* (Springfield, Mo.: Gospel, 1977).

[80] Jürgen Moltmann, *The Church in the Power of the Spirit*, trans. Margaret Kohl (New York: Harper and Row, 1977).

[81] Additional representative resources that treat ecclesial theology are Donald F. Durnbaugh, *The Believers' Church* (New York: Macmillan, 1968); Edward Farley, *Ecclesial Man* (Philadelphia: Fortress, 1975); François G. Gérard, *The Future of the Church: The Theology of Renewal of Willem Adolf Visser't Hooft* (Pittsburgh: Pickwick, 1974); and John P. Schanz, *A Theology of Community* (Washington: University Press of America, 1977). For a portrait of the view of ecclesial community taken by the Church of the Saviour in Washington, D. C., see Elizabeth O'Conner, *The New Community* (New York: Harper and Row, 1976).

[82] See the definition of classical Protestantism in the glossary at the end of this chapter.

[83] See A. James Rudin and Marcia R. Rudin, *Prison or Paradise? The New Religious Cults* (Philadelphia: Fortress, 1980), pp. 15–16, "After an extensive study, Drs. Egon Mayer and Laura Kitch, sociologists at Brooklyn College, concluded that since 1956 more than thirteen hundred new religious groups have appeared in America." Also, "Flo Conway and Jim Siegelman, authors of *Snapping* [(New York: J. B. Lippincott, 1978), p. 12], assert there are perhaps as many as 3 million past and present cult members in America alone."

[84] Joel McCollam, *Carnival of Souls* (New York: Seabury, 1979).

[85] Herbert F. Beck, *How to Respond to the Cults* (St. Louis: Concordia, 1977).

[86] See Ronald Enroth, *The Lure of the Cults* (Chappaqua, N.Y.: Christian Herald Books, 1979); James W. Sire, *Scripture Twisting: Twenty Ways Cults Misread the Bible* (Downers Grove: InterVarsity, 1980); and Jack Sparks, *The Mind Benders* (Nashville: Nelson, 1977). For a treatment of heterodoxy throughout the world, e.g., Kimbanguism in Africa, the Iglesia ni Christo in the Philippines, and the United Pen-

[87] tecostal Church (Jesus Only) in South America, see David J. Hesselgrave, ed., *Dynamic Religious Movements* (Grand Rapids: Baker, 1978). Two sources for this type of Christian apologetics are: Spiritual Counterfeits Project, Box 4308, Berkeley, CA 74704; and InterVarsity Press, Downers Grove, IL 60515.

[87] See "Cracking Down on the Big Ones," *Time* (December 31, 1979), p. 63; and "Küng Unrepentant," *Time* (January 21, 1980), p. 50.

[88] See the glossary at the end of this chapter for the Chalcedonian Symbol.

[89] Edward Schillebeeckx, *Jesus: An Experiment in Christology*, trans. John Bowden (New York: Seabury, 1980). Schillebeeckx's eucharistic creed, in the epilogue of his book, has this paragraph on Jesus Christ: "I believe in Jesus Christ, the only-beloved Son of God. For love of all of us, he has willed to share our history, our existence with us. I believe that God also wanted to be our God in a human way. He has dwelt as man among us, a light in the darkness. But the darkness did not overcome him. We nailed him to the cross. And he died and was buried. But he trusted in God's final word, and is risen, once and for all; he said that he would prepare a place for us, in his Father's house, where he now dwells" (p. 847).
Cf. the Chalcedonian Symbol, in the glossary at the end of this chapter, for traditional affirmations missing in the above statement.

[90] Hans Küng, *On Being a Christian*, trans. Edward Quinn (Garden City: Doubleday, 1976), p. 449.

[91] Ibid., pp. 449–50.

[92] Karl Rahner, *Theological Investigations*, trans. David Bourke, 16 vols. (New York: Seabury, 1975), 13:213–19. Also, see his *Foundations of Christianity*, trans. William V. Dych (New York: Seabury, 1978); and Rahner and William Thüsing, *A New Christology*, trans. David Smith and Verdant Green (New York: Seabury, 1980).

[93] Walter Kasper, *Jesus the Christ*, trans. Verdant Green (London: Burns and Oates, 1976), p. 247.

[94] John E. Hartley and R. Larry Shelton, eds., *Wesleyan Theological Perspectives*, 3 vols. (Anderson: Warner). Volume 1, *An Inquiry into Soteriology from a Biblical Theological Perspective*, was published in 1981. Volume 2 will be on hermeneutics, and volume 3 on pneumatology.

[95] Joseph Blenkinsopp, *Prophecy and Canon* (Notre Dame: University of Notre Dame Press, 1977), p. 142.

[96] See K. Grobel, "Biblical Criticism," in *The Interpreter's Dictionary of the Bible*, ed., George Arthur Buttrick, 4 vols. (New York: Abingdon, 1962), 1:407–13. Also, S. J. DeVries, "History of Biblical Criticism," *Interpreter's Dictionary of the Bible*, 1:413–18.

[97] For an introduction to form criticism, see K. Grobel, "Form Criticism," *Interpreter's Dictionary of the Bible*, 2:320–21. "Form criticism . . . is a method of dealing with folk material, whether written down or not, which for some part of its existence was oral tradition" (p. 320).

[98] For an introduction and full discussion of redaction criticism, see Norman Perrin, *What Is Redaction Criticism?* (Philadelphia: Fortress, 1969). Redaction criticism "is concerned with studying the theological motivation of an author as this is revealed in the collection, arrangement, editing, and modification of traditional material and in the composition of new material or the creation of new forms within the traditions of early Christianity" (p. 1).

[99] For a conservative critique of biblical criticism, see R. K. Harrison et al., *Biblical Criticism: Historical, Literary and Textual* (Grand Rapids: Zondervan, 1978); and Gerhard Maier, *The End of the Historical-Critical Method* (St. Louis: Concordia, 1977).

[100] Blenkinsopp, *Prophecy and Canon*, p. 139.

[101] Ibid., pp. 151–52.

[102] George W. Coats and Burke O. Long, eds., *Canon and Authority* (Philadelphia: Fortress, 1977), p. x. Other contributors to this volume include Peter R. Ackroyd of University of London, Bernhard W. Anderson of Princeton Seminary, Ronald E. Clements of Cambridge, Paul D. Hanson of Harvard, Rolf P. Knierim and James A. Sanders both of Claremont, Wayne Sibley Towner of Union in Virginia, and Gene M. Tucker of Emory.

[103] Bernhard W. Anderson, "A Stylistic Study of the Priestly Creation Story," in Coats and Long, *Canon and Authority*, p. 162.

[104] Ibid., p. 161.

[105] Bernhard W. Anderson, *The Living Word of the Bible* (Philadelphia: Westminster, 1979), p. 29. In a rhetorical question about preaching on Genesis 22, the story of Abraham's testing, Anderson asks, "Would you say that you are taking your text from the Elohist, though admitting to yourself (not to the congregation!) that the document is a reconstruction from fragments and, if it existed, may not actually reflect the historical situation of Elijah's time? Would you say that you are going back, via form criticism, into the preliterary stages of tradition and concentrating on one of the presumed layers of tradition?"

[106] David H. Kelsey, *The Uses of Scripture in Recent Theology* (Philadelphia: Fortress, 1975), p. 106.

[107] Coats and Long, *Canon and Authority*, p. x.

[108] An example is Robert Duncan Culver, *The Life of Christ* (Grand Rapids: Baker, 1976).

[109] An example is Norman Perrin, *The New Testament: An Introduction* (New York: Harcourt, Brace Jovanovich, 1974).

[110] An example is Sam Keen, *Apology for Wonder* (New York: Harper and Row, 1969) and *To a Dancing God* (1970). For a short introduction to Keen's

perspective, see Sutphin, *Options in Contemporary Theology*, pp. 13-19.

[111] Two examples, the first systematically oriented and the second canonically oriented, are: W. T. Purkiser, Richard S. Taylor and Willard H. Taylor, *God, Man, and Salvation: A Biblical Theology* (Kansas City: Beacon Hill, 1977); and Brevard S. Childs, *Introduction to the Old Testament as Scripture* (Philadelphia: Fortress, 1979). See also Paul J. Achtemeier, *The Inspiration of Scripture: Problems and Proposals* (Philadelphia: Westminster, 1980); Sidney Greidanus, *Sola Scriptura: Problems and Principles in Preaching Historical Texts* (Toronto: Wedge, 1979); and James D. Smart, *The Past, Present, and Future of Biblical Theology* (Philadelphia: Westminster, 1979).

[112] Smart, *Past, Present, and Future*, p. 148.

[113] Childs, *Introduction to the Old Testament as Scripture*, p. 16. See also his earlier *Biblical Theology in Crisis* (Philadelphia: Westminster, 1970).

[114] Paul Tillich, *Systematic Theology*, 3 vols. (Chicago: University of Chicago Press, 1951-1963), 1:235ff.

[115] Kaufman, *Essay on Theological Method*, p. 64.

[116] Purkiser, Taylor, and Taylor, *God, Man, and Salvation*, p. 43.

[117] For a discussion of dogmatic or confessional theology, see Paul G. Schrotenboer, "The Role of Theology in the Church (a Reformed understanding)," in *The Nature of the Church and the Role of Theology* (Geneva: World Council of Churches and the Reformed Ecumenical Synod, 1976), pp. 25-27.

[118] Carl F. H. Henry, *God, Revelation and Authority*, 4 vols. (Waco: Word, 1976), 1:215.

[119] Ibid., p. 216.

[120] Kaufman, *Essay on Theological Method*, p. 38. Cf. pp. xi, 6, 15, 55, and 64. Cf. his earlier *Systematic Theology: A Historicist Perspective* (New York: Scribner, 1968), chap. 2 on "The Concept of Revelation."

[121] Ibid., p. 43.

[122] Tracy, *Blessed Rage for Order*, p. 32.

[123] Langdon Gilkey, *Message and Existence: An Introduction to Christian Theology* (New York: Seabury, 1979), p. 59.

[124] Ibid.

[125] Ibid.

[126] See especially Wolfhart Pannenberg, *Basic Questions in Theology: Collected Essays*, trans. George H. Kehm, vol. 1 (Philadelphia: Westminster, 1968); Wolfhart Pannenberg, ed., *Revelation as History*, trans. David Granskou (New York: Macmillan, 1968).

[127] E. Frank Tupper, *The Theology of Wolfhart Pannenberg* (Philadelphia: Westminster, 1973), pp. 20-21. Cf. Clark H. Pinnock, "Pannenberg's Theology: Reasonable Happenings in History," *Christianity Today*, vol. 21, no. 3 (November 5, 1976): 19 [147]; and "No-Nonsense Theology: Pinnock Reviews Pannenberg," *Christianity Today*, vol. 21, no. 4 (November 19, 1976): 14[218]. Also cf. Laurence W. Wood, "Presidential Address: History and Hermeneutics: A Pannenbergian Perspective," *Wesleyan Theological Journal*, vol. 16, no. 1 (Spring 1981): 7-22.

[128] For general introductions to political theology, see André Dumas, *Political Theology and the Life of the Church*, trans. John Bowden (Philadelphia: Westminster, 1978); Alfredo Fierro, *The Militant Gospel: A Critical Introduction to Political Theologies*, trans. John Drury (Maryknoll: Orbis, 1977); Alistair Kee, ed., *A Reader in Political Theology* (Philadelphia: Westminster, (1974); Dorothee Sölle, *Political Theology*, trans. John Shelley (Philadelphia: Fortress, 1974); Theology in the Americas, *Is Liberation Theology for North America? The Response of First World Churches* (New York: Theology in the Americas, 1978); and Sergio Torres and Virginia Fabella, eds., *The Emergent Gospel: Theology from the Underside: Papers from the Ecumenical Dialogue of Third World Theologians, Dar es Salaam, August 5-12, 1976* (Maryknoll: Orbis, 1978). For a Wesleyan critique, see Harold B. Kuhn, "Liberation Theology: A Semantic Approach," *Wesleyan Theological Journal*, vol. 15, no. 1 (Spring 1980): 34-45.

[129] For a full discussion, see Peter Hebblethwaite, *The Christian-Marxist Dialogue: Beginnings, Present Status, and Beyond* (New York: Paulist, 1977).

[130] For example, see James H. Cone, *God of the Oppressed* (New York: Seabury, 1975).

[131] See discussion in Gustavo Gutiérrez, *A Theology of Liberation*, trans. and ed., Sister Caridad Inda and John Eagleson (Maryknoll: Orbis, 1973), especially pp. 3-13. For a critique of the position taken by G. Gutiérrez, see Juan Gutiérrez, *The New Libertarian Gospel: Pitfalls of the Theology of Liberation*, trans. Paul Burns (Chicago: Franciscan Herald, 1977), especially pp. 1-36.

[132] An example of a severe critique of capitalism is William R. Coats, *God in Public: Political Theology Beyond Niebuhr* (Grand Rapids: Eerdmans, 1974).

Much third-world theology is predicated on the conscious need to distance indigenous theology from Western theology; for example, see Gerald H. Anderson, ed., *Asian Voices in Christian Theology* (Maryknoll: Orbis, 1976); Choan-Seng Song, *Third-Eye Theology: Theology in Formation in Asian Settings* (Maryknoll: Orbis, 1979); John S. Pobee, *Toward an African Theology* (Nashville: Abingdon, 1979); and Kofi Appiah-Kubi and Sergio Torres, eds., *African Theology en Route, Papers from the Pan-African Conference of Third World Theologians, December 17-23, 1977, Accra, Ghana* (Maryknoll: Orbis, 1979).

[133] An example is Julio de Santa Ana, *Good News*

to the Poor: The Challenge of the Poor in the History of the Church (Maryknoll: Orbis, 1979). Also see Santa Ana, ed., *Separation Without Hope: The Church and the Poor During the Industrial Revolution and Colonial Expansion* (Maryknoll: Orbis, 1980).

[134]Cf. Coats, *God in Public*, pp. 157-73.

[135]For an analysis, see J. G. Davies, *Christians, Politics and Violent Revolution* (Maryknoll: Orbis, 1976).

[136]For an introduction to these and other leaders, see Rosino Gibellini, ed., *Frontiers of Theology in Latin America*, trans. John Drury (Maryknoll: Orbis, 1979).

[137]See Gayraud S. Wilmore and James H. Cone, *Black Theology: A Documentary History, 1966-1979* (Maryknoll: Orbis, 1979).

[138]For a general discussion of liberation theology from various perspectives—black, feminist, native American, and others—see Gerald H. Anderson and Thomas F. Stransky, *Mission Trends No. 4: Liberation Theologies in North America and Europe* (New York: Paulist, 1979). See especially pp. 175-243 for a feminist perspective and bibliographical data.

GLOSSARY OF SPECIAL TERMS

Chalcedonian Symbol (451) refers to the formal statement issued by the Fourth Ecumenical Council in 451, regarding the humanity and divinity of Jesus Christ. It reads as follows:

> In agreement, therefore, with the holy fathers, we all unanimously teach that we should confess that our Lord Jesus Christ is one and the same Son, the same perfect in Godhead and the same perfect in manhood, truly God and truly man, the same of a rational soul and body, consubstantial with the Father in Godhead, and the same consubstantial with us in manhood, like us in all things except sin; begotten from the Father before the ages as regards His Godhead; and in the last days, the same, because of us and because of our salvation begotten from the Virgin Mary, the *Theotokos*, as regards His manhood; one and the same Christ, Son, Lord, only begotten, made known in two natures without confusion, without change, without division, without separation, the difference of the natures being by no means removed because of the union, but the property of each nature being preserved and coalescing in one *prosopon* and one *hupostasis*—not parted or divided into two *prosopa*, but one and the same Son, only-begotten, divine Word, the Lord Jesus Christ, as the prophets of old and Jesus Christ Himself have taught us about Him and the creed of our fathers has handed down. [Quoted from J. N. D. Kelly, *Early Christian Doctrines*, 2nd ed. (New York: Harper and Row, 1960), pp. 339-40.]

Classical Protestantism as it is used here refers not only to those churches having their ecclesiastical inception in the sixteenth-century Reformation (e.g., Lutheran, Reformed) but also all those churches of later ecclesiastical origin (e.g., Methodist, Disciples, Pentecostals) that, even though stressing additional doctrinal emphases, nevertheless remain true to basic Protestant positions.

Ecclesial Communities is a term used in this chapter to refer to any type of Christian fellowship that takes institutional form—whether denominations, movements, hierarchies, brotherhoods and or sisterhoods, trans-, non-, or undenominational organizations. It refers to any kind of institutional form that church life takes.

Orthodoxy means belief that is considered by a particular ecclesial community to be not only right, but officially approved. More particularly, Christian orthodoxy refers to the central tenets of faith held by all three major branches of the church—Roman Catholic, Eastern Orthodox, and Classical Protestant. (See a delineation of these central tenets in the text of this chapter, Part II, Section C.)

Systematic Theology as it is used in this chapter refers to the contemplative, analytical, and holistic study of the God concept as set forth in Scripture, variously interpreted by the church throughout history, experienced in the community of faith, and critically reviewed in light of contemporary concerns both pastoral and societal. (See the discussion of theology in the text of this chapter, Part II, Section B.)

DISCUSSION QUESTIONS

1. What is your understanding of the starting point for that form of theological thinking that is distinctively Christian? Is it the teaching ministry of your ecclesial community? the Bible? Christ? the historic confessions of the church? Christian experience? contemporary thought? philosophical analysis? the phenomenology of life? history? some other?

2. At the beginning of the chapter it was suggested that the challenge facing contemporary theologians is to determine which interfacing perspectives discussed call for exclusive demarcation, which call for complementation, and which call for integration. As you view these contemporary frontiers, discuss particular needs for exclusive demarcation, for complementation, and for integration.
3. Concerning the matter of interest in the historical events spoken of in the Bible, what is the basic difference between a Fundamentalist's aim and that of a Pannenbergian?
4. In your view, what is the relationship between pastness, presentness, and futurity in biblical religion?
5. Discuss the values and the problems of process thought in the light of biblical understandings.
6. To what extent do you agree or disagree with the view of the theologians of radical secularization that the world has "come of age" and is consequently responsible to take care of itself, rather than being dependent on God?
7. According to your understanding of Wesleyan theology, what is the relationship between the objectification of the gospel (the out-there-ness) and the subjectification of it (the in-here-ness)? What would you say about the relationship of the two as evidenced in the congregational life of Wesleyan-oriented churches? Are any correctives needed?
8. What degree of apartness among believers makes their witness to the gospel ineffective? What degree of togetherness compromises too many convictional and doctrinal matters?
9. Discuss the importance of christology in relationship to ecclesiology, soteriology, pneumatology, and eschatology.
10. Discuss whether in your view your own ecclesial community is sufficiently appreciative of essential Christian orthodoxy so that it is sensitive to heterodoxical positions that seriously compromise the essence of Christian thought. Does there seem to be more concern in your community over essentially Wesleyan (or Lutheran, Reformed, Anglican, Catholic, as the case may be) denominational orthodoxy? What place should right doctrine play in the life of the church?
11. In your view, to what extent are the historical-critical method of biblical scholarship and canonical (i.e., biblical) theology compatible or incompatible? Must one of them inevitably compromise the other?

RECOMMENDATIONS FOR FURTHER READING

Anderson, Gerald H., ed. *Asian Voices in Christian Theology*. Maryknoll: Orbis, 1976.

Appiah-Kubi, Kofi, and Torres, Sergio, eds. *African Theology en Route*. Maryknoll: Orbis, 1979.

Coats, George W., and Long, Burke O., eds. *Canon and Authority*. Philadelphia: Fortress, 1977.

Coats, William R. *God in Public: Political Theology Beyond Niebuhr*. Grand Rapids: Eerdmans, 1974.

Culp, John. "A Dialog with the Process Theology of John B. Cobb, Jr.," *Wesleyan Theological Journal*, vol. 15, no. 2 (Fall 1980): 33-44.

Ford, Lewis S. *The Lure of God: A Biblical Background for Process Theism*. Philadelphia: Fortress, 1978.

Gundry, Stanley N., and Johnson, Alan F. *Tensions in Contemporary Theology*. Chicago: Moody, 1979.

Hall, Thor. "Does Systematic Theology Have a Future?" *The Christian Century* (March 17, 1976), pp. 253-56.

Heron, Alasdair. *A Century of Protestant Theology*. Philadelphia: Westminster, 1980.

Kantzer, Kenneth S., and Gundry, Stanley N., eds. *Perspectives on Evangelical Theology*. Grand Rapids: Baker, 1979.

Kuhn, Harold B. "Liberation Theology: A Semantic Approach," *Wesleyan Theological Journal*, vol. 15, no. 1 (Spring 1980): 34-45.

MacCollam, Joel A. *Carnival of Souls: Religious Cults and Young People*. New York: Seabury, 1979.

Meeks, M. Douglas. *Origins of the Theology of Hope*. Philadelphia: Fortress, 1974.

Neville, Robert C. *Creativity and God: A Challenge to Process Theology*. New York: Seabury, 1980.

Oden, Thomas C. *Agenda for Theology*. San Francisco: Harper and Row, 1979.

Peterson, Michael L. "Orthodox Christianity, Wesleyanism, and Process Theology," *Wesleyan Theological Journal*, vol. 15, no. 2 (Fall 1980): 45-58.

Ryan, Michael D., ed. *The Contemporary Explosion of Theology*. Metuchen, N.J.: Scarecrow, 1975.

Smart, James D. *The Past, Present, and Future of Biblical Theology*. Philadelphia: Westminster, 1979.

Staples, Rob L. "The Present Frontiers of Wesleyan Theology," *Wesleyan Theological Journal* 12 (Spring 1977): 5-15.

Sutphin, Stanley T. *Options in Contemporary Theology*. Washington: University Press of America, 1979.

Thielicke, Helmut. *The Evangelical Faith*. Vol. 1: *Prolegomena: The Relation of Theology to Modern Thought-Forms*. Trans. and ed. Geoffrey W. Bromiley. Grand Rapids: Eerdmans, 1974.

Tupper, E. Frank. *The Theology of Wolfhart Pannenberg*. Philadelphia: Westminister, 1973.

Wilmore, Gayraud S. and Cone, James H. *Black Theology: A Documentary History, 1966-1979*. Maryknoll: Orbis, 1979.

BIBLIOGRAPHY

The rationale for the following entries is that these works introduce one to the broad dynamics of the theological frontiers identified in this chapter. Instead of listing in this bibliography the significant works of the contemporary theologians under consideration, they are referred to throughout the whole chapter, either in the text or in the documentations within the framework of the relevant discussion.

Anderson, Gerald H., ed. *Asian Voices in Christian Theology*. Maryknoll: Orbis, 1976.

Anderson, Gerald H., and Stransky, Thomas F. *Mission Trends No. 4: Liberation Theologies in North America and Europe*. New York: Paulist, 1979.

Appiah-Kubi, Kofi, and Torres, Sergio, eds. *African Theology en Route*. Maryknoll: Orbis, 1979.

Barr, James. *Fundamentalism*. Philadelphia: Westminster, 1978.

Berger, Peter L. and Neuhaus, Richard John. *Against the World for the World: The Hartford Appeal and the Future of American Religion*. New York: Seabury, 1976.

Bloesch, Donald G. *The Invaded Church*. Waco: Word, 1975.

Brown, Robert McAfee. *Frontiers for the Church Today*. New York: Oxford University Press, 1973.

Childs, Brevard S. *Biblical Theology in Crisis*. Philadelphia: Westminster, 1970.

Coats, George W., and Long, Burke O., eds. *Canon and Authority*. Philadelphia: Fortress, 1977.

Coats, William R. *God in Public: Political Theology Beyond Niebuhr*. Grand Rapids: Eerdmans, 1974.

Cobb, John B., Jr., and Griffin, David Ray. *Process Theology: An Introductory Exposition*. Philadelphia: Westminster, 1976.

Conn, Harvie M. *Contemporary World Theology: A Layman's Guidebook*. Nutley, N.J.: Presbyterian and Reformed, 1973.

Cox, Harvey. *The Seduction of the Spirit: The Use and Misuse of People's Religion*. New York: Simon and Schuster, 1973.

Culp, John. "A Dialog with the Process Theology of John B. Cobb, Jr.," *Wesleyan Theological Journal*, vol. 15, no. 2 (Fall 1980): 33-44.

Curtis, C. J. *Contemporary Protestant Thought*. New York: Bruce, 1970.

Davies, J. G. *Christians, Politics and Violent Revolution*. Maryknoll: Orbis, 1976.

Dumas, Andre. *Political Theology*. Translated by John Bowden. Philadelphia: Westminster, 1978.

Fierro, Alfredo. *The Militant Gospel: A Critical Introduction to Political Theologies*. Translated by John Drury. Maryknoll: Orbis, 1977.

Ford, Lewis S. *The Lure of God: A Biblical Background for Process Theism*. Philadelphia: Fortress, 1978.

Gibellini, Rosino, ed. *Frontiers of Theology in Latin America*. Maryknoll: Orbis, 1979.

Griffin, David Ray, and Altizer, Thomas J. J., eds. *John Cobb's Theology in Process*. Philadelphia: Westminster, 1977.

Grounds, Vernon C. *Revolution and the Christian Faith*. Philadelphia: Lippincott, 1971.

Gundry, Stanley N., and Johnson, Alan F. *Tensions in Contemporary Theology*. Chicago: Moody, 1979.

Hall, Douglas John. *Lighten Our Darkness: Toward an Indigenous Theology of the Cross*. Philadelphia: Westminster, 1976.

Hall, Thor. "Does Systematic Theology Have a Future?" *The Christian Century,* vol. 93, no. 9 (March 17, 1976): 253–56.

Hartt, Julian N. *Theological Method and Imagination.* New York: Seabury, 1977.

Healey, F. G., ed. *Preface to Christian Studies.* London: Lutterworth, 1971.

Hebblethwaite, Peter. *The Christian-Marxist Dialogue: Beginnings, Present Status, and Beyond.* New York: Paulist, 1977.

Heron, Alasdair. *A Century of Protestant Theology.* Philadelphia: Westminster, 1980.

Herzog, Frederick, ed. *The Future of Hope.* New York: Herder and Herder, 1970.

Hesselgrave, David J., ed. *Dynamic Religious Movements.* Grand Rapids, Baker, 1978.

Hordern, William. *New Directions in Theology Today.* Philadelphia: Westminster, 1976.

Houlden, J. L. *Patterns of Faith: A Study in the Relationship between the New Testament and Christian Doctrine.* Philadelphia: Fortress, 1977.

Jossua, Jean-Pierre, and Metz, Johann Baptist, eds. *Doing Theology in New Places.* New York: Seabury, 1979.

Kantzer, Kenneth S., and Gundry, Stanley N., eds. *Perspectives on Evangelical Theology.* Grand Rapids: Baker, 1979.

Kaufman, Gordon D. *An Essay on Theological Method.* Rev. ed. Missoula, Mont.: Scholars, 1979.

Kee, Alistair, ed. *A Reader in Political Theology.* Philadelphia: Westminster, 1974.

Kelsey, David H. *The Uses of Scripture in Recent Theology.* Philadelphia: Fortress, 1975.

Kuhn, Harold B. "Liberation Theology: A Semantic Approach," *Wesleyan Theological Journal,* vol. 15, no. 1 (Spring 1980): 34–45.

MacCollam, Joel A. *Carnival of Souls: Religious Cults and Young People.* New York: Seabury, 1979.

McCool, Gerald A., ed. *A Rahner Reader.* New York: Seabury, 1975.

Macquarrie, John. *Existentialism.* Philadelphia: Westminster, 1972.

McFadden, Thomas M., ed. *Liberation, Revolution, and Freedom: Theological Perspectives.* New York: Seabury, 1975.

McKelway, Alexander, and Willis, E. David. *The Context of Contemporary Theology: Essays in Honor of Paul Lehmann.* Atlanta: John Knox, 1974.

Meeks, M. Douglas. *Origins of the Theology of Hope.* Philadelphia: Fortress, 1974.

Metz, Rene, and Schlick, Jean, eds. *Liberation Theology and the Message of Salvation.* Translated by David G. Gelzer. Pittsburgh: Pickwick, 1978.

Miller, Randolph Crump. *The American Spirit in Theology.* Philadelphia: Pilgrim, 1974.

The Nature of the Church and the Role of Theology: Papers from a Consultation between the World Council of Churches and the Reformed Ecumenical Synod, Geneva 1975. Geneva: World Council of Churches and the Reformed Ecumenical Synod, 1976.

Neville, Robert C. *Creativity and God: A Challenge to Process Theology.* New York: Seabury, 1980.

Oden, Thomas C. *Agenda for Theology.* San Francisco: Harper and Row, 1979.

Peterson, Michael L. "Orthodox Christianity, Wesleyanism, and Process Theology," *Wesleyan Theological Journal,* vol. 15, no. 2 (Fall 1980): 45–58.

―――――. "Theology and Linguistic Analysis in the Twentieth Century," *Western Theological Journal,* vol. 15, no. 1 (Spring 1980): 19–33.

Pinson, William M., Jr., and Fant, Clyde E., Jr., eds. *Contemporary Christian Trends: Perspectives on the Present.* Waco: Word, 1972.

Pobee, John S. *Toward an African Theology.* Nashville: Abingdon, 1979.

Rogers, Jack B., and McKim, Donald K. *The Authority and Interpretation of the Bible: An Historical Approach.* San Francisco: Harper and Row, 1979.

Rudin, A. James, and Rudin, Marcia R. *Prison or Paradise? The New Religious Cults.* Philadelphia: Fortress, 1980.

Ryan, Michael D., ed. *The Contemporary Explosion of Theology.* Metuchen, N.J.: Scarecrow, 1975.

Sider, Ronald J., ed. *The Chicago Declaration.* Carol Stream, Ill.: Creation, 1974.

Smart, James D. *The Past, Present, and Future of Biblical Theology*. Philadelphia: Westminster, 1979.

Song, Choan-Seng. *Third-Eye Theology: Theology in Formation in Asian Settings*. Maryknoll: Orbis, 1979.

Song, Choan-Seng, ed. *Doing Theology Today*. Madras: The Christian Literature Society, 1976.

Staples, Rob L. "The Present Frontiers of Wesleyan Theology," *Wesleyan Theological Journal* 12 (Spring 1977): 5-15.

Sutphin, Stanley T. *Options in Contemporary Theology*. Washington: University Press of America, 1979.

Swidler, Leonard, ed. *Consensus in Theology? A Dialogue with Hans Küng and Edward Schillebeeckx*. Philadelphia: Westminster, 1980.

Sykes, Stephen. *An Introduction to Christian Theology Today*. Atlanta: John Knox, 1971.

Thielicke, Helmut. *The Evangelical Faith*. Vol. 1: *Prolegomena: The Relation of Theology to Modern-Thought-Forms*. Translated and edited by Geoffrey W. Bromiley. Grand Rapids: Eerdmans, 1974.

Tracy, David. *Blessed Rage for Order: The New Pluralism in Theology*. New York: Seabury, 1975.

Tupper, E. Frank. *The Theology of Wolfhart Pannenberg*. Philadelphia: Westminster, 1973.

Wiles, Maurice. *What Is Theology?* London: Oxford University Press, 1976.

Wilmore, Gayraud S., and Cone, James H. *Black Theology: A Documentary History, 1966-1979*. Maryknoll: Orbis, 1979.

Wingren, Gustaf. *Creation and Gospel: The New Situation in European Theology*. New York: Mellen, 1979.

Wood, Laurence W. "Presidential Address: History and Hermeneutics: A Pannenbergian Perspective," *Wesleyan Theological Journal*, vol. 16, no. 1 (Spring 1981): 7-22.

CHAPTER 2

HISTORICAL AND MODERN SIGNIFICANCE OF WESLEYAN THEOLOGY

Richard S. Taylor

Richard S. Taylor is a retired pastor, evangelist, missionary, and seminary professor. He received the M.A. degree from Pasadena College and the Th.D. degree from Boston University School of Theology. He spent eight years as founder and head of the Nazarene Bible College in Australia and sixteen years as Professor of Theology and Missions at Nazarene Theological Seminary in Kansas City, Missouri.

Dr. Taylor has written a number of books including the following: A Right Conception of Sin, The Disciplined Life-Style, Miracle of Joy, Life in the Spirit, Biblical Authority and Christian Faith, *and* Return to Christian Culture. *He has also written numerous articles on the Christian life. At the present time he is completing his editorial work on the* Beacon Dictionary of Theology. *He is a member of the Christian Holiness Association, the Evangelical Theological Society, and the Wesleyan Theological Society.*

CONTENTS

INTRODUCTION / 55

  I. THE HOLINESS MOTIF BEFORE WESLEY / 56
  - **A.** Apostolic Fathers / 56
  - **B.** Later Church Fathers and Movements / 57
  - **C.** The Medieval and Reformation Periods / 59

  II. TRIBUTARY STREAMS IN THE HOLINESS QUEST / 62
  - **A.** Puritanism / 62
  - **B.** Pietism / 62
  - **C.** Arminianism / 63

  III. A MEDIATING THEOLOGY / 64

  IV. WESLEYAN THEOLOGY IN MODERN TIMES / 65

  V. SOME SUMMARY OBSERVATIONS / 66
  - **A.** The Universal Instinct for Holiness / 66
  - **B.** A Second Crisis Normative / 66
  - **C.** Holiness and Revival / 67
  - **D.** Holiness and Social Reform / 67
  - **E.** Holiness and Education / 67
  - **F.** The Contemporary Challenge / 67

NOTES / 68

DISCUSSION QUESTIONS / 70

RECOMMENDATIONS FOR FURTHER READING / 70

BIBLIOGRAPHY / 71

Historical and Modern Significance of Wesleyan Theology

INTRODUCTION

In order to trace the historical significance of Wesleyan Theology it will be helpful to encapsulate it into a single motif. R. Newton Flew identified this as "perfection" and traced it superbly in his classic volume, *The Idea of Perfection in Christian Theology*.[1] His subtitle reveals his concept of perfection—"An Historical Study of the Christian Ideal for the Present Life." In a masterly way Flew succeeded in demonstrating that the idea of perfection is neither an aberration nor an appendage in the Christian religion but lies at the very heart of the New Testament and of Christian thought at its best, from the apostles to Wesley.

In her *Theology of Love* Mildred Bangs Wynkoop has attempted in more recent times to compress Wesleyanism into the motif of love, or at least to see love as the hermeneutical principle for determining the lines of authentic Wesleyan theology. In an admirable way she has distilled the essence of Wesley's moral concern, viz., that religion must be moral and that Christians must be holy not merely by imputation but in reality. Her approach may have oversimplified Wesley, however, resulting in less than justice to some facets of Wesley's thought, such as his rigorous belief in original sin as an inherited defect in human nature as fallen.

Any such attempt to see Wesleyanism through a single lens runs the risk of distorting or excluding important strands of doctrine. Wesley himself insisted that his doctrines were not novel nor deviant but basic historical and biblical Christianity. Yet there were special emphases and tenets that marked them off from pure Lutheranism, Calvinism, or even Anglicanism. Philip S. Watson summarizes normative Wesleyanism by four propositions: (1) All men need to be saved; (2) all men can be saved; (3) all men can know they are saved; and (4) all men can be saved to the uttermost.[2]

If one proposition more than another most uniquely charts Wesley's lifelong emphasis it is the fourth. It was his faith in the sufficiency of grace to save from all sin, in this life, that drew much of the persecution and wrath that was heaped on him. It is still the battleground.

But for Wesley the uttermost salvation required a second great change, which he called the great salvation, holiness, entire sanctification, or Christian perfection.

Wesleyan theology is mutilated if its doctrine of a "second blessing" is severed. This was the kind of holiness Wesley had in mind when he declared that God had raised the Methodists up "to spread scriptural holiness over the land."[3] And it was what he had in mind when he said that for Methodists repentance was the porch of religion, faith the door, but holiness religion itself.[4] As Harald Lindstrom has shown in his thorough and definitive study, *Wesley and Sanctification,* the doctrine of sanctification was much more pivotal in Wesley's thought than has usually been recognized. Rarely, he says, "has the significance, for Wesley's total view of salvation, of the principle of entire sanctification, been clearly expounded."[5]

While both *perfection* and *love,* therefore, are legitimate motifs of Wesleyan theology, there is sound basis for preferring *holiness.* To seek to read "Wesleyan theology" back into church history would be anachronistic, but if we inquire into the historical significance of holiness, we are on sure ground.

I. THE HOLINESS MOTIF BEFORE WESLEY

In thinking of holiness in history we must distinguish between (1) holiness as an ethical standard by which Christians are expected to live, (2) holiness as a personal quest, (3) holiness as a professed experience, and (4) holiness as defined and articulated doctrine. As an ethical standard and as personal quest, holiness has been confluent with church history, though at times a minor stream in the midst of the broader current of nominal or corrupt ecclesiasticism. As a professed experience holiness has seldom been without its witnesses (though the witness has been given in greatly diverse forms). As to doctrinal formulation, precursors of the Wesleyan movement go back to the church fathers, though by no means with equal clarity and precision.

A. Apostolic Fathers

A careful reading of these ancient homilists, who were so close to the apostles, will impress one with their primary concern, the holiness of the church. This holiness was expounded by frequent references to apostolic Scriptures and reflected the same high standard: abstention from the works of the flesh, and fullness of love and righteousness. Instructions, as in the *Didache,* have suggested to some a works righteousness, as if a new law were being substituted for justification by faith. The internal evidence does not support this but shows rather a fear of a mechanical and superficial faith. Their exhortations were warnings against what a later prophet (Bonhoeffer) would call "cheap grace." Hence they warned against fleshly sins, against wavering, and against double-mindedness. Pleading for a "single mind," Clement of Rome urges, "Wherefore let us not be double-minded, neither let our soul indulge in idle humours respecting His exceeding and glorious gifts."[6] In writing to the Ephesians Ignatius is anxious that "no herb of the devil be found" in them, but that they "in all purity and temperance abide . . . in Christ Jesus," both with their "flesh" and with their "spirit."[7]

The doctrine of holiness found in the apostolic fathers is thoroughly "Wesleyan" in two very significant respects. For one thing, there is no hint of a reliance on an imputed righteousness that is not personally real. Not the slightest vestige of anything that would savor of antinomianism or of the false comfort of supposing that God sees us as holy in Christ even when we are not can be found. Ignatius warns against those who "hawk about the Name, while they do certain other things unworthy of God."[8] He says, "For when no lust is established in you . . . then truly ye live after God"; and, "They that are of the flesh cannot do the things of the Spirit, neither can they that are of the Spirit do the things of the flesh; even as faith cannot do the things of unfaithfulness, neither unfaithfulness the things of faith."⁹

The second respect in which these early writers were "Wesleyan" is their undeviating assumption that if the believer is finally to make it to heaven, he must while on earth persevere in faith, obedience, and righteousness. They knew nothing of a "locked-in" security based on divine election or a "finished salvation" based on an unconditional, totally objective atonement. The hope of the resurrection, declares Clement, belongs only to "them that have served Him with holiness in the full assurance of a good faith,"¹⁰ and "what world will receive any of them that desert from His service?"¹¹

The writer of the Epistle of Barnabas warns against presuming that the covenant of grace is inviolable. He speaks of those who "pile up sin upon sin, saying that our covenant remains to them also."¹² But he reminds his readers of the Israelites who lost their covenant "in this way." "Wherefore," he says, "Let us take heed. . . . For the whole time of our faith shall profit us nothing" unless we, "as becometh sons of God," resist the "Black One." For:

> The Lord judgeth the world without respect of persons; each man shall receive according to his deeds . . . lest perchance, if we relax as men that are called, we should slumber over our sins, and the prince of evil receive power against us and thrust us out from the kingdom of the Lord. . . . When ye see that after so many signs and wonders wrought in Israel, even then they were abandoned, let us give heed, lest haply we be found, as the scripture saith, *many called but few chosen*.¹³

It is clear that Wesley's qualified synergism, which postulates a true free agency through prevenient grace and which prevails throughout the entire stretch of earthly probation, is much more in harmony with primitive Christianity than with any form of inflexible monergism. Persons are accountable for their sins, accountable for their repenting or not repenting, and accountable for their preseverance in "faith working through love" (Gal. 5:6). Only on this basis can the plan of salvation be thoroughly moral and the terms *holiness* and *righteousness* bear their full and proper meaning. Lindstrom enunciates true Wesleyanism in saying:

> This view of salvation as something also dependent on human decisions is emphasized by the idea of repentance before faith as a condition of justification and repentance after faith as a condition of perfect sanctification. In accordance with his Arminian view of election Wesley thus rejects the idea of a *gratia irresistibilis*. Grace, that is, does not operate irresistibly; its effectiveness is dependent on human cooperation. In consonance with this basic idea he dismissed the doctrine of an unconditional perseverance. Thus those who believe in Christ are not regarded as incapable of apostasy. A believer whose faith is wrecked, is *ipso facto* no longer a child of God.¹⁴

B. Later Church Fathers and Movements

A brief and partial chronological synopsis will be illuminating. In addition to the apostolic fathers, the second century witnessed the preaching of the apologists and the reform movement of Montanism. Tatian, an apologist of Mesopotamia, preached what Turner believes could have been the "first sermon on Christian perfection . . . in which he expounded the conversation between Jesus and the rich young ruler."¹⁵ The rigorous moralism of the Montanists, especially Tertullian, while mixed with fanaticism and heresy, was really a protest against the laxity into which the church had already fallen, and a call to holy living. Otto W. Heick goes so far as to say that Montanism "paved the way for a series of movements which have continued down through the history of Christianity, such as those of the Novatians, the Donatists, the Waldensians, the radicals of the Reformation period (Mennonites and others), and the modern Pentecostal and Holiness churches."¹⁶ However, we must resist any covert insinuation in Heick's statement that holiness is in any sense a maverick emphasis instead of the heart of Christian faith—even if it has not always been seen as such by the majority of Christendom.

The most representative "personality in the second-century Church," according to Flew, was Irenaeus, whose doctrine of recapitulation was essentially "a doctrine of perfection."[17] The goal of our being is "to be in Christ, and having received the Spirit, living in communion with God, we are well on our way to that goal."[18] Flew quotes Irenaeus's own summary: "The Son of God appeared on earth and was conversant with men: that man might be after the image and likeness of God."[19]

The third century was stamped by Clement of Alexandria and Origen, among others, with their advocacy of holy living in contrast to the looseness of paganism and nominal Christianity. It was Origen's passion for personal holiness that prompted him to emasculate himself as a young man—an action that, while heroic, indicated a failure to grasp the available moral power in God's sanctifying grace.

Clement's three treatises are all expositions of the possible attainment of holiness through Christ. According to Flew, the perfection "contemplated by the *Paedagogus* is the perfection of all genuine religious experience, when the soul meets God. The perfection to which believers are called by the *Stromateis* . . . is a full unification of the powers of the soul. There is knowledge in it, but there is also love, complete harmony of purpose and desire."[20] It was Clement's description of a Christian that was Wesley's inspiration for his tract on the character of a Methodist.

Many of the controversies of this century were attempts to purify the church and to know what to do with Christians who relapsed into sin. These attempts reflected deep concern for the preservation of Christian sanctity. Henry Chadwick says:

> From the third century the question was being put with steadily increasing pressure whether the Church could occupy a position of influence in high society without losing something of its moral power. . . . The primitive Church had imposed high demands and strict discipline—so strict that in the second century it had to face painful controversy about the very possibility of repentance for sins committed after baptism. The debates about the holiness of the Church as an empirical society ended in the defeat of rigorism when Novation was rejected at Rome in 251. . . . But the old ideal was never lost, and could be reasserted without creating a schism.[21]

The student of Wesleyanism is struck by the similarity of this third-century struggle with the battle of Wesley and his co-workers to extricate the church of eighteenth-century England from its captivity to the decadence of its social environment.

The fourth century saw the flight of the hermits into the desert and the rise of monasticism—both movements as attempts to achieve holiness. Harnack calls this "the greatest organized quest for perfection in history."[22] According to Christensen, tens of thousands took up the hermitic or monastic life in the deserts of Egypt and the Near East.[23] While, as Turner points out, much of this was a threat to biblical holiness in its lopsided asceticism, it was nevertheless a quest for holiness.

The most famous ascetic was Anthony (Antony) of Egypt, whose biography written by Athanasius was a direct influence in the conversion of Augustine. In the words of Christensen, "As Augustine heard how Anthony had forsaken all to live a life of utter devotion to God in the desert, he was deeply moved."[24] Moreover, it was a "holiness text" of Scripture that God used to activate his faith and bring peace. The passage was: "Let us behave properly as in the day, not in carousing and drunkenness, not in sexual promiscuity and sensuality, not in strife and jealousy. But put on the Lord Jesus Christ, and make no provision for the flesh in regard to its lusts" (Rom. 13:13-14).

As to Augustine's own influence, he affected holiness doctrine both positively and negatively. His *Confessions* breathe a continuous acknowledgment of holiness as the longing of the soul. Even when before his conversion he prayed, "Make me pure, but not now," the very prayer testified that holiness was the goal. Early in his career he theorized that complete victory over all sin was possible, but later in his controversy with Pelagius he retreated from this optimism, and settled for a more pessimistic view of sin and grace. The human race was literally a *massa peccati* (mass of sin). This endemic sin manifested itself as pride and also as concupiscence. Augustine desires, says Harnack, "to retain the 'amor sui' as the principal conception of sin, but in reality he ranks concupiscence above it."[25] Since concupiscence is strong sexual desire and arises spontaneously, apart from the will, it taints the marriage relation and in procreation transmits its own corruption. By thus linking sexual appetite to original sin, Augustine in effect denigrated marriage and sexual union, associated sinfulness with the body, and equated carnality with the natural appetites. This confusion became an incubus on holiness concepts for over a thousand years—until Wesleyanism restored a more biblical optimism about both sin and holiness.

A more positive influence of the third century was Cyprian of North Africa, one of the four great Latin fathers, bishop of Carthage. From him comes what Turner terms perhaps "the most explicit witness to the baptism of the Spirit which cleanses from sin and fills with love. . . . He testified to his own experience of deliverance and exhorted others to seek the fullness of the blessing of the gospel of God."[26]

In the fourth century there was Basil (c. 330-379), one of the four fathers of the Greek church, whose pious life and teachings influenced John Chrysostom and influenced also St. Benedict in the development of the Benedictine Order. Of Basil, William Greathouse declares, "There can be no doubt that Basil believed that the heart could in this life be purified from sin and that the commandments of love could be kept." Greathouse also quotes W. K. Lowther Clarke's claim that Basil "believes intensely in sanctification. In and by the Spirit, the Christian living under the favourable conditions of a monastery, can avoid sin."[27] Centuries later John Wesley would magnify divine grace even more by affirming that one can avoid sin even in the unfavorable conditions of a British colliery.

Gregory of Nyssa and Macarius the Egyptian also belong to the fourth century. Albert Outler designates Gregory as "the greatest of all Eastern Christian teachers of the quest for perfection."[28] His constant theme was the possibility and necessity of believers being like Christ, but that this required the cleansing of the dual nature within them. He says, "The definition of peace is the harmony of dissonant parts. Once the civil war in our nature is expelled, then we become peace and reveal our having taken on the name of Christ as true and authentic."[29]

Wesley was so influenced by Macarius that he included a portion of his *Homilies* in *A Christian Library* (vol. 18).[30] In Wesley's diary is this entry: "I read Macarius and sang!" It was Macarius who more than any of the ancient fathers associated sanctification with the baptism with the Spirit. However, his understanding of this baptism fell short of instantaneous cleansing from all sin.

C. The Medieval and Reformation Periods

In the long centuries of the Middle Ages the light burned dim but was never extinguished. Flew lists Bernard of Clairvaux and Thomas Aquinas as being in the holiness (or perfection) succession. William S. Deal emphasizes the contributions of the Christian mystics, among whom were Thomas à Kempis, Savonarola, and John Wycliffe.[31] A man who had been a nominal Catholic and had led a thoroughly pagan life told this writer that after his conversion it was through the reading of

The Imitation of Christ, placed in his hands by a priest, that he was led into entire sanctification—this as a profoundly radical and thorough experience, without benefit of doctrinal aid. It could have been a passage such as this that especially influenced him:

> Thou must divest thyself of self in all things. For how canst thou be Mine and I thine, unless, both inwardly and outwardly, thou be stripped of all self-will? . . . Forsake thyself, resign thyself, and thou wilt enjoy great inward peace. Give all for all; ask for nothing; require nothing back; abide purely and unhesitatingly in Me, and thou will possess Me. Then shalt thou be free in heart, and no darkness shall burden thy spirit.[32]

Other spiritual leaders within the Catholic tradition were St. Francis of Assisi (13th century, Italy), St. Teresa of Avila (16th century, Spain), "Brother Lawrence" (17th century, France),[33] Madam Guyon, and Bishop Fenelon. Bishop Fenelon was led by Madam Guyon into heart holiness, and in turn Fenelon wrote much on the subject of Christian perfection. His writings are still read with delight and have permeated the thinking of holiness people.[34]

On the other side of the ecclesiastical line were the Reformers. While John Calvin fell short of a clear doctrine of entire sanctification as a second work of grace, he was by no means an antinomian or indifferent to practical holiness. Rather he believed that only a life of righteousness and obedience could constitute the evidence of one's eternal election. Good works, he says, "are proofs of God dwelling and reigning in us."[35] Yet because our righteousness can never be perfect, or completely free from sin, the perpetuity of our justification must be based, not on personal holiness, but on the continuous imputation to us of Christ's righteousness, and by "the constant remission of sins."[36] Having adopted the Augustinian concept of sin and accepted the consequent limitations on grace, and having also developed a supralapsarian doctrine of predestination, carrying with it irresistible grace and infallible perseverance, Calvin is trapped into a disjunction between declarative grace and operative grace. This means that the Atonement assures the final justification of the elect in spite of the shortcoming of operative grace in bringing about true personal holiness. Yet personal holiness is still the goal. What grace cannot accomplish in life will be accomplished in death. Such is the implication of Calvin's statement:

> Our imperfection and impurity, covered with this [Christ's] purity, are not imputed, but are as it were buried, so as not to come under judgment until the hour arrives when the old man being destroyed, and plainly extinguished in us, the divine goodness shall receive us into beatific peace with the new Adam, there to wait [in the Intermediate State] the day of the Lord, on which, being clothed with incorruptible bodies, we shall be translated to the glory of the heavenly kingdom.[37]

Thus complete cleansing that Wesleyanism believes is available now is in Calvinism available only at death. Wesleyanism magnifies grace, in that instead of grace being captive to sin, sin is captive to grace. Grace is able not only to deliver us from sin's consequences in eternity but also to break its power in time and enable us to be holy in the arena of our earthly warfare. God is more glorified by true holiness in the presence of evil than by holiness that can exist only in a perfect, heavenly environment.

Luther is generally supposed to have been weak in his concept of sanctification, but the German Lutheran theologian Adolf Köberle says, "He [Luther] wanted to distinguish between 'external' righteousness and 'inner' sanctification but without separating them from each other."[38] Sanctification was real in that it produced a true change of life and character. Like Wesley, Luther saw love as the essence of Christian ethics. But it was a love that always fell short of perfection. Sanctification could never in any sense be said to be entire except in the sense of imputation. "On this side of eternity the Christian is *simul justus et peccator,* both righteous and a sinner, holy and profane, an enemy of God and yet a child of God."[39]

The three doctrines of predestination, inalienable sin while in the body, and severance of justification from obedience as the basis of final salvation together inevitably breed antinomianism and moral laxity. Both Calvinism and Lutheranism (at their best) have found themselves almost continually doing battle against the logical implications of their own systems. In the Lutheran camp the Formula of Concord (1576) was that church's early effort to safeguard against certain misunderstandings, including antinomian tendencies. While insisting that "justification before God" is not dependent on "subsequent new obedience," the writers hasten to qualify this disjunction by adding, "Yet we are not to imagine any such justifying faith as can exist and abide with a purpose of evil, to wit: of sinning and acting contrary to conscience."[40] Other disclaimers follow:

> That faith is such a confidence in the obedience of Christ as can abide and have a being even in that man who is void of true repentance, and in whom it is not followed by charity, but who contrary to conscience perseveres in sins.[41]

There seems, indeed, to be a repudiation of any illusion of unconditional security and the postulation of a certain contingency in "election":

> We believe, therefore, teach, and confess that when it is said that the regenerate do good works of a free and spontaneous spirit, this is not to be so understood as that it is left to the regenerate man's option to do well or ill whenever it may seem good to him, so that he retains faith, even though of set purpose he perseveres in sins.[42]

Elsewhere the Formula declares that "men may incur damnation no less by an Epicurean persuasion concerning faith than by a Pharisaic and Papistic confidence in their own works and merits."[43] The peril of fatal backsliding could scarcely be expressed more pointedly than in this paragraph:

> Moreover, we repudiate and condemn that dogma that faith in Christ is not lost, and that the Holy Spirit, even though a man sin wittingly and willingly, nevertheless dwells in him; and that the holy and elect retain the Holy Spirit, even though they fall into adultery or other crimes, and persevere in the same.[44]

Thus did Lutheranism attempt to forestall antinomianism. The fact remains, however, that because both Calvinism and Lutheranism radically limit the degree of holiness possible in this life, the consequence is a reduction of the believer's expectation. On the one hand are the deeply entrenched concepts of (1) sin as appetitive and (2) the sufficiency of imputed righteousness to compensate for inadequate personal righteousness, and on the other hand is the vigorous rejection of any notion of cleansing from original sin. These twin faith-depressants are devastating in their practical effects.

Moreover, since sin is seen not only as willful transgression but also as any falling short of absolute perfection, it becomes consistent in one and the same breath to repudiate willful sinning and declare that we "sin in thought, word, and deed every day"—and therefore stand in need of continual forgiveness.

It cannot be denied that there is here a kinship with Wesleyanism. No one conceded more willingly to the imperfections of the sanctified than Wesley, and that through infirmity even the entirely sanctified fall short and therefore stand in continuous need of the Atonement. But Wesley refused to call these shortcomings sins and refused to assume that in possessing infirmities believers were thereby demonstrating the remains of inbred sin. Neither perfect cleansing nor perfect love were incompatible with remaining scars and defects that, while the product of the Fall, were qualitatively different from original sin seen as pride and self-willfulness.

II. TRIBUTARY STREAMS IN THE HOLINESS QUEST

"There is a river whose streams make glad the city of God" (Ps. 46:4). It is increasingly apparent that the holiness made available to God's people in Christ is such a river. The scope of this study does not permit detailed tracing of the minor tributary streams that during the Middle Ages and the Reformation centuries flowed into this mighty, lifegiving river. These streams include the Waldensians, the Brethren of the Common Life, and the Moravians.

A. Puritanism

In Britain such a tracing would include George Fox and the Society of Friends. Fox's doctrine, at its clearest and best, was remarkably similar to Wesley's yet antedated it by one hundred years. Unfortunately, by Wesley's day Quakerism's holiness emphasis was largely diluted by materialism and little was left but its eccentricities. Wesley seemed to sense little affinity with the Quakers. Following Wesley, however, a revitalization occurred that brought large segments of Quakerism into the main stream of the so-called Holiness Movement. Nevertheless, Wesley himself was far more influenced by Puritanism. He found himself at home with Puritanism's rugged moral earnestness. He was influenced in his early years by the intense single-mindedness and purity of intention expounded by Jeremy Taylor and William Law. He shared with Puritans their insistence on repentance and sanctification and borrowed from their genius in teaching growth in grace.

Robert C. Monk traces in great detail Wesley's interaction with the Puritans. Wesley thought so highly of their writings that in his *Christian Library,* a series of fifty volumes, which he edited specifically for his Methodists, he included selected writings of thirty-two Puritans out of a total of sixty authors.[45] Monk believes that Wesley's concept of perfection may have been drawn from John Preston's *New Covenant,* in which perfection is presented, says Monk, as "perfection of the heart: that is, a heart dedicated singularly and solely to God."[46] Wesley included an abridgment of this work in his *Library*. In Volume IV of the *Library* he explains why he favors certain Puritans (as quoted by Monk):

> They are continually tearing up the very roots of Antinomianism, by shewing at large, from the oracles of God, the absolute necessity, as of that legal repentance which is previous to faith, so of that evangelical repentance which follows it, and which is essential to that holiness, without which we cannot see the Lord.[47]

But Wesley did not borrow from Puritan writings uncritically. In abridging the material he deleted the unacceptable outcroppings of hyper-Calvinism. Monk summarizes:

> The theological considerations which guided Wesley's omissions and modifications indicate several areas of divergent opinion. These are primarily in their respective understandings of God's election of the believer, man's active role in salvation, the perseverance of the saints, and the extent of man's perfectibility.[48]

B. Pietism

A second tributary to the formulation of Wesley's theological views was Pietism, primarily the influence of Count von Zinzendorf's Moravians. Peter Bohler and his associates became midwife not only to Wesley's revised concept of evangelical faith but also to his personal conversion as he "broke the faith-barrier" on May 24, 1738. From the Moravians he learned the privilege of the witness of the Spirit and the importance of vital personal experience and at times he caught glimpses of the teaching of a pure heart. Yet gradually he recoiled from elements among the Moravians of quietism, of disparagement of the sacraments and means of grace, and the incipient if not practicing antinomianism;

and certainly he rejected Zinzendorf's notion of the simultaneity of entire sanctification with regeneration. Monk believes that Wesley's reaction to Moravianism was what drove him closer to the writings of the Puritans.[49]

C. Arminianism

The third—and at the same time central—influence on Wesleyanism was and is Arminianism. Many interpreters discount this influence, in fact they seem embarrassed over it.[50] It is true that Arminianism in the Church of England of Wesley's day was often humanistic, Pelagian, and latitudinarian. From these strands Wesley was forever dissociating himself. Yet the attempt to label Wesley as more Calvinist than Arminian, as many have done, is squelched by the simple fact that Wesley called his periodical *The Arminian Magazine;* and it cannot be overlooked that his only controversy with his dear friend Whitefield was over Arminian vs. Calvinistic principles. Obviously Wesley considered himself an Arminian, whether his interpreters are happy about going along with that identification or not. No clearer disquisition could be found than Wesley's own summary of both sides in his essay, "The Question, 'What Is an Arminian?' Answered. By a Lover of Free Grace." After scorning certain popular but incorrect allegations, Wesley states very briefly the identity of *Jacobus Arminius* and the events that resulted in the pitting of Arminianism against the Canons of Dort —which were Calvinism's violent reaction to the budding protest movement in Holland. Wesley says:

> The errors charged upon these (usually termed *Arminians*) by their opponents, are five: (1.) That they deny original sin; (2.) That they deny justification by faith; (3.) That they deny absolute predestination; (4.) That they deny the grace of God to be irresistible; and, (5.) That they affirm a believer may fall from grace.

Wesley roundly declares "Not guilty" to the first two charges. He gladly admits the truth of the next three charges but denies that they are errors. Both the clarity and the importance of his summary justify its inclusion here:

> But there is an undeniable difference between the Calvinists and Arminians, with regard to the three other questions. Here they divide; the former believe absolute, the latter only conditional, predestination. The Calvinists hold, (1.) God has absolutely decreed, from all eternity, to save such and such persons, and no others; and that Christ died for these, and none else. The Arminians hold, God has decreed, from all eternity, touching all that have the written word, "He that believeth shall be saved: He that believeth not, shall be condemned:" And in order to this, "Christ died for all, all that were dead in trespasses and sins;" that is, for every child of Adam, since "in Adam all died."
>
> The Calvinists hold, Secondly, that the saving grace of God is absolutely irresistible; that no man is any more able to resist it, than to resist the stroke of lightning. The Arminians hold, that although there may be some moments wherein the grace of God acts irresistibly, yet, in general, any man may resist, and that to his eternal ruin, the grace whereby it was the will of God he should have been eternally saved.
>
> The Calvinists hold, Thirdly, that a true believer in Christ cannot possibly fall from grace. The Arminians hold, that a true believer may "make shipwreck of faith and a good conscience;" that he may fall, not only foully, but finally, so as to perish for ever.
>
> Indeed, the two latter points, irresistible grace and infallible perseverance, are the natural consequence of the former, of the unconditional decree. For if God has eternally and absolutely decreed to save such and such persons, it follows, both that they cannot resist his saving grace, (else they might miss of salvation,) and that they cannot finally fall from that grace which they cannot resist. So that, in effect, the three questions come into one, "Is predestination absolute or conditional?" The Arminians believe, it is conditional; the Calvinists, that it is absolute.[51]

In addition therefore to the main doctrines of the Reformation, these are the special influences that helped to form

Wesley's thinking. We can say, therefore, that all of these streams contributed to the swelling tide that covered the land in the sweeping Wesleyan revival overflowing to the Continent and to America, becoming the mighty Methodist confluence of movements, touching and reshaping throughout the nineteenth century the whole of American religious history, as well as other English-speaking areas of the world.

III. A MEDIATING THEOLOGY

Wesley revolted against a doctrine of sovereignty that impugned the divine benevolence, and doctrines of sin and grace that implied inadequate grace—that it availed to save sinners in their sins but not from them. Wesleyanism brings need and possibility together. The need, and the natural hunger of the awakened and regenerate heart, is not only for forgiveness but also for moral power.

John Wesley did not set out to develop a mediating theology, but that is what he accomplished. This was the result of close study of Scripture, rigorous logic, personal experience, and evangelistic passion. Since seldom does truth lie in either extreme of the pendulum, it is well that the truth of the center was found and theological thinking liberated from the implications of divine arbitrariness, with humanity as the pawn, and from humanistic sufficiency, with Christ as dispensable.

The mediating position of Wesleyan Theology is between Pelagianism and Augustinianism (without falling prey to semi-Pelagianism), between theological determinism and humanistic autonomy, and between a totally objective view of the Atonement and a totally subjective one.

The crux of the issue is the relation of persons as moral agents to the will of a sovereign God. This issue affects radically one's concepts of sin, holiness, and grace. If God is the only actor (ultimately); if the action is on the human will, creating infallibly a domino effect of repentance, faith, and obedience; and if even the selection of recipients is entirely an action of God's will, then the moral value of human response is diluted and holiness loses its moral reality. Car drivers can talk about the responsiveness of a car, and speak of it as being smooth, gentle, firm, or lively, but they cannot meaningfully call it holy.

Of course the analogy is not fully apt because the secondary holiness of persons or objects derived from a specific relationship to Deity (e.g., "holy ground," Exod. 3:5) is a biblical concept. But the Bible never permits the mind to rest here; it demands holiness of persons themselves—a holiness that is real because it is chosen in freedom. Such a holiness consists of choosing Christ as Savior and choosing His full will and the full power of the Spirit to change us at the very root of our being. But it is not a once-for-all, nonnegotiable choice that controls irrevocably all subsequent choices, but a continuous choosing that becomes at once a habitual action of the will and a state of character. The import of this is that pure monergism makes full holiness impossible, and the holiness concepts of such a theology are inevitably tainted with an element of make-believe.

If, on the other hand, to preserve the moral content of holiness as a reality of the heart we assert the unimpaired free will, we minimize the reality of sin, the absolute need for grace, and the indispensability of the Atonement.

Wesleyan theology avoids either error by its doctrine of prevenient grace. This is seen not as a grace operative in the elect alone, but a universal benefit of the Atonement, removing the racial guilt related to Adam's sin, making all men salvable, assuring the salvation of infants and irresponsibles, and restoring a sufficient degree of moral ability to permit moral action in real freedom, either to respond to the convicting of the Spirit or to resist. The grace is indispensable but not irresistible. God's will is that all should respond, but His will has elected to permit people not to respond. He would rather have some choose Him freely and serve Him because they love Him than to have the elect serve Him on a predetermined, puppetlike basis or to have *all* flock to Him on a morally unconditioned basis.

While Wesleyanism's doctrine of sin is essentially Augustinian, there is nevertheless a radical difference. The essence of sin is seen as unbelief, pride, self-sovereignty, self-idolatry—not the sex urge per se. Original sin as an infection of the race is not physical or biological in nature—even though transmitted by parents—but spiritual and psychic. Therefore its correction is not dependent on death, but is possible now, by faith in the inward operation of the Holy Spirit on the self. This difference changes the pessimism of both Lutheranism and Calvinism, respecting possibilities of grace, into a God-honoring optimism. Faith is encouraged to lay hold of present power for present purity, rather than being compelled to resign the deepest need to future hope.

Wesleyanism's doctrine of sin is Augustinian in respect to humanity's extensive, though not intensive, total depravity and moral inability. Apart from grace persons are unable, even disinclined, to turn to God. No one, according to Wesley, is born only in a state of fallen nature—though he is that—but already in grace. This grace will shepherd one to repentance, regeneration, entire sanctification, and final perseverance if not resisted and rejected somewhere along the way. Thus Wesleyanism's synergism is qualified. Grace is prior; the initiation is God's and also the enabling. No one who understands Wesleyanism will call it Pelagian, or accuse it of magnifying man rather than God. How could God be more magnified than by a plan of salvation that offers full salvation from all sin to all people in the arena of this life?

IV. WESLEYAN THEOLOGY IN MODERN TIMES

From Wesley's day until now the basic concern for holiness—and also the articulation of the doctrine—has been a steadily enlarging stream. Many have traced the development through the nineteenth century, as the holiness emphasis found its expression (though not fully Wesleyan) in the Keswick movement of England; then in the distinctly Wesleyan Salvation Army; the mighty camp-meeting surge of America; the great Palmerite revival that touched David Updegraf, Thomas Upham, and dozens more, from a score of denominations; the National Holiness Association (now Christian Holiness Association); and the holiness denominations, such as Wesleyan, Free Methodist, and Church of the Nazarene. The story has been told by George Turner, Delbert Rose, Timothy Smith, Leo Cox, Leslie Wilcox, William Deal, William Greathouse, M. E. Dieter, and doubtless many others.

The most impressive bibliographical survey has been published by Charles Edwin Jones, a volume of over nine hundred pages.[52] Merely browsing through the table of contents reveals the astonishing spread of the holiness movement, a movement represented by hundreds of distinct agencies, by a world-wide and extensive missionary activity, by huge publishing interests, and by numerous colleges, Bible institutes, and seminaries. Obviously holiness is not an offbeat concern. And while the relevance of holiness teaching needs no defense, the statement by Timothy Smith in the foreword of Jones's volume is pertinent:

> The fascination with extra-rational experience which one finds in modern art and poetry as well as in the drug culture and the revival of the occult is matched by a rationalized and somewhat puritan commitment of increasing numbers of Christian groups to the search for a Christian discipline which eventuates in personal holiness.[53]

The growing interest in holiness is by no means parochial within formal Wesleyanism. The revival spirit of our day is marked by a spate of books and articles on the subject of holiness written by Calvinists and Lutherans. "An important development in recent theology is a renewal of interest in sanctification," writes William E. Hordern in the first volume of the series, *New Directions in Theology Today*.[54] The trend is illustrated by Dietrich Bonhoeffer's *Cost of Discipleship,* Emil Brunner's third volume of *Dogmatics,* Tillich's book *The New Being,* and Karl Barth's major treatment of the subject in his *Church Dogmatics,* volume four—one of the most extensive "since the work of John Wesley."[55] Not that these treatments are Wesleyan, but they illustrate the converging interest of the church at large in the question of personal holiness.

V. SOME SUMMARY OBSERVATIONS

In evaluating the significance of holiness as seen in church history and currently, six observations may be in order.

A. The Universal Instinct for Holiness

The instinct for holiness imbedded in the Christian faith is obvious. The reach for holiness is endemic to spiritual life, certainly by no means an interest artificially worked up by an isolated segment of Christendom. No matter how desolate the religious landscape, men and women who have desired God have desired to be holy and have seen holiness as elementary to biblical faith. This holiness would universally, in any age, have certain irreducible notes: pure morals, right relationships with others, and a walk with Christ in faith, obedience, and love.

B. A Second Crisis Normative

It is surprising how often the personal pilgrimage of the saints has involved a profound crisis and change at some point after first believing on Christ. Many can identify with St. Teresa of Avila, who because of her doublemindedness went through a deep spiritual struggle. In her autobiography she writes, "I spent nearly twenty years on that stormy sea, often falling in this way and each time rising again, but to little purpose, as I would only fall once more."[56] But in her forty-first year the conflict ceased, a "new peace" came to her, and a new and deeper life of prayer.

Remarkably clear also was the experience of John Woolman, a Quaker, who during an illness had a vision of struggling, lost humanity and of his call to blend himself with them, not seeking to save his life. In the vision the angel said, "John Woolman is dead." Christensen writes:

> When he came to himself, and was informed by those around him that he was really John Woolman, he found himself repeating the verse of Scripture, "I am crucified with Christ, nevertheless I live; yet not I, but Christ liveth in me." He then understood that what the angel had been announcing was the death of John Woolman's *will.* He was no longer to live for himself, but as a wholly dedicated servant of God.[57]

While cases cited are usually not as dramatic or mystical as Woolman's experience, this "secondness" of full salvation is supported by numerous authors. George Allen Turner in *Witnesses of the Way* describes, frequently in their own words, the deeper crisis experiences of one hundred famous persons, from Clement of Rome to Julian C. McPheeters.[58] V. Raymond Edman, former chancellor of Wheaton, provides a more detailed account of the second crisis experiences of outstanding evangelical leaders of modern times—some Wesleyan but many non-Wesleyan; yet in the focus on "dying out to self" and being filled with the Spirit, there was remarkable similarity among their experiences.[59] This is a grace that is found not only among those who articulate a specific doctrine in Wesleyan terms, for the simple reason that it is basic to Christian experience itself, and when believers follow the Spirit, this is the direction in which they will be led.

Revival often breaks out of dogmatic straitjackets, and people seek and find a walk with God that their creeds did not encourage them to expect. The implication of this for the validation of holiness theology cannot be missed. The church has an obligation to endeavor to formulate the doctrinal expression that matches what the Spirit does, and that serves as a guide to blessing rather than a roadblock to be overcome.

C. Holiness and Revival

While true revival movements have always fostered holy living, the deep search for holiness by the few has times without number ignited revival. It is when God's people "get right," when they pursue "peace with all men, and the sanctification without which no one will see the Lord" (Heb. 12:14), when they die out to self, and, filled with the Spirit, are set ablaze with holy love for God and souls—it is then that revival fires become mighty conflagrations, purifying the church and reaching sinners with new power. According to the four pastors chiefly instrumental in the sweeping revival of 1972 in Canada, that was a holiness revival—not charismatic, but consciously and deeply holiness.[60]

D. Holiness and Social Reform

Not only is a holiness emphasis the vanguard of revival but it is the soil out of which social reform springs. In respect to America Timothy Smith has traced this generative and fertile power in his classic *Revivalism and Social Reform*. After a thorough analysis of the "revival measures and perfectionist aspiration" that flourished between 1840 and 1865, he was able to say:

> The quest for personal holiness became in some ways a kind of plain man's transcendentalism, which geared ancient creeds to the drive shaft of social reform. Far from disdaining earthly affairs, the evangelists played a key role in the widespread attack upon slavery, poverty, and greed. They thus helped prepare the way both in theory and in practice for what later became known as the social gospel.[61]

In England the far-reaching effects of the Wesleyan revival on the social structures were incalculable. Wesley saw clearly the social implications of holiness and refused to allow men to separate what God had joined together—faith and good works. It was the preaching of righteousness combined with the social conscience of Methodism (both Arminian and Calvinistic branches) that produced the Clapham Sect, an informal group of reform-minded Evangelicals. The group included William Wilberforce, who more than any other one person led in the fight against slavery. Wesley's last letter, written four days before his death, was to Wilberforce, encouraging him to press on in his courageous fight.[62] Other reforms resulting from the Evangelical Revival included the Sunday school movement, prison reform, child protection laws (including protection for the chimney sweeps), debt reform, medical aid to the poor, better housing, and the founding of public schools.

E. Holiness and Education

The history of holiness doctrine and movements shows that such a teaching has salutary cultural, educational, and intellectual effects. Wherever holiness people have gone, schools have been founded. Only aberrant pockets of fervent but misguided holiness advocates have at times been anti-intellectual. The holistic tendency of holiness doctrine fosters loving God with all the mind as well as with all the heart, soul, and strength. As Turner says, "Both in individuals and in groups, a revival of vital salvation brings an intellectual stimulus." He also calls attention to the "multiplication of books and tracts which Wesley urged his preachers to use and distribute."[63]

F. The Contemporary Challenge

Perhaps a personal word of exhortation is justified. Across the centuries God has always had a witness to His justifying and sanctifying grace. Hundreds of devout saints have struggled to understand their privileges in Christ, in order that this good news might be clearly conveyed to others. Out of the confusing and faulty articulations of the past God in His providence has brought forth in the last two and a quarter centuries a more adequate view of the possibilities of grace. This is a heritage that brings great blessings and privileges, but also with these it brings awesome responsibilities. We are in a critical day. On one side are the charismatics whose emphasis is more on what we feel and what we can do than what we are, and who appeal to those whose hearts are hungry but whose carnality gravitates to the showy more than the holy. On the other side is the great non-Wesleyan evangelical world, active, fervent, overpowering, marching numerically, but whose message boils down to a promise of heaven through Christ that falls short of an offer of present holiness through Christ. As a consequence much of the religious stir abroad today is sadly superficial. It is lacking in ethical depth, devotional power, and healthy discipline. Without radical repentance, without the teaching of the absolute indispensability of holy living and personal obedience for *salvation itself,* there cannot but be a religious life that is more sound and fury than substance.

We are in an age of large evangelizing activity that results in small change. But Christianity that does not change people through and through, both in heart and in lifestyle, will in the end precipitate a backlash that will set the cause of so-called evangelical Christianity back three hundred years.

Therefore it falls upon the adherents and advocates of Wesleyan theology to guard its purity during these days of theological dilution and to keep steady hands on the pilot wheel of the theological enterprise as it plies its way through the strong crosscurrents and shifting winds of these contemporary seas.

NOTES

[1] R. Newton Flew, *The Idea of Perfection in Christian Theology* (1934; reprint ed., Oxford: Clarendon, 1968).

[2] Philip S. Watson, *The Message of the Wesleys* (New York: Macmillan, 1964), p. 35.

[3] *The Works of John Wesley,* 14 vols. (Kansas City, Mo.: Nazarene, reprint of authorized edition published by the Wesleyan Conference Office in London in 1872), 8:299.

[4] *Works,* 8:472. "Our main doctrines," he says, "which include all the rest, are three,—that of repentance, of faith, and of holiness." In this context Wesley defines holiness (or "religion itself") as "the love of God and of all mankind." Elsewhere he explains that such holiness in its available fullness is not experienced in the new birth, but some time after, when believers have seen "the ground of their heart" (*Works,* 11:380–81 et al.). Cf. A. Skevington Wood, *The Burning Heart: John Wesley, Evangelist* (Grand Rapids: Eerdmans, 1967), pp. 260–69.

[5] Harald Lindstrom, *Wesley and Sanctification* (London: Epworth, 1946), p. 15.

[6] J. B. Lightfoot, *The Apostolic Fathers,* ed. and completed by J. R. Harmer (Grand Rapids: Baker, 1962), p. 23.

[7] Ibid., p. 66.

[8] Ibid., p. 65.

[9] Ibid.

[10] Ibid., p. 24.

[11] Ibid., p. 25.

[12] Ibid., p. 139.

[13] Ibid., p. 140.

[14] *Wesley and Sanctification,* p. 214.

[15] George Allen Turner, *Christian Holiness* (Kansas City, Mo.: Beacon Hill, 1977), p. 23.

[16] Otto W. Heick, *A History of Christian Thought,* 2 vols. (Philadelphia: Fortress, 1965), 1:79.

[17] Flew, *Idea of Perfection,* pp. 124, 126–27. Irenaeus's theory of Recapitulation was the belief that the Logos passed through every phase of human experience, by means of which He was able to reverse the damage done by sin and win complete salvation for the human race.

[18] Ibid., p. 127.

[19] Ibid., p. 128.

[20] Ibid., p. 141.

21. Henry Chadwick, *The Early Church* (Grand Rapids: Eerdmans, 1968), p. 175.

22. Quoted by Turner, *Christian Holiness*, p. 23.

23. Bernhard Christensen, *The Inward Pilgrimage* (Minneapolis: Augsburg, 1976), p. 17.

24. Ibid., p. 12.

25. Adolf von Harnack, *Outlines of the History of Dogma*, trans. Edwin Knox Mitchell (New York: Funk and Wagnalls, 1893), p. 374.

26. Turner, *Christian Holiness*, p. 23.

27. William M. Greathouse, *From the Apostles to Wesley* (Kansas City, Mo.: Beacon Hill, 1979), p. 55.

28. Ibid., p. 59.

29. From his chapter "On Perfection," in *St. Gregory of Nyssa Ascetical Works*, trans. Virginia Callahan (Washington, D.C.: The Catholic University of America, 1967), p. 103. Quoted by Greathouse.

30. William S. Deal, *The March of Holiness Through the Centuries* (Kansas City, Mo.: Beacon Hill, 1978), p. 32.

31. Ibid., pp. 43-51.

32. Thomas à Kempis, *The Imitation of Christ* (Philadelphia: Porter and Coates, n.d.), pp. 180-81.

33. Actually Nicholas Herman, born in Lorraine, France, 1611.

34. E.g., *Christian Perfection* (New York: Harper, 1947).

35. John Calvin, *The Institutes of the Christian Religion*, 3 vols., trans. Henry Beveridge (Edinburgh: Calvin Translation Society, 1845), 1:370.

36. Ibid., 1:362.

37. Ibid., 1:364. Cf. 1:118 where Calvin discusses the "two principles" in the believer, due to the fact that "we are never so well in the course of the present life as to be entirely cured of the disease of distrust." Cf. also 1:166 where the Spirit's ministry in bringing about our sanctification is affirmed, but no hope is held out for the Spirit's complete success, since, "though purged by his sanctification, we are still beset by many vices and much weakness, so long as we are enclosed in the prison of the body." Therefore we must be "daily struggling with the evil by which we are entangled."

38. Adolf Köberle, *The Quest for Holiness*, trans. John C. Mattes (Minneapolis: Augsburg, 1936), p. 93. In analyzing the respective emphases of those days, Köberle makes this neat summary: "We can perhaps formulate it thus: for grace, Melanchthon says forgiveness; Luther says forgiveness and sanctification; Osiander, sanctification and forgiveness. The Roman Church for grace, says only sanctification" (p. 94).

39. Heick, *Christian Thought*, 1:358.

40. Philip Schaff, *The Creeds of Christendom*, 3 vols., 4th ed. (1877; reprint ed., Grand Rapids: Baker, 1969), 3:118.

41. Ibid., p. 119.

42. Ibid., p. 124.

43. Ibid., pp. 125-26.

44. Ibid., p. 126.

45. Robert C. Monk, *John Wesley: His Puritan Heritage* (Nashville: Abingdon, 1966), p. 38. In a footnote Monk adds: "According to a cursory count of the pages of the second edition . . . Puritan materials constitute some 7,200 pages, whereas the Church of England materials make up only 3,900."

46. Ibid., p. 113.

47. Ibid., pp. 118-19.

48. Ibid., p. 63.

49. Ibid., p. 118.

50. A. Skevington Wood in *Burning Heart*, scarcely mentions Wesley's connection with Arminianism in 286 pages, except to quote a denial by James Orr (p. 240) and cast his own doubt on the matter in a footnote. See Lindstrom, *Wesley and Sanctification*, pp. 1-14, where he notes this strange reticence.

51. *Works*, 10:358-61.

52. Charles Edwin Jones, *The Holiness Movement* (Metuchen, N.Y.: Scarecrow, 1974; published jointly with The American Theological Library Association).

53. Ibid., p. vii.

54. William E. Hordern, *New Directions in Theology Today*, 6 vols. (Philadelphia: Westminster, 1966), 1:95.

55. W. T. Purkiser, in an unpublished manuscript, "Exploring Christian Holiness."

56. Quoted by Christensen, *The Inward Pilgrimage*, p. 57.

57. Ibid., p. 97.

58. George Allen Turner, *Witnesses of the Way* (Kansas City, Mo.: Beacon Hill, 1981).

59. V. Raymond Edman, *They Found the Secret* (Grand Rapids: Zondervan, 1968).

60. Reported to me by the pastors themselves. A remarkable "by-blessing" of the revival was the experience of Shirwood E. Wirt, which he recounts in his book, *Afterglow: The Excitement of Being Filled With the Spirit* (Grand Rapids: Zondervan, 1975). Wirt's experience provides another confirmation of the thesis that a second crisis is so natural to the Christian life that it occurs to hungry-hearted believers whose doctrinal frame of reference may be non-Wesleyan.

61. Timothy L. Smith, *Revivalism and Social Reform* (New York: Abingdon, 1957), p. 8.

62. *Works*, 13:153.

63. *Christian Holiness*, p. 32.

DISCUSSION QUESTIONS

1. As Wesley used the terms *perfection, love,* and *holiness,* would they be equally acceptable as the "motif" for Wesleyan theology?
2. Is there biblical ground for preferring the term *holiness*?
3. Why are the apostolic fathers not more precise in spelling out a second work of grace?
4. What is the significance of the absence from the apostolic fathers of any hint of the so-called doctrine of eternal security?
5. Why did the hermits and monks suppose that holiness could be found only in solitude or in a monastery?
6. Why did concupiscence loom so large in Augustine's thinking?
7. Has the modern holiness movement departed from the rugged self-abnegation urged in *The Imitation of Christ,* by Thomas à Kempis?
8. Did John Calvin teach that entire sanctification was not necessary or only not possible now?
9. Why do the doctrines of predestination, inalienable sin while in the body, and severance of justification from continued obedience breed antinomianism?
10. Did Puritanism include both Calvinistic and Arminian strains?
11. Which is the more prominent emphasis in Wesleyanism—the witness of the Spirit or sanctification? Which is the more important emphasis?
12. According to Wesley, Arminianism agrees with Calvinism at what points? Disagrees at what points?
13. Why is the designation Augustinianism sometimes used instead of Calvinism?
14. What is meant by "mediating theology"? Is it an attempt
    a. to compromise?
    b. to effect a truce?
    c. to eliminate or discount differences?
    d. to find the middle ground on which the errors of both extremes can be avoided and the truth of both extremes be retained?
15. Why is Wesleyanism's synergism called a *qualified* synergism?
16. What are the "irreducible notes" of holiness broadly conceived? What is the additional teaching essential to making it Wesleyan?
17. How can the guarding of Wesleyanism's purity, as advocated in the last section, be implemented?

RECOMMENDATIONS FOR FURTHER READING

Carter, Charles W. *The Person and Ministry of the Holy Spirit: A Wesleyan Perspective.* Rev. ed. Grand Rapids: Baker, 1977.

Christensen, Bernhard. *The Inward Pilgrimage.* Minneapolis: Augsburg, 1976.

Deal, William S. *The March of Holiness Through the Centuries.* Kansas City, Mo.: Beacon Hill, 1978.

Dieter, Melvin E. *The Holiness Revival of the Nineteenth Century.* Metuchen, N.J.: Scarecrow, 1980.

Edman, V. Raymond. *They Found the Secret.* Grand Rapids: Zondervan, 1968.

Finney, Charles G. *The Promise of the Spirit.* Compiled and edited by Timothy L. Smith. Minneapolis: Bethany, 1980.

Flew, R. Newton. *The Idea of Perfection in Christian Theology.* Oxford: Clarendon, 1968.

Greathouse, William M. *From the Apostles to Wesley.* Kansas City, Mo.: Beacon Hill, 1979.

Hordern, William E. *New Directions in Theology Today.* Philadelphia: Westminster, 1966. Volume 1.

Jones, Charles Edwin. *The Holiness Movement.* Metuchen, N.Y.: Scarecrow, 1974. Published jointly with The American Theological Library Association, 1974.

Köberle, Adolf. *The Quest for Holiness.* Minneapolis: Augsburg, 1938; copyright 1936. A Lutheran view.

Lightfoot, J.B. *The Apostolic Fathers.* Edited and completed by J.R. Harner. Grand Rapids: Baker, 1962.

Lindstrom, Harald. *Wesley and Sanctification.* London: Epworth, 1946.

Monk, Robert C. *John Wesley: His Puritan Heritage.* Nashville: Abingdon, 1966.

Smith, Timothy L. *Revivalism and Social Reform.* New York: Abingdon, 1957.

Turner, George Allen. *Christian Holiness: In Scripture, in History, and in Life.* Kansas City, Mo.: Beacon Hill, 1977.

_____. *The Vision Which Transforms.* Kansas City, Mo.: Beacon Hill, 1964.

Wilcox, Leslie D. *Be Ye Holy.* Cincinnati, Ohio: Revivalist, 1965.

Wynkoop, Mildred Bangs. *Foundations of Wesleyan-Arminian Theology.* Kansas City, Mo.: Beacon Hill, 1967.

_____. *Theology of Love.* Kansas City, Mo.: Beacon Hill, 1972.

BIBLIOGRAPHY

Calvin, John. *The Institutes of the Christian Religion.* 3 vols. Translated by Henry Beveridge. Edinburgh: Calvin Translation Society, 1845.

Carter, Charles W. *The Person and Ministry of the Holy Spirit: A Wesleyan Perspective.* Rev. ed. Grand Rapids: Baker, 1977.

Christensen, Bernhard. *The Inward Pilgrimage.* Minneapolis: Augsburg, 1976.

Deal, William S. *The March of Holiness Through the Centuries.* Kansas City, Mo.: Beacon Hill, 1978.

Dieter, Melvin E. *The Holiness Revival of the Nineteenth Century.* Metuchen, N.J.: Scarecrow, 1980.

Edman, V. Raymond. *They Found the Secret.* Grand Rapids: Zondervan, 1968.

Finney, Charles G. *The Promise of the Spirit.* Compiled and edited by Timothy L. Smith. Minneapolis: Bethany, 1980.

Flew, Newton R. *The Idea of Perfection in Christian Theology.* 1934. Reprint. Oxford: Clarendon, 1968.

Greathouse, William M. *From the Apostles to Wesley.* Kansas City, Mo.: Beacon Hill, 1979.

Harnack, Adolf von. *Outlines of the History of Dogma.* Translated by Edwin Knox Mitchess. New York: Funk and Wagnalls, 1893.

Hordern, William E. *New Directions in Theology Today.* Philadelphia: Westminster, 1966. Volume 1.

Jones, Charles Edwin. *The Holiness Movement.* Metuchen, N.J.: Scarecrow, 1974. Published jointly with The American Theological Library Association.

Kempis, Thomas à. *The Imitation of Christ.* Philadelphia: Porter and Coates, n.d.

Köberle, Adolf. *The Quest for Holiness.* Translated by John C. Mattes. Minneapolis: Augsburg, 1936.

Lightfoot, J.B. *The Apostolic Fathers.* Edited and completed by J. R. Harmer. Grand Rapids: Baker, 1962.

Lindstrom, Harald. *Wesley and Sanctification.* London: Epworth, 1946.

Monk, Robert C. *John Wesley: His Puritan Heritage.* Nashville: Abingdon, 1966.

Schaff, Philip. *The Creeds of Christendom,* 3 vols. 4th ed. 1877. Reprint. Grand Rapids: Baker, 1969.

Smith, Timothy L. *Revivalism and Social Reform.* New York: Abingdon, 1957.

Turner, George Allen. *Christian Holiness.* Kansas City, Mo.: Beacon Hill, 1977.

_____. *The Vision Which Transforms.* Kansas City, Mo.: Beacon Hill, 1964.

_____. *Witnesses of the Way.* Kansas City, Mo.: Beacon Hill, 1981.

Watson, Philip S. *The Message of the Wesleys.* New York: Macmillan, 1964.

Wilcox, Leslie D. *Be Ye Holy.* Cincinnati: Revivalist, 1965.

Wynkoop, Mildred Bangs. *Foundations of Wesleyan-Arminian Theology.* Kansas City, Mo.: Beacon Hill, 1967.

_____. *A Theology of Love.* Kansas City, Mo.: Beacon Hill, 1972.

CHAPTER 3

A HISTORICAL AND CONTEMPORARY APPRAISAL OF WESLEYAN THEOLOGY

Timothy L. Smith

Timothy L. Smith is Professor of History and Director of the Program in American Religious History at the John Hopkins University and an ordained minister in the Church of the Nazarene. He is a graduate of the University of Virginia and earned his Ph.D. at Harvard University.

He is the author of Called Unto Holiness: The Story of the Nazarenes *and* Revivalism and Social Reform in Mid-Nineteenth-Century America. *He is also editor of* Promise of the Spirit: Charles G. Finney's Lectures on Sanctification. *Among his numerous articles in scholarly journals is a recent series on aspects of the history and theology of John Wesley's movement, most of them published in the* Wesleyan Theological Journal. *Dr. Smith has served pastorates in the Church of the Nazarene in Virginia, Massachusetts, Maine, and Colorado and from 1971 to 1975 was preacher to the congregation located on the campus of Eastern Nazarene College. He taught at Eastern Nazarene College, East Texas State College, and the University of Minnesota before joining the John Hopkins faculty in 1968. He appears frequently to lecture and preach on Christian college campuses and presents several papers each year to scholarly societies. He has directed his graduate students in four major research programs, each occupying several years, under the sponsorship of the U.S. Office of Education, the Lilly Endowment, the Fund for the Advancement of Education, and the National Endowment for the Humanities.*

CONTENTS

I. INTRODUCTION / 77
II. THE FORMATION OF WESLEYAN DOCTRINE / 78
III. THE WESLEYAN REVIVAL, 1758–1790 / 83
IV. WESLEYAN THEOLOGY IN AMERICA DURING THE NINETEENTH CENTURY / 88
V. THE HOPE OF HOLINESS IN AN AGE OF DESPAIR / 94

NOTES / 98
DISCUSSION QUESTIONS / 100
RECOMMENDATIONS FOR FURTHER READING / 101

A Historical and Contemporary Appraisal of Wesleyan Theology

I. INTRODUCTION

The notion that Wesleyan theology has no systematic structure rests on the myth that the only theology worthy of the name is Calvinist. Those who cling to this myth have been unable or unwilling to bear John Wesley's insistence that the doctrine of salvation is the heart of Christian theology and sanctification the essence of salvation. The doctrine of Christian perfection was indeed the centerpiece of Wesley's religious thought. Neither his own experience nor those of his followers formed the basis of that doctrine, however—though for a century the impulse to modernism among Methodists has fed on the legend that they did. Rather, Wesley believed that clear reasoning about the plain meanings of Scripture would be illuminated by the Holy Spirit and so by grace bring knowledge of the truth. From this sprang conviction both of one's own sin and of God's supreme love for sinners, as well as the persuasion that the divine purpose was to renew His obedient children in purity and perfect love. Christian experience began, as Jesus had said, in knowing the truth; and it enabled believers, the apostle Paul said, to do the truth.

Wesley's system of theology, therefore, was thoroughly biblical. He came very early to believe that the only proper way to approach the Scriptures, and the only means of grasping their unity, was through the hermeneutic of holiness that he derived from studying them. The command and the promise that we should love God with all our hearts and serve Him in holiness and righteousness all the days of our lives was to Wesley the central theme of every part of the Bible, whatever the immediate setting and purposes of its many books. He was certain, moreover, that the system of biblical theology that emerged from close study of the texts guided by that hermeneutic was best and most scripturally communicated by preaching. He never composed a creed for Methodists, being content with the Anglican and the ancient ones. And he set forth the classic Christian doctrines in sermons, hymns, and evangelical tracts. In these, however, he dealt carefully with every major topic in systematic theology. He proclaimed the faith, as Moses and the prophets and Jesus

---

All rights reserved by the author.

and the apostles had, in situations framed by his intention to bring men and women to the experience of it.¹

For all these reasons, Wesleyan Christianity was a model of modern evangelical faith. Scripture was its basis, the new birth to a life of righteousness and love its central theme, and evangelism its governing mission.

II. THE FORMATION OF WESLEYAN DOCTRINE

The genesis of the evangelical awakening came in that moment when, while they were students at Oxford, John Wesley and his younger brother Charles set out in scriptural study to find "the holiness without which no man shall see the Lord." That initial insight into what they soon concluded was the Bible's central promise and the conviction of their freedom and responsibility under grace to seek it were rooted in the evangelical piety that permeated their Anglican heritage. That piety was especially intense in their mother, Susannah Wesley. Little wonder, therefore, that in the early years of their search the two brothers leaned heavily on the famous volumes written by Bishop Jeremy Taylor in the previous century, *The Rule and Exercises of Holy Living* and *The Rule and Exercises of Holy Dying*, and the writings of their contemporary, William Law. Law's *Practical Treatise Upon Christian Perfection* and *Serious Call to a Devout and Holy Life* were published in 1726 and 1728, respectively.

The Wesleys were also deeply affected by Thomas à Kempis's *Imitation of Christ*, a classic of pre-Reformation Catholic piety popular with many Anglicans, and by Scottish Henry Scougall's *Life of God in the Soul of Man*, representing the best of Calvinist piety. All of these made the Old and New Testament Scriptures the foundation of faith and stressed their call to personal holiness and their promise to fallen humanity of renewal in the image of God. All declared that love is the essence of the moral law and that the impartation of divine love is the source of the power to keep the law. Two Anglicans, Taylor and Law, spoke strongly for the doctrine of universal redemption and, therefore, of the freedom and responsibility of individuals to respond to grace.²

John Wesley was certainly not conscious of any break from the traditions of these writers when in 1728 he determined to make the Bible his "chief study." The fruit of that study is clear in his early sermon "The Circumcision of the Heart," preached at Oxford University January 1, 1733. It anticipated in every major respect, except the idea of two moments of conscious assurance of saving and sanctifying grace, all that John Wesley was to preach in the years after his famous Aldersgate experience of "salvation by faith" on May 24, 1738. Other sermons of the early years, printed by mistake in 1816 under the name of Charles Wesley, but recently discovered to have been John's, are almost equally clear in their perception of the biblical promise of a new covenant of grace, through the hallowing Spirit, to fulfill the law of holiness and perfect love.³

To be sure, the depth of their education in the Latin classics, the early church fathers, and the Greek and Hebrew Bible impelled the Wesleys and the small circle of students who joined them in Oxford's "Holy Club" to grapple earnestly with the whole range of doctrines set forth in the historic creeds of Christendom. Clearly, however, their personal quest for "the righteousness which is by faith," for renewal in God's image, was the governing impulse of their religious thought. After pursuing that quest in heroic habits of devotion and self-discipline for seven years, the two Wesleys led several of the Holy Club, including George Whitefield, to Georgia, where they intended to minister to both the Indians and the first English settlers there. During their journeys, all of them came into contact with German Pietists from the missionary community of Herrnhut in Moravia. The Moravians played a crucial role in shaping the Methodist understanding of what Scripture taught about the experience of salvation, namely, that a seeker is born again in a moment of renewal through "living faith." John Wesley defined the latter many times as an inward evidence and conviction, wrought by the Holy Spirit, that Christ had forgiven that person's sins and given him or her new life. When Wesley returned from Georgia in mid-winter in early 1738, the Moravian Peter Böhler told him that true faith in Christ always produced "dominion over sin, and constant peace from a sense of forgiveness"—that is, the assurance of adoption and a radical beginning of sanctification as well. Convinced by a careful rereading of the Gospels and Acts and by further conversations with Böhler, Wesley realized he had not found such faith and resolved not to preach again until he possessed it. Böhler advised him, however, to "preach faith *till* you have it; and then, you will preach it *because* you have it." By April 22, Wesley's *Journal* tells us, passages whose meaning he "had been long since taught to construe away" affirmed the Moravian understanding that true faith is a "sure trust and confidence" that the believer's "sins are forgiven," that both happiness and holiness are "fruits of this living faith," and that "the Spirit itself beareth witness with our spirit that we are the children of God."[4]

All that remained was the startling proposition that such faith was received in a moment, an instant of grace. Searching again the Book of the Acts of the Apostles, Wesley said, he "found scarce any instances" of conversion that were not instantaneous. The next day, his *Journal* reads, "I could now only cry out, 'Lord, help thou my unbelief!'" Ten days later, Wesley organized the first Methodist Society at Fetter-Lane, which brought together Londoners who were seeking the new life of the Spirit. Certain of the trustworthiness of Scripture, he preached this "new gospel" with such fervor that he was excluded from three Anglican pulpits in London a fortnight before he received at a Moravian prayer meeting in Aldersgate Street the assurance of his own salvation, "by grace, through faith." From this word of Paul in Ephesians 2:8 Wesley preached at Oxford two weeks later the sermon "Salvation by Faith," which some have made the beginning point of the evangelical awakening.[5]

George Whitefield, however, had been preaching precisely the same promise of regeneration, of being "born of the spirit" to a life of victory over sin, for at least a year before that time—first in England while Wesley was in Georgia, and then in America, after Wesley had left for home. The evidence is not only Whitefield's account in his youthful autobiography, published in 1744, but his sermon *On the Nature and Necessity of Regeneration or New Birth in Christ Jesus,* published in mid-summer, 1737. Indeed, in Whitefield's autobiography, possibly shaped by subsequent experience, he attributed the extensive revivals that broke out under his ministry in Bristol, Gloucestershire, and London on the eve of his first departure for Georgia to his ringing preaching of the scriptural promises that that sermon declared. Its text, "If any man be in Christ he is a new creature" (2 Cor. 5:17), was the one that Peter Böhler pressed upon John Wesley in February 1738. That text, construed as a promise to be fulfilled in an undefined process of discipline and devotion, had long preoccupied Wesley and it dominated his thinking about salvation for the next year and a half. During the spring and summer of 1739, Whitefield's sermons on the new birth (especially "The Indwelling Spirit," published at the height of the great revivals that he and the Wesleys conducted in Bristol and London) and John Wesley's several sermons on that subject, some of them from the same texts, made the doctrine of the presence and sanctifying work of the Holy Spirit in regeneration the scriptural foundation of the evangelical revival.[6]

At this point Wesleyan, Calvinist, and Moravian doctrines converged. The eighteenth-century consensus about Scripture, spiritual experience, and evangelism remains to this day the defining mark of evangelicalism in every Christian tradition. Two ideas defined the distinctively Wesleyan version of this evangelical consensus: Wesley's firm rejection of the doctrine of predestination and the emergence in the fall of 1739 of his conviction that the Scriptures taught that a second "moment" of hallowing grace was crucial to the process by which the Holy Spirit perfected God's children in righteousness and love.

Wesley's understanding of that second moment of sanctifying grace also rested on Scripture rather than on either his experience or the experiences of his converts. This fact has escaped scholarly notice because so many have dated the crystallization of the doctrine of Christian perfection eighteen months later than its actual occurrence. The evidence for the earlier date comes chiefly from John Wesley's "Diary" and *Journal* entries for November 7 and 17, 1739, and from the preface he wrote to his and his brother's second volume of *Hymns and Sacred Poems*, published during the first half of 1740.[7] Supporting evidence appears in the correspondence of George Whitefield, written from Boston and Philadelphia in September and November 1740, both to his Calvinist friends in England and to John and Charles Wesley, in response to letters dated six months or more earlier. Whitefield expressed surprise and dismay that the two brothers had embraced what he always thereafter called the doctrine of "sinless perfection." These facts leave us every reason to conclude that the sermon on Christian perfection that Wesley tells us in his "Diary" and *Journal* he composed in early November 1739 and began preaching at once in Bristol and elsewhere was substantially the same one that he published under that title early in 1741, a few weeks before Whitefield arrived from America in the hope of setting his friends straight.[8]

Wesley's earliest sermon on the second work of grace may indeed have been the one published in 1748 as the third of his twelve discourses on the Sermon on the Mount. Late in the summer of 1739, Wesley tells us, he "began expounding a second time" Christ's teachings in Matthew 5 in a series of sermons at a small town near Bristol.[9] The first and second discourses, "Blessed are the poor in spirit" (whom Wesley made out to be the repentant seekers) and "Blessed are they that mourn" (whom he understood to be born-again Christians suffering temptations to doubt and fear until they are assured by "a fresh manifestation of His love" of their continued acceptance in Christ) conform closely to the preface Wesley wrote a few months later for the second volume of *Hymns and Sacred Poems*. The third discourse of the series was on the texts "Blessed are the pure in heart" and "Blessed are those who hunger and thirst after righteousness." In the preface to that discourse and, a bit later, in his tract *Character of a Methodist*, Wesley laid out precisely what he believed to be the nature of entire sanctification.

The preface of 1740 later became the centerpiece of Wesley's *Plain Account of Christian Perfection*. In it he wrote that Christians are enabled, because of the reassurance of God's forgiving love, to bear the disclosure of the "desperate wickedness" that lies deep in their hearts. From that moment they earnestly desire "to be renewed after the likeness of Him that created us," to have "the whole mind which was in Christ," to be "joined unto the Lord in one spirit," to "walk in the light as God is in the light," and to be "purified even as He is pure." In the third discourse on the Sermon on the Mount, Wesley stressed the promise of Jesus that "those who hunger and thirst after righteousness shall be filled." He insisted that those who are in Christ would then love their neighbors as themselves, live beyond all unkindness, pride, self-serving anger, and evil thoughts and believe, hope, and endure all things. In the preface he declared that in response to such seeking God remembers His holy covenant and He giveth them a single eye and a pure heart; He stamps upon them His own image and superscription; He createth them anew in Christ Jesus; He cometh unto them with His Son and blessed Spirit, and, fixing His abode in their souls, bringeth them into the rest which remaineth for the people of God.[10]

Wesley's expositions of the Old and New Testament texts cited in this sentence were central in his preaching and in the hymns he and his brother published in 1740. These texts remained the foundation of his doctrine of Christian perfection to the end of his life.

This earlier dating of Wesley's first preaching on entire sanctification also makes it clear that his teaching was hammered out of Scripture during the growing controversy with the London Moravians that began in early fall, 1739. Several of the Moravians, moving well beyond Peter Böhler, taught the converts of Wesley and Whitefield that seekers were not truly born again until they were entirely free of all doubt and fear, as well as of guilt and sin. Moreover, nothing a seeker could or should do by way of self-discipline, repentance, prayer, Christian service, or attendance upon preaching and the sacraments would hasten his or her experience of such Christian holiness as the Scriptures promised. This doctrine of "stillness" Wesley had not perceived at Herrnhut when he visited the Moravians there in the August following Aldersgate. A year later, however, it had so pervaded the London congregation that by early November 1739 Wesley did not find "one woman of the society" who was not "upon the point of casting away her confidence in God." A long conference with Bishop Spangenburg on November 7 made it clear that the Moravians would continue to insist that persons still "liable to any doubt or fear" were not born of God and ought, therefore, to abstain from the Lord's Supper. Precisely at this point, Wesley's "Diary" and *Journal* tell us, he wrote a sermon on Christian perfection and returned to Bristol preaching it. Its import was both to reassure believers and deepen their hunger for inward holiness.[11]

During the following eight months of controversy with the Moravians, Wesley preached a succession of new sermons from texts that he always thereafter used to proclaim the promise of purity of heart and perfect love. Among these were 2 Peter 1:4; 1 John 2:12; 4:7; Ephesians 4:23-24; Hebrews 4:9; 10:19. He first preached on Hebrews 4:9, explaining "the rest which remaineth for the people of God," at the Kingswood School June 1, 1740, and later that same day, out of doors, before six or seven thousand of the miners of that East Bristol town. He returned to London at the end of June and stood by helplessly as the Fetter-Lane Society was divided. Those who stood with him, definitely a minority, fitted out a place to worship in an old foundry. Wesley's inaugural sermon there was on the Kingswood text, Hebrews 4:9. Nine days later he urged the congregation to "press forward for the prize of their high calling (Phil. 3:14), even a clean heart, thoroughly renewed after the image of God, in righteousness and true holiness (Eph. 4:24)." At the end of September he began at the foundry chapel his discourses on the Sermon on the Mount. We can be reasonably sure that this time around, the doctrine of entire sanctification they set forth attained the scriptural wholeness displayed in their published version.[12]

Occasionally, during the next few years, Wesley sought to minimize public discussion of this distinctive teaching. He insisted he was simply explaining the meaning of scriptural promises and revitalizing the teaching of historic Christianity. In fact, however, the doctrine of "perfect love," of full inward renewal in God's image and cleansing from all the corruption of "inbred sin," was for the remaining fifty years of his life the center of his thinking, whatever the subject of his preaching or writing. It gave logical and scriptural coherence to the stream of tracts that followed, notably his *Appeal* and *Farther Appeal to Men of Reason and Religion* and his long *Letter to Dr. Con-*

yers Middleton. It pervaded the third volume of *Hymns and Sacred Poems,* as its preface announced in 1742. It illumined all the later hymnbooks, including the volume for Pentecost published in 1746 under the title *Hymns of Petition and Thanksgiving for the Promise of the Father.* It is the hermeneutic key to such sermons as "Scriptural Christianity," which he knew would be the last one he preached at Oxford because the university officials would not bear his insistent question whether they were "filled with the Holy Spirit," as the text of Acts 4:31 suggested all believers should seek to be.[13]

The breadth of biblical vision that permeated the hymns as well as every page of their tracts and sermons shows both Wesleys to have been preeminently biblical theologians. In recent decades, however, scholars have reflected the growing interest in the history of the Enlightenment by realizing that Wesley stressed reason, along with Scripture and experience, as an indispensable element in Christian theology. And even more recently, Professor Albert Outler has highlighted Wesley's deep devotion to the historic traditions of the Christian church, from the early fathers to the sixteenth-century composers of the Anglican creed, homilies, and *Book of Common Prayer.*[14] But the notion of a "Wesleyan quadrilateral," in which Scripture, experience, reason, and tradition stand as the four cornerstones of faith, will scarcely fit the facts.

Concerning experience, Wesley's doctrine of entire sanctification was hewn entirely out of Scripture before any of his followers began to profess that grace. And for the rest of his life he sought purity of heart but did not seem ever to believe he had received it. A powerful testimony to the primacy of Scripture in Wesley's theology of salvation is the fact that despite this unsatisfied quest he preached the promise of perfect love incessantly and counseled and encouraged several thousands of his followers who he believed had experienced it.

As for reason, Wesley, as John Fletcher did after him, insisted that the most acute intellect he had encountered in all of human literature was, save for Jesus, that of the apostle Paul. The firm conviction of both the Wesleys that the Holy Spirit must illuminate God's Word and by regenerating grace restore the "spiritual senses" by which human beings can understand it was a fundamental challenge to enlightenment rationalism. To be sure, many years later in his sermon "The Case of Reason Impartially Considered" he explained that sound reasoning can help us understand "the essential truths" about the way of salvation that are set forth in the Bible. But "true religion stands upon the oracles of God," he declared. "It is built upon the prophets and apostles, Jesus Christ himself being the chief cornerstone." Reason cannot produce either the faith or the hope in Christ from which love flows; these are the gift of grace. God alone, he cried, can "shed his love abroad in your heart by the Holy Ghost given unto you."[15]

Likewise, Wesley subjected both ancient and Anglican traditions to the test of Scripture. In his important *Address to the Clergy,* published in 1756, he urged all to acquire a knowledge of the early church fathers because they are "the most authentic commentators on Scripture, as being both nearest the fountain, and eminently endued with the Spirit by whom all Scripture is given." Years later he took public pride in the "known principle of the Church of England" that "nothing is to be received as an article of faith, which is not read in the Holy Scriptures, or to be inferred therefrom by just and plain consequences." He wrote in the preface to his *Notes Upon the New Testament* that the Old and New Testaments set forth "a most solid and precious system of divine truth. Every part thereof is worthy of God; and altogether are one entire body, wherein is no defect, or excess. It is the foundation of heavenly wisdom, which they who are able to taste prefer to all writings of men, however wise or learned or holy."[16]

III. THE WESLEYAN REVIVAL, 1758–1790

The second decade of Methodist history, from 1748 to 1758, witnessed continuing public controversy about the doctrines of John Wesley and some inner tensions in the movement itself. The latter were complicated by the huge embarrassment of John Wesley's sudden and, as events turned out, unhappy marriage and by the seeming resistance of many of his preachers to seeking or encouraging their people to seek the blessing of heart purity. Wesley published a third volume of his sermons in 1750. In it he completed the series on the Sermon on the Mount, adding an ecumenical appeal for holiness in one entitled "A Catholic Spirit." He struck powerful blows against antinomianism and disdain for the Old Testament by a sermon on the nature and use of the law and another, his second on the subject, "The Law Established Through Faith." In 1754 he set to work in earnest writing his *Explanatory Notes Upon the New Testament*. He intended this two-volume work not as a learned commentary, something he was entirely capable of writing, but as an aid to his preachers who were not blessed with an education in Greek and Hebrew. He wanted the *Notes* simply to give them the sense of what the Scriptures actually say. During this decade he also answered with growing power the serious theological critiques of Methodism made by Calvinists, rationalists, and Anglican moralists such as the Lord Bishop of Exeter. In the midst of completing the *Notes*, he wrote a long treatise entitled *The Doctrine of Original Sin, According to Scripture, Reason, and Experience*.

These tasks behind him, Wesley seems to have developed in 1757 a renewed sense of urgency to preach the gospel of sanctification by faith and to lead his people into that experience. The texts of his great sermons "Scripture Way of Salvation," "The Repentance of Believers," and "The Lord Our Righteousness," published separately at the height of the revival that ensued, appear repeatedly in his Sermon Register for 1758 and 1759, as do the texts of "On Zeal" and "The End of Christ's Coming." The first two laid out with special care the precise parallels between the two moments of hallowing grace. Both regeneration and entire sanctification were grounded in repentance—in the first instance for sinful deeds and in the second for the ugly reality of the remains of inbred sin. Both were brought to pass through faith in Christ—in the one case for forgiveness and new life and in the other for inward cleansing and perfect love. The two sermons entitled "The Lord Our Righteousness" and "The End of Christ's Coming" affirmed what all the Methodists knew had been Wesley's teaching from the beginning: that salvation was by grace alone, through faith, and that all the believer's righteousness, both imparted and imputed, stemmed from Christ's atonement.[17]

The immense range of Wesley's sermon texts during this period, however, makes clear the breadth of the theological instruction he thought necessary to sustain the renewal of primitive Christianity he believed the Wesleyan revival was called to bring about. During the long period from late February to mid-November of each year, he preached his way across England, Ireland, and Scotland, visiting nearly every Methodist society. He often recorded in his sermon register as many as six sermons a day, nearly always beginning with one before daybreak in the open air near a town or village center and ending with a Bible exposition at an evening meeting of one of his local societies.

Wesley began in 1758 to inquire closely concerning the progress the members of each society were making toward the experience of perfect love. When he found persons who professed that grace he questioned them carefully and, though himself apparently still seeking the blessing, recorded in his *Journal* generous judgments of their lives and testimonies. Everywhere they went, the two Wesleys used the most pointed of their earlier hymns to proclaim the promise of sanctifying grace.

The result of all this, by the year 1759, was a spreading revival in which testimonies to purity of heart were central. To Wesley's surprise, young people barely in their teens seemed to have experienced that grace, with its attendant fruits of rejoicing always, praying without ceasing, and in everything giving thanks (1 Thess. 5:16-18). He urged the preachers in the conferences he held on each circuit to seek it earnestly. In 1760 Wesley published in his fourth volume of sermons the tract entitled *Thoughts on Christian Perfection,* the record of his conversations with his ministers on the subject. A condensation of it filled an important section of his classic *Plain Account of Christian Perfection,* first published in 1766.

The great surge of seeking holiness that took place in 1761 and 1762 reminded Wesley that years before, in a moment of discouragement, his brother Charles had told him that his Pentecost had not yet fully come. When it did, Charles said, they would "hear of persons sanctified, as frequently as . . . of persons justified." Looking back over the previous twelve months, Wesley wrote in his *Journal* for October 28, 1762, that "any unprejudiced reader" would "observe that it was now fully come."[18] Although a grievous outbreak of self-righteousness and fanaticism about the second coming of Christ followed soon after in the London congregation, it did little to slow the momentum of the revival. The preaching of Christian holiness continued to flourish throughout the 1760s.

Indeed, the publications of that decade greatly clarified all the major points of Christian doctrine that the Wesleyan movement stood for. Chief among these, of course, was that of entire sanctification. The volume of John Wesley's sermons published in 1760 contained such classics on the subject as "The Wilderness State," "Heaviness Through Manifold Temptation," "Original Sin," and "Self-Denial." All these emphasized the distinction between human frailty and sin and, concerning the latter, between evil acts and the underlying disposition to evil called "inbred sin." And they stressed the duty of Christians both before and after their experience of heart purity to discipline themselves, seek righteousness, and, as Paul put it, work out their salvation with fear and trembling (Phil 2:12). In succeeding years, Wesley published in separate pamphlets his greatest holiness sermons: *On Sin in Believers* (1763), *Scripture Way of Salvation* (1765), and *The Repentance of Believers* (1768). Passages in all these continued his lifelong effort to clarify the relationship between the instantaneous and the progressive aspects of sanctification. Wesley had always viewed human beings as dynamic and their relationship with God as a living one, depending moment by moment on their continuing faith and commitment and the continuing work of the Holy Spirit. In these sermons, therefore, as in his correspondence and tracts of the period, Wesley scarcely ever mentioned entire sanctification without stating, usually in the same sentence, that growth in holiness was both a necessary and joyous fruit of the experience of perfect love. Such growth must continue to the end of life, he urged, and perhaps on into eternity, until all the works of the devil were done away, including the marks of sin on personality, disposition, and judgment.

One notable development was Wesley's increasing use of the language and the events of Pentecost to expound Christian perfection. From the beginning of his preaching that doctrine, he had used Pentecostal terms, as indeed the New Testament does, to refer to both regeneration and entire sanctification, since in his view both experiences took place on that day. During the months after Aldersgate, he and his brother often clothed the promise of the new birth in Pentecostal language, as Whitefield did. Their primary challenge was to persuade doubting Anglicans that the gift of the life-changing power of the Holy Spirit was promised to all believers in all times and not simply to the apostles.

Peter had declared that promise to repentant Jews at the close of his sermon on Pentecost Day.[19]

Being faithful to what Acts 2 declares happened to the 120 believers earlier that day, however, the two brothers seem never to have used the phrase or idea of being *filled* with the Holy Spirit to describe believers not yet made pure in heart. John's *Explanatory Notes Upon the New Testament,* especially his comments on John 14-17, describing Jesus' promise of the abiding Holy Spirit to His believing but anxious disciples, greatly reinforced the teaching of his last Oxford sermon on this point. His *Thoughts on Christian Perfection,* cast in the form of answers he gave in 1758 and 1759 to various "objections" raised against this doctrine, repeatedly used such phrases as "filled with pure love" or "filled with the love of God" to refer to entire sanctification; and toward the end of that writing he described those who enjoyed that grace as "indeed full of His Spirit."[20] On March 16, 1771, he wrote an inquiring Joseph Benson that he believed "one that is *perfected in love,* or *filled with the Holy Ghost,* may be properly termed a *father*" in Israel, a term from 1 John 2:13 that he used throughout his life to refer to those who experienced perfect love. "This we must press both babes and young men to aspire after," Wesley continued, "yea, to expect. And why not now?"[21]

Equally important to Wesley during that decade was his continuing emphasis on the doctrine of the Holy Spirit's work in regeneration. As always, he strenuously resisted any tendency in the preaching of entire sanctification to minimize that measure of holiness granted in the new birth, as until the first decades of the twentieth century his followers nearly always did. The issue was crucial to his long crusade against antinomianism and crucial also to his ability to maintain his tacit alliance with George Whitefield. Both men stood firm against those who would corrupt the evangelical awakening by preaching that faith and grace make void the moral law. Hence the importance Wesley attributed to the sermons on regeneration he published in pamphlet form during the decade: *The Lord Our Righteousness* (1766), affirming *imputed* on the ground of *imparted* holiness, and a second discourse on *The Witness of the Spirit* (1767).

In the early years of the decade both Wesley and Whitefield wrote long responses to the garbled attack that William Warburton, Anglican Bishop of Worcester, had recently published against their teachings about the Holy Spirit. Wesley stressed the scriptural promise and the Anglican doctrine that the gift of the Spirit empowers those who are born again to live a righteous life. Whitefield was even more explicit on the sanctification that flows from regeneration. He declared that all Christians "do now and always will" stand in as much need of the "transforming influence of the Spirit of Jesus Christ" as did the first apostles. Only the Spirit's abiding presence, he wrote, can make them truly Christian, "by beginning, carrying on, and completing that holiness in the heart and life of every believer, in every age, without which no man living shall see the Lord."[22] Here, revived, was the language of Whitefield's earliest sermons. Shortly afterward Whitefield wrote to a friend concerning Lady Huntington, praising her "laudable ambition" to lead the Christian vanguard. "O for a plerephory [that is, a fullness] of faith! To be filled with the Holy Ghost," Whitefield exlaimed. "This is the grand point. God be praised that you have it in view."[23]

These developments opened the possibility of even closer fellowship between Wesleyans and those Calvinists who took the call to holiness seriously. John Fletcher—a Methodist who had grown up in the French-speaking Reformed Church of Switzerland, migrated to England, and was ordained Anglican rector at the parish of Madeley—sensed this opportunity. A pastor of poor workers in the Severn Valley, cradle of the industrial revolution, Fletcher shared with the Wesleys the spiritual ambitions Whitefield has praised in Lady Huntington. With John Wesley's blessing, he accepted the countess's invitation to preside over the college called Trevecca that she had founded in South Wales, in the hope of uniting the youthful followers of both Wesley and Whitefield. What seems in retrospect a sad misunderstanding, occasioned by Wesley's "unguarded" remarks on good works at his conference of 1770, dashed all these hopes, and Fletcher and Joseph Benson left Trevecca.

Nevertheless, when the news reached England in 1770 that George Whitefield had died and been buried at Newburyport, Massachusetts, John Wesley preached, as his friend had requested, a memorial sermon in Whitefield's London pulpit. In it, Wesley declared that the two men had never differed on the central doctrine of the evangelical awakening: that the gift of the Holy Spirit in the experience of regeneration delivered believers from both the dominion and the guilt of sin and enabled them to "walk as Christ also walked." Both men had also consistently taught that the sanctification begun in the moment of regeneration must be thereafter progressive. But Wesley did not mention on this occasion what everyone present knew: that he had very early gone beyond Whitefield in his conviction that the Bible promised a second instant of grace that would cleanse believers from all inward sin and thereby make God's hallowing process more effective in their "outward" lives.[24]

In the early 1770s, John Fletcher emerged as the theologian of Wesleyan perfectionism, with the founder's full blessing. In a series of seven volumes called *Checks to Antinomianism,* originally prompted by attacks on Wesley by champions of antinomian Calvinism that Whitefield would not have countenanced, Fletcher presented in systematic form the doctrines of free will, free grace, and perfect love. These volumes, published over a period of five years, deepened the Wesleyan estrangement from contemporary Calvinism. But their major accomplishment, particularly in Fletcher's *Essay on Truth* (the center-piece of his *Equal Check to Phariseeism and Antinomianism*), was to ground Wesleyan doctrine in the scriptural promises that denied both legalism and the tendency of those who believed in salvation "by faith alone" to minimize the righteousness that came by grace through that faith.

In the process, Fletcher reiterated John Wesley's doctrine of prevenient grace. This teaching protected evangelical Arminianism from a merely human moralism. Wesley understood the Fall of humanity to have brought extensive total depravity. God's promise of redemption, however, was certified by His gift to all human beings, prior to faith, of the power to know right from wrong; to hear God's voice in conscience, Scripture, and the Holy Spirit; to acknowledge responsibility for their sins; and in repentance to seek righteousness and love. In the experience of salvation, the gift of the Holy Spirit brought believers the assurance of forgiveness and moral strength to overcome both outward and inward sin. Thereafter, the "faith that works by love" would keep them "more than conquerors" so long as they continued to exercise those "holy tempers" the Spirit had given: poverty of spirit (repentance), mourning (for God's continued presence), meekness (entire dependence on God), hungering and thirsting after righteousness, and loving those who persecuted or abused them.[25]

Fletcher's special contribution, however, was to press for a fuller and more persistent use of the events and the language of Pentecost to declare the promise of heart purity. At first Fletcher seems to have thought he was improving Wesley's doctrine. He had not paid close attention either to the founder's last Oxford sermon, "Scriptural Christianity," or to the passage on the dispensations of grace and the promise of the Spirit that Wesley laid out in his comments on John 7:38–39 in his first sermon on Christian perfection and in his *Notes* on the New Testament. Fletcher seems to have supposed that Charles

Wesley alone was the author of the Pentecost hymns the two brothers had published together in 1746. Indeed, during the five years he spent writing the first six of his *Checks to Antinomianism* Fletcher occasionally suggested that receiving the gift of the Holy Spirit, when one was in the moral condition of the three thousand God-fearing Jews converted on Pentecost Day, was virtually identical to the apostles' experience earlier that day of being filled with the Spirit.[26]

Wesley thought such a view minimized the gift of the presence and power of the Holy Spirit in regeneration. Their difference of opinion, however, did not seem great to either man. During this time Wesley repeatedly urged Fletcher to leave his parish and travel with him so as to become the aging founder's successor at the head of Methodism. Moreover, Wesley closely edited and published his young friend's *Essay on Truth,* which first laid out completely, though briefly, Fletcher's notion of what happened at Pentecost.

The crucial fact is that Wesley himself published Fletcher's *Last Check to Antinomianism* and in private letters also gave it his full blessing. In this final work in the series Fletcher adopted the founder's language and made it plain that he did not think the converts at Pentecost were filled with perfect love on that day simply because they had received the gift of the Holy Spirit. The language of the *Last Check* thus conformed perfectly with the view expressed in Wesley's last Oxford sermon, that the multitude of those converted at Pentecost were filled with the Holy Spirit at some later time, many of them on the day when Peter and John returned from their first hearing before the Sanhedrin. Wesley's text for that Oxford sermon was taken from the account of the prayer meeting that followed that event when, as Acts 4:31 declares, "they were all filled with the Holy Spirit." Fletcher cited that sermon and Wesley's other writings on the point in his footnotes to the *Last Check.*

All this fit logically into the fact that Wesley had throughout his life affirmed that those who believed on Christ before Pentecost were truly born again. He often used Mary's words of praise, "My soul doth magnify the Lord, and my spirit hath rejoiced in God my Savior," and Thomas's confession, "My Lord and my God," to depict the witness of the Spirit to regeneration. He also frequently alluded to Peter's word concerning Cornelius's household, that the Holy Spirit there had "fallen upon them as upon us at the beginning, purifying their hearts by faith," as testimony to what the apostles believed happened to them at Pentecost, and as proof of the universal availability of entire sanctification.[27]

The result of this fine tuning of the Wesleyan exegesis of the Scriptures was that in the later years of the eighteenth century and throughout the nineteenth, Methodists who sought and experienced perfect love tended more and more to use Fletcher's language of Pentecostal grace and to identify being baptized with being filled with the Spirit of holiness and love. The evangelical revival had from the beginning centered on the promise of the indwelling Spirit. In the Wesleyan extension of it, that promise, fulfilled at Pentecost, affirmed both regenerating and wholly sanctifying grace.

In retrospect, we know that the system of biblical theology Wesley and Fletcher expounded was centered in the experience of righteousness through faith. It proclaimed the renewal of individuals, of the church of Jesus Christ, and, at last when Christ should return, of all nature in the holiness for which God had created them. Moreover, the early Wesleyans did not ignore other major tenets of Christian doctrine but incorporated them into their theology of salvation. The two Wesleys and the tiny company of Anglican clergymen who joined the Methodist societies taught their followers to reverence the sacraments and to embrace the doctrines set forth in the Anglican creed and in the Apostle's Creed. Although they made Scripture, understood according to what they thought was its own hermeneutic of holiness, the source and test of doctrine, the early Methodists in England and America neither disdained reason nor rejected the traditions of the early church and the Protestant Reformation.

Wesley labored throughout his life to provide substitutes for the theological education his lay preachers had been denied and of which he thought many clergymen in the Church of England had failed to take full advantage. The publication of his library of devotional classics, his and his brother's sermons and hymns, his *Journal* and tracts, and his *Notes* on both the Old and New Testaments expressed their broad aim to raise up ministers rich in spiritual, biblical, and historical understanding. Amid the sweeping revival of the early 1760s, John Wesley found time to pull together and publish a two-volume *Compendium of Natural Philosophy* for his preachers. It is rarely studied because, being largely an abridgement of the works of others, it was never published with his other writings. Nevertheless, a third American edition had been published by 1823. The work helps us understand the importance Wesley assigned to both history and nature in his several short tracts and one sermon dealing with the history of God's dealings with humanity and in his later sermons dealing with the doctrine of the Second Coming and the renewal of the earth. In them Wesley affirmed history to be, in biblical terms, the continuing story of God's striving with humankind to restore all that sin had taken away. His sermons on last things declared God's intention to bring all who would have faith in Him (and at last, because of their faith, all of created nature) back to the beauty and perfection of His original purpose.[28]

Wesleyans have always thought themselves, therefore, devoted to the "fundamental doctrines of Christianity," as believed in all times and places by those who followed closely the teachings of Scripture under the illumination of the Holy Spirit. They have feared, as Wesley did, that the high Calvinist doctrines of predestination and assured final perseverance would undermine the call to righteousness that they believed was the center of biblical religion in both the Old and the New Testaments. Covenant, Cross, and Comforter —Father, Son, and Hallowing Spirit— call us to holiness, they declared, and promise grace to fulfill that call.

IV. WESLEYAN THEOLOGY IN AMERICA DURING THE NINETEENTH CENTURY

By the close of the American Revolutionary War Francis Asbury, whom John Wesley had sent to help his other preachers in America in 1771, was superintending a movement that was expanding rapidly in the towns between Baltimore and Boston as well as in rural and frontier regions of the former colonies. Wesley granted the American Methodists their independence in 1784, and the preachers at once elected Asbury their bishop, a title Wesley had never considered. However, in the few years of Wesley's life that remained, the growth of the American denomination delighted him. American Methodism was soon to witness the emergence of two independent black Methodist denominations and a white one as well. The last, protesting Asbury's dominance, called itself "Republican Methodist."

The long-held view that the doctrine of Christian perfection did not flourish in America during these years because the circuit riders were so busy seeking the conversion of sinners is no longer tenable. Asbury's sermon texts and the substance of his preaching as recorded in his journals and letters followed the example John Wesley set during the great revival of entire sanctification that occurred between 1757 and 1767. It was during that decade that the young Methodist had come to maturity in England. And the Methodist preachers in America in Thomas Jefferson's day earnestly sought the experience of perfect love. The United States version of the *Arminian Magazine* carried sermons, testimonies of Christian experience, and records of revivals that proclaimed holiness of heart just as Wesley's English magazine did. The *Plain Account of Christian Perfection* appeared in all the editions of the *Book of Discipline* from 1785 to 1795. After 1795 it was printed separately for convenience and sold everywhere. Several of John Fletcher's essays and two complete American editions of his works were printed before 1810, as were many editions of Wesley's hymnbook, sermons, and tracts on free grace and perfect love. The only ominous event was the lapse in enforcement and, eventually, the repeal of the rules forbidding Methodist laypersons to own slaves. Asbury resisted this for a long time, fearing correctly that it would undermine the ethics of perfect love, but finally acquiesced. Nevertheless, as compared with what happened among English Wesleyans, where Joseph Benson and other leaders muted the founder's emphasis on purity of heart, the American conferences remained substantially devoted to that doctrine.[29]

Some time after 1815, renewed calls to seek entire sanctification began in the conference centered in New York City and spread rapidly to New England and Pennsylvania. The preachers organized "select bands" of believers committed to seeking inward holiness, on Wesley's earlier model, and promoted in each conference an annual camp meeting where the promise of that experience was proclaimed. Nathan Bangs, the most influential leader in the American church during the period, and Wilbur Fisk, Methodism's most prominent educator, promoted it faithfully from the 1820s onward. In 1835 Sarah Lankford and her sister Phoebe Palmer organized their famous "New York Tuesday Meeting for the Promotion of Holiness." It ministered first to the wives of Methodist leaders in New York, then, for over forty years, to the leaders themselves and to Methodist ministers visiting New York from all over the nation. In 1839 Timothy Merritt began publishing in Boston the monthly *Guide to Holiness*. After 1840 George O. Peck, editor in turn of *The New York Christian Advocate* and *The Methodist Quarterly Review*, opened the columns of those journals to the holiness witness. In the 1850s Daniel Wise, editor of the Methodist abolitionist weekly in Boston, *Zion's Herald*, heartily encouraged it. Under Phoebe Palmer's inspiration, and often led by their wives, several future bishops and a great number of pastors, lay leaders, and professors in Methodist colleges entered by faith into the experience of heart purity and became ardent champions of it. Meanwhile, camp meetings and revivals all over the expanding church and nation encouraged public testimony to what one of Mrs. Palmer's books called entire devotion.[30]

The revival of Christian holiness in Methodism was accompanied after 1835 by a parallel awakening in Congregationalist and Presbyterian circles, led by Charles G. Finney, Asa Mahan, and the faculty of Oberlin College. Mahan's book, *The Scripture Doctrine of Christian Perfection,* published in 1839, and Finney's lectures on sanctification, printed in the *Oberlin Evangelist* the same year, helped inspire George Peck to write and publish a landmark volume with the same title as Mahan's. The Oberlin writers encouraged Methodists in their growing use of the experience of the 120 who were filled or baptized with the Holy Spirit on the Day of Pentecost as a model of entire sanctification. The publication in 1832 of Thomas Jackson's recent fine edition of the complete works of Wesley and, in 1833, of a third American edition of the works of John Fletcher helped quicken the holiness movement. Phoebe Palmer's several books and Thomas C. Upham's volumes *The Life of Faith, The Interior Life,* and the *Life of Madam Guyon* (Guyon was a Catholic mystic) helped spread the doctrine far beyond Methodist and Oberlin circles. Indeed, the growing influence of the holiness movement strengthened the optimism of Americans about what their experiment in democracy might make possible in the political as well as the moral and religious spheres.³¹

Little wonder, then, that by the mid-1850s the idea of evangelical perfection had taken root in all Christian communions. In New England, Lyman Beecher and Nathaniel W. Taylor, though attuned to patterns of thought coming out of the Calvinist tradition, affirmed almost as heartily as Methodists did free grace, free will, and the power of the Holy Spirit to make the law of love effective in human lives. George Peck welcomed Mahan and Finney as champions of perfectionism without quibbling over the details of their language and logic. In the mid-1850s Phoebe Palmer freely corresponded with Frederick Dan Huntington, Professor of Morals and preacher in the Appleton Chapel at Harvard, who was soon to forsake Unitarian for Trinitarian beliefs. She explained that the sanctifying fullness of the Holy Spirit is not to be received mystically, but morally and rationally. Presbyterian William E. Boardman published his best-selling volume called *The Higher Christian Life* in the midst of the nationwide revival of 1857–1858. Boardman chose language, both in his title and in his text, that he thought would get around sectarian prejudices against Methodist terminology; but he acknowledged that the doctrine and experience the book proclaimed was what Wesley and the American Methodists taught. Isaac Hecker, reared a Methodist and nurtured for a time in Boston transcendentalism, became a priest in the Roman Catholic church, where he joined one of Charles G. Finney's former converts, Clarence Walworth, in founding the Paulist Fathers. The two spent the rest of their lives preaching sanctification through grace, and grace mediated necessarily but by no means exclusively through the sacraments of the Roman Catholic church.³²

After the Civil War, the holiness movement became a crusade within Methodism, led by the National Campmeeting Association for the Promotion of Holiness, parent to the present-day Christian Holiness Association and its offspring, the World Gospel Mission. After 1880, however, an undercurrent of opposition began to surface. The bishops of both the Northern and Southern Methodist churches warned of the excesses of the movement, and a full-scale doctrinal debate broke out in the Methodist press. Pastors and scholars writing from the perfectionist viewpoint quickly won the argument as to which side was faithful to Wesley; but Wesley's convictions notwithstanding, some of the intellectual and many of the episcopal leaders of the denomination drew away from the doctrine of Christian holiness. For a time, some of them made the experience of the witness of the Holy Spirit to a radical experience of regeneration the distinctive doctrine of Methodist faith, and Methodist theologians in many places gradually accepted this view.

The controversy had important effects. It encouraged the Wesleyan Methodist and Free Methodist denominations, whose origins lay in both the antislavery and the holiness movements before the Civil War, to make their faithfulness to the doctrine of entire sanctification the centerpiece of their appeal to Methodists still loyal to Wesley's teaching. It also nurtured the conviction, born in the spread of holiness teachings outside of Methodism, that the movement was grounded in the Bible and belonged to all Christian denominations. In the 1890s the National Holiness Association abandoned its exclusive identification with Methodism. Doctrinally, the growing conflict produced a hardening of both language and temper that affected the substance and the spirit of holiness preaching and eventually muted the traditional Wesleyan emphasis on the growth in holiness that every Christian should enjoy both before and after the experience of being cleansed from inward sin.

Partly as a result of the controversy, several new holiness denominations emerged, ranging from the antiecclesiastical Church of God Reformation Movement, centered in Anderson, Indiana, to

A. B. Simpson's loosely organized Christian and Missionary Alliance, and the Salvation Army, which William and Catherine Booth had established in Great Britain and exported to the United States and Canada. What was soon to become the largest of these, the Church of the Nazarene, drew together during the years 1907 to 1914 four small organizations, one from the northeastern, one from the southeastern, one from the southwestern, and one from the far western sections of the United States. The last, led by Phineas Bresee, Methodist pastor and presiding elder in Los Angeles, gave the Nazarenes their name and much of their ability to combine the efficiency of Methodist superintendency with the freedom of lay persons to call their pastors and share in the administration of both local and denominational affairs. The Nazarene leaders, like those of other holiness communions, aimed their chief efforts at the conversion of the largely poor and uprooted people who had recently migrated from the countryside to American cities. Bresee, like the Nazarenes from other sections of the country, stood with Wesley in refusing to part company with other Christians over "mere opinions," insisting only that all be willing for their hearts to be set right by being filled with divine love.[33]

The Keswick movement that emerged in England after 1874 paralleled these American developments. Holiness evangelists from the United States made important tours of the British Isles after 1850, among them Finney, Phoebe Palmer, Boardman, Mahan, and, later, the Philadelphia Quakers Robert Pearsall and Hannah Whitall Smith. When Dwight L. Moody went to London for his first great revival there in 1872, Boardman and the Smiths followed him, conducting in London and other places prayer meetings devoted to the higher Christian life. The American evangelists won a surprisingly positive response. This stemmed in part from the influence of Christian idealism in recent English and German thought. Their basic appeals, however, were to the popular image of Christ and to the hunger for inward peace and purity that pervades human consciousness in every age and place.

The Keswick Convention for the Promotion of Holiness met annually after 1875 in the little town of Keswick, in the lake country of Wordsworth. It became the English equivalent to the American National Campmeeting Association. The differences lay chiefly in the earlier explicit commitment of the Keswick movement to a nondenominational stance and in the persistence of its leaders in teaching that inbred sin, though overwhelmed and made utterly powerless by the baptism and fullness of the Holy Spirit, is not entirely cleansed away. The influence of the Keswick Convention spread rapidly throughout Great Britain and, eventually, to the far corners of the British Empire. This was due largely to early leadership of the Americans Asa Mahan and Hannah Whitall Smith, the recruitment of numerous able clergymen from the Church of England, and the development of affiliate assemblies and publications in several cities of that country and, eventually, in Canada, South Africa, and Australia.[34]

What appraisal can we fairly make, in a few paragraphs, of the theological developments in this wide-ranging nineteenth-century movement to promote Christian holiness? To what extent were its leaders true to John Wesley's vision, and in what ways do they seem to have departed from it?

Certainly in its broadly ecumenical outreach—for example, both borrowing from and contributing to Roman Catholic traditions of saintliness—the nineteenth-century holiness movement seemed to fulfill Wesley's call for a rebirth of the catholic spirit in Christianity. Throughout his life, Wesley resisted narrow and sectarian definitions of Christian doctrine. He claimed to champion only the great essentials set forth in Scripture and enshrined in the major creeds of Christendom. He drew continuously on the Puritan sources his parents had honored, welcomed the influences of continental Pietism that touched him first through his mother and then through Peter Böhler and the Moravians, and defined on the narrowest possible ground the points of his disagreement with Calvinist Evangelicals. He wished to unite all Christians in the quest of righteousness through grace.

Viewed in this perspective, Wesley's nineteenth-century heirs understood his ecumenicity in ways the modern interchurch movement, Methodist or otherwise, does not. For like both Wesley and Whitefield, they realized that the prayer of Christ that His followers should be one was grounded in the promise of the Father that they should be sanctified in the truth. And God's Word—in Scripture as well as in the revelation of the Son and the guidance of the Holy Spirit—is truth. Wesley's famous sermon entitled "Catholic Spirit" stemmed from his lifelong commitment to this central promise of Scripture. He believed that it shines through the veils of historical circumstance, cultic ritual, and literary convention that we encounter in reading the varied parts of the Word of the Lord. George Peck and Asa Mahan, Phoebe Palmer and William Boardman, and Daniel Steele and Andrew Murray all shared Wesley's faith in the scriptural covenant of holiness and love. It was sealed in the blood that cleanses from all sin, they declared, and, thereafter, it is inspired moment by moment by the hallowing fullness of the Spirit. The living and inward experience of that covenant would unite true believers in such love to God and their fellow human beings as to make righteousness and *shalom* embrace each other and the kingdom of God to come on earth.[35]

The beliefs about sanctification that Wesley set forth were all cardinal ideas among the nineteenth-century holiness advocates. Like him, they stressed ethical righteousness, defined by Christ's example and wrought by the Holy Spirit through faith. Popular critics made them out to be simply moralistic Puritans. Yet their sermons, tracts, and autobiographies, from Finney to Phineas Bresee, stressed the fallenness of human beings. Humanity's only hope lay in the prevening grace that enabled sinners to hear the gospel, repent, and believe on Christ Jesus for the gift of spiritual life. They taught, as Wesley did, that neither justification nor sanctification came by "faith alone," but in the experience by grace of a "living faith" that is the gift of the Holy Spirit and produces works of love. The holiness movement's understanding of the order or stages of "full salvation" was also Wesley's: awakening to repentance; saving faith, certified in the witness of the Spirit; growth in holiness through good works and the ministry of the Spirit; the experience of a second moment of inwardly purifying grace; and, thereafter, continuous growth in holiness and love. The ultimate goal was the perfection of personality, knowledge, and disposition that, at the end of their days on earth and in larger measure after their entrance to heaven, would fulfill all God had promised to His children.

For them, as for Wesley, the proof of heart purity was both inwardly and outwardly evident: loving God entirely and loving one's neighbors ethically. John A. Wood, leader in the National Holiness Association, wrote a classic work called *Perfect Love*. Scholarly Daniel Steele, professor at Syracuse and Boston universities, wrote another classic work called *Love Enthroned*. The care for the poor and compassion for black people that had flowered before the Civil War continued afterwards, illustrated best in the teachings of the Salvation Army heroine Catherine Booth and in the ministry of the Church of God (Anderson, Indiana) Reformation Movement among Alabama blacks. Amanda Smith, a colored evangelist, was almost as famous on both sides of the Atlantic as Hannah Whitall Smith, who taught two generations of holiness people that *The Christian's Secret of a Happy Life*, as the title of her book put it, was to let the Holy Spirit fill one's hardest days with thoughts and deeds of love.

Their only distortion of Wesley's theology of salvation lay in their tendency to minimize the sanctifying power of the Spirit that began in the experience of the new birth. This was especially evident among the non-Wesleyans in the Keswick movement. The denial that the baptism with the Holy Spirit brought entire deliverance from inbred corruption prompted its leaders to identify that second experience with deliverance from evil acts and intentions. For the rest, all parties of American Wesleyans followed John Wesley closely. They drew from his sermons on sanctification their understanding of the nature of repentance, both in sinners and in believers; of the divine source of that faith by which alone we can please God; of the Holy Spirit's authorship of all that is good and true; and of the necessity of growth in holiness, both before and following the experience of the "second blessing."[36]

This was especially the case with Phoebe Palmer. True, Nathan Bangs appeared at her Tuesday meeting in 1857 to read a chastening comment on what he feared was her overemphasis on the exercise of faith in seeking holiness. He thought she had muted Wesley's doctrine that the Holy Spirit must both grant that faith and bear inward witness to the experience.

In his statement Bangs truly stood with Wesley; but so did Phoebe Palmer. She never doubted that inward assurance, or the witness of the Spirit, is the indispensable mark that a seeker's faith had been grounded in the promises of God and exercised by His grace, as Wesley taught in his great sermon "Scripture Way of Salvation." Indeed, her encouragement to seekers to exercise faith seems never to have gone a step beyond the words Wesley used in the closing paragraphs of that same sermon. Wesley had urged those praying for purity of heart to look "every day, every hour, every moment" for "this great work in the soul" to be accomplished. "Certainly you may look for it now, if you believe it is by faith," he cried.

If you seek it by faith, you may expect it *as you are;* and if as you are, then expect it *now*. . . . Stay for nothing. Why should you? Christ is ready; and He is all you want. He is waiting for you. He is at the door! Let your inmost soul cry out, "Come in, come in, thou heavenly Guest! Nor hence again remove; but sup with me, and let the feast be everlasting love."[37]

Third, the general doctrine of the Holy Spirit that nineteenth-century holiness preachers proclaimed reflected Wesley's interpretation of Scripture. True, they used freely the Pentecostal language Fletcher had popularized, which Wesley had endorsed but did not often use. However, the central theological aim of John Wesley's and George Whitefield's preaching was to proclaim the promise of the gift and fullness of the Holy Spirit to all who would repent, believe, and obey Christ. The holiness movement's celebration of the Spirit's work was at least as much a fulfillment of the vision of Wesley and Whitefield as a response to the soaring ideals and the sobering fears of the nineteenth century. The multiplying evils of an industrial and democratic society, the crisis over slavery and festering urban poverty were the catalysts that renewed their interest, as they had sparked Wesley's, in the promise of His outpouring in the "last days."

Moreover, Wesley taught that the doctrine of the Holy Spirit was central to the teachings of the Scripture about the Trinity. Those who declared the hallowing power of the Spirit in the nineteenth century believed they were resisting both the tri-theism that pervaded evangelical folk theology and the Christ-Unitarianism that was incipient in the popular phrase, "Christ only, and Him crucified." Their use of the language of Pentecost to describe the work of God's grace in the human soul affirmed the sovereignty of God without denying the responsibility of human beings to "work out their own salvation with fear and trembling." Seekers must not only choose to hear the gospel; after they receive both the gift and the fullness of the Spirit they must continue to deny themselves and take up their cross daily to follow Christ. This affirmation of both God's sovereignty and human accountability helped Christians of Dwight Moody's era to escape the temptations to antinomianism that have for decades threatened to overwhelm twentieth-century Evangelicals in many other traditions besides the Wesleyan.[38]

Finally, the nineteenth-century holiness preachers combined the eschatology of spiritual and social hope with the responsibilities of evangelism, just as John Wesley did. They shared his view of the link Jesus made between the great commission and the "promise of the Father" to fill believers with the Spirit of love and holiness. Not only among American Wesleyans but also in the English Keswick conferences the new dispensationalist ideas about the Second Coming that the Plymouth Brethren and others taught were excluded, almost to the end of the century.

V. THE HOPE OF HOLINESS IN AN AGE OF DESPAIR

The present century, which idealists in both liberal and conservative circles hoped would be the Christian century, has indeed been remarkable for the persistent growth of evangelical faith. But the growth has taken place amid growing gloom about the future of the church, and now of the human race, on earth. World War I, the shattered dreams of first the League of Nations and then of the United Nations, and the world-wide social problems of poverty, racial conflict, industrialization, and uprootedness sapped the optimism of the previous era. The barbarism of World War II, the Nazi and Stalinist programs of mass destruction of Jews and political dissidents, the American use of nuclear weapons against Japan, and the growing dependence of the world ever since upon a fragile balance of nuclear terror crushed hopes everywhere. Evangelical Christianity itself witnessed the emergence of new movements that posed substantial challenges to the ideals of Wesleyan faith. And the tendency of all Evangelicals to yield to the twentieth-century passion for freedom from moral constraints on individual behavior, particularly biblical ones, threatened for a time to divorce the faith and righteousness that Scripture always binds together.

The complexity of modern evangelicalism was itself a source of confusion. Since it formed the religious environment in which Wesleyan faith persisted, however, that complexity needs to be understood before we go further.[39]

The several millenarian movements in America—those of the Adventists, Mormons, and Jehovah's Witnesses—all responded in one way or another to the dispensational theology of the Plymouth Brethren. But the spreading influence of premillennialism in Baptist, Presbyterian, and Congregationalist circles at the turn of the century opened wider opportunities for the dispensationalism of the Brethren. This, in turn, gave rise to the Fundamentalist movement and greatly affected the beginnings of the Pentecostal movement as well. Fundamentalism also borrowed heavily from the resistance to modern learning and culture that conservative Calvinists displayed at the end of the nineteenth century and from the idea of the literal inerrancy of Scripture in matters of science and history, as well as faith and ethics. The result was the Fundamentalist campaign against all forms of modernism, not only in theology but also in science, politics, and education. The Pentecostal movement, whose founders were convinced that the baptism of the Holy Spirit, attested to by speaking in "unknown" tongues, was both a sign and a promise of the Last Days, was born in the first year of the century. It spread slowly across America for a time, then burst into flame in the national and international response to the famous revival at a mission on Azusa Street, Los Angeles, in 1906.[40]

Conservative Calvinists, deeply entrenched in numerous Presbyterian denominations, were guided intellectually by professors at Princeton Theological Seminary who left that institution in 1928 to found Westminster. They stood apart from Fundamentalism's premillennial doctrines but shared many of its other concerns. For a brief time they challenged the modernists for control of the Presbyterian Church in the United States, the major northern denomination of that tradition. Southern Baptists, generally Calvinist but in the early years of the century not usually dispensationalists or predestinarians, multiplied their evangelistic efforts and agencies. They combined the doctrines of free grace and final perseverance so as to affirm that persons truly born again could not lose their standing before God in imputed righteousness, despite the persistence of sin in their thoughts, words, and deeds. By mid-century, the Southern Baptists had become America's largest denomination and were spreading, with the migration of southerners, all over the United States.

The most conservative wing of Alexander Campbell's followers, called Churches of Christ, stood sharply isolated from other Evangelicals. So did the growing community called "Christians," who stood midway between the Churches of Christ and the liberal leaders of the denomination usually called Disciples of Christ. Both of these evangelical "Restorationist" groups maintained what they believed was Campbell's devotion to the biblical ideas of radical obedience, free will, the new birth, and the exclusive character of the believers' church. They both grew rapidly, though without much public attention, particularly in the Mississippi Valley and the Great Southwest. So did the conservative branches of the German and Scandinavian Lutherans and of the German Reformed, Dutch Reformed, and other denominations that served recent immigrants.

Meanwhile, the holiness movement, challenged by leaders in the principal branches of Methodism who denied Wesley's doctrine of a second work of grace and preached only a progressive sanctification, spawned several new denominations, as we have seen. It also deeply influenced others, notably the Brethren in Christ, whose Pennsylvania-German heritage went back to the colonial settlement of Brethren and Mennonites, and the Ohio, Kansas, and Oregon yearly meetings of the Society of Friends. Meanwhile, the Wesleyan-holiness denominations, including the Wesleyan Methodist Church (founded 1843), and the Free Methodist Church (founded 1860), and to some extent the Evangelical United Brethren, African Methodist Episcopal, African Methodist Episcopal (Zion), and Colored Methodist churches, placed a larger emphasis on the doctrine of Christian perfection. This was consistent with their traditions and it offered discontented Methodists an alternative to joining one of the newer holiness denominations. All these Wesleyan bodies, however, sensed a continuing challenge to their central doctrine from the other expanding evangelical movements, whether Baptist, Calvinist, Pentecostal, Lutheran, or Restorationist. So did the great company of holiness people who remained in the northern and southern branches of the white Methodist Episcopal denomination.

All this tended among Wesleyan-holiness bodies to produce what is sometimes called a "fortress mentality," or a degree of defensiveness. This pessimistic outlook, stemming from the Fundamentalist-Modernist encounter as much as from anything else, spread through all the evangelical movements. It reinforced their increasing isolation not only from the old-line denominations but also from one another. It affected deeply those leaders of the holiness movement who determined to continue the struggle within Methodism from their bases at Asbury College, Taylor University, and other such schools. The social pessimism that pervaded the culture seemed to justify and certainly nurtured this defensive attitude. The result was a significant alteration of the spiritual outlook and the doctrinal emphases of all those who claimed to stand in the radical Wesleyan tradition. In the new organizations, belief in or testimony to entire sanctification became a means of recruiting members and, hence, of defining the boundaries of separation from the world.

Pastors and bishops in the Methodist communions who had not been a part of the holiness movement but who wished to remain in a general way loyal to their founder's teachings complained that the holiness preachers and denominations had narrowed Wesley's doctrine of sanctification and subordinated it to organizational or sectarian purposes. As time passed, certain developments gave some justice to these complaints. Many holiness evangelists became preoccupied with defining ever more sharply the distinctions between the two works of grace and with identifying the precise nature and immediate consequences of each of them. This minimized the emphasis both Wesley and the nineteenth-century preachers had placed on the process by which the Holy Spirit led seekers toward perfection in Christ before, between, and after the experience of the new birth and of cleansing from all sin. The tendency to elevate righteousness in external matters of dress and behavior over other more basic fruits of inward grace was apparent to the holiness leaders themselves, as it had been to their Methodist forbears. The increasing confinement of Pentecostal imagery and exposition to the second work of grace was magnified when Wesleyans who had defected to the Pentecostals began to proclaim that the event of Pentecost pointed to a baptism of the Spirit that followed sanctification, or what was known as a third work of grace. The result was to modify the emphasis Whitefield and the Wesleys had placed on the large measure of sanctification that the Holy Spirit brought in the experience of the new birth.

More serious, however, was the impact on Wesleyan idealism of the growth of antinomianism, that is, opposition to the law, in twentieth-century culture and religion. Every evangelical tradition gave way at some point before it. For some, the adjustment was doctrinal: to picture law and grace as polar opposites and to deride as salvation by works the righteousness that every tradition had long declared to be the necessary fruit of faith. For others, whether in the Pentecostal movement at one extreme or in liturgical churches at the other, the notion of psychic blessedness gained ground against the moral view of sanctification. Whether through the ecstasy of the unknown tongue or the mystery and beauty of the mass and the holy communion, the cultivation of warm feelings often displaced the quest of justice, purity, and love.

Intellectual leaders in several evangelical traditions quailed before the derision that Karl Barth and Reinhold Niebuhr heaped upon the easy optimism of perfectionism, whether social or individual. Christian realism, these and other neo-orthodox thinkers said, must embrace the biblical testimony that demonic powers rule over both culture and history, that humanity is in sin and sin is pervasive in humanity, and that whatever the Scriptures promise of actual holiness lies beyond history in the eschaton. Such reasoning sustained, at the popular level, the view of many Southern Baptists and Fundamentalists that sinning in word, thought, and deed was inescapable in this life, even though persons who are truly born again cannot really fall from grace. Finally, the dispensationalist view of the Second Coming gave to a widening circle of preachers and evangelical lay persons a vivid expectation of being caught up and made righteous in the rapture of the saints. In all quarters, the faith of believers in what Christ had done or was about to do *for them* tended to obscure faith for what He had, in Scripture, promised to do *in them,* here and now.

Twentieth-century Wesleyans did not escape the impact of antinomianism, despite the stout resistance of their pastors and theologians. The substitution of inward feelings of peace and comfort for the realities of a heart made pure and a life empowered for righteousness occurred increasingly often. It constituted a corruption by sentiment of the central teaching of the Bible: that God's purpose was to renew His children, in this present world, in His own moral image. A second corruption was sustained by the first: to allow mechanical metaphors to obscure the actual reality of heart cleansing. The notion of the eradication of the taproot of sin —a notion that was certainly indebted to Scripture as Wesley expounded it— complemented an equally mechanical idea of the nature of saving or sanctifying faith. Seekers were taught that God's promise to sanctify their hearts must, on account of His faithfulness in that promise, be automatically fulfilled whenever believers "met the conditions" of consecration and the mental exercise of an act of faith. The tendency of this notion to diminish reliance on the Holy Spirit in seeking both regeneration and entire sanctification, and thus to weaken spiritual witness to those two works of grace, became widely apparent. The result was increasing neglect of the doctrine of the witness of the Spirit, at least in the form the Wesleys taught it.

In these several omissions and distortions of Wesleyan doctrine lay the faults of the "folk theology" of which theologians in the Wesleyan denominations have recently complained. These distortions developed in the early twentieth century, however, far more than in the nineteenth. Responsibility for them rests not with our grandfathers' generation but our own.

For all these reasons, the rediscovery of John Wesley's way of preaching and expounding the biblical promise of Christian holiness has been of great theological significance to his modern followers. In the years since 1965, the Wesleyan Theological Society (founded in that year) and its *Wesleyan Theological Journal,* both sponsored by the Christian Holiness Association, have provided a forum for many of the scholars engaged in this recovery. Equally important has been the scholarly thought, writing, and preaching of various qualified and able theologians of such Wesleyan-holiness denominations as the Church of the Nazarene, the Wesleyan Church, the Free Methodist Church, and various others. Outstanding contributions to this contemporary renewed emphasis have been the colleges and graduate theological seminaries of these denominations and movements. Among the latter are Asbury Theological Seminary, founded by H. C. Morrison in 1923, Nazarene Theological Seminary, Anderson Seminary, and Western Evangelical Seminary.

An appraisal of the implications of this renewal for Wesleyan theology today will form the summary and conclusion of this essay. For one thing, the rereading of Wesley helped to restore the biblical emphasis on the process of sanctification in which, as Wesley taught, the two moments called regeneration and entire sanctification were indispensable. The use of the word *process* seemed ominous both to old-timers who remembered the turn-of-the-century effort to substitute moral growth for radical cleansing and to younger scholars, both of whom rejected the implicit atheism of the emerging school of "process theology." The latter rooted faith in human experience, not Scripture, and made the processes of history, not the wonder of divine intervention in them, the ground of hope. To avoid these two positions, while expounding the biblical teaching that a moment-by-moment growth in the uprightness and love that flows from the presence of God's hallowing Spirit in the life of believers, has become the major task of Wesleyan theology.

The last two decades have also witnessed a growing evangelical awareness of the dangers of twentieth-century antinomianism, which makes Wesley suddenly relevant to all Bible-believing Christians. Richard Lovelace, a leading exponent of Reformed theology, and John R. W. Stott, a British teacher nurtured in his youth in InterVarsity circles, have both stressed the necessity of radical righteousness to oppose the gross evils that entwine human culture. With many others, they have sparked renewed interest in sanctification among a broad spectrum of English and American Evangelicals. Likewise, Evangelicals in the historic peace churches—Friends, Mennonites, Brethren, and the Brethren in Christ—have found in the biblical promise of holiness a basis on which to proclaim radical love as the antidote to the violence not only of war but also of the exploitation of the poor peoples of the world by the rich.

Meanwhile, Old Testament scholars such as Brevard Childs, E. P. Sanders, and James A. Sanders have helped Wesleyan and other students of the New Testament to recover the reverence for the law that permeates Jesus' teachings in the Gospels and in the epistles of James, Peter, and Paul. Daniel Fuller, a professor at the theological seminary founded by his father, radio evangelist Charles E. Fuller, published in 1980 his book *Gospel and Law: Contrast or Continuum.* It became immediately a focal point of discussion at the national meeting and several regional meetings of the Evangelical Theological Society. Accordingly, thoughtful Wesleyans are now realizing that John Wesley's profound study of the whole Bible sustained his lifelong antipathy to antinomianism in all its forms. He understood and proclaimed from his earliest years that the ethical teachings of Jesus and Paul bound together both the Old and the New Testaments and that on the two great commandments—to love God with all our hearts and our neighbors as ourselves—"hang all the law and the prophets."

Finally, the rediscovery of Wesley is also beginning to undergird the recovery of the doctrine of the Holy Spirit in twentieth-century Christian theology. The growing interest in that doctrine in other circles has proceeded from many causes, and among these are the impact of the Pentecostal and charismatic movements, the modernist search for a biblical rationale for progressive revelation, and the Protestant search for a biblical substitute for the Catholic doctrine of natural law. Lack of interest in these broader issues may have contributed to the hesitancy of Wesleyan scholars to turn to the question. However, a careful reading of the earlier sermons of the two Wesleys and of George Whitefield and of the three early volumes of the Wesleys' *Hymns and Sacred Poems,* published in 1739, 1740, and 1742, makes clear the central preoccupation of the evangelical revival with the "promise of the Father" to pour out His sanctifying Spirit in believers' hearts and on the church of Christ. That promise shaped the spiritual and intellectual climate in which the Wesleys preached and wrote for the next half century. In it Wesley saw that what he had long known was the central biblical call—to a godliness modeled by the incarnate Christ—was to be fulfilled through the gift of the sanctifying Spirit in the experience of regeneration and, through His hallowing fullness, in the experience of perfect love.

NOTES

[1] Timothy L. Smith, "John Wesley and the Wholeness of Scripture," presented before the Evangelical Theological Society, Toronto, December 27, 1981.

[2] Martin Schmidt, *John Wesley: A Theological Biography: Volume I,* tr. Norman P. Goldhawk (New York: Abingdon, 1963), pp. 52-58, 73-84, 106-14.

[3] In Charles Wesley, *Sermons . . . with a Memoir of the Author* (London, 1816); see especially those entitled "Winning Souls" (July 12, 1731, from Proverbs 11:30), "Love of God and Neighbour" (Sept. 15, 1733, from Mark 12:13), "The One Thing Needful" (May, 1734, from Luke 10:42), and "A Single Intention" (February 4, 1736, from Matthew 6:22-23). They are identified by John Wesley's handwriting and dating of the manuscript copies at the Methodist Archives and Research Center, the John Rylands Library, The University of Manchester, England, Box John Wesley IV.

[4] John Wesley, *Journal,* ed. Nehemiah Curnock, 8 vols. (London, 1909-16), entries for March 19 and 23, and April 22, 1738.

[5] Ibid., April 23, and May 3, 7, 9, 14, 19, and 24, 1738.

[6] I have spelled out the evidence for all of this in my unpublished paper, "George Whitefield on John Wesley's Perfectionism," presented before the American Academy of Religion in December 1982.

[7] Not in 1742, as Wesley mistakenly recalled in his *Plain Account of Christian Perfection* (London, 1766), in John Wesley, *Works . . .* , 14 vols. (1872, reprint ed., Kansas City, Mo.: Beacon Hill, 1978), 11:380-81.

[8] George Whitefield, *Letters . . . Written to His Most Intimate Friends . . .* , 3 vols. (London, 1772), 1:209-13, 219, containing letters to John Wesley dated September 25 and November 9, 1740. Cf. George Whitefield, *Journals,* ed. Arnold Dallimore (London, 1960), entry for September 20, 1740; John Wesley, "Diary," entry for November 7 and 9, 1739, and *Journal,* entry for November 15, 1739.

[9] Wesley, *Journal,* entries for July 21-23, 26, 1739.

[10] John Wesley, "Sermon on the Mount—Discourse III," in *Works,* 5:278-79, 282-85, 293; and the preface in *Works,* 14:326-27.

[11] Wesley, *Journal,* entries for November 1-7, 15, 1739, and "Diary," (printed with the *Journal*), Nov. 7.

[12] Wesley, *Journal,* entries for January 9 and 15, March 5 and 28, April 14, May 5, June 1, August 1, and September 28, 1740.

[13] Timothy L. Smith, "The Holy Spirit in the Hymns of the Wesleys," *The Wesleyan Theological Journal* 16 (Fall 1981): 32-37; and John Wesley, sermon, "Scriptural Christianity" (Oxford, August 17, 1744, from Acts 4:31), *Works,* 5:8, and passim.

[14] Albert C. Outler, *John Wesley,* "Library of Protestant Thought" (New York: Oxford, 1964), pp. 14-17, 135.

[15] John Wesley, sermon, "The Case of Reason Impartially Considered" (July 6, 1781, on 1 Cor. 14:20), *Works,* 6:351, 354, 358.

[16] John Wesley, *Address to the Clergy* (London, 1756), *Works,* 10:484; John Wesley, "The Advantage of the Members of the Church of England, Over Those of the Church of Rome," in *Works,* 10:133-34; John Wesley, *Explanatory Notes Upon the New Testament,* 2nd ed. (1760; reprint ed., London, 1976), preface, p. 9., quoted here from his *Works,* 14:238.

[17] Timothy L. Smith, "Chronological List of John Wesley's Sermons and Doctrinal Essays," *Wesleyan Theological Journal* 16 (Fall 1982). This article is aimed to make possible more precise estimates of the context of each of his writings.

[18] Wesley, *Journal,* October 28, 1762.

[19] John Wesley, *A Farther Appeal to Men of Reason and Religion,* Part I (London, 1745), *Works,* 8:76-111; John and Charles Wesley, *The Pentecost Hymns of the Wesleys . . .* , ed. Timothy L. Smith (Kansas City, Mo.: Beacon Hill, 1982).

[20] John Wesley, "Thoughts on Christian Perfection," in Outler, *John Wesley,* 283-97. Cf. Timothy L. Smith, "Notes on the Exegesis of John Wesley's 'Explanatory Notes Upon the New Testament,'" *Wesleyan Theological Journal* 16 (Spring 1981): 107-8.

[21] John Wesley, Chester, 16 March, 1771, to Joseph Benson, in *Letters,* ed. John Telford, 7 vols. (London, 1938), 5:228-29.

[22] George Whitefield, *Observations on . . . "The Office and Operations of the Holy Spirit,"* ed. William Warburton (London and Edinburgh, 1764), p. 16.

[23] George Whitefield, Tottenham Court (London), December 20, 1766, to "W—P—, Esq.," in Whitefield, *Letters,* 3:342-43.

[24] John Wesley, sermon, "On the Death of the Rev. Mr. George Whitefield . . ." (November 8, 1770, from Numbers 23:10) (London, 1770), in *Works,* 6:177-80.

[25] Harald Lindström, *Wesley and Sanctification, a Study in the Doctrine of Salvation* (1946; reprint ed., Wilmore, Ky.: Asbury, 1982, with an introduction by Timothy L. Smith), pp. 44-49.

[26] This and the following paragraphs rest on Timothy L. Smith, "How John Fletcher Became the Theologian of Wesleyan Perfectionism, 1770-1776," *Wesleyan Theological Journal* 14 (Spring 1980): 72-74.

[27] Timothy L. Smith, "Notes on the Exegesis of John Wesley's 'Explanatory Notes Upon the New Testament,'" *Wesleyan Theological Journal* 15 (Spring 1981): 111.

[28] John Wesley, sermons, "The General Deliverance" (Nov. 30, 1781, from Romans 8:19-22), "The General Spread of the Gospel" (April 22, 1783, on Isaiah 11:9), "The New Creation (November 1785, on Revelation 21:5), in *Works,* 6:241-52, 277-96.

[29] Francis Asbury, *Journals and Letters,* ed. J. Manning Potts and others, 3 vols. (Nashville: Abingdon, 1958), passim, but esp. in 2:435, 443, 447, 450, 455, 459, 465, 468-69, 475, 483, 494, 499-500, 506, 520-21.

[30] Timothy L. Smith, *Revivalism and Social Reform in Mid-Nineteenth-Century America* (Nashville: Abingdon, 1957), 114-34; idem, "Righteousness and Hope: Christian Holiness and the Millennial Vision in America, 1800-1900," *The American Quarterly* 31 (Spring 1979): 21-45.

[31] Smith, *Revivalism and Social Reform,* pp. 103-13; Charles G. Finney, *The Promise of the Spirit, Lectures on Sanctification,* ed. Timothy L. Smith (Minneapolis: Bethany, 1980, from *The Oberlin Evangelist* for 1839), 9-28.

³²Smith, *Revivalism and Social Reform*, pp. 135-47; Jay Dolan, *Catholic Revivalism in the United States, 1830-1900* (South Bend, Ind.: Notre Dame, 1978), preface; John Farina, *An American Experience of God: The Spirituality of Isaac Hecker* (New York: Paulist, 1981), 9-30, 46-60, 118-31.

³³The foregoing paragraphs are based on Timothy L. Smith, *Called Unto Holiness: The Story of the Nazarenes* (Kansas City, Mo.: Beacon Hill, 1963), pp. 15-52; and Emory Stevens Bucke, ed., *The History of American Methodism*, 3 vols. (Nashville: Abingdon 1964), 2:611-27.

³⁴Smith, *Called Unto Holiness*, pp. 15-52.

³⁵John Wesley, sermon, "Catholic Spirit" (September 8, 1749, from 2 Kings 10:15), in *Works*, 5:492-504.

³⁶See the selections and the notes and commentary in Timothy L. Smith, ed., *Nineteenth-Century Popular Holiness Classics* (Kansas City, Mo.: Beacon Hill, forthcoming).

³⁷Cf. John Wesley, sermon, "Scripture Way of Salvation," (May 22, 1758, from Eph. 2:8), in *Works*, 6:53-54; Phoebe Palmer, *Incidental Illustrations of the Economy of Salvation . . .* (1855; reprint ed., New York: Palmer, 1875), 36-41, quoting the same sermon and other of Wesley's writings on the controverted point.

³⁸Selections from works cited in Smith, *Called Unto Holiness*, pp. 38-47, illustrating these points, also will appear in Smith, *Holiness Classics*, forthcoming. Cf. Smith, "How John Fletcher Became the Theologian of Wesleyan Perfectionism," pp. 72-82.

³⁹The following descriptions are based largely on historical essays prepared by Timothy L. Smith and others, *The American Evangelical Mosaic*, forthcoming in 1984.

⁴⁰George M. Marsden, *Fundamentalism in American Culture: The Shaping of Twentieth-Century Evangelicalism, 1870-1925*, (New York: Oxford, 1980).

DISCUSSION QUESTIONS

1. To what extent, and on what authority, were the principles of Wesleyan theology worked out before John and Charles Wesley experienced "salvation by faith" in May 1738?
2. What were the circumstances surrounding the discovery by the two Wesleys in the fall of 1739 that the Bible taught a second moment of sanctifying grace, beyond regeneration?
3. Explain why the doctrine of the Holy Spirit held such a central place in their theology of salvation.
4. How, in John Wesley's matured view, do reason, experience, and Christian tradition sustain the fundamental authority of Scripture in all things necessary to faith and righteousness?
5. How did the doctrine of prevenient grace make possible a degree of reconciliation between Wesleyans and Calvinists?
6. What did John Fletcher actually contribute to the Wesleyan understanding of the Pentecostal experience of being filled with the Holy Spirit?
7. Contrast John Wesley's view of the future of the earth and the second coming of Christ with modern premillennial and postmillennial views.
8. Explain why the preaching of entire sanctification did not die out in early American Methodism.
9. Evaluate the evidence that the holiness revival that began in New England and New York around 1820 depended heavily on a renewal of historic Wesleyan teachings.
10. Discuss why you think nineteenth-century American Wesleyans did not find it necessary to alter significantly John Wesley's doctrine of sanctification by grace through faith.
11. Weigh the positive and negative results of the controversy over the experience and the promotion of entire sanctification that broke out in late nineteenth-century Methodism.
12. In the light of the resurgence of evangelicalism generally during the twentieth century evaluate the alterations of John Wesley's doctrine of salvation that seem to have occurred among twentieth-century Wesleyans.
13. How do you think the current revival of the study of the original content and form of John Wesley's understanding of scriptural Christianity can contribute to a more saving encounter of modern Wesleyans with modern culture?
14. In retrospect, what is the usefulness of knowing the Wesleyan tradition of biblical interpretation to one who seeks to work out by scriptural study a fully biblical doctrine of salvation?

RECOMMENDATIONS FOR FURTHER READING

Cattell, Everett Lewis. *The Spirit of Holiness.* Grand Rapids: Eerdmans, 1963.

Dieter, Melvin. *The Holiness Revival of the Nineteenth Century.* Metuchen, N.J.: Scarecrow, 1980.

Knight, John Allen. *The Holiness Pilgrimage: Reflections on the Life of Holiness.* Kansas City, Mo.: Beacon Hill, 1973.

Lindström, Harald. *Wesley and Sanctification.* 1946. Reprint ed. Wilmore, Ky.: Asbury, 1982.

Outler, Albert, ed. *John Wesley,* in A Library of Protestant Thought. New York: Oxford University Press, 1964.

Rose, Delbert R. *A Theology of Christian Experience: Interpreting the Historic Wesleyan Message.* Minneapolis: Bethany, 1965.

Smith, Timothy L. *Called Unto Holiness: The Story of the Nazarenes.* Kansas City, Mo.: Nazarene, 1963.

———. *Revivalism and Social Reform: American Protestantism on the Eve of the Civil War.* 1957. Reprint ed. Baltimore: Johns Hopkins, 1980.

Smith, Timothy L., ed. *Charles G. Finney on Christian Holiness: The Promise of the Spirit.* Minneapolis: Bethany, 1980.

———. *Nineteenth-Century Popular Holiness Classics.* Kansas City, Mo.: Beacon Hill, forthcoming.

Turner, George Allen. *The More Excellent Way.* Winona Lake, Ind.: Light and Life, 1952.

Wesley, John. *A Plain Account of Christian Perfection.* Kansas City, Mo.: Beacon Hill, 1983.

Wood, Lawrence W. *Pentecostal Grace.* Wilmore, Ky.: Asbury, 1980.

Wynkoop, Mildred Bangs. *A Theology of Love: The Dynamics of Wesleyanism.* Kansas City, Mo.: Beacon Hill, 1972.

CHAPTER 4

THEISM:
The Eternal, Personal, Creative God

Albert Truesdale

Albert Truesdale is Associate Professor of Philosophy of Religion and Christian Ethics at Nazarene Theological Seminary. He received his B.D. degree from Nazarene Theological Seminary and his Ph.D. degree in Systematic Theology from Emory University. For a number of years he served as minister in various Nazarene churches. Later he held the positions of Assistant Professor in the department of Religion at Eastern Nazarene College and Dean of the College at Olivet Nazarene College.

Dr. Truesdale's Ph.D. dissertation was entitled "A Tillichian Analysis of White Racism in the South." He has contributed chapters to the following books: Discipleship: Your New Life in Christ; Tough Questions: Christian Answers; *and* Finding Your Ministry: The Fruit and Gifts of the Holy Spirit *and has written articles for the* Wesleyan Theological Journal *and* Preacher's Magazine *(a Church of the Nazarene publication). He is a member of the American Academy of Religion.*

CONTENTS

I. INTRODUCTION / 107
    A. Theological Methodology / 107
    B. The Essentials of a Wesleyan Doctrine of God, and the Spirit of Wesleyan Catholicity / 108
    C. The Biblical Norm for the Doctrine of God / 109
    D. Epistemological Considerations / 110

II. THE CHRISTIAN UNDERSTANDING OF GOD / 111
    A. The Living God / 112
    B. God Is Holy / 116
    C. God Is Love / 120
    D. The Attributes of God / 122
        1. Sovereignty / 122
        2. Omnipotence / 124
        3. Eternity / 124
        4. Immutability / 125
        5. Omnipresence / 126
        6. Omniscience / 126
        7. Wrath / 127
    E. God Is Triune / 127

III. THE WORK OF GOD / 129
    A. The Work of God in Creation / 130
        1. God creating / 130
        2. God preserving / 132
        3. God directing / 133
    B. The Work of God in Revelation and Redemption / 133
    C. The Work of God in Hope / 134

NOTES / 137

DISCUSSION QUESTIONS / 140

RECOMMENDATIONS FOR FURTHER READING / 140

BIBLIOGRAPHY / 141

THEISM

The Eternal, Personal, Creative God

I. INTRODUCTION

A. Theological Methodology

Whatever the theological tradition in which a Christian theologian works, that theologian must take cognizance of the ferment that characterizes the present social, religious, and intellectual scene. The degree to which a theologian is in direct dialogue with the present milieu depends in part on his or her purposes for doing theology, on the methodology, and on the particular theological tradition out of which he or she speaks. By definition, some theological positions depend a great deal on the secular context for an interlocutor, others only moderately so. Still, other theological stances face the modern era in only a polemical relationship.

Some theologians, believing the God of the Bible and classical Christian faith to be thoroughly anachronistic, abandon all efforts to do theology within the context of a confessing community (e.g., the radical theologians).

Other theologians, no less aware of the importance of modern pluralism, strive to restate the classical Christian faith by using linguistic and conceptual vehicles that on the surface sound foreign to the traditional language of the church. We call these people apologists because they try to "answer for" the Christian faith to those outside the confessing community who challenge the veracity of its faith. The work of the apologist, as the Christian church has sometimes forgotten, is very important to the Christian message, even though it is risky. Theological dialogue with the major intellectual, religious, and cultural moods of the day is essential for the ongoing life of the church and the fulfillment of its mission.

Sometimes a theologian utilizes a contemporary philosophical conceptualization of reality to provide a credible intellectual structure through which a Christian can understand his or her own faith. An example of this is John Cobb's work in *A Christian Natural Theology*.[1]

Other theologians are more *kerygmatic* in their approach. While perhaps not depreciating the apologetic task, they engage primarily in articulating the message of God's self-disclosure as it is attested in the Bible and in the faith and ministry of the church. The kerygmatic theologian is not immediately interested in using language drawn from the contemporary social and

107

intellectual milieu, even though he or she may be fully conversant with it. Rather, this approach relies heavily on the language of faith as it is spoken in the Bible and in the faith and practice of the church. The kerygmatic theologian is a proclaimer, i.e., one who strives to state the message of revelation systematically.

All of these approaches are important for the church's message that Jesus is Lord.

In this chapter the kerygmatic approach will be taken. This is by no means, however, intended to belittle other theological methodologies. Although here we must engage in some discussion with the modern temper and although no theological approach can fail to be cognizant of the milieu in which it works, dialogue with the major thought forms of our day is not our *principal* goal.

B. The Essentials of a Wesleyan Doctrine of God, and the Spirit of Wesleyan Catholicity

This chapter attempts to give a systematic statement of the doctrine of God in a manner that expresses and is consistent with the essential doctrinal commitments of the Wesleyan tradition. In regard to the doctrine of God, briefly stated, these commitments are (1) belief in the reality of the one God to whom the Bible bears witness; (2) belief that holiness and love are essentially constituent of His being; (3) belief in the one God as essentially, eternally Triune—Father, Son, and Holy Spirit; (4) belief in God's sovereignty as the sovereignty of His love; (5) belief that God has freely manifested Himself as Creator and Redeemer and that this manifestation or revelation constitutes a unique history of salvation (definitively culminated in God's incarnation in Jesus of Nazareth) that can be traced through the Old and New Testament records; and (6) belief in the scope or range of God's saving activity on man's behalf as being universal in provision.

Wesleyan theology is thoroughly evangelical, i.e., from beginning to end salvation is from God alone, as a free gift to the believer. Justification by grace through faith alone is its soteriological cornerstone. Furthermore the grace of God is preveniently extended to all people to prompt them to repentance and reconciliation. In the Wesleyan doctrine of God there is a profound optimism of grace as it relates not only to individual existence but also to social existence. The whole tenor of Wesleyan theology is expressed in the Pauline affirmation that God was in Christ reconciling the world to Himself (Col. 1:20).

John Wesley's theology, as has been extensively demonstrated by a host of interpreters, was in no way sectarian or provincial. Wesley was a determined catholic-spirited Christian. Many of his writings appeared as defenses against charges that the Methodists were an aberrant form of Christianity. Other writings opposed sectarian or heretical tendencies within Methodism. In one of his most irenic pieces, an open "letter" written in 1749 to a small, unidentified group of Irish Catholics, Wesley articulated what he believed to be the truly "catholic spirit" of Protestant theology:

> I am assured that there is an infinite and independent Being and that it is impossible that there should be more than one, so I believe that this one God is the Father of all things, especially of angels and men; that he is in a peculiar manner the Father of those whom he regenerates by his Spirit, whom he adopts in his Son as co-heirs with him and crowns with an eternal inheritance; but in a still higher sense, the Father of his only Son, whom he hath begotten from eternity. . . .
>
> I believe that Jesus of Nazareth was the Savior of the world, the Messiah so long foretold; that, being anointed with the Holy Ghost, he was a *prophet*, revealing to us the whole will of God; that he was a *priest*, who gave himself a sacrifice for sin, and still makes intercession for transgressors; that he is a *king*, who has all power in heaven and in earth, and will reign till he has subdued all things to himself. . . .[2]

Wesley believed that what he taught about the doctrine of God was contained within the Bible and embraced by the faith of the Christian church. This was his conviction notwithstanding his running battles with the Calvinists over predestination. Consequently the person who goes to John Wesley's theology expecting to find an esoteric or eccentric, sectarian or provincial doctrine of God will be thoroughly disappointed.

As Frank Baker, Albert Outler, W. R. Cannon, and many others have shown, John Wesley believed that the evangelical faith he preached, and that gave Methodism its life, was a faithful declaration of the meaning of Anglican (and by that he meant Protestant) doctrine.

The danger of becoming theologically sectarian, of losing doctrinal comprehensiveness, plagues the theological and devotional descendants of any great Christian leader. Those who are deeply influenced by the theology of John Wesley are not excepted. One danger is that, while trying to be faithful to the theological vision bequeathed us and that grasps us with conviction, we may fail to maintain the spirit of learner and pilgrim that characterized such giants as Luther, Calvin, and Wesley. John Wesley was not just a teacher, he was also a prodigious learner, as anyone familiar with the diversity of his reading and the influence these readings had on his writings can attest.

Therefore, a doctrine of God written in the spirit of John Wesley will not only have certain distinguishing features, it will also be marked by an openness to what Christ, through the Spirit, teaches the church catholic. I hope that my treatment of the doctrine of God will not only express the characteristic Wesleyan doctrinal commitments but will also be guided by the classical Christian tradition.

So, to do theology within a Wesleyan context does not mean that we woodenly repeat Wesley. Such a procedure would grossly violate the man's spirit and could not possibly serve the Christian faith today. Living theological traditions do not retain their power to inspire by becoming lost in obscurantism, but they do so through constant testing, interchange, and an inner dynamic that allows them to maintain identity and continuity even while undergoing growth and change.

Theologians who consciously work within the Wesleyan tradition and have the task of identifying the continuing theological dynamic of Wesleyan thought, stating it, and enriching it as Wesley would have done through dialogue with contemporary theological interests. According to Wesley's pattern of critiquing and drawing on the diverse theological currents of his day, this chapter will draw on some of this century's major shapers of Christian thought.

C. The Biblical Norm for the Doctrine of God

Fundamental to Protestant Christianity is the primacy of the Old and New Testament Scriptures for all matters of faith and practice. The Bible is the fundamental and decisively authoritative message concerning God—His person and His creative and saving acts in the world. It is the book of the mighty acts of God.

The primacy of Scripture is thoroughly characteristic of Wesleyan theology. At no point is its Protestant identification more clearly shown. To one James Hervey, John Wesley said that theological ideas not supported by Scripture "weigh nothing with *me*. I allow no other rule, whether of faith or practice, than the Holy Scriptures."[3] Wesley would have agreed with Emil Brunner's statement that

> the church has always called the Scriptures of the Old and New Testaments the "word of God." In so doing the church expresses the fundamental truth of the Christian faith, namely, that in these books the historical self-manifestation of God is offered to faith in an incomparable, decisive, and unique manner; this means that no Christian faith can either rise or be preserved which ignores "Holy Scripture."[4]

The importance of the Bible for Christian doctrine and practice was the central issue that sparked the sixteenth-century Protestant Reformation. *Sola Scriptura* and *sola fide* are the material and formal principles of Protestant theology. They were also fundamentals in Wesley's doctrine of authority. Gerhard Ebeling says that for Martin Luther "theology consisted of the interpretation of the Holy Scripture. . . . He never doubted that the will of God was revealed and comprehensible to man solely through the Holy Scriptures."[5] Although John Wesley interpreted *solus* to mean "primarily" rather than "solely" or "exclusively," what Ebeling says of Luther is no less true of him, the man of "one book."[6]

The decisive authority of the Old and New Testament Scriptures distinguishes the Christian faith from all quasi-Christian movements that superimpose on the Bible de facto, if not de jure, alleged superior revelations and criteria by which the Bible must be interpreted. The church refers to the Bible as the "Word of God" and declares that it is the basic source of theology. But the phrase the "Word of God" should not be simply equated with the Bible. John's Gospel proclaims that Jesus the Christ, the One in whom God was incarnate, is *the* Word of God (John 1:1-5). *He* has made the Father known (John 1:18). The "Word of God" is He who reveals the living God to us through His creating and saving deeds. "For the church of the New Testament the final, historical, saving act, and the final word of divine revelation, is simply and solely Jesus Christ himself, as the absolute personal self-manifestation of God."[7]

God is spoken of in the Bible, says Karl Barth, and we must listen to what is said of Him there. "He who is to be seen and heard there is God."[8]

D. Epistemological Considerations

The Bible makes clear that, regarding knowledge of God, religious epistemology and soteriology intersect. We know God at the point where we meet Him as the One who qualifies us ultimately. Under these conditions the "god" who can be the object of man's investigations and predetermined means of verification vanishes, and the Holy One who confronts us as the "Divine Thou" cannot be doubted. In the name of the evangelical character of the faith to which the New Testament bears witness, *all* attempts to separate knowledge of God from salvation must be rejected. Knowledge of God can be received only in the presence of salvation, a creative and transforming participation in Him who is to be known.

The mode of knowing any object must be appropriate to that object. This is surely no less true of God. He is not a being that submits to microscopic analysis, nor a research subject that leaves the researcher subjectively independent of the object under investigation. To insist that He who is from eternity, who is *Being Itself,* and who gives existence to the world must Himself be discovered as an amoeba or a social grouping in Southeast Asia is discovered is extreme epistemological arrogance.

If the eternal God is to be known, He must set the conditions. John Hick argues this forcefully.[9] And God has clearly done this as is recorded in the history of His self-disclosure; the history of His self-revelation is the history of salvation. No one has stated this intersection of epistemology and soteriology more clearly than has Karl Barth in his discussion of the *analogia fidei* (analogy of faith). We are enabled to speak of God where He grasps human language and makes it the bearer of divine revelation.[10]

The desire for epistemological independence is as surely a mark of man's sinfulness as is his overt self-worship. Some day we will see how foolish it was to limit knowledge to what can be empirically verified or falsified. We will see how restricted life really is when the method of scientific investigation, wholly appropriate in the empirical sciences, is improperly used in the dimensions of the human spirit, where it does not belong. Knowledge of the God who inhabits eternity is surely one such area. "The heart" said Pascal, "has reasons that the mind knows not of."

Already the epistemological arrogance of positivism and neopositivism is under heavy attack from within and outside philosophy, from within and outside the empirical sciences. Huston Smith says that a scientific world view in which this world, this ontological plane, "is the only one that is genuinely countenanced," is, strictly speaking, "a contradiction in terms. The reason is that science does not treat of the whole world; it treats of a part only."[11] Walter Kaufmann, after carefully noting the positive contributions made by language analysts such as A. J. Ayer, says that on the whole they have "ignored large areas of experience and dealt very partially with art, religion, and morality." Empiricism, he says, has become empiricide. Instead of employing their critical acumen and scrupulous precision to sift the wheat from the chaff, too often the analysts have "abandoned any effort to grow wheat."[12]

The scandal of the Cross so directly embraced by the New Testament is no less a scandal in our day. It is both (1) an epistemological scandal—to know God only through faith in Jesus Christ scandalizes the criteria of empirical epistemology—and (2) a religious scandal—to hold that the only Begotten Son of the Father who became incarnate in Jesus of Nazareth is the *One* who makes the Father known scandalizes man's own ability to discover God.

So be it. The scandal of the Incarnation and the Cross, through which God definitively discloses Himself, is authored by God. No Christian theologian, regardless of how much the scandal displeases him, has any warrant to tamper with it. It is still true that, "God chose the foolish things of the world to shame the wise; . . . the weak things of the world to shame the strong" (1 Cor. 1:27 NIV). Christ is the power and wisdom of God. Through its own wisdom the world did not know God. It pleased Him that through the folly of the proclamation of Jesus Christ as Lord, God's righteousness, sanctification, and redemption would be known (1 Cor. 1:18-31).

II. THE CHRISTIAN UNDERSTANDING OF GOD

The Christian concept of God is not simply a continuation or enrichment of the ideas about God that have come to us through philosophy and religions other than Judaism and Christianity. "God," says Karl Barth, "is not to be found in the series of gods. He is not to be found in the pantheon of human piety and religious inventive skill."[13] Rather, when Christian faith speaks of God, it means that *Wholly Other One* who has freely chosen to disclose Himself as Creator and Redeemer, a disclosure whose faithful narration is the biblical record. Wesleyan theologian H. Orton Wiley succinctly states this more formally: "God is a Spirit, holy in nature and attributes, absolute in reality, infinite in efficiency, perfect in personality, and thereby the ultimate ground, adequate cause and sufficient reason for all finite existence."[14] This affirmation stands solidly against the claim that God is but the product of subjective projection by the human ego or corporate consciousness as has been taught by Ludwig Feuerbach, Karl Marx, and Sigmund Freud, among others. The Scriptures teach, and Wesleyan theology believes, that God as the infinite and eternal Spirit "has real and substantial existence."[15]

Although this chapter does not examine the question of God from a philosophical perspective, it should at least be affirmed that in the Christian doctrine of God the absolute of philosophy, the ultimate logos of philosophical inquiry, finds its highest expression and complete identification. The philosophical question of "being as such," or "reality as a whole," is definitively answered at the point at which the God who is *Being Itself* becomes redemptively manifest in Jesus of Nazareth.

A. The Living God

The God who meets us in the biblical record is the one eternal, living God. "I am the Lord, and there is no other, apart from me there is no God" (Isa. 45:5 NIV). "I am the Lord, who made all things, who alone stretched out the heavens, who spread out the earth by myself" (Isa. 44:24 NIV). "I am the first and I am the last; . . . is there any God besides me? No, there is no other Rock; I know not one" (Isa. 44:6, 8 NIV).

As to His identity, the Bible says that God is Spirit (John 4:24). That God is Spirit (*ru'ach,* Hebrew; *pneuma,* Greek) is the most all-embracing, unrestricted designation of divine life. As Spirit, God absolutely unites power and meaning in personal life; but what this unity means can be grasped only by examining the content of the Christian affirmation about God.

YHWH (called the *tetragrammaton* and usually pronounced *Yahweh*), the name[16] by which God identified Himself to Moses (Exod. 3:14), is a form of the verb *to be,* as active rather than static. The Bible is not primarily concerned with who God *is* but with what He *does*. In this is manifested who He *is*. He is known by what He does. The name Yahweh indicates God's action and presence in historical affairs, a living God who discloses His will to man. The tetragrammaton is variously translated as "I am who I will be," "I am what I am," and "I will be what I will be." The name discloses God's exclusive claim to freedom and sovereignty. It probably signifies the God whose reality is expressed in His living presence among His people, the living, sovereign God who is manifest in their midst as "deliverer, guide, and judge, and who is accessible in worship."[17]

As living, God proclaims His name through His presence. He is free to be present as He will be present and to show mercy on whom He will show mercy (cf. Exod. 33:19). Moses was given an answer to his question, Who is God? not through an abstract discussion of God's nature and not by being called to renounce the arena of life so that he might eventually become absorbed in absolute, impersonal being, but through God's living, creative, and redemptive activity in the world. Moses was sent back to Pharaoh and the slaves, where he learned who God is.

The Old and New Testaments constitute the narrative of God's self-manifestation as the living God. All human history is a theater of His self-disclosure, and nature is His handiwork.[18] At the center of this narrative stands the unquestioned superiority of the living God over the lifeless, defenseless gods of the nations.

In the most definitive instruction about how to refer to God, Jesus said we should call Him Father, and it is clear that the language addressed to Him is appropriate only in an atmosphere of life. But God does not simply share life with man as though it were a common property between them. He *is* life, and only where He *gives* life can there be life besides Him. The world is absolutely dependent on Him for its life. Jesus says, "I am the . . . truth and the life" (John 14:6 NIV). He is "the bread of life" (John 6:35). "In him was life, and that life was the light of men" (John 1:4 NIV). He came to *give* what God *is*—life, eternal life (3:15-16). Jesus said that the Father has *life in Himself,* that He has given His life to the Son, and that apart from the Father who is in the Son there is no life (John 5:26, 40).

The God of the Bible stands in bold contrast to the inert, so-called gods people worship. Unlike Him, they have no life whatever. They are false, and their falsity is exhibited in their inability to save themselves, to be their own source and guarantee of life. In their moment of greatest crisis they have to be carried by their hapless worshipers. Those who make and worship them cannot see that the living God gave life to the wood out of which the idols are made (Isa. 44). Yahweh is the absolute source of life. There is no God besides Him (Isa. 44:8).

The God of whom the Old and New Testament Scriptures speak is also clearly different from the supposed causes for the world found in most Eastern religions and philosophies. Brahman, the world soul of Hinduism (the religious and philosophical absolute), is not a living God. Nor is the Buddha Essence that lies behind the redemptive work of the Boddhisattvas in Mahayana Buddhism. The eternal Tao (the way) of Taoism is impersonal and impassive, never to be addressed as a living God.

The God of Israel, the Father of our Lord, trivializes the multitude of demigods and other mythical figures of the Babylonian myths and Greek religions whose own "existence" is often contingent on other gods. For example, the great God of the Enuma Elish, Marduk, was created, "engendered," as a result of a conflict between the older divinities.[19] By contrast, the biblical God is the "source" of His own life. We speak of God's *aseity;* His being is from Himself.

Finally, the *theos* in Aristotle's highly developed theology is not a living God in the biblical sense, even though as the world's *final* cause—i.e., its lure—he moves it to its "perfection." But never is he directly engaged with the world as is the God of the Bible, whose own life is in no way jeopardized by direct involvement with it.[20]

Perhaps the most outstanding Old Testament vindication of God as living occurs in the contest on Mount Carmel between the prophets of Baal and the prophet Elijah (1 Kings 18). The question was, Who has the power to control rain and fertility and who really gives life to the earth and to man, Baal or Yahweh? In this epic contest Baal could not respond. Only He who answered by fire, who by His own will brought an end to the earth's infertility (drought), is God. "Yahweh, He is God!" the people cried (v. 39).

Central to the New Testament message stands the resurrection of Jesus Christ. Because the living God willed Jesus' resurrection, even the powers of death and chaos had to bow before Him. By the power of the living God Jesus is "designated Son of God . . . according to the Spirit of holiness by his resurrection from the dead . . ." (Rom. 1:4, RSV).

The living God is both transcendent and immanent. He is immediately and constantly present to and active in His world. But His presence in the world does not exhaust His being. Neither is He dependent on it for His own being. He is both *Deus Revelatus* and *Deus Absconditus*.

Belief in God's transcendence and immanence stands against deism and pantheism, both of which claim to make positive statements about the being of God. But each position sacrifices an essential element in the Christian doctrine of God. While attempting to maintain God's transcendence, deism sacrifices the immanence or presence of God in the world. On the other hand, pantheism wishes to protect God's immanence but it does so at the expense of His transcendence. According to Baruch Spinoza (1632-1677), the world is but an attribute of God.

To the deist, God is far removed from human history and everyday human cares, unapproachable and impassive. It follows that there is no place for direct divine revelation or self-disclosure. What needs to be known about God can be gained through the exercise of man's rational powers and through the observation of nature.

The church has had to struggle against deistic tendencies, from the Greek concept of a God whose being is endangered by contact with the world to the deism spawned by the Age of Reason in the eighteenth century.[21] Deism viewed the world as an orderly universe governed by fixed laws set in motion by God but not requiring His presence to sustain them. Deism can be more consistently expressed than can pantheism. (Of course in our day naturalistic views of the world have largely, but not completely, replaced deism. Philosophical naturalists believe that the being of God is no longer necessary to account for the world. Whereas for the deists reason demonstrated the existence of God, for naturalists reason demonstrates just the opposite.)

Pantheism understands God's immanence in such a way that the distinction between God and the world, the human and the divine, are either blurred or disappear altogether. Although pantheism does not simply mean that the world is God, it is very difficult to identify in what way God is "more" than the sum of His expressions in the world. Pantheism appears in the thought of Spinoza (1632-1677), and at least pantheistic tendencies appear in Georg Frederick Hegel (1770-1831) and more recently in Thomas Altizer.

Of the Eastern religions, Hinduism and Buddhism exemplify pantheism. However, in these religions few adherents are capable of consistently conceptualizing God and the world pantheistically. Consequently, efforts to think of absolute reality as in some way personal is tolerated. Over a period of time the avatars, or epiphanies, of absolute reality became almost innumerable, as exemplified in the many personifications of Brahman.

In the Christian doctrine of God, both His transcendence and immanence are held in tension, without sacrificing either. The God who sustains the world by the word of His power, in whom all things cohere (Col. 1:17), nevertheless is above His creation in the sense that His being cannot be identified with or derived from it. He is the absolute ontological *prius* of the world's origin and the source of its continuation. God's question to Job is paradigmatic for the whole creation: "Where were you when I laid the earth's foundation?" (Job 38:4 NIV). He *is* in the full perfection of His being before the universe came into existence.

When Christian faith speaks of "the living God," it intends to say that He is *essentially* personal and that He is properly addressed as a "Thou." God is He who according to the holy Scriptures exists, acts, and makes Himself known.

He who calls us to live righteously and justly before Him meets us in an existential relationship that is a profound I-Thou encounter. To speak of God as personal brings out vividly the voluntary and captive character of the idea of God and thus guards it from two tendencies: the transformation of the conception of God into an abstract idea, and the identification of God with some force in nature, thus obscuring the fact that God's power is nothing else than the power of love.[22]

The Bible knows nothing of a God whose being is endangered by ascribing to Him the characteristics of personhood. Such a God would indeed be a very poor one, according to the biblical understanding. The Bible does not place God beyond knowing, feeling, willing, and loving.

The personhood of God must be understood in terms of His self-disclosure. This means that (1) we do not impose human concepts of personhood on Him, for He defines not only His own "personhood" but ours as well, and (2) it is futile to seek a higher and more complete understanding of God as did Hegel in his lectures on the philosophy of religion and most completely in *The Phenomenology of Mind*. For Hegel religious language (which is *pictorial*) must be transcended, although not completely replaced, by philosophical language. Hegel's error is still with us today in those theologians who look to philosophy for a description of God that is at least implicitly judged superior to biblical faith. Contrary to this view, Christian theology insists that what we learn about God in the Old and New Testaments can never be transcended by philosophy. The Bible is the only adequate record of God's self-disclosure. Since God is the content of revelation and since the biblical record is the definitive testimony to this self-manifestation, any attempt to transcend it is a failure of faith, if not an act of idolatry.

Ludwig Feuerbach, in *The Essence of Christianity*,[23] maintained that belief in the reality of God as personal results from a process by which man's own noble characteristics are projected into infinite dimensions and then posited in a divine being in whom they cohere in perfect expression. The truth about theology, Feuerbach argued, is that it is in fact anthropology. God, he said, is man's highest predicate. Now that we know the truth about religion, the study of God should become the study of man, and our energies should be committed to achieving on earth our unlimited potential for love in community.

The highest perfection, according to Feuerbach, is not the God affirmed by Christian faith, but Intellect, Will, and Love, which together constitute human essence; they are unique to the human species and they are its greatness. Our problem, Feuerbach says, is that we have thrown our greatness away by projecting man's essence into a fictional divine person—God—who perfectly embodies Intellect, Will, and Love. This "waste," Feuerbach believed, must be reversed.[24] The friends of God must now become, instead, the friends of man.

But the Bible knows nothing of such a process. In fact it stoutly rebukes all efforts to measure God in human dimensions, for the personhood of God is not the result of human projection. To the contrary, the personhood of man is made possible by and is a reflection of the personhood of God. "God created man in His own image, in the image of God he created him" (Gen. 1:27 RSV).

There is probably no way—and certainly no need—to refute Feuerbach rationally and empirically. The personhood of God and the creatureliness of man is an affirmation of faith that results from our being grasped by the Creator/Redeemer God. When the Holy God about whom the Bible speaks confronts man, there can no longer be any question about God's existence. Instead, the doubt concerns man: can he exist in the presence of the wholly-other One (Isa. 6:3–5)?

The event of redemption, as the Bible and Christian experience testify, carries absolutely compelling conviction. The "god" that answers to Feuerbach's anthropocentric definition is not the personal God of revelation. The Holy One who inhabits eternity does not simply fulfill human expectations. He shatters our designs about what He should be, defines Himself, and in the process redefines man as well. God's self-disclosure to faith is the high epistemological ground for a knowledge of His existence and of what it means to speak of Him as person. To depart from this foundation undermines belief in God's reality.

Some theologians believe that we should not speak of God as "a person," but as "personal." Since the term *person* as we commonly use it carries definite spatial and temporal limitations, to speak of God as "a person," it is argued, fixes in our mind an anthropomorphic concept of God as a superhuman, yet located, being. He is thus conceived as one cosmic "thing" among other, though greatly diminished, "things." To avoid this misconception, some say, we should refer to God as "personal" and thereby retain the authentic personal qualities of the God whose being is not to be spoken of in the spatio/temporal terms that characterize finite existence.

Although the term *person* is not applied to God in the New Testament (where He is spoken of as Spirit [John 4:24]), it does use terms such as *Lord* and *Father* to reveal His name. These can have a content that is neither more nor less than personal. When Jesus refers to the Father's relation to the world, He uses the language of personhood. He is the Father who rejoices over the return of a wayward son. Nowhere is there any indication that such language is inadequate for comprehending the central truth about God's nature. Christian theology must not depart from this language to secure a supposedly higher vantage point for understanding God. God is neither the impersonal Brahman of Hinduism, the "One" of Neoplatonism, nor the Absolute Spirit of Hegel's philosophy. He is the One whom Jesus called "Father." Anything that can be properly said about Him must be governed by Jesus' "I-Thou" discourse with the Father.

When we say that God is personal, we are speaking analogously, but not by use of the analogy of being (*analogia entis*). Were the latter true, we would gain our knowledge of God primarily from a human reference; we would look for the traces of the divine in man, who was created in God's image and in nature. We would say, "God is like this, but He is far more because *man* and *God* are not univocal terms [i.e., having exactly the same meaning]." Karl Barth saw that the analogy of religious language is an analogy of faith (*analogia fidei*). By this he meant that we can properly speak of God only where He, through His own self-disclosure, grasps human language, transforms it, and empowers it to carry the content of revelation. Then such words as father, son, love, spirit, fellowship, life, hope, and knowledge receive a content they could not otherwise have. But the meaning supplied by the faith-event is certainly not unrelated to our common use of such words. Otherwise, they would communicate nothing. Transformed, they convey the meaning of revelation.[25]

Just such a transformation of language happens to the word *person* in the event of God's incarnation in Jesus of Nazareth. The person, the being, of the Christ magnificently and transparently reveals the personhood of God and in the process reveals what human personhood should and can be. Only through the event of redemption and the life of the Spirit in the community of faith can this meaning in its fullness be ascertained.

As personal, God is fully conscious not only of Himself but also of His creation. He freely acts in harmony with His purposes. Unlike Aristotle's God with whom communion is impossible, *Yahweh* can be addressed. He is the divine *Thou* over against the human subject with whom He carries on conversation. And the Bible is the record of this divine-human dialogue. Any doctrine of God that jeopardizes the free dialogic character of His reality should not be allowed to pass as Christian.

B. God Is Holy

The whole of the Old and New Testaments is the revelation of the God who *is* holiness and love. Together holiness and love constitute the essential being of God. They are not attributes of God, but His essence, on which such concepts as omniscience and omnipotence are predicated. The meaning of God's holiness is completed in the meaning of His love, and the meaning of His love is completed in his holiness. Unless these two are kept in balance, God's holiness may be distorted into a harsh, threatening transcendence, and His love may dissipate into aimless sentimentality. God's revelation of Himself is the revelation of His holiness and love. Therefore every affirmation about Him should be an affirmation about His holiness and love. "The indissoluble connection between holiness and love," Emil Brunner says, "is the characteristic and decisive element in the Christian idea of God."[26] Although in the Old Testament there seems to be a greater emphasis on the holiness of God and in the New Testament a greater emphasis on His love, it is a serious error to isolate these two qualities as if they belong only to their respective Testaments. The gracious self-giving love of God does not first appear in the New Testament but in His initial creative activity on the world's behalf. He who *is* holiness and love creates *in* holiness and love, and the unity of these qualities is not one bit diminished in the fullness of God that is embodied in our Lord.

First we consider God as holy and, second, as love.

Holiness (*qadosh*, Hebrew; *hagios* Greek) is the very nature of God. It means "God-ness." It is a distinction of the divine essence that God shares with none other, except derivatively as He freely sanctifies that which belongs to Him, such as places (Isa. 11:9), people (Exod. 19:6), and things (e.g., the temple). "Hallowed [holy] be your name" is the prayer taught by our Lord to His disciples (Matt. 6:9). "Holy and awesome is His name" (Ps. 111:9). "Your ways, O God, are holy" (Ps. 77:13). God swears by His holiness (Amos 4:2 NIV).

One of the most significant developments in Christian theology and liturgy in this century has been a recovery of the biblical meaning of God's holiness. This has been due largely to the work of such people as P. T. Forsyth,[27] Rudolph Otto,[28] Karl Barth, Emil Brunner, Albert C. Knudson,[29] and Norman H. Snaith.[30] Of no small importance was the influence of Søren Kierkegaard's book *Fear and Trembling*.

Prior to this recovery two errors had become associated with the idea of God's holiness. The first was that holiness is an attribute of God, rather than His essence.[31] The second was that God's holiness is primarily a moral category, rather than a religious one. The second error came into the stream of Protestant theology largely through the influence of Immanuel Kant.

Snaith says that holiness "is the most intimately divine word of all. It has to do . . . with the very Nature of Deity. . . ."[32] The root *q-d-sh* refers positively to what is uniquely God's, to the essential difference between God and man. He is Yahweh, and His glory He does not share with any other (cf. Isa. 40:18, 25; 42:8). Holiness distinguishes Him from everything else. It is the central meaning of His transcendence, the sublimity of God as contrasted with human creatureliness. He exhausts the meaning of the term *God;* His kind and character are incommensurable with our own: "before [Him] we recoil in a wonder that strikes us chill and numb."[33] The only appropriate disposition in His presence is worship. Before Him man responds with absolute awe and fascination (attraction), "a strange harmony of contrasts" to which the biblical record bears witness.

Scholars such as Snaith, Otto, and Brunner agree that at first the word had no direct ethical connotation. It communicated that mysterious, indefinable, awe-inspiring quality that differentiates God from man and the rest of creation. But although holiness stands for the difference between God and man, it should not be viewed as distance from man. God is different from His creation but He is assuredly always near to it. Therefore the meaning of God's holiness points not only to the infinite qualitative difference between God and man but also to the fact that God is present as the life-giving ground or source of creaturely existence. He is both transcendent and immanent. He is at once God in the Highest, God Almighty, and God the Creator, Sustainer, and Redeemer.

Among the Hebrews the use of the word *qadosh* in its personal sense came to refer to Yahweh exclusively (e.g., "Who can stand in the presence of the LORD, this holy God?" [1 Sam. 6:20 NIV] and Isa. 5:16, where the title "Yahweh of hosts" is paralleled with "El, the Holy One": "The LORD of hosts is exalted in justice, and the Holy God shows himself holy in righteousness," RSV). In Isaiah 40:25 the designation "the Holy One" is used as a synonym for the divine Name. This is also true in Leviticus 18:21 (LXX, "the Holy Name of thy God"); Job 6:10; Hosea 11:9; Habakkuk 3:3. In Isaiah the phrase "the Holy One of Israel" occurs frequently (e.g., 1:4; 5:19; 10:20; 30:11; 43:3, 14; 48:17; 60:9). When Amos says that God "has sworn by His holiness" (4:2), he means that Yahweh "has sworn by His deity, by Himself as God, and the meaning is therefore exactly the same as in Amos 6:8, where Amos says that 'the Lord God has sworn by Himself.'"[34]

Holiness, therefore, characterizes all of God's self-manifestations. In Hebrew thought holiness comes to represent the positive activity of that Personal Other whom the Hebrews recognized as Yahweh (Deut. 33:2; Ps. 50:2; 80:1; Isa. 10:17).

Largely under the impact of the eighth-century B.C. prophets there occurs a distinctive development in the Hebrew understanding of God's holiness, the association of holiness and righteousness (cf. Isa. 5:16). Now holiness comes to include righteousness as the main element of its content. Although holiness had already indicated the inner nature of God, the moral element of God's holiness reaches its highest expression under the impact of Isaiah, Amos, Hosea, and Micah (and later, Jeremiah). Snaith argues that the moral content of God's holiness as preached by the eighth-century prophets is distinctive, completely without parallel among the religions of Canaan and Mesopotamia and in the moral ideas of the Greeks. Although these prophets, except for Isaiah, do not often use the words *qodesh* ("holiness") and *qadosh* ("holy") (Micah does not use the word at all), "all four prophets combine into a solid unanimity in repeatedly reiterating the fact that Jehovah by His very Nature demands right conduct from His worshippers and will be content with nothing less."[35] These prophets explicitly connect holiness and righteousness (*tsedaqah;* e.g., Isa. 5:16; 6:1-5).

In their ministry righteousness comes to have special reference to the needs of the poor, the widow, and the orphan, that is, the exploited and helpless ones. According to these prophets, the sanctifying or hallowing of the name of God "is to be done in righteousness." The holiness of Yahweh will be seen by the exaltation of righteousness in their midst. In Isaiah's temple experience there is an unmistakable connection between God's holiness and His righteousness. The vision of the Holy One convinces Isaiah of his and his people's sin: "Woe to me! . . . I am ruined! For I am a man of unclean lips, and I live among a people of unclean lips" (Isa. 6:5).

The ethical standards of these prophets —Amos's condemnation of the rich for oppressing the poor, Hosea's charge of untrustworthiness among the people, Micah's tirades against the city dwellers who exploited the rural poor, and Isaiah's "chorus of protest" against the general wickedness of Jerusalem—issued from what they knew of the nature of God. They rested their vision of righteous conduct on their knowledge of God, not on some abstract or culturally conditioned ethical code. The Holy One is He who acts justly and loves mercy, who does not "acquit a man with dishonest scales" (Mic. 6:8, 11 NIV).

In His relationship to mankind God models the substance and meaning of what He wills for His creation. His dealings with Israel exhibit the judgment and righteousness, the mercy and love that should characterize all ethical relationships among His people (Amos 5:24). God has shown Himself to be the champion of the defenseless: "The Lord works righteousness and justice for all the oppressed" (Ps. 103:6, NIV). The moral, then, is what Judah has seen in God's covenantal faithfulness. The Decalogue (the Ten Commandments) is surely misconstrued unless it is understood as the consistent expression of God's own self-disclosure, His own nature as it bears on His will for Israel—His covenantal partner—and all mankind.

Preéminently in the New Testament God models what He wills as the ethical norm by reaching out to us in creative justice instead of distributive justice. He has not dealt with us according to our sins: "While we were still sinners, Christ died for us" (Rom. 5:8 NIV). "When we were God's enemies, we were reconciled to him through the death of his Son" (Rom. 5:10 NIV). The ethic of the New Testament derives not from speculation about morality, and not from the issuance of a new moral code, but from the way God has forgiven and restored us who can make no just claim on Him.

The eighth-century B.C. prophets judged their hearers sinners not *primarily* because they had broken an ethical code, but because their flagrant injustices committed against the defenseless revealed hearts far advanced in insurrection against the holy God, whose being they were supposed to manifest and whose will they were to obey. Authentic *hesed* ("steadfast love") will take every opportunity to evidence the content of God's holiness through justice and mercy. Therefore, sin is not to be viewed primarily as an ethical but as a religious matter, a matter of relationship to the holy God. The unrighteousness of Israel and Judah show that they had forsaken their knowledge of God's nature and the claim He made on them. They rejected His teaching and despised His Word (Isa. 1:24).

The righteousness of God as manifested in the moral design that He has set for man, John Wesley says, is

> an incorruptible picture of the High and Holy One that inhabiteth eternity. . . . It is the face of God unveiled; God manifested to his Creatures as they are able to bear it; manifested to give and not to destroy, life—that they may see God and live. It is the heart of God disclosed to man.[36]

The moral law that we ascribe to God is the expression of His will. But it must be remembered, Wesley says, that God's will and His nature cannot be separated. William R. Cannon summarizes Wesley's position in this way: "Nature and will stand together, and divine creativity is that which defines right and that which gives good its meaning. . . . God abides by that which he has defined and remains loyal to that which he has given."[37]

Wesley's words are reflected in those of twentieth-century theologian Gustaf Aulen who says that a proper understanding of God's holiness acts as a sentinel to insure that every affirmation about God retains its purely religious character.[38] Aulen says that there are four ways in which a proper understanding of God's holiness monitors our affirmations about Him.

First, it guarantees that abstract and superfluous speculations will not encroach on the biblical concept of God and that religion will not be reduced to moralism or ethics. This was true of Albrecht Ritschl, for whom the Christian religion was fundamentally defined in ethical categories.[39]

Second, the holiness of God guards against all anthropocentric explanations of the Christian faith that view God as a projection of the human mind. "He is the divine *Thou,* upon whom human existence is wholly dependent."[40] It also dispels all anthropocentrism that masquerades in the robes of religion. This was one of the fundamental criticisms leveled at nineteenth-century liberal theology by the neo-Reformation theologians.

Third, the holiness of God proclaims His unfathomableness and completely frustrates all rationalistic efforts to encompass the being of God. Knowledge of Him is not gained through finite ingenuity. The free, holy God sets the conditions by which He can be known. The neutral ground of the independent observer completely passes away. "To meet God as the Holy One is to be placed under a supreme compulsion, and to be confronted by a power advancing in sovereign majesty . . . we are in his power, not he in ours."[41]

Finally, the holiness of God utterly resists all forms of mysticism that obliterate the distinction between the human and the divine. Both rationalism and mysticism try to do this, but in different ways and, on the surface at least, for different reasons. When the goal of mysticism is identity with and absorption by the human into the divine, God reasserts His Wholly Otherness. Before Him creaturely consciousness is never erased.

But this is a promise, not a threat. By the clear expression of His will for the world and the moral content of the righteousness that should characterize human life, we know what is God's appraisal of and will for this world: it is an appropriate place for life and human fulfillment to occur. The secular, or the "profane," is not simply secular. It is far more; it is the place graced by God's sanctifying presence, where people are to "do justice, and to love kindness, and to walk humbly with [their] God" (Mic. 6:8 RSV). He who worships the holy God will know that in human society "justice [should] roll on like a river, righteousness like a never-failing stream" (Amos 5:24 NIV).

We see therefore that even though the holiness of God must be contrasted with the secular, His holiness does not exclude the secular or profane. The word *profane* has assumed the connotation of unclean, but this is not a necessary part of its definition. It means "in front of the doors" of the holy. The German word *profan* retains the neutrality. The secular is the realm of the finite, the created order. It can be made sacred, sanctified by the holy. This may be called "transitive holiness."

The incarnation of the holy God in Jesus of Nazareth forecloses all negative appraisals of the world. John, writing against first-century proto-Gnosticism, which disdained all things material, insisted that the antichrist is precisely he who denies that Jesus is come in the flesh (1 John 2:22). Despair about the world is much more in harmony with Hinduism or Buddhism—for whose adherents the world and distinct individuality are illusory—than it is with Christian faith. In the Christian doctrine of God and His relationship to the world, there is no necessary ontological incongruity. He is not one bit diminished by contact with it. The world is not inherently evil or defective, making the rejection of it necessary for knowledge of God. The creation can and ought to be the bearer of the divine imprint. It is the place where God initiates a covenantal relationship with man that includes the whole creation. Everything secular is potentially sacred, open to consecration; God's holiness can be, and is, expressed through the secular.[42]

The whole world, all of life, can have sacramental significance. The children of Israel were to be "a people holy to the Lord [their] God" (Deut. 14:2; 28:9; 30:2, 10; Lev. 20:26). Jesus prayed for the sanctification of His church, the instrument of His holiness (John 17:7-19). Those who are raised to new life in Christ are holy, "saints" (*hagioi,* 1 Cor. 1:2; 1 Peter 2:9). Paul's writings show an abundant awareness that God's holiness can be expressed through the secular. He declared that life lived *in* the flesh can nevertheless be lived *according to* the Spirit: "Therefore, I urge you, brothers, in view of God's mercy, to offer your bodies as living sacrifices, holy and pleasing to God—which is your spiritual worship" (Rom. 12:1 NIV).

C. God Is Love

The writer of 1 John says simply, "God is love. Whoever lives in love lives in God, and God in him" (1 John 4:16 NIV). The apostle Paul speaks of God as the "God of love and peace" (2 Cor. 13:11). Love is not primarily what God *does* but what He *is.* He does what He is.

To say that God is love expresses the center of John Wesley's doctrine of God. His vision of normative Christian life is that it is lived in an acceptable worship of God that seeks to "imitate" the One who is worshiped. This includes God's justice, mercy, and truth. But, Wesley says, the most essential imitation, the one that is more expressive of the essential being of God, is love.[43]

God has shown the character of His love to be universal, generous, and disinterested. It springs from no view of advantage to itself. "It soars above all . . . scanty bounds, embracing neighbors and strangers, friends and enemies; yea, not only the good and gentle but also the froward, the evil and unthankful." God's love is demonstrated in "the constant care" with which He still attends the world, the "work of his own hand."[44] Wesley would have agreed with Luther who said that in Jesus Christ God has shown Himself to be "an abyss of eternal love that can never be plumbed by the most elevated religious awareness."

When speaking of God's love, the New Testament uses the word *agape* in contrast to *eros,* a love that is derived from, or evoked by, the beautiful or valuable in the object of love.[45] God's love as *agape* is love for that which is unlovely, that which in itself does not evoke from the lover attraction or appreciation. It creates or gives value where there was none. Unlike a love sparked by faithfulness, beauty, and purity, God's love extends to the faithless, to those who have spurned His love. It strives to achieve reconciliation and even creates the conditions by which alienation can be overcome. Through love, God freely reconciles sinners to Himself and transforms them in the image of His dear Son. This is *euangelion,* the "good news," of the New Testament (Luke 4:43; Rom. 15:20; 1 Cor. 15:1). In His person Christ flawlessly embodies the content and meaning of God's love. He *is* the "good news," *doing* among us, the prodigals, what God *is,* love.

God's love is always prevenient; that is, it reaches out to the beloved long before the gift of love is or can be reciprocated.[46] In the interest of life, *agape* cuts through death; in the interest of reconciliation, it conquers alienation. For forgiveness it breaks the kingdom of guilt; for holiness it cleanses from sin, and for wholeness it overcomes fragmentation. "How great is the love the Father has lavished on us, that we should be called children of God!" (1 John 3:1 NIV). "Because of his great love for us, God, who is rich in mercy, made us alive with Christ even when we were dead in transgressions—it is by grace you have been saved" (Eph. 2:4–5 NIV). "This is love: not that we loved God, but that he loved us and sent his Son as an atoning sacrifice for our sins" (1 John 4:10 NIV; cf. Rom. 6:23; Luke 19:10; Titus 3:5).

The parables of Jesus repeatedly exhibit the love of God as He freely reaches out in saving mercy to the unlovely, the lost, and the hopeless. Many people encountered and were transformed by *agape* in Jesus' ministry: Zacchaeus (Luke 19:1–10), the woman taken in adultery (John 8:3–11), the woman at the well (John 4:7–42), the thief on a cross (Luke 23:43), lepers (Luke 17:11–19), the incurably sick (e.g., John 5:5–14), and even some who were dead (e.g., John 11:1–44). Always He is the one who speaks with authoritative love: "If therefore the Son shall make you free, you shall be free indeed" (John 8:36) and "Whoever believes in me, . . . streams of living water will flow from within him" (John 7:38 NIV).

Discussion of God's love cannot be limited to the New Testament. The One who loved the world and gave His own Son for it also displayed an intense love for Israel. His deeds in the Old Testament are consistent with His deeds in the New even though in the New Testament His love achieves a universal expression perhaps not fully realized in the Old. But perhaps even this may be explained by Israel's failure to fulfill its calling as a "missionary nation" charged with the responsibility of universalizing God's love. This is the central message of the Book of Jonah.

God's love (Hebrew, *ahavah*) for Israel displays a content identical with that of *agape* in the New Testament. In the Old Testament we are told that God did not set His love upon Israel or choose them because they were more in number than any other people. In fact, they were the fewest of all the nations. The reason is totally gracious: "But it was because the Lord loved you . . . that he brought you out with a mighty hand and redeemed you from the land of slavery, from the power of Pharaoh king of Egypt" (Deut. 7:8 NIV; cf. v. 7; Deut. 10:15; 23:5).

Perhaps the most sublime Old Testament depiction of God's love and the clearest parallel to the New Testament is found in the Book of Hosea. This is a parable of Israel's faithlessness and of God's love extended to her even after she had loved other gods. Gomer, Hosea's unfaithful wife, is nevertheless loved by him. Just so, God's love for the people of Israel is based on no quality in them, but comes solely from His redemptive election of them.

One of the most incomprehensible features of God's love is its vulnerability. He loves with an unqualified love even though there is no certainty that His love will be reciprocated. Herein is the sovereignty of God exhibited, not in frightful, coercive power, but in a self-giving love that takes the awesome risk of rejection. Before such power the neck of rebellion is broken, and *hesed,* the steadfastness and trustworthiness of true covenantal love, takes root in the human spirit. God excites a faithfulness, or loyal love, in the beloved that binds them together in the most complete of relationships.[47]

Such a posture by God toward the world would be unthinkable for Aristotelian or Neoplatonic thought. Even though there is no clearly developed theology in Plato, it would be inconceivable for him that the "good," which is finally the most comprehensive of the ideas, would "pursue" what is its contrary. In Aristotle's more highly developed theology God thinks the highest and best, and since God is all-perfection and fullness, He thinks only Himself. To even conceive of God loving the unlovely would mean the undoing of Aristotle's God. To think the lesser, to be conscious of the ugly for example, would jeopardize God's own perfection. The *One* in Neoplatonism is beyond being; it is in no sense directly engaged in the world that emanates from *being*, the One's first emanation. The world participates less and less in being as its parts descend the scale of being. Hence, direct saving contact between the One and sinful man as is exhibited in God's love for the world is unthinkable in this scheme. In none of these instances is it possible to speak of "God in search of man."[48]

God's love must be understood as the power of His being, His sovereignty, His freedom. Even before the divine life and love are manifest in and to the creation they are manifest in the Trinity—in the Father, Son, and Holy Spirit, whose oneness is partly their community of love. Divine love characterizes triune life: the Father gives Himself to the Son and to the Spirit, the Son to the Father and the Spirit, and the Spirit to the Father and the Son.

We can get some indication of this by the way the Father speaks of the Son at Jesus' baptism and by the Holy Spirit's presence in this event. In addition, Jesus says that the Father loves the Son and shows Him all things (John 5:20). This love may also be seen in the way the Son speaks of the Father and the Spirit in His high-priestly prayer (John 17).

Therefore, when love (*agape*) appears as God giving life, renewal, and redemption to the world, no fundamentally new character is added to it. When He creates and redeems, God is truly manifesting Himself. Love is ultimate; God as love constitutes the nature of ultimate being.[49] He acts out of complete concern not only for all, but also for all dimensions of life, for the conditions that sustain, promote, and enhance life, including new life and new conditions of life. His love even carries to the point of redemptive participation in creaturely suffering as seen in the Incarnation and the Cross.

This love that the Father has for the church, Jesus says, will be of one kind with the love that the Father and Son have for each other (John 17:23). This kind of love will be the church's distinguishing feature as well. *Agape* at work in us who believe—a love that extends to our neighbor's—is God's presence in us (1 John 4:12). By disclosing the character of the Father's love, the Son reveals the content of the Father's own being, His name; the two are the same (John 17:26).

D. The Attributes of God

After having considered God as living, as holy, and as love, we are now prepared to consider His attributes, which are consistent expressions of His being. Consequently, God's attributes ought not to be discussed apart from holiness and love. When they are, on the basis of metaphysical speculation about what "ought to be," for example, they distort the biblical doctrine of God.

In his sermon "The Unity of the Divine Being" John Wesley gives six attributes of God. But, he says, "only some of His attributes He hath been pleased to reveal to us in His word."[50] Although some standard attributes of God are normally treated by theologians, there seems to be no universally accepted "list" of His attributes. Our treatment of His attributes will include His sovereignty, omnipotence, eternity, immutability, omnipresence, omniscience, and His wrath.

1. Sovereignty God's sovereignty means that He is absolutely free from creaturely restraints; that is, He is free to be who He is, the God who is holiness and love. As we have seen, this is probably the meaning of the *tetragrammaton* (Exod. 3:14). He is Lord above all. But we must keep in mind that His freedom is always an expression of who He is; His sovereignty is the power of holiness and love, expressed not oppressively or repressively, but in a most magnificent array of creating, saving, forgiving, and merciful deeds. This is but another way of restating John Wesley's insistence that "the sovereignty of God [must] never be brought to supersede His justice."[51] This is one of Wesley's chief arguments against the Calvinist doctrine of unconditional election and reprobation. Said he, "It flatly contradicts, indeed utterly overthrows, the Scripture account of the justice of God."[52] Wesleyans prefer to define God's sovereignty according to His victorious involvement *in* the world.[53]

Consequently, common meanings of sovereignty, power, and strength as they appear in ordinary human language may not apply to God at all. Where they are employed they must be carefully governed by His self-disclosure. His is not a sovereignty that wins allegiance from His subjects through brute strength and threat, but through self-giving and self-sacrificing love. (This is certainly not unique to Wesley.)

God's *fundamental* designs of creation and redemption cannot be finally frustrated. In His world God has shown and will show Himself to be the Creator-Redeemer God. Even those who reject Him, who, as Karl Barth says, commit the "possible impossibility" of rejecting eternal life, bear witness to God's holiness and love. The Bible leaves absolutely no doubt about the present and final demonstration and vindication of God's sovereignty, understood as the freedom of His holiness and love. Often Christians have expressed faith in God's sovereignty when almost all the political, social, and economic indicators seem to present telling arguments against it. Although exiled in harsh surroundings by the power of Rome, John nevertheless offered an uninhibited doxology—"to [God] be glory and power for ever and ever! Amen" (Rev. 1:6 NIV). This burst of praise, characteristic of Christian faith, was occasioned by John's knowledge of the God whose sovereignty finally brackets or makes relative the power of imperial Rome: "'I am the Alpha and the Omega,' says the Lord God, 'who is and who was and who is to come, the Almighty'" (Rev. 1:8).

Not only did John know of the history of God's sovereign redemptive deeds in Israel's behalf, he also knew that even the powers of death, hell, sin, and the grave had been unable to stay God's sovereign holiness and love. By His sovereignty God had raised Jesus from the dead. Now there is no reason to fear: "I am the Living One; I was dead, and behold I am alive forever! And I hold the keys of death and Hades" (Rev. 1:18 NIV). Of Christ, John says, "In him was life, and the life was the light of men. The light shines in the darkness, and the darkness has not overcome it" (John 1:4-5 RSV). In this statement the manifestation of God's sovereignty reaches its clearest and highest manifestation, in His gracious conquest of sin and alienation.

From the human side the sovereignty of God is most immediately encountered in the event of faith; here the gracious God arrests the sinner, breaks his bondage to the law of sin and death, and freely reconciles the penitent to Himself. His sovereignty is encountered by us as that power by which we become children of God (John 1:12). "For John Wesley," says Albert Outler, "the sovereignty of God is most perfectly displayed as the sovereignty of His grace by which He effects full salvation in the believer."[54]

The presence of evil in the world cannot be reconciled with an understanding of God's sovereignty viewed primarily as unrestricted, coercive strength, as will to power. If this were the proper understanding of God's sovereignty, then there would either be no evil in the world or there would be no God. God would either have to eliminate evil or surrender His claim to sovereignty. But power as the power of God's love can be reconciled with the presence of evil in the world and at the same time express His active opposition to it. Only sovereign love can brook a challenge to itself and thereby demonstrate its supremacy over that which challenges it. Through a display of unrestricted and coercive power, external allegiance may be won, but only through love is the whole disposition of the human spirit brought into harmony with God's will. Love is evil's most formidable enemy.

2. Omnipotence (infinite power). When discussed apart from His holiness and love, God's omnipotence appears both frightening and despotic. Many of the problematic questions about God's omnipotence arise completely outside the range of His holiness and love. He is not a heavenly magician engaged in bizarre exhibitions of power that dazzle onlookers. His omnipotence doesn't mean that "God can do anything." It has nothing to do with logical contradictions. That which is flawed by illogic remains so even when the word *God* is attached to it. His omnipotence is a matter of the power of His holiness and love in a world that is the object of His care and keeping. It is displayed in creation, redemption, and eschatological hope. To look for it elsewhere is futile. For the New Testament writers God's omnipotence is centrally manifest in the resurrection of Christ, as the power "of his mighty strength, which he exerted in Christ when he raised him from the dead and seated him at his right hand in the heavenly realms" (Eph. 1:19-20 NIV).

We cannot too strongly emphasize that God's omnipotence is demonstrated not in His power to threaten man's feeble hold on finite life but precisely in His power and willingness to make room for it. Omnipotence is God's guarantee that His covenantal promises to His creation will be fulfilled, preeminently in a real "I-Thou" communion. Charles Hartshorne says that God's omnipotence means His supreme creativity, a creativity that makes room for lower (contingent) forms of creativity. He is the sole source of creative freedom.[55]

Therefore, divine omnipotence does include the radical contingency of the world. God is the sole ground of the world's existence. "God . . . gives life to everything" (1 Tim. 6:13 NIV) and "in him all things hold together" (Col. 1:17 NIV). All powers other than His own are derived ones; that is, nothing has ontological independence from Him. Therefore He makes all other so-called gods ridiculously superfluous. Even that which stands against Him, and thereby seems to be independent of Him, can exist only as a perversion or distortion of His gift of life. Evil has no ontological independence of its own. God is certainly not the author of evil; this must be clearly understood. But evil's "No!" to God presupposes God's gift of an ontological foundation from which the no is spoken. God makes even the no of evil to praise Him.

3. Eternity In the Bible the eternality of God is usually spoken of as (1) His being from everlasting to everlasting ("from everlasting to everlasting Thou art God" [Ps. 90:2; cf. 41:13]) and (2) His name, His being, which will endure forever (Ps. 72:17). The eternity of God should be viewed as the sovereignty of divine holiness and love in relationship to time. Time is a category appropriate to derived or contingent being, not to Him who *is* life and being. The world *exists,* and therefore the categories of space and time properly apply to it; they characterize its finitude. But God *is.* As regards time, He is the absolutely noncontingent One.

Let us be careful to note, however, that God's eternality does not shut Him out of space and time. As the history of salvation clearly shows, especially the *kenosis* passage of Philippians 2:5-11, He who creates the heavens and the earth is capable of intense involvement with it. The Incarnation is the definitive expression of this fact.

God's eternality may be glimpsed in Paul's statement, "love never ends" (1 Cor. 13:8 RSV). Love's constancy reveals that absolute dependability of God's own being. His is an everlasting righteousness (Ps. 119:142); His kingdom, power, and glory are forever (Matt. 6:13). Although He takes human history seriously, makes it the arena of His own presence and the object of His care, temporal contingency cannot be imposed on Him. He *is* eternal life, eternal love.

4. Immutability (unchangeableness). In few places has Greek metaphysics had so much undesirable impact on the doctrine of God as in the attribute of immutability. For Aristotle change is a part of the process of coming to be and passing away. God, who is absolutely perfect, cannot be subject to change—not even that which comes by thinking about an object—else He would also be subject to decay. So He thinks the most perfect: He thinks Himself.

The One in Neoplatonism is also beyond the process of coming to be and passing away because He is beyond *being,* beyond all contact with what we call existence. He is outside history, outside the entire sphere of mutability, having no contact with it.[56] This is the so-called *apathia* of God.[57]

Too often the Greek paradigm has determined our view of God's immutability. When this happens, Christian thought departs from the biblical doctrine of the living God who is intimately involved in the affairs of His creation and who is noticeably impacted by this involvement. Biblical descriptions of God's intimacy with the world—e.g., His weeping over Israel in the person as well as the presence of Hosea—ought not be dismissed as a concession to those who have limited theological insight. Of course, neither we nor Hosea believe that God is a physical being with tear ducts. But Christian theology knows of no superior understanding of God that advances beyond Him who is vitally engaged in communion with His world to a "more mature" view of Him as impersonal and impassive. He who is most truly the living God loves, hopes, and rejoices over reciprocated love, and hurts in the presence of faithlessness.

The world makes a difference to God, else His love loses all meaning for us. Jesus says that there is rejoicing in heaven over a sinner who repents, who turns to the Father. When Jesus describes the joy of the father who meets the returning prodigal, He means to say something perfectly accurate about the character of God's relationship to us.

If we take seriously these indications of God's relationship to us, then His immutability cannot mean the same as it does for Aristotle or Plotinus. Rather, God's immutability signifies His absolute constancy, His faithfulness to Himself and to His creation. He does not and will not fail to be Himself; He will be holy love. But this is far different from the idea of a static deity who sits unmoved and unfeeling in the heavens, unaffected by worship and rejection or by the fulfillment of value in the world.

A distinction must be made between God's unchangeable nature and His freedom for enriching His own experience as a result of His very real interaction with us. As Creator and Sustainer, God extends to us aims or goals that reflect His purposes for us. Achievement of these aims fulfills the potential for value. Achievement of God's aims is neither a vacuous exercise nor a matter of playing out a preordained script. Through God's grace something novel and beautiful actually comes into being. This is God's doing, but it occurs through obedient human response.

Does this have no positive, enriching bearing on God's own range of experience? In the Wesleyan doctrine of God's activity in the world, grace makes possible a divine-human synergism. God really does take man seriously; He takes seriously the world as a place where love creates the new, the valuable, the beautiful. God is not a static Aristotelian perfection unengaged in these happenings. He experiences achievement (satisfaction) of value also, and He is enriched by it. When God creates, He creates additional contents of His own awareness.

If we cannot say that God's experience

of the world—of His children as they respond to Him in faith and love—enriches His own life in some significant way, then we will have to surrender our claim to understand what it means to speak of the relationship between God and man as a loving one (cf. Eph. 1:18). In all of our experiences of love those who participate in it are enriched by it.

The Greek concept of God's immutability is extremely difficult to dislodge from Christian thought. On this matter, normally there is a major disjunction between one's devotional encounter and his or her reflective concepts of God.

5. Omnipresence Viewed from the being of God as holy love, omnipresence means nothing less than the ability of divine love to maintain itself everywhere unhindered by limitations of space.[58] God's omnipresence has nothing to do with how a physical entity can nevertheless be unbounded by spatial restrictions. God is Spirit and those who worship Him must worship Him "in Spirit and truth" (John 4:23).

6. Omniscience (infinite knowledge). Debates about the meaning of God's omniscience have been extensive and inconclusive. Speculation about whether God's knowledge includes not only the past and present but also the future, about how extensive is His knowledge of the future, and the bearing God's knowing of the future would have on human freedom has not produced any general theological consensus. But most of us can agree that God's purposes involve the future, that He takes seriously man's freedom and his involvement in the realization of these purposes, and that whatever the extent of God's knowledge it must be consistent with His love.

Charles Hartshorne is very helpful at this point. Since God is the all-inclusive reality, His knowledge, unlike our fragmentary knowledge, must be all-inclusive. His awareness includes all that can be known, or, to put it another way, nothing that can be known remains outside the sphere of His awareness. We are wise to leave the dimensions of "what can be known" up to God. Whatever He knows does not violate His commitment to take finite freedom seriously. This affirmation should be enough to satisfy our understanding of God's omniscience. Nothing is gained by endless wrangling over whether God knows all the details of future events.

It is a mistake to think that God's own being is somehow endangered or diminished unless He knows the future absolutely as though it were the past. God is love and love makes true novelty possible. God knows that what He purposes for the world will not be finally frustrated. His kingdom will come with power and glory.

In the Bible God's omniscience is a profound comfort to the righteous and a source of fear for the wicked. Testimony to His omniscience is extensive. One of the most penetrating and yet simple assertions about God's omniscience is made by Hagar. Exiled, frightened, and apparently alone, she is met by the angel of the Lord who cares for her. Hagar responds, "You are the God who sees me" (Gen. 16:13 NIV) or "Thou art the God of seeing" (RSV). The Scriptures tell us that God knows "the hearts of all men" (1 Kings 8:39 NIV; cf. 2 Chron. 6:30). He "searches all hearts, and understands every intent of the thoughts" (1 Chron. 28:9; cf. Luke 16:15; Acts 1:24). He is perfect in knowledge, Job tells us (Job 37:16). All our ways are known to Him (Ps. 119:168; 139:1-16); He declares the end from the beginning (Isa. 46:10). "Nothing in all creation is hidden from God's sight. Everything is uncovered and laid bare before the eyes of him to whom we must give account" (Heb. 4:13 NIV).

All of these statements about God's omniscience result from encounter with Him through faith and grace. They testify to the unerring righteousness of God's judgments. His omniscience bespeaks His all-seeing eye of love, which sees everything in crystal-clear light.[59]

7. Wrath God wills to be Lord in His world, to declare His glory among us. His is not a complacent and indulgent love. Sin is a radical challenge to God's being Lord in His world, and He does not meet it with a chuckle and a wink. Sin is insurrection against God's holiness and love, and its goal is nothing short of God's extinction, His *absolute* frustration. Sin, said Karl Barth, is "hell's beachhead in God's universe of order." Sin is not simply a matter of aiming at the mark and missing it, but of aiming at the wrong mark and hitting it every time.

The wrath of God is a consistent expression of His love, it is divine love opposing that which opposes love, and its satisfaction can be nothing less than defeat of what promotes chaos, alienation, and death. In *The Essentials of Wesleyan Theology* Paul A. Mickey says that according to Wesleyan theology "the sovereign God is the God who lovingly gathers the world into final righteousness through the outworking of His righteous wrath against all that is evil."[60]

God cannot dismiss His wrath without trivializing His love. Sometimes wrath is dismissed as being incommensurate with God's love. But this is not so. A love incapable of expressing radical opposition to love's opponents is not love at all. It then becomes powerless sentimentality. God's love drives toward wholeness, life, and communion. It is powerful, active, and disciplinary.

Divine wrath conceived of apart from love can only be misconceived. Then wrath becomes fury, tyrannical destruction, and despotic vengeance, inspiring fear and hate. God's wrath serves His love; its *telos* is redemptive.

So intense is God's wrath that sinful man cannot stand before it, cannot bear its vented judgment. In the death of Jesus Christ, the God who is holy love takes on Himself the abyss of His wrath. In this event the wisdom of God is demonstrated and a full expression of His love occurs. Man's pride and insurrection broken, sinful but repentant, he stands utterly humbled before that event in which the wrath of God is turned away, is freely absorbed by Him who knew no sin but who became obedient to the Father, even to death on the cross.

In this one sublime event we learn the character of God's holiness and love and the nature of sin. "Christian identity," says Jürgen Moltmann, "can be understood only as an act of identification with the crucified Christ." We must accept the proclamation that in Christ God has graciously identified Himself with us, the otherwise hopeless ones. The Cross is at once an expression of God's unwavering fidelity to Himself as holy love, to His unremitting opposition to that which opposes love, and the definitive demonstration of the extent to which He is willing to go to overcome the antagonism, alienation, and guilt brought on by sin.

E. God Is Triune

For the Christian, no less than for the Jew, the confession commonly called the *Shema'*, Hebrew "hear": "Hear, O Israel! The LORD is our God, the LORD is one!" (Deut. 6:4ff.) is the core of our religious faith. It stands indisputably against all forms of polytheism, dualism, and henotheism.

Monotheistic faith is at the heart of Wesleyan thought about God. For John Wesley God "is one in essence, in knowledge, in will, and in . . . testimony."[61] "The One God," Wesley said, "is the Father of all things." He is the One infinite and independent Being. "It is impossible there should be more than one."[62]

Any departure from monotheistic faith fails to comprehend the central element of our faith. God has revealed Himself as one God and the *content* of His disclosure as we have encountered it testifies to this.

Equally central to Christian faith is the confession that the one God is triune—Father, Son, and Holy Spirit. The doctrine of the Trinity maintains the definitive Christian confession that Christ is Lord, and it maintains also our confession in one God. Universally, Christians affirm:

> We believe in one Lord, the Father All-sovereign, maker of heaven and earth . . . and in one Lord Jesus Christ, the only begotten Son of the Father, . . . true God of true God, . . . of one substance with the Father, through whom all things were made; . . . and in the Holy Spirit, the Lord and the life-giver, that proceeds from the Father, who with the Father and Son is worshiped together and glorified together. . . .[63]

John Wesley unambiguously affirmed "faith in the Holy Trinity."[64] Though he declined to speculate about the dogma of the Trinity, to offer a "rational explanation" of it, Wesley thought "constantly in trinitarian terms and used every instance possible to stress [the] doctrine of a triune God and its immediate importance for religious experience."[65]

But although Wesley accepted the orthodox Western formulations regarding the Trinity and used such words as *Trinity* and *person* "without any scruple," he did not insist on anyone's using these words. They are not scriptural terms.[66] "Wesley," says Colin Williams, "sought to keep attention directed toward Christian life and to prevent it from running off into a speculative concern for right formulation."[67] Since no completely adequate explanation of the doctrine of the Trinity can be produced, Wesley did not believe it important to accept any particular explanation of it. What is important for him is that we honor the Son, the Holy Spirit, and the Father as one God.[68] According to Wesley, whatever tentativeness there may be about the doctrine of the Trinity does not lie in its *fact*, but altogether in its *manner*.[69] What is essential for Christians is that they know the fact of the doctrine.[70]

In Wesleyan theology affirmation of the doctrine of the Trinity is not fundamentally grounded in theological or philosophical speculation but in the character and content of the Christian community's redemptive encounter with God. Doctrinal definition proceeds from the examination of Christian experience.[71] Lycurgus Starkey, Jr., provides an excellent example of how Wesleyan thought about the Trinity proceeds:

> The doctrine of the Holy Spirit and the triune nature of God arose out of the religious experience of the early Christian community. The first Christians shared the faith of Israel in a creator God in covenant with his people. In Jesus of Nazareth they were challenged and claimed for discipleship with a new covenant by this same God. It was their experience that God was redemptively present as Saviour and Lord in Jesus the Christ. After Jesus' physical departure, they experienced a continuing sense of his abiding presence in their fellowship, the Christlike presence of God bringing pardon and power for moral transformation in their personal and corporate life. In its own experience the church knew God in three ways. Its members gave expression to this as they invoked the blessing of Father, Son, and Holy Spirit upon one another. How were they to explain this experience of knowing God in three ways? How were they to hold to their Jewish inheritance of monotheism and yet give honest expression to their conviction that Jesus was divine? After many attempts to solve the doctrinal problem by compromising the testimony of experience, the church, at Nicaea and subsequent ecumenical councils, formulated the paradoxical theological definition we know as the doctrine of the Trinity.[72]

Although Wesley believed that a clearly stated doctrine of the Trinity is more characteristic of "fathers in Christ" than of "babes," he nevertheless maintained that he did not know how anyone could

> be a Christian believer till he "hath," as St. John speaks, "the witness in himself;" till "the Spirit of God witnesses with his Spirit, that he is a child of God;" that is, in effect, till God the Holy Ghost witnesses that God the Father has accepted him through the merits of God the Son: and, having this witness, he honours the Son, and the blessed Spirit, "even as he honors the Father."[73]

Wesley adds that he does not see how it is possible for any person to have vital religion who "denies that these Three are One."[74]

As soon as the New Testament attests that "Jesus is Lord" and that "God sent forth the Spirit of his Son into our hearts, crying, '*Abba,* Father!'" (Gal. 4:6), the question of the Trinity is raised. We know that Jesus is to be invoked as Lord and also that there is only one Lord, He who has created the heavens and the earth. He who was born of the Virgin Mary, baptized by John the Baptist, who took the form of a servant, and became obedient to death is the One in whom "all the fullness of Deity dwells in bodily form" (Col. 2:9). "He is the image of the invisible God" (Col. 1:15).

This is no less true of the Holy Spirit. His deity is unquestioned in the New Testament, even though the testimony of the Holy Spirit is consistently oriented to the person and work of our Lord. Christ manifests the Father, but it is the Holy Spirit who manifests Christ to us. We are in the Father, through the Son, by the Holy Spirit. Paul plainly identifies the Holy Spirit as the Spirit of Him who raised Jesus from the dead (Rom. 8:9, 11). He sheds abroad in the believer's heart the love of God manifest in Jesus Christ (Rom. 5:5). Through the Spirit of holiness the Son was declared to be the Son of God with power (Rom. 1:4). Life in Christ is life according to the Spirit.

The doctrine of the Trinity, the Christian faith confesses, is the only adequate way of articulating the content of God's self-disclosure. It is not, as many think, the product of arbitrary speculation and it is certainly not a doctrine whose intent and end is to confuse the faithful. The Bible teaches, and the faith encounter of the Christian church confirms, that God is one and that the one God is essentially, eternally Father, Son, and Spirit.

III. THE WORK OF GOD

Biblical faith is faith in the God whose works are of such a nature as to call forth praise from those who observe His deeds. "I will praise thee; for I am fearfully and wonderfully made: marvelous are thy works: and that my soul knoweth right well" (Ps. 139:14 KJV). "That I may publish with the voice of thanksgiving, and tell of all thy wondrous works" (Ps. 26:7 KJV; cf. 92:4; 111:2). Accordingly, God's name and power are manifest in His works. "We give thanks to Thee, O God; we give thanks, for Thy name is near; men declare Thy wondrous works" (Ps. 75:1). "For the word of the LORD is upright; and all his work is done in faithfulness" (Ps. 33:4 RSV).

Nature and human history are His arenas of activity and God's familiarity with His world seems to be so complete and natural that it doesn't surprise those who observe His doings. The world is His, and He is at home here. There is not the slightest hint in the Bible of a metaphysical dualism that pits a material world, essentially evil, against God and the human spirit who are essentially good. When He was creating, God delivered a positive appraisal of what He created. He called it good (Gen. 1:10, 12, 18, 21)—and thereby forever set the cast against all negative evaluations of the world that view it as essentially opposed to Him. "God made the earth by his power; he founded the world by his wisdom, and stretched out the heavens by his understanding" (Jer. 10:12 NIV). The world is His. It can bear His presence.

The same positive appraisal of the creation is continued in the New Testament. Here we find that He through whom the Father created is also He through whom the Father redeems and through whom He sustains the world by the word of His power. The world is infused with God's presence, His works. This fact stands as a formidable opponent to all gnosticizing tendencies, both ancient and modern, that despair of the world.

In his doctrines of creation and providence John Wesley was faithful to the Bible's affirmation about the world's essential ontological status vis-à-vis the goodness of God. For Wesley, says W. R. Cannon, everything inasmuch as it is the product of God's hand expresses in its nature His design and His purpose. Nothing, therefore, in itself is evil. . . . When God had finished His creation of the heavens and the earth, it pleased Him to pass sentence upon it and to say, in regard to every particular object, that it was good.[75]

We may distinguish between the work of God (1) in creation, (2) in revelation and redemption, and (3) in hope. These distinctions allow us to discuss the various aspects of God's work. But we should keep in mind that His work is all of one fabric—it reveals His Name and glory; all of His works are revelatory in character.

A. The Work of God in Creation

Both the Old and New Testaments affirm that God creates, sustains, and directs His world. John Wesley thought that when we speak of God from the perspective of His relationship to the world, He should be viewed under a "two-fold character": God as Creator and God as Governor.[76] In this section I will make a similar distinction but will treat Wesley's second element under two headings: God preserving and God directing.

1. God creating All religions have as part of their belief structure some account of how man and the world came into being or of what principle moves the world's cycles even if it is taken to be eternal. Christian faith believes that man and the world are radically contingent on the creative will and activity of God. In sharp contrast to some accounts that see the world as eternal or as the result of conflict among the gods or as the product of a demigod who shapes formless matter and thereby shapes the world, Christian faith affirms that man and the world are the result of the creative word of God. God created the cosmos in the beginning and on His sovereign will all creatures, terrestrial and celestial, depend for their being.

There is a difference of opinion among conservative scholars on the duration of the initial creative period. But belief in God as creator and sustainer of His world does not necessitate acceptance of a particular idea about *how* God created, except that original creation involved a divine act. That God created the world is a fundamental matter of faith with which theology is concerned.

It cannot be too strongly emphasized that Christendom's affirmation that the God it worships is this world's Creator arises not *primarily* on the basis of rational arguments or empirical considerations, but is compellingly elicited by the biblical witness and by the character of the church's redemptive encounter with Him. He who redeems thereby displays His creativity—a creativity that convinces us not only of our, but also the whole world's, radical dependence on Him. We know that He is the absolute ground of all human and cosmic existence. The power and love of the One who meets us in Jesus the Christ through the testimony of the Holy Spirit, the Scriptures, and the church, compels us to affirm that "without him nothing was made that has been made," that in Him is life, and that He alone is the light of men (John 1:3-4). The writer to the Hebrews says plainly, "By faith we understand that the universe was formed at God's command, so that what is seen was not made out of what was visible" (Heb. 11:3 NIV).

Because of their encounter with the One who accomplishes His purposes in history and who has control over the world in which history occurs, the ancient Hebrews confessed God to be the Creator. What they saw Him do and what they learned about Him made such a confession necessary.

The New Testament basis for asserting that God is Creator is not substantially different from the Old Testament basis. The glorious might by which the Father prepares the church "to share in the inheritance of the saints," by which He "has rescued us from the dominion of darkness and brought us into the kingdom of the Son he loves" is the sure ground on which we know that in Christ "all things were created." These are "things in heaven and on earth, visible and invisible, whether thrones or powers or rulers or authorities; all things were created by him and for him" (Col. 1:12-13, 16 NIV).

The act of redemption is no less overwhelming than the act of creation. It is a "new creation" (2 Cor. 5:17). He who successfully struggles with and subdues the hostile and chaotic powers of the universe is of such a magnificence that only He could account for the being and continued existence of the world.

For many people the existence of the world (the cosmological argument), the suggestions of intelligent design that we observe in the world (the teleological argument), the need to account for the ultimate seriousness of the moral imperative (the moral argument), and what is believed to be an immediate awareness of the absolute ground of being that completely qualifies all finite existence (the ontological argument) are strong and convincing reasons for belief in the sort of creator-God spoken of in the Bible. For many others these arguments carry no such conviction. In the modern era, belief in God as creator, sustainer, and director of the world has met intense opposition. Whereas the classical arguments for God's existence were once believed to be self-evidencing proofs, now this is no longer true. No modern theologian who is alert to the debate about God's existence maintains that the cosmological, teleological, ontological, and moral arguments for God do more than indicate and support His existence. Now it is generally recognized by theologians and philosophers alike that belief, or at least the disposition to believe, is brought to the arguments.

The present value of the "arguments" is in one or more of the following: (1) to raise the question of God's existence, (2) to show that the idea of God is rationally defensible, (3) to show that the world itself is best understood theistically, or (4) to act as confirmatory considerations that present themselves to us when we bring belief in God to our considerations of the world and human life. F. R. Tennant, for example, believed that "the multitude of inter-woven adaptations by which the world is constituted a theater of life, intelligence, and morality cannot reasonably be regarded as an outcome of mechanism, or of blind formative power, or of ought but by purposive intelligence." But Tennant knew that the best his "wider teleology" can deliver is a high degree of probability for God's existence.[77]

The psalmist believed that if only people would open their eyes to nature's message, they too would be compelled to say, "The heavens declare the glory of God; the skies proclaim the work of his hands. Day after day they pour forth speech; night after night they display knowledge" (Ps. 19:1-2 NIV). The apostle Paul echoed the belief that the world itself gives clear indication of the God who alone could account for its being: "Since the creation of the world God's invisible qualities—his eternal power and divine nature—have been clearly seen, being understood from what has been made, so that men are without excuse" (Rom. 1:20 NIV).

Regardless of what the world should be able to tell us about its Creator the intellectual climate no longer exists in which the arguments for demonstrating the world's radical dependence on God can be appealed to with conclusive authority.

Christians should not expect too much from the arguments for God's existence. H. Orton Wiley says that

> there is a limit to their power of demonstration, and indeed they are more properly regarded in this light, as probable rather than demonstrative arguments. . . . In either case they require the enforcement of the Holy Spirit's influence as divine credentials and must in every case derive their strength from the further revelation of God as to His own essence and perfections.[78]

At best, therefore, the arguments stand in the service of faith. Knowledge of God's reality and His work as Creator is fundamentally grounded in His work as Redeemer; such knowledge is primarily soteriological. However, the prevenient grace of God that reaches all people, whose purpose is to draw us to the Father in repentance and renewal, should be sufficient to impress on the open mind the reality of God. But self-imposed blindness, as Paul notes in Romans 1:20-23, has stifled this witness; it is a blindness promoted in large part by a thoroughly naturalistic view of the world that holds the allegiance of many. Seldom does the naturalist admit that his denial of God is supported by arguments that are no more rationally demonstrable than are the traditional theistic arguments for God's existence. But in our time doubt seems to pass as proof, whereas belief is given no such privilege.

God's sovereignty as Creator reaches its highest expression in the creation of man (understood as male and female). Man, the crown of God's creation, plays a special role in God's world. He was created in the "image of God." If man's primary identification is theological, then his fundamental orientation should not be to the created order but to God. Therefore, in Christian theology, *man* is first of all a theological category or a religious concept, and not a psychological, physical, or sociological one. Christian faith boldly declares that these latter dimensions lose their way apart from the first order of orientation.

The Christian doctrine of creation uses the phrase *creatio ex nihilo* (creation out of nothing). This doctrine guards against all forms of metaphysical dualism, and against any form of creaturely independence from God. The God whom we are to worship is the One on whom man and the world depend absolutely. Apart from His gift of being there is nothing, absolutely nothing.[79]

2. God preserving (providence). Just as the "new creation" (the content of salvation) is not limited to the past but continues as the active work of God, just so creation is a continuing work. The Bible gives abundant testimony to the preserving activity of God in His world. It speaks of His preservation of the physical world. But much more often testimony is given to God's unfailing "watchcare" over His people. "The eyes of the Lord range throughout the earth to strengthen those whose hearts are fully committed to Him" (2 Chron. 16:9 NIV). After the exiles had returned to Jerusalem from the land where they were held captive, they sang the following song:

> Blessed be your glorious name, and may it be exalted above all blessing and praise. You alone are the LORD. You made the heavens; even the highest heavens, and all their starry hosts, the earth and all that is on it, the seas and all that is in them. You give life to everything, and the multitudes of heaven worship you" (Neh. 9:6 NIV).

"The LORD Almighty is with us; the God of Jacob is our fortress" (Ps. 46:7 NIV). So man and the world do not receive life as a *substance* from God and then become free from His continued provision of life as did Pinocchio in his famous independence from old Geppetto.

Only because of God's unceasing gift of being to the world is the world able to escape the clutches of chaos and nothingness. God is its permanent creative Being.[80] John Wesley believed that God is never absent from His creation. He sustains its being and its processes. What God has called into existence through the power of His sovereign will "must likewise be supported and preserved through the power of his governing providence."[81] H. Orton Wiley specifically identifies Christ, the *logos,* as the one through whom "nature receives its substantiality and order" and through whom man receives his "personal consciousness."[82]

The doctrine of God's preserving presence in the world was clearly taught by Augustine and the Reformers and was magnificently expressed by Jonathan Edwards (1703-1758) as the doctrine of God's continuing creativity. Edwards taught that the existence of created substance, in each successive moment, must be the effect of the immediate agency, will and power of God. . . . God's *preserving* created things in being is perfectly equivalent to a *continued creation,* or to him creating those things out of nothing at each moment of their existence. If the continued existence of created things be wholly dependent on God's preservation, then those things would drop into nothing, upon the ceasing of the present moment, without a new exertion of the divine power to cause them to exist in the following moment.[83]

The continued creativity of God is, Jonathan Edwards says, as it was in the beginning, through Christ.

3. God directing In opposition to a secularistic world view that denies purposiveness to the world, and in opposition to any philosophy that regards human existence as meaningless, Christian theology believes that the world and human life do have a *telos* or purpose. The world is the subject of God's guidance. He infuses it with purpose and works to satisfy His aim for it.

The New Testament expresses the belief that the whole creation participates in God's redemptive scheme. The physical world, as well as those who through the Spirit have tasted the firstfruits of redemption, anticipates the consummation of God's purposes (Rom. 8:19-23).

B. The Work of God in Revelation and Redemption

Because the doctrines of revelation and redemption will be systematically treated in chapters 7, 11, and 12, only a preliminary statement appears here. However, such a statement is needed to complete the systematic discussion of the Christian doctrine of God.

The God about whom the Bible speaks and whom Christians worship has chosen to reveal Himself, to make Himself known. Revelation (*apokalypsis*) means the unveiling of the veiled. In the Christian doctrine of revelation it means God's own self-disclosure (Luke 2:32; Gal. 1:12).

In the Old and New Testaments "divine revelation" means God's entire activity by which He discloses Himself as Creator and Redeemer. It means the whole story of the "acts of God," which disclose His nature and will. In the Bible, says Father Sergius Bulgakoff (1871-1944), revelation is

> the personal act of a personal deity . . . which takes place "face to face". . . . It is a dialogue, a colloquy between God and His creation, angels and men. . . . Revelation represents a divine-human communion, an act of God within man, and the consequent acceptance of God by man. Revelation implies an encounter and a conversation, God's covenant with man. Man is a personal being, and revelation proceeds from the *Person* of God to the *person* of man.[84]

"Revelation," says Emil Brunner, "is something that *happens,* the living history of God in His dealings with the human race; the history of revelation is the history of salvation, and the history of salvation is the history of revelation."[85]

For Wesleyan theology the doctrine of revelation is christocentric; the doctrine of God proceeds from and is governed by our knowledge of Him who "is the radiance of God's glory and the exact representation of his being" (Heb. 1:3 NIV). It is thoroughly guided by the Johannine affirmation that "the only Son, who is at the Father's side has made [the Father] known" (John 1:18 NIV). All other aspects of the doctrine of revelation must be informed by christology. Wiley warns that unless this is the case, it is always difficult to lift our understanding of God "to a standard which is fully and consistently Christian."[86] In Scripture "the living and abiding word of God" is expressly identified as "the word which was preached to you" (1 Peter 1:23, 25). We know that the New Testament identifies our Lord as the Good News, the One who inaugurates the new reality.

In Wesleyan theology the whole of God's self-disclosure has as its purpose not only to declare God's name but to establish and commune with man the creature. In part, the *telos* or design of revelation is redemption, and for Wesleyan theology its scope is universal. Every person is a subject of God's redemptive intent.

C. The Work of God in Hope

The last work of God to be considered is the creation of hope. Recently we have witnessed a renewed theological interest in the meaning and importance of Christian hope. In the Old Testament, but with much greater richness and intensity in the New, hope is a central part of God's work. Although hope is discussed last, the Christian understanding of hope must in no sense be viewed as a distant expectation tacked onto the end of Christian theology. Rather, it is central to the meaning of our faith. Christian theology lives from and advances to Christian hope.

Hope is an essential fruit of knowing who God is and of participating in His redemption. It is the profoundly comprehensive realization that the many threats to our precarious hold on finitude and meaning, our awesome awareness of contingency and estrangement from God, are not the final words about human existence. Christian hope infuses life with meaning even in the presence of external occurrences that seem to count against it. Christian hope is both the present realization of redemption and a joyous anticipation of its fulfillment. Christianity, says Emil Brunner, taught man how to hope.

Never has humankind been able to achieve so much in the way of material possessions, technological inventiveness, medical knowledge, and the understanding of nature's processes. Paradoxically, perhaps never have we been so profoundly aware of how utterly contingent and unfulfilling these things really are for human existence. They can't deliver what the eighteenth and nineteenth centuries led us to expect from them.

In this century we watched as a civilization rich in art, philosophy, music, religion, and technological brilliance, yet lacking in needed moral strength, stood paralyzed before a clique of power-crazed Nazis bent on plunging the whole world into war and on exterminating European Jewry. Today two military powers, unprecedented in war-making abilities, stand poised with nuclear weapons at their command, neither quite certain of the other's intentions.

At a time when the achievements of education and technological research should have delivered their great dividends of human happiness and social stability, we are beset with a moral and spiritual vacuum that threatens to collapse the fabric of Western society. *Hope* is a word often on our lips, but thoroughly lacking in spendable currency.

The malaise of the human spirit that has characterized most of this century followed on the heels of a period of almost unbounded optimism about the "perfectibility of man." In the eighteenth century, Rousseau (1712-1778), French philosopher and a principal representative of the Age of Reason, spoke of the perfectibility of man. He was sure that the power of reason, the knowledge gained thereby, and improved ways to apply it would result in unambiguous good results. Added to this in the nineteenth century was Charles Darwin's theory of evolution, which profoundly influenced philosophy, religion, political theory, and science to believe that Rousseau's expectations were realistic. For many thinkers, such as Goethe, Schiller, Ranke, and Marx, this was an optimism that could support itself without recourse to God.

But two world wars, totalitarian revolutions, and the development of awesome means for using reason in the service of destruction profoundly shook this optimism. Some thinkers say that in light of the sobering and chastening impact these events have had on our optimism we should now speak of ours as the "postmodern era."[87]

Awareness of mankind's meager hold on life and hope is by no means of recent origin. The pre-Socratic philosophers, such as Thales of Miletus, Anaximander, Anaximenes, and the Pythagoreans, looked for the *really real,* for that which persists in the midst of decay and change. Those early Greeks, says Frederick Copleston, were not simply happy and careless children of the sun. "They were very conscious of the dark side of our existence on this planet, for against the background of sun and joy they saw the uncertainty and insecurity of man's life, the certainty of death, the darkness of the future."[88]

They too were haunted by the paradox of human existence: a profound awareness of our finitude and an equally persistent knowledge that there is another dimension in us that simply cannot be reduced to temporal and passing categories.

Outside the Bible there is no more profound statement of the belief that man is more than simply a child of nature than Plato's *Phaedo.* Facing the sentence of death handed down by the Athenians, Socrates tells his friends that after his death he expects to find himself among good men.

> I shall find there divine masters who are supremely good. That is why I am not so much distressed as I might be, and why I have a firm hope that there is something in store for those who have died, and, as we have been told for many years, something much better for the good than for the wicked.[89]

The later Stoics, such as Seneca (d. A.D. 65), Epictetus (A.D. 50-138) and Marcus Aurelius (A.D. 121-180), believed that ultimately the structure of reality is meaningful, i.e., that it has a *logos* structure, and that the anxiety of both life and death can be overcome by this meaning.[90]

Always there have been those who argued that hopes like those expressed by Socrates are simply futile but necessary burdens not required of the lower forms of animal existence. Man's burden is all the greater, they say, because he is aware of his finitude and because it is possible for him to imagine himself or some form of being as free from death's imminent foreclosure on life. But finally, according to this appraisal, man's aspirations toward the eternal mock and elude him.

In much of the existentialist literature there is a paradoxical awareness not only of man's magnificent capacity for love and beauty, for creating and projecting meaning into life, but also of the inescapable appointment with death that will trivialize and mock him. Human life is finally an encounter with nothingness.[91]

The late Jean Paul Sartre was profoundly impressed by *forlornness:* "Man is absolutely alone in the world; there is no God and no meaning other than what man can create. Man must write, he is writing, his own destiny." Human existence is finally absurd.[92] It is very distressing, Sartre says, that God does not exist, "because all possibility of finding values in a heaven of ideas disappears along with Him; there can no longer be an *a priori* good, since there is no infinite and perfect consciousness to think it."[93] As a result, man is forlorn. Neither within nor without does he find anything to which he can cling. We are now condemned to be free; this is the source and limit of our greatness and hope.

Man feeds on the "wine of the absurd" and the "bread of indifference," says Albert Camus. In a world absolutely lacking in final meaning, "man has forgotten how to hope. This hell of the present is his kingdom at last."[94] What should we do? According to Camus, neither hope nor suicide, but *revolt,* is the answer; this is our proper mode of life. We must live in revolt against the absurd. In this way we can expect to carve out some temporary meaning. We must not make the mistake of hoping that the world finally has some comprehensive and lasting meaning. The world is absurd, and the absurd must be kept alive. Camus, like Sartre, admits to an appetite for the absolute and for unity, but he is equally certain that these do not exist. "Hope . . . means nothing within the limits of my condition."[95]

But not all who believe that we live in a world without God are as limited in their expectations as are Sartre and Camus. Although they perceive no comprehensive meaning for the world, many people believe that man now has placed before him broad and unprecedented opportunities for achievement and happiness. The "absence of God," they say, should not be met by forlornness as Sartre and Camus believed, but with a sense of great freedom and confidence that the problems of existence and the anxieties of fate can be conquered.

People such as Sydney Hook, B. F. Skinner, Paul Kurtz, Kai Neilson, and Brand Blanshard are optimistic about the measure of meaning that can be achieved in a world where belief in the reality of God is dead. These secular humanists argue that in a world where six million defenseless people could die in gas chambers and slave camps, it is now senseless to speak of God—His governance of history, His love and care for us. We have seen absolutely no reason, they insist, to believe that God gives meaning to life. Such "vacuous language," they say, must be put behind us, and we must all now lend our strength to achieving a truly humane pattern of life for everyone. "Humanist Manifesto II" says in part, "We can discover no divine purpose or providence for the human species. While there is much that we do not know, humans are responsible for what we are or will become. No deity will save us; we must save ourselves."[96]

This position is reiterated in the sequel to Humanist Manifesto II, "The Secular Humanist Declaration, 1981," initially signed by fifty-eight leading secular humanists. The declaration says in part,

> We consider the universe to be a dynamic scene of natural forces that are most effectively understood by scientific inquiry.... We find that traditional views of the existence of God either are meaningless, have not yet been demonstrated to be true, or are tyrannically exploitative. Secular humanists ... believe that men and women are free and are responsible for their own destinies and that they cannot look toward some transcendent Being for salvation.[97]

The Bible is not a stranger to the question of whether human life has a meaning or of whether there is any legitimate reason for human hope. It candidly chronicles man's questions about the meaning of life, about whether despair is finally his last habitat. In some instances even those who have soared to great heights of faith are plunged into the depths of despair. So, while the Bible is a faithful record of God's self-disclosure and love, it does not diminish or cover up the ambiguities of human existence. It is a drama of concern about the purpose and value of life.

But neither is the Bible ambiguous in its answer. The world apart from God is finally meaningless—it is hopeless. But the stalwart affirmation in the Old and New Testaments is that God does not leave the world alone. He graciously gives Himself to it and thereby gives it meaning and hope. "Blessed is the man who trusts in the LORD," says Jeremiah, and "whose confidence is in him" (Jer. 17:7 NIV; cf. Prov. 16:20).

The exultant tone of hope in the New Testament is made possible by the fact that in Jesus, who is the Christ, a reason for hope—rather, He who is hope—has appeared. In Him the hopelessness of guilt and death are broken. Because of Him, there is no oppression or futility that can stand before us as an ultimate threat. Those who knew the crushing weight of despair, or the absurd, heard Jesus gladly. And what they heard was good news, a reason for hope.

To proclaim and embody God's deed of hope that has appeared in Christ is alone the charter for the church's existence. Its life and message must be "good news" to the world. "Blessed be the Lord God of Israel, for He has visited us and accomplished redemption for His people. And has raised up a horn of salvation for us" (Luke 1:68-69).

Contrary to the conclusions reached by people like Sartre and Camus, despair does not appear as the last actor on the stage, but the One who says, "Do not be afraid. I ... am the living One; I was dead, and behold I am alive for evermore, and I have the keys of death and Hades" (Rev. 1:17–18). He has *gained* the right to speak, to say, "I am the Alpha and the Omega, the first and the last, the beginning and the end" (Rev. 22:13). He is the bread of life, the light of the world, the door, the good shepherd, the resurrection, the way, the truth, and the life (John 6:35; 8:12; 10:7, 11; 11:25; 14:6).

The apostle Paul knew what the risks are if the words of Jesus are not true. If Christ has not been raised from the dead by the power of the God who is life and who gives hope, then we who have believed "are of all men most to be pitied" (1 Cor. 15:19). But Christ's words are not in error. The God of all hope did raise Jesus from the dead and now, because of this, "neither death, . . . the present nor the future, nor any powers, neither height nor depth, nor anything else in all creation, will be able to separate us from the love of God that is in Christ Jesus our Lord" (Rom. 8:38–39 NIV).

He it is who shines into the world's hopelessness, whatever its guise may be, and overcomes it, for He is life and light (John 1:4–5). The good news of the Christian gospel is that there is reason for hope! Jesus' words to the world are simple and direct. "If any man is thirsty, let him come to me and drink" (John 7:37). Those who come to Him sing this doxology, "Praise be to the God and Father of our Lord Jesus Christ! In his great mercy he has given us new birth into a living hope through the resurrection of Jesus Christ from the dead" (1 Peter 1:3 NIV).

Therefore the work of God as giving hope is not a deferred promise that we impatiently anticipate as might children who have been promised a gift. Hope is the sum of Christian faith and life. It is God's gift of Himself to us through the Spirit here and now. The kingdom has come in Christ; He is the *eschaton*. The meaning of life and the center of history have appeared in Him. The last and guiding word about the being of the world and the purpose of human existence has been spoken in His person.

Christian hope is also anticipatory. We do await the consummation of His kingdom, but not as something that will be significantly different from the hope we now have through God's presence. Nevertheless, the church does live between the kingdom that has already come and the kingdom that is to come in its fullness. We live between the already and the not yet.

But anticipation does not mean suspended animation. The God of hope is the God of the future and He calls His church into His future.

NOTES

[1] John Cobb, Jr., *God and the World* (Philadelphia: Westminster, 1965). See also Cobb's *Christian Natural Theology: Based on the Thought of Alfred North Whitehead* (London: Lutterworth, 1966).

[2] John Wesley, "A Letter to a Roman Catholic," in *The Works of John Wesley,* 14 vols. (1872; reprint ed., Kansas City: Nazarene, n. d.), 10:81.

[3] Letter to James Hervey, March 20, 1739, in *John Wesley,* ed. Albert C. Outler (New York: Oxford University Press, 1964), pp. 70–73.

[4] Emil Brunner, *Revelation and Reason: The Christian Doctrine of Faith and Knowledge,* trans. Olive Wyon (Philadelphia: Westminster, 1946), p. 118.

[5] Gerhard Ebeling, *Luther: An Introduction to His Thought,* trans. A. Wilson (Philadelphia: Fortress, 1970), p. 96.

[6] Outler, *John Wesley,* p. 28.

[7] Brunner, *Revelation and Reason,* p. 119.

[8] Karl Barth, *Dogmatics in Outline* (New York: Harper and Row, 1959), p. 37.

[9] John Hick, ed., *The Existence of God, Problems of Philosophy Series* (New York: Macmillan, 1969), pp. 256–57.

[10] Hans Urs von Balthasar, *The Theology of Karl Barth,* trans. John Drury (Garden City, N.Y.: Doubleday, Anchor, 1972), pp. 70–138.

[11] Huston Smith, *Forgotten Truth: The Primordial Tradition* (New York: Harper and Row, 1976).

[12] Walter Kaufmann, *Critique of Religion and Philosophy* (Princeton: Princeton University Press, 1958), pp. 34-35. See also Antony Flew and Alasdair MacIntyre, ed., *New Essays in Philosophical Theology*, paperback ed. (New York: Macmillan, 1964); Richard Rorty, *The Linguistic Turn: Recent Essays in Philosophical Method* (Chicago: University of Chicago Press, 1975); J. H. Randall, Jr., *The Role of Knowledge in Western Religion* (Boston: Beacon, 1956); R. B. Braithwaite, *An Empiricist's View of the Nature of Religious Belief* (Cambridge: University Press, 1955); John Hick, ed., *Classical and Contemporary Readings in the Philosophy of Religion* (Englewood Cliffs, New Jersey: Prentice-Hall, 1970); and Paul Van Buren, *The Secular Meaning of the Gospel* (New York: Macmillan, 1963).

[13] Barth, *Dogmatics in Outline*, p. 36.

[14] H. H. Orton Wiley, *Christian Theology*, ninth printing (Kansas City, Mo.: Beacon Hill, 1960), 1:218.

[15] Ibid., p. 252.

[16] The appearance of the name *Yahweh* in the Old Testament is preceded by the name *Elohim;* e.g., Genesis 1:1.

[17] Bernhard W. Anderson, *Understanding the Old Testament*, 3rd ed. (Englewood Cliffs, N.J.: Prentice-Hall, 1975), p. 55.

[18] Ibid., p. 9.

[19] See James B. Pritchard, ed., *Ancient Near Eastern Texts Relating to the Old Testament* (Princeton: Princeton University Press, 1969); *Enuma Elish*, pp. 60-72; *The Gilgamesh Epic*, pp. 73-99.

[20] G.E.R. Lloyd, *Aristotle: The Growth and Structure of His Thought* (Cambridge: Cambridge University Press, 1968), pp. 133-47.

[21] See C. R. Cragg, *The Church and the Age of Reason: 1648-1789* (Baltimore: Penguin, 1970).

[22] Gustaf Aulen, *The Faith of the Christian Church*, trans. Eric H. Wahlstrom, 1st paperback ed. (Philadelphia: Fortress, 1973), p. 136.

[23] Ludwig Feuerbach, *The Essence of Christianity*, trans. George Eliot, with an introductory essay by Karl Barth and a foreword by H. Richard Niebuhr (New York: Harper and Row, 1957).

[24] Ibid., preface.

[25] Balthasar, *Theology of Karl Barth;* see also Paul Tillich's discussion of religious symbols in *The Dynamics of Faith* (New York: Harper and Row, 1957).

[26] Emil Brunner, *Dogmatics: The Christian Doctrine of God*, trans. Olive Wyon (Philadelphia: Westminster, 1950), p. 49.

[27] P. T. Forsyth, *God the Holy Father*, (London: Independent, 1897).

[28] Rudolph Otto, *The Idea of the Holy: An Inquiry Into the Non-Rational Factor in the Idea of the Divine and Its Relation to the Rational*, trans. John W. Harvey, (London: Oxford University Press, 1970).

[29] Albert C. Knudson, *The Religious Teaching of the Old Testament*, (New York: Abingdon, 1918); *The Doctrine of God* (Nashville: Abingdon-Cokesbury, 1930), pp. 335ff.

[30] Norman H. Snaith, *The Distinctive Ideas of the Old Testament* (London: Epworth, 1944).

[31] Aulen, *Faith of the Christian Church*, p. 103.

[32] Snaith, *Distinctive Ideas*, p. 21.

[33] Otto, *Idea of the Holy*, p. 28.

[34] Snaith, *Distinctive Ideas*, p. 43.

[35] Ibid., p. 53.

[36] John Wesley, "The Original Nature, Property, and Use of the Law," in *Works*, 5:438.

[37] William Ragsdale Cannon, *The Theology of John Wesley* (Nashville: Abingdon-Cokesbury, 1946), p. 175.

[38] Aulen, *Faith of the Christian Church*, p. 104.

[39] Albrecht Ritschl was heavily influenced by Immanuel Kant's *Critique of Practical Reason*, trans., with introduction, by Lewis White Beck (New York: Bobbs Merrill, 1956).

[40] Anderson, *Understanding the Old Testament*, p. 305.

[41] Aulen, *Faith of the Christian Church*, p. 105.

[42] This view of God's relationship to the world is thoroughly characteristic of Wesley's understanding of God's presence in His creation. "As the true God, He is also the Supporter of all the things that He hath made. He beareth, upholdeth, sustaineth, all created things by the word of His power, by the same powerful word which brought them out of nothing. As this was absolutely necessary for the beginning of their existence, it is equally so for the continuance of it; were His almighty influence withdrawn, they could not subsist a moment longer" (*Works*, 6:426).

[43] John Wesley, "A Plain Account of Genuine Christianity," in Outler, *John Wesley*, p. 184.

[44] Ibid., pp. 184-87.

[45] The most important book in this century to explore the distinctive meaning of *agape* for the Christian understanding of God is by the Swedish Lundensian theologian, Anders Nygren, *Eros and Agape*, trans. by Philip S. Watson (Philadelphia: Westminster, 1953).

[46] Aulen, *Faith of the Christian Church*, p. 113.

[47] Anderson, *Understanding the Old Testament*, p. 287.

[48] Abraham J. Heschel, *God in Search of Man: A Philosophy of Judaism* (New York: Harper and Row, 1966).

49 Nels Ferre, *The Christian Understanding of God* (New York: Harper and Row, 1951), p. 116.

50 John Wesley, "The Unity of the Divine Being," in *Works,* 7:265.

51 John Wesley, "Predestination Calmly Considered," in *Works,* 10:221.

52 Ibid.

53 Outler, *John Wesley,* p. 426.

54 Ibid., p. 253.

55 Hartshorne, *A Natural Theology for Our Time,* pp. 119-20.

56 For an excellent discussion of Neoplatonism and its divergence from Christian theology see Etienne Gilson, *Being and Some Philosophers* (Toronto: Pontifical Institute of Mediaeval Studies, 1952), pp. 1-40.

57 Aulen, *Faith and the Christian Church,* p. 127.

58 Ibid., p. 128.

59 Ibid., p. 129.

60 Paul A. Mickey, *Essentials of Wesleyan Theology* (Grand Rapids: Zondervan, 1980), pp. 36-37.

61 John Wesley, *Explanatory Notes on the New Testament,* comments on 1 John 5:8.

62 John Wesley, "A Letter to a Roman Catholic," in *Works,* 10:81.

63 "The Creed of Nicea," *Documents of the Christian Church,* ed. Henry Bettenson (London: Oxford University Press, 1971).

64 John Wesley, sermon "On the Trinity," in *Works,* 6:199-206.

65 Lycurgus M. Starkey, Jr., *The Work of the Holy Spirit: A Study in Wesleyan Theology* (Nashville: Abingdon, 1962), pp. 26-27.

66 Wesley, "On the Trinity," 6:201.

67 Colin W. Williams, *John Wesley's Theology Today* (Nashville: Abingdon, 1960), p. 93.

68 Cannon, *Theology of John Wesley,* p. 160.

69 Wesley, "On the Trinity," 6:204.

70 Williams, *John Wesley's Theology Today,* p. 95.

71 Starkey, *The Work of the Holy Spirit,* p. 24.

72 Ibid., p. 23.

73 Wesley, "On the Trinity," 6:205.

74 Ibid., p. 206.

75 Cannon, *Theology of John Wesley,* pp. 163-64.

76 Ibid., p. 162.

77 F. R. Tennant, *Philosophical Theology,* 2 vols. (Cambridge: Cambridge University Press, 1928-30), 2:121.

78 Wiley, *Christian Theology,* 1:232.

79 Paul Tillich, *Systematic Theology,* 3 vols. (Chicago: University of Chicago Press, 1951), 1:253-54.

80 Ibid., 1:262-63.

81 Cannon, *Theology of John Wesley,* pp. 169, 171.

82 Wiley, *Christian Theology,* 1:251.

83 Sydney E. Ahlstrom, ed., *Theology in America: The Major Voices from Puritanism to Neo-Orthodoxy,* The American Heritage series (New York: Bobbs Merrill, 1967), p. 165.

84 John Baillie and Hugh Martin, ed., *Revelation* (London: Faber and Faber, 1937), pp. 126-27.

85 Brunner, *Revelation and Reason,* p. 8.

86 Wiley, *Christian Theology,* 1:222.

87 See Carl E. Braaten, *The Future of God: The Revolutionary Dynamics of Hope* (New York: Harper and Row, 1969); Fredrick Herzog, ed., *The Future of Hope: Theology as Eschatology* (New York: Herder and Herder, 1970); Douglas M. Meeks, *Origins of the Theology of Hope* (Philadelphia: Fortress, 1974).

88 Frederick Copleston, *A History of Philosophy: Greece and Rome,* vol. 1, part 1 (Garden City, N.Y.: Image, 1962), 1:33.

89 Edith Hamilton and Huntington Cairns, eds., "The Phaedo," in *Plato: The Collected Dialogues* (Princeton: Princeton University Press, 1969).

90 Paul Tillich, *The Courage to Be* (New Haven: Yale University Press, 1952); see also Copleston, *History of Philosophy,* vol. 1, part 1.

91 See William Barrett, *Irrational Man: A Study in Existential Philosophy* (New York: Doubleday, 1962).

92 See Jean-Paul Sartre, *Being and Nothingness: An Essay on Phenomenological Ontology,* trans., with introduction, by Hazel E. Barnes (New York: Philosophical Library, 1956).

93 Jean-Paul Sartre, *Existentialism and Human Emotions* (New York: Philosophical Library, 1957).

94 Albert Camus, *The Myth of Sisyphus and Other Essays,* trans. Justin O'Brien (New York: Random, 1955), p. 33.

95 Ibid., p. 38.

96 Paul Kurtz, "Humanist Manifesto II," first appeared in *The Humanist* (Sept./Oct. 1973). It is reprinted in Roger Eastman, ed., *The Ways of Religion* (San Francisco: Carfield, 1975), pp. 534-41.

97 Full text located in *Free Inquiry* 1 (Winter 1980-81): 3-6.

DISCUSSION QUESTIONS

1. What impact should the "secular evaluation of the world" and its current "reevaluation" have on the way Wesleyan theology is done today?
2. Of what importance for Wesleyan and contemporary theology is the creative tension between "Wesleyan distinctives" and "Wesleyan catholicity" as they relate to the doctrine of God? (See Colin W. Williams, *John Wesley's Theology Today* [Nashville: Abingdon, 1960].)
3. Discuss the meaning of the assertion that in Wesleyan theology "religious epistemology and soteriology intersect." Why is this so critically important for what we believe about "knowledge of God"? Could this assertion be understood in a manner that results in counterproductive religious subjectivism?
4. Why is it so important to distinguish the "wholly otherness" of God from what might be psychological, sociological, or cultural projections of who He "is"?
5. How does the Christian doctrine of God differ essentially from the concepts of God that come from Plato, Aristotle, and the major Eastern religions?
6. What are some of the dangers to Christian life and thought posed by pantheism and deism?
7. Why is it so critical that the language we use to speak of God be transformed and guided by what we know of God's self-disclosure in Jesus, who is the Christ?
8. Why is it important that theologians and the church establish a proper understanding of God's holiness? What essential place does a correct view of God's holiness have in defining Judeo/Christian monotheism?
9. What critical importance for our doctrines of creation, salvation, and Christian ethics can we expect the Wesleyan understanding of God as holiness and love to have?
10. What dangers occur when our beliefs about God's attributes are not consistently guided by His being as holiness and love?
11. While there is absolutely no tentativeness in Wesley's belief that the one God is also triune—Father, Son, and Holy Spirit, there is a certain tentativeness in his insistence that such words as "Trinity" and "persons" be used. Why is this true? Should this still be true of those who are significantly influenced by Wesley's theology? What are the strengths (or weaknesses) of the Wesleyan approach to the doctrine of the Trinity?
12. A correct understanding of God's positive appraisal of His creation is of major importance for our doctrines of salvation and ecclesiology and for Christian ethics. Discuss the implications of its importance for these parts of Christian faith.
13. Discuss the relationship between God's work as Redeemer and our faith in Him as Creator.

RECOMMENDATIONS FOR FURTHER READING

Baker, Frank. *John Wesley and the Church of England.* Nashville: Abingdon, 1970.
Barth, Karl. *Evangelical Theology: An Introduction.* New York: Holt, Rinehart and Winston, 1963.
Henry, Carl F. H., ed. *Basic Christian Doctrines.* Grand Rapids: Baker, 1962.
Herzog, Fredrick. *Understanding God.* New York: Scribner, 1966.
Kelly, J. N. D. *Early Christian Doctrines.* New York: Harper and Row, 1960. Pp. 109-37; 252-79; 459-89.
Lawson, John. *Comprehensive Handbook of Christian Doctrine.* Englewood Cliffs, N.J.: Prentice-Hall, 1967.
MacQuarrie, John. *Principles of Christian Theology.* New York: Scribner, 1966. Chaps. 5, 9, 11.
Outler, Albert C. "John Wesley: Folk Theologian," *Theology Today* 34 (July 1977): 150-60.
Prestige, G. L. *God in Patristic Thought.* London: SPCK, 1969.
Schmidt, Martin. *John Wesley: A Theological Biography,* 2 vols. Nashville: Abingdon, 1973.
Thielicke, Helmut. *The Evangelical Faith.* Grand Rapids: Eerdmans, 1974. Vol. 1.
Wood, Laurence W. "Wesley's Epistemology," *The Wesleyan Theological Journal* 10 (September 1975): 48-59.

BIBLIOGRAPHY

Ahlstrom, Sydney F., ed. *Theology in America: The Major Voices from Puritanism to Neo-Orthodoxy.* The American Heritage Series. New York: Bobbs-Merrill, 1967.

Anderson, Bernhard W. *Understanding the Old Testament.* 3rd ed. Englewood Cliffs, N.J.: Prentice-Hall, 1975.

Aulen, Gustaf. *The Faith of the Christian Church.* Translated by Eric H. Wahlstrom. First paperback ed. Philadelphia: Fortress, 1973.

Baillie, John and Hugh Martin, eds. *Revelation.* London: Faber and Faber, 1937.

Balthasar, Hans Urs von. *The Theology of Karl Barth.* Translated by John Drury. Garden City, N.Y.: Doubleday, 1972.

Barrett, William. *Irrational Man: A Study in Existential Philosophy.* New York: Doubleday, 1962.

Barth, Karl. *Dogmatics in Outline.* New York: Harper and Row, 1959.

Berger, Peter. *A Rumor of Angels.* Garden City, N.Y.: Anchor Books, 1970.

Bettenson, Henry, ed. *Documents of the Christian Church.* London: Oxford University Press, 1971.

Bonhoeffer, Dietrich. *Ethics.* Edited by Eberhard Bethge. New York: Macmillan, 1978.

Braaten, Carl E. *The Future of God: The Revolutionary Dynamics of Hope.* New York: Harper and Row, 1969.

Braithwaite, R. B. *An Empiricist's View of the Nature of Religious Belief.* Cambridge: Cambridge University Press, 1955.

Brunner, Emil. *Dogmatics: The Christian Doctrine of God.* Translated by Olive Wyon. Philadelphia: Westminster, 1950.

———. *Faith, Hope and Love.* Philadelphia: Westminster, 1956.

———. *Revelation and Reason: The Christian Doctrine of Faith and Knowledge.* Translated by Olive Wyon. Philadelphia: Westminster, 1946.

Camus, Albert. *The Myth of Sisyphus and Other Essays.* Translated by Justin O'Brien. New York: Vintage, 1955.

Cannon, William R. *The Theology of John Wesley.* Nashville: Abingdon-Cokesbury, 1946.

Cobb, John, Jr. *A Christian Natural Theology: Based on the Thought of Alfred North Whitehead.* London: Lutterworth, 1966.

———. *God and the World.* Philadelphia: Westminster, 1965.

Copleston, Frederick. *A History of Philosophy: Greece and Rome,* vol. 1, part 1. Garden City, N.Y.: Image, 1962.

Cousins, Ewert H., ed. *Process Theology.* Toronto: Newman, 1971.

Cox, Harvey. *The Secular City.* New York: Macmillan, 1965.

Cragg, C. R. *The Church and the Age of Reason: 1648–1789.* Baltimore: Penguin, 1970.

Ebeling, Gerhard. *Luther: An Introduction to His Thought.* Translated by R. A. Wilson. Philadelphia: Fortress, 1970.

Eliade, Mircea. *The Sacred and the Profane: The Nature of Religion.* Translated by Willard R. Task. New York: Harcourt, Brace and World, 1959.

Ellul, Jacques. *The New Demons.* N.Y.: Seabury, 1975.

Ferre, Nels. *The Christian Understanding of God.* New York: Harper and Row, 1951.

Feuerbach, Ludwig. *The Essence of Christianity.* Translated by George Eliot, with an introductory essay by Karl Barth and a foreword by A. Richard Niebuhr. New York: Harper and Row, 1957.

Flew, Antony, and MacIntyre, Alasdair, eds. *New Essays in Philosophical Theology.* New York: Macmillan, 1964.

Forsyth, P. T. *God the Holy Father.* London: Independent, 1847.

Gilkey, Langdon. *Naming the Whirlwind: The Renewal of God Language.* New York: Bobbs Merrill, 1969.

———. "Theology for a Time of Troubles," *The Christian Century* 98 (April 29, 1981): 474–79.

Gilson, Etienne. *Being and Some Philosophers.* Toronto: Pontifical Institute of Mediaeval Studies, 1952.

A CONTEMPORARY WESLEYAN THEOLOGY

Greeley, Andrew M. *Unsecular Man: The Persistence of Religion*. New York: Schocken, 1974.

Hamilton, Edith, and Huntington, Cairns, eds. *Plato: The Collected Dialogues*. Princeton: Princeton University Press, 1969.

Hartshorne, Charles. *A Natural Theology for Our Time*. LaSalle, Ill.: Open Court, 1973.

Herzog, Fredrick, ed. *The Future of Hope: Theology as Eschatology*. New York: Herder and Herder, 1970.

Heschel, Abraham Joshua. *God in Search of Man: A Philosophy of Judaism*. New York: Harper and Row, 1966.

Hick, John. *The Existence of God*. New York: Macmillan, 1969.

Huxley, Julian. *Religion Without Revelation*. New York: New American Library, 1957.

Kant, Immanuel. *The Critique of Practical Reason*. Translated, with an introduction, by Lewis White Beck. New York: Bobbs-Merrill, 1956.

Kaufmann, Walter. *Critique of Religion and Philosophy*. Princeton: Princeton University Press, 1958.

Knudson, Albert C. *The Religious Teaching of the Old Testament*. New York: Abingdon, 1918.

――――. *The Doctrine of God*. Nashville: Abingdon-Cokesbury, 1930.

Küng, Hans. *Does God Exist?: An Answer for Today*. Translated by Edward Quinn. Garden City, N.Y.: Doubleday, 1980.

Kurtz, Paul. "The Humanist Declaration" *Free Inquiry* 1 (Winter 1980-81): 3-6.

Lloyd, G. E. R. *Aristotle: The Growth and Structure of His Thought*. Cambridge: Cambridge University Press, 1968.

Marias, Julian, *History of Philosophy*. New York: Dover, 1967.

Meeks, Douglas M. *Origins of the Theology of Hope*. Philadelphia: Fortress, 1974.

Mickey, Paul A. *Essentials of Wesleyan Theology*. Grand Rapids: Zondervan, 1980.

Moltmann, Jürgen. *Theology of Hope*. New York: Harper and Row, 1967.

Niebuhr, Reinhold. *The Nature and Destiny of Man*. New York: Scribner, 1941-43.

Noss, John B. *Man's Religions*. 5th ed. Rev. New York: Macmillan, 1974.

Nygren, Anders. *Eros and Agape*. Translated by Philip S. Watson. Philadelphia: Westminster, 1953.

Otto, Rudolf. *The Idea of the Holy: An Inquiry into the Non-rational Factor in the Idea of the Divine and Its Relation to the Rational*. Translated by John W. Harvey. London: Oxford University Press, 1970.

Outler, Albert C. *John Wesley*. New York: Oxford University Press, 1964.

Pritchard, James B., ed. *Ancient Near Eastern Texts Relating to the Old Testament*. Princeton: Princeton University Press, 1969.

Randall, J. H., Jr. *The Role of Knowledge in Western Religion*. Boston: Beacon, 1958.

Ricouer, Paul. *The Symbolism of Evil*. Translated by Emerson Buchanan. Boston: Beacon, 1967.

Rorty, Richard. *The Linguistic Turn: Recent Essays in Philosophical Method*. Chicago: University of Chicago Press, 1975.

Runyon, Theodore, Jr. "Friedrich Gogarten," *A Handbook of Christian Theologians*. Edited by Dean E. Peerman and Martin E. Marty. New York: World, 1965.

Sartre, Jean-Paul. *Being and Nothingness: An Essay on Phenomenological Ontology*. Translated, with an introduction, by Hazel E. Barnes. New York: Philosophical Library, 1956.

――――. *Existentialism and Human Emotions*. New York: Philosophical Library, 1952.

Schumacher, E. F. *A Guide for the Perplexed*. New York: Harper and Row, 1977.

Smith, Huston. *Forgotten Truth: The Primordial Tradition*. New York: Harper and Row, 1976.

Snaith, Norman H. *The Distinctive Ideas of the Old Testament*. London: Epworth, 1944.

Starkey, Lycurgus, Jr. *The Work of the Holy Spirit: A Study in Wesleyan Theology*. Nashville: Abingdon, 1962.

Swinburne, Richard. *The Coherence of Theism*. Oxford: Clarendon, 1977.

Teilhard de Chardin, Pierre. *The Phenomenon of Man*. Translated by Bernard Wali, with an introduction by Julian Huxley. New York: Harper and Row, 1959.

――――. *Science and Christ*. New York: Harper and Row, 1965.

Tennant, F. R. *Philosophical Theology*. 2 volumes. Cambridge: Cambridge University Press, 1928–30.

Tillich, Paul. *The Courage to Be*. New Haven: Yale University Press, 1952.

_____. *Systematic Theology,* 3 volumes. Chicago: University of Chicago Press, 1951–63.

Tracy, David Wesley. *The Analogical Imagination: Christian Theology and the Culture of Pluralism*. New York: Crossroad, 1981.

_____. *Blessed Rage for Order*. Chicago: University of Chicago Press, 1972.

Van Buren, Paul. *The Secular Meaning of the Gospel: Based on an Analysis of Its Language*. New York: Macmillan, 1963.

Wesley, John. *Explanatory Notes Upon the New Testament*. Reprint ed., London: Epworth, 1954.

_____ . *The Works of John Wesley,* 14 vols. 1872. Reprint edition. Kansas City, Mo.: Nazarene, n.d.

Wiley, H. Orton. *Christian Theology,* 3 vols. Kansas City, Mo.: Beacon Hill, 1960.

Williams, Colin W. *John Wesley's Theology Today*. Nashville: Abingdon, 1960.

CHAPTER 5

COSMOLOGY:
The Handiwork of God in Creation

Eugene E. Carpenter

Eugene E. Carpenter is Professor of Old Testament, Wheaton College. He received the M.Div. degree from Associated Mennonite Biblical Seminaries, Elkhart, Indiana, and the Ph.D. degree from Fuller Theological Seminary. He taught at Bethel College, Mishawaka, Indiana, for several years before assuming his present position.

Dr. Carpenter has written a number of articles for a church magazine and for the International Standard Bible Encyclopedia. *He is a member of the following organizations: Chicago Society of Biblical Literature, Society of Biblical Literature, Northern Indiana Fellowship of Professors of Religion, and American Theological Society. He is an associate member of the Wesleyan Theological Society.*

CONTENTS

INTRODUCTION / 149

I. COSMOLOGY IN THE ANCIENT NEAR EAST AND IN THE OLD TESTAMENT / 149
    A. Literary Genre of the ANE Accounts of Cosmology / 150
    B. ANE Concepts of Cosmology / 151
        1. Preexistence of matter, chaos, or primeval ocean in ANE cosmology / 151
        2. Theogony as a vital part of ANE cosmology / 151
        3. Instrumental means of "creation" in ANE cosmology / 151
        4. The theology of ANE cosmology / 152
        5. Man's place in ANE cosmology / 153
        6. Moral concepts in ANE cosmology / 153
        7. The polemical nature of ANE cosmology / 154
        8. Some philosophical implications of ANE cosmology / 154
    C. Literary Genre of the Old Testament Account of Creation / 154
    D. The Old Testament Concept of Creation / 156
        1. Preexistence of God alone / 157
        2. Creation ex nihilo / 157
        3. Instrumental means of creation in Old Testament cosmology / 158
        4. The theology of Old Testament cosmology / 159
        5. Man's place in Old Testament cosmology / 161
        6. The intrinsic moral nature of Old Testament cosmology / 162
        7. The polemical nature of Old Testament cosmology / 163
        8. Some philosophical implications of Old Testament cosmology / 165
        9. The Old Testament concept of the new creation / 166
        10. Some observations on science and Old Testament cosmology / 167
    E. Comparison and Contrast of ANE and Old Testament Accounts (with chart) / 167

II. COSMOLOGY IN THE INTERTESTAMENTAL LITERATURE: BRIEF OVERVIEW / 168
    A. The Literature / 168
    B. The Connecting Link Between the Old Testament and the New Testament / 169

III. COSMOLOGY IN THE NEW TESTAMENT / 170
    A. Pagan Cosmology Unchanged in Essence / 170
    B. The New Testament Affirms Old Testament Cosmology / 171
    C. The New Testament Contribution to Cosmology / 171
    D. The New Creation (Cosmology) of the New Testament / 173
        1. Its basic features / 173
        2. Cosmology and eschatology / 174

IV. WHY A BIBLICAL VIEW OF COSMOLOGY? / 174
  A. Positive Clear Presentation of a Basic Cosmology Found in Scripture / 174
  B. Biblical Cosmology Vital to a Christian World View / 175
  C. Failure of Nonbiblical Views to Explain the Cosmos in Essential Areas / 175
  D. Its Relevancy and Sufficiency / 176

V. SOME WESLEYAN OBSERVATIONS ON COSMOLOGY / 176
  A. Introduction / 176
  B. Early Wesleyan Views on Cosmology / 177
  C. Contemporary Wesleyan Views on Cosmology / 177
  D. Concluding Observations / 178

NOTES / 179

DISCUSSION QUESTIONS / 186

RECOMMENDATIONS FOR FURTHER READING / 187

BIBLIOGRAPHY / 187

COSMOLOGY

The Handiwork of God in Creation

INTRODUCTION

This Christian cosmology presents an account of the inspired biblical writer's revelatory concepts about the origin, nature, purpose, and goal of the created order by making use of relevant historical background and linguistic study. In the origin, nature, purpose, and goal of biblical cosmology we discover the intrinsic value of God's creation, which bears the imprint of the creative Word of God. Man is declared, moreover, to bear the image of the Creator in his being. The New Testament declares that the creative Word of God was, is, and continues to be none other than Jesus Christ. In Him all things find their ultimate meaning (John 1:1–14; Col. 1:15–20; Heb. 1:1–3).

The biblical account of creation is amazing and striking in many ways. Its revelatory character is clearly demonstrated when it is placed among its nonbiblical counterparts, both ancient and modern. God's creation receives His stamp of approval from the beginning and God's redemptive activities in respect to the cosmos are a testimony to the inherent value God placed on His original creation. In a real sense, everything rests on a Christian cosmology. What God has begun to do, He will bring to completion.

Wesley and contemporary Wesleyan theology realize the great necessity to interpret correctly God's activities in the beginning of all things. God's major goal in creation past and present is to create His own people and an appropriate environment for them. The essential goal of people of God is to bear their Creator's image in holiness, righteousness, love, and wisdom in an environment "in which righteousness dwells." This is the positive goal of all creation and history. Mankind's present potential renewal in the image of God was stressed by Wesley and is also stressed by modern Wesleyan writers. And, not only man, but all creation finds its end in Jesus Christ, who is none other than God Himself.

I. COSMOLOGY IN THE ANCIENT NEAR EAST AND IN THE OLD TESTAMENT

Since the first half of the nineteenth century, phenomenal archaeological finds have occurred in the Near East. Some of these discoveries have increased our understanding of the Ancient Near East—the place of origins of the Old Testament—to the extent never thought possible even during the last half of the nineteenth century. Old Testament scholars have found certain of these archaeological materials of inestimable value for understanding the Old Testament in its own world.[1] Especially the written documents that have been discovered and deciphered have proved helpful. The historical and cultural background, and all that this entails, of the Old Testament has become discernible to the modern biblical and Ancient Near Eastern scholar. The value of some of the finds unearthed for grasping the ancient concept of cosmology is priceless. Several documents that refer to cosmology, even though incidentally, help us to catch a glimpse of what the ancient Hebrews' neighbors taught about this subject. The ideas held about cosmology in several of these nonbiblical sources will be examined briefly in order to present some representative examples of cosmology from the Ancient Near East. The examination will demonstrate the background against which, and the milieu and ambience within which, the Old Testament creation account arose. Some similarities and differences will be noted between the Old Testament revelatory Scriptures and the Ancient Near Eastern stories in order to discern the unique place that the Old Testament cosmology holds among these ancient materials.

A. Literary Genre of the ANE Accounts of Cosmology

One of the vital questions to be asked before interpreting a written document concerns its literary genre: What kind of document is it? A document's literary genre largely determines how it is to be interpreted. It is somewhat surprising that there are no creation stories per se among the nonbiblical Ancient Near Eastern texts thus far unearthed.[2] The leitmotifs in the diverse texts recovered center around themes *other than* creation and/or the creation concept itself and are *subordinated* to personal, political, cultural, or ethnically narrow religious purposes. This literary situation can be demonstrated by referring to several of the significant literary works stemming from the Ancient Near East, which are often termed "creation stories" or "creation epics."

Perhaps the best known nonbiblical ancient text is the *Enuma Elish,* the so-called Babylonian creation account.[3] The first presentation of this account in English was made by George Smith in 1876 in his *Chaldean Account of Genesis.* The main purpose of the document is to establish Babylon as the capital of the nation and to establish the city's chief god, Marduk, as supreme among all gods. Little emphasis is given to creation, but much is given to the establishment of Babylon and its pantheon as supreme among the nations and the gods of the world. Only one-sixth or less of the entire account containing seven tablets treats cosmology in a significant way.[4] Hence, the designation of the *Enuma Elish* as a creation account is misleading. It is more correctly seen as an ethnically centered political document that subordinates creation and religious matters to cultural, ethnic, political, and national goals, to say nothing about its failure to present a concept of true "creation."

Space permits brief reference to only one more major Ancient Near Eastern "creation account,"[5] and little needs to be said about its design and goal in order to recognize that its purpose is not the presentation of cosmology per se, but the exaltation of an ancient capital of Egypt during the First and Second Dynasties (ca. 3100–2680 B.C.). This document is named "The Theology of Memphis," and its specific goal is to exalt the leading god of the Memphite pantheon to first rank among all gods.[6] As the *Enuma Elish,* the Memphite text uses mythology to demonstrate the supremacy of the god Ptah, and, hence, of Memphis, even going so far as to suggest that Upper and Lower Egypt were first united at Memphis. This creation story is not continuous; none of the Egyptian cosmology accounts are. They all fall into a generic category other than creation stories. The Memphite text subordinates creation to cultural, ethnic, political, and national purposes. The center of political power changed hands numerous times throughout Egypt's history, and each time a new propagandistic account was prepared in order to elevate a given local deity (e.g., at Thebes, Memphis, and Heracleopolis) to national religious prominence. Along with this, "a new legend about creation was coined."[7] None of the accounts can be termed a true "creation account," but they are rather mythical[8] and legendary accounts politically and religiously based to accomplish a narrow national and ethnic purpose.

B. ANE Concepts of Cosmology

Although there are no creation accounts per se among the Ancient Near Eastern texts deciphered so far, various significant and essential concepts about cosmology are found in diverse places in these documents. The following observations attempt to indicate some of the more important ideas that are found. These ancient writings are not systematic in their presentation of material—at least not to the Western mind; hence, the reader should realize that the thoughts presented here are found scattered throughout numerous sections of this ancient literature with which we are dealing.[9]

1. Preexistence of matter, chaos, or primeval ocean in ANE cosmology A regular feature of these texts is the original presence of something variously labeled chaos, primeval hillock, primeval ocean, cosmic egg, and/or an originally repelled water monster.[10] However and whenever these terms may be used, they indicate a conviction that in the distant past a source, or élan vital of some kind, was there. In Egypt the abysmal waters were referred to as Nun, the waters of chaos. In Babylonian literature, the beginning is connected organically with the appearance of earth (most often), water, and time.[11] The threat of the orderly creation again returning to its chaotic state is evident in both Egyptian and Babylonian literature.[12] This original beginning or "source of 'beginning'" is always prior to any gods that subsequently appear on the scene and who are responsible for the origin(s) of the habitable world of man and other created creatures.

2. Theogony as a vital part of ANE cosmology Theogony is an interesting and startling feature of the Ancient Near Eastern accounts of creation. By theogony we mean the generation of the gods. Yet, on the other hand, this is a logical result of concluding that "something" lies behind everything—even behind the gods themselves.

The following lines from the *Enuma Elish* make this fact candidly and frankly:

> When no gods whatever had been brought into being, Uncalled by name, their destinies undetermined—Then it was that the gods were formed within them.[13]

The "them" mentioned in the last line is a personification of Apsu and Tiamat, fresh waters and salt waters respectively.

Theogony played an important part in Egyptian cosmology. It was noted above that Atum sprang from or was identified with a primeval hillock.[14] Re and, hence, Atum-Re, sprang from the waters of chaos, according to one account. From Atum was engendered the ennead, or nine gods, according to Heliopolitan cosmology.[15] At Hermopolis, chaos existed in the beginning, but from original chaos the ogdoad, or eight gods, was produced. At Memphis a later development made the god Ptah, the chief god of Memphite theology, the progenitor of the other gods who were a mishmash of the Heliopolitan ennead and the Hermopolitan ogdoad. In numerous Ancient Near Eastern theogonies, some gods are personified forces or elements of nature or the world.

3. Instrumental means of "creation" in ANE cosmology The means of "creation" in the Ancient Near Eastern texts are all ultimately oriented to a physical or material basis. A few claimed exceptions do not seem to stand up to close scrutiny. In one Egyptian report, Atum and/or Atum-Re sputtered or spit forth Shu and Tefnut (god of air and goddess of moisture respectively) and put his *Ka*[16] into them. As noted above, this productive activity by the gods included the naming and the appearance of various subsequent gods who then proceeded to create by various ways. Re created by masturbation, according to some reports.[17] In all of this there is a generated power and informing source at work apart from the purely voluntary thoughts and desires of the gods. Ptah, chief god of Memphis, engages in a partially intellectual process of creation; but, even in this case, the ultimate informing source is the *senses,* which gather all of the necessary information and report to the heart. The tongue then puts forth an utterance that produces a created entity.[18]

The same basic physical or materialistic ideas of cosmology are found in the Mesopotamian sources, including the very ancient Sumerian texts. For the Babylonian, the substance of the world is eternal.[19] Hence, any productive acts by the gods are only secondary. "Creation" is really only fashioning and ordering what is there. Nothing is narrated about the means (if there was one) used to bring matter (*physis*) into existence. Everything is subsequent to matter and, hence, all future "creative" activity is informed by the generative power residing in eternal matter. The instrumental means of creation as found in Mesopotamian literature are applied in a secondary way to what has inexplicably already been created—or always existed. In some cases magic was possibly involved, and this further involved the behavior of already-existing matter or an appeal to a *nonrational element* to effect the desired object. The creative word in Mesopotamian literature is impotent in the face of some situations and is always accompanied by other means of ordering.

4. The theology of ANE cosmology
Perhaps the most striking fact to those who are acquainted with the Judeo-Christian idea of God is the Ancient Near Eastern pantheon of gods. Polytheism was without exception the religious view of the nonbiblical Old Testament world. James lists about one hundred *major* deities mentioned in ancient Egyptian texts.[20] Just as many can be listed for Mesopotamian texts.[21] Hundreds and even thousands of minor deities existed.

None of these gods existed at some time in the past, but came into being. In Egyptian theology, even Re (Atum-Re) asserts that he came into existence by himself.[22] He is the father of the gods. However, as has been incidentally noted before, Re and many of the original gods were generated by a prior source. Ptah seems to be everything; all Egyptian gods are in him. Ptah is sometimes indicated to be a principle "life force" rather than a god with personality.[23] Many gods are identified with various elements of the natural world and are given appropriate names to indicate this fact.[24] Perhaps because the gods are never conceived of as prior to chaos, or matter, they are never portrayed as omnipotent *in toto*. Some things remain ambiguous and mysterious to them. They are called on to fight against forces and expend and enervate themselves.[25] On the other hand, everything is made for the benefit and enjoyment of the gods.

As in Greek mythology, these gods are anthropomorphized and are guilty of all of the faults of mankind. Battles among the gods are frequent and baleful. The gods are potentially immortal, but many of them are killed in vicious battles with other gods.[26]

The stated relationships among some of these gods are simply impossible for Western minds to comprehend. In Egyptian thought, Seth can be both the brother and uncle of Horus. Gods begot gods and goddesses, and these gods and goddesses intermarried and produced other offspring.[27] At different times in Egyptian and Mesopotamian history the gods of the various local places were identified with one another in various ways.²⁸

5. Man's place in ANE cosmology

The place accorded to man and his creation is relatively insignificant compared to the space given to other subjects of ancient cosmology. The gods and all that they had created for their enjoyment had to be cared for by someone, and man was, therefore, created. Because of this task, his functional purpose made him important.

In Egypt man's origin was conceived of in various ways. He came into being from the tears that the god Re shed, according to one account. In another account, he came forth from Re's eyes, but tears are not mentioned. Another text mentions man as the product of the tears of the Creator-god.²⁹ In one cultic hymn, the Creator-god brings forth man by speaking.³⁰ Mesopotamian concepts of man's creation are diverse. In the Sumerian "Hymn to the Mattock," people spring from the ground,³¹ and in a Sumerian myth, people are brought forth from clay.³² In other Mesopotamian texts, man is made from the blood of gods, from clay, and in other texts, from clay mixed with the blood of a god. Magic is evidently used, and several gods are involved in man's creation. Creation by word is always aided by various other means and processes.³³

It has been noted already that man was created to serve the gods, to feed and care for them; his tasks are menial, but important to the gods. In Egypt, it is recorded that man's end is destruction, for he is rebellious against the gods. He is saved from annihilation by Re.³⁴ He is also termed the cattle of the gods.³⁵ Similar statements are made about man in Mesopotamian literature: man is to help the gods, and in the *Enuma Elish* man is made so that rebellious gods may be set free from punishment.³⁶

Man's nature is mortal; he is not created to live forever, but *naturally* suffers death. He is in the gods' image with all of the gods' frailties, but not blessed with possible immortality. It is clear, too, that being in the gods' image does not entitle man to any fellowship or any kind of essential equality with the gods. In a sense, man occupies one of the lowest positions in the nonbiblical Ancient Near Eastern orders of cosmology.

6. Moral concepts in ANE cosmology

It is difficult to discuss morality in the Ancient Near Eastern literature because no consistent ethical system is evident unless, perhaps, we might think of some kind of polytheistic naturalism.³⁷ At any rate, in this discussion we are concerned with the values as they follow from the nature of the original creation—"the value significance of cosmic entities."³⁸

The phenomenon of death is an anomalous feature of the world of the gods. The gods fight, they die, they perform all of the "immoral" acts of mankind. In fact, the social life of the gods is a reflection of the life of mankind. The gods are, in one sense, "in man's image." However, the potential for eternal life does exist for the gods.

Evil in many forms, both natural and moral, was present from the beginning. Such evils as sorrow, pain, distress, jealousy, killing, and hatred exist for both gods and people. Man is naturally mortal and death is part and parcel of his lot through no fault of his own; death is not occasioned because of moral failure. The gods find no serious moral problems with man but are sufficiently angry with him to destroy him when he becomes too noisy or will not perform his menial tasks for them. In general, a man's future hope (if any) lies in the preponderance of good works over evil deeds in his life. In Egypt an impersonal concept of *maat* (righteousness) was pursued. Demons afflict man, and disease and pain are woven into the original order of cosmology.³⁹ Man's highest duty and goal is menial—to preserve and please the gods. The gods' supreme goal is functional —to preserve order. Back of gods and men lies chaos. Natural disorders are a result of disharmony or anger among the gods. But "nature" itself can threaten the gods.⁴⁰

No categorical moral qualities are attributed to the creation, and the threat of a return to chaos—the ultimate destiny of everything, according to some texts—negates any assignment of an ultimate goal or purpose to cosmology. Although everything is created for the gods, even the gods are mere products of an unknown generative force that may or may not relapse into chaos. The ultimate source and nature of all things are therefore ambiguous and not determinative for ultimate and purposive values.[41]

7. The polemical nature of ANE cosmology The major polemical purpose of the Ancient Near Eastern cosmological texts is political. As noted above, the capital of Egypt changed numerous times through her long history. Each time a new local city achieved prominence as Egypt's capital, its political and religious hegemony was authenticated by asserting that it was the original site of creation.[42] And, in general, throughout Egypt's history creation stories were used to establish the royal power of the rulers. This same observation is valid for cosmological materials throughout the Mesopotamian world; it is true in all of the Ancient Near East. In the Assyrian version of the Babylonian "Creation Epic," Marduk, the chief god of the Babylonian pantheon, is replaced by Ashur, the chief god of Assyria. Hence the polemics involved in these accounts are evident.

This last observation underlines the fact that throughout the Ancient Near East there were no serious challenges to the generally accepted concepts of original cosmology. The particular activities of certain gods, names of the gods, the location of primeval creation, the chosen ethnic group, some of the trivial concepts of cosmology—these could all change as circumstances dictated, but the basic philosophical and theological principles involved remained amazingly constant. A common world view is evident—a solidarity of polytheistic naturalism and materialism.[43]

8. Some philosophical implications of ANE cosmology Most of what can be said about the philosophical bases and the resultant world view(s) of the Ancient Near East has already been stated. A few summary statements may be helpful.

Some type of materialism lies at the root of Ancient Near Eastern cosmology; however, some kind of "divine" élan vital is inherent or comes to be within this primeval eternal matter, and as a result gods are generated. Hence, a primitive or incipient vitalism was nearly affirmed. Sometimes the original primeval matter is personified as god(s), for example, Apsu and Tiamat. Polytheistic naturalism is a paradoxical term, but the mythical and nonlogical concepts of creation that are presented seem to require some such term. There is an interesting mixture of divine and naturalistic elements in the Ancient Near Eastern world view. Creation is a process of forming and molding what exists. Evil is present in this cosmology, and not as an entirely foreign element. The ultimate base of the universe is evidently amoral, and evil consists basically of disorder in some sphere of cosmology.

Man is a finite being made by the gods, but he does not share in the gods' life—he is mortal. His chief value is not in himself or his nature, but in his function of serving the gods. His knowledge of and fellowship with the gods is minimal. The sphere of the gods is beyond him.[44] Evil spirits and demons are part of the cosmos and great evil is caused by them.[45] The basic goal of the cosmos is to continue as it is.[46] No other specific goal or teleology is inherent in the world views presented by the texts.

C. Literary Genre of the Old Testament Account of Creation

The literary style, content, and purpose of Genesis 1-2, the primary creation Scripture in the Old Testament, identify these chapters as creation accounts per se; their aim is to relate the origin(s) of all things.

This ancient Hebrew document of the cosmos is the creation account par excellence that has come down to us from the Ancient Near East. That its provenience is the Ancient Near East is evidenced by much of its literary style and cultural tone, but at the same time it is *sui generis* and is clearly the product not only of man but also of divine revelation. The account cannot be considered a mere product of the Ancient Near Eastern culture.[47] It is clear that the inspired writer has been informed by God's revelation as to the nature, purpose, and goal of the world and of man. Hence, he is enabled to present to his readers a true understanding of the beginning of all things. He presents this report in the language of his day.[48] Especially noteworthy and essential is the theological perspective of this report about the origin of the cosmos. From the theological foundation of all things comes the significance of all things.

Although it shares many of the common cultural elements of the Ancient Near East, the Genesis account of creation presents its report with content and emphases that result in a unique biblical account of origins.[49] Not only is the objective reality of the cosmos truly declared, but the value of cosmic realities is also emphatically stated. Not merely the "thatness" but also the intrinsic value of that which exists is given. Genesis 1-2 must not be read merely as a straightforward declaration of God's objective creation, but also as a religious—a theological—statement that conveys to faith the origin of all things (Heb. 11:3);[50] not merely the existence of the atom, but the basis for the existence of morals, values, religion—for the world as we know it. Any account of the origin of all things should provide the basis for a holistic interpretation of the cosmos. Genesis 1-2 does this well.

We cannot expect the biblical writer, writing within the space of two chapters, to deal in detail with the *how* of the Creator's work except in large outline. Within the space of a few verses, we read in phenomenological language[51] a profound report about creation that is satisfactory at every level at which we may investigate it: scientific, religious, psychological, philosophical, sociological, and anthropological. Its truth creates its effectiveness.

This account of creation is universal in scope and presents a universal Creator. The provincialism of the nonbiblical materials that deal with the origin of the cosmos is entirely lacking in Genesis 1-2. Its view of the original creation is one in which God brings forth perfection and that which is "very good" in every way. Man is created upright (Eccl. 7:29) and is free to use his *imago Dei* (image of God) capabilities to follow his Creator in truth or to pursue his own exaltation in falsehood. The original perfection of the creation is highly important theologically and, of course, biblically.

God's future involvement in and relation to His created order is established because of the nature of His cosmos. The Creator is capable of a relationship with His creation because He has given it the potential to respond to Him. All things are declared good, and God cares for what He has created. The later redemptive processes of God, as He deals with a fallen creation, are a result of the values and goals that He caused to adhere in His original creation, as well as a result of His own nature. Redemption flows from the Creator to His creation (Neh. 9:6-8). God will perfect that which He has begun and, therefore, values.

Space will not permit a full discussion of the literary nature of Genesis 1-2, but a few remarks are in order. First of all, Genesis 1-2 gives complementary reports about origins told from two perspectives, not two contradictory accounts.[52] Creation themes per se are much more prevalent in Genesis 1 but are present in Genesis 2 also. Because of not taking into sufficient consideration the change of purpose that the writer pursues in these two chapters, many scholars argue for two creation accounts on the basis of the formal principle of "change of style demands a change in author." The goal and purpose of chapter 1 is to give us a magnificent comprehensive overview of God the Creator calling all things into existence. By the use of the Hebrew word *bara* the writer identifies God's activities in Genesis as *without human analogy*. There is little story narration, but there is a developed sequential narrative[53] and a series of commands by God that effect the beginning of all things. Genesis 2 has a different purpose and is a literary unit with chapter 3f. Man's intimacy with his Creator is brought out through anthropomorphisms,[54] but all of the basic truths of chapter 1 are presupposed and some are developed further. A historical drama begins to take place in chapter 2, and new themes are treated that find no correspondence in chapter 1.[55] However, just because of the necessary change in perspective and purpose of the writer and a resultant change in style of chapter 2 (and 3f.), there is no need to posit two separate accounts and two authors for the present accounts. In numerous ways chapters 1 and 2 interlock and many so-called contradictions between 1 and 2 are produced by critics' methodologies and presuppositions rather than posited by the text itself.[56] When allowing a literary document to interpret itself, we must let it dictate to us the kind of literature it is and how it is to be understood and, finally, what it means by what it says.[57]

The actual classification of the literary style of Genesis 1-2 is difficult, but the style involves exalted Hebrew prose.[58] The consecutive *waw* of Hebrew is used throughout Genesis 1-2 but in genuine Hebrew poetry it is usually missing.

The definite sequential pattern of these verses, the use of the sign of the direct object in Hebrew and the use of "these are the generations of" to introduce these momentous events in a way parallel to following clearly historical events in Genesis affirms that we are dealing basically with Hebrew prose and, hence, with accounts of historical, factual material about creation.[59]

However, the fact that these verses reflect exalted Hebrew prose and make use of some poetry and rich symbolism taken from the Ancient Near East establishes the fact that the writer intends to present more than a mere "scientific"[60] account of creation and that he intends to speak to the spiritual, moral, theological, and religious dimensions of the cosmos as well.

In the remaining pages we will examine these chapters and numerous other Old Testament Scriptures that deal with creation. We will consider these under the same eight categories used in investigating the background material of the Ancient Near Eastern concepts of cosmology. Indeed this will have to be an overview of the Old Testament concept of creation, for Genesis 1-2 alone is sufficient to demand a whole book. And, because of the limited space not all of the ramifications of the Old Testament cosmology can be presented.[61]

D. The Old Testament Concept of Creation

Genesis 1-2 presents to us a concentrated and complete story of the origins of the cosmos, but scattered throughout the Old Testament many other Scriptures speak to the subject that we are considering. The revelatory material subsequent to the Mosaic period confirms and clarifies the basic outline of creation presented in Genesis 1 and 2. Some points are made more explicit. The new element of cosmology that will be encountered in the prophets is the demise of the first creation along with its restoration into a new heaven and a new earth, a new creation. Not all of these issues can be treated thoroughly, but it is hoped that the essentials of an Old Testament concept of the cosmos will be presented. Wesley was correct when he said, "The Scriptures were written, not to satisfy our curiosity, but to lead us to God."[62] It will help readers to grasp the uniqueness of the biblical account of creation if they keep in mind the comments made earlier under a given area in regard to Ancient Near Eastern thinking.[63]

1. Preexistence of God alone When Genesis 1–2 is seen in its Ancient Near Eastern setting, the purpose of the order of the creative events is clear. The gods of the Ancient Near Eastern creation views are *absent* in the primeval beginning; they themselves are generated from some original source. To the biblical writer God is prior to the cosmos; nothing precedes Him (Gen. 1:1).[64] He is prior in time, power, and wisdom, indeed *in all ways;* this fact will become evident as we continue our discussion. Nothing lies back of God, according to the Hebrew account of creation. The writer stresses this fact laconically, but emphatically, by placing God Himself and His creative activity first in his account. All things of the cosmos have a beginning, but the biblical writer knew that his God did not "come to be." He was always there (cf. Pss. 90:2; 102:24). The writer does not make a futile attempt to explain the origin of God, but he does affirm the fact of God (cf. Heb. 11:2).[65] Hardly a more effective polemic could be devised to denigrate the pagan accounts about the origin of their gods. The clear implication of the biblical writer is that God has "no beginning" that is analogous to the origin of the created order that man knows. No Scripture even hints at a beginning of God. Even the chaotic state of the original matter out of which He frames the material world is declared to be a creation of God.[66]

In Ancient Near Eastern creation accounts chaos was sometimes represented as a foe of god, a monster to be overcome.[67] In Genesis 1 the original state of the material universe is described as waste and desolate (*tohu wabohu*), but it is simply God's lifeless, inert creation, unable to produce order or life until God speaks.[68] The chaotic state of God's original creation obeys Him precisely as He speaks to it. It offers no threat to Him, and clearly God precedes it.

God, a personal God, lies behind creation and is its basis; its basis is not some impersonal force or material.[69] Since God is prior to all things, it follows that all things have come to be because of His will, and His spoken word is absolute proof of His will.[70] There is no other causative factor involved in the original motivation to create except God's will informed by His power and wisdom, since He is supreme and prior to all (Ps. 104:25; Rev. 4:11).

The fact that God is prior in all ways to all things has many ramifications for the biblical view of creation, some of which will be discussed. An important corollary of the fact of God's complete priority to the cosmos is the biblical doctrine of creation ex nihilo.

2. Creation ex nihilo The Christian understanding of the origin of all things has traditionally been that God brought the cosmos into existence without the use of prior materials. This is expressed technically as creation ex nihilo, or creation out of nothing.[71] This is clearly taught in the New Testament, but is also deducible from what the Old Testament says about the subject.[72] As was noted above, in section 1, God is assumed by the biblical writer to be prior to all things. No state of original chaotic matter preceded Israel's God.

Again the dissimilarity of the Genesis creation accounts to other pagan accounts of the cosmos is evident. In all of their accounts, as noted above, something precedes the gods—water, land, sea, air, sky, or some other matter. In Genesis everything comes into being only *after* God speaks or acts it into being. The creation of matter is generally termed primary creation and the following process of bringing an orderly world out of chaotic matter is secondary creation. However, in *both* cases God brings about something totally dependent on His having acted. Before God spoke, matter did not have the ability to produce life. The Hebrew word *bara* is characteristic of Genesis 1. Although this word does not in itself teach creation ex nihilo, it does denote that which is brought about by the activity of divinity—by God only. Hence, there is no analogical activity that man engages in. When God creates (*bara*) something, He does that which has no human parallel. Never is it mentioned that God uses a preexistent material. His word or creative power effects His will, even creating the necessary material of which an object is to consist. Nothing is beyond the purview of God.

God is totally aware of and knows all that has come into being, for He is its divine Author. The biblical God indeed shapes effortlessly, for that which He shapes is not foreign to Him but bears His creative logos. He knows that which He shapes and conforms it to His will.

The biblical account of creation allows for no "given" that exists from eternity with God and that, as a result, is not totally comprehended by God or totally dependent on Him.[73] Because God is the Author of all things, He stands in complete control of all things. No mysterious power lurks behind God nor behind anything He has created. God's total wisdom and power manifest over the cosmos is the outcome of all of this.

The concept of creation ex nihilo of course means that the cosmos had a beginning. Aristotle as well as Ancient Near Eastern religions taught the eternity of matter, a fact also believed vehemently by some astronomers during the twentieth century.[74] The simple yet profound statement that "in the beginning God created" is being found amazingly suggestive by some modern astronomers who are now on the verge of declaring that, indeed, the cosmos had a beginning. Creation ex nihilo is a doctrine adhered to by most evangelical scientists.[75]

3. Instrumental means of creation in Old Testament cosmology The Old Testament prepares the reader for the New Testament. One effective way this is accomplished is by intimating, foreshadowing, predicting, or partially revealing that which comes to full fruition only in the New Testament. Nowhere is this done more effectively than in the concept of "word" creation presented in Genesis 1. It is simply at the expression of the divine will through God's word that the cosmos becomes a reality. There is no exact parallel to this in the other Ancient Near Eastern religions.[76] The psalmist sings in praise in Psalm 33:6-9:

> By the *word* of the Lord the heavens were made, and by the *breath* of His mouth all their host. He gathers the waters of the sea together as a heap; He lays up the deep in storehouses. Let all the earth fear the Lord; let all the inhabitants of the world stand in awe of Him. For He spoke, and it was done; He commanded, and it stood fast.

The literary structure of Genesis 1 emphasizes creation by divine command. Repeatedly one meets the simple but powerful statements: "God said," "Let there be," "it was so," "God called," and "blessed." There is no hint by the biblical writer that any effort is expended by God other than whatever is involved in His speaking His word.[77] Genesis 2 with its different perspectives assumes the initial creation of Genesis 1 and aims to present God as acting with regard to three areas: (1) the formation of man and animals, (2) the formation of the Garden of Eden for man, and (3) the formation of woman. The center of attention in Genesis 2 is man, and the fact that man is a unique creature sharing intimately with the Creator is emphasized. Man is, however, not a product of natural forces, but only as God's "breath of life" is imparted to him by his Maker does he exist as a living being, as man (in fact, creation ex nihilo).

God's forming man in Genesis 2 and creating him in Genesis 1 involves no contradiction for the biblical writer, for the distinction between word and deed in the Ancient Near East and in the Bible was not natural nor were the terms mutually exclusive. In biblical thought God's word (*dābār*) and God's deed (*dābār!*) are one and the same. Especially is this evident with respect to God, for His word is His creative word. To do was to speak, to speak was to do. God's word resulted in action. These two accounts, therefore, basically agree, although each has its own perspective. However, Genesis 1 clearly and effectively implies creation ex nihilo, whereas Genesis 2 clearly affirms man's origin in respect to his physical and psychical nature. Man is not an angel. The characteristic word for man's formation in Genesis 2 is *yaṣar* (to form, mold, shape). Its purpose is to indicate God's special care and concern for man and His intimate relationship to him. Man's life is from God. Man's uniqueness is demonstrated by his dominion over the animals and in his intimate relationship to his Creator, all of which is predicated of man since he is in God's image.

Also to be affirmed as an active force in the original creation is God's Spirit (Gen. 1:2; Ps. 33:6).[78] In the Old Testament the Holy Spirit is a term for God's outgoing energy, creative and sustaining (Ps. 104:30; Job 26:13; 33:4). The connection between the working of the word and the Spirit is obscure in Genesis 1–2, but the creative activity of the Spirit appears to effect the commanded word. The Spirit's "brooding" over the original created matter made the command effective to shape and order the cosmos. "As in the new birth the Spirit is the source of life, so in creation was the Spirit the source of vitality and life."[79] With God the Father acting through the word and the power of His Spirit (Zech. 4:6) the triune God creates His cosmos. Although this fact is evident only in germ here in these verses, it does provide for the revelation yet to come.

This concept of creation by word and Spirit in the Old Testament lays the background for the salvation that would be revealed in the New Testament, especially through the Word by whom the worlds were made and who would make the new creation. This doctrine of creation will be picked up and developed when we consider the New Testament materials on creation. Numerous theological and philosophical implications flow from creation by word and Spirit and some are pointed out below. Here it should at least be noted that the word of God is not to be equated with Hellenistic concepts of an impersonal logos or reason permeating the cosmos. We have to do here rather with the word of a living personal God being stamped upon creation. That creation is orderly is indeed self-evident, but that it has a personal dimension to it is revealed to us. The order of the world, its intrinsic goodness and meaning, comes about because of a faithful Creator who watches over it and owns it all through His word.[80]

4. The theology of Old Testament cosmology The paramount message of Genesis 1 and 2 and all other essential Old Testament creation narratives is that all things come from the *Creator*. All things come to be through Him, and apart from His activity nothing comes to be (cf. John 1:1). There is *one* Creator, not many, *one* God, not many. In a few short verses the polytheism of all other Ancient Near Eastern religions, past and present, is rendered inane and fatuous. Not only is the one God clearly affirmed, but His unity is evident. He is not divided and He is Lord over all aspects of the cosmos. There is not a god of the seas and a god of the plains, according to Genesis 1. *One* God in His *unity* has created and ordered the universe.

His origin is not to be explained. He is the one inexplicable fact that explains all others. His beginning is not recounted, for He had none. He is self-revealed, for no man has seen Him at any time (John 1:18). His activity in the Old Testament clearly shows that He is all-powerful, all-wise, all-good, and sufficiently present in every area of His creation in order to sustain and preserve it (Gen. 1–2; Neh. 9:6; Pss. 104:1–10; 147:17–19).

His will determines all things (Rev. 4:11), and the Genesis 1 account uses the concept of creation by word as an expression to indicate that the will of the Creator was effected. There is no indication anywhere in the Old Testament that Israel's God (1) was under compulsion to create the cosmos or (2) labored in the creative activity in any way.[81]

The biblical God is a God of order, and

His closest relationship is with man, the being highest in the order of creation even to the point of being *sui generis*. Man is His supreme creation and not only stands the highest in the created order but is absolutely unique in bearing the Creator's image. The Creator's purpose is plain in the sequence of creation. He is desirous of creating beings in His image who will share with Him. All of creation is geared to serve the Creator and thereafter *man*. That God is personal is evident, for He speaks, thinks, acts, and has fellowship with a personal being of His own creation. Man, bearing God's image, is indeed a son of God.[82] God desires fellowship and relationship to both man and the rest of His creation, but He desires a unique relationship to man, His image.

Although Genesis 1-2 and the rest of the Old Testament do not purport to declare the being of God, they do use language taken from the sphere of mankind to talk about the Creator. The anthropomorphic language used in Genesis 1 and 2 testifies to the fact that those terms that describe man are those that best describe the Creator.

An important theological insight is at hand here, for God is One who is available and can be known relationally by the being man, who is in His image.[83] The Creator cannot be proved scientifically, but He can be affirmed by faith (Heb. 11:3; 2 Peter 3:5). He cannot be found under the microscope, but He can be *known* by the searching of the heart of man (Jer. 29:13). He expects obedience from His creation and disobedience results in separation between God and man (Gen. 2:16; 3:23). As an object of scientific research God is not available; as a personal being to be experienced, He is as near as life itself (Gen. 2:8; Acts 17:28). It is fitting that the being that exemplifies personhood best —man—be the supreme creation of the personal God. Since God is the base on which all rests, all things are declared, in Genesis 1-2, to have a personal intelligent being as their basis. There is, from one perspective, little wonder that because of God's investment in His original creation, redemption has become a reality. In fact Scripture is clear that God is the God of redemption *because* He is the Creator who knows all (Isa. 40).

As to the nature of the cosmos, it is clear that it bears the imprint of His creative word; hence, it is good (Gen. 1:4, 10, 12, 18, 21, 25, 31). Since all creation is a product of the Creator's activity, it is *merely* a created thing. Creation stands in awe of its Creator, according to the biblical writer (Neh. 9:6; Pss. 8; 148:35). Indeed, while pagans worshiped the heavenly bodies, the biblical writer declares that the sun, moon, and stars worship God. The original creation was totally good. Evil in no way marred the cosmos. Again the extreme dissimilarity of the Genesis report on original creation in comparison to Ancient Near Eastern creation material is astounding. Wherever and whenever evil did arise, it did not arise within God Himself, nor was it intrinsic to His original creation.[84]

Because the created order bears the imprint of the creative word, it is, of course, expected that it will show order and form. Indeed it does do this.[85] From a biblical theistic point of view this phenomenon of order and form in the universe is seen as a result of the will of the biblical God. Science as pure science investigating the natural world is simply man "thinking God's thoughts" after Him.[86] Much more could be said in this area.

To go beyond Genesis 2 is to begin to talk about, not creation, but pollution—the destruction of God's original perfect creation. For this topic see the chapter on hamartiology.[87]

One further important topic remains to be discussed under the heading of theology of the Old Testament cosmology. This is generally termed providence, or God's continued watchful sovereignty and lordship over His created order.

God's ability to create and destroy is dramatically set forth in Genesis 1-9. The order of the antediluvian world was demolished, but the order and habitable nature of the postflood world is maintained by Him (8:20-21; 9:8-17). The present observable order of the cosmos is recognized as coming from and presently sustained by His word and His Spirit (Ps. 33:6-9). His ability, however, to remove the current heavens and earth and replace them is clear in Isaiah 24-27; 65:17. His sovereignty over His creation is clearly indicated as He directs the course of history (Gen. 37:1-50; Jer. 18:1-12; Dan. 4:19-28), and the great eschatological and apocalyptic passages of the Old Testament indicate His omnipotence as He brings history and the cosmos to its end (*telos*) (Ezek. 37-39; Isa. 24-27; 65-66; Dan. 7).

God's continued response and preservation of His creation is not, however, mechanical, but based on moral and religious principles in which the action and beliefs of mankind as free moral agents play a vital role (Dan. 4:19-28; Jer. 18:1-12). This lays great stress on the fact that God's relationship to the cosmos is one that is based on moral and religious principles. God's providence, His sovereignty and lordship, is exercised in a manner that demonstrates this. This indicates that the teleology of God's providential relationship to His creation is moral and religious. Ideally His providence desires to be a response to a cosmos in which He finds righteousness. Any deistical, mechanical doctrine of providence is plainly excluded.

That God's providence is highly teleological, moral, and religious is a dimension of biblical cosmology that is largely beyond the purview of the relationship of the gods of the Ancient Near East and their creative order. But it is a central constant observation of Scripture.

5. Man's place in Old Testament cosmology Since an entire chapter is given to anthropology in this book, only a few comments will be made about the creation and place of man in the biblical cosmology.

The psalmist was undoubtedly considering the Genesis 1 creation account when he penned:

What is man, that thou dost take thought of him?
And the son of man, that thou dost care for him?
Yet Thou hast made him a little lower than God.[88]
And dost crown him with glory and majesty!
Thou dost make him to rule over the works of Thy hands;
Thou hast put all things under his feet.

(Ps. 8:4-6)

The importance of man in the creation account in Genesis 1 and 2 is clear. His lowly position in the nonbiblical creation materials has been demonstrated (see above, p. 153. In Genesis 1 the vertical creation line is from the lowest entity, chaos, to the highest entity, man; from the least organized creation to the most highly complex and organized creation—man. The creation (*bara*) of mankind is recorded in Genesis 1:27[89] as two beings, male and female, both bearing God's image. Man does not come forth from a previously existing being; there is *no mediate creation* discernible in these verses. Man is the direct creation of God. It is clear in Genesis 1 that the creation, excepting man, was made for the benefit and use of man (Gen. 1:27-31). In Genesis 2 man stands, not at the apex of this narrative, but at its center—as its central concern. Genesis 1 has stressed the spiritual aspect of man (*imago Dei*); Genesis 2 affirms his solidarity with the animal creatures as a living being. God's original intention for man is not complete until woman, man's equal companion, is created and the basic social unit of mankind, the family, is completed. Any attack on the family structure is an attack on God's greatest human institution. God's original, perfectly good human pair is provided an ideal environment in which to relate to their Creator and to each other.

Man is unique in both Genesis 1 and 2. In Genesis 1 this uniqueness is expressed in man's bearing the divine image (Gen. 1:26-27; 5:1; 9:6). The fact that he bears God's image entitles him to be the lord of God's created cosmos (Gen. 1-2). Indeed, the functional component of bearing the Creator's image lies precisely in the dominion that man exercises over all the rest of creation. Dominion is the result, not the essence, of the image of God. However, the ability to exercise dominion assumes all of the attributes necessary to carry out this stupendous task. Man, as God's ambassador and agent, is to rule His creation as God rules all things—with wisdom, love, holiness, and righteousness. The outworking of the *imago Dei* in man is concretely demonstrated in Genesis 2 when man exercises his dominion over all other creatures[90] and over the elements.

That man does not come from, nor develop from, any previously created being is evident in the majestic way both Genesis 1 and 2 present God's creation. Man alone is the creature of address in Genesis 2. In Genesis 1 the writer indicates that special deliberation is held in the heavenly council before God's greatest creation occurs. The absolute "otherness" of man from the animal creation could not be stressed more strongly than is done in Genesis 2:18–20; man has no companionship among the animals. Man, in God's creation, is *sui generis*. He alone bears the divine image and shares a personal relationship with the Creator; he alone requires the "building" of a mate like him.[91] He is enabled to fulfill the divine image by means of living out through personality (all aspects physical and nonphysical) his essential nature as God's image; he is to be a being of love, wisdom, righteousness, and holiness in order to be a true child of God.[92]

Man is, according to Genesis 1 and 2, not a product of the forces of nature, but a creation of God who acts in order to bring man into existence. Man indeed shares on one level physical and psychical life with the animal creation,[93] but his uniqueness also contributes to his true essence. Man was formed from the *dust* of the ground (Gen. 2:7) and he became a "living being" just as the animals did. God's breathing into man demonstrates God's intimate care for His unique creature made in His image. The breath of life is merely a way of saying that man was animated by God's impartation of breath. The Hebrew word *nismāh* does not denote some divine element that God imparted to Adam. God did not impregnate an already living being with divine elements in order to make man. Nowhere is "dust" used to indicate a previously living being.[94]

The fact that man shares some physical characteristics with certain primates is totally irrelevant (but true according to Genesis 2) as to his essential nature.[95] Man is God's image and God is a spirit. And because man was glorious and his nature so blessed, his fall was so tragic.

In the New Testament doctrine of man and man's restoration, the concept of the *imago Dei* and its essence becomes extremely important. Moreover, it is clear, as James Orr noted long ago, that the fact that man was in the *imago Dei* is the presupposition for the incarnation of God *in His own image*.[96]

6. The intrinsic moral nature of Old Testament cosmology The general fact of the value significance of God's created cosmos is found throughout Genesis 1. The nature of God's creation *before the fall* should be carefully compared to the nonbiblical ideas of original creation. The difference is to be found in kind, not in degree. The two concepts of original creation on the moral level are totally irreconcilable. The revelation account in Genesis stands out like a jewel among pebbles. In this section we will talk about the moral quality of the Old Testament cosmology as it is pictured and delineated in the original creation.

Nothing could be more clear than that a good Creator has created a good cosmos. The Genesis 1 account stresses this fact (Gen. 1:10, 12, 18, 21, 26, 31). Genesis 1:31 emphasizes that it was *very good (tov me'od)*. The Hebrew word *tov* is used here in a comprehensive sense,[97] but clearly the moral and religious dimensions of the word are paramount. God created no evil in any way in His created work. This sublime teaching removes God from any blame for the presence of evil in the cosmos.[98] It clearly teaches that the material world is not in itself evil, but good; capable of knowing its Creator. To the biblical writer the impersonal nature of God's creation was not as strong as it is with us, with our modern impersonal scientific view of the cosmos. The cosmos bore the imprint of the word of a personal Creator.[99]

Man, the moral being, displays his nature in three ways: (1) in his relationship to the creation, (2) in his relationship to his fellow man, and (3) in his relationship to his Creator. These are not mutually exclusive; one affects the other. Man's relationship to the rest of creation is stated. He has dominion over all things but he is to care for all things as a worthy steward, as one standing in God's place. He may use the created world for his sustenance, but not abuse it. He is to recognize his Creator as his God and recognize His word as a final and supreme guide for his conduct.

From the beginning the essential moral nature of man is indicated by God's instructions to man. Hence, man's moral nature is a vital part of the *imago Dei*.[100] There are right actions and bad actions; the ultimate source for knowing the right is God's will, informed by His infinite and infallible wisdom as to the nature, goal, and purpose of His cosmos. Man, being finite, needs directives; he cannot grasp all of God's creation. The essence of morality for man was to act in a "right relationship" to God and the cosmos as a free moral agent.

The amazing truth about Genesis 1 and 2 is the insight it gives about the essential moral nature of creation.[101] Everything centers around good and evil (response or lack of response to the Creator's word). The future of creation hangs on man's fulfilling his moral, religious, and theological purpose—obedience to and correct relationship to his Maker.[102] The creation finds its goal in the destiny of man (cf. Rom. 8:19–25). The most devastating tragedy conceivable for the "good" cosmos was that the moral-religious quality of it (including its nature and relationship to God) be disrupted—and this is precisely what happened. The essential religious, theocentric, moral fiber of the creation was corrupted. As to the original creation, God is its perfect Creator; as to the restoration and redemption of that original creation, He becomes its new Creator or, as more commonly termed, its Redeemer. God's new creation, as we shall see, is very much related in nature, purpose, and goal to His first creation. Many of the original conditions present in the original creation are present again in the new creation. This will become evident when the New Testament materials are discussed.

The inability of atheistic evolution to provide a satisfactory explanation of the intrinsic moral nature of man is a serious shortcoming. The biblical model of a good creation, with man bearing God's image, is wholly capable of providing to the believer a satisfactory explanation of the moral quality of life, both metaphysically and relationally. This dimension of the cosmology in Genesis is an essential element in helping one form a proper and satisfactory Christian perspective of "men and things." It is vital for a true understanding of biblical cosmology in the Old Testament (and elsewhere) that one see the pertinence with which these accounts speak to the natural sciences but also, and perhaps more importantly, as the "battle for man" is being waged, to all of the humanities—the whole sphere of life.

7. The polemical nature of Old Testament cosmology As has been already stated, the truths of Genesis 1 and 2 and other Old Testament Scripture regarding creation constitute the polemic of these narratives. A sufficient presentation of truth amid error is adequate polemic in itself. However, it is also true that the Genesis account does have the task of refuting error as it presents the truth. The polemic of Genesis is as relevant today *mutatis mutandis* as it was when it was first written. An examination of a few items at random in the account will perhaps be sufficient to demonstrate how Genesis served (and still serves) as a piece of polemical writing. Of course Genesis 1 and 2 is not a mere piece of polemical writing, but one function of its presentation is to vindicate truth over against untruth.[103] A few of these points have been made incidentally already.[104]

The God of the Bible has no beginning. This is a simple and clear truth. Although it was unique among the religions of the Ancient Near East, the superiority of this concept has become common among most people today. For the Sumerians, Akkadians, and Assyrians there were many gods; for Israel one God, who had no beginning. The many features of nature caused the natural religions of the various Ancient Near Eastern nations to conceive of a multiplicity of divisions among their gods, ascribing various functions and different manifestations to certain gods. For Israel God was a *unity* (Deut. 6:4). He, and He alone, functioned as God throughout the cosmos. The various manifestations of nature were not different aspects of God.

The existence of light was an enigma to many of the ancient people, as it still is to modern science. It was commonplace among the Babylonians to hold that light dwells with the gods. Light, the opposite of darkness, was an entity of great power and wisdom. Some gods were conceived of as light or dwelling in the light. Light emanates from the gods, and the tendency to worship light itself, especially in the form of the sun disc, was always present. As Heidel has pointed out, Marduk was a solar deity, and light was thought to proceed from him as an attribute.[105] In the biblical account, light is God's creation, not an attribute of the Creator.[106] Today modern science conceives of light as possibly the basic "given" of the universe, and, of course, considers light as a puzzling combination of energy and matter. Light, an awesome concept in the Ancient Near East and a puzzling entity in the modern world, was, whatever its essence, created by God. It is a created thing, and as such the biblical God has total control of it.[107]

The Babylonians and numerous other ancient people worshiped the sun and the moon. These "gods" were given names. *Shamash* was the Ancient Near Eastern name of both the sun god and the physical orb. The biblical narrative presents these bodies as simply created entities of the all-powerful God. They are not personified or divinized and are not to be worshiped. They have their purposes: to mark our times and seasons of the year and to give light on the earth. The biblical writer does not even use the technical names for these heavenly bodies, but simply calls them the greater and the lesser lights, a procedure that a votary of Shamash would not have appreciated. The stars were astral deities of the Babylonians and other peoples, with names; the biblical writer laconically states that God "made the stars also." In a few words Scripture disavows astrology.

Many ancient cosmologies record the existence of one or more original chaos monsters[108] with whom the gods fought in order to bring about order, but Genesis merely reports, "And God created the great sea monsters" (Gen. 1:26-27). Even this awesome creature was only a creation of God. As Kidner has pointed out, in God's kingdom there may be "rebels, but no rivals."[109]

The power of reproduction was a mystery to ancient man, and fertility cults that involved the worship of both male and female genital organs and that engaged in debauchery in its rituals were widespread. Canaan was permeated by fertility cults. But the gift of fertility, of reproduction, was no mysterious power to be worshiped. It was a gift the Creator bestowed on man. Israel was to worship the Giver of the gift, not the gift (Gen. 1:22, 28).

The high position of man in Genesis and his bearing of the divine image certainly effectively contested the deplorable views of man held in pagan cultures. In Genesis 1 the concept of the *imago Dei* is democratized and all men and women are made in

His image.[110] The fact that woman shares in the divine image is unique among the Ancient Near Eastern creation materials as far as I am aware (Gen. 1:26–27). Even the serpent in Genesis 3 is a created creature and not a being outside of the pale of God's creative activity.[111] The clear way in which the biblical writer condemns bestiality in Genesis 2 and polytheism hardly needs comment.

Indeed Genesis 1 and 2 are both statements of truth and, hence, a powerful polemic for the Hebrew and Christian view of cosmology.

8. Some philosophical implications of Old Testament cosmology Several philosophical implications of the cosmology of the Old Testament have already been mentioned. A few summary statements can be given here by way of review and a few additional points considered.

Perhaps the most vexing problem of philosophy is the problem of evil. The Genesis perspective on creation speaks to this issue both directly and indirectly. The biblical account is unequivocal in affirming the fact that the original creation was "very good." Wherever evil originated, it did not arise as a necessary ingredient of God's perfect cosmos. The Creator is cleared in these accounts from any blame for evil. The material universe is not evil, but good in its original state. This truth is still effective even now (Rom. 14:14). The ultimate foundation of all things is God (see below for the New Testament way of stating this, pp. 171–74) and God is a morally responsible being, as is clearly implied and affirmed by the Old Testament writer. The present state of the cosmos was not the original state. There was no intrinsic evil; the environment itself in which man was placed was perfect, and man was capable of obeying his Creator,[112] but he was endowed with free will. Given man's early condition and environment, his decision to disobey was indeed a free decision of his will, not enforced in any way according to the biblical text.[113] That God created a free moral person was considered good by the inspired biblical writer, whatever the outcome.

Therefore, given the original state of creation, it is clear that death, sickness, pain, and disorders in both the personal and natural world are intruders into God's original creation and not intrinsic or natural to it. This is in strong disagreement with both the Ancient Near Eastern views of the topics and modern man's nonbiblical beliefs, in which evil is "natural." In the new creation these intruders are removed (Isa. 65:17; see below for New Testament materials). Moreover, man's wrong moral decision caused the entry of these evils into the personal life and environment of man. Even the creature who tempted man was depicted by the biblical writer as a creature of God.[114] However, given the fact that God has created all things good, it seems to be clear that evil arose originally in one of God's creatures endowed with free will.[115] In the conception of God's original creation, all things are implicated in failure and frustration in some way (Gen. 3:8–24).

The present state of the creation reflects the condition of what is related in Genesis 3. The relationship between man and God, man and the cosmos, and the very being of the created natural order (Gen. 3:8–24), including man's nature (Gen. 3:22–24; 5:6; 8:21; Jer. 17:19), are depicted in Genesis 3, but only *after* establishing the original perfect creation of Genesis 1 and 2.

God does not do things without a purpose, and that there was a purpose and goal in His creation is clear if only from the fact that after the Fall its goal and purpose is being reestablished through God's redemptive activities. Science has little if anything to say about the goal and purpose of creation. Genesis has this concern as a major motif. The original creation enjoyed a relationship and standing before the Creator not now evident to man, but made clear by the biblical writer.

The account of creation by word (Gr. *logos;* Heb. *dabar*) is important in establishing at least the following: A triangular relationship is created and the possibility of God and man's relating to one another and both relating appropriately to the cosmos is evident. All of God's creation bears the stamp of God's creative word; hence, it is orderly and capable of being understood. Man, who is commanded to have dominion over all things, is endowed with the ability to understand creation because he is made in the divine image. He is capable of grasping and administering God's logos creation. Through the *imago Dei* he is a creature who not only relates to the cosmos as its lord, but also to God as the One who made him in His image. Man has the possibility of communion with God. His essential nature is fulfilled when he is like his God (holy, loving, righteous, wise).

Of no small importance is the Old Testament's clear affirmation of a real world, an objective creation apart from God Himself. In philosophical terminology this view of the cosmos is dualistic.[116] There is a cosmos over which man can exercise dominion, and natural science is a possibility because there is an objective world created by God to measure, touch, and explore. Genesis 1 clearly lays the groundwork for the possibility of natural science. The *imago Dei* of man makes it a reality. From a biblical perspective modern science should be a tool through which man exercies his dominion over the cosmos. But to exercise dominion correctly man must exercise his original perfect nature concomitantly—that is, he needs to administer all things lovingly, wisely, righteously, and in holiness.

It is imperative that responsible Christian scholars discern the relevance of Genesis 1 and 2 not only to the natural sciences but also, in the present *Zeitgeist* (spirit of the times), to the humanities. Only a meticulous reading of the profound biblical documents can give this result.

9. The Old Testament concept of the new creation A Christian cosmology must also deal with God's promised new heaven and new earth. This creative work indeed is equal to and surpasses the original work of creation. The whole biblical scheme of cosmology might have a sequence such as the following: (1) the original creation with God's original purposes (OT), (2) the failure and fall of the original creation (OT), (3) the demise of the old creation since God's goals and purposes were temporarily thwarted (OT), (4) the promise of a new creation with the regaining of God's original purposes (OT), (5) the beginning realization of the new creation (NT), and (6) the full realization of the goals and purposes of God in the completed new heaven and new earth (NT).[117] Eschatology becomes a dominant theme in the prophets along with the new creation because there is an organic connection between eschatology and creation. Eschatology is the fulfillment of God's goals and purposes for His creation both old and new, as reward or judgment (Isa. 54:21-22). The old order will be dissolved, but a new one will be established (Isa. 41:20; Jer. 31:22, 31; Ezek. 11:19; 18:31; 36:26).

The Hebrew term *bara* clusters in the Bible in Genesis 1-2 and in Isaiah. It is this word that indicates the creation of the new heaven and new earth. The feature of this creation will be righteousness (cf. 2 Peter 3:13).

The ex nihilo aspect of this new heaven and new earth is evident, for all the former things pass away while God creates (*bara*) new things. The ex nihilo nature of the new heaven and earth confirm that the first creation was considered to have been created ex nihilo, for it is on the fact of God's former creative activity (*bara* is used in Isa. 40:26, 28; 42:5; 43:1, 7, 15; 45:8, 12, 19) in the creation of the first heavens and earth that the new creation is predicated. This new creation entails a new covenant and a new man to enter into that covenant, as well as to inhabit the new creation (Jer. 31:22, 31; Ezek. 11:19; 18:31; 36:26). It is clear in all of this that God's original purposes will yet be accomplished—on the one hand, by renewal of some aspects of the old creation and, on the other hand, by the creation of totally new things.

It is worth noting that the cosmology of the new creation is not open to the investigation of natural science. It may be open to some searching by the humanities (sociology, psychology, anthropology), for only the beginning of the new creation is now evident. Eschatology, or, much better, God's teleology, will perfect all things.

10. Some observations on science and Old Testament cosmology Perhaps something can be said about the physical and space-time aspects of Genesis 1 and 2. The issue of science and Genesis became a major issue after Wesley's biblical commentaries, but the challenge of modern science for our generation cannot go unanswered. A few general observations are offered here.

First of all it is most important to let the biblical writer speak. If this is done, it is evident that he did not major in minors, such as how long the original "day" was as depicted in Genesis[118] or the exact date of creation.[119] Hence a proper summary of Genesis 1–2 should stress the themes that the writer of Genesis stresses. To debate the length of the days in Genesis is *not unimportant* but it often engenders strife, not edification (1 Tim. 1:4), and causes more important items to go unexamined. Second, one must ask what scientific picture of the universe is to be used when discussion takes place. The "Big Bang" theory of the origin of the universe is presently favored by most scientists.[120] However, it could go into oblivion overnight. Science is in a state of flux. To my knowledge no definitive explanation of creation outside of the Bible is available. There is much *truth,* and scientific truth does help illuminate a few points in Genesis, and vice versa. However, any view of cosmology that does not do justice to the major motifs and affirmations of Genesis cannot be acceptable.

Only if man were to attain a definitive explanation of the cosmos *and* a perfect exegesis of Genesis could a legitimate comparison be made between the two. The Christian is confident that they would be in agreement at every point where they touch base. However, no perfect explanation is at hand, and no exegete is errorless.[121] Hence, the writer of Hebrews calls us all to awe and humility before Genesis 1 and 2 (Heb. 11:3), and 2 Peter 3:13 reminds us to remember the Genesis record.

Kidner makes a penetrating observation about the scientific accounts of the universe: "The scientific account of the universe, realistic and indispensible as it is, overwhelms us with statistics that reduce our apparent significance to the vanishing point."[122] There is a distinct contrast between modern science's cosmology as opposed to the Genesis view in which God, man, and personal relationships are paramount and where morality and values are preeminent in the discussion.

Another point needs to be made in regard to the scientific views stated or implied in Genesis and the rest of the Old Testament. It is manifestly incorrect to hold as Speiser does that the ancient Hebrews succumbed to the pseudo-science of the Babylonians and accepted their views as valid depictions of some aspects of the universe.[123] As Payne has pointed out, there are no grotesque "scientific" ideas of the Ancient Near East included in Genesis 1 and 2.[124] By noting the Ancient Near Eastern survey offered above, the reader can discern the weight of truth in Payne's statement.

Many interesting and *helpful* articles and books are available for those who care to pursue the ongoing consideration of Genesis in the light of modern science. Some relevant comments have been made on the historical significance of Genesis 1 and 2 in section I. C. above.

E. Comparison and Contrast of ANE and Old Testament Accounts The tendency in the past has been for most scholars to delineate the similarities between Genesis 1 and 2 and the Ancient Near Eastern materials. This discussion has shown that the similarities are helpful if not taken too far. The likenesses tend to be on a more or less superficial level (but they are not unimportant). Kenneth A. Kitchen, a leading Egyptologist, has referred to the parallels and similarities between Genesis and pagan accounts of creation as constituting the "banalities" of creation.[125] This is overstating the case, but it is certain that the differences between the biblical accounts and the Ancient Near Eastern materials go to the core of the issue and concern essential cosmological concepts. Heidel and Speiser record the analogies that may be seen between Genesis and the Babylonian account of creation.[126]

We have noted many differences, and even the "similarities" highlight some basic differences (note especially items 1, 2, and 3 below) aside from what we have said about the creation of man and the monotheism of Genesis versus the polytheism of the nonbiblical accounts. A few contrasts are noted here in chart form for convenience. Many more could be added.

These issues could be multiplied, but the point is clear.

II. COSMOLOGY IN THE INTERTESTAMENTAL LITERATURE: BRIEF OVERVIEW

A. The Literature

The intertestamental literature spanning the years from ca. 300 B.C. to the New Testament era is the production of various factors that were shaping Judaism and forcing it to express itself.[127] The Old Testament remained the major source of information about the cosmos during these centuries; therefore, most of the cosmology of the Old Testament is affirmed.[128] However, various forces influenced the writers of this uninspired, pedestrian, non-canonical literature. The apocrypha, the pseudepigrapha, some Qumran writings, the Elephantine papyri, and other writings that stem from this period show various influences including Persian (Zoroastrian

---

ANE ACCOUNTS

1. Matter is first, eternal, uncreated.
2. Gods were created or generated.
3. "Creation," is the forming of preexistent matter.
4. Deity is polytheistic.
5. Matter (élan vital?) generates the gods.
6. "Creation" is imperfect.
7. Man is a lowly servant of little value.
8. Man is mortal, dies.
9. Creation is defiled by inherent evil.
10. The created order is worshiped.
11. There is little moral value.
12. The cosmos is not "good."

GENESIS ACCOUNTS

1. Matter is created.
2. God is uncreated, eternal.
3. Matter was called into existence and formed.
4. Deity is monotheistic.
5. The Spirit of God broods over created matter.
6. Creation is perfect.
7. Man was made in God's image and is of great value.
8. Man is potentially immortal, lives.
9. No evil was inherent in the creation.
10. The created order is to be used for sustenance.
11. Moral order is paramount.
12. All is "very good."

thought), Greek (which is especially strong), Roman, Babylonian, and Egyptian. The Jews were increasingly exposed to foreign religious doctrines and philosophies. But, as noted above, this influence was still *secondary* to the Old Testament itself, although at times the syncretistic phenomenon practically negates the uniqueness of the biblical material. There is little to state that is especially *de novo*, except for the Greek "way of philosophy" with its stress on rational thought about cosmology.[129] Certain concepts and tendencies can be mentioned, however, and will lead us into and illuminate the New Testament canonical literature.

In the apocryphal books the doctrine of creation ex nihilo is affirmed (2 Macc. 7:28),[130] as is creation by God's word (Sir. 43:26; W. Sol. 9:1). There is an unfortunate tendency for the writers to hypostasize certain Old Testament concepts, such as wisdom, along philosophical lines. Proverbs 8:30 speaks of wisdom through personification, but Wisdom of Solomon 7:22; 9:4, 9–10; and Enoch 42:1 turn wisdom into an entity separate from God, making wisdom a craftsman (*teknites*) alongside of God. Wisdom is not a mere attribute of God, but becomes an independent being. In some pseudepigraphal books the Torah is conceived of as the means by which the cosmos was created. This, of course, creates theological problems in regard to the unity and primal place of God.

God is referred to as the "Lord of spirits" numerous times in pseudepigraphal literature (e.g., Enoch 47:4; 61:11) and in certain Dead Sea Scroll writings (esp. Hymn of Thanksgiving 1:5–29). This coincides with a general tendency during this period to see God as transcendent in relationship to the creation, with many spirits serving as intermediaries between the creation and its Creator (cf. Enoch 60:11–24). In line with Greek rationalism there was a tendency to stress the natural law of the universe. In Enoch certain stars are punished because they strayed from their appointed courses. This is a concept discernible but not stressed in the Old Testament. There is a slight tendency to depersonalize the concept of God's constant providence and turn it into a natural law that keeps all things in order.

The purpose of creation was discussed by these writers and, based on the Old Testament, was said to have a twofold purpose: the cosmos is for the sake of man, and all things were created solely for God's glory (Gen. 1:26; Ps. 8; 2 Esds. 6:46; 2 Bar. 15:7).

B. The Connecting Link Between the Old Testament and the New Testament

The tendency of intertestamental literature to hypostasize certain elements of the Old Testament creation accounts is instructive, especially for understanding the significance of the New Testament concept of Christ as Creator, the personification of God's wisdom, word, law, and mediation. Wisdom of Solomon has several passages (1:7; 7:22, 26) declaring "wisdom" to be "that which holds things together," "an image of His goodness," "eternal," and the "fashioner of all things." In Sirach 43:26 God's word holds all together and wisdom is eternal (24:9). *The New Testament consummates this search for the key to creation.* Also, in Christ the goal and purpose of God's creation is clearly recognized. These intertestamental attempts to draw out the *sensus plenior* (the fuller meaning) of Old Testament cosmological concepts are failures, for creation is a secret hidden from man. It must be accepted and "understood" from the perspective of faith. Without divine revelation to aid man he would never arrive at the New Testament's amazing completion of the Old Testament cosmology, which is summed up in Christ.

In respect to the creation of man the intertestamental literature has a few comments. The Wisdom of Solomon states that God made man "in the image of His own eternity" (2:23); futhermore He made man immortal in righteousness, in a righteous environment (1:13-15). God did not make death. Man's nature now is subject to death because of the Devil (2:24). Man's purposes are to be wise, righteous, loving (merciful), and holy (9:1-3). Sirach 17:3 affirms that man was appropriately clothed in strength and made in the divine image, but is also dust (33:10-11). These are basically observations based on the Old Testament's affirmation of man's creation, but Wisdom of Solomon tends to have a philosophical ring[131] to it not present in Genesis, and man's moral failure and degeneration is not sufficiently affirmed.

One must enter the world of the New Testament before one is able to encounter a satisfactory teleological commentary and development of Old Testament cosmology.

III. COSMOLOGY IN THE NEW TESTAMENT

It is true that the New Testament affirms Old Testament cosmology and in this way does not affirm a new doctrine of creation. However, it is also true that without the New Testament's development of Old Testament cosmology in the light of the Christ-event we would still be producing speculations about the Old Testament's cosmology that are now not necessary because of the revelatory account in the New Testament. Here we see the *sensus plenior* of the Old Testament developed in an authoritative way.

A. Pagan Cosmology Unchanged in Essence

In the New Testament era, which we might set at ca. 40 B.C.-A.D. 100, the influence of pagan religious views on the biblical writers was undoubtedly great; however, these writers resisted this influence and penned the amazing statements about origins that we find in their writings. Pagan cosmology had not changed *in essence,* although it had grown more sophisticated, and in many countries a tendency toward unifying the ancient views of the gods was evident.[132] Certainly the Grecian philosophical movement, which peaked in the writings and teachings of Aristotle and Plato, was a revolutionary emphasis. Nature became an impersonal entity apart from the gods and operated by natural law to some extent.[133] The use of reason was emphasized, and many writers such as Philo and Josephus attempted to reconcile the teachings of the Old Testament with Greek philosophical schools.[134] Aristotle's unmoved Mover and Plato's World-Soul or Creator Artisan[135] replaced the primeval forces (élan vital) of the older Ancient Near Eastern cosmological thought. However, Plato and Aristotle did not deny the gods, but for these philosophers "the existence of the world from eternity is a basic presupposition" as is noted by Walther Eichrodt.[136] The unaided reason and/or emotions of man did not attain, even by New Testament times, a view of cosmology that did not reflect the *basic* principles noted above in Ancient Near Eastern cosmology.

The Epicureans and the Stoics (Acts 17:16-33) were typical of the type of reform that the new philosophers were creating. The Epicureans attributed everything to the chance combination of atoms, and the Stoics, thoroughly pantheistic, coined a universal concept that they called the logos, which was wholly impersonal and served as an impersonal world principle.[137]

Philo of Alexandria developed a logos concept that adumbrated some of the New Testament affirmations about Christ, the Logos of God,[138] and Plato required that the cosmos be rational (*logikos*). However, as will be noted, the authentic background for the New Testament *logos* is the Old Testament. It is the New Testament that gives an inspired development and interpretation of the Old Testament "word" (*logos*) of creation.

The concept of wisdom (Prov. 8) is developed and hypostasized and personified by the writer of Wisdom of Solomon (esp. 6-9), who teaches the cardinal virtues of Plato and the Stoics (8:2-16). The New Testament development of Proverbs 8 culminates instead in Christ.

The difference in kind between the pagan and biblical concepts of creation remain, even in New Testament times, a clear "dividing line between revelation and unrevealed religion."[139] In my opinion the New Testament succeeds in making more emphatic the dividing line between a revealed cosmology and a natural cosmology based on unaided speculation or philosophizing.

B. The New Testament Affirms Old Testament Cosmology

The New Testament is a monument to the truth contained in Genesis 1 and 2 and in other Old Testament affirmations on creation. Let me explain this briefly. God the Father is affirmed as the originator and creator of all things.[140] Creation ex nihilo is not only implied but clearly stated (Heb. 11:3; Rev. 14:7),[141] and creation by God's word is a leitmotif in the New Testament (2 Cor. 4:6; Heb. 11:3; 2 Peter 3:5). The fact that the original creation was good is implied in Romans 5:12-21 and affirmed in 1 Timothy 4:3-4. God is both distinct from His creation in His transcendence and immanent in it (Acts 18:18; Col. 1:17). But by far the major theme of the original creation is again man *made in the image of God*. This thought is expressed in various ways in the New Testament (see Matt. 19:4; Mark 10:6; Acts 17:25-28; 1 Cor. 11:7; James 3:9).

The historical factual nature of the events in Genesis 1 and 2 is affirmed, for numerous concepts found in those verses are quoted or alluded to; for example, Adam is a historical figure (Matt. 19:4; Rom. 5:12ff.; 1 Cor. 11:9; 15:45, 47; 2 Cor. 4:6; 1 Tim. 2:12; 4:3-4). Romans 5:12ff. also declares that the present state of affairs in regard to the cosmos has occurred just as Genesis 3 indicates. The fall was a fact in history. Indeed, the answer to man's dilemma and the dilemma of the cosmos (Rom. 8:28ff.) is predicated on the fact that Genesis 1-3 is true in the picture it presents of the original creation and its subsequent fall. The moral dimension of creation is recognized in the New Testament as it was in the Old Testament, for the moral failure in Genesis 3 that corrupts the original creation is recognized as the cause that produced the present tragic state of affairs. As we will see, the way out of this degenerated cosmos is by way of reversing some of the events in Genesis, and, more precisely, the original disobedience of the first man must be overcome before a regeneration of man, indeed, of all things, can begin. Man in the New Testament, as in the Old Testament, becomes the focal point of God's concern from the side of creation, especially the New Man, Christ, and the new man in Christ. As the first man's decision determined all, so the second Adam's decision determines all. The key to New Testament cosmology can be summed up in two words—Jesus Christ.[142] From the divine side, the focal point in the New Testament becomes the kingdom of God—all to His glory in the end, the goal of the original creation.

C. The New Testament Contribution to Cosmology

The unique event that determines the revelation of the New Testament in the area of cosmology is the unfolding of the significance of Christ for all things. He is revealed as creation's source, creator (Word), Lord, preserver, redeemer, goal, and purpose—all creation, in a word, is summed up in Him. The Christian doctrine of creation is a mystery revealed to us by God in the Scriptures—a naturalistic scientific method cannot uncover it. The inspired and revelatory nature of the Bible is nowhere more clear than is this area, for no human reason or wisdom could have discovered or explicated the intimate relationship that in fact exists between Christ and the cosmos.

Christ, as depicted in the New Testament, is indeed the creator and source of all things. John's striking words (John

1:1-4) "In the beginning was the Word" (John 1:1) are clearly parallel to Genesis "In the beginning." However, the subject of John's sentence is none other than Jesus Christ, the Word of God (John 1:14), who took on flesh and blood. This beginning in John's Gospel predates the beginning of Genesis 1:1, which declares the inception of the cosmos. John 1:1 refers to an absolute beginning to which no time speculations are relevant. "The Word was God" (John 1:1) is a clear affirmation of the fact that God and the Word are one in essence.

The relevance of the Old Testament background is evident, for in some way the word of God spoken of in Genesis 1 is related in an intimate way to the Word of the New Testament. The point is clear. For John, Jesus Christ was the creative Word of God, and in a clear sense the Creator of all things (John 1:10). Is anything, therefore, too hard for the Lord who has created all things? Hebrews 11:3 and 2 Peter 3:5 affirm the concept of word creation, but John gives us the ultimate insight into the nature of that Word. It not only bore the marks of being personal, but was in fact Jesus Christ in His preincarnate state. As the Old Testament taught that God was before all things, so do these verses and others (John 17:5, 24) teach that Christ, the Word, was before all things. Colossians 1:16-17 also delineates the "cosmic Christ" as the Creator of all things (also Rom. 11:36).[143]

With Christ the new heavens and the new earth, which includes the new man, are beginning to be realized. Hence, the Holy Spirit, the generative power of God in the Old Testament, has now set the creative regenerative processes in order. Indeed the Holy Spirit is, along with Christ, the agent of the new order of things. In the incarnation (Matt. 1:18, 21) and supremely in the resurrection of Christ (Rom. 1:4), the shift from God's great creative acts in the first creation to the new creation through Christ and the Spirit is effected. The new cosmos is in process of actualization now.[144]

Christ is designated as the one *through* whom all things were made (John 1:3; RSV, NIV) and apart from (without) whom nothing came to be (John 1:3). The Christian, born of the Spirit, is a creation of the Creator, Christ. In Revelation 3:14 Christ is explicitly referred to as the beginning of God's creation in the sense that He is the *principle* and *source* of all things (also John 1:3; Col. 1:15, 18 [less clearly its source]).

Christ is not only the above, but is indeed the Lord of all. All things are subservient to Him and He rules over all with all authority (1 Cor. 8:6; Col. 1:15, 17-18). The corresponding position of God in the Old Testament is evident and more correspondences are forthcoming. Christ is also the preserver of all things (Col. 1:17) in the sense that in Him all things "hold together" (*synestēken*). That the perspective of the Scriptures is different from that of natural science is manifest. The personal care of Christ, the Creator, is pronounced here, and His immanence is understood in His work as preserver *in this instance*. In Hebrews 1:3 it is stated that Christ is "sustaining [*pherōn*] all things by his powerful word." The evident value of the concept of the "word of God" in creation is manifest, for in His divine wisdom He has constituted His universe in such a way that His word (Word) is the preserving and ordering element of the cosmos. The implication of this for understanding the cosmos is evident (see above, pp. 164-66). The fact that in Christ we find our wisdom, understanding, and the meaning of all things (He is truth) becomes a logical corollary to His place in the cosmos.

The fact that Christ is the Redeemer of creation hardly needs emphasizing, but the point is clear in Colossian 1:20. This concept is closely related to the new creation and will be discussed below.

In the Old Testament discussion of cosmology we noted that from Genesis 1-2 it was clear that God's goal and purpose in creation was to create a people after His own image. In the New Testament this is explicit, and Christ is the One in whom, by whom, and through whom God's purposes are realized. The original creation's purposes are effected in Him—all creation is summed up in Him: "He made known to us the mystery of His will, according to His kind intention which he purposed in Him with a view to an administration suitable to the fulness of the times, *that is,* the summing up of all things in Christ" (Eph. 1:9-10).[145] Ephesians 1:5 is more explicit as to God's goal for humankind: "to be adopted as his sons through Jesus Christ." Those who become sons of God will become so through God's predestined method —adoption as children through Christ. Colossians 1:16 notes that all things are "for him," and Colossians 1:20 notes again that all things will find their reconciliation *to* Him and also *through* Him.

The development of the concept of wisdom found in Proverbs 8:22-36 by Wisdom of Solomon was noted. Proverbs clearly identifies wisdom in a personal way and personifies it as God's master workman in creation (Prov. 8:30).[146] Christ is the One who becomes the wisdom of God in the New Testament, and His part in creation is evident (1 Cor. 1:24, 30; Col. 2:3). Christ, the Creator, created with all the wisdom of God. That Christ is the wisdom of God is important to note, especially in the new creation when man is restored and created anew in God's image.

Certainly the concern of biblical cosmology is not with the nature of molecules and the physical essence of things, but with that dimension of cosmology that will not pass away but will be summed up in Christ. The moral structure and matrix of the cosmos is, according to the Bible, its most essential feature, which, when out of order, subjects the entire creation to futility. Thus Christ restores and redeems the cosmos on the vital level. And when this is accomplished fully, then Romans 8:28-30 will become a complete reality.

D. The New Creation (Cosmology) of the New Testament

1. Its basic features In the preceding Old Testament section a brief discussion was given concerning God's drastic solution to the problem of His fallen creation. There it was noted that such prophets as Isaiah, Jeremiah, and Ezekiel clearly saw the failure of man before God, the consequent pollution of the present heaven and earth, and God's determination to create a new heaven and a new earth (e.g., Isa. 63:17). These themes are picked up in the New Testament and fulfilled. Their fulfillment is effected through the Christ-event, which includes His incarnation, resurrection, and restoration of all things (Col. 1:20). No Christian cosmology would be complete without indicating what Scripture says about the new cosmos that He will make, for the present cosmos will be "restored" and "pass away," while a qualitatively new cosmos will appear. In the process Christ is the connecting link between creation and consummation. The only adequate way of ascribing these events is to say as Revelation 21:5 says, "He who was seated on the throne said, 'I am making everything new!'" This is a clear echo of the words of the One who made all things in the beginning and of the One through whom all things come (John 1:3).

In regard to the new creation, as was the case with the first creation, the how of this new creative work of God is not stressed, except that it is created (*ktizo*)[147] in, by, through, and for Him, and that its goal and purpose is the glory of God through the Son (Rev. 22:15).

The new heavens and new earth are alluded to by Christ as "my Father's kingdom" and "the kingdom of God" (Matt. 26:29; Mark 14:25). The major goal of God in the new heavens and new earth is the revealing of the "sons of God" (Rom. 8:19), but also involved in this will be the fact that "the creation itself also will be set free from its slavery to corruption into the freedom of the glory of the children of God" (Rom. 8:21). The new creation *has begun* in the renewal of man in the "image of God" in righteousness and true holiness (2 Cor. 3:18; Eph. 4:24; Col. 3:10) by means of his being in Christ who is the "express image" of God (Heb. 1:3; cf. 2 Cor. 4:4; Col. 3:10) and the perfect example of Man who is righteous, holy, loving, and wise.[148] The key to the renewal of this creation and the creation of the new man is made possible through Christ's *obedience,* a moral action (Rom. 5:18–21; 1 Cor. 15:45-50). Through Christ's moral action the moral decline of this creation has been potentially reversed. Man can be a new creation now.[149] This has much to say about the purpose, nature, and goal of the new heavens and earth.

The moral quality of the new heavens and new earth is emphasized; 2 Peter 3:13 indicates that it is "a place in which righteousness dwells" (as opposed to the old creation after the Fall, where wickedness dwells [Gen. 6:5-6; 8:21; Jer. 7:12; 17:9]). It is imperishable and not subject to corruption (1 Cor. 15:50). No evil or wickedness will enter it *again* (Rev. 21:27; 22:15). Man, as noted above, will be and is being created anew as an appropriate inhabitant (2 Cor. 5:17; Gal. 6:15; Eph. 2:15; 4:24). The nature of the new heavens and new earth and their inhabitants can only be described as a totally new creation by *God through Christ* (Rev. 21:1ff.; 22:1ff.).

2. Cosmology and eschatology Cosmology and eschatology are closely connected in the Scriptures, for the final description of the new heaven and new earth is reminiscent of the original perfect creation by the Creator. The difficulty of describing events that are not presently observable, such as original creation and the final consummation effected in the new heavens and new earth, is evident. How does one describe such unique events? He does so biblically through revelation and inspiration on the divine side and by the necessary use of rich symbolic language from the human author's standpoint, but in any case he uses language that indicates the true nature of things.

Christ is the new and perfect Adam, His environment is perfect and His relationship to God and His fellow man is ideal (Rev. 21; 22:1). The appearance of "a river of water of life" (Rev. 22:1) and the reappearance of the tree of life (22:2) are clear allusions to language in Genesis. The likenesses are there, but differences are evident in that the new heaven and new earth are of an imperishable nature, as is man's spiritual body. No night is there and the natural luminaries are not necessary any longer (Rev. 22:1–5). *Eschatology* is an unfortunate term used to describe God's activity in bringing all things to their proper fulfillment (*telos*). *Teleology* would be a better term, as it treats the goal and purpose of things and would better describe the true nature of what occurs in the end. The teleology or goals and purposes inherent in God's original perfect creation are effected by His sovereign activity in conjunction with man as a free moral agent. Christian cosmology is thoroughly teleological. The "good" of the old creation finds itself fulfilled and improved in the new heavens and new earth. The wicked features of the fallen creation are also brought to their end (*telos*); their proper goal is assigned by the Creator.

The *nature* of the new heavens and new earth is not entirely susceptible to the investigation of science or other spheres of human endeavor (1 Cor. 2:9, a quote of fulfillment from Isa. 64:4; 65:17), "*but God has revealed it to us by his Spirit*" (1 Cor. 2:10) in language that speaks to the whole man. And thereby we affirm that God is indeed presently successful and will continue to be successful in creating children of God who do not presently, but some day will, live in an environment that is "the home of righteousness."

IV. WHY A BIBLICAL VIEW OF COSMOLOGY?

A. Positive Clear Presentation of a Basic Cosmology Found in Scripture

Little effort needs to be spent in affirming the presence of a cosmology in broad outline in the Scriptures. The subject of creation permeates *all* of the biblical books in some way or the facts of creation are merely presupposed. The texture and nature of the cosmos as presented in Genesis 1-2 are the great presuppositions of the entire Bible. The Bible begins with God's creative acts and ends with the completion of the new creation. The doctrine of creation as presented in Genesis 1-2, with man created in God's image and all creation bearing His creative *logos* (word), *is the necessary postulate of the Christian faith.* Anything less will not do. The redemptive processes of God are predicated on His initial performance in creation (Isa. 40; Heb. 11:1-3; 2 Peter 3:13-15). The emphasis, therefore, that Scripture places on biblical cosmology is a sufficient reason for every serious Christian to come to an understanding about the Creator and His creation.

B. Biblical Cosmology Vital to a Christian World View

Man does *not* naturally understand the cosmos in any sense of knowing the reason for its existence. As was noted above, Kidner has pointed out the way in which man is dwarfed and reduced to the vanishing point by some scientific view of the cosmos. Jean Paul Sartre and Albert Camus have at least shown the fruitlessness and nihilism that faces man in our modern age, but they find no satisfactory explanation as to the purpose of all things. The *why* of things as well as the *thatness* of things is precisely the value and purpose of a Christian cosmology.

James Orr, writing in 1893, discussed the necessity for a Christian world view (*Weltanschauung*) that would satisfy the longings of men's *minds* and *hearts*. The need of a Christian world view is evident again ninety years later. However, Orr's sketch of a Christian world view is still relevant today, and his first three foundational points are in essence concerned with cosmology—the biblical view of creation:

I. First, then, the Christian view affirms the existence of a Personal, Ethical, Self-revealing God. It is there at the outset a system of Theism, and as such is opposed to all systems of Atheism, Agnosticism, Pantheism, or mere Deism.

II. The Christian view affirms the creation of the world by God, His immanent presence in it, His transcendence over it, and His holy and wise government of it for moral ends.

III. The Christian view affirms the spiritual nature and dignity of man—his creation in the Divine image, and destination to bear the likeness of God in a perfected relation of sonship.[150]

C. Failure of Nonbiblical Views to Explain the Cosmos in Essential Areas

The failure of nonbiblical world views lies in one area especially: the explanation of man. How man, the religious and moral being, is to be explained is still an enigma to atheistic evolutionism, as well as to theistic evolution. The answer to the enigma of man is penetrated greatly by the biblical cosmology. The most consistent particular failure of non-Christian views of man consists in their persistent attempts to explain man from a nonholistic point of view. Naturalism, rationalism, and idealism all fail in the end because of their attempt to explain mankind from a position that is too narrow. Naturalism is unable to account adequately for morality, mind, and spiritual dimensions of man, while rationalism denies the very reality of the material creation.[151] And perhaps an even greater failure of nonbiblical world views is their strong opposition to anything supernatural in the true biblical sense, even though man himself is aware of a supernatural dimension of his own life.

Man experiences himself as a complex multifaceted being and the Christian Scriptures present a model of man that both *describes* and *predicts* him accurately: it gives a realistic, but holistic picture of man as he came from the hands of the Creator and as he subsequently experienced himself after his fall. The *imago Dei* concept as the unique aspect of man from which righteousness, holiness, love, and wisdom become concrete realities through personhood adequately models man as the supreme, unique creature in the universe, while the concept that man on the physical side is merely another living being (*nephesh*) as are all other animals explains the physical affinities of man with the animal kingdom. The negative side of man, shown in rebellion, is sufficiently accounted for by the biblical model of humankind. Man's unique nature (essence) and existence is matched by his unique *origin,* which is recounted only in biblical cosmology.

However, nonbiblical views of the origin of the cosmos and of its nature fail to explain the phenomena that are apparent in the cosmos as man experiences it. The phenomenon of mind itself has long been an enigma to both scientists and philosophers. The biblical concept of word-creation, as presented above, offers some helpful insights.

God did not create arbitrarily. He created the material in the beginning that would be receptive to His further designs and goals: life, mind, personality, morality, religion, and more. Hence the logos-bearing matter of God's creation is not mere unresponsive matter, but is capable of being a vehicle for mind for all of the manifold dimensions of creation. As the *imago Dei* is the presupposition for the Incarnation, so the concept of Word Creation is the presupposition that helps explain the potential of created matter to bear, on the material side, mind, personality, and emotion—even the *imago Dei.*

D. Its Relevancy and Sufficiency

Some observations should be made of the relevancy and sufficiency of the biblical view of the cosmos. The biblical concept of cosmology has been seen to indicate clearly from a revelatory point of view why the cosmos is rational and comprehensible. It is so because it is a product of the Word of God Himself and bears the imprint of the creative spoken word. Biblical cosmology suggests that phenomena in various fields of research should be expected by the Christian investigator. The transcendent dimension of man discussed in nearly all philosophies is suggested by the *imago Dei* dimension of man. The uniqueness of man as the "religious animal" was predicted (thousands of years ago), although comparative religious study has established this as an *empirical* fact only during the past century. The sociological phenomenon of man as the "gregarious animal" is readily predicted on the basis of the biblical affirmation of man's nature as one that needs companionship. These observations could be extended into psychology and man's striving for perfection (Creation) while he is frustrated by guilt and anxiety (the Fall). In fact, there is no truer or more relevant and sufficient view of the cosmos than that which is recorded in the biblical concept of creation and subsequent recreation.

V. SOME WESLEYAN OBSERVATIONS ON COSMOLOGY

A. Introduction

To many people cosmology is an uninteresting topic to deal with, but to those who have attempted any systematic thinking about a Christian *Weltanschauung,* cosmology assumes a place of importance second only to the doctrine of God. However, the above study has shown the importance of a "right conception of creation." Purkiser has stated well some of the issues that make an encounter with Christian cosmology vital and experientally relevant:

> Cosmology sounds cold and forbidding, but it ceases to be an impersonal set of theories when it is brought under the purview of Christian theology. In a Christian perspective, cosmology becomes a consideration of God's relation to the world. The relation is personal and religious. In God's world— and that this is God's world is the basic

assumption of Christian cosmology—there are actually no impersonal or nonreligious problems.[152]

In addition to Purkiser's emphases it has been seen that cosmology is an investigation of the nature of the world in light of the fact that God created it and does relate to it. In addition to God's religious relation to the world, He has a vital moral relation to it and concern for it, and this indicates the essential moral essence of man and even of other cosmic entities, if not in themselves at least in the way they relate to other moral components of the cosmos. Just as Israel's absolutely unique revealed religion is moral in its essence,[153] so a true Christian cosmology should reflect and does reflect the basic moral nature of God's creation. Wesleyan theology must concern itself with this side of cosmology *without* losing sight of other issues that are pressing, such as scientific challenges to biblical creation. A correct view of God's political creation asserts that when the moral and religious level of the cosmos, its essential essence, is disrupted, a moral and religious solution to the problem is the correct response—precisely what is provided in the doctrine of the new creation.

It will be helpful now to look briefly in closing at some more representative examples of Wesleyan scholarship that treat the doctrine of cosmology.

B. Early Wesleyan Views on Cosmology

Frank Collier wrote a book in 1928 that he entitled *John Wesley Among the Scientists*.[154] This book helps put Wesley's concept of creation into perspective. Wesley himself wrote a natural philosophy. He entitled it *A Survey of the Wisdom of God in the Creation*.[155] The goal of this work is clearly moral and religious. Wesley wanted to see the Creator displayed in "the invisible things of God, his power, wisdom and goodness." Wesley saw man as the epitome of God's creation in a state of original perfect moral rectitude. This fact provided Wesley with the cutting edge of his definition of sin.[156] Wesley traced nearly all wrong conceptions of evil to a wrong conception about the nature of God's creation, for originally creation was good.[157] It could justly be said that the *purpose* of the biblical account of creation is to lead us to God.[158] Wesley thought of scientists as doing an honorable work and as interpreters of the divine language written in nature, including the moral dimension of man.[159]

Adam Clark's commentary[160] marked a distinct advance over Wesley by displaying a more scientific exegesis that was beginning to be informed and influenced by Ancient Near Eastern materials and sciences. However, he does not lose Wesley's religious and moral concerns as he applies himself to the exegesis process. He understands the original creation of light to refer to "caloric or latent heat" and argues for the translation of *rāqîa'* in Genesis 1:6 as expanse rather than firmament. Still he does not treat the Ancient Near Eastern materials sufficiently, but in his day this was only beginning to be a factor in the exegesis of the Old Testament. But most important he discerned the importance of the perfect state of God's original creation and man's original state of righteousness, holiness, and true knowledge.[161]

Finney offers little if anything on cosmology, but his concerns lay elsewhere, as was the case with Clark and Wesley, but he affirms the good teleology of the creation on the basis of a good God and His institution of moral government over it.[162]

All three of these men stress the *moral* and religious dimensions of creation, a fact that I have found to be basic and thoroughly biblical in comprehending God's cosmos. In all three, man is written large in cosmology, for he is the moral and religious being par excellence.

C. Contemporary Wesleyan Views on Cosmology

Wesleyan scholars have not produced any extensive investigation of cosmology. This is probably true for at least two reasons. First, Wesley's theology is centered around practical pastoral issues and, second, Wesleyan theology has been intensely concerned with man; it is, in a good sense, man-centered. As a result of these two situations, cosmology in its broader aspects has not been of major concern. Howard Snyder demonstrates the pastoral and ecclesiastical way Wesley used the concept of man in the *imago Dei*. And, of course, Snyder also sees this high conception of man and his renewal in the image of God as a vital part of church renewal.[163]

However, some of the contemporary writers on cosmology demonstrate their realization of the need of Christian cosmology to interact and take the best of modern science and Ancient Near Eastern studies. Ancient Near Eastern studies have demonstrated the uniqueness of biblical cosmology and hence help make concrete its revelatory and inspired nature.

Herbert Livingston effectively illuminates the biblical text for his readers through the use of Ancient Near Eastern literature both in his work on Genesis for the *Beacon Bible Commentary* and in his helpful book *The Pentateuch in Its Cultural Environment*. One might have hoped for a little more stress on the moral and religious nature of the cosmos, but for the Ancient Near Eastern contributions made one can only express appreciation.

Haines complements Livingston well through his interaction with concepts of modern science in his *Wesleyan Bible Commentary* on Genesis.[164] He effectively keeps the matters of most importance in the forefront of his discussions. His comments point out some vital philosophical and theological implications of Genesis. However, great caution must be taken in advocating a modern scientific theory, for even the big-bang theory is highly speculative and does not necessarily lead to conclusions consonant with biblical theism.

In the systematic field of theology a similar step forward has been taken in the way that the authors interact with modern science and Ancient Near Eastern materials.

H. Orton Wiley demonstrates great acumen in his theological insights into cosmology. He does, however, tend to spend too much time relating science and Christianity, even drawing in the outdated gap theory of Genesis 2 in order to harmonize natural science and Scripture. He could have set biblical cosmology more effectively in a historical background, but he does give it adequate interaction with contemporary teachings. He also draws out significant ethical and moral concerns with regard to the new heaven and the new earth. His discussion of the providence of God in His creation is excellent.[165]

D. Concluding Observations

Wesleyan theology has stressed the original righteousness (moral rectitude) of God's crowning creation—man. This moral dimension of God's supreme creation needs to be seen and stressed in cosmological studies as a whole; the intrinsic moral and religious value of all cosmic entities should be taken into account, for the aim of the new heaven and the new earth is a perfectly righteous setting. In the end when the kingdom of God is realized, it is the moral and religious dimension of the cosmos that will engulf every other dimension of existence as God creates a cosmos that is "a place in which righteousness dwells."

Wesleyan theology is in a position to respond effectively to the challenges of secular thought not only in the natural sciences and Ancient Near Eastern studies but also in the humanities. In the humanities it is the nature of man that is being debated; the "battle for man," who he is both individually and collectively, is the question of the day. For if he is not who and what Scripture declares he is, the teleology of the cosmos is shown to be vacuous. Indications of a Wesleyan answer to this type of challenge has been indicated above briefly. God's intention in creating man must be affirmed—a son, bearing the imprint of his Father, bearing His image in wisdom, righteousness, love, and holiness.

NOTES

[1] A few of the books that demonstrate the relevance of Ancient Near Eastern materials for illuminating and understanding the Old Testament are: D. Winton Thomas, ed., *Documents from Old Testament Times* (New York: Harper and Row, 1961); K. A. Kitchen, *Ancient Orient and Old Testament* (Downers Grove, Ill.: InterVarsity, 1966); idem, *The Bible in Its World* (Downers Grove, Ill.: InterVarsity, 1977); Walter Beyerlin, ed., *Near Eastern Religious Texts Relating to the Old Testament* (Philadelphia: Westminster, 1978); Edwin Yamauchi, *The Stones and the Scriptures* (Grand Rapids: Baker, 1972); Alexander Heidel, *The Babylonian Genesis*, 2nd ed. (Chicago: University of Chicago Press, 1961); Alexander Heidel, *The Gilgamesh Epic and Old Testament Parallels*, 2nd ed. (Chicago: University of Chicago Press, 1949); J. Barton Payne, ed., *New Perspectives on the Old Testament* (Waco: Word, 1970). Many other books could be listed, but the definitive work in this field is James B. Pritchard, ed., *Ancient Near Eastern Texts Relating to the Old Testament*, 3rd ed. with suppl. (Princeton, N.J.: Princeton University Press, 1969). This excellent work gives the reader a chance to read representative primary texts of literature from the Ancient Near East. This work will be referred to as *ANET*. Any adequate introduction to the Old Testament must deal with the extrabiblical materials stemming from the world of the Old Testament.

[2] William W. Hallo and William Kelly Simpson, *The Ancient Near East: A History* (New York: Harcourt Brace Jovanovich, 1971), pp. 163-72. These pages contain a brief but helpful summary of the literary genres of Mesopotamian texts. Pages 196-98 do the same for Egyptian materials; also see pp. 201-98 passim. Hallo and Simpson classify the Babylonian *Enuma Elish* as a myth recounting the "epic of creation" (p. 166). Kitchen, *Ancient Orient*, pp. 88-90, discusses the different aims of Genesis 1 and 2 and the Ancient Near Eastern texts. Note how the various ancient texts are classified as to genre in the introductory sections of *ANET*. See T.G.H. James, *An Introduction to Ancient Egypt* (New York: Farrar Straus Giroux, 1979), pp. 97-148, for a further discussion of types of ancient Egyptian texts. See also Kitchen, *Bible in Its World*, pp. 26-27. We will have to await the possible contribution that the Ebla texts can make in this area. Various unsubstantiated claims have already been presented. For some orientation to Ebla discoveries see Chaim Bermant and Michael Weitzman, *Ebla: A Revelation in Archaeology* (New York: Time Books, 1979), p. 164, passim. See also relevant issues of *The Biblical Archaeologist* and of *Biblical Archaeology Review*.

[3] The text may be found in *ANET*, pp. 60-72, 514. Portions of it dealing with creation are in Beyerlin, *Near Eastern Religious Texts*, pp. 80-84. The date of the text is generally placed either ca. 12th century B.C. (late dating) or ca. first quarter of the second millennium B.C. See Heidel's discussion also, *Babylonian Genesis*, pp. 13-14. Heidel agrees with the early dating.

[4] Beyerlin, *Near Eastern Religious Texts*, p. 81, says that in the *Enuma Elish* "emphasis was laid less on creation . . . than on Marduk's victory." See further Kitchen, *Ancient Orient*, p. 89, and Heidel, *Babylonian Genesis*, pp. 10-11.

[5] The reader is referred again to the English translations offered in *ANET* and Beyerlin, *Near Eastern Religious Texts*, for further reading in this area. The Sumerian literature and "The Atrahasis Epic" will be important. The following articles are excellent: J. Laessøe, "The Atrahasis Epic: A Babylonian History of Mankind," *Bior* 13 (1956): 90-102; W.G. Lambert, "A New Look at the Babylonian Background of Genesis," JTS, N.S. 16 (1965): 287-300; D. Hämmerly-Dupuy, "Some Observations on the Assyro-Babylonian and Sumerian Flood Stories," *AUSS* 6 (1968): 1-18; A. R. Millard, "A New Babylonian 'Genesis' Story," *Tyndale Bulletin* 18 (1967): 3-18; W. G. Lambert and A. R. Millard, *Atra-hasis: The Babylonian Story of the Flood* (Oxford, 1969).

[6] *ANET*, pp. 4-6; Beyerlin, *Near Eastern Religious Texts*, pp. 3-5. The extant text probably dates from 700 B.C. but may go back to ca. 2800 B.C., although scholarly estimates vary greatly. Beyerlin notes that the text presents a "polemically shaded theology," (p. 4). Some Egyptologists are especially concerned to assert the influence of Egyptian cosmology on biblical cosmology; e.g., see James Hoffmaier's paper on this topic (Wheaton College).

[7] James, *Ancient Egypt*, pp. 130, 146.

[8] The definitions of "myth" offered by scholars are many. Here the term is being used as a "story about the gods"; however, these stories are being used as propaganda. Samuel N. Kramer, ed., *Mythologies of the Ancient World* (Garden City, N.Y.: Doubleday, 1961), p. 40, says of the Heliopolitan, Egyptian cosmology, "I think that the genuine purpose of the . . . cosmogony . . . was to prove the divine character of the king and not to interpret the coming into existence of world and kingship."

[9] See notes 1 and 5 above for information about where to find these texts translated into English. Also use the bibliographies and footnotes found in the various works mentioned in notes 1 and 5. Nothing will take the place of reading these materials first hand in a good English translation. Some experts in these ancient texts are quite pessimistic about the possibility of presenting adequately the religious and cosmological view of these defunct civilizations. For instance, see A. Leo Oppenheim, *Ancient Mesopotamia* (Chicago: University of Chicago Press, 1964), pp. 7-30, 171-287. Other scholars are more

optimistic. See H.W.F. Saggs, *The Greatness That Was Babylon* (New York: Hawthorne, 1962), pp. 299-444.

[10]Mary K. Wakeman, *God's Battle With the Monster* (Leiden: Brill, 1973). This work provides an excellent study of biblical imagery and the purpose of the Ancient Near Eastern myths. See pp. 3-6 esp. For primary materials see: *ANET* pp. 3-5, 6, 8-9, 368, 417, 501-2, 515. See also the relevant notes to these texts, e.g., p. 4, note 7. Cf. Beyerlin, *Near Eastern Religious Texts,* pp. 6-7, 11-12; Kramer, *Mythologies,* pp. 38ff.

[11]For comments about Atum see Kramer's reference above. Atum is there identified, according to Kramer, with the hillock. For the model of time as the essential element of creation see Wakeman, *God's Battle,* p. 42. Also see Lambert, "A New Look," pp. 292-93.

[12]*ANET,* pp. 9, 42-44, 72-79, 450.

[13]*ANET,* p. 61. See also pp. 445, 517-18. Beyerlin, *Near Eastern Religious Texts,* pp. 82-83, 104.

[14]See note 10 above.

[15]*ANET,* pp. 3-4, 6-7. James, *Ancient Egypt,* pp. 145-46. For a list of about one hundred principal Egyptian gods see pp. 149-54.

[16]*ANET,* pp. 3, 4, 6. Cf. also Beyerlin, *Near Eastern Religious Texts,* pp. 24-25.

[17]*ANET,* p. 6.

[18]*ANET,* p. 5. col. 1, pp. 55-60; pp. 37-38, 74. Beyerlin, *Near Eastern Religious Texts,* pp. 4-5. Some have made a favorable analogy between the creation method of Ptah and the Christian Logos doctrine; however, the difference in kind between the two is evident. Other occurrences of fiat creation are found in Egyptian literature. See Hoffmaier's paper cited above (n. 6).

[19]For more on this see Heidel, *Babylonian Genesis,* p. 89 and pp. 89-122 passim.

[20]James, *Ancient Egypt,* pp. 145, 149-54; *ANET,* 3-7, 8-10, 168-69; Kramer, *Mythologies,* p. 39; Beyerlin, *Near Eastern Religious Texts,* p. 26. See also Sir Alan Gardiner, *Egypt of the Pharaohs* (New York: Oxford University Press, 1961), pp. 214ff. The so-called monotheism of Amenophis IV (Akhenaten) is far from strict monotheism.

[21]*ANET,* pp. 27ff., 60-99, 517-18; Beyerlin, *Near Eastern Religious Texts,* pp. 82-83, 104-5. Henotheism is merely an adjustment within a still polytheistic world view.

[22]*ANET,* pp. 4, 6.

[23]Ibid., pp. 4-6.

[24]See further comments by Heidel, *Babylonian Genesis,* pp. 96-97.

[25]Heidel, *Babylonian Genesis,* pp. 126-27. Marduk in the *Enuma Elish* approaches omnipotence. However, even the power that he does possess is vested in him by the other gods who willingly let him become their ruler.

[26]*ANET,* pp. 66-67.

[27]Hallo and Simpson, *Ancient Near East,* pp. 196, 212, 217; James, *Ancient Egypt,* pp. 145-48.

[28]Gardiner, *Pharaohs,* pp. 214-16.

[29]*ANET,* pp. 6, 8, 11, 266.

[30]*ANET,* p. 271; Beyerlin, *Near Eastern Religious Texts,* p. 26. See note 18 above on creation by word in the Memphite Theology. Various other references to man's formation in the god's (gods') image and his being "formed" (cf. Gen. 2) can be found in Hoffmaier's paper (n. 16 above). However, the content of "image" in the Bible vs. ANE literature is vital.

[31]Beyerlin, *Near Eastern Religious Texts,* pp. 75-76, note 6.

[32]Ibid., pp. 76-77; *ANET,* p. 74.

[33]*ANET,* pp. 68, 99-100; Beyerlin, *Near Eastern Religious Texts,* p. 84; Heidel, *Babylonian Genesis,* pp. 118-22.

[34]*ANET,* pp. 8, 11.

[35]Ibid., p. 417.

[36]Ibid., pp. 68, 99; Beyerlin, *Near Eastern Religious Texts,* p. 76. Cf. also *ANET,* p. 59.

[37]Heidel, *Babylonian Genesis,* pp. 139-40, has some perceptive comments in this area.

[38]James Oliver Buswell, Jr., *A Christian View of Being and Knowing* (Grand Rapids: Zondervan, 1960), p. 120.

[39]*ANET,* pp. 327, 334, 346, 348, 589, 604. Maat was also mentioned as a god in Egyptian religion.

[40]This point is strongly felt in the Gilgamesh Epic. See Heidel, *Gilgamesh,* pp. 84-88.

[41]Regarding these comments see *ANET,* pp. 3-10, 42, 60-99, 100, 104-6, 501, 503, 512. A broad reading in these materials is necessary in order to get a feel for the moral dimensions of creation in the *ANET* texts. See relevant texts in Beyerlin, *Near Eastern Religious Texts.*

[42]*ANET,* pp. 4, 8. Note the purpose of the account about "The Memphite Theology" and "Thebes as the Place of Creation." Also James, *Ancient Egypt,* pp. 130, 145-49.

[43]The religious revolution of Amenophis IV (1379-1362 B.C.) has not been sufficiently shown to negate this type of statement. His reform faltered both on religious and political grounds. Probably more on the latter. For a summary of Amenophis's attempted "monolatry" see Thomas, *DOTT,* pp. 142-50, esp. p. 144. Also *ANET,* 169-71.

[44]See, for example, Thomas, *DOTT,* pp. 97-103, 162-67; *ANET,* pp. 405-7, 601-4.

[45]*ANET,* pp. 6, 64, 109-10, 328, 348, 589, 604.

[46]In effect the ANE texts present what might be

called an "ontic" view of cosmology—a cosmos whose goal is to continue the status quo.

[47]Unfortunately, Genesis 1-2 has been reduced to this level by some, especially in the past, when they claimed it was merely a Hebrew adaptation of other ANE cosmologies. The differences, however, are essential, the likenesses are "banalities." Kitchen, *Bible in Its World*, pp. 26-27; Kitchen, a leading Egyptologist, feels that any real relationship between Genesis 1-2 and Babylonian materials is in doubt, *Ancient Orient*, p. 90. For a helpful summary of comparisons and contrasts between Genesis and ANE materials see G. H. Livingston, *The Pentateuch in Its Cultural Environment* (Grand Rapids: Baker, 1974), pp. 138-41. See also Harold G. Stigers, *A Commentary on Genesis* (Grand Rapids: Zondervan, 1976), pp. 51-52.

[48]I would like to credit Dr. Fred Bush of Fuller Theological Seminary for directing my thinking on some of the thoughts contained in the preceding sentences.

[49]The author used *some* literary devices, such as style, language, and symbolism, but historicized the material and did not produce an account of origins essentially similar to its ANE rivals.

[50]H. Orton Wiley calls Genesis 1 a "hymn of creation" and "a religious document" and says that it is "not a scientific statement in any modern sense," but "the Christian view is that the Mosaic account represents true history concerning the origin of the world." Paul T. Culbertson, ed., *Introduction to Christian Theology* (Kansas City, Mo.: Beacon Hill, 1959), pp. 135-36. Cf. James O. Buswell, Jr., *A Systematic Theology of the Christian Religion* (Grand Rapids: Zondervan, 1962). Buswell, approaching the issue from a different perspective, says its structure is "mnemonic," for memorizing easily (p. 140). However, determinative for the Christian is the acceptance of the historical nature of Genesis 1-2 by other biblical persons, including Jesus (e.g., Hosea 6:7; Ezek. 28:15; Matt. 19:9; 1 Cor. 11:3; 15:45; Jude 14).

[51]"Phenomenological" language as used here means the language that man uses in describing events without recourse to technical jargon, e.g., "The sun rises."

[52]William H. Green, *The Unity of the Book of Genesis* (1895; reprint ed., Grand Rapids: Baker, 1979), pp. 1-41. Green gives a detailed account of the unitary nature of Genesis 1 and 2. I have not seen it done any better by more recent authors.

[53]Cf. J. Barton Payne, *The Theology of the Older Testament* (Grand Rapids: Zondervan, 1962), p. 136. Payne finds that the "most striking feature of the Biblical record of creation is its progressiveness" (p. 136). More will be noted about this issue.

[54]As used here, anthropomorphism means talking about God by attributing to Him, for the sake of discussion, human attributes and features.

[55]R. K. Harrison, *Introduction to the Old Testament* (Grand Rapids: Eerdmans, 1969), calls these early chapters of Genesis "religious drama" (pp. 553-57). Various ways of describing these chapters are permissible, so long as no one way claims to have a corner on the truth contained in the documents.

[56]Green, *Unity of Genesis*, pp. 1-41, gives probable translations of the Hebrew words in Genesis 2 to solve the alleged sequential problems found there. However, it is clear that the sequential problem was not of the essence of the matter for the Genesis composer.

[57]See the following commentaries, which stress the early date and unity of Genesis: George Herbert Livingston, *Genesis, Beacon Bible Commentary* (Kansas City, Mo.: Beacon Hill, 1969), pp. 23-42; Lee Haines, *Genesis and Exodus, The Wesleyan Bible Commentary* (Grand Rapids: Eerdmans, 1967), pp. 1-34; Umberto Cassuto, *A Commentary on the Books of Genesis*, trans. Israel Abrahams, 2 vols. (Jerusalem: Magnes, 1961-1964); Derek Kidner, *Genesis: An Introduction and Commentary* (Chicago: InterVarsity, 1967). In my opinion an indispensible book for the study of Genesis is an older book: William Henry Green, *The Unity of the Book of Genesis* (1895; reprint ed., Grand Rapids: Baker, 1979). The early pages of this book give some convincing argumentation for considering Genesis 1 and 2 as complementary chapters.

[58]Not surprisingly, in Genesis 1:27 the writer does present a perfect piece of Hebrew poetry with its balanced thought and emphasis through *parallelismus memborum* (parallelism of the members). Read this verse in several versions.

[59]See also section I.D. 10 below. A helpful chapter has been written concerning these issues: Walter C. Kaiser, "The Literary Form of Genesis 1-11," in *New Perspectives on the Old Testament*, ed. J. B. Payne (Waco: Word, 1970), pp. 48-65.

[60]Those who want to read Genesis 1-2 as a *purely* scientific treatise commit two errors: (1) they limit the goal and purposes of these inspired chapters and (2) they usually assume that the particular scientific world view that they are working with is absolutely correct.

[61]Although not all of the following references can be treated, they are offered here for the convenience of the reader or student: Genesis 1:1-2, 25; 5:1-2; 6:7; Deut. 4:32; Neh. 9:6; Job 11:8-9; 26:10; 33:4; 36:32; 38:4, 7-8, 11; Ps. 8; 19:1, 6; 24:1-2; 33:6-9; 74:16-17; 89:11; 90:2; 100:3; 102:25; 104; 119:73; 121:2; 125:5-9; 146:6; 147:8; 148:3-5; Prov. 8:22-31; Eccl. 3:11; 12:7; Isa. 40:12-14, 18, 22-23, 25-26, 28; 42:5; 44:24; 45:12, 18; 64:8; 65:17-18; Jer. 5:22; 10:12; 31:35; 51:15-16; Amos 4:13; Zech. 12:1; Mal. 2:10. Of course, this list is not exhaustive, but all of the major principles involved in Old Testament biblical cosmology are touched on in these verses.

[62]John Wesley, *Explanatory Notes Upon the Old*

Testament (1755; reprint ed., Salem, Ohio: Schmul, 1975), p. 6.

[63] E. J. Young, one of the most respected and learned conservative scholars of this century, said, "There is deep need for a thorough study of the relation of the early chapters of Genesis to the cosmogonies of antiquity, a study that will proceed from the assumption that Genesis is sacred Scripture, the inerrant revelation of the triune God. Only upon such a basis can the true relation be established." ("A New Tour of Genesis," *Christianity Today* [Dec. 23, 1966], p. 26.)

[64] The fact of the universe's having a beginning, but not God, will become more clear in Section I.D. 2 below where creation ex nihilo is presented.

[65] Man has yet to solve by natural reason and science the question of which came first, the chicken or the egg.

[66] The human mind sees similarities between things easily, but must be trained to see differences readily. The contrast between Genesis 1 and other ANE creation stories becomes strikingly evident in the first three verses.

[67] Cf. Livingston, *Pentateuch*, p. 138, for some general background, and Wakeman, *God's Battle*, for a full discussion. Also refer to summary comments above in ANE section. See also Kitchen, *Bible in Its World* and *Ancient Orient* for discussion and bibliography.

[68] The nonmythical usage of these words of the Bible can be discussed by carefully reading the following passages with the aid of proper exegetical tools: Deut. 32:10; 1 Sam. 12:21; Job 6:18; 26:7; Isa. 24:1, 10; 24:11; 29:21; 45:18; Jer. 4:23.

[69] The terms for God in Genesis 1–2 are themselves indications of the personal aspect of God. In Genesis 1 *elohim*, "God," is used to depict the Creator of all things. In chapter 2 the term *YHWH* (*Yahweh*, translated LORD in NASB, RSV, NIV) is used to refer to the LORD of Creation who enters into covenantal fellowship with man. Many times in Genesis the context reveals why *elohim* "God" or YHWH ("LORD") is used by the Hebrew writer. See Umberto Cassuto, *The Documentary Hypothesis and the Composition of the Pentateuch*, trans. Israel Abrahams, 1st Eng. ed. (Jerusalem: Magnes, 1961).

[70] Adam Clarke, *Commentary on the Holy Bible*, abridged ed. (reprint ed., Kansas City, Mo.: Beacon Hill, 1967), p. 16. Clark's commentary has many helpful insights.

[71] Possibly the first *explicit* statement of creation ex nihilo is found in 2 Maccabees 7:28, "God made them out of things that did not exist."

[72] "Creation ex-nihilo is," according to Robert W. Gleason, "implicit in the Genesis recital of the world." See Robert W. Gleason, *Thought* 37, no. 147 (Winter 1962): 528. For a comprehensive study see N.H. Ridderbos, "Genesis 1:1 und 2," *Oudtestamentische Studien XII* (Leiden: Brill, 1958), p. 222 esp. The exegesis of Genesis 1–2 by the prophets and psalmists indicates that they felt that creation ex nihilo was taught in Genesis 1–2. The translation of Genesis 1:1 as "In the beginning God . . ." is supported by all the ancient versions and is grammatically possible and contextually probable. Finally, it is theologically preferable.

[73] If something is coeternal with God, it is clear that God's omnipotence, omniscience, and omnipresence are impossible.

[74] Robert Jastrow, *God and the Astronomers* (New York: Warner, 1978). Robert Jastrow, *Until the Sun Dies* (New York: Warner, 1977). These two books are excellent reading for acquiring a current survey of what is believed about evolution and astronomy. It was Einstein, among others, who would not contemplate the absurdity of the cosmos having a beginning until the big-bang theory of the universe was accepted as a possible explanation of all things.

[75] E.g., R.J. Barry, *Adam and the Ape* (London: Falcon, 1975), pp. 32–33. See the relevant special volume "Origins and Change," *Journal of the American Scientific Affiliation*, spec. vol. (1978).

[76] See above, pp. 151–52. It should always be kept in mind that formal parallelism is not at all the same as material (content) parallelism. The latter is nearly always lacking in the ANE parallels to the Old Testament.

[77] One does not have to believe that an audible sound is produced in God's speaking. Genesis 1 uses anthropomorphic language in order to communicate to his reader as does Genesis 2. In fact Genesis 1:26–27 uses the most radical anthropomorphic language found in Genesis 1–2.

[78] For the concept of Spirit of God in Genesis 1:2 as opposed to wind, force, etc., see Sabatino Moscati, "The Wind in Biblical and Phoenician Cosmogony," *JBL* 66 (1947): 305–10.

[79] Stigers, *Commentary on Genesis*, p. 52.

[80] For a penetrating study see James H. Olthuis, *The Word of God and Creation* (Toronto, Canada: Institute for Christian Studies), p. 11, passim. This entire study of fifteen pages is helpful. Nor should the Spirit of God be thought of as Hegel's spirit (mind) seeking realization.

[81] Cf. Wiley, *Introduction*, p. 134.

[82] Sonship is defined essentially as bearing the image of another (Gen. 5:1–3).

[83] John Wesley, "The General Deliverance," in *The Works of John Wesley* (Grand Rapids: Zondervan), 47:249.

[84] Cf. above, pp. 153–54, on moral concepts in ANE cosmology.

[85] The tendency of natural science from a non-Christian perspective to reduce this component of the cosmos to a mere natural law is, of course, too impersonal for the biblical theistic point of view.

[86]Michael Polanyi, *Science, Faith and Society* (Chicago: University of Chicago Press, 1946), speaks of scientific discovery as "guided not so much by the potentiality of a scientific proposition as by an aspect of nature seeking realization in our minds" (p. 35).

[87]Of course, man's being a part of the original creation must be considered here as well.

[88]It should be noted that this is another way of saying that man is in God's image.

[89]*Bara* is used in Genesis to indicate (1) the creation of the primal elements (Gen. 1:1), (2) the great reptiles (tannânîm) "and every living creature" (Gen. 1:21), (3) man (Gen. 1:27; 5:1-2), and (4) to summarize all of God's creative acts (Gen. 2:3-4). Writers often fail to observe the inclusive use of *bara* in point 4. It is important.

[90]Especially the naming of the animals is indicative of man's dominion over them.

[91]Psychologists are tending to stress the "differences" between man and woman. However, Genesis is mainly concerned with their sameness. It is evident, by the way, that the supernatural production of Eve confutes theistic evolution. It is worth noting also that man bears the *imago Dei* from the beginning, even in the very earliest stages of his historical and political development (Gen. 4-5).

[92]Popular science writers such as Carl Sagan stress the intellectual superiority of man as his goal. This is not the case in Genesis. Man has intellect only as one aspect of his total personality and through it and by means of it he is to express himself as the *imago Dei*, though personality (including intellect) is also a functional aspect of the *imago Dei*.

[93]Science will be unable to uncover the real essence of man as long as it studies his material and psychical side only. On the other hand, it is amazing that well-educated secular writers can be so uninformed about the clear scriptural declaration that man shares his physical side with the animals (cf. Peter Farb, *Humankind* [New York: Bantam, 1980], p. 3).

[94]Stigers, *Commentary on Genesis*, pp. 42-43, presents some very helpful points against a theistic evolutionary approach to the creation of man. In Genesis the antiquity of man is not the essence of the matter.

[95]It is highly significant that in no ANE account is man ever derived from previously existing animals. See ANE section above on man.

[96]James Orr, *God's Image in Man* (London: Hodder and Stoughton, 1907), pp. 270-71.

[97]E. A. Speiser, *Genesis,* Anchor Bible Series, ed. W. F. Albright and D. N. Freedman (Garden City, N.Y.: Doubleday, 1964), p. 5.

[98]Wesley, "On Eternity," *Works*, vol. 6, p. 214, states that "evil *must* exist only in the *present* state of things."

[99]Cf. Henry Frankfort, *The Birth of Civilization in the Near East* (Garden City, N.Y.: Doubleday, 1956).

[100]Wesley, *Notes Upon the Old Testament*, p. 7, finds that the image of God in man lay chiefly in his moral correspondence to the Creator, specifically in man's purity and rectitude. See also Wesley, "Original Righteousness," *Works*, p. 34, "These texts, therefore, do manifestly refer to personal internal holiness; and clearly prove, that this is the chief part of the 'image of God' in which man was originally created." The holiness of God is emphasized throughout the Old Testament, and Ecclesiastes 7:29 states the original uprightness of man. Cf. Orr, *God's Image*, pp. 58, 156ff.

[101]Buswell, *Systematic Theology*, p. 66, is excellent on pointing out the way in which ethics is to be derived from the nature of God's creation.

[102]Both Clarke and Wesley see the significance of the tree of the knowledge of good and evil lying in the challenge of obedience that it presented to Adam and Eve. Cf. Wesley, *Notes Upon the Old Testament,* p. 5, and Clarke, *Commentary,* p. 20. For man's "whole duty" see Ecclesiastes 12:13-14.

[103]See Lee Haines, *Genesis and Exodus, The Wesleyan Bible Commentary,* 6 vols. (Grand Rapids: Eerdmans, 1967), 1:22, for similar comments.

[104]Gerhard Hasel, "Polemical Nature of the Genesis Cosmology," *EvQ* 46 (1974): 81-102. The polemical purpose of Genesis 1-2 simply cannot be denied. And there is reason to believe that the Hebrews would have needed this polemic upon entering Canaan or even much earlier (in Egypt?).

[105]Heidel, *Babylonian Genesis*, pp. 101-2; *ANET*, pp. 62, 368-69.

[106]Of course "light" when used in a religious or moral sense is said to be characteristic of God. It is interesting that Clark calls the creation of light in Genesis the production of "caloric heat." This comment reveals the impact that early nineteenth-century science was having on him.

[107]See I.D. 10 below for additional comments.

[108]Wakeman, *God's Battle,* passim. This work offers a comprehensive study of this area.

[109]The Hebrew word *tannânîm* (Gen. 1:21) is a difficult word to translate. It certainly does not mean whale and is probably a biblical clue to understanding the great lizards and serpents that once roamed the earth. Cf. Derek Kidner, *Genesis,* p. 49.

[110]In the nonbiblical ANE records the image of God is limited (1) as to its content—it is hardly significant; (2) as to its application, for woman is not mentioned and the image of God was normally related only to kings or idols of the gods; (3) as to its origin; that is, man in the *imago Dei*, is a sociological or a political phenomenon. In the Bible it is a "theological" fact of creation and is predicated of all

mankind. These comments are from my unpublished study "Man as the Imago Dei."

[111]For a short note on God's creation of beings other than man see below, note 114.

[112]This is the necessary conclusion of God's holding man responsible for obeying His words.

[113]For a discussion of man's sinful plight see the chapter on hamartiology, pp. 237ff.

[114]Certain Old Testament Scriptures imply and certain New Testament Scriptures affirm that a "fall" of some kind occurred among spirit creatures of God's creation. However, this fall did not necessarily implicate man in disobedience, but did provide the possibility of man's testing. Nowhere are we told the exact nature of angels. They are not stated to be "in the image of God," an honor seemingly belonging only to man and possibly explaining why fallen angels are not redeemable.

[115]According to Augustine, to ask the origin (cause) of an original evil decision by a free will is nonsensical. The will is its own adequate cause. Its function is "to will."

[116]Monism is an unacceptable philosophical view that asserts that all things are ultimately merely expressions of one homogeneous substance. Pantheism, for example, follows from monism and states that God is all. See Warren C. Young, *A Christian Approach to Philosophy* (Grand Rapids: Baker, 1954), pp. 199-223, for a presentation of Christian Realism as a Christian world view.

[117]Here are a few Scriptures to consider in this scheme of things: destruction of the original creation (Isa. 24:19-20, 23; 34:4; 51:6; 54:10); certain things remain and are merely renewed (Isa. 24:23); the new heavens and the new earth will be present (Isa. 65:17; 66:22).

[118]I have commented on this briefly above, see pp. 154-56. For additional bibliography see Samuel Schultz, *The Old Testament Speaks*, 3rd ed. (New York: Harper and Row, 1980), p. 13. A strong argument for twenty-four-hour days is found in Henry Morris, ed., *Scientific Creationism* (San Diego, Calif.: Creation Life, 1974), pp. 221-30. P. J. Wiseman argues for the revelation of creation to the biblical writer during a six-day period. See P. J. Wiseman, *Clues to Creation in Genesis* (London: Marshall, Morgan and Scott, 1977).

[119]Wesley, though prescientific, stated that God began His creation when He saw fit. (Robert W. Burtner and Robert E. Childs, eds., *A Compend of Wesley's Theology* [Nashville: Abingdon, 1954], p. 56.)

[120]See Jastrow, *God and Astronomers*, for an agnostic's evaluation.

[121]See R. Laird Harris, "The Bible and Cosmology," *BETS* 5 (1962): 11-17; idem, "The Mist, the Canopy, and the Rivers of Eden," *BETS* 11 (1968): pp. 178-79. Harris makes a necessary beginning to correct the improper exegetical results of numerous exegetes. A faulty biblical cosmology is often the result of inadequate exegesis.

[122]Kidner, *Genesis*, p. 57. For a discussion of evolution and creation, along with material concerning the date of earth and man, see Kidner, pp. 26-31 and Stigers, *Genesis*, pp. 40-43. Adam Clarke, *Commentary*, notes some linguistic problems in translating certain passages in Genesis 1-2, e.g., "firmament," as opposed to "expanse."

[123]Speiser, *Genesis*, p. 11.

[124]Payne, *Theology of the Older Testament*, p. 134.

[125]Kitchen, *Bible in its World*, p. 26.

[126]Speiser, *Genesis*, p. 10; Heidel, *Babylonian Genesis*, p. 120.

[127]*The New Oxford Annotated Bible* contains the apocrypha and excellent short introductions to these books. For the Dead Sea Scrolls see Theodore H. Gaster, *The Dead Sea Scriptures*, 3rd ed. (New York: Anchor, 1976). R. H. Charles's excellent sampling of the pseudepigraphal literature is still the best place to get at the primary literature of Judaism, *Apocrypha and Pseudepigrapha of the Old Testament*, vol. 2 (Oxford: Clarendon, 1913). See also for the Dead Sea Scrolls: Geza Vermes, *The Dead Sea Scrolls in English*, 2nd ed. (New York: Penguin, 1975). Especially helpful for the doctrines of Qumran is Helmer Ringgren, *The Faith of Qumran: Theology of the Dead Sea Scrolls* (Philadelphia: Fortress, 1963). Ringgren presents the theology of the community in standard theological terminology. Finally, very helpful is a book by David N. Freedman and Jonas Greenfield, eds., *New Directions in Biblical Archaeology* (Garden City: Doubleday, Anchor, 1971).

[128]The reader can note the following passages as illustrations of the cosmological views of various books of the apocrypha: Tobit 8:6; Judith 9:12; 13:19; 16:14; Wisdom of Solomon 1:14; 2:23-24; 6:22; 7:22; 9:1-3, 9, 17; 10:1; 11:17, 24-26; 12:1; 13:3; 15:11; 18:15; 19:6; Sirach 15:14; 16:26-30; 18:1-3; 23:20; 24:8-9; 33:10-11; 36:15; 39:16, 18, 33; 41:10; 43:5-9, 26. This list is merely a sampling from a few books but is indicative of what can be found.

[129]For a full discussion of Plato's cosmology see I. M. Crombie, *An Examination of Plato's Doctrines*, vol. 2 *International Library of Philosophy and Scientific Method* (New York: Humanities, 1963), pp. 197-246. Immediately the reader will become aware of the difference between the Craftsman of Plato, who shapes (demiorgeo) as he is allowed to by the primal material, and the Creator of Genesis 1-2. For an excellent presentation of the Greco-Roman model of the world and an illustration of the religious syncretism of the Greco-Roman era see David R. Cartlidge and David L. Dungan, *Documents for the Study of the New Testament* (Philadelphia: Fortress,

1980), pp. 243-51, esp. p. 246. See also Frederick Copleston, *A History of Philosophy: Greece and Rome* (vol. 1), pts. 1-2 (Garden City, N.Y.: Doubleday, Image, n.d.).

[130] W. Sol. 11:17 does not seem to deny this as Gaster claims. These verses contain an affirmation of God's creative activity after creating "formless matter" (*ex amorphou ules*).

[131] This is evident, for example, in W. Sol. 7:24, where wisdom is said to be superior to any motion. This is clearly a polemical statement, for motion was deemed an important primal component of the universe and basic to all things in certain Greek philosophical views.

[132] This is clear in nearly all nations. See John B. Noss, *Man's Religions*, 6th ed. (New York: Macmillan, 1980), pp. 40-53, and K. L. McKay, "Creation," *The New Bible Dictionary*, ed. J. D. Douglas et al. (Grand Rapids: Eerdmans, 1962), pp. 272-73.

[133] Noss, *Religions*, pp. 52-53.

[134] Josephus, *Antiq.* 1.7; Samuel Sandmel, *Philo of Alexandria* (New York: Oxford University Press, 1979), pp. 52-55, 94-101.

[135] Noss, *Religions*, p. 52.

[136] Walther Eichrodt, *Theology of the Old Testament*, trans. J. A. Baker (Philadelphia: Westminster, 1967), p. 104, n. 3; Crombie, *Plato's Doctrines*, p. 200.

[137] McKay, "Creation," *NBD*, p. 273. In this same volume see the articles on "Logos," "Stoics," and "Epicureans."

[138] Sandmel, *Philo*, pp. 52-55, 94-101.

[139] Wiseman, *Clues to Creation*, p. 227.

[140] Acts 7:49-50; 14:15; 17:25-28; Rom. 11:36; 1 Tim. 4:3-4; Heb. 1:2; 11:3; Rev. 14:7.

[141] It is clear that a total biblical view of creation demands creation *ex nihilo*, whatever the possible ambiguities of Genesis 1:1-2. See above, pp. 157-58.

[142] It is worth noting that the New Testament does not concern itself with the length of days in Genesis, when creation took place, etc. It accepts and deals with "the fact of God's creation" and the emphases that are found in the Genesis 1-2 accounts, as we have noted earlier.

[143] Buswell, *Systematic Theology*, p. 138, note, "It should be clear that these references to the Son as Creator do not exclude the Father, but they do indicate that the Son is just as truly the Creator as the Father."

[144] Livingston, *Genesis*, p. 38, points out that the center of things has been shifted from original creation to the event of the Resurrection. However, it is in and through the Incarnation and Resurrection that the *new creation* has now become the focal point.

[145] God's will in regard to creation is *declared* plainly to us; it is *that all things be summed up in Christ*. No eternal decree of individual predestination is revealed, but God's major purpose of creation is given to us through the inspired writer.

[146] The translation of the Hebrew is difficult here, but the overall tenor of these verses requires a translation along the line suggested by "workman" or "technician."

[147] *Ktizō*. This is the New Testament equivalent of *bara*, but its usage is wider.

[148] The goal of man in creation is to be a righteous, loving, holy, and wise son of God, in His image. This biblical concept can be compared to some modern scientific statements on the nature, goal, and destiny of man (cf. Carl Sagan, *The Dragons of Eden* [New York: Random, 1977], p. 197). Man's goal is intellect or "intelligence," according to most of these observations. According to a Christian view, intellect is subordinated to man's goal to be a righteous, holy, loving, and wise being. Intellect is merely one component of man's unified personality by which he can express his essential nature.

[149] The second law of thermodynamics may demonstrate a physical effect of the Fall. The decrepit and degenerating moral nature of man shows clearly a more significant and biblically important effect. Man is degenerating morally and religiously.

[150] Orr, *Christian View of God and the World*, p. 37. It is unfortunate that no work comparable to Orr's has been *attempted* by Wesleyan-Arminian scholars.

[151] Young, *Christian Approach to Philosophy*, pp. 38-43, presents a helpful succinct review of "assumptions and world-views." H. Orton Wiley, *Christian Theology*, 3 vols. (Kansas City, Mo.: Beacon Hill, 1940), 1:440-87, discusses world views under the heads of mechanical theory, eternal creation, natural evolution, and continuous creation (pp. 442-46). See also the discussion in Clark Pinnock, *Reason Enough* (Downers Grove: InterVarsity, 1980); Donald Bloesch, *The Ground of Certainty* (Grand Rapids: Eerdmans, 1971); Colin Brown, *Philosophy and the Christian Faith* (Downers Grove: InterVarsity, 1968); Yandall Woodfin, *With All Your Mind* (Nashville: Abingdon, 1980).

[152] W. T. Purkiser, *Exploring Our Christian Faith* (Kansas City, Mo.: Beacon Hill, 1960), p. 145.

[153] This is clearly seen, for instance, in the fact that no idol of God was placed in the ark of the covenant but the tablet of stones bearing God's moral commands.

[154] Frank W. Collier, *John Wesley Among the Scientists* (New York: Abingdon, 1928).

[155] The full title and publication data as given in Collier, *John Wesley Among the Scientists*, p. 179, is *John Wesley, A Survey of the Wisdom of God in the Creation, or, A Compendium of Natural Philosophy. In Five Volumes. The Third Edition, enlarged. By John Wesley, A.M. London: Printed by J. Fry and

Co., in Queen Street, and sold at the Foundry, Upper Moorfields, and by the Booksellers in Town and Country, 1777. 12 mo, pp. 369, 335, 369, 348, 331.

[156] Collier, *Wesley Among the Scientists,* p. 80.

[157] This is pointed out all too briefly in Martin Schmidt, *John Wesley: A Theological Biography,* trans. Denis Inman (Nashville: Abingdon, 1973), pp. 90, 105; see also Wesley, *Works,* 6:213-14.

[158] Wesley's Hebrew exegesis was terribly faulty, and his introduction to Genesis in his *Notes Upon the Old Testament* reflects bad principles as well as bad facts. However, he wrote before the archaeology explosion of the Ancient Near East began in the nineteenth century.

[159] Collier, *Wesley Among the Scientists,* pp. 85-86.

[160] Clark, *Commentary.* Finished in 1826.

[161] Ibid., p. 18. His exegesis of *nephesh* in Genesis 2 is, however, faulty.

[162] Charles Finney, *Finney's Systematic Theology* (Minneapolis: Bethany, 1976), pp. 150-59.

[163] Howard Snyder, *The Radical Wesley* (Downers Grove: InterVarsity, 1980), pp. 47, 76.

[164] Haines, *Genesis.*

[165] Wiley, *Christian Theology,* 1:440-87. Wiley discusses cosmology on pages 440-49, 461, 463-67, 470, 472-77, 483. His view of Genesis 1 as "poetry" is not sufficiently true to the nature of the Genesis narrative. His discussion of the "nebular hypothesis" and "the planetesimal explanation" of original light attempts too much in the way of substantiating scientifically the claim of the creation story (p. 466). See also H. O. Wiley and Paul R. Culbertson, *Introduction to Christian Theology* (Kansas City, Mo.: Beacon Hill, 1959).

DISCUSSION QUESTIONS

1. How can Wesleyan theology help present a biblical view of man in the face of humanism, science, atheism?
2. Does the modern scientific approach to creation (even the approach in many Christian works) fail to treat the religious and moral implications of Creation adequately?
3. What is the value of discerning the genre of a piece of literature before interpreting it?
4. How is cosmology important in forming a Christian world view (*Weltanschauung*)? in forming Christian ethics?
5. Is God's providence in caring for His creation of theoretical, practical, and pastoral value?
6. Why is it vitally important that God precede everything in every way?
7. How does a comparison of the biblical account of creation with ANE accounts and modern accounts demonstrate in a concrete, comprehensible way the concepts of revelation and inspiration?
8. What does it mean to say that the biblical writer was able by divine inspiration to grasp the real nature, meaning, goal, and purpose of the cosmos?
9. Is the Genesis creation account helpful for our understanding the alien nature of sin and death in the human race? in the cosmos?
10. How does the biblical model of man in the *imago Dei* help to explain the presence of elements of religion in all known human societies?
11. How does the *logos* ("word") concept of creation predict the probability of natural science?
12. How is man's capability of having dominion over the cosmos to be explained biblically?
13. What was and is God's ultimate goal for His creation? as a whole? what is His goal for now?
14. What helpful insights into cosmology are gleaned from the intertestamental literature?
15. How can the biblical concept of cosmology help to inform a Christian perspective on the humanities?
16. The new creation will result in man's attaining what status with regard to his religious and moral condition?
17. What is the essential feature of the new heavens and the new earth, according to Isaiah and 2 Peter?
18. Why does redemption follow from the nature of creation?
19. Why have science and biblical theism often been at loggerheads?
20. How do some modern scientific theories parallel ancient concepts of cosmology?
21. Is there a distinctive contribution by way of emphasis or singularity that Wesleyan theology gives to Christian cosmology?

RECOMMENDATIONS FOR FURTHER READING

Aalders, G. C. *Genesis*. Vol. 1. Translated by William Heynen. 1918. Reprint. Grand Rapids: Zondervan, 1981. This is a translation of this great Dutch scholar's excellent conservative work on Genesis.

Barcus, Nancy. *Developing a Christian Mind*. Downers Grove: InterVarsity, 1977.

Beyerlin, Walter. *Near Eastern Religious Texts Relating to the Old Testament*. Translated by John Bowden. Philadelphia: Westminster, 1978.

Biblical Account of Man's Creation. A study report (unpublished) submitted to H. T. Armerding, President, Wheaton College, Wheaton, Illinois, 1965.

Brandon, S.G.F. *Creation Legends of the Ancient Near East*. Aylesbury, Bucks: Hodder and Stoughton, 1963.

Clark, Adam. *Christian Theology*. 2nd ed. Cincinnati: Swormstedt and Poe, 1835.

Douglas, J. D., ed. *The New Bible Dictionary*. Grand Rapids: Eerdmans, 1962.

Eichrodt, Walther. *Theology of the Old Testament*. Vol. 2. Translated by J. A. Baker. Philadelphia: Westminster, 1967.

Haines, Lee. "Genesis," in *The Wesleyan Bible Commentary*. Vol. 1. Grand Rapids: Eerdmans, 1967.

Harris, R. L. "The Bible and Cosmology." *BETS* 5 (1962): 7–17.

———. "The Mist, the Canopy, and the Rivers of Eden." *BETS* 11 (1968): 177–79.

The following issues of the *Journal of the American Scientific Affiliation*, Elgin, Illinois, will be helpful: "Origins and Change" (1978, special issue); vol. 14, no. 2 (June 1962); vol. 17, no. 2 (June 1965); vol. 28, no. 4 (Dec. 1976).

Morris, Henry. *Scientific Creationism*. San Diego: Creation-Life, 1974.

Purkiser, W. T., ed. *Exploring Our Christian Faith*. Kansas City, Mo.: Beacon Hill, 1960.

Orr, James. *The Christian View of God and the World*. Edinburgh: Andrew Elliot, 1893.

Ridderbos, H. N. *Is There a Conflict Between Genesis One and Natural Science?* Grand Rapids: Eerdmans, 1957.

Sire, James, W. *The Universe Next Door*. Downers Grove: InterVarsity, 1976.

Skinner, J. A. *A Critical and Exegetical Commentary on Genesis*. 2nd ed. Edinburgh: T. & T. Clark, 1930.

Thomas, D. W. *Documents From Old Testament Times*. New York: Harper and Row, 1961.

Thurman, T. Duane. *How to Think About Evolution*. 2nd ed. Downers Grove: InterVarsity, 1978.

Wiley, H. Orton. *Christian Theology*. Vol. 1. Kansas City, Mo.: Beacon Hill, 1940.

Young, E. V. *The Relation of the First Verse of Genesis One and Natural Science?* Grand Rapids: Eerdmans, 1957.

BIBLIOGRAPHY

The following bibliography is divided into two main sections, *General Works* and *Science and the Bible*. Those works within the first section will at least have relevant sections in them that can be consulted to the reader's great benefit.

GENERAL WORKS

Allis, Oswald T. *The Old Testament: Its Claims and Its Critics*. Grand Rapids: Baker, 1972.

Armerding, Hudson T., ed. *Christianity and the World of Thought*. Chicago: Moody, 1968.

Barcus, Nancy B. *Developing a Christian Mind*. Downers Grove: InterVarsity, 1977.

Beyerlin, Walter, ed. *Near Eastern Religious Texts*. Philadelphia: Westminster, 1978.

Bloesch, Donald. *The Ground of Certainty*. Grand Rapids: Eerdmans, 1971.

Brown, Colin. *Philosophy and the Christian Faith: A Historical Sketch from the Middle Ages to the Present Day*. Downers Grove: InterVarsity, 1968.

Burtner, Robert W., and Chiles, Robert E., eds. *A Compendium of Wesley's Theology*. New York: Abingdon, 1954.

Buswell, James Oliver. *A Christian View of Being and Knowing*. Grand Rapids: Zondervan, 1960.

⸺⸺⸺. *A Systematic Theology of the Christian Religion*. Vol. 1. Grand Rapids: Zondervan, 1962.

Carter, Charles, ed. *The Wesleyan Bible Commentary*. Vol. 1, part 1. Grand Rapids: Eerdmans, 1967.

Cassuto, U. *A Commentary on the Book of Genesis*. Vol. 1. Translated by Israel Abrahams. Jerusalem: Magnus, 1978.

Cartlidge, David R., and Dungan, David T. *Documents for the Study of the Gospels*. Philadelphia: Fortress, 1980.

Childs, Brevard S. *Introduction to the Old Testament as Scripture*. Philadelphia: Fortress, 1979.

Clarke, Adam. *Christian Theology*. Cincinnati: Swormstedt and Poe, 1856.

⸺⸺⸺. *Commentary on the Holy Bible*. Abridged by Ralph Earle. Kansas City, Mo.: Beacon Hill, 1972.

Collier, Frank. *John Wesley Among the Scientists*. New York: Abingdon, 1928.

Crombie, I. M. *An Examination of Plato's Doctrines*. Vol. 2. Plato on Knowledge and Reality. International Library of Philosophy and Scientific Method. Edited by A. J. Ayer. London: Routledge & Kegan Paul, 1963.

DeGraff, Arnold H., and Olthuis, James H. *Toward a Biblical View of Man: Some Readings*. Toronto: Institute for Christian Studies, 1978.

Driver, S. R. *The Book of Genesis*. 15th ed. London: Methuen, 1948.

Dyrness, William. *Themes in Old Testament Theology*. Downers Grove: InterVarsity, 1979.

Eckelmann and Newman. *Genesis and the Origin of the Universe*. Downers Grove: InterVarsity, 1977.

Eichrodt, Walther. *Theology of the Old Testament*. Vol. 2. Translated by J. A. Baker. Philadelphia: Westminster, 1967.

Eissfeldt, Otto. *The Old Testament*. Translated by Peter Ackroyd. New York: Harper and Row, 1966.

Eliade, Mircea. *Gods, Goddesses and Myths of Creation: A Thematic Source Book of the History of Religions*. Part 1. New York: Harper and Row, 1967.

Erdman, Charles R. *The Book of Genesis*. New York: Revell, 1940.

Ferré, Frederick. *Basic Modern Philosophy of Religion*. New York: Scribner, 1967.

Finney, Charles. *Finney's Systematic Theology*. Edited and abridged by J. H. Fairchild. Minneapolis: Bethany, 1976.

Frazer, Sir James George. *The New Golden Bough*. Edited by Theodor H. Gaster. New York: Mentor, 1964.

Gordon, Cyrus H. *The Ancient Near East*. 3rd rev. ed. New York: Norton, 1965.

Green, William Henry. *The Unity of the Book of Genesis*. Grand Rapids: Baker, 1979.

Guthrie, Donald. *New Testament Introduction*. 3rd rev. ed. Downers Grove: InterVarsity 1970.

⸺⸺⸺. *New Testament Theology*. Downers Grove: InterVarsity, 1980.

Hallo, William W., and Simpson, William Kelley. *The Ancient Near East: A History*. New York: Harcourt Brace Jovanovich, 1971.

Harrison, R. K. *Introduction to the Old Testament*. Grand Rapids: Eerdmans, 1969.

Heidel, Alexander. *The Babylonian Genesis: The Story of Creation,* 2nd ed. Chicago: University of Chicago Press, 1972.

⸺⸺⸺. *The Gilgamesh Epic and Old Testament Parallels*. Chicago: University of Chicago Press, 1946.

Jastrow, Robert. *God and the Astronomers*. New York: Warner, 1978.

Jonas, Hans. *The Gnostic Religion: The Message of the Alien God and the Beginnings of Christianity*. 2nd ed., revised. Boston: Beacon, 1963.

Kaiser, Walter C., Jr., ed. *Classical Evangelical Essays in Old Testament Interpretation*. Grand Rapids: Baker, 1972.

Keil, C. F., and Delitzsch, F. *Biblical Commentary on the Old Testament*. Vol. 1. Translated by James Martin. Grand Rapids: Eerdmans, 1949.

Kidner, Derek. *Genesis*. The Tyndale Old Testament Commentaries. Downers Grove: InterVarsity, 1977.

Kitchen, K. A. *Ancient Orient and Old Testament*. Downers Grove: InterVarsity, 1977.

_____. *The Bible in Its World: The Bible and Archaeology Today.* Downers Grove: InterVarsity, 1977.

Kramer, Samuel Noah. *History Begins at Sumer.* New York: Doubleday, 1959.

_____, ed. *Mythologies of the Ancient World.* Garden City, N.Y.: Doubleday, 1961.

_____. *The Sumerians.* Chicago: University of Chicago Press, 1963.

Levitt, Zola. *Creation: A Scientist's Choice.* Wheaton: Victor, 1971.

Leupold, H. C. *Exposition of Genesis.* Vol. 1. Grand Rapids: Baker, 1942.

Livingston, G. Herbert. *The Pentateuch in Its Cultural Environment.* Grand Rapids: Baker, 1977.

McDonald, H. D. *The Christian View of Man.* Westchester: Crossway, 1981.

McKenzie, John L. *Second Isaiah.* The Anchor Bible. Edited by William Foxwell Albright and David Noel Freedman. Garden City: Doubleday, 1968.

Noss, John B. *Man's Religions.* 6th ed. New York: Macmillan, 1980.

Oppenheim, A. Leo. *Ancient Mesopotamia.* Chicago: University of Chicago Press, 1965.

Orr, James. *The Christian View of God and the World.* Edinburgh: Elliott, 1893.

Payne, J. Barton. *The Theology of the Older Testament.* Grand Rapids: Zondervan, 1962.

Pinnock, Clark H. *Reason Enough: A Case for the Christian Faith.* Downers Grove: InterVarsity, 1980.

Pritchard, James B., ed. *Ancient Near Eastern Texts.* 3rd ed. with supplement. Princeton: Princeton University Press, 1969.

Purkiser, W. T., ed. *Exploring Our Christian Faith.* Kansas City, Mo.: Beacon Hill, 1968.

Ringgren, Helmer, and Strom, Ake V. *Religions of Mankind: Today and Yesterday.* Edited by J.C.G. Grieg. Translated by Niels L. Jensen. Philadelphia: Fortress, 1967.

Saggs, H. W. *The Greatness That Was Babylon.* New York: Hawthorne, 1962.

Sandmel, Samuel. *Philo of Alexandria.* New York: Oxford University Press, 1979.

Schmidt, Martin. *John Wesley: A Theological Biography.* Vol. 2, part 2. Translated by Denis Inman. New York: Abingdon, 1973.

Schultz, Samuel. *The Old Testament Speaks.* 3rd ed. San Francisco: Harper and Row, 1980.

Sheed, F. J. *Genesis Regained.* New York: Sheed and Ward, 1969.

Sire, James W., ed. *The Universe Next Door: A Basic World View Catalog.* Downers Grove: InterVarsity, 1976.

Smart, Ninian. *The Religious Experience of Mankind.* 2nd ed. New York: Scribner, 1976.

Snyder, Howard A. *The Radical Wesley and Patterns for Church Renewal.* Downers Grove: InterVarsity, 1980.

Speiser, E. A. *Genesis.* Garden City: Doubleday, 1964.

Sproul, Barbara C. *Primal Myths: Creating the World.* San Francisco: Harper and Row, 1979.

Stigers, Harold G. *A Commentary on Genesis.* Grand Rapids: Zondervan, 1976.

Thomas, D. Winton, ed. *Documents From Old Testament Times.* New York: Harper and Row, Torchbook, 1961.

Vawter, Bruce. *On Genesis: A New Reading.* Garden City: Doubleday, 1977.

Von Rad, Gerhard. *Genesis.* Translated by John H. Marks. Philadelphia: Westminster, 1961.

Wesley, John. *Explanatory Notes Upon the Old Testament.* Vol. 1. Salem, Ohio: Schmul, 1975.

_____. *The Works of John Wesley.* Vols. 5, 6, 7, 9. 1872. Reprint. Grand Rapids: Zondervan, n.d.

Westerman, Claus. *Creation.* Translated by John J. Scullion. Philadelphia: Fortress, 1971.

_____. *The Genesis Accounts of Creation.* Edited by John Reumann. Translated by Norman E. Wagner. Biblical Series. Vol. 7. Philadelphia: Fortress, 1964.

Wiley, H. Orton, and Culbertson, Paul T. *Introduction to Christian Theology.* Kansas City, Mo.: Beacon Hill, 1959.

Wilkes, Peter, ed. *Christianity Challenges the University.* Downers Grove: InterVarsity, 1981.

Wolff, Hans Walter. *Anthropology of the Old Testament.* Philadelphia: Fortress, n.d.

Woodfin, Yandall. *With All Your Mind: A Christian Philosophy.* Nashville: Abingdon, 1980.

Young, Warren G. *A Christian Approach to Philosophy.* Grand Rapids: Baker, 1954.

Young, Edward J. *An Introduction to the Old Testament.* Grand Rapids: Eerdmans, 1973.

SCIENCE AND THE BIBLE

Alexander, Denis. *Beyond Science.* Philadelphia: Holman, 1972.

Berry, R. J. *Adam and the Ape: A Christian Approach to the Theory of Evolution.* London: Falcon, 1975.

Bube, Richard H., ed. *The Encounter Between Christianity and Science.* Grand Rapids: Eerdmans, 1968.

Buswell, J. O. "A Creationist Interpretation of the Prehistoric Man," in *Evolution And Christian Thought Today.* Edited by R. L. Mixter. Paternoster, 1959.

Custance, Arthur C. *Noah's Three Sons.* The Doorway Papers. Vol. 1. Grand Rapids: Zondervan, 1975.

Eliade, Mircea. *Cosmos and History: The Myth of the Eternal Return.* Translated by Willard R. Trask. New York: Harper and Row, 1959.

England, Donald. *A Christian View of Origins.* Grand Rapids: Baker, 1972.

Flanagan, Dennis, ed. *The Solar System.* San Francisco: Freeman, 1975.

Friar, Wayne, and Davis, P. William. *The Case for Creation.* Chicago: Moody, 1972.

Jenkins, D. *What Is Man?* London: SCM, 1970.

Kerkut, G. A. *Implications of Evolution.* London: Pagamen, 1960.

Klotz, John W. *Genes, Genesis and Evolution.* St. Louis: Concordia, 1970.

Kofahl, Robert E., and Segraves, Keldy L. *The Creation Explanation: A Scientific Alternative to Evolution.* Wheaton: Harold Shaw, 1975.

Loewenberg, Bert James. *Darwinism: Reaction or Reform?* Source Problems in World Civilizations. New York: Holt, Rinehart and Winston, 1966.

Moore, John N., and Slusher, Harold S., eds. 2nd ed. *Biology: A Search for Order in Complexity.* Grand Rapids: Zondervan, 1974.

Morris, Henry M. *Evolution and the Modern Christian.* Grand Rapids: Baker, 1977.

———. *Scientific Creationism.* San Diego: Creation-Life, 1975.

Morris, Henry M., and Patten, Donald W., eds. *A Symposium on Creation.* Vols. 1–6. Grand Rapids: Baker, 1968–1977.

Olthuis, James H. *The Word of God and Creation.* Toronto: Institute for Christian Studies, 1975.

Polanyi, Michael. *Science, Faith and Society.* Chicago: University of Chicago Press, 1964.

Ramm, Bernard. *The Christian View of Science and Scripture.* Grand Rapids: Eerdmans, 1955.

Reid, James. *God, the Atom, and the Universe.* Grand Rapids: Zondervan, 1968.

Smith, A. E. Wilder. *The Creation of Life: A Cybernetic Approach to Evolution.* Wheaton, Ill.: Harold Shaw, 1970.

Thurman, L. Duane. *How to Think About Evolution and Other Bible Science Controversies.* Downers Grove: InterVarsity, 1978.

Whitcomb, John C., Jr. *The World That Perished.* Grand Rapids: Baker, 1973.

Whitcomb, John C., Jr., and Morris, Henry M. *The Genesis Flood.* Grand Rapids: Baker, 1961.

Willis, David L., ed. *Origins and Change.* Elgin, Ill.: American Scientific Affiliation, 1978.

CHAPTER 6

ANTHROPOLOGY:
Man, the Crown
of Divine Creation

Charles W. Carter

Charles W. Carter is Scholar-in-Residence and Professor of Religion and Missions at Marion College, Marion, Indiana. He holds the following degrees: Th.M., Christian Theological Seminary; B.D., D.D., Asbury Theological Seminary. He served pastorates in several mid-Western churches; was missionary to Sierra Leone, Africa, for three terms as principal of the Clarke Memorial Biblical Seminary; and Professor of Philosophy and Missions, and Chairman of the Division of Philosophy and Religion, Marion College, for eleven years; he was Professor of Philosophy and Religion at Taylor University for twelve years. He taught theology and ethics in Taiwan for four years and was lecturer and/or visiting professor at colleges and seminaries in other areas of the world. He was a cofounder of the Wesleyan Theological Society and was editor of the Wesleyan Theological Journal *for seven years.*

Dr. Carter is author of fifteen books, including A Half Century of American Missions in West Africa, Road to Revival, The Person and Ministry of the Holy Spirit, *and* Missionaries Extraordinary. *He was general editor and contributor to the* Wesleyan Bible Commentary *(7 volumes) and has contributed to the* Zondervan Pictorial Encyclopedia of the Bible, *the* Wesleyan Theological Journal, *and other scholarly journals. He is a member of the American Association of University Professors, the Metaphysical Society of America, the Mid-Western Fellowship of Professors of Missions, the Evangelical Theological Society, and the Wesleyan Theological Society.*

CONTENTS

- I. THE PLACE OF HUMANITY IN THE UNIVERSE / 195
- II. HUMANITY AS *HOMO SAPIENS* / 196
- III. THE BIBLICAL VIEW OF HUMANITY'S ORIGIN AND NATURE / 197
- IV. THE UNIQUE CHARACTERISTICS OF HUMANITY / 199
  - A. Humanity's Unique Physical Characteristics / 199
  - B. Humanity's Unique Ethico-Religious Characteristics / 201
- V. THE DIVINE ANTECEDENT OF HUMANITY / 201
- VI. THE BIBLICAL FOUNDATION OF THE HUMAN RACE / 202
- VII. THE PRIOR CREATIVE ACTIVITY OF GOD / 203
- VIII. THE CREATION OF ANIMALS AND HUMAN BEINGS / 204
- IX. GOD'S PLAN FOR HUMANITY / 208
  - A. Humanity's Relationship to God / 208
  - B. Humanity's Relation to the Rest of Creation / 209
- X. THE GENIUS OF HUMANITY / 210
  - A. The Basis of Human Genius / 210
  - B. The Extent of Human Genius / 211
  - C. The Use and Misuse of Human Genius / 213
- XI. MARRIAGE AND THE FAMILY IN GOD'S CREATIVE PLAN / 214
  - A. The Relationship of Man and Woman in God's Plan / 214
  - B. The Place of Marriage and the Family in God's Creative Plan / 215
    1. Marriage, God's plan as the basis of the family / 215
    2. Marriage constitutes the human family / 216
    3. Marriage complements the sexes / 217
    4. The family provides for the nurture of the young / 219
    5. A New Testament prescription for the Christian family / 220

XII. JOHN WESLEY'S EVALUATION OF HUMANITY / 220

    A. Wesley's View of Degenerate Humanity in Eighteenth-Century Britain / 220
    B. Wesley's View of the Physical Aspects of Humanity / 221
    C. Wesley's View of Human Rationality / 222
    D. Wesley's View of Human "Liberty" and the "Will" / 222
    E. Wesley's View of Death / 223
    F. Wesley's View of Faith Versus Sense Knowledge / 223
    G. Wesley's View of God's Design in the Creation of Humanity / 223
    H. Wesley's View of the Original State of Humanity / 223
    I. Wesley's View of the Fall of Humanity / 224
    J. Wesley's View of Humanity in Distinction From Animals / 224
    K. Wesley's Scriptural Method of Solving the Riddle of Humanity / 225
    L. Wesley's View of the Duration of Humanity / 225

XIII. THE MINUS AND PLUS FACTORS OF HUMANITY / 226

    A. Humanity, Person or Animal? / 226
    B. The Fatal Deficiency / 227
    C. The Hope for Humanity Through the Remnant / 228

NOTES / 229

DISCUSSION QUESTIONS / 230

RECOMMENDATIONS FOR FURTHER READING / 231

BIBLIOGRAPHY / 231

ANTHROPOLOGY

Man, the Crown of Divine Creation

I. THE PLACE OF HUMANITY IN THE UNIVERSE

Then God said, "Let Us make man in Our image, according to Our likeness; and let them rule over the fish of the sea and over the birds of the sky and over the cattle and over all the earth, and over every creeping thing that creeps on the earth." And God created man in His own image, in the image of God He created him; male and female He created them. And God blessed them; and God said to them, "Be fruitful and multiply, and fill the earth, and subdue it; and rule over the fish of the sea and over the birds of the sky, and over every living thing that moves on the earth." Then God said, "Behold, I have given you every plant yielding seed that is on the surface of all the earth, and every tree which has fruit yielding seed; it shall be food for you; and to every beast of the earth and to every bird of the sky and to every thing that moves on the earth which has life, I have given every green plant for food"; and it was so (Gen. 1:26-30).

Augustine somewhere said, "Man wonders over the restless sea, the flowing waters, the sight of the sky, and forgets that of all wonders, man himself is the most wonderful."

The term *anthropology* derives from two Greek words, namely: *anthropos* ("man") and *logos* ("discourse," or "science"). Thus, anthropology is concerned with a discourse about, or the science of, man as humanity—man being thus generic rather than masculine per se. There are three main branches of anthropology: archaeology, physical anthropology, and cultural anthropology. This study is concerned primarily with the last two branches only, from both Wesley's and a contemporary perspective.

Physical anthropology deals with the physical structure and nature of humanity, as also with human psychological processes. *Cultural anthropology* is concerned with the customs and patterns of social behavior. By definition, "culture is the integrated system of learned behavior patterns which are characteristic of the members of a society and which are not the result of biological inheritance."[1] Culture includes, in the words of Tylor, all the "capabilities and habits acquired by man as a member of society."[2]

Mankind as a whole will be considered holistically as human persons in the totality of their being from the following three points of view: (1) humanity in relation to God and the universe; (2) humanity and its unique characteristics; and (3) the future of the human race in the universe, as viewed by Wesley in the eighteenth century and from a contemporary perspective.

II. HUMANITY AS *HOMO SAPIENS*

Humanity in relation to the universe is distinctive—in fact, humanity is unique in the universe. As far as man's knowledge of himself goes, he is, and always has been, man. If there ever was a time when man, as he knows himself now, was not man, then he was *not man,* and thus nothing is known about him before he became man. So-called prehuman skeletal remains are too indecisive and imaginatively speculative to afford any convincing evidence for a pre-*homo sapiens* ancestry.

The earliest valid knowledge that we have about humanity from the anthropological perspective is that left to us by early primitive people who drew pictures of themselves and of animals on the walls of ancient caves. In these pictures they distinguished themselves from the animals they drew. Of course, it is taken for granted that it was *people* who drew pictures of themselves and the animals, and not *animals* who drew pictures of themselves and people. Incidentally, this early-person pictography is a clear indication that early people were *artists* from the time of the first knowledge that we have of them. No other creature has even communicated a purposeful objective record of itself to its posterity. It is well known that primitive art is remarkably sophisticated, thus reflecting a high degree of intelligence on the part of the early primitive person. G. K. Chesterton has put it thus:

> It is the simple truth that man does differ from the brutes in kind and not in degree; and the proof of it is here; that it sounds like a truism to say that the most primitive man drew a picture of a monkey and that it sounds like a joke to say that the most intelligent monkey drew a picture of a man.[3]

Another important postulate concerning people in the universe is that as long as they have been known, they have belonged to *homo sapiens;* that is, man regarded as a biological species and thus capable of subracial crossbreeding with the production of fertile offspring. If one objects that a species cannot be certainly known, then we may reply that it cannot really be known that any new species has ever evolved. Carl F. H. Henry supports this conclusion when he says, "In fact, contemporary science seems less and less sure how to define a species, the human species included."[4]

On the unity of the human race, Edwin G. Conklin has observed that anthropologists are generally agreed that people have had a common origin at some remote time in the past and that the development of the different subraces was from a common source as a result of mutations and separations occasioned by geographical barriers. Further, Conklin notes that all races (subraces) are now so similar that intermarriage with the resultant production of fertile offspring is both possible and actual. Conklin asserts that there is no justification whatsoever for the view that any one subrace is potentially superior to another, though there are apparently superior and inferior individuals among all subracial groups.[5] However, there is no *known time* when this similarity did not exist.

Thus the present solidarity of *homo sapiens* is apparently acknowledged by most, if not all, anthropologists. That certain racial subdivisions do exist is, of course, common knowledge. However, that their differences are superficial and not essential or fundamental cannot be successfully denied in the light of modern scientific knowledge.

How and when *homo sapiens* ultimately originated, as far as anthropology is concerned, is shrouded in the remote mystery of a timeless past that compels an inescapable agnostic conclusion. Many highly speculative and imaginative theories based on certain dubious carbon-14 datings of fragmentary skeletal findings, plus possible unwarranted inferences drawn from the application of the genetic theory, have led to a rather wide variety of scientific speculations regarding the origin and age of humanity, few if any of which are satisfactory.

Thus it becomes evident that anthropology has little of certainty or significance to teach us concerning the ultimate origins of *homo sapiens,* and if we are to take these anthropological speculations seriously, we are left in hopeless agnosticism concerning man's origin and nature.

On the unreliability of the carbon-14 method of dating, William F. Albright, one of the world's most distinguished archaeologists who served as Professor of Semitic Languages at Johns Hopkins University from 1929 to his retirement in 1958 and is the author of *From the Stone Age to Christianity* and a contributor to thousands of scholarly volumes, said as late as January 1963:

> Carbon 14 is almost totally useless in dating bones, which contain a minimum of carbon. We now have many thousands of carbon dates from all over the world, but dating material by inscriptions is nearly always more accurate than the use of radiocarbon.[6]

When we turn from these largely fruitless speculative theories to a consideration of humanity as revealed in the Bible and as historically known, we realize greater scholarly fruitfulness. What is designated prehistoric, if the etymology is to be taken seriously, relates to that which antedates historical information and record.

III. THE BIBLICAL VIEW OF HUMANITY'S ORIGIN AND NATURE

On the biblical origin of humanity Wesley remarks:

> None of our senses, no not the sight itself, can reach beyond the bounds of this visible world. They supply us with such knowledge of the material world as answers all the purposes of life. But as this was the design for which they were given, beyond this they cannot go. They furnish us with no information at all concerning the invisible world.
>
> But the wise and gracious Governor of the worlds, both visible and invisible, has prepared a remedy for this defect. He hath appointed *faith* to supply the defect of sense; to take us up where sense sets us down, and help us over the great gulf. Its office begins where that of sense ends. Sense is an evidence of things that are seen; of the visible, the material world, and the several parts of it. Faith, on the other hand, is the "evidence of things not seen;" of the invisible world . . . faith is an evidence to me of the existence of that unseen thing, my own soul. Without this I should be in utter uncertainty concerning it. I should be constrained to ask that melancholy question:—"Hear'st thou submissive, but a lowly birth, Some separate particles of finer earth?" But by faith I know it is an immortal spirit, made in the image of God; in his natural and moral image; "an incorruptible picture of the God of glory."[7]

Adam Clarke states:

> *Gregory Nyssen* has very properly observed that the superiority of man to all other parts of creation is seen in this, that all other creatures are represented as the effect of God's *word,* but man is represented as the *work* of God, according to plan and consideration: "Let us *make* MAN *in our* IMAGE, *after our* LIKENESS."[8]

H. Orton Wiley takes a similar view of humanity's origin when he says:

> No longer do we have the words, "Let there be," which involves the immediacy of the creative fiat in conjunction with secondary causes; but "Let us make man in our image, after our likeness"—an expression which asserts the power of the creative word in conjunction with deliberative counsel. This counsel, involving as it does the doctrine of the holy Trinity, becomes explicit only as read in the light of added revelation.

Thus Wiley sees humanity as the culmination and climax of God's entire creative acts, related to them as the crown of creation, but nevertheless "distinct from them as a new order of being. In him [man] the physical and the spiritual meet. He is at once a creature and a son."[9]

While man's physical being was related to the earth, he became a spiritual being or person as a result of the breath of God. Thus man became a creature of two worlds—the natural and the spiritual. There is a very real sense in which by creation mankind is both racial and individual.

In the final analysis the doctrine of special creation rests on faith in God's word and action, which are not subject to empirical evidence (Heb. 11:3). Empirical science can neither verify nor successfully deny creation by the divine fiat. Likewise what is presently known about humanity corresponds with the record given in the Scriptures.

History, as such, reveals nothing concerning humanity in regard to basic physiological and psychological constitution that is essentially different from humanity as known today. That a great variety of cultural patterns are in evidence is clearly revealed by the historical perspective; but that such variety is still in evidence in the human race is also common knowledge. However, whereas the physiological natures of people are essentially the same, their cultures are relative and widely variant.

On the dangers of a naturalistic downgrading of humanity, Peter A. Bertocci, Borden Parker Bowne Philosopher at Boston University, says:

> The task before contemporary Christianity is . . . to find a new *whole* [person] which is more completely rededicated to God.
>
> A human being . . . is not an animal with rationality added. He is not a mere plastic set of needs and wants, which allow him more possibility than animals enjoy. He is not an animal with more choices, made possible by his capacity for self-conscious reflection and symbolization. He is not an unconscious wasteland of nonmoral desires insecurely tied down by a superego which automatizes the predential bargaining of his ego with the surrounding culture. Nor is homo sapien a creature who is one-third animal, one-third man, and one-third God, full of anxiety about the monstrosities which may be produced from such a union. . . .
>
> We would suggest that man is a creature whose desires even are none of them like those of animals when seen *within the context of his whole being*. The very fact that man can think, that he feels obligation, that he can will, that he appreciates beauty, is stirred by the holy—these facts transform his most physical demands . . . making them different from those of animals. . . .
>
> If we leave God out of account and start with physical and biological evolution, then we say: Since man emerges from the animal, he must be conceived thus and so! What I plead for is . . . that we see man for what he is and . . . ask what light *his* nature throws, along with the physical and animal world, on the structure of reality.[10]

George W. Forell states, concerning the dignity of persons:

> Because of our alienation from our Creator, classical Protestantism asserts, we turn love into hate and freedom into slavery. Whatever we do works our destruction. Yet the destruction of the image of God in people does not turn them into animals. Even the enslaved human being is still human. Even a person who is full of hate is still a person. People cannot escape their humanity. They can try to escape, but they never succeed.[11]

In his sermon based on Psalm 8:4, entitled "What Is Man?" Wesley gives an interesting, though prescientific from the present point of view, treatment of man from several perspectives. These include such aspects as the physical, the rational, the emotional, and the volitional. He treats also the destiny of humanity.[12] Further attention will be given to these considerations later.

By nature, people have from the beginning realized themselves to be creatures of destiny. They seem always to have realized, at least vaguely, that the natural order was intended for their conquest and use. At no time in human history have beasts conquered people and ruled over them as their hapless prey. At no time has the plant kingdom conquered and ruled people. Indeed, we speak of people in our industrialized era as the slaves of the machine, but in our sober moments we are aware that people make the machines and operate them, and not vice versa, and this extends to the most sophisticated computers. God's first great commission to mankind was to "be fruitful and multiply, and fill the earth, and subdue it." Man was to "rule over" the created order (Gen. 1:28; cf. Ps. 8:3-8). The history of humanity reveals a progressive accomplishment of this God-given commission to conquer and use the created natural order, notwithstanding failures and tragedies throughout the ages.

Not all of nature has yet been brought under human control through the application of the known principles of science; but in the short period of known human history, human progress in the conquest of nature has been amazing. It is important to note that while *people* have made progress in the conquest of nature, all other creatures remain largely the slaves of their environment, as they have been from the unknown past.

The one factor that most accounts for humanity's phenomenal progress in the conquest of nature is the disposition to transcend, to rise above and conquer the obstacles and make them servants. Within humankind there appears to be a sense of destiny—a sort of teleology, or purpose, that ever spurs them on toward the mastery of the natural order. People know that they cannot achieve this God-implanted purpose singlehandedly, and therefore they, already unified as families, also develop clans, evolve nations, and organize empires—political, social, economic, and industrial—that they may cooperatively accomplish what they could not do individually (Gen. 4:17; 11:4).

The universality of religion and ethics as human characteristics and experience are evidences of humanity's transcendent destiny. Religion is a person's recognition of, and sense of dependence on, the supernatural, Friedrich Schleiermacher informs us (this is at least a partial truth, though an inadequate definition). Thus people in religion witness to their human limitations and consequent dependence on God, however divinity may be defined, for help in their transcendent quest. Ethics, supported by religious beliefs, gives normative directives to individual and social conduct.

The foregoing establishes human beings in the universe as intelligent, transcendent creatures who in human ethical cooperation and religious dependence strive ever onward and upward toward the God-ordained conquest and lordship of the created order. People are creatures of four worlds: (1) the world of unaided sense, (2) the microscopic world, (3) the telescopic world, and (4) the metaphysical world. Without a consciousness of the latter, man is, as one has defined the atheist, "a person without invisible support." These four factors constitute the universe to which people find themselves related.

IV. THE UNIQUE CHARACTERISTICS OF HUMANITY

What are the unique universal characteristics that distinguish human beings from all other creatures in the universe and enable them to transcend the natural order?

A. Humanity's Unique Physical Characteristics

Though people have many physical characteristics in common with certain other creatures, they also have certain physical characteristics that clearly distinguish them from all other beings. In fact, the differences are greater than the similarities. We will note here a few of the most significant differences.

The Hebrews well understood the physical uniqueness of humanity. The psalmist sang the praises of God in recognition of His wonderful work in humanity's unique physical constitution thus:

> You created my inmost being; you knit me together in my mother's womb. I praise you because I am fearfully and wonderfully made; your works are wonderful, I know that full well. My frame was not hidden from you when I was made in the secret place. When I was woven together in the depths of the earth, your eyes saw my unformed body (Ps. 139: 13-16 NIV).

Concerning the psalmist's expression, "I was woven together in the depths of the earth," Wesley thinks that meaning to be in a secret place remote from human sight even as are the lowest parts of the earth.[13]

Clarke has an interesting comment on this passage in the Psalms as rendered in the KJV: "Thou hast possessed my reins." "As the Hebrews believed that the *reins* were the first part of the human fetus that is formed, it may here mean, thou hast laid the foundation of my being."[14]

Nowhere in the sacred Scripture is there such a description of the animal kingdom. Although man is sometimes said to belong to the animal kingdom, he is of an immensely higher order. Human beings differ physically from animals not so much in chemical content as in the intricate and purposeful manner in which they are fashioned and compounded. That Christ in His incarnation should assume a human body while He executed redemption for humanity, instead of taking the form of an angel, or otherwise manifesting Himself, suggests the uniqueness of mankind's physical being.

Among the characteristics that distinguish human beings from all other creatures is a *natural* upright posture, the free flexible fingers and the prehensible thumb, the complete rotation of the arm socket, a larger head and brain with a more complex and intricate nervous system than is found in animals.

In addition to the unique physical characteristics, people are so constituted as to be able to symbolize their ideas and translate them into articulate speech and written languages. Together the spoken word and the written word are the principal conveyers of human culture. Likewise, inventiveness and cultural growth differentiate mankind from the rest of creation.

Again, the development of cooperation in increasingly larger groups has enabled humanity to advance in social and political organization, agriculture, industry, education, science, religion, and even in ethics in the better periods. All of this has been made possible by increasingly specialized division of labor—from that of primitive men and women in hunting, gathering, and fishing, to that of present-day highly skilled technicians organized into labor unions.

An important social characteristic of people is their ability to develop and carry on commerce and administer justice. People alone among the creatures of earth have developed a system of the interchange of goods, either in kind or in cash. And, of all known creatures, only people have founded, organized, and administered laws and courts of justice. In these socio-ethical institutions people have probably risen to their highest human ideal, short of religion.

Important as the preceding human distinctives are, more important is the fact that man stands alone under God in the universe as the only known personal being created in the image of God. Persons are so constituted as to be able to communicate personally with God. A person bears, in his or her finitude, the essential notes of the infinite, divine Person. These notes, as we are able to know them, are what make man a unitary spiritual being characterized by moral intelligence or rationality, moral freedom, emotional capacity, spiritual and moral sensibilities, and a sense of moral responsibility. These are essential notes of a unitary personality with their respective functions. They are not parts of a compounded personality. They correspond in their finitude to the essential notes of the infinite personality of God. It does not follow, however, that one's personality is of the same essence as God's. Such a conclusion would make man divine.

Animals are conscious of their environment. There is, however, little if any evidence of true self-consciousness. Self-consciousness is essentially a human distinctive. As self-conscious persons, people are capable of memory and imagination. Thus the past lives in the present, and the present is projected into the future; or perhaps it may be said that one brings the future into the present experience. The beginnings and ends of time meet on the pivot of the verb *to be*. Humanity is capable of transcending chronological time through the grasp of conceptual time (in Greek known as *kairos,* as distinguished from *chronos*). Thus, a person is both conscious and conscious of the fact that he or she is conscious. In these facts of consciousness and self-consciousness lies a person's cognitive ability—the ability to know.

Beyond the consciousness of selfhood, a person is characterized by the power to choose and to implement his or her decisions within certain limitations. But one's freedom, ethically and physically, is always in proportion to one's intelligence. No one is freer than the degree to which one is intelligent.

As persons, people have artistic ability and aesthetic appreciation. They are capable of creating artifacts—of projecting their personalities into works of art—and then objectively viewing these works with aesthetic appreciation. In this respect, humanity stands alone among the known creatures of the earth.

Certainly one of the most distinctive characteristics of persons is in their God-given power of procreation. It is probably in the sex experience with the intent of procreation that they realize their highest humanity and make their nearest approach to God. Here they are creators, in a very real sense, not of a natural universe, but of a new everlasting *potentially immortal personality.* Indeed, animals reproduce themselves, but only to live and die within the time boundaries of the natural world, while persons are timeless.

B. Humanity's Unique Ethico-Religious Characteristics

Among the greatest, if not indeed the greatest, of human distinctives are man's universal and incurable religious and ethical quests and aspirations. That these impulses are of the fundamental drives of human personality can hardly be denied on empirical or rational grounds. All people are ethico-religious, and nothing else on earth is ethico-religious. These drives may of course be misdirected toward false ends, resulting in idolatry and ending in futility. However, when they are directed toward the true God, as He is revealed in Christ, in love for God and fellow beings, then they fulfill their God-intended purpose.

How inspiring are the views of the author of the letter to the Hebrews concerning the Christian's future prospect, when he says, "You have come . . . to the spirits of righteous men made perfect" (Heb. 12:23; cf. vv. 18–24 NIV).

The unfinished conquest of the natural world lies before the human race as a challenge to the fuller development of its human potential realizable through cooperation with the God of the universe. Do people fear the future in the light of the rapid population increase? Let them bring the subterranean waters to the surface of the Sahara Desert, an area about twice the size of India, where about a fourth of the present human race dwells, and by irrigation convert the greatest wasteland of the earth into a fertile field that might well provide for the nutritional needs of the present entire population of the earth. When this supply has been outgrown, perhaps an exodus to some outer planet can be arranged for the population overflow—and then another, and another.

Persons, and persons only, have the intelligence potential, and only they have access to a personal relationship with the righteous God of the universe—a relationship that will enable them to realize the spiritual, ethical, and temporal goals God has set for them in the universe.

V. THE DIVINE ANTECEDENT OF HUMANITY

"What is man that you are mindful of him, the son of man that you care for him?" (Ps. 8:4 NIV). Any adequate understanding of the biblical account of humanity must first take note of God and His creative activities and plans for the universe as a home and habitat for mankind, the crown of His creative work. According to the biblical account, all of God's plans and creative activities were enacted with a view to God's purpose and plans for persons whom He was to create in His own image (the *imago Dei*) and place over the works of His hands. To this the Genesis account testifies when, following the account of the completion of all the rest of God's creative works, it states:

> And God created man in His own image, in the image of God He created him; male and female He created them. And God blessed them; and God said to them, "Be fruitful and multiply, and fill the earth and subdue it and rule over . . . every living thing that moves on the earth" (Gen. 1:27, 28).

Likewise, the psalmist testifies to this divine purpose, extending it to the entire created universe:

> When I consider Thy heavens, the work of Thy fingers, the moon and the stars, which Thou hast ordained; What is man, that Thou dost take thought of him? . . . Yet Thou hast made him a little lower than God [Elohim—possibly angels], and dost crown him with glory and majesty! Thou dost make him to rule over the works of Thy hands; Thou hast put all things under his feet (Ps. 8:3-6).

The author of the Epistle to the Hebrews takes up this refrain from the psalmist and expresses it in this way:

> "WHAT IS MAN, THAT THOU REMEMBEREST HIM? OR THE SON OF MAN, THAT THOU ART CONCERNED ABOUT HIM? . . . THOU HAST CROWNED HIM WITH GLORY AND HONOR, AND HAST APPOINTED HIM OVER THE WORKS OF THY HANDS; THOU HAST PUT ALL THINGS IN SUBJECTION UNDER HIS FEET." For in subjecting all things to him, he left nothing that is not subject to him (Heb. 2:6-8a).

The author of this Epistle then qualifies this statement in the light of man's Fall and finitude and the necessity of Christ, the perfect God-Man, to complete, through His redemptive work, what man has failed to do in the execution of God's plan for him. Thus, he states, "But now we do not yet see all things subjected to him" (Heb. 2:8).

In the light of the biblical account of God's original purpose for humanity, the entire universe (Gr. *kosmos*) was created by God as a habitat for the human race that had not as yet been created and with a view to man's creation to be God's vice-regent over His entire natural universe. To "subdue and rule over" all creation was God's first great commission to our first ancestors. It is beyond human imagination to understand what the ultimate eventuation of the created order under humanity's dominion would have been had not the Fall occurred.

VI. THE BIBLICAL FOUNDATION OF THE HUMAN RACE

Genesis is the first and foundational book of both the Pentateuch and the entire biblical record. Genesis is, in fact, the epitome of God's entire revelation as it relates to human beings and the created universe over which they were commissioned by God to be the subsovereign custodians. Here we have a statement of the biblical account of the origin of the human race together with God's purpose and plan for that race.

The word *Genesis* means "first," "beginning," or "origin." It is closely related to the scientific terms *genetics* and *genes*. Remove the Genesis record, and the rest of the Bible would be meaningless. From the Genesis record all else in the Bible issues. Without it the Bible would be like a building without a foundation. With the validity of the Genesis record, the orthodox Judeo-Christian faith stands or falls. The Bible is a record of humanity's creation, Fall, and divine redemption. This entire record is explicit or implicit in Genesis.

Source-critical scholarship has denied the Mosaic authorship of Genesis, regarding it rather as the work of a redactor or redactors, designated "R," who compiled it from a variety of extant literary sources designated "J" (*Jahweh*), "E" (*Elohim*), "D" ("hortatory and legal materials"), and "P" ("priestly materials"). Leupold agrees with the *Interpreter's Bible,* however, that source criticism has had its day during the past fifty years with meager fruits to show in constructive interpretation.[15] While the Mosaic authorship of Genesis is not explicit in the Bible, the implications for that fact are many. Admittedly, Moses could not have written the early portions of Genesis that antedated his own lifetime, or those portions of the Pentateuch that followed his death, except by direct divine revelation or, in the case of the former, from received reliable traditions, either or both of which is possible. Therefore, we assume, with traditional conservative scholarship, that Moses wrote, or at least compiled, the major part, if not the whole, of Genesis, using oral traditions and direct personal knowledge as he was moved and directed by the inspiration of God's Spirit (cf. Exod. 17:14; 24:4, 7; Num. 33:2; Deut. 17:18; 27:1-8; 31:9, 24; John 5:46-47; 2 Peter 1:20-21). Kevan states that "no reason has yet been produced which categorically requires that the belief in Mosaic authorship should be abandoned."[16] The Book of Genesis, however, gives no indication of the time when it was written, beyond the internal evidence that it was in the patriarchal era.

Indeed, there are various scientific and naturalistic speculations concerning the ultimate origin and age of the universe and the human race. These range from the ancient and more modern naturalistic evolutionary speculations, through theistic evolution, to the recent big-bang theory and other speculations. None of these speculations, however, are anything more than people's subjective interpretations of uncertain piecemeal data. Likewise, the age of humanity is left in total uncertainty, notwithstanding the various anthropological and archaeological attempts to establish reliable data. Even available inscriptions tell us little concerning the antiquity of human beings.

VII. THE PRIOR CREATIVE ACTIVITY OF GOD (Gen. 1:1-2)

The opening words of Genesis, "In the beginning God created the heavens and the earth," are a statement given by divine revelation and accepted by human faith. It is beyond the province of empirical science to either prove or disprove them. No equivalent theory of ultimate origins has ever been offered. This utterance stretches the mind back to the threshold of eternity, beyond which it is impossible to go, for the ultimate mystery of eternity belongs to God. No other dating of creation is given in Scripture.

The priority of God to all creation is highly significant. It precludes the errors of such "eternal" dualistic theories as spirit and matter, good and evil, and God and Satan. It precludes atheism, agnosticism, polytheism, naturalistic evolution, and monistic pantheism. Positively, it predicates the reality, personality, and eternity of God. It affords the mind an ultimate starting point—an ultimate reality and frame of reference for thought and faith. These words, "In the beginning God created," suggest God's unitary nature, self-existence, sovereignty, intelligence, and power manifest in His purposeful creative energy and activity.

Although God is referred to by different names in Scripture—names that reflect His various characteristics—in Genesis 1 He is called in Hebrew *Elohim* or *Alehim*. Though *Elohim* is a plural noun, when used of the one true God it is always joined with singular verbs and adjectives.[17] Thus plurality in the Godhead is indicated in a manner that is distinguished from the plurality of pagan polytheism. This trinitarian plurality is essential to the very existence of God. St. Augustine is represented as having said that "if God is love, then in God there must be a Lover, a Beloved, and the Spirit of love, for there can be no love without a lover and a beloved."[18]

Genesis represents God as active. He "created the heavens and the earth." If

God is love, as the Scriptures make abundantly evident (e.g., 1 John 4:8), then He is necessarily active, for love is an active verb expressive of personal relationships (John 3:16). But, it may be asked, where was the personal object of God's love in His creation of the material heavens and the earth? The answer is found in God's "ultimate object in creation," human beings, yet to be created and given dominion over all creation (Gen. 1:27-28; Ps. 8).

The sovereignty of God is displayed in His creation of the heavens and the earth ex nihilo, "out of nothing." The Hebrew verb *bara,* used here for creation, sometimes means other than creation ex nihilo; but, like any other word, its meaning is determined by the context in which it is used. Nor is the idea of creation ex nihilo dependent only on the word *bara.* As noted by another, that doctrine "is implied rather, (1) in the words, 'in the beginning,' (2) in the total absence of any suggestion of anything uncreated upon which God worked, (3) in reference to the divine *fiat* as causative, and (4) in the way in which the record was understood by the later writers of the Scriptures."[19] Confirmation of this understanding of creation is found in many subsequent biblical passages (cf. Isa. 42:5; 45:18; John 1:1-3; Heb. 11:3).

It is of special interest that God first created the heavens, and second the earth. Rather than ascending from nature to nature's God, as naturalism attempts to do, the order is reversed. It is descent from God to God's works of nature. The Creator first speaks of creation, rather than creation first speaking of the Creator, or the gods, as is the case with the naturalistic accounts of origins.

Although "the heavens" may denote the atmosphere, the stellar system, God's dwelling place, or the blessed home of the soul, when "the heavens" are joined with "the earth," the totality of the universe is suggested.

God's first creative act produced the substance, the *prima materia,* or first elements. This substance was formless and void (Hebrew, *tohu* and *bohu,* "confusion, disorder, chaos"), or a waste and emptiness enshrouded in utter darkness.

VIII. THE CREATION OF ANIMALS AND HUMAN BEINGS (Gen. 1:20-2:3)

On the fifth creative day, aquatic creatures and fowls were created. Their creation represents a definite progression over the appearance of the plant kingdom, a sequence with which science is in agreement. Here, as previously, the Hebrew word *bara* expresses creation of these forms of animal life by divine fiat. Whether God used some intermediate instruments such as the sea and land in His creation of this life is not clear from the record. In any event, it came forth at the creative command of God, not by a process of blind naturalistic, or impersonal pantheistic, evolution.

On the sixth day, land animals and man were created. The land animals apparently shared God's commission to "be fruitful and multiply," as they, too, were to serve the needs of human beings, next to be created.

The creation of persons marks the crown of God's handiwork. Only here does there occur a trinitarian consultation preceding creation: "Let Us make man in Our image, according to Our likeness." Thus, man is, in a very real sense, the child of God by creation, bearing as he does, the natural, moral, and political image of God.

While sex is implied in the multiplication of the aquatic creatures, the birds, and the animals to "fill" their respective habitats, only to people does God give the command to procreate themselves and "fill" the earth (Gen. 1:27-28). But the crowning honor conferred on human beings by God, which they share with no other creature, is dominion over the created realms as God's viceroys (Gen. 1:28; cf. Ps. 8).

The statement that "God . . . rested on the seventh day from all His work" obviously suggests the perfection of creation, rather than rest from weariness. Further, it was designed to exemplify God's plan for humanity of six days of work and one of rest (Exod. 20:8–11). (This does not mean that God has been inactive since that seventh day, for God is always active in His universe [John 5:17 NIV].) Again, God hallowed, or sanctified and blessed, the seventh day (the Sabbath) for humanity's benefit. Six days of work and one day of rest were necessary for production and spiritual, mental, and physical renewal. Since Christ's resurrection, Christians rest and worship on the first day of the week, Sunday, instead of on the seventh, the Sabbath.

According to Wesley's view of the *imago Dei*, based on Genesis 1:26–27, God created human beings

> not barely in His *natural image*, a picture of His own *immortality*; a spiritual being, indued with understanding, freedom of will, and various affections;—nor merely in His *political image*, the governor of this lower world, . . .—but chiefly in His *moral image*; which, according to the Apostle, is "righteousness and true holiness" (Eph. 4:24) . . . "God is love:" Accordingly, man at his creation was full of love; which was the sole principle of all his tempers, thoughts, words, and actions. God is full of justice, mercy, and truth; so was man as he came from the hands of his Creator. God is spotless purity; and so man was in the beginning pure from every sinful blot; otherwise God could not have pronounced him, . . . "very good" (Gen. 1:31).[20]

It is of special interest, especially in light of the position held by some that in the Fall humanity lost the image of God in its entirety, that Wesley views this matter otherwise.

> The Scriptures do say, "God created man in his own image" (Gen. 1:27). But whatever that phrase may mean here, it doubtless means the same in Genesis 9:6: "Whoso sheddeth man's blood, by man shall his blood be shed: For in the image of God made he man." Certainly it has the same meaning in both places; for the latter plainly refers to the former. And this much we may fairly infer from hence, that "the image of God," whereinsoever it consisted, *was not utterly effaced* in the time of Noah. Yea, so much of it will always remain in all men, as will justify the furnishing murderers with death. But, we can in no wise infer from hence, that the entire image of God, in which Adam was at first created, now remains in his posterity.[21]

It is obvious that if human beings had become intensively totally depraved or had lost the total image of God in the Fall, then there would have been no point of contact at which God could have reached or communicated with them. They would have been as the beasts in relation to God.

To argue that the entire image of God was lost in the Fall and that it is only the "prevenient grace" of God that accounts for fallen humanity's moral sense, is to face another dilemma beyond that previously posed by Wesley. Certainly, if people were totally devoid of the moral image of God, there could be no suffering in hell, as there could be no knowledge of right and wrong; and it is unlikely that anyone would wish to charge God with the unthinkable cruelty of extending "prevenient grace" to those damned in hell that they might have moral knowledge in order to suffer there forever. The Scriptures clearly teach that hell is "outer darkness," and since "God is light and in him there is no darkness at all" (1 John 1:5), God cannot be present in the darkness of the world of the damned to sustain them with His prevenient grace (cf. Luke 16:19–31).

H. Orton Wiley writes convincingly that "since there was a declaration of the divine purpose in humanity before even the creative fiat was executed, this image must belong to his inmost creaturely constitution."[22]

Concerning the divine image (the *imago Dei*) in humanity, William Burton Pope says, "As such it was *essential* and *indestructible;* the self-conscious and self-determining personality of man, as a spirit bearing the stamp of likeness to God—a reflection in the creature of the divine nature."[23]

While a variety of views concerning the

terms *image* and *likeness* have been held by theologians from the days of the early church, in general Protestant theologians have regarded the two terms as synonymous and as simply explanatory of each other.

Wiley holds that the *natural* or *essential image* of God in man consisted of his basic original constitution that made him man per se and distinguished him from the rest of creation. The *moral* image consists of the use of the powers with which God endowed him at creation. The first constitutes his personality; the second, his moral likeness to God, or divine holiness.[24]

The natural image of God consists of *spirituality*, which is a person's most intimate likeness to God (Heb. 12:9); *cognition*, or the ability to know (Col. 3:10); and *everlasting personal existence*. While immortality is frequently used synonymously with everlasting existence, technically this is incorrect. While all persons are so constituted as to exist forever, whether for weal or woe, in heaven or hell, only believers in Christ have the life of God, which is immortality. Paul declared that God "alone possesses immortality" (1 Tim. 6:16), and, while God in Christ gives His life to believing persons (John 10:28; 17:3), His presence is not with the lost in the world of doom.

Since a person's spiritual nature characterizes his or her personality, this personality per se is not subject to mortality. Indeed, though the bodily form in which the personality expresses itself will fall away, the person will live on endlessly. The life Christ promised to believers was qualitative—not simply quantitative. While all unbelievers, as well as believers, have life in the latter sense, only believers in Christ have it in the former.

In distinguishing the *natural* from the *moral image*, Wiley summarizes as follows:

> The natural image of God in man has reference to personality, by which he is distinguished from the lower animal creation; while the moral image refers to the character or quality of his personality. The first has to do with the constitution of man as possessing self-consciousness and self-determination; the second has to do with the rightness or wrongness of the use of these powers. The natural image gives him his natural ability and moral responsibility; the moral image gives him his moral ability and makes possible a holy character.[25]

Since humanity was originally created in the perfect image of God but lost that image in part, it remained for the perfect image to be manifest anew in God's son, Jesus Christ, the perfect God-man. Nowhere is this perfect image better expressed than in the Epistle to the Hebrews: "He [Christ] is the radiance of His glory and the exact representation of His nature" (Heb. 1:3). Thus Jesus Christ restored to human beings in His person the perfect divine image in which they were created, but which was marred in the Fall and was not known again until Christ came.

The sullying of humanity's *imago Dei* through the Fall made necessary the renewed, perfect *imago Dei* in the God-man, Christ Jesus, in order that humanity might be restored to God and His original image might be restored in humankind. Thus, the *imago Dei,* both in its pristine glory at creation, though marred in the Fall, and in its manifestation in the perfect man Christ Jesus, are essential to the entire redemptive plan. Only Christ, as the re-manifested *imago Dei* could show to fallen humanity what God intended it to be as created in His image. Likewise, only the moral image of God in Christ could provide the power of divine righteousness necessary for personal salvation. Paul clearly saw this and declared, "I am not ashamed of the gospel [of Jesus Christ], for it is the power of God for salvation to everyone who believes. . . . For in it the righteousness of God is revealed" (Rom. 1:16–17). To deny the *imago Dei* in humanity at creation is to deny the Fall of humanity; to deny the Fall is to make unnecessary the redemption of humanity through Jesus Christ.

Likewise, Carl Henry reminds us that "Hebrew-Christian theology frames the doctrine of the *imago Dei* in the setting of divine creation and redemption."[26] He then quotes David Cairns as saying:

> The gist of the doctrine of Creation is surely this [in respect to the imago Dei], that man's being, though linked with the divine, is itself essentially not divine, but created, and thus dependent on God, and of a different order from His own being though akin to it.[27]

Any attempt to deny God's image in humanity results automatically in some form of idolatry, and idolatry is a violation of the First Commandment and an insult to God. Since the *imago Dei* was marred in the Fall, human beings naturally tend toward idolatry as a substitute for the perfect *imago Dei* in which they were created. Thus the only hope of deliverance from that idolatrous tendency is to find a personal identity in a personal saving relationship with the *imago Dei* as personified in Jesus Christ.

Since the political image, like the natural, was marred in the Fall, humanity has as a result formed a great variety of marital, domestic, national, and perhaps also ecclesiastical organizations that have tended to divide rather than unify humankind. While some of these organizations and institutions have been better than others in the interest of humanity, none have approximated the divinely ordained order that existed before the Fall. Some, such as communism and other forms of totalitarianism, have so distorted the political image that no place for the divine order whatsoever has been allowed. Necessary as is some form of the political image for the preservation of society, nevertheless the perfect political order cannot be realized short of its execution in and through the revealed political image of God in Jesus Christ. Thus, notwithstanding the utopian dreams of the political, economic, and social philosophers of the ages, until the kingdom of God is ultimately established under the governorship of Jesus Christ, who bears the perfect image of God, this order of humanity will continue to reflect the marred political image. Doubtless Aristotle was correct when he saw government as the highest temporal good, since it insures all of humanity's rights, privileges, opportunities, provisions, and protections. What he failed to see, however, as all humanist thinkers have likewise failed to see, was that humanity is in a fallen state and unable to attain that perfection of government that is in the best interest of all humankind. That ideal government remains for the kingdom of God under Christ's lordship.

The *imago Dei* is reflected in a threefold manner, namely: personal, moral, and political. As personal, people were created rational, volitional, emotional, responsible, physico-spiritual individuals. As moral, they were endowed with the Spirit of God's own righteousness. As political beings, they possessed the attribute of social organization, which extends all the way from the family, as the basic unit of society, through the clan, the tribe, nation, and and the empire, even to the United Nations. While these attributes are infinite in God's personality, in humanity they are finite as originally given and are further limited by the effects of the Fall.

Man's political image is reflected in the creation of woman who complemented man, and thus together the man and the woman formed the basic and indispensable unit of all society, the "family." When God looked upon His finished universal creation, He pronounced it "very good," or complete—perfect (Gen. 1:31). Before the creation of woman, however, God said it was "not good" (or perfect) "for the man to be alone" (Gen. 2:18). The fact that God created them "male and female" signifies, first, that women, as well as men, bear the image of God; and second, it establishes the personal equality of women with men.

Man's creation relates him to two worlds—the world of "dust" (finest earthly elements) and the "breath of life breathed into" him by God. Thus, he is a synthesis and a citizen of two worlds, and during earthly time his life is incomplete if deprived of the blessings of either. God's provision of "a garden" afforded him his relationship to and dependence on nature for subsistence on the one hand and meaningful employment on the other. Both are essential to human fulfillment.

IX. GOD'S PLAN FOR HUMANITY

A. Humanity's Relationship to God (Gen. 1:26-31)

Then God said, "Let Us make man in Our image, according to Our likeness" (Gen. 1:26). Having completed man's temporal habitat and having pronounced it good, according to the divine plan, God proceeded to create His final and most important creature, a human being (Heb., *adham*), the climax and "crown" of all His handiwork. All other creation was preparatory for persons, whose creation was the completion of God's plan and purpose. At the conclusion of each previous work of creation, God pronounced it "good," but at the completion of the creation of man, God pronounced it "very good" (Gen. 1:31), or "completed," "finished," "perfect."

Man's uniqueness among all creatures is suggested by the thrice-repeated, and thus emphasized, Hebrew verb *bara* in his creation (Gen. 1:26-27), signifying creation by a divine fiat. That the divine Trinity is suggested here in the creation of man, in the plural expressions "Let Us . . . in Our image" (Gen. 1:26), is quite in harmony with the plural form of God's name *Elohim* in verse 1 and elsewhere. That the idea of Trinity is but implicit and undeveloped here is obvious.

As previously noted, human beings bear the divine image in at least three respects, namely, the personal, the moral, and the political. As created in God's image, people bear the essential notes of God's personality. These consist of rationality, sensibilities, volition, and moral responsibility. God's moral image in people is His righteousness, thus enabling them to conform to the "Word" and "will" of the Creator. The political image consists of the ability to subdue, organize, and govern the created universe over which God made men and women subsovereigns, or viceroys (Gen. 1:26). The genius of people in the exercise of the political aspect of God's image is reflected in their organizational and governmental ability. Only the government of the universal kingdom of God is reserved for God Himself.

Finally, humanity bears God's image in the everlastingness of His being, something not characteristic of any other creature unless it should be the angelic order. However, while humanity reflects God's image in all these, and perhaps yet other characteristics, they are finite in persons, whereas with God they are infinite.

Scientific progress witnesses the extent to which humanity has, across the ages, fulfilled the divine commission to *subdue* and *rule over* God's creation (cf. Ps. 8:5, 6; Heb. 2:6-8). Great as has been man's scientific achievement toward the fulfillment of his God-given commission, he has failed woefully in ethical self-conquest and government. Humanity stands in grave danger of destroying itself by its own achieved scientific powers.

That God created human beings distinct from all other creatures is evident from their unique characteristics. As also previously noted, they are physically unique. Socially and psychologically they are unique in their capability of progressive social development domestically, in groups, and politically; in their ability to symbolize feelings and thoughts and communicate them through oral and written languages; and in their capacity for music and art, among other characteristics. Spiritually, persons are unique in knowledge of God and the universal disposition to worship. Ethically, they are the only known creatures capable of moral knowledge with the ability to make moral decisions and choices with the consequent sense of moral responsibility to God, themselves, and their fellows.

Man was created a heterosexual being: "Male and female He created them." Indeed, sexual distinction was implied in the created animal kingdom when God commissioned them to multiply. The complementariness and equality of responsibility the man and woman shared together in God's plan is indicated by His having "blessed them" and commissioned them to "be fruitful," to "multiply," to populate or "fill the earth," "subdue it," and "rule over" it jointly as man and woman (Gen. 1:28). God's parental care is seen in His provision of a thoroughly furnished home for the human race—the garden of Eden.

God called the entire universe to witness the artistic beauty and perfection of His six-day masterpiece in the words "behold, it was very good" (Gen. 1:31 KJV) and then announced the end of special creation at the close of the sixth day (Gen. 1:31; 2:1).

B. Humanity's Relation to the Rest of Creation (Gen. 2:7–9)

At the end of the sixth day, or before the beginning of the seventh (Heb. *shabboth,* "to cease," or "desist"), God declared "the heavens and the earth . . . completed, [with] all their hosts" (Gen. 2:1). Thus, what had been created in essence at the outset (Gen. 1:1) is now completed in finished form. That these words suggest an original creation by a divine fiat of all things in essence, followed by their completion or perfection during the subsequent five days, is favored by certain reputable scholars, and seems most likely. Even the "fine dust" from which man's body was formed on the sixth day was created originally with the earth (Gen. 1:1). "The heavens and the earth and all their hosts" (Gen 2:1) is translated meaningfully by the Septuagint as "cosmos" (Gr. *pas ho kosmos autōn*), literally, "all their ornaments," "a decorated or adorned whole or system."[28] The expression "hosts" suggests a regulated army of soldiers under the general command of God (cf. Isa. 6:3). "Universe" is the English equivalent of the Greek *kosmos* and means literally all things turning in perfect harmony as *one*—unity in diversity. Thus, it is quite improper to speak of universes in this sense, as there is but one universe, though many worlds.

Whereas in Genesis 1 a general overview of divine creation is given, chapter 2 details that work, particularly as it relates to humanity, the crown of God's handiwork. Chapter 2 does not give, as some interpreters have supposed, a second and different account of creation from that of chapter 1.

Genesis 2:7 gives three details concerning man's creation. First, man is related to the earth by the fact that "the LORD God" (Heb. *Yahweh-Elohim,* the majestic Trinity) "formed" his body "of dust from the ground" (Heb. *apar* or *aphar* = "a damp mass of the finest earth"; cf. Jer. 10:10–12).[29]

"Formed" suggests the work of the skilled potter molding the vessel to conform to the pattern of his highest ideal (cf. Exod. 25:40; Heb. 8:5). However, it also relates man to all other forms of earthly life (2:19) and accounts for his finitude (cf. 2 Cor. 4:7). Man's earthly kinship is further emphasized by the similarity of his Hebrew name "Adam" to "earth" (Heb. *adamah*).

Second, man is related to God and the spiritual realm by reason of the fact that the Lord God (*Yahweh-Elohim*) breathed into his nostrils the breath of life (*nishmath chaiyim,* "the breath of LIVES, i.e., animal and intellectual"[30] (cf. 1 Kings 17:17–23; 2 Kings 4:34–36; Acts 20:9–10).

The "breath of life" breathed by God into man's material form is not, according to Leupold, man's distinctive characteristic, as it is essentially the same as all other animal life (Gen. 7:22). Neither does the expression "a living soul" (KJV and ASV), or person, indicate man's distinguishing characteristic, as the same term is used for other animate beings in Genesis 1:24. Rather it is the manner of its impartation that denotes man's special dignity.[31]

It is God's image in human beings (the

imago Dei) above all else, that distinguishes them from all other creatures. Indeed, God's Spirit animates the souls of persons in a higher sense than in other creatures who do not possess His Spirit. The Aristotelian view was that the soul is not the total human nature, since *person* is the composite of matter informed by the soul.

> The soul is the principle of life; it is the "primary actualization of a natural organic body." But souls differ from one another in the variety and complexity of the functions they exercise, and this difference in turn corresponds to differences in the organic structures involved. Fundamental to all . . . physical activities are the functions of nutrition, growth and reproduction, which are possessed by all living beings, plants as well as animals. Next come sensation, desire, and locomotion, exhibited in animals in varying degrees. Above all are deliberative choice and theoretical inquiry, the exercise of which makes the rational soul, peculiar to man among the animals.[32]

The more satisfactory English designation of man, in his total psycho-physical being, is "person," or "individual" (Gr. *ego*), hence a self-conscious, rational human individual. However, the time-honored term *soul* will probably persist, and in reference to the "*ego-psychē*" it seems to be quite adequate. In any event, the "man" God created is a personal unitary being who in God's image is an everlasting, indestructible entity, whether for weal or woe. As a person, man is a holistic being—a composite being—but so harmonized as to function as a unit.

In the third instance God placed Adam and Eve in most pleasant and advantageous circumstances—"a garden toward the east, in Eden" (Gen. 2:8). This special provision for them was severalfold. First of all, the created earth was their special habitat (their "paradise," Septuagint). Second, its beauty was designed to satisfy their aesthetic appreciation. Third, its fruitage provided amply for their nutritional demands. Fourth, the special "tree of life" and the "tree of knowledge of good and evil" afforded adequate ethical "provision" and "prohibition"—what they could and should not do, both of which were for their personal well-being. Fifth, God gave them the occupation of cultivating the garden—an occupation that was both self-fulfilling and productive. Finally, He charged them with the ethical responsibility of keeping, guarding (protecting), preserving, and developing their paradise (Gen. 2:8, 9, 13-17; cf. Gen. 13: 10; Isa. 51:3; Ezek. 28:13).

X. THE GENIUS OF HUMANITY

A. The Basis of Human Genius

The genius of humanity is suggested in the Bible by man's relationship to God. Man (generic) was created in the image of God—the *imago Dei* (Gen. 1:26-27). As such he bears a Godlikeness, or a relationship to God, notwithstanding his fallen nature. Even in his fallen condition, to declare his independence of God and assert his boasted self-sufficiency (humanism), he is in effect acknowledging his relationship to God. Further, when he attempts to deny the very existence of God (atheism), he is in a certain sense unwittingly acknowledging God's existence. In a *certain sense* the etymology of the word atheist implies God's existence. It derives from the Greek negative particle *a*, meaning *not*, plus the noun *theos* (God), thus "not God" or "God is not." The very assertion, however, is based on the assumption that God does exist, at least in the idea of the one making the denial, though not an ontological admission. It is as much as to say, "God, You do not exist." It is more than passing strange that three of the world's most renowned atheists, namely, Friedrich Nietzsche (1844-1900), Jean-Paul Sartre (1905-1980), and Madelyn Murray O'Hair should have devoted their lives and talents in efforts to disprove that in which they professed not to believe. Without the assumption of God's existence there would be no point in an attempted denial. Little wonder that the psalmist twice states, "The fool has said in his heart, 'There is no God'" (Pss. 14:1; 19:1-6; 53:1). Man can no more divest himself of his consciousness of God than can a person completely divest himself of his family heritage. He is always attached to his *roots.* So does the genius of human beings stem from their divine origin. The universality of religion, man's sense of dependence on the supernatural and his disposition to worship, further indicates this human-divine relationship. The divine image, no matter how sullied, is still in man and ever will be.

Jesus seems to suggest this inescapable relationship in His parables as recorded in Luke 15. The coin long lost, but sought and found by the woman, even though it may have been corroded, still bore the identifiable image of Caesar (Luke 15:8-9). The lost sheep, though but one of a hundred and possibly injured, was still identifiable by its owner (Luke 15:4-6). Even the prodigal in his extreme dissipation and degeneracy was identified by his father as a family member as the father exclaimed in ecstasy, "*This son of mine was dead, and has come to life again; he was lost, and has been found*" (Luke 15:24). Notwithstanding the *extensive* depravity of human beings, they are never quite *intensively* or entirely depraved. Man is still man, even in his fallen condition, and he knows in his sober moments that he belongs to God—that God has a claim on his life. This seems to account for the fact that the universality of religion testifies to mankind's search for God, although on its own terms of reconciliation. Augustine is reported to have said that man is born with salt on his tongue for God. He has an insatiable thirst for the divine—a homesickness for his heavenly Father.

From God's perspective, the psalmist saw humanity as related to God and as the chief object of God's concern when he said:

> What is man, that Thou dost take thought of him? And the son of man, that Thou dost care for him? Yet Thou hast made him a little lower than God, and dost crown him with glory and majesty! Thou dost make him to rule over the works of Thy hands; Thou hast put all things under his feet (Ps. 8:4-6).

B. The Extent of Human Genius

When God gave to mankind at creation the commission to "be fruitful and multiply, and fill the earth, and *subdue it,*" and to "*rule over . . .* every living thing that moves on the earth" (Gen. 1:28), He implied the genius of humanity and presented a challenge for the exercise of the genius that humanity bore in its relationship to God.

Human beings have exercised their genius in a number of universal achievements expressed in their life and culture. Apart from and in addition to certain constitutional physical and psychological common characteristics of mankind, there are those *universal cultural characteristics* that witness to humanity's achievements in the purpose and plan of God.

Among humanity's cultural achievements throughout the ages has been the development of agriculture from the primitive methods of Cain and Abel to the sophisticated methods of modern times. That such development was the purpose of God is evident from the beginning when God placed our foreparents in Eden with the commission "to cultivate it and keep it" (Gen. 2:15). Likewise from the first architectural beginnings by Cain—whether he built a city or a house (since its name Enoch [Heb. *chanoch*] is sometimes used for the dedication of a house [Deut. 20:5])—to the present city skyscrapers, people have developed remarkable architectural skill.

From the earliest recorded metallurgy of "Tubal-Cain, the forger of all implements of bronze and iron" (Gen. 4:22) to the present industrial age with its automation, humanity has developed its mechanical ingenuity and achievements. From Jabal, who "was the father of those who dwell in tents and have livestock" (Gen. 4:20), the domestication of animals has become practically a universal cultural achievement with their present marketable values.

Jubal, the brother of Jabal, was "the father of all those who play the lyre and pipe" (Gen. 4:21). From that primitive beginning music has become universal, in one form or another, all the way to the great symphonies of the world such as those of Bach and Beethoven.

Art and craftmanship have likewise characterized the cultural accomplishments of humanity from the skills of Bezalel (Exod. 31:3-5) to the highly sophisticated achievements of modern times. Dress and ornamentation have developed from the simple garments our foreparents wore when they were expelled from Eden (Gen. 3:7, 21) to the present multifold stylistic creations.

Economics is yet another cultural universal achieved by humanity. This is in evidence all the way from primitive blind barter to the great international banking institutions and exchange systems of modern times.

Certainly one of humanity's greatest universal cultural achievements has been the development of articulate speech, or language, for the oral communication of symbolized sensations and ideas. While not all people have developed a written language, none are devoid of spoken communication, and all languages are capable of translation for intercommunication with peoples of a different language. The origin of this cultural universal is seen when God "brought them [the various creatures] to the man [Adam] to see what he would call them; and whatever the man called a living creature, that was its name. And the man gave names to all the cattle, and to the birds of the sky, and to every beast of the field" (Gen. 2:19-20). Here is the basis of all scientific classification. That God's formation of "every beast of the field and every bird of the sky" (Gen. 2:19) was for humanity's benefit is evident from His challenge to Adam to name them. As names are the means by which people know and control the objects of their environment, we see here a reemphasis of God's command to "subdue" and "rule over" every living thing (Gen. 1:28). Three things are important to note here. First, Genesis 2 is not to be regarded as a chronological account, as though man and woman were created (Gen. 1:27) before the animal kingdom (Gen. 1:20-25). Second, it is not stated or implied that Adam named all members of the animal kingdom at this time—for instance, no mention is made of aquatic creatures in 2:19. Third, here is a challenge to humanity's intellectual capacity to develop a language for purposes of knowledge and communication. Man gave the names, perhaps in keeping with observed characteristics of the creatures, and God approved his denominations (Gen. 2:19-20). Thus, this does not evince an original given language, as some have supposed.

Here Wesley remarks on the naming of the nonhuman creatures: ". . . either by the ministry of angels [which seems doubtful since angels are not mentioned], or by a special instinct, . . . and so might give a proof of his knowledge, the names he gave them being expressive of their inmost natures."[33]

Social and political organizations, elsewhere dealt with, are among the universal cultural developments of the human race for the preservation and orderly control and ongoing of society. Likewise law in some form of expression is as universal as the human race—a cultural development without which society could not exist.

Both Wesley and Clarke take an exceedingly dim view of humanity as depicted in Psalm 8. They were probably greatly influenced toward an unduly pessimistic estimation of humanity by the indescribable degeneracy of their eighteenth-century English environment, even as every person's evaluations are to some extent influenced by his environment. A more realistic view of the psalmist's evaluation of mankind and its achievements is given by a contemporary Wesleyan scholar who writes of God's evaluation of humanity in Psalm 8 as follows:

Man's position is potentially higher even than the angels, for a ministry unto redeemed man is one of their duties (Heb. 1:14). While believing men are sons (1 John 3:2), angels are but servants.

God made man in His own image (Gen. 1:26, 27). Although the moral aspect of that image was lost in the fall, the natural image of God, though weakened and marred, still remains (Jas. 3:9). One evidence of God's continuing image in man is seen in his continued ability to rule over "all sheep and oxen, yea, and the beasts of the field, the birds of the heavens, and the fish of the sea" (cf. Gen. 1:27, 28; 9:2). Through science, man is continuing the conquest of earth, even observing it from the vantage point of outer space. . . .

Man must recognize that his own greatness, though real, is derived. Man's glory is but the reflected splendor of Him who rules all things. "O Jehovah, our Lord, how excellent is thy name in all the earth!" In the final analysis, man's greatest glory lies not in his ability to dominate the earth, but in his right to look up and say "Our Lord" and "How excellent is thy name!"[34]

The psalmist's evaluation of mankind in Psalm 8 appears to be fourfold: (1) He extols the greatness and majesty of God; (2) he depicts the God-ordained dignity, glory, and majesty of man as created in God's image and having a position but little lower than God (NIV margin); (3) he shows the weakness and inadequacy of humanity in its fallen state; and, (4) in the thought of certain scholars, there is a subtle hint that the weakness of humanity is to be remedied by the perfection of the God-man, Jesus Christ (Ps. 8:2). One commentator states of this psalm that it

> is based upon the story of creation (Gen. 1:26–28), and sets forth the ideal dignity of man. V. 6 is applied in 1 Cor. 15:27, Eph. 1:22 to the exaltation of Christ, in whom alone the ideal is realized. In Heb. 2:6–8 the same thought is expressed in another way, man's failure to attain to full dominion being contrasted with the supremacy Christ has won.[35]

Archdeacon Aglen states that the answer to the question "'What is man?' must always touch the two poles, of human frailty on the one hand, and the glory of human destiny on the other," following which he quotes Pascal as saying, "O the grandeur and the littleness, the excellency and the corruption, the majesty and the meanness, of man."[36]

On the one hand it boggles the human mind to contemplate what humanity, in God's ordained plan, would have achieved in the universe had the Fall not occurred; while on the other hand the mind of man falls short of comprehending the extent of human depravity in the fallen state. While cultural and scientific achievements have attained astronomical heights, humanity has suffered from a fatal spiritual and moral deficiency because of the sinful nature. Man may be an intellectual and cultural giant, but without God he is in his sinful state in grave danger of destroying himself and his civilization by his own achievements. Will Durant has stated:

> Science tells us how to heal and how to kill; it reduces the death rate in retail and kills us wholesale in war; but only wisdom [God-given wisdom, we may add]—desire coordinated in the light of all experience—can tell us when to heal and when to kill.[37]

C. The Use and Misuse of Human Genius

Important as the foregoing universal cultural achievements are, they in no way exhaust the list. They do, however, clearly indicate the genius of humanity created in the image of an all-wise God. That these cultural achievements have often been perverted and turned to selfish interests is but an indication of man's fallen condition. Of all the perversions to which mankind has turned its God-given talents, the near-universal practice of warfare has probably been the most self-destructive. Few if any of the universal human achievements have been absent, in one form or another, from the practice of warfare.

Only as people return to God from their alienation and experience the restoration of the moral image in which they were originally created will their cultural

XI. MARRIAGE AND THE FAMILY IN GOD'S CREATIVE PLAN
(Gen. 2:21-25)

A. The Relationship of Man and Woman in God's Plan

Genesis 2:18-25 gives the origin of the human family, which is the foundation of all societies. The Lord God declared, "It is not good for man to be alone." The created man was "good," but it was not in God's general plan for man to be celibate. Marriage is God's plan for the human race. Thus God purposed to make for man a "corresponding" and "complementary" companion—for a companionship infinitely superior to that afforded by animals (cf. 1 Cor. 11:8-9). This is not, of course, a denial that God calls certain exceptional individuals to celibate lives for special vocations or for other justifiable reasons. However, this is not a justification for the institution of a celibate clergy.

Wesley's remarks at this juncture are interesting: "Though there was an upper world of angels, and a lower world of brutes, yet there being none of the same rank of being with [man] himself, he might truly be said to be alone."[38]

The "deep sleep" under which God placed Adam, necessary for the production of woman, was neither swoon nor ecstasy. The Hebrew word *tsela*, sometimes translated *rib*, is better understood as "part of Adam's side," including both *bone and flesh* (Gen. 2:23). Created with and from Adam, woman bore the same nature, the same flesh and blood, and the same constitution; she had equal faculties, powers, and rights, though with certain anatomical and temperamental distinctions. Thus woman corresponded to and complemented man. Adam Clarke says:

> Adam was convinced that none of these creatures [the animals] could be a suitable companion for *him*, and that therefore he must continue in the state that *was not good*, or be a farther debtor to the bounty of his maker; for among all the animals which he had named *there was not found a help meet for him.*[39]

Wesley remarks:

> This lovely creature, now presented to him, was a piece of himself, and was to be *his companion, and wife of his covenant*—In token of his acceptance of her, he gave her a name, not peculiar to her, but common to her sex, she shall be called *woman* . . . a *she-man*, differing from man in sex only, not in nature; made *of man*, and joined *to man*.[40]

Genesis 2:24 indicates, first, a more intimate relationship between man and wife than between parents and children. When children become mature, they leave their parents, but the man-wife relationship continues. Second, the ultimate "essential unity" of man and wife is realized, not in the sometimes temporary marital and sex relationships, important as they are with all of their fringe benefits, but in the offspring that bears characteristics of both parents. Together they constitute the family that is the basic unity of society. The offspring is in itself a new and ultimately independent and indissoluble personal entity (cf. Matt. 19:5; Mark 10:7, 8; 1 Cor. 6:16; Eph. 5:31).

Third, verse 24 suggests a "permanent, monogamous relationship," providing a family and home conducive to the nurture and well-being of the human offspring.

Wesley says,

> The sabbath and marriage were two ordinances instituted in innocency, the former for the preservation of the church, the latter for the preservation of mankind. It appears by Matt. xix. 4, 5 that it was God himself who said here, a man must leave all his relations to cleave to his wife. . . . The virtue of a divine ordinance, and the bonds of it, are stronger even that those of nature.[41]

The man and the woman were naked but unashamed (Gen. 2:25), for before the Fall there had been no misuse or perversion of

God's provisions. Their perversion was expressed in disobedience. Shame is always due to misuse of what is intended for a good purpose. When Adam and Eve misused God's intended provision in partaking of the forbidden fruit, they became unduly self-conscious of their bodies with the result that shame replaced innocence. This need have no sexual implications.

This is to be understood symbolically in that sin exposes its own nature—*shame*. Obviously this is not related to sex or nudity per se under proper circumstances. Wesley's comment is interesting:

> They were *both naked,* they needed no clothes for defense against cold, or heat, for neither could be injurious to them: they needed none for ornament. *Solomon in all his glory was not arrayed like one of these, nay,* they needed none for decency, they were *naked,* and had no reason to be ashamed. *They knew not what shame was,* so the *Chaldee* reads it.[42]

B. The Place of Marriage and the Family in God's Creative Plan

1. Marriage, God's plan as the basis of the family Marriage is both an institution and a relationship that forms the basis for the family. Marriage is as universal and as ancient as the known human race itself. The renowned anthropologist Robert H. Lowie regards so-called group marriage among certain primitive peoples as a purely fictitious nonentity. He sees marriage as a universal human practice and institution, and monogamous marriage as a possibility among any people. This authority notes that

> man shares with other animals the sexual urge, but differs in discriminating between proper, less proper, and improper relations resting on it. . . . Every community regards as superior a relatively permanent bond between permissible mates, and this is marriage; on the other hand, it condemns other forms of relationship as vicious. . . .
>
> Promiscuity in the scientific sense is not mere looseness but a hypothetical condition in which society is indifferent as to the mating habits of its members. . . . Such license, however, occurs nowhere, and there is no evidence of its former existence on the human level. Societies differ in the restrictions they impose, but all of them somehow limit the choice of mates. . . .
>
> Marriage being a permanent bond with fixed mutual rights and obligations, there is no such thing as group marriage anywhere . . . a purely hypothetical condition.[43]

Since Judeo-Christian is the qualifying designation in the present consideration of marriage, it is obvious that the Judeo-Christian Scriptures should afford the primary source for the divine origin and purpose of the institution and relationship of marriage. This is a fact that has always been officially recognized by the Christian church. The following is typical of modern, standard Christian marriage rituals bearing on the basic reason for the institution of marriage.

> We are gathered together in the sight of God and in the presence of this company, to join together this man and this woman in holy marriage. This is an honorable estate, *instituted by God* in the time of man's innocency, *confirmed by the teaching and hallowed by the presence of our blessed Lord,* and *likened by St. Paul to the holy union that exists between Christ and his Church,* and therefore is not by any to be entered into unadvisedly, but reverently, discreetly, and in the fear of God. Into this holy estate, these two persons are come to be joined (italics added).[44]

Although specific marriage rituals are neither prescribed nor exemplified in the Old or New Testaments, divinely instituted monogamous marriage is clearly revealed in the Bible as the will and purpose of God from the beginning of the human race.[45] W. Melville Capper and Morgan H. Williams make the following significant statements concerning God's plan for marriage.

> The Bible glorifies marriage and sexual love in itself . . . and the family. It contradicts any idea that sex is bad. The Bible . . . suggests that [the] man who keeps this instinct [sex] in its right perspective has more gratification and pleasure from it than

those who inflame and excite it. . . . For . . . [the basic relationship between man and woman] we have to go back to the very beginning of the Bible. . . . In simple words, the Bible asserts that men and women are different from the animals in possessing a spirit capable of fellowship with God. Adam was also instructed in the fundamental relationship that exists between man and woman. Some of us are so conditioned in our thinking by the scientific approach that we are unable to discern the true nature of this [Genesis] record.[46]

R. Payne Smith observes that

every step and stage in this [Genesis] description is intended for the enoblement of the marriage. . . .

The great and primary object of this part of the narrative is to set forth marriage as a Divine ordinance. . . . He who at the beginning made them male and female pronounced the Divine marriage law that man and wife are *one flesh*.[47]

The Genesis account of the origin of woman and her union with man at the hand of God is the basis of the entire biblical teaching concerning marriage, notwithstanding the deviations from and perversions of this original divine purpose that are sometimes encountered in the Scriptures. Monogamous marriage eventuating in the family is clearly an institution planned, initiated, and sanctioned by God.

2. Marriage constitutes the human family The prime purpose of marriage is to establish the family and home. Although marriage ceremonies, families, and homes differ in various cultures, they hold in common the fact that they are the smallest universal unit of society. The relationship of marriage to the family is of prime consideration as defined anthropologically:

The bond between spouses emphatically differs from that of lovers in implying mutual obligations apart from sex life. . . .

The total of sentimental, economic and legal ties between spouses, parents and children, and between siblings makes the family a very strong social unit.[48]

Paul H. Landis asserts:

Marriage and family are not optional; they are necessary. They meet man's deepest needs. New conditions bring changes, but if history teaches any lesson it is that the family is as durable as man. . . .

The family is one institution that will never die.[49]

E. Adamson Hoebel states that

the family is the most fundamental of all social groups, and it is universal in its distribution. . . .

The conjugal family, consisting of married spouses and their offsprings, performs at least four basic functions: (1) the institutionalization of mating with its attendant controls over sexual outlet; (2) cooperative division of labor between male and female; (3) nurture of the young in an atmosphere of intimacy; (4) basic enculturation of the oncoming generation.[50]

This somewhat complex social unit implies recognized roles and division of labor within the family, both on the part of the husband and wife and on the part of the offspring. Thus the male assumes the dual major role of husband and father, while the female contracting party in the marriage assumes the dual role of wife and mother, though she may often be independently involved in extradomestic duties.

It is of importance to note that while the individual human family is the most brittle, and perhaps least permanent, unit of the social organization, it is at the same time the most persistent social institution. It is much easier to dissolve a family than a clan, a tribe, a nation, or an empire. Through all the vicissitudes of social change from the primitive clan system to a modern democracy, the family unit persists; nor is there sufficient evidence to indicate that it will ever be supplanted by another institution or form of social organization. Attempts to eliminate the family in Communist Russia, in the People's Republic of China, and in certain Western communes, have ended in failure.

Turning more specifically to the religious emphasis on the family, it is noteworthy that in the Judeo-Christian, or biblical, context the family plays a basic role in God's plan for the human race. From their beginning at creation, throughout the patriarchal era, the period of the Judges, the monarchy, the captivity, the restoration, and in the New Testament era in the teachings of Christ and the apostles, marriage and the family have consistently played a major role in society and the plan and purpose of God for the human race.

The Judeo-Christian insistence on the importance of the family as a God-ordained social institution [relationship] is well described by John Charles Wynn in the following manner:

> The family is the custodian and only true example of life's highest known ideal. It is the one institution in which it is possible to say "we" without any loss of individuality. . . . To say "we" and to mean it, is a very great spiritual achievement. . . . A family in which each does what he can and each receives what he needs, wholly without financial calculation of earning or merit, represents the highest known ideal, our only true approximation to the Kingdom of God. . . . This is a foretaste of what the world ought to become.[51]

Dark and foreboding as the picture may be for marriage and the family in the present generation, we may be certain that they will survive. Since marriage and the home, like the church, is a relationship instituted by God from creation, it has stood the test of the past ages and it will stand the vicissitudes of the ages to come until it realizes its ultimate fulfillment in the kingdom of our Lord and Savior Jesus Christ.

3. Marriage complements the sexes
Marriage is the only satisfactory provision for the complementation of the sexes. This is cogently set forth in Genesis 2. "But for Adam there was not found a helper suitable for him" (v. 20) suggests the incompleteness of his being and life as he stood alone to become God's delegated sovereign over the created natural order (see Gen. 1:26-30; cf. Ps. 8:4-8; Heb. 2:5-8). The domestication of certain animals and their reduction to Adam's servitude, and even their friendship, could not supply his need for personal, spiritual companionship. Thus to meet his essential personal need (also for the procreation of the human race), God formed a woman from the very *side* or *flank* (Vulgate, *costa*) of Adam, not from one of his several ribs the loss of which he would not feel. Smith remarks, "She [woman] is one side of man; and though he may have several sides to his nature and character, yet without woman one integral portion of him is wanting."[52]

Smith remarks further that the woman's

> formation is described [v. 22] as requiring both time and care on the heavenly artificer's part. Thus the woman is no casual or hasty production of nature; but is the finished result of labour and skill. Finally, she is brought with special honour to the man as the Creator's last and most perfect work. . . . Woman is not made from the *adamah* but from Adam. She is something that he once had, but had lost; and while for Adam there is simply the closing of the cavity caused by her withdrawal, she is moulded and refashioned, and built up into man's counterpart. She brings back more than the man parted with, and the creator Himself leads her by the hand to her husband. The anthropomorphic language of these early chapters is part of that condescension to human weakness which makes it the rule everywhere for inspiration to use popular language. . . . At last . . . he [Adam] found one standing by him in whom he recognized a second self, and he welcomed her joyfully, and exclaimed, "This at last is bone of my bones, and flesh of my flesh." That is, she is man's counterpart, not merely in feeling and sense—his flesh—but in his solid qualities. . . . The words . . . *man* and *woman* (perhaps womb-man), represent with sufficient accuracy the relation of the words in the original.[53]

In commenting on a rather difficult passage from the writings of the apostle Paul dealing with the subject of marriage (1 Cor. 7:3-7), an eminent contemporary British writer remarks:

> Paul strikes a supremely great principle. Marriage is a partnership. The husband cannot act independently of the wife, nor the

wife independently of the husband. They must always act together. The husband must never regard the wife simply as a means of self-gratification; he must regard the whole marriage relationship, both in its physical and spiritual sides, as something in which both find their gratification and both find the highest satisfaction of all their desires.[54]

Wood likewise sees the fulfillment of the complementariness of the sexes as one of the highest aims of marriage when he asserts that "the finest and most complete union of personality is the real end and aim of marriage."[55] Capper and Williams record Augustine as having remarked concerning marriage as the complementation of the sexes:

> If God had meant woman to rule over man, He would have taken her out of Adam's head. Had he designed her to be his slave, from his feet. But God took woman out of man's side, for He made her to be a helpmate and an equal to him.[56]

The most complete oneness of a man and a woman in love with each other cannot be realized short of the marital relation. Even though the engaged couple experiences unbelievable happiness, there will eventually arise within them a deep desire for a fuller mutual self-giving. Capper and Williams state:

> They will—for the most part unconsciously—come more and more under the spell of the ultimate purpose of marriage. . . . Poetry, music and art have all failed to give adequate expression to this sublime experience. . . . Man should realize his imperfection, finding completion only in his "helpmate" or complement. The divine order was, and still is, that God gave man and woman one to the other in companionship so close and enduring that they would become one flesh and that the closeness and permanence of their relationship should outstrip all other human ties.[57]

Monogamy, not polygamy or polyandry or any other form of group marriage, was God's plan for humanity from the beginning of time. He made them *man and woman*. Repeatedly the Scriptures speak plainly to this point, beginning from Genesis 2:24: "For this cause a man shall leave his father and his mother, and shall cleave to his wife, and they shall become one flesh." Matthew expands this pronouncement, saying:

> Have you not read, that He who created them from the beginning MADE THEM MALE AND FEMALE, and said "FOR THIS CAUSE A MAN SHALL LEAVE HIS FATHER AND MOTHER, AND SHALL CLEAVE TO HIS WIFE; AND THE TWO SHALL BECOME ONE FLESH"? (Matt. 19:4, 5).

Mark likewise records this divine pronouncement (Mark 10:6-8), and Paul uses the monogamous relationship as a basis for both the Christian family and the church as the bride of Christ (Eph. 5:22-33).

Wesley's comment on this issue is especially significant:

> The sabbath and marriage were two ordinances instituted in innocency, the former for the preservation of the church, the latter for the preservation of mankind. . . . The virtue of a divine ordinance, and the bonds of it, are stronger even than those of nature.[58]

Clarke's observation goes somewhat beyond Wesley when he says:

> These words may be understood in a twofold sense. 1. *These two shall be one flesh,* shall be considered as one body . . . each being equally interested in all things that concern the marriage state. 2. These two shall be one *for the production of one flesh;* from their union a posterity shall spring, as exactly resembling themselves as they do each other. . . .
>
> We have here the first institution of marriage, and we see in it several particulars worthy of our most serious regard. . . . God pronounces the state of celibacy to be a *bad state,* or, if the reader please, *not a good one;* and the Lord God said, *It is not good for man to be alone.* This is GOD'S judgment. Councils, and fathers, and doctors, and synods, have given a different judgment; but on such a subject they are worthy of no attention. The word of God abideth for ever.[59]

The principle of complementariness in marriage is not limited in its expression to sex fulfillment in the narrower sense, important as that is in itself with its extra procreation benefits. Sexual division of labor, witnessed in all societies, likewise eloquently testifies to this principle, as does the necessity of the cooperation of male and female for the procreation of the human offspring and the care and nurture of the children. The sociological tendency to support homogamy, or the opposing psychoanalytic disposition to support heterogamy, have not succeeded in denying the complementariness of the sexes nor making the complementariness an expression of perversion.[60] Both lesbianism and male homosexuality are clear witnesses to the expressed need for sexual complementariness, though both practices are perversions of the natural functions and stand condemned by God's righteous judgment. The inspired Scripture is explicit in regard to these unnatural practices.

> God gave them over to degrading passions; for their women exchanged the natural function for that which is unnatural, and in the same way also the men abandoned the natural function of the woman and burned in their desire toward one another, men with men committing indecent acts and receiving in their own persons the due penalty of their error . . . and, although they know the ordinance of God, that those who practice such things are worthy of death, they not only do the same, but also give hearty approval to those who practice them (Rom. 1:26-27, 32; cf. 1 Cor. 6:9; 1 Thess. 4:3-5; Lev. 18:22; 20:13).

Certainly there is hope in the power of the gospel for those who are guilty of this kind of sinful perversion or of other forms of vice. The apostle said, "I am not ashamed of the gospel, for it is the power [Gr. *dynamis*] of God for salvation to *everyone* who believes" (Rom. 1:16).

4. The family provides for the nurture of the young The nurture of the young is one of the most important provisions of the family. There can be no adequate substitute for the function of the family in the development of the child. The noted anthropologist Margaret Mead has paid high tribute to the family in this important function. She wrote:

> It has been . . . effectively demonstrated that children do not thrive, in spite of good physical care, if kept as young infants in impersonal institutions and that separation from the mother—especially at certain periods—has serious deleterious effects on the child. Retardation, failure to learn to talk, apathy, regression, and death all appear as accompaniments to institutionalization when no mother surrogate is provided.[61]

Landis adds his testimony to that of Mead on the importance of the home in providing for the nurture of the young child:

> Psychologists now believe that our feelings of security and belonging which are basic to the way we respond to other people throughout our lifetime, are established to a considerable extent by relationships with our mothers during the first two or three years of life. If a mother, by affection and care, makes a child feel that he is wanted, that he belongs, this carries over to the other relationships. If, on the other hand, she is irritable or indifferent and makes him feel that he is unwanted, he develops a sense of insecurity that is difficult to eradicate in later years.[62]

Of course the father plays an equally important role in the development of the personality traits of the child, though the mother's influence may be greater in the earlier stages. A warm family environment in which love and directive discipline are wisely but freely administered provides the rich soil in which the young human plant will grow and develop into a healthy and strong personality. This family training will express itself in a kind but firm and positive program of child nurture about which the parents have mutual understanding and agreement. Such training will be directed toward the goal of the child's independent, creative action rather than the personal pleasure of the parents. Children will be incorporated into the family as members in full standing where cooperation and confidence are the true goals of family living. Here they will find health and nurture for their growing bodies, answers to the questions of their inquiring minds, and wholesome nurture in their developing social consciousness and relationships. Individual differences and needs will be noted and provided for by wise Christian parents (cf. Heb. 12:5-11). The ultimate goal of family child nurture will be the healthy, independent, and mature personality of the child in adulthood. Wynn records that

> the stability of the modern family is dependent upon the child's spiritual development or failure to develop spiritually. Just as we parents and our society have the obligation to assure our child the best possible physical health of which he is capable, the best possible intellectual development, and the best possible social and emotional development, so we are obligated to see about his spiritual inheritance.[63]

5. A New Testament prescription for the Christian family (Eph. 5:21-6:4) In his Epistle to the Ephesians Paul presents a threefold formula for the Christian family's life in Christ. This formula consists of the Christian wife's duties to her husband, the Christian husband's duties to his wife, and the mutual obligation of the parents and their children.

XII. JOHN WESLEY'S EVALUATION OF HUMANITY

A. Wesley's View of Degenerate Humanity in Eighteenth-Century Britain

Among the several factors that influenced Wesley's theological evaluation of humanity, in addition to the Bible, were the social, politico-economic, and prevailing moral degeneracy of the people of the British Isles in the eighteenth century. In all of these respects the British Isles had descended to the lowest moral level in their entire history.

Indeed, Britons had an enviable Christian heritage and, notwithstanding the general degeneracy that characterized them, they still considered themselves Christian. The English had been among the first pagan nations of Europe to receive the gospel at an early date, possibly as early as the middle of the second century.

The degenerate moral conditions that characterized the England of Wesley's time, however, gave a bad complexion to the church and the Christian religion, and indeed to mankind in general. The pulpit was by this time largely silent on moral issues, and the conscience of society was stultified, if not radically perverted, as it condoned the prevailing personal and social evils of the day.

The nefarious African slave trade in which England had become involved blinded the minds and hardened the hearts of society to human concern and compassion. In degrading other human beings to the status of slaves, the English had degraded themselves.

The moral degeneracy extended to the so-called nobility, and even to the Royal Crown. George I (1714-1727) openly practiced concubinage and allowed his mistresses to influence the official affairs of the nation.

In habits of speech Wesley declared there was no other nation on earth as profane as the British. Regarding this, he said:

> Permit me to touch on one article more, wherein indeed, we excell all the nations upon earth. Not one nation under the canopy of heaven can vie with the English in profaneness. Such a total neglect, such an utter contempt, of God is nowhere else to be found.[64]

Again, Wesley said:

> We daily curse and swear, and blaspheme the Most High, merely by way of diversion, almost from the highest to the lowest. Nobility, gentry, tradesman, peasants, blaspheme the worthy name whereby we are called, without provocation, without remorse. Sloth and luxury we allow are general among us; but profaneness is well nigh universal. Whoever spends but a few days in any of our large towns, will find abundant proof, that senseless, shameless, stupid profaneness is the true characteristic of the English nation.[65]

The English people were inundated with intoxicating liquor in Wesley's day. He saw the drunkard as a beast rather than a man as he staggered under the influence of liquor. According to Bready, England was producing no less than 11 million gallons of gin annually by 1750. A typical example of British corruption was Sir Robert Walpole, Britain's Prime Minister from 1721 to 1742. He was a gross and sensual glutton and drunkard who lived in adultery without shame or public censure. His lifestyle was reflected in his official duties as he practiced bribery, duplicity, and general political corruption.

An impassable gulf existed between the rich and the poverty-stricken, leaving the latter in unthinkable and hopeless destitution. Rich and poor alike, however, manifested similar immoral and even brutal characteristics, though each level operated in its own area of sinful activities, including gambling and brutal sports.

There was the notoriously inhumane treatment of prisoners in Britain's appalling prison houses. Added to all this was the use of child labor in factories, depriving young children of health, happiness, and education.

Under these circumstances, Wesley saw England in particular, and humanity in general, as so extensively depraved that it is not surprising he should on occasion have concluded that humanity as represented by his native England had become so degenerate as to have totally lost the image of God. Yet at other times, in his more reasoned theological judgment, he could say that only the moral image of God was lost while there remained the natural and political image in man, though even these were sullied by the Fall.

Further, it must be remembered that Wesley was primarily an evangelist and moral reformer, rather than a systematic theologian per se. As such, he, like all reformers, found it necessary to paint the picture of gross sinfulness in the darkest hues in order to awaken the consciences of sinful and degenerate Britons. Thus Wesley used theological terminology in a manner best suited to the needs of his audiences for the accomplishment of his evangelistic purposes. In this sense Wesley was pragmatic, rather than systematic. If he sometimes appears to have been inconsistent in his use of terminology, he was nevertheless consistent in his purpose and aims to win people to Christ and reform the moral conditions of humanity.

B. Wesley's View of the Physical Aspects of Humanity

There appear to be few, if any, aspects of humanity, from creation to eternity, that Wesley did not consider and on which he did not write. In his sermon "What Is Man?" based on Psalms 8:4, Wesley delineates the various aspects of humanity.[66]

Two things must be taken into account in understanding Wesley's view of the physical aspects of humanity. First, it is evident that he was influenced by the early Greeks in his concept of the components of man's physical being. He sees these physical elements as fourfold—namely, "earth" (matter), "air," "water," and "fire." Wesley held a view of man's physique not greatly different from that of the "pluralistic" Greek philosophers, especially the Pythagoreans.[67]

In a somewhat similar manner, but perhaps with a more mechanical emphasis, Wesley describes the human body, which he designates "a curious machine." He states:

> It is a little portion of earth, the particles of which cohering, I know not how, lengthen into innumerable fibers, a thousand times finer than hairs. . . . In order to the continuance of , . . circulation, a considerable quantity of air is necessary. And this is continually taken into the habit, by an engine fitted for that very purpose. But as a particle of ethereal *fire* is connected with every particle of air, (and a particle of water too,) so both air, water, and fire are received into the lungs together; where the fire is separated from the air and water, both of which are continually thrown out; while the fire extracted from them, is received into, and

mingled with, the blood. Thus the human body is composed of all the four elements, only proportioned and mixed together; the last which constitutes the vital flame, whence flows the animal heat.[68]

Wesley sees the component of fire, contained in the blood and assisted by the elastic force of the arteries, as effecting the circulation of the blood. He argues that the heart of a strong man would be unable to lift the weight of 3,000 pounds, whereas it would require a force equal to 100,000 pounds to circulate the blood through the human body.[69]

Second, it must be remembered that Wesley lived and thought in a relatively prescientific age and consequently reflects the science of his day.

C. Wesley's View of Human Rationality

In addition to the four elements of earth, water, air, and fire that Wesley saw as constituting the physical body, he recognized an additional factor not akin to any of these or a combination of them. He says, "I find something in me that thinks . . . something which sees, and hears, and smells, and tastes, and feels; all which are so many moods of thinking."[70] Then Wesley continues that when objects are perceived by any one of a person's senses, he forms ideas, and this thinking being formulates judgments, either negative or positive. The mind then proceeds to reason on the basis of these judgments, inferring one proposition from another. The mind reflects on its own operations—it is endued with memory and imagination. Wesley believes that any of the mind's operations may be subdivided into other operations.

Thinking as he does of a compounded or composite being, rather than seeing persons holistically as they are generally viewed today, Wesley faces the same question that a dualistic view of human nature has always faced—how can this spiritual mind interact with a material body? Since, to Wesley, mind does not pervade the body, he concludes that the thinking, governing principle must be in the "head; but whether in the pineal gland [as Descartes believed], or any part of the brain, I am not able to determine."[71]

This inner thinking principle, Wesley thinks, is capable of such emotions as "love, hatred, joy, sorrow, desire, fear, hope, etc., and a whole train of other inward emotions."[72] Wesley then proceeds to identify the emotions with "will" and says, "They [the emotions] seem to be the only spring of action in that inward principle I call the soul."[73]

Since Wesley sees the physical components of earth, fire, air, and water as purely passive in themselves, they cannot be the soul, he concludes. "But my soul has from Him an inward principle of motion, whereby it governs at pleasure every part of the body."[74] In the face of this statement, however, Wesley makes certain exceptions. He wrote, "The dilation and contraction of the lungs, the systole and diastole of the heart, the pulsation of the arteries, and the circulation of the blood. These are not governed by me at pleasure: They do not wait the direction of my will";[75] they are involuntary.

Wesley regards the soul as distinct from the body, and this is an assurance of immortality: "When my body dies, I shall not die. I shall exist as really as I did before."[76] He admits that the body and soul are intimately connected for the present and will be again in the resurrection.

D. Wesley's View of Human "Liberty" and the "Will"

Wesley sharply distinguishes between "freedom" and "will." In his view the "will" seems to belong to the emotions, which are associated with the physical part of man, whereas "freedom" is a property of the soul—"a power of self-determination."[77] At this point it seems difficult to follow Wesley's distinction between "freedom" and "will," as "freedom" is said to extend over the bodily functions and would thus be master of the will, which belongs to the emotions.

E. Wesley's View of Death

Death, Wesley declares, "is properly the separation of the soul from the body."[78] While the fact of death is certain, the evidence of death is an uncertain matter for Wesley, even as it is to the present. Neither cessation of breathing, arrested heartbeat, nor arrested circulation of the blood are certain evidences of death, he thinks. From any or all of these, people have been revived, he notes. Of one thing Wesley is certain: death occurs when the soul is separated from the body. The exact time when this occurs, it seems, God only knows.[79]

F. Wesley's View of Faith Versus Sense Knowledge

Wesley's views on sense knowledge, as far as they go, do not differ substantially from the present generally accepted view. He recognizes the limitations of sense knowledge in the present temporal world:

> None of our senses, no, not the sight itself, can reach beyond the bounds of this visible world. They [the senses] supply us with such knowledge of the material world as answers to all the purposes of life. But as this was the design for which they were given, beyond this they cannot go. They furnish us with no information at all concerning the invisible world.[80]

On the other hand, Wesley understands humanity to be endowed by the Creator with the ability to transcend the empirical world—this he calls faith. He says:

> He [God] hath appointed *faith* to supply the defect of sense; to take us up where sense sets us down, and help us over the great gulf.... Faith ... is the "evidence of things not seen," of the invisible; of all those invisible things which are revealed in the oracles of God.[81]

At this point Wesley fears the subjective aspects of divine revelation when he says, "But indeed they reveal nothing, they are a mere dead letter, if they are not mixed with faith in those that hear them."[82] He further argues that he could not even know that he had a soul, except by faith.

Wesley understands that the origin and the everlastingness of the soul are to be accepted by faith. Again he believes in the existence of "millions" of other spirits, both good and bad, in our world, though they are not subject to discernment by the physical senses. God, he holds, is a necessary object of faith and is not empirically known. To Wesley the invisible world is as real as, even more real than, the world of sense experience, when apprehended by faith (cf. Heb. 11).[83]

G. Wesley's View of God's Design in the Creation of Humanity

Wesley asks, "For what end is life bestowed upon the children of men? Why were we sent into the world?[84] He answers by saying it was for one purpose only, and that "to prepare for eternity." He argues that we live for this purpose alone, and for this purpose is "life either given or continued." This, he says, "was the end [purpose] of his creation . . . that he might know, and love, and enjoy, and serve his great Creator to all eternity."[85] By this, however, Wesley does not mean that humanity should not live in and enjoy the present life, for he says, "It pleased the all-wise God, at the season which he saw best, to arise in the greatness of his strength, and create the heavens and the earth, and all things therein. *Having prepared all things for him*, He 'created man in his own image, after his own likeness.'"[86] Thus it was for humanity's benefit and well-being, that God created the natural world, so that through its use humanity should glorify God.

H. Wesley's View of the Original State of Humanity

Wesley understands that man in the original state was in God's image, as holy as God was holy, as merciful as God was merciful, and as

> perfect as his Father in heaven is perfect. As God is love, so man, dwelling in love, dwelt in God, and God in him. God made him to be an image of his own eternity, an incorruptible picture of the God of glory. He was accordingly pure, as God is pure. . . . He knew not evil in any kind or degree. . . . He loved the Lord his God with all his heart, and with all his mind, and soul, and strength.[87]

God gave to this perfect personal creature a perfect law to which He required perfect obedience so long as he should live in this world. To the law of love in the heart of man God added the law of prohibition against eating from the tree of the knowledge of good and evil, and to this prohibition He attached the penalty of death. By obedience to the law of love human beings experienced life everlasting, since they participated in the eternal life of God Himself.[88]

I. Wesley's View of the Fall of Humanity

Since this subject has been dealt with in chapter 7, on hamartiology, little need be said here.

Humanity's fall was occasioned by the misuse of the power of moral choice when Adam and Eve disobeyed the specific command of God not to eat the fruit of the tree of the knowledge of good and evil. It was right and proper that they should have intellectual knowledge of evil as well as of good and make a clear distinction between the two. This they evidently had or they would not have been responsible for their disobedience. It was when they desired and consequently decided to acquire experiential knowledge of these distinctions that they identified with the evil through disobedience and thus fell under the judgment of God. Wesley says, "He [man] wilfully and openly rebelled against God, and cast off his allegiance to the majesty of heaven. Hereby he instantly lost both the favor of God, and the [moral] image of God wherein he was created."[89]

Wesley goes so far as to say that humanity, through the fall, "became lower than even the beasts that perish."[90] Such a statement can stand only in the sense that the power of free moral choice that Adam and Eve were given enabled them to depart from their Maker, whereas beasts have no such ability but are determined to serve their own Maker in the realm of His will. Beyond this the reader is referred to chapter 7 for the nature and effects of the Fall.

J. Wesley's View of Humanity in Distinction From Animals

Wesley states that "man was the channel of conveyance between his creator and the whole brute creation . . . man was God's vicegerent upon earth, the prince and governor of this lower world; and all the blessings of God flowed through him to the inferior creatures."[91]

Wesley regards the beasts as originally having had, in common with man, what he calls "an innate principle of self-motion; and that, at least, in as high a degree as they enjoy it at this day." Further, he saw them as "endued with a degree of understanding; no less than they are possessed of now."[92]

He states that

> they had also a will, including various passions, which, likewise, they still enjoy: And they had liberty; —a power to choose; a degree of which is found in every living creature. Nor can we doubt but their understanding too was, in the beginning, perfect in its kind. Their passions and affections were regular, and their choice always guided by their understanding.[33]

Wesley then raises the question of the difference between humans and brutes, as he chooses to call them, and discusses the line that brutes cannot pass. He says that the distinct characteristic of humans is not reason, by which he means "understanding." Positively, he states:

> But it is this: man is capable of knowing God; the inferior creatures are not. We have no ground to believe that they are, in any

degree, capable of knowing, loving, or obeying God. This is the specific difference between man and brute; the great gulf which they cannot pass over. And as loving obedience to God was the perfection of man, so a loving obedience to man was the perfection of brutes.[94]

Wesley goes so far as to say that animals were not only happy and fully provided for under the government of persons before the Fall but they also possessed "some shadowy resemblance of even moral goodness." Doubtful as this statement concerning animals may be, as are also certain others Wesley makes concerning their kind, it would appear that Wesley overstates his case when he says, "And they too were immortal: For God made not death; neither hath he pleasure in the death of anything."[95]

Genesis 1:27-30, when considered in the light of Genesis 4:2, 4, 20 compared with 9:2-3, seems to indicate that God intended animals as food for man, and thus they were subject to death. Likewise God Himself slew animals to provide covering for Adam and Eve. Thus, there would seem to be no basis here for strict vegetarianism.

K. Wesley's Scriptural Method of Solving the Riddle of Humanity

Wesley ridicules the wisdom of men who tried in vain for ages to reconcile the greatness and the littleness, the achievements and the failures of humanity. He then turns to the Scriptures for the answer to this puzzle. He declares that

> what all the wisdom of man was unable to do, was in due time done by the wisdom of God. When it pleased God to give an account of the origin of things, and of man in particular, all the darkness vanished away, and the clear light shone.[96]

The "clear light," of which Wesley speaks, was the light of God's Word revealing the fact of humanity's creation in His image. It is this fact that accounts for "the greatness, the excellency, the dignity of man."[97]

In contrast, "the littleness and baseness of man," in which, as Wesley sees him, "he is sunk even below the beasts that perish," is a result of the loss of his relationship with God. Wesley declares that "no beast is fallen so low as man." Then he states that

> by considering . . . these things in one view [or together],—the creation and the fall of man,—all the inconsistencies of his nature are easily and fully understood. The greatness and littleness, the dignity and baseness, the happiness and misery, of his present state, are no longer a mystery, but clear consequences of his original state and his rebellion against God. This is the key that opens the whole mystery, that removes all the difficulty, by showing what God made man at first, and what man has made of himself."[98]

Wesley does not, however, completely despair of fallen humanity. He proceeds to say, "It is true, he may regain a considerable measure of the image of God wherein he was created: But still, whatever we regain, we shall have this treasure in earthen vessels."[99]

L. Wesley's View of the Duration of Humanity

After having considered the finitude of man, his brief and often miserable duration during this life, Wesley turns to a more optimistic view of human duration. Indeed, he sees the brevity of the physical life in comparison to the eternity of God. The fear and anxiety that accompany the brevity of life in time are dispelled by realizing

> that the body is not the man; that man is not only a house of clay, but an immortal spirit; a spirit made in the image of God; an incorruptible picture of the God of glory; a spirit that is of infinitely more value than the whole earth, . . . yea, than of the whole material creation. Consider that the spirit of man is not only of a higher order, of a more excellent nature, than any part of the visible

world, but also more durable, not liable either to dissolve or decay.[100]

Wesley then says in support of his optimistic conclusion concerning the duration of humanity:

> We know all the things "which are seen are temporal;"—of a changing, transient nature;—but "the things which are not seen" (such as is the soul of man in particular) "are eternal." "They shall perish," but the soul remaineth. "They shall wax old as a garment; but when heaven and earth pass away, the soul shall not pass away."[101]

Thus Wesley rightly bases his faith and hope on the eternal God of the universe and on persons who bear the personal image of God Himself. Thus it becomes evident that while Wesley has an element of pessimism in his understanding of fallen humanity, that pessimism is overcome through faith in Christ's redemptive work and the Christian hope of the resurrection and life everlasting with God in heaven. Wesley is neither a stark pessimist nor a blind optimist; rather, he is a Christian realist.

XIII. THE MINUS AND PLUS FACTORS OF HUMANITY

A. Humanity, Person or Animal?

While evolutionary views of the origin and development of humanity and the universe date back to the early Greeks of more than 2,500 years ago, the attempted scientific development of the theory of evolution found its principal modern impetus under the influence of Charles Darwin's *Origin of the Species* published in 1859. By this time the modern scientific era was coming into its own. The colonies of North and South America had gained their independence in the late eighteenth and early nineteenth centuries and their future development promised bright hope of cultural advancement. The Deistic philosophy of the late seventeenth and eighteenth centuries had set God apart from His government of the universe and left it to operate according to its established mechanical laws. Humanity, liberated from the ecclesiastical strictures of the Middle Ages by the Renaissance and subsequently liberated spiritually by the Protestant Reformation, could then say with William Ernest Henley (1849-1903) in his "Invictus": "I am the master of my fate; I am the captain of my soul."[102]

Ralph Waldo Emerson (1803-1882), disillusioned with the futility of his ministry in the Unitarian church, "left that church with a sigh," and became one of America's most noted and influential literary philosophers. Emerson's optimistic pantheism was best expressed in three of his famous essays.[103] The first was entitled *Nature*, in which God was reduced to the vital, impersonal principle of nature, and in which humanity itself became an essential part of nature. In his second essay, *Self Reliance*, Emerson instructed humanity to discover its own inherent divinity rather than whine at the footstool of an imagined transcendent deity that had no existence in objective reality. His third essay, *Transcendence*, promised humanity its own conquest of all obstacles to progress and the ultimate perfection of the human race and civilization itself.

William James (1842-1910) became America's most influential pragmatic philosopher-psychologist, who envisioned the progress and inevitable perfection of humanity and civilization through the exercise of the human will to believe in the possibilities of all desired and invisioned goals.[104]

The mainline Christian denominations, by and large, became enamored of the optimistic spirit of the era. Theologically adulterated by German rationalism and higher criticism, they lost their theological rootage and swung into the movement toward humanistic perfectionism. God was removed from His transcendent throne and was made the divine "ground of man's being," to borrow an expression from Paul Tillich. Thus God was created in the image of man, and "divine humanity" marched forth to create a millennium on earth during the present era. Earth and time became

ANTHROPOLOGY

humanity's envisioned heaven, and the doctrine of divine retribution was relegated to the attic of medieval superstition, while sin became social maladjustment to be cured by psychiatric treatment. In fact, in the words of Bishop William Cannon of the United Methodist Church, "the church substituted the psychiatrist's couch for the mourner's bench."[105]

The extent to which some churchmen have become humanistic is revealed in an article entitled "Humanism and the Churches," which appeared in *Christianity Today:*

> When *Time Magazine* spoke about the return of God to the center of the stage, the Rev. A. E. Potts of Knoxville, Tennessee, wrote the editor: "I must disagree wholeheartedly with your thesis that God is coming back to life, but I would definitely agree that man is rediscovering his own humanity. For most of the people with whom I work, and for myself, God is an obsolete piece of baggage belonging to man's past. But our humanity most certainly is not."[106]

John Dewey (1859-1952) became America's most influential humanistic educator. He refined James's pragmatic philosophy and combined it with all of the previous humanistic movements and made them into his so-called progressive education, otherwise known as instrumentalism. Dewey's new brand of secular education became the instrument through which Western mankind was thoroughly humanized.

By the beginning of the twentieth century Western man was confident of his ability, quite independent of reliance on or assistance from any supernatural power, to solve all of his problems and attain the goal of inevitable universal perfection. Humanity had come of age through the evolutionary process and no longer needed the assistance of God, it was thought. *Eternity Magazine* records that in 1973 the "Humanist Manifesto II," which was molded after John Dewey's "Humanist Manifesto" (1933), promised the fulfillment of the American utopian dream. Malefyt wrote of the Second Manifesto:

One hundred and twenty religious leaders, philosophers, scientists, writers and social scientists signed "Manifesto II." These included Andrei D. Sakharov, the dissident Soviet physicist; B. F. Skinner, Harvard psychologist; Sidney Hook, professor emeritus of philosophy at New York University; Rabbi Mordecai Kaplan, founder of the Jewish Re-constructionist Movement; and Carliss Lemont, chairman of National Emergency Civil Liberties Union.

Anti-religious in tone, it denounced "traditional dogmatic or authoritarian religions that place revelation, God, ritual or creed above human needs and experience." Because "promises of immortal salvation or fear of eternal damnation are both illusory and harmful," they should be condemned. They perform a disservice to the human species because "they distract humans from present concerns, from self-actualization and from rectifying social injustices," it warned. The Manifesto asserted in a hollow way that the good life is here and now. Indeed, "reason and intelligence are the most effective instruments that mankind possesses."[107]

Thus it is evident that modern humanity has repeated the error of our first parents in declaring their independence from God and attempting to live their lives and run the affairs of the universe in divorcement from the Creator God who assigned them stewards, not lords, over God's heritage.

B. The Fatal Deficiency

That great material progress has been realized during the past two centuries of optimistic self-reliance toward the envisioned utopian perfection of the human race is not to be denied. The one fatal deficiency of this grand utopian dream, however, is the failure to acknowledge God as the Creator and providential governor of the universe. The result is a tragic "ethical lag" in the midst of temporal, materialistic progress.

From 1914 through 1918 the First World War struck a near-fatal blow to this utopian dream of the preceding decades. A ten-year period of recovery followed the end of that war in 1918. By the close of the

1920s the world was plunged into a deep, dark world-wide depression that lasted until the outbreak of the Second World War in 1939—a war that lasted until 1945 and caused incredible human carnage. This in turn was followed by the Korean and Viet Nam wars, the latter ending in one of history's most infamous fiascoes. Thus one world war, a ten-year worldwide depression, and another world war, followed by yet more futile wars designed to restore humanity's hopes for a utopian civilization, resulted in utter frustration as people contemplated another humanistic unfinished Tower of Babel. All of this was followed by the youth rebellion, secular theology, situation ethics, and the God-is-Dead movement of the 1960s and early 1970s. Still humanity had not learned the lesson of the inadequacy of human depravity in the absence of divine grace.

Few today, or in any day, would openly deny the existence of God. The majority, however, live as though God does not exist. Humanity in general has committed again the error committed at the outset of the human race. They have substituted an anthropocentric universe for the theocentric. They have created their gods in the image of men and thus have further sullied the *imago Dei*.

C. The Hope for Humanity Through the Remnant

Notwithstanding the failures and tragedies of a godless humanistic society, there is help for the present and hope for the future of the human race. God has not forsaken "the crown of His creation." Within the human race there is today, as there ever has been, a faithful righteous remnant in and through which God is working out His purpose and plan. Isaiah saw this in the midst of Israel's degeneracy and departure from God in his day and, looking beyond the dark picture of human degeneracy, he announced, "I saw *also the Lord* . . . high and lifted up" (Isa. 6:1, KJV). Again the prophet said, "A remnant will return, the remnant of Jacob, to the mighty God. For though your people, O Israel, may be like the sand of the sea, only a remnant within them will return" (Isa. 10:21-22). The apostle Paul saw this truth and, quoting Isaiah, said, "It is the remnant that will be saved" (Rom. 9:27); and yet again he declared, "There has also come to be at the present time a remnant according to God's gracious choice" (Rom. 11:5). Martin Luther saw this in his day of awful depravity and through faith in God became the divine instrument in precipitating the Protestant Reformation. John Wesley saw this in spite of the human degeneracy of England in the eighteenth century, and the British people gained a new lease on life through the righteous remnant that made possible the spiritual and moral reformation of his day. Martin Marty has seen this renewed hope for humanity through God's dealings with the remnant within the eroded religion of our day.[108]

God is not finished with humanity in spite of failure and apostasy. He has now, as always, a faithful, righteous remnant. Through that faithful remnant He is working out His purpose of world evangelism and the building of His righteous kingdom that will endure forever. God is creating anew, in His own image, a new humanity through the redemptive power of His Son Jesus Christ (Eph. 2:10; 4:23-24; Col. 3:10; Rev. 1:5-6). Man is still man, and humanity is still human, and one day all who identify with and submit to the lordship of the perfect God-Man, Christ Jesus, in His redemptive work will be restored to the perfect *imago Dei* in which God originally created humanity in the person of Adam.

NOTES

[1] E. Adamson Hoebel, *Anthropology: The Study of Man*, 4th ed. (New York: McGraw, 1972), p. 6.

[2] Robert H. Lowie, *An Introduction to Cultural Anthropology* (New York: Farrar and Rinehart, 1940), p. 3.

[3] G. K. Chesterton, *The Everlasting Man* (New York: Dodd, Mead, 1925), p. 16.

[4] Carl F. H. Henry, "Man," in *Baker's Dictionary of Theology*, ed. Everett F. Harrison (Grand Rapids: Baker, 1960), p. 338.

[5] Edwin G. Conklin, *Man, Real and Ideal* (New York: Scribner, 1943), p. 24.

[6] William F. Albright, *Christianity Today* (January 18, 1963), p. 4.

[7] John Wesley, *The Works of John Wesley*, 3rd ed., 14 vols. (reprint ed., Grand Rapids: Baker, 1978), 3:232 (hereinafter referred to as *Works*).

[8] Adam Clarke, *Clarke's Commentary: "A Commentary and Critical Notes,"* 6 vols. (New York-Nashville: Abingdon-Cokesbury, n.d.), 1:38.

[9] H. Orton Wiley, *Christian Theology*, 3 vols. (Kansas City, Mo.: Nazarene, 1941), 2:9.

[10] Peter A. Bertocci, *Free Will, Responsibility, and Grace* (New York: Abingdon, 1957), pp. 87-94.

[11] George W. Forell, *The Protestant Faith*, rev. ed. (Philadelphia: Fortress, 1975), pp. 126-27.

[12] Wesley, *Works*, 7:225-30.

[13] John Wesley, *Explanatory Notes Upon the Old Testament* (reprint ed., Salem, Ohio: Schmul, 1975), 3:1819.

[14] Clarke, *Clarke's Commentary*, O.T., 3:664.

[15] H. C. Leupold, *The Zondervan Pictorial Encyclopedia of the Bible*, ed. Merrill C. Tenney (Grand Rapids: Zondervan, 1975), 2:680.

[16] E. F. Kevan, *The New Bible Commentary*, ed. F. Davidson (Grand Rapids: Eerdmans, 1954), p. 75.

[17] Andrew Jukes, *The Names of God in Holy Scripture* (1888; reprint ed., Grand Rapids: Kregel, 1967), p. 16.

[18] Ibid., p. 20.

[19] J. Oliver Buswell, *Baker's Dictionary of Theology*, p. 146.

[20] Wesley, *Works*, 6:66; see also pp. 269-71.

[21] Wesley, *Works*, 9:291.

[22] Wiley, *Christian Theology*, 2:29.

[23] William Burton Pope, *Compendium of Christian Theology*, 3 vols. (New York: Philips and Hunt, 1881), 1:423.

[24] Wiley, *Christian Theology*, 2:32.

[25] Ibid., p. 38.

[26] Henry, *Baker's Dictionary of Theology*, pp. 338-39.

[27] David Cairns, *The Image of God in Man* (New York: Philosophical Library, 1953), p. 63.

[28] Clarke, *Clarke's Commentary*, 1:41.

[29] H. C. Leupold, *Exposition of Genesis*, 2 vols. (Columbus, Ohio: Wartburg, 1942), 1:115.

[30] Clarke, *Clarke's Commentary*, 1:42.

[31] Leupold, *Exposition of Genesis*, 1:116.

[32] Dagobert D. Runes, *The Dictionary of Philosophy* (New York: Philosophical Library, 1942), p. 88; cf. pp. 20-23.

[33] Wesley, *Old Testament Notes*, p. 13.

[34] W. Ralph Thompson, *The Wesleyan Bible Commentary*, ed. Charles W. Carter (reprint ed., Grand Rapids: Baker, 1979), 2:189.

[35] J. R. Dummelow, ed., *A Commentary on the Holy Bible by Various Writers* (1908; reprint ed., New York: Macmillan, 1951), p. 332.

[36] Archdeacon Aglen, *Ellicott's Commentary on the Whole Bible*, ed. Charles John Ellicott (Grand Rapids: Zondervan, n.d.), 4:97. See also William R. Taylor et al., *The Interpreter's Bible* (New York-Nashville: Abingdon, 1955), 4:48-52.

[37] Will Durant, *The Story of Philosophy* (Garden City, N.Y.: Garden City, 1933), p. 2.

[38] Wesley, *Old Testament Notes*, 1:13.

[39] Clarke, *Clarke's Commentary*, 1:45.

[40] Wesley, *Old Testament Notes*, 1:13.

[41] Ibid.

[42] Ibid., pp. 13-14.

[43] Lowie, *An Introduction to Cultural Anthropology*, pp. 230, 245, 250.

[44] David G. Wylie, *The Minister's Companion* (New York: Nelson, 1911), p. 31.

[45] See especially Gen. 2:18-24; Prov. 31:10-31; Matt. 19:3-9; Eph. 5:23-33.

[46] W. Melville Capper and Morgan H. Williams, *Toward Christian Marriage* (Chicago: InterVarsity, 1958), pp. 119-20.

[47] R. Payne Smith, *Ellicott's Commentary on the Whole Bible*, 1:22-23.

[48] Lowie, *An Introduction to Cultural Anthropology*, pp. 246, 252.

[49] Paul H. Landis, *Your Marriage and Family Living*, 2nd ed. (New York: McGraw, 1954), p. 3.

[50] E. Adamson Hoebel, *Man in the Primitive World*, 2nd ed. (New York: McGraw, 1958), pp. 318-19.

[51] John Charles Wynn, *Sermons on Marriage and Family Life* (New York, Nashville: Abingdon, 1956), pp. 18-19.

⁵²Smith, *Ellicott's Commentary*, p. 22.

⁵³Ibid., pp. 22-23.

⁵⁴William Barclay, *The Letters to the Corinthians*, 2nd ed., The Daily Bible Study Series (Philadelphia: Westminster, 1956), p. 67.

⁵⁵Leland Foster Wood, *Harmony in Marriage*, rev. ed. (New York: Round Table, 1955), p. 73.

⁵⁶Capper and Williams, *Toward Christian Marriage*, p. 66.

⁵⁷Ibid., pp. 59, 61.

⁵⁸Wesley, *Old Testament Notes*, 1:13.

⁵⁹Clarke, *Clarke's Commentary*, O.T., 1:46.

⁶⁰See Robert F. Winch, *Mate Selection: A Study of Complementary Needs* (New York: Harper and Brothers, 1958), chapter 1.

⁶¹Margaret Mead, "Some Theoretical Considerations on the Problem of Mother-Child Separation," *The American Journal of Orthopsychiatry*, 24 (1954): 474.

⁶²Landis, *Your Marriage and Family Living*, p. 282.

⁶³Ibid., p. 299.

⁶⁴Wesley, *Works*, 7:407.

⁶⁵Wesley, *Works*, 11:148.

⁶⁶Wesley, *Works*, 7:225-30.

⁶⁷Herbert Ernest Cushman, *A Beginner's History of Philosophy*, 2 vols. (New York: Houghton Mifflin, 1946), 1:45.

⁶⁸Wesley, *Works*, 7:225-26.

⁶⁹Ibid.

⁷⁰Ibid.

⁷¹Ibid.

⁷²Ibid., p. 227.

⁷³Ibid.

⁷⁴Ibid.

⁷⁵Ibid.

⁷⁶Ibid.

⁷⁷Ibid., p. 228.

⁷⁸Ibid.

⁷⁹Ibid., p. 232.

⁸⁰Ibid.

⁸¹Ibid.

⁸²Ibid.

⁸³Ibid., pp. 233-38.

⁸⁴Ibid., p. 129.

⁸⁵Ibid.

⁸⁶Ibid.

⁸⁷Ibid., 5:54.

⁸⁸Ibid.

⁸⁹Ibid., 7:230.

⁹⁰Ibid., pp. 229-30.

⁹¹Ibid.

⁹²Ibid.

⁹³Ibid.

⁹⁴Ibid.

⁹⁵Ibid., p. 245.

⁹⁶Ibid., p. 344.

⁹⁷Ibid.

⁹⁸Ibid., pp. 344-45.

⁹⁹Ibid., p. 345.

¹⁰⁰Ibid., p. 171.

¹⁰¹Ibid.

¹⁰²William Ernest Henley, "Invictus," *One Hundred and One Famous Poems* (Chicago: Cable, 1929), p. 95.

¹⁰³Gordon S. Haight, ed., *The Best of Ralph Waldo Emerson: Essays-Poems-Addresses* (New York: Van Nostrand, 1941).

¹⁰⁴William James, *The Will to Believe and Other Essays in Popular Philosophy* (New York: Longmans, Green, 1939).

¹⁰⁵Bishop William Cannon, from a statement made in a lecture delivered at Taylor University.

¹⁰⁶"Humanism and the Churches," *Christianity Today* (April 10, 1970), pp. 30, 31.

¹⁰⁷Calvin S. Malefyt, "The Dream That Went Phtt!," *Eternity*, vol. 25, no. 7 (July 1974): 7.

¹⁰⁸Martin Marty, *The New Shape of American Religion* (New York: Harper and Brothers, 1959), pp. 118ff., 134ff.

DISCUSSION QUESTIONS

1. What specifically is meant by the *imago Dei*, and how does it distinguish humanity from all other created beings?

2. What are the main components of the *imago Dei*? Which of those components were lost in the Fall? What effect did the Fall have on the remaining components?

3. Consider the nature and extent of the responsibility over God's creation that was delegated to humanity upon its creation.

4. In what way was the woman's creation included in the man's? Was she in all respects equal to the man? In what respect did she differ from him?
5. Consider the universal characteristics of humanity that are not shared with any other creatures.
6. Consider the Fall and its effects on people's relation to themselves, to God, and to society.
7. What hope did God afford fallen humanity from its otherwise hopeless condition, and how was that plan of redemption executed?
8. What was John Wesley's view of humanity's condition in eighteenth-century England?
9. Consider Wesley's understanding of human liberty in relation to human will.
10. What were Wesley's views on the future of humanity in this life and the next?

RECOMMENDATIONS FOR FURTHER READING

Bertocci, Peter A. *Free Will, Responsibility, and Grace.* New York: Abingdon, 1957.
Bready, John Wesley. *England Before and After Wesley.* New York: Russell and Russell, 1971.
Burtner, Robert W. and Childs, Robert E. *A Compend of Wesley's Theology.* Nashville: Abingdon, 1954.
Cannon, William R. *The Theology of John Wesley.* Nashville: Abingdon, 1946.
Chesterton, G. K. *The Everlasting Man.* New York: Dodd, Mead, 1925.
Conklin, Edwin G. *Man, Real and Ideal.* New York: Scribner, 1943.
Forell, George W. *The Protestant Faith.* Rev. ed. Philadelphia: Fortress, 1975.
Grunlan, Stephen A., and Mayers, Marvin K. *Cultural Anthropology: A Christian Perspective.* Grand Rapids: Zondervan, 1979.
Nida, Eugene A. *Customs, Culture, and Christianity.* London: Tyndale, 1954.
Outler, Albert C., ed. *John Wesley.* New York: Oxford University Press, 1964.
Tournier, Paul. *The Meaning of Persons.* Perennial Library, New York: Harper and Row, 1957.
Tuttle, Robert G., Jr. *John Wesley, His Life and Theology.* Grand Rapids: Zondervan, 1978.
Wynkoop, Mildred Bangs. *Foundations of Wesleyan Arminian Theology.* Kansas City, Mo.: Beacon Hill, 1967.

BIBLIOGRAPHY

Astley, H.J.D. *Biblical Anthropology.* London: Oxford University Press, 1929.
Barclay, William. *The Daily Bible Study.* 17 vols. Philadelphia: Westminster, 1958–1960.
Bertocci, Peter A. *Free Will, Responsibility, and Grace.* New York: Abingdon, 1957.
Bready, John Wesley. *England Before and After Wesley.* New York: Russell and Russell, 1971.
Brown, Colin, ed. *The New International Dictionary of New Testament Theology.* 3 vols. Grand Rapids: Zondervan, 1978.
Brown, Ina Corinne. *Understanding Other Cultures.* Englewood Cliffs, N.J.: Prentice-Hall, 1963.
Bruce, F. F. *The Epistle to the Hebrews.* NLC. Grand Rapids: Eerdmans, 1964.
Burtner, Robert W., and Chiles, Robert E. *A Compend of Wesley's Theology.* Nashville: Abingdon, 1954.
Cannon, William R. *The Theology of John Wesley.* Nashville: Abingdon, 1946.
Carter, Charles W., ed. *The Wesleyan Bible Commentary.* 7 vols. Grand Rapids: Baker, 1964–1969.
Chesterton, G. K. *The Everlasting Man.* New York: Dodd, Mead, 1925.
Clarke, Adam. *Clarke's Commentary: A Commentary and Critical Notes.* 6 vols. Nashville: Abingdon-Cokesbury, n.d.
Conklin, Edwin G. *Man Real and Ideal.* New York: Scribner, 1943.
Cushman, Herbert Ernest. *A Beginner's History of Philosophy.* 2 vols. New York: Houghton Mifflin, 1946.

A CONTEMPORARY WESLEYAN THEOLOGY

Davidson, F., ed. *The New Bible Commentary*. Grand Rapids: Eerdmans, 1954.

Dummelow, J. R., ed. *A Commentary on the Holy Bible*. New York: Macmillan, 1951.

Fletcher, John. *The Works of the Reverend John Fletcher*. 4 vols. Reprint ed. Salem, Ohio: Schmul, 1974.

Forell, George W. *The Protestant Faith*. Rev. ed. Philadelphia: Fortress, 1975.

Frost, S. E. *The Basic Teachings of the Great Philosophers*. Philadelphia: Blackstone, 1942.

Gamertsfelder, S. J. *Systematic Theology*. Harrisburg, Pa.: Evangelical, 1921.

Gardner, Helen. *Art Through the Ages*. New York: Harcourt, Brace, 1926.

Glenn, Paul. *Dialectics*. St. Louis, Mo.: Herder, 1939.

Grunlan, Stephen A., and Mayers, Marvin K. *Cultural Anthropology: A Christian Perspective*. Grand Rapids: Zondervan, 1979.

Gundry, Stanley N., and Johnson, Allen F., eds. *Tensions in Contemporary Theology*. Chicago: Moody, 1976.

Hand, John Raymond. *Why Accept the Genesis Record*. Wheaton, Ill.: VanKampen, 1955.

Harrison, Everett F., ed. *Baker's Dictionary of Theology*. Grand Rapids: Baker, 1960.

Hoebel, E. Anderson. *Anthropology: The Study of Man*. 4th ed. New York: McGraw, 1972.

Jukes, Andrew. *The Names of God in Holy Scripture*. 1888. Reprint ed. Grand Rapids: Kregel, 1967.

Kane, J. Herbert. *A Global View of Christian Missions*. Grand Rapids: Baker, 1975.

Ladd, George Eldon. *A Theology of the New Testament*. Grand Rapids: Eerdmans, 1974.

Lowie, Robert H. *An Introduction to Cultural Anthropology*. New York: Rinehart, 1940.

Meyer, Edward M., ed. *The Illustrated Library of the Natural Sciences*. 4 vols. New York: Simon and Schuster, 1958.

Nida, Eugene A. *Customs, Culture, and Christianity*. London: Tyndale, 1954.

Outler, Albert C., ed. *John Wesley*. New York: Oxford University Press, 1964.

Parker, Piercy Livingston, ed. *The Journal of John Wesley*. Chicago: Moody, 1950.

Plumb, J. H. *England in the Eighteenth Century*. Baltimore, Md.: Penguin, 1968.

Purkiser, W. T. et al. *God, Man, and Salvation*. Kansas City, Mo.: Beacon Hill, 1977.

Runes, Dagobert D. *The Dictionary of Philosophy*. New York: Philosophical Library, 1942.

Sandmel, Samuel. *The Hebrew Scriptures: An Introduction to Their Literature and Religious Ideas*. New York: Knopf, 1963.

Schmidt, Martin. *John Wesley: A Theological Biography*. 2 vols. Nashville: Abingdon, n.d.

Souter, Alexander. *A Pocket Dictionary to the Greek New Testament*. Oxford: Clarendon, 1916.

Southey, Robert. *The Life of Wesley, and Rise and Progress of Methodism*. 2 vols. New York: Harper and Brothers, 1847.

Tenney, Merrill C., ed. *The Zondervan Pictorial Encyclopedia of the Bible*. 5 vols. Grand Rapids: Zondervan, 1975.

Thiessen, Henry C. *Lectures in Systematic Theology*. Grand Rapids: Eerdmans, 1979.

Tillich, Paul. *The Dynamics of Faith*. New York: Harper and Brothers, 1957.

Tuttle, Robert G., Jr. *John Wesley, His Life and Theology*. Grand Rapids: Zondervan, 1978.

Van Baalen, Jan Karel. *The Chaos of Cults*. 14th ed. Grand Rapids: Eerdmans, 1951.

Vos, Geerhardus, *Biblical Theology: Old and New Testaments*. Grand Rapids: Eerdmans, 1948.

Wesley, John. *The Works of John Wesley*. 3rd ed., Complete and Unabridged. 14 vols. Reprint ed. Grand Rapids: Baker, 1978.

Wiley, H. Orton. *Christian Theology*, 3 vols. Kansas City, Mo.: Nazarene, 1940.

Wynkoop, Mildred Bangs. *Foundations of Wesleyan Arminian Theology*. Kansas City, Mo.: Beacon Hill, 1967.

CHAPTER 7

HAMARTIOLOGY:
Evil, the Marrer
of God's Creative
Purpose and Work

Charles W. Carter

Charles W. Carter is Scholar-in-Residence and Professor of Religion and Missions at Marion College, Marion, Indiana. He holds the following degrees: Th.M., Christian Theological Seminary; B.D., D.D., Asbury Theological Seminary. He served pastorates in several mid-Western churches; was missionary to Sierra Leone, Africa, for three terms as principal of the Clarke Memorial Biblical Seminary; and Professor of Philosophy and Missions, and Chairman of the Division of Philosophy and Religion, Marion College, for eleven years; he was Professor of Philosophy and Religion at Taylor University for twelve years. He taught theology and ethics in Taiwan for four years and was lecturer and/or visiting professor at colleges and seminaries in other areas of the world. He was a cofounder of the Wesleyan Theological Society and was editor of the Wesleyan Theological Journal *for seven years.*

Dr. Carter is author of fifteen books, including A Half Century of American Missions in West Africa, Road to Revival, The Person and Ministry of the Holy Spirit, *and* Missionaries Extraordinary. *He was general editor and contributor to the* Wesleyan Bible Commentary *(7 volumes) and has contributed to the* Zondervan Pictorial Encyclopedia of the Bible, *the* Wesleyan Theological Journal, *and other scholarly journals. He is a member of the American Association of University Professors, the Metaphysical Society of America, the Mid-Western Fellowship of Professors of Missions, the Evangelical Theological Society, and the Wesleyan Theological Society.*

CONTENTS

I. INTRODUCTION / 237

II. KINDS OF EVIL IN THE WORLD / 238
  A. Moral Evil / 238
  B. Cosmic or Natural Evil / 238

III. SIN AND EVIL PER SE / 239
  A. The Origin of Evil / 239
  B. Extrabiblical Philosophic and Rationalistic Theories / 239
    1. Evil as an eternal principle / 239
    2. Evil as a dysteleological surd / 240
    3. Evil as a characteristic of human finitude / 241
    4. Evil as the necessary antithesis of good / 242
    5. Evil as the expression of the *physical* nature in opposition to the *spiritual* / 242
    6. Evil as the expression of moral ignorance / 243
    7. Evil as the absence of adequate experience / 244
    8. Evil as the residue of the evolutionary process / 244
    9. Evil as the residue theory in creation / 245
    10. Evil as a cultural creation / 245
    11. Evil as an economic creation / 246

IV. THE BIBLICAL VIEW OF THE ORIGIN OF EVIL / 246

V. THE TEMPTATION AND FALL OF HUMANITY / 248
  A. The Battle Royal in Eden / 248
  B. The Necessity and Nature of Temptation as a Moral Test / 248
  C. The Failure of Humanity in the Moral Test / 249
  D. The Results of Humanity's Failure in the Moral Test / 250
    1. God's first covenant with humanity / 250
    2. Humanity's breach of the first covenant / 251
    3. Immediate effects of the broken covenant / 252

VI. EFFECTS OF THE FALL ON ADAM'S DESCENDANTS / 253
  A. The Birth and Occupations of Adam's Sons / 253
  B. The Worship of Adam's Sons / 254
  C. The Violence Among Adam's Descendants / 256
  D. A Divine Ray of Hope for Fallen Humanity / 257

VII. THE VICTORY OF CHRIST'S TEMPTATION / 257
  A. The Necessity of Christ's Temptation / 257
  B. The Process of Christ's Temptation / 258

VIII. THE BASIC NATURE OF SIN / 259
  A. Sin as Unbelief / 259
  B. Sin as Pride / 260
  C. Sin as Rebellion / 260
  D. Sin as Alienation / 260
  E. Sin as Moral Corruption / 261
  F. Sin as a Universal Malady / 262
   1. Depravity is universal / 262
   2. Depravity is personal deprivation / 262
  G. Sin Against the Holy Spirit / 263

IX. JOHN WESLEY'S UNDERSTANDING OF SIN / 265
  A. Introduction / 265
  B. The Wesleyan Doctrine of Original Sin / 266
   1. John Wesley's views on original sin and inherited guilt / 266
   2. Wesley's views on inherited guilt and prevenient grace / 267
   3. Wesley's views on *extensive* versus *intensive* total depravity / 268
   4. Wesleyan views on the transference of original sin to Adam's descendants / 270
   5. Wesley's views on active or overt sin / 270

X. A GENERAL OVERVIEW OF SIN, FROM CHRIST TO THE LATE NINETEENTH CENTURY / 272
  A. Sin as Characterized by Christ and Paul / 272
  B. Sin as Understood in the Middle Ages / 272
  C. Sin as Understood From the Reformation to Wesley / 273
  D. Sin as Understood in the Nineteenth Century / 273
  E. Sin as Understood in the Twentieth Century / 273
  F. Sin as Understood in the Twentieth-Century Neoorthodox Movement / 274
   1. Evil in the theology of Karl Barth / 274
   2. Evil in the theology of Paul Tillich / 274
   3. Evil in the theology of Reinhold Niebuhr / 274
   4. Evil in the theology of Emil Brunner / 275
   5. Evil in the theology of Rudolf Bultmann / 275
  G. Sin as Understood in the Rise of Radical Secularism / 275
  H. God's Remedy for Humanity's Sin / 276

NOTES / 276

DISCUSSION QUESTIONS / 278

RECOMMENDATIONS FOR FURTHER READING / 279

BIBLIOGRAPHY / 279

HAMARTIOLOGY

Evil, the Marrer of God's Creative Purpose and Work

I. INTRODUCTION

Of all the theological problems, in fact of all the problems confronting humanity, evil is the most universal, vexing, and enigmatic. It has occupied and perplexed the minds of men and women from the greatest to the least throughout human history.

The intellectual giants and saints of the ages—the ancient Hebrew prophets, the eminent Greek philosophers, Paul, St. Augustine, the early church fathers, Dante, Calvin, Aquinas, Luther, Milton, Wesley, C. S. Lewis (especially in *Screwtape Letters*), and Edwin Lewis (in *Creator and the Adversary*)—have all struggled to understand, explain, and find a solution to the problem of evil. Even Christ asked, "Why . . . ?" as He hung on the cross (Matt. 27:46).

While evil is multifold in its manifestation and treatment in the Scriptures, neither evil in general nor sin as moral evil per se are ever defined in the Old or New Testaments. Kenneth Kinghorn is correct when he says, "There is no precise biblical *definition* of sin. The Bible is concerned more with the remedy for sin than with a definition of sin."[1] Neither has any solution to the problem of evil ever been found outside of the Judeo-Christian Scriptures.

Man alone, the crown and perfection of God's creation, bore the very image of his Creator. Thus he possessed the potential for the highest moral creative genius of all God's creation. He has made noble achievements in science, art, literature, music, and material civilization. He has developed elaborate and sometimes admirable systems of humanistic religion and ethics. The psalmist extolled the greatness of humanity when he exclaimed in Psalm 8:3-5:

> When I consider Thy heavens, the work of Thy fingers, the moon and the stars, which Thou hast ordained; what is man, that Thou dost take thought of him? And the son of man, that Thou dost care for him? Yet Thou hast made him a little lower than God [Elohim—possibly angels], and dost crown him with glory and majesty.

Great as is this *crown* of divine creation, humanity suffers from a fatal (from a human point of view) and incurable physical, spiritual, and moral malady, which the Bible calls *sin*. This deplorable condition has been depicted in the great literary tragedies from Homer, Dante, Shakespeare *(Hamlet)*, and Milton *(Paradise*

Lost) to C. S. Lewis *(Pilgrim's Regress)*, and Jean-Paul Sartre *(No Exit)*. It is prominent in all the great religions of mankind from primitive magic to Christian theism. It has been manifest in all the wars and human conflicts of the ages, from Cain's murder of his brother to Viet Nam and beyond. It has been recognized by all but the most blindly optimistic philosophers and theologians of the ages from Plato to Karl Barth. It is evidenced in the contemporary greed, hostility, avarice, dishonesty, strife, violence, political corruption, human suffering, and moral callousness of the present age.

II. KINDS OF EVIL IN THE WORLD

Generally speaking, there are two types of evil in the world—namely, moral and cosmic, the latter sometimes designated natural evil.

A. Moral Evil

Although moral evil will be dealt with more fully later in this chapter, it is important to note here that moral evil is that type of evil for which humanity is directly or indirectly responsible. While the evil one, Satan, existed before the creation of the first human pair and was the instrument of their temptation and fall, they were nevertheless responsible for disobeying God and yielding to the temptation that brought the Fall and so brought down the human race, of which they were the head. Thus the first tragic human sin was committed in Eden by Adam and Eve. This was properly speaking, the *original sin,* as far as humanity is concerned; and it was the sin that infected the entire human race of which they were the head and foundation.

At their creation Adam and Eve shared the perfect holiness of their Creator; however, they were only potentially ethical, not yet having confronted an ethical situation where they were faced with the necessity of choosing between good and evil. When, however, that ethical situation confronted them in the light of God's specific command, and they made their choice, wrong as it was, their ethical eyes were opened and they knew the shame of their wrong choice. Thus they were culpable and fell under divine condemnation for their sin. Had they made the right choice, they would likewise have become *actually ethical* as the clear light of God would have shown upon the evil they had rejected and would have approved the choice they made. Thus from the moment of the rational free choice in Eden made by the first pair, the human race has borne its ethical responsibility before God, their fellow beings, and themselves.

There are many different kinds of sin and evil to be dealt with later in this chapter, but clearly the decision and misdeed of Adam and Eve in Eden was properly *sin,* as a willful act of disobedience against the clearly known will of God. An ethical situation always involves three factors, namely: (1) a knowledge of what is right and wrong, (2) freedom to choose between the alternatives, and (3) moral responsibility for the choice made. Adam and Eve failed the test and thus were morally condemned both by their own consciences and by their righteous Creator to whom they were responsible. This was the first human sin per se. In this act they lost the favor and presence of God's righteous Spirit (the *moral* image in which they were created) from their lives. Thus, deprived of God's righteousness, they became depraved in their moral natures, and this depravity has been passed on to every member of the human race of which Adam was God's appointed head.

B. Cosmic or Natural Evil

God's pronouncement of the curse on Satan and the first pair in Eden for their willful act of disobedience included much more than that expressed in the account given in Genesis 3:14-19. Involved in the Fall and the divine curse that followed were all the disorders that have characterized an originally perfect cosmos, throwing it out of balance and subjecting it to further disorders by Satan, who had usurped man's control over nature as well as God's control over humanity.

The evidences for this conclusion are many, both in Scripture and in nature itself. The first natural disruption resulting from the Fall is clearly stated by God Himself (Gen. 3:16-19):

> To the woman He said, "I will greatly multiply your pain in childbirth, in pain you shall bring forth children, yet your desire shall be for your husband, and he shall rule over you." . . . Then to Adam He said, . . . "Cursed is the ground because of you; in toil you shall eat of it all the days of your life. Both thorns and thistles it shall grow for you; and you shall eat the plants of the field; by the sweat of your face you shall eat bread, till you return to the ground, because from it you were taken; for you are dust, and to dust you shall return."

This curse was the earliest of the disorders brought by man's sin; worse disorders were to follow. The question may be fairly asked, however, whether these natural disorders and disruptions represent God's direct arbitrary pronouncement of a curse on nature or whether they were the consequences of man's loss of control over the natural order that God had placed under Adam's stewardship (cf. Gen. 1:27-30; 2:15, 19-20; 3:22-24).

In other words, may this simply be a way of saying that since man was God's vice-regent over nature and had betrayed his trust, in his fall he took his realms down with him to suffer the consequences of his failure? May Adam not be comparable to a sea captain who, in disobedience to the nautical rules of the sea, wrecks his ship, and as it sinks he takes with him the vessel, the crew, and the passengers, for all of which he bears the responsibility? If this is so, then the curse on nature was a consequence of the Fall, rather than an arbitrary pronouncement of divine punishment on nature. Further, in the fallen condition of man and nature, Satan himself had gained a certain limited advantage over the natural order. In fact, Paul refers to Satan as "the prince of the power of the air, . . . the spirit that is now working in the sons of disobedience" (Eph. 2:2). Likewise, it appears to have been this satanic power that caused the enemies and the elements to destroy Job's property and the lives of his children and servants (Job 1:12-19; cf. Eph. 6:12).

To what extent Satan is responsible for natural disorders and destruction the Scripture does not reveal, but that he exercises such powers within divine limitations is evident from the biblical record. That he may be responsible for many occasions of disruptive and destructive natural disasters today is certainly possible. If these deductions are valid, then satanic interference in the natural order may be responsible for many of the destructive volcanic eruptions, earthquakes, tidal waves, typhoons, tornados, cyclones, floods, and droughts that produce so much human misery and suffering.

Certainly when God created humanity, as well as all of nature, perfect (Gen. 1:31), it was not His will that human diseases and maladies such as cancer, polio, retardation, decimating epidemics, and death itself should be the experience of the human race. While we cannot say that such afflictions are necessarily the *direct* result of personal sin, it is evident that they are the indirect result of the Fall, and thus a consequence of moral evil. They are not morally evil in themselves, however, since nature is impersonal and consequently incapable of moral evil.

III. SIN AND EVIL PER SE

A. The Origin of Evil

In order to better understand the biblical account of the origin of sin and evil, it may be helpful to see it against the backdrop of certain nonbiblical theories.

B. Extrabiblical Philosophic and Rationalistic Theories

1. Evil as an eternal principle Perhaps no other system furnishes a better example of evil as an eternal principle than does the

Zoroastrian religion. The Zoroastrian religion teaches that good and evil have coexisted from all eternity. This is religious dualism per se. Robert Ernest Hume states that

> an aboriginal and distinctive feature of Zoroastrianism among all the religions of the world is this doctrine of a fundamental cosmological dualism of a good God and a wicked devil fighting against one another. These two cosmic powers are co-equal from the beginning of time, and they will continue to limit each other until the end of the world.[2]

Likewise, another eminent authority states:

> The conflict between Ahura Mazda [the good god, or principle] and the Daevas [the evil spirit or principle] . . . form the continuing subject of his [Zoroaster's] verse. The . . . two primordial spirits . . . are *eternally* hostile to each other, the Good against the bad. Ahura Mazda, the Wise Lord, is often identified with Spenta Mainyu, the Holy Spirit; Angra Mainyu, the Evil Spirit, is also called Druj—that is, the Lie.[3]

While Zoroastrianism has at least a semipersonal concept of these two eternal deities, Hinduism, on the other hand, conceives of a monistic pantheism in which evil, though illusory, as is all else in Hinduism, is nevertheless an essential characteristic of the eternal *world soul,* "the individual self *(Atman)* . . . the Brahman (the universal self).''[4] Thus neither Zoroastrianism nor Hinduism (nor Buddhism, which in this respect is identical with Hinduism, from which it sprang) attempts to give any explanation of the origin of evil. Evil is simply taken for granted.

Platonia dualism and especially Neo-Platonism likewise afford no explanation of the origin of evil beyond the fact that it inheres in matter and is therefore as eternal as the matter itself.

Gnosticism, which invaded the Christian church as early as the first century and gave the Christian apostles serious trouble, held that evil inhered in matter and could be terminated only with the destruction of the body, by which the spirit or soul could then be set free. Gnosticism, which issued from Alexandrian influence, gave rise to various forms of asceticism, including monasticism and celibacy in the Roman Catholic church, as means to holiness of life—a form of *works righteousness.*

Certain forms of Gnosticism issued in libertinism with a view to the destruction of the evil body by excessive indulgences in sinful pleasures.[5]

These Gnostic heresies were revived in the church by Manes in the third century and appeared again in the Paulican heresy of the twelfth century. Traces of it are even found in contemporary Christianity.

Of Gnosticism in the Post-Apostolic Era (100-170), Lars P. Qualben states:

> Two primary and equal Powers, Good and Evil, were recognized. The latter was co-eternal with the former; hence the marked dualism in all gnostic systems. . . . Sin was conceived of as residing in matter, or the body, and not as the [orthodox] Christians believed, in the heart or in the moral nature of man. The Fall was identified with the incorporation of material substance in the universe, and the fall of man simply consisted in the incarnation of spirits in material bodies, where these spirits were held as in a prison house. Redemption consisted in the liberation of the spirit from the [evil] material body. The resurrection of the body was emphatically denied.[6]

Even in the latter half of the first century Paul was struggling against this heresy that had invaded the church at Corinth as he wrote his defense of the resurrection of the body in First Corinthians 15. Likewise, the presence of Gnosticism is evident in the church of the Colossians, to which he wrote his letter in the early sixties.

2. Evil as a dysteleological surd A contemporary theory concerning the origin of evil, a theory that was advanced by Edgar Sheffield Brightman of Boston University, is that evil is a dysteleological surd. Mathematically considered, a surd is a quantity not expressible in rational terms. In a value-theory context, however, a surd is a *nonvalue,* or something not reducible to *good,* or a value. Thus, it is basically an irreducible nonvalue. A surd is that which has no value—it is purposeless and thus nonteleological.

After having discussed several other types of evil, such as "a will that is more or less incoherent," "the intellectual evil of ignorance," "maladjustment . . . [as] an intrinsic evil," and "incompetence . . . [as a] type of evil," Brightman says that

> these . . . types may sometimes be superseded by internal development; an incoherent will may become relatively more coherent; ignorance may be enlightened; maladjustment may be overcome by proper relationships; and incompetence may be supplanted by skill. But a dysteleological surd is a type of evil which is inherently and irreducibly evil and contains within itself no principle of development or improvement.[7]

While Brightman admits that it is debatable whether a dysteleological surd is a valid concept, he considers it nevertheless conceivable that such does exist, as for instance in the case of an imbecile. While imbecility is valueless in itself, he thinks, nevertheless, it may serve to inspire pity and even encourage psychiatry. "Yet, [he says,] if it be an incurable condition, there remains in it a surd evil embodied in the intrinsic worthlessness of the imbecile's existence and the suffering which this imposes on others."[8]

3. Evil as a characteristic of human finitude The position that evil is a characteristic of human finitude says that because mankind is not infinite as God Himself is infinite, he is evil. This is, of course, a direct contradiction of God's own evaluation of humanity when He finished His creative work with man and pronounced it "very good," or perfect (Gen. 1:27, 31).

This theory says that because humanity is not infinite, the absence of infinitude is evil. It is evil because it has no existence. However, if a thing does not exist, how can it be considered evil? The very statement that evil is the absence of good is to assign evil existence to the supposed nonexistent. This position is the very acme of nonsense.

There is, however, another version of man's finitude that is designated evil. In this view, God is "all being" and therefore, the *perfect good.* Evil is the minus factor in humanity in that it is "the not-yet-complete or not-yet-perfect being" in a *becoming process.* Thus evil is neutral rather than either negative or positive. Clearly this is the humanistic existential theory well represented by the atheistic philosophy of Jean-Paul Sartre (1905–1981). Sartre places "existence before essence." Thus he begins with "nothing" and moves existentially toward authentic existence. If man were authentic, however, he would be absolutely perfect, and such perfection is impossible. Therefore, man, if indeed he can be denominated man, is ever striving toward becoming an authentic being, which becomes unauthentic as he moves toward this subjectively projected goal of authenticity. It is as though he were moving toward a mirage that ever fades into nothingness as he approaches it. Beginning with nothing, he ends with nothing. This is the basis of Xenophanes' axiom in his doctrine of the eternity of matter, which in application is *ex nihilo nihil fit* ("from nothing nothing comes"). This turns out to be a dream in the absence of a dreamer. Sartre saw the folly of this reasoning and called it *nullity*—nothingness.

Indeed, man is a "becoming" creature, but as such he is a "created being" and, notwithstanding the Fall, he is still man in the image of God who created him, however sullied that image may be. Redeemed man is ever progressing toward the restoration of that perfect image in which he was created before the Fall. Though the moral image was lost in the Fall and the natural and political image was sullied, yet in Christ "we all, with unveiled face beholding as in a mirror the glory of the Lord, are being transformed into the same image from glory to glory, just as from the Lord, the Spirit" (2 Cor. 3:18; Col. 1:15).

Again, the apostle says of the redeemed that they "have put on the new [renovated] self who is being renewed to a true knowledge according to the image of the One who created him" (Col. 3:10).

In the light of this, man's perfection is relative to God's perfection, just as the perfectly well and healthy child's perfection is relative to that of the parent. His "child perfection" is not, however, a deficiency or evil in his being; it is simply *his perfection*. This is what Christ meant when He said, "Therefore you are to be perfect, as your heavenly Father is perfect" (Matt. 5:48). This is an exhortation to human Christian perfection, not to the absolute perfection of God. God created mankind finite, and a perfect God could not create an evil person. This theory of the evil of finitude is in every respect false.

4. Evil as the necessary antithesis of good Whether Wilhelm Fredric Hegel (1770-1831) originated or taught the dialectical theory is controversial in present scholarship. In any event, it is the theory per se that we are here concerned with and not its originator or chief exponent.

Although variously interpreted and applied, the dialectic consists in essence of the synthesis of opposites. The formula is simply expressed as *thesis* (the positive factor), *antithesis* (the negative or opposite factor), and *synthesis,* which is the merging factor in which the opposites of thesis and antithesis are blended into *one,* which in itself becomes a new thesis. Thus when this system is applied theologically, evil becomes the necessary antithesis to good in which the two are blended into a synthesis in which it is impossible to designate anything bad in opposition to a good. In other words, white and black merge into gray—a color that can be called neither white nor black. Thus a sort of moral neutrality results. Although there appears to be a contrariety between evil and good, there is no real contradiction in the synthesis of the opposites. This philosophy has had a profound influence on liberal theology in which evil and good are but two aspects of the same thing—two sides of one and the same theological coin.[9]

In the dialectical theory all progress is based on action overcoming inertia, reaction, or resistance. Personality develops toward perfection, morally and personally, by overcoming its antagonist—evil propensity or opposition. Thus evil when thought of as the antithesis of good becomes a necessity, and this in effect makes evil a good, or at least essential to the good. Paul counters this false theory as follows:

> But if our unrighteousness demonstrates the righteousness of God, what shall we say? The God who inflicts wrath is not unrighteous, is He? . . . May it never be! For otherwise how will God judge the world? But if through my lie the truth of God abounded to His glory, why am I also still being judged as a sinner? And why not say (as we are slanderously reported and as some affirm that we say), "Let us do evil that good may come"? Their condemnation is just (Rom. 3:5-8).

5. Evil as the expression of the *physical* nature in opposition to the *spiritual* This view is indeed very similar to the Gnostic view in that it regards evil as inhering in matter, or the physical body. It presupposes the antagonistic, dualistic nature of humanity. The human body is, in this view, empirical and belongs to the empirical world. The spirit is idealistic and consequently belongs to the ideal world. Plato represented this theory by imagining two horses hitched to the same chariot. One was a winged steed with a nature that disposed it to wish to fly upward. The other was a common steed of the earth and was disposed to forage on the grass of the earth. Thus the two were in continual tension. The only hope of resolving the problem rested in the death of the earthbound steed so that the winged one might fly away and realize its independence from the other. Out of this notion came the doctrine, held by certain segments of Christianity, that humanity's ultimate release from sin rests in the death of the body.

The fallacies of the foregoing theory are obvious from the Scriptures, as well as from reason. First, the Bible represents man as a unitary rather than a dualistic or compounded being (1 Thess. 5:23). Second, contemporary psychology views a person as unitary, or holistic, in nature. Third, the Bible represents evil as inhering in the person's spiritual nature, though it may be expressed through the physical body. Fourth, the greatest evils of humanity are spiritual, rather than physical—such as unbelief, pride, malice, envy, anger, hatred, and selfish ambition (cf. Matt. 15:18-19; Mark 7:14-23). Fifth, this theory makes the spirit subservient to the flesh, or body. Sixth, if this theory were true, then with age and declining physical health and desires the person would automatically become more righteous, which of course, is not true to either Scripture or human experience.

In a somewhat pessimistic mood the writer of Ecclesiastes contradicts this theory when he says, "Remember your Creator in the days of your youth, before the days of trouble come and the years approach when you will say, 'I find no pleasure in them'" (Eccl. 12:1 NIV). Another translator graphically depicts this human decline thus: "when old age fears a height, and even a walk has its terrors, when his hair is almond white, and he drags his limbs along, and the spirit flags and fades. So man goes to his long, long home" (Eccl. 12:5, Moffatt).

6. Evil as the expression of moral ignorance The view that evil is the expression of moral ignorance is as old as Socrates (c. 470-399 B.C.) and as modern as John Dewey. Basically, with Socrates, it says that the good life is ethical, and the ethical life is attained by self-knowledge through which the universal innate moral laws are discovered. When, as Socrates thought, these innate moral laws are discovered through self-examination, the person will automatically obey them. Out of this theory came Socrates' famous dictum: "Virtue is knowledge." This means that if one knows what is right, one will automatically act in accordance with the good, or right. Consequently, all evil is the result of ignorance, in this view.

Socrates' theory is pantheistic in that it holds the human mind to be infinite because it possesses all knowledge innately, though this may not be realized by reason of ignorance. This theory is also rationalistic in harmony with Stoicism by reason of its assumption that the human mind, when enlightened, is capable of solving all its own problems. Again, the Socratic view fails to consider fallen man's propensity toward evil and to consider the weakness of the human will in the face of temptation to do what is known to be wrong. Even Plato reminded Socrates that we see people flying in the very face of what they know to be right.

B.A.G. Fuller says of Socrates' theory of good:

> If . . . self-knowledge was the beginning of wisdom and virtue, it might also be regarded as the end thereof. Since man was a rational being, and presumably actuated by self-interest, he would naturally do what was best for him if he but knew what that best was. Virtue, then, from start to finish depended on knowledge, and could be defined as such. So we reach the famous Socratic assertion that *virtue is knowledge*, and that if only men can be brought to see what the better course is they will spontaneously follow it.[10]

Fuller criticizes Socrates' position by saying:

> He did not give sufficient weight to the power of instinct, and passion, and the desire of the moment to fly in the face of the true good, even when our best interests in the long run are clearly perceived. Over and over again, we do wrong knowingly. As the poet Ovid sings, we know and approve the better course, but follow the worse.[11]

If Socrates' doctrine were true, then it would seem logical that the wisest would be the most virtuous and the ignorant would be the greatest sinners. History and experience, as well as the Scriptures have proved this to be false. Paul declared that "the world through its wisdom did not come to know God" (1 Cor. 1:21) and then he told the Corinthian Christians, their "faith should not rest on the wisdom of men, but on the power of God" (1 Cor. 2:5). This Socratic dictum has influenced the human race across the ages to the present time, especially in the realm of secular education. The Surgeon General's announcement that cigarette smoking is a cause of lung cancer has not been effective in diminishing the habit, and the published information that about 25,000 people die on the American highways annually because of drinking drivers has not diminished the death rate from this cause. While it is necessary to know what is morally right in order to do it, it simply is not true that to know right is to do what is right. More than knowledge is necessary for a person to be virtuous.

7. Evil as the absence of adequate experience A rather similar view, though in certain respects different from that of Socrates, is that evil is the lack of experience. This view was advocated by the American educator John Dewey (1859–1952). The principal difference between Socrates and Dewey was that the latter emphasized evil as due to the absence of experience, whereas Socrates credited it to the lack of knowledge.

Although Dewey minimized the importance of traditional educational methods and subject matter per se, he advocated the attainment of knowledge through the interaction of the organism with its environment, or "learning by doing." This became known as the genetic method of attaining knowledge. Dewey held that from the attainment of pleasure or pain through the trial and error of experience one learns what is right or wrong in moral conduct. The learned experience that affords the greatest degree of pleasure or sense of satisfaction is right and consequently it is ethical. Thus for Dewey the only evil is ignorance that results from the absence of adequate experience. In this he closely approximates Socrates, though the route of attainment and the source of knowledge are different. Dewey's theory became known as instrumentalism, and his educational system as progressive education. Every branch of learning and every area of life and activity in America came under the influence of Dewey's philosophy to some extent during his long educational career. In more recent times his theory has invaded the Orient and is of great influence there also. In some ways Dewey's philosophy may become a form of hedonism, since the pleasure or satisfaction derived from the experience determines what is right.

There are three important respects in which the theories of Socrates and Dewey must be judged to be wrong.

First, history, experience, and the Bible all witness to the fact that intellectually attained knowledge of right and wrong, whether by self-examination as with Socrates or by experiential knowledge as with Dewey, gives no assurance that a person will act in accordance with his knowledge.

Second, knowledge of what is right is not adequate to counterbalance the perverted desires and weakened will of fallen humanity.

Third, the theories of both Socrates and Dewey are purely humanistic and thus leave no place for God in the life of humankind. Accordingly, both leave human beings at the mercy of their inadequate fallen natures.

8. Evil as the residue of the evolutionary process This theory, as taught by some, holds that evil is the savage remnant of humanity's animalistic ancestry. Moral evil, in this view, represents an ethical lag in humanity's evolutionary climb physically and mentally. When man's ethical lag catches up with his psychological and physical advance he will become morally good. Borden Parker Bowne (1847–1910) wrote that evil is a relic of the animal not yet outgrown, a resultant of the mechanism of appetite and impulse and reflex action for which the proper inhabitants are not yet developed. Only slowly does it grow into a consciousness of itself as evil.[12]

Bowne's theory, like those of all other committed evolutionists, denies the *imago Dei* in man and relegates him to the position of a more advanced animal than his contemporaries. The question of why other animals in a similar climate with equal opportunities did not advance is left unanswered. This theory denies the reality of moral evil and is characteristic of the unfounded and now exploded optimism of the late nineteenth century. Along with the whole optimistic evolutionary structure, it has suffered the fate of disillusionment precipitated by the twentieth-century wars and human tragedies.

The theistic evolutionary theory of recent times affords little if any ethical improvement over naturalistic evolution. The idea that at some stage of animalistic evolution God intervened and imparted a higher kind of life and personhood to certain members of the more advanced animal kingdom while by-passing the rest of the common herd leaves many unanswered questions. Neither has there been any reliable scientific, anthropological, archaeological, or biblical evidence for this theory.

9. Evil as the residue theory in creation The residue theory, as the term connotes, has to do with "that which is left after part has been taken away; remainder; rest" *(New World Dictionary of the American Language)*. In this sense, evil in the world and humanity consists of the imperfect remnants after God had completed His otherwise perfect creative work. Evil is perhaps something like the chippings from the sculptor's marble when he has finished his masterpiece. The principal objections to this theory are that (1) there is no biblical evidence for it; (2) it reflects upon God as being responsible for something valueless in His creation, or at best imperfect; and (3) such a concept of evil would in reality be amoral and consequently eliminate the necessity for the substitutionary atonement of Jesus Christ, leaving His death of no more than "moral influence" significance, if indeed of any significance whatsoever.

It is only fair to note, however, that Edwin Lewis in his work *The Creator and the Adversary* gives a somewhat different interpretation to this "residue" theory. He says:

> It provides the "substance" of whatever is created but it never increases or diminishes in its total quantity. There is as much now as there ever was, and there will never be any less or more than there is now. It is residual because it is that form of the primal self-differentiation which enters into neither the divine nor the demoniac. It is a constant just because it is eternal and uncreated. . . . The qualities and disqualities inhere in a common base, which in itself has neither quality nor disquality. . . . It creates nothing, but it provides a condition without which creation would be impossible.[13]

Thus understood, this theory seems to make the "residue" a neutral, eternal, unchanging constant out of which both good and evil issue or are created. Consequently this would posit an eternal dualism between God and the morally neutral "residue" out of which God created all that exists, with the result that God would be responsible for both the good and the evil in His created works, however that evil may be regarded.

10. Evil as a cultural creation Among the several advocates of the theory that evil is a cultural creation was Jean Jacques Rousseau (1712-1778). Rousseau believed in the essential goodness of man and human nature. He thought that "primitive" people were the most moral of mankind. This view gave rise to the "noble savage" theory, which has long since been abandoned by most philosophers following anthropological investigations of the culture of primitive peoples. Rousseau theorized that the development of civilization and culture corrupted the morals of primitive humanity. Consequently, evil is a social creation. It must be acknowledged that there is some truth in Rousseau's theory. There is much in modern culture that is vicious and tends to further corrupt the morals of humanity. When this is recognized, however, the question arises as to who created the corrupting culture? Since only humanity has culture, there was of necessity evil in humanity that corrupted the culture. Thus Rousseau's theory resolves itself into cyclical reasoning and loses its significance.

11. Evil as an economic creation The most influential economic-evil theory of modern times has been Marxism, or possibly it is better designated Leninism. While Karl Marx (1818-1883) and Frederick Engels (1820-1895) were the cofounders of this theory, it was Vladimir Ilyich Lenin (1870-1924) who became the chief exponent of dialectic materialism that was based on the *thesis, antithesis, synthesis* view, which found expression in Russian Communism.

Karl Marx had reasoned that economic inequality resulted in social injustice, which in turn brought about class struggles. Since economic inequality produced social injustice, injustice is the meaning of evil. It is interesting that Marx reasoned that social injustice was the original sin of humanity. Only persons were created in economy this primary accumulation plays much the same part that is played by original sin in theology."[14]

This humanistic theory denies the biblical account of original sin, substituting for it social injustice. It robs humanity of self-determination and thus enslaves people to their environment. It leads directly to totalitarianism by making society per se an entity and it tends to destroy individuality and personal initiative. It denies a personal deity and deifies the state. Thus in the end the evil of Leninism is totalitarianism.

IV. THE BIBLICAL VIEW OF THE ORIGIN OF EVIL

The biblical view of the origin of sin and evil presupposes the uniqueness of humanity. This is especially true because the Bible represents evil at the outset as an immoral act of disobedience, rather than a cosmic accident. There seems to be no biblical evidence that any other being was created in *the same ethical sense* as was humanity. Only persons were created in God's image, and thus people were capable of exercising moral cognition, freedom to choose, and a sense of moral responsibility for their decisions and actions, with all else that characterizes morality. Thus in this sense humanity is responsible for its own destiny. The Scriptures are replete with instances of humanity's obediences and disobediences to the known will of God—of choices between what was clearly known to be right or wrong. Animals choose by instinct or training, human beings by rational moral knowledge and freedom with a consequent sense of moral responsibility.

Indeed, the temptation to sin by an external agent (Satan, as represented by the serpent) clearly indicates the existence of evil prior to the fall of humanity. This, however, was both prior and external to human involvement in evil. The history, nature, and experience of this extrahuman being will be dealt with in the chapter "Angelology and Demonology." It is sufficient here to note that Peter says, "God did not spare angels when they sinned, but cast them into hell and committed them to pits of darkness, reserved for judgment" (2 Peter 2:4), while Jude declared, "Angels who did not keep their own dominion, but abandoned their proper abode, He has kept in eternal bonds under darkness for the judgment of the great day" (Jude 6).

Whoever Satan may have been, or whatever may have been the nature of his fall, it was with the temptation and fall of Adam and Eve in Eden that sin and evil had their origin in the human race, according to the Scriptures. Paul makes this clear when he says, "through one man [Adam], sin entered into the world, and death through sin, and so death spread to all men, because all sinned" (Rom. 5:12). John Wesley has an interesting comment on this passage:

> As by one man—Adam: who is mentioned, and not Eve, as being the representative of mankind. *Sin entered into the world*— Actual sin, and its consequence, a sinful nature. And *death*—with all its attendants. It *entered into the world* when it entered into being; for till then it did not exist. By *sin*— Therefore it could not enter before sin.[15]

Thus Wesley understood Paul to mean that until the fall of Adam and Eve sin did not exist in the experience of humanity. Sin originated in the human race with the Fall. The Fall occurred as the result of the disobedience of the first human pair. Their disobedience was in the clear knowledge of God's prohibitive command and as a specific act of their uninhibited volition. Thus the sin of the human family was in a certain sense a creative ethical enactment. It was not a substance that they took into their experience. It was an act of disobedience that they performed—it was an unethical act. Consequently the original human sin, and all subsequent sin per se, in its basic nature, falls into the category of ethics. That there were many consequences of this original sin and that there are many secondary types of sin is evident in the Scriptures and in the experience of humanity. These will engage our consideration presently.

It is necessary here to note that all sin as moral evil per se is primarily against God. This is accounted for by the fact that man bears the image of God. Therefore any sin is a violation of that sacred image, whether it be against fellow beings or against oneself. Sin mars God's image in man, and that is an offense against the One whose image is represented in humanity. David recognized this truth, and, though he had sinned against Bathsheba, her husband, and his kingdom in his immoral deeds, he realized that his offense was primarily against God, and he cried out, "Against you, you only, have I sinned and done what is evil in your sight, so that you are proved right when you speak and justified when you judge" (Ps. 51:4 NIV). Another translation has, "It is against thee I have sinned, I have done evil in thy sight. Yes, thou art just in thy charge, justified in thy sentence" (Moffatt). David is in no sense denying his offense against Bathsheba with whom he had committed adultery, against her husband whom he had killed, or against the kingdom over which he ruled. He is forthrightly admitting that since God is the creator of all, any offense against God's creation is primarily an offense to God Himself, who created all, and whose it is. This utterance of David reveals one of the deepest theological insights in all the Bible. To deny the existence and creatorship of God is to deny the possibility of sin. Indeed, there may be tort, or an offense against another person, or a crime that is an offense against society, but there can be no sin per se in the absence of a *personal, holy God;* and there can be no true repentance of sin apart from an acknowledgment that the offense is primarily against God Himself.

Of whatever nature Satan may have been before his expulsion from heaven, along with a third of the angels that followed him, his sin was such as to close the door of possible redemption against himself forever. Beyond this, divine revelation is silent on the existence of evil before the Fall in Eden, and beyond this all human speculation is futile.

If, as some have assumed, the Genesis account of the Fall (Gen. 3:1–24) is a myth, it would be utterly meaningless unless it portrayed the reality of a historical human experience. If, on the other hand, it portrays the reality of such a human experience, it is then true to human experience and thus would be human history in any event, no matter in what figure of speech it might be expressed. Thus, either way, the historicity of the account is valid. In fact all language is figurative, as words are but necessarily symbols of ideas designed to express those ideas. To deny the historicity of the essential biblical accounts is in effect to deny universally recognized valid human experience. There had to be a *first* in the life of someone somewhere for every valid human experience. Until someone can invent a superior representation of such experiences than those recorded in the Bible, it would seem that we cannot do better than accept the biblical accounts as valid and trustworthy. Human speculations and imaginations have not so far been able to equal the biblical accounts, nor do they give promise of doing so in the future.

V. THE TEMPTATION AND FALL OF HUMANITY

A. The Battle Royal in Eden

The temptation of Adam and Eve in Eden, like the temptation of Jesus Christ in the wilderness, may be rightly called *The Battle Royal*. As Adam (a generic name) was created in God's own image—the *imago Dei,* he was the rightful son and heir of God. The created universe was willed to him as his inheritance at his creation (Gen. 1:26-31). Thus creation was bequeathed to Adam, the princely son, by his Father, the King of all creation. God *rested* when He had finished His creative work and placed the governorship of that creation under the control of His created son, Adam (Gen. 2:1-3). (Incidentally it may be seriously questioned whether the term *son* belongs to any other creature than humanity and Christ.)

After having received his glorious heritage, his right of possession and rulership was contested by another prince, whom Paul calls "the prince of the power of the air, the spirit that now worketh in the children of disobedience" (Eph. 2:2 KJV); and whom Christ called "the prince of this world" (John 13:30 NIV; cf. Matt. 9:34; 12:24; Mark 3:22; John 16:11).

This would-be usurper, who had lost his previous heritage through rebellion against God, the King of the universe, subtly embodied himself in the serpent, a native creature of Adam's own realms, and engaged this prince of God, from within, on his own territory in the first great Battle Royal for the possession of all creation. The story of this conflict to the death is told in Genesis 3:1-7. Satan won that battle and gained limited control over humanity and creation. Adam lost the battle, surrendered his realms to the victor, was imprisoned within his lost domain, and so subjected himself and his entire posterity to the status of vassals to "the god of this world" (2 Cor. 4:4; Eph. 2:1-3).

The rest of the Bible is devoted to an account of God's endeavor to recapture and restore humanity and their lost realms to their original state under the new federal headship of Jesus Christ who, when redemption should be completed, would become, in the words of John the Revelator, "the faithful witness, the firstborn of the dead, and the ruler ['prince,' KJV] of the kings of the earth" (Rev. 1:5). This however, is another story yet to be told as the result of a future greater Royal Battle.

B. The Necessity and Nature of Temptation as a Moral Test

To ask how perfectly holy persons, created in God's own image, as Adam and Eve were, could be tempted to disobey God and fall into sin, is to ignore the ethical constitution of humanity. Though untested before the Fall, Adam and Eve were created potentially ethical with the personal characteristics of moral cognition, freedom to choose, and a sense of responsibility for the choices they would make. None of these ethical characteristics, essential as they are to true personhood, could be realized without an opportunity to test them. No one knows his own physical strength or mental ability until an opportunity presents itself to test these qualities. It was Socrates who said, "There is no real philosophy until the mind turns around and examines itself.... *Know thyself.*"[16] "The celebrated inscription on the temple of Apollo at Delphi, 'Know thyself,' was the beginning of wisdom."[17] Paul wrote to the Corinthians, "Test yourselves to see if you are in the faith; examine yourselves! Or do you not recognize this about yourselves, that Christ Jesus is in you—unless indeed you fail the test?" (2 Cor. 13:5). God designed His people to be a tried people; and James explicitly says, "Blessed is the man that endureth temptation, for when he is tried, he shall receive the crown of life, which the Lord has promised to them that love him" (James 1:12 KJV). Loving devotion and loyalty to a person or a cause derive their meaning from freedom to make alternate choices. God did not create people as robots but as ethical persons capable of realizing their full divinely intended potential, designed of God for that purpose.

C. The Failure of Humanity in the Moral Test

The first problem that confronts the serious theologian is this: Was *enticement* to do evil necessary to the trial of our first parents' love for and loyalty to God in Eden—or is it in fact necessary in any temptation? God did not entice them to disobey, for as James says, "Let no man say when he is tempted, 'I am being tempted by God'; for God cannot be tempted by evil, and He Himself does not tempt anyone" (James 1:13).

Apart from the mystery of the existence and activities of Satan, our first parents were placed in a situation in which, even without the enticements of Satan, they were confronted with the necessity of making a moral decision to obey or disobey God. This constituted the test of their loyalty to their Creator. Had there been no Satan present to entice them, they would still have had the choice to make between obedience and disobedience to God. What choice they would have made in the absence of the enticements of Satan we do not know, but that a choice had to be made was inevitable since they were ethical beings. That the enticements of Satan greatly intensified their temptation to disobey God is without question. If, however, we say that Satan's enticements were essential to their temptation, then we make evil a necessity in the plan and purpose of God. To do this is to make God responsible for evil, and such a conclusion would cancel out the perfection of God, or at best create a *necessary dualism* of good and evil. The Judeo-Christian religion does not allow for such an ethical dualism.

James doubtless gives the best definition of temptation presented in the Bible when he says, "Each one is tempted when he is carried away and enticed by his own lust," or as stated in another version: "Every man is tempted, when he is drawn away of his own *lust,* and enticed" (James 1:14 KJV). The problem here is with the Greek word *epithumias,* which is translated "lust." This Greek word, however, does not of necessity carry an evil meaning, though when translated "lust" in English, it does have such connotation. Alexander Souter translates *epithumeō,* "I seek after, search for, make inquiries about"; and *epithymia* he translates as "eager (passionate) desire, passion."[18] Henry Thayer says that *epithyméo* is "to set one's heart upon, to have a desire for, long for."[19] In the context of James 1:14, this word does not appear to convey an *evil* desire, but rather in itself a strong though legitimate desire. John Wesley says of James 1:14:

> He is drawn away. . . . By his own desire —we are therefore to look for the cause of every sin, not out of ourselves. Even the injections of the devil cannot hurt before we make them our own. And everyone has desires arising from his own constitution, tempers, habits, and way of life. And enticed in the progress of the temptation, catching at the bait: so the original word signifies.[20]

Such a desire, characteristic of all the natural constitutional human drives, becomes evil only when it is misdirected toward an illegitimate object or is allowed to overpower reason in its quest for satisfaction. In the latter circumstance, the illegitimate object toward which it is directed becomes an enticement that serves to unite the strong desire with the forbidden object resulting in sin that effects spiritual death.

James draws his figure expressive of temptation from the life cycle. He continues, "when lust has conceived [or when the strong desire unites with the illegitimate object], it gives birth to sin; and when sin is accomplished, it brings forth [or issues in spiritual] death" (James 1:14-15). While James does not mention Satan in this connection, it is granted that Satan may, and often does, use and amplify the forbidden object to intensify the human desire. What does seem evident is that temptation may possibly take place and result in sin without the tempting agency of Satan, though this was not the case in Eden. If such were not possible, it would be difficult, if not impossible, to account for the fall of Satan himself, who must have been a perfectly holy being as he came from the hand of God, and that with no existing evil to entice him. Here, however, there are unresolved mysteries in the absence of any clear divine revelation.

Olin A. Curtis lists four elements in the original Fall: (1) physical craving, (2) a cosmic curiosity, (3) an individual drive toward self-expression, and (4) social influence.[21] All of these elements come to clear light in the process of the temptation in Eden. The fourth fact mentioned by Curtis, the influence of social pressure, was of course limited to the mutual moral support of Adam and Eve in Eden, which in the end proved inadequate.

The actual process of the temptation in Eden was somewhat as follows: (1) The environment was favorable, a beautiful environment of pleasure and plenty—the Garden of Eden. (2) Adam and Eve had a clear knowledge of the will of God. (3) They had normal, God-given desires, or appetites. (4) Their appetites were stimulated by the objects they saw. (5) They desired the fruit, though it was forbidden. (6) Satan injected a doubt into their minds concerning God's motives and the veracity of His prohibitive command and its certain results. (7) They gave heed to Satan's suggestions. (8) Weakened by doubt and confused by satanic rationalization, they blindly followed his suggestions and partook of the forbidden fruit.

D. The Results of Humanity's Failure in the Moral Test

1. God's first covenant with humanity (Gen. 2:15-17) The very creation of human beings in God's personal moral image constituted them ethical beings, and their ethical nature they did not share with any other creature.

God's purpose for human beings is indicated by His placing them in the garden previously prepared for them (Gen. 2:8; cf. Ps. 1). "God put him into the garden of Eden" literally means "He made him rest," that is, "He gave it to him as his permanent and settled dwelling."[22] But the state of human beings was not to be inactivity. Rather, they were charged with responsibility for "working" the garden productively and "watching" it guardingly—"to cultivate it and keep it" (Gen. 2:15; cf. 1 Thess. 1:9-10). To cultivate *(abhadh)* signifies to serve and thus indicates humanity's subordination to the Creator who gave man the garden for provender and pleasure. To "keep" *(shamar)* signifies "to watch," "to look after," or "have charge of," indicating man's stewardship under God, well-illustrated by Joseph's stewardship under Egyptian rulers (Gen. 40:2-6; 41:38-45).

The garden with its idyllic environment was designed by God to meet and satisfy every basic need of humanity. As such, it represented in miniature all creation.

Beyond the responsibilities of occupancy and stewardship for Adam and Eve in Eden, there existed two special trees—the "tree of life," designed for their immortality and to which they had free access until the Fall (Gen. 3:22-24), and "the tree of the knowledge of good and evil," as a challenge to their ethical potential. The tree of life was constantly accessible to Adam and Eve as their only means of sustaining their God-given immortality. There were, however, both permissions and prohibitions placed on them. Thus "the tree of the knowledge of good and evil" had a disciplinary purpose and function in their lives. Otherwise stated, everything beneficial and necessary to them was permitted; that which was destructive was forbidden.

Until Adam and Eve were faced with the necessity of making a moral decision to obey or disobey the command of the Creator, they were perfectly holy as the holy God had created them, but they were only potentially, rather than actually, ethical. Thus, confronted with God's negative command, having clear knowledge of the character of the tree, knowing the divinely stated consequences of disobedience, and having an unsullied mind and conscience, they made the first moral decision as the representatives of the human race. It was in this momentous decision that their moral consciousness came to birth. The threefold requirement of an ethical situation—knowledge of right and wrong, freedom to choose between the alternatives, and responsibility for the consequences of the decision—were met. The future of all mankind hinged on the outcome of their decision. Would it be "life" or "death"?

The sentence pronounced by God on their disobedience was certain and awful—*death*! Adam Clarke's rendering is specific: "Thou shalt not only die spiritually, by losing the life of God, but from that moment thou shalt become mortal, and shalt continue in a *dying state* till thou die."[23] God's first covenant with humanity, like all subsequent covenants, had its conditions of reward and retribution.

2. Humanity's breach of the first covenant (Gen. 3:1-6) Much speculation has surrounded the serpent of Genesis 3. In any event, subsequent inspired writers identified the serpent with Satan (2 Cor. 11:3; 1 Tim. 2:14; Rev. 12:9; 20:2). Whether the serpent walked on legs before the Fall as other animals did or was capable of speaking, we cannot be certain; at any rate these speculations are unimportant to an understanding of Eve's temptation. That he was a real, crafty representative of the Evil One, rather than a product of a collection of primitive myths or an allegory, as certain critics have supposed, is surely in keeping with the biblical account of the nature and work of Satan. Thus it is best to accept the account as an inspired historical record reflecting highly significant symbolisms (cf. Job 1:6-19; 2:1-7; 31:33; Hos. 6:7; John 8:44; Rom. 5:12; 1 Cor. 15:22; Eph. 6:12; 1 Thess. 3:5). If the temptation experience itself is true to life, as most will testify, then there seems to be no logical reason to deny the validity of the first account, especially since there had to be "a first."

During the first half of the twentieth century many theologians scoffed at the idea of a personal devil. With the publication of C. S. Lewis's masterpiece on the craftiness of the devil, *The Screwtape Letters* (1943), the religious climate relative to a real devil changed radically. Today there are probably few Christians who would deny the reality of the devil's existence, and not a few apostates have even resorted to Satan worship.

The effectiveness of the serpent's subtle approach to his unsuspecting victim is evident in the inspired record. It is instructive to compare Eve's temptation with that of Christ's in Matthew 4:1-11. First, the tempter injected a doubt into Eve's mind concerning the correctness of her understanding of God's command, designed to confuse her: "Indeed, has God said, 'You shall not eat from any [or 'every'] tree of the garden?'" (cf. Matt. 4:3). This is followed with a direct contradiction of God's warning: "You surely shall not die!" Herein is an age-long deception of Satan foisted upon God's people: that disobedience to God's will may result in the loss of grace, but not in the loss of one's relationship with God. This is, in turn, followed by a slanderous insinuation against the character of God Himself—that He is robbing man of a deserved benefit (Gen. 3:5).

Weakened by doubt and confused by uncertainty, Eve allowed physical appeal and personal pride to take precedence over faith in and obedience to God, and she yielded to the tempter's enticements (Gen. 3:6). Nor was she satisfied to depart alone from obedience to God; "she also gave some to her husband, who was with her, and he ate it" (cf. Rom. 1:32 NIV). Thus the tragic drama of temptation ended in the catastrophic wreckage of God's perfect creation. John summarizes the temptation drama as "the lust of the flesh and the lust of the eyes and the boastful pride of life" (1 John 2:16; cf. James 1:13-15).

3. Immediate effects of the broken covenant (Gen. 3:7-8) The immediate effects of the breach of the divine covenant were (1) the loss of innocence: "their eyes were opened"; (2) guilty shame: "they knew that they were naked"; (3) fearful alienation: they "hid themselves from the presence of the LORD God"; (4) attempted compensation: "they sewed fig leaves together and made themselves loin coverings"; and (5) projection: "the woman whom Thou gavest to be with me, she gave me from the tree, and I ate" (Gen. 3:12). The results were much more far-reaching.

Innocence does not necessarily presuppose the absence of intellectual knowledge of evil. In fact, such knowledge is both beneficial and necessary for us to understand the nature of evil. Innocence does, however, mean the absence of "experiential knowledge" of evil. Adam and Eve were well acquainted with the tree of the knowledge of good and evil, though they probably lacked knowledge of the far-reaching effects of disobedience to God's command. Their moral eyes were opened to see guilt when they identified with evil through their experience of disobedience to God.

To Adam and Eve, as to all who follow their example, disobedience brought a personal sense of guilt and shame as a result of the perversion, or misuse, of what was intended by God for their benefit and welfare. It is probable that the customary time of worship for Adam and Eve was the breezy eventide in the garden where God met and communed with them daily. But after the Fall they were absent from worship, and the voice of God summoned them to account: "Where are you?" This is not a question concerning physical location, but spiritual, designed to renew their frame of reference and thus enable them to locate themselves morally and spiritually (cf. Luke 15:11-17).

Spiritual loss, like all losses, results in a sense of deficiency that automatically seeks compensation. Having lost their original innocence, Adam and Eve sought to compensate for this loss by the artificial means of making fig-leaf clothing. Rather than indicating that sex was associated with the Fall, as some have mistakenly supposed, their shame-consciousness was in the realm of their highest God-given abilities—procreative reproduction—and they devised a kind of artificial, substitutionary covering for their sin. It remained for God to provide "a blood-atonement covering" for them. The revealed presence of the holy God could do no less than intensify their sense of guilt and fear, with the result that they sought refuge in the forest from God's presence.

Arraigned before God, Adam sought justification for his sin through psychological projection revealed in his response to God: "The woman whom Thou gavest to be with me. . . ." This was a twofold implied accusation; first, against God, who gave him the woman, and, second, against the woman whom God gave him. Thus God and His gift to Adam are blameworthy, not Adam himself. In turn, Eve projected her sin on the serpent in order to escape the consequent guilt (Gen. 3:13). True as her accusation was, nonetheless she bore her own guilt for allowing herself to be deceived, even as did Adam for following his wife's lead.

Their perverted moral thinking is evident in their total reaction. No longer was Eve Adam's God-given bosom companion, corresponding to and complementing him—"bone of my bones and flesh of my flesh; . . . called 'woman,' because she was taken out of man" (Gen. 2:23). At the arraignment Adam disowned Eve and judged her to be an unworthy and unappreciated imposition from God, who had thus caused his downfall, and therefore God, and not man, is ultimately responsible for all human sin and woe. This is a human device to escape guilt—a device perpetuated to the present time. Such is sinful man's perverted thinking.

Contrary to much confused thinking about conscience, it is, in the final analysis, simply the mind's qualitative judgments in moral matters—a God-given aspect of the constitutional nature of human beings—and not something capable of being added to or subtracted from their being (cf. Rom. 2:14-15). Indeed, if the inherent human mind is capable of improvement or perversion, so is the conscience as the moral judging function of the mind. Thus sin clouded and confused Adam's moral judgment. Such perverted judgment led, and leads, to all sorts of perverted moral thinking and conduct (see Rom. 1:18-32).

Likewise Eve's disposition to rationalize is evident from her reply to God: "The serpent deceived me, and I ate" (Gen. 3:13). True, but in the pristine purity of her primitive mind and in the light of God's clear command, she need not have allowed herself to be deceived.

God traces sin to its "ultimate source" in the tempter and pronounces a curse on him commensurate with his evil nature and deed (Gen. 3:14). Clarke remarks, "He [the tempter], cannot roll the blame on any other; *self-tempted he fell,* and it is natural for him, such is his enmity, to deceive and destroy all he can. His fault admits of no excuse, and therefore God begins to pronounce sentence on *him* first'"[24] (cf. John 16:11).

Adam's sin divided the human race and set enmity (Heb. *ebhab,* "a moral characteristic") between the unrighteous and the righteous to the end of the age, beginning with the first offspring of Adam and Eve.

The natural cosmos itself appears to have suffered a cataclysmic disturbance with the fall of man. How else may we account for such cosmic evils as destructive weather disturbances (cf. Job 1:16, 18-19; 1 Cor. 2:6; Eph. 2:2), earthquakes, decimating famines, epidemics, polio, cancer, and a thousand other occurrences of suffering and misery.

Added to the innumerable cosmic evils are the moral evils of humanity—greed, lust, envy, hatred, deceptiveness, violence, bloody wars, broken homes, child abuse, robbery, murder, rape, suicides—and inevitable death for all. These and many others are the fruits of humanity's disobedience to God's will.

In the midst of the dark night of apparent utter despair there arose a bright star of hope. God announced that in spite of the enmity and suffering caused by the Fall, as Satan bruised the heel of Eve's posterity, the seed of woman would eventually bruise Satan's head (Gen. 3:15). Here is found the first evangel (Gr., *protevangelium*), the first promise of the Redeemer. It is significant that it is to be the woman's seed (singular in the original, with the masculine pronoun *he*), not Adam's, who will destroy Satan. It was of the woman (Mary), without the concurrence of man, that the Savior was to be born. In His suffering and death the Savior's "heel" was bruised by Satan, but in His victory over death through the resurrection, Christ the Savior crushed *(shuph)* the serpent's head—destroyed the power of Satan forever (Rom. 16:20; 1 Cor. 15:20-28).

In merciful kindness God prevented the ultimate consequences of humanity's sinful disobedience by prefiguring the substitutionary atonement for sin, to be offered by a Savior to come, when He slew animals to provide a covering for man's guilt (Gen. 3:21).

VI. EFFECT OF THE FALL ON ADAM'S DESCENDANTS

A. The Birth and Occupations of Adam's Sons (Gen. 4:1-2)

Although the Bible account of the Fall is limited to Genesis 3, the results of that sad event pervade the Judeo-Christian Scriptures and human history and are the theme of much of the world's greatest literature and philosophy. Sin, like an infectious plague, cannot be confined. The conflict between Cain and Abel reflects the first racial effects of the Fall. In the Fall Adam and Eve sinned against God, the most fundamental of all sins. In fact, sin against God is generic to all sin—the taproot of all evil (cf. Ps. 51:4).

No other personal intimacy equals that expressed by the English word *knew,* inadequate as that word may be. The expression "the man had relations with his wife Eve" is unsatisfactory. Perhaps Moffatt's plain language is best understood: "Now the man had [sexual] intercourse with his wife Eve." Conception resulted from their union, and in due time Eve gave birth to Cain, whom she regarded as a special gift from God, perhaps reassuring her of God's continued favor, or possibly an expression of gratitude for divine assistance in the ordeal of childbirth (cf. Gen. 3:16). The word *manchild* (Heb. *ish*) suggests a "man endued with immaterial and personal existence."[25]

In any event, the first male child is an Oriental's greatest honor and as the firstborn male he would carry the family's name on to future generations. Some have even seen a possible hint in Eve's exclamation of faith that God was fulfilling His promise of Genesis 3:15, that her seed would crush the head of the tempter. Evidently it indicated her personal restoration to God following her sin.[26]

In due time, Eve's second son, Abel, was born. His name *(Hebhel)* means "breath," "vapor," or "vanity," and may suggest a note of disillusionment with life as the consciousness of the effects of the Fall began to dawn on Adam and Eve, but especially as they were barred from Eden and the tree of life (Gen. 3:22-24).

Cain and Abel had their respective occupations. Abel was "a keeper" of flocks, perhaps small cattlelike sheep and goats, in which he may have been a follower of Adam (cf. Gen. 3:21). "Cain was a tiller of the ground" (Gen. 4:2) or literally, "a server of the soil," an occupation God had approved (Gen. 3:17, 18, 23). Neither occupation was inferior to the other, and both were God-ordained, honorable, and life-sustaining. Both occupations by these first sons of Adam and Eve contradict the evolutionary theory that herdsmanship and agriculture were later developments.

B. The Worship of Adam's Sons (Gen. 4:3-7)

There is no scriptural evidence that God commanded sacrifice of Adam and Eve or of their sons. Nor is there reason to suppose that the sacrifices mentioned in Genesis 4:3-4 were the first that they ever offered. In fact, Cain's and Abel's sacrifices may well have been their regular means of worshiping God and may have originated with their father, Adam. Sacrificial worship is both natural and beneficial to man and is, in fact, universal in some form among humanity. Moses later codified the sacrifices people were offering. The word *offering (minchah,* "a gift of gratitude") may signify any kind of gift to God.

Much difference of opinion exists among interpreters concerning the offerings of Cain and Abel. The record simply states that "Cain brought an offering to the Lord of the fruit of the ground," whereas "Abel . . . brought of the firstlings of his flock and of their fat portions" (Gen. 4:3-4). Obviously, each offered from the products of his chosen and legitimate occupation, and both kinds of offerings were subsequently made to God and approved by Him, as recorded in the Old Testament.

The main problem arises over the reason for God's acceptance of Abel's offering and His rejection of Cain's. One authority thinks the difference lay in the liberality and quality of Abel's offering, as suggested by the words "the finest," as given in some versions, literally, "of their fattest parts,"[27] in contrast to Cain's merely bringing "an offering to the Lord." Several modern scholars, including Speiser and Leupold, reject completely the traditional view that God's acceptance of Abel's offering and His rejection of Cain's was because Abel made a "blood sacrifice," signifying atonement for sin, whereas Cain's offering lacked that essential quality. However, several older scholars, including Clarke and Wesley, hold, with some good reasons, that the difference actually lay in the nature of their sacrifices and that Abel's "blood offering" suggested atonement for sin. Especially in favor of this view is the fact that God had previously rejected Adam and Eve's leaf-coverings, and slew animals to provide coverings for their shame and guilt (Gen. 3:21).

R. Payne Smith's interpretation has much to commend it. He says it was a combination of factors that made the difference, including the following: (1) Abel offered "a more excellent sacrifice" because it was done in faith (Heb. 11:4); (2) in unbelief Cain may have offered "a scanty present of common produce, and not of first fruits," whereas Abel offered "firstlings [first-fruits], and of their fat portions," the choicest portions; (3) "Abel may also have shown a deeper faith in the promised Deliverer by offering an animal sacrifice"; (4) "certainly the acceptance of his sacrifice quickened among men the belief that the proper way of approaching God was by the death of a victim"; and (5) "Cain's unbloody sacrifice had also a great future before it. It became the *minchah* of the Levitical law, and under the Christian dispensation is the offering of prayer and praise, and especially the Eucharistic thanksgiving."[28]

God's rejection of Cain's offering and His acceptance of Abel's had the effect of arousing within Cain a twofold reaction; namely, anger at God for His rejection, and jealousy of Abel because of his acceptance by God. Observing the change in Cain's countenance (cf. Prov. 15:13; 25:23; Isa. 3:9), God asked him three questions, followed by a severe warning and certain wise counsel.

God's first question to Cain was, in fact, twofold: "Why are you angry?" seems designed to bring him to face reality (Cain knew he was angry, though he did not admit it). The second, "Why has your countenance fallen?" (Gen. 4:6), revealed the evidence that prevented Cain from denying the fact of his anger. God well knew why Cain was angry, but Cain needed to face this fact. God's further question, "If you do well, will not your countenance be lifted up?" appears designed to force Cain to an acknowledgment of what he already knew within himself: that his worship had been defective and thus rightfully rejected by God.

God's searching questions are followed by a solemn and severe warning against Cain's jealous anger. Like a ferocious hungry beast, sin was "crouching" just outside Cain's door awaiting his exit in order to devour him. Here is the first mention of sin (*chatta'th*, "missing the mark") by name in the Bible, and God's depiction of it as a devouring beast is most graphic. Sin lurks in the jealous and angry mind of Cain, not as the crafty serpent that deceived his mother, but as a devouring beast striving to get at him, hungry for the kill (1 Peter 5:8; cf. Prov. 6:34; Song of Sol. 8:6). Satan's manifestations are many, subtle, and varied (cf. 2 Cor. 11:14).

God does not promise Cain exemption from temptation to jealous wrath, but He does admonish him to "master it" (Gen. 4:7). This is neither a suggestion of mastery over sin by suppression or works-righteousness. Rather, it places Cain under obligation, as it does all believers, to exercise vigilant self-discipline, especially in the areas of recognized personal weaknesses (cf. 1 Peter 5:8-9). There appears to be a hint here that Cain's outburst of jealous rage against his brother had been smoldering for some time as he had witnessed Abel's advance over him. Possibly his jealousy involved a fear that he would lose his rights of primogeniture to his younger brother, even as Esau later did to Jacob (cf. Gen. 25:33-34; Deut. 21:15-17; 1 Chron. 5:1-2; Heb. 12:

16-17). In any event, God did not leave Cain in hopelessness, but encouraged him to master his problem. This does not imply humanism per se, in the sense that Cain, or anyone, could master his evil propensities without the help of God, but simply that self-discipline was necessary.

C. The Violence Among Adam's Descendants (Gen. 4:8-13)

In Genesis 4:8 is the first recorded homicide in biblical history. The opinions of scholars concerning verse 8 are many and varied. That Cain and Abel were in the field where Abel was possibly lured by his brother and that Cain "told Abel" something, possibly what God had said to him, or possibly how he felt toward his brother, seems reasonably certain. That Cain's smoldering jealousy erupted into volcanic wrath and that he slew his brother (how we do not know) is certain. The beastly sin that crouched at his door had sprung on him and made him the first murderer.

God's second encounter with Cain demanded a responsible accounting for his violent deed (Gen. 4:9). Cain's reply is characteristic of his state of mind in the face of his deed. First, he boldly and insultingly lied to the omniscient God: "I do not know." Second, he disowned responsibility for his brother: "Am I my brother's keeper?" Here is the first, but by no means the last, disclaimer of social responsibility that has caused so much human misery across time and history. God's question, "What have you done?" was designed to awaken Cain's conscience to the realization of the enormity of his crime. This is enforced by God's disclosure that Cain's crime had already been detected: "The voice of your brother's blood is crying to Me from the ground" (Gen. 4:10). Likely, to hide his deed, Cain had buried Abel's body in the field where the murder was committed. The body may have been found later by members of his family. Possibly the voice of Abel's blood was echoed to God by the sad wail of his widow and children.

Adam's body was molded from the earth, God commissioned him to till the earth, his sustenance came from the earth, and now Cain had polluted his own homeland, of which he was a cultivator, by his younger brother's blood in homicide. Thus his fields rebelled, under divine impulse, against his attempt to gain a livelihood from them: "The ground . . . shall no longer yield its strength to you." Cain, unable to make a living any longer on the land and haunted by the shadow of his evil deed, became a vagabond, "a vagrant and a wanderer" (Gen. 4:12)—a disreputable, lonely, remorseful, guilt-ridden fugitive. Little wonder that Cain cried out: "My punishment is too great to bear" (v. 13). In fear of "blood vengeance" from members of Abel's household or line, and bereft of God's "face" and protection, he complained, "It will come about that whoever finds me will kill me" (Gen. 4:14; cf. 9:5-6). In mercy God established a protective sign over Cain's life. One of the saddest lines in the Bible is this: "Then Cain went out from the presence of the Lord," plaintively wailing, "My punishment is too great to bear!" (Gen. 4:13, 16). Parallel to this is the statement concerning Judas's betrayal of Christ: "He went out immediately; and it was night" (John 13:30).

Rather than "settled" (as in NASB), Cain "lived in the land of Nod, east of Eden" (Gen. 4:16 NIV). Since "Nod" means "wandering," Cain's lot seems to have been that of a forlorn wanderer without friends and ever fearful that vengeance was pursuing him (Gen. 4:14). Where Cain got his wife is unanswered in the Bible. It is possible that he acquired her in the land of Nod; however, the Bible does not state this. Rather, it simply states that he "lay with his wife, and she became pregnant and gave birth to Enoch. Cain was then building a city, and he named it after his son Enoch," which may indicate his search for security (v. 17 NIV), even as in the case of Abraham, of whom it is said, "He was looking forward to the city with foundations, whose architect and builder is God" (Heb. 11:10 NIV; cf. v. 16; 12:22-24).

Across the ages, since their first departure from God, people have sought in vain for security in cities. While Abraham chose to dwell in temporary tents until he should occupy the city "whose architect and builder is God" (Heb. 11:10, 16), Cain, an exile by divine justice, built a city and named it after his son Enoch, but he found no resting place there. Ever since then, people have sought in vain for refuge in cities. Uncounted millions have migrated to great centers of population where indescribable poverty, evil, violence, and frustration characterize the populations.[29]

D. A Divine Ray of Hope for Fallen Humanity (Gen. 12:1-3)

Out of the dark night of humanity's fall and despair there arose a bright star of hope, namely, God's choice of Abraham to become the father of the redemptive people, the Hebrews.

Abraham entered into a faith relationship with God in obedience to his call from idolatrous Ur. This relationship was based on a sevenfold divine promise. First, God promised to make him great, not only in worldly estimation, but in the provision through him of a Messiah-Savior for all mankind. Second, God would "bless" him in material prosperity, but far more in becoming the forerunner of the Savior. Third, He would make his name "great"—great as the "friend of God" (Gen. 12:2; James 2:23). Fourth, he would be a blessing, both by divine sanction and by divine command. Fifth, God promised to "bless those who bless" Abraham, and thus there seems to be a sense in which even those outside of the covenant people will benefit from their contribution to the messianic hope within the covenant line. Sixth, God's protective wrath would be exercised over Abraham by cursing those who oppose him. Finally, God's promise to Abraham rises to its grand messianic climax in assuring him that "all the families of the earth shall be blessed" in him. Thus God's veiled promise of a Redeemer from the Fall (Gen. 3:15) is sharply accented in this clear promise to Abraham. Thus the Book of Genesis is concerned with the total scope of God's created work from the beginning of time to the ultimate redemption of mankind.

VII. THE VICTORY OF CHRIST'S TEMPTATION

A. The Necessity of Christ's Temptation

There is a close parallel in certain respects between the temptation of our foreparents in Eden and the temptation of Christ in the wilderness, as recorded in Matthew 4:1-11, though the outcome in Christ's case was entirely different.

When John hesitated to baptize Jesus in the Jordan River, Jesus replied, "Let it be so now; it is proper to do this to fulfill all righteousness" (Matt. 3:15). Another version is more specific; it says, "Let it be so for the present; we do well to conform in this way with all that God requires" (NEB). Wesley comments:

> The particular meaning of our Lord seems to be, that it becomes us to do (Me to receive baptism, and you to administer it) in order to fulfill, that is, that I may *fully perform, every part of the righteous law* of God, and the commission He hath given me.[30]

If it was imperative that Christ be baptized to fulfill the Law, it was equally necessary that He be subjected to temptation. It was as necessary as it had been for Adam and Eve, though for a different reason, and it had vastly different results. They had failed under trial and subjected themselves and their realms to Satan's dominion. Christ's mission was to deliver them and their subjugated realms from the power and usurped authority of Satan, who had defeated them in Eden. Before He could make atonement for the sins of humanity on the cross, it was necessary that He confront the challenges of Satan, who had usurped this authority, and defeat him on his own terms. Thus Christ came as the Son of God, in the express image of God (Heb. 1:1), but in the form of man—the unique God-Man—to win back what humanity had lost in Eden. As perfect Man, as well as perfect God, He, the Second Adam, was under necessity of proving Himself superior to Satan and defeating him in the contest of temptation where the first Adam had been defeated by Satan.

B. The Process of Christ's Temptation

Matthew's account of Christ's temptation (Matt. 4:1-11) reveals the following process: First, His temptation was necessitated by the will of God, though not executed by God: "Jesus was led up by the Spirit into the wilderness to be tempted by the devil" (v. 1). Second, He was prepared for the ordeal by hunger, or intense physical desire, by forty days and nights of fasting (v. 2). Third, He met the enemy in a bleak wilderness alone, with neither such mutual human support nor pleasant circumstances as Adam and Eve had in Eden. Fourth, though He knew the will of the Father and His own mission, He was not buttressed by any specific commands of "You shall" and "You shall not," such as Adam and Eve had. Fifth, He met Satan in a face-to-face, fearful confrontation, whereas the pair in Eden were approached by a subtle, disguised creature who proffered his assistance to deliver them from their illusions and lead them into an existence of enlightenment and freedom from the ulterior motives of their selfishly evil deity.

Sixth, Satan's appeal to Christ, like that in Eden, was in the area where he supposed Him to be most vulnerable—His appetite. Calling attention to the scattered stones resembling small Oriental loaves of bread, Satan first attempted to inject into the mind of Christ a doubt concerning His divine identity: "If you are the Son of God," and then proceeded to remind Him of His intense hunger by saying, "Command that these stones be made bread" (v. 3). In other words, if Christ could not perform a miracle to satisfy His hunger pains, He certainly was not divine, and if He was not divine, Satan could exercise the same authority over Him that he exercised over the rest of humanity that he had already defeated and captured in Adam. Christ's answer to this first challenge of Satan is highly significant. It simply defines priority values. While He does not deny the importance and even the necessity of physical nourishment, He denies that it is right to trade spiritual nourishment for the physical, as Esau did with Jacob (Gen. 25:29-34; cf. Heb. 12:15-17); and further it reflects Christ's devotion to one of life's greatest values, namely, loyalty to God and His truth. Thus He simply says, "IT IS WRITTEN, 'MAN SHALL NOT LIVE ON BREAD ALONE, BUT ON EVERY WORD THAT PROCEEDS OUT OF THE MOUTH OF GOD'" (v. 4). In these words Christ gives priority to God and spirituality over the material in life.

Seventh, Satan next appealed to the religious instincts of Christ in relation to His life's mission. Having quickened Christ's imagination to a position of messiahship among His own people, who had for so many centuries prayed and expectantly waited for the Messiah, Satan bade the Christ to cast Himself down from the pinnacle of the temple into the midst of the worshiping throng, and they would hail Him as the fulfillment of their age-long dreams (vv. 5-6).

It seems there had been a long-standing belief among the Jews that their Messiah would suddenly appear at one of their great annual feasts in some such spectacular manner and that He would be accepted accordingly. Indeed, to allay any fear that Christ might suffer injury in such an event, Satan assured Him of divine support and protection, if in reality He was the Son of God (v. 6). This aspect of the temptation was threefold in nature. Like the others, it was prefaced by an implied doubt, "If you are the Son of God." But this temptation was psychological in that it strongly appealed to His heightened imagination as Satan depicted the expectant worshiping Israelitish throng in the Jerusalem temple

(v. 5). Again the assurance of physical protection, based on misquoted divine support, is falsely assured Him (v. 6). Jesus, however, counters this approach with corrected scriptural rebuke: "It is written, 'Do not put the the LORD YOUR GOD TO THE TEST'" (Matt. 4:7 NIV). Jesus well knew that God does not extend His miraculous power for the exercise of spectacular demonstrations to fulfill the wishes of mistaken religious fanaticism (cf. Acts 1:6-8). Divine miracles always have a moral value, and they must be judged accordingly.

Eighth, defeated in each of the preceding battles of the great war of the ages, Satan attempts one last master stroke of his military strategy. Again with a psychological appeal to Christ's imagination in the light of His redemptive purpose in coming into the world, Satan "showed Him all the kingdoms of the world, and their glory" (v. 8). Was it not for the very purpose of conquering and ruling the hearts and lives of all peoples that Christ took on human form? Satan well knew that this was the mission of Jesus Christ. He possibly also knew, however, that it was to be accomplished through his own defeat through the Cross. Thus he offers Christ all that He came for, minus His suffering and death on the cross if He would but follow the example of the first Adam, and fall down and worship him (v. 9) or recognize his sovereignty and become his vassal. This was by far the most subtle and effective strategy of the Battle Royal. Later, in Christ's most severe trial, as He faced the cross, He cried out in His humanity, "Father, if it is possible, let this cup [the cup of suffering and death] pass from Me." Then, gathering the full force of His courage, He continued, "Yet not as I will, but as Thou wilt" (Matt. 26:39). So He set His face toward the Cross and fixed His purpose to meet the last great battle of the ages against the usurper of God's and humanity's realms. Looking ahead to that final victory on Calvary, Christ rebuked Satan with the words, "Begone, Satan! For it is written, 'YOU SHALL WORSHIP THE LORD YOUR GOD, AND SERVE HIM ONLY'" (Matt. 4:10).

Then, thoroughly defeated and routed, "the devil left Him; and behold, angels came and began to minister to Him" (v. 11). While the first Adam lost the Battle Royal and slunk away in defeat and shame, only to be discovered and condemned by God for his failure, the Second Adam emerged from His Battle Royal, with the prince of darkness, unscathed, triumphant, and approved by God. Then God sent His ministering angels to commend Christ for His glorious victory, while Satan slunk away in shameful defeat to hide himself in the wilderness of Judea.

These are the accounts of the two greatest temptations of the ages—the one ending in ignominious defeat, the other in the greatest victory of the ages. The first Adam lost his kingdom and his spiritual freedom. The Second Adam won His conflict against the usurper and regained the losses of the first Adam and qualified to become the Savior and Lord of all mankind and of the universe itself (Rom. 8:19-26).

VIII. THE BASIC NATURE OF SIN*

A. Sin as Unbelief

In the religious or theological sense sin is unbelief (John 16:8-9). It is a rejection of God's saving work. The Gospel of John emphasizes that belief in the Father and the Son is the condition for salvation. This involves a personal commitment to Jesus (John 3:16; 8:31, 32; 20:31). To "believe in" Jesus Christ involves a personal relationship with Him and participation in His life. The basic sin in the Gospel of John, then, is unbelief. This is a refusal to affirm and accept the interpersonal or

---

*I am indebted to Dr. Larry Shelton of Seattle Pacific University for much of the treatment of sin under section VIII, "The Basic Nature of Sin," which is included here, with certain modifications, by permission of Dr. Shelton.

covenant relationship with Christ. A refusal to come to Christ the incarnate Word means a deprivation of "life" (John 5:40).[31]

The Reformers stressed that sin is the opposite of man's appropriate relationship with God. The Reformation theocentric emphasis thus focused on sin as failure to believe in the personal God and saw man as either in a state of faith, the proper relationship to God, or in a state of sin, the improper relationship to God.[32] Sin is thus religious and affects one's relationship to God rather than being only the transgression of the law. It is personal-theological, not simply legal. Such unbelief distrusts God's integrity and rejects His wisdom.[33] The logical consequence, then, is to turn to oneself in pride.

Furthermore, Jesus emphasizes that being children of God is not based on traditional or genealogical foundations. He says, "But as many as received Him, to them He gave the right to become children of God, even to those who believe in His name, who were born not of blood, nor of the will of the flesh, nor of the will of man, but of God" (John 1:12–13). Thus Jesus has done a new thing by showing that salvation is based on belief, and those who do not receive Him are not children of God (John 1:11). Unbelief, then, frustrates the purposes of Christ's new covenant.

B. Sin as Pride

Understood in terms of personality, sin is pride. It is the self-centeredness that results from unbelief and issues in rebellion against God.[34] John Wesley asserts that the root of all sin is the desire to be independent of God.[35] Independency and self-sufficiency result in an aversion to God's will[36] and an insistence on finding one's own fulfillment in the created order rather than in God (Rom. 1:25).[37] When the self becomes thus enthroned, it becomes characterized by fleshly mindedness *(sarkikos)*, which opposes the mind of the Spirit (Rom. 7:14, 23). The whole person in bondage to the flesh is separated from God and placed in submission to that which is creaturely and fallen.[38] The covenant obligations of submission to the Creator are broken.

C. Sin as Rebellion

The pride of self-sufficiency leads to rebellion against the covenant of God. In contradiction to the order of creation, the self seeks defiantly to reverse this order. The result of this defiance is a break in communion with God while the self attempts to become independent of Him. The irony, however, is that in attempting to be independent of God, in whom is ultimate freedom, man becomes dependent on his own limitations and is thus enslaved to the very self he sought to make free. His desire for autonomy thus is a denial of God. Instead of accepting his life from the Creator, man in revolt leaves the wholeness with which he was created and the fellowship with God that is his reason for existence.[39] This propensity Wang calls a law because its function is both uniform and predictable. He describes this sort of sinfulness as "a predictable and spontaneous contrariness toward the law of God uniformly present in human nature as now constituted."[40] Richard S. Taylor says that since the "law of God" is an extension of His own mind and self; sin is thus contrariness against the self of God. Lawlessness *(anomia)* is essentially, then, rebellion against God.[41]

D. Sin as Alienation

Since man is not in the relationship with God that was intended by creation, he is homesick. His alienation from God stirs within him what Brunner calls an "unrest of heart," which leaves him with an inner tension, a sense of being "out of place" and far from home.[42] This desperate nostalgia is reflected in Augustine's famous words, "Our hearts are restless until they find their rest in Thee, Lord." Sin becomes, as Wiley says, "self-separation from God in the sense of decentralization, the place which should be occupied by God being assumed by the self."[43] Thus man, who was created to be in fellowship with God, is left alone with himself. The resulting existential loneliness calls forth the poignant reminder of Paul, "Remember that at that time you were separate from Christ, excluded from the commonwealth of Israel and strangers to the covenants of promise, having no hope and without God in the world" (Eph. 2:12).

E. Sin as Moral Corruption

Wiley points out that the consequences of the Fall were external in that man became alienated from God and enslaved to Satan. Internally, however, man lost the divine grace and became subject to physical and moral corruption. Since the inspiring presence of the Holy Spirit was lost, man had no organizing principle for the harmonious integration of his personality. Therefore, he became morally disintegrated with the results of blindness of heart, a tendency toward concupiscence, and a moral inability to overcome sin. Deprived of the gracious work of the Holy Spirit, he became depraved in his moral perception and being.[44]

The nature of this moral corruption is different from physical depravity, or the limitation and disintegration of human nature. Sin is not to be confused with humanness, however deteriorated the latter may become. If moral corruption becomes confused with physical limitations, it becomes impossible to maintain any consistent biblical view of victory over sin. If human weakness is understood as sin, as so often happens in Augustinian theological systems, then moral corruption is seen to be intrinsic to human nature. The biblical understanding, however, sees man's sinfulness as the result of moral eccentricity, a self-centeredness that grows out of a willful and dynamic resistance to God-centered obedience. Moral corruption is thus a rejection of proper covenant partnership. It is not an ontological essence that cannot be separated from the physical body and that thus can be escaped only at death.[45]

The sin that makes salvation necessary must be understood as a corruption of the proper covenant relationship with God. It is not to be conceived of as an independent metaphysical entity. The Augustinian tendency to identify sin with physical being leads to a materialistic understanding that attributes a sort of tangibility or "thingness" to it. Such biblical terms as those translated literally "flesh" (Gal. 5:19, 24), "carnal mind" or "the mind of the flesh" (Rom. 8:6–7), "carnal" (Rom. 7:14; 1 Cor. 3:1, 3–4), "the body of this death" (Rom. 7:24), "the old man" (Rom. 6:6; Eph. 4:22), and "the body of sin" (Rom. 6:6) tend to become interpreted as having material reality.[46] It must be understood that language uses symbols or metaphors to communicate nontangible realities. Although metaphors are useful, they may mislead the thought processes if their function is not understood. A metaphor is intended to suggest a likeness between two realities, not the identification of them. If a metaphor is identified with the reality it describes, the abstract qualities that the metaphor represents tend to become reified, or substantialized. The tendency for reification, or "thing thinking," is to conceive of all reality as existing only in things that can be weighed, measured, or located in space. If the concept of sin as moral corruption is reified, it then becomes inextricably identified with the physical body, with the result that the covenantal or relational reality of sin becomes obscured. Sin is in fact a moral reality that exists only in the distorted relationships between God and fallen humanity. Like love, sin is interpersonal. As Corlett says, "Carnality has no capital of its own."[47] In the biblical sense, sin or corruption is a moral and relational concept. It does not inhere in matter. As G. Ernest Wright notes, "Sin is the violation of the covenant and rebellion against God's personal lordship. . . . It is a violation of relationship, a betrayal of trust."[48]

It is this rebellious violation of trust that stands in need of redemption.[49]

F. Sin as a Universal Malady

The question of the scope and degree of fallenness has occupied theologians for centuries. If salvation is necessary because mankind has repudiated the covenant relationship with God, to what extent is all humanity implicated in this alienation? The problem has often been labeled "original sin." To what degree does it affect man? Wiley defines the issue thus:

> "Original Sin" or "Inherited Depravity" are terms applied to the subjective moral state or condition of man by birth, and therefore *express the moral condition of man in his natural estate*. This depravity must not, however, be regarded as a physical entity or any other form of essential existence added to man's nature. It is, rather, as its name implies, a deprivation or loss.[50]

1. Depravity is universal Paul indicates the universality of depravity as follows:

> Therefore, just as through one man sin entered into the world, and death through sin, and so death spread to all men, because all sinned . . . the many were made sinners, even so through the obedience of the One the many will be made righteous (Rom. 5:12, 19).

The issue here is that the consequences of the Fall affect the entire race, "death spread to all men." The spiritual death and depravity that characterize the race are described by Jesus and Paul as "flesh" *(sarx)*. Jesus says:

> Unless one is born of water and the Spirit, he cannot enter into the kingdom of God. That which is born of the flesh is flesh; and that which is born of the Spirit is spirit (John 3:5-6).

Man's moral condition requires the work of salvation. Paul also says as much:

> For those who are according to the flesh set their minds on the things of the flesh, but those who are according to the Spirit, the things of the Spirit. . . . For if you live according to the flesh, you must die (Rom. 8:5, 13).

As Wiley points out, "The term flesh as here used, is representative of the fallen estate of mankind generally—not the destruction of any of its essential elements, but the *deprivation* of its original spiritual life, and hence the *depravation* of its tendency."[51] The consensus of orthodox scholars has been that the effects of the Fall are universal. In some way, all persons were deprived of God's gracious Spirit and thus depraved as a result of Adam's sin. With the exception of Pelagian and Semi-Pelagian approaches, which have denied original sin or depravity in any general sense, the *consensus omnium* has affirmed the depravity of all.[52]

2. Depravity is personal deprivation If the universality of depravity has received general consensus, the question of the extent and nature of the depravity in the individual certainly has not. It is clear that because of the disobedience of man in eating of the forbidden fruit, a cleavage has occurred in the original harmonious relationship between God and creation. When man in his high-handedness has been left to himself, he deteriorates morally: Cain killed his brother, Lamech loved war, and sin reigns in the human heart. Genesis 6:5 declares, "The LORD saw that the wickedness of man was great on the earth, and that every intent of the thoughts of his heart was only evil continually." The sin that started with the first couple continued in their descendants and was expressed in the corruption of their moral life.[53]

The disagreement over the extent of depravity revolves around two issues: the nature of the depravity itself and the extent of its effects on the human personality.

The nature of original sin is seen by Arminius primarily as deprivation rather than depravation. Actual sins committed by individuals are the result of the deprivation that issues from original sin. He feels that if our first parents had lived obediently within the covenant given by God, the gifts of eternal life and fellowship would have been given to all their posterity. The Fall resulted in man's becoming devoid of the gift of the Holy Spirit, with the consequent deprivation of the (moral) image of God. Thus, for him, original sin (a term he used reluctantly) is the absence of original righteousness,[54] but not the imputation of guilt for Adam's sin.

Calvin goes much further in his insistence that original sin, or depravity of nature, is (intensively) total and involves real sin and guilt. He says:

> Original sin, therefore, seems to be a hereditary depravity and corruption of our nature, diffused into all parts of the soul, which first makes us liable to God's wrath. . . . We are so vitiated and perverted in every part of our nature that by this great corruption we stand justly condemned and convicted before God, to whom nothing is acceptable but righteousness, innocence and purity.[55]

Even infants carry this condemnation from the womb, and their entire nature is sinful and their iniquity is not considered by God to be simply the lack of original righteousness, but positive and active perversity, which continually bears new fruit.[56] Thus there is no distinction between inherited depravity and guilt for sin. With Calvin, even an infant stands guilty and condemned for its original sin.

The position of Arminius is similar to that of Zwingli, the Zurich Reformer, who refuses to admit that original sin is properly sin in the sense of transgression of the law. Although mankind is without a birthright to immortality, original sin does not involve culpability.[57]

Wesley admits that moral depravity is entire and that man cannot cooperate with God's grace for salvation while enslaved to this sin. However, Wesley appears to refuse to assign guilt to this depravity and teaches that on the basis of Christ's redemption, man is given prevenient grace by the Holy Spirit to enable him to cooperate with God's work of salvation.[58] Thus Wesley, as well as Richard Watson and other Wesleyan-Arminians such as H. Orton Wiley, sees original sin as a depravity that results from deprivation. It is a loss of original righteousness and involves guilt only in the sense of culpable liability to punishment. This depravity affects the entire person and therefore vitiates every part of the intellect, feelings, and will. Man is incapable in himself of moral righteousness. The Wesleyan-Arminian position also affirms, however, the function of the grace of God to enable all who choose to turn from sin to belief and cleansing.[59]

The Augustinian-Calvinist position, in contrast, sees depravity as total and intensive. Every aspect of the personality is so corrupted that it can never respond to grace apart from divine election and effectual calling.[60] (Some present-day Calvinists would prefer to say "apart from regeneration and effectual calling.") This depravity also bears guilt in that the sinner was represented in Adam. Thus, for Calvinism, original sin or depravity is total, intensive, and culpable.

Both Calvinists and Wesleyan-Arminians, however, agree that the sin that afflicts mankind and annuls the relationship between Creator and creature requires an act of salvation whereby this breach of covenant may be restored.

G. Sin Against the Holy Spirit

There appears to be but one sin spoken of in the Bible that is unforgivable. That is the sin against the Holy Spirit. Various views on this sin have been advanced by scholars.

Some believe that the unforgivable sin against the Holy Spirit is to assign to Him the work of Satan. In Matthew's Gospel, the Pharisees said of Christ, "He casts out the demons by the ruler of the demons" (Matt. 9:34). It was in reply to this accusation, made again in Matthew 12:24, that Jesus gave the following answer:

> Therefore I say to you, any sin and blasphemy shall be forgiven men, but blasphemy against the Spirit shall not be forgiven. And whosoever shall speak a word against the

Son of Man, it shall be forgiven him, but whosoever shall speak against the Holy Spirit, it shall not be forgiven him, either in this age, or in the age to come (Matt. 12:31-32).

This is one of the most awe-inspiring statements in the entire Judeo-Christian Scriptures—or, indeed, in all literature. William Barclay calls these words "the most terrifying thought in the New Testament."[61] Mark's version of this statement of Christ is equally solemn and awe-inspiring (see Mark 3:28-30). Luke and John pass over the incident in silence. Harris says of the word *blaspheme:*

> . . . to speak evil of someone. The Greek blasphemeō is usually translated "blaspheme," but also "defame," "rail on," "speak evil of," etc. . . . The law of blasphemy of Lev. 24:11-16 prescribed death for the man in Israel who "cursed" the name of the Lord or blasphemed (nāqab).[62]

Matthew's version makes clear that this sin consists in ascribing to the Holy Spirit the work of Satan, for this was the occasion of Christ's rebuke to the Pharisees. The convincing logic and divine authority of Christ's rebuke consists in the fact that Christ is the only Savior of mankind. The Holy Spirit alone is the administrator of Christ's saving provisions. Satan is the sworn enemy of Christ and His redemptive work. In Satan there is no hope of salvation. Thus to ascribe to Satan the work of the Holy Spirit is to take from Christ His saving mission. This in turn cuts off any access of God to man, and man to God. Thus man is left in an utterly hopeless position in relation to God. This was in effect what these Pharisees were doing when they said, "This man [Christ] casts out demons only by Beelzebub, the ruler of the demons" (Matt. 12:24). Thus they were denying in fact that Christ had conquered Satan in His temptation (Matt. 4:1-11) and were assigning to Satan the superior power over Christ, making Him the servant of Satan to do his work. Christ shows the illogic of their accusation when He says, "Any kingdom divided against itself is laid waste; any city or house divided against itself shall not stand. And if Satan casts out Satan, he is divided against himself; how then shall his kingdom stand?" (Matt. 12:25-26). Wesley succinctly remarks: "Does not that subtle spirit [Satan] know this is not the way to establish his kingdom?"[63]

William Barclay has an interesting view on this unforgivable sin which, if correct, is most helpful in solving the problem. He thinks that the expression "son of man" in Matthew's account may not be in reference to Christ, but that it may mean any human person. In this view it is understandable that blasphemy against a fellow person would be forgivable, and the distinction between sin against Christ as Son of God and Son of Man and a sin against the Holy Spirit would disappear.[64]

Barclay, however, has a further significant view on this incident. He thinks that the sin against the Holy Spirit may consist in resisting His striving until a person becomes totally insensitive to His appeals. This view finds support in the Genesis account of men's wickedness before the Flood. There God said, "My Spirit shall not strive with man forever" (Gen. 6:3). It seems likely that it is this sin of which John speaks when he says, "There is a sin leading to death [spiritual and moral death]. I do not say that he should make request for this" (1 John 5:16).

Barclay is on a solid basis when he says that the person who fears he has committed the sin against the Holy Spirit is one who has not done so.[65] If a person has actually committed this sin, he has probably lost his moral consciousness of sin by reason of having deadened his moral and spiritual sensibilities. If one realizes himself to be a sinner, he cannot have committed the sin against the Holy Spirit, because it is the Spirit Himself who brings conviction for sin (John 16:8).

Somewhere in his autobiography, entitled *The Words,* the world-renowned existential atheist Jean-Paul Sartre reflects on a previous encounter he evidently had with the God in whom he professed not to believe, and in crude language says, "I collared the Holy Ghost in the basement and threw him out the window." It will be remembered that Sartre knew well the Christian religion, having been raised by a Christian grandfather. Could his adamant persistence in atheism have been the result of his earlier encounter with and resistance to the Holy Spirit?

IX. JOHN WESLEY'S UNDERSTANDING OF SIN

A. Introduction

The dual emphases of John Wesley's preaching and theology consisted of humanity's sin and Christ's salvation. Wesley was first and foremost an evangelistic reformer. As a theologian he was biblical rather than systematic. Theology, for Wesley, was ever practical rather than speculative. Wesley's theology was designed to serve the practical end of bringing conviction for sin to the lives of people and the redemptive grace of Christ for their salvation and sanctification both for righteous living here and for preparation to meet God in peace hereafter. Wilber T. Dayton says:

> John Wesley was primarily an evangelist. His theology left him no alternative and his evangelism demanded his theology for a rationale. To him the very gist of the gospel was to call sinners to repentance and faith. Everything else must be understood in this light and not vice versa. As A. Skevington Wood says, "Wesley's theology was practical and occasional rather than theoretical and systematic."[66]

Wesley used theological terminology as best suited his evangelistic purposes in winning people to Christ. This sometimes led him, when occasion seemed to demand, to emphasize the sinfulness of humanity by stressing *total intensive depravity* to the point that mankind was something less than the animal kingdom.[67] At other times he recognized that while human beings had largely lost the *moral image* of God in the Fall, they retained the sullied natural and political image. He realized that otherwise there could be no point of contact in humanity to which the gospel could appeal. This *intensive total depravity* emphasis characterized the earlier thinking of Karl Barth and led him to conclude that man's depravity is such that there is no tangent point at which God could contact fallen man. This, in turn, landed him in a type of divine determinism, wherein salvation became an imposition on man, even against his will. It is well known that Barth saw the error of this extreme position later and modified his theology considerably.

Wesley's practical biblical theology has led certain scholars to believe that he was a man of religious experience *only,* and not a theologian per se. William Hordern, a noted Lutheran scholar, says, "I was raised on the assertion that Wesley had no theology and that he taught a religion of experience alone, but it is now evident that Wesley was a powerful theologian."[68] Hordern further admits that in more recent times there have been significant trends within Methodism toward a rediscovery of Wesley's theological significance. Among these trends is the work of George C. Cell, *The Rediscovery of John Wesley,* published in 1935,[69] and *The Theology of John Wesley,* by Bishop William R. Cannon of the United Methodist Church, published in 1946.[70] Cell notes that Wesley's own theology—and, incidentally, later Wesleyanism—has been misunderstood as a brand of liberal Arminianism that has departed far from the Reformation theology. Many other scholars, both Wesleyan and non-Wesleyan, have rediscovered the genius of John Wesley as a theologian in recent times.

Cell asserts he discovered that instead of departing from the essentials of the Reformers' theology, Wesley was reaffirming the main principles of Reformation theology, and by doing so he counteracted and arrested the decline of Christianity, which was being so seriously eroded by the influences of the Enlightenment.[71] While it must be admitted that Cell's interpretation of Wesley's position goes beyond Wesley's intent in relation to Lutheran/Calvinist theology, at the same time his recognition of the importance of Wesley's theology is highly significant. Bishop William Cannon presents a wholesome corrective of Cell's misunderstanding of Wesley's position in relation to Reformation theology.[72]

Likewise A. Skevington Wood points up that "*sola gratia* and *sola fide* were the twin watchwords of the Reformation, and they found an echo in Wesley's preaching."[73]

That for Wesley original sin was man's basic problem is evident throughout his writings. In fact, this malady disenabled humanity from making any contribution to its salvation.[74] What, then, is the Wesleyan doctrine of original sin?

B. The Wesleyan Doctrine of Original Sin

Two things must be frankly admitted from the outset. First, while Wesley held tenaciously to the doctrine of original sin in all humanity, he obviously wavered on the question of the extent of the effect of that malady on the nature of mankind. He sometimes even appears to make conflicting statements. This issue will be dealt with presently. Second, while in contemporary Wesleyan scholarship the doctrine of original sin, or inherent depravity, is solidly maintained by conservative Evangelicals, there is not unanimity of opinion on the exact nature and extent of that condition. This may be due in part to the lack of clarity on the issue in Wesley's own writings and in part to the late development of a contemporary Wesleyan theology. It may also stem in no small measure from the fact that a great percentage of contemporary Wesleyan scholars are the products of non-Wesleyan theological training, especially on the graduate level. Thus it should not be surprising that on this issue the present writer holds certain positions with which some other Wesleyan scholars may not fully agree.

1. John Wesley's views on original sin and inherited guilt This item raises three issues: the meaning of original sin, the effect of original sin on Adam's descendants, and the condition of fallen humanity in relation to the gospel of redemption.

Since the present work is within the Wesleyan theological context, definitions and treatment will be confined mainly to that context. Having earlier distinguished between original sin in the sense of the first sin and original sin as the fall of our foreparents with its effects on them and their posterity, we will examine Wiley's definition of original sin.

Orton Wiley, a leading contemporary Wesleyan theologian, offers the following definition:

> We believe that original sin, or depravity, is the corruption of the nature of all the offsprings of Adam, by reason of which everyone is very far gone from original righteousness or the pure state of our first parents at the time of their creation, is averse to God, is without spiritual life, and is inclined to evil, and that continually; and that it continues to exist with the new life of the regenerate, until eradicated by the baptism with the Holy Spirit (Article I).[75]

Three items in this definition give rise to certain divergent views among Wesleyan scholars. First, the definition does not mention "inherited guilt" from Adam's sin. Second, the term *eradication* is used to denote the purification of the fallen nature from inherited corruption. Third, the purification of the believer's sinful nature is said to be effected by the baptism of the Holy Spirit.

Although it is unlikely that any evangelical Wesleyan scholar would deny the inheritance of a corrupt nature from the fall of Adam as the federal head of the human race, many would differ on the doctrine of *inherited guilt,* on both scriptural and ethical grounds. It is not a question as to whether Wesley taught this doctrine, for he obviously did on occasion. In Wesley's argument with one Dr. Taylor, he says, "God does not look upon infants as innocent, but as involved in the guilt of Adam's sin; otherwise death, the punishment denounced against that sin, could not be inflicted upon them."[76] The question is, rather, was Wesley correct, either scripturally or ethically, in this particular teaching?

It is obvious that Wesley was influenced by Calvinism to a greater extent than he may have realized in regard to the doctrine of inherited guilt. To argue that because Adam was the head of the human race and that all humanity was in him and shared the *effects* of the Fall through inherited depravity is not the same as saying that all participated in Adam's act of disobedience and consequently incurred the guilt of his fall. This would be no more logical than to conclude that a child or children inherit the guilt of a parent for a heinous sin or crime committed by that parent before the child was born or was even conceived. A child might well inherit a propensity to evil or even a disease from the parent's sin, but *guilt stems from a culpable act traceable to the unethical conduct of a morally responsible person*. The logical corollary and consequent of this position, that all actually sinned in Adam and thus inherit his guilt, would be that all are likewise included in the Second Adam, Jesus Christ, and through His atonement are automatically absolved of their guilt. This would lead inevitably to universalism, which of course neither Wesley nor his present-day followers would accept—notwithstanding the fact that some non-Wesleyan scholars have misunderstood Wesleyanism to teach universalism. Wesley himself said, *"Nothing is sin strictly speaking, but a voluntary transgression of a known law of God"* (italics added).

Concerning the question of *eradication* as a theological term describing the crisis experience of sanctification, there is also a divergence of opinion among contemporary Wesleyan scholars. While an exegetical case may well be made for this term, many prefer the use of such biblical terms as *cleansing, purification,* and *purging* because of the unfortunate connotation the word *eradication* has for many people. In fact, for many it seems to suggest that sin is some sort of a material substance that may be rooted out of a person in crisis sanctification. Apparently, Wesley did not use the word eradication, though he may well have approximated it. The index to the fourteen-volume unabridged *Works of John Wesley* (third edition), does not list eradication.

Again, certain Wesleyan scholars, apparently influenced by Reformed theology, deny the identity of the baptism in the Holy Spirit with the crisis experience of sanctification, electing to relate it to the conversion experience, as is common in Reformed theology.[77] (See vol. 2, chapter 10, "Hymnology: The Theology of the Wesleyan Hymns," by Timothy Smith.)

2. Wesley's views on inherited guilt and prevenient grace While Wesley has written explicitly on this point, as previously noted, again he seems to modify his views somewhat elsewhere, if indeed he does not waver in this conviction, when he writes:

> And yet it is allowed, *we are not so guilty by nature, as a course of actual sin afterward makes us*. But we are, antecedent to that course, "children of wrath;" *liable to some degree of wrath and punishment*. Here, then, from a plain text, taken in its obvious sense, we have a clear evidence both of what Divines term, *original sin imputed*, and of original sin inherited. *The former is the sin of Adam, so far reckoned ours as to constitute us in some degree guilty;* the latter, a want of original righteousness, and a corruption of nature; whence it is, that from our infancy we are averse to what is good, and propense to what is evil.[78]

Two things are noteworthy in the preceding quote. First, in this passage Wesley is obviously following "St. Augustine, and other Christian writers of his time [who] brought . . . [this doctrine] into common use."[79] This in itself shows that to some extent at least Wesley was influenced by St. Augustine and others of this school whose doctrine of intensive total depravity led them inescapably into a form of divine determinism expressed in divine election and predestination—some to eternal life and others to eternal damnation. Again Wesley's less rigid expressions here concerning guilt betray a certain hesitation on his part to go all the way with the doctrine of inherited guilt.

Wesley makes a distinction between "original sin *imputed* and original sin *inherited,*" the former of which is an expression of divine wrath against Adam's offspring because of Adam's sin, while the latter appears to be a natural consequence of Adam's sin.

In an earnest attempt to absolve God of injustice in the imputation of guilt to Adam's descendants, certain recognized contemporary Wesleyan theologians have emphasized Wesley's doctrine of prevenient grace. Briefly stated, by prevenient grace in this connection Wesley meant the grace of God that precedes, or goes before, and absolves Adam's descendants of the guilt imputed to them by God because of Adam's sin. This prevenient grace is made possible by the atonement of Jesus Christ that is made available to all people. For infants unaware of their inherited guilt from Adam, it automatically atones for their guilt. For others aware of this inherited guilt, repentance and faith in Christ's merits for salvation are required. This means that though infants were damned by reason of their inherited guilt, they are now, by reason of God's prevenient grace, not damned.

For some, this appears to be a perfectly satisfactory way of resolving the problem. To certain others who are more aware of the ethical implications inherent in the imputation of guilt to those who have not by personal choice sinned against God, this answer is less satisfactory. It seems to say that by inheritance from Adam a person both *is* and *is not* guilty. If the ethical implications could be resolved, the prevenient grace solution might be more theologically palatable. The Augustinian/Calvinist position that this apparent contradiction is a divine mystery, hidden in the inscrutable knowledge and will of God, beyond man's comprehension, is not satisfactory to many, though it apparently is to some. This problem seems to have played a major role in the Barthian and Neoorthodox conclusion concerning the paradoxical nature of the Bible and theology. What Neoorthodoxy designated paradoxes, however, were in reality unresolvable contradictions. This was well illustrated in a lecture by Barth, heard by the writer, when he said, "Metaphysically the devil does not exist; but practically you cannot escape him."

The inheritance of a sullied nature from the Fall poses no serious problem for evangelical Wesleyans. The theory of the inheritance of *guilt* from Adam's sin, for many others, however, remains an unsatisfactory doctrine when considered in the light of its ethical implication in relation to divine justice. To conclude with Calvin, as understood by Cannon, that "God's justice lies beyond the scope of man's free inquiry,"[80] is for many not a satisfactory answer to humanity's ethical or theological quest. Cannon quotes W. R. Moltby as saying:

> Our theological coat, in the spirit if not in the language of Wesley, "was cut for the figure of total [intensive] depravity, but when it was tried on, it was found not to fit any kind of human nature. Accordingly, we let out a seam in the back, as far as it would go, and the margin thus gained, with the stitches still showing, we called prevenient grace."[81]

3. Wesley's views on *extensive* versus *intensive* total depravity There were occasions in which Wesley, confronted with the deep depravity of eighteenth-century British society and likely influenced by Reformed theology from which he was not far removed in certain respects, would see humanity as totally intensively depraved. This was especially true in his evangelistic preaching. In his sermon "The Way to the Kingdom," he says:

> Know that thou art corrupt in every power, in every faculty of thy soul; that thou art totally corrupted in every one of these, all the

foundations being out of course. . . . Such is the inbred corruption of thy heart, of thy very inmost nature.[82]

Indeed, Wesley saw humanity created in the *natural, political,* and *moral image* of God; but, he says, when Adam sinned,

> so had he lost both the knowledge and love of God, without which the image of God could not subsist. Of this, therefore, he was deprived at the same time, and became unholy as well as unhappy. In the room of this, he had sunk into pride and self-will, the very image of the devil; and into sensual appetites and desires, the image of the beasts that perish.[83]

Elsewhere, however, Wesley admits that there does remain in unregenerate humanity the natural and political image of God, though these are seriously sullied. Wesley says:

> The Scriptures do say, "God created man in his own image" (Gen. i:27). But whatever that phrase means here, it doubtless means the same in Gen. ix 6: "Whoso sheddeth man's blood, by man shall his blood be shed; For in the image of God made he man." . . . Certainly the latter plainly refers to the former. And thus we may fairly infer from hence, that *"the image of God,"* wherein "man was" at first created, whereinsoever it consisted, *was not utterly effaced in the time of Noah. Yea, so much of it will always remain in all men, as will justify the punishing murders with death.* But we can in nowise infer from hence, that *the entire image of God,* in which Adam was first created, now remains in all his posterity (italics added).[84]

Since Wesley here clearly admits the continued existence of the *imago Dei* in fallen humanity, however sullied it may be, he certainly did not believe in the *intensive total depravity* of humanity, though he apparently regarded mankind as *extensively totally depraved.*

In the light of these and other apparently conflicting statements by Wesley on this issue, it is clear that he found it difficult to be strictly consistent when treating this issue. These inconsistencies may be best understood in the light of his times, when eighteenth-century England had sunk to incomprehensible depths of degeneracy. Thus, when Wesley looked at degenerate humanity about him, he saw them as lower than the amoral beasts—*intensively totally depraved.* But in his sober moments of biblical and theological reflection, he realized that, depraved though they were, human beings still retained the marred image of their Creator. Like the psalmist, when he looked at sinful mankind, he saw them pessimistically. "Until I went into the sanctuary of God: then understood I" (Ps. 73:17 KJV). Even David said on one occasion, "I said in my haste, 'All men are liars'" (Ps. 116:11 KJV). Then, realizing that he was caught in his own syllogism, he modified his evaluation. If all men were liars, and David was a man, then David would himself be a liar, and consequently he would not be telling the truth about all men being liars. His words "I said in my haste" imply his recognized mistake.

A further factor bearing on Wesley's theological thinking was his involvement in the Anglican church in which he had been nurtured. He was too close, in time, to the Lutheran/Calvin theological climate to be completely free from those influences in this respect.

Wesley realized that in order for the gospel to reach people, they still had to be human; and the *imago Dei* in humanity, no matter how sullied or perverted, is an essential ingredient of human nature that still distinguishes man from all other creation. What mankind lost in the Fall was the *moral image* of God—God's own righteous Spirit. When Adam disobeyed, God's Spirit was evicted from his life and he fell away from God into his own inadequate humanity. What he did not lose in the Fall was his essential humanity—the natural and political image of God in which he was created, but even these aspects of the *imago Dei* were seriously damaged by that Fall, and so they will ever remain sullied in humanity until, through the redemptive work of Christ on mankind's behalf, they have "put on the new self who is being renewed to a true knowledge according to the image of the One who created him" (Col. 3:10).

4. Wesleyan views on the transference of original sin to Adam's descendants This issue constitutes one of the most difficult problems in Judeo-Christian theology, and it is a problem on which there has emerged no ultimately satisfactory answer. Various theories have been advanced, some of which are interesting if not fully satisfying.

One of the oldest theories of the transference of original depravity is known as "creationism," which must be distinguished from the original creation of the universe. This view is especially characteristic of Roman Catholicism but is also held by some Protestants. It may be explained as follows.

Parents procreate the bodies of their children. At or before conception, God creates and gives to the woman the spiritual soul of the child. Since God is altogether holy, only that which comes from Him is holy. In some mysterious way depravity is passed from the parents to their offspring in physical procreation via the human nature. When the pure spirit of the child is united with the humanly procreated body in the womb of the woman at conception, it is contaminated by that union and participates in the fallen human nature.

Certain criticisms of the creationist theory may be considered. First, this is a dualistic view of humanity that divides the person into matter and spirit. Thus it does not accord with the contemporary *holistic* concept of man. Second, it reflects on God as a participant in the creation of a new, unholy entity by communicating a perfectly holy spirit-child to an unholy human nature, or body, in the womb of a woman. A further, and yet more serious objection, to this position occurs when, for instance, a gangster copulates with a harlot, with the biological consequent being conception and the birth of a child brought into a situation in which it is terribly disadvantaged socially and morally from birth. This would obviously place God in a serious ethically questionable position.

Another more satisfactory suggestion of the transmission of depravity is the theory of *traducianism*. This view lends itself to the holistic or unitary concept of the person. As such, it holds that God created the first pair and committed to them the responsibility of procreating themselves in their offspring. The parents procreate a total offspring as a holistic person, conveying to the child their own natures combined into a new personal entity. Thus in a sense, the offspring is an emergent from the parents. Perhaps this is what the Scriptures mean in saying that "they [the man and the woman in the marital relation] shall become one flesh" (Gen. 2:24; Matt. 19:5; Mark 10:8), essentially one in the offspring. Certainly childless couples have a certain unity, but not that in which they are essentially and irreducibly one in the offspring.

The advantages of the traducianist view are several: (1) The parents, and not God, bear responsibility for the begetting and nurture of the child (see Gen. 1:27-28). (2) Human depravity is transmitted through the parents to a unitary or holistic offspring. (3) This view lends itself to the genetic theory of inheritance, if indeed that theory is valid. (4) It avoids any notion of dualism in humanity. (5) It places parents under heavy responsibility for the proper begetting and nurture of children within the marital bonds and the home. Limitations of space prohibit a fuller treatment of this issue. Orton Wiley has discussed a number of different theories in "The Origin and Transmission of Original Sin," to which the interested reader is referred.[85]

5. Wesley's views on active or overt sin In a letter to a Mrs. Bennis, Wesley makes crystal clear his definition of sin per se—in distinction from the broader view of sin held by Calvinists. He says:

Nothing is sin, strictly speaking, but a voluntary transgression of a known law of God. Therefore, every voluntary breach of the law of love is sin; and nothing else, if we speak properly. To strain the matter farther is only to make way for Calvinism. There may be ten thousand wandering thoughts and forgetful intervals without any breach of love, though not without transgressing the Adamic law. But Calvinists would fain confound these together. Let love fill your heart, and it is enough (italics added).[86]

In the foregoing definition of "sin, strictly speaking," Wesley makes clear the following issues: First, there may be, and frequently are, many human imperfections and unintentional offenses that do not fall into the category of "sin, strictly speaking." He allows that "there may be ten thousand wandering thoughts and forgetful intervals without any breach of [the law of] love." Here, however, he distinguishes between "sin, strictly speaking," and "the transgression of the Adamic law." By the latter he evidently refers to the various nonmoral imperfections of humanity resulting from the Fall that characterize all of Adam's race—the regenerated as well as the unregenerated. Evidently Wesley is thinking here of the solidarity of the human race under the headship of Adam in which all sinned *in* and *with* Adam, thus making all people sinners. Wesley would exclude "sin, strictly speaking" from this category. On the other hand, he sees Calvinism as viewing sin in a much more comprehensive way, to include all human imperfections and involuntary transgressions. Indeed, much confusion exists at this point over the distinction between the Calvinist and Wesleyan concepts of sin. If the Calvinist position is accepted, then indeed sin is inevitable, even in the lives of sanctified Christian believers. On the other hand, Wesley's position allows for the inevitable imperfections and involuntary transgressions without categorizing them as "sin, strictly speaking."

In fact, Wesley says:

In speaking from those words, "In many things we offend all," I observed (1) as long as we live, our soul is connected with the body; (2) as long as it is thus connected it cannot think but by the help of bodily organs; (3) as long as these organs are imperfect we are liable to mistakes, both speculative and practical; (4) yea, and a mistake may occasion my loving a good man less than I ought, which is a defective, that is, a wrong temper; (5) for all these we need the atoning blood, as indeed for every defect or omission. Therefore (6) all may have need to say daily, "Forgive us our trespasses."[87]

Second, Wesley is defining "sin, strictly speaking" in a much more limited sense. In fact, he is giving sin a strictly ethical definition. Sin, in Wesley's definition, presupposes a knowledge of what is right and what is wrong—the sinner knows obedience to the law of God to be right and disobedience of that law to be wrong. Sin is "a transgression of a *known* law of God." Again, however, in Wesley's definition, "sin, strictly speaking" presupposes the existence of a morally free agent and involves the exercise of that agent, for it is "a *voluntary* transgression of a known law of God." This is not a "sin of ignorance" that Wesley is defining, nor is it a situation in which there is only one choice, which incidentally is no choice at all. Where there is no alternative choice, there is no ethical principle involved. That kind of situation is deterministic. In the third instance, Wesley defines sin as a violation or transgression of God's law of love. Since "God is love" (1 John 4:8), all His laws, negative and positive, are expressions of His essential character, which is love. Even God's justice is but the other side of the coin of His love. All "sin, strictly speaking" is a violation of man's love relationship with God. This places sin, as defined by Wesley, directly in the area of motive, and that is where Wesley intends to categorize "sin, strictly speaking." Thus, with Wesley, sin is sin whether in intent or action, when it violates the love principle in regard to God or other human beings created in His image. Therefore Wesley could teach the doctrine of perfect love, or Christian perfection, when understood within his definition of "sin, strictly speaking." Sin, as thus defined by Wesley, is never a necessity, since it involves the intelligent volition of an ethical agent. Were it a *necessity per se*, then God and not man would be responsible for sin, and such would relegate sin to divine determinism and consequently make God its author. This would in turn abrogate the holiness of God and make Him a devil, except that of course then there would be no holy God to make possible sin or the devil. Only in the light of God's holy love can there be sin, as defined by Wesley.

If Wesleyans and Calvinists better understood the manner in which the theology of each defines sin, it is entirely possible that the gap between their theological positions on sin and salvation would be greatly narrowed. Wesley himself said that there is but a hair's breadth between Calvinism and Wesleyanism.

X. A GENERAL OVERVIEW OF SIN, FROM CHRIST TO THE LATE NINETEENTH CENTURY

A. Sin as Characterized by Christ and Paul

Sin was clearly characterized as moral evil both by Christ and Paul. This is not to say the other New Testament writers, as also those of the Old Testament, do not clearly denominate sin as moral evil, for they certainly do. Rather, the source and nature of sin are more succinctly treated by Christ and Paul than by other writers of the sacred Scriptures.

Jesus located the source of sin in the moral nature of humanity when He said, "Out of the heart come evil thoughts, murders, adulteries, fornications [sexual immorality], thefts, false witness, slanders. These are the things which defile the man" (Matt. 15:19-20). However, Jesus probed deeper into the source of sin when He designated the work of the Spirit thus: "And He [the Spirit], when He comes, will convict the world concerning sin, and righteousness, and judgment; concerning sin, because they do not believe in me . . ." (John 16:8-9). *Failure to believe* in Christ, who revealed the Father to mankind (John 1:14), is the taproot from which all these fruits of evil spring.

Likewise Paul graphically depicted the moral nature of sin in humanity's progressive degeneracy and departure from faith in the holy and righteous God. (See his unequaled description of that fatal malady in Romans 1:18-32.) Of the awful final consequence of that fatal course of departure from the knowledge of God Paul stated, "Although they know the ordinance of God, that those who practice such things are worthy of death, they not only do the same, but also give hearty approval to those who practice them" (v. 32). Likewise in his Galatian letter Paul cataloged the manifestations of sin as moral evil as follows:

> Now the deeds of the flesh are evident, which are: immorality [*sexual immorality*], impurity, sensuality, idolatry, sorcery, enmities, strife, jealousy, outbursts of anger, disputes, dissensions, factions [*heresies*], envyings, drunkenness, carousings, and things like these, of which I forewarn you just as I have forewarned you that those who practice such things shall not inherit the kingdom of God (Gal. 5:19-21; cf. 1 Cor. 6:9-10, 18; 2 Cor. 12:20-21; James 3: 14-16; Rev. 21:8).

B. Sin as Understood in the Middle Ages

Following the Edict of Toleration by Constantine in A.D. 313 vast numbers of unconverted pagans professed conversion and took refuge in the church. Naturally they brought with them pagan beliefs and practices that tended to corrupt the purity of the Christian faith and doctrine concerning God's holy nature and the earlier clear concept of sin. This situation developed progressively until the church was plunged into the Dark Ages of spiritual and moral degeneracy.

For some 1,200 years, from Constantine to the Protestant Reformation in about A.D. 1517, Christianity became structured, formalized, and in large measure crystallized under the dominion of the Roman church. Ritual was substituted for righteousness, ecclesiastical authoritarianism and tradition took precedence over the authority of the Bible, the pope supplanted Christ in the main, the church altar with its sacramentalism replaced the efficacy of Christ's cross, penance replaced repentance, the sale of indulgences replaced divine forgiveness, works righteousness replaced the saving grace of Christ, the monastery replaced the mission field, and purgatorial purification replaced Christian sanctification (even some of the popes required purgatorial purification, according to Dante). General moral degeneracy obscured God's holiness and humanity's sin. This is not to say that the light of the gospel was entirely extinguished. The faith was kept alive in the monasteries, from which truth was disseminated to many peoples of Europe and Asia.

C. Sin as Understood From the Reformation to Wesley

The Reformation with its strong emphasis on the sinfulness of humanity and on justification through faith in the atonement of Jesus Christ reawakened anew in the conscience of humanity the reality of sin as moral evil and the need of repentance and personal salvation through faith in Jesus Christ.

Important as was the Reformation in renewing humanity's consciousness of sin and Christ's adequacy for salvation, doctrinal disputes dulled the cutting edge of the gospel truth. The church ultimately identified itself with the state and was reincarnated in the political structure, in which it was formalized and made authoritarian, both in Europe and in the Church of England. Thus evil was politicized and humanity's sense of moral responsibility was transferred from God to the state. The descent continued until the moral conscience of man was once again awakened under the influence of German Pietism and the eighteenth-century Wesleyan revival. This revival of the consciousness of sin and a vital salvation in Christ spread to the colonies and the far reaches of the world.

D. Sin as Understood in the Nineteenth Century

The nineteenth century saw the rise of naturalistic evolution under the influence of the thought of Herbert Spencer and the work of Charles Darwin, with the resultant liberation of humanity from divine responsibility.

If mankind is the product of naturalistic evolution, then there is no ethical responsibility to a personal holy God, and consequently there is no sin per se. German rationalism and higher criticism of the Bible undermined faith in the authority of divine revelation. In America, Ralph Waldo Emerson's pantheistic transcendentalism identified the goodness of God with both nature and humanity and thus in effect denied moral evil in human experience, while the Social Gospel Movement under the influence of Walter Rauschenbusch (1861–1918) arose to supplant sin as personal moral evil with the concept of social evil. These factors contributed to the liberalizing of the Christian faith and the dimming of the concept of sin as moral evil.

E. Sin as Understood in the Twentieth Century

The late nineteenth and early twentieth centuries witnessed the socialization of education, economics, labor, utilities, medicine, and even religion to a considerable degree. Under the Social Gospel Movement, sin as moral evil suffered demise and the remaining evil of humanity was socialized. Environmental and behavioristic psychology, of the Thorndike and Watsonian brands, made man the product of a combination of his environment and his glandular functions. Thus man became a determined being helplessly molded by factors from without and within over which he had no control and for which he was not morally responsible. Sigmund Freud (1856-1939) applied his theory of subjectivistic projectionism to all areas of religious claims and made both God and sin the products of human imagination. Thus, whether in its original Freudian form or in its contemporary Neo-Freudian cloak, sin, like all other religious claims, became an illusion. On the other hand, scientism became the god of twentieth-century humanity, promising to solve all human problems and create the millennium envisioned by liberal Christianity. The liberal church capitulated to scientific socialism, which buried the decaying corpse of original sin. Humanity, now free of that wearisome burden of past ages, was prepared to realize the utopian dream of the humanistic inevitable perfectibility of mankind envisioned by such influential pragmatic thinkers as William James (1842-1910) and John Dewey (1859-1952).

F. Sin as Understood in the Twentieth-Century Neoorthodox Movement

Two world wars and a great depression, followed by yet more wars, revolutions, riots, and a recrudescence of violent crime and political corruption, rudely awakened twentieth-century humanity from its pleasant utopian dream of the inevitable perfectibility of humanity and once again revealed man to be the hopelessly fallen creature that he is without God. C. S. Lewis brought the devil and his cohorts out of hiding with his insightful work *Screwtape Letters* published in 1941 during the carnage of the Second World War. Once again sin was recognized to be humanity's number one enemy.

1. Evil in the theology of Karl Barth Karl Barth (1886-1968), originally a Christian Socialist in Switzerland, was jarred out of his illusion and reverted to a radical emphasis on Reformed theology and became the king of the neoorthodox theological movement. No one of this school went so far in his emphasis on the intensive total depravity of humanity as did Barth in the early years of his reversal. Sin became sin once again under the Barthian influence, though he later modified his radical views.

2. Evil in the theology of Paul Tillich Paul Tillich (1886-1965), who founded the Christian Socialist Movement in Germany with the hope of Christianizing his German compatriots and perhaps the rest of mankind, ran afoul of Hitler in 1933. With the help of Barth he barely escaped with his life before coming to America.

First at Union Theological Seminary in New York, then at Harvard University, and later at the University of Chicago, Tillich brought God down from His personal transcendence and made Him the *foundation* and *depth* of humanity's essential being. Thus in his theology there is no real sin as moral evil in the absence of a transcendent holy God. Tillich may be best characterized as a pantheistic existentialist. He disclaimed neoorthodoxy per se. He was more philosophical than theological, though he wrote a voluminous systematic theology that few, even of the professionals, have been able to understand. In typical dialectical fashion, Tillich made sin a logical divine necessity, though there appeared to be no personal god to necessitate it. His emphasis on idolatry would have been welcomed had he posited any clear concept of a personal holy God.

3. Evil in the theology of Reinhold Niebuhr Reinhold Niebuhr (1892-1971) instituted a type of Christian socialism through his ministry to the working class in the Detroit, Michigan, area. Here he championed the cause of the working man but eventually became disillusioned and discouraged with his results. Niebuhr was then drawn toward the positions of Søren Kierkegaard and Karl

Barth, especially in their uncompromising attacks on humanism and their unqualified *no* to sin. In *Moral Man and Immoral Society* (1930), Niebuhr held that people may be moral individually, but that they become immoral when acting in groups. Thus he reflected something of the influence of Rousseau's philosophy of social environmentalism. He did not despair of humanity in its sin of selfish self-love. He concluded that sin is rooted deep in man's nature as a result of the Fall. Man is not wholly degraded, in Niebuhr's view, however. He is both noble and ignoble— both angel and beast. The doctrine of sin leads to a demoniac view of life, but not to fatalism, he reasoned. He believed there was a remedy through encounter with God. Niebuhr failed to go on to a complete remedy for sin, however.

Later in his Gifford Lectures, Niebuhr restored the concept of sin to a respectable place in modern theology. He concluded that man is neither beast nor angel, and that the Christian is no better than a worldly sinner. He simply has the advantage of knowing that he is guilty and can be repeatedly forgiven. According to Niebuhr, pride and sensuality are the expressions of sin. The Christian's pride of being good is as bad as the pride of independence from God. The Christian's morality is no better than that of the world—Christians only have the advantage of living in an attitude of repentance.

4. Evil in the theology of Emil Brunner Emil Brunner (1889–1966), while usually classified as a Neoorthodox, took a more moderate position with regard to human depravity than other neoorthodox leaders. While he held that the "formal image" of God in man remains, the content of that image was lost in the Fall. Divine love restores the content of the formal image. Brunner held that depravity expresses itself either in license or in legalism. The natural man follows the law for the law's sake, not for the love of God. This is legalism. Legalism is impersonal and produces pharisaic pride. With Brunner, the natural man is in revolt against God, but he is not fully irresponsible. He is, however, able to respond to God. Man is not extinguished by the Fall. He is still a person, a responsible human being. He is an idolator, but not *intensively* totally depraved. If he were so, he would have no sense of guilt. Thus, in regard to his view of sin in the natural man, Brunner is not far removed from the position of Wesley.

5. Evil in the theology of Rudolf Bultmann Rudolf Bultmann (1884–1976), while perhaps not properly classified as a neoorthodox theologian, was certainly one of the most influential New Testament scholars of modern times. Bultmann demythologized sin in the Bible along with the historical redemptive accounts. To Bultmann, the Fall was not an actual historical event in human experience and history. Nonetheless when the biblical myth of the Fall is demythologized, it is existentially reenacted in the experience of all humanity, and thus man knows himself to be a guilty sinner, though he may be left to wonder how and why.

Overall, the neoorthodox movement made a valuable contribution to the renewing of humanity's consciousness of the reality of sin, even if it failed to offer a satisfactory remedy for that moral malady. Neoorthodoxy was more diagnostic than curative, and in this respect it revealed itself to be a religious expression of modern existentialism. Again, the neoorthodox movement broke the backbone of earlier theological liberalism and restored Christian theology to a place of scholarly respectability. Further, it greatly deepened theological interest and scholarship.

G. Sin as Understood in the Rise of Radical Secularism

The 1960s saw the rise of radical secularism under the leadership of such noted thinkers as Bishop John A. T. Robinson. Concerning Robinson's book *Honest to God* (1963), C. S. Lewis is reported to have said he would rather be honest *with*

God. This was followed in turn by Thomas Altizer's *Christian Atheism* (1966) and a number of other works in this secular vein by such men as William Hamilton, Joseph Fletcher, and various other theological pallbearers. Thus, with the demise of a transcendent God and the deification of humanity, man was relieved of his personal moral responsibility to God, and the deceptive mirage of sin faded before the rising sun of the new brand of secularistic humanism. The bright hopes of humanistic salvation had little more than made their appearance when the dark clouds of human evil obscured those hopes and religious secularism went into eclipse, only to reappear later in a new garb. Thus the pages of history are strewn with the humanistic *unfinished Towers of Babel.*

H. God's Remedy for Humanity's Sin

Today there is in evidence a recrudescence of sin in both human nature and human conduct. The beast that was wounded has revived. Notwithstanding the contemporary efforts to make sin a sickness or disease subject to remedy by medical or psychiatric treatment, it continues to be sin, issuing in crime that overcrowds prisons and sends fear into the hearts of people. It will continue to be sin, whether in individuals or in society, until the remedy is found in the cross of Christ. As that remedy was found in early Christianity and the eighteenth-century revival of Wesley's day and other days of revival, it can always be found where the redemptive work of Jesus Christ is clearly and dynamically presented and appropriated through repentance and saving faith in the cross and resurrection of Christ. Vital faith in the cross and resurrection of Jesus Christ is and ever has been the only known remedy for the fatal moral malady of humanity that the Bible calls sin. In Christ, and in Him only, is humanity's hope of deliverance from sin and restoration to divine favor. Paul expressed this hope confidently and succinctly in his Epistle to the Romans: "For I am not ashamed of the gospel, for it is the power of God for salvation to every one who believes" (Rom. 1:16) and, in contrasting God's saving provisions in Christ with sin's deadly work in the experience of humanity: "For the wages of sin is death, but the free gift of God is eternal life in Christ Jesus our Lord" (Rom. 6:23). In Christ, and in Him only, humanity's remedy for sin is found. Jesus is "the Lamb of God who takes away the sin of the world" (John 1:29).

NOTES

[1] Kenneth Kinghorn, "Biblical Concepts of Sin," *Wesleyan Theological Journal,* vol. 1, no. 1 (Spring 1966): 21.

[2] Robert Ernest Hume, *The World's Living Religions* (New York: Scribner, 1947), pp. 203-4.

[3] S. Vernon McCasland et al., *Religions of the World* (New York: Random, 1969), p. 131.

[4] Ibid., p. 382.

[5] See William Barclay, *The Letters of John and Jude,* The Daily Bible Study Series (Philadelphia: Westminster, 1960), pp. 221-39.

[6] Lars P. Qualben, *A Short History of the Christian Church,* rev. ed. (New York: Thomas Nelson, 1942), pp. 76-77.

[7] Edgar Sheffield Brightman, *A Philosophy of Religion* (New York: Prentice-Hall, 1940), pp. 244, 246.

[8] Ibid., pp. 245-46.

[9] See "The Hegelian Dialectical Method," in *The Dictionary of Philosophy,* Dagobert D. Runes, ed. (New York: Philosophical Library, 1942), pp. 123-24.

[10] B.A.G. Fuller, *A History of Ancient and Medieval Philosophy,* 3rd ed., 2 vols. (New York: Holt, Rinehart, and Winston, 1955), 1:113.

[11] Ibid. (See also Will Durant, *The Story of Philosophy* [1926; reprint ed., New York: Garden City, 1943], pp. 7-13, for further treatment of the Socratic Doctrine.)

[12] Borden Parker Bowne, *The Atonement* (New York: Eaton and Mains, n.d.), p. 69.

[13] Edwin Lewis, *The Creator and the Adversary* (New York: Abingdon-Cokesbury, 1948), p. 143.

[14] Mary F. Thelen, "Man as Sinner" in *Contemporary American Realistic Theology* (New York: King's Crown, 1946), p. 35.

[15] John Wesley, *Explanatory Notes Upon the New Testament* (reprint ed., London: Epworth, 1954), p. 539, n. 12.

[16] Durant, *The Story of Philosophy* (reprint ed., New York: Garden City, 1943), p. 9.

[17] Fuller, *A History of Ancient and Medieval Philosophy*, 1:55.

[18] Alexander Souter, *A Pocket Lexicon to the Greek New Testament* (reprint ed., Oxford: at the Clarendon Press, 1916, 1966), p. 92.

[19] Joseph Henry Thayer, *A Greek Lexicon of the New Testament* (1886; reprint ed., New York: American, n.d.), p. 238.

[20] Wesley, *Notes Upon the New Testament*, pp. 857-58.

[21] Olin A. Curtis, *The Christian Faith: Personally Given in a System of Doctrine* (1905; reprint ed., Grand Rapids: Kregel, 1978), pp. 195-96.

[22] R. Payne Smith, *Ellicott's Commentary on the Whole Bible*, 8 vols. (Grand Rapids: Zondervan, n.d.), 1:21.

[23] Adam Clarke, *A Commentary and Critical Notes*, 6 vols. (New York: Abingdon-Cokesbury, n.d.), 1:44.

[24] Ibid., 1:52.

[25] Robert Baker Girdlestone, *Synonyms of the Old Testament* (1897; reprint ed., Grand Rapids: Eerdmans, n.d.), p. 45.

[26] H. C. Leupold, *Expositions of Genesis*, 2 vols. (Grand Rapids: Baker, 1942), 1:189-90.

[27] E. A. Speiser, "Genesis," *The Anchor Bible* (Garden City, N.Y.: Doubleday, 1964), 1:30.

[28] Smith, *Ellicott's Commentary*, 1:28.

[29] The place of the city in the history of humanity and God's redemptive plan for the city is graphically described in Roger S. Greenway, ed., *Discipling the Cities: Theological Reflection on the Urban Mission* (Grand Rapids: Baker, 1979).

[30] Wesley, *Notes Upon the New Testament*, p. 24.

[31] George A. Turner, "Soteriology in the Gospel of John," in *An Inquiry into Biblical Soteriology*, vol. 1, Wesleyan Theological Perspectives (Anderson, Ind.: Warner, 1981), pp. 87-91.

[32] Emil Brunner, *The Christian Doctrine of Creation and Redemption*, trans. Olive Wyon (Philadelphia: Westminster, 1952), pp. 115-16.

[33] Merne Harris and Richard S. Taylor, "The Dual Nature of Sin," in *The Word and the Doctrine* (Kansas City, Mo.: Beacon Hill, 1965), p. 108.

[34] William M. Arnett, "The Wesleyan-Arminian Teaching on Sin," in *Insights into Holiness* (Kansas City, Mo.: Beacon Hill, 1963), p. 59.

[35] Wesley, *Notes Upon the New Testament*, p. 857.

[36] Harris and Taylor, "Dual Nature of Sin," p. 108.

[37] George Eldon Ladd, *A Theology of the New Testament* (Grand Rapids: Eerdmans, 1974), p. 400.

[38] H. Orton Wiley, *Christian Theology*, 3 vols. (Kansas City, Mo.: Beacon Hill, 1940), 2:94.

[39] Brunner, *Christian Doctrine*, pp. 91-93, 125.

[40] Joseph Wang, "Soteriology in the Synoptic Gospels," in *An Inquiry into Biblical Soteriology*, John Hartley and Larry Shelton, eds. (Anderson, Ind.: Warner, 1981), p. 59.

[41] W. T. Purkiser, Richard S. Taylor, and Willard H. Taylor, *God, Man, and Salvation* (Kansas City, Mo.: Beacon Hill, 1977), pp. 292-93.

[42] Brunner, *Christian Doctrine*, p. 127.

[43] Wiley, *Christian Theology*, 2:84.

[44] Ibid., p. 65; Harris and Taylor, "Dual Nature of Sin," p. 107.

[45] Harris and Taylor, "Dual Nature of Sin," pp. 101-11.

[46] W. T. Purkiser, *Sanctification and Its Synonyms* (Kansas City, Mo.: Beacon Hill, 1961), pp. 50, 55.

[47] Lewis T. Corlett, "Holiness and Nervous Reactions," in *Future Insights Into Holiness*, K. Geiger, ed. (Kansas City, Mo.: Beacon Hill, 1963), pp. 51, 57.

[48] G. Ernest Wright and Reginald K. Fuller, *The Book of the Acts of God* (Garden City, N.Y.: Doubleday, 1960), p. 94.

[49] John Wesley discusses the need for salvation in his sermon, "Original Sin," in *The Works of John Wesley*, 14 vols., 3rd ed. (Grand Rapids: Baker, 1978), 6:54-65.

[50] Wiley, *Christian Theology*, 2:119.

[51] Ibid., p. 100.

[52] For further discussion of the scope of original sin, see Wiley, *Christian Theology*, 2:100-19; John Calvin, *Institutes of the Christian Religion*, 1, Library of Christian Classics, vol. 20, ed. John T. McNeill (Philadelphia: Westminster, 1960), II.1. 241-50; John Wesley, "Original Sin," 6:54-65, 67; Richard Watson, *Theological Institutes* (New York: Mason and Lane, 1936), 2:73-83; Julius Muller, *The Christian Doctrine of Sin*, vol. 2, trans. William Urwick (Edinburgh: T & T Clark, 1885), pp. 328-30; Brunner, *Christian Doctrine*, pp. 95-100.

[53] T. C. Vriezen, *An Outline of Old Testament Theology* (Newton Center, Mass.: Bradford, 1958), pp. 26-27. See Wang, "Soteriology," p. 63. For discussion of the universality of sin in Judaism, see Gustar Stahlin and Walter Grundmann, "The Concept of Sin in Judaism," in *Theological Dictionary of the New Testament*, ed. by Gerhard Kittel, vol. 1, G. W. Bromiley, trans. and ed. (Grand Rapids: Eerdmans, 1962), pp. 290-91.

[54] Carl Bangs, *Arminius: A Study in the Dutch Reformation* (Nashville: Abingdon, 1971), pp. 338-40; see *The Writings of James Arminius*, 3 vols. (Grand Rapids: Baker, 1956), 1:253, and other notes cited by Bangs.

[55] John Calvin, *Institutes*, II. 1. 8. 251.

[56] Ibid., pp. 51-52.

[57] Wiley, *Christian Theology*, 2:107.

[58] Ibid., p. 108; Wesley, "Original Sin," 6:63-65.

[59] Wiley, *Christian Theology*, 2:128-29.

[60] Calvin, *Institutes*, I. 1. 2. 241-89.

[61] William Barclay, *The Promise of the Spirit* (London: Epworth, 1960), p. 24.

[62] R. Laird Harris, *Baker's Dictionary of Theology* (Grand Rapids: Baker, 1960), pp. 97-98.

[63] Wesley, *Notes Upon the New Testament*, p. 63.

[64] Barclay, *The Promise of the Spirit*, pp. 27-29.

[65] Ibid.

[66] Wilber T. Dayton, "A Wesleyan Note on Election," in *Perspectives on Evangelical Theology*, Kenneth S. Kantzer and Stanley N. Gundry, eds. (Grand Rapids: Baker, 1979), pp. 98-99.

[67] Wesley, *Works*, 7:229-30.

[68] William Hordern, "Recent Trends in Systematic Theology," *Canadian Journal of Theology*, vol. 7, no. 2 (1961): 87.

[69] George C. Cell, *The Rediscovery of John Wesley* (New York: Henry Holt, 1935), 1:189-90.

[70] William R. Cannon, *The Theology of John Wesley* (Nashville: Abingdon, 1946), pp. 61, 105, 116.

[71] Ibid.

[72] Ibid., pp. 105-18.

[73] A. Skevington Wood, *John Wesley: The Burning Heart* (Grand Rapids: Eerdmans, 1967), p. 220.

[74] Ibid., p. 230.

[75] Wiley, *Christian Theology*, 2:121.

[76] Wesley, *Works*, 9:316; see also pp. 420, 426, 428.

[77] For a discussion of this issue see the chapters "Entire Sanctification," and "Hymnology," in this work, vol. 2, and Charles W. Carter, *The Person and Ministry of the Holy Spirit*, rev. ed. (Grand Rapids: Baker, 1977), pp. 157-90; Howard Marshall, "The Significance of Pentecost," The Asbury Seminarian, vol. 32, no. 2 (April 1977): 17-39.

[78] Wesley, *Works*, 9:420.

[79] Ibid., p. 415.

[80] Cannon, *Theology of John Wesley*, p. 199.

[81] Ibid., p. 200, quoted from an article published in the *Methodist Recorder*, December 1916.

[82] Wesley, *Works*, 5:82.

[83] Ibid., 6:66-68.

[84] Ibid., 9:291.

[85] Wiley, *Christian Theology*, 2:109-30.

[86] Robert W. Burtner and Robert E. Chiles, *A Compend of Wesley's Theology* (New York-Nashville: Abingdon, 1954), p. 177.

[87] Ibid.

DISCUSSION QUESTIONS

1. How does sin per se differ from the general concept of evil?
2. What are some of the principal problems inherent in the ultimate origin of evil in the universe?
3. What is meant by cosmic or natural evil and what are some of its manifestations?
4. Discuss some of the extrabiblical theories concerning the origin of evil.
5. Discuss the biblical view of the origin of evil and consider how it differs from the naturalistic views.
6. Discuss the temptation and fall of humanity: how it occurred and its immediate and far-reaching effects on humanity.
7. Discuss the similarities between the temptation of the first pair in Eden and Christ's temptation in the wilderness.
8. Discuss the six different views of the basic nature of sin listed under section VIII, pp. 259-65, and consider which are the most important.
9. Discuss John Wesley's understanding of original sin.
10. What are the differences between *extensive* and *intensive* total depravity and how do they influence the question of salvation?
11. Discuss the problem of inherited depravity and how it differs from inherited guilt.

12. How is the depraved nature of mankind transmitted to posterity?
13. What seems to be the main reason that John Wesley sometimes appears to be inconsistent in his theological statements, especially concerning human depravity?

RECOMMENDATIONS FOR FURTHER READING

Agnew, Milton. *More Than Conquerors*. Kansas City, Mo.: Beacon Hill, 1977.

Bangs, Carl. *Arminius: A Study in the Dutch Reformation*. Nashville: Abingdon, 1971.

Binney, Amos, and Steel, Daniel. *Binney's Theological Compend Improved*. Nashville: Abingdon, 1902.

Brunner, Emil. *The Christian Doctrine of Creation and Redemption*. Translated by Olive Wyon. Philadelphia: Westminster, 1952.

Carter, Charles W. *The Person and Ministry of the Holy Spirit: A Wesleyan Perspective*. Grand Rapids: Baker, 1977.

Carter, Charles W., and Earle, Ralph. *The Acts of the Apostles*. Rev. ed. Grand Rapids: Zondervan, 1973.

Cox, Leo G. *Wesley's Concept of Perfection*. Kansas City, Mo.: Beacon Hill, 1964.

Grider, J. Kenneth. *Entire Sanctification: The Distinctive Doctrine of Wesleyanism*. Kansas City, Mo.: Beacon Hill, 1980.

Hamilton, Kenneth. *God Is Dead: The Anatomy of a Slogan*. Grand Rapids: Eerdmans, 1966.

─────. *Revolt Against Heaven*. Grand Rapids: Eerdmans, 1965.

Hume, Robert Ernest. *The World's Living Religions*. New York: Scribner, 1947.

Leupold, H. C. *Expositions of Genesis*. Grand Rapids: Baker, 1942. Vol. 1.

Lewis, C. S. *The Screwtape Letters*. New York: Macmillan, 1946.

Marty, Martin E. *The New Shape of American Religion*. New York: Harper and Brothers, 1958.

Metz, Donald S. *Studies in Biblical Holiness*. Kansas City, Mo.: Beacon Hill, 1971.

Niebuhr, Reinhold. *Moral Man and Immoral Society*. New York: Scribner, 1970.

Outler, Albert C., ed. *John Wesley*. New York: Oxford University Press, 1964.

Parker, Percy Livingston, ed. *The Journal of John Wesley*. Chicago: Moody, n.d.

Smith, Timothy L. *Revivalism and Social Reform in Mid-Nineteenth Century America*. Nashville: Abingdon, 1957.

Taylor, Richard S. *A Right Conception of Sin*. Kansas City, Mo.: Beacon Hill, 1939.

Tillich, Paul. *The Dynamics of Faith*. New York: Harper and Brothers, 1957.

Tuttle, Robert G. *John Wesley, His Life and Theology*. Grand Rapids: Zondervan, 1978.

Wood, A. Skevington. *John Wesley: The Burning Heart*. Grand Rapids: Eerdmans, 1967.

Wynkoop, Mildred Bangs. *Foundations of Wesleyan Arminian Theology*. Kansas City, Mo.: Beacon Hill, 1967.

BIBLIOGRAPHY

Agnew, Milton S. *More Than Conquerors*. Kansas City, Mo.: Beacon Hill, 1977.

Arnett, William M. "The Wesleyan/Arminian Teaching on Sin," *Insights Into Holiness*. Kansas City, Mo.: Beacon Hill, 1980.

Ashcraft, Morris. *Rudolf Bultmann*. Waco: Word, 1972.

Bangs, Carl. *Arminius: A Study in the Dutch Reformation*. Nashville: Abingdon, 1971.

Barclay, William. *The Daily Bible Study Series*, 17 vols. Philadelphia: Westminster, 1956-60.

─────. *The Promise of the Spirit*. London: Epworth, 1960.

Berkouwer, G. C. *Sin*. Translated by Philip C. Holtrop. Grand Rapids: Eerdmans, 1971.

A CONTEMPORARY WESLEYAN THEOLOGY

Binney, Amos, and Steel, Daniel. *Binney's Theological Compend Improved.* New York-Nashville: Abingdon, 1902.

Blake, Robert J. *Secular Theology and God Who Acts.* Grand Rapids: Eerdmans, 1970.

Bowne, Borden Parker. *The Atonement.* New York: Eaton and Mains, n.d.

Brightman, Edgar Sheffield. *A Philosophy of Religion.* New York: Prentice-Hall, 1940.

Brown, Colin, ed. *The New International Dictionary of New Testament Theology.* 3 vols. Grand Rapids: Zondervan, 1975-78.

Brunner, Emil. *The Christian Doctrine of Creation and Redemption.* Translated by Olvie Wyon. Philadelphia: Westminster, 1952.

Bultmann, Rudolf. *Jesus Christ and Mythology.* New York: Scribner, 1958.

Burtner, Robert W., and Chiles, Robert E. *A Compend of Wesley's Theology.* New York-Nashville: Abingdon, 1954.

Buttrick, George Arthur, ed. *The Interpreter's Bible.* 12 vols. New York-Nashville: Abingdon, 1952.

——— . *The Interpreter's Dictionary of the Bible.* 4 vols. New York-Nashville: Abingdon, 1962.

Calvin, John. *Institutes.* I.1; II.1, 8.

Cannon, William. *The Theology of John Wesley.* Nashville: Abingdon, 1946.

Carter, Charles W. *The Person and Ministry of the Holy Spirit: A Wesleyan Perspective.* Grand Rapids: Baker, 1974.

Carter, Charles W., ed. *Wesleyan Bible Commentary.* 7 vols. Grand Rapids: Eerdmans, 1964-1969.

Carter, Charles W., and Earle, Ralph. *The Acts of the Apostles* (1959). Rev. ed. Grand Rapids: Zondervan, 1973; reprint ed. Schmul, 1983.

Cell, G. C. *The Rediscovery of John Wesley.* New York: Henry Holt, 1935.

Chapman, James B. *The Terminology of Holiness.* Kansas City, Mo.: Beacon Hill, 1947.

Clarke, Adam. *Christian Theology.* Reprint ed. Salem, Ohio: Convention Book Store, 1967.

——— . *A Commentary and Critical Notes.* 6 vols. Nashville: Abingdon-Cokesbury, n.d.

Cook, Thomas. *New Testament Holiness.* 16th ed. London: Epworth, 1963.

Cox, Leo G. *Wesley's Concept of Perfection.* Kansas City, Mo.: Beacon Hill, 1964.

Corlett, Lewis T. "Holiness and Nervous Reactions," in *Further Insights Into Holiness.* Edited by Kenneth Geiger. Kansas City, Mo.: Beacon Hill, 1963.

Curtis, Olin A. *The Christian Faith, Personally Given in a System of Doctrine.* 1905. Reprint ed. Grand Rapids: Kregel, 1978.

Dayton, Wilber T. "A Wesleyan Note on Election," in *Perspectives on Evangelical Theology.* Edited by Kenneth Kantzer and Stanley N. Gundry. Grand Rapids: Baker, 1979.

Demaray, Donald E. *Basic Beliefs: An Introductory Guide to Christian Theology.* Grand Rapids: Baker, 1958.

Durant, Will. *The Story of Philosophy* (1933). Reprint ed. New York: Garden City, 1943.

Ellicott, Charles John, ed. *Ellicott's Commentary on the Whole Bible,* 8 vols. Grand Rapids: Zondervan, n.d.

Fletcher, John. Reprint ed. *The Works of the Reverend John Fletcher.* Salem, Ohio: Schmul, 1974.

Fletcher, William. *The Moderns: Molders of Contemporary Theology.* Grand Rapids: Zondervan, 1962.

Fuller, B.A.G. *A History of Philosophy.* 3rd ed. 2 vols. New York: Holt, Rinehart, and Winston, 1955.

Gamertsfelder, S. J. *Systematic Theology.* 1921. Reprint ed. Harrisburg, Penn.: Evangelical, 1952.

Girdlestone, Robert Baker. *Synonyms of the Old Testament* (1897). Reprint ed. Grand Rapids: Eerdmans, n.d.

Greenway, Roger S. *Discipling the Cities: Reflections on the Urban Mission.* Grand Rapids: Baker, 1979.

Grider, J. Kenneth. *Entire Sanctification: The Distinctive Doctrine of Wesleyanism.* Kansas City, Mo.: Beacon Hill, 1980.

Gundry, Stanley, and Johnson, Alan, eds. *Tensions in Contemporary Theology.* Chicago: Moody, 1976.

Hamilton, Kenneth. *God Is Dead: The Anatomy of a Slogan.* Grand Rapids: Eerdmans, 1966.

——— . *Revolt Against Heaven.* Grand Rapids: Eerdmans, 1965.

_____. *What's New in Religion: A Critical Study of New Theology, New Morality and Secular Christianity.* Grand Rapids: Eerdmans, 1968.

Harris, Merne, and Taylor, Richard. "The Dual Nature of Sin." *The Word and the Doctrine.* Kansas City, Mo.: Beacon Hill, 1965.

Harrison, Everett F., ed. *Baker's Dictionary of Theology.* Grand Rapids: Baker, 1960.

Henry, Carl F. H. *Frontiers in Modern Theology.* Chicago: Moody, 1965.

Hills, A. M. *Fundamental Christian Theology: A Systematic Theology.* Salem, Ohio: Schmul, 1980. Vol. 1.

Hordern, William. *A Layman's Guide to Protestant Theology.* New York: Macmillan, 1955.

_____. *New Directions in Theology Today,* 7 vols. Philadelphia: Westminster, 1966.

_____. "Recent Trends in Systematic Theology," *Canadian Journal of Theology.* Vol. 8, No. 2 (1961).

Hume, Robert Ernest. *The World's Living Religions.* New York: Scribner, 1947.

Jewett, Paul K. *Emil Brunner.* Chicago: InterVarsity, 1961.

Kinghorn, Kenneth. "Biblical Concepts of Sin," *Wesleyan Theological Journal.* Vol. 1. No. 1 (Spring 1966).

Kittel, Gerhard, ed. *Theological Dictionary of the New Testament.* Translated by Geoffrey W. Bromiley. 10 vols. Grand Rapids: Eerdmans, 1965–1975.

Ladd, George Eldon. *Rudolf Bultmann.* Chicago: InterVarsity, 1964.

_____. *A Theology of the New Testament.* Grand Rapids: Eerdmans, 1974.

Leitch, Addison. *Winds of Doctrine.* Old Tappan, N.J.: Revell, 1966.

Leupold, H. C. *Expositions of Genesis.* 2 vols. Grand Rapids: Baker, 1942.

Lewis, Edwin. *The Creator and the Adversary.* New York: Abingdon, 1948.

McCasland, M. et al., *Religions of the World.* New York: Random, 1969.

McDonald, H. D. *Living Doctrines of the New Testament.* Grand Rapids: Zondervan, 1972.

MacGregor, Geddes. "The Mystery of Evil," in *Introduction to Religious Philosophy.* Boston: Houghton Mifflin, 1959.

Marty, Martin E. *The New Shape of American Religion.* New York: Harper and Brothers, 1958.

Metz, Donald S. *Studies in Biblical Holiness.* Kansas City, Mo.: Beacon Hill, 1971.

Meynell, Hugo. *The New Theology and Modern Theologians.* London: Sheed and Ward, 1967.

Moltmann, Jurgen, et al. *The Future of Hope: Theology as Eschatology.* New York: Herder and Herder, 1970.

Mueller, David L. *Karl Barth.* Waco: Word, 1972.

Niebuhr, Reinhold. *Moral Man and Immoral Society.* New York: Scribner, 1960.

Orr, James, ed. *International Standard Bible Encyclopedia.* 5 vols. 1939. Reprint ed. Grand Rapids: Eerdmans, 1957.

Outler, Albert C., ed. *John Wesley.* New York: Oxford University Press, 1964.

Parker, Percy Livingston, ed. *The Journal of John Wesley.* Chicago: Moody, n.d.

Purkiser, W. T. *Sanctification and Its Synonyms.* Kansas City, Mo.: Beacon Hill, 1961.

Purkiser, W. T. et al. *God, Man and Salvation: A Biblical Theology.* Kansas City, Mo.: Beacon Hill, 1977.

Qualben, Lars P. *A Short History of the Christian Church.* Rev. ed. New York: Thomas Nelson, 1942.

Ridderbos, Herman. *Bultmann.* Translated by David H. Freeman. Philadelphia: Presbyterian and Reformed, 1960.

_____. *Paul: An Outline of His Theology.* Translated by John R. De Witt. Grand Rapids: Eerdmans, 1975.

Roark, Dallas M. *Dietrich Bonhoeffer.* Waco: Word, 1972.

Ruth, C. W. *Entire Sanctification Explained.* Kansas City, Mo.: Beacon Hill, 1939.

Schmidt, Martin. *John Wesley: A Theological Biography.* Translated by Norman P. Goldhawk. 2 vols. Nashville: Abingdon, n.d.

Seeburg, Reinhold. Reprint ed. *The History of Doctrine.* Translated by Charles E. Hay. Grand Rapids: Baker, 1977.

Smith, Timothy L. *Revivalism and Social Reform in Mid-Nineteenth Century America.* New York-Nashville: Abingdon, 1957.

Smith, Timothy L., compiler and editor. *Charles G. Finney on Holiness: The Promise of the Spirit.* Minneapolis: Bethany Fellowship, 1980.

Southey, Robert. *The Life of Wesley.* 2 vols. New York: Harper and Brothers, 1847.

Speiser, E. A. *Genesis,* vol. 1. *The Anchor Bible.* Garden City, N.Y.: Doubleday, 1964.

Stott, John R. W. *Basic Christianity.* Rev. ed. Grand Rapids: Eerdmans, 1971.

Stolz, Karl R. *The Psychology of Religious Living.* New York: Abingdon-Cokesbury, 1936.

Souter, Alexander. *A Pocket Lexicon to the Greek New Testament.* 1916. Reprint ed. Oxford: Clarendon, 1966.

Taylor, Richard S. *A Right Conception of Sin.* Kansas City, Mo.: Beacon Hill, 1939.

Tenney, Merrill C., ed. *The Zondervan Pictorial Encyclopedia of the Bible.* 5 vols. Grand Rapids: Zondervan, 1975.

Thayer, Joseph Henry. *A Greek Lexicon of the New Testament.* 1886. Reprint ed. New York: American, n.d.

Thelen, Mary F. "Man As Sinner." In *Contemporary American Realistic Theology.* New York: Kings Crown, 1946.

Thiessen, Henry C. *Lectures in Systematic Theology.* Revised by Vernon D. Doerksen. Grand Rapids: Eerdmans, 1979.

Tillich, Paul. *The Dynamics of Faith.* New York: Harper and Brothers, 1957.

Trench, Richard C. *Synonyms of the New Testament.* 1880. Reprint ed. Grand Rapids: Eerdmans, 1980.

Turner, George Allen. "Soteriology in the Gospel of John." In *An Inquiry Into Biblical Soteriology.* Anderson, Ind.: Warner, 1981. Vol. 1.

Tuttle, Robert G. *John Wesley, His Life and Theology.* Grand Rapids: Zondervan, 1978.

Vos, Geerhardus. *Biblical Theology: Old and New Testament.* Grand Rapids: Eerdmans, 1948.

Wang, Joseph. "Soteriology in the Synoptic Gospels." In *An Inquiry Into Biblical Soteriology.* John Hartley and Larry Shelton, eds. Anderson, Ind.: Warner, 1981.

Wesley, John. *Explanatory Notes Upon the New Testament.* Reprint ed. London: Epworth, 1954.

_____. *Explanatory Notes Upon the Old Testament.* 1765. Reprint ed. 4 vols. Salem, Ohio: Schmul, 1975.

_____. *The Works of John Wesley.* 3rd ed. 14 vols. 1892. Reprint ed. Grand Rapids: Baker, 1978.

Wiley, H. Orton. *Christian Theology.* 3 vols. Kansas City, Mo.: Beacon Hill, 1940.

Wood, A. Skevington. *John Wesley: The Burning Heart.* Grand Rapids: Eerdmans, 1967.

Wright, G. Ernest, and Fuller, Reginald. *The Book of Acts of God.* Garden City, N.Y.: Doubleday, 1960.

Writings of James Arminius, The. Translated by James Nichols and W. R. Bagnall. 3 vols. Reprint ed. Grand Rapids: Baker, 1956.

Wynkoop, Mildred Bangs. *Foundations of Wesleyan-Arminian Theology.* Kansas City, Mo.: Beacon Hill, 1967.

_____. *John Wesley: Christian Revolutionary.* Kansas City, Mo.: Beacon Hill, 1970.

_____. *The Theology of Love.* Kansas City, Mo.: Beacon Hill, 1972.

CHAPTER 8

REVELATION AND INSPIRATION:
The Spoken Word of God

Ralph Earle

Ralph Earle is Distinguished Professor Emeritus of New Testament at Nazarene Theological Seminary. He received his M.A. degree at Boston University, his B.D. and Th.D. degrees at Gordon Divinity School, and his D.D. degree at Eastern Nazarene College. He did postgraduate studies at Harvard and Edinburgh universities.

Dr. Earle is the author of forty books. Among them are How We Got the Bible, What the Bible Says About the Second Coming, Know Your New Testament, *and* Story of the New Testament. *In addition, he has contributed to some twenty reference works. He has preached, lectured, and taught in many countries of the world. He is a member and past president of the Evangelical Theological Society and a member of the American School of Oriental Research, the American Academy of Religion, and the Wesleyan Theological Society.*

CONTENTS

I. REVELATION / 287
  A. Definition / 287
  B. General Revelation / 288
  C. Special Revelation / 289
   1. John Wesley on the Scriptures / 289
   2. The content of the Scriptures / 289
   3. The finality of the Scriptures / 290
   4. The canon of the Scriptures / 291
      a. The Old Testament / 291
      b. The New Testament / 292
   5. The nature of the Scriptures / 293
   6. The acceptance of the Scriptures / 294
   7. The value of the Scriptures / 294

II. INSPIRATION / 295
  A. Definition / 295
  B. Biblical Doctrine / 295
  C. Communication / 297
  D. History of the Doctrine / 298
   1. The early church / 298
   2. The Reformers / 299
   3. The Protestant creeds / 300
   4. The Reformed view / 301
   5. The Neoorthodox view / 303
   6. The Arminian-Wesleyan view / 303
  E. The Bible, a Divine-Human Book / 318
  F. Conclusion / 319

NOTES / 321

DISCUSSION QUESTIONS / 324

RECOMMENDATIONS FOR FURTHER READING / 324

BIBLIOGRAPHY / 324

REVELATION AND INSPIRATION

The Spoken Word of God

I. REVELATION

A. Definition

In the King James Version the verb *reveal* occurs some fifty-one times (22 in the Old Testament and 29 in the New). In the Old Testament it translates the Hebrew *galah* (Aramaic *gelah*). In the New Testament it is normally the rendering of the Greek *apocalyptō*, which literally means "uncover"—from *calyptō* ("cover") and *apo* ("away from"), and so means "take the cover off."

However, in 2 Thessalonians 1:7 and 1 Peter 4:13 the Greek noun *apocalypsis* is used, from which we get "apocalypse"—an uncovering, and so a disclosure. The reason the last book of the Bible is called "Revelation" is that the first word of that book is *apocalypsis*. In that book we find a supernatural disclosure of the actual prevailing conditions in the seven churches of Asia and also an uncovering of the future, which could be known only by divine revelation.

The noun *apocalypsis* occurs eighteen times in the New Testament. Twelve of these times it is translated "revelation." In several places it refers to the return of Christ (e.g., 1 Cor. 1:7; 1 Peter 1:7). It is also used for special divine "revelations" given to, or claimed by, members of the early church (1 Cor. 14:6, 26; Gal. 2:2). We will note later its use for the revelation of God's truth in the written Word.

We get our English word *reveal* from the Latin *revelo*. J. I. Packer says that the Hebrew, Greek, and Latin terms "all express the same idea—that of unveiling something hidden, so that it may be known for what it is."[1] It is a divine disclosure of divine truth.

Bernard Ramm makes this interesting observation: "*Revelation is the autobiography of God,* i.e., it is the story which God narrates about himself. It is that knowledge *about* God which is *from* God."[2]

A good compact definition of revelation is that given by C. M. Horne:

> Revelation is God's disclosure of Himself through creation, history, the conscience of man and Scripture. It is given both in event and word.... Revelation has to do with the unveiling, uncovering and manifesting of something or someone previously veiled or covered.[3]

In addition, it must be noted that God's final and fullest revelation was in the person of His Son Jesus Christ (John 1:1–14; Heb. 1:1). Horne also writes:

> Revelation must be understood in terms of three factors: (1) *The revealer*—in this case God; (2) *The instruments of the revelation*—in this case Scripture speaks of various modalities such as vision, dream, deep sleep, urim and thummim, the lot, theophanies, angels, divine speaking, historical event, and the incarnation resulting in *a product,* namely the Word of God (the Bible). Up to this point we have revelation only objectively conceived. (3) Finally, we have the *receiver*—in this case men who respond in faith to the One of whom the message testifies. This is revelation subjectively conceived.[4]

B. General Revelation

Some scholars (e.g., Karl Barth) have protested that there is no such thing as general revelation; there is only special revelation. But the Bible itself contradicts this view.

In Psalm 19 we have a most striking combination of general and special revelation. The former is depicted graphically in verses 1–6, the latter in verses 7–11.

In the first of these we have the revelation of God in nature. I quote verses 1–4 from the New International Version, which reflects the poetic structure of the original Hebrew:

> The heavens declare the glory of God;
>   the skies proclaim the work of his hands.
> Day after day they pour forth speech;
>   night after night they display knowledge.
> There is no speech or language
>   where their voice is not heard.
> Their voice goes out into all the earth,
>   their words to the ends of the world.

The implications of this passage are immense and inspiring. To get a meaningful glimpse of divine revelation, all we have to do is to look up at the heavens, for they "declare" God's glory. And this declaration or proclamation (line 2) goes on day and night (v. 2). Still more striking, if possible, is the fact that nature speaks of God in a universal language, understood by people of all nations and tongues. If this is not "general revelation," what does that expression mean?

Then the psalmist, who loved to meditate daily on the sacred Scripture available at that time, turns to the special revelation in God's Word (vv. 7–11). Verses 7–9 (NIV) read as follows:

> The law of the LORD is perfect,
>   reviving the soul.
> The statutes of the LORD are trustworthy,
>   making wise the simple.
> The precepts of the LORD are right,
>   giving joy to the heart.
> The commands of the LORD are radiant,
>   giving light to the eyes.
> The fear of the LORD is pure,
>   enduring forever;
> The ordinances of the LORD are sure
>   and altogether righteous.

This psalm alone should teach us the importance of holding to *both* general and special revelation. Even the most devout student of the Bible can find his knowledge and appreciation of God enhanced by taking time to view the divine handiwork in nature.

It has sometimes been said that we may see a revelation of God's greatness and power by viewing His creation but that is as far as it goes. However, when we turn to the New Testament we see an extension of what may be known by general revelation.

In the latter part of Romans 1 Paul describes the sins of the Gentiles, who had no knowledge of God's Word. He says:

> The wrath of God is being revealed from heaven against all the godlessness and wickedness of men who suppress the truth by their wickedness, since what may be known about God is plain to them, because God has made it plain to them. For since the creation of the world God's invisible qualities—his eternal power and divine nature—have been clearly seen, being understood from what has been made, so that men are without excuse (Rom. 1:18–20 NIV).

General revelation stretches back to the time of Creation, long before Moses began the writing of the sacred Scriptures. God is justified in condemning unbelieving people for their sins, because He has given them a revelation of Himself.

Still, we must ask how these people would have a consciousness of sin. Paul answers that specifically:

> Indeed, when Gentiles, who do not have the law, do by nature things required by the law, they are a law for themselves, even though they do not have the law, since they show that the requirements of the law are written on their hearts, their consciences also bearing witness, and their thoughts now accusing, now even defending them (Rom. 2:14-15 NIV).

Conscience, then, is a very important aspect of general revelation. God has planted a conscience in every human being, and those who disobey its voice are guilty of sin.

With regard to the relationship between general and special revelation, Benjamin B. Warfield writes:

> But, though thus distinguished from one another, it is important that the two species or stages of revelation should not be set in opposition to one another, or the closeness of their mutual relations or the constancy of their interaction be obscured. They constitute together a unitary whole, and each is incomplete without the other.[5]

Warfield goes on to say:

> Without special revelation, general revelation would be for sinful men incomplete and ineffective, and could issue, as in point of fact it has issued wherever it alone has been accessible, only in leaving them without excuse (Rom. 1:20). Without general revelation, special revelation would lack that basis in the fundamental knowledge of God as the mighty and wise, righteous and good maker and ruler of all things, apart from which the further revelation of this great God's intervention in the world for the salvation of sinners could not be either intelligible, credible or operative.[6]

C. Special Revelation

1. John Wesley on the Scriptures

George Turner asserts, "That the Bible is the unique revelation of God was one of the two most fundamental convictions in Wesley's theological outlook . . . there is a God, and God has revealed Himself in a Book."[7] Turner goes on to say: "In his view of the Bible as revelation, Wesley was in line with the classic view of Augustine and the Reformers, but out of line with the rationalists of his day."[8]

The truth of Turner's assessment can be easily documented from Wesley's own writings. For instance, in the preface to his *Explanatory Notes Upon the New Testament* (1755) he says:

> Concerning the Scriptures in general, it may be observed, the word of the living God, which directed the first patriarchs also, was, in the time of Moses, committed to writing. To this were added, in several succeeding generations, the inspired writings of the other prophets. Afterwards, what the Son of God preached, and the Holy Ghost spake by the apostles the apostles and evangelists wrote. This is what we now style the Holy Scripture: this is that "word of God which remaineth for ever"; of which, though "heaven and earth pass away, one jot or tittle shall not pass away." The Scripture, therefore, of the Old and New Testament is a most solid and precious system of divine truth. . . . It is the fountain of heavenly wisdom, which they who are able to taste prefer to writings of men, however wise or learned or holy.[9]

> An exact knowledge of the truth was accompanied, in the inspired writers, with an exactly regular series of arguments, a precise expression of their meaning, and a genuine vigour of suitable affections. . . .

> In the language of the sacred writings we may observe the utmost depth, together with the utmost ease. All the elegancies of human composures sink into nothing before it: God speaks not as man, but as God. His thoughts are very deep, and thence His words are of inexhaustible virtue.[10]

2. The content of the Scriptures

In his book *Special Revelation and the Word of God* Bernard Ramm declares, "The Scripture is fundamentally *gospel*."[11] Then he gives a threefold enlargement of this. First, he says, "As fundamentally gospel, the *graphe* is the transcript of the great Triune God in the great act of creation and in the continued act of providence and preservation. It is, more correctly, the record of all that this Triune God has done for the salvation of man."[12] Second, he asserts, "The Scripture is the transcript of man in the light of revelation."[13] In the third place, "Scripture is the transcript of Jesus Christ. He is the hidden reality of the Old Testament and the revealed Lord of the New."[14]

This shows why special revelation was an absolute necessity as a supplement to general revelation. The central message of the Bible is God's redemption of mankind. This could be understood only as it was spelled out in the written Word.

3. The finality of the Scriptures The question is often raised, "Are we sure that we have in the Bible God's complete written revelation to man?" What about futher revelations? Why should the canon of Scripture stop with the first century?

Probably the best answer to all of this is found in Hebrews 1:1-2. Let us look at this passage. The Epistle to the Hebrews is written in the most lofty—almost classical—style of all books of the New Testament. This is reflected in its striking introduction, expressed in what has been described as "sonorous and dignified" language. F. W. Farrar says, "It is hardly possible in a translation to preserve the majesty and balance of this remarkable opening sentence of the Epistle. It must be regarded as one of the most pregnant and noble passages of Scripture."[15]

The very opening words are (in Greek): *Polymeros kai polytropos*—two adverbs connected by *kai* ("and"). *Poly,* as we know from our English use of it as a prefix, means "many." *Meros* means "part"; *tropos* means "way" or "manner." So the literal translation would be: "In many parts and in many ways."

On the first word Farrar makes this comment:

> The first great truth which God prominently revealed was His Unity; then came the earliest germ of the Messianic hope; then came the Moral Law; then the development of Messianism and the belief in Immortality.[16]

On the second adverb that we find here Farrar makes this observation:

> The "many manners" of the older revelation were Law and Prophecy, Type and Allegory, Promise and Threatening; the diverse individuality of many of the Prophets, Seers, Warriors, Kings, who were agents of the revelation; the method of various sacrifices; the messages which came by Urim, by dreams, by waking visions, and "face to face".... The mouthpiece of the revelation was now a Gentile sorcerer, now a royal sufferer, now a rough ascetic, now a polished priest, now a gatherer of sycamore fruit. Thus the separate revelations were not complete but partial; and the methods not simple but complex.[17]

B. F. Westcott has this to say about the significance of these two adverbs:

> The variety of the former revelation extended both to its substance and to its form. The great drama of Israel's discipline was divided into separate acts: and in each act different modes were employed by God for bringing home to His people various aspects of truth. Thus the "many parts" of the preparatory training for Christianity may be symbolized (though they are not absolutely coincident with them) by the periods of the patriarchs, of Moses, of the theocracy, of the kingdom, of the captivity, of the hierarchy, as Israel was enabled to assimilate the lessons provided providentially in the national life of Egypt, Canaan, Persia, Greece. And the many "modes" of revelation are shadowed forth in the enactment of typical ordinances, in declarations of "the word of the Lord," in symbolic actions, in interpretations of the circumstances of national prosperity and distress.[18]

Marcus Dods notes that the alliteration used here for the two adverbs is characteristic of the author of Hebrews. He then goes on to say:

> *Polymeros* points to the fragmentary character of former revelations. They were given piece-meal, bit by bit, part by part, as the people needed and were able to receive them. The revelation of God was essentially

progressive; all was not disclosed at once, because all could not at once be understood. One aspect of God's nature, one element in His purposes, reflected from the conditions of their time the prophets could know; but in the nature of things it was impossible they should know the whole. They were like men listening to a clock striking, always getting nearer the truth but obliged to wait till the whole was heard. . . . His speaking was also *polytropos* . . . not in one stereotyped manner but in modes varying with the message, the messenger, and those to whom the word is sent. Sometimes, therefore, God spoke by an institution, sometimes by parable, sometimes in a psalm, sometimes in an act of righteous indignation. . . . These features of previous revelations, so prominently set and expressed so grandiloquently, cannot have been meant to disparage them, rather to bring into view their affluence and pliability and many-sided application to the growing receptivity and varying needs of men. He wins his readers by suggesting the grandeur of past revelations.[19]

In contrast to the past revelations, we are told that "at the last of these days"—in the Messianic Age—God has spoken to us "by *his* Son" (KJV). The Greek literally says "in a son." Dods says, "*En whio* without the article [the Greek language has only a definite article, not an indefinite] must be translated, 'in a son' or 'in one who is a son,' indicating the nature of the person through whom this revelation was made. . . . This revelation was final because made by one who in all He is and does reveals the Father."[20]

The importance of the contrast between verses 1 and 2 of the first chapter of Hebrews can hardly be overemphasized. After the divine revelation in many parts and in many ways, God spoke "in a son." An impersonal revelation of a person must always be incomplete and imperfect. Only a personal revelation of a person can be a perfect revelation. This is logical.

And so God finally spoke "in a son"—in His Son. Jesus declared, "Anyone who has seen me has seen the Father" (John 14:9 NIV). These are either the words of the world's worst egotist or they are the expression of One who was fully conscious of His deity. Two thousand years of history have confirmed that it was the latter. The fact that practically all nations use the chronology of B.C. (before Christ) and A.D. (anno Domini, "in the year of our Lord") shows that Jesus Christ has proved to be the Lord of all history, standing at the divinely ordained division of time.

All of this emphasizes the finality of God's revelation in Christ. It is the revelation of divine nature. And it is also, at Calvary, the revelation of divine redemption. There can be no further revelation to this world until the end of time. And the record of that revelation in Christ, found in our New Testament, is God's final written revelation. There can be no other.

4. The canon of the Scriptures Our word *canon* comes directly from the Greek word *canon*. Originally this term meant "a rod or bar"; later it came to mean "a measuring rule." As we use it here, it means the official list of books accepted by the church as constituting the Bible.

a. The Old Testament The Protestant canon of the Old Testament is the same as the Hebrew canon accepted by the Jews as their complete "Holy Scriptures." The Roman Catholic canon is longer. It includes fourteen books (or parts of books) that are not included in the Protestant Old Testament, though they were in the original King James Version.

The Jews divide their Hebrew canon into three parts: (1) the Law, (2) the Prophets, and (3) the Writings. The Law, or Torah, was the name given to the first five books. We usually call them the Pentateuch (from *pente,* the Greek word for "five").

The Prophets were divided by the Jews into the Former Prophets and the Latter Prophets, each containing four books. The Former Prophets consisted of Joshua, Judges, Samuel, and Kings. In the Hebrew text Samuel and Kings (as also Chronicles) are each one book. The Hebrew alphabet has no vowels. When the Hebrew Old Testament was translated into Greek (the

Septuagint) in 250-150 B.C., the Greek vowels expanded the text, making it too long for a single scroll of Samuel or Kings. So these were expanded into two scrolls each.

We list these four books among the "Historical Books" (Joshua—Esther). But the Jews wisely saw that these books contain prophetic history—God's dealings with His people.

The Latter Prophets consisted of Isaiah, Jeremiah, Ezekiel, and the Twelve Prophets (our "Minor Prophets"—Hosea through Malachi).

The Writings included all the other books of our Old Testament. These were often divided into the three Poetical Books (Psalms, Proverbs, Job), the Five Rolls (Song of Solomon, Ruth, Lamentations, Ecclesiastes, Esther), and the three Historical Books (Daniel, Ezra–Nehemiah, Chronicles).

We find this threefold division of the Hebrew canon clearly reflected in one passage in the New Testament (Luke 24:44): Jesus said, "Everything must be fulfilled that is written about me in the Law of Moses, the Prophets and the Psalms" (NIV). Since the third division, the Writings, began with the Book of Psalms, the whole group could be referred to as "the Psalms." The Jews counted twenty-four books in their canon. But these included all the thirty-nine books included in our Old Testament.

The limits of the Hebrew canon were fixed at the Council of Jamnia, about A.D. 90. The Jews had lost their temple in A.D. 70, when it was destroyed by the Romans. All that was left was their synagogues, where the rabbis taught the Scriptures every Sabbath Day. So the Jews became "the people of the Book." It was essential that the canon should be fixed, especially as Christian writings began to appear.

We have already noted that the Roman Catholics have a larger Old Testament canon than Protestants have. The fourteen additional books (or parts of books) that Catholics accept are referred to as the Apocrypha—a Greek term that means "hidden." This term reflects the ancient tradition that these books contained secret wisdom, which could be known only to the initiated.

These books are in the Greek Septuagint and the Latin Vulgate. Why, then, do Protestants reject them from their Bibles?

As early as the fourth century Jerome, who produced the official Bible translation of the Roman Catholic church called the Latin Vulgate, said that the apocryphal books were good for edifying but were not authoritative. In its Thirty-nine Articles the Church of England took the same stand. Because of these and other influences, in 1827 the British and Foreign Bible Society voted not to use any of its funds in publishing the Apocrypha. Gradually it was excluded from the King James Version.

Was this a mistake? I believe not. Anyone can satisfy his own mind by reading these books for himself. Several popular English translations of the Apocrypha are available today.

Actually there are numerous things in these books that do not fit in with the sacred Scriptures. The worst example is the statement in Tobit that almsgiving atones for sin. The uniform teaching of the Bible is that we cannot buy our way into God's favor. Salvation is the free gift of God, given to those who believe and obey.

b. The New Testament The New Testament consists of four Gospels, Acts (which forms a logical link between the Gospels and the Epistles), thirteen Pauline Epistles, Hebrews, seven General Epistles, and Revelation. Probably all of these twenty-seven books were written in the second half of the first century.

Some scholars have suggested an early date of about A.D. 45 for the Epistle of James, because of its strongly Jewish character. But probably a date in the 50s is more accurate. Several contemporary scholars think that the Epistle to the Galatians was written around A.D. 48, but many other scholars hold that 1 Thessalonians (A.D. 50) is the first book of the New Testament to appear. Perhaps all of Paul's thirteen letters were written in the 50s and 60s.

Hebrews is usually dated somewhere in the middle 60s. The same can be said of 1 and 2 Peter. All of John's writings—the Gospel, three Epistles and Revelation—were probably written about A.D. 95, in the time of the Emperor Domitian. The dating of the synoptic Gospels is much debated. I would place Mark in the 50s, and Matthew and Luke in the early 60s. This would mean that the entire New Testament was written within a period of fifty years, whereas the writing of the Old Testament stretched out over a thousand years—about 1400-400 B.C. Thus the sixty-six books of the Bible appeared, one by one, during a period of fifteen hundred years. And yet the unity of emphasis—on God's redemptive work for mankind—points to the inspiration of the Holy Spirit.

We have already noted that the canon of the Hebrew Scriptures (the Old Testament) was fixed by the Jewish rabbis about the end of the first century A.D. The limits of the New Testament canon were not officially declared until the end of the fourth century.

About A.D. 140 in Rome the heretic Marcion adopted as his New Testament ten epistles of Paul (excluding the Pastorals) plus a mutilated Gospel of Luke (with the first two chapters missing, because they emphasized the humanity of Jesus). Marcion was Gnostic in his ideas—only spirit is good; all matter is evil.

It is clear that by the end of the second century the Christian church was using essentially the same New Testament that we have today (though not bound in one volume). This is shown by comparing the writings of Irenaeus in Gaul (France), Clement of Alexandria (Egypt), and Tertullian of Carthage (North Africa). It is significant that Irenaeus had come from Asia Minor, lived in Rome, and finally moved to Gaul. So he represented the church from east to west.

During the third century and early fourth century there was some dispute about the canonicity of seven of the New Testament books—Hebrews, James, 2 Peter, 2 and 3 John, Jude, and Revelation. The first exact list of the present twenty-seven books is in the Easter letter of Athanasius, in A.D. 367. Finally, near the close of the fourth century, in A.D. 397, the Council of Carthage decreed that only "canonical" books should be read in the churches. It then listed the twenty-seven books that are now included in the New Testament. Anyone who reads Edgar Hennecke's two-volume *New Testament Apocrypha* (Philadelphia: Westminster, 1963-65) will surely agree that the many noncanonical writings certainly do not belong in the New Testament.

5. The nature of the Scriptures That humanity needed a special revelation from God is obvious. But what kind of revelation would meet human need? The following is a good, comprehensive statement of the necessity and the nature of God's special revelation:

> Concerning a divine revelation, we remark that, 1. It is possible. God may, for aught we know, think proper to make known to his creatures what they before were ignorant of; and, as a Being of infinite power, he cannot be at a loss for means of communication. 2. It is desirable; for while reason is necessary to examine the matter of revelation, it is incapable, unaided, of finding out God. 3. It is necessary; for without it we can attain to no certain knowledge of God, of Christ, and of salvation. 4. Revelation must, to answer its ends, be sufficiently marked with internal and external evidences. These the Bible has. 5. Its contents must be agreeable to reason. Not that everything revealed must be within the range of reason; but this may be true, and yet there be no contradiction. To calm, dispassionate reason there is nothing in doctrine, command, warning, promises, or threatenings which is opposed thereto. 6. It must be credible; and we find the facts of Scripture supported by abundant evidence from friend and foe. 7. Revelation also must necessarily bear the prevailing impress of the circumstances and tastes of the times and nations in which it was originally given. The Bible, however, though it bears the distinct

impress of Asiatic manners, as it should do, is most remarkable for rising above all local and temporary peculiarities, and seizing on the great principles common to human nature under all circumstances; thus showing that as it is intended for universal benefit, so will it be made known to all mankind. The language of the Bible is the language of men, otherwise it would not be a divine revelation to men. It is to be understood by the same means and according to the same laws by which all other human language is understood. It is addressed to the common-sense of men, and common-sense is to be consulted in its interpretations.[21]

6. The acceptance of the Scriptures One of the most encouraging trends of the past thirty years has been the increased interest in the study of the Bible. During the first half of the twentieth century (1900-1949) only about half a dozen significant new series of English commentaries on the Bible (or New Testament) appeared. But in the following ten years (1950-1959) no fewer than ten new series were begun. This trend has continued through the 60s and 70s. There are probably more Bible study classes held every week in the United States than at any other time in its history. This new interest in the Bible has been stimulated, in part, by the appearance of several good English translations of the Bible that help the Word of God to be understood more clearly and accurately.

In his preface to a recent book Raymond Abba has this to say:

> Recent years have witnessed a complete change of emphasis in biblical studies. The new attitude, while accepting substantially the earlier work of biblical criticism, which is still valued and continued, seeks to transcend it by constructive theological exposition. Critical and historical analysis are seen as *prolegomena* to biblical theology. While recognizing the human element in the Bible, the emphasis is placed upon its significance as the living and abiding Word of God. That is the background of this book. It springs from the conviction that the Bible is authoritative as the primary witness to the events in time in which the Eternal God has visited and redeemed His people; that it is both the record and the instrument of a unique divine revelation, given through the history of Israel, culminating in Jesus Christ, interpreted by the Church, and authenticated in religious experience. The written Word mediates the authority and saving power of the Word made flesh. The Bible is the Word of God because through it God Himself speaks to each generation of men.[22]

In past years there has been much discussion as to whether the Bible is a divine revelation or a record of such a revelation. The fact is that it is both. The New Testament, for instance, records the revelation of God in Christ. But it also gives us a Spirit-inspired revelation of the meaning and application of this in the Christian life.

James Orr makes this interesting observation:

> We have now found that the line between revelation and its record is becoming very thin, and that, in another true sense, *the record,* in the fulness of its contents, *is itself for us the revelation.* There are parts of the revelation—some of the prophetic discourses, *e.g.,* or the Epistles—which never existed in any but written form. But the record as a whole is the revelation—God's complete word—for us. Its sufficiency is implied in the fact that beyond it we do not need to travel to find *God's whole will* for our salvation.[23]

7. The value of the Scriptures How do we measure the value of a thing? By the question, "What would be our loss if we did not have it?"

Alan Richardson observes, "But to say that the Bible contains the highest ideas about God which man can attain does not satisfy us; we do not want ideas about God, we want God."[24] He goes on to say:

> The question which our generation asks is not where the highest human wisdom about God can be found, but whether there is any place in which God Himself speaks to us. . . . Now the uniqueness of the Bible does not consist in the excellence of its theological or moral teaching, but in its claim to record the message of God to the world.[25]

At the very center of our Bibles we find the longest chapter in the Bible—Psalm 119. It is perhaps not without significance that its main subject is the Word of God, spoken of as "the law of the Lord" (v. 1), "his statutes" (v. 2), "his ways" (v. 3), "precepts" (v. 4), "decrees" (v. 5), "commands" (v. 6), and "word" (v. 9).

Psalm 119:9 points up one of the most important practical values of the Scriptures. It reads (in the NIV):

How can a young man keep his way pure?
By living according to your word.

The only way we can live as God wants us to live is by living according to His Word. That means, among other things, that we must read it carefully each morning and then seek to order our lives by it that day. We must hide it in our hearts by memorizing it (v. 11). We must meditate on it to understand it well (v. 15). (Someone has said that meditation is mental mastication.) We must delight in it and not neglect it (v. 16). And we should pray before we read it (v. 18). This is the safe way to live.

II. INSPIRATION

A. Definition

The word *inspiration* comes from the Latin *inspiratio,* which basically means the act of breathing in or breathing into. As we shall see later, this is perhaps not the best concept of what we mean by biblical inspiration. Webster's dictionary gives as the theological definition of inspiration, "a supernatural divine influence on the prophets, apostles, or sacred writers, by which they were qualified to communicate truth without error."[26] Carl Henry puts it this way: "Inspiration is a supernatural influence of the Holy Spirit upon divinely chosen men in consequence of which their writings became trustworthy and authoritative."[27] This definition closely follows that of Benjamin Warfield.[28]

In his essay "The Communication of Revelation" Kenneth Kantzer says:

All of Scripture was produced by human authors whose writings reflect throughout the individual personality and linguistic habits of each particular Biblical author. At the same time the Spirit of God so worked upon the Biblical author that what he wrote is also exactly that message which God wishes to convey to man. Biblical inspiration may be defined, therefore, as that work of the Holy Spirit by which, without setting aside their personalities and literary or human faculties, God so guided the authors of Scripture as to enable them to write exactly the words which convey His truth to men, and in doing so preserved their judgments from error in the original manuscripts. Or, inspiration is the work of the Holy Spirit by which He employed the instrumentality of the whole personality, literary talents, and various faculties of their human authors to constitute the words of the Biblical autographs as His written Word to men and, therefore, of divine authority and without error in faith (what we ought to believe) and practice (what we ought to do).[29]

The important point to note is that when we speak of the inspiration of the Bible, we mean something different from the inspiring effect of great literature on those who read it. Biblical inspiration has to do with the origin of the Bible itself.

B. Biblical Doctrine

It is universally recognized that there are two main passages in the New Testament relating to the subject of inspiration. They are 2 Timothy 3:16 and 2 Peter 1:21.

In the King James Version the first part of 2 Timothy 3:16 reads: "All Scripture is given by inspiration of God." The last part, "given by inspiration of God," is all one word in Greek—*theopneustos* (used only here in the New Testament), which means "God-breathed." So the whole clause can simply be translated: "All Scripture is God-breathed" (NIV).

The KJV goes on to say, "and is profitable...." The ASV renders the text in this way: "Every scripture inspired of God is also profitable." But the RSV reads: "All scripture is inspired by God and profitable." Which is right?

The simple fact is that the Greek text of verse 16 has no verb at all. But in English we have to insert a verb ("is") to make any sense. It seems logical, then, to make *theopneustos* a predicate adjective. Since all Scripture is "God-breathed," it is (also) useful. Walter Lock favors the translation: "All Scripture is inspired by God . . . and therefore useful."[30] And E. K. Simpson gives four good reasons for rejecting the ASV rendering and adopting the NIV reading, "All Scripture is God-breathed and is useful."[31]

Concerning the force of *theopneustos*, Warfield writes:

> What it says of Scripture is not it is "breathed into by God" or is the product of the Divine "inbreathing" into its human authors, but that it is breathed out by God, "God-breathed," the product of the creative breath of God. In a word, what is declared by this fundamental passage is simply that the Scriptures are a Divine product, without any indication of how God has operated in producing them.[32]

We turn now to the second passage, 2 Peter 1:21. The preceding verse reads, "Knowing this first, that no prophecy of the scripture is of any private interpretation" (KJV). This has often been taken to mean that we are not to give *our* private interpretation to Scripture passages. But the Greek literally says, "Every prophecy of Scripture does not come [*ginetai*] of one's own interpretation." This is spelled out more specifically by the NIV: "Above all, you must understand that no prophecy of Scripture came about by the prophet's own interpretation." This gives a logical introduction to verse 21: "For the prophecy came not in old time by the will of man: but holy men of God spake as they were moved by the Holy Spirit" (KJV). The second half of this does not very well represent the Greek, which literally reads, "But men, being carried along by the Holy Spirit, spoke from God" (cf. NASB, NIV).

This tells us a bit more clearly how inspiration took place. The writers of sacred Scripture were picked up, as it were, and carried along *(pheromenoi)* by the Holy Spirit. It was more than a process of increased understanding or vivid insight. They were moved supernaturally so that they were able to speak "from God" the words He wanted them to say.

Joseph B. Mayor makes a further observation: "The position of *anthropoi* at the end of the sentence next to *theou* is emphatic. Though the prophets were men, yet their prophecies came not from human impulse, but proceeded from God."[33]

On the idea of being "carried along" Warfield writes:

> The term used here is a very specific one. It is not to be confounded with guiding, or directing, or controlling, or even leading in the full sense of the word. It goes beyond all such terms, in assigning the effect produced specifically to the active agent. . . . The men who spoke from God are here declared . . . to have been taken up by the Holy Spirit and brought by His power to the goal of His choosing. The things which they spoke, under this operation of the Spirit were therefore His things, not theirs.[34]

The two definite statements in the New Testament about the divine inspiration of the Old Testament are well supported by the testimony of the Old Testament writers themselves. David, who wrote about half of the Psalms—if we may trust the headings—declares:

> The Spirit of the LORD spoke through me;
> his word was on my tongue.
> (2 Sam. 23:2 NIV)

Isaiah, the prince of prophets, begins his great book of prophecy with these words:

> Hear, O heavens! Listen, O earth!
> For the LORD has spoken.
> (Isa. 1:2 NIV)

In Isaiah 3:15 a quotation is documented with the words "declares the Lord, the LORD Almighty." The next verse begins with this introduction to another quotation: "The LORD says." A much longer oracle is introduced with these words: "The LORD Almighty has declared in my hearing" (Isa. 5:9 NIV). In connection with Isaiah's vision is this introductory formula: "Then

I heard the voice of the Lord saying " (6:8 NIV). In 7:7 the introduction reads: "Yet this is what the Sovereign LORD says" (NIV). Chapter 8 begins with the words "The LORD said to me." A longer quotation is preceded by "The LORD spoke to me again" (v. 5). Then Isaiah says in verse 11: "The LORD spoke to me with his strong hand upon me" (NIV) and proceeds to share the message of warning that God gave him. Another long quotation is introduced with the words "This is what the Sovereign LORD, the Holy One of Israel, says" (30:15 NIV).

As every student of the Bible knows, the most common phrase in the prophetic books of the Old Testament is "Thus saith the LORD" (KJV), which occurs some 359 times. In the NASB this is modernized to "Thus says the LORD." But since the word *thus* is not in good style in contemporary English, the NIV has "This is what the LORD says."

It should be obvious that the use of this term over and over again amounts to no less than a firm declaration of divine inspiration. The prophetic writers claim to be speaking directly for God. And the centuries have vindicated their claims. Not only do we find in the prophetic books the highest moral teaching of ancient times, but their messianic predictions have been fulfilled (in Christ's first coming to earth) with startling accuracy. Nothing but a divine revelation could have brought this about.

Jeremiah is even more detailed than Isaiah in asserting the direct divine inspiration of his prophecies. In the first chapter of his book he declares, "The word of the LORD came to me" (vv. 4, 11, 13), "The LORD said to me" (vv. 7, 12), and "declares the LORD" (vv. 15, 19). Most striking of all is this introductory formula: "Then the LORD stretched out His hand and touched my mouth, and the LORD said to me" (v. 9). In Jeremiah 5:14 we read, "Therefore this is what the LORD God Almighty says," and in 13:12: "This is what the LORD, the God of Israel, says" (NIV). Similar introductory formulae occur frequently throughout the Book of Jeremiah, as well as the Minor Prophets. These men spoke from God and for God.

C. Communication

Inspiration is primarily a matter of communication. The inspiration of the Bible is an expression of God's effort to communicate His eternal truth and sovereign will to man.

Eugene Nida, vice-president in charge of translating for the American Bible Society, delivered a series of lectures some time ago on the general subject of the problem of communication. He pointed out the important fact that all effective communication involves three factors—the source, the message, and the receptor. It is not enough for the source to produce a message. That message must finally reach the receptor before communication has actually taken place.

Neoorthodoxy has emphasized the idea that inspiration is primarily, if not altogether, a subject-to-subject relationship. God the subject speaks to man the subject. The Word of God is not the Bible but the voice of God speaking directly to people today.

Obviously the neoorthodox theologians have left out one essential factor. Communication is not just a subject-to-subject relationship, but a subject-object-subject process. It is God the subject reaching man the subject by way of the Bible, the object. Without any written revelation the door is thrown wide open for all kinds of fanatical vagaries to be proposed as God's will and word for man. God must speak to me. But He has chosen to speak to me primarily through the Bible.

While neoorthodoxy has tended to bypass, or at least minimize, the authority of the mediating object, the written Word, too often evangelical scholars have been guilty of neglecting the third factor. They have made inspiration merely a subject-object relationship, failing to recognize that communication is not completed until the object has effectively and effectually reached the final subject. The Bible as the written Word of God does not communicate until it conveys God's truth accurately and meaningfully to modern man.

In his helpful essay, from which I quoted earlier, Kenneth Kantzer underscores this third phase. He calls it "illumination" and defines it this way: "By illumination is meant the work of the Holy Spirit by which He enables man to recognize the divine revelation in act or word, and to respond to it with appropriate acceptance."[35] He then goes on to say, "By the twentieth century writers of orthodox persuasion, the Biblical doctrine of illumination has been largely neglected. . . . Without the illumination of the Holy Spirit all direct personal relationship to God would be lost."[36]

Kantzer also gives a threefold application of this whole picture of communication. He writes:

> By revelation God communicates Himself and His truth to man through His (wordless) acts and through His (acts of communication by) words. The Bible provides the record of these acts of God in the past; and thus it may be said correctly: "The Bible *contains* the Word of God."
>
> By inspiration God also saw fit to provide His own divinely guided prophetic and apostolic Word about the revelatory acts and words of God given in history. Scripture, therefore, is the divinely guaranteed record of God's words and acts provided by human authors who were so motivated, guided and taught by the Spirit that they convey exactly that which God wishes to say to men. It may thus also be said quite correctly: "The Bible *is* the Word of God."
>
> By illumination, God enables men to recognize the Jesus Christ of Holy Scripture as their present living Lord and Saviour, and to recognize and receive Holy Scripture for what it is—God's Word. . . . It may thus, finally, be said correctly and with full Biblical warrant: "The Bible *becomes* the Word of God."[37]

D. History of the Doctrine

1. The early church Clement of Rome's First Epistle to the Corinthians is the earliest extant Christian writing outside the New Testament and possibly the only such document from the first century. This letter is filled with quotations from the Old Testament, frequently introduced by such expressions as "the Holy Spirit says," or "God said," as well as the typical New Testament phrase "It is written." Clement has this to say to his readers: "Ye have searched the scriptures, which are true, which were given through the Holy Ghost; and ye know that nothing unrighteous or counterfeit is written in them."[38]

Ignatius and Polycarp both quote copiously from the Scriptures, especially from the New Testament. The latter in his epistle to the Philippians refers to the New Testament as "scriptures."[39]

A little later Justin Martyr says in his *Dialogue with Trypho:*

> If a Scripture which appears to be of such a kind be brought forward, and then if there be a pretext (for saying) that it is contrary (to some other), since I am entirely convinced that no Scripture contradicts another, I shall admit rather that I do not understand what is recorded, and shall strive to persuade those who imagine that the Scriptures are contradictory to be rather of the same opinion as myself.[40]

That has always been the attitude of faith.

Justin deals more definitely with the manner of inspiration in his *Hortatory Address to the Greeks*. He says that the writers of Scripture presented "themselves pure to the energy of the Divine Spirit, in order that the divine plectrum itself, descending from heaven, and using righteous men as an instrument like a harp or lyre, might reveal to us the knowledge of things divine and heavenly."[41]

Irenaeus writes, "The Scriptures are indeed perfect, since they were spoken by the Word of God and His Spirit."[42]

It should be noted that the early church fathers use the expression "the Word of God" for the eternal Logos more than for the Bible. Inspiration is the Logos of God speaking through the Holy Spirit to the writers of sacred Scripture. Hippolytus (third century) stressed this idea of the living Word expressing Himself through the written Word. Using the same figure that Justin had adopted a century earlier, he says of the writers of the Old Testament: "For these Fathers were furnished with the Spirit, and largely honoured by the Word Himself; and just as it is with instruments of music, so had they the Word always, like the plectrum . . . and when moved by Him, the prophets announced what God willed."[43] The divine Logos is compared to the plectrum, with which one would pluck the strings of the lyre to produce music. The figure is suggestive but inadequate, for the writers of Scripture were not passive instruments.

As we have seen, the familiar word *theopneustos* ("God-breathed") is used of the Old Testament Scriptures in 2 Timothy 3:16—"All Scripture is breathed out by God." The first to apply this term to the New Testament is Clement of Alexandria (second century) who speaks of "the inspired scriptures."[44] It is also used by Origen (third century), who refers to "the divine inspiration of the holy Scriptures."[45] Again he writes, "The sacred books are not the compositions of men, but they were composed by inspiration [*epipnoias*] of the Holy Spirit."[46]

Clement of Alexandria, as quoted by Eusebius, also uses a very interesting phrase. He says that John, in composing his Gospel, was "divinely moved by the Spirit"[47]—*pneumati theophorethenta*, literally "having been God-borne in spirit (by the Spirit)." The language is reminiscent of that in 2 Peter 1:21: "But men spoke from God, being borne along by the Holy Spirit" (. . . *hypo pneumatos hagiou pheromenoi*).

In recent years there has been a running debate over the question as to whether the early church fathers believed in verbal inspiration. Though many writers have denied that they did, it is significant that Alan Richardson, who himself discounts the doctrine, nevertheless declares, "From the second century to the eighteenth this theory was generally accepted as true."[48] William Sanday supports this position.[49]

He also says specifically, "Both Irenaeus and Tertullian regard Inspiration as determining the choice of particular words and phrases."[50]

We have looked briefly at what some church fathers of the second and third century have to say on the subject of inspiration. Now it is necessary to see what Augustine, the leading figure of the fourth century, has to say.

A. D. R. Polman has made a careful survey of Augustine's thought on this subject. He writes:

> Together with the entire Church of his day, St. Augustine was firmly convinced that the Bible was divinely inspired, and he was greatly heartened in his belief by the unanimous witness of the Church from Apostolic times onwards. . . . St. Augustine would often gainsay opponents of his doctrine on divine inspiration by pointing out this strange unanimity of the Universal Church.[51]

After citing numerous examples from Augustine's works, Polman adds:

> However it remains a strange fact that St. Augustine very rarely proved the inspiration from Scripture itself. He simply took it for granted. To him, "the Holy Scriptures were the work of God's fingers, because they have been completed by the operation of the Holy Ghost, who worketh in the holy authors." Hence he called Scripture "the Word of God," "a kind of bond of God's, which all who pass by, might read," "the divine books," "the divine Scripture," "the holy Scripture," "the scripture of God," "letters of that city, apart from which we are wandering," "the divine oracles."[52]

2. The Reformers When the Bible was rediscovered in the Protestant Reformation, it was only natural that the subject of inspiration should come to the fore again. Luther declared the full divine authority of "the Scriptures alone,"[53] in contrast to the traditions that "have been invented by men in the Church."[54] Yet Luther has left us no clearly defined doctrine of inspiration. That seems sufficiently evident from the fact that both extreme liberals and ultraconservatives have quoted him in support of their opposing views.

A typical assertion is that of Kramm, in his book *The Theology of Martin Luther:* "Protestant theology after Luther developed the doctrine of 'verbal inspiration.'"[55] In the same vein James Mackinnon writes, "The theory of verbal inspiration of Scripture is a product not of Luther, but of the later Lutheran orthodoxy."[56] It is difficult, however, to harmonize that with another statement that Mackinnon makes:

> Luther has an unbounded veneration for the Bible as the God-inspired book. His veneration embraces its language as well as its contents. In the Bible we have the very utterance of God, or the Spirit of God or of Christ.[57]

Perhaps Luther should be allowed to speak for himself. In his *Commentary on the Psalms* he says of Psalm 90: "We must, therefore, believe that the Holy Spirit Himself composed this Psalm."[58] That sounds very much like verbal inspiration!

Incidentally, Kramm is very fair in his description of what is meant by verbal inspiration. He writes:

> This does not necessarily imply a mechanical theory of dictation; the differences in the gifts of the individual authors can be used by the Holy Spirit for His purpose. But it would mean that the authors were inspired to write down these very facts and thoughts. In this case each sentence, thought, and even word of the original texts has its meaning and was inspired by the Holy Ghost.[59]

Calvin was much more of a systematic theologian than was Luther. It is not surprising, therefore, to find him more specific in his doctrine of biblical inspiration. The following statement in his *Institutes* seems to assert nothing less than verbal inspiration:

> Since we are not favoured with daily oracles from heaven, and since it is only in the Scriptures that the Lord hath been pleased to preserve his truth in perpetual remembrance, it obtains the same complete credit and authority with believers . . . as if they heard the very words pronounced by God himself.[60]

Perhaps Calvin's greatest contribution in this field was his emphasis on the validation of the divine authority of the Bible to the individual believer by the inner witness of the Spirit. Here is the way he expresses this great truth: "It is necessary, therefore, that the same Spirit, who spake by the mouths of the prophets, should penetrate into our hearts, to convince us that they faithfully delivered the oracles which were divinely intrusted to them."[61] It is only this inner certification of the Holy Spirit to our spirits that can give complete conviction of His inspiration, and so of the divine authority, of books written by many men long ago.

Calvin also wrote:

> For as God alone can properly bear witness to His own words, so these words will not obtain full credit in the hearts of men, until they are sealed by the inward testimony of the Spirit. . . . Let it therefore be held as fixed, that those who are inwardly taught by the Holy Spirit acquiesce implicitly in Scripture. . . . Enlightened by Him, we no longer believe, either on our own judgment or that of others, that the Scriptures are from God; but, in a way superior to human judgment, feel perfectly assured—as much so as if we beheld the divine image visibly impressed on it—that it comes to us, by the instrumentality of men, from the very mouth of God.[62]

The major problem in Calvin's treatment of Scripture relates to his frequent statements that God "dictated" to the writers of Scripture and his references to them as "clerks" and "penmen." Kenneth Kantzer made a careful study of the phenomenon and came up with this conclusion: "Calvin's rather loose usage of the word 'dictate' corroborates the suggestion that he did not conceive of dictation in any mechanical sense."[63]

3. The Protestant creeds After the Reformation came the Protestant creeds. It seems somewhat surprising that the Augsburg Confession (1530) has no article on the Bible. The French Confession of Faith (1559) lists the books of both Old and New Testaments (Article III), certifies their canonicity (Article IV), and then goes on to say in Article V: "We believe that the Word contained in these books has proceeded from God, and receives its authority from him alone, and not from men."[64]

The language used here reminds one of a heated debate carried on in this century. Is it correct to say that the Bible *is* the Word of God or that it *contains* the Word of God? The simple fact is that both statements are true. It is not a case of either/or but of both/and.

The Belgic Confession (1561) is a bit more explicit, making pointed reference to the passage in 2 Peter. It devotes five articles to the Bible. The Thirty-nine Articles of the Church of England lists the canonical books but contains no statement on inspiration. The Irish Articles of Religion (1615) constitutes the first creed, as far as we can discover, that uses the term *inspiration*. It begins with the statement, "The ground of our religion and the rule of faith and all saving truth is the Word of God, contained in the holy Scripture," and then, after listing the canonical books, adds: "All which we acknowledge to be given by the inspiration of God, and in that regard to be of most certain credit and highest authority."[65]

The fullest creedal statement about the Scriptures is found in the Westminster Confession of Faith (1647). Ten articles are devoted to it. The canonical books are listed, and the statement added: "All which are given by inspiration of God, to be the rule of faith and life."[66] Here also one finds the following beautiful passage, which cannot be quoted too often:

> The heavenliness of the manner, the efficacy of the doctrine, the majesty of the style, the consent of all the parts, the scope of the whole (which is to give all glory to God), the full discovery it makes of the only way of man's salvation, the many other incomparable excellencies, and the entire perfection thereof are arguments whereby it doth abundantly evidence itself to be the Word of God.[67]

It is obvious that the early Protestant creeds lack any clear statement about verbal inspiration. Their emphasis regarding the Bible was rather on canonicity. In view of the Catholic acceptance of the authority of the apocryphal books and church tradition this attitude can well be understood. It would appear that biblical inspiration was not questioned and so needed neither defense nor explanation.

4. The Reformed view Reformed theologians of the past one hundred years have made up for this deficiency. Perhaps the most widely acknowledged compend is the three-volume *Systematic Theology* by Charles Hodge, who for fifty years was a professor at Princeton Theological Seminary. Here we find a statement of inspiration that is clear-cut and definite. Hodge writes:

> The sacred writers were the organs of God, so that what they taught, God taught. It is to be remembered, however, that when God uses any of his creatures as his instruments, He uses them according to their nature. . . . The church has never held what has been stigmatized as the mechanical theory of inspiration. The sacred writers were not machines. Their self-consciousness was not suspended; nor were their intellectual powers superseded. It was . . . living, thinking, willing minds, whom the Spirit used as his organs. The sacred writers impressed their peculiarities on their several productions as plainly as though they were the subjects of no extraordinary influence. . . . Nevertheless, and none the less, they spoke as they were moved by the Holy Ghost, and their words were his words.[68]

Interestingly Hodge labels this view "plenary inspiration."[69] But many today distinguish between plenary *verbal* inspiration and plenary *dynamic* inspiration. The latter is the view of many thoroughly evangelical scholars.

An outstanding defender of verbal inspiration in the past generation was Benjamin B. Warfield, a giant intellectual who taught at Princeton for a third of a century. He writes that the church

> has always recognized that this conception of co-authorship implies that the Spirit's superintendence extends to the choice of the words by the human authors (verbal inspiration), and preserves its product from everything inconsistent with a divine authorship—thus securing, among other things, that entire truthfulness which is everywhere presupposed in and asserted for Scripture by the Biblical writers (inerrancy).[70]

Two members of the Evangelical Theological Society have in recent years written excellent, scholarly treatises in explanation and defense of the doctrine of verbal inspiration: *Inspiration and Canonicity of the Bible,* by Laird Harris, and *Thy Word Is Truth,* by Edward J. Young. They were both published in 1957.

The former gives the following definition: "By verbal inspiration we merely mean that God superintended the process of writing so that the whole is true—the historical, the doctrinal, the mundane, the minor, the major."[71] Surprisingly, this statement contains no specific reference to the exact *words* of Scripture. As it stands it would be fully acceptable to those who hold to a plenary dynamic view but who prefer to avoid the use of the expression "verbal inspiration" because of what they feel to be an inevitable mechanical implication.

Young has placed all of us deeply in debt to him by his very thorough discussion of contemporary issues relating to biblical inspiration. The current crisis is reflected in the large place (three entire chapters) given to the question of the inerrancy of the original manuscripts.[72] It would seem that one purpose for writing the book was to defend the sole doctrinal statement of the Evangelical Theological Society: "The Bible is the Word of God written, and so inerrant in the original autographs."

Young begins with a discussion of inspiration. He translates *theopneustos* as "that which is breathed out by God."[73] Inspiration he defines as follows: "According to the Bible, inspiration is a superintendence of God the Holy Spirit over the writers of the Scriptures, as a result of which these Scriptures possess Divine authority and trustworthiness and, possessing such Divine authority and trustworthiness, are free from error."[74] He also asserts, "We are convinced that the Scriptures do indeed claim to be the Word of God, and since they are from Him and find their origin in Him, are therefore infallible and entirely free from error of any kind."[75]

Surprisingly, the term *verbal* is not used in these statements. Young is mainly concerned about the matters of infallibility and inerrancy. But he finally does say, "If, therefore, the inspiration of the Bible is plenary, it should be evident that it is one which extends to the very words. . . . It is, to state the matter boldly, a verbal inspiration."[76]

Laird Harris, for whom I have profound respect, also holds to the idea of verbal inspiration. He also is aware of the problems involved. In his essay "The Problem of Communication" he deals very helpfully and reasonably with the matter of the different meanings of a given word. He writes, "It is possible to think that words never express exact thoughts but always mean one thing to the speaker and a different thing to the hearer."[77] He goes on to say, "Every translator knows that words have not one simple meaning, but usually an area of meaning. They may have a formal sense, a slang sense, a particular sense in certain phrases and a technical sense in the jargon of a special profession."[78]

After quoting Warfield's statement of verbal inspiration—which I have already cited—Harris observes, "This doctrine does not say that every sentence is spoken with a precision sometimes not possible for our ideas, to say nothing of our words. God's purpose was evidently to convey ideas within acceptable limits of accuracy."[79] He adds, "Precision and accuracy are not terms exactly equivalent to truth. The fact that a word cannot be exhaustively and precisely defined does not mean that it cannot be used appropriately to convey an idea, otherwise one should never be able to order a meal in a restaurant."[80]

Laird concludes his discussion of this particular point with a quotation from the Westminster Confession:

> All things in Scripture are not alike plain in themselves, nor alike clear unto all; yet those things which are necessary to be known, believed, and observed, for salvation, are so clearly propounded and opened in some place of Scripture or other, that not only the learned, but the unlearned, in a due use of the ordinary means, may attain unto a sufficient understanding of them.[81]

This is a very reasonable and realistic statement. It seems to me to accord well with a plenary dynamic theory of inspiration.

How does Laird Harris define verbal inspiration? Here is his statement: "By verbal inspiration we merely mean that God superintended the process of writing so that the whole is true—the historical, the doctrinal, the mundane, the minor, and the major."[82]

5. The Neoorthodox view Karl Barth emphasizes the fallibility of the Bible. He declares that the prophets and apostles were "sinful in their action, and capable and actually guilty of error in their spoken and written word."[83] He does not stop there, but asserts, "The vulnerability of the Bible, i.e., its capacity for error, also extends to its religious or theological content."[84] Barth also asserts, "No human word, no word of Paul is absolute truth. In this I agree with Bultmann—and surely with all intelligent people."[85]

After noting Barth's views on the humanity and fallibility of the Bible, Klaas Runia writes, "We begin our critique by expressing our cordial *agreement* with Barth's great stress upon the *humanity* of the Bible."[86] He goes on to say:

> Admittedly some of the Early Fathers and some of the Lutheran and Reformed theologians of the seventeenth century came dangerously near to a mechanical conception, and in some cases even transgressed the limit. In general, however, Reformed theology adopted a more "organic" view of inspiration, according to which the Holy Spirit acted upon the authors in harmony with the laws of their own being. They were not passive, but active.[87]

But, against Barth, Runia argues strongly that the humanity of the Bible does not mean its fallibility. He writes:

> Here we strongly disagree with Barth. In our opinion Barth is guilty of a leap of thought which has no adequate grounding. Humanity and fallibility may indeed coincide on the purely human level, as we all experience daily, but this gives us no right to draw the same conclusion with regard to the Bible. For—and this is the decisive point—we are not on a *purely* human level here. We have to do with the inspired Word of God, i.e., with the Word that came into being not by human activity only, but in and through this human activity by the operation of the Holy Spirit. There is therefore no ground for such a straightforward identification of humanity and fallibility.[88]

Brunner is just as outspoken as Barth in his opposition to any idea of an infallible Bible. He writes, "The doctrine of the divine infallibility of Scriptural texts is a clear parallel to the doctrine of the infallibility of the Pope."[89]

John Baillie, late principal of New College, Edinburgh, agrees with the neoorthodox position that the Bible is not the divine revelation, but only a witness to it. He says, "The witness itself is a human activity and as such fallible."[90] He also stresses the subject to subject concept of revelation[91] and further declares, "Revelation has place only within the relationship between the Holy Spirit of God and the individual human soul. Nothing is the vehicle of revelation for me unless I hear God speaking to me through it."[92]

6. The Arminian-Wesleyan view James Arminius was a Dutch theologian who was born in 1560 and died in 1609. With regard to the Bible he wrote, "We now have the infallible word of God in no other place than in the Scriptures."[93]

The most specific statement that Arminius makes about inspiration is as follows:

> The primary cause of these books is God, in his Son, through the Holy Spirit. The instrumental causes are holy men of God, who, not at their own will and pleasure, but as they were actuated and inspired by the Holy Spirit wrote these books, whether the words were inspired into them, dictated to them, or administered by them under divine direction.[94]

This passage suggests three degrees of inspiration for different parts of the Bible. First, there is eternal truth "inspired into"; that is, breathed out of God and into the hearts and minds of the writers. Second, some parts of Scripture seem actually to have been dictated—as the law given to Moses at Sinai. But, third, other parts of the Bible were simply "administered by them under divine direction." These include the genealogical tables and other historical documents that the authors were led by the Spirit to copy and to incorporate into their writings.

It was John Wesley in the eighteenth century who took the theology of James Arminius and made it the powerful force for precipitating the greatest revival England has ever seen. In the preface to his *Explanatory Notes Upon the New Testament* he says of sacred Scripture: "Every part thereof is worthy of God; and all together are one entire body, wherein is no defect, no excess."[95]

In the same connection he writes, "The language of His messengers, also, is exact in the highest degree: for the words which were given them accurately answered to the impressions made upon their minds."[96]

Commenting on 2 Timothy 3:16, Wesley writes: "The Spirit of God not only once inspired those who wrote it [the Scriptures], but continually inspires, supernaturally assists, those that read it with earnest prayer."[97] Thus Wesley showed his awareness of the problem of communication. God's Word must reach man today.

Adam Clarke is universally recognized as the leading Wesleyan commentator. In his "Introduction to the Four Gospels and to the Acts of the Apostles" section 1 is entitled: "Concerning the Manner in which Divine Inspiration was granted to the sacred writers." Early in this discussion Clarke writes, "I beg leave to make a few extracts from Dr. Whitby, who has written excellently on this point."[98] Since Adam Clarke presents this material as expressing his own views, I will quote the most significant part of it.

> To proceed then to the consideration of the distinction made by some, viz. Of inspiration by suggestion, and inspiration of direction only: I say, then,
>
> First, Where there is no antecedent idea or knowledge of the things written for the good of others to be obtained from reason, or a former revelation, there, any inspiration of suggestion must be vouchsafed to the apostles, to enable them to make them known unto the world. But where there is an antecedent knowledge of the things to be indited, it can only be necessary that God should either immediately, or by some special occasions, excite them to indite those things, and should so carefully preside over and direct their minds, whilst writing, as to suggest, or bring into their memories, such things as his wisdom thought fit to be written; and should not suffer them to err in the delivery of what was thus indited in his name, or which they had written as apostles of God the Father, and our Lord Jesus Christ.
>
> Secondly, In all their revelations of mysteries, or things which could not otherwise be made known to them, either by natural reason or antecedent revelation, they must be acknowledged to have had them by an immediate suggestion of the Holy Spirit....
>
> Thirdly, As for those things which they did know already, either by natural reason, education, or antecedent revelation, they needed only such an assistance, or direction in them, as would secure them from error in their reasonings, or in their confirmation of their doctrines by passages contained in the Old Testament; and therefore, a continual suggestion must be here unnecessary....
>
> Fourthly, In writing the historical parts of the New Testament, or matters of fact relating to themselves, or others, it is only neces-

sary that what is there delivered as matter of fact should be truly performed, as it is said to have been done: but it is not necessary that they should be related in that order of time in which they were performed, unless that also be affirmed of them; for this must be sufficient to assure us of the truth of what they thus delivered.

Moreover, in writing the discourses contained in these books, it is not necessary that the very words should be suggested, or recorded, in which they were first spoken, but only that the true intent and meaning of them should be related, though in diversity of words. . . .

Lastly, From what is thus discoursed, it may appear that I contend only for such an inspiration, or Divine assistance of the sacred writers of the New Testament, as will assure us of the truth of what they wrote, whether by inspiration or suggestion, or direction only; but not for such an inspiration as implies that even their words were dictated, or their phrases suggested to them by the Holy Ghost.[99]

The first point made by Whitby, and endorsed by Adam Clarke, is that direct suggestion of new truth had to be made to writers of Scripture, when there was no previous knowledge of it. But when there was previous knowledge of it, God needed only to direct them in writing what they already knew.

In his second point Whitby reinforced the first part of this by asserting that we must recognize an immediate suggestion of the Holy Spirit for new material. But for previously known truth, in the third place, there was needed only such direction as would keep them free from error in what they wrote.

The fourth point takes care of the differing chronological order of events that we find, for instance, in the synoptic Gospels. Such order was not necessary. Also the discourses of the Gospels do not need to be in the exact original words, as long as their true intent and meaning is conveyed.

In his final point Whitby comes out very clearly for dynamic, rather than verbal, inspiration. This has always been the Arminian view.

The greatest Methodist theologian of the nineteenth century was W. B. Pope. In his three-volume *Compendium of Christian Theology* (first published in 1875–76) he devotes thirty-seven pages to inspiration. He writes of the Bible:

> Its plenary inspiration makes Holy Scripture the absolute and final authority, all-sufficient as the Supreme Standard of Faith, Directory of Morals, and Charter of Privileges to the Church of God. Of course, the Book of Divine revelations cannot contain anything untrue; but its infallibility is by itself especially connected with religious truth. . . . It is comparatively silent as to human science . . . it quotes traditions and admits records as testimony without pledging itself to their exactness. It does not profess to be divine in any such sense as should remove it from human literature: a Bible of that kind would be something very different from what we have. It is after all, a Divine-human collection of documents: the precise relation of the human to the Divine is a problem which has engaged much attention, and has not yet been, though it may yet be, adequately solved. But in the domain of religious truth, and the kingdom of God among men, its claim to authority and sufficiency is absolute.[100]

Speaking for his day, Pope makes these further observations:

> Most orthodox churches have more recently endeavoured to maintain a doctrine of Plenary inspiration in harmony with the notion of different DEGREES. Rejecting the terms MECHANICAL and VERBAL, as both inconsistent with the human element, they have sometimes used DYNAMICAL, as indicating that the inspiring influence was not so much UPON as IN and THROUGH the writers: the result, however, being the infallible Rule of Faith delivered by the instrumentality of men acted upon according to the laws of their own nature. This has required the distinction of SUGGESTION, the direct revelation of things otherwise unknown; ELEVATION, providing for the due preparation of the instruments; and SUPERINTENDENCY, as guarding the processes from the intrusion of error. . . . The Inspiration is PLENARY, as making the Holy Spirit responsible for the truth of all the

matter; but not VERBAL, as if He dictated the very words, which in some cases are lost with the autographs of Scripture.[101]

Pope has stated the case well: plenary inspiration, yes; verbal inspiration, no. Rather, the inspiration was dynamic, the Holy Spirit suggesting new truths and guiding the biblical writers so completely that they correctly conveyed these truths without error.

He then makes a significant point: We do not have the autographs of Scripture books and in some cases we can never be certain about the original wording. But we have the assurance that divine truth has been communicated to us accurately.

On the matter of verbal inspiration Pope speaks out with even more definiteness. He says:

> Many of the arguments urged against the inspiration of Scripture are really directed against a false or exaggerated notion of its verbal character, and consequently fall away before a freer theory. That many words and sentences were given or suggested to the writers cannot be doubted by anyone who considers the solemn importance of some of the leading terms of Scripture. But to assert that every word was put into the mind of every writer on every subject is to lay on our doctrine a burden too heavy to be borne. It is hard to suppose that the very words in that case would not have been protected for ever. And such inspiration would have been too mechanical to harmonize with the obvious and undeniable range given to the human faculties. But the chief point is that this notion furnishes ground of opposition which it is difficult to resist. Very many instances occur in the Gospels of variation in the reports of our Lord's words, on the most solemn occasions, which in no case affect their sacred spirit and eternal meaning, but are absolutely incompatible with verbal inspiration. Our Lord could not have spoken the several exact words placed in His lips: what they severally mean He did speak.[102]

For a good example of differing words clearly spoken at the same time Pope cites Matthew 26:28; Mark 14:24; Luke 22:21; 1 Corinthians 11:25. These are Jesus' words instituting the Lord's Supper—a truly solemn occasion.

I will discuss these differences in wording later, when comparing the parallel accounts of Jesus' sayings in the synoptic Gospels. There we will see that Pope's arguments against verbal inspiration are well taken. The phenomena of the Gospels do not accord with the verbal theory.

In the preface to his *Elements of Divinity,* Thomas Ralston describes his work as "a text-book of Wesleyan Arminian Theology." In it he deals at some length with the subject of the inspiration of the Bible. He writes:

> Inspiration, in this plenary sense, is not contemplated as applying to the writers as a *personal illumination,* rendering them infallible and free from error, as individuals, but as a spiritual influence, guiding, directing and controlling . . . their pens as they write the Scriptures, so that all they thus . . . write shall be free from error, and just as God would have it.[103]

Ralston names several of the writers of Bible books and then goes on to say:

> This inspiration did not destroy their *individuality.* They were not used by the divine Spirit as mere machines, so as thus to blot out or suspend their moral agency or intellectual character; hence we find in the inspired writers the same variety in style and manner by which other authors are distinguished.[104]

After discussing this matter further, Ralston finally comes to what sounds very much like verbal inspiration:

> But, according to the view of inspiration we have presented, it seems the very *words,* as well as the *thoughts,* must have been inspired. This is precisely the doctrine we maintain. The Bible is the "word of God." What the Bible says, God says; what the Bible declares to be true, is true; what it declares to be right, is right; what it declares to be wrong, is wrong. What it teaches is to be believed, not on the authority of Moses, of Paul, or of other inspired men, but on the authority of God. The Bible is inspired, not as to *ideas* merely, but as to *words* also.[105]

Ralston does not label his theory verbal inspiration. But it seems to be precisely that. At least it borders heavily on it.

John Miley points out the problems of a mechanical theory of verbal inspiration. Perhaps unfortunately, he identifies the two ideas of mechanical and verbal inspiration as being the same. Under the heading "The Mechanical Theory" his first statement is: "This is the theory of verbal inspiration."[106] Since contemporary exponents of verbal inspiration deny that it was mechanical, we refrain from repeating his arguments.

So we turn to his elucidation of the "Dynamical Theory." He treats it under four headings as follows:

1. *Sense of the Theory.* There is a supernatural operation of the Spirit within the consciousness and appropriate faculties of the mediate agent, yet not such as reduces him to the office of a mere instrument. He remains self-conscious and personally active in the use of his own faculties. Yet through the agency of the Holy Spirit he is so enlightened and possessed of the truth, and so guided in its expression, that the truth so given forth, whether by the spoken or written word, is from God. Through this agency the true and sufficient authorship of the Scriptures is with the Holy Spirit.

2. *Place for the Human Element.* We previously noted this manifest element in the construction of the Scriptures, and also pointed out its irreconcilable contrariety to the theory of a common verbal inspiration. The dynamical theory gives a proper place to this element, yet in a sense entirely consistent with such an inspiration as secures to the Holy Spirit the proper authorship of the Scriptures.

3. *Clear of Serious Difficulty.* This theory avoids the insuperable difficulties of a common verbal inspiration, as previously noted. Nor are there others of trying force. Surely there is none in the notion of such an agency of the Spirit as the theory alleges, real and sufficient as it is for the purpose of a divine revelation. If any finite mind is within the reach of an immediate divine influence, the human soul, made in the image of God, must be open to his inspiration. Otherwise, he has never exerted, and never could exert, any direct influence upon a single soul to enlighten and quicken it, to renew and lift it up, to guide and help it in the moral exigencies of life. Then, while through some means God might still speak to the ear or symbolize truth to the eye, he could not by any immediate interior influence open the mind for the reception of truth, or communicate truth to it, or make it the mediate agent of truth to others. Such an implication of divine impotence accords with a denial of the divine personality, but can have no place in a scheme of truth grounded in Christian theism.

4. *Sufficient for a Revelation.* The Scriptures are as really a divine revelation on this theory as they could be on that of verbal inspiration. This can be true, and is true, because an exact set of words, dictated by the Spirit, is not necessary either to the truthful expression of the divine mind or to the divine authorship of the Scriptures. The sufficiency of the theory is manifest as we group its facts. Through an interior illumination the Holy Spirit prepared the minds of the mediate agents for the reception of divine truth, and then communicated the necessary truth to them, and finally so directed them as to secure a proper expression of this truth, and also the selection and use of such other truths as might be proper for the Scriptures. These facts meet all the requirements of a divine revelation, and determine the truths so uttered to be in a very profound sense the word of God.[107]

These three men—Pope, Ralston, and Miley—all lived through most of the nineteenth century. Now we turn to a prominent twentieth-century Wesleyan.

After quoting half a dozen definitions of inspiration—from Webster's to Hodge's—A. M. Hills spells out what we do *not* mean when we say that the Bible is divinely inspired. Among other things, he says this:

Inspiration did not imply or involve any suppression or setting aside of the natural power and faculties of the writers. It did not destroy their individuality, nor restrain the free play of their thoughts and feelings. The natural poet, when inspired, still wrote as a poet. The logician, when inspired, did not forget his logic. The clear thinker, when inspired, lost none of his lucidity. God used the men as intelligent, voluntary agents, and his inspiration neither made them unconscious nor irrational. Each author preserved his peculiar style and mode of expression, yet God used the authority to record his own thought. Hence the marvelous variety of the sacred writings, and their perfect adaptation to interest all classes of minds and meet the needs of every condition of men. The human and the Divine are so inextricably blended that it is impossible to separate them or discriminate between them.[108]

Hills then discusses several views of inspiration. The first one he takes up is "the theory of plenary inspiration." Here is what he says about it:

> This regards the inspiration as extending to all parts of the Scripture, whether prophetical, doctrinal, or historical. It is held to cover, also, all the separate books, and all the subjects discussed, and all the statements made. So that every statement is always to be looked upon as true and authoritative.[109]

He next discusses "the theory of verbal inspiration." He quotes Hannah as saying, "By Verbal Inspiration is meant that the inspired servants of God, while they retained the proper use of their powers and faculties, were always guided, or assisted to use such language as would convey 'the mind of the Spirit' in its full and unimpaired integrity."[110]

Hills goes on to show that "there is much in the Scripture to support" this view. "A large portion of the entire Bible consists in direct messages from God."[111] He cites as examples "a large part of Exodus, most of Leviticus, much of Deuteronomy and Numbers," and the greater part of the prophetic books, as well as the words of Jesus. He concludes on this point: "From these statements of the Bible writers themselves it is evident that very much at least of the Bible is verbally inspired, so that the authors recorded the very words God would have them use."[112]

The fourth theory that Hills discusses is the Dynamical Theory, "which holds that there is a supernatural operation of the Spirit within the consciousness and appropriate faculties of the mediate agent." He continues:

> Through the agency of the Holy Spirit he is so enlightened and possessed of the truth, and so guided in its expression, that the truth so given forth, whether by the spoken or written word, is from God. Through this agency, the true and sufficient authorship of the Scriptures is with the Holy Spirit. This Dynamical theory leaves a proper place for the human element, yet in a sense entirely consistent with the true and proper authorship of the Holy Spirit.[113]

It is this plenary dynamic view of inspiration that is held most widely by Wesleyan scholars in our day. It affirms that the whole Bible is inspired dynamically by the Holy Spirit.

It is generally agreed that the greatest Wesleyan theologian of this century was the late H. Orton Wiley. Asked by his denomination to prepare a work on systematic theology, he spent nearly twenty years of intensive labor in carrying out this assignment. The result is his monumental, three-volume *Christian Theology,* published in 1940.

In the first volume is a chapter entitled "The Inspiration of the Scriptures." After quoting definitions of inspiration from seven outstanding theologians, he offers his own. It is this: "By *Inspiration* we mean the actuating energy of the Holy Spirit through which holy men were qualified to receive religious truth, and to communicate it to others without error."[114]

How did this take place? Wiley suggests three "factors" that he considers essential. He defines them as follows:

> The first is "superintendence," by which is meant a belief that God so guides those chosen as the organs of revelation, that their writings are kept free from error. Following this is the factor of "elevation," in which the minds of the chosen organs are granted an enlargement of understanding, and an elevation of conception beyond the natural measure of man. The highest and most important is the factor of "suggestion," by which is meant a direct and immediate sug-

gestion from God to man by the Spirit, as to the thoughts which he shall use, or even the very words which he shall employ, in order to make them agencies in conveying His will to others.[115]

The word Wiley uses to describe his understanding of the inspiration of the Bible is *plenary*. Here is the way he puts it:

> For this reason we conclude that the Scriptures were given by plenary inspiration, embracing throughout the elements of superintendence, elevation and suggestion, in that manner and to that degree that the Bible becomes the infallible Word of God, the authoritative rule of faith and practice in the Church.[116]

Wiley does not treat "plenary" as one of the theories of inspiration, but as a necessary, inescapable fact. He then goes on in the rest of the chapter to discuss various theories of inspiration. The first is the mechanical or dictation theory, which makes the writers of the Bible mere amanuenses or penmen. He quotes Hooker, who writes, "They neither spoke nor wrote any word of their own, but uttered syllable by syllable as the Spirit put it into their mouths." The second theory is the intuition theory, according to which inspiration is only the natural insight of men lifted to a higher plane of development. The third is the "dynamical" theory, which preserves both the divine and human factors in the inspiration of the Scriptures. Wiley adds that this theory "has been held by such standard theologians as Pope, Miley, Strong, Watson, Wakefield, Summers, Ralston and Hills, and with some modification by Curtis, Sheldon, Martensen and Dorner."[117]

A. H. Strong, the noted Baptist theologian, agrees with James Arminius and Adam Clarke in differentiating three kinds or degrees of inspiration. Some parts of the Bible are verbally inspired. At other times there was an illumination or quickening of the writers' natural faculties in recording truth that they were familiar with. In other cases it was merely a guidance in copying or adapting materials already available.[118]

We wish now to turn to the biblical evidence that seems to support a dynamic theory of inspiration rather than a verbal theory. Inasmuch as my main field of competence is the New Testament, this discussion will mostly be limited to that part of the Bible.

One of the most significant areas of evidence is to be found in the parallel accounts of Jesus' words as recorded in the synoptic Gospels. It begins with the first preaching in Jesus' public ministry. According to Matthew 4:17, He said, "The kingom of heaven [literally "of the heavens" *(tōn ouranōn)*] is near." According to Mark 1:15 Jesus declared, "The kingdom of God [*tou theou*] is near." Which *did* He say? Actually, we find the expression "kingdom of heaven" thirty-two times in Matthew but *never* in Mark or Luke. Mark has "kingdom of God" fifteen times, and Luke thirty-three times. For some unknown reason Matthew does have this expression five times (6:33; 12:28; 19:24; 21:31, 43).

Sometimes in the sayings of Jesus in Matthew and Luke—where they are found far more copiously than in Mark—we discover parallel sayings of considerable length that are verbatim except for one difference: Matthew has "kingdom of heaven" where Luke has "kingdom of God." And sometimes the parallel sayings were clearly uttered at the same time and in the same setting, so that we cannot take refuge in the alibi: "He used one expression sometimes and the other expression at other times." Facing the facts, we have to say that Jesus said it only one way in the given situation—probably "kingdom of God." But since the Jews preferred to use euphemisms for God, Matthew, because he was writing his Gospel for the Jews, used "heaven" so that his Jewish readers would not be offended. There seems to be no other explanation that fits the facts.

A good example of the Jewish use of "heaven" for "God" is found in the parable of the prodigal son. The penitent returnee said, "Father, I have sinned against heaven" (Luke 15:18). What he meant was: "I have sinned against God."

All this seems to suggest that the important thing was the correct thought rather than the specific word. This phenomenon of equivalent thought but difference in wording occurs over and over again in the parallel passages in the synoptic Gospels.

Another example is the first word Jesus said to the paralytic let down through the roof. In Mark 2:5 it is *teknon,* "child." In Luke 5:20 it is *anthrōpe,* "man." Most scholars agree that Jesus probably spoke in Aramaic. But even there we would find a distinction between the words for "man" and "son."

The most striking contrast comes in the so-called Beatitudes in the Sermon on the Mount. The first beatitude reads in Matthew (5:3):

> Blessed are the poor in spirit,
> for theirs is the kingdom of heaven.

In Luke 6:20 it reads:

> Blessed are you who are poor,
> for yours is the kingdom of God.

Is Matthew interpreting Jesus' words by adding "in spirit"? We have no way of knowing. In any case we could believe that Matthew was led by the Holy Spirit to make this interpretation.

The fourth beatitude in Matthew (second in Luke) reads:

> Blessed are those who hunger and thirst for righteousness,
> for they will be filled (5:6 NIV).

In Luke 6:21 (NIV) it is much shorter:

> Blessed are you who hunger now,
> for you will be satisfied.

It is obvious that Luke's form of this Beatitude is economic in thrust: Those who are physically hungry will be fed. But Matthew, again, gives a spiritual interpretation, for both the need and the provision.

Less striking, but still interesting, is the second Beatitude in Matthew (third in Luke). In Matthew 5:4 (NIV) we read:

> Blessed are those who mourn,
> for they will be comforted.

In Luke 6:21 (NIV) this reads:

> Blessed are you who weep now
> for you will laugh.

The closing verse (v. 48) of Matthew 5 reads, "Be perfect, therefore, as your heavenly Father is perfect" (NIV). This comes as the climax of Jesus' emphasis on loving our enemies (vv. 43–47). Luke gives a similar, though somewhat different, account of this (Luke 6:27–35). But he has Jesus saying at the close: "Be merciful, just as your Father is merciful." Matthew clearly indicates that the perfection Jesus requires of us is perfection in love, but Luke's version emphasizes one aspect of love, namely mercy.

Both Matthew and Luke close their accounts of the Sermon on the Mount with Jesus' words about the wise and foolish builders (Matt. 7:24–27; Luke 6:47–49). A careful comparison of these two accounts will show that the same truth is spelled out in practically the same way. And yet there are some striking differences in the exact wording. This is the phenomenon that we find over and over again in the synoptic Gospels. It seems to accord better with plenary dynamic inspiration than plenary verbal inspiration.

To be perfectly fair we must note that some New Testament scholars label Luke 6:17–49 "The Sermon on the Plain" on the basis of "a level place" in verse 17. But this could well be a small plateau "on a mountainside" (Matt. 5:1). It is true that Jesus doubtless repeated His important teachings on different occasions, and perhaps in different form. But we do get the impression that exact agreement in wording is not the basic requirement in the synoptic Gospels. And of course in John's Gospel there are striking spiritual interpretations of Jesus' teachings.

We find these differences in exact wording to be frequent also in the parables of Jesus. The most striking example is in the parable of the sower (Matt. 13:3–8; Mark 4:2–8; Luke 8:5–8), especially the careful explanation of its meaning given by Jesus (Matt. 13:18-23; Mark 4:14-20; Luke 8:11-15).

The first difference occurs in the identification of the birds that ate up the seed that fell along the hard-surfaced path. Matthew says they represent "the evil one" (v. 19); Mark says "Satan" (v. 15); and Luke, "the devil" (v. 12). Which did Jesus say? Apparently that is not the important question. All three expressions refer clearly to the same person, and that is all that matters. The thought is the same; the words are different. This accords with dynamic inspiration but hardly with verbal inspiration. It is this truth that forced itself on me when, many years ago, I first went through a harmony of the synoptic Gospels in Greek, underlining in blue the words that are the same and in red the words that are different. The results were impressive.

We find a still greater variation in the explanation of the seed that fell among thorns. Matthew names two things that kept the seed from producing a good crop: "the worries of this life, and the deceitfulness of wealth" (v. 22 NIV). Mark repeats these two and then adds a third: "the desires for other things" (v. 19). Luke also has three, but expresses them more simply: "life's worries, riches and pleasures" (v. 14). Again, the thought is basically the same, but the words differ. This is true also in the concluding clause of this part of the explanation. Literally Matthew says, "It chokes the word, and it becomes unfruitful"; Mark reads, "They choke the word, and it becomes unfruitful"; and Luke has "They are choked and do not mature." Again we ask, "Which did Jesus say?" Obviously, the exact wording is not a necessary criterion of inspiration.

During the last week of His public ministry Jesus was questioned three times by the Pharisees or Sadducees. Finally, in return Jesus asked the Pharisees how the Messiah could be both David's son (descendant) and David's Lord. In connection with this Jesus quoted Psalm 110:1 (in all three Synoptics). Matthew's introduction to this quotation is framed differently from Mark's and Luke's; so it will be omitted. Mark has (literally): "David himself said in the Holy Spirit" (12:36). Luke has: "David himself says in the Book of Psalms" (20:42). These two statements complement each other very significantly (divine authority and human authorship). But which did Jesus say?

In the institution of the Lord's Supper we find a typical slight variation in wording, as reflected in NIV. Giving the disciples the cup, Jesus said to them, "Drink from it, all of you" (Matt. 26:27). Mark has no words of Jesus at this point. He simply says, "And they all drank from it" (Mark 14:23). Luke has Jesus saying, "Take this and divide it among you" (Luke 22:17). The meaning is the same, but the words are different.

Following this, Jesus told His disciples that He would not again drink of this fruit of the vine "until that day when I drink it new with you in my Father's kingdom" (Matt. 26:29). Mark has "until that day when I drink it new in the kingdom of God" (Mark 14:25). Luke says it more briefly: ". . . until the kingdom of God comes" (Luke 22:18). The thought is equivalent, but the words differ somewhat.

Examples like these could be exhibited almost endlessly. But these are enough to show that equivalence of thought was more essential to the biblical writers than exact sameness of words. As we have noted, the giving of the Ten Commandments was apparently by verbal inspiration. I would also use this designation for the writings of the Old Testament prophets when they say repeatedly, "Thus says the LORD." But it is surely significant that the three synoptic Gospels report the same sayings of Jesus with some variation in wording.

Commenting on this phenomenon, even including all four Gospels, Augustine wrote:

> On this question we ought not to suppose that any one of the writers gave an unreliable account, if, when several persons recall some matter either heard or seen by them,

they fail to follow the very same plan, or to use the very same words, while describing, nevertheless, the selfsame fact. This is absolutely impossible, since the truth of the Gospel, conveyed in that word of God which abides eternal and unchangeable above all that is created, but which at the same time has disseminated throughout the world by the instrumentality of temporal symbols, and by the tongues of men, has possessed itself of the most exalted height of authority.[119]

In his same work Augustine made his point even more strongly when he wrote:

> From these varied and yet not inconsistent modes of statement adopted by the Evangelists, we evidently learn a lesson of the utmost utility, and of great necessity—namely that in any man's words the thing which we ought narrowly to regard is only the writer's thought which was meant to be expressed, and to which the words ought to be subservient; and further that we should not suppose one to be giving an incorrect statement, if he happens to convey in different words what the person really meant whose words he fails to reproduce literally. And we ought not to let the wretched cavillers at words fancy that truth must be tied somehow or other to the jots and tittles of letters; whereas the fact is, that not in the matter of words only, but equally in all other methods by which sentiments are indicated, the sentiment itself, and nothing else, is what ought to be looked at.[120]

Probably most Arminian scholars would agree in general with Augustine's statement. No one should assume that Augustine was ignoring the divine inspiration of the biblical writers, for this great church father speaks in strongest terms of the Holy Spirit's part in the production of the Holy Scriptures.

There is another important area where variation of wording plays a significant part. I refer to quotations of the Old Testament that are found in the New Testament. This is an extensive field to cover. But I want to note a few examples that are particularly impressive.

Before citing specific examples, I should point out that about 80 percent of the Old Testament quotations in the New are drawn from the Septuagint.[121] In the majority of these instances there is little or no disagreement between the Septuagint and the Masoretic Hebrew text. But in some cases they do differ significantly, and "there are numerous instances in which a New Testament writer obviously follows the Septuagint in distinction from the Hebrew."[122]

One of the best known and most striking of these instances is found in Hebrews 10:5. It is a quotation from Psalm 40:6, which in the Hebrew reads literally, "Ears you have opened [dug] for me." But the Septuagint says, "A body you fitted [shaped] for me." How can we reconcile these two? Westcott insists that the Septuagint rendering must be taken as "a free interpretation of the original text." He explains it this way: "The 'body' is the instrument for fulfilling the divine command, just as the 'ear' is the instrument for receiving it."[123] Marcus Dods says of the two renderings: "The meaning is the same. The opened ear as the medium through which the will of God was received, and the body by which it was accomplished, alike signify obedience to the will of God."[124] Alford writes, "How the word *soma* came into the LXX, we cannot say: but being there, it is now sanctioned for us by the citation here: not as the, or even a, proper rendering of the Hebrew, but as a prophetic utterance, equivalent to and representing that other."[125] Lenski puts it this way:

> "To do, God, thy will" in holy obedience (v. 7) remains the contrast to the earthly sacrifices, whether we have the Hebrew's "ears" opened to hear God's will or the LXX's "body" to respond to that will. . . . Delitzsch is probably right: the LXX sought to make "digged my ears for me" more intelligible to their Greek readers by translating "shaped a body for me" by which to obey.[126]

All of this fits perfectly into the theory of plenary dynamic inspiration but is hard to explain on a verbal theory. Once more we note that it is the thought that is infallibly conveyed; apparently the exact choice of words is left to the writer. We may very well assume that the inspiring Holy Spirit led the author of Hebrews to quote the Septuagint rather than the Hebrew text, in order to make the truth of the passage more clear to his Christian readers in the first century.

There is another quotation from the Epistle to the Hebrews that follows the Septuagint rather than the Hebrew Masoretic text. It is found in Hebrews 1:6. The line quoted there—"Let all God's angels worship him" (NIV)—does not appear in the Masoretic Hebrew text. But it is found in the Septuagint (in Codex Vaticanus) and in the Dead Sea Scrolls. So this involves the matter of textual criticism. But, again, we may believe that the Holy Spirit led the writer of Hebrews to quote it from the Septuagint.

Sometimes the New Testament writers departed from both the Septuagint and the Hebrew text. One example of this is found in Matthew 11:10. It reads (NIV):

> I will send my messenger ahead of you,
> who will prepare your way before you.

This is a quotation from Malachi 3:1, which says: "See, I will send my messenger, who will prepare the way before me"NIV). Why the change from "me" to "you"? A. B. Bruce says that it is "to make the Messianic reference apparent."[127]

In 1 Peter 2:6 the apostle quotes from Isaiah 28:16 in these words (NIV):

> See, I lay a stone in Zion,
>   a chosen and precious cornerstone,
> and the one who trusts in him
>   will never be put to shame.

When we turn back to Isaiah, however, we find it worded in a slightly different way:

> See, I lay a stone in Zion,
>   a tested stone,
> a precious cornerstone for a sure foundation;
>   the one who trusts will never be dismayed.

Actually, Peter has given us a very free quotation, which does not agree exactly with either the Hebrew or the Septuagint. But the meaning is essentially the same.

One of the weaknesses, of course, of the theory of verbal inspiration lies in the fact that we do not have the autograph of a single book of the Bible. We have only copies. The books of the Old Testament were copied by hand for two thousand and more years—until printing began about 1456. The books of the New Testament were copied for about fourteen hundred years. Practically speaking, it is almost impossible for anyone to copy any lengthy book of the Hebrew Old Testament or the Greek New Testament without making some mistakes. We have over five thousand manuscripts of the Greek New Testament, in whole or in part, and it is generally agreed that no two of them are exactly alike. Only by carefully comparing them can we arrive at a high degree of certainty as to the original text.

Let us look first at the Old Testament. Fortunately the Jews, at least in later times, had such a high regard for the exact words of Scripture that they copied them with meticulous care. So the manuscripts of the Masoretic Hebrew text agree more closely than do the Greek manuscripts of the New Testament.

Years ago negative critics openly asserted, "Our oldest Hebrew manuscript of the Book of Isaiah comes from the tenth century A.D. How do we know that it has the same text as in the time of Christ, to say nothing of what Isaiah wrote way back there?" (Of course they held that he wrote only the first thirty-nine chapters, in the eighth century B.C.).

Fortunately, no scholar today can ask that upsetting question. In 1947 an Arab shepherd boy discovered the first of what came to be known as the Dead Sea Scrolls. The most important of these was the scroll of Isaiah, dated by paleographers at about 125 B.C. When it was compared with our Masoretic text from the Middle Ages, it was found to agree very closely. So we are justified in holding that we have a reliable Hebrew text for the Old Testament.

However, in a dozen or more places there is a somewhat different wording. The Revised Standard Version complete Bible was published in 1952. The careful reader will discover some fourteen footnotes beginning with: "One ancient Ms." Some of the footnotes read: "One ancient Ms Gk." The latter are cases where the Dead Sea Scroll of Isaiah agrees with the Septuagint against the Masoretic Hebrew text. Since the Septuagint and the Dead Sea Scroll of Isaiah both appear to have come from the second century B.C., it seems reasonable and logical to accept their combined testimony against that of a much later Masoretic text.

The situation is somewhat complicated. But we might note some passages where one word is significantly different. In the NIV the second line of Isaiah 49:24 reads:

or captives rescued from the fierce?

A footnote on "fierce" explains: "Dead Sea Scrolls, Septuagint, Vulgate and Syriac; Masoretic Text *righteous*." The NASB has:

Or the captives of a tyrant be rescued?

It carries this footnote: "So ancient versions and DSS; MT reads, the *righteous*." The RSV also has "tyrant." Is it "lawful man" (KJV) or "tyrant" (two opposites)? We can never be absolutely certain.

In the KJV of Isaiah 33:8 the fifth poetic line reads:

he hath despised the cities.

The RSV has:

witnesses are despised.

Similarly the NIV reads:

its witnesses are despised.

The footnote on "witnesses" informs us: "Dead Sea Scrolls; Masoretic Text / *the cities*." The NASB translators chose to retain "cities." It is obvious that we cannot be totally sure as to which was in the original Hebrew text of Isaiah.

Another interesting passage is Isaiah 21:8. In the KJV the first part reads:

And he cried, A lion.

The NASB has:

Then the sentry called *like* a lion.

The RSV reads:

Then he who saw cried.

The NIV says:

And the lookout shouted.

A footnote in the NIV explains, "Dead Sea Scrolls and Syriac; Masoretic Text *A lion*."

In Isaiah 14:4 the last clause reads in the KJV:

the golden city ceased!

The RSV has:

the insolent fury ceased!

Both the RSV and the NIV read "fury." The latter has the footnote: "Dead Sea Scrolls, Septuagint and Syriac; the meaning of the word in the Masoretic Text is uncertain."

It is obvious that we cannot be completely certain about the exact wording of the original Hebrew text of the Old Testament. And this is even more true of the Greek text of the New Testament. It should be quickly said, however, that the basic meaning of the passages involved is still clear. It is the exact words that we cannot always be sure of.

Soon after the discovery of the first Dead Sea Scrolls was made public in 1948, evangelical scholars rejoiced that the essential reliability of the Masoretic Hebrew text had been confirmed beyond cavil. By allowing these manuscripts to be discovered, God effectively shut the mouths of negative critics!

It is hard to understand the very different reaction regarding New Testament discoveries. The KJV is basically a translation of Erasmus's Greek text (slightly revised). Erasmus had only six Greek manuscripts: two of the Gospels, two of Paul's epistles, one of Acts and the General Epistles, and one of Revelation. And not one of them was older than the tenth century A.D. In 1859 Tischendorf discovered Codex Sinaiticus on Mount Sinai. He later persuaded the Roman Catholics to furnish a photographic copy of Codex Vaticanus, which was kept in the Vatican library at Rome. Both of these manuscripts were from the fourth century. In about 1935 a second momentous discovery began to take place: Seventy-five papyrus Greek manuscripts of books of the New Testament have been found, most of them coming from the third century. We now have over five thousand manuscripts of the Greek New Testament, in whole or in part. One would think that all Bible-loving Christians would rejoice over these very significant discoveries, as they did over the Dead Sea Scrolls. But instead of being thankful that we now have much older witnesses to the ancient text of the New Testament, some Fundamentalists have denounced these very early Greek manuscripts as being worthless. For instance, some insist that Textus Receptus, based on medieval manuscripts, is more accurate than Papyrus 66, which gives us most of the text of John's Gospel from about A.D. 200, only about a hundred years after that Gospel was written near the end of the first century. Most reasonable-minded people would agree that Papyrus 66 is apt to be more reliable than one from the thirteenth century that is a result of a thousand years of copying and recopying. Yet some assert that the Textus Receptus is the Word of God verbatim, that it is exactly the same, word for word, as the autographs of the first century. And so they stand by the KJV and condemn almost all recent translations.

All of this brings up another subject closely related to inspiration—that of inerrancy. Every year, as is required when we pay our dues, the members of the Evangelical Theological Society sign a statement declaring that the Bible is the Word of God written and so inerrant in the original autographs. I believe that statement to be true.

But the facts of the case are that we do not have any of the original autographs. Furthermore, we do not have today a completely inerrant text of either the Old Testament or the New Testament. So a not unreasonable question is: "How can we speak of our Bible today as being inerrant?" That it is the infallible Word of God every true evangelical Christian believes. It infallibly teaches us the way of salvation and instructs us in living the Christian life. But we know that there are many passages, especially in the New Testament, where we cannot be certain as to the exact wording of the original text. This does not detract from the religious authority of the Bible, that is, from its infallibility. But it does raise questions as to its inerrancy.

That is why I feel that it is unfortunate that some make the term *inerrancy* the touchstone of orthodoxy, the main criterion as to whether a person is a true Evangelical or not. What more do we need, or should we expect, than an infallible Bible to guide us safely?

Scrivener puts it well. He deals realistically with the methods by which Scripture has been preserved and handed down to us. Here is what he says:

> God *might,* if He would, have stamped His revealed will visibly on the heavens, that all should read it there: He *might* have so completely filled the minds of His servants the Prophets and Evangelists, that they should have become mere passive instruments in the promulgation of His counsel, and the writings they have delivered to us have borne no traces whatever of their individual characters: but for certain causes that we can perceive, and doubtless for others beyond the reach of our capacities, He has chosen to do neither the one nor the other.[128]

Scrivener then deals with "the relation our existing text of the New Testament bears to that which originally came from the hands of the sacred penmen." He says:

> Their autographs *might* have been preserved in the Church as the perfect standards by which all accidental variations of the numberless copies scattered throughout the world should be corrected to the end of time: but we know that these autographs perished utterly in the very infancy of Christian history.[129]

We know that the autographs were not preserved. But how about the copyists? Scrivener deals realistically with this question also. He writes:

Or if it be too much to expect that the autographs of the inspired writers should escape the fate which has overtaken that of every known relique of ancient literature, God *might* have so guided the hand or fixed the devout attention of copyists during the long space of fourteen hundred years before the invention of printing, and of compositors and printers of the Bible for the last four centuries, that not one jot or tittle should have been changed of all that was written therein. Such a course of Providential arrangement we must confess to be quite possible, but it could have been brought about and maintained by nothing short of a continuous, unceasing miracle: by making fallible men (nay, many such in every generation) for one purpose absolutely infallible.[130]

Of course the facts, as we know full well, are that God did not operate that way. Men made mistakes as they copied the sacred Scriptures over the centuries.

We have already noted the fact that the personalities of the various writers are clearly imprinted on what they wrote. Scrivener has a very good discussion of this point:

God willed that His Church should enjoy the benfit of His written word, at once as a rule of doctrine and as a guide unto holy living. For this cause He so enlightened the minds of the Apostles and Evangelists by His Spirit, that they recorded what He had imprinted on their minds or brought to their remembrance, without the risk of error in anything essential to the verity of the Gospel. But this main point once secured, the rest was left, in a great measure, to themselves. The style, the tone, the language, perhaps the special occasion of writing, seem to have depended much on the taste and judgment of the several penmen.[131]

Then Scrivener goes into more detail concerning the specific differences among the New Testament authors. He expresses it this way:

Thus in St. Paul's Epistles we note the profound thinker, the great scholar, the consummate orator: St. John pours forth the simple utterings of his gentle, untutored, affectionate soul: in St. Peter's speeches and letters may be traced the impetuous earnestness of his noble yet not faultless character. Their individual tempers and faculties and intellectual habits are clearly discernible, even while they are speaking to us in the power and inspiration of the Holy Ghost.[132]

Any thoughtful reader of the Bible cannot but be impressed with the accuracy of this characterization. It comes through most strikingly and fully in the Greek. But even in the contemporary style of a good English version today it is very apparent.

In his article "Inspiration and Revelation" in Hasting's *Dictionary of the Apostolic Church,* Sanday begins his discussion of inspiration by citing 1 Corinthians 2:7-16 as "the fundamental passage" on the subject. I will quote from it these verses.

Paul has just affirmed (v. 6) that he speaks a message of wisdom among the mature, but that it is not the wisdom of this age. Then he goes on to say, "No, we speak of God's secret wisdom, a wisdom that has been hidden and that God destined for our glory before time began. None of the rulers of this age understood it, for if they had, they would not have crucified the Lord of glory" (vv. 7-8 NIV). Paul here claims to have a revelation of divine secret wisdom.

How did this revelation come to him? Paul tells us (in vv. 9-10a NIV):

However, as it is written:
  "No eye has seen,
    no ear has heard,
  no mind has conceived
    what God has prepared for those who love him"—
but God has revealed it to us by his Spirit.

Paul declares that he received the revelation of divine wisdom by inspiration of the Holy Spirit. This is the basic truth in the doctrine of inspiration.

The apostle goes on to say in verse 10b: "The Spirit searches all things, even the deep things of God" (NIV). As Sanday notes, we frequently have the problem, in reading Paul's epistles, of knowing when to capitalize the Greek word *pneuma,* since the Greek has no way of indicating this. But rather clearly "Spirit" is correct here.

The contrast between the human spirit and the Holy Spirit is brought out specifically in verse 11: "For who among men knows the thoughts of a man except the man's spirit within him? In the same way no one knows the thoughts of God except the Spirit of God" (NIV). We cannot think God's thoughts except by the help of the Holy Spirit.

Verse 12 carries Paul's argument a step further: "We have not received the spirit of the world but the Spirit who is from God, that we may understand what God has freely given us" (NIV). The apostle constantly needed the help of the Holy Spirit to understand the divine truth that God was giving him.

Then comes the climax, in verse 13: "This is what we speak, not in words taught us by human wisdom but in words taught by the Spirit, expressing spiritual truths in spiritual words" (NIV). Admittedly the last clause may be translated several different ways, as one will quickly see by comparing recent versions.

Sanday discusses at considerable length the significance of this passage. After noting that inspiration has to do both with facts and with the interpretation of facts, he writes:

> We begin by observing that the passage is descriptive specifically of the Christian or apostolic inspiration. It is, indeed, possible to generalize from it and to treat it as applying to the inspiration of the Old Testament as well as the New Testament. Yet the passage implies throughout what we have called the Christian facts—the whole historical series of revelations culminating in Jesus Christ.[133]

Again we face the question of the source of this inspiration. Sanday observes, "If it is asked how he came by his knowledge, the answer is that it was imparted to him by the Holy Spirit acting upon his own spirit."[134]

Then Sanday faces up to the matter we have been discussing at some length: how this inspiration of the Holy Spirit actually takes place. He writes:

> When it is said that the Spirit searches the deep things of God and then bestows a knowledge of these deep things on men, it is not meant that there is a mechanical transference of information. The process is dynamic, and not mechanical. What is meant is that the same Holy Spirit which mirrors, as it were, the consciousness of Deity, so acts upon the human faculties, so stimulates and directs them, as to produce in them a consciousness of God which is after its own pattern.[135]

This pattern is such a suggestion and superintendence of the Spirit of God that the result is the infallible Word of God. This has always been the firm belief of the true church of Jesus Christ, as reflected in the New Testament and repeated by the great fathers of the church.

There is another passage in Paul's epistles that bears on this matter of the divine revelation and so the divine authority of what Paul preached and wrote. In Galatians 1:11–12 (NIV) the apostle declares, "I want you to know, brothers, that the gospel I preached is not something that man made up. I did not receive it from any man, nor was I taught it; rather, I received it by revelation from Jesus Christ."

It is generally recognized that the leading theologian in the New Testament is the apostle Paul. It is his divinely revealed theology on which the church, particularly the Protestant church, has built so heavily across the centuries. And Paul asserts most emphatically that it was not something he thought up; rather, it was God-given. It was of divine, not human, origin; and so it is of full divine authority.

The last three words of verse 12 in the Greek are *apocalypseōs Iesou Christou*. "Jesus Christ" is in the genitive case, which is used several ways. One of the greatest problems that plagues exegetes of the New Testament is the question as to whether a genitive case in any given passage is to be taken as an objective genitive—in this case, revealing Jesus Christ—or as a subjective genitive: Jesus

Christ's revealing the gospel message. Burton prefers the former.[136] Other good commentators opt for the latter. Since we can never be certain as to which Paul intended here, it seems to me the part of wisdom to take it both ways. Jesus Christ had revealed to Paul through the Holy Spirit that He was Son of God and Savior, and this is the heart of the gospel.

In the last discourse of Jesus in the Upper Room the night before His crucifixion, the Master said to His disciples: "All this I have spoken while still with you. But the Counselor, the Holy Spirit whom the Father will send in my name, will teach you all things and will remind you of everything I have said to you" (John 14:25-26 NIV). This was, among other things, the divine guarantee of the inspiration of the Holy Spirit for writing the Gospels of Matthew and John. But this inspiration, the true church has always held, was extended to all writers of the New Testament. And such phrases as "Thus saith the Lord" and "The Lord spoke to me, saying" assure us of the divine inspiration and authority of the Old Testament as well.

E. The Bible, a Divine-Human Book

The Bible is a divine-human book, as Christ is the divine-human Person. This is the key that unlocks the door to an understanding of the true nature of the Scriptures.

God could have sent His Son in adult human form without a human birth. Jesus' body would then have been simply a shell in which was encased the divine nature.

But God in His wisdom did not choose to do it that way. Rather, He caused His Son to be born of a woman. Jesus thus partook of the personality characteristics of His mother—psychologically as well as physically. He not only bore resemblance to her in His facial features but He was influenced by the intellectual and social atmosphere of the home. He was the son of Mary as well as the Son of God.

So it was with the Bible. God could have sent down the Book all inscribed with the complete revelation, bound in black leather, divinity circuit, gold-edged, silk-sewn, India paper. But He did not choose to do so. Instead the light of divine revelation broke in on the soul of Moses, of Samuel, of David, of John. The result is a divinely inspired, humanly written revelation of God's truth for man.

The human authors wrote on sheepskin and goatskin, on papyrus and parchment. They wrote the thoughts of God as best they could understand them by the help of the Holy Spirit.

Just as sunlight when conducted through a prism is broken down into its various rays, so the light of God's truth when filtered through the prisms of human personalities took on the varying slants and interests of those personalities. That is shown not only in the language used—both vocabulary and style—but also in actual thought-forms, in ways of approach, in diversity of emphasis. The Holy Spirit used the varying interests and emphases of the different writers to convey the total of divine revelation in the Bible.

It is unfortunate that too often we see only one side of a truth, and so we actually have only a half-truth. Ask some Evangelicals, "Was Jesus divine or human?" and they will answer emphatically, "Divine!" Ask a humanist the same question and the reply will be, "Human." Both are right and both are wrong. The opposition between Jesus' deity and His humanity exists only in false theological thinking. Jesus was, and is, both human *and* divine.

The same situation is true in regard to the Scriptures. Some conservatives emphasize the *divine* source of the Bible to the extent that they neglect the *human* origin. Some liberals stress the latter and forget—if not actually deny—the former. The Bible did have a human origin; it came from the hands of the men who wrote it. But its ultimate source was divine; the Holy Spirit inspired the writers. It is this that gives it its unique authority as the Word of God.

One person sees only the scribe sitting at a desk, pen in hand, writing the words of Scripture, and he declares, "The Bible is a human book." Another sees only the inspiring Spirit hovering overhead, and he cries, "It is divine!" What we need is to see the whole picture, not just one part of it. The Bible is a divine-human book.

F. Conclusion

After making this examination of a vast subject, I will add a few observations in closing.

1. Just as there is some measure of truth in all theories of the atonement—satisfaction, substitutionary, ransom, governmental, moral influence—and yet no one of these by itself is adequate, so no single view of inspiration conveys the total, and so true, picture. Paul said, "Now I know in part."[137] A like humility should characterize theologians today. At best we see "enigmatically" and we should use caution in speaking dogmatically, lest we go beyond what is written.

2. It seems to me that the idea of illumination is properly included in the understanding of inspiration. Runia says, "The theology of the Reformation, however, has never seen this special operation of the Holy Spirit in the subject as part of inspiration, but always conceived it as a separate work of the Spirit and called it *illumination*."[138] Still, he says, in a "broader sense it would also be possible to call the illumination *inspiration*."[139] But this, he holds, is not the same thing as the inspiration of the Bible. "While the latter refers to the origin of the Scripture, to the *communication* of the revelation, the former or 'subjective' inspiration refers to the *reception* of Holy Scripture, the hearing and understanding of the revelation."[140]

But perhaps Barth has something to say at this point that will be of profit and enrichment to us. He distinguishes two phases in inspiration. The first came when the books of the Bible were written. The second comes when the books are read. And so he concludes:

> The circle which led from the divine benefits to the Apostle instructed by the Spirit and authorized to speak by the Spirit now closes at the hearer of the Apostle, who again by the Spirit is enabled to receive it as is necessary. The hearer, too, in his existence as such is part of the miracle which takes place at this point.[141]

This leads us back to what we noted earlier—that communication involves a full-rounded circuit of subject-object-subject. Without disparaging the authority of the Bible as itself a divine revelation —as Barth does—we yet need to recognize that revelation is not complete unless and until God's Word actually reaches us through the help of the Holy Spirit. The object, the Bible, does not exist for its own sake, but only that it may be a medium of revelation from God to all people. The Scripture is in itself a revelation. But also, and just as importantly, it is a *means* of revelation. The failure to give this aspect its proper place is one of the faults of much of the discussion in evangelical circles. Just as the Bible is both divine and human, so it is both a revelation and a medium of revelation. As noted above, it is correct to say that the Bible *is* the Word of God and also that it *contains* the Word of God. We get further ahead intellectually and spiritually if we use both tracks of truth and do not try to ride a monorail.

3. It seems to me that recognition should be given to the idea of "degrees of inspiration." Reid, in his book *The Authority of Scripture*, rejects the validity and worth of this proposal. He says, "God cannot be thought of as granting greater and smaller quantities of inspiration, if they are inspired words that we have in the Bible."[142] But this appears unrealistic. Certainly a greater measure of inspiration would be required for helping in the writing of lofty passages in Isaiah or Paul's epistles than in guiding a scribe to copy the long genealogical tables of 1 Chronicles.

4. The related questions of inerrancy and infallibility need to be handled with great care, for there is considerable difference of opinion among Evangelicals who

are equally loyal to the inspiration and authority of the Scriptures.

A mediating view that seems to commend itself is expressed thus by a leading Wesleyan theologian, A. M. Hills:

> What is the infallibility we claim for the Bible? It is infallible as regards the purpose for which it was written. It is infallible as a revelation of God's saving love in Christ to a wicked world. It infallibly guides all honest and willing and seeking souls to Christ, to holiness, and to heaven.[143]

In 1938 Samuel Cartledge put out a book entitled *A Conservative Introduction to the New Testament.* In it he says, "The Conservative believes that inspiration guarantees the infallible accuracy of the Scriptures in matters of faith and practice."[144]

In his later work, *The Bible: God's Word to Man,* he pursues this point at considerable length. He asks this question: "Does perfection and final authority extend beyond matters of faith and practice to every other area as well?" His answer is negative. He allows for errors in the Bible in the realms of rhetoric—this seems to me largely irrelevant—history, and science.[145] My own reaction is that Cartledge has made more concessions than the data demands. He confesses contradictions in places where it seems that the historical accounts can be harmonized by careful hermeneutics.

Nevertheless—and this is the point I wish to make here—the real importance of the infallibility of the Bible attaches to its teaching in the field of religion. It is true that it is historically grounded and its history is certainly far from being unimportant. But the real issue is this: Does the Bible infallibly give us the truth in relation to man's salvation? Cartledge would say yes, and so would all Evangelicals.

5. We come finally to the matter of verbal versus dynamic inspiration. One finds this amazing confession from Karl Barth in his commentary on Romans:

> From the preface to the first edition onwards, I have never attempted to conceal the fact that my manner of interpretation has certain affinities with the old doctrine of Verbal Inspiration. As expounded by Calvin, the doctrine seems to me at least worthy of careful consideration as capable of leading to spiritual apprehension and I have already made it clear how I have, in fact, made use of it. Is there any way of penetrating the heart of a document—of any document—except on the assumption that its spirit will speak to our spirit through the actual written words?[146]

The expression "verbal inspiration" does not mean the same thing to all. Cartledge observes that it may be used in two senses. He writes, "To some people it means complete inerrancy or even dictation, but to others it means simply that God's inspiration took care of the words as well as the ideas back of the words."[147] He adds, "It is almost impossible to express any ideas without words, even between two people living at the same time."[148]

Nida, in his lectures already referred to, pointed out the important truth that no one word ever means the same thing to two people. Everyone who has worked much with languages knows that no word means exactly the same thing when translated into another language. Nida declared that on the basis of tests it has been ascertained that people operating with exactly the same symbols achieve only about 80 percent of perfect communication. Then he made this significant observation: "Formal equivalence cannot be achieved. All we can hope for is a dynamic equivalence."

All this seems to be wholly relevant to the problem of inspiration. What we should look for in the Scriptures is not a formal equivalence but a dynamic equivalence. The *words* are not the ultimate reality, but rather the *thoughts* that they are intended to convey.

No one can read Paul's epistles carefully, especially in the Greek, without sensing his acute struggle, almost an agonizing one at times, to try to find words accurate and adequate enough to express the great eternal truths that crowded into his mind under the inspiration of the Spirit.

This rather apparent phenomenon accords well with the view of plenary dynamic inspiration—much better than it does with plenary verbal inspiration.

That is why some prefer the term "plenary inspiration" to "verbal inspiration." It conserves the full divine authority of the Bible while at the same time avoiding the almost inevitable mechanical implications, or at least overtones, that attach themselves to the word *verbal*.

We live in a complex day. Too many people feel that there are only two alternatives in an evaluation of the Scriptures. One alternative is a fatalistic skepticism, or a wholesale negative criticism that amounts to the same thing. The other is taking false refuge in oversimplification.

But is there no third alternative? Can we not face fully and realistically the complicated and often confusing data that confronts us and find by faith and the honest, strenuous use of the minds God has given us a sane solution in an insane age?

Humbly let us say with John Wesley:

> I have thought, I am a creature of a day, passing through life as an arrow through the air, I am a spirit come from God, and returning to God. . . . I want to know one thing—the way to heaven; how to land safe on that happy shore. God himself has condescended to teach the way: For this very end he came from heaven. He hath written it down in a book. O give me that book! At any price, give me the book of God! I have it: Here is knowledge enough for me. Let me be *homo unius libri*.[149]

NOTES

[1] J. I. Packer, "Revelation," in *The New Bible Dictionary*, ed. J. D. Douglas (Grand Rapids: Eerdmans, 1962), p. 1090.

[2] Bernard Ramm, *Special Revelation and the Word of God* (Grand Rapids: Eerdmans, 1961), p. 17.

[3] C. M. Horne, "Revelation," in *The Zondervan Pictorial Encyclopedia of the Bible*, ed. Merrill C. Tenney, 5 vols. (Grand Rapids: Zondervan, 1975), 5:86.

[4] Ibid., p. 88.

[5] Benjamin B. Warfield, "Revelation," in *The International Standard Bible Encyclopaedia* (hereafter, ISBE), ed. James Orr, rev. ed., 5 vols (1929; reprint ed., Grand Rapids: Eerdmans, 1960), 4:2575.

[6] Ibid.

[7] George A. Turner, "John Wesley as an Interpreter of Scripture," in *Inspiration and Interpretation*, ed. John F. Walvoord (Grand Rapids: Eerdmans, 1957), p. 159.

[8] Ibid., p. 160.

[9] John Wesley, *Explanatory Notes Upon the New Testament* (reprint ed., London: Epworth, 1941), pp. 8-9.

[10] Ibid., p. 9.

[11] Bernard Ramm, *Special Revelation and the Word of God* (Grand Rapids: Eerdmans, 1961), p. 185.

[12] Ibid.

[13] Ibid., p. 186.

[14] Ibid.

[15] F. W. Farrar, *The Epistle of Paul the Apostle to the Hebrews*, Cambridge Greek Testament (Cambridge: Cambridge University Press, 1894), p. 24.

[16] Ibid., p. 25.

[17] Ibid.

[18] B. F. Westcott, *The Epistle to the Hebrews*, 2nd ed. (London: Macmillan, 1892), p. 5.

[19] Marcus Dods, "The Epistle to the Hebrews," *The Expositor's Greek Testament* (Grand Rapids: Eerdmans, n.d.), 4:247-48.

[20] Ibid., p. 249.

[21] John McClintock and James Strong, eds., *Cyclopaedia of Biblical, Theological and Ecclesiastical Literature*, 12 vols. (reprint ed., Grand Rapids: Baker, 1970), 8:1061.

[22] Raymond Abba, *The Nature and Authority of the Bible* (Philadelphia: Muhlenberg, 1958), p. xi.

[23] James Orr, *Revelation and Inspiration* (reprint ed., Grand Rapids: Baker, 1969), p. 159.

[24] Alan Richardson, *Preface to Bible Study* (Philadelphia: Westminster, 1944), p. 36.

[25] Ibid., p. 37.

[26] Webster's *New International Dictionary of the English Language*, 2nd ed. (Springfield, Mass.: Merriam, 1943), p. 1286.

[27] Carl F. H. Henry, "Inspiration," in *Baker's Dictionary of Theology*, ed. E. F. Harrison (Grand Rapids: Baker, 1960), p. 286.

28. Benjamin B. Warfield, *The Inspiration and Authority of the Bible* (Philadelphia: Presbyterian and Reformed, 1948), p. 131.

29. Merrill C. Tenney, ed., *The Bible—The Living Word of Revelation* (Grand Rapids: Zondervan, 1968), p. 75.

30. Walter Lock, *A Critical and Exegetical Commentary on the Pastoral Epistles,* The International Critical Commentary (Edinburgh: T. & T. Clark, 1924), p. 110.

31. E. K. Simpson, *The Pastoral Epistles* (Grand Rapids: Eerdmans, 1954), p. 150.

32. Benjamin B. Warfield, "Inspiration," in ISBE, 3:1474.

33. Joseph B. Mayor, *The Epistle of St. Jude and the Second Epistle of St. Peter* (Grand Rapids: Baker, 1965), p. 115.

34. Warfield, *Inspiration and Authority,* p. 137.

35. Tenney, ed., *The Bible,* p. 75.

36. Ibid., p. 79.

37. Ibid., pp. 78–79.

38. "The Epistle of S. Clement to the Corinthians," chap. 45, *The Apostolic Fathers,* ed. J. B. Lightfoot (London: Macmillan, 1893), p. 76.

39. Polycarp, "Epistle to the Philippians," chap. 12, *The Apostolic Fathers,* ed. J. B. Lightfoot (London: Macmillan, 1893), p. 181.

40. Justin, "Dialogue with Trypho," LXV, *The Ante-Nicene Fathers* (reprint ed., Grand Rapids: Eerdmans, 1979), 1:230.

41. Ibid., 1:276.

42. Irenaeus, "Against Heresies," III.16.2. *Ante-Nicene Fathers,* 1:444.

43. Hippolytus, "Christ and the Antichrist," 2. *Ante-Nicene Fathers,* 5:204.

44. Clement, "Stromata," VII.16. *Ante-Nicene Fathers,* 2:553.

45. Origen, "De Principus," IV.1.8. *Ante-Nicene Fathers,* 4:335–36.

46. Ibid., IV.1.9. *Ante-Nicene Fathers,* 4:357.

47. Eusebius, *Ecclesiastical History,* VI.14.7.

48. Alan Richardson, *Preface to Bible Study* (Philadelphia: Westminster, 1944), p. 25.

49. W. Sanday, *Inspiration,* 3rd ed. (London: Longmans, Green, 1896), pp. 392–93.

50. Ibid., p. 34.

51. A. D. R. Polman, *The Word of God According to St. Augustine,* trans. A. J. Pomerans (Grand Rapids: Eerdmans, 1961), p. 40.

52. Ibid., pp. 41–42.

53. Martin Luther, *Works* (Philadelphia: United Lutheran Publication, 1915–32), 3:337.

54. Ibid., 2:261.

55. H. H. Kramm, *The Theology of Martin Luther* (London: James Clark, n.d.), p. 117.

56. James Mackinnon, *Luther and the Reformation* (London: Longmans, Green, 1930), 4:303.

57. Ibid.

58. Martin Luther, *Works,* ed. J. Pelikan (St. Louis: Concordia, 1956), 13:81.

59. Kramm, *Theology of Martin Luther,* p. 117.

60. John Calvin, *Institutes of the Christian Religion,* trans. John Allen (Grand Rapids: Eerdmans, 1949), I, vi, 2 (1:82).

61. Ibid., I, vii, 4 (1:90).

62. Ibid., I, vii, 1.

63. Kenneth S. Kantzer, "Calvin and the Holy Scriptures" in *Inspiration and Interpretation,* ed. John F. Walvoord (Grand Rapids: Eerdmans, 1957), p. 140, n. 97.

64. Philip Schaff, *The Creeds of Christendom* (New York: Harper and Brothers, 1878), 3:362.

65. Ibid., pp. 526–27.

66. Ibid., p. 602.

67. Ibid., p. 603.

68. Charles Hodge, *Systematic Theology* (Grand Rapids: Eerdmans, 1940), 1:156–57.

69. Ibid., p. 165.

70. Benjamin B. Warfield, *Inspiration and Authority of the Bible,* ed. Samuel G. Craig (Philadelphia: Presbyterian and Reformed, 1948), p. 173.

71. R. Laird Harris, *Inspiration and Canonicity of the Bible* (Grand Rapids: Zondervan, 1957), pp. 83–84.

72. Edward J. Young, *Thy Word Is Truth* (Grand Rapids: Eerdmans, 1957), chaps. 5–7.

73. Ibid., p. 20.

74. Ibid., p. 27.

75. Ibid., p. 45.

76. Ibid., pp. 48–49.

77. R. Laird Harris, "The Problem of Communication," in *The Bible—The Living Word of God,* ed. Merrill C. Tenney (Grand Rapids: Zondervan, 1968), p. 89.

78. Ibid., p. 90.

79. Ibid.

80. Ibid., p. 91.

81. Ibid.

82. Harris, *Inspiration and Canonicity,* pp. 83–84.

83. Karl Barth, *Church Dogmatics* (New York: Scribner, n.d.), 1:520.

84. Ibid., 1:509.

85. Karl Barth, *Epistle to the Romans,* trans. Edwyn C. Hoskyns (London: Oxford University Press, 1933), p. 19.

86. Klaas Runia, *Karl Barth's Doctrine of Holy Scripture* (Grand Rapids: Eerdmans, 1962), p. 65.

87. Ibid.

88. Ibid., p. 74.

89. Emil Brunner, *The Divine-Human Encounter*, trans. A. W. Loos (Philadelphia: Westminster, 1943), p. 172.

90. John Baillie, *The Idea of Revelation in Recent Thought* (New York: Columbia University Press, 1956), p. 111.

91. Ibid., p. 32.

92. Ibid., p. 119.

93. James Arminius, *Writings*, trans. James Nichols and W. R. Bagnall (Grand Rapids: Baker, 1956), 2:15.

94. Ibid., 2:16.

95. John Wesley, *Explanatory Notes Upon the New Testament* (London: Epworth, 1941), p. 9.

96. Ibid.

97. Ibid., p. 794.

98. Adam Clarke, *The New Testament of Our Lord and Saviour Jesus Christ* (New York: Methodist Book Concern, n.d.), 1:8.

99. Ibid., pp. 9-10.

100. W. B. Pope, *Compendium of Christian Theology*, 2nd ed. (New York: Phillips and Hunt, 1881), pp. 174-75.

101. Ibid., pp. 182-83.

102. Ibid., p. 189.

103. Thomas N. Ralston, *Elements of Divinity*, rev. ed. (Nashville: Cokesbury, 1924), p. 597.

104. Ibid., p. 598.

105. Ibid.

106. John Miley, *Systematic Theology* (New York: Eaton & Mains, 1894), 2:484.

107. Ibid., pp. 486-87.

108. A. M. Hills, *Fundamental Christian Theology* (1931; reprint ed., Salem, Ohio: Schmul, 1980), 1:119.

109. Ibid., p. 123.

110. Ibid., p. 124.

111. Ibid.

112. Ibid., p. 126.

113. Ibid., p. 127.

114. H. Orton Wiley, *Christian Theology* (Kansas City, Mo.: Beacon Hill, 1940), 1:169.

115. Ibid., p. 171.

116. Ibid.

117. Ibid., pp. 176-77.

118. Augustus Hopkins Strong, *Systematic Theology* (Philadelphia: Judson, 1907), 1:196.

119. Augustine, *De Consensu Evangelistarum*, II, 28.

120. Ibid., p. 67.

121. Robert H. Pfeiffer, *Introduction to the Old Testament* (New York: Harper and Brothers, 1941).

122. D. Moody Smith, Jr., "The Use of the Old Testament in the New," in *The Use of the Old Testament in the New and Other Essays,* ed. James M. Efird (Durham, N.C.: Duke University Press, 1972), p. 9.

123. B. F. Westcott, *The Epistle to the Hebrews*, 2nd ed. (London: Macmillan, 1892), p. 308.

124. Marcus Dods, "The Epistle to the Hebrews," *The Expositor's Greek Testament* (Grand Rapids: Eerdmans, n.d.), 4:343.

125. Henry Alford, *The Greek Testament,* rev. E. F. Harrison (Chicago: Moody, 1958), 4:188.

126. R. C. H. Lenski, *The Interpretation of the Epistle to the Hebrews and of the Epistle of James* (Columbus, Ohio: Wartburg, 1946), p. 328.

127. A. B. Bruce, "The Synoptic Gospels," *The Expositor's Greek Testament* (Grand Rapids: Eerdmans, n.d.), 1:172.

128. Frederick H. Scrivener, *A Plain Introduction to the Criticism of the New Testament* (Cambridge: Deighton, Bell, 1861), p. 2.

129. Ibid.

130. Ibid., pp. 2-3.

131. Ibid., pp. 1-2.

132. Ibid., p. 2.

133. William Sanday, "Inspiration and Revelation," in *Dictionary of the Apostolic Church,* ed. James Hastings (New York: Scribner, 1919), 1:614.

134. Ibid.

135. Ibid.

136. Ernest DeWitt Burton, *A Critical and Exegetical Commentary on the Epistle to the Galatians,* The International Critical Commentary (Edinburgh: T. & T. Clark, 1921), pp. 41-43.

137. 1 Corinthians 13:12.

138. Klaas Runia, *Karl Barth's Doctrine of Holy Scripture* (Grand Rapids: Eerdmans, 1962), p. 145.

139. Ibid., p. 146.

140. Ibid.

141. Karl Barth, *Church Dogmatics* (New York: Scribner, n.d.), 1:516.

142. J. K. S. Reid, *The Authority of Scripture* (London: Methuen, 1957), p. 161.

143. A. M. Hills, *Fundamental Christian Theology* (Pasadena: Kinne, 1931), 1:134.

144. Samuel A. Cartledge, *A Conservative Introduction to the New Testament* (Grand Rapids: Zondervan, 1938), p. 193.

[145] Samuel A. Cartledge, *The Bible: God's Word to Man* (Philadelphia: Westminster, 1951), pp. 35-36.

[146] Karl Barth, *The Epistle to the Romans,* trans. Edwin C. Hoskyns (London: Oxford University Press, 1933), p. 16.

[147] Cartledge, *The Bible,* p. 57.

[148] Ibid.

[149] John Wesley, *Works,* 14 vols. (Grand Rapids: Zondervan, n.d.), 5:3.

DISCUSSION QUESTIONS

1. What do we learn about God from general revelation?
2. Why do we need a special revelation?
3. In what way does the Bible differ from all other books?
4. How can we know that the Bible is the inspired Word of God?
5. Why was it necessary to fix the canon of both the Old and New Testaments?
6. What do we mean by divine inspiration?
7. How does the Holy Spirit help us as we read the Scriptures?
8. How should we pray each time before we begin reading the Bible?
9. In what ways is the neoorthodox view of inspiration deficient?
10. Why is a high view of inspiration important?
11. In what ways is the Bible human?
12. In what ways is it divine?

RECOMMENDATIONS FOR FURTHER READING

Abba, Raymond. *The Nature and Authority of the Bible.* Philadelphia: Muhlenberg, 1958.

Baillie, John. *The Idea of Revelation in Recent Thought.* New York: Columbia University Press, 1956.

Cartledge, Samuel. *The Bible: God's Word to Man.* Philadelphia: Westminster, 1951.

Harris, R. Laird. *Inspiration and Canonicity of the Bible.* Grand Rapids: Zondervan, 1957.

Orr, James. *Revelation and Inspiration.* Reprint ed. Grand Rapids: Baker, 1969.

Sanday, William. *Inspiration,* 3rd ed. London: Longmans, Green, 1896.

Tenney, Merrill C., ed. *The Bible—The Living Word of Revelation.* Grand Rapids: Zondervan, 1968.

Warfield, Benjamin B. *The Inspiration and Authority of the Bible.* Philadelphia: Presbyterian and Reformed, 1948.

Young, Edward J. *Thy Word Is Truth.* Grand Rapids: Eerdmans, 1957.

BIBLIOGRAPHY

Abba, Raymond. *The Nature and Authority of the Bible.* Philadelphia: Muhlenberg, 1958.

Alford, Henry. *The Greek Testament.* Revised by E. F. Harrison. Chicago: Moody, 1958.

Arminius, James. *Writings.* Translated by James Nichols and W. R. Bagnall. Grand Rapids: Baker, 1956.

Baillie, John. *The Idea of Revelation in Recent Thought.* New York: Columbia University Press, 1956.

Barth, Karl. *Church Dogmatics.* New York: Scribner, n.d.

_____. *Epistle to the Romans.* Translated by Edwyn C. Hoskyns. London: Oxford University Press, 1933.

Bruce, A. B. "The Synoptic Gospels," *The Expositor's Greek Testament*. Grand Rapids: Eerdmans, n.d.

Brunner, Emil. *The Divine-Human Encounter*. Translated by A. W. Loos. Philadelphia: Westminster, 1943.

Burton, Ernest DeWitt. *A Critical and Exegetical Commentary on the Epistle to the Galatians,* The International Critical Commentary. Edinburgh: T. & T. Clark, 1921.

Calvin, John. *Institutes of the Christian Religion*. Translated by John Allen. Grand Rapids: Eerdmans, 1949.

Cartledge, Samuel. *A Conservative Introduction to the New Testament*. Grand Rapids: Zondervan, 1938.

———. *The Bible: God's Word to Man*. Philadelphia: Westminster, 1951.

Clarke, Adam. *The New Testament of Our Lord and Saviour Jesus Christ*. New York: Methodist Book Concern, n.d.

Dods, Marcus. "The Epistle to the Hebrews," *The Expositor's Greek Testament*. Grand Rapids: Eerdmans, n.d.

Farrar, F. W. *The Epistle of Paul the Apostle to the Hebrews,* Cambridge Greek Testament. Cambridge: University Press, 1894.

Harris, R. Laird. *Inspiration and Canonicity of the Bible*. Grand Rapids: Zondervan, 1957.

———. "The Problem of Communication," *The Bible—the Living Word of God*. Edited by Merrill C. Tenney. Grand Rapids: Zondervan, 1968.

Henry, Carl F. H. "Inspiration." In *Baker's Dictionary of Theology*. Edited by E. F. Harrison. Grand Rapids: Baker, 1960.

Hills, A. M. *Fundamental Christian Theology*. 1931. Reprint ed. Salem, Ohio: Schmul, 1980.

Hodge, Charles. *Systematic Theology*. Grand Rapids: Eerdmans, 1940.

Horne, C. M. "Revelation." In *The Zondervan Pictorial Encyclopedia of the Bible*. Edited by Merrill C. Tenney. Grand Rapids: Zondervan, 1975.

Kantzer, Kenneth S. "Calvin and the Holy Scriptures." In *Inspiration and Interpretation*. Edited by John F. Walvoord. Grand Rapids: Eerdmans, 1957.

Kramm, H. H. *The Theology of Martin Luther*. London: James Clarke, n.d.

Lenski, R. C. H. *The Interpretation of the Epistle to the Hebrews and of the Epistle of James*. Columbus, Ohio: Wartburg, 1946.

Lightfoot, J. B., ed. *The Apostolic Fathers*. London: Macmillan, 1893.

Lock, Walter. *A Critical and Exegetical Commentary on the Pastoral Epistles,* The International Critical Commentary. Edinburgh: T. & T. Clark, 1924.

Luther, Martin. *Works*. Philadelphia: United Lutheran Publication, 1915–32.

McClintock, John, and Strong, James, eds., *Cyclopaedia of Biblical, Theological and Ecclesiastical Literature*. Reprint ed. Grand Rapids: Baker, 1970.

Mackinnon, James. *Luther and the Reformation*. London: Longmans, Green, 1930.

Mayor, Joseph B. *The Epistle of St. Jude and the Second Epistle of St. Peter*. Grand Rapids: Baker, 1965.

Miley, John. *Systematic Theology*. New York: Eaton & Mains, 1894.

Orr, James. *Revelation and Inspiration*. Grand Rapids: Baker, 1969. Reprint.

Packer, J. I. "Revelation," *The New Bible Dictionary*. Edited by J. D. Douglas. Grand Rapids: Eerdmans, 1962.

Pfeiffer, Robert H. *Introduction to the Old Testament*. New York: Harper and Brothers, 1941.

Polman, A. D. R. *The Word of God According to St. Augustine*. Translated by A. J. Pomerans. Grand Rapids: Eerdmans, 1961.

Pope, W. B. *Compendium of Christian Theology*. 2nd ed. New York: Phillips & Hunt, 1881.

Ralston, Thomas N. *Elements of Divinity*. Rev. ed. Nashville: Cokesbury, 1924.

Reid, J. K. S. *The Authority of Scripture*. London: Methuen, 1957.

Richardson, Alan. *Preface to Bible Study*. Philadelphia: Westminster, 1944.

Runia, Klaas. *Karl Barth's Doctrine of Holy Scripture*. Grand Rapids: Eerdmans, 1962.

Sanday, William. *Inspiration,* 3rd ed. London: Longmans, Green, 1896.

Schaff, Philip. *The Creeds of Christendom*. New York: Harper and Brothers, 1878.

Scrivener, Frederick H. *A Plain Introduction to the Criticism of the New Testament*. Cambridge: Deighton, Bell, 1861.

Simpson, E. K. *The Pastoral Epistles*. Grand Rapids: Eerdmans, 1954.

Smith, D. Moody, Jr. "The Use of the Old Testament in the New." In *The Use of the Old Testament in the New and Other Essays*. Edited by James M. Efird. Durham, N.C.: Duke University Press, 1972.

Strong, Augustus Hopkins. *Systematic Theology*. Philadelphia: Judson, 1907.

Tenney, Merrill C., ed. *The Bible—The Living Word of Revelation*. Grand Rapids: Zondervan, 1968.

Turner, George A. "John Wesley as an Interpreter of Scripture." In *Inspiration and Interpretation*. Edited by John F. Walvoord. Grand Rapids: Eerdmans, 1957.

Warfield, Benjamin B. *The Inspiration and Authority of the Bible*. Philadelphia: Presbyterian and Reformed, 1948.

———. "Revelation." In *The International Standard Bible Encyclopaedia*. Rev. ed. Chicago: Severance, 1929.

Wesley, John. *Explanatory Notes Upon the New Testament*. London: Epworth, 1941. Reprint.

———. *Works*. Grand Rapids: Zondervan, n.d.

Westcott, B. F. *The Epistle to the Hebrews*. 2nd ed. London: Macmillan, 1892.

Wiley, H. Orton. *Christian Theology*. Kansas City, Mo.: Beacon Hill, 1940.

Young, Edward J. *Thy Word Is Truth*. Grand Rapids: Eerdmans, 1957.

CHAPTER 9

CHRISTOLOGY:
The Incarnate Word of God

Charles R. Wilson

Charles R. Wilson is Professor of Religion at Taylor University, Upland, Indiana. He has the following degrees: M.A. from Syracuse University and Ph.D. from Vanderbilt University, Nashville, Tennessee. Before taking up his present position, he served as a pastor in Wesleyan churches in Oklahoma, Kansas, and Ohio and taught courses in Houghton College, Houghton, New York.

Dr. Wilson has written part 2 of volume 1 of the Wesleyan Bible Commentary. *He is a member of the Wesleyan Theological Society and the Society of Biblical Literature.*

CONTENTS

INTRODUCTION / 331

I. BIBLICAL EVIDENCE / 331
    A. The Scripture / 331
        1. The identity of Jesus Christ in the Gospels / 331
        2. The claim that Jesus Christ is the unique God-man / 332
            a. Jesus' self-understanding / 333
            b. Jesus' extraordinary vocation / 335
        3. The testimony of the Epistles and Revelation / 338
    B. John Wesley and the Evidence From Scripture / 338

II. HISTORICAL CONTROVERSY / 339
    A. Developments in the Christological Controversy / 339
    B. Decision of Chalcedon in A.D. 451 / 340

III. JOHN WESLEY'S CHRISTOLOGY / 342
    A. The Historical Setting / 342
        1. The English Reformation / 342
        2. The Enlightenment / 343
    B. John Wesley's Experience of Christ / 344
    C. John Wesley's Teaching Concerning Christ / 346
        1. He adhered to the Chalcedonian creed and to the Thirty-nine Articles of the Church of England / 346
        2. He set the person of Christ always in the context of the work of Christ / 347
        3. He linked the person of Christ with the distinctive Wesleyan teaching, namely, Christian perfection / 348

IV. CONTEMPORARY CHRISTOLOGY / 350
    A. Methods of Research and Study / 351
        1. The traditional method of orthodoxy / 351
        2. The historical-criticism method of liberalism / 351
        3. The radical "form criticism" method in biblical studies / 352
    B. Christology in Crisis / 353

- **C.** A Contemporary Christology With a Wesleyan Influence / 356
  1. The experience of salvation by faith in Jesus Christ / 356
  2. The tradition of connecting salvation and christology / 357
  3. The importance of the Incarnation for christology / 362
  4. The offices of Christ / 363
     a. The prophetic office / 364
     b. The priestly office / 364
     c. The kingly office / 364
  5. The estates of Christ / 364
     a. The state of humiliation / 364
     b. The state of exaltation / 365

NOTES / 367

DISCUSSION QUESTIONS / 368

RECOMMENDATIONS FOR FURTHER READING / 368

BIBLIOGRAPHY / 369

CHRISTOLOGY

The Incarnate Word of God

INTRODUCTION

Essential to the study of christology, that is, the person of Christ, is faith in the biblical sources as reliable and authoritative. Anselm expressed the approach of the mainstream of Christianity in this way: "I believe, in order that I may understand." Faith is that personal activity that is more than sense experience. "Faith is being sure of what we hope for and certain of what we do not see" (Heb. 11:1).*

Viewing the Bible as the Word of God in the words of men, as George E. Ladd proposes, has two important implications for our study.[1] First, the Bible in the words of men implies a historical and human element, which is open to historical inquiry. Second, the Bible as the Word of God implies that transcendent, divine element, which is recognized by faith.

In like manner, christology is a study of the Word of God incarnate, namely, that which is historical and human as well as that which is transcendent and divine. The authoritative source for the knowledge of Christ, the living Word, is the Bible, the written Word. Study of the Bible requires intense and disciplined exegesis and includes the responsive activity of faith, rather than doubt and skepticism. Disciplined study may require rational deliberation in arriving at conclusions and decision. Included in the discipline of study is the activity of faith.

I. BIBLICAL EVIDENCE

A. The Scripture

Our particular study, christology, is dependent on the evidence from biblical sources. This study is brought to its sharpest focus by the question, Who is Jesus Christ?

1. The identity of Jesus Christ in the Gospels Jesus Christ is the name of that particular person born of Mary, who was betrothed to Joseph. His name Jesus refers to the specific characteristic of human nature. His name Christ designates Him the "Anointed One," the Hebrew term being *Messiah*. In the Old Testament there is the expectation of the coming of the Lord's Anointed One, the *Messiah* of God. In the

---

*The New International Version is the source of Scripture quotations in this chapter. Used by permission.

New Testament this expectation is expressed by the Greek term *Christos,* that is *Christ.*

Christology begins with the advent of Deity into humanity. Incarnation is the divine act of taking on flesh, or, to put it more adequately, taking on human nature. The prologue of the Gospel of John states, "The Word became flesh and lived for a while among us" (John 1:14; cf. 2 Cor. 5:19; Phil. 2:6, 7; 1 John 1:1–2). Incarnation is Deity joined in inseparable union with humanity, God joined with man in one person.

The four Gospels are very instructive regarding the identity of Jesus Christ. The first three Gospels are designated synoptic Gospels for a very definite reason, namely, they all portray Jesus from a common or similar point of view. That similar viewpoint may be identified as one that gives emphasis to the historical and the human. Jesus was a human being who lived during a specific period in history. The reason for this emphasis of the Synoptics was the need in the early church for recording the historical account that was proclaimed orally by those who had been eyewitnesses of Jesus and His work or who had heard about Him from eyewitnesses. Emphasis was given to the fact that Jesus was a person firmly rooted in the historical and living a true humanity. This was not to be indifferent to acknowledging Jesus as the divine Christ, for that was affirmed without equivocation.

The point of view of the fourth Gospel has never been identified with that of the Synoptics. The distinctly different point of view of this Gospel is clearly expressed in the key verses:

> Jesus did many other miraculous signs in the presence of his disciples, which are not recorded in this book. But these are written that you may believe that Jesus is the Christ, the Son of God, and that by believing you may have life in his name (John 20:30–31; cf. 21:25).

John's Gospel views the historical Jesus as the divine Christ. When this emphasis given by the fourth Gospel is joined with the emphasis given by the Synoptics, there is the clear portrayal by the four Gospels of Jesus being fully human and fully divine.

Having noted that the purpose of the fourth Gospel is to set forth Jesus as truly divine, we turn to note the purpose of one of the Synoptics, namely, Luke. He writes:

> Many have undertaken to draw up an account of the things that have been fulfilled among us, just as they were handed down to us by those who from the first were eyewitnesses and servants of the word. Therefore, since I myself have carefully investigated everything from the beginning, it seemed good also to me to write an orderly account for you, most excellent Theophilus, so that you may know the certainty of the things you have been taught (Luke 1:1–4).

It is clear that Luke intends to give a historical emphasis to his account. Although Matthew and Mark lack the explicitness of Luke, we assume that, because they are Synoptics, their purpose is the same as Luke's, with some expected variations.

2. The claim that Jesus Christ is the unique God-man In the light of the purpose of the fourth Gospel and the purpose of the Synoptics, we are confronted with the claim of the four Gospels that Jesus Christ is the unique God-man. At this point it is necessary to recognize that there exists in modern scholarship of the Bible a major controversy regarding the interpretation of the evidence we are about to consider. On the one hand, there is the orthodox critical view, which regards highly the inspiration of the Bible and declares that the evidence of Jesus' self-understanding comes directly from Jesus Himself through reliable Gospel accounts written by faithful eyewitnesses under divine inspiration. On the other hand, there is the modern radical critical view, which proposes that the evidence regarding Jesus' self-understanding is really evidence regarding the understanding the early church had concerning Jesus. This understanding, this view declares, has been projected back to Jesus by the Gospel writers as though the understanding had originated with Him, whereas, in fact, it originated with the early church. Accordingly, the Gospels record merely the understanding the early church had of Jesus. The result of this radical critical view is that there is no record of the understanding that Jesus had of Himself.

a. Jesus' self-understanding The evidence we are about to examine will be viewed in the light of the orthodox critical view rather than the radical modern critical view. This evidence may be conveniently considered under two points: (1) the names He applied to Himself and (2) the "I am" sayings, which are found in John's Gospel but do not appear in the Synoptics.

Turning to the first point, namely, the names Jesus applied to Himself, we discover that He used the name *Son of Man* more frequently than any other. In fact, it appears to have been His favorite. This name appears approximately seventy times in the Synoptics. It was on the lips of Jesus from the beginning of His public ministry (Mark 2:10), and its usage increased in frequency as Jesus neared the end of His ministry. After the great confession of Peter (Mark 8:29) the name had increasing significance.

From where did Jesus get this name? Jesus Himself has not indicated. The name appears in Ezekiel some ninety times, where it refers to the prophet himself. It also appears in Daniel where the prophet's vision is recorded. Daniel said that he saw one like a Son of Man, who was given a kingdom (Dan. 7:13). We do not know with certainty from where Jesus got this name; however, H. D. McDonald considers that Daniel 7:13 is accepted by general consent to be the source.[2] McDonald's own view seems less precise: "The truth is, perhaps, that Jesus derived it partly from the Old Testament and partly from His own messianic consciousness."[3]

It is obvious that such a title as Son of Man would identify Jesus as a member of the human race. Yet in the Old Testament the name has more than one meaning. This makes for ambiguity. One meaning is found in the Psalms, where the psalmist exclaims, "What is man that you are mindful of him, the son of man that you care for him?" (Ps. 8:4; cf. Heb. 2:6). The obvious meaning is a reference to the human race. A second meaning is found in Daniel 7:13: "In my vision at night I looked, and there before me was one like a son of man, coming with the clouds of heaven. He approached the Ancient of Days and was led into his presence." Here, the name evidently refers to the LORD's Messiah.

In addition to the fact that this name has multiple meanings, it appears that it had a multiple use by Jesus' contemporaries. Thus there was a fluidity about its meaning. It provided Jesus with a name that He could give new messianic meaning and apply to Himself.

During the Old Testament period the term *Messiah* and its reference to the Anointed One anticipated a divinely anointed leader who would usher in the kingdom of God and rule as the LORD's Anointed. The popular conception of the Messiah among the contemporaries of Jesus was that of a political and military leader in the tradition of the great King David. This new leader would bring in the new age in which God would reign. In fact, it was this expectation that was the unifying feature in all messianic expectations.

In the light of this popular contemporary expectation of the Messiah, Jesus entered His ministry intent on revealing Himself as the Messiah. Yet He was widely misunderstood. His family, His friends, His enemies—all misunderstood Him. An example of this misunderstanding is evident in a study of Mark 8–10, where Jesus is shown teaching His disciples the meaning of His messiahship, for they were continually misinterpreting Him. Another example of His disciples' misinterpreting Him is recorded in the Book of Acts. When Jesus spoke about the kingdom of God,

His disciples thought of an earthly kingdom, so they asked, "Lord, are you at this time going to restore the kingdom to Israel?" (Acts 1:6).

Because of this dominant contemporary expectation of the Messiah and an earthly kingdom, Jesus was required to reveal His identity discreetly. Furthermore, He found it necessary to instruct His disciples concerning His interpretation of His messiahship before declaring to them that He was the Messiah. In Mark's Gospel there is a progressive unfolding of the messiahship of Jesus. First, it is revealed at His baptism (Mark 1:11). Second, it is revealed to a man who had an evil spirit (Mark 1:24; cf. 3:11). Third, it is revealed on the occasion of Peter's great confession at Caesarea Philippi (Mark 8:27-33). Fourth, it is revealed to His disciples as a group (Mark 8:31; 9:31; 10:33). Fifth, it is revealed on the day of the triumphal entry into Jerusalem in the shouts of the multitude as they cried, "Hosanna! Blessed is he who comes in the name of the Lord! Blessed is the coming kingdom of our father David!" (Mark 11:9-10). Sixth, it is revealed at the trial of Jesus before the high priest:

> Again the high priest asked him, "Are you the Christ, the Son of the Blessed One?"
>
> "I am," said Jesus. "And you will see the Son of Man sitting at the right hand of the Mighty One and coming on the clouds of heaven" (Mark 14:61-62).

In the light of this evidence in Mark's Gospel it can be said that for Jesus the name Son of Man meant someone quite different from the expectation of His contemporaries. According to the account, Jesus interpreted the role of the Messiah as one of suffering and death, as well as victorious triumph. It was the suffering and humiliation of the Messiah that was totally unacceptable and utterly abhorrent to Jesus' contemporaries. Even Peter, who had declared Jesus to be the Messiah, bluntly contradicted Him, and for this Jesus sharply rebuked and deliberately reprimanded Peter. Also, Jesus purposefully set about to fulfill the will of God.

Jesus had an extraordinary understanding of Himself. He saw Himself, paradoxically, as the sovereign Messiah with regal authority as well as a suffering Servant, and these two aspects of His person are clearly depicted in Isaiah (cf. Isa. 42:1-9; 49:1-9; 50:4-9; 52:13-53:12). The following passages support the fact that in Jesus the two contrasting characteristics of sovereignty and suffering meet: First, there are passages where the characteristic of suffering is emphasized (Matt. 12:40; 17:9, 12, 22; 20:18; 26:2, 24; 9:9, 12, 31; 10:33; 14:21, 41; Luke 9:22; 11:30; 18:31; 22:22, 48) and second, there are passages where the characteristic of sovereignty is emphasized (Matt. 13:14; 16:27-28; 24:27, 37, 39, 44; 25:31; 26:64; Mark 8:38; 13:26; 14:62; Luke 9:26; 12:40; 17:24, 26; 18:8; 21:27, 36). This is impressive evidence of how Jesus saw Himself in terms of the Son of Man.

There is another name that helps in our study of Jesus' self-understanding. That name is the *Son of God*. The historical event at Caesarea Philippi is very instructive for us regarding this. It was there that Jesus was positively and dramatically declared to be the Son of God. On that occasion Peter was the spokesman (Matt. 16:13ff.; Mark 8:27ff.; Luke 9:18ff.). According to the fullest account, that of Matthew, Jesus asked, "Who do people say the Son of Man is?" (Matt. 16:13). His disciples answered that some believed that He was John the Baptist, others believed He was Elijah, and still others believed He was Jeremiah or another prophet.

Then Jesus put the question to His own disciples. It was a crucial moment in His public ministry. As far as is known, they had not been explicit regarding this matter prior to this time. Now, however, the moment of truth is at hand. Peter arose to the momentous occasion with the unequivocal declaration: "You are the Christ, the Son of the living God" (Matt. 16:16).

In His reply to Peter, Jesus referred to God as His Father. He said, "Blessed are you, Simon son of Jonah, for this was not revealed to you by man, but by my Father in heaven'' (Matt. 16:17). Here, Jesus is setting forth a distinctive Father-Son relationship between God and Himself.

In Peter's great confession Jesus is identified as the Son of God. Because of this the confession by Peter is of highest importance. Jesus openly accepted Peter's declaration and then stated clearly that God was His Father. For orthodox scholarship, the incident at Caesarea Philippi is real history and, as such, is the subject of critical historical inquiry. In addition, the incident is the occasion for divine revelation verified by One who was qualified to declare that a revelation had occurred. For radical modern scholarship, historical criticism provides a differing understanding of the incident. What is revealed by the incident is the view of Jesus that the earliest Christians developed according to their own subjective faith. This view was projected back to Jesus and declared to be the faith of Christianity.

The Gospel of John is another valuable source for evidence explicitly setting forth the truth that Jesus is the Son of God (e.g., John 1:18, 34, 49; 3:16, 18, 35, 36; 5:9, 20, 21, 22, 23, 25, 26; 8:35, 36; 10:36; 11:4, 27; 14:13; 17:1; 20:31).

Not only do the names that Jesus used to show His self-understanding (Son of Man and Son of God) help in a right interpretation of His identity, but so also do His well-known "I am" sayings. These sayings are found in the Gospel of John and set forth Jesus' conscious self-identity and His extraordinary claims. The phrase *I am* suggests to one who is aware of the "I AM" who revealed Himself to Moses (Exod. 3:14) that Jesus, in some way, identified Himself with the great "I AM." In a dramatic way this self-understanding of Jesus is revealed: "I am the bread of life" (John 6:35); "I am the light of the world" (8:12); "I am the door of the sheep" (10:7); "I am the good shepherd" (10:11); "I am the resurrection and the life" (11:25); "I am the way and the truth and the life" (14:6); "I am the true vine" (15:1).

It has been my intent to consider the claim of the four Gospels that Jesus Christ is the unique God-man. Up to this point, we have considered that claim in the light of Jesus' own self-understanding, which is evidenced by the names He used, namely, Son of Man and Son of God, and by the "I am" sayings recorded in the fourth Gospel.

b. Jesus' extraordinary vocation We will now consider Jesus' disclosure of His vocation or calling as it contributes to interpreting correctly the claim of Jesus that He is the unique God-man. It is clear that to Jesus His vocation involved the disclosure of the kingdom of God. The theme of the kingdom of God is deeply rooted in the Old Testament. It provided great expectations for the Jews in the time of Jesus. The popular understanding of the kingdom of God in Jesus' time was that it was a coming restoration or reconstruction of the Old Testament kingdom that David had established in the tenth century B.C.

According to Mark's Gospel, Jesus began His popular Galilean ministry with the proclamation of the kingdom of God: "After John was put in prison, Jesus went into Galilee, proclaiming the good news of God. 'The time has come,' he said. 'The kingdom of God is near. Repent and believe the good news!'" (Mark 1:14–15). This theme is central in the life and teachings of Jesus as recorded in the Gospels. It was predominant throughout His earthly ministry. Even during the forty days following His resurrection, Jesus kept this theme before His disciples. "He appeared to them over a period of forty days and spoke about the kingdom of God" (Acts 1:3).

The Gospel of Matthew has thirty-three references to "the kingdom of heaven" and four to "the kingdom of God," all thirty-seven being references to the same "kingdom." Viewing this Gospel as written primarily to the Jewish Christians, who used the word *heaven* as a substitute for the name of God, we understand that Matthew is referring to the same kingdom as Mark and Luke. Mark and Luke prefer the phrase "the kingdom of God," Mark using it fourteen times, and Luke thirty-two times. The sum total of these references to the kingdom of God in the synoptic Gospels is impressive.

Throughout the Synoptics where the kingdom theme is mentioned, it is highly significant that Jesus did not interpret the kingdom of God according to the popular view of the restoration of David's earthly kingdom. Instead of making the kingdom concept a slogan to rally followers, as the would-be messiahs of that time attempted to do, Jesus used it in the prayer He taught His followers. The petition concerning the kingdom may well be the most important petition in the Lord's Prayer:

> Your kingdom come,
> your will be done
> on earth as it is in heaven.
> (Matt. 6:10)

If that petition is studied as a poetic parallelism, it becomes clear that the petition is a synonymous parallelism, giving an illuminating definition of the kingdom of God. The petition considers the kingdom of God synonymous with the will of God. Jesus came to declare the will of God and to call His hearers to follow Him.

Jesus' contemporaries were so committed to the coming of a tangible, earthly kingdom that they gave little attention to any other kind of kingdom. The Jews were obsessed with the hope of a nationalistic kingdom. They strongly resented Roman domination and control. Also, they had strong desires for liberation and for the restoration of the earthly nation of Israel. Great emphasis was given to the hope of a "kingdom," but there was little vital faith in God. God seemed distant and compassionless. The restoration of the nation seemed impossible.

Then Jesus arrived and made this theme dominant in His life and teachings. Jesus was of course more than a human leader, yet it can be said of Him, as it can be said of every influential leader who has towered high among the members of the human race and who has had a great impact on human affairs, that a great theme possessed Him. For Socrates the theme was "immortality of the soul"; for Buddha, "renunciation of life"; for Alexander the Great, "I shall conquer the world"; for Muhammad, "There is no God but Allah, and Muhammad is his prophet"; for Luther, "justification by faith"; for John Wesley, "Christian perfection"; and for Jesus Christ, "the kingdom of God." Jesus took a lifeless and earth-bound slogan of Judaism and gave it breath from heaven.

In the light of the events in the life of Jesus as recorded in the Gospels, the expectations of a nationalistic and earthly kingdom rose spectacularly in Judaism. However, these expectations were soon shattered as Jesus refused to be identified with such a conception of the kingdom of God. What was Jesus' interpretation of the kingdom of God? In the rabbinic literature of the intertestamental period the distinctive phrase "This age and the age to come" was in common usage. This expression was taken with utmost seriousness by Jesus. He used it in His teaching about the unpardonable sin: "Anyone who speaks a word against the Son of Man will be forgiven, but anyone who speaks against the Holy Spirit will not be forgiven, either in this age or in the age to come" (Matt. 12:32). He also used it in His discussion with His disciples following the encounter with the rich young ruler (Mark 10:17-31; cf. Luke 18:18-30):

> "I tell you the truth," Jesus replied, "no one who has left home or brothers or sisters or mother or father or children or fields for me and the gospel will fail to receive a hundred times as much in this present age (homes, brothers, sisters, mothers, children and fields—and with them, persecutions) and in the age to come, eternal life" (Mark 10:29-30).

Jesus sets "the age to come" over against "this present age," and therefore "the age to come" is not a future era within the "present age" but a whole new order of existence. This contrast provides the framework for Jesus' explanation of the kingdom.

The Jews generally recognized that the kingdom of God manifested sovereign power. With its coming all opposition would be destroyed. It was associated with "the day of the Lord," and was viewed eschatologically. Prophets of the Old Testament and apocalyptic literature of the intertestamental period looked forward to this revelation. This is the eschatological interpretation of the kingdom viewed as the triumph of the "age to come" over "this present age."

However, Jesus set forth the kingdom of God not only in terms of the coming age but also in terms of the present age. For example, in the following statement He affirmed that the kingdom of God was present in His work: "But if I drive out demons by the Spirit of God, then the kingdom of God has come upon you" (Matt. 12:28). Jesus rejected the allegation of His accusers that He was using satanic power to drive out demons; instead, He explained His work as the power of God. This was evidence that the kingdom of God was present. For Jesus, the kingdom of God was no mere formal expectation without power and life; rather, there is divine power active in this age.

Jesus' message, which was supported by His miraculous works, was that the satanic evil of this present age was being defeated by the sovereign power of God. In addition to this message, Jesus declared that in the age to come the power of God will destroy Satan as well as sin and death. This message was a radical modification of the popular view in Judaism, which viewed the kingdom of God as a future, earthly nation brought into being by the power of God.

Jesus' message concerning the kingdom of God included an emphasis on its presence in this age. Experiencing the kingdom of God in this present age consists, in the first place, of the realization of divine power. There is spiritual conquest over evil spiritual forces. In the second place, there is the realization that this divine power brings salvation to everyone who believes, and it brings it now.

Jesus also taught that the kingdom of God is a future event that will bring an end to this present age. In His highly important eschatological discourse (Matt. 24-25; cf. Mark 13; Luke 21) Jesus revealed that the conquest of this present evil age by the coming kingdom age will be catastrophic. Furthermore, He revealed that people must respond to His message of the present kingdom of God if they expect to be in the coming kingdom of God, which will overpower this present age. Jesus did not proclaim two kingdoms of God; rather, He proclaimed that the kingdom of God has two manifestations. In the present manifestation of the kingdom of God there is a suffering Messiah revealing the will of God in power. In the future manifestation there will be a sovereign Messiah who will establish His reign.

The parables of Jesus are very instructive regarding the close relationship He perceived existing between these two manifestations of the kingdom of God. Matthew's Gospel has an outstanding chapter on parables of the kingdom (Matt. 13). The first parable in this collection depicts the presence of the kingdom of God in this present age. Some people, like some kinds of soil, are not receptive; other people, like good soil, are receptive and become productive. They experience salvation. Another parable in this collection sets forth the problem of identifying who in this present age belongs to the kingdom of God and who does not. However, according to the parable, the problem will be resolved at the end of this age when the harvest will occur. Then the wheat will be harvested, but the tares will be burned. These parables provide a sampling of the way Jesus viewed the kingdom of God: a reality that will be the manifestation of God at the end of this present historical reality but already has penetrated this present age to bring salvation.

It is evident that an authentic human being made this extraordinary disclosure, namely, that the kingdom of God has come. Yet it is inconceivable that He is no more than a mere human being. Some of Jesus' contemporaries became convinced that Jesus was deceiving His hearers and they stopped short of nothing but revolt against Rome to do away with Him. Others were convinced that Jesus was who He claimed to be and they experienced the life and power of the kingdom of God.

3. The testimony of the Epistles and Revelation The Epistles give witness to christology. In the important passage of Philippians 2:5-11 Paul affirms the incarnation of Christ in Jesus. According to the passage, the preexisting Christ became man and lived in obedience to God. His obedience even led to death on the cross.

According to Colossians 1:15-20, Christ participates in divine creation and providence. In 2 Corinthians 5:17-19 the incarnation is given as the reason for a person becoming "a new creature." God was in Christ for the purpose of reconciliation.

In the Epistle to the Hebrews there are references to the human existence of Jesus, such as His faithfulness (3:6), His prayers (5:7), His subjection to temptation (2:18), and His submission to suffering and death (2:9). However, there are also references in which Jesus is said to transcend His human existence, such as the superiority of His priesthood (4:14-15) and His presence at creation (1:2-3).

Revelation sets forth christological truth in the central figure of the Lamb who executes judgment. Indeed, John said that he saw one like the Son of Man among the candlesticks (1:12-16). Moreover, the name of this one in His time of judgment is "The Word of God" (19:13), and this relates to the prologue of John's Gospel where John writes, "The Word was God" (1:1).

B. John Wesley and the Evidence From Scripture

John Wesley, founder of the movement in theology that is recognized as Wesleyan theology and one of the original leaders of the movement known as Methodism, stands in the tradition of those who believe that Jesus was who He claimed to be, namely, the God-man. In a significant note on John 1:1 in his *Explanatory Notes Upon the New Testament* he wrote:

> The other evangelists aim at this—to prove that Jesus, a true man, was the Messiah. But when at length some from hence began to doubt of His Godhead, then St. John expressly asserted it, and wrote in this book as it were a supplement to the Gospels, as the Revelation to the prophets.[4]

The following excerpt from Wesley's "Sermon CXLI" is an accurate summary statement of his orthodox view of Jesus Christ as the God-man:

> In the beginning, the heavenly Word,—being a Spirit that issued from the Father, and the Word of his power,—made man an image of immortality, according to the likeness of the Father; but he who had been made in the image of God, afterwards became mortal, when the more powerful Spirit was separated from him. To remedy this, the Word became Man, that man by receiving the adoption might become a son of God once more; that the light of the Father might rest upon the flesh of our Lord, and come bright from thence unto us; and so man, being encompassed with the light of the Godhead, might be carried into immortality. When he was incarnate and became man, he recapitulated in himself all generations of mankind, making himself the center of our salvation, that what we lost in Adam, even the image and likeness of God, we might receive in Jesus Christ. . . .
>
> Christ is not only God above us; which may keep us in awe, but cannot save; but he is Immanuel, God with us, and in us. As he is the Son of God, God must be where he is; and as he is in the Son of man, he will be with mankind; the consequence of this is, that in the future age 'the tabernacle of God will be with men,' and he will show them his glory; and, at present, he will *dwell* in their hearts by faith in his Son.[5]

John Wesley was in harmony not only with the synoptic Gospels regarding Jesus Christ as human but also with the fourth

Gospel regarding the divinity of Christ. In addition to that, Wesley implicitly grasped the truth of Jesus' teaching about the kingdom of God that it is not only the coming age but also a present experience by faith. See also chapter 10, pages 386–88, concerning the deity of Christ.

II. HISTORICAL CONTROVERSY

A. Developments in the Christological Controversy

Christology in the Wesleyan tradition is founded not only on biblical authority but also on the ancient creeds of the church. In particular, there is the Chalcedonian Creed of 451 A.D. This creed was formed because of controversies that occurred after the Council of Nicea in 325.

At the Council of Nicea the assembled church leaders approved the statement called the Nicene Creed, which set forth the doctrine of the Trinity. This doctrine included the affirmation that Christ was truly divine. However, the Nicene Creed did not resolve the question as to whether Christ was truly human.

This unresolved question became the center of the christological controversy that extended from the latter part of the fourth century through the first half of the fifth century. There were periods during this time when the controversy became so violent as to threaten the very survival of the church.

Fueling the fires of controversy were three heretical viewpoints regarding whether Christ was truly human: (1) Apollinarianism, (2) Nestorianism, and (3) Eutychianism. I will give a description of each of these heresies in its historical setting.

Apollinarianism, the first view, was developed in the latter part of the fourth century by Apollinaris, bishop of Laodicea in Asia Minor. Apollinaris regarded human nature as having three parts; namely, body, soul, and spirit. For him, this was established by Paul, who had written in 1 Thessalonians 5:23, "May the God who gives us peace . . . keep your whole being, spirit, soul, and body . . .'' (TEV). Apollinaris, on the basis of his belief that the Bible taught that a human being is a trichotomy, proposed the view that the divine Christ became incarnate in a human body with its animal soul. In the place of the human spirit was the divine Logos. According to Apollinaris's view, the result was a trichotomous being having a human body and soul and a divine spirit.

Controversy erupted, with opponents claiming that Apollinaris sacrificed the true humanity of Christ by denying that Christ had a total human nature. This was the essential element of heresy in Apollinaris. Therefore his view was rejected by the church.

Nestorianism, the second view, was developed in the early part of the fifth century. Nestorius, bishop of Constantinople in Asia Minor, rejected Apollinarianism and affirmed that Christ was fully human as well as fully divine. When he declared that Mary was not to be called *Theotokos* ("mother of God"), he precipitated vigorous controversy. Nestorius declared that Mary was the mother of Christ's human nature, but she could not have been the mother of His divine nature. So, according to the Nestorian view, Christ was composed of a divine person, who was not subject to birth and whose mother was not Mary, and a human person, who suffered for the salvation of humanity, while the divine person did not. Christ was not the God-man but a God-bearing man. This view of Christ made Nestorius subject to the accusation that he explained the possibility of salvation by means of the human nature of Christ; he excluded the divine nature from the plan of salvation. The church leaders viewed Nestorianism as heresy and rejected it at the general church council held at Ephesus in 431.

Eutychianism, the third view, developed as an overreaction to Nestorianism. During the fourth century, Eutyches, who headed a monastery in Constantinople, proposed a view that was in direct opposition to Nestorianism. Affirming the reality of the Incarnation, Eutyches theorized that when the divine nature became incarnate in the human nature, the human nature became divine. The human nature was absorbed into the divine nature as a drop of syrup is absorbed into the ocean. Such a metaphor indicated clearly that just as the syrup no longer remained a drop of syrup when put in the ocean so the human nature of Christ no longer remained a distinguishable human nature when the divine nature became incarnate.

On the one hand, Nestorius had so insisted on keeping the human and divine natures in Christ separated that he sacrificed the oneness of Christ's person. On the other hand, Eutyches so insisted on maintaining the unity of Christ's person that he sacrificed the human nature of Christ. He even went so far as to deify both the human nature and the body of Christ.

Because of the ongoing controversy regarding the relationship between the two natures of Christ and the conflicting heretical views injected into it, a general council of the church was held at Chalcedon in Asia Minor in 451. The council addressed itself to the single question that had been the cause of the controversy: How were the divine and human natures of Christ brought together to form one person?

The council explicitly tried to avoid two extreme and heretical views: (1) the heresy that the two natures were brought alongside each other but were not actually united together and (2) the heresy that the two natures were actually so united together that a new third nature was formed, Christ being neither truly divine nor truly human.

B. Decision of Chalcedon in A.D. 451

The following is the text of the Chalcedonian Creed of 451 as given by Henry Bettenson:

> Therefore, following the holy fathers, we all with one accord teach men to acknowledge one and the same Son, our Lord Jesus Christ, at once complete in Godhead and complete in manhood, truly God and truly man, consisting also of a reasonable soul and body; of one substance [$\acute{o}\mu oo\acute{u}\sigma\iota o\varsigma$] with the Father as regards his Godhead, and at the same time of one substance with us as regards his manhood; like us in all respects, apart from sin; as regards his Godhead, begotten of the Father before the ages, but yet as regards his manhood begotten, for us men and for our salvation, of Mary the Virgin, the God-bearer [$\theta\epsilon o\tau\acute{o}\kappa o\varsigma$]; one and the same Christ, Son, Lord, Only-begotten, recognized in TWO NATURES, WITHOUT CONFUSION, WITHOUT CHANGE, WITHOUT DIVISION, WITHOUT SEPARATION; the distinction of natures being in no way annulled by the union, but rather the characteristics of each nature being preserved and coming together to form one person and subsistence [$\acute{u}\pi\acute{o}\sigma\tau\alpha\sigma\iota\varsigma$], not as parted or separated into two persons, but one and the same Son and Only-begotten God the Word, Lord Jesus Christ; even as the prophets from earliest times spoke of him, and our Lord Jesus Christ himself taught us, and the creed of the Fathers has handed down to us.[6]

This brings into focus the important question: How true to the Bible is this creed? While it is necessary to acknowledge that this creed does not have the quality of inspiration and canonicity that we affirm inheres in the Bible, it does affirm orthodoxy. While this creed is not a replacement for the Bible, it is the interpretation that the church has given regarding the biblical account of Christ. Admittedly, the christological controversy was marred by developments that were unbecoming to Christianity, to say the least; however, in spite of such developments and shortcomings, the church has confidently affirmed that the Holy Spirit was at work in the effort to distinguish truth from error.

Underlying the work of the council at Chalcedon was the concern regarding the necessary requirements Christ must fulfill in order to be the author of salvation. None of the church leaders has expressed that concern better than Irenaeus, bishop of Lyons in southern Gaul during the latter part of the second century A.D., two and one-half centuries before the council at

Chalcedon. The concern of Irenaeus was the continuing concern of orthodoxy. The following celebrated passage from Irenaeus articulated this concern regarding our salvation and sets forth Christ as both divine and human in order to accomplish our salvation:

> Now it has been clearly demonstrated that the Word which exists from the beginning with God, by whom all things were made, who was also present with the race of men at all times, this Word has in these last times, according to the time appointed by the Father, been united to his own workmanship and has been made passible man. Therefore we can set aside the objection of them that say, "If he was born at that time it follows that Christ did not exist before then." For we have shown that the Son of God did not then begin to exist since he existed with the Father always; but when he was incarnate and made man, he recapitulated [or summed up] in himself the long line of the human race, procuring for us salvation thus summarily, so that what we had lost in Adam, that is, the being in the image and likeness of God, that we should regain in Christ Jesus.[7]

The leaders of the council at Chalcedon were concerned to resolve the christological controversy by affirming both the divinity and humanity of Christ. In so affirming, the council faced questions such as the following: How can Christ have a divine nature and a human nature and yet be only one person? If Christ is only one person, is the divine nature humanized or the human nature deified? Did the union of the two natures result in a third nature constituting the person of Christ?

Since the Bible does not give direct answers to such questions as these, the Christian community has had to construct its distinctive doctrine and creed as it responded to various views that were rejected as heretical. The Chalcedonian creed regarding christology has been the most influential interpretation of the person of Christ. This interpretation is the view of orthodox Christianity.

The creed distinctly affirms the full divinity of Christ. Accordingly, Arian christology was excluded from orthodoxy because Arius, the proponent of this view, denied the full divinity of Christ. The Chalcedonian creed also affirms the full humanity of Christ. Accordingly, Apollinarian christology is excluded because it denies Christ a fully human mind. Furthermore, the creed affirms the personal oneness of the divine and human natures. According to the Chalcedonian creed, Christ is regarded as one person having two natures, the divine and the human. Consequently, Nestorian christology, which regarded Christ as two persons, and Eutychian christology, which regarded the human nature becoming deified and identified with the divine nature, were both excluded from the orthodox doctrine concerning the person of Christ.

The Chalcedonian creed stands as the best interpretation of the Bible regarding the person of Christ. In the midst of religious controversy and political intrigue, Christians exercised both their faith and their reason in sorting out the various views and excluding the heretical ones. It is imperative to believe that the Holy Spirit was present at Chalcedon in order that orthodoxy might be established.

From the human point of view, the key motivating dynamic at Chalcedon was the deep religious concern to view Christ as the appropriate and sufficient Savior to accomplish our salvation. There was a keen awareness that Christ must have a truly divine nature and a truly human nature existing in one personality. Only such a Christ can accomplish the salvation revealed in the Bible and interpreted by the orthodox tradition as expressed in the creeds.

In the first century A.D. the apostle Paul stated the matter with clarity but without any depth analysis:

> Therefore, if anyone is in Christ, he is a new creation; the old has gone, the new has come! All this is from God, who reconciled us unto himself through Christ and gave us the ministry of reconciliation: that God was reconciling the world to himself in Christ, not counting men's sins against them (2 Cor. 5:17–19).

In the second century the church father Irenaeus gave more depth analysis in articulating why God was in Christ. According to Reinhold Seeberg's account:

> Irenaeus described the work of Christ under various aspects. The premise is always the reality of the divinity and humanity of the Saviour. Only upon this basis could he furnish certain deliverance and deliver the particular race of man. . . .
>
> Christ, therefore, became man in order to recapitulate the whole human race in himself. . . . He embraces in himself the entire human race and all human life: "When he became incarnate and was made man, he recapitulated in himself the long line of men, standing surety in compendium for our salvation, so that what we lost in Adam, i.e., our being in the image and likeness of God, this we might receive in Christ Jesus."[8]

In keeping with the minds of Paul, Irenaeus, and the host of Christians concerned that Christ be declared a sufficient Savior, the council at Chalcedon wrote the creed in the light of the imperative of maintaining an inextricable relation between Christ and our salvation. The creed affirms Christ to be who He is because our salvation requires it.

III. JOHN WESLEY'S CHRISTOLOGY

A. The Historical Setting

From Christianity in the fifth century we turn now to Christianity in the eighteenth century in England when John Wesley lived. Two background developments provide perspective on Wesley's christology: one was the English Reformation and the other was the influence of the Enlightenment on the Church of England. A brief study of each of these will be helpful, but it will not be possible to be exhaustive in this chapter.

1. The English Reformation Roman Catholicism prevailed in England until the fifteenth century. By that time there had developed such a strong national identity and consciousness that the nation and its sovereigns were wholly opposed to foreign impositions. Their opposition was extended even to the impositions of the Roman papacy. The decisive step was taken during the reign of Henry VIII when the English Parliament passed the Act of Supremacy in 1534. This action made the English sovereign the only supreme head of the Church of England.

This separation from Roman Catholicism during the reign of Henry VIII did not, however, result in extensive reformation in doctrine or practice. The really formative developments occurred during the reign of Queen Elizabeth from 1558 to 1603. During these forty-five years, two actions taken by the English Parliament contributed enormously to the religious identity of the Church of England. In 1563 the Thirty-nine Articles were adopted at the meeting of Convocation. In 1571 the clergy as well as degree candidates at the universities were required by the action of Parliament to subscribe to all thirty-nine articles.

The Thirty-nine Articles are not so much a confession of faith as a response to the Reformation. This document reflects the spirit of controversy that was in evidence at that time. It may be summarized as follows: the first five articles present Christianity in terms of the doctrine of the Trinity; articles 6 through 8 declare the Bible to be the rule of faith and refer to the appropriate creeds of early Christianity; articles 9 through 18 refer to individual religion in terms of sin and grace and corresponding Reformation issues; articles 19 through 36 discuss the church and the sacraments with special references to the differences of the Church of England from Roman Catholicism; articles 37 through 39 relate church and state.[9]

For our particular christological study, the second article is necessarily relevant. It reads as follows:

> Of the Word or Son of God, which was made very Man. The Son, which is the Word of the Father, begotten from everlasting of the Father, the very and eternal God, and of one substance with the Father, took Man's nature

in the womb of the blessed Virgin, of her substance: so that two whole and perfect Natures, that is to say, the Godhead and the Manhood, were joined together in one Person, never to be divided, whereof is one Christ, very God, and very Man; who truly suffered, was crucified, dead, and buried, to reconcile his Father to us, and to be a sacrifice, not only for original guilt, but also for actual sins of men.[10]

As this article is compared with the Chalcedonian creed, it becomes obvious that it is derived from the creed. In the spirit of the Reformation the Church of England reflected its adherence to historic orthodox Christianity. This was the legacy John Wesley received as a member of the clergy of the Church of England in the eighteenth century. He embraced the christology of the church.

During the reign of Queen Elizabeth, the second event that contributed to the identity of the Church of England was the adoption of the revised *Book of Common Prayer* by the Act of Uniformity of 1559. All worship in the Church of England was to be in accordance with the liturgical forms in this book. Both the ancient tradition of the church and the interpretations provided by the Reformation were included in the book. Prayers and liturgical forms of worship dating from the early history of Christianity were included. Also, the Bible was an important authority for determining what should and should not be included. There was a broad and comprehensive expression of the Christian faith embodied in the *Book of Common Prayer*.

2. The Enlightenment Developments in science and philosophy were foundations for the emergence of the Enlightenment, a movement that dominated the atmosphere during the eighteenth century. During the sixteenth and seventeenth centuries, Copernicus and Galileo had formulated the heliocentric view of the universe. During the latter part of the seventeenth century, the English philosopher John Locke had proposed that all claims to knowledge be subject to reason based on experience.

The Enlightenment penetrated the Church of England and furthered rationalism in religion. This was one of the most important results of the spirit of the Enlightenment in its influence on the Church of England. This cultural movement was a conscious effort to apply the rule of reason to all individual and social matters. It was based on the assumption that through reason all of life could become understandable.

Theologically the Enlightenment was of great importance in England because it brought a new alternative to orthodoxy. By assuming the sufficiency of reason, theologians and philosophers affirmed that necessary religious insights could be obtained through the use of reason. Therefore the orthodox idea of revelation was no longer held to be distinctive. Rather, because of the power of reason, revelation merely confirmed what was understandable through reason. Revelation was merely the handmaid of reason. Christianity increasingly became merely a rationalistic form of religion. Essentially Christianity was a reasonable religion.

The impact of the Enlightenment during the latter part of the seventeenth and first part of the eighteenth centuries had a great influence on the Church of England. That influence exerted itself in three phases.[11] During the course of the first phase there was the recognition of the supernatural character of Christianity and Christian revelation and the affirmation that revelation was in accord with reason. For example, it was recognized that prophecy and miracle were supernatural evidences for Christianity. This evidence was considered an essential, reasonable fact. Since prophecy and miracle were submitted as evidence that Jesus was the Messiah, such proof was declared to be reasonable.

During the course of the second phase the Christian religion was considered an illustration of natural religion, that is, a religion that conformed to the natural order of things and to reason. For natural religion meant religion according to reason and compatible with religion in general.

In the course of the third phase there was open opposition to the supernatural character of Christianity. Prophecy and miracle were declared unacceptable to the reasonable understanding of Christianity. The Bible became the focal point of controversy. It was attacked as being unacceptable to reason. There emerged an antagonistic deism that had a devastating influence on the spiritual life of the Church of England.

The concept of revelation was very important in the orthodox understanding of Christianity. Revelation made possible the communication of the supernatural to mankind. Deism, however, because its primary principle was the ultimate authority of reason, attacked revelation as the communicator of the supernatural. According to deism, reason required only the natural. This was a radical break with orthodoxy. It opened up a new alternative to orthodoxy.

This new alternative to orthodoxy became dominant in the Church of England during the time of John Wesley. It appealed to human reason. Yet, increasingly, it was met with growing indifference. More than rational Christianity was needed to meet the needs of England. The Church of England had its orthodoxy in the Book of Common Prayer and the Thirty-nine Articles. Here was to be found correct doctrine. However, the Enlightenment and its rational principle had so deprived the doctrine of any vital content that Christianity in the church was nothing more than "a form of godliness" without its power (2 Tim. 3:5).

B. John Wesley's Experience of Christ

While at a meeting of a religious society in Aldersgate Street, London, on the evening of May 24, 1738, John Wesley had an experience that changed his life. That experience has been recorded in classic sentences by Wesley himself:

> In the evening I went very unwillingly to a society in Aldersgate-Street, where one was reading Luther's preface to the Epistle to the Romans. About a quarter before nine, while he was describing the change which God works in the heart through faith in Christ, I felt my heart strangely warmed. I felt I did trust in Christ, Christ alone for salvation: And an assurance was given me, that he had taken away *my* sins, even *mine*, and saved *me* from the law of sin and death.[12]

When Wesley recorded his Aldersgate experience, he included much more than the pinpoint of 8:45 p.m. on Wednesday evening, May 24. What occurred that evening was for the first time in his life a sure feeling that he trusted in Christ alone for salvation, that his sins were taken away, and that he was saved from the power of sin and death. However, that sure feeling of faith was not something that occurred in a vacuum nor was it unrelated and irrelevant to what had occurred prior to that time. Rather, that experience involved a whole lifetime and a process that came to the moment of crisis on that eventful evening.

The account of Aldersgate that Wesley gives in his *Journal* begins with his infancy and reviews his spiritual life up to Aldersgate, when he was thirty-four years of age. His account refers to the diligent spiritual nurture he received at home as well as at institutions of learning. It includes references to his efforts at morality and "works" such as prayer, Bible reading, social work, preaching, and even going as a missionary to a foreign land. It also includes reference to his involvement in mysticism and spiritual exercises to induce spiritual ecstasy. Yet his spiritual life was a failure, for he was filled with fear, doubt, and conviction of sin. He was afraid of death and realized he was under the wrath of God.

Throughout his life Wesley had never realized a satisfying religious experience. Even though he had Christian parents and the influence of Christian upbringing, even though he was among the elite as a Fellow of Lincoln College, Oxford University, and even though he had been a minister in the holy orders of the Church of England for over a dozen years, John Wesley had a desolate and sin-sick soul.

Wesley writes about his meeting Peter Bohler earlier in 1738. In the conversation, Bohler affirmed that victory over sin and peace coming from the realization of forgiveness are the two fruits that result in true faith in Christ. When Bohler made this affirmation, it astonished Wesley:

> So that when Peter Bohler, whom God prepared for me as soon as I came to London, affirmed of true faith in Christ, (which is but one,) that it had those two fruits inseparably attending it, "Dominion over sin, and constant Peace from a sense of forgiveness," I was quite amazed, and looked upon it as a new Gospel. If this was so, it was clear I had not faith. But I was not willing to be convinced of this. Therefore, I disputed with all my might, and laboured to prove that faith might be where these were not; especially where the sense of forgiveness was not: For all the Scriptures relating to this I had been long since taught to construe away; and to call all Presbyterians who spoke otherwise. Besides, I well saw, no one could, in the nature of things, have such a sense of forgiveness, and not *feel* it. But I felt it not. If then there was no faith without this, all my pretensions to faith dropped at once.[13]

In subsequent conversations with Peter Bohler, Wesley came to realize his need for faith in Christ. He writes of his resolve in his *Journal:*

> I was now thoroughly convinced; and, by the grace of God, I resolved to seek it unto the end, 1. By absolutely renouncing all dependence, in whole or in part, upon *my own* works or righteousness; on which I had really grounded my hope of salvation, though I knew it not, from my youth up. 2. By adding to the constant use of all the other means of grace, continual prayer for this very thing, justifying, saving faith, a full reliance on the blood of Christ shed for *me;* a trust in Him, as *my* Christ, as *my* sole justification, sanctification, and redemption.[14]

The catalyst for Wesley's awakening regarding faith in Christ in order to have the feeling of forgiveness was Peter Bohler. He was used of the Lord in bringing the gospel to a sin-smitten, desolate soul. This awakening of Wesley in March, 1738, was followed by the assurance of forgiveness at Aldersgate on May 24. In all of the developments involved, the focus of Wesley's faith was Christ.

Without detracting in any way from the emphasis that so many studies of Wesley's Aldersgate experience make regarding the subjective aspect of that experience, it is relevant in this study to place the emphasis on the objective aspect, namely, the Christ who warmed the heart of Wesley. Wesley did not experience a fantasy or merely human emotion. Objectively, he experienced the One whom Saul of Tarsus experienced on the Damascus road and the One whom anyone can experience in forgiveness by truly believing and trusting.

The important point here is that in the midst of a natural religion that was bringing the touch of death to the Church of England, there occurred to a clergyman of the Church a supernatural heartwarming experience that was to bring what Williston Walker terms "The Evangelical Revival in Great Britain."[15] Such an analysis may be considered too simplistic and too much prejudiced in favor of orthodoxy by some. Contemporaries of Wesley who were highly skeptical of feeling and emotion in matters of religion thought Wesley was irrational. For years Wesley was charged with "enthusiasm," or fanaticism, a charge against which he defended himself often. The rationalistic deism that engulfed the Church of England in the eighteenth century vigorously rejected the view that God could actually enter a person's life and transform him. The Aldersgate experience of feeling the peace of God's forgiveness through faith in Christ was a compelling response to the prevailing rational view. In 1738, in the midst of the prevailing deistic religion of the Church of England in the eighteenth century, the alternative of the heart of an individual feeling the peace of God's forgiving love in Christ dramatically altered the course of Christianity in England.

These alternatives offered different answers to the all-important question that Jesus asked of His disciples at Caesarea Philippi: "Who do you say I am?" (Mark 8:29). Peter's answer that Jesus was the Christ is capable of being variously interpreted. Orthodox interpretation, arrived at by rejecting heretical views, declared Christ to be truly God and truly man. The Enlightenment and its emphasis on a reasonable religion at the expense of revelation, viewed Christ as an ideal human teacher of morals and conduct. At Aldersgate, Wesley experienced divine forgiveness as he trusted in Christ. The skeptic views Wesley's experience as a subjective emotion; however, the believer views such an experience as based on the objective reality of God in Christ who gives peace to the trusting soul.

C. John Wesley's Teaching Concerning Christ

1. He adhered to the Chalcedonian creed and to the Thirty-nine Articles of the Church of England In what is a clear and loyal expression of the orthodox view concerning Christ, Wesley wrote a letter to a Roman Catholic in which he set forth his view:

> I believe that Jesus of Nazareth was the Saviour of the world, the Messiah so long foretold; that, being anointed with the Holy Ghost, he was a Prophet, revealing to us the whole will of God; that he was a Priest, who gave himself a sacrifice for sin, and still makes intercession for transgressors; that he is a King, who has all power in heaven and in earth, and will reign till he has subdued all things to himself.
>
> I believe that he is the proper, natural Son of God, God of God, very God of very God; and that he is the Lord of all, having absolute, supreme, universal dominion over all things; but more peculiarly our Lord, who believe in him, both by conquest, purchase, and voluntary obligation.
>
> I believe that he was made man, joining the human nature with the divine in one person; being conceived by the singular operation of the Holy Ghost, and born of the blessed Virgin Mary....
>
> I believe he suffered inexpressible pains both of body and soul, and at last death, even the death of the cross, at the time that Pontius Pilate governed Judea, under the Roman Emperor; and his body was then laid in the grave, and his soul went to the place of separate spirits; that the third day he rose again from the dead; that he ascended into heaven; where he remains in the midst of the throne of God, in the highest power and glory, as Mediator till the end of the world, as God to all eternity; that, in the end, he will come down from heaven, to judge every man according to his works; both those who shall be then alive, and all who have died before that day.[16]

Much of this quotation reflects the Apostles' Creed. However, it also reflects the Chalcedonian creed and the second article of the Thirty-nine Articles. Although Wesley's writings that treat christology specifically are not dominant, yet there can be no question that Christ was central in his theology and essential to every other doctrine.

There is an entry in his *Journal* made on April 5, 1768, that reflects the centrality of Christ:

> About noon I preached at Warrington; I am afraid, not to the taste of some of my hearers, as my subject led me to speak strongly and explicitly on the Godhead of Christ. But that I cannot help; for on this I *must* insist, as the foundation of all our hope.[17]

Wesley's experience of feeling Christ's forgiveness at Aldersgate was an extraordinary deterrent to acquiescing to the deistic view that Christ was nothing more than a moral teacher. At the same time, that experience was highly significant in giving orthodoxy newness of life and vitality. It is a lamentable commentary on the Church of England that the churches were closed to the changed Wesley who had a new message, which he proclaimed with a new power. Notwithstanding this rejection, Wesley took to the open places. On the streets and in the field he preached to throngs who came to hear him. This resulted in many becoming believers and experiencing the reality of the new life that Wesley was preaching.

2. He set the person of Christ always in the context of the work of Christ The renewed Wesley, like the historic orthodox believers of the Chalcedonian view, saw the person of Christ in terms of His qualifications to accomplish divine salvation for humanity. Accordingly the orthodox view of the person of Christ was that He was truly God and truly man in order to qualify as Savior.

This view was reached by the early church and its councils through the process of eliminating those views of the person of Christ that were declared to be in error. The views of Nestorianism, Apollinarianism, and Eutychianism, mentioned on pages 339–40, were inadequate to explain Him as the Savior of the world.

It was precisely at this point that deism was inadequate and consequently heretical, according to the qualifications required in orthodoxy. According to deism, the Christ of the New Testament was merely a noble human being who taught an impressive morality. He was in no way essential to salvation, unless by way of His moral influence.

The power of Wesley's view of Christ was in his affirmation and proclamation that Christ is the Redeemer. He is the answer to "the human need." In the following quotation from Wesley's *Explanatory Notes Upon the New Testament* he clearly sets forth Christ as meeting the human need:

> It may be further observed, that the word Christ in Greek, and Messiah in Hebrew, signify "Anointed"; and imply the prophetic, priestly, and royal characters which were to meet in the Messiah. Among the Jews, anointing was the ceremony whereby prophets, priests, and kings were initiated into those offices. And if we look into ourselves, we shall find a want of Christ in all these respects. We are by nature at a distance from God, alienated from Him, and incapable of a free access to Him. Hence we want a Mediator, an Intercessor; in a word, a Christ in His priestly office. This regards our state with respect to God. And with respect to ourselves, we find a total darkness, blindness, ignorance of God, and the things of God. Now here we want Christ in His prophetic office, to enlighten our minds, and teach us the whole will of God. We find also within us a strange misrule of appetites and passions. For these we want Christ in His royal character, to reign in our hearts, and subdue all things to Himself.[18]

According to Wesley in this quotation, humanity needs One who is prophet, priest, and king. Deism could offer only another human being, since it was beyond the bounds of reasonable Christianity to view Christ as supernatural and divine. The new Wesley, filled with the positive assurance of forgiveness and salvation, unequivocally declared that Christ was as truly God as He was man. For Wesley, it was faith in Christ so understood that accomplished the change in his life. This was his experience, and the Scripture supported his experience.

In the sermon "Justification by Faith," Wesley quotes the Bible to show that salvation is by Christ:

> By the sin of the first Adam, who was not only the father, but likewise the representative, of us all, we all fell short of the favour of God; we all became children of wrath; or, as the Apostle expresses it, "judgment came upon all men to condemnation." Even so, by the sacrifice for sin made by the Second Adam, as the Representative of us all, God is so far reconciled to all the world, that he hath given them a new covenant; the plain condition whereof being once fulfilled, "there is no more condemnation" for us, but, "we are justified freely by his grace, through the redemption that is in Jesus Christ."[19]

What is highly significant for our purpose in this quotation is that salvation is possible through Christ, and the qualifications that Christ has, though not explicitly listed here but cited by Wesley elsewhere as necessary qualifications, are His divinity and His humanity.

This leads to a consideration of how Wesley viewed the coming together of the divine and the human in one person. Nothing less than a true incarnation is sufficient. This is evident in the following quotation:

> In the beginning, the heavenly Word,—being a Spirit that issued from the Father, and the Word of his power,—made man an image of immortality, according to the likeness of the Father; but he who had been made in the image of God, afterwards became mortal, when the powerful Spirit was separated from him. To remedy this, the Word became Man, that man by receiving the adoption might become a son of God once more; that the light of the Father might rest upon the flesh of our Lord, and come bright from thence unto us; and so man, being encompassed with the light of the Godhead, might be carried into immortality. When he was incarnate and became man, he recapitulated in himself all generations of mankind, making himself the center of our salvation, that what we lost in Adam, even the image and likeness of God, we might receive in Christ Jesus. By the Holy Ghost coming upon Mary, and the power of the highest overshadowing her, the incarnation of Christ was wrought, and a new birth, whereby man should be born of God, was shown; that as by our first birth we did inherit death, so by this birth we might inherit life.
>
> This is no other than what St. Paul teaches us: "The first man, Adam, was made a living soul, but the Second Adam was made a quickening spirit." All that the first man possessed of himself, all that he has transmitted to us, is "a living soul;" a nature endued with an animal life, and receptive of a spiritual. But the Second Adam is, and was made to us, "a quickening spirit;" by a strength from him as our Creator, we were at first raised above ourselves; by a strength from him as our Redeemer, we shall again live unto God.[20]

In a very compelling and moving passage Wesley sets forth the incarnate Christ by means of the memorable fifty-third chapter of Isaiah:

> Man did disobey God. . . . And in that day he was condemned by the righteous judgment of God. . . . His soul died. . . . And being already dead in spirit, dead to God, dead in sin, he hastened on to death everlasting. . . . Thus, "through the offence of one," all are dead, dead to God, dead in sin, dwelling in a corruptible, mortal body, shortly to be dissolved, and under the sentence of death eternal. . . .
>
> In this state we were, even all mankind, when "God so loved the world, that he gave his only-begotten Son, to the end we might not perish, but have everlasting life." In the fulness of time he was made Man, another common Head of mankind, a second general Parent and Representative of the whole human race. And as such it was that "he bore our griefs," "the Lord laying upon him the iniquities of us all." Then was he "wounded for our transgressions, and bruised for our iniquities." "He made his soul an offering for sin:" He poured out his blood for the transgressors: He "bare our sins in his own body on the tree," that by his stripes we might be healed: And by that one oblation of himself, once offered, he hath redeemed me and all mankind; having thereby "made a full, perfect, and sufficient sacrifice and satisfaction for the sins of the whole world."[21]

For Wesley, the Incarnation meant that the Word of God entered into the Servant described in Isaiah. The Servant suffered for the transgressors and became an offering to God in their behalf. There can be no doubt that Wesley's christology was interpreted according to his interpretation of biblical salvation and his own salvation experience.

3. He linked the person of Christ with the distinctive Wesleyan teaching, namely, Christian perfection In order to make explicit the link between Wesley's understanding of the person of Christ and his view of Christian perfection, it is necessary to consider *A Plain Account of Christian Perfection* as believed and taught by the Reverend Mr. John Wesley from the year 1725 to the year 1777. For the record, the title to this work does not imply that after 1777 Wesley must have changed his views, for the evidence is clear and unequivocal that he made no change.

In this particular writing Wesley sets forth his view of Christian perfection and the consistency with which he adhered to that view, notwithstanding the storms of controversy and ridicule it created. In order to provide a context he sets forth a series of developments. Throughout these developments he maintains he consistently adhered to the essential truth of Christian perfection. The series begins in 1725 with Wesley's reading and being deeply moved by Bishop Taylor's writing regarding purity of intention in "Rules and Exercises of Holy Living and Dying." Consequently Wesley made a commitment to which he was faithful through the years with determined consistency.

In 1726 Wesley saw in a new way the nature and extent of inward religion and realized that such religion requires giving all of one's heart to God. This came about as he read Thomas à Kempis's "Christian's Pattern." Within two years, Mr. Law's "Christian Perfection" and "Serious Call" made Wesley determined to be devoted totally to the Lord. In the light of these events, Wesley wrote in *A Plain Account of Christian Perfection:* "Will any considerate man say, that this is carrying matters too far? or that anything less is due to Him who has given himself for us, than to give him ourselves, all we have, and all we are?"[22]

It is obvious that these rhetorical questions are intended to support the validity of the essential truth in the teaching of Christian perfection. In 1729 Wesley devoted himself to intensive Bible reading:

> In the year 1729, I began not only to read, but to study, the Bible, as the one, the only standard of truth, and the only model of pure religion. . . . And this was the light, wherein at this time I generally considered religion, as an uniform following of Christ, an entire inward and outward conformity to our Master. Nor was I afraid of anything more, than of bending this rule to the experience of myself, or of other men; of allowing myself in any the least disconformity to our grand Exemplar.[23]

In the light of renewed Bible study Wesley realized more than ever that Christian perfection was living according to the example of Christ. Then, in 1733, he preached a very important sermon in St. Mary's church at Oxford University entitled "The Circumcision of the Heart." The following quotation includes excerpts from the conclusion of that sermon:

> Let your soul be filled with so entire a love to Him, that you may love nothing but for his sake. . . . Have a pure intention of heart, a stedfast regard to his glory in all your actions. For then, and not till then, is "that mind in us, which was also in Christ Jesus," when in every motion of our heart, in every word of our tongue, in every work of our hands, we "pursue nothing but in relation to him, and in subordination to his pleasure"; when we too neither think, nor speak, nor act, to fulfil "our own will, but the will of Him that sent us"; when, "whether we eat or drink, or whatever we do, we do it all to the glory of God."[24]

In his *Plain Account of Christian Perfection* of 1777, Wesley wrote concerning the sermon "The Circumcision of the Heart":

> It may be observed, this sermon was composed the first of all my writings which have been published. This was the view of religion I then had, which even then I scrupled not to term *perfection*. This is the view I have of it now, without any material addition or diminution. And what is there here, which any man of understanding, who believes the Bible, can object to? What can he deny, without flatly contradicting the Scripture? what retrench, without taking from the word of God?[25]

The point in giving this series of quotations from Wesley's *Plain Account of Christian Perfection* is that the essential truth of Christian perfection was very clear to him and it was scriptural. As Wesley draws his account to a close, he presents with extraordinary sensitivity a summation of the scriptural truth of Christian perfection:

> I found it in the oracles of God, in the Old and New Testaments when I read them with no other view or desire but to save my own soul. But whosoever this doctrine is, I pray you, what harm is there in it? Look at it again; survey it on every side, and that with

the closest attention. In one view, it is purity of intention, dedicating all the life to God. It is giving God all our heart; it is one desire and design ruling all our tempers. It is the devoting, not a part, but all our soul, body, and substance to God. In another view, it is all the mind which was in Christ, enabling us to walk as Christ walked. It is the circumcision of the heart from all filthiness, all inward as well as outward pollution. It is a renewal of the heart in the whole image of God, enabling us to walk as the full likeness of Him that created it. In yet another, it is the loving God with all our heart, and our neighbour as ourselves. Now, take it in which of these views you please, (for there is no material difference,) and this is the whole and sole perfection, as a train of writings prove to be a demonstration, which I have believed and taught for these forty years, from the year 1725 to the year 1765.[26]

Having set forth Wesley's teaching on Christian perfection, it is now possible to establish the link between this distinctive Wesleyan teaching and the person of Christ. Wesley is explicit in making the connection in his *Plain Account of Christian Perfection:*

In every state we need Christ in the following respects. (1.) Whatever grace we receive, it is a free gift from him. (2.) We receive it as his purchase, merely in consideration of the price he paid. (3.) We have this grace, not only from Christ, but in him. For our perfection is not like that of a tree, which flourishes by the sap derived from its own root, but, as was said before, like that of a branch which, united to the vine, bears fruit; but, severed from it, is dried up and withered. (4.) All our blessings, temporal, spiritual, and eternal, depend on his intercession for us, which is one branch of his priestly office, whereof therefore we have always equal need.[27]

Not only is Wesley explicit in making the connection between Christian perfection and the person of Christ with the analogy of the vine and the branches but he also makes the connection between Christian perfection and a moment-to-moment dependence on Christ:

The holiest of men still need Christ, as their Prophet, as "the light of the world." For he does not give them light but from moment to moment: The instant he withdraws, all is darkness. They still need Christ as their King; for God does not give them a stock of holiness. But unless they receive a supply every moment, nothing but unholiness would remain. They still need Christ as their Priest, to make atonement for their holy things. Even perfect holiness is acceptable to God only through Jesus Christ.[28]

Wesley's christology was more than the orthodoxy of the Church of England. His was a christology that made real the experience of Christian perfection. The Christ whom Wesley proclaimed had come with power to save and to make people like Himself. Christ present in a believer is the potential for the quality of perfection that Christ makes possible. Wesley was wholly committed to becoming what the power of the indwelling Christ could accomplish. As dominant as any note he sounded was Wesley's declaration that a Christian grows in grace and exhibits the perfect qualities of Christ. The reason supporting him in this declaration was that the power and presence of Christ were in the Christian to accomplish this work of grace.

IV. CONTEMPORARY CHRISTOLOGY

Contemporary christology is in crisis because three impressive methodologies are in confrontation in scholarly studies. There are other methods, but it seems adequate for a work of this nature to discuss three major ones. These methods open up christology by giving options regarding the person of Christ.

The first method is that which has been and continues to be used by orthodox scholarship, which accepts the historical reliability of the Gospel records and the authoritative interpretation provided by the ancient creeds of Christendom. The second method has roots in the Enlightenment of the eighteenth century with its scientific method for gaining knowledge.

Liberalism, a dominant nineteenth- and twentieth-century theological movement in Christendom, has employed science in the study of the historical accounts provided by the Gospels for the purpose of setting forth the life of the "Jesus of history." The third method is the most recent of the three. It is used by those biblical scholars who study the Gospels historically, not by seeking to discover the literary sources after the manner of the liberal scholars, but by seeking to explain the historical account as composed of "forms," such as teaching, miracle, and parable, with older forms considered more reliable in expressing the earliest apostolic preaching, that is, the *kerygma*.

The second and third methods have roots in the Enlightenment with its reliance on reason and natural science. By contrast, the first method has a long tradition that extends back to the Bible itself and the ancient creeds of the Christian church. It is obvious that the second and third methods are deeply influenced by modern thought with its scientific emphasis. It is incumbent on adherents to the first method to give serious consideration to developments in modern thought in order to maintain relevancy and to engage in meaningful dialogue. In order to gain understanding regarding the options in christology that exist in our time, it is necessary to consider each of these methodologies.

A. Methods of Research and Study

1. The traditional method of orthodoxy It has been axiomatic for this method that the Bible is inspired and that the ancient creeds are authoritative regarding Christian doctrine. In addition, this method has approached the Gospels as historical and has viewed the history of the Gospels as reliable concerning Jesus Christ. Moreover, this method recognizes that the Gospels have a theological as well as a historical concern; that is, they refer to God as well as to history. According to the traditional method, God is transcendent in the sense of being supernatural, and God is also immanent in the sense of being active in creation and becoming incarnate.

Included in the traditional method is the exercise of faith as well as reason, with reason exercising the supportive role in relation to faith. Faith is to be distinguished clearly and emphatically from credulity, by which is meant a disposition to believe without any justification. The faith of which I speak is defined as follows: "Now faith is being sure of what we hope for and certain of what we do not see" (Heb. 11:1).

This characterization of the traditional method may appear simplistic and naïve in relation to the sophisticated methods determined by modern thought. In fact, it may be offensive to some. Therefore, some sincere effort is necessary to characterize modern thought.

2. The historical-criticism method of liberalism The long shadow of the influence of eighteenth-century rationalism as produced by the Enlightenment extended to the nineteenth century and produced the movement called liberalism. Accompanying the rational emphasis of the Enlightenment in the pursuit of knowledge were the new discoveries being made in the natural world. Empirical evidence that was submitted to rational and critical study produced impressive progress in understanding.

The study of history came within this development. To study history scientifically as the empirical world was studied came to mean the study of historical events and their causes. It was held that rational, scientific study could through critical inquiry uncover the empirical causes of historical events. The Enlightenment produced an optimism regarding progress in obtaining knowledge of nature and history.

It was inevitable, it seems, that this method would sooner or later be used in the study of the history recorded in the Gospels. It appears that in the process of establishing the primacy of reason, the advocates of reason came to regard the matter of the inspiration of Scripture as expendable, since it was not subject to rational study that was concerned with empirical evidence. Without regard for the inspiration of Scripture, the historians of the Gospels set out to discover through scientific study of the Gospels the "Jesus of history."

Consistent with the scientific method, the rational historians studied the Gospels for empirical evidence regarding the "Jesus of history." In his study of liberal methodology as used by Adolf Harnack and others, Donald Guthrie comments:

> The result was that the portrait of Jesus was conformed to the contemporary pattern of nineteenth century life. . . . It must be recognized that these principles were affected by the earlier rationalism, the attempt to pass all the gospel materials through the sieve of what is intelligible to reason.[29]

In his important book *God Was in Christ,* Donald Baillie has given a clear and cogent treatment of the liberal "Jesus of history" method.[30] According to Baillie, this method was a natural result in an era that was conscious of a new critical approach in the search for knowledge. Using modern historical methods with scientific efficiency, liberal scholars set out to discover the true historical person called Jesus. The result was that the "Jesus of history" whom the liberal scholars produced stood out among men as He had never stood out before, since it was the custom to emphasize the divinity of Christ in church dogma. By way of modern historical study, liberal studies viewed Jesus in terms of His humanity.

Not only scholars, but also lay persons were greatly influenced by this approach. It seemed correct to begin the study of the Gospels with the intent of discovering Jesus as He really was while on earth. Such a study could be so much more rewarding than the study of the Christ of the creeds, who seemed so mysterious and unapproachable. It would enable one to discover Jesus and then believe on Him. This was the promising and hopeful expectation that the liberal method offered regarding Jesus.

Notwithstanding this expectation, there was the severe limitation of the strictly historical perspective, a perspective controlled by the scientific method of studying history. Consequently the liberal method produced only a human portrait of Jesus. In the light of this, it is with great interest that we consider the next method, for proponents of this method find the liberal method inadequate to provide a portrait of the central personality of the Gospels.

3. The radical "form criticism" method in biblical studies At the end of the nineteenth century, there was considerable optimism that historical-critical studies would provide a portrait of the true historical Jesus. However, the twentieth century was just well under way when Albert Schweitzer's book *The Quest of the Historical Jesus* appeared in German in 1906. This study was a shattering blow to the optimism regarding the results of historical criticism. The conclusion of the study was that historical criticism, instead of portraying "Jesus of history" as a human being acceptable to the rational thought of the nineteenth century, actually disclosed an apocalyptic Jew who made fanatical messianic claims and died disillusioned and mistaken.

With the failure of the historical criticism of liberalism to make it possible to discover the "Jesus of history," a new method known as the form-criticism method appeared in the early part of the twentieth century. Advocates of this method have proposed that the historical accounts that the Gospels give are not concerned with the empirical "facts" of objective history. Liberalism had proposed that the Gospels did provide enough "facts" about the human Jesus that He could be discovered in the Gospels by means of historical criticism. However, the liberal proposal was shown to be defective, according to modern scholarship.

The advocates of form criticism view

the Gospels differently from the way the liberals view them. Rather than viewing the Gospels as containing "facts," they view the Gospels as colored by the faith of the early Christian community. The Gospels, for the form critic, are not factual accounts of the "Jesus of history" but are faith testimonies regarding the "Christ of faith." The proposed end result of the form-criticism method is the coming to a knowledge of what the early Christian community believed and witnessed concerning Christ. This is to say, in effect, that this method offers nothing more than the knowledge of the faith of the early Christians. By using this method we have no way to come to a knowledge of Christ as He is in Himself.

In his analysis of this method, Donald Baillie refers to assumptions that are far-reaching but far from self-evident.[31] One assumption is that the Gospels are not based on "source-documents" but were composed of "forms" by their authors. A second assumption is that the authors used "forms" because these authors had no historical interest. Rather, their interest was theological as well as christological. A third assumption is that during the period when the forms were originating there were no eyewitnesses of Jesus' life and work. A fourth assumption is that the situation *(Sitz im Leben)* of any of the sayings or events recorded in the Gospels must be a situation in the early Christian community and not in the actual life of Jesus.

All of this seems to point out that the form-criticism method approaches the Gospels in search of the witnessing, that is, the *kerygma,* of the early Christians, and not in search of what Jesus Christ actually said and did and meant. Rudolf Bultmann is one of the outstanding form critics of the twentieth century. Norman Perren has been a well-known Bultmannian in the United States. These theologians represent a radical twentieth-century reaction to nineteenth-century historical criticism. They propose a christology based on the faith of the early church. This method is so radical that it results in a christology lacking any historicity but aimed at being acceptable to modern thought.

B. Christology in Crisis

It is clear in our time that methods of scholarship have great influence in the interpretation of the Gospel accounts of Jesus Christ. Therefore, some understanding of contemporary methodology is essential in order to understand contemporary christology.

For John Wesley in the eighteenth century the issue was between an orthodox christology that lacked spiritual vitality and a rational christology influenced by the Enlightenment but untrue to the Gospels. His experience at Aldersgate brought Christ and life to Wesley's orthodoxy. He experienced newness of life by Jesus Christ.

In our time, the issue is more complex. There is the traditional method, which sets forth the Jesus Christ of the Bible and tradition. This includes the acceptance of the Gospel accounts as given by eyewitnesses and as reliable historically. It also includes the acknowledgment of the correctness of interpretation of christology as provided by the Chalcedonian creed; that is, that Jesus Christ was truly God and truly man. Wesleyan christology is, according to the traditional method, coupled with the emphasis on the experience of Jesus Christ in the life of one who truly believes.

Involved in the traditional methodology is a frame of mind that is open to the supernatural and to the revelation of the supernatural in the realm of the natural. Quite frankly, this openness is vulnerable because of the obvious and self-evident fact of the human predicament involving limitations and perversions. Consequently, human responses to the supernatural and to revelation can err. In the Judeo-Christian orthodox tradition there is acknowledgment that even before the Fall the response of Adam and Eve to the

Creator was wrong. Instead of obeying the divine prohibition, they disobeyed it. Yet, Christian orthodoxy recognizes Peter's confession at Caesarea Philippi as right. In answer to Jesus' question, Peter said, "You are the Christ" (Matt. 16:16). Then Jesus replied, "Blessed are you, Simon son of Jonah, for this was not revealed to you by man, but by my Father in heaven" (Matt. 16:17).

To be open to the revelation of God in Christ requires the venture of faith. Human reason and understanding have the ability to exercise an intellectual assent, but this is not equivalent to the total personal trust that the term *faith* symbolizes, as we are using the term. Faith, as understood by orthodox Christianity, involves a total personal trust in the supernatural God. This characteristic of an orthodox Christian is resisted by the modern mind, either as it is under the influence of the rationalism of the Enlightenment and liberalism, or as it is found reacting to that rationalism by way of twentieth-century existentialism or mysticism. In either case, the modern mind finds its haven in the natural dimension. For some this is satisfying, while for others it is bitterly frustrating.

Having considered the christology that the traditional method of orthodoxy sets forth, we now turn to the christology of a liberal historical methodology used within naturalism. In the nineteenth century, the liberal movement in Christianity employed the historical criticism method to project a new interpretation of christology on the scene. In a way, the christology of liberalism was a reaction to the christology of orthodoxy. Liberalism viewed the christology of orthodoxy as inclined toward "docetism"; that is, the inclination to emphasize the divinity of Christ to the extent that the humanity of Christ was only an appearance. Although Jesus appeared to be a man, underneath the appearance he was God. He really had none of the limitations of humanity.

So when the historical criticism method of studying the Gospels showed unmistakably that Jesus was truly human, liberalism declared that it had rediscovered the "Jesus of history." Historical study showed that He not only had a human body, but that He also had limited knowledge, just like other human beings. He really was tempted and frustrated. He really experienced hunger and anger.

Having rediscovered the Jesus of history, liberalism had little more than that to say about Him. It considered the historical facts of the Gospels as of primary importance and did not consider theological references to His being more than a man relevant to the portrait of Him. He was merely humanity at its best. His teachings and example were the primary sources for moral instruction and enlightenment.

This view of Jesus significantly altered the view of salvation as held by the orthodox. Jesus was irrelevant as Savior and Reconciler. Instead, He was the great moral leader and example. Jesus was an example of being conscious of God. He has given an example for all to follow. In following Jesus in this experience of the consciousness of God, we find reconciliation with God.

Dissatisfaction with the results of liberal historical criticism because of the resulting inaccurate picture of the "Jesus of history" caused New Testament scholars to propose another reason for the Gospels being written than to record history. The new proposal of the twentieth century is to consider the Gospels for just what the term *gospel* suggests—"good news." According to the proposed explanation for writing the Gospels, they were not written to present historical events but to declare the Christian faith of the early Christian fellowship in which they originated. Rather than study the Gospels to discover the "Jesus of history," we should study them to discover the "Christ of faith" as that faith professed by the early Christians was incorporated into the Gospels.

Proponents of this method term it "form criticism" because it studies the Gospels as composites of "forms" that may be studied for understanding and knowledge of what the early Christians believed. It is the beliefs of these early Christians that the form critics of this century claim present the "Christ of faith." So when we are given the results of form-criticism research, we are given knowledge of what the early Christians believed concerning Christ, and no more.

Immediately we are aware that we are confronting a whole new way of looking at christology. We are challenged about how much we can really know about what really happened in the land of Palestine nineteen centuries ago by way of historical criticism. This radical historical criticism offers such a radical christology because its advocates consider themselves guided by modern thought. In the light of this guidance, they subject the Gospel records to modern methods of criticism and see orthodoxy as antiquarian in its methods of historical research.

This rejection of orthodox christology is explicit in the contemporary volume entitled *The Myth of God Incarnate,* edited by John Hick, Professor of Theology, Birmingham University, England. The writers of that book are convinced that the time has come in this last part of the twentieth century for a major development in christological understanding. This development must involve the recognition that Jesus was a mere man whom God approved for a special role. The conception of Jesus as God incarnate, which developed among the early Christians after the time of Jesus, is now to be interpreted as merely a mythological or poetic way of referring to Jesus.

This is a radical reinterpretation of the historical Incarnation. It is viewing the Incarnation as the product of wish-fulfillment and imagination. The whole concept is swept out of objective reality into subjective myth.

At this point it is pertinent to recognize the Gospels as historical and the historical character of the origin of Christianity. The Judeo-Christian tradition makes most seriously this fact of history. The Old Testament history includes important references to divine theophanies—that is, God-manifestations. The New Testament history pivots on important references to divine incarnation. It is this New Testament concept to which the fourth Gospel makes reference in the prologue: "In the beginning was the Word . . . and the Word was God. . . . The Word became flesh and lived for a while among us" (John 1:1, 14). Paul inextricably intertwines this New Testament concept with the biblical concept of reconciliation, that is, salvation: "God was reconciling the world to himself in Christ" (2 Cor. 5:18).

It is true that the concept of incarnation may not be acceptable to modern thought, which is not inclined to go beyond the realm of nature. It is also true that incarnation (the Incarnation) is unequivocally indispensable to a christocentric Christianity. The proposal of an incarnation does not conform to modern critical thought with its limitations set by reason. Yet, the issue is enormous, for essential truth concerning Christianity is involved.

It appears to me a strange turn of events that the very environment out of which the modern era emerged with all its remarkable characterizations was a Christianized environment. The Renaissance, the Enlightenment, the modern sciences as well as the arts, industry and technology, modern medicine and education, rationalism and existentialism have all flourished in that part of the world that has been Christianized.

However, if modern thought with its naturalistic limits predominates in the open arena of the free exchange of ideas, traditional orthodox Christianity will be under constraint, in order to be acceptable to the modern-mind syndrome, to undergo transformation. Traditional biblical truth and traditional Christian orthodoxy face transmutation. Christology will have a radical reconstruction.

In the light of that eventuality, Christian scholarship is confronted with a hard question of extraordinary seriousness: Can genuine, authentic Christianity survive the radical transmutation that the modern mind requires for acceptability and understandability? There is no guarantee that change will always be for the better, in fact the chances are that it will be for the worse, our human reason being limited and inclined toward perverseness as it is. Modern rational thought has yet to prove itself capable of the task of translating ancient Christian truth and communicating it to the rational mind.

At the same time, the traditionally minded Christian scholar faces an extraordinary responsibility regarding his relationship to the modern mind. It is our inescapable lot that we live our life in the modern era, rather than in some era more to our fancy. We have no choice regarding our time of life in this natural order. Our time is now, and the challenge and responsibility are truly significant.

C. A Contemporary Christology With a Wesleyan Influence

In order to set before our generation a christology with roots in the Scripture and the creeds of the early Christians and with the relevance that the prophets of the Old Testament and the apostles of the New Testament, as well as Wesley of the eighteenth century, had to their contemporaries, we propose to start with Christian experience.

1. The experience of salvation by faith in Jesus Christ Since the entire New Testament was written by those who experienced salvation, our endeavor to set forth a christology begins with their witness to this experience. An extraordinary example is Paul. He frankly admitted his zeal for the law and its traditions until he experienced Christ in his life. He testifies:

> I have been crucified with Christ and I no longer live, but Christ lives in me. The life I live in the body, I live by faith in the Son of God, who loved me and gave himself for me (Gal. 2:20).
>
> But by the grace of God I am what I am, and his grace to me was not without effect (1 Cor. 15:10).
>
> So from now on we regard no one from a worldly point of view. Though we once regarded Christ in this way, we do so no longer. Therefore, if anyone is in Christ, he is a new creation; the old has gone, the new has come! All this is from God, who reconciled us to himself through Christ and gave us the ministry of reconciliation (2 Cor. 5:16-18).

Paul consistently proclaimed that his experience of salvation changed his understanding of Christ. This was the experience of the first Christians, for Christianity originated among the Jews. It was inevitable that the early Christian believers would make a great effort to give some account of who Jesus was and how it was that by Him individuals experienced salvation.

Peter's outstanding effort on the day of the observance of the Jewish Pentecost was accompanied by the power of the Holy Spirit. The throng attending the festival of Pentecost was aroused by the phenomena of sights and sounds in the midst of the 120 Christian believers who had been waiting for the fulfillment of the promise Jesus had made to His apostles before He ascended. "Amazed and perplexed, they asked one another, 'What does this mean?'" (Acts 2:12).

Peter responded:

> "Fellow Jews and all of you who are in Jerusalem, let me explain this to you; listen carefully to what I say. . . . Jesus of Nazareth was a man accredited by God to you by miracles, wonders and signs, which God did among you through him, as you yourselves know. This man was handed over to you by God's set purpose and foreknowledge; and you, with the help of wicked men, put him to death by nailing him to the cross. But God raised him from the dead, freeing him from the agony of death, because it was impossible for death to keep its hold on him. . . .
>
> "Therefore let all Israel be assured of this: God has made this Jesus, whom you crucified, both Lord and Christ" (Acts 2:14, 22-24, 36).

From the throng of people came the appeal for help: "Brothers, what shall we do?" (Acts 2:37). Peter replied, "Repent and be baptized, every one of you, in the name of Jesus Christ so that your sins may be forgiven'' (v. 38). According to the account, there were about three thousand who received the message and were baptized.

This experience of salvation that occurred to so many people that day is not an isolated phenomenon. John, writing in the prologue of his Gospel, offers it to everyone:

> He was in the world, and though the world was made through him, the world did not recognize him. Yet to all who received him, to those who believed in his name, he gave the right to become children of God—children born not of natural descent, nor of human decision or a husband's will, but born of God.
> The Word became flesh and lived for a while among us. We have seen his glory, the glory of the one and only Son, who came from the Father, full of grace and truth (John 1:10-14).

The writings of the New Testament rest on the belief that the experience of salvation by faith in Jesus Christ is a genuine experience that happens in this life. This experience is not a dream; it is not wishful thinking; it is not emotion. It is a conscious, historical event in a person's life.

By what authority does the validity of the New Testament rest on this belief? The answer is important. According to the historical evidence, Jesus, the man, claimed to be God. Also, according to the evidence, Peter confessed that he believed Jesus was God. In addition, the historical evidence reveals the violence and criminal activity of Jesus' contemporaries against Him for His claim. Matthew's historical account of Jesus' trial before the Sanhedrin reports the actions of this powerful Jewish institution:

> The high priest said to him, "I charge you under oath by the living God: Tell us if you are the Christ, the Son of God."
> "Yes, it is as you say," Jesus replied. "But I say to all of you: In the future you will see the Son of Man sitting at the right hand of the Mighty One and coming on the clouds of heaven."
> Then the high priest tore his clothes and said, "He has spoken blasphemy! . . . What do you think?"
> "He is worthy of death," they answered.
> Then they spit in his face and struck him with their fists. Others slapped him and said, "Prophesy to us, Christ. Who hit you?" (Matt. 26:63-68).

Self-evident in the claim of Jesus that He was God is the theological truth called the Incarnation. This term is of Latin origin from the words *in carnus* ("in flesh"). The most vivid New Testament statement expressing this truth is "The Word became flesh" (John 1:14). Traditional orthodoxy views the theological truth of the Incarnation with awesome respect. Supernatural Deity projecting Himself into the natural order of which humanity is a part is beyond the power of the natural order. Yet this is what the New Testament writings affirm without hesitation or equivocation. The Incarnation is necessary for our salvation. This is the view of the New Testament and is affirmed in the traditional interpretation of orthodox Christians.

2. The tradition of connecting salvation and christology Inherent in Christianity throughout its existence is the great concern regarding the salvation of humanity. The simple yet sublime language of the "golden text of the Bible" expresses that concern: "For God so loved the world that he gave his one and only Son, that whoever believes in him shall not perish but have eternal life" (John 3:16).

The concern regarding the salvation of humanity is indissolubly connected with christology. It comes out of the New Testament and continues in an unbroken tradition in the history of Christianity. It cannot be made irrelevant to Christianity without changing essentially the true character of original Christianity and the Christian understanding of salvation.

It is to the credit of Irenaeus of the second century A.D. that he was the first of the church fathers following the apostolic period to consider this connection thoroughly and explicitly (see the reference to Irenaeus on pp. 340-42). Furthermore, he is truly representative of orthodox Christianity in concentrating on the central ideas of the Christian faith itself. He did not approach Christian thought along some philosophical line. The following quotation from Seeberg illuminates the approach of Irenaeus to this connection between salvation and christology, which is our immediate concern:

> This union of God with the human nature, for Irenaeus, is of the greatest religious significance. Thus God himself has entered the race and become an active force in it. Inasmuch as the Logos assumed flesh of our flesh, he united all flesh to God. From this point of view we must interpret the life of our Lord: "For in what way could we have been able to be the partakers of this adoption as sons, unless through the Son we had received from him that communion which brings us to him—unless his Word, made flesh, had communicated it to us? Wherefore he comes also to every age, restoring to all that communion which brings to God" (iii. 18.7; 19.1; v. 14.2).[32]

For Irenaeus, with his practical religious interest, christology is intimately bound up with salvation. The reality of salvation depends on God's becoming true man and experiencing human existence. By maintaining a hold on this connection between salvation and christology, Irenaeus maintained an orthodox christology.

He was able to avoid the misunderstanding that Jesus was only God and not man. The New Testament writings clearly state that Jesus was a man. Irenaeus was able to avoid the misunderstanding that Jesus was some kind of an intermediate being between God and man, as Arianism maintained. He avoided the misunderstanding that in Jesus God only appeared to be a man. This was the error of Docetism and Apollinarianism. Finally, we may note that Irenaeus avoided the heresy that Jesus as man became divine. This is the error of Adoptionism.

We must emphasize that the approach to christology that keeps it connected with soteriology—that is, salvation—has the strength and resource for determining erroneous understandings of christology. Beginning with the recognition of the priority of faith, Irenaeus accepted three norms for doctrinal statements. He accepted the "rule of faith," that is, the acknowledged and accepted tradition of apostolic teachings. He also recognized the bishops of the church as the ongoing custodians of the Christian teachings. Finally, he acknowledged the canon of Scripture as authoritative.

The main challenge that faced Irenaeus was Gnosticism, and the main issue in the challenge was the matter of salvation. Gnosticism with its first principle being a dualistic view of reality, with matter being the realm of evil and spirit being the realm of good—God being the unapproachable supreme Good—viewed salvation as escape from matter. Irenaeus set forth an extraordinary alternative view of salvation. Supported by the New Testament and emphasizing the connection between salvation and christology, he established the orthodox interpretation of christology. He was decisively influential in the Chalcedonian council of the fifth century, so sound was the view he had set forth some two and one-half centuries earlier.

For our purposes, there is nothing noteworthy in the development of christological interpretation until the sixteenth century when Luther experienced the biblical doctrine of salvation. This occurred after years of gigantic struggles in his soul about his salvation. It was during the years 1505-1508, as a monk in the monastery at Erfurt, that Luther groped in spiritual darkness. It was his spiritual goal to attain divine favor through the good works of his monastic life. Yet he came to the fearful conclusion, after years of effort, that all his good works at the monastery had not brought him salvation.

In 1508 Luther was called to teach at the University of Wittenberg, where Johannes von Staupitz was dean. Staupitz was not only a scholar but also a true shepherd of souls. He urged the spiritually distraught Luther to look to the wounds of Christ and see them as the expression of God's love for the sinner. He showed Luther that a sinner's penitence is not the doing of penance as an effort at good works but a change of mind and heart toward God's love as revealed in the wounds and blood of Christ.

During 1513-1515, Luther was lecturer on the Psalms at Wittenberg. It is evident from his lectures that he had experienced a new understanding of salvation. His biblical exegesis involved looking at a passage in four different ways. First, the literal and historical way—applying the passage to Christ, since Christ was the focal point of the Bible, the Old Testament as well as the New. Second, the allegorical way—applying the passage to God's activity in the church. Third, the spiritual way—applying the passage to God's activity in the individual soul. Fourth, the mystical way—applying the passage to God's activity in the last days. Not every passage could be studied in these four ways, but Luther used them as they were applicable.

By this fourfold method, Luther prepared his lectures on the Psalms. As he studied Psalms 22 and 31 he applied the passages to Christ and His bleeding, wounded body. Then he applied them to his own suffering soul. As he became aware of Jesus' faith in God during the agonizing passion of the crucifixion, he began to realize the meaning of salvation. While he studied the Psalms, he also studied Romans. The following words took on increasing significance for him: "For in the gospel a righteousness from God is revealed, a righteousness that is by faith from first to last, just as it is written: 'The righteous will live by faith'" (Rom. 1:17).

Illumination came to Luther as he realized that there was a connection between "the righteousness from God" and the "faith" that a believer exercises for righteousness and salvation. That "righteousness from God" is what Jesus and His wounds accomplished. It is faith in Christ rather than merit of good works that saves. God's way of making righteous is Christ and His crucifixion.

Formerly Luther had understood the "righteousness of God" as God's expectation that everyone become righteous before Him by doing good works. At the monastery at Erfurt Luther had tried as hard as he could, but he found no relief from the agony of his soul. With the new understanding of the "righteousness of God," that God's way of making righteous is by Jesus Christ and His wounds, Luther experienced an inexpressible love for the "righteousness of God." What had formerly terrorized Luther's soul now became an occasion of love.

In 1515-1516, Luther lectured on Romans at the University of Wittenberg. He opened his lectures with this emphasis:

> The sense and substance of this letter is: to pull down, to pluck up, and to destroy all wisdom and righteousness of the flesh . . . no matter how heartily and sincerely they may be practiced, and to implant, establish, and make large the reality of sin (however unconscious we may be of its existence).[33]

It was very clear to Luther that human efforts to be right with God could never succeed:

> For God does not want to save us by our own but by an extraneous righteousness which does not originate in ourselves but comes from beyond ourselves, which does not arise on our earth but comes from heaven. Therefore, we must come to know this righteousness which is utterly external and foreign to us. . . .
> For even if by his native and spiritual gifts a man is wise, righteous, and good in the sight of men, he is not so regarded by God, especially if he himself considers himself as such. . . .
> For we all hope and wish our own achievements to be accepted by God and rewarded by him. But it remains forever true: "It is not of him that wills, nor of him that runs, but of God that has mercy" (Rom. 9:16).[34]

Luther's treatment of salvation cannot be separated from the orthodox view of christology without destroying both the understanding and the experience of salvation. To Luther salvation was an act of God accomplished through faith in Christ. The following quotation is as explicit a statement on Christ as anything else that Luther wrote:

> This is the chief doctrine of the Christian faith. The sophists have completely obliterated it, and today the fanatics are obscuring it once more. Here you see how necessary it is to believe and confess the doctrine of the divinity of Christ. When Arius denied this, it was necessary also for him to deny the doctrine of redemption. For to conquer the sin of the world, death, the curse, and the wrath of God in Himself—this is the work, not of any creature but of the divine power. Therefore it was necessary that He who was to conquer these in Himself should be true God by nature. For in opposition to this mighty power—sin, death, and the curse—which of itself reigns in the whole world and in the entire creation, it is necessary to set an even higher power, which cannot be found and does not exist apart from the divine power. Therefore to abolish sin, to destroy death, to remove the curse in Himself, to grant righteousness, to bring life to light (2 Tim. 1:10), and to bring the blessing in Himself, that is, to annihilate these things and to create those—all these are works solely of the divine power. Since Scripture attributes all these to Christ, therefore He Himself is Life, Righteousness, and Blessing, that is, God by nature and in essence. Hence those who deny the divinity of Christ lose all Christianity and become Gentiles and Turks through and through.
>
> As I often warn, therefore, the doctrine of justification must be learned diligently. For in it are included all the other doctrines of our faith; and if it is sound, all the others are sound as well. Therefore when we teach that men are justified through Christ and that Christ is the Victor over sin, death, and the eternal curse, we are testifying at the same time that he is God by nature.[35]

Two things are perfectly clear in this quotation: First, salvation is the work of Christ, and the work of no one else. Second, salvation is organically and inseparably connected with the person of Christ. It is this connection that is decisive in the tradition of orthodoxy for the understanding of christology. Christ is who He is because of the salvation He provides humanity. This important connection must always be in evidence in formulating christological interpretations.

In surveying the highlights of the tradition that connects salvation and christology, we pass from Martin Luther of the sixteenth century to John Wesley of the eighteenth century. The obvious point of contact is Luther's preface to the Epistle to the Romans. This preface was read at the service at Aldersgate on May 24, 1738, in the presence of John Wesley, whose heart was strangely warmed. For years, Wesley had had an intense desire to have the certainty of salvation but he could not attain it.

He had believed that salvation was by way of good works and moral goodness. In his effort to gain salvation, he did good works in England. Then in 1735, he left England as a missionary to the American Indians in Georgia: "Our end in leaving our native country was not to avoid want, . . . but singly this,—to save our souls; to live wholly to the glory of God."[36]

Wesley went out to do good works, but he came back disillusioned; on February 29, 1738, he wrote:

> It is now two years and almost four months since I left my native country, in order to teach the Georgian Indians the nature of Christianity: But what have I learned myself meantime? . . .
>
> This, then have I learned in the ends of the earth—That I "am fallen short of the glory of God:" That my whole heart is "altogether corrupt and abominable;" and, consequently, my whole life; . . . That "alienated" as I am from "the life of God," I am "a child of wrath," an heir of hell: That my own works, my own sufferings, my own righteousness are so far from reconciling me to an offended God, so far from making any atonement for the least of my sins, . . . I have no hope, but that of being justified freely, "through the redemption that is in Jesus:" I have no hope, but that if I seek I shall find Christ, and "be found in him not having my own righteousness, but that

which is through the faith of Christ, the righteousness which is of God by faith." (Phil. iii.9.)[37]

It shocked Wesley greatly as he came to realize his missionary zeal and his "good work" of going to Georgia as a missionary, instead of assuring him of salvation, actually shattered any sense of assurance and security regarding the matter of his salvation. He experienced utter hopelessness regarding his ability to merit salvation by good works.

In the extremity of spiritual frustration and defeat, Wesley went "very unwillingly" to a meeting at Aldersgate on May 24, 1738. Apparently he had no awareness of how close he was to the time when he would experience salvation through faith in Jesus Christ. He already clearly understood salvation by faith intellectually. He even preached this teaching to others in the months prior to May 24. Yet he had no conscious awareness that he had experienced personal salvation. Therefore, his conscious experience of the warming of his heart by faith in Christ was of the greatest importance. It was the confirmation in concrete experience of what God promised through Christ, as that promise was given in the Bible. In sincere honesty, Wesley wrote that he felt that he trusted in Christ alone for salvation. What happened as the result of his trusting Christ is beyond explanation in terms of human reason: "An assurance was given me, that he had taken away *my* sins, even *mine,* and saved *me* from the law of sin and death."[38]

In the remarkably eloquent and also exceedingly clear conclusion of his outstanding sermon "Justification by Faith," Wesley sets aside all human effort and looks to Christ alone for salvation:

> For he that cometh unto God by this faith, must fix his eye singly on his own wickedness, on his guilt and helplessness, without having the least regard to any supposed good in himself, to any virtue or righteousness whatsoever. He must come as a *mere sinner,* . . . Thus it is, and thus alone, when his *mouth is stopped,* and he stands utterly *guilty before* God, that he can *look unto Jesus,* as the whole and sole *Propitiation for his sins.* Thus only can he be *found in him,* and receive the "righteousness which is of God by faith . . . Thus *look unto Jesus!* There is *the Lamb of God,* who *taketh away* thy *sins!* . . . Plead thou, singly, the blood of the covenant, the ransom paid for thy proud, stubborn, sinful soul.[39]

It is essential in Wesley's view of salvation that Christ be a sufficient Savior. Therefore, because salvation is a supernatural event in the life of one who believes in Christ, there must be a supernatural explanation of how salvation is accomplished. Wesley stands squarely in the orthodox tradition as he affirms a christology that is adequate to explain soteriology. In the following quotation he shows the necessity of the Incarnation for Jesus Christ to be true God and true man:

> In this state we were, even all mankind, when "God so loved the world, that he gave his only-begotten Son, to the end we might not perish, but have everlasting life." In the fulness of time he was made Man, another common Head of mankind, a second general Parent and Representative of the whole human race. And as such it was that "he bore our griefs," "the Lord laying upon him the iniquities of us all." Then was he "wounded for our transgressions, and bruised for our iniquities." "He made his soul an offering for sin:" He poured out his blood for the transgressors: He "bare our sins in his own body on the tree," that by his stripes we might be healed: And by that one oblation of himself, once offered, he hath redeemed me and all mankind; having thereby "made a full, perfect, and sufficient sacrifice and satisfaction for the sins of the whole world." . . . So that, for the sake of his well-beloved Son, of what he hath done and suffered for us, God now vouchsafes, on one only condition, (which himself also enables us to perform,) both to remit the punishment due to our sins, to reinstate us in his favour, and to restore our dead souls to spiritual life, as the earnest of life eternal.[40]

Because Jesus Christ is God and man, He has accomplished our salvation. Because of a genuine Incarnation, we experience a genuine salvation when we believe in the incarnate One and His work of salvation for us.

This review of the highlights of the orthodox tradition that consistently associates christology with soteriology discloses a high christology in which Jesus Christ is understood as truly God and truly man because the salvation of humanity is possible in no other way and by no other means. It is the neglect of this connection of christology with soteriology that has opened christology to unorthodox interpretations. The nineteenth and twentieth centuries exhibit such developments. On the one hand, the liberal source-critical view, dominant in the nineteenth century, interpreted christology within the framework of the "Jesus of history," while, on the other hand, the more radical form-critical view, made impressive in the twentieth century by such critics as Rudolf Bultmann, interpret christology within the framework of the existential meaning of the "Christ of faith," severed from all historical roots of the first century.

3. The importance of the Incarnation for christology The central problem in christology, from the viewpoint of traditional orthodoxy, is not the reality of the supernatural in relationship with the natural but our concept of this reality and our attempts to communicate this concept. In traditional orthodoxy we say that Jesus Christ is both God and man. Why do we make that statement and what do we mean by it? How do we explain the occurrence of this unique fact?

A helpful analogical approach to christology is a consideration of the experience with which every true Christian is familiar: a person's awareness that every good thing about him or her in the Christian life is not because of the human person but because of God. Paul puts it so well: "I no longer live, but Christ lives in me. The life I live in the body, I live by faith in the Son of God" (Gal. 2:20).

The true Christian knows as well as anyone else that he or she is free to choose. In a sense, everything depends on the choices we make. When we make the wrong choice, we carry the full responsibility of making such a choice. Yet when we make the right choice, the true Christian realizes, it is not simply a basis for human merit. Rather, the Christian acknowledges a prevenient grace. The right choice is possible because it is God's will that it be. Granted that this is the experience that Christians have, the intellectual concept and the verbal communication of such an experience is difficult to achieve and easily misunderstood.

Applying the realization that Paul describes in terms of "I live . . . yet not I but Christ" to the life of Jesus in relation to the Father, we find that John's Gospel records extraordinary claims of Jesus. These claims help us to understand christology. On the one hand, Jesus claims to make human choices: "I always do what pleases him" (John 8:29). "I lay down my life. . . . I lay it down of my own accord" (John 10:17-18). "I have brought you glory on earth by completing the work you gave me to do" (John 17:4). On the other hand, Jesus affirms that His choices depend on the Father: "By myself I can do nothing" (John 5:30). "The words I say to you are not just my own. Rather, it is the Father, living in me, who is doing his work" (John 14:10). Here is the experience of the One who is the very essence of Christianity experiencing both humanity and divinity.

If the question be raised by historical scholarship as to how accurate the Johannine discourses are in giving the exact words of Jesus, the responses, predictably, will vary according to the method used. Liberal historical criticism of the "sources" will answer that the discourses disclose only what the human Jesus could claim within the limits of His humanity. Radical modern historical criticism of the "forms" will answer that the discourses disclose only what the early church claimed about Jesus, not what Jesus claimed. Traditional orthodoxy will answer that the Johannine discourses are accepted as historically reliable and they disclose in Jesus both humanity and divinity.

As we recognize the different answers, we respect all the more a central clue in all of this, namely, Jesus' own experience. What Jesus was experiencing included the humanity of the natural order and the deity of the supernatural order. This explanation of Jesus' experience, which is along the lines of orthodoxy, is in harmony with our own finite Christian experience, where our humanity is in such a relationship with Christ that we honestly and truly say, "I live; yet not I, but Christ liveth in me" (Gal. 2:20 KJV).

This leads to an important point, namely, the incarnation of Christ, rather than being clarified by the analogy from our own finite experience of "Christ in me," is in some sense the prototype of the Christian experience. This would suggest that the incarnation of Christ provides a divinely revealed model in Christian experience.

It is realistic to state that the central problem of christology—that is, how Jesus could be both human and divine—is continually exposed to erroneous interpretation by an emphasis of the divine over the human, or vice versa. The error is to minimize either the transcendent divinity or the historical humanity of Jesus Christ so that He is neither fully God nor fully man. In early Christian thought, the adherents of Adoptionism and Ebionism regarded Jesus as a man who achieved such remarkable goodness that He was exalted to deity. On the other hand, Docetism and Apollinarianism regarded Jesus as God disguised in the form of a man.

Christology is continually with us because of the timeless relevance of the question Jesus asked the disciples: "Who do you say I am?" (Mark 8:29). It is an intensely personal question. It involves much more than human scholarship because it has an intimate connection with the matter of our salvation. When the matter of salvation is treated with indifference or even outright rejection, we become more keenly aware of the importance of a high understanding of christology.

The concern for salvation and for a Christ who is sufficient for our salvation is evident in the tradition of orthodoxy, as Paul, Irenaeus, Luther, Wesley, and contemporary orthodox theologians show. Essential for meeting that concern is an understanding of christology that reflects in our concept of who Christ is. He is not a mere concept of human experience and understanding. His identity is of greatest concern to the scholarly Christian. The Bible discloses with vivid clarity to believers that Jesus is who He claims to be, namely, Son of God and Son of Mary. The creed of Chalcedon declares Jesus to be of two natures—the one fully divine and the other fully human. Jesus Christ is God incarnate. For those with the twentieth-century naturalistic mind-set, the great problem regarding christology is how to make it intelligible and acceptable. That Jesus could have two natures, one of the natural order and the other of the supernatural order, is inconceivable because the naturalistic mind does not accept the supernatural, which is discarded as superstition, wishful thinking, and imaginative conjecture.

In the arena of sophisticated modern scholarship, my point of view may appear naïve and simplistic to some, but I see a need for the opening of our minds to the supernatural. I see a need for an enormous and "agonizing reappraisal" of the modern mind-set with its criteria for knowledge deeply imbedded in the natural order. I see the need for a faith in the incarnate Christ, who makes known God, and in the supernatural not as mere wishful thinking but as true reality.

4. The offices of Christ Christ, having divine and human natures, is the only sufficient Mediator between God and humanity. By reason of His being a Mediator, Christ has functions, or offices. Traditionally, these have been identified as those of prophet, priest, and king. In Eusebius's *Ecclesiastical History* (I.3.8–9), written in the fourth century, these offices are given prominence. John

Calvin has made significant use of them in his *Institutes*. The sermons of John Wesley reflect the importance he attached to these offices. His sermon "The Law Established Through Faith: 2" is exemplary: "To preach Christ, as a workman that needeth not to be ashamed, is to preach him, not only as our great High Priest . . . but likewise as the Prophet of the Lord . . . yea, and as remaining a King forever."[41]

a. The prophetic office As Prophet, Christ communicates the Word of God to us. Like the prophets of the Old Testament, whose messages included both "forthtelling" and foretelling as they served as mediators between God and Israel, Christ is Mediator in declaring God's Word for both the present time and the future. As the incarnate Word, He is the perfect Prophet. An impressive example of His prophetic authority is the Sermon on the Mount (see especially Matt. 5:22, 28, 32, 34, 39, 44).

b. The priestly office As Priest, Christ appears in the presence of God for us. He is the representative of all humanity. Great emphasis is given this office in the Epistle to the Hebrews. The author of this epistle skillfully presents Christianity as superior to all other faiths. For him the greatest reason for the superiority of Christianity is that Christ is the superior Priest. Christ has offered to God an atoning sacrifice that is sufficient for the salvation of all believers (Heb. 2:17).

In this epistle, Christ is also presented as the sufficient sacrifice, which He offered in His own person on the cross (Heb. 9:26, 28). In addition to offering Himself as a sacrifice, Christ offers continual intercession to God for the purpose of providing for the continual bestowal of the blessings of His salvation on His redeemed ones (Heb. 7:25-27; 9:24-28). This is of great comfort to those who trust in Christ as their Priest. It is clear that Christ needs to be both divine and human as the Priest who appears in the presence of God on our behalf.

c. The kingly office As King, Christ exercises the right to reign. His ascension marked His entrance into royal splendor. It is in Revelation that strong biblical evidence for Christ's kingship is given. It is summed up in the dramatic title: "KING OF KINGS AND LORD OF LORDS" (Rev. 19:16). Revelation recounts how it will come about that "The kingdom of the world has become the kingdom of our Lord and of his Christ" (Rev. 11:15).

5. The estates of Christ During the christological controversy in the early church, it was recognized that Jesus has two natures and, also, that He existed in two states, namely, those of humiliation and exaltation. It is necessary to recognize this. There is confusion if the study of the two natures is not clearly distinguished from the study of the two estates. The two estates refer to Christ's rank or position. They give recognition to the varying emphases on His two natures as we perceive them in relationship to each other.

The Scriptures portray Jesus Christ in positions of striking contrast. Old Testament expectations as well as the historical accounts in the Gospels and the Christian eschatology of the entire New Testament reinforce this contrast. Jesus Christ is presented both in the state of humiliation and in the state of exaltation.

a. The state of humiliation A major reason for the opposition Jesus encountered during His earthly life was His humble estate. In addition to the opposition from His contemporaries, Jesus suffered intense humiliation in His passion week, when He was tried, beaten, and crucified. The sheer quantity of data in the Gospels testifies to the importance of the Passion Week. Approximately one-half of John, one-third of Mark, and one-fourth of both Matthew and Luke present the passion narrative.

For Jesus to be subjected to the state of humiliation was essential for the redemption of mankind. Paul's language is clear:

> For the message of the cross is foolishness to those who are perishing, but to us who are

being saved it is the power of God. For it is written:

> "I will destroy the wisdom of the wise;
> the intelligence of the intelligent I will frustrate."

Where is the wise man? Where is the scholar? Where is the philosopher of this age? Has not God made foolish the wisdom of the world? For since in the wisdom of God the world through its wisdom did not know him, God was pleased through the foolishness of what was preached to save those who believe. Jews demand miraculous signs and Greeks look for wisdom, but we preach Christ crucified: a stumbling block to Jews and foolishness to Gentiles, but to those whom God has called, both Jews and Greeks, Christ the power of God and the wisdom of God (1 Cor. 1:18–24).

In this discussion on the humiliation of Christ, we should continually recognize the risk of overemphasizing the humanity of Christ. In His humiliation, Jesus was fully God. It is not merely His humanity that endured the state of humiliation; rather, it was His person that endured. He was no less a person in His humiliation. He remained fully God and fully man. Our salvation requires this.

The following Scripture sets forth the nature of the humiliation clearly:

> Your attitude should be the same as that of Christ Jesus:
>
> Who, being in very nature God,
> did not consider equality with God something to be grasped,
> but made himself nothing,
> taking the very nature of a servant,
> being made in human likeness.
> And being found in appearance as a man,
> he humbled himself
> and became obedient to death—
> even death on a cross!
> Therefore God exalted him to the highest place
> and gave him the name that is above every name,
> that at the name of Jesus every knee should bow,
> in heaven and on earth and under the earth,
> and every tongue confess that Jesus Christ is Lord,
> to the glory of God the Father.
>
> (Phil. 2:5–11)

It is evident in this portion of Scripture that Paul refers to Christ's state of exaltation as well as His state of humiliation. However, we must avoid understanding the humiliation as depicting the human nature of Jesus Christ. Rather, the Incarnation occurred when the divine person, the Son of God, who possesses the divine nature, took the nature of man into personal union with His divine nature. In doing this, the divine Son entered into the consciousness of temptations and sufferings that are like ours. Here is an important truth regarding the Incarnation: it was a divine act, not a human act. In that divine act, the divine Son entered personally into human nature in such a manner as to be conscious of the trials and hurts and experiences that we have.

Traditional orthodoxy needs to give emphasis to the christological truth that both the divine nature and the human nature of Christ enter into the consciousness of His person in the ordeal of His suffering and death. If the human nature alone were involved in the humiliation, Jesus Christ would not be the Savior we need. We need the God-man for our salvation.

b. The state of exaltation Paul makes it clear in the portion of Philippians quoted above that Jesus Christ, the incarnate One, was first in the state of humiliation and then in the state of exaltation. Although there is no explicit reference to the Resurrection in the passage, it was that event that brought Jesus out of the state of humiliation; at the same time, that event certainly was a part of the state of exaltation. Traditional orthodoxy declares that the Resurrection was a historical fact.

The enemies of Jesus resist this view. From their point of view, there is no place for the resurrection of Jesus. In fact nature itself testifies that resurrection is superstition or myth. Notwithstanding these and other factors opposed to the Resurrection as historical fact, this event is indispensable in the life of the incarnate Christ. Its absolute necessity is asserted by Paul:

> And if Christ has not been raised, your faith is futile; you are still in your sins. Then those who have fallen asleep in Christ are lost. If only for this life we have hope in Christ, we are to be pitied more than all men (1 Cor. 15:17-18).

Evidence for the Resurrection can be ignored, distorted, or ridiculed. It cannot be refuted. Of exceptional importance is the fact that on the Day of Pentecost, which was just fifty days after the Crucifixion, the apostolic preaching of Jesus' resurrection convinced thousands. The enemies of Jesus heard the preaching concerning the Resurrection but they could not refute it. The apostles were preaching historical truth.

The supreme proof of the Resurrection is the person of Jesus Christ. Although the disciples had great difficulty at first because of the staggering blow of the Crucifixion, they came to see that, Jesus being who He was, it was inevitable that He would rise again. Peter, preaching at Pentecost, declared: "But God raised him from the dead, freeing him from the agony of death, because it was impossible for death to keep its hold on him" (Acts 2:24).

Included in the exaltation is Jesus Christ's ascension to the right hand of God. The proof of this is the descent of the Holy Spirit on the Day of Pentecost. Peter made this very clear:

> God has raised this Jesus to life, and we are all witnesses of the fact. Exalted to the right hand of God, he has received from the Father the promised Holy Spirit and has poured out what you now see and hear. . . . God has made this Jesus, whom you crucified, both Lord and Christ (Acts 2:32-33, 36).

At the Ascension, Jesus had promised His disciples that He would send them the Holy Spirit. The fulfillment of that promise was evidence that Jesus was truly the exalted One. In fact, He is Lord. Peter referred to Christ as Lord, the equivalent to the "I AM" by which God revealed Himself to Moses (Exod. 3:14).

More than this, the exaltation of Christ is to reach its consummation with His second coming. During Passion Week, Jesus had talked with His disciples about the future. In His famous eschatological discourse, He told them of His coming. It would be so public that there would be no doubt about it:

> For as the lightning comes from the east and flashes to the west, so will be the coming of the Son of Man. . . .
> No one knows about that day or hour, not even the angels in heaven, nor the Son, but only the Father. As it was in the days of Noah, so it will be at the coming of the Son of Man. . . .
> Therefore keep watch, because you do not know on what day your Lord will come. . . . So you also must be ready, because the Son of Man will come at an hour when you do not expect him (Matt. 24:27, 36-37, 42, 44).

Paul also has words to say concerning the second coming of Christ. This is a dominant theme in his correspondence to the young Christian church at Thessalonica:

> According to the Lord's own word, we tell you that we who are still alive, who are left till the coming of the Lord, will certainly not precede those who have fallen asleep. For the Lord himself will come down from heaven, with a loud command, with the voice of the archangel and with the trumpet call of God, and the dead in Christ will rise first (1 Thess. 4:15-16).

It is the Book of Revelation that gives the fullest and most dramatic disclosure of the second coming of Christ. The theme of the book is phrased accurately in the following words:

> The kingdom of the world has become the
> kingdom of our Lord and of his Christ,
> and he will reign for ever and ever.
> (Rev. 11:15)

He will reign as King of kings and Lord of lords. His sovereign rights have come at the cost of great humiliation. He who shall march on as invincible Lord will do so because He "took a towel" and became a servant. If He is King, it is because He willingly endured crucifixion. As the risen, ascended, and reigning King at the right hand of God, Jesus is Lord of heaven and earth. He will return to earth as He promised.

The Book of Revelation is clearly christological. It gives unequivocal evidence of Jesus as a historical person. He is of the Jewish race (5:5); He had twelve apostles (21:14); He was crucified in Jerusalem (11:8). Moreover, Jesus rose from the dead (1:5, 18) and is now exalted (3:21). The entire Book of Revelation discloses the authority of Jesus Christ over history, which is set forth by the One whom John referred to as being "like a son of man" (1:13). This One spoke to John:

> I am the First and the Last. I am the Living One; I was dead, and behold I am alive for ever and ever! And I hold the keys of death and Hades. . . .

> Write, therefore, what you have seen, what is now and what shall take place later (Rev. 1:17-19).

Jesus Christ is presented as the Lamb (5:6); as the Lion of Judah and heir to the throne of David (5:5); as the conquering Son of Man (14:14-15); and as the Word of God (19:13). He is the guardian of the church (1:12-20) and He is the final judge of the earth (22:12). He is the shining light of the final city of God (21:23). The main theme of Revelation is the second coming of Christ.

The supreme proof that makes Revelation credible is the person of Jesus Christ. He is the incarnate God-man, having two complete natures in one person. By Him the incredible becomes credible, and the impossible, possible. John heard the enthroned Sovereign say, "I am making everything new! . . . It is done. I am the Alpha and the Omega, the Beginning and the End" (Rev. 21:5-6).

NOTES

[1] George Eldon Ladd, *The New Testament and Criticism* (Grand Rapids: Eerdmans, 1967), p. 14.

[2] H. D. McDonald, *Jesus—Human and Divine* (Grand Rapids: Zondervan, 1968), p. 45.

[3] Ibid., p. 46.

[4] John Wesley, *Explanatory Notes Upon the New Testament* (London: Epworth, 1948), p. 302.

[5] *The Works of John Wesley*, 14 vols. (1872; reprint ed., Grand Rapids: Zondervan, n.d.), 7:513.

[6] Henry Bettenson, *Doctrines of the Christian Church* (New York and London: Oxford University Press, 1943), pp. 72-73.

[7] Ibid., p. 42.

[8] Reinhold Seeberg, *Textbook of the History of Doctrines* (Grand Rapids: Baker, 1956), p. 129.

[9] Jerald C. Brauer, ed., *The Westminster Dictionary of the Church* (Philadelphia: Westminster, 1971), p. 819.

[10] Philip Schaff, *Creeds of Christendom*, 3 vols., 4th ed. (New York: Harper and Brothers, 1919), 1:488.

[11] John Dillenberger and Claude Welch, *Protestant Christianity* (New York: Scribner, 1955), pp. 127-29.

[12] *The Works of Wesley*, 1:103.

[13] Ibid., 1:101-2.

[14] Ibid., 1:102.

[15] Williston Walker, *A History of the Christian Church* (New York: Scribner, 1959), p. 454.

[16] *The Works of Wesley*, 10:81-82.

[17] Ibid., 3:315.

[18] John Wesley, *Explanatory Notes*, p. 16.

[19] *The Works of Wesley*, 5:55-57.

[20] Ibid., 7:51-53.

[21] Ibid., 5:55.

[22] Ibid., 11:367.

[23] Ibid.

[24] Ibid., 11:368-69.

[25] Ibid., 11:369.

[26] Ibid., 11:444.

[27] Ibid., 11:396.

[28] Ibid., 11:417.

[29] Donald Guthrie, *A Shorter Life of Christ* (Grand Rapids: Zondervan, 1970), p. 34.

[30] D. M. Baillie, *God Was in Christ* (New York: Scribner, 1948), pp. 30ff.

[31] Ibid., p. 56.
[32] Seeberg, *History of Doctrines*, p. 125.
[33] Martin Luther, *Lectures on Romans*, trans. and ed. Wilhelm Pauck (*Library of Christian Classics*, 26 vols., Philadelphia: Westminster, 1961), 15:3.
[34] Ibid., 15:5-6.
[35] *Luther's Works*, 54 vols., ed. Jaroslav Pelikan (St. Louis: Concordia, 1963), 26:282-83.
[36] *The Works of Wesley*, 1:17.
[37] Ibid., 1:76-77.
[38] Ibid., 1:103.
[39] Ibid., 5:63-64.
[40] Ibid., 5:55.
[41] Ibid., 5:461-62.

DISCUSSION QUESTIONS

1. What scriptural evidence can be cited in support of Jesus' claim that He was the God-man?
2. What was the heresy in each of the following: Apollinarianism, Nestorianism, and Eutychianism?
3. Summarize the essential content of the Chalcedonian Creed.
4. Characterize the eighteenth-century Enlightenment, which was contemporary with John Wesley.
5. Give the highlights of John Wesley's teaching concerning Jesus Christ.
6. Distinguish the following methods used in the study of christology: (1) the traditional method of orthodoxy, (2) the historical criticism method of liberalism, and (3) the radical form-criticism method in biblical study.
7. Summarize the present crisis in christological study.
8. Discuss the impact that the experience of salvation by faith in Jesus Christ has on the study of christology.
9. Discuss the significance of the connection between salvation and christology.
10. List and explain the offices and estates of Christ.
11. Explore the reasons for errors in christological thought.
12. Set forth the biblical teaching on christology.
13. Of what importance is christological doctrine today?
14. Is it possible for a person to be saved if he or she is in error regarding Jesus Christ?

RECOMMENDATIONS FOR FURTHER READING

D. M. Baillie, *God Was in Christ* (New York: Scribner, 1948), pp. 9-132.

Hendrikus Boers, "Where Christology Is Real: A Survey of Recent Research on New Testament Christology," *Interpretation*, vol. 26, no. 3 (July 1972): 300-27.

Robert W. Burtner and Robert E. Chiles, eds., *A Compend of Wesley's Theology* (New York and Nashville: Abingdon, 1954), pp. 71-88.

William Ragsdale Cannon, *The Redeemer* (New York and Nashville: Abingdon-Cokesbury, 1951), pp. 7-224.

Donald G. Dawe, "Christology in Contemporary Systematic Theology," *Interpretation*, vol. 26, no. 3 (July 1972): 259-77.

S. J. Gamertsfelder, *Systematic Theology* (Harrisburg, Pa.: Evangelical, 1921), pp. 223-72.

H. D. McDonald, *Jesus—Human and Divine* (Grand Rapids: Zondervan, 1968), pp. 11-140.

John Miley, *Systematic Theology*, 2 vols. (New York: Eaton and Mains, 1894), 2:1-62.

James Orr, *The Christian View of God and the World* (New York: Scribner, 1893), pp. 213-84.

Clark H. Pinnock, "Chalcedon: A Creed to Touch Off Christmas," *Christianity Today*, vol. 24, no. 21 (Dec. 12, 1980): 24-28.

James S. Stewart, *The Life and Teaching of Jesus Christ* (Nashville: Abingdon, 1978), pp. 1-241.

H. Orton Wiley, *Christian Theology*, 3 vols. (Kansas City, Mo.: Beacon Hill, 1941), 2:143-216.

BIBLIOGRAPHY

Baillie, D. M. *God Was in Christ.* New York: Scribner, 1940.
Bauman, Edward W. *The Life and Teaching of Jesus.* Philadelphia: Westminster, 1960.
Bettenson, Henry. *Documents of the Christian Church.* New York and London: Oxford University Press, 1943.
The Book of Common Prayer. Cambridge: Printed by J. Smith, Printer to the University, 1821.
Brunner, Emil. *The Mediator.* New York: Macmillan, 1934.
Burtner, Robert W., and Chiles, Robert E. *A Compend of Wesley's Theology.* New York and Nashville: Abingdon, 1954.
Cannon, William Ragsdale. *The Redeemer.* New York and Nashville: Abingdon-Cokesbury, 1951.
―――. *The Theology of John Wesley.* New York and Nashville: Abingdon-Cokesbury, 1946.
Dillenberger, John, and Welch, Claude. *Protestant Christianity.* New York: Scribner, 1955.
Gamertsfelder, S. J. *Systematic Theology.* Harrisburg, Pa.: Evangelical, 1921.
Goguel, Maurice. *The Life of Jesus.* New York: Macmillan, 1933.
Guthrie, Donald. *A Shorter Life of Christ.* Grand Rapids: Zondervan, 1970.
Hick, John, ed., *The Myth of God Incarnate.* Philadelphia: Westminster, 1979.
Hunter, A. M. *The Work and Words of Jesus.* Philadelphia: Westminster, 1950.
Ladd, George Eldon. *The New Testament and Criticism.* Grand Rapids: Eerdmans, 1967.
―――. *A Theology of the New Testament.* Grand Rapids: Eerdmans, 1974.
Luther, Martin. *Lectures on Romans.* Translated and edited by Wilhelm Pauck. Philadelphia: Westminster, 1961.
Luther's Works. Edited by Jaroslav Pelikan. 54 vols. St. Louis: Concordia, 1963.
Marshall, I. Howard. *I Believe in the Historical Jesus.* Grand Rapids: Eerdmans, 1977.
McDonald, H. D. *Jesus—Human and Divine.* Grand Rapids: Zondervan, 1968.
Miley, John. *Systematic Theology.* 2 vols. New York: Eaton and Mains, 1892.
Orr, James. *The Christian View of God and the World.* New York: Scribner, 1893.
Pannenberg, Wolfhart. *Jesus—God and Man.* Translated by Lewis L. Wilkins and Duane A. Priebe. Philadelphia: Westminster, 1968.
Pope, William Burton. *Compendium of Christian Theology.* 3 vols. New York: Phillips and Hunt, 1881.
Ralston, Thomas N. *Elements of Divinity.* Edited by T. O. Summers. Nashville: Cokesbury, 1924.
Schaff, Philip. *The Creeds of Christendom.* 3 vols. New York: Harper and Brothers, 1884.
Schweitzer, Albert. *The Quest of the Historical Jesus.* New York: Macmillan, 1968.
Seeberg, Reinhold. *Textbook of the History of Doctrines.* Translated by Charles E. Hay. Grand Rapids: Baker, 1956.
Stevens, George Barker. *The Theology of the New Testament.* New York: Scribner, 1899.
Stewart, James S. *The Life and Teaching of Jesus Christ.* Nashville: Abingdon, 1978.
Taylor, Vincent. *The Life and Ministry of Jesus.* Nashville: Abingdon, 1955.
Theological Dictionary of the New Testament. Edited by Gerhard Kittel and translated by Geoffrey W. Bromiley. 10 vols. Grand Rapids: Eerdmans, 1964.
Walker, Williston. *A History of the Christian Church.* New York: Scribner, 1959.
Watson, Richard. *Theological Institutes.* 2 vols. New York: Lane and Scott, 1851.
Wesley, John. *Explanatory Notes Upon the New Testament.* London: Epworth, 1948.
―――. *The Works of John Wesley.* 14 vols. 1892. Reprint ed. Grand Rapids: Zondervan, n.d.
Wiley, H. Orton. *Christian Theology.* 3 vols. Kansas City, Mo.: Beacon Hill, 1946.
Willey, Basil. *The Eighteenth Century Background.* London: Chatto and Windus, 1940.
―――. *The Seventeenth Century Background.* London: Chatto and Windus, 1934.
Wingren, Gustaf F. *Theology in Conflict.* Translated by Eric H. Wahlstrom. Philadelphia: Muhlenberg, 1958.

CHAPTER 10

THE HOLY TRINITY:
The
Triune God

J. Kenneth Grider

J. Kenneth Grider, Professor of Theology, Nazarene Theological Seminary, holds the following degrees, among others: M.A., M. Div., Drew University, and Ph.D., University of Glasgow, Scotland. He did postdoctoral studies at Oxford (England) and Claremont.

Dr. Grider has written Repentance Unto Life: Taller My Soul; *and* Entire Sanctification: The Distinctive Doctrine of Wesleyanism. *He has contributed to various commentaries and has had numerous articles published in various periodicals and in reference works. He is a member of the following societies: the American Theological Society, the Wesleyan Theological Society, the American Academy of Religion, and the Kansas City Society for Theological Studies.*

CONTENTS

INTRODUCTION / 375

   I. EXPLANATION OF THE DOCTRINE / 375

  II. A REVEALED MYSTERY / 378

 III. THE TEACHING OF SCRIPTURE / 379
- A. The Unity of God / 380
    1. Reasons for its emphasis in the Old Testament / 380
    2. Evidence of the unity in the Old Testament / 380
    3. The New Testament emphasis / 381
    4. The significance of God's oneness / 381
- B. The Threeness of God / 382
    1. The threeness in the Old Testament / 382
    2. The threeness in the New Testament / 385
- C. The Deity of Christ / 386
- D. The Deity of the Holy Spirit / 388

 IV. THE TRINITY IN THE CREEDS / 391
- A. The Apostles' Creed / 391
- B. The Nicene Creed / 392
- C. The Nicene-Constantinopolitan Creed / 392
- D. The Athanasian Creed / 392
- E. The Augsburg Confession (1530) / 393
- F. The Formula of Concord (1576) / 393
- G. The Westminster Confession of Faith (1647) / 393
- H. The Thirty-nine Articles (1562) / 393
- I. The Belgic Confession (1561) / 393

  V. THE PROCESSION OF THE HOLY SPIRIT / 394

 VI. THE PRIORITY OF THE FATHER / 397

VII. THE QUESTION OF PERSON / 400

VIII. OPPOSITION TO THE TRINITY DOCTRINE / 402

 IX. SIGNIFICANCE OF THE DOCTRINE / 403
- A. It Presupposes Various Beliefs / 403
- B. It Helps Our Worship / 404
- C. It Helps in Evangelism / 405
- D. Its Importance Is Seen in Christianity's Past / 405

NOTES / 406

DISCUSSION QUESTIONS / 408

RECOMMENDATIONS FOR FURTHER READING / 408

BIBLIOGRAPHY / 408

The Triune God

INTRODUCTION

The audacious Christian view of God is that He is three persons existing eternally in one nature or essence. That is, He is three distinct persons, three centers of self-consciousness, in one underlying nature. The oneness is so real that it flows into the three persons, interpenetrating them, so that, while they are distinct as persons, they are one in substance—in the fundamental nature that the three possess.

I. EXPLANATION OF THE DOCTRINE

This oneness is not that of mere arithmetic. It is instead the kind of oneness that obtains in an organism when all its "systems" interpenetrate each other and work together. This organismic kind of oneness in God constitutes an intensification of oneness. Therefore the oneness is not sacrificed because of the three personal distinctions in God.

This understanding of the Trinity, with all its ramifications in Christian theology,

---

All rights reserved by the author.

including its spillover into the area of redemption, is the "central doctrine of our faith."[1] This doctrine of

> The Immortals of the eternal ring,
> The Utterer, the Uttered, Uttering,

to quote Gerard Manley Hopkins, is "at once the ultimate mystery and the supreme glory of the Christian Faith."[2] Lowry further says, "The doctrine of the Trinity is the most comprehensive and most nearly all-inclusive formulation of the truth of Christianity. It is in and of itself a not inadequate summation of the principal teachings of the Christian religion."[3]

No wonder that in 1961, at the New Delhi meeting of the World Council of Churches, a certain change was made in the one doctrinal requirement for denominations—there are over 250 of them—that would continue to be, or become, members. The requirement had been belief in Jesus Christ as "God and Savior." This was almost tantamount to affirming the doctrine of the Trinity because, through the centuries, almost all outstanding theologians and all significant denominational groups who have admitted Christ's deity have also admitted the Holy Spirit's deity. There have been no significant binitarian theologians or Christian groups. The option has been between Unitarianism and Trinitarianism—and the Unitarians, of course, are not part of the World Council of Churches. What the change in the WCC at New Delhi in 1961 meant, therefore, is that, first, the ninety-person Central Committee, and then the WCC itself, followed through with the logic of the WCC's earlier confessional statement. From belief in Jesus Christ as "God and Savior," it went on to express faith in "the Trinity according to the Scriptures."

This attempt at a brief explanation of the doctrine of the Trinity, however, including the capsule reference to the doctrine in the WCC membership requirements, is entirely inadequate—as, indeed, all explanations are. This is so because, as relates to this doctrine (as to some others, such as the Incarnation), the doctrine is a revealed mystery. That is, it is something that by its very nature, and by our very nature, we cannot figure out by our observations or by our rational processes.

A psalm writer was talking about God's omniscience, and not, of course, about the doctrine of the Trinity, when he said, "Such knowledge is too wonderful for me; it is too high, I cannot attain to it" (Ps. 139:6). Yet what he said about God's knowing capacity could be said about the doctrine of the Trinity—with the revelation of God that we now have and with the Spirit-guided church formulations that relate to this doctrine. The doctrine of the Trinity is a high and holy doctrine; we cannot attain to it, unaided.

Since Scripture clearly teaches that the Father and the Son and the Holy Spirit are all divine and also that there is but one God, it evidently teaches what the church later put into its creedal formularies: that God is both three and one, both one and three.

Some, confronted with this "bad arithmetic," have simply discounted and even slurred this Christian teaching. Thomas Jefferson, a deist, discounted it as "incomprehensible jargon." Matthew Arnold, a late-nineteenth-century poet and literary critic, who often felt free to make liberal theological observations, slighted the Trinity doctrine as "the fairytale of the three Lord Shaftesburys." This actually misses the point, because God really is only one God, while three humans would not be one, but would be simply three in number. Christians, from the early centuries until now, have thankfully received the doctrine as a revealed mystery.

Jesus said, "If any man is willing to do His will, he shall know of the teaching, whether it is of God, or whether I speak from Myself" (John 7:17). So to really know a doctrine such as this, a person needs to *do,* to perform, in his life what God's will is. Obedience, rapt adoration of the Trinity, and an ear attuned to the speaking God will all help in understanding the one God's tripersonal nature.

Thomas Aquinas talked about the liberating effect of accepting by faith in revelation such doctrines as that of the Trinity, which cannot be attained to by reason. He said that mere reason chains us down to what is merely logical—to what our own mental capacities can deduce. Aquinas was correct. Human beings have the capacity to venture, to soar. And when by faith, which is one of the highest and most creative capacities we possess, we accept a revelation from God, we do ourselves the favor of permitting ourselves a certain luxury that is not otherwise open to people. We have the capacity for "opticality" as well as for logicality, as the Old Testament prophets such as Ezekiel had. We, too, are seers. As such, when we "see" the truth of the Trinity, we are "in possession of a prize of rare and marvelous beauty."[4]

Scripture does not specifically seek to support the doctrine of the Trinity any more than it does God's existence. It simply states, over and over, that there is but one God; but, nonetheless, as will be treated specifically later, it often speaks of the Father and the Son and the Holy Spirit. The ingredients of the doctrine, therefore, are in Scripture, but the written Word itself does not use the ingredients to construct the Trinity doctrine. That was left to the church during the early centuries of our era.

A number of the early Fathers sought to explain the doctrine. Tertullian (c. 165-220), a theologian of the West who wrote mostly in Latin, was the earliest of the church fathers both in the West and in the East to attempt a careful explanation of the doctrine. Tertullian might or might not have been the first to use the term *trinitas,* or "trinity." Yet he wrote a significant treatise on the subject and was certainly the earliest church father to describe God as one in substance and, at the same time, three persons. If Tertullian was not the first to use *trinitas,* he was probably the first to use *persona* for "person" and *substantia* for "substance"—the terms later appearing in the creeds that officially explain the orthodox Trinity doctrine.

In his important treatise *Against Praxeas,* which is the earliest extant treatment of the Trinity, Tertullian explains: "This . . . [is] unity in trinity, . . . Father, Son, and Spirit—three . . . but one nature and of reality and of one power, because there is one God."[5]

Emphasizing God's threeness but maintaining at the same time His oneness, Tertullian says that "unity, deriving trinity from itself, is not destroyed by it, but made serviceable."[6]

The most influential church father of all, Augustine (354-430), contributed significantly to the doctrine of the Trinity. He said that "no one" should "wonder and think it absurd that we should call the Father God, the Son God, the Holy Spirit God, and that nevertheless we should say that there are not three Gods in that Trinity, but one God and one substance."[7]

Speaking of "the Trinity, one God, of whom are all things,"[8] he explains, "Thus, the Father and the Son and the Holy Spirit, and each of these by Himself, is God, and at the same time they are all one God; and each of them by Himself is a complete substance, and yet they are all one substance."[9]

Augustine also said, "To all three belong the same eternity, the same unchangeableness [a questionable matter, I feel], the same majesty, the same power"[10]—which is the usual Christian view.

Later others also at least attempted to explain the Trinity doctrine. The evangelical Protestant theologian Henry Thiessen says, "In Christian theology, the term 'trinity' means that there are three eternal distinctions in the one divine essence, known respectively as Father, Son, and Holy Spirit."[11] Thiessen further explains, "These three distinctions are three persons, and one may speak of the tripersonality of God."[12]

A number of analogies have been offered in attempting to explain the doctrine of the Trinity. In his treatise *On Christian Doctrine,* Augustine used a tree, with its root, trunk, and branches, as an analogy. He writes:

> But in the case of that Trinity, we have affirmed it to be impossible that the Father should be sometime the Son, and sometime the Holy Spirit: just as, in a tree, the root is nothing else than the root, and the trunk (*robur*) is nothing else than the trunk and we cannot call the branches anything else than branches; for what is called the root cannot be called trunk and branches; and the wood which belongs to the root cannot by any sort of transference be now in the root, and again in the trunk, and yet again in the branches, but only in the root; since this rule of designation stands fast, so that the root is wood, and the trunk is wood, and the branches are wood, while never-the-less it is not three woods that are thus spoken of, but only one.[13]

Augustine seems to temper his use of this and other physical analogies by saying that they probably tend to depict the oneness of God more adequately than they do His threeness. In this connection he explains:

> But these examples in things (*corporalia exempla*) have been adduced not in virtue of their likeness to that divine Nature, but in reference to the oneness which subsists even

in things visible, so that it may be understood to be quite a possibility for three objects of some sort, not only severally, but also all together, to obtain one single name.[14]

Numerous other analogies have been used to illustrate the Christian doctrine of God as both three and one. A family composed of a father and a mother and a child has often been cited as an illustration of the Trinity. This is perhaps a serviceable analogy for instructing small children in the doctrine but, like most analogies, it serves better to illustrate threeness than oneness. The shamrock, with its three petals extending from one petiole has sometimes been used. The triangle has sometimes served as an analogy, there being one triangle, with three sides. Some have used the prism, in which there is a oneness, along with three kinds of light. Water has been used, as well; it possesses a oneness as water but is found in three states: ice, liquid, and vapor. This last illustration tends to suggest modal understanding, in which the three exist successively, not at the same time. Others, as I have suggested, tend to be particularly inadequate at the point of oneness, because three humans, e.g., are not one in the sense that God is; but the other illustrations are also inadequate for depicting God's threeness, because the three are all impersonal.

The special reason for the inadequacy of the various analogies of the Trinity is that they are all more or less physical, while God is not physical in nature; and in the analogies we are trying to rise from physical to spiritual verities. There is simply nothing in the physical world that is actually analogous to the threeness-in-oneness, the oneness-in-threeness, of the Trinity.

II. A REVEALED MYSTERY

The above treatment discusses attempts to explain the doctrine of the Trinity, including the use of analogies in order to do this. But these attempts are admittedly inadequate, because the doctrine of the Trinity is to Christians a revealed mystery.

Here the ground Christians stand on is holy (Exod. 3:5). Moses could not explain how a bush could burn without being consumed, but still he witnessed what was happening; so too we cannot explain the doctrine of the Trinity but affirm it audaciously. As Paul had "heard things which cannot be told, which man may not utter" (2 Cor. 11:2-4 RSV), so it is with us in regard to this doctrine. It is "better felt than telt," as has been said of Christian experience.

As we humans, finite and fallen, open up to God on our godward sides, He opens up to us the very nature of His existence. As we look and listen, we learn what He is like. As a person, as indeed tripersonal, God would be able to keep from us what His existence is really like. A person can clam up, and not let you in on what he is like, what his feelings are like. A spouse can keep a marriage partner in the dark about his or her feelings. Since God is a person—tripersonal—He would be able to shut us off from what He is really like; but He elects to disclose Himself to those who are opened up to Him. And He discloses to us that He is three persons in one underlying nature. He put all this in a Book but in such a way that we are expected to glean it from raw material given us in the Book.

It has been said that while one may be in danger of losing his soul by denying the doctrine of the Trinity, he is in equal danger of losing his wits if he tries to understand it. Thus John Miley, widely read in the Holiness Movement during the early decades of our century, said that this doctrine "is exclusively a question of revelation."[15] Similarly Thomas Aquinas (1225-1274) said that the "truth that God is three and one is altogether a matter of faith."[16] Thus Karl Rahner speaks of "the revelation of the Trinity,"[17] and calls it a "mystery."[18] He even says, "The dogma of the Trinity is an *absolute mystery* which we do not understand even after it has been revealed."[19]

Thiessen calls this doctrine "the greatest mystery of all revealed truth."[20]

He suggests, however, that even though it is a mystery, this "should offer no objection to a doctrine [such as this] based on revelation."[21] He says it is altogether understandable, if the nature of God, the Infinite One, should "present mysteries to the finite mind."[22]

In connection with the doctrine's being a mystery, Augustine said that it is the pure in heart to whom it is given to "see God" in this way. He says:

> For these things cannot be seen except by the heart made pure; and (even) he who in this life sees them "in part," as it has been said, and "in an enigma," cannot secure it that the person to whom he speaks shall also see them, if he is hampered by impurities of heart. "Blessed," however, "are they of a pure heart, for they shall see God."[23]

Augustine goes on to say that although "it is our duty to enjoy the truth . . . the soul must be purified that it may have the power to perceive that light, and to rest in it when it is perceived."[24]

While Christians have readily admitted that the doctrine is a mystery, we have not usually been willing to say that it is contrary to reason. Above reason, yes, but not contrary to it. Thus Theissen says:

> Revelation concerning a trinity of Persons related in one Essence contradicts no absolute truth. It is evident that as to wholly separated and individually identified subjects, one is not three, nor are three one. Such is a contradiction. The doctrine of the Trinity asserts no such inconsistency.[25]

But why is this doctrine a mystery? Why has God seemed to reveal Himself as a tri-unity, three in one and one in three? And why is it so difficult for us to understand what the existence of this tripersonal God is like? Why can we not figure it out, to our greater satisfaction? On this, Augustine had some devout things to say. He was referring in part to the revealed doctrine of the Trinity and the difficulty we have in trying to understand it when he wrote:

> And I do not doubt that all this was divinely arranged for the purpose of subduing pride by toil, and of preventing a feeling of satiety in the intellect, which generally holds in small esteem what is discovered without difficulty.[26]

By reason, we exist. By observation, we exist. By revelation, we live. And, in order to our "living," as creatures under God, He has revealed Himself to us as one God who is at the same time Father and Son and Holy Spirit.

III. THE TEACHING OF SCRIPTURE

As mentioned, Scripture does not teach the doctrine of the Trinity as such. It speaks of the Father and the Son and the Holy Spirit, with varying names for the three; and the three seem to be in a wholly unique relationship. There are even several passages, as we shall see, that mention the three in a brief compass—sometimes in a single verse of Scripture. But it is never stated that the three are one. It does happen that in the King James Version both the threeness and the oneness are mentioned: "For there are three that bear record in heaven, the Father, the word, and the Holy Ghost: and these three are one" (1 John 5:7).

But it is well known that this verse is not in any of the older extant New Testament Greek manuscripts. Nor is it in any of the early Latin codices. It is never quoted by any orthodox Greek or Latin father—and surely it would have been, had it been available. Tertullian's teaching, however, is so similar to it that some scholars think his teachings presuppose his knowledge of the passage. Since it is not in any of these manuscripts, it is assumed by most scholars, even by those who are profoundly evangelical and conservative, that this was a verse added by a later editor of 1 John—added, perhaps, after that editor had known about the doctrine of the Trinity that had developed among Christians. An interesting aspect of this matter is that the addition did, strangely, get into the Latin Vulgate version. Another interesting matter is that Erasmus seems to have been pressured into including it in the third edition of his Greek New Testament. It is in the Textus Receptus, the received text, the one used by the translators of the 1611 King James Version. Erasmus seems to have been "pressured" because, knowing it was not in the early extant Greek manuscripts, he wanted to omit it in his Greek New Testament, but persons with vested interest in the Latin version seem to have exacted a promise from him that he would insert the "Trinity" passage if he were shown even one Greek manuscript in which the passage was found. A very late manuscript was shown him, and he inserted the questionable passage.

Without the KJV addition, entering in great part through Erasmus's Greek text, the passage reads differently in other versions. In the NIV we read, "For there are three that testify: the Spirit, the water and the blood; and the three are in agreement." In the RSV, a revision of the KJV (and the ASV), verses 7-8 read: "And the Spirit is the witness, because the Spirit is the truth. There are three witnesses, the Spirit, the water, and the blood; and these three agree." In so strategic a "Trinity" passage, the NASB, a revision of the ASV, should also be noted. It reads, "And it is the Spirit who bears witness, because the Spirit is the truth. For there are three that bear witness, the Spirit and the water and the blood; and the three are in agreement" (vv. 7-8). Only the KJV includes the reference to heaven and to the Father and the Son (who dwell there). The doctrine of the Trinity is a correct, basic understanding of Christians generally. But it is a doctrine based on Scripture teaching as later interpreted. Only in 1 John 5:7 in the KJV is it taught in roughly the same way that it came to be taught a few centuries later; but that passage seems to have been an editorial revision added to the inspired original writing of the apostle John.

With all this said about 1 John 5:7, the doctrine of the Trinity—that God is both three and one, three persons in one nature—is taught in Scripture clearly enough for Christians to have affirmed it since the early centuries as perhaps our most fundamental doctrine.

A. The Unity of God

The unity of God—His oneness—is an emphasis of Scripture, in both of the Testaments. It is certainly an emphasis of the Old Testament Scriptures. The central text most singularly supportive of it is Deuteronomy 6:4, where we read, "Hear, O Israel! The LORD is our God, the LORD is one!" Another supportive passage is Isaiah 45:18, where God says through the prophet, "'I am the LORD, and there is none else.'" Later in the same chapter God again says through Isaiah, "Turn to Me and be saved, all the ends of the earth; for I am God, and there is no other" (Isa. 45:22).

1. Reasons for its emphasis in the Old Testament God's unity was exceedingly important to the Jewish mind. Faith-filled Jews were to teach this to their children more than any other doctrine.

This emphasis was made for two special reasons. One reason is the prevalent extra-Israelitish worship of local baals. Since the peoples who had occupied various areas of Palestine had earlier worshiped these local deities, it was of paramount importance that the new settlers, the Israelites, be taught God's oneness and that other gods are not really gods and cannot hear the supplicators' requests. It is Yahweh alone, the living God, the one who really exists, who is the one and only God.

A second important reason for the Old Testament's emphasis on God's unity is Israel's nationalism. This was valid even after the division of the kingdom in 933 B.C. at Solomon's death. In this connection A. C. Knudson says, "The pronounced nationalism of their religion made it impossible that there should at any time have been any serious peril from poly-yahwism."[27] One nation, so one God!

2. Evidences of the unity in the Old Testament As there are two basic reasons why Israel emphasized God's unity, there are at least two basic evidences of that emphasis. One is the centralization of worship. A longstanding emphasis, opposed especially by Jeremiah, was that everyone was to worship God in one place: the temple at Jerusalem. Unity of sanctuary helped the popular mind to conceive of the unity of God, possibly because one could expect only one kind of action—just and wise action—from the one God worshiped at the one place. Thus the oneness of sanctuary at least served in a secondary way the emphasis on the oneness of God's being.

The other special evidence of God's oneness in Old Testament times is in the fact that there was no sexual distinction in the Hebrew understanding of God. Yahweh had no feminine counterpart as did at least some of the baals. Actually the Hebrews seem to have been the only people of those times who did not differentiate the Deity sexually. C. H. Cornill, in *The Prophets of Israel*, says, "Israel is the only nation we know of that never had a mythology, the only people who never differentiated the Deity sexually."[28] In fact the Hebrew language did not even contain a word for "goddess." This oneness of the deity, with no sexual distinction, contributed to the high moral tone of Jewish life. By contrast the Greeks taught that the gods loved each other much as humans do in sexual ways and that they even cohabited with humans. This contributed to a low moral tone in Greek life. Yet the more basic advantage of the Hebrew understanding that there is no feminine counterpart to Deity is that the Deity is characterized by unity.

3. The New Testament emphasis The New Testament also teaches that there is but one God. The Socinian Racovian Catechism bases its teaching of God's oneness on three particular passages: John 17:3; 1 Corinthians 8:6; and Ephesians 4:6. Trinitarians, no less than Unitarians, believe there is but one God and likewise support the doctrine of God's oneness in part on the basis of these passages.

The John 17:3 passage is a part of Jesus' priestly prayer, in which He says, "This is eternal life, that they may know Thee the only true God, and Jesus Christ whom Thou hast sent." When Jesus speaks of the Father as "the only true God," He is not saying that He and the Holy Spirit were not divine persons of the Godhead. He was distinguishing God from the so-called gods that are idols made with men's hands. Other things Jesus says show that He and the Father are one, such as: "He who has seen Me has seen the Father" (John 14:9); "I and the Father are one" (John 10:30); and "The glory which Thou hast given Me I have given to them; that they may be one, just as We are one" (John 17:22). When He said that "the Father is greater than I" (John 14:28), He was not denying His substantial oneness with the Father; He was instead speaking of a certain priority that the Father has in authority and other functions, which will be discussed later.

In 1 Corinthians 8:6 Paul says, "Yet for us there is but one God, the Father, from whom are all things, and we exist for Him; and one Lord, Jesus Christ, through whom are all things and we exist through Him." Trinitarians believe this as heartily as Unitarians do. The New Testament usually means the "Father" when it speaks of "God." And God is one, though Christ is divine. Besides, this very passage implies Christ's deity by what it says of Him. Other passages also clearly state His deity.

Paul speaks similarly in Ephesians 4:4-6: "There is . . . one Lord, one faith, one baptism, one God and Father of all who is over all and through all and in all." Again, the clear statements elsewhere, that Jesus is divine, help us to see that Paul means to say here only that the Father is the person of priority in the Godhead.

The unity of God is also taught when Paul says, "Now to the King eternal, immortal, invisible, the only God, be honor and glory forever and ever" (1 Tim. 1:17).

4. The significance of God's oneness This discussion of God's oneness began with the implication that God's oneness and His unity are the same thing; and this is not incorrect. But when we are thinking theologically about the meaning of unity, unity means more than mere oneness. Karl Rahner, perhaps the most distinguished Roman Catholic theologian of our time, makes a helpful distinction. He distinguishes between unicity (a word he coined) and unity. By God's unicity he refers to the oneness of essence of the three persons of the Trinity. And by unity he means the agreement, the "teamwork," the organismic working together of the three persons. He says that "this treatise [the book he is writing at the time] does not speak only of God's essence and its unicity, but of the unity of the three divine persons, of the unity of the Father, the Son, and the Spirit, and not merely of the unicity of the divinity."[29]

It is difficult for Jews and Moslems and Unitarians to understand what Christians mean by God's oneness. They think we sacrifice God's oneness when we teach that the Son and the Spirit are deity even as God the Father is. They think we are talking mumbo-jumbo when we say that there are three divine persons but only one divine being. They cannot conceive of three divine persons unless they are three Gods. Christians should respect their zealousness for God's oneness. In fact we are as zealous for teaching God's oneness as they are. We would be just as much opposed to any multiple-Gods teaching as they are. We also want our children to hear that *Yahweh* our *Elohim* is one *Yahweh*. We marshal all the Old Testament and all the New Testament passages that emphasize that there is but one God. As James Denney says:

> The apostles were all Jews—men, as it has been said, with monotheism as a passion in their blood. They did not cease to be monotheists when they became preachers of Christ, but they instinctively conceived God in a way in which the old revelation had not taught them to conceive him.[30]

Actually Christians, with a Trinitarian view of God, emphasize God's oneness more than Jews or Moslems or Unitarians emphasize it. The reason why we emphasize the oneness more than they do—the numerical oneness of essence, of nature, of substance, of kind of being—is that, as mentioned above, we also emphasize what Rahner calls the unity of the three persons. We emphasize what Oxford's Leonard Hodgson does in his book on the Trinity: that the three are one as an organism is one. And that is more of oneness than mere numerical oneness is. A stick is not one to the extent that an organism is—whose respiratory and digestive and reproductive systems work together in organic unity. Three divine persons who share one nature and who work together so that there is a complete and perfect cooperation between the three, without any bickering or jealousy whatever, but only a harmony that is absolutely perfect, are more one than a unipersonal being would be. Thus Chafer writes, "To acknowledge the triune mode of existence, does not impair, diminish, or complicate the doctrine of the *one God,* or lessen the obligation to uphold it."[31] Chafer also calls God's oneness "a fundamental theme which he [the Christian] is appointed to exhibit and defend."[32]

B. The Threeness of God

Even as God is absolutely one, He is absolutely three. Even as He is one in nature, He is tri-personal—three infinite and eternally existing centers of self-consciousness.

1. The threeness in the Old Testament

Admittedly, God's threeness is not clearly taught in the Old Testament as it is in the New Testament. Yet the Old Testament teaches some things that are indications of the threeness of God as found in the New Testament. One such indication is what might well be implied by the fact that the name for God as the God of power, the generic name for God, is *Elohim*—found hundreds of times in the Old Testament and usually found in this plural form (not simply in the singular *El*). While it regularly appears with a singular verb and while it might indicate merely a plurality in God's powers and only possibly indicates plurality and not threeness as such, it is still taken by many Christians as a foregleam of the later revelation of God as tripersonal.

Somewhat more significant than the plural name *Elohim* are the Old Testament references to God in the clearly plural form. This appears in Genesis 1:26 where we read, "Then God said, 'Let Us make man in Our image, in Our likeness.'" The "Us" and the "Our" imply plurality. Genesis 3:22 likewise contains a plurality reference. There we read, "Then the LORD God said, 'Behold, the man has become like one of Us, knowing good and evil.'" This implied plurality also appears in Genesis 11:5–7: "And the LORD came down to see the city and the tower which the sons of men had built. And the LORD said, '. . . Come, let Us go down and there confuse their language, that they may not understand one another's speech.'" Another reference to plurality is in Isaiah 6:8: "Then I heard the voice of the LORD, saying, 'Whom shall I send, and who will go for Us?'"

Still more significant as a first installment on the New Testament's revelation of God's threeness are the threefold distinctions in God in certain Old Testament passages. In Psalm 33:6 reference is made to the "word of the LORD," and thus also to "the LORD," and also possibly to the Spirit in "the breath [Spirit] of his mouth." It reads, "By the word of the LORD the heavens were made, and by the breath of His mouth all their host." This vague reference to threeness, used in connection with the creation, is in agreement with other quite clear and not-so-clear references to the persons of the Trinity as participating in the creation. Of course, God the Father creates. He is at least included in the plural *Elohim* in Genesis 1:1: "In the beginning God created the heavens and the earth." If the "word of the LORD" in Psalm 33:6 is a reference to Christ, often called the Word in the New Testament, this would agree with John's Gospel's including Christ, the Word, as figuring in the creation. There we read, "All things came into being through Him [the Word, v. 1]; and apart from Him nothing came into being" (John 1:3). In that Gospel we also read that "the world was made through Him [the Word]" (1:10). Psalm 33:6 is also in agreement with Colossians 1:16 where Paul says, "For by him [Christ] all things are created" (NIV). Since the Psalm 33:6 passage refers to "the breath" or "the Spirit," "of his [God's] mouth," it might be in agreement with the vague reference to the Spirit's figuring in creation, according to the Genesis account. Right after the Genesis 1:1 reference to God's creation we read, "And the earth was formless and void, and darkness was over the surface of the deep; and the Spirit of God was moving over the surface of the waters" (v. 2). There is a possible indirect reference to threeness in Isaiah 61:1: "The Spirit of the Sovereign LORD is on me, because the LORD has anointed me . . ." (NIV). Here the "Spirit" might be the Holy Spirit, the "Sovereign LORD" might be Christ, and the "LORD" might be the Father. Such a passage, also, is Isaiah 63:9–12. There the "Holy Spirit" is twice mentioned (vv. 10–11), there being only one other instance of the appearance of these two words in all the Old Testament (Ps. 51:11). The Father is clearly referred to in the passage. And Christ might appear in verse 9 in the reference to "the angel [messenger] of His presence."

It is also entirely possible that there is Trinitarian anticipation in Isaiah's reference to God as thrice holy in 6:3: "Holy, Holy, Holy, is the LORD of hosts."[33]

Besides the plural form *Elohim*, the references to God in plural pronouns, and the "threeness" references to God, there is some support for the doctrine of the Trinity in the Old Testament references to the Spirit, or to the Holy Spirit, and in its possible references to Christ.

The three Old Testament uses of the designation "Holy Spirit" have just been mentioned. But the Old Testament makes numerous references to the "Spirit of God" (e.g., Gen. 1:2; Judg. 3:10; 6:34; 14:6; 15:14; 1 Sam. 11:6; Pss. 33:6; 104:33; 139:7; Job 26:13; 27:3; 32:8; 33:4; Isa. 40:7, 13; 59:19). God's Spirit, in these and other passages, is the source of blessings, gifts, courage, bodily strength, etc.

The Old Testament probably refers to Christ many times. Some theologians, such as H. Orton Wiley, think that each reference to *Yahweh* in the Old Testament is a reference to Christ. Wiley says, "Christ was the Jehovah [*Yahweh*] of the Old Testament."[34] The view of Augustine, however, seems preferable: that Yahweh might be any one of the persons of the Trinity, or all three conceived of as God, according to indications in the context.[35]

Even if the many references to *Yahweh* are not necessarily references to Christ, many other passages probably do refer to Him. Christ is possibly referred to when, many times, God is said to have created the world through the word—a word that is more of a power than a mere voice (see Gen. 1:3ff.; Pss. 147:18; 148:8; Joel 2:11).

In addition, the Old Testament's personifications of wisdom might be vague references to Christ. The most vivid such personification is in Proverbs 8:12ff. There, wisdom is an "I," who dwells "together with prudence" (v. 12). This "I" possesses "knowledge and discretion" (v. 12). By him "kings reign" and "rulers decree justice" (v. 15). Of this wisdom we read, "The LORD possessed me at the beginning of His way, before His words of old" (v. 22). Of him it is also said, "From everlasting I was established, from the beginning, from the earliest times of the earth" (v. 23). Of wisdom we also read, "When He established the heavens, I was there. . . . Then [at the creation] I was beside Him, as a master workman" (vv. 27, 30). Some scholars of Platonic leanings, who believe that concepts such as wisdom are eternal, interpret this hymn about wisdom as referring to an eternal "wisdom" concept or idea that God followed when He created the world. Those of us who do not believe that beauty, goodness, etc., are eternally existing concepts and who believe that Scripture does not teach such, tend to interpret this lengthy "wisdom" passage in Proverbs as a reference to Christ. It fits in with many things we read elsewhere about Christ, such as His figuring so significantly in creation and His being with God "in the beginning" (see also John 1:1)—i.e., eternally.

A similar reference to wisdom as figuring in creation and possibly referring to Christ is in Proverbs 3:19: "The Lord by wisdom founded the earth." Another such possible reference is in Jeremiah: "It is He who made the earth by His power; who established the world by His wisdom" (10:12; 51:15).

As wisdom might refer to Christ in certain places in the Old Testament, the angel of *Yahweh,* the angel of *Elohim,* or the messenger of the covenant might also in certain places refer to Him. The phrase often refers simply to an angel (e.g., 1 Kings 19:5-7; Dan. 3:25, 28; 6:23; 10:13). But certain other instances of the phrase might well refer to Christ. Malachi 3:1 surely does: "And the Lord, whom you seek, will suddenly come to His temple; and the messenger of the covenant, in whom you delight, behold, He is coming, says the LORD of Hosts." This messenger and the LORD are used synonymously of a distinctly different being, "the LORD of Hosts" being a reference to God the Father. Of many of the instances of "the angel of Yahweh," Herman Bavinck says that "though distinct from Jehovah [a different way of transliterating the Hebrew for *Yahweh*] this Angel of Jehovah bears the same name, has the same power, effects the same deliverance, dispenses the same blessings, and is the object of the same adoration."[36] Such mentions of the angel of *Yahweh* are found in numerous Old Testament passages, including Job 33:23; Psalm 34:7; Proverbs 8:22ff.; 30:4; Isaiah 9:5; Micah 5:6; Zechariah 1:8-14.

2. The threeness in the New Testament If Augustine and Barth and others could say with sound basis that, in general, what is concealed in the Old Testament is revealed in the New—the doctrine of the Trinity would be most certainly included in that observation. What is concealed about God's threeness in the Old Testament—concealed by being only germinally indicated—is made plain in the New Testament. At least it is made sufficiently plain for the church to take the data and construct the doctrine that the one God is tripersonal.

The baptismal formula, coming from Jesus Himself, found in what we call the Great Commission, and constituting one aspect of Jesus' instituting of the sacrament of baptism (Barth says He instituted it also by being Himself baptized), is a most significant aspect of this New Testament revelation. "Go therefore and make disciples of all the nations," Jesus said, "baptizing them in the name of the Father and the Son and the Holy Spirit" (Matt. 28:19).

Paul's benediction, found at the close of 2 Corinthians and used widely in closing worship services, is another significant "threeness" passage. Paul concludes this second epistle to the Corinthian church—perhaps actually the third one he wrote to them—by saying, "The grace of the Lord Jesus Christ, and the love of God, and the fellowship of the Holy Spirit, be with you all" (2 Cor. 13:14). Here the inspired apostle links the Son and the Spirit with the Father as though they are of equal status with Him—as though they share fully in His divine nature.

The three are mentioned in Ephesians 4:4-6 as though, again, the Spirit and the Son are in the same class with the Father: "There is one body and one Spirit, just as also you were called in one hope of your calling; one Lord, one faith, one baptism, one God and Father of all who is over all and through all and in all." While Arians (to be discussed later) view this as saying that Christ and the Spirit are not divine, Trinitarians read it as teaching that they are divine, just as the Father is, but that there is a priority in the Trinity that belongs to the Father.

The three are mentioned again in 2 Thessalonians 2:13: "But we should always give thanks to God [the Father] for you, brethren, beloved by the Lord [Christ], because God has chosen you from the beginning for salvation through sanctification by the Spirit and faith in the truth." And again, the passage could be read with an Arian or a Unitarian frame of mind as teaching that only the Father is divine since the Son and the Spirit are not called God. But the Father is the one normally called God in the New Testament. He is the one we are to pray to, and prayer to Him is mentioned in this verse. He does enjoy a status of priority over the others within the Godhead. At the same time, the Son and the Spirit are mentioned along with God the Father, as though they too are divine. And if it is not clear from this and other passages that they are also divine, there are certain other passages, as we shall soon see, that declare outright that the Son is divine (e.g., John 1:1; 20:28) and imply that the Holy Spirit also is (Heb. 9:14).

The apostle Peter, one of those closest to Jesus during the Lord's public ministry, spoke of the Father and the Son and the Spirit in one verse, as though the Son and the Spirit were of the same nature with the Father. Writing to Christians generally, "God's elect," he says they had been, "chosen according to the foreknowledge of God the father, by the sanctifying work of the Spirit, that you may obey Jesus Christ and be sprinkled with His blood" (1 Peter 1:2).

And John the apostle, closest to Jesus of all the Twelve, likewise links together the three persons of the Trinity in 1 John 5:4-7. In that passage the Father is referred to in the phrase "born of God." In it he speaks of "Jesus" as "the Son of God" and of "Jesus Christ" who "came by water and blood." He also refers to the Holy Spirit saying, "And it is the Spirit who bears witness because the Spirit is the truth." Again the three are not here declared to be one. Such specific declaration, regarding all three, is not found in Scripture but only in the creeds—e.g., the Athanasian Creed (more clearly than in either the Apostles' or Nicene creeds). But this linking of the three, again taken together especially with such passages as John 1:1 and John 20:28 where Christ is referred to as "God," indicates the sameness of nature of the three as expressly stated and restated in the fifth-century Athanasian Creed.

C. The Deity of Christ

It is the New Testament's clear teaching of the deity of Christ, along with its at-least-implied teaching of the deity of the Holy Spirit, that is the strongest biblical support of all for the doctrine of the Trinity. The threeness passages just discussed do not in any instance declare outright that the Son or the Spirit is divine. The deity of the Son and the Spirit is only implied when they are spoken of and lauded in the same inspired breath with mentions of God the Father. It is especially the New Testament's teaching of Christ's deity that nudged the Christians of the very early centuries to yield their unipersonal view of God and to begin the long process whereby they came to teach officially the threeness as well as the oneness.

And it was not especially Christ's miraculous works that "declared" Him to be divine. Some early Fathers did indeed feel that Christ's works were proof of His deity. Many theologians and church leaders have felt the same way, including John Wesley. But Christ prayed to the Father to raise Lazarus and to do other such stupendous works. And Christ declared that He could not do them of Himself—evidently because of His taking on human nature and holding in reserve His divine attributes. So the miracles were not proof as such of His deity. Yet they were indicators of it. This is in part because of the wondrousness especially of some of the miracles—among them the turning of water into wine, the feeding of five thousand persons by beginning with only a small amount of bread and fish. Peter and Paul and others prayed, and God the Father did miraculous things especially in physical healings. But those did not display the divine power quite so wondrously as, say, turning water into wine.

More significant than Christ's miraculous works as indicators of His deity are certain names given Him. Names such as Jesus and Christ are not particularly significant here. His being called Lord so frequently *is* significant, for that is the word that translates especially two frequently used Hebrew words designating God: *Yahweh* and *Adonai*. Jesus is referred to in prophecy as "Immanuel," which means "God with us," and this name is certainly supportive of His deity (see Isa. 7:14). Some scholars feel that when Peter and others called Christ "the Son of God," they indicated His deity, and this might be so; yet this should not be rated as highly as "Lord" and "Immanuel," since the New Testament also calls believers sons of God (e.g., John 1:12; 1 John 3:1).

It is when the New Testament actually calls Jesus "God" *(theos)* that we have its most important support of Christ's diety—and, finally, of the doctrine of the Trinity. There are two passages that might or might not do this, depending on how they are translated and interpreted. One of them is Titus 1:3, where Paul speaks of "God our Savior," but it might refer to God the Father. The other is Hebrews 1:8: "But about the Son he says, 'Your throne, O God, will last for ever and ever'" (NIV). This is part of a more lengthy quote from Psalm 45:6-7, and the writer of Hebrews seems to be saying that that passage in the Psalms refers to God's Son, Jesus Christ.

A few other passages also refer to Jesus Christ in such a way that His deity is clearly indicated. One such is in Colossians 1:13-20. There the "Son" (v. 13) is declared to be "the image of the invisible God"—the one who as enfleshed was the very image of God. This is a closer

THE HOLY TRINITY

"image" than that in which man was made, for Paul also here says, "For it was the Father's good pleasure for all the fulness to dwell in him" (v. 19). Besides, man was "made," according to Genesis 1:26–27—he was created, that is, out of nothing—whereas Christ was "begotten," the "only begotten" (John 1:18; 3:16; 1 John 4:9ff.). He was begotten eternally. Origen interpreted the *monogenēs* (only begotten) passages as meaning "eternally begotten," and the church has in general accepted the interpretation. Thomas Aquinas added what is not in Scripture: that the Son is eternally generated from the Father's intellect (and that the Holy Spirit proceeds eternally from the love existing between the Father and the Son).

One of the strongest supports of the deity of Christ in all of Scripture, and therefore one of the Bible's strongest supports of the later-developed doctrine of the Trinity, is John 1:1. There the apostle begins his Gospel by saying, "In the beginning was the Word, and the Word was with God, and the Word was God." John says that the Word, Christ, existed "in the beginning." It probably denotes the Word's eternality. Chafer suggests, "The phrase *in the beginning,* as used here by John, could hardly be a reference to aught else than the eternity past which was prior to the event mentioned in the next verse, namely, 'All things were made by him.'"[37] Besides, this "Word," Christ, as God's message to us, simply "was" —that is, He existed eternally. And He was "with God," the word here *(pros)* meaning near to, in the vicinity of, God. Not only that, however. This Word "was God" (John 1:1). There it is! That is one of the most anti-Arian statements in the Bible. It does not say that Christ was like God. It states that he indeed "was God." It matters not that the definite article does not appear before *theos,* here. In abstract nouns such as God, love, etc., the definite article might or might not appear in the Greek. The Jehovah's Witnesses, who do not believe in Christ's deity or, of course, in the Trinity, translate it as saying Christ was "a god." This is about all they can do when such a strong declaration of Christ's deity appears in Scripture.

Another similarly strong support of the deity of Christ—and finally of the doctrine of the Trinity—is also in John's Gospel (20:28). There Thomas, the one who had been most prone to doubt Christ's resurrection, declares, "'My Lord and my God!'" Actually, this declaration of Christ's deity is the earliest such statement in Scripture. It was made shortly after the resurrection of Christ, perhaps some sixty years before the John 1:1 statement was written and earlier than those in Hebrews, Colossians, and elsewhere. The one most prone to doubt became the first person we know of to express the highest, most profound faith in Christ—that He is *theos,* God.

Christ is also called God in Romans 9:5, where Paul says of the Jews, "Theirs are the patriarchs, and from them is traced the human ancestry of Christ, who is God over all, forever praised" (NIV).

In two other passages it seems that Christ is called God. In 1 John 5:20 we read, "And we know that the Son of God has come, and has given us understanding, in order that we might know Him who is true, and we are in Him who is true, in His Son Jesus Christ. This is the true God and eternal life." This seems to say that Christ is the "true God." The other such passage is Revelation 1:8, 17. In verse 8 we read, "'I am the Alpha and the Omega,' says the Lord God, who is, and who was, and who is to come, the Almighty." This is in a context that is clearly speaking of Christ, who "released us from our sins by His own blood" (v. 5); and who "is coming with the clouds, and every eye will see Him, even those who pierced Him" (v. 7). Besides, in verse 17 of this chapter "the First and the Last," who would be the "Alpha and the Omega" of verse 8, is clearly Christ, for of this "Living One" we read, "'I was dead, and behold, I am alive forevermore'" (v. 18).

It is also probable that Christ is called

God in two other places. One of them is in Peter's words in his second epistle: "Simon Peter, a bond-servant and apostle of Jesus Christ, to those who have received a faith of the same kind as ours, by the righteousness of our God and Savior, Jesus Christ" (2 Peter 1:1). "God," here, does not seem to mean the Father, but Christ. Another text is Titus 2:13, where Paul speaks of "the glory of our great God and Savior, Jesus Christ."

Besides all these scriptural supports of Christ's deity, there are many others, even though some of them are not quite as clear and direct as these.

Some of the others cluster around Christ's eternality. He is "the first-born of all creation" (Col. 1:15), meaning that He was not formed or made, but born—that is, begotten, eternally begotten. Jesus Himself said, "Before Abraham was born, I am" (John 8:58), suggesting His eternality. Christ also prays, "'And now, glorify Thou Me together with Thyself, Father, with the glory which I ever had with Thee before the world was'" (John 17:5). Later in the same prayer Jesus speaks of "'the glory you have given me because you loved me before the creation of the world'" (v. 24 NIV). If some of these passages could be taken as teaching only Christ's preexistence, they may be interpreted as teaching His eternal preexistence because there are passages, as shown, that teach that the preexistence was eternal.

One other "deity-of-Christ" passage is Philippians 2:6, where the KJV reads, "Who, being in the form of God," the NASB has "who, although He existed in the form of God," and the NIV reads "who, being in very nature God." This not only declares Christ's deity, it is also a scriptural support of the view later developed that the Son (and the Spirit too) is of the same nature or substance with the Father.

Still other suggestions of Christ's deity are His statements "Even as the Father knows me and I know the Father" (John 10:15) and "No one knows the Son, except the Father, nor does anyone know the Father, except the Son, and anyone to whom the Son wills to reveal Him" (Matt. 11:27). In these passages Jesus says He knows the Father in most special ways. In the former He declares that He even knows the Father as intimately as the Father knows Him, and this can be true only if Jesus is divine.[38]

On the deity of Christ see also chapter 9, pages 331–38.

D. The Deity of the Holy Spirit

Along with or shortly after the dawning realization that Christ is divine came the apostolic and early church's understanding that the Holy Spirit is also divine. Already in what C. H. Dodd liked to call the beforehand times of the "older Testament," glimmers of light begin to appear that are pointers to the much clearer New Testament revelation regarding the deity and personality of the Holy Spirit. Only three times is He designated the "Holy Spirit" in all the Old Testament—once is in what is probably a Davidic psalm (Psalm 51) written after the king's sin with Bathsheba and before he had received the forgiveness he so expressly describes in Psalm 32. The Spirit even in those not-yet times was at His good work of convincing people of the sinfulness of sin. David pleads for "mercy" (v. 1) and for cleansing (vv. 2, 7) and prays, "Do not cast me from your presence or take your Holy Spirit from me" (v. 11). The King James Version does not capitalize "Holy Spirit" here, but some versions, such as the NASB and the NIV, do—indicating the translators' understanding that He is the divine person we have come to call the third person of the Trinity.

The other two instances of "Holy Spirit" in the Old Testament, as mentioned in an earlier discussion, are in Isaiah 63:10–11. In these instances the KJV capitalizes only "Spirit" in the phrase, but again the NASB and NIV capitalize "Holy" also. Isaiah would not have known how truly he was speaking. He would hardly have been intending to speak of a distinct person of the Godhead other than the one we have come to call God the Father. But since this Holy Spirit was inspiring such prophets to say what they had to say, we are given here a pointer that occasions our saying, "Aha, here is a foregleam of what our New Testament Scriptures make much more clear." Isaiah says the people "rebelled and grieved His Holy Spirit" (63:10). The Spirit's being "grieved" is in specific keeping with the New Testament teaching about Him, because Paul urges the Ephesians (and other area churches, if Ephesians is a circular letter): "And do not grieve the Holy Spirit of God" (Eph. 4:30)—the "of God" here probably meaning "who proceeds eternally from the Father" (see John 15:26).

The designation "Holy Spirit" in Isaiah 63:11 seems to refer to a being distinct from God the Father—although, again, Isaiah was probably saying more than he realized he was saying. He asks, "Where is He [God] who put His Holy Spirit in the midst of them?"

The Old Testament also indicates the Holy Spirit's deity by speaking of "The Spirit of the LORD [*Yahweh*]" (Isa. 11:2), and "the Spirit of God [*Elohim*]" (Exod. 31:3). Without the New Testament revelation, we would say these passages are speaking of *Yahweh's* Spirit or *Elohim's* Spirit—meaning simply the spiritual being sometimes called *Yahweh* and sometimes called *Elohim*. But passages such as Romans 8:9, where Paul speaks of "the Spirit of God," which we take to mean the Holy Spirit who proceeds eternally from God (John 15:26), interpret the Isaiah and Exodus passages as perhaps referring to the Holy Spirit.[39]

Another such passage is Isaiah 6:5-9, compared with Acts 28:25. In Isaiah 6:9 it is "the LORD," *Yahweh*, who says to Isaiah "'Go, and tell this people: Keep on listening, but do not perceive . . .'"; and in Acts 28:26 this is quoted, and it is prefaced by the statement that "the Holy Spirit" said it: "'The Holy Spirit rightly spoke through Isaiah the prophet to your fathers'" (Acts 28:25).

Also, in Exodus 17:7 we read that "they tested the LORD [*Yahweh*]," and Hebrews 3:7-9 implies that it was "the Holy Spirit" whom they had tested.

Further, in Jeremiah 31:31-35 we read, "'Behold, days are coming,' declares the LORD [*Yahweh*], 'when I will make a new covenant with the house of Israel and with the house of Judah'" (v. 31); and Hebrews 10:15-18 quotes this but says it is the Holy Spirit who says it: "The Holy Spirit also bears witness to us; . . . saying, 'This is the covenant that I will make with them after those days. . .'" (vv. 15-16).

While it is conceivable that in such references as these the New Testament writers mean only that the Holy Spirit says these things, because they know He helped the Old Testament people say and write things, what is said is actually more than that. *Yahweh* sometimes seems to be the same as the Holy Spirit. Passages such as these and those that equate Christ with especially *Yahweh* occasioned Augustine's correct view, mentioned earlier, that *Yahweh* was sometimes a reference to the entire Trinity and at other times to any one of the three persons of the Trinity. Even so, it seems that both *Yahweh* and *Elohim*, used so often in the Old Testament, ordinarily refer to God the Father.

In the New Testament, of course, we have numerous passages such as the baptismal formula of Matthew 28:19 and the benediction of 2 Corinthians 13:14 that link the Holy Spirit with the Father and the Son and that therefore imply His deity. But the New Testament contains much more than this.

In denying the deity of the Holy Spirit liberals also denied His personality, saying more or less that He was an influence. Therefore, before we discuss "deity" passages, let us note that the New Testament portrays the Holy Spirit as a person. Although in Greek *pneuma* ("Spirit") is neuter in gender, personal pronouns are used with reference to the Holy Spirit. Thus Jesus says, "He [the Holy Spirit] will bear witness of Me" (John 15:26). Thus Jesus also says:

But when he, the Spirit of truth, comes, he will guide you into all truth. He will not speak on his own; he will speak only what he hears, and he will tell you what is yet to come. He will bring glory to me by taking what is mine and making it known to you (John 16:13–14 NIV).

Besides, His personality is implied when He is called a "Counselor" (John 15:26) and "another Counselor" (John 14:14–16). More than this, He does what only persons do. He searches (1 Cor. 2:10–11), judges (Acts 15:28), hears (John 16:13), speaks (Rev. 2:7), and intercedes (Rom. 8:27).

Suggestive of the Holy Spirit's deity is the fact that it is one and the same thing if God speaks to us or indwells us or is resisted by us (Ps. 95:7–8; cf. Heb. 3:7–9; Rom. 8:9–10; 1 Cor. 3:16; Eph. 3:22; also Isa. 6:9; cf. Acts 28:25).

In addition, divine attributes are ascribed to the Holy Spirit. In Hebrews 9:14 He is called "the eternal Spirit." According to 1 Corinthians 2:1–11, He is omniscient: "The Spirit searches all things, even the depths of God" and "The thoughts of God no one knows except the Spirit of God." He seems to have all power even as God has because Paul says, "Now there are varieties of gifts, but the same Spirit. . . . There are varieties of effects, but the same God who works all things in all persons" (1 Cor. 12:4–6).

The Spirit's deity is implied when Paul says, "Do you not know that you are a temple of God and that the Spirit of God dwells in you?" (1 Cor. 3:16). The Spirit's living in us seems to be what makes us God's temple. (Cf. 2 Cor. 6:16: "For we are the temple of the living God.")

Although the Holy Spirit is not clearly called "God" *(theos)* in the New Testament, He is said to be eternal, has divine attributes, and does works that only a divine person could do. And since Christ is clearly called "God" *(theos)* in the New Testament and the Spirit is often spoken of along with the Father and the Son, the clear implication is that the Holy Spirit is divine.

This is the way in which the church has conceived of the Holy Spirit across the centuries—as a person who is divine. The very first Christians, soon after Pentecost, baptized only in the name of Jesus according to the Book of Acts, seeming not to have remembered Jesus' statement that baptism should be in the name of all three divine persons (Matt. 28:19). But after the Gospel of Matthew was written and disseminated, probably in the 60s, the baptismal formula in the Great Commission of Matthew 28:19 became a kind of first creed for Christians. It helped them toward the consciousness that the Holy Spirit was divine. The earliest church discipline, the *Didache,* written somewhat before or somewhat after A.D. 100 and purporting to teach what the apostles did, calls attention to this baptismal formula.[40] Clement of Rome implies the Spirit's deity,[41] as does Ignatius.[42] Justin Martyr refers to the Trinity,[43] as does Theophilus.[44] Tertullian taught it, as discussed earlier, in his *Against Praxeas*; as did Origen.[45] Later, Cyprian (d. 257) mentions the baptismal formula, and says "the Three are one."[46] Athanasius taught the deity of the Holy Spirit, although his emphasis was on the Son's deity. He said there is "one Godhead in Trinity."[47] Augustine often taught the Spirit's deity expressly, as when he wrote, "The Holy Spirit, who is not of a nature inferior to the Father and the Son, but, so to say, consubstantial and coeternal. . . ."[48] Actually, in general, the Fathers of the East and the West taught the Spirit's deity and the doctrine of the Trinity, such as Gregory Nazianzen,[49] Gregory of Nyssa,[50] and Basil,[51] to mention a few. Some aspects of their teachings needed ironing out (such as the Trinity's being analogous to three humans) but in general the Trinitarian doctrine was the teaching of the Fathers. However, there were denials of the Spirit's deity (and of that of the Son) on the part of some often-devout persons, as we will see when we trace heretical views.

The Nicene Creed of 325 mentions the Holy Spirit as though He is divine—along with its clear teaching of Christ's deity. At Constantinople in 381 the Holy Spirit's deity was expressly stated, because some had begun to deny it. The Athanasian Creed, which seems to be of the late fifth century (subsequent to the Council of Chalcedon of 451), states and restates the Holy Spirit's deity. It declares, "We worship one God in the Trinity, and the Trinity in unity; we distinguish among the persons, but we do not divide the substance. . . . The entire three persons are coeternal and coequal with one another, so that . . . we worship complete unity in Trinity and Trinity in unity."

But this discussion of the diety of the Holy Spirit in the early centuries of the church's history gravitates us toward the creeds of the church; and the creeds need to be discussed from the wider standpoint of their declarations regarding the doctrine of the Trinity as such.

As mentioned, the baptismal formula was a kind of early creed and implied the threeness of the Godhead without actually stating that the Son and the Spirit are divine. Also, it says nothing about the oneness of the three. In this connection Emil Brunner says, "Very early the Christian Church had fixed the main content of its faith in a threefold 'triadic' baptismal formula as a kind of creed."[52]

The Apostles' Creed, most of its clauses dating to around A.D. 150,[53] is constructed on a kind of Trinitarian outline. But it is not clearly Trinitarian, since the Son and the Spirit are not declared to be divine. Since it calls the Father "God" and does not say that the Son and Spirit are divine, it could be taken as not teaching their deity. Yet it should not be expected to be specifically Trinitarian, because the problems and heresies regarding the Trinity had not yet arisen. And the apostolic Fathers, writing in the post-apostolic era, are themselves not very clear on the Trinity.

On the deity of the Holy Spirit see also chapter 11, pages 416–17.

IV. THE TRINITY IN THE CREEDS

While there are several capsule statements in Scripture of what is truly believed among Christ's people (e.g., 1 Cor. 15:3), these statements are not creeds of the church as such.

A. The Apostles' Creed

The earliest of the actual creeds is the Apostles' Creed. This statement of belief, so named because it purports to teach, in brief compass, what the twelve apostles taught, dates perhaps to about the middle of the second century A.D. Although no copy of it exists from that early a time, historians such as Adolph Harnack and A. C. McGiffert say not only that such a creed existed at that time, but that, from the writings of the period, we can be quite confident about what clauses it then contained and which ones (such as reference to Christ's descent into Hades) were added at a later time.

Even in that early time, however, the creed seems to have been divided roughly into three parts—relating to the Father, the Son, and the Holy Spirit.

Yet, although it lists the three persons of the Trinity and is a kind of extension of the baptismal formula mentioned in Matthew 28:19, it is not at all an adequate Trinitarian statement. Only the Father is said to be divine; only He is called "God." "I believe in God the Father Almighty," we say. We go on to say that Christ is God's "only Son," but that does not necessarily express confidence in the Son's deity. Nor does anything else in this creed necessarily do this. Still less is said of the Holy Spirit that might imply His deity. Of Him, besides saying, "I believe in the Holy Spirit," this creed states only something merely functional: that Christ was "conceived by the Holy Spirit."

It is important to notice one other inadequacy of the Apostles' Creed's statement of the Trinity: it says nothing whatever about the oneness of the Father and the Son and the Spirit.

Still, the Apostles' Creed is about as Trinitarian as we could expect it to be, dating as it does to so early an era. At the time when it was basically composed, the church had not as yet been confronted with many of the heresies—which the later creeds were in great part devised to combat. Sabellianism-Monarchianism, Arianism, Macedonianism-Pneumatomachiniasm, etc. (which will be discussed later), were all of later vintage, and there was no way for the writer or writers of the early form of the Apostles' Creed to know that they needed to express Christian faith in a way that would avoid what came to be heretical understandings.

B. The Nicene Creed

This is historically the second of the ancient Christian creeds. It is based on the decisions of the first of the seven early ecumenical (East and West combined) councils—the council that met at Nicea, in Bithynia, during May or June of A.D. 325. There, some 300 bishops (318, according to some accounts)—from both the East and the West, i.e., from the Greek-speaking and the Latin-speaking areas—were called together by Emperor Constantine, who presided. Present were probably over a thousand persons—including such persons as presbyters and deacons, none of whom had a vote. Among the deacons was the young Athanasius, who had already written his *Concerning the Incarnation of the Word of God,* to this day one of the most significant books ever written on the Incarnation. Athanasius helped his bishop (from Alexandria) and, of course, defended the teaching of Christ's deity, so crucial for the Trinitarian understanding. Only perhaps twenty bishops were either Arians (very few in number), who stressed Christ's nature as unlike that of the Father, or Eusebians, who believed that Christ's nature was like *(homoiousia)* that of the Father.

As is well known, and as is so crucial to Trinitarian doctrine and to the Christian religion as such, the Athanasian view won out. The council declared that Christ is of the same substance *(homo ousia)* with the Father: "of one substance with the Father," "Very God of Very God." He is the "only begotten Son of God," "not made" as the world was made. After the Synod of Toledo in 589 it was changed to double procession to read, for the West, that the Holy Spirit "proceedeth from the Father and the Son."

C. The Nicene-Constantinopolitan Creed

Partly since the Holy Spirit's deity was not controverted at the Council at Nicea, His status was not defined. The Pneumatomachians latched onto this and began to teach a kind of binitarianism, in which only the Father and the Son were divine but not the Holy Spirit. Their teaching occasioned the next ecumenical council, the one that met in 381 at Constantinople and made the Holy Spirit's deity quite express, adding to the Nicene Creed that, "with the Father and the Son," He "is to be worshipped." It also added that He is "the Lord and Giver-of-Life, who proceeds from the Father." The Nicene Creed, with these additions, came to be known as the Nicene-Constantinopolitan Creed.

D. The Athanasian Creed

This creed was named for the fourth-century defender of orthodoxy, Athanasius, but (as seems evident from some of its wording) was written by an unknown person or persons some time after the Council of Chalcedon of A.D. 451. The first mention of it is at a synod held some time between 659 and 670. It was no doubt written in the West and in Latin. Over and over, much as an anthem asserts and reasserts something, it teaches that the Father and the Son and the Holy Spirit are all divine and that they share one nature so that they constitute one God. It reads that "we worship one God in Trinity, and Trinity in Unity; neither confounding the

Persons: nor dividing the Substance." It further reads, "So likewise the Father is Almighty, the Son Almighty: and the Holy Ghost Almighty. And yet there are not three Almighties: but one Almighty." It has in it the double procession of the Spirit, reading, "The Holy Ghost is of the Father and of the Son." It further states that "the Trinity in Unity is to be worshipped." Interestingly, it stated that one needed to believe precisely what it stated in order to be saved: "He, therefore who will be saved must thus think of the Trinity."[54]

E. The Augsburg Confession (1530)

This early Lutheran confession expresses full agreement with "the decree of the Nicene Synod concerning the unity of the divine essence and of the three persons . . . : to wit, that there is one divine essence which is called and is God . . . ; and that yet there are three persons of the same essence and power, who are also coeternal, the Father, the Son, and the Holy Ghost."[55]

F. The Formula of Concord (1576)

This late Lutheran confession expresses full agreement with all three of the ancient Christian creeds, which means that the Lutherans are located full-fledgedly not only with the Nicene Creed, but also with the official developments of doctrine, including Trinitarian doctrine, all the way through the rather late Athanasian Creed. Of ". . . the Apostles', the Nicene, and the Athanasian Creeds," it states: "We publicly confess that we embrace them, and reject all heresies and all dogmas which ever have been brought into the Church of God contrary to their decision."[56]

G. The Westminster Confession of Faith (1647)

This creed, official for Presbyterian denominations of various types, likewise affirms the doctrine of the Trinity in its classical purity. Interestingly, it begins with a lengthy statement about the Scriptures, which are not discussed at all in any of the ancient creeds. Then on the Trinity it states:

> In the unity of the Godhead there be three persons, of one substance, power, and eternity: God the Father, God the Son, and God the Holy Ghost. The Father is of none, neither begotten nor proceeding; the Son is eternally begotten of the Father; the Holy Ghost eternally proceeding from the Father and the Son.[57]

Here again the deity of all three and the Spirit's double procession are affirmed.

H. The Thirty-nine Articles (1562)

This creed, the official statement of the Church of England (and Episcopalianism generally), is of course classical on the doctrine of the Trinity. On this doctrine it reads:

> There is but one living and true God, everlasting, without body, parts, or passions; of infinite power, wisdom, and goodness; the Maker, and Preserver of all things both visible and invisible. And in unity of this Godhead there be three Persons, of one substance, power, and eternity: the Father, the Son, and the Holy Ghost.[58]

I. The Belgic Confession (1561)

While the Heidelberg Catechism (1563) only implies the doctrine of the Trinity by its lengthy articles "Of God the Father," and "Of God the Son," and "Of God the Holy Ghost"; and while the Canons of the Synod of Dort (1618–1619),[59] dealing as it does only with the Calvinistic-Arminian controversy, does not treat the doctrine of the Trinity, one of the important confessions official for Reformed branches of Christianity, the Belgic Confession, does indeed treat the doctrine of the Tri-Unity. It reads, "According to . . . this Word of God, we believe in one only God, who is one single essence, in which are three persons, really, truly, and eternally distinct, . . . The Father, and the Son, and the Holy Ghost."[60] But since the faithful are guided to use as a package of official creeds the Heidelberg Catechism, the Canons of Dort, and the Belgic Confession, it does not matter if any of them omits what another of them includes.

We shift, now, to a somewhat detailed study of the principal problem of the centuries among believers in the Trinity: whether the Holy Spirit proceeds only from the Father or from both the Father and the Son.

V. THE PROCESSION OF THE HOLY SPIRIT

While the Son is generated eternally (from the Father), the Holy Spirit eternally proceeds—either from the Father only or from both the Father and the Son (see John 15:26; Rom. 8:9, etc.).

The Nicene, or Ecumenical, Creed agreed on by the First Ecumenical Council (Nicea, 325) had stated simply, "And [we believe] in the Holy Spirit."

The Second Ecumenical Council (Constantinople, 381) had expanded this to include: "And in the Holy Spirit, the Lord and the Giver-of-Life, who proceeds from the Father. . . ." This Nicene-Constantinopolitan Creed was received in the West as well as the East as the official Christian creed.

Somewhat later the Third Ecumenical Council (Ephesus, 431) prohibited any creed that was different from the Nicene Creed itself; but the Fourth Ecumenical Council (Chalcedon, 451) refers to the Nicene-Constantinopolitan Creed as official—not the Nicene. So it was permitted, even in the East, to change the Nicene Creed by adding that the Holy Spirit "proceeds from the Father."

However, Augustine (354–430), before the third and fourth ecumenical councils had met, in his lengthy treatment of the doctrine of the Trinity, *Concerning the Trinity*, and elsewhere in his writings, had taught that the Holy Spirit proceeds from the Son as well as from the Father. Augustine had added a four-syllable Latin word to what the official Nicene-Constantinopolitan Creed taught: *filioque*, meaning "and the Son."

Since Augustine came to enjoy wide respect, especially in his own area of the church, the West, his teaching was promulgated by various Western theologians of the next few centuries.

A certain statement of belief (the *Quicumque* creed), perhaps originating in Gaul around 500, from an unknown author, was expressly Augustinian, and contained the addition "and the Son." Individuals of the West began to use this creed; and its addition of the *filioque* worked its way into the decrees of certain Spanish councils. In a short time, this creed's *filioque* phrase got added to the text of the Ecumenical Creed itself—although, of course, without official papal or ecumenical-council approval. So popular did the *filioque* view become that various popes taught it during the centuries immediately following these developments, although they did not at that time want to alter the Ecumenical Creed by adding to it the phrase "and the Son." These popes, including Leo III (795–816), and Western theologians generally, did not understand that the phrase "and the Son" constituted a material change in what was being taught. They tended to believe that this phrase was consistent with, and not necessarily divergent from, the teaching of the Ecumenical Creed that the Holy Spirit "proceeds from the Father."

By the time of the Carolingian era, at the beginning of the ninth century, the acceptance of the orthodoxy of the *filioque* had become widespread in the West.

At this time, Pope Leo III, who believed in the *filioque* doctrine but opposed its addition to the Ecumenical Creed (partly because he did not believe he had the authority to alter that creed), at first seemed not to disapprove of the addition of "and the Son" to the "creed" liturgy, which the Western monks sang during their worship.

Then some of these Western monks made a pilgrimage to Jerusalem and, in worshiping on Mt. Olivet with Eastern monks, shocked the latter by singing "and the Son" in the process of their liturgical worship when they sang the Ecumenical Creed.

At about 790 or 791 a certain creed (the *Libri Carolini*) was devised, probably written mostly by Theodulf of Orleans (and not Alcuin), since it shows the influence of the Spanish developments favorable to the *filioque*—including the teachings of Isadore of Seville (as well, naturally, as of the earlier Augustine). In this creed support for the addition of "and the Son" is based significantly on the view that otherwise the Holy Spirit would be only a creature, and not divine. Its author says that if Christians were to teach, as the East suggested we should, that the Holy Spirit proceeded from the Father "through the Son," the Holy Spirit would be said to have His existence the same way Scripture (John 1:3, 10) says the created world does: through the Son. This would tend to suggest that the Holy Spirit is a creature. This author also supports his view in the way Augustine had done, and as numerous other Western writers had done and were doing: by saying that Christ's breathing on the disciples and saying, "Receive the Holy Spirit," suggests that the Spirit proceeds from Christ. But this is a poor support, surely, since the passage obviously refers only to Christ's figuring in the Spirit's ministry, or His coming, at that time or at Pentecost and not to the manner of His eternal origination.

This writer appeared, actually, to believe that the *filioque* was in the Ecumenical Creed—whereas it was at that time only in the Athanasian Creed, to which he also clearly refers. This incorrect understanding on the part of a person who was probably a Spaniard, seems to have had a certain significance in the acceptance of the *filioque* on the part of the leading Franks of the time.

Soon Paulinus, who had been made Patriarch of Aquileia by Charlemagne, was commissioned by the Council of Frankfurt (794) to refute the Adoptianism of certain Spaniards. He convoked a council (796 or 797), but it actually considered, mainly, the matter of the addition of the *filioque* to the Ecumenical Creed.

Paulinus said that, while nothing is to be added to the Nicene-Constantinopolitan Creed, the *filioque* can and should be a part of that creed because (1) it does not add anything, since he thinks it is implied in what was said, and (2) it does not contradict anything in that creed.

Paulinus argued for his view in the way that many other Westerners did, particularly in the upcoming debates (e.g., with Ratramnus). He said that since the Second Ecumenical Council, at Constantinople (381), had added something ("who proceeds from the Father") to the Nicene Creed (of 325), a precedent was started for additions such as the *filioque*. He says that the Holy Fathers were entirely correct in saying what they said about the Son's deity at Nicea; that they were correct in what they added at Constantinople about the Spirit's proceeding from the Father; and that later Fathers—and Christians of his own time—were also correct in confessing "that he [the Holy Spirit] proceeds from the Father and the Son."[61] Paulinus continues, "'He is truly and properly the Holy Spirit, not born, not created, but proceeding eternally and inseparably from the Father and the Son.'"[62]

Then Paulinus did something that was of special significance in the establishment of the *filioque* understanding in the West: he added to his treatment of the matter a liturgy that contained the *filioque* addition to the Creed and sent copies to Charlemagne and Alcuin (the emperor's right-hand theologian). Alcuin was pleased, told Charlemagne and Paulinus so, and, with the emperor's full approval, caused the creed to be distributed and propagated with this addition in the Carolingian West.

But something happened that occasioned a serious controversy between the Carolingian West and the Byzantine East. As mentioned earlier, Frankish monks made a pilgrimage to Jerusalem and at Mt. Olivet shocked the Eastern monks, there, by singing the liturgy with the "and the Son" added to the Ecumenical Creed.

To these Eastern monks, and to the East generally, this was an utterly serious matter: a heresy of the first magnitude. Many of them even felt that a person who accepted such an aberration of the Ecumenical Creed would be denied heaven in the next life. It is of course in part because of this difference of view regarding the procession of the Spirit that the East and West officially divided much later (many authorities give 1054 as the date, while others make it twelfth century).

Patriarch Thomas of Jerusalem wrote Pope Leo III about this incident, the letter not now being extant. The pilgrim Frankish monks also wrote the Pope. Leo III forwarded both letters to Charlemagne. He also wrote a letter to "'all the churches of the East.'"[63] In the letter Pope Leo says, "The Holy Spirit proceeds equally from the Father and the Son and is consubstantial and co-eternal with the Father and the Son. The Father is fully God in himself, the Son born of the Father is fully God. The Holy Spirit, proceeding from the Father and the Son, is fully God."[64] Even so, Pope Leo III soon made it clear that he was opposed to the actual addition of the *filioque* to the Ecumenical Creed.

Charlemagne then charged his scholars to prepare a reply to the Jerusalem monks, and they did so—supporting the Western view.

Ratramnus especially contributed to the West's view at this point. Like Augustine and Paulinus, Ratramnus (strangely) used Christ's breathing on the disciples and saying "Receive the Holy Spirit" (John 20:22) as supportive of the West's predilection. Likewise, as Paulinus had done, he argued that the Roman Christians should have the right "'through the authority of Scripture'" to add to the creed, even as Constantinople had done in 381. He said that when Constantinople had declared that the Spirit proceeds from the Father, it had not at all denied that He proceeds from the Son as well.

Meantime Photius, the Patriarch of Constantinople (858-867; 878-886), had entered into the foray, on the side of the East. This was notably after he was deposed by Emperor Leo VI in 886 from his second term as the Patriarch, at which time he wrote *Mystagogia,* on the procession of the Spirit. He felt that the *filioque* teaching leads toward such heresies as Sabellianism and Macedonianism, and even to paganism. He also believed that, rather than leading to triadology, it leads to both tetralogy (strangely) and dyadology.[65]

Pope Nicholas I (858-867), like Leo III, came to accept the *filioque* addition but, again, he did not endorse its addition to the creed. However, Ratramnus assumed that he had endorsed this, since he had expressed belief in it. Ratramnus discussed the view, therefore, and urged it as though it was then the official one. This error on Ratramnus's part seems to have contributed to a widespread belief in the West that the addition of the *filioque* to the creed was official. Indeed, this contributed to its becoming official, being papally sanctioned (as it is to this day in the Roman Catholic church).

Since Protestants broke off from the Roman Catholic West and not from Eastern Orthodoxy and since the *filioque* was not a special issue in the Reformation, Protestants have usually accepted the double procession of the Holy Spirit. At the same time, they have not usually viewed the matter as of grave significance, as the Eastern Church did.

The Lutheran Church itself officially accepted the *filioque* addition. This can be said because, besides the six Lutheran confessions, it accepts as official the three ancient creeds—the Apostles', the Nicene, and the Athanasian (quasi-ancient)—and because the last of these decidedly supports the *filioque* phrase. This acceptance of the Athanasian Creed is shown in the Formula of Concord of 1576, which speaks of the "primitive Church symbols," which "contained the unanimous consent of the Catholic Christian faith, and the confession of the orthodox and true Church (such as are the Apostles', the Nicene, and the Athanasian Creeds)''; and it adds that ''we publicly profess that we embrace them, and reject all heresies and all dogmas which have ever been brought into the Church of God contrary to their decision.''[66]

Likewise, as noted earlier, whereas the Canons of Dort (1619) do not take up the matter of the Trinity at all the earlier Belgic Confession (1561) had declared of ''the Holy Ghost'' that He ''is the eternal Power and Might, proceeding from the Father and the Son.'' The Westminster Confession of Faith of 1647, official (along with a statement of 1967) for Presbyterians, speaks of ''the Holy Ghost eternally proceeding from the Father and the Son.'' And the Thirty-nine Articles of the Anglican Church (1562) speak of ''the Holy Ghost, proceeding from the Father and the Son.''[67]

Wesleyan theologians, and indeed Calvinistic and Lutheran ones as well, have generally understood that the Holy Spirit proceeded from both the Father and the Son. Protestants in general have taught in this way largely because they broke off not from Eastern Orthodoxy but from Roman Catholicism and did not find adequate reason to take a different position from that of Roman Catholicism on this issue that had earlier been so divisive.

VI. THE PRIORITY OF THE FATHER

Within the Trinity there is a certain priority that belongs to God the Father. He is the first-named member of the Trinity; the Son, the second; and the Holy Spirit, the third. When the three are named in Scripture, as in the baptismal formula (Matt. 28:19), the Father is usually named first—an exception to this being in that benediction where the Son is named first as Paul closes 2 Corinthians by saying, ''The grace of the Lord Jesus Christ, and the love of God, and the fellowship of the Holy Spirit be with you all.''

All three members of the Trinity are deity. All possess attributes that are divine. For example, all have existed eternally, a matter on which Scripture is clear; e.g., the Father: ''The eternal God is your refuge'' (Deut. 33:27); the Son: ''But of the Son He says, 'Thy throne, O God, is forever and ever'' (Heb. 1:8); and the Holy Spirit: ''. . . who through the eternal Spirit offered Himself without blemish to God'' (Heb. 9:14). Yet Scripture describes the Godhead in such a way as to make it clear that the Father holds a place of priority.

A certain priority of the Father seems to be suggested in the fact that while Paul states that we have *koinonia* (''fellowship'') with Christ and with the Holy Spirit, he nevers says we have this kind of close sharing with the Father. John, however, does say we have fellowship with the Father (1 John 1:3).

Paul also indicates the Father's priority in 1 Timothy 6:16, where he says of the Father, ''. . . who alone possesses immortality and dwells in unapproachable light, whom no one has seen or can see.'' This is said of ''God, who is the blessed and only Sovereign'' (1 Tim. 6:15). Since God the Father did not incarnate Himself, no one has actually seen Him. He dwells transcendently in ''unapproachable light.'' This cannot be said of the Son; and it would not be said of the self-effacing Holy Spirit.

Paul even more clearly teaches the Father's priority in other passages. One is in 1 Corinthians 11:3 where he says, ''But I want you to understand that Christ is the head of every man, and the man is the head of the woman, and God is the head of Christ.'' And this is a teaching Paul wants the Corinthians to hold onto, for the previous verse reads, ''I praise you for remembering me in everything and for holding on to the teaching.''

Paul also seems to suggest a priority of the Father in 1 Corinthians 8:6 when he says, ''Yet for us there is but one God, the Father, from whom are all things, and we exist for Him; and one Lord, Jesus Christ, through whom are all things, and we exist through Him.'' Here the word *Theos*

("God") refers expressly to the Father, as is usual in the New Testament as a whole. And the Father, here, has a priority, for it is from Him that all things came. This includes the eternal origination of Christ, as Jesus says, "For just as the Father has life in Himself, even so He gave to the Son also to have life in Himself" (John 5:26). In this verse it is evident that the Father has priority not only in giving life eternally to the Son but also in giving authority to the Son. Jesus continues by saying, "And He gave Him authority to execute judgment, because He is the Son of Man" (v. 27).

The fact that to Paul the first-named person of the Trinity is "the God and Father of our Lord Jesus Christ" (Eph. 1:3) suggests the Father's priority. If He is the Father of Christ, and Christ is the Son, this is logical and originative priority—though not chronological priority.

And in Paul's writings the Father has a priority as the One who plans the future. Thus, speaking of God, meaning the Father, Paul says that we were chosen to be in Christ "according to the plan of him who works out everything in conformity with the purpose of his will, in order that we, who were the first to hope in Christ, might be for the praise of his glory" (Eph. 1:11-12 NIV). This is in keeping with Christ's oft-used statement that the Father had sent Him and that He had come to do the will of the one who had sent Him.

Paul reveals a priority of the Father when he, as do other New Testament preachers (e.g., Peter in Acts 2) and writers, says that it is the Father who by His great power raised Jesus from the dead. Thus Paul speaks of God's "mighty strength, which he exerted in Christ when he raised him from the dead and seated him at his right hand in the heavenly realms" (Eph. 1:19-20 NIV). And "God [the Father] placed all things under his [Christ's] feet and appointed him to be head over everything for the church" (Eph. 1:22 NIV). And clear priority is shown when Paul speaks of "one Lord [Christ], one faith, one baptism; one God and Father of all, who is over all through all and in all" (Eph. 4:5-6).

And although Christ had been "in the form of God" and on a plain of "equality with God" (Phil. 2:6), it is "God" the Father who by Christ's resurrection "highly exalted Him, and bestowed on Him the name which is above every name" (v. 9).

The Father's priority in the Godhead is so often implied and stated in the New Testament generally and in Paul's writings particularly that it does not need much elucidation. Yet it does need to be pointed out. This is so because in much of evangelicalism there is a tendency to give Christ the first position in the Trinity. This tendency is present in part because Evangelicals have needed to be protective of the doctrine of Christ's deity, since liberals have denied it. It is present also in part because it is Christ who tabernacled among us and died on a Roman crossbar for us, becoming the One who provided for the redemption the Father gives us. But Paul and the other writers would have us keep in mind that Christians are not "unitarians of the Son," that we are not "Jesus only" people. Paul and the others make it clear that a kind of important priority is the Father's. It always has been, since the Son is eternally generated from His nature as the light has always issued from the sun, and the Father always will have the priority. Fundamentalist Evangelicals like to say that any priority there seems to be was in effect only during the period of the Son's incarnation. When I gave a paper on the doctrine of the Trinity at Gordon Theological Seminary (now Gordon-Conwell) several years ago at a national meeting of the Evangelical Theological Society, certain fundamentalist scholars argued in this way. They objected to my agreement with James Arminius who said that Christ is not *autotheos,* God of Himself, since Christ originated eternally from the Father. They even said the *monogenēs* ("only begotten") passages of the New Testament refer to Christ's being begotten of Mary. Nonetheless, Scripture makes the

Father's priority clear. Paul and the others imply it and state it hundreds of times. And one of the strongest of these, one that shows that the priority of the Father will obtain eternally, is what Paul says in 1 Corinthians 15:27–28:

> For he "has put everything under his feet." Now when it says that "everything" has been put under him, it is clear that this does not include God himself, who put everything under Christ. When he has done this, then the Son himself will be made subject to him who put everything under him, so that God may be all and in all (NIV).

So everything is put under Christ, but Christ is somehow "under" God the Father, that the Father might be "all and in all."

And it is subsequent to the years of Christ's enfleshment that Paul says, "But I want you to understand that Christ is the head of every man, and the man is the head of a woman, and God is the head of Christ" (1 Cor. 11:3). That is just the way it is, with all our proneness to give Christ the place of priority. He is fully divine, "very God of very God" as the creed says. He is co-eternal with the Father. But in the Godhead He is the Christian's Blessed Number Two.

There is reason and order and beauty in this, but many of us Evangelicals don't want an Incarnation after we have been given one. We would like to make of Christ another heavenly Father, but that spoils the plan and beauty and order of it all. It presses too far in the direction of opposing the liberals who have, by their denial of Christ's deity, occasioned our pressing. We tend to swing the pendulum to the opposite extreme from the liberals, when Scripture would have us place it somewhere between the two extremes.

While recent fundamentalism has been prone to make the Son the number one member of the Trinity, the church historically has not done this. From the earliest centuries it has understood that there is in the Godhead a priority of the Father. In the earliest extant treatise on the Trinity, Tertullian's *Against Praxaeas,* the early Latin father taught the Father's priority in several ways. Even as in his use of the terms *"trinitas,"* "person," and "substance" he taught what was later accepted by the church generally, so with the Father's priority. Tertullian gave several analogies to prove this: a shrub's root, the shrub, and its fruit; a river's source, the river, and the channel of the river; the sun, its rays, and what the rays strike. And in each case, he says in effect that there is firstness and secondness and thirdness. In one rather lengthy passage he groups these three analogies together and speaks of them in one rounded discussion:

> Therefore according to the pattern of these examples I declare that I speak of two, God and His Word, the Father and His Son. The root and the shrub are also two things, but joined together; the source and the river are two forms, but undivided; the sun and the ray are two forms, but they cleave together. Everything that proceeds from something, must be second to that from which it proceeds, but it is not therefore separated. Where, however, there is a second, there are two, and where there is a third, there are three. The Spirit is third with respect to God and the Son, even as the fruit from the shrub is third from the root, and the channel from the river is third from the source, and the point where the ray strikes something is third from the sun.[68]

Tertullian also writes, "So also the Father is other than the Son; since He is greater than the Son, since it is one that begets, another that is begotten; since it is one that sends, another that is sent; since it is one that acts, another through whom action takes place."[69]

Tertullian goes on to speak of "'the Holy Spirit,' the third name of divinity and the third stage of majesty."[70] He saw things scripturally, even at so early a time.

Augustine (354–430), who wrote the next really influential work on the Trinity, likewise clearly taught the Father's priority. He quoted and elucidated this biblical passage: "'All things are yours, and ye are Christ's, and Christ is God's'" (1 Cor.

3:22-23 KJV). Augustine also refers to other priority-of-the Father Scripture passages, without giving references (chapters and verses were not invented for the New Testament books until the thirteenth and sixteenth centuries respectively). He says:

> "For the Father is greater than I"; and, "The head of the woman is the man, the Head of the man is Christ, and the Head of Christ is God:" and, "Then shall He Himself be subject unto Him that put all things under Him:" and, "I go to my Father and your Father, my God and your God:" together with some others of like tenor.[71]

Then, about these, he comments:

> Now all these have had a place given them, (certainly) not with the object of signifying an inequality of nature and substance; for to take them so would be to falsify a different class of statements, such as, "I and my Father are one" *(unum);* and, "He that hath seen me hath seen my Father also;" and, "The Word was God,"—for He was not made, inasmuch as "all things were made by Him;" and, "He thought it not robbery to be equal with God:" together with all the other passages of a similar order.[72]

One can readily see that Augustine understands that the Scriptures teach the Father's priority and that the most influential of all the church fathers accepted it fully.

Through all the eventful and less eventful centuries of our Christian era, the church has taught the Father's priority. The Apostles' Creed implies it by beginning with the Father and by referring only to Him as "God." The other ancient creeds both imply it and assert it. In general, too, the Fathers, the Scholastics, and the Reformers have viewed the Trinity in this way.

In our time Karl Rahner has taught this imaginatively. He does so by calling the Father "the simply unoriginate God."[73] He implies that Christ and the Holy Spirit originated from the Father, but that the Father had His origination from no one. Similarly, he speaks of "the unoriginatedness of the Father."[74] He explains:

> The bond between the original self-communicator and the one who is uttered and received, a bond which implies a distinction, must be understood as "relative" (relational). This follows simply from the sameness of the "essence."[75]

To see the priority of the Father, with its ramifications, puts the student of the doctrine of the Trinity into the vestibule where he can then begin to roam around in the large-dimensioned room that is the Trinity doctrine. It will help a Christian to see that he is, at least usually, to direct his prayer to the Father; to thank the Father for the redemption He grants through the Son's provision and through the Holy Spirit's gentle nudges and powerful persuasions. It will help him better to conceive of the one-God doctrine of Trinitarianism, since there is one primal unoriginated source of the other two fully-divine persons—so that nothing like any Tritheism is even skirted.

VII. THE QUESTION OF PERSON

Whereas the principal problem shortly after the doctrine of the Trinity had developed had to do with the Spirit's procession, the principal problem within this doctrine in recent times has to do with whether or not the Father and the Son and the Spirit should be called persons. Karl Barth, for example, who is profoundly Trinitarian, believes that it is a bit misleading to call them persons. He uses the term *persons* for the Three, occasionally, as when he says that "the Father, the Son, and the Holy Spirit in the Bible's witness to revelation are the one God in the unity of their essence, and the one God is the variety of His Persons: the Father, the Son, and the Holy Spirit."[76] Yet Barth does not like to call them persons, for he thinks that that term suggests tritheism to people. Barth prefers to call them "Modes" instead of persons. But he avoids the ancient heresy of Modalism by saying that the three Modes exist simultaneously, not successively.

Karl Rahner also prefers not to refer to

the Three as persons, though he does not object as strongly as Barth does. He seems to be accepting of the word *person* when he says, "We do not agree with Karl Barth that the word 'person' is ill adapted to express the intended reality and that it should be replaced in ecclesiastical terminology by another word which produces fewer misunderstandings."[77] In this context he admits some problems with the word, but adds: "Yet the word 'person' happens to be there, it has been consecrated by the use of more than 1500 years, and there is not really a better word, which can be understood by all and would give rise to fewer misunderstandings."[78] However, in the same book, Rahner shows that he prefers to speak of "three distinct manners of subsisting." He says that "the Father, Son, and Spirit are the one God each in a different manner of subsisting and in this sense we may count 'Three' in God."[79] Rahner also says:

> But even so there are advantages in speaking of the "distinct manner of subsisting" or of God in three distinct manners of subsisting, rather than of person. "Three persons" says nothing about the unity of these three persons, so that this unity must be brought from outside to the word by which we designate the three persons.[80]

Rahner's own substitution "distinct manners of subsisting," will surely be more unclear to people than "persons" is, yet, interestingly, his chief reason for opting to use the difficult-to-understand phrase is to make more clear what we mean by persons.

So one of the reasons for urging some other term than *persons* is to avoid tritheism, and another is to make more clear what we mean when we refer to God's threeness. Still another reason why some, such as Paul Tillich, like to avoid the use of "persons" for the Three is that humans are persons, and this is to talk about the Ground of our existence in terms of our own human existence. Thus it is an affront to our God of greatness, even as it is an affront to Him, for Tillich, to say that He exists. We exist, and if we say that God exists, we are not saying enough about Him. One can see a good motive in this kind of reticence to designate the Three as persons. But it surely avoids something that Scripture writers do not see the need to avoid, for they often speak of God as being like humans: with psychological anthropomorphisms such as jealousy; and with physical ones, so that He is said to have a hand, feet, a back, a face, etc.

Yet a further reason why people urge a change is that the literal meaning of "person" might not be what we would want to be saying about God. "Person," not found either in the Hebrew Old Testament or the Greek New Testament, is from the Latin, *persona,* which means "mask (especially one worn by an actor), actor, role, character, person."[81] Although such as this is included in the literal meaning, it is doubtful whether people in general know this. Thus it is doubtful whether by "persons," in reference to the Three of the Trinity, they would be bothered by such meanings as masks and actors. Actually, since "role" is close to the "modes" Barth likes, and since "person" is certainly one of the meanings of *persona*, the term does not in any special way miss the mark of what we mean when we refer to the Three as persons. Each of the Three does have a role in creation and in redemption; and each is a person in the ancient Aristotelian meaning of "person" as characterized by intellect, feeling, and will.

With all this said, it must be added that by the "persons" of the Godhead we do not mean three beings, such as three human beings are. There are in God, as stated earlier, three centers of self-consciousness;[82] but these so interpenetrate each other that a oneness of being obtains that does not obtain in the case of three human individuals.

The use of "persons" in referring to Father, Son, and Spirit has a long history in Christianity—and this augurs for its continued use. Tertullian spoke of God's "Triune Personality."[83] Yet he may have gone too far when he said of Christ that "a wholly different 'Self' has stepped into the scene with *his* own validity."[84] The phrase "wholly different" is perhaps too much, since the Three are one in nature.

The three-person language was used in early credal statements, such as the most significant one of all, that of Chalcedon in 451, that we are not to divide "the substance" nor confuse "the persons." It is the language of the centuries; and the word *persons,* it seems, best describes the distinctions in the Godhead described in Scripture.

VIII. OPPOSITION TO THE TRINITY DOCTRINE

As might be expected, the doctrine of the Trinity has had numerous opposers as the centuries have passed. Any doctrine as significant as this would quite naturally be conceived of in certain aberrant ways that, after the church had declared itself in official councils, constituted them heresies. Often those offering aberrant interpretations were bishops who were most devout and altogether well-intended.

Praxeas, against whom Tertullian wrote so early, was a kind of monarchian, conceiving that the Father and the Son and the Spirit are actually one and the same. Tertullian says, "So Praxeas managed two pieces of the devil's business at Rome: he drove out prophecy and brought in heresy, he put the Paraclete to flight and crucified the Father."[85] "Crudely expressed, his [Praxeas's] position was that the Father alone was God, and that all the experiences undergone by Jesus in His earthly life were undergone by the Father."[86]

Sabellius taught that the Father, Son, and Spirit are one God, one Person, manifested in three successive modes or fashions. His teaching was called Modalism, because the three were conceived of as three modes instead of three persons; or monarchianism, because God consisted of only one, and not three, and so was like a monarch who is a sole ruler.

The chief heresy of all was Arianism. It was more significant than any of the others because it was the greatest threat of them all. The Council of Nicea, the first of the seven early general councils was called in A.D. 325 to decide whether or not Arius was right, and it decided that he was not. The Council stated that Christ was *homoousios,* of the same substance with the Father (not *homoiousus,* of like substance; nor was His substance or nature unlike that of the Father). The position of Athanasius had won out, as mentioned earlier. Alexander, bishop of Alexandria, voiced Athanasius's view, and it carried the day. Yet not all was settled. Several times, in the nearly fifty years of his life after that time, Athanasius, then bishop, was sent into exile—at such times as it seemed it would be more politically cementing for the empire if the church were Arian. In 336, Arius, who had been excommunicated, was to be brought back into the church as a member the next day; and that night he died. But he had many followers, and that for centuries.

Arius has been described as "a tall, spare man, ascetic in habits and dress, with long, tangled hair, and a curious practice of twisting about, withal of fascinating manners and address, and not without a considerable mixture of craft and vanity."[87] In about A.D. 318 Arius, a leading presbyter at Alexandria, came into conflict with his bishop in his Trinity doctrine. He said that Christ, the Son, was a created being, made "out of nothing," that He was the greatest of the creatures and that through Him the rest of the universe was made, that He was not eternal, but only preexistent, that He was not of divine nature or substance, and that He was not able to comprehend the Father.[88] Whereas Origen had taught that there never was a time when the Son was not, Arius said, "There was when he was not." And Arius taught that the Holy Spirit is a still less exalted creature than Christ was and that He was created by the Son even as the rest of creation was.

Historian Gibbon has made light of the whole world being convulsed about a diphthong, feeling that not much was at stake in the Arian controversy. Yet Adolph Harnack, James Orr, and other historians of doctrine view the matter very differently—as exceedingly important.[89]

While in medieval times Roscellinus was accused of being a tritheist, and Peter Abelard a Sabellian, most theologians accepted the doctrine of the Trinity as described in the Nicene-Constantinopolitan Creed and in the more elucidated Athanasian Creed. The really big issue was whether the Spirit proceeded only from the Father or from both the Father and the Son, as discussed earlier in this chapter. But in the main, in the East and the West during these centuries the Monarchian-Sabellian heresies were squelched, and Arianism was at least altogether unofficial.

The Reformers had no special differences with the just-earlier Scholastics on the matter of the Trinity. Servetus (d. 1553) suffered death within the Reformation for teaching pretty much what came to be Unitarianism (and Universalism). Faustus Socinius (d. 1604) taught a kind of anti-Trinitarianism, which came to be known as Socinianism and which also was a precursor of Unitarianism. In important ways, too, Socinianism-Unitarianism is a revival of ancient Arianism.

Also opposed to the doctrine of the Trinity were the English Deists such as Lord Herbert and John Locke; and their view spread to Germany (from England to Germany!), where we know it as the Enlightenment, represented by such men as Leibnitz and Wolff. The great triumvirate of German philosophical theology—Immanuel Kant, Friederick Schleiermacher, and Friederick Hegel—all denied the doctrine of the Trinity. In fact, all the Rationalists and the Modernists have denied the doctrine, teaching in general that Christ was only a man, albeit a good and great man, and that the Holy Spirit is an influence and not a divine person. One of them, William Adams Brown, a liberal theologian of America, figured that the threeness is simply the way we think about God, not the way He exists.[90]

One of the main recent oppositions to the doctrine of the Trinity has come from another teacher at Union Theological Seminary (in New York), Cyril C. Richardson, in his *Doctrine of the Trinity*. Richardson likes to speak of the three as "symbols,"[91] not persons. Frequently he calls them "terms."[92] He supposes that the doctrine of the Trinity "often beclouds[93] . . . the vital concerns of the Christian faith." To him, the doctrine is "an artificial threefoldness."[94]

Richardson properly credits Oxford's Leonard Hodgson with giving us one of our excellent recent studies of Trinitarian doctrine. But while Hodgson says that there are three centers of consciousness in God and that this makes for a more intensive unity, Richardson admits the possibility of three making a more intensified unity but asks why Hodgson stops with three centers of consciousness. Richardson says, "The logic of this should perhaps have driven Hodgson to posit an *infinite* number of persons in the Trinity." The reason of course why Hodgson posits only three—and this might sound strange to Richardson—is that both the Bible and the creeds stop at three.

IX. SIGNIFICANCE OF THE DOCTRINE

The doctrine of the Trinity in the Christian faith holds a place of primal importance among the doctrines.

A. It Presupposes Various Beliefs

The doctrine of the Trinity presupposes various doctrines that relate to God the Father, but it is more inclusive than those doctrines. For example, it presupposes the existence of God and the doctrines of creation, God's sovereignty, and providence, as well as others—doctrines that relate somewhat more particularly to God the Father than to the other two persons of the Trinity.

It presupposes the deity of Christ, but includes more than that. It presupposes the

Virgin Birth of Christ, since the Virgin Mary's conceiving Jesus by the Holy Spirit instead of by a human male is what founds Jesus in Deity; but it is far more inclusive than the Virgin Birth doctrine. It presupposes the Incarnation, since that is Deity's becoming enfleshed; but it is more inclusive than the Incarnation doctrine.

Likewise, the doctrine of the Trinity presupposes various aspects of the doctrine of the Holy Spirit. It fundamentally presupposes the Spirit's deity and His being a person. It presupposes His work as executor of the Godhead, who implements the Father's grace—prevenient, justifying, sanctifying, sustaining. It presupposes His work in the inspiration of Scripture.

This doctrine of the Trinity, so fundamental to Christian faith and so elemental, might be thought of as analogous to the air we breathe. As the air is more basic than even food or water, the doctrine of the Trinity, so inclusive, so ramified, is more basic than any other Christian doctrine.

B. It Helps Our Worship

One of the most important reasons why we Christians should hold a correct view of the doctrine of the Trinity is that we may worship God more correctly and more fulfillingly than would otherwise be possible.

For example, since it is God the Father who has the priority among the persons of the Trinity, and since it is the Father who actually answers our prayers, it is to Him that we ought to address our prayers. All the actual prayers of Scripture are addressed to the Father; only one is addressed to God the Son, and that is Stephen's one-sentence "prayer" in Acts 7:59: " 'Lord Jesus, receive my spirit' "; and none are addressed to God the Holy Spirit. The Son and the Spirit are divine, so they could hear our prayers. They have divine attributes, so they would be powerful enough and wise enough to answer them. But we do not normally address them because we are taught in Scripture to address the Father instead. And we do not normally address them because their peculiar functions are what Scripture says they are: the Son's to intercede with the Father for us; and the Holy Spirit's to nudge us toward prayer and help us in all sorts of ways during prayer.

Not only will a correct understanding of the doctrine of the Trinity help us in our worship by assuring that we address the Father in our prayers and that we at the same time understand what the functions of the Son and the Spirit are, but it will also help us in praising God in our worship. We will be helped to direct our praise to the Father, since He is the One we address directly. It will help us to articulate what we praise the Son and the Spirit for. We will tell the Father we are thankful for His sending Christ the Son into the world, for the Son's permitting people to hang Him on a Roman crossbar, and for the Father's great power by which the crucified Christ was raised bodily from among the dead.

Worshiping more or less correctly, we will tell or at least signal to the Father that we are thankful for the Holy Spirit's special and gracious ministries to us. We will become filled with praise for the Holy Spirit's ministries of conviction, and of guidance, and of illumination; for His function in the conception of Jesus Christ in Mary's womb; for His function in inspiring the many and diverse writers of Holy Scripture. We will praise the Father for the Holy Spirit's using specific persons and specific events and circumstances to urge us toward justifying and sanctifying grace.

The fact that a more or less correct theology is important for the purpose of a more or less correct worship of God is pointed up by the root meaning of the word *orthodoxy*. *Ortho* means "straight." Thus an orthodontist is a straightener of teeth, and an orthopedist is a straightener of the back. The rest of that Greek word is from *dokeō*, meaning "to think." Thus our word *orthodoxy* means "correct thinking," or "straight doctrine." The reason for this is that especially in the early

Greek-speaking East, Christians felt that the chief purpose of correct doctrine is for the purpose of a correct worship of God.

C. It Helps in Evangelism

Another important significance of a more or less correct understanding of the doctrine of the Trinity is in order to a proper and effective evangelism servanthood to Christ. Evangelism, of course, is the main mission of the church. It is the church's most elemental, most basic work in God's world. Christ's church, as a saved community, is a saving community. And in this ministry to the unsaved it is important that we understand God's oneness and His threeness as we present the Good News of redemption to people. Here it is not so much the ontological Trinity as the economic Trinity that surfaces. We do not so much explain to the unsaved how God exists in Himself as three persons in one nature. Rather, we explain to them the economic Trinity: the three persons in their special functions—especially, in their redemptive functions.

We might well begin with the Good News about the redemption made provisional through Jesus Christ. We announce to the unevangelized that Jesus Christ, God's eternal son, left the glory He had with the Father and came into this world to save sinners; that He died on the cross to soften the Father's holy wrath against sin and to make it possible for the Father to forgive those who repent and believe and still remain a just God; and that God the Father raised this really crucified God-man, Jesus, from the dead, making Jesus a savior instead of a martyr.

We explain to the unevangelized the place of the Holy Spirit in redemption. We tell them to look for His nudges, for His wooings, for His inwardly moving convincings of who Jesus is and of the sinfulness of sin.

We need to tell the unevangelized about the Father also. We need to tell them that He has the most basic function of all, in the offer of redemption: it is He who sent the Son; it is He who makes the latent offer of redemption to anyone at all who will repent and believe; it is He who actually does the forgiving and, later, the cleansing from original sin through Jesus Christ's baptism with the Holy Spirit.

D. Its Importance Is Seen in Christianity's Past

If the doctrine of the Trinity is not important, then why did the early Greek and Latin fathers and the councils engage themselves so much with it as Christianity began to win its good way in the Roman Empire of the early Christian centuries? If it is not important, why were people baptized in the name of the three persons of the Trinity? If it is not important, why did the Father and the Son and the Spirit form the basic three-point division of the earliest ecumenical creed—the Apostles' Creed? If it is not significant, why were the other two early ecumenical creeds, the Nicene and the Athanasian, constructed around the doctrine? And why, otherwise, do the first twenty-eight of the forty-four numbered statements in the Athanasian Creed have to do with the Trinity, and why are they the first twenty-eight of the forty-four? And otherwise, why are statements twenty-nine to thirty-seven of that creed on Christ's incarnation and His status; and number thirty-eight, on His atonement and resurrection; and number thirty-nine on His ascension; and number forty on His second coming?

Off with our shoes, then, Wesleyans, and Christians generally, for the teaching of the Trinity is holy ground. Off with our shoes, so that believing may come readily, when we stand in rapt adoration of the One-in-Three God, the Three-in-One God, who offers us undeserving humans healing and wholeness and heaven.

NOTES

[1] G. A. F. Knight, *A Biblical Approach to the Doctrine of the Trinity* (Edinburgh: Oliver and Boyd, 1953), p. 1.

[2] Charles W. Lowry, *The Trinity and Christian Devotion* (New York: Harper and Brothers, 1946), p. xi.

[3] Ibid., p. 79.

[4] Ibid., p. 54.

[5] See Tertullian, *Against Praxeas,* trans. A. Souter (New York: Macmillan, 1920), p. 30.

[6] Ibid., p. 31.

[7] Augustine, *On Christian Doctrine* (Edinburgh: T. & T. Clark, 1892), pp. 359-60.

[8] Ibid., p. 10.

[9] Ibid.

[10] Ibid.

[11] Henry Thiessen, *Lectures in Systematic Theology* (Grand Rapids: Eerdmans, 1979), p. 90.

[12] Ibid.

[13] Augustine, *Christian Doctrine,* p. 359.

[14] Ibid., pp. 359-60.

[15] John Miley, *Systematic Theology,* vol. 1 (New York: Methodist Book Concern, 1892), p. 272.

[16] Thomas Aquinas, *The Trinity and the Unicity of the Intellect,* trans. Sister Rose Emmanuel à Brennan (St. Louis: Herder, 1946), p. 42.

[17] Karl Rahner, *The Trinity* (New York: Seabury, 1974), p. 7.

[18] Ibid.

[19] Ibid., p. 50.

[20] Thiessen, *Lectures,* p. 273.

[21] Ibid.

[22] Ibid.

[23] Augustine, *Christian Doctrine,* p. 365.

[24] Ibid., p. 13.

[25] Thiessen, *Lectures,* p. 274.

[26] Augustine, *Christian Doctrine,* p. 37.

[27] A. C. Knudson, *The Religious Teachings of the Old Testament* (New York: Abingdon, 1918), p. 73.

[28] C. H. Cornill, *The Prophets of Israel* (Chicago: Open Court, 1895), p. 23.

[29] Rahner, *Trinity,* pp. 45-46.

[30] James Denney, *Studies in Theology* (Grand Rapids: Baker, 1976), p. 70.

[31] Lewis Sperry Chafer, *Systematic Theology,* vol. I (Dallas: Dallas Seminary Press, 1947), p. 287.

[32] Ibid.

[33] It is unlikely that the three angels who appeared to Abraham, according to Genesis 18, were the three members of the Trinity, as some have suggested.

[34] H. Orton Wiley, *Christian Theology,* vol. 2 (Kingshighway, 1941), p. 173.

[35] I have discussed this with Dr. Wiley considerably and corresponded with him on it. In a letter he indicates that Augustine's view would be entirely acceptable to him. He was working on a revision of his *magnum opus* at the time of his death and was considering this and numerous other changes that I suggested to him.

[36] Herman Bavinck, *The Doctrine of God,* trans. William Hendriksen (1895-1899; reprint ed., Grand Rapids: Baker, 1951), p. 257. This book is a reprint of a large section of Bavinck's *magnum opus, Gereformeerde Dogmatiek.* Although I found an occasional incorrect Scripture reference in it, it was the most helpful of all my sources on the doctrine of Trinity in Scripture.

[37] Chafer, *Systematic Theology,* p. 297.

[38] For the same view on the impact on these passages see ibid., p. 296.

[39] The Son is also sometimes called "God" *(El)* in the Old Testament, as in Isaiah 9:6, where it is said that the "child" to be born will be called "Wonderful Counselor, Mighty God," and in Psalm 68:18: "When you [Christ] ascended on high [after the Resurrection], you led captives in your train; you received of men, even from the rebellious—that you, O LORD God, might dwell there" (NIV).

[40] *Didache or Teaching of the Twelve Apostles* in *The Fathers of the Church* (New York: Címa, 1947), 1:177.

[41] Clement of Rome, "The Letter to the Corinthians," in *Fathers of the Church,* 1:54.

[42] St. Ignatius of Antioch, "Letter to the Smyrnaeans," in *Fathers of the Church,* 1:119.

[43] Justin Martyr, "First Apology," in *Ante-Nicene Fathers,* ed. Alexander Roberts and James Donaldson, 10 vols. (Buffalo: Christian Literature, 1886), 1:164, 185.

[44] Theophilus, "The Autolycus," in *Ante-Nicene Fathers,* 2:101.

[45] Tertullian, "Against Praxeas," in *Ante-Nicene Fathers,* 4:598.

[46] Cyprian, "To Jubarian," in *The Fathers of the Church,* ed. Roy Deferrari, 69 vols. (Washington, D.C.: Catholic University of America Press, 1946), 51:271, 275.

[47] Athanasius, "Discourse I Against the Arians," in *A Library of Fathers of the Holy Catholic Church,* 41 vols. (London: Rivington, 1844), pp. 205-6.

[48] Augustine, *Christian Doctrine,* p. 357.

[49] Gregory Nazianzen, "Funeral Oration," in *The*

Fathers of the Church, ed. Roy Deferrari, 69 vols. (New York: Fathers of the Church, 1953), 22:86.

[50] Gregory of Nyssa, "On Perfection," in *Fathers of the Church,* ed. Deferrari, 59:106.

[51] Basil, "To Meletius, Bishop of Antioch," in *Fathers of the Church,* ed. Deferrari, 13:267.

[52] Emil Brunner, *Christian Doctrine of God (Dogmatics,* vol. I), trans. Olive Wyon (Philadelphia: Westminster, 1950), p. 220.

[53] See Wiley, *Christian Theology,* 1:40.

[54] Paul T. Fuhrmann, *An Introduction to the Great Creeds of the Church* (Philadelphia: Westminster, 1966), pp. 49-50.

[55] Philip Schaff, *Creeds of Christendom,* 3 vols. (Grand Rapids: Baker, 1977), 3:7.

[56] Ibid., pp. 93-95.

[57] John Leith, *Creeds of the Churches* (Richmond, Va.: John Knox, 1973), p. 197.

[58] Ibid., pp. 487-88. Quoted from the 1801 American revision, which is identical to the 1562 original on the doctrine of the Trinity but which updates the English.

[59] Schaff, *Creeds of Christendom,* 3:581-97. Of special interest to Arminian-Wesleyans is the fact that the Synod of Dort refers repeatedly to the Arminians as the "calumniators" and warns them "to consider the terrible judgment of God which awaits them."

[60] Ibid., p. 389.

[61] Richard Haugh, *Photius and the Carolingians: The Trinitarian Controversy* (Belmont, Mass.: Nordland, 1973), p. 58.

[62] Ibid.

[63] Ibid., p. 68.

[64] Ibid.

[65] Ibid., p. 147.

[66] Schaff, *Creeds of Christendom,* 3:93-95.

[67] Ibid., p. 489.

[68] Tertullian, "Against Praxeas," p. 45.

[69] Ibid., pp. 46-47.

[70] Ibid., p. 116.

[71] Augustine, *Christian Doctrine,* p. 361.

[72] Ibid.

[73] Rahner, *Trinity,* p. 84.

[74] Ibid., p. 78.

[75] Ibid., pp. 102-3.

[76] Karl Barth, *Church Dogmatics,* ed. G. W. Bromiley and T. F. Torrance (Edinburgh: T. & T. Clark, 1936-69), p. 353.

[77] Rahner, *Trinity,* p. 44.

[78] Ibid.

[79] Ibid., p. 114.

[80] Ibid., p. 111.

[81] *Webster's New International Dictionary, Unabridged* (Springfield, Mass.: Merriam, 1961).

[82] Some scholars, such as Karl Rahner, teach differently. Others teach this profoundly, e.g., Lowry in *Trinity and Christian Devotion,* pp. 79ff.

[83] Tertullian, "Against Praxeas," p. 256.

[84] Ibid. Karl Rahner disagrees with this. He says, "Thus, as we said above, when nowadays we hear of 'three persons,' we connect, almost necessarily, with this expression the idea of three centers of consciousness and activity, which leads to a heretical misunderstanding of the dogma" (*Trinity,* pp. 56-57). Rahner also says, "But there are not three consciousnesses; rather, the one consciousness subsists in a threefold way. There is only one real consciousness in God, which is shared by the Father, Son, and Spirit, by each in his own proper way. Hence the threefold subsistence is not qualified by three consciousnesses" (ibid., p. 10). Many scholars disagree with Rahner on this matter. One of them is Lowry, *Trinity and Christian Devotion.* Another is John Lawson, who writes about "person": "In usage it has become enriched since then, and one might say that as used in the trinitarian formula it includes the conception of self-consciousness, but not that of exclusiveness. We may symbolize the Three as 'knowing' one another, but not as 'shutting one another out.' The divine persons are not exclusive, like human personalities, but are inclusive" (John Lawson, *Introduction to Christian Doctrine* [Wilmore, Ky.: Asbury, 1980], p. 123).

[85] Tertullian, "Against Praxeas," p. 27.

[86] Ibid., xvii.

[87] James Orr, *The Progress of Dogma* (London: Hodder and Stoughton, 1897), p. 108.

[88] Ibid., p. 113.

[89] Ibid., p. 109.

[90] Ibid., p. 113.

[91] Cyril C. Richardson, *The Doctrine of the Trinity* (New York: Abingdon, 1958), p. 111.

[92] See ibid., p. 98.

[93] Ibid., p. 114.

[94] Ibid., p. 15.

DISCUSSION QUESTIONS

1. Is it tritheistic to understand that in the Godhead there are three centers of self-consciousness?
2. Just why is it that the various analogies of the Trinity such as the triangle or the human family are always inadequate?
3. In what ways does Scripture teach Christ's deity?
4. In what ways does Scripture teach the Holy Spirit's deity?
5. In what ways does Scripture teach the unity—the oneness—of God?
6. How should a knowledgeable person discuss 1 John 5:7 with an older saint who questions making any changes in what the King James Version states?
7. Would we today consider it an important matter whether the Holy Spirit proceeds only from the Father (Eastern view) or from both the Father and the Son (Western view)?
8. Is it proper to say that the Father has a certain priority in the Godhead?
9. Should we normally address our prayers to God the Father? Why or why not?
10. Is it correct to refer to the Father, Son, and Spirit as persons?
11. What would have been the result if Arianism had won out?
12. Is a denomination a Christian group if it denies the doctrine of the Trinity? What of the Jehovah's Witnesses? the Unitarians? the Jesus-Only Pentecostals?

RECOMMENDATIONS FOR FURTHER READING

Augustine. *On Christian Doctrine*. Edinburgh: T. & T. Clark, 1892.

Bavinck, Herman. *The Doctrine of God*. Edited by W. Hendriksen. Grand Rapids: Baker, 1951.

Brunner, Emil. *Christian Doctrine of God (Dogmatics*. Vol. I.). Translated by Olive Wyon. Philadelphia: Westminster, 1950.

Denney, James. *Studies in Theology*. Grand Rapids: Baker, 1976.

Knight, G. A. F. *A Biblical Approach to the Doctrine of the Trinity*. Edinburgh: Oliver & Boyd, 1953.

Lowry, Charles. *The Trinity and Christian Devotion*. New York: Harper and Brothers, 1946.

Rahner, Karl. *The Trinity*. New York: Seabury, 1974.

Richardson, Cyril C. *The Doctrine of the Trinity*. New York: Abingdon, 1958.

Schaff, Philip. *Creeds of Christendom*. Vol. III. Grand Rapids: Baker, 1977.

Tertullian. "Against Praxeas." In *The Ante-Nicene Fathers*. Vol. IV. Edited by A. Souter. New York: Macmillan, 1920.

BIBLIOGRAPHY

Athanasius. "Discourse I Against the Arians." In *A Library of Fathers of the Holy Catholic Church*. Vol. 18. London: Fathers of the Church, 1953.

Aquinas, Thomas. *The Trinity and the Unicity of the Intellect*. Translated by Sister Rose Emmanuell à Biennan. St. Louis: Herder, 1946.

Augustine. *On Christian Doctrine*. Edinburgh: T. & T. Clark, 1892.

Barth, Karl. *Church Dogmatics,* I. Edited by G. W. Bromiley and T. F. Torrance. Edinburgh: T. & T. Clark, 1936-1969.

———. *Theology and Church*. New York: Harper and Row, 1962.

Basil, "To Meletius, Bishop of Antioch." In *The Fathers of the Church*. Vol. 13. Edited by Roy Deferrari. New York: Fathers of the Church, 1953.

Bavinck, Herman. *The Doctrine of God*. Edited by W. Hendriksen. Grand Rapids: Baker, 1951.

Brunner, Emil. *Christian Doctrine of God (Dogmatics)*. Vol. I.). Edited by Olive Wyon. Philadelphia: Westminster, 1950.

Chafer, Lewis Sperry. *Systematic Theology*. Vol. I. Dallas: Dallas Seminary Press, 1954.

Clement of Rome. "The Letter to the Corinthians." In *The Fathers of the Church*. Vol. I. New York: Cima, 1947.

Cornill, C. H. *The Prophets of Israel*. Chicago: Open Court, 1895.

Cyprian. "To Jubarian." In *The Fathers of the Church,* Vol. 51. Edited by Roy Deferrari. Washington, D.C.: Catholic University of America Press, 1946.

Denney, James. *Studies in Theology*. Grand Rapids: Baker, 1976.

"Didache or Teaching of the Twelve Apostles." In *The Fathers of the Church*. Vol. 1. New York: Cima, 1947.

Fuhrmann, Paul T. *An Introduction to the Great Creeds of the Church*. Philadelphia: Westminster, 1950.

Gregory, Nazianzen. "Funeral Oration." In *The Fathers of the Church*. Vol. 22. Edited by Roy Deferrari. New York: Fathers of the Church, 1953.

Gregory of Nyssa. "On Perfection." In *The Fathers of the Church*. Vol. 58. Edited by Roy Deferrari. New York: Fathers of the Church, 1953.

Haugh, Richard. *Photius and the Carolingians: The Trinitarian Controversy*. Belmont, Mass.: Norland, 1973.

Ignatius of Antioch. "Letters to the Smyrnaeans." In *The Fathers of the Church*. Vol. 1. New York: Cima, 1947.

Justin Martyr. "First Apology." In *The Ante-Nicene Fathers*. Vol. 1. Edited by Alexander Roberts and James Donaldson. Buffalo: Christian Literature Publishing Co. 1886.

Knight, G. A. F. *A Biblical Approach to the Doctrine of the Trinity*. Edinburgh: Oliver & Boyd, 1953.

Knudson, A. C. *The Religious Teachings of the Old Testament*. New York: Abingdon, 1918.

Lawson, John. *Introduction to Christian Doctrine*. Wilmore, Ky.: Asbury, 1980.

Leith, John. *Creeds of the Churches*. Richmond, Va.: John Knox, 1973.

Lowry, Charles. *The Trinity and Christian Devotion*. New York: Harper and Brothers, 1946.

MacGregor, Geddes. *The Nicene Creed*. Grand Rapids: Eerdmans, 1980.

Miley, John. *Systematic Theology*. Vol. 1. New York: Methodist Book Concern, 1892.

Orr, James. *The Progress of Dogma*. London: Hodder and Stoughton, 1897.

Purkiser, W. T.; Taylor, Richard S.; and Taylor, Willard H. *God, Man and Salvation*. Kansas City, Mo.: Beacon Hill, 1977.

Rahner, Karl. *The Trinity*. New York: Seabury, 1974.

Richardson, Cyril C. *The Doctrine of the Trinity*. New York: Abingdon, 1958.

Schaff, Philip. *Creeds of Christendom*. Vol. III. Grand Rapids: Baker, 1977.

Tertullian. "Against Praxeas." In *The Ante-Nicene Fathers*. Vol. IV. Edited by A. Souter. New York: Macmillan, 1920.

Theophilus, "The Autolycus." In *The Ante-Nicene Fathers*. Vol. II. New York: Macmillan, 1920.

Thiessen, Henry. *Lectures in Systematic Theology*. Grand Rapids: Eerdmans, 1979.

Webster's New International Dictionary, Unabridged. Springfield, Mass.: G. and C. Merriam Co., 1961.

Wiley, H. Orton. *Christian Theology*. Vol. II. Kansas City, Mo.: Beacon Hill, 1941.

CHAPTER 11

PNEUMATOLOGY:
The Doctrine of the Holy Spirit

Milton S. Agnew

Milton S. Agnew is a colonel in the Salvation Army. He has been a Salvation Army officer for fifty-four years, having received his commission from the Salvation Army School for Officers' Training in Chicago in 1929. In 1955 he received his B.D. degree from Northern Baptist Seminary. He is presently on the faculty of the School for Officers' Training in Los Angeles, where he teaches theology. He had held various administrative positions and, especially since his retirement in 1970, has conducted Holiness Institutes with officers in many parts of the world.

Colonel Agnew is the author of several books, including Manual of Salvation; Security of Believers; Transformed Christians; *and* The Holy Spirit: Friend and Counselor. *He is a member of the Christian Holiness Association and a charter member of the Wesleyan Theological Society.*

CONTENTS

I. **THE HOLY SPIRIT POSSESSES A PERSONALITY** / 415
    A. The Holy Spirit Is an Active Person / 416
    B. The Holy Spirit Is a Divine Person / 416

II. **THE HOLY SPIRIT IS IN THE DIVINE TRINITY** / 417
    A. The Old Testament Scriptures Imply His Trinitarian Relationship / 417
    B. The New Testament Scriptures Confirm His Trinitarian Relationship / 417

III. **THE HOLY SPIRIT IS SYMBOLIZED IN THE SCRIPTURES** / 417
    A. He Is Symbolized as Breath, or Wind / 417
    B. He Is Symbolized as Water / 417
    C. He Is Symbolized as Fire / 418
    D. He Is Symbolized as Oil / 418
    E. He Is Symbolized as a Dove / 419
    F. He Is Symbolized as a Seal / 420

IV. **THE HOLY SPIRIT REPRESENTS BOTH THE OLD AND THE NEW ERAS** / 420
    A. This Is True Regarding the *Presence* of the Spirit / 420
    B. This Is True Regarding the *Purpose* of the Spirit's Presence / 420

V. **THE ADMINISTRATIVE WORK OF THE HOLY SPIRIT BEGAN BEFORE PENTECOST** / 421
    A. He Was the Divine Creative Agent / 421
    B. He Was the Divine Author of the Scriptures / 421
    C. He Was Active in the Redemptive Life and Ministry of Jesus / 423

VI. **THE HOLY SPIRIT HAS BECOME THE ADMINISTRATOR OF THE DIVINE PLAN OF REDEMPTION UNDER THE NEW COVENANT** / 425
    A. All Members of the Trinity Are Involved in Man's Salvation / 425
    B. All Members of the Trinity Are Involved in the Life of Holiness / 426
    C. The Spirit Governs the Type of Action in All Aspects of Salvation / 427
    D. The Holy Spirit Is Our Witness / 427

VII. **JESUS PRESENTS UNMISTAKABLE TEACHINGS REGARDING THE HOLY SPIRIT** / 427
    A. The Holy Spirit Is Now *Present* With Every Believer / 427
    B. The Holy Spirit Is Now *Available* to Every Believer in a New and Different Way / 428
    C. Consider Christ's Paraclete Teachings / 430
    D. Jesus Will Baptize With the Holy Spirit / 435
    E. The Holy Spirit, as Administrator, Will Be Associated With the Church / 438

VIII. "THE PROMISE OF THE FATHER" IS CENTRAL TO THE TEACHING OF THE SPIRIT / 438
    A. This Effusion of the Spirit Has Several Titles / 439
    B. The "Promise of the Father" Was to Be Fulfilled Subsequent to Conversion / 439
    C. The Message of 1 Corinthians 12:13 Examined / 442
    D. Water Baptism and Spirit Baptism in the Scriptures / 445

IX. THE CHURCH IS ESTABLISHED BY THE HOLY SPIRIT / 447
    A. God's Long-Range Plan Fulfilled / 447
    B. Several Titles Become Proper for God's Family / 448
    C. The Jerusalem Church Exhibited Essential Characteristics / 448
    D. The Holy Spirit Has Continued to Work in the Church / 448

X. THE HOLY SPIRIT BESTOWS GIFTS / 449
    A. The Gifts of the Spirit Defined / 449
    B Underlying Principles Regarding Gifts / 449
    C. There Are Hazards in Gifts / 450
    D. There Are Basically Four Lists of Gifts in the Scriptures / 451
    E. The Scriptural List of Gifts May Not Be Sacrosanct / 452
    F. Christ's Teachings Regarding the Gifts of the Spirit / 453

XI. THE HOLY SPIRIT PRODUCES FRUIT / 454
    A. Fruit That Remains Is Engendered by a Mystical Union / 454
    B. Fruit Requires Cultivation / 454
    C. Fruit Is Developed by the Indwelling Spirit / 455
    D. Fruit Is Produced by the Planting of Seed / 455

XII. MINISTRIES, FRUIT, AND GIFTS OF THE SPIRIT COMPARED / 456

XIII. SUMMARY HISTORY OF THE DOCTRINE OF THE HOLY SPIRIT / 457
    A. The Early-Church Controversies Concerning the Spirit / 457
    B. The Medieval Church Fostered Bitter Disputes / 458
    C. The Reformation Reopened a Channel for the Holy Spirit to Work / 460
    D. The Eighteenth and Nineteenth Centuries Saw the Rise of Counter Developments / 460
    E. The Twentieth Century Marks a Revival of the Holy Spirit in the Church / 461

NOTES / 463

DISCUSSION QUESTIONS / 465

RECOMMENDATIONS FOR FURTHER READING / 465

BIBLIOGRAPHY / 466

PNEUMATOLOGY

The Doctrine of the Holy Spirit

I. THE HOLY SPIRIT POSSESSES A PERSONALITY

The reality of a living Holy Spirit must be established or His credibility, His indispensability, His unmatched importance cannot be accepted. This is not altogether easy to accomplish. For one thing there is the haunting specter of a Ghost—from the old English of the King James Version of the Bible. There is the oft-repeated Apostles' Creed, which has, for centuries, brought to the church service the sacred and stately: "I believe in the Holy Ghost," and for some three centuries the doxology has closed with "Praise Father, Son, and Holy Ghost."

Those of the Wesleyan persuasion will recognize the frequency with which Charles Wesley's hymns open with the phrase "Come, Holy Ghost." A survey of one hymnal disclosed that more than thirty songs include this name.

For the mature, or at least the older, Christian frequent use has accommodated the title "The Holy Ghost" to that which is sacred, dignified, and precious. But to the younger, to the immature, to the non-church-goer, it is still, and will remain, obscure, unreal, and misleading.

It must be admitted that the word *Spirit* is not much more helpful or definite. The dictionary refers one abruptly from "Holy Spirit" to "The Holy Ghost." In turn "The Holy Ghost" is succinctly defined as "The third person of the Trinity: also called Holy Spirit." Further search discloses that "spirit" is "the vital essence or animating force in living organisms. In the Bible, the [Holy Spirit is the] creative, animating power or divine influence of God."[1] "Vital essence!" "Animating power!" "Divine influence!" These do not spell out to the casual reader the divinity of the Third Person of the Trinity. They give no hint of the intimate touches of His personality. They do not speak of the indispensable Administrative Agent of the Godhead. Little wonder that it is in this insipid, impersonal, ineffectual light that the world generally views the Holy Spirit! "This reflects the liberal and the neoorthodox point of view [comments Charles Ryrie]. Most neoorthodox writers deny the distinct personality of the Spirit. He is regarded as more of an activity of God than a person of the Godhead."[2]

It is true that until the Incarnation the Holy Spirit had never been disclosed clearly as the third Person of the Trinity.

He had been frequently identified as "the Spirit of God" (Gen. 1:2), as "the Spirit of the LORD" (Judg. 3:10), as "Thy Spirit" (Ps. 139:7), as "My Spirit" (Isa. 44:3), and as "His Spirit" (Isa. 48:16). But only three times in the Old Testament is He termed "Holy Spirit" (Ps. 51:11; Isa. 63:10-11), and even then as "Holy Spirit" or "His Holy Spirit." As H. Orton Wiley has observed:

> Consequently the term is used relatively and not in the absolute sense. The full disclosure of His personality and perfections was not made until the set time for His inauguration. Only when Christ had been fully glorified at the right hand of the Father could the Holy Spirit come in the fullness of His pentecostal glory.[3]

Herbert Lockyer comments, "The error of treating the Spirit in an impersonal way can be traced back to the third century when the theory was advanced that the Holy Spirit was a mere influence, an exertion of divine energy and power, an emanation from God."[4]

A. The Holy Spirit Is an Active Person

1. Personal attributes are ascribed to Him He is an intelligent person, possessing a mind, containing knowledge (Rom. 8:27; 1 Cor. 2:11). He is a communicative person, possessing a vocabulary (1 Cor. 2:13). He is a volitional person with a will of His own (1 Cor. 12:11). Comments Ralph Herring:

> As to the Spirit's powers of volition, the remaining and perhaps the most conspicuous attribute of personality, Jesus himself gives us the best illustration. "The wind bloweth where it will," He said to Nicodemus, "so is every one that is born of the Spirit" (John 3:8). In other words, the Spirit is free as the wind. He is utterly sovereign. . . . He refuses to be bound by precedent and, in every new circumstance, remains at liberty to work his own good pleasure.[5]

Possibly most important of all, Jesus carefully identifies Him as a person by using the personal pronoun, "He," even though "spirit" in the Greek is neuter in gender (John 14:17, 26; 16:13-15). Furthermore, Jesus recognizes Him as a person in referring to Him as "another Comforter," where *allos*, "another of the same sort," identifies Him with Himself as a person.

2. Sensitivity is ascribed to Him He possesses the sensitivities of a person. He exerts love as a person (Rom. 15:30). He can be insulted (Heb. 10:29), lied to (Acts 5:3), and resisted (Acts 7:51). He can be grieved (Eph. 4:30).

B. The Holy Spirit Is a Divine Person

1. Divine attributes confirm His divinity He is omnipresent (Ps. 139:7); omniscient (Isa. 40:13-14; 1 Cor. 2:10); and omnipotent as reflected in the new birth (John 3:6) and as reflected in the resurrection, first of Jesus, then of His people (Zech. 4:6; Rom. 8:11); He is eternal (John 14:16; Heb. 9:14).

2. Divine titles confirm His divinity He has an imposing list of titles that identify Him with Deity. These include Helper (John 14:16), the eternal Spirit (Heb. 9:14), Holy Spirit (Ps. 51:11; Eph. 1:13; 4:30), power of the Most High (Luke 1:35), the Spirit of Christ (1 Peter 1:11), the Spirit of the LORD (Isa. 11:2), the Spirit of glory (1 Peter 4:14), the Spirit of God (Gen. 1:2), the Spirit of grace (Zech. 12:10), the Spirit of holiness (Rom. 1:4), the Spirit of the Lord GOD (Isa. 61:1), the Spirit of life (Rom. 8:2), the Spirit of your Father (Matt. 10:20), and the Spirit of His Son (Gal. 4:6).

3. Supernatural activities confirm His divinity He is credited with activities that only a person of divinity could accomplish. He teaches (John 14:26), guides (John 16:13), intercedes (Rom. 8:26), bears witness (John 15:26), convicts (John 16:7-8), strives (Gen. 6:3), and directs (Acts 8:29).

4. Divine personal sensitivity confirms His divinity Only as a divine person could He be sinned against in this sense (Ps. 51:4; Matt. 12:31).

5. Apostolic pronouncements confirm His divinity The divinity of the Holy Spirit is clearly taught by Peter when he confronted Ananias with the charge that when he lied to the Holy Spirit he lied to God (Acts 5:3–4). His divinity is clearly indicated by Jesus when He identifies blasphemy against the Holy Spirit as being comparable to blasphemy against Himself (Matt. 12:31–32).

See also chapter 10, pages 388–91, concerning the divinity of the Holy Spirit.

II. THE HOLY SPIRIT IS IN THE DIVINE TRINITY

Herbert Lockyer points out that "the term Trinity is . . . a nonspiritual one. It was first formally used in the Synod of Alexandria in 317 A.D. and was coined to express the doctrine tersely. It signifies threefoldness, and is not, as sometimes stated, an abbreviation of ''tri-unity.''"[6]

A. The Old Testament Scriptures Imply His Trinitarian Relationship

It is true there is no clear-cut statement of the Trinity in the Old Testament. Implications appear in such verses as Numbers 6:24–27; Isaiah 6:3; 48:16. It is in Luke 4:18–21 that Jesus identifies the prophecy of Isaiah 61:1–2 as being fulfilled in Him.

B. The New Testament Scriptures Confirm His Trinitarian Relationship

It is in the New Testament that the Trinity is made explicit, thus identifying the Holy Spirit as a member of the Trinity. This is true in the account of the baptism of Jesus (Matt. 3:16–17), in the Great Commission (Matt. 28:19), in Paul's benediction (2 Cor. 13:14), and in the account of the death of Stephen (Acts 7:55–60).

III. THE HOLY SPIRIT IS SYMBOLIZED IN THE SCRIPTURES

The reality of the Holy Spirit, furthermore, is viewed from several angles in the various symbols used of the Spirit. The very word *symbol,* derived from the Greek *sym* (''with'') and *ballien* (''to throw or put''), carries the meaning of ''something chosen to stand for or represent something else; especially, an object used to typify a quality.'' Thus the reality of the Spirit as more than ''an animating power'' or ''a divine influence'' is clarified by symbols.

A. He Is Symbolized as Breath, or Wind

The Spirit is identified as breath that God breathes and as the wind that blows. The Hebrew word *ruach* and the Greek word *pneuma* are variously translated—as ''breath'' in Genesis 2:7 and Acts 17:25; as ''wind'' in Genesis 8:1 and John 3:8; as ''Spirit'' in Genesis 1:2 and John 3:8. Thus there is presented the fact in Genesis 2:7 that, as applying to none of the animals, God breathed into man His Spirit to make for Himself a unique creation in His likeness—an immortal soul. And thus there is delicately described by Jesus the new birth: ''The wind blows where it wishes and you hear the sound of it, but do not know where it comes from and where it is going; so is every one who is born of the Spirit'' (John 3:8). In this sense the Spirit is invisible, heavenly, powerful, and sovereign.

Consider also the exciting account of ''the valley of dry bones'' in Ezekiel. ''Thus says the Lord God to these bones, 'Behold, I will cause breath to enter you that you may come to life.' . . . Say to the breath, 'Thus says the Lord God, ''Come from the four winds, O breath, and breathe on these slain, that they come to life''''' (Ezek. 37:5, 9).

B. He Is Symbolized as Water

The Holy Spirit is symbolized by John as water. Jesus declared, ''He who believes in Me, as the Scripture said, 'From his innermost being shall flow rivers of living water.'" Then the elderly John, from many years of personal experience, explained, "But this He spoke of the Spirit, whom those who believed in Him were to receive; for the Spirit was not yet given, because Jesus was not yet glorified" (John 7:38-39). This is the water of the birth of the Spirit from above—available to the unregenerate for their regeneration (John 3:5-6). This is the water that, in its fullness, is the baptism of the Spirit—available to the regenerate (Acts 1:5, 8; 2:1-4) for their sanctification (John 17:17, 20; Acts 15:8-9). This is the living water that alone will satisfy man's deepest needs and will be an overflowing artesian well springing up for the sanctifying and empowering of believers (cf. John 4:13-17; 7:38-39). This is the water of life that is inexhaustible (Rev. 7:17); the water that makes life fruitful (Rev. 22:1-2); and the water that the thirsty may receive freely (Rev. 22:17; also see Isa. 44:1-5; Ezek. 36:25-27; Joel 2:28).

C. He Is Symbolized as Fire

Fire, as a symbol of the Spirit in the Old Testament, represents the Lord in His holy presence (Exod. 3:2), in His approval (Lev. 9:24), in His protection (Exod. 13:21), in His judgment (Lev. 10:2), and in His cleansing (Isa. 6:1-8). The Old Testament gives way to the New Testament representation of the Holy Spirit as fire of burning, brilliance, and purging (Matt. 3:11-12). Matthew 3:11 records John as declaring, "As for me, I baptize you in water for repentance; but He who is coming after me is mightier than I, and I am not even fit to remove His sandals; He Himself will baptize you with the Holy Spirit and fire." There being but one participle, the two objects of that participle, "Holy Spirit" and "fire," are synonymous, not sequential.

This is the fire of cleansing ("for our God is a consuming fire" [Heb. 12:29]); the fire of proving ("gold . . . tested by fire" [1 Peter 1:7]); the fire that ignites, kindles, and inflames ("who makes His . . . ministers a flame of fire" [Heb. 1:7]); the fire of purification ("And there appeared to them tongues of fire distributing themselves, and they rested on each one of them" [Acts 2:3]).

Under the chapter "Red-hot Religion," Samuel Brengle in his *Resurrection Life and Power* presents a vivid description of this stirring subject.

> One of the unsolved problems of science is to produce a physical light that is cold. The problem which religion has solved, and must solve, is to produce a spiritual light that is hot, which is nothing other than the old-time religion. Jesus said of His forerunner, John the Baptist, "He was a burning and shining light." He shone until Jerusalem and all Judea and all the regions around Jordan were startled and awakened by the light, and went out to see and to hear; and he burned into their hard, cold hearts until the multitudes confessed their sins, and the King Herod himself and his adulterous wife were so scorched by the heat of the burning herald of righteousness that Herod shut him up in prison, and beheaded him.
>
> John burned his way into the dulled consciences of the men of his day, and stirred all Palestine.
>
> Stephen burned into the guilty souls of priests and rulers until their wrath knew no bounds, and they cast him out and sent him to Heaven in a shower of stone.
>
> The apostles burned their way into idolatrous cities and into a pagan civilization reeking with unmentionable lusts and unspeakable cruelties (Rom. 1:22-32) until the world was transformed.
>
> What is this fire? It is God the Holy Ghost burning in and through humble, holy, faithful men . . . They hungered and thirsted for Him, and found Him. And when they found Him they *burst into flame*. "Our God is a consuming fire," and holy fire kindles in every soul that lives with Him.[7]

D. He Is Symbolized as Oil

There is, in oil, a threefold symbol of the Holy Spirit.

1. He is represented as anointing oil

The anointing with oil authenticates, dedicates, empowers. In this the Old Testament merges with the New. The priest was consecrated (Exod. 29:7), the authority of the king confirmed (1 Sam. 12:3-5). By His anointing, Jesus was prepared for His ministry with the oil of the Spirit (Luke 4:18; Acts 10:38). Thus was Jesus established as the promised "Messiah," "the Christ," "the anointed One." For the Hebrew *mashiach* (Ps. 2:2; Isa. 45:1 KJV) and the Greek *chrio* (Luke 4:18) mean "to anoint" or "the anointed One" from which come "Messiah" (Ps. 2:2; Dan. 9:25) and "Christ" (John 1:41).

It is to the same "oil" of the Spirit that Paul refers when he declares of God's children, "Now He who establishes us with you in Christ and anointed us is God" (2 Cor. 1:21), while John encourages his people with the assurance, "But you have an anointing from the Holy One. . . . And as for you, the anointing which you received from Him abides in you . . . as His anointing teaches you about all things" (1 John 2:20, 27).

2. He is represented as medicinal oil

This is the oil that heals. Mark 6:13 says of the Twelve, sent by Christ on a mission: "They were . . . anointing with oil many sick people and healing them" (see also Luke 10:34; James 5:14). The Holy Spirit heals many wounds and diseases of the body, but also of the soul and the mind.

3. He is represented as illuminating oil

There is the oil that illuminates, as declared by William Biederwolf:

> Oil is an illuminator and so is the flame of spiritual life kindled within and kept burning by the oil of the Spirit, illuminating the conscience and dispelling the moral darkness of the heart, shining out into the world through the light of Christian character unto the glory of the Christian's Father.[8]

The ten virgins of Matthew 25:1-12 depended on oil for light from their lamps when the bridegroom should come. It is recorded that the wise took extra oil "in flasks along with their lamps" but "when the foolish took their lamps, they took no oil with them." The *glory* of that midnight hour is found in the simple statement regarding the prudent who possessed the needed supply of oil: "Those *who were ready* went in with him to the wedding feast." The *tragedy* of that hour is in the futility of the cry of the foolish, *who were not ready:* "Our lamps are going out." The *finality* of that hour is succinctly declared: "And while they were going away to make the purchase [of oil] . . . *The door was shut."* A desperate appeal to the bridegroom only brought the stern reply, "Truly I say to you, I do not know you," and they were consigned to "outer darkness."

What can this say to us but to underscore the admonition given by Paul: "Understand what the will of the Lord is . . . and be filled with the Spirit" (Eph. 5:17-18), where "be filled" is in the present tense of continuous action—"keep filled." This is a continuing responsibility of the child of God. Paul gave warning of a tragic possibility when, using the Greek verb found in Matthew 25:8, *sbenumi* ("are going out"), he admonished the believer, "Do not quench the Spirit" (1 Thess. 5:19). He can be "quenched"!

E. He Is Symbolized as a Dove

It was as a dove that the Holy Spirit came upon Jesus at His baptism. Matthew 3:16 records: "And after being baptized, Jesus went up immediately from the water; and behold, the heavens were opened, and he saw the Spirit of God descending as a dove, and coming upon Him."

Now the first reference to a dove in the Scriptures is in the account of Noah and the Flood (Gen. 8:8-10), where the dove is identified for its loving, tender characteristics. The next is as a sacrifice (Gen. 15:9), which is described more fully in Leviticus 1:14-17; 14:4-8. It is intriguing that a pair of doves was included in the sacrifice offered at the dedication of the child Jesus (Luke 2:24), when His parents could not afford a lamb (see Lev. 12:6-8)! Jesus' own reference to doves (Matt. 10:16) identifies them as "innocent."

How appropriate, then, that the Spirit of God, at the launching of Christ's ministry descended on Him "as a dove"—loving and tender in nature, sacrificial in purpose and task, innocent and sinless in character!

F. He Is Symbolized as a Seal

The symbolism of the Spirit as a seal, promised to the believer, attributes some important characteristics to the Holy Spirit. "In Him, you also, after listening to the message of truth, the gospel of your salvation—having also believed, you were sealed in Him with the Holy Spirit of promise" (Eph. 1:13).

The order of the Ephesians' entry into the promises of God is both interesting and instructive. First, they heard ("after listening"); second, they believed ("having also believed"); and third, they "were sealed" with the Holy Spirit. There is here both an order and a progression. Each step is dependent on the preceding one. It is believers who are to be sealed. Is this not, for example, a picture of the progression recounted for the Ephesian twelve in Acts 19:1-7?

A seal has a threefold significance. It indicates ownership. Paul confidently declared, "For I bear on my body the brand-marks of Jesus" (Gal. 6:17). Again, a seal suggests authority. The official seal on a passport gives validity to that document. Ralph Earle suggests that "the ring given the repentant son (Luke 15:22) probably was the father's official signet ring with which he stamped the soft sealing wax on letters. The son was thereby authorized again to do business in his father's name."[9] So the Spirit-sealed Christians bear a mark of divine authority and ownership on their lives. They are authorized "to do business" in the Father's name. (See Luke 19:13.)

A seal also suggests preservation or security. However, such a preservation depends on satisfactory preparation, and the center of that preparation is purification, cleansing, sanctification. As observed by Charles W. Carter: "Thus these Gentile believers had heard the gospel preached, they had believed it as the word of truth, and they were made sons of God, in consequence of which God purified their hearts through the baptism with the Holy Spirit, and sealed them as His own possession."[10]

Thus through these several channels and in these several aspects, the *reality* of the Holy Spirit is established, His *viability* is disclosed, and the *vitality* of His Person is revealed. He is real as a person, real in His divinity, and real as a full-fledged member of the Trinity.

IV. THE HOLY SPIRIT REPRESENTS BOTH THE OLD AND THE NEW ERAS

A. This Is True Regarding the *Presence* of the Spirit

Under the Old Covenant, God exercised His sovereign choice in the selection of the recipients of the Spirit, but under the New Covenant *all believers* are indwelt by the Holy Spirit (Rom. 8:9; 1 Cor. 6:19)—even though they may not be Spirit-filled (1 Cor. 3:1). All believers *on their request* may be baptized and filled with the Spirit and may receive "the promise of the Father" (Luke 11:13; Acts 2:38; 11:15-16; Eph. 5:18).

B. This Is True Regarding the *Purpose* of the Spirit's Presence

Under the old covenant the Spirit energized people who would fulfill a task. Balaam was chosen to speak a parable (Num. 24:2-9); Bezalel, to build the tabernacle and its furniture (Exod. 31:3-5); Gideon, to deliver his nation from their enemies (Judg. 6); David, to give leadership to his people (1 Sam. 16:13); Ezekiel, to prophesy to the nation in the distress of their captivity (Ezek. 2:1-7); and holy men, that they might write the Scripture (2 Peter 1:20-21).

Under the old covenant there was also the less defined purpose of spiritual quickening. The Holy Spirit strove with men (Gen. 6:3), worked a spiritual transformation in Saul (1 Sam. 10:6-9), proved Himself to be an essential presence in the repentance of David (Pss. 51:9-11; 143:10), and admonished God's people through the prophets (Neh. 9:30). However, this purpose was not then paramount.

Under the new covenant the primary purpose of the Spirit is ethical. He is the Spirit of truth (John 15:26-27; 16:12-13), of holiness (Gal. 5:22-23), and of power (Acts 1:8). He is the One who expedites the plan of redemption in all its aspects, the One who establishes and maintains the church. He empowers believers to be "more than conquerors" in their Christian lives. In an important yet secondary role, the Holy Spirit in this dispensation enables His people to perform tasks, to fulfill assigned areas of work, to bring in the kingdom of God through gifts and enablements, and to be effective in their witness.

The movement in the method of choice and in the purpose of operation of the Spirit from the old covenant to the new largely typifies the two dispensations and will become more evident as we proceed.

Not everyone, however, is in accord on the present dispensation. Calvinists accept the fact of the presence of the Holy Spirit in every believer but look doubtfully on the believer's privilege of requesting and receiving the Spirit in the fullness of a baptism in the Spirit, and on the purpose of the baptism. The Charismatics agree on the availability of the Spirit to the believer in a baptism in the Spirit but find the first evidence of this to be that of gifts of the Spirit, especially tongues, and power to perform these gifts. These points of difference will be explored more fully later on.

V. THE ADMINISTRATIVE WORK OF THE HOLY SPIRIT BEGAN BEFORE PENTECOST

Each member of the Godhead has a definite and distinctive area of responsibility; this will become most evident under an examination of the plan of redemption as outlined in the New Testament. But that the Holy Spirit has always carried the responsibility of administration was evident from the beginning.

A. He Was the Divine Creative Agent

The Holy Spirit was, from the beginning, the divine Administrator in Creation. The writer of Genesis 1:1-2 declares that "in the beginning God created the heavens and the earth." He also points out that "the Spirit of God was moving over the surface of the waters," referring obviously to the primal substance of the universe.

The Genesis record states, "Then the LORD God formed man of dust from the ground, and breathed into his nostrils the breath of life; and man became a living being" (2:7). This is obviously referred to by Elihu when he declared, "The Spirit of God has made me, and the breath of the Almighty gives me life. . . . Behold, I belong to God like you; I too have been formed out of the clay" (Job 33:4-6). Indeed, the Holy Spirit, as the breath of God, acted as the divine Executive in the creation of both that which is physical and that which is spiritual.

Samuel Chadwick comments:

> Breath is the word for Spirit. It is a picture word. God does not breathe. The Spirit is not wind. It is a figure of speech to illustrate the fact that God communicated to man the life which was within Himself. God breathed into man. His Spirit and man became a living soul. It was by the Spirit of God that man was made in the image of God, and it was by the Breath of God in His Son that there was given unto man again the gift of the Holy Ghost.[11]

B. He Was the Divine Author of the Scriptures

The Holy Spirit was the administrative Author of the Scriptures. In a very pertinent statement David owned this to be true. "The Spirit of the Lord spoke by me, and His word was on my tongue'' (2 Sam. 23:2). The prophets were very conscious of this ministry of inspiration. Micah states:

> On the other hand I am filled with power—
> With the Spirit of the LORD—
> And with justice and courage
> To make known to Jacob his rebellious act,
> Even to Israel his sin.
> (Mic. 3:8)

Ezekiel presents a truly dramatic setting for the guidance of the Spirit:

> Then He said to me, ''Son of man, stand on your feet that I may speak with you!'' And as He spoke to me the Spirit entered me and set me on my feet; and I heard Him speaking to me. Then He said to me, ''Son of man, I am sending you to the sons of Israel, to a rebellious people who have rebelled against Me; they and their fathers have transgressed against Me to this very day. . . . But you shall speak My words to them whether they listen or not, for they are rebellious'' (Ezek. 2:1-3, 7).

Again, Ezekiel says:

> And it came about in the sixth year, on the fifth day of the sixth month, as I was sitting in my house with the elders of Judah sitting before me, that the hand of the Lord GOD fell on me there. Then I looked, and behold, a likeness as the appearance of a man. . . . And He stretched out the form of a hand and caught me by a lock of my head; and the Spirit lifted me up between earth and heaven and brought me in the visions of God to Jerusalem. . . . And behold the glory of the God of Israel was there, like the appearance which I saw in the plain (Ezek. 8:1-4).

Could it not be that Peter had the vivid imagery of Ezekiel in mind when he penned these words: ''But know this first of all, that no prophecy of Scripture is a matter of one's own interpretation, for no prophecy was ever made by an act of human will, but men moved by the Holy Spirit spoke from God'' (2 Peter 1:20-21)?

Now the verb ''moved'' *(pherō)* is a verb of active conveyance. It is translated ''carry'' in Luke 23:26 and Acts 5:6, and ''take'' in John 2:8. Thus men of God were figuratively ''carried,'' ''taken,'' and ''moved'' by the Holy Spirit as they recorded the Scriptures.

John Williams comments:

> Peter's careful use of language here recognizes both the divine and the human aspects of Scripture. He allows for the conscious involvement of men with all their individuality, yet underlines the sovereignty and surveillance of God, which guarantees us the inerrancy of Scripture.[12]

The symbolic use of the ''breath'' of God is plainly declared in the basic statement of 2 Timothy 3:16: ''All Scripture is God-breathed and is useful for teaching, rebuking, correcting and training in righteousness, so that the man of God may be thoroughly equipped for every good work'' (NIV).

The authorship of the Scriptures by the Holy Spirit was not confined to the Old Testament. Jesus promised His disciples, ''But the Helper, the Holy Spirit, whom the Father will send in My name, He will teach you all things, and bring to your remembrance all that I said to you'' (John 14:26); and again, ''But when He, the Spirit of truth, comes, He will guide you into all the truth; for He will not speak on His own initiative, but whatever He hears, He will speak; and He will disclose to you what is to come'' (John 16:13).

Even the very vocabulary from which Paul drew in his New Testament writing is identified by him in his Corinthian correspondence: ''And my message and my preaching were not in persuasive words of wisdom but in demonstration of the Spirit and of power, that your faith should not rest on the wisdom of men, but on the power of God'' (1 Cor. 2:4-5). Then, speaking also for the other apostles, Paul comments on the hidden mysteries of God:

> For to us God revealed them through the Spirit; for the Spirit searches all things, even the depths of God. For who among men knows the thoughts of a man except the spirit of the man, which is in him? Even so the thoughts of God no one knows except the Spirit of God. Now we have received, not the spirit of the world, but the Spirit who is

from God, that we might know the things freely given to us by God, which things we also speak, not in words taught by human wisdom, but in those taught by the Spirit, combining spiritual thoughts with spiritual words (1 Cor. 2:10-13).

Thus Paul identifies the very words he chooses in presenting God's Word as having been selected from a vocabulary he learned from the Holy Spirit. In this Paul was rich. This makes a fascinating study, even if Peter did say that some of Paul's writings contain some things "hard to understand" (2 Peter 3:14-16).

In the matter of the inspiration of the Scriptures by the agency of the Holy Spirit Andrew Blackwood makes an interesting observation:

> All Christians agree that in some sense the Bible is inspired. The verb "inspire" means literally "breathe in." It suggests that the Holy Spirit has "breathed" life into the Scripture as once He breathed into man the breath of life when man became a living soul. For the word "inspiration" is found only twice within the Bible.
>
> The Holy Spirit inflamed the hearts of men, giving them intense concern about serious problems. Then the Holy Spirit, working usually through "natural" channels, guided human minds toward solutions. As Luke tells us, the historian had to look up his references. The poets of the Bible, like poets today, doubtless had to pace the floor, biting their fingernails, while searching for the word that would express a meaning with precision. But in all their writings is more than the honest search for clarity and beauty. The Biblical writers themselves believed that God had "showed" (e.g., Micah 6:8) or "spoken" (Isaiah 46:11).[13]

C. He Was Active in the Redemptive Life and Ministry of Jesus

The Holy Spirit was the divine Administrator in the life of Jesus in all its facets.

1. He effected the incarnation of Jesus Christ The Incarnation, the clothing of divinity with humanity or "flesh" *(carnis)*, is delicately but straightforwardly told by Luke the physician: "And the angel answered and said to her, 'The Holy Spirit will come upon you, and the power of the Most High will overshadow you; and for that reason the holy offspring shall be called the Son of God'" (Luke 1:25). This was confirmed to Joseph, with added information, as recorded in Matthew 1:22-23: "Now all this took place that what was spoken by the Lord through the prophet might be fulfilled, saying, 'BEHOLD, THE VIRGIN SHALL BE WITH CHILD, AND SHALL BEAR A SON, AND THEY SHALL CALL HIS NAME IMMANUEL,' which translated means, 'GOD WITH US.'"

Matthew twice records that Jesus was born without the concurrence of a human father: "Mary . . . was found to be with child by the Holy Spirit" (Matt. 1:18) and "that which has been conceived in her is of the Holy Spirit" (1:20). Thus, the truth of God's plan of redemption hangs on the acceptance or rejection of the activity of the Holy Spirit in the divine Incarnation. It is the very heart of the Christian faith—the life-giving principle. Charles Ryrie has aptly outlined the import of this point:

> The result of the virgin birth was the incarnation. A human nature was conceived, not a person, for the Second Person existed always. With the conception of the human nature the God-man came into existence, and it was a perfect humanity. This means that although the components of humanity were present, it was a sinless human nature, not merely a sanctified human nature. But the incarnation also brought limitation—not a limitation of a moral nature but only those amoral limitations of humanity. In other words, nothing was missing from His humanity which is essential to humanity and nothing was added which was non-human.[14]

The theological importance of this work of the Holy Spirit is immense. Being man, but without any sin of His own, Jesus could make atonement for sinful human beings as only one of their own could do. He was identified with sinful humanity in an undeniable fashion for the thorough reconciliation and the complete regeneration of sinful mankind. Cecil Frances Alexander expressed it thus:

> There was no other good enough
> To pay the price of sin;
> He only could unlock the gate
> Of Heaven, and let us in.

Being God, His atonement was sufficient and had infinite redemptive value, and the union He effects between God and man is complete (see 2 Cor. 5:19-21). As God alone, Jesus would not be identified with mankind. As man alone, His death would be insufficient in value and significance for the Atonement.

As to the significance of the Incarnation to the disclosure of the Holy Spirit Himself, H. Orton Wiley has made certain significant statements:

> The mystery of the Incarnation made possible the unveiling of the Holy Spirit as the Third Person of the Trinity. Until the Annunciation the Holy Spirit had never been revealed as a distinct Personal Agent. Never before had He been called by His own name. Previous to that time He was always mentioned in connection with the other Divine Persons. In the penitential Psalm it is *take not thy holy spirit from me* (Psalms 51:11); and in Isaiah, *they rebelled, and vexed his holy Spirit* (Isa. 63:10). Consequently the term is used relatively and not in the absolute sense. The full disclosure of His personality and perfections was not made until the set time for His inauguration. Only when Christ had been fully glorified at the right hand of the Father could the Holy Spirit come in the fullness of His pentecostal glory.[15]

2. He anointed Christ for His mission Jesus was anointed at the time of His baptism as the Holy Spirit descended in bodily form like a dove (Luke 3:21-22), thus fulfilling prophecies by Isaiah (11:1-2; 42:1). Note that the office and work of the Messiah, which were defined by Isaiah, were repeated by Jesus (Luke 4:18-19) and amplified by Peter (Acts 10:38).

Observe that, in line with Isaiah, both Jesus and Peter call this encounter with the Holy Spirit an "anointing," not a "baptism." Wiley makes a cogent commentary on this:

> While it is recorded that Jesus was baptized with water by John it is not stated that He was baptized with the Holy Spirit. This is significant. The reason is plain—baptism implies cleansing, and Jesus had no sin from which to be cleansed; neither could He in this sense be filled with the Spirit, for the Spirit already dwelt in Him without measure. But he was anointed with the Spirit at the time of His baptism by John, and thereby inducted into the office and work of the Messiah or Christ.[16]

The anointing of Jesus for His messianic office qualified Him in two particulars: (1) It was the source of His own enduement with power. And why should Jesus, the divine One, require this? It was not as the divine One that He was anointed, but as the human one, notwithstanding His divine-human consciousness. (2) The Holy Spirit's coming upon Him in fullness also qualified Him to bestow the Holy Spirit on His own disciples (Matt. 3:11; John 20:22; Acts 1:5).

3. He directed and sustained Jesus Christ in His temptation The Holy Spirit also acted as God's administrative agent in Christ's temptation. Luke records: "And Jesus, full of the Holy Spirit, returned from the Jordan and was led about by the Spirit in the wilderness for forty days, while tempted by the devil" (Luke 4:1-2). The Spirit did not desert Him in His hour of need, but consoled and strengthened Him while He was being tempted of the devil. But was there more?

Mark indicates some kind of pressure, in that "immediately the Spirit impelled Him to go out into the wilderness" (Mark 1:12). This suggests that for some reason there was an urgency in the Spirit's leading. But did the Spirit actually lead Him *into* temptation? Matthew says so. "Then Jesus was led up by the Spirit into the wilderness *to be tempted* by the devil" (Matt. 4:1). Dana and Mantey would term this a "purpose" infinitive, "used to express the aim of the action denoted by the finite verb."[17] (See Matt. 2:2; 5:17; Luke 1:77.) Since Jesus had come "to fulfill all righteousness" (Matt. 3:15), it is suggested that the wilderness temptation was essential to this accomplishment. Indeed, it is because of this that it could later be said, "For we do not have a high priest who cannot sympathize with our weaknesses, but one who has been tempted in all things as we are, yet without sin. Let us therefore draw near with confidence to the throne of grace, that we may receive mercy and find grace to help in time of need" (Heb. 4:15–16); and "Since He Himself was tempted in that which He has suffered, He is able to come to the aid of those who are tempted" (Heb. 2:18).

4. He empowered Jesus Christ for His redemptive work Furthermore, the Holy Spirit imparted power to Christ. It was in the *fullness* of the Spirit that He went into the wilderness (Luke 4:1) and it was "in the *power* of the Spirit" (4:14) that He returned from the wilderness, having performed His first miracle, the miracle of meeting and resisting the devil. It was in this power that He went forth into His life's work (Luke 4:18–19; Acts 10:38) and that He cast out demons (Matt. 12:28).

5. He directed Jesus in giving orders to His disciples The specific directions given by Jesus to His followers at the end were by the supervision of the Holy Spirit, so that, right up to His ascension, Jesus was under the guidance of the Spirit (Acts 1:1).

6. He endorsed the divinity of Jesus Christ by sealing The Holy Spirit brought to Jesus' life a "sealing" that marked His heavenly origin, as it is recorded in John 6:27. Jesus declared of Himself: "On Him the Father, even God, has set His seal." Of this statement by Christ Julius Mantey makes an interesting comment: "This corresponds to the rabbinic practice of stamping approved meats as *kosher,* officially endorsed for use. Jesus presented Himself thus with the Father's seal of approval; He was *kosher.*"[18]

7. He shared the victory of Jesus Christ The Spirit was used to bring joy into the life of Jesus. "At the very time [of the return of the seventy with their report of victories on the field] He rejoiced greatly in the Holy Spirit" (Luke 10:21; cf. Heb. 12:1). How delightful to see Him participating "greatly" in this fruit of the Spirit! It was a precious moment of self-revelation when the disciples saw "the man of sorrows" surfeited with joy. Surely in this His children may share!

8. He enabled Jesus Christ in His death and resurrection In God's will the Holy Spirit was the agent both in Christ's death and in His resurrection. The author of Hebrews states, "Christ . . . through the eternal Spirit offered Himself without blemish to God" (Heb. 9:14). Paul proclaims that "His Son . . . was declared with power to be the Son of God by the resurrection from the dead, according to the Spirit of holiness" (Rom. 1:4). And Peter declares, "Christ . . . was put to death in the body but made alive by the Spirit" (1 Peter 3:18–19 NIV).

VI. THE HOLY SPIRIT HAS BECOME THE ADMINISTRATOR OF THE DIVINE PLAN OF REDEMPTION UNDER THE NEW COVENANT

Although implied under the old covenant (Gen. 6:3; 1 Sam. 10:6–9; Neh. 9:30; Pss. 51:9–11; 143:10), the clear mandate regarding the Holy Spirit in God's redemptive plan was not fully disclosed until after Pentecost. Indeed, it was only then that full disclosure was made of the responsibilities assumed by the various members of the Trinity in the reclamation of mankind.

A. All Members of the Trinity Are Involved in Man's Salvation

God the Father *planned* it. "This is good and acceptable in the sight of God our Savior, who desires all men to be saved and to come to the knowledge of the truth" (1 Tim. 2:3-4; see also 2 Peter 3:9). God the Son *purchased* it: "For there is one God, and one mediator also between God and men, the man Christ Jesus, who gave Himself a ransom for all, the testimony borne at the proper time" (1 Tim. 2:5-6). From the very event of man's fall God expressed His will, and set forth a plan that included His Son (see Gen. 3:15; 12:3; Isa. 53; Matt. 20:28; Rom. 5:6-8). It was in an early dated divine conference that Christ accepted a human body and presented it as a sacrifice for the sins of mankind according to eternal counsel (see Heb. 10:4-10).

The role of God the Holy Spirit in *administering* this plan of redemption was proclaimed in a clear and forthright fashion only after the Day of Pentecost.

Mark the marvelous unity of planning and efficiency in recalling man from his pitifully sinful state. Ralph Herring summarizes it: "The Father thought it, the Son bought it, the Holy Spirit wrought it."[19]

The Spirit, with the help of the church, gently invites and woos the sinner (Rev. 22:17). He awakens the sinner's sleeping conscience (John 16:8). Then, in an orderly and totally inclusive fashion, the Spirit puts the divine plan of redemption into action in all its aspects.

He is the agent for *justification,* which includes a free pardon for sins committed (1 Cor. 6:11). He is the agent for *regeneration,* the doctrine of the new birth (John 3:3, 6-7; see also 2 Cor. 3:6; Titus 3:5). He is the agent for *adoption,* that blessing of being made a bona fide member of the family of God, with its privileges and its responsibilities (Gal. 4:5-6). He is the agent also for *sanctification,* that provision for cleansing included in God's great plan for man's reclamation (2 Thess. 2:13).

B. All Members of the Trinity Are Involved in the Life of Holiness

Victorious living is an integral part of the plan of redemption and of full salvation, and in no way is it the product of any one member of the Godhead alone.

God the Father *planned* it. Before history began His purpose was clear. He desired a holy people, created in His likeness, with whom He could fellowship, and from whom He could accept worship. Paul expresses it thus: "He chose us in Him before the foundation of the world, that we should be holy and blameless before Him" (Eph. 1:4; see also 1 Thess. 4:1-3, 7). God the Son *purchased* it. As truly as He died on the cross that man's sins might be forgiven, that man might become a new creature, that he might be a child of God, so truly did He die that the believer might become holy: "Therefore Jesus also, that He might sanctify the people through His own blood, suffered outside the gate" (Heb. 13:12; see also Eph. 5:15-27; Heb. 10:10, 14).

It is God the Holy Spirit who *administers* this sanctification in all its apsects (Rom. 15:16). He is the agent for *initial* sanctification, as illustrated by the Corinthians who, "by the Spirit of our God," had, at the time of their conversion, been "sanctified" from those outer and coarse sins of the flesh (1 Cor. 6:9-11). This is accomplished by the *presence* of the Spirit. (Note 1 Cor. 6:19.) He is also the agent for *entire* sanctification. (See Acts 15:7-9 in connection with Acts 2; and 11:15-17.) This is accomplished by the *baptism* and the fullness of the Spirit. The Spirit is also the agent for that life of holiness known as *progressive* sanctification, termed variously "walking according to the Spirit," "setting the mind according to the Spirit," and being "led by the Spirit" in such passages as Romans 8:4-5 and Galatians 5:16, 18, 25. This is accomplished by the *abiding fullness* of the Spirit. The progress is beautifully expressed by Paul: "But we all, with unveiled face beholding as in a mirror the glory of the Lord, are being transformed into the same image from glory to glory, just as from the Lord, the Spirit" (2 Cor. 3:18).

C. The Spirit Governs the Type of Action in All Aspects of Salvation

It is instructive to observe the pattern of God's movements in the hearts of people as the Holy Spirit performs His administrative work of redemption. There is the action of *an event,* sometimes known as "point action," governed by the *aorist* tense in the Greek. This is found in the verses previously quoted, which identify the work of the Holy Spirit in justification ("were justified" [1 Cor. 6:11]), in regeneration ("is born," "be born" [John 3:3, 6-7]), in adoption ("might receive" [Gal. 4:5, 6]). This point action is also found in identifying the work of the Spirit in initial sanctification ("were sanctified" [1 Cor. 6:11]) and in entire sanctification ("suddenly . . . appeared . . . rested . . . filled" [Acts 2:2-4], "fell . . . gave" [Acts 11:15-17], "giving . . . cleansing" [Acts 15:7-9; 1 Thess. 5:23]).

However, the action of the Spirit becomes *a process,* as governed by the *present* tense in the Greek, depicting a continued, flowing action in all those verbs connected with progressive sanctification, as in Romans 8, Galatians 5, and 2 Corinthians 3. It is *a life* of holiness that he sponsors in the believer.

D. The Holy Spirit Is Our Witness

God leaves no believer in uncertainty of his standing. The Holy Spirit is His messenger of assurance:

> For all who are being led by the Spirit of God, these are the sons of God. For you have not received a spirit of slavery leading to fear again, but you have received a spirit of adoption as sons by which we cry out, "Abba! Father!" The Spirit Himself bears witness with our spirit that we are children of God" (Rom. 8:14-16).

Note that God declares, not "bears witness *to*" but bears witness *"with."* The Greek verb is *summartureo* (*sum* = "with"; *martureo* = "to witness"). Bagster suggests "to bear witness together with another."[20] Walter Conner elaborates on this theme:

> It is the Spirit of God conjointly with my spirit that bears testimony that I am a child of God. It is not the divine Spirit saying *to* me that I am a child of God; it is rather the divine Spirit saying *along with* my spirit that I am a child of God. It is the indwelling and creative Spirit enabling me to realize for myself that I have this relationship with God.[21]

The happy fact is that the Holy Spirit and the believers' spirits commune together, adding one to another their testimonies, and agreeing that they are God's children. What a lovely testimony meeting! What an abiding assurance! Thus the Spirit has been revealed in a much broader role since His advent on the day of Pentecost and He continues in an emphasized position in the present world. In view of this let us study with interest, first, the teachings of Jesus regarding the Spirit, then the development of the Spirit's ministry under the new covenant, as recorded in Acts and expounded in the New Testament Scriptures.

VII. JESUS PRESENTS UNMISTAKABLE TEACHINGS REGARDING THE HOLY SPIRIT

It would be folly to overlook, or to minimize, the teachings of Jesus regarding the Holy Spirit. Some of these are implicit, some explicit. All are vastly important.

A. The Holy Spirit Is Now *Present* With Every Believer

1. Paul taught this It is evident in the teachings of Paul that the Holy Spirit is now present with every believer. He frankly declares, "If anyone does not have the Spirit of Christ, he does not belong to Him" (Rom. 8:9); and again, "Or do you not know that your body is a temple of the Holy Spirit who is in you, whom you have from God, and that you are not your own?" (1 Cor. 6:19). There is no exception, even with the unspiritual believers, as the Corinthians were.

2. This had been implicit in the teachings of Jesus

Speaking to believers through His disciples, Jesus declared of the Spirit, "He abides with you" (John 14:17). He had implied this in conversation both with Nicodemus and with the woman at the well. The new birth was to be "of the Spirit." The "living water" that He offered would be "in [the believer] a well of water springing up to eternal life." As the giver of life and as the enricher of life, the Holy Spirit is now present with every believer.

It may well be that the Holy Spirit always had been with all believers, although explicit Scripture supporting this is not common. J. C. Ryle declares, "He was ever in the hearts of the Old Testament believers. No one ever served God acceptably, from Abel onward, without the grace of the Holy Ghost."[22] Quoting Hebrews 1:1–2 and 10:1 in support, Charles Carter notes that "the pre-Christian believers became partakers of the messianic blessing of salvation through anticipatory faith in Christ inspired in their hearts by the Holy Spirit."[23] On the other hand Merrill Tenney avers that "nowhere in Judaism was taught the coming of the Spirit upon all men for their personal regeneration."[24]

B. The Holy Spirit Is Now *Available* to Every Believer in a New and Different Way

This was implied by Jesus in His full statement to the disciples: "He abides with you, and will be in you" (John 14:17).

1. He is available now in a life-sharing way (John 7:37–39)

The Holy Spirit should so fill the believer that He will overflow in blessing to others. The occasion mentioned in John 7:37–39 had been a joyous, yet awesome one. The Feast of Tabernacles was always impressive. It was associated with the study of the law, and on each of the several days included a procession of priests carrying water from the pool of Siloam to the altar of burnt offering, as the people chanted from Isaiah, "Therefore you will joyously draw water from the springs of salvation" (Isa. 12:3), and again, "For in the wilderness shall waters break out, and streams in the desert" (Isa. 35:6 KJV). Arriving at the altar, the priest poured out the water onto it. This ceremony had a twofold significance. The occasion was a memorial of God's provision of water for the thirsty Israelites in the time of their desert wanderings and it was an appeal for rain to bring in the next harvest.

On this occasion Jesus was present. It was the last day, "the great day of the feast," a day when no water was carried to the altar. Suddenly, unannounced, Jesus stood to His feet and called out loudly to the throng of people: "If any man is thirsty, let him come to Me and drink. He who believes in Me, as the Scripture said, 'From his innermost being shall flow rivers of living water'" (John 7:37–38). Undoubtedly the startled crowd was perplexed. It is questionable that even His own followers knew fully what He meant. But, from the vantage point of the many intervening years and events, John added when he wrote this some thirty or more years later: "But this He spoke of the Spirit, whom those who believed in Him were to receive; for the Spirit was not yet given, because Jesus was not yet glorified" (v. 39).

An abundant supply of the Spirit was to be available to that believer who was minded to receive Him. The Spirit was to be available, not just for the satisfaction of his own thirst, but for sharing with the thirsty throngs about him. The Spirit was to be available in a life-sharing way. Thus Spirit-filled persons were to be a blessing to others. This, however, was not to be until after Jesus was "glorified." The full disclosure of the Holy Spirit was to await the completion of Jesus' ministry, His death, resurrection, and ascension. And thus it was so reflected in the events of the Book of Acts. Note that the Spirit is to be "received" by believers. As explained more fully later (pp. 431–32), "receive" *(lambanō)* here has the sense of an active and volitional verb often translated "take" (see John 10:17-18).

The observation by Laurence Wood is worthy of note at this juncture:

> "Receiving the Spirit" means a receiving of *the fulness* of the Spirit. I most certainly affirm that every believer in Christ has experienced the transforming power and presence of the Holy Spirit in his life, but not every believer has "received [the fulness of] the Spirit." This distinction can popularly be expressed this way: "Every believer has the Holy Spirit, but the Holy Spirit does not fully have every beleiver." Hence "to receive the Spirit" is the biblical phrase to describe the believer who has fully appropriated the fulness of Pentecostal grace.[25]

2. He is available now upon the request of the believer Jesus was next to make a most startling declaration. Remember that through the preceding centuries the Spirit had "come upon," or "clothed Himself with," people *He* chose. In no wise was He available *on the request* of a believer. None dared to ask for Him. But now Jesus made the surprising announcement: "If you then, being evil, know how to give good gifts to your children, how much more shall your Heavenly Father give the Holy spirit to those who ask Him?" (Luke 11:13).

G. C. Morgan says, "This was a purely dispensational and Jewish statement; and the men never asked and never received."[26] Dale Brown declares, "After Pentecost only the disciples of John were advised to pray for the baptism with the Holy Ghost."[27] However, it is hard to reconcile the thrust of these statements with the recorded facts. This admonition came at the conclusion of our Lord's discourse on prayer, when His disciples had asked Him, "Lord, teach us to pray just as John also taught his disciples" (Luke 11:1). This He did, dwelling on the contents (vv. 2-3), the urgency (vv. 4-8), the persistence (vv. 9-10), and the rewards (vv. 11-12) of effective prayer. In conclusion He announced that the gift of the Holy Spirit would be the Father's supreme reward of such prevailing prayer.

Obviously this prayer pattern belonged to Christendom and not just to a group of twelve disciples, and it has been so accepted through the centuries. How strange and absurd to identify the pinnacle, the climax of the prayer with the charge of its being "purely dispensational and Jewish" and "only for the disciples of John."

Then examine the prayer meeting on the eve of Pentecost as recorded in Acts 1:13-14: "These all with one mind were continually devoting themselves to prayer." What prayer? Frederick Bruner states that the Holy Spirit was not mentioned, and expresses doubt that He was even thought of.[28] However, it is instructive to note that in the Greek text there is an untranslated "the," so that it really says "devoting themselves to *the* prayer." Could this not have been "the prayer" to which they had been directed by Jesus? Indeed, Jamieson comments: "They prayed for the promised baptism, the need of which in their orphan state would be increasingly felt."[29] And could it not again have been this prayer that was so effective throughout the days of the early church on such occasions as those described in Acts 4:31; 8:15; and 9:11?

Michael Harper points out: "The Father was ready to give you the power of the Holy Spirit from the very moment you entered his family. It was never intended to be an optional extra or a bonus for good behaviour." And again, "The Holy Spirit is given 'to those who ask the Father,' not to those who are worthy."[30]

Indeed, He *is* ready and eager. Jesus said, "How much more. . . ." However, it is also emphatically evident that God does not give His "Gift" lightly or casually. There must be urgency, persistence, a specific request. "The promise of the Father" is not an "incidental benefit" distributed in a careless fashion to an indifferent recipient. Indeed, in the Matthew account of the same incident regarding prayer, Jesus is recorded as saying, "Do not give what is holy to dogs, and do not throw your pearls before swine" (Matt. 7:6). This is shocking language. Yet how many of God's people through the years have missed this available blessing by treating God's Gift casually and indifferently?

Herbert Lockyer emphasizes the positive in observing, "As believers, then, we have the Spirit through the joint prayers of Jesus (John 17) and ourselves (Luke 11)."[31] From a previous generation, A. W. Tozer challenges us:

> That every Christian can be and should be filled with the Holy Spirit would hardly seem to be a matter for debate among Christians. Yet some will argue that the Holy Spirit is not for plain Christians, but for ministers and missionaries only. Others hold that the measure of the Spirit received at regeneration is identical with that received by the disciples at Pentecost. A few will express a languid hope that some day they may be filled.
>
> I want here boldly to assert that it is my happy belief that every Christian can have a copious outpouring of the Holy Spirit in a measure far beyond that received at conversion.[32]

C. Consider Christ's Paraclete Teachings

The teachings of Jesus regarding the Holy Spirit have been considered essentially in the chronological order chosen by Christ. It was at the close of His ministry that Jesus presented this choice cluster of teachings contained in John 14, 15, and 16, known as the Paraclete Sayings. Included in them are incisive truths, important announcements, and significant guideposts. There are no more meaningful teachings regarding the Spirit than these.

The translation "Comforter" in the King James Version is unfortunate. "Comfort" today has the significance of "coziness," while "comforter" in the United States means a long woolen scarf, or a thick quilted bedcover, and, in England, a child's pacifier. In the days of King James "comfort" referred to the "strength" and "counsel" of an almighty God. The meaning has changed. For this reason "Helper," "Advocate," "Counselor," "Intercessor," "Strengthener," and "Standby" are variously used.

The Greek word is *Paraklētos*. In itself the word is *para* ("alongside") and *klētos* ("called"). Thus He is One who may be "called alongside," to comfort, to strengthen, to guide, to counsel, to intercede, to witness. It is a term in contrast to *katēgoros*, "an accuser" as used in Acts 23:3, 35. Thus, by antonym, it takes to itself the description of one who exonerates, vindicates, acquits (1 John 2:1).

William Barclay comments:

> To call the Holy Spirit *paraklētos* is to say that the Holy Spirit is the person who enables a man to meet four-square and erect the sorrows, the struggles, the burdens of this world, the person who nerves the feeble for the battle and who makes the coward brave. When we think of all that, we can do no other than pray: "God, send Thy Holy Spirit upon *me!*"[33]

There are four Paraclete sayings, namely, John 14:15-17, 25-26; 15: 26-27; 16:7-15. They are unique, for no one else termed Him "the Paraclete." Consider now the several teaching aspects Jesus presents.

1. The Holy Spirit is the Gift of God "And I will ask the Father, and He will give you another Helper, that He may be with you forever" (John 14:16). The Holy Spirit is God's Gift, requested by Jesus. "It is well to remember that the possession of the Holy Spirit is a gift, and not an achievement," warns Barclay.[34] Thus He is not to be "earned," "deserved," or "merited." Yet, as a gift, He is not presented to believers unwanted or unsought. As a gift, He is priceless and must thus be yearned for, diligently sought, highly valued, and warmly received.

2. He will be "another" Helper He is identified as "another," *allos,* another of a similar nature, in contrast to *heteros,* another of a different nature. (See Acts 2:4; Gal. 1:6.) The "other" Helper is identified in 1 John 2:1, the only other place in the Scriptures that *paraklētos* is used. This of course refers to Jesus and is here translated "Advocate." Thus Jesus is "one-called-alongside" God the Father as our Advocate. Thus the believer has two similar *paraklētoi*. The Holy Spirit represents the Father to believers, while Jesus represents believers before the Father. There He defends us against accusations, as One who Himself has faced all the temptations we face. George Williams suggests that "as a Priest He deals with the guilt of sin; as an Advocate, with the restoration of the soul."[35]

3. He will be an abiding Helper There are those who see in this an eternal-security assurance. They therefore say that David's cry "Do not take Thy Holy Spirit from me" (Ps. 51:11) is limited to the old covenant and has no place in the Christian's prayer. But actually Jesus is not giving the promise of eternal security to a Spirit-filled believer. Rather He is contrasting two facts—that He Himself is departing and that the Spirit is remaining. This is the age of the Holy Spirit for the church. The majority of commentators agree with Bishop Ryle who declares that as an abiding Helper "He will not, like Christ after His resurrection, return to the Father, but will always be with God's people until Christ comes again."[36] His abiding quality applies to the dispensational plan, not necessarily to the individual believer in his spiritual state before God.

4. He is the Spirit of truth He is "the Spirit of truth, whom the world cannot receive, because it does not behold Him or know Him, but you know Him because He abides with you, and will be in you" (John 14:17). John's favorite title for, and description of, the Spirit is "the Spirit of truth" (John 14:17; 15:26; 16:13). This in itself is informative and interesting. But here there is, with the noun, the article *the*—He is "the Spirit of *the* truth." Regarding such an expression Julius Mantey declares:

In Greek, when it is desired to apply the sense of an abstract noun in some special and distinct way the article accompanies it. Thus *alētheia,* truth, means anything in general which presents a character of reality and genuineness, but *hē alētheia,* as used in the New Testament, means that which may be relied upon as really in accord with God's revelation in Christ.[37]

With that in mind let us remember that Jesus presented Himself as "the truth," while Pilate simply cried out in his dilemma, "What is truth?" The Holy Spirit is the Spirit of *the* truth—of the truth that may be relied on as really in accord with God's revelation in Christ; indeed, of Jesus Himself.

5. He cannot be received by the world, but only by the believer Herein is embodied information of vital importance. To "receive" the Holy Spirit is one of the great privileges of the child of God—a privilege denied the ungodly. It was to believers that Jesus said, "Receive the Holy Spirit," a privilege fulfilled after He was glorified. Now, the word *receive (lambanō)* is not a verb of passive acceptance nor of automatic, indifferent acquiescence. It depicts rather an assertive act, a conscious choice. It is sometimes translated "take." For example, "Let the one who wishes take the water of life without cost" (Rev. 22:17; see also Matt. 5:40; 8:17; 25:1, 3, 4; 26:17; 27:24).

Its meaning is well described thus:

The action indicated by *lambanō* ("to receive") is normally active and volitional. When we read in John 1:12 "To all who receive him," we are certainly to understand that a deliberate taking of Jesus is meant; the reference is not to passive recipients but active acceptors, who believe on Jesus in the sense that they choose to take him as Christ and Lord. It is justifiable to interpret Paul in the same sense in his forceful questioning of the Ephesians. "Did you receive the Holy Spirit, having believed?" (Acts 19:2 NASB), meaning, "Did you *take* the Holy Spirit?" When Jesus "breathed" on His disciples and said "Receive the Holy Spirit" (John 20:22), it was not the immediate impartation of the Spirit but a command to *take* the Spirit. The verb is ingressive aorist active imperative, hence a command to incisive action, not a statement of present fact. The command bears a close relationship to Luke 24:49.[38]

Laurence Wood perceptively points out that "there are twelve places in the New Testament where 'receiving the Spirit' is used as descriptive of Pentecostal fulness, namely, John 7:39; 14:17; 20:22; Acts 1:8; 2:38; 8:14-15; 8:17; 8:19; 10:47; 19:2; Galatians 3:2, 14." He then observes impressively: "I most solemnly affirm that every believer has the transforming power and *presence* of the Holy Spirit in his life, though he may not have 'received [the fullness of] the Spirit.'"[39] How true this has been, both in the early church of the Book of Acts and in the church through the centuries.

Now, although the child of God is invited, indeed urged, to receive the Holy Spirit, Jesus clearly states that the world is not only *not invited*, but also *not able* to receive Him.

Andrew Blackwood has aptly observed, "When the Savior tells us that the world cannot receive the Holy Spirit, He is drawing a distinction between the natural man and the redeemed man. Both were born 'of the flesh.' The redeemed man is also born 'of the Spirit.'"[40] To this we add, only he who is born of the Spirit can receive the Spirit. Thus Spirit-birth is a prerequisite to Spirit-baptism. Paul witnessed to the same truth when he compared himself as the Spirit-filled writer of Scripture with the barren "man of the world," the "natural man":

> Now we have received, not the spirit of the world, but the Spirit who is from God, that we might know the things freely given to us by God. . . . But a natural man does not accept the things of the Spirit of God; for they are foolishness to him, and he cannot understand them, for they are spiritually appraised (1 Cor. 2:12, 14).

W. T. Purkiser comments, "To receive ('welcome with open arms, acknowledge His lordship') the Comforter, one must in some measure know Him,"[41] while A. T. Robertson points out, "The world lacks spiritual insight *(ou theorei)* and spiritual knowledge *(oude ginōskei)*. It failed to recognize Jesus (1:10), and likewise the Holy Spirit."[42] To this may be added the realization that the world lacks any urgency, any eagerness, any persistence in prayer required by God for the receiving of the Spirit. It is foolishness to the unregenerate.

6. He will give a teaching ministry

"These things I have spoken to you, while abiding with you. But the Helper, the Holy Spirit, whom the Father will send in My name, He will teach you all things, and bring to your remembrance all that I said to you" (John 14:25-26).

Jamieson declares of this verse: "On this rests the credibility and ultimate Divine authority of the gospel history."[43] Indeed, the Spirit gives not only credibility to the gospel history that writers will record but also authority to the doctrinal truths that they will proclaim. "For, indeed, the Spirit searches all things" and thus knows "even the depths of God" (1 Cor. 2:10). What new insights and confidences of God they were to receive after Pentecost! What Spirit-given influence there would be in the world of believers! However, this work of the Spirit is not confined to the disciples of that century. His teaching ministry is a ministry of *interpretation* of the same Scriptures to the Spirit-filled disciple of today!

7. He will be an effectual co-witness with the believer

> "When the Helper comes, whom I will send to you from the Father, that is the Spirit of truth, who proceeds from the Father, He will bear witness of Me, and you will bear witness also, because you have been with Me from the beginning." (John 15:26-27).

The requirement for two witnesses had long been established. "A single witness shall not rise up against a man on account of any iniquity or any sin which he has committed" said the law; but "on the evidence of two or three witnesses a matter shall be confirmed" (Deut. 19:15). Jesus, in a new covenant view, declared, "And if your brother sins, go and reprove him in private; if he listens to you, you have won your brother. But if he does not listen to you, take one or two more with you, so that BY THE MOUTH OF TWO OR THREE WITNESSES EVERY FACT MAY BE CONFIRMED" (Matt. 18:15-16).

Indeed, Jesus said of Himself:

> If I alone bear witness of Myself, My testimony is not true. There is another who bears witness of Me; and I know that the testimony which He bears of Me is true. You have sent to John and he has borne witness to the truth. . . . But the witness which I have is greater than that of John; for . . . the Father who sent Me, He has borne witness of Me (John 5:31-37. See also John 8:12-18).

Paul added: "EVERY FACT IS TO BE CONFIRMED BY THE TESTIMONY OF TWO OR THREE WITNESSES" (2 Cor. 13:1).

Thus may be seen the importance of the corroborating witness of the Spirit to the witness of God's children. The believer's witness will not stand alone but will actually be preceded by the witness of the Spirit as He lays the groundwork for the believer. Likewise, however, the witness of the Spirit does not stand alone, but seeks the support of the believer!

Supported by A. T. Robertson,[44] the NIV recognizes in verse 26 the emphatic masculine pronoun He *(ekeinos)* and the future active of *martureō* as stressing the mission of the Paraclete: "The Spirit of truth . . . he will testify of me." Then, in verse 27 it projects the present active imperative form of *matureō* as describing *our* mission as being a "command" performance: "but you also must testify." He will; we must. It is interesting to hear Peter declare regarding "two or three witnesses" as himself, John, and the Holy Spirit: "And we [you and I] are witnesses of these things; and so is the Holy Spirit" (Acts 5:32).

There follows the fourth "Paraclete Statement" of John 16:7-15, governed by the three verbs *elenchō, hodēgeō, doxadzō*—"convict," "guide," and "glorify," which affect respectively the world, the believer, and Jesus. It is introduced by a proclamation of general information and genuine importance: "But I tell you the truth, it is to your advantage that I go away; for if I do not go away, the Helper shall not [a future imperative with a strong double negative] come to you; but if I go, I will send Him to you" (John 16:7). Now what could be more important to the disciples than the Lord's presence? He was their inspiration, their guide, their discipline, their hope of greatness! His departure was more important, because that meant the coming of the Paraclete. The Spirit's presence was all-important. For a new dispensation was upon them—the age of the Holy Spirit. With that as foremost, Jesus gave the reasons for the importance of this drastic change. These reasons are expressed in three areas of our Lord's teaching regarding the Spirit.

8. He will convict the ungodly

> And He, when He comes, will convict the world concerning sin, and righteousness, and judgment; concerning sin, because they do not believe in Me; and concerning righteousness, because I go to the Father, and you no longer behold Me; and concerning judgment, because the ruler of this world has been judged (John 16:8-11).

"He" *(ekeinos)*—an emphatic demonstrative pronoun—identifies an exclusive duty. There is no one, other than the Holy Spirit, who can accomplish this. The church cannot convict the world. Preaching cannot. Organization cannot. Education cannot. He, the Holy Spirit alone, can convict of sin, righteousness, and judgment. Yet there *is* an adjunctive source of conviction. It is when He has "come to you" (v. 7) that this will be accomplished. God has chosen to work through people—through Spirit-filled men and women. It is the principle just established of co-witnessing. Indeed, there is not an incident in the Book of Acts of someone being convicted of sin and won to Christ, except through some *one*. This has been, and still is, God's pattern. God needs Spirit-filled believers! R. A. Torrey observes, "If Peter had preached that same sermon the day before Pentecost, there would have been no results; but now he and the hundred twenty 'were all filled with the Holy Spirit'" (Acts 2:4).[45]

"He . . . will convict the world." The verb is *elenchō*, which, according to G. Abbott-Smith, is "a rebuke which brings conviction."[46] (See Matt. 18:15; John 8:46; Titus 1:9.) This is in contrast to *epitimaō*, expressing simply a rebuke, which may be undeserved (Matt. 16:22) or ineffectual (Luke 23:40). The Paraclete is the One, indeed the only one, who will bring effectual conviction to the world regarding three important facts.

"He will convict the world concerning sin." The world does not want to hear of sin—of error perhaps, or misunderstanding, of "sickness," or even of crime, but not of sin. Yet one of the greatest needs of the present day is a conviction of sin. Indeed, the average person has no realization of the awfulness of sin, of its penalty, and of its cure. And what is the chief sin—murder? immorality? dishonesty? Not really. The chief sin, the basic sin, is unbelief—or more accurately, unwillingness to believe. It is a refusal to believe Christ, to believe Him to be the Son of God, to believe His message. That is basic, but it is more than that.

Pisteuō, translated here and in John 3:16 as "believe," is translated in John 2:24 as "entrust." *Eis*, translated here as "in," is a preposition of penetration, translated generally as "into" (John 3:4). Of this preposition Gresham Machen points out, "It must not be supposed, however, that the preposition *eis* with the accusative here really means *in* like *en* with the dative. Rather it is to be said that the Greek language merely looks at the act of believing in a different way from the English; Greek thinks of putting one's faith *into* some one."[47] Thus saving faith is more than an entrustment of one's very life into the care or the hands of a loving Lord. Andrew Blackwood has accurately commented, "The difference between 'belief about' and 'belief in' lies in commitment. . . . Christianity is the commitment of self to Christ."[48] John 3:16 might well read, "Whosoever entrusts/commits himself into Him need not perish. . . ." Thus the world's basic sin is failure to *entrust* itself *into* the care of Christ. Of this the Spirit will convict the world.

He "will convict the world [also] . . . concerning righteousness, because I go to the Father, and you no longer behold me" (John 16:8, 10). Whereas His enemies thought Jesus was entirely discredited by the shameful death on the cross, it would become evident that His death was a victorious return to the Father of "the Holy and Righteous One" (Acts 3:14). His spotless righteousness would be vindicated by His being "glorified," a righteousness that He had displayed on the earth in a sinless life.

And finally, "He will convict the world . . . concerning judgment, because the ruler of this world has been judged." In apparent victory Satan has actually met judgment, and is condemned to defeat. There *is* a place of eternal punishment "prepared for the devil and his angels." Hell is as real as heaven. However, judgment means not just condemnation and defeat. The first meaning of the Greek word *krisis* is "a separating."[49] The world will see the contrast between the stark emptiness of sin and the shining reality of righteousness, and it will see that between sin and righteousness there is a defined separation. There *are* established moral standards in God's economy, both in the "here" and in the "hereafter."

Thus the world will be convinced that there *will be* a day of accounting and of separation, as announced by Jesus in Matthew 25:32, by Peter in Acts 17:30-31, and by Paul in Romans 14:10-12, and that conviction will come to the world through Spirit-filled believers—by human agency.

As R. A. Torrey put it:

To sum it all up then; it is the work of the Holy Spirit to convict men of sin, and of righteousness, and of judgment. It is not our work but His. But please notice very carefully that, WHILE IT IS THE HOLY SPIRIT WHO CONVICTS MEN OF SIN, AND OF RIGHTEOUSNESS, AND OF JUDGMENT, HE DOES IT THROUGH US, i.e., THROUGH THOSE WHO ALREADY BELIEVE ON JESUS CHRIST. . . . What a solemn thought that is![50]

9. He will enlighten the believer

I have many more things to say to you, but you cannot bear them now. But when He, the Spirit of truth, comes, He will guide you into all the truth; for He will not speak on His own initiative, but whatever He hears, He will speak; and He will disclose to you what is to come (John 16:12-13).

There will be new, deep spiritual realities that the Spirit will reveal as His followers can "bear" them. Samuel Chadwick suggests, "Divine truth is not of grammar, of learning, or of logic, but of the Holy Spirit of God. He is given to reveal 'the deep things of God.'"[51] This is to be a growing, expanding experience. The Spirit will not blind with total light at one flash, but will enlighten with a gently growing intensity. In this the Spirit will not project Himself but Christ and His message.

10. He will glorify Jesus

"He shall glorify Me; for He shall take of Mine, and shall disclose it to you. All things that the Father has are Mine; therefore I said, that He takes of Mine, and will disclose it to you" (John 16:14-15).

This is possibly the pinnacle of the accomplishments of the Holy Spirit. He does it by disclosing Christ's thoughts to the believer. He does it by keeping Himself in the shadows and Jesus in the light. He does it, possibly most importantly, in that He carries out in a quiet but efficient manner as God's Administrator the redemptive work planned by the Father and purchased by the Son. He woos the sinner, brings him to a conviction regarding spiritual realities, leads him into a new life in Christ, projects him into an experience of purity and holiness, then gently guides him into the fullness "of the knowledge of the glory of God in the face of Christ" (2 Cor. 4:6).

D. Jesus Will Baptize With the Holy Spirit

Luke records Jesus' teaching on this important subject of the baptism with the Holy Spirit twice, in his Gospel and in the Book of Acts. "And behold, I am sending forth the promise of My Father upon you; but you are to stay in the city until you are clothed with power from on high" (Luke 24:49), and "He commanded them not to leave Jerusalem, but to wait for what the Father had promised, 'Which,' He said, 'you heard of from Me; for John baptized with water, but you shall be baptized with the Holy Spirit not many days from now.'" He then continued, "You shall receive power when the Holy Spirit has come upon you; and you shall be My witnesses both in Jerusalem, and in all Judea and Samaria, and even to the remotest part of the earth" (Acts 1:4-5, 8).

1. The Father promised Now "the promise of the Father" had been established many years before. Through Joel in the eighth century before Christ, God had given this ringing assurance:

And it will come about after this that I will pour out My Spirit on all mankind; and your sons and daughters will prophesy, and your old men will dream dreams, your young men will see visions. And even on the male and female servants I will pour out of My Spirit in those days (Joel 2:28-29).

About a century later the Father spoke again through Isaiah: "Until the Spirit is poured out upon us from on high, and the wilderness becomes a fertile field and the fertile field is considered as a forest" (Isa. 32:15). Through Isaiah this promise was renewed several times as in 34:16; 44:3; 59:21. Finally, about a century after Isaiah's day, once more the Father spoke:

"And I will put My Spirit within you and cause you to walk in My statutes, and you will be careful to observe My ordinances" (Ezek. 36:27).

It was a promise that the disciples had previously heard from Jesus (Acts 1:4). Undoubtedly He had referred to these great passages from the Old Testament. Had He not also referred to such a "promise of the Father" when He declared, "He who believes in Me, as the Scripture said, 'From his innermost being shall flow rivers of living water' " (John 7:38)? And was He not alluding to such a promise of the Father when He assured His disciples, "If you then, being evil, know how to give good gifts to your children, how much more shall your Heavenly Father give the Holy Spirit to those who ask Him?" (Luke 11:13; see also John 14:16–18).

2. Jesus endorsed the promise and identified it as the baptism with the Spirit The terminology of such a baptism was introduced by John the Baptist in a prophetic announcement some three years before (Matt. 3; Mark 1; Luke 3; John 1). John identified Jesus as "the one who baptizes in the Holy Spirit" (John 1:33). As John Stott points out, "This use of the present participle is timeless. It describes, not the single event of Pentecost, but the distinctive ministry of Jesus."[52]

During the months that followed John's announcement Jesus had established the necessity of the sinner being "born of the Spirit" if he is to enter the kingdom of God (John 3). He had spoken of the availability to the believer of the overflowing presence of the Spirit after He Himself should be glorified (John 7), and He had identified the means of securing the abundance of the Spirit as an earnest, searching request by the child of God to his heavenly Father (Luke 11). Then, somewhere in the course of time, Jesus had brought into His vocabulary "the baptism with the Spirit" for Peter later "remembered the word of the Lord, how He used to say, 'John baptized with water, but you shall be baptized with the Holy Spirit' " (Acts 11:16). It was now, however, in the closing days or hours of His ministry that Jesus finally became specific in identifying "the promise of the Father" as the baptism with the Holy Spirit (Luke 24:49; Acts 1:4–5). God's plan of the centuries was becoming clear.

At this point, however, mention should be made that to some there is a confusion of identifying *baptism* with the Spirit with *birth* by the Spirit. H. Orton Wiley presents a helpful analysis:

> There are certain other acts or functions of . . . (the Spirit's) administrative work which . . . pertain especially to the work of salvation, and may be classified broadly under two general heads—the Holy Spirit as "Lord and Giver of Life," and the Holy Spirit as "a sanctifying Presence." To the former belongs the "birth of the Spirit" or the initial experience of salvation; to the latter, the "baptism with the Spirit"—a subsequent work by which the soul is made holy . . . known as entire sanctification.[53]

3. Jesus presented certain truths regarding the baptism with the Spirit

a. He taught that it is vital and urgent Our Lord's specific teaching regarding this baptism per se is limited. Only in this verse in Acts is He quoted on the subject. However, the association with His teaching regarding the Paraclete, as recorded in John 14–17, is marked and inescapable. The Holy Spirit "coming on" His followers was the fulfillment of "the promise of the Father," which is now clearly identified by Jesus with the baptism with the Holy Spirit. And this is vital and urgent.

b. He implied that there is relationship between being filled and being baptized with the Spirit The promised "baptism with the Holy Spirit" was recorded by Luke as being "filled with the Spirit" (Acts 2:4) but was identified later by Peter as the "baptism" with the Spirit (Acts 11:15–16).

It should be noted, however, that becoming "filled with the Spirit" is not always the same as being "baptized with," or "receiving" the Spirit. There *is* an original filling with the Spirit available to every believer, as on the day of Pentecost, which constitutes our Lord's baptizing the believer with the Spirit. However, Scripture records indicate that believers may then be recurrently filled with the Spirit (Acts 2:4; 4:8, 31; 9:17; 13:9) or may be continually full of the Spirit (Luke 4:1; Acts 6:3, 5, 8; 7:55; 11:24). God's children are urged, indeed, to keep filled with the Spirit (Eph. 5:18) where "be filled" is in the present tense of continuous action. With spiritual growth, capacity enlarges. In carrying out Christian duties, there is a "giving out" that calls for the Spirit to be replenished. Note the experience of Jesus in Luke 6:19 and 8:46 when He became aware that "power" had gone out of Him. Furthermore, the believer is not a vessel to contain the Spirit, but a channel through whom He will flow (John 7:38). It has thus been rightly suggested that Christ offers one baptism—but many fillings.

c. Christ taught that His baptism is marked by power This is to be a baptism of strength and vitality. What are the implications of this? It says that God cannot countenance weak, defeated Christians. It says there is power available to be "more than conquerors" in the battles of life against sin and Satan. John gives us the encouragement. "Greater is He who is in you than he who is in the world" (1 John 4:4). The marginal note of Acts 1:8 in the KJV gives the alternate translation: "Ye shall receive the power of the Holy Ghost coming upon you." "The power of the Holy Ghost" speaks of the indomitable strength of the divine Administrator as He represented the Trinity in the writing of the Scriptures, in inspiring the prophets of old, in ushering Christ Himself into the world and in anointing Him for His ministry, in applying the awesome provision of redemption to mankind through the centuries. It speaks of the deep reservoir of power residing in the Paraclete as He is called alongside to comfort, to counsel, to enlighten. It is of this immeasurable power that the believer may receive!

d. He taught that His baptism is marked by testimony "You shall be my witnesses," Christ declared. "Not 'Ye shall witness unto me,'" observes Dick Mohrman. "Notice," he says, "that the emphasis is not on *doing* witnessing but on *being* witnesses."[54] But actually, witnessing should be both. It can be verbal and visual. When the early disciples shook Jerusalem by their witness, they were asked, "By what power, or in what name, have you done this?" (Acts 4:7). The answer came in two ways. First, it was visual: "Now as they observed the confidence of Peter and John, and understood that they were uneducated and untrained men, they were marveling, and began to recognize them as having been with Jesus" (v. 13). Their lives reflected the Master. They were *being* witnesses. But the answer was also verbal: "With great power the apostles were giving witness to the resurrection of the Lord Jesus" (4:33). It was *doing* witnessing. It was what they said "with great power."

Of this power to witness Samuel Brengle has observed:

> If you ask how the Holy Spirit can dwell within us and work through us without destroying our personality, I cannot tell. How can the electric fluid fill and transform a dead wire into a live one, which you dare not touch? How can a magnetic current fill a piece of steel, and transform it into a mighty force which by its touch can raise tons of iron, as a child would lift a feather? How can fire dwell in a piece of iron until its very appearance is that of fire, and it becomes a fire-brand? I cannot tell.
>
> Now, what fire and electricity and magnetism do in iron and steel, the Holy Spirit does in the spirits of men who believe in Jesus, follow Him wholly, and trust Him intelligently. He dwells in them, and inspires them till they are all alive with the very life of God. The transformation wrought in men by the baptism with the Holy Ghost, and the power that fills them, are amazing beyond measure.[55]

The purposefulness of all this is manifest in Christ's delineation of the program. For this witnessing is to be done in ever-widening circles, "both in Jerusalem, and in all Judea and Samaria, and even to the remotest part of the earth." *Power, program,* and *progress* are the keys to the Book of Acts, to the expansion of Christ's church.

e. Christ established that baptism with the Spirit is the divinely appointed means to sanctification and victorious living On the eve of His crucifixion, Jesus' paramount burden was the sanctification, not only of His disciples who were then with Him, but also of all believers, in all parts of the world, for all time (John 17:17-20). This was so much the key to His continued ministry that He specifically excluded "the world" from those prayers (John 17:9). Manifestly this was of paramount importance in the mind of our Lord as an anticipated result of the forthcoming outpouring of the Spirit, of the fulfillment of the age-long "promise of the Father." Indeed, there is no more important result of the believers' receiving of the Spirit under the new covenant than this!

E. The Holy Spirit, as Administrator, Will Be Associated With the Church

One more teaching by Jesus regarding the Holy Spirit is an inference fulfilled only after Christ's ascension, rather than an announcement regarding an occurrence that began during His lifetime. It had been during the second year of His teaching, at the conclusion of what is known as His Galilean Ministry, that Jesus in His first announcement regarding His forthcoming passion, made the profound, if enigmatic prediction, "Upon this rock I will build My church; and the gates of Hades shall not overpower it" (Matt. 16:18). On only one other occasion did Jesus speak of the church (Matt. 18:17), and then possibly more in the sense of a local assembly than of the body of Christ.

The relationship of the Holy Spirit to the church will be explored later, under the proper heading. But Christ's present announcement gives evidence that even at that time He had the full knowledge of divine plans, which would be disclosed in the fullness of time, of the continued ministry of the Holy Spirit in the ages to come.

VIII. "THE PROMISE OF THE FATHER" IS CENTRAL TO THE TEACHING OF THE SPIRIT

There are divisions of interpretation regarding the baptism with the Spirit and fillings with the Spirit among the Calvinist, the Wesleyan, and the charismatic—divisions that will be identified in two areas.

For the evangelical Calvinist the baptism with the Holy Spirit is a prime experience, associated with conversion. Other fillings are to be expected in the days that follow. The fullness of the Spirit is the consequence of the baptism with the Spirit, a unique initiatory experience. The fullness is intended to be continuous, the permanent result, the norm. As an initiatory event, the baptism is not repeatable and cannot be lost, but the fillings can be repeated.

Furthermore, the baptism with the Spirit is not an ethical experience. John Williams summarizes this in his statement thus: "Spirituality was neither the prerequisite for Spirit baptism nor the inevitable result of it. The gift of the Holy Spirit is the unconditional blessing of all who are believers in Christ."[56] To suggest this he refers to the "unspiritual" Corinthian church (1 Cor. 3:1; 12:13). This will be considered later (see p. 442).

For the charismatic and the Wesleyan the baptism with the Holy Spirit is an experience subsequent to conversion, usually identifiable by a distinct and important evidence, and is available to that believer who will earnestly seek it. Again, with numerous fillings, fullness of the Spirit should be a normal experience. For the Wesleyan particularly, the baptism with the Spirit is an ethical experience of the first magnitude.

A. This Effusion of the Spirit Has Several Titles

The terms are herewith listed, not necessarily in order of their importance, but in the order of their first appearance in the Scriptures: to be "baptized with" or "in" the Holy Spirit (Matt. 3:11; Mark 1:8; Luke 3:16; John 1:33; Acts 1:5; 11:16; 1 Cor. 12:13); to "receive" the Holy Spirit (John 7:39; 14:17; 20:22; Acts 2:38; 8:15, 17, 19; 10:47; 19:2; Gal. 3:2); to claim "the promise of the Father" (Luke 24:49; Acts 1:4; 2:39); to have the Spirit "come upon" one (Acts 1:8; 19:6); to be "filled with" the Holy Spirit (Acts 2:4; 9:17; 13:52—these constitute in each case a first filling); to have Him "pour out" or "pour forth" His Spirit (Acts 2:17–18; 10:45); to receive "the gift" of the Holy Spirit or have the Holy Spirit "given" (Acts 2:38; 5:32; 8:18; 10:45; 11:17; 15:8; 2 Tim. 1:6–7); to have the Holy Spirit "fall upon" them (Acts 8:16; 10:44; 11:15). Laurence W. Wood, in his article "Exegential-Theological Reflections on the Baptism With the Holy Spirit," astutely observes that "these are equivalent phrases *in these particular* passages to denote the reality of Pentecost, either in reference to the day of Pentecost or to subsequent occasions similar to the day of Pentecost" (italics his).[57]

These terms are all deftly woven together in the Word. Christ equates "the promise of the Father" (Acts 1:4) with "being baptized with the Holy Spirit" (v. 5) and "being filled with the Spirit" (Acts 2:4). Peter equates "being baptized with the Spirit" (Acts 11:16) with "the gift of the Spirit" (v. 17), with the Spirit "being poured out" (Acts 10:45), and with "receiving" the Spirit (v. 47). They are clearly all equivalents.

Furthermore, this effusion by the Spirit is connected by Jesus to sanctification (Acts 1:4–5 and John 17:17) and by Peter to cleansing (Acts 11:15–17; 15:8–9). It surely is an ethical experience of the first magnitude!

B. The "Promise of the Father" Was to Be Fulfilled Subsequent to Conversion

1. There is a division of opinion between theologies on this point R. A. Torrey declares straightforwardly: "The Baptism with the Holy Spirit is a work of the Holy Spirit distinct from and additional to His regenerating work. In other words it is one thing to be born again of the Spirit, and quite another thing to be baptized with the Holy Spirit."[58]

Robert Mattke agrees: "All Christians are born of the Holy Spirit; all may be baptized or filled with the Spirit, subsequently."[59]

Richard Taylor comments with customary insight:

> This promised baptism with the Holy Spirit is not the same as the birth of the Spirit, about which Jesus talked to Nicodemus. . . . In the birth of the Spirit we have the beginning of the spiritual life, but in the baptism with the Spirit we have the flowering of the fullness of spiritual life. This fulfills the Old Testament promise and also characterizes the New Testament standard.[60]

On the other hand, John Stott says frankly, "The forgiveness of sins and the 'gift' or 'baptism' of the Spirit are received together."[61] Frederick Bruner holds that "the Holy Spirit is received *with* the forgiveness of sins. Neither Paul nor anyone else will ever be more worthy of the Holy Spirit than when God has washed away his sin."[62] And John Williams declares, "The baptism of the Spirit took place historically on the day of Pentecost. Each believer enters into the good of this at conversion."[63]

2. Nevertheless, Jesus taught this as a subsequent experience It is surely evident that Jesus proclaimed that the baptism with the Holy Spirit is subsequent to conversion. He taught clearly that the Holy Spirit comes in His fullness only on those who are already forgiven and regenerate.

Consider, for example, the "Paraclete Sayings." To whom were they directed? Not to the unbeliever. The world is not able to receive the Holy Spirit, nor the related promises. The "you" of these sayings referred first to the disciples. And the time was "not many days from now." But it surely was not confined to the Twelve, nor to the Day of Pentecost. The "you" of the total address was believers, and believers of all time. For example, consider these words of Jesus, surely directed to us as well as to them.

> Let not your heart be troubled; believe in God, believe also in Me. In my Father's house are many dwelling places; if it were not so, I would have told you; for I go to prepare a place for you. And if I go and prepare a place for you, I will come again, and receive you to Myself; that where I am, there you may be also (John 14:1-3).

Thus such a promise as "I will send Him unto you, and when He is come . . ." refers not only to the Twelve, and not only to the 120 on the Day of Pentecost, but to believers of all time. Certainly Peter understood this when he declared, "For the promise is for you and your children, and for all who are far off, as many as the Lord our God shall call" (Acts 2:39). Furthermore our Lord's promise was not to people *when they became* believers, but to those who *already were believers*. Jesus promised it, not as a primal blessing, but as a subsequent privilege. He was referring not to the *presence* of the Spirit, which brought new birth, but to an *advent* of the Spirit in His fullness as believers might "receive" Him in faith—and this advent brought sanctification.

Consider also the designated recipients of our Lord's high-priestly prayer. He prayed not "on behalf of the world, but of those whom Thou hast given Me; for they are Thine" (John 17:9). Again, He said, "I do not ask in behalf of those alone, but for those also who believe in Me through their word" (v. 20). Furthermore, Christ dismissed any doubt whatsoever regarding the spiritual purpose of the baptism when He centralized His prayer on their sanctification.

But why did God plan it this way? We cannot fully read His mind. But there are evidences that He knew there would be "unspiritual" believers, like those in Corinth—and like the disciples themselves—who, although children of God, still had jealousy, strife, and divisiveness in their lives and still were weak and vacillating in their faith. There were two things God might do about this. He might condone such conduct as unfortunate, but "human" and "natural." Or He might condemn it and offer corrective measures. This, of course, He has done in that the Holy Spirit is made available in His sanctifying presence to all believers, not only on the Day of Pentecost, but as they might seek Him on their own day of Pentecost throughout the centuries.

3. The history of the early church confirms this Consider the repeated evidence of God's pattern at work as recorded in the Book of Acts. In each case, consistently, the gift of the Spirit is subsequent to the act of believing. In the light of our Lord's enunciation of divine policy it would be absurd if it were otherwise. Now the word *subsequent* speaks, not so much of the length of the time interval, but of the order of occurrence—"following in time, or as a result." If subsequent, the question may be, "By how long?" The answer is, God is ready when the believer is. There is a law of readiness. There is also a law of responsibility. Man is subject to both.

First, there were the eleven disciples on the Day of Pentecost (Acts 2:1-4), men whose "names are recorded in heaven" (Luke 10:20), who belonged to God and to Jesus (John 17). Of them Samuel Chadwick has written:

> It is puerile to say they were not already saved. Our Lord places that question for ever beyond doubt in His intercession for them on the eve of His Passion. They were His. He had kept them by His power, given them the eternal Word, and they were not of the world even as He was not of the world.[64]

Then there were the rest of the 120 (Acts 2:1-4). Who would doubt their salvation?

"These all with one mind were continually devoting themselves to prayer, along with the women, and Mary the mother of Jesus, and with His brothers" (Acts 1:14). The effusion of the Spirit upon them was definitely subsequent to their conversion.

The three thousand converts of Acts 2:37-39 are not classified so specifically. There is not a statement, for example, that they actually "received the promise," though they were urged to do so. But the spiritual warmth of the church thereafter testifies to it (Acts 2:41-47). However, note that Peter's response to them, "You shall receive the gift of the Holy Spirit," was properly in the same tense as their question—the future tense, not of *prediction*, "What will we do?" but of *requirement*, "What shall [must] we do?" And this is in line with the volitional nature of the verb "receive"—"You shall" [must] reach out and "take the gift of the Holy Spirit." Note also that this was a second command, subsequent to "repent . . . for the forgiveness of sins." Laurence Wood suggests that the two acts exist "in a *continuum*."[65] As Ralph Herring puts it, "Two things are promised: first, the remission of sins; second, the gift of the Holy Spirit. One follows upon the other. All who have dealt faithfully with the sin question through genuine repentance are in a position to claim the gift of the Spirit. It is a part of the same promise."[66]

The Samaritans of Acts 8:14-17 offer a clear case of subsequent Spirit baptism. They had believed and had been baptized, but the Holy Spirit "had not yet fallen upon any of them" until the visit of Peter and John.

The case of Saul of Tarsus (Acts 9:1-18) seems less evident and possibly presents a case of simultaneous action. However, Paul's conversion has always been known as a "Damascus-Road experience," not as a "Street-Called-Straight experience." Paul's account before king Agrippa (Acts 26:12-19) establishes this. Here Paul testifies to the very commission he received *on the Damascus Road*, clearly indicating his own spiritual redemption was at that time, *before* receiving the baptism in the Spirit some three days later.

Acts 10:44 presents the experience of Cornelius and his household. The subsequent nature of the coming of the Holy Spirit is identified by Peter in using the aorist participle in his likening the event to Pentecost: "God therefore gave to them the same gift as He did to us also *after believing* in the Lord Jesus Christ" (Acts 11:17, italics added). See also, "God . . . bore witness to them, giving them the Holy Spirit, *just as He also did to us* [as believers]" (Acts 15:8, italics added).

Acts 13:48-52 describes the action at Antioch, where "Gentiles . . . believed." Then they became disciples who were, as believers, "continually filled with joy and the Holy Spirit." Or, treating this as *an imperfect of repeated action* (see Williams on Acts 8:17; also on Luke 14:7; John 19:3) the disciples were one by one being filled with joy and the Holy Spirit.

The twelve disciples in Ephesus (Acts 19:1-7) had failed to receive the Holy Spirit "when they believed" or, as in the KJV, "since they believed." In Scripture, "disciples," unless associated with a person as in "disciples of John," always indicates disciples of Christ. And their lack of knowledge of the Spirit is only too common, even today, among believers. Thus the question is significant—and timeless. Paul knew that there were disciples in those days also who, though believers, had not yet received the baptism in the Holy Spirit. It would have been an absurd question if this were not so. The question was an evangelistic challenge to believers then, as it should be now. "Having believed, have *you* received the baptism in the Holy Spirit?"

Furthermore, there are at least twice as many instances of conversion recorded in the Book of Acts *with no mention being made of the Holy Spirit* being poured out as of conversions in which the Holy Spirit is mentioned. Why should the Spirit be identified in these several instances, but not in all, if the baptism with the Spirit was enjoyed as an initial experience by all?

The pattern of conversion is set in Acts 2:47: "And the Lord was adding to their number day by day those who were being saved." The individual accounts, as examples, specify that they "believed" (4:4); "a large number who believed turned to the Lord" (11:21); many "were believing and being baptized" (18:8). But, as I already mentioned, the Bible only occasionally declares that the converts were also filled with the Spirit.

Furthermore, it is apparent that not every believer was Spirit filled. It was necessary to institute a "search" to find seven men "full of the Spirit" to care for the widows. Barnabas was set apart among believers as "a good man, and full of the Holy Spirit" (Acts 11:24). An entire church was classified as being "unspiritual" (1 Cor. 3:1). And does Galatians 6:1, "you who are spiritual," imply that some in that church were not spiritual?

Thus, that the special infusion of the Holy Spirit was to be a subsequent experience to conversion is evident by the clear teaching of Jesus, by the teaching of the apostles, by the spiritual needs of the children of God, and by the universal experience of the early church as recorded in Acts and indicated in the epistles.

However, the manner of His coming will vary as it did then—in the dramatic setting comparable to the Day of Pentecost; in the quiet visit from a godly messenger as Ananias to Saul; in a small, solemn gathering as to the Twelve in Ephesus. The principles of expectant faith, surrender, and request remain the same. But is there a precise pattern? No, not really. This would lead to artificial stimuli, to demands for certain signs from God, to a presumption of achievement based often on physical or emotional signs.

We recall our Lord's reminiscence: "The wind blows where it wishes and you hear the sound of it, but do not know where it comes from and where it is going; so is every one who is born of the Spirit" (John 3:8). And so it is with everyone who is baptized with the Spirit.

C. The Message of 1 Corinthians 12:13 Examined

When one verse appears to contradict the general flow of Scripture, the teaching of Jesus and the apostles, or the experience of the early church, an examination is in order.

On the general subject W. T. Purkiser declares frankly: "One must be born of the Spirit before he can be baptized or filled with the Spirit. It is only to those regenerated by the Spirit that He becomes the sanctifying Lord (2 Cor. 3:17-18)."[67] However, the interpretation often given 1 Corinthians 12:13 does not agree with this conclusion.

This verse is identified by many as the induction of the believer, upon his conversion, into the body of Christ through baptism by the Spirit. Charles Ryrie succinctly states, "The baptism of the Spirit *makes us members of the body* of Christ."[68] John Stott observes, "The baptism of the Spirit in this verse . . . is, in fact, the means of entry into the body of Christ. . . . The baptism of the Spirit is not a second and subsequent experience enjoyed by some Christians, but the initial experience enjoyed by all."[69]

But surely such an interpretation is taking the verse out of context. In this section of the epistle Paul is warmly pleading for *unity within,* not for an *entrance into,* the body of Christ. This thought is reflected in the preceding verses, which speak of "the same Spirit . . . the same Lord . . . the same God" and of many members but one body. It is also reflected in the verses that follow, identifying the numerous members of the body as being related to one another in usefulness through unity and harmony among themselves: "that there should be no division in the body." They do not speak of the members *becoming part* of the body. Surely, then, verse 13 is announcing an outpouring of the Spirit, an outpouring that has already baptized into one body those believers who experienced it, although they were of widely divergent backgrounds.

Charles W. Carter has made a cogent observation on 1 Corinthians 12:13:

> In a previous section Paul has emphasized the variety of spiritual gifts. He now emphasizes the unity within that variety. The Corinthian church prided itself in its great variety of gifts. It had little to boast about in its unity. Paul seeks to show that without the unity the multiplication of gifts is meaningless.... The Church is made a spiritual body through the baptism in the Spirit. Through that glorious baptism Jews and Greeks, slaves and freemen, women and men, wise and simple, rich and poor, are all made one in the body of Christ—each in his respective place and fulfilling his respective function—because each has become a partaker of the spiritual water of life (cf. John 7:37-39).[70]

Actually there are two verses in this passage to be considered together: "For by one Spirit we were all baptized into one body, whether Jews or Greeks, whether slaves or free, and we were all made to drink of one Spirit.... Now you are Christ's body, and individually members of it" (1 Cor. 12:13, 27).

1. There is a *contrast of persons* in verses 13 and 27 The personal pronouns, "we" in verse 13 and "you" in verse 27, are emphasized. In Greek the personal pronoun in the nominative case is included in the verb. When the pronoun is also used separately, it is for emphasis, because the personal pronoun is a repetition of the subject already expressed in the verb. But, when two such pronouns are used in the same passage, it is for *contrast*—a common and important practice.[71] Paul uses such contrast dramatically in the same letter: *"We* are fools for Christ's sake, but *you* are prudent in Christ; *we* are weak, but *you* are strong; *you* are distinguished, but *we* are without honor" (1 Cor. 4:10, italics added here and following). All the Gospel writers use it in contrasting the baptisms of John and Jesus: "As for me, *I* baptize you in water for repentance; but He who is coming after me is mightier than I, and I am not even fit to remove His sandals; *He* Himself will baptize you with the Holy Spirit and fire" (Matt. 3:11; see also Mark 1:8; Luke 3:16; John 1:26-27). The antithesis holds even in widely separated verses, as in John 18:31, 38; 19:6: "Pilate therefore said to them, 'Take Him *yourselves,* and judge Him.... *I* find no guilt in Him.'" "'Take Him *yourselves* ... for *I* find no guilt in Him.'"*

Then who are the "we" of verse 13 and the "you" of verse 27 who are in contrast? And how are they in contrast? The "you" of verse 27 are the believers who made up the church in Corinth—"Christ's body, and individually members of it." They had been brought into membership in the church on the very terms Jesus Himself had set for such membership, *without any mention of a baptism with the Holy Spirit*. "And the Lord was adding to their number day by day those who were being saved" (Acts 2:47). It is recorded, then, of the Corinthians: "Many of the Corinthians when they heard were believing and being baptized" (Acts 18:8). It is specifically declared that the Holy Spirit had taken up His abode in their hearts (1 Cor. 6:19); but it is just as specifically stated in the same epistle that, although they were Christians, they were not "spiritual" (3:1), not Spirit-filled, not baptized with the Spirit as Jesus defined the baptism of Pentecost (Acts 1:4-5; 2:2, 4). And their mode of life bore out that poverty of Spirit in carnality, childishness, envying, strife, and divisiveness.

Antithetically, the "we" of verse 13 are also believers, but believers who *additionally* and subsequently had been baptized with and received the Spirit, indeed, who had been "made to drink" of, and

---

*Other examples of contrast are numerous: Matt. 8:7, 9; Luke 22:32; John 4:38; 5:35; 7:8; 8:13-15; 8:23; 8:41, 44; 13:33; 15:5, 16; 16:7, 8; Acts 9:5; 13:33; 22:8; 26:15; 1 Cor. 1:12; 3:4; Heb. 1:5; 5:5; James 2:3; 1 John 4:4-6; 4:19. Thus the use of two personal pronouns in the same passage to identify a contrast is a frequent occurrence, sometimes with important insights but with limited facility within the English language of adequate expression.

were manifestly "filled with," the Spirit. It is generally agreed that this being baptized and the drinking are equivalent expressions.[72] This was an experience reserved for the believer subsequent to his conversion, according to Jesus (John 14:17; 20:22) and according to the universal experience of the early church, as discussed above.

Thus here the *hēmeis* ("we") of verse 13 is *in contrast* to the *humeis* ("you") of verse 27. The contrast is simply between two sets of believers, those who have been baptized with the Holy Spirit and those who have not been so baptized and are not Spirit-filled. That makes the difference.

John Williams makes a great deal of the *all* who were baptized:

> The word "all" is particularly significant in the context of this Epistle to the church at Corinth since the Corinthians were not only spiritually immature . . . but culpably immature. Now if it is true that the baptism of the Spirit is the exclusive province and blessing of the spiritual man how is it that Paul, writing to deliberately carnal Christians, can remind them that they *all* were baptized in the Spirit? Obviously Paul was as thoroughly informed about the condition of the Corinthians as he was about the doctrine of the Holy Spirit. The answer is plain. For Paul, as for the other New Testament writers, spirituality was neither the prerequisite for Spirit baptism nor the inevitable result of it. The gift of the Holy Spirit is the unconditional blessing of all who are believers in Christ.[73]

However, an examination of the verse will indicate that the "all" does *not* refer to all *individuals,* but to all *types* or kinds of Christians—all nationalities "whether Jews or Greeks," all strata of society "whether slaves or free." God is no respecter of persons in the baptism with the Holy Spirit. Jesus had promised, "How much more will the Father give the Holy Spirit to those who ask Him?" Peter caught the vision on the Day of Pentecost: "For the promise is for you [largely Jews], and your children [all future generations], and for all who are far off [all nationalities], even as many as the Lord our God shall call to Himself" (Acts 2:39).

Spirituality indeed *was* and *continues to be* the inevitable result of our Lord's baptizing the believer with the Holy Spirit. The tragic fact was that the Corinthians *had not* been so baptized. The glorious fact was that throngs of believers of all nationalities and of all strata of society *had been* so baptized and so were cleansed spiritually and brought into spiritual unity.

2. There is also a *contrast of purpose* in verses 13 and 27 Note that the central theme of the entire passage is unity. The Spirit-baptism is not, then, an entrance into *"the* body" of Christ, but a baptism into *"one* body." The body should be a unity—one. "There should be no division in the body" (v. 25). In diversity, illustrated by the diverse members of a body (vv. 12–27), there is unity *if the unifying force of the Holy Spirit knits it together* into a useful and harmonious whole (v. 13).

Membership in the body of Christ came to *us,* implies Paul, in the same way as to *you* Corinthians—through faith and acceptance of Christ. Unity, however, came upon *us all*—Jews or Greeks, slave or free—as believers, in spite of our diverse background and origin, only through the cleansing, sanctifying baptism of the one Spirit. In Galatians 3:27–28 Paul adds, "For all of you who were baptized into Christ have clothed yourselves with Christ. There is neither Jew nor Greek, there is neither slave nor free man, there is neither male nor female; for you are all one in Christ Jesus."

Here in the Corinthian epistle was a skillfully devised charge by Paul to a schismatic church to come into the harmony, the oneness, enjoyed by so many others through the baptism and fullness of the Holy Spirit. It was a oneness enjoyed by diversified Christians of all types—Jews and Greeks, slave and free, male and female. "Come into that fellowship," he invited.

The oneness, repeatedly prayed for by

Jesus for His church (John 17), will be achieved only when Christians are sanctified (v. 17) through the one baptism that is uniquely Christian, the baptism with the Holy Spirit (Acts 1:4-5).

3. Shall it be "by" or "in" the one Spirit? Every baptism requires a *recipient,* an *agent,* and a *medium.* The phrase "by one Spirit" identifies the Spirit as the *agent,* the one who does the baptizing. But there is thus provided no medium or element in which to be baptized. This is confusing, if not totally incomprehensible. And the frequently used religious shibboleth "the Holy Spirit baptizing believers into the body of Christ" is incongruous and meaningless. Baptizing with what?

The participle "by" is from *en,* which often carries the sense of "agency" as in 1 Corinthians 6:2: "the world is judged by you." But in every text regarding baptism, save this one, it carries the sense of being "a medium," as in Matthew 3:11: "I baptize you in water . . . He shall baptize you with the Holy Spirit" (see also Mark 1:8; Luke 3:16; Acts 1:5; 11:16). Change this verse to *"in* the one Spirit," as do NEB, RSV, Weymouth, Goodspeed, NASB (Margin), and the Holy Spirit is the *medium,* Christ becomes the *agent,* and the believer is the *recipient.* The verse then becomes meaningful.

The following is a suggested change of order, quite compatible with the Greek, which may clarify the meaning of this passage: "For in one Spirit we, whether Jews or Greeks, whether slaves or free, were all baptized into one body, and were all made to drink of one Spirit."

D. Water Baptism and Spirit Baptism in the Scriptures

Is there a relationship between water baptism and Spirit baptism? If so, to what extent and how? Does "baptize," unless another medium is announced, always presuppose the medium of water? Indeed, are there effusions of the Spirit that are not always recognized as such?

John the Baptist announced the contrasting baptism of the Holy Spirit that Jesus would inaugurate (Matt. 3:11). When he said, "I have need to be baptized by You, and do You come to me?" (v. 14), did he imply that, if it were possible, he would desire this Spirit-baptism from Jesus? It is difficult to give an unequivocal answer. But the possible implication of John's statement is too often overlooked. After all, the One who will be baptizing "is mightier than I, and I am not even fit to remove His sandals" (v. 11). John's thought was "Why should I not seek, from the greater Baptizer, the greater baptism?"

The statement that "Jesus Himself was not baptizing, but His disciples were" (John 4:2) draws varied comment. A. T. Robertson suggests that "it is possible that Jesus stopped baptizing because of the excitement and the issue raised about his Messianic claims till after his resurrection when he enjoined it upon his disciples as a rule of public enlistment in his service."[74]

George Turner says that "Jesus did not perform the mechanics of baptizing; the disciples did it in his name. It was customary for the rabbis to have their pupils baptize proselytes."[75]

However, Michael Harper declares, "Jesus did not come to baptize people in water but *in the Spirit.* . . . The element which he would use, from Pentecost onwards, was Spirit not water."[76]

Is it significant that Paul, the most effective implement of the Great Commission, had so indifferent an attitude toward water baptism (1 Cor. 1:13-17), but so positive a teaching regarding baptism with the Spirit? (1 Cor. 12:13; Eph. 4:5). When Paul wrote of baptism, to which baptism was he referring?

Consider, for example, two texts written by Paul: Romans 6:3-8 and Colossians 2:12. Was it to water baptism or to Spirit baptism he referred? H. Orton Wiley points out that "the argument for immersion rests entirely upon the words 'buried with him *by* or *in* baptism' [in these texts]; and it is assumed that the apostle is here speaking of water baptism, and therefore defining the mode." Dr. Wiley then apparently commits himself to baptism in the *Spirit* in both of these texts by saying, "That these texts have no reference either to water baptism or to its mode is ably and concisely stated by Dr. Wakefield." He then quotes Wakefield (*Christian Theology,* p. 582), who, in substance, declares:

> We conclude, therefore, from a very careful examination of the whole subject, that in the passages under consideration the apostle has no allusion whatever either to water baptism itself or to its mode; but is speaking of a *spiritual* death, burial, resurrection, and life. . . . Indeed, the whole argument of the apostle shows that he is speaking of the work of the Spirit, and not of water baptism. . . . Can water baptism accomplish the moral change of which the apostle is here speaking? Surely no one will affirm this, unless he has adopted the wild notion that "immersion is the regenerating act."[77]

To this we would add a survey of the relative pronoun *hosoi,* a selective or excluding word, translated in KJV as "as many as." Paul uses it in Romans 2:12: "For as many as have sinned without law shall also perish without law: and as many as have sinned in the law shall be judged by the law"; and in Romans 8:14: "For as many as are led by the Spirit of God, they are the sons of God" (KJV). *Hosoi* thus indicates a selection, an exclusion. Thus in Romans 6:3 Paul declares, "Know ye not that so many of us as were baptized into Jesus Christ were baptized into his death?" (KJV). Apparently some of the believers had not been so "baptized." And was that missing, transforming baptism in water, or in the Holy Spirit? Dr. Wakefield challenges, "Can water baptism accomplish the moral change of which the apostle is here speaking?"

It is interesting to discover the same pronoun, *hosoi,* in Galatians 3:27: "For as many of you as have been baptized into Christ have put on Christ" (KJV).

This brings us to a consideration of the "one baptism" of Ephesians 4:5. Reformed scholars, holding that baptism with the Spirit is an *initial* experience, common to all, tend to make it a combination water-Spirit event. Says Frederick Bruner: "The baptism with the Holy Spirit and baptism, they knew, belonged together in such a way as to form the 'one baptism.'"[78] John Williams observes, "In all probability both are in Paul's thinking, since for the early church they were practically simultaneous. The one was the outward expression of the other, which was an inner reality."[79]

A liturgical view holds that the one baptism is that of "the sacrament." "Baptism is specified, being the sacrament whereby we are incorporated into the 'one body'."[80]

George Williams expresses a pertinent, nonsacramental viewpoint:

> There are not two Spirits or two Lords or two Gods, and there are not two Hopes, or two Faiths, or two Baptisms.
> All here is in the spiritual realm. The one Lord, the one Revelation and the one Baptism are all on the same spiritual plane. The subject of the passage is the unity of the Spirit. So this one and unifying baptism is objective, spiritual, and divine; as are also the one Lord and the one Revelation. Many assume the baptism here is to be baptism into water. But that baptism is physical and subjective—it has to do with discipleship in the earth, and is limited and local, for the climate makes it universally impossible; but this one baptism is that of the Spirit baptizing both Jew and Gentile into one body. There are not two baptisms. There were two in John iv but that into water ceased and that of the Holy Spirit abides.[81]

Actually the one baptism must be that of the Spirit, first of all because, compared to the other baptisms—in the cloud, in water, of suffering—Spirit-baptism is obviously the chief, the most important. Of this Robert Mattke writes:

> While emphasizing the superiority of the baptism of the Holy Spirit, care must be taken not to minimize John's baptism. It fills a very important place in God's redemptive plan. Jesus' submission to John's baptism is a testimony to its own merit and validity. It must not be discounted or depreciated.

As important as John's baptism is in its own right, the truth remains that it is not the ultimate in baptisms; it is not the final baptism in God's redemptive order. The baptism of the Holy Spirit is the baptism of baptisms; it is the one baptism spoken of by Paul in company with "One Lord, one faith. . . . One God and Father of all, who is above all, and through all, and in you all" (Eph. 4:5,6; 1 Cor. 12:13).[82]

Again, of the various baptisms, baptism with the Spirit is clearly the only one that is distinctly Christian. Ralph Earle declares:

> In view of the clear assertion of John the Baptist here, it is difficult to understand the almost universal neglect in the Christian Church of the baptism with the Holy Spirit. There was nothing particularly unique about John's method of water baptism. Judaism baptized new converts with water. Water baptism is thus not distinctively a *Christian* rite. The only distinctive and utterly unique Christian baptism is the baptism with the Holy Spirit. That cannot be duplicated by any other religion. It is peculiarly Christ's: *"He* shall baptize you with the Holy Spirit" (Mark 1:7-8).[83]

Finally, the "one baptism" must be the baptism with the Holy Spirit in that, in and of itself, water baptism does not confer grace. As a sign and a seal it witnesses to it. "Baptism symbolizes . . . regeneration through union with Christ."[84] On the other hand Christ clearly related the grace leading to the sanctification that He petitioned for His disciples (John 17:17) and for all believers (John 17:20) to baptism with the Spirit (Acts 1:5), and baptism with the Spirit to spiritual power and effectual witnessing (Acts 1:8). Peter clearly identified the Pentecostal baptism with the Spirit to the experience of cleansing and sanctification that came on the disciples in Jerusalem and on the Gentiles in Caesarea (Acts 11:15-17; 15:1-9).

The baptism with the Holy Spirit then, for the believer, is a transforming experience of grace, planned by God the Father (Eph. 1:4), purchased by God the Son (Eph. 5:25-27), and produced by God the Spirit (Eph. 5:18; 2 Thess. 2:13b).

IX. THE CHURCH IS ESTABLISHED BY THE HOLY SPIRIT

A. God's Long-Range Plan Fulfilled

Jesus, of course, had proclaimed: "Upon this rock I will build My church; and the gates of Hades shall not overpower it" (Matt. 16:18). Under the title *ekklēsia*—"called out ones"—our Lord would establish an impregnable body of believers. Augustine may have been the first to refer to the Day of Pentecost as "the birthday of the Church," for it brought together believers from "every nation under heaven" into one great mystical body. John Williams suggests, "The mission of Jehovah's servant, so perfectly begun by Him during the days of His flesh, would now be maintained by Him through His mystical body, the Church" (Acts 1:1).[85]

A better designation, however, for Pentecost might be "the inauguration of the church," since the church was already in existence. It was not a new designation for God's people. Stephen spoke about "the congregation [*ekklēsia*] in the wilderness" (Acts 7:38) in direct reference to the "congregation" of Israel. Ralph Earle observes that Acts 7:37 is a quotation of Deuteronomy 18:15. "Right following that, in Deuteronomy 18:16, *ekklēsia* is used in the Septuagint for the congregation of Israelites assembled at Sinai to receive the Law. So it is properly applied to God's people in Old Testament times."[86] Charles W. Carter suggests, "Moses was a part of the true church of God in the wilderness, which culminated in Christ the Messiah."[87]

Just as Israel, delivered from Egypt by the shed blood of the Passover lamb, was molded into a theocracy by the giving of the law at Sinai, so believers, delivered from sin by the shed blood of Jesus, our Passover Lamb, were molded into the Christian church at Pentecost. The law of Sinai, written on stone, was replaced by the law of Calvary, written on tables of the heart. Thus the Holy Spirit not only united individual believers to Christ in a sacred union, but He also unites the body of believers to each other in that sacred union known as the Christian church. As H. Orton Wiley declares, "Formerly there was isolation, every man for himself; now it is an organic union of all the members under their one Head. This is the difference between the days before and after Pentecost."[88]

B. Several Titles Become Proper for God's Family

"The church," the entire company of Christians "in one Spirit," came to be known also as "fellow-citizens with the saints," "God's household," "a holy temple in the Lord," and "a dwelling of God" (Eph. 2:18-22), as "one body in Christ" (Rom. 12:5; 1 Cor. 12:27; Eph. 1:23; 4:12; Col. 1:24; 2:19) and as His bride (Rev. 18:23; 21:2, 9; 22:17).

C. The Jerusalem Church Exhibited Essential Characteristics

Established through the memorable outpouring of the Spirit, the first church was in many ways a model for other congregations.

1. It was a teaching church (Acts 2:42) The desire to learn must ever characterize true members of His church. As Charles Carter observes, "All progress in grace will be accomplished by new and progressive knowledge received through a faithful and diligent search for truth."[89] There was no disregard of human teaching because the Holy Spirit had promised "to reveal all things."

2. It was a fellowshiping church (vv. 42, 46) They fellowshiped in the happy sharing, both of meals and of prayer. Indeed, the *koinōnia,* literally the "having things in common" with the Holy Spirit (2 Cor. 13:14) as well as with the believers, came to be an earmark of Christianity.

3. It was a worshiping church (v. 43) For worshipers, "a sense of awe" combined with "wonders and signs." Reverence was mingled with the miraculous. The spectacular climaxed the reverential, leading to a practical application of power and authority to the worshipfulness of the service.

4. It was a sharing church (vv. 44-47a) The Spirit did not inspire them to give in a spectacular fashion for the sake of giving. It was as needs appeared that "they began selling their property and possessions, and were sharing them with all, as anyone might have need." Here was a practical concern for the needs of others. Samuel Chadwick comments, "The Kingdom of God henceforth is a new theocracy, permeated, dominated, sanctified in the Spirit of Pentecost."[90] Michael Harper states, "We suddenly become aware of the large family into which we have been born. The natural instinct man has to belong to something bigger than himself is satisfied. We are part of the Body of Christ."[91]

5. It was a Spirit-filled, Spirit-baptized church (vv. 37-47) In the light of the dismal record of the Corinthian church it is refreshing to discover the warm spiritual climate binding the believers together in the Spirit in Jerusalem.

6. It was an evangelizing church (v. 47) Note that the consistency of the church's growth was under the Lord's tutelage, based on an evangelistic outreach but motivated by the Spirit's presence in dedicated church members.

D. The Holy Spirit Has Continued to Work in the Church

1. In the realm of intercessory prayer Romans 8:26-27; Ephesians 2:18; 6:18-19; and Jude 20 together establish the assuring fact that in understanding, in expression, and in warm affection the Spirit will help our infirmity in the area of intercessory prayer.

2. In counsel and approval The church had come together in conference. Important issues of policy and doctrine were to be considered and decided. After careful and prayerful consideration the church was able to write, "For it seemed good to the Holy Spirit and to us . . ." (Acts 15:28). Thus was set for all generations the pattern of the counsel of the Spirit in church policies. This pattern has never been withdrawn.

3. In constraint and restraint Acts 13:2-4 and 16:6-7 establish that sometimes the Spirit says "go" and sometimes "no." The church was under the constraint and the restraint of the Spirit.

4. In the setting of standards Paul witnessed, "For we are the true circumcision, who worship in the Spirit of God, and glory in Christ Jesus and put no confidence in the flesh" (Phil. 3:3). Again he advises, "And do not get drunk with wine, for that is dissipation, but be filled with the Spirit, speaking to one another in psalms and hymns and spiritual songs, singing and making melody with your heart to the Lord; always giving thanks for all things in the name of our Lord Jesus Christ to God, even the Father; and be subject to one another in the fear of Christ" (Eph. 5:18-21).

Thus it is a Spirit-empowered church that Christ foresaw, Spirit-filled, Spirit-guided, Spirit-restrained, Spirit-enlightened, against which the gates of Hades should not prevail.

X. THE HOLY SPIRIT BESTOWS GIFTS

The subject of the gifts of the Spirit is truly a contemporary aspect of theology. As late as 1950 major theological works, a standard dictionary, a several-volume encyclopedia, and most books on the Holy Spirit were silent on the subject of the charismatic gifts.

In the early years of the church, clericalism, one of the less desirable results of the legalization of the church by Constantine in the fourth century, had sown the seed for this omission. In order to supply suitable and official representatives to the state, the church stimulated hierarchical development. Bishops, presbyters, and deacons, who had already in a great measure gained supremacy over laymen, became more authoritative after the union with the state at the close of the century. Thus the clergy became the officials of the church, and a stratification set in. They became the official voice of the church. In particular, the sacraments became the sole responsibility of the clergy. The layman's access to God was through the church and through the clergy. As a result the layman became in practice a worshiper and not an active participant in church activities. The majority of Christians became "unemployed." The church had discarded the proper use of the gifts of the Spirit.

The awakening was a long time coming, but it has arrived. Today, possibly as never before since the first century, we are in the age of the Holy Spirit, and the gifts of the Spirit are being emphasized.

A. The Gifts of the Spirit Defined

The gifts of the Spirit are identified in Scripture as *charismata,* or gifts of grace, *charis.* H. Orton Wiley suggests that "the gifts are the divinely ordained means and powers with which Christ endows His church in order to enable it to properly perform its task on earth."[92] They are given for service. They may be described as the varied manifestation of the Holy Spirit in the ever-varying human personality, with no two exactly the same, differing largely according to the person's natural abilities and talents. They are given to each believer "according to his own ability," said Jesus.

B. Underlying Principles Regarding Gifts

1. Gifts have a diversity of pattern and purpose There are "varieties of gifts" (1 Cor. 12:4), gifts "that differ" (Rom.

12:6), and are given in a sovereign fashion by the Spirit, "distributing to each one individually just as He wills" (1 Cor. 12:11). Gifts cannot be merited or earned, but are given by grace. Kenneth Kinghorn suggests, "He offers to each Christian the gifts best suited to his personality."[93]

2. All Christians are gifted (1 Cor. 12:7; Eph. 4:7; 1 Peter 4:10) However, Christians differ in gifts (Rom. 12:4-6a; 1 Cor. 12:8-10, 29-30), and thus no one possesses all the gifts (1 Cor. 12:29-30). This is illustrated by Paul in likening the church to the human body, with various members that are quite distinct in appearance and function, but all necessary.

3. Gifts are distributed to benefit the entire body of believers The Scriptures say manifestations of the Spirit are given "for the common good" (1 Cor. 12:7); "for the equipping of the saints for the work of service, to the building up of the body of Christ" (Eph. 4:12); that each may "employ it in serving one another" (1 Peter 4:10), so that none is for private benefit. John Stott points out, "The gifts of the Spirit are given to the individual believers, but they are given for the healthy growth of the church."[94] W. T. Purkiser has aptly observed:

> One clear implication of Romans 12:3-8 and 1 Corinthians 12:12-26 (where gifts are placed in the context of the body life) is that in every local congregation there are people with gifts to accomplish all that congregation ought to be doing in the kingdom of God. Every true function of the body of Christ has a "member" to perform it, and every member has a function to perform.[95]

4. Gifts must be discovered This must be done before development, for gifts are not achieved but received. Every Christian should take an inventory to discover his gift or gifts.

5. Gifts require development They may be developed by the Holy Spirit. W. T. Purkiser suggests, "Effectiveness depends on the energy of the Spirit channelled through it."[96] He who gives the gift is interested in developing it. Gifts may be improved by the possessor. In the parable of the talents each possessor was responsible for enlarging his possession. "Burying" the gifts by idle possession will not prove fruitful. Charles Ryrie helpfully observes:

> Although the Spirit is the source of spiritual gifts, the believer may have a part in the development of his gifts. He may be ambitious in relation to his own gifts to see that they are properly developed and that he is doing all he can for the Lord (1 Cor. 12:31). To covet the better gifts is not a matter of sitting down and conjuring up enough faith to be able to receive them out of the blue. It is a matter of diligent self-preparation. For instance, if one covets the gift of teaching, he will undoubtedly have to spend many years developing that gift. The Holy Spirit is sovereign in the giving of gifts, but in the development of them He works through human beings with their desires, limitations, ambition, and the like.[97]

Gifts may be neglected just as truly as they may be improved. Timothy was warned, "Do not neglect the spiritual gift within you" (1 Tim 4:14). C. Peter Wagner has warned, "Every spiritual gift we have is a resource that we must use and for which we will be held accountable at the day of judgment. . . . Stewards are held responsible for what the master has chosen to give them."[98] Kenneth Kinghorn suggests:

> Neglect of spiritual gifts stems from any of several causes:
> (1) *Ignorance* of God's provision for equipping the church with gifts.
> (2) *Lethargy* concerning God's working in our lives.
> (3) *Unwillingness* to respond to some aspect of God's call to service and ministry. The neglect of spiritual gifts will stifle personal growth and cripple the ministry of the church.[99]

C. There Are Hazards in Gifts

With all the unmistakable benefits of gifts, there are also warnings to be sounded. The example of the Corinthian church identifies several of these.

1. Dangers of independence and jealousy This is implied in 1 Corinthians 12:15-21: "Because I am not a hand, I am not a part of the body . . . I have no need of you."

2. Sense of superiority Verses 22-24 speak of "members of the body which we deem less honorable."

3. Divisiveness Arrogance can lead to the divisiveness Paul observed in verses 25-27.

4. Inversion of importance There can be the real danger of discarding the order of importance established in verse 28, placing spectacular gifts in the place of undue importance.

5. One gift may be cited as the evidence of the Holy Spirit The truth must be jealously guarded that the possession of any gift is, by itself, no evidence of the baptism with the Spirit, or even of any degrees of spirituality. The Corinthian church again gives an unhappy evidence of this error.

D. There Are Basically Four Lists of Gifts in the Scriptures

1. 1 Corinthians 12:1-11 presents one list Some twenty gifts are itemized by Paul in four different Scripture passages. The first list was given to the Corinthians because of a serious misunderstanding regarding the gifts of the Spirit. "Now concerning spiritual gifts, I do not want you to be unaware (or, more accurately in deference to the present tense, "to *continue* to be unaware"). In their ignorance they had even given credit to the Spirit for inspiring someone to declare, "Jesus is accursed." Furthermore, Paul instructs them that "no one can say, 'Jesus is Lord,' except by the Holy Spirit."

In the light of this fact he advises them: "There are varieties of gifts, but the same Spirit." Then, *in a plea for unity,* he lists several gifts, all distributed "by the same Spirit." These are "the word of wisdom," "the word of knowledge," "faith," "gifts of healing," "effecting of miracles," "prophecy," "the distinguishing of spirits," "kinds of tongues," and "the interpretation of tongues."

Following this listing he continues his plea for the unity that binds together entirely dissimilar types of people through the baptism with the one Spirit and for the unity that is illustrated by many disparate members united in the one body by interrelated responsibilities (1 Cor. 12:12-27).

2. 1 Corinthians 12:28-31 presents a second list In this latter part of the chapter Paul enumerates "appointments in the church" made by God, listed now in a diminishing order of importance that is instructive—"first apostles, second prophets, third teachers," then four others, with "various kinds of tongues" listed last. ("Interpretation of tongues" is omitted.) In doing this he repeats four gifts given in the first list but adds four others—the first- and third-place "apostles" and "teachers," then "helps" and "administrations." He thus has established "the greater gifts"—and the lesser ones.

Then, anxious to clear the facts that *all cannot claim to possess the same particular gift* and that *no one possesses all the gifts,* Paul asks a series of questions governed by the Greek *mē,* a negative particle that, used in a question, expects a negative answer:

> All are not apostles, are they? All are not prophets, are they? All are not teachers, are they? All are not workers of miracles, are they? All do not have gifts of healings, do they? All do not speak with tongues, do they? All do not interpret, do they? But earnestly desire the greater gifts.

This led very naturally into the announcement: "And I show you a still more excellent way"—more excellent even than the "greater gifts"—the way of love, which is not really a "gift of the Spirit" but a "fruit of the Spirit." Paul had difficulty with these unspiritual Corinthians. Their shallow, unethical practices were reflected in their emphasis on gifts *(charismata)* (1 Cor. 1:7) and in their unwise evaluation and choice of the various gifts. There was "a still more excellent way."

Reflecting on this, a comment by Kenneth Kinghorn is meaningful:

> The presence of a spiritual gift in a Christian does not "prove" his spirituality or his maturity. God gives spiritual gifts (as he gives natural talents) assuming the risk that we might apply them wrongly. Through immaturity, ignorance, or self will, one may misuse his spiritual gift.[100]

3. Romans 12:3-8 contains a further list of gifts

4. Ephesians 4:7, 11-16 completes the listing The lists in Romans 12 and Ephesians 4 are interrelated. To the Roman and Ephesian churches Paul is evidently writing to more mature Christians. Further, he repeats the three gifts he told the Corinthians were the more important ones—namely apostles, prophets, and teachers. But none of the other Corinthian gifts is here repeated. Some of the omissions are significant. The additions likewise are significant for their practical nature. To the Romans he presents the additional gifts of "service," "exhortation," "giving," "leading," and "showing mercy"; and to the Ephesians, "evangelists" and "pastors." W. T. Purkiser reminds us that "the Roman list deals with gifts that are part of the everyday life of the Christian community [while] the Corinthians list deals with gifts that are more exceptional, more transitory, less universal."[101] At any rate, the change in tenor from Corinth to Rome and Ephesus is noteworthy.

Several years later Peter gave an epilogue to the discussion of gifts with his practical and applicable exhortation, "As each one has received a special gift, employ it in serving one another, as good stewards of the manifold grace of God" (1 Peter 4:10). It is notable that the verb "serving" *(diakoneō)* is the same word for service that Jesus used to describe His own ministry in the washing of the feet of the disciples at the Passover supper: "I am among you as the one who serves" (Luke 22:27). Each gift should be a "serving gift" with practical application.

E. The Scriptural List of Gifts May Not Be Sacrosanct

1. There may be additional gifts Most would agree with Peter Wagner when he declares, "The Bible does not lock us into tight restrictions as to the number of gifts."[102] Indeed, he finds four other gifts to be celibacy (1 Cor. 7:7), voluntary poverty and martyrdom (1 Cor. 13:3), and hospitality (1 Peter 4:9-10). It is suggested that Charles Wesley's ability as a hymnist was as much a gift as was his brother John's gift of evangelism. Indeed, who is the more "gifted," Billy Graham or Beverly Shea? In reviewing the Great Commission (Matt. 28:18-20), might we wonder if he who "disciples" all the nations is not as gifted as he who "teaches" them? And what of the gift of "preaching" (Rom. 10:14-15; 1 Cor. 1:17; 2 Tim. 4:2)?

2. Gifts may be temporary Some consider that from time to time they have received all the gifts, given for the moment of need, then withdrawn until needed again.[103] In light of Scriptures just examined, however, this may be seriously questioned.

Richard Taylor suggests:

> It is better to think of these gifts as occasional enduements to meet emergencies, not necessarily permanent endowments. Peter may not always have been able to "see through" people as he did Ananias and Sapphira. Paul was not always able to exercise the gifts of healing (2 Tim. 4:20).[104]

Charles Ryrie proposes:

> The Scriptures teach that the Spirit has not given all the gifts to every generation. There were foundation gifts of apostles and prophets (Eph. 2:20), which gifts do not

appear in the periods of building the superstructure of the church. . . . Actually, it is no argument to say that every gift must appear in every generation of the history of the church so that no generation will be slighted.[105]

3. Gifts may be withdrawn Charles W. Carter, in referring to 1 Corinthians 13:8–12, feels that these are temporary gifts and will eventually cease "when the perfect is come, namely, the completion of the New Testament."[106]

John Stott expresses doubts that there are "apostles" and "prophets" in today's church, stating that the Twelve "have no successors today" as apostles, and that, as to prophets, "there is no longer anyone in the church who may dare to say 'The word of the Lord came to me, saying . . .', of 'Thus says the Lord.'"[107] Again, of course, this depends on one's definition of "apostle" and "prophet."

F. Christ's Teachings Regarding Gifts of the Spirit

1. The relationship between gifts and talents Many agree that Jesus made reference to gifts of the Spirit in His parable of the talents, though the gifts are not specifically thus identified. "For it is just like a man about to go on a journey, who called his own slaves, and entrusted them . . . to one . . . five talents, to another, two, and to another, one, each according to his own ability . . . and he went on his journey" (Matt. 25:14–15). It was for the time of His absence, it was to His own servants (believers), and it was according to His own choice that He gave His own possessions (gifts) as the suitable talents to each. After that, each servant was on his own but was expected to produce.

Peter Wagner says, "God takes a natural talent in an unbeliever and transforms it into a spiritual gift when that person enters the Body of Christ."[108] Likewise, John Stott says, "The God of creation gives talents to *all* men and women. . . . yet He bestows 'spiritual gifts' only upon His *redeemed* people. . . . We should be slow to deduce that there is no link whatever between the two."[109] W. E. Vine points out that "the talent *(talanton),* denoting something weighted, has provided the meaning of the English word as a gift or ability, especially under the influence of the Parable of the Talents."[110]

Thus it appears that it was the gifts of the Spirit that Jesus was identifying, with the reward of "Well done, good and faithful slave . . . enter into the joy of your master" to the productive; and the designation of "worthless" and the condemnation into "outer darkness" to the unresponsive and irresponsible slave.

Jesus warns us that there *is* a responsibility to being "gifted."

2. An anointing of the Spirit makes effective the gifts of the Spirit Gifts are spiritually effective only following an anointing of the Spirit. "You will be my witnesses," said Jesus. These persons were termed "prophets" by Joel (Acts 2:17–20) but "witnesses" by Jesus (Acts 1:8). Now these new witnesses were to appear, to establish His church, and to spread the gospel from Jerusalem to Judea, to Samaria, and even to the remotest part of the earth. Possessing only in a dormant state their gifts of the Spirit, which they had received when they became believers, the disciples were not ready to witness. Jesus knew this when He said, "You shall receive power when the Holy Spirit has come upon you." This was the key to Pentecost, to the new church, to the surging breakthrough of early Christianity. Until, as believers, they had received the Holy Spirit, or until as H. Orton Wiley put it, they were "anointed with the Spirit," or indeed until they had experienced their Pentecost, their witness was ineffectual and empty, a mere profession.[111] Baptized with the Spirit, they would witness with power, vitality, and effectiveness, utilizing the gifts in a soul-winning ministry. The trumpet call to the anointed would set on fire the dormant gifts of the Spirit through effective witnessing. It was, and still is, Spirit-filled, Spirit-anointed men and women *only* whom God can fully use. The finest gifts in the world are empty, false, and useless unless fired by the Spirit. The Corinthian church is a sad evidence of this. Their vaunted gifts were ineffectual because they lacked the anointing of the Spirit. The Jerusalem church is a glorious evidence of God's plan working through Spirit-anointed believers.

> And when they had prayed, the place where they had gathered together was shaken, and they were all filled with the Holy Spirit, and began to speak the word of God with boldness. . . . And with great power the apostles were giving witness to the resurrection of the Lord Jesus, and abundant grace was on them all (Acts 4:31, 33).

The child of God who would put his gifts from the Spirit to work must by all means make a thorough study of the gifts of the Spirit. He should search out and identify those that are his, and develop them by his own ministry and application. But, above all, these gifts must be dedicated in a fiery baptism of the Pentecostal flame. Jesus said His disciples would receive power when the Holy Spirit would come upon them (Acts 1:8). Only then, through their own witness, could God make full use of the gifts He had entrusted to them. "'Not by might nor by power, but by My Spirit' says the LORD of Hosts'' (Zech 4:6).

It is instructive to note that even Jesus embarked on His mission of productive witnessing *only after the anointing of the Spirit* (Luke 4:16–32; Acts 10:38). Surely "a slave is not greater than his master" (John 15:20).

XI. THE HOLY SPIRIT PRODUCES FRUIT

Fruit is the true measure of spirituality, of Christian vitality. As John Williams has expressed it, "It is in these spiritual fruits and moral values that we discern true spirituality."[112]

There are essentially four Scripture passages that deal with fruit. There is Jesus' parable of the true vine, Peter's dissertation regarding the prevention of fruitlessness, Paul's description of the fruit of the Spirit, and Jesus' profound statement regarding buried grain.

A. Fruit That Remains Is Engendered by a Mystical Union (John 15)

Our Lord projected this truth through His parable of the true vine. Without specifically mentioning the Holy Spirit, He presented God as the vinedresser, Christ as the vine, and the believer as the branch. Christians are grafted into the vine that they may be fruitful. A vine branch really has but one purpose, and that is to bear fruit. George Turner sees four requirements.[113] The condition of fruit bearing is an abiding life. The cost of fruit-bearing is purging or pruning. All that is bad should be pruned away. But much that is good also must be cut away to provide the ultimate in fruitfulness.

Merrill Tenney observes that the word *abide,* which occurs ten times in this passage, "means the maintenance of an unbroken connection rather than repose, and bespeaks the necessity of a constant active relationship."[114] Increasing success is marked by "fruit," "more fruit," and "much fruit." This fruit may essentially be that of reproduction of the Christian into the lives of others, but it also represents the fruit of Christian character, expected of us all.

B. Fruit Requires Cultivation (2 Peter 1:4–8)

Peter emphasizes the necessity of cultivation if fruitfulness is to be realized. There is a progressive pattern. He starts with conversion—"having escaped the corruption that is in the world by lust" (v. 4)—and points toward the goal of becoming "partakers of the divine nature," which is His holiness, His purity, His power for victorious and fruitful living. He then gives the needful steps for cultivation, accompanied by the admonition "applying all diligence," for people have a responsibility. God does not do for people what they can do for themselves. The eight steps to this goal are mutually dependent: faith, moral excellence, knowledge, self-control, perseverance, godliness, brotherly kindness, and Christian love. The process begins in faith and ends in love, Christian love.

C. Fruit Is Developed by the Indwelling Spirit (Gal. 5:22–23)

Paul takes up the theme by announcing the ninefold characteristics of the resulting fruit from the abiding Spirit. However, he heightens this by first recounting the "deeds of the flesh"—gross, impure, ungodly. They speak of the revolting nature of the "flesh"—"human nature when infected and corrupted by sin"[115]—in contrast to the winsome nature of the fruit of the Spirit.

"Love" crowns the manifold characteristics of the fruit of the Spirit and permeates the whole. There are, in Greek, several kinds of love. *Eros,* found in the English word *erotic,* is generally used to describe sexual love, but it is not found in the Scriptures, although it was, in the pagan Greek community at that time, the most commonly used of the various words. *Philia* (or *philos*), found today in "Philadelphia," speaks of brotherly love and is frequently found in Scripture, both in combination and alone. In combination it is found in 2 Peter 1:7, where it is translated "brotherly kindness." By itself it is found in James 4:4 as "friendship" and "friend." *Storgos* is used only in a compound as *astorgos*—a ("without") *storgos* ("natural affection") (Rom. 1:31 KJV). But *agape,* the word used in Galatians 5:22, is the choice word for "Christian love." "God is *agape*" (1 John 4:8). God thus loved the world. It was then an almost unknown word, but it became literally "born within the bosom of revealed religion." Dick Mohrman has commented with insight: "You and I are capable of producing *eros, phileo,* and *storgos* love, but we are incapable of producing *agape* love.... God's love has been given to us."[116]

In defending his doctrine of Christian Perfection John Wesley said, "Loving God with all our heart, mind, soul and strength is Christian Perfection. This implies that no wrong temper, none contrary to love, remains in the soul; and that all the thoughts, words, and actions are governed by pure love."[117]

It is generally agreed that the singular noun "fruit" is associated directly with "love." "All the other qualities listed are aspects of love" suggests John Williams.[118] He then goes on to identify the aspects of the fruit under three headings of three virtues each: (1) "inward virtues" of love, joy, and peace; (2) "manward virtues" of longsuffering, gentleness, and goodness; and (3) "outward virtues" of faithfulness, meekness, and temperance. Charles W. Carter classifies the same triad as (1) "the state of the believer's relationship to the Spirit"; (2) "the Spirit's outworking activities through the believer's *patience, kindness* and *goodness*"; and (3) "the fruit of the Spirit's influence upon the character of the believer is faithfulness, gentleness, and self-control."[119]

Gradual maturity is an obvious message of the figure of the ripening fruit and is a wholesome fact in the Christian's life. However, although it takes months to mature the fruit, it took the action of a moment to plant the seed that produces the tree. This truth is reflected in the fourth Scripture.

D. Fruit Is Produced by the Planting of Seed (John 12:23–24)

Jesus answered...., "The hour has come for the Son of Man to be glorified. Truly, truly I say to you, unless a grain of wheat falls into the earth and dies, it remains by itself alone; but if it dies, it bears much fruit."

The primary application of this imagery was to Christ Himself. In the Greek it is "the" grain of wheat rather than "a" grain. *He* was that grain. Unless *He* would die, He would be fruitless. As Bishop Ryle put it: "'I am that corn of wheat,' Jesus seems to say. 'Unless I die, whatever you in your private opinion may think, my purpose in coming into the world will not be accomplished. But if I die, multitudes of souls will be saved.'"[120]

The secondary application must be to the Christian. For *him* there also comes a time, a moment, to die—to die to sin. Unless *he* dies, he will be fruitless. In his case the fruit is twofold.

Unless he dies, he remains by himself—alone. What a tragic possibility! Entering heaven—but by himself. A moment of utter loneliness. But if he dies, he bears much fruit in souls won for Christ.

For the believer, it is the cultivation both of the quality of life outlined as "the fruit of the Spirit," and of the reproductive life of the fruitful vine.

In both of these the Christian can be either barren, or fruitful. It depends on his willingness, at a God-given moment, to join Christ in death—"dead to sin, but alive to God in Christ Jesus" (Rom. 6:4, 10-11).

In order to share this fruitfulness with their Lord,

> believers must do more than associate themselves with Calvary as those who look upon the Sin-bearer who suffers *for* them there. They are called to identify themselves with Him *on* the Cross, as being crucified *with* Him and fully united with Him, and He with them, so that His death means the death of their old nature, leading to a new life in the power of the Resurrection.[121]

In declaring, "I have been crucified with Christ; and it is no longer I who live, but Christ lives in me" (Gal. 2:20), Paul was giving his own witness that a time had come in his life when he faced up to spiritual reality and, as an earnest believer, joined Christ on the cross. As he put it, regarding Spirit-baptized believers: "Our old self was crucified with Him, that our body of sin might be done away with, that we should no longer be slaves of sin" (Rom. 6:6). Indeed, fruit is produced *only* by the planting of seed.

XII. MINISTRIES, FRUIT, AND GIFTS OF THE SPIRIT COMPARED

The Spirit's relationship to the believer comes under three headings—His ministries, His fruit, and His gifts.

In His *ministries,* as the administrator of the Godhead, the Holy Spirit invites the sinner, brings him under conviction, and leads him into justification, regeneration, adoption, and sanctification. He transforms (2 Cor. 3:18), assists in prayer (Rom. 8:26), leads (Rom. 8:4-5), and establishes worship patterns (Eph. 5:18-20). Since these ministries are essential to God's plan of salvation, continued rejection of the Holy Spirit is an unpardonable sin. On the other hand, all these ministries are available and necessary to every member of the human race.

The *fruit* of the Spirit is the harvest. It evinces growth and maturity and is expected, in every aspect, in every believer. The word signifies ethical character and holiness in thought, word, and action. Since fruit—in contrast to individual gifts—is the common mark of Christ's followers everywhere, it produces unity in His body, the church.

Gifts of the Spirit are skills that the Spirit gives to believers to enable them, when properly used, to serve others, to edify the church, and to witness to the unconverted. Since God, through His Spirit according to His sovereign will, chooses to give different gifts to different believers, the result is a healthy and useful diversity in the church. Thus gifts vary from believer to believer. To none does the Spirit bestow all His gifts; no gift does He confer on all. God is wise and providential in providing a Christian with these three aspects of the Spirit's relationship to him as a child of God! How foolish one can be if he allows these to assume improper perspective one to another! Each must be cherished for its purpose and value.

Since ministries and fruit are essential and available in their totality to every believer, it is illogical to make gifts more important than these. Since gifts can more easily be "counted for credit" and are often more dramatic, exciting, and spectacular, they can easily take precedence over ministries and fruit.

Here the Wesleyan viewpoint contrasts with that often found in the charismatic movement. The very title *charismatic* means gifted. By its fundamental doctrines the name *Wesleyan* signifies holiness. These two are not mutually exclusive, but the center of emphasis must be recognized by the nomenclature. The Wesleyan emphasis is on the unobtrusive, purifying, and perfecting work of the Spirit-baptism and the continuing purifying work of the Spirit's presence, on the power that makes holiness in conduct possible in those whom He has made "more than conquerors," and on the cultivation of the fruit of the Spirit—all of which should be the experience of every Christian.

By its name the charismatic emphasis, on the other hand, is frankly on the gifts of the Spirit, and not infrequently on the dramatic gifts of tongues, healing miracles (associated with physical manifestations), and ecstatic speaking.

For example, charismatics will commonly hold that speaking with tongues is the initial evidence of the baptism with the Spirit and that baptism with the Spirit provides power for service.[122] As to tongues, however, Wesleyans will remember that Paul wrote, "All do not speak with tongues, do they?" They will remember that Peter, in mentioning the Spirit-baptism shared jointly by the disciples in Jerusalem and the Gentiles in Caesarea, emphasized *heart cleansing* as *the evidence* of the Spirit's effluence in both groups (Acts 11:12-17; 15:5-9) and ignored entirely their speaking in tongues as apparently of secondary importance. They will remember, however, that Peter declared that this outpouring was "just as He also did to us," implying that the "tongues" at Caesarea also were known, understandable languages as on the Day of Pentecost, serving again the evangelical purpose that was evident in Jerusalem, with no translators needed.

As to power, the Wesleyans will not deny its being given for service, especially as that applies to such service gifts as teaching, helps, evangelism, encouragement, preaching. But they will remember that the Spirit provided power first for witnessing from victorious lives. Wesleyans will continue to remember that Paul, recognizing that the Corinthians favored "gifts" as their pattern of life, showed them the "still more excellent way," the way of Christian love and all that this implies.

XIII. SUMMARY HISTORY OF THE DOCTRINE OF THE HOLY SPIRIT

A. The Early-Church Controversies Concerning the Spirit

From the New Testament times the church has given honor and praise to the Holy Spirit as well as to the Father and the Son. Although theologians during the first centuries of the Christian era were slow to formulate exact language describing the person and work of the Spirit, He was specifically recognized along with the Father and the Son in the baptismal formula, in early hymns and liturgies, and in the negative response of the church to tendencies to downgrade His role in the Godhead. The devotional language and the actual worship in the early church were in advance of the doctrinal system developed by the theologians.

Controversies concerning the Holy Spirit were not as conspicuous during these early centuries as the furious struggles concerning the person of the Son. However, erroneous concepts concerning the Son often resulted in errors concerning the Spirit. For instance, those who denied that the Son is fully God almost invariably denied that the Spirit is fully God as well. As theologians groped for a precise statement concerning the person and work of the Holy Spirit several misconceptions developed:

1. A denial that the Godhead consists of three Persons The Sabellian heresy held that there is only one person in the Godhead. The designations "Father, Son, and Holy Spirit" signify merely three "modes of manifestation."

2. Assignment of the Spirit to a lesser place The Arian heresy accepted the divinity and personhood of the Son and the Spirit, but assigned them a lesser place than the Father. Thus the formidable Arian heresy held that both the Son and the Spirit are created beings.

3. Inferiority of some members of the Godhead to others There arose the belief that the Son is inferior to the Father, and the Spirit is inferior to both the Father and the Son, perhaps a creation of the latter. This hierarchical approach to the Godhead was congenial to Gnosticism and other systems with concepts of a series of divine beings in descending order of power and importance.

4. The Holy Spirit is not divine and is inferior Some claimed that both the Father and the Son are fully God but that the Holy Spirit is inferior to both. They said that the Spirit is only one of the ministering spirits, different only in degree from the angels. These people were called Pneumatomachians—"fighters against the Spirit."

The Holy Spirit and His gifts received at least a great deal of publicity through the doctrines and activities of the Montanist sect. Montanus (born c. 150) and his "prophetesses" claimed to be mouthpieces of the Holy Spirit, the Paraclete, who revealed through them new truths on a par with Scripture. Their intense religious excitement and their rigorous intolerance toward "erring" Christians provoked opposition. Some of their beliefs and practices were rightly condemned, especially their claims to special revelations apart from Scripture. However, the Montanists did keep alive the conviction that the Spirit continues to be active in the world. In contrast, the church hierarchy took the stand that extraordinary gifts are not promised the church as a permanent legacy.

The fourth-century Arian heresy claimed that the "begotten" Son had not existed from eternity and was thus inferior to the Father. The bitter agitation that split the church climaxed at the Council of Nicea in 325, which formulated the creed that spelled out in detail the orthodox position concerning the eternal nature and full divinity of the Son. Acceptance of the Son's full divinity facilitated the same acceptance concerning the Spirit. In regard to the latter, however, the creed stated simply, "I believe in the Holy Spirit" without giving further detail. Apparently the council was content to make a full statement regarding the principal object in dispute, the doctrine concerning the Son. The brevity of the council's reference to the Spirit may, on the other hand, also reflect lack of mature understanding at this time of the nature and work of the Spirit.

In its action concerning this continuing fourth-century controversy, the Council of Constantinople in 381 added to the creed's affirmation regarding the Holy Spirit the words "the Lord and Giver of Life; who proceedeth from the Father, who with the Father and Son together is worshipped and glorified; who spake by the prophets." While this statement does not categorically state that the Spirit is of the same substance with, and equal to, the Father and the Son, the belief is strongly implied by the parallel structure of the articles on the Father, Son, and Spirit, and seemed to settle the question for the church.

B. The Medieval Church Fostered Bitter Disputes

The words "proceedeth from the

Father" just mentioned were the focus of another bitter dispute, the *"filioque"* controversy, which troubled the church for centuries. Does the Spirit proceed from the Father *alone,* from the Father *through* the Son, or from the Father *and* the Son? A council in Toledo, Spain, in 589, representing only the Western church, brought the dispute to a head by adding to the creedal words "proceedeth from the Father" the words "and the Son." This unilateral action in the West understandably antagonized the Eastern churches, which from this time on denied the procession of the Spirit from the Son. The resultant doctrinal strife, which involved primarily the "monarchy" of the Father and the place of the Son in the Godhead rather than the Holy Spirit per se, was one of the factors in the eventual permanent break between the Eastern and Western churches.

The Christian writer who exerted the most powerful influence on the Western church throughout the Middle Ages and on into the Reformation was Augustine of Hippo (354–430). He taught the divinity and personhood of the Holy Spirit and emphasized His work and gifts in the life of the believer. He taught, however, that God does not extend His grace directly, but indirectly through the church. The specific medium of grace is the sacraments, through which the Spirit is conveyed to the communicant. Only the clergy may administer the sacraments. Augustine's teachings on the meaning of human history, on the origin of evil, on grace, free will, the church, and the sacraments shaped the whole central tradition of medieval theology and exercised a profound influence on both Luther and Calvin.

These teachings presented some serious problems with regard to a valid doctrine of the Holy Spirit. Since Augustine found it difficult to leave room in his doctrine of grace for a genuine free response by man to the Spirit's gift of salvation, the role of the Spirit became part of his rigorous doctrine of predestination. This doctrine, however, was soft-pedaled in the Middle Ages in favor of Augustine's teaching regarding the sacraments, leading to an excessive preoccupation with sacramental forms. Salvation, rather than being the work of the Spirit, became in practice a matter of performing certain rituals. Also, since the clergy alone could administer the sacraments, the whole theological system channeled the network of the Spirit through the clergy. The church denied that the Spirit could teach all Christians directly through the Word of God. Thus, although the thousand years of the Middle Ages saw a great outpouring of theological discussion and writing, development of a rounded doctrine of the Holy Spirit had no high place on the theological agenda.

On the other hand, the medieval period also saw a reaction against the cold formalism, dialectic reasoning, and worldly involvement of the church establishment. Seekers after a more genuine spiritual life sought a more vital and intimate relationship to God, which often took the form of highly individualized mystical experience—a thread entwined in the history of the church from New Testament times to the present. The Spirit was pictured as the "soul" of the church—its interior principle of life, growth, unity, and holiness.

Medieval mysticism showed wide variations and contrasts—from the Christ-centeredness of Bernard of Clairvaux and the all-absorbing spiritual devotion of Thomas à Kempis to the radical concepts of Joachim of Fiore (c. 1135–1202). Joachim combined stress on the equality of the three persons of the Trinity, with division of history into an "Age of the Father," an "Age of the Son," and an imminent "Age of the Holy Spirit" when the monastery would embrace all mankind. Joachim's ideas influenced clamorous fringe groups of the late Middle Ages and thus contributed to the turbulent religious climate of the day.

In the post-Reformation period mysticism at its best was represented by Jacob

Bohme (1575-1624), who, at a time of cold religious dogmatism, was cheered by the assurance in God's Word that God is willing to give His Holy Spirit to those who ask Him. His sincere piety gave credence to his belief that in the illumination of the Spirit he could discern directly the realities of the life in God. However, mystics might easily—and frequently did—elevate feeling above knowledge and personal experience and mystical "revelations" above the Word of God. They were not apt to develop a well-balanced doctrine of the Holy Spirit understandable to the general body of Christ.

C. The Reformation Reopened a Channel for the Holy Spirit to Work

Although the person and work of the Holy Spirit were not directly a major issue in the Reformation, that movement's "three cardinal principles" were in effect a milestone in the history of the doctrine of the Spirit. The Reformation denied to the clergy the role of mediator between man and God and thus reopened the channel through which the Spirit might work directly in the heart and mind of the believer. It denied the efficacy of works in human salvation and thus revived the doctrine of regeneration by the Spirit. It stressed that the Scriptures, illuminated by the Spirit, are the only infallible authority for faith and practice, and thus it opened to laymen as well as clergy the biblical teachings regarding the person and work of the Spirit.

Protestant churches of the Reformation period and after were (and are) far from consistent in applying these cardinal truths, but on balance the Reformation was an important step in giving the Spirit His rightful place in the life of the individual and the church. In words of Protestant confessions, the Spirit draws people to God, grants saving faith, effects regeneration, works sanctification, gives assurance, and furnishes the believer with the power to live a godly life.

D. The Eighteenth and Nineteenth Centuries Saw the Rise of Counter Developments

The eighteenth century saw developments moving in diametrically opposite directions—the antibiblical rationalism of the so-called Enlightenment and the Evangelical revivals occurring under the auspices of the Holy Spirit.

The Enlightenment, or Age of Reason, rejected what cannot be grasped through man's unaided reasoning faculties. It thus rejected the supernatural—not only the supernatural events recorded in the Scriptures but the supernatural origin of the Scriptures themselves. Its God was the remote unitarian "Supreme Architect" who had created the universe but then had withdrawn from active, immediate contact with the world of men. Such a system, of course, could have no place whatever for the person of the Holy Spirit. Its effect was spiritual poverty.

But the eighteenth century also saw great revivals on the European continent, in Great Britain, and in America. In discussing these revivals in the present context—the history of the doctrine of the Holy Spirit—the most obvious and profound comment is that the revivals themselves were the work of the Spirit. Nothing else can explain their spread and power.

In contrast to the harsh and rigid dogmatism characterizing the German church at the time, Pietist movements, such as the Moravian, stressed personal faith in the triune God, the new birth as a work of the Holy Spirit, the Spirit-directed life, and a warm evangelical zeal. The role of the Holy Spirit in these revivals is well illustrated by a memorable gathering in the Moravian community of Herrnhut in Saxony in 1727. When the gathering was threatened with disunity, the Holy Spirit Himself (in the words of one of those present) made them one by an outpouring of "new love and faith toward the Savior and likewise with a burning love toward one another." A similar event took place in London twelve years later in a meeting attended by the Wesleys, George Whitefield, the Moravian leader Benjamin Ingham, and others.

The crucial role of the Holy Spirit in Wesleyan theology is well known to readers of this volume and it would be redundant to endeavor to detail it here. The earlier Arminianism had been accused, justly or unjustly, of downgrading the role of the Spirit by placing excessive faith in human ability to contribute to man's redemption. Not even its bitterest critics will claim, however, that Wesleyan doctrine deemphasizes the role of the Holy Spirit. That doctrine not only teaches that salvation is the free gift of God communicated by the Holy Spirit (an emphasis shared by all other Evangelical groups) but by its distinctive teachings concerning a second work of grace and Christian perfection brought to the church a new and greater recognition of the power and benefits of the Spirit.

The new attention to the person and work of the Holy Spirit promoted by the eighteenth-century revivals was not, however, confined to the Pietist and Methodist movements. It was evidenced also in important circles in the Church of England, in Reformed churches of Europe, and in the powerful thrust of the Great Awakening in America.

The main outline of the eighteenth-century developments just described was, in a sense, repeated in the divergent religious and cultural movements of the nineteenth century. On the one hand, advances in science and technology and the dramatic success of new inventions in improving the quality of material life produced an excessive faith in the ability of human minds and hands to produce a new Eden on earth without reliance on the Spirit of God. On the other hand, the work of the Holy Spirit was supremely evident in the great nineteenth-century revivals led by Finney, Moody, the Methodists, and others in the inauguration of the American Holiness movement and in the birth of a number of new international organizations such as the Salvation Army, the Wesleyan church, the Pilgrim church and the Church of the Nazarene, all of which strongly stressed the unique work of the Holy Spirit. This recognition of the Spirit bore fruit in the advance of the missionary thrust around the world. This was also a time when the doctrine of the Holy Spirit received new attention from theologians and biblical scholars, some of whose works still hold a high place in our studies today.

E. The Twentieth Century Marks a Revival of the Holy Spirit in the Church

The twentieth century's most noteworthy development in the history of the doctrine of the Holy Spirit has been the appearance and growth of the Pentecostal, or charismatic, movement.

Born around the turn of the century, this movement has been predominantly (but not invariably) orthodox in its beliefs concerning the major Christian doctrines. Its distinctive doctrines involve the work of the Holy Spirit in the individual and in the church. The term *Pentecostal* suggests its dynamic accent on the experience of the early Christians on the Day of Pentecost described in Acts 2. The term *charismatic* (which usually has wider application) refers to a new emphasis on the gifts *(charismata)* of the Holy Spirit, particularly speaking in tongues and divine healing. The terms also suggest a more uninhibited style of worship than is countenanced by many churches.

The movement includes new, distinctly charismatic denominations but also elements within older denominations that seek renewal of the church through fostering the gifts of the Spirit. Consequently no precise statement of doctrine applies to all groups within the movement. Most, however, consider speaking in tongues the outward sign of the baptism or infilling of the Spirit and tend to divide believers into two groups—those who are "Spirit-baptized" and those who are not.

The movement has grown phenomenally in the second half of the century, expanding from the older Pentecostal denominations to aggressive elements within the older Protestant denominations and, surprisingly, the Roman Catholic church. The movement has also experienced a remarkable geographic expansion in North America and Europe and especially through indigenous churches in Africa and Latin America. It has been described as a "fourth strand" in the Christian community, alongside Roman Catholicism, Eastern Orthodoxy, and traditional Protestantism. The growth has been attributed to the enthusiastic vitality engendered by its adherents' experience of the Holy Spirit, to the appeal of the spontaneous style of worship, to evangelistic zeal, and to freedom from the restraints of an established church hierarchy.

On the other hand, the movement has been severely criticized for its alleged divisiveness, its excessive emphasis on emotion and outward physical manifestations, its doctrinal haziness, and its failure to appreciate the debt owed to noncharismatic believers in the history of the church.

At the opposite end of the theological spectrum are the twentieth-century theological liberals. Since they deny the authoritativeness of the Scriptures, they conduct their theological studies within a frame of reference different from that of Evangelical scholars. Priding themselves on intellectual freedom, they have not developed a consistent pattern of belief regarding the Holy Spirit. Their tendency, however, has been toward a unitarian position: God is one, though His manifestations are many. As in past centuries, denial of the deity of Christ has inevitably led to denial of the personhood of the Holy Spirit. The divinity of both Son and Spirit has typically been seen as a later mutation of the primitive experience of God in Christ. Attributing personhood to the Spirit may be merely a "figure of speech" on a level with personification of qualities such as Love and Truth. Or the words "Father, Son, and Holy Spirit" may be merely theological terms for the Christian's personal experience of God. Rather than recognizing the supernatural work of the Spirit, liberals tend to seek psychological or other human explanations for mental or emotional states. The spiritual paucity of such beliefs regarding the Spirit has contributed to much disillusionment with the entire liberal position in recent years.

Noeorthodoxy developed as a conscious reaction to the theological flimsiness of extreme liberalism and occupies a theological position somewhere between liberalism and traditional Christianity. Since most of these scholars do not accept the absolute authority of the Scriptures, they have been free to develop their own doctrines of the Holy Spirit. Many use the terms of traditional Christianity but give them new meanings. Some affirm the deity of the Spirit in much the same way as the early Fathers did. Others reject His personhood in much the same way as do the liberals. Neoorthodox theologians have tended to concentrate on the person of Christ to the exclusion of the Spirit. With the passing from the theological scene of many of its celebrated spokesmen, neo-orthodox influence has tended to wane.

Like the believers of the first century, Christians today know the Father as the Planner, not only of creation but also of the divine pattern for human redemption. They know the Son as the Purchaser, who carried through that plan on the cross and who lives today as the heavenly Intercessor. And today they, like the believers of two thousand years ago, know the Holy Spirit as the Implementer of that plan. They are conscious of a Friend who drew them to the Savior and walks beside them and makes available in their daily lives the resources of divine grace.

NOTES

[1] *Funk & Wagnalls Standard College Dictionary* (New York: Funk & Wagnalls, 1977).

[2] Charles Caldwell Ryrie, *The Holy Spirit* (Chicago: Moody, 1973), p. 119.

[3] H. Orton Wiley, *Christian Theology* (Kansas City, Mo.: Beacon Hill, 1960), 2:308.

[4] Herbert Lockyer, *The Holy Spirit of God* (Nashville: Thomas Nelson, 1981), p. 22.

[5] Ralph A. Herring, *God Being My Helper* (Nashville: Broadman, 1955), p. 7.

[6] Lockyer, *Holy Spirit of God*, p. 26.

[7] Samuel L. Brengle, *Resurrection Life and Power* (Atlanta: The Salvation Army, 1978), p. 107.

[8] William Edward Biederwolf, *A Help to the Study of the Holy Spirit* (Grand Rapids: Zondervan, 1936). p. 101.

[9] Ralph Earle, *Wesleyan Bible Commentary* (Grand Rapids: Eerdmans, 1965), 4:296.

[10] Charles W. Carter, *Wesleyan Bible Commentary* (Grand Rapids: Eerdmans, 1965), 5:384.

[11] Samuel Chadwick, *The Way to Pentecost* (Fort Washington, Pa.: Christian Literature Crusade, 1976), p. 25.

[12] John Williams, *The Holy Spirit, Lord and Life-Giver* (Neptune, N.J.: Loizeaux, 1980), p. 69.

[13] Andrew W. Blackwood, Jr., *The Holy Spirit in Your Life* (Grand Rapids: Baker, 1961), pp. 25, 27.

[14] Ryrie, *Holy Spirit*, p. 45.

[15] Wiley, *Christian Theology*, 2:308.

[16] Ibid., 2:324.

[17] H. E. Dana and Julius R. Mantey, *A Manual Grammar of the Greek New Testament* (New York: Macmillan, 1947), p. 214.

[18] George Turner and Julius R. Mantey, *The Gospel of John* (Grand Rapids: Eerdmans, 1964), p. 159.

[19] Herring, *God Being My Helper*, p. 18.

[20] *The Analytical Greek Lexicon* (New York: Harper and Brothers, n.d.), p. 382.

[21] Walter Thomas Conner, *The Work of the Holy Spirit* (Nashville: Broadman, 1940), p. 95.

[22] J. C. Ryle, *Ryle's Expository Thoughts on the Gospels* (Grand Rapids: Zondervan, 1956), 4:303.

[23] Charles W. Carter, *The Person and Ministry of the Holy Spirit* (Grand Rapids: Baker, 1974), p. 90.

[24] Merrill C. Tenney, *John: The Gospel of Belief* (Grand Rapids: Eerdmans, 1951), p. 87.

[25] Laurence W. Wood, *Pentecostal Grace* (Wilmore, Ky.: Asbury, 1980), p. 17.

[26] G. C. Morgan, *The Spirit of God* (Grand Rapids: Eerdmans, 1948), p. 109.

[27] Dale W. Brown, *Flamed by the Spirit* (Elgin, Ill.: Brethren, 1978), p. 45.

[28] Frederick Dale Bruner, *A Theology of the Holy Spirit* (Grand Rapids: Eerdmans, 1970), pp. 162, 171.

[29] Jamieson, Fausset, and Brown, *Commentary on the Whole Bible* (Grand Rapids: Zondervan, n.d.), p. 174.

[30] Michael Harper, *Live by the Spirit* (Ann Arbor, Mich.: Servant, 1979), p. 20.

[31] Lockyer, *Holy Spirit of God*, p. 67.

[32] A. W. Tozer, *The Divine Conquest* (Old Tappan, N.J.: Revell, 1950), p. 121.

[33] William Barclay, *The Promise of the Spirit* (Philadelphia: Westminster, 1960), p. 34.

[34] Ibid., p. 35.

[35] George Williams, *The Student's Commentary on the Holy Scriptures* (Grand Rapids: Kregel, 1949), p. 1011.

[36] Ryle, *Expository Thoughts on the Gospel*, 4:303.

[37] Dana and Mantey, *A Manual Grammar*, p. 486.

[38] W. T. Purkiser, Richard S. Taylor, and Willard H. Taylor, *God, Man, and Salvation: A Biblical Theology* (Kansas City, Mo.: Beacon Hill, 1977), p. 486.

[39] Wood, *Pentecostal Grace*, p. 15.

[40] Blackwood, *Holy Spirit in Your Life*, p. 146.

[41] W. T. Purkiser, *Proclaiming the Spirit* (Kansas City, Mo.: Beacon Hill, 1975), p. 100.

[42] Archibald Thomas Robertson, *Word Pictures in the New Testament* (New York: Long and Smith, 1932), 5:253.

[43] Jamieson, Fausset, and Brown, *Commentary*, p. 156.

[44] Robertson, *Word Pictures*, 5:264.

[45] R. A. Torrey, *The Holy Spirit* (Old Tappan, N.J.: Revell, 1927), p. 51.

[46] G. Abbott-Smith, *Manual Greek Lexicon of the New Testament* (Montreal [unlisted publisher], 1936), p. 144.

[47] J. Gresham Machen, *New Testament Greek for Beginners* (New York: Macmillan, 1947), p. 85.

[48] Blackwood, *Holy Spirit in Your Life*, p. 69.

[49] Abbott-Smith, *Manual Greek Lexicon*, p. 258.

[50] Torrey, *Holy Spirit*, p. 59.

[51] Chadwick, *Way to Pentecost*, p. 79.

[52] John R. W. Stott, *Baptism and Fullness* (Downers Grove, Ill.: InterVarsity, 1977), p. 48.

[53] Wiley, *Christian Theology*, 2:321.

54. Dick Mohrman, *Let It Show* (Chappaqua, N.Y.: Christian Herald, 1979), p. 51.

55. Samuel L. Brengle, *When the Holy Ghost Is Come* (Atlanta, Ga.: Salvation Army, 1978), p. 55.

56. Williams, *Holy Spirit, Lord and Life-Giver,* p. 184.

57. Laurence W. Wood, "Exegetical-Theological Reflections on the Baptism with the Holy Spirit," *Wesleyan Theological Journal,* vol. 14, no. 2 (Fall 1979), p. 53.

58. Torrey, *Holy Spirit,* p. 112.

59. Robert A. Mattke, "The Baptism of the Holy Spirit as Related to the Work of Entire Sanctification," *Wesleyan Theological Journal,* vol. 5, no. 1 (Spring 1970), p. 28.

60. Richard S. Taylor, *Life in the Spirit* (Kansas City, Mo.: Beacon Hill, 1966), p. 79.

61. Stott, *Baptism and Fullness,* p. 29.

62. Bruner, *Theology of the Holy Spirit,* p. 216.

63. Williams, *Holy Spirit, Lord and Life-Giver,* p. 185.

64. Chadwick, *Way to Pentecost,* p. 36.

65. Wood, *Pentecostal Grace,* p. 33.

66. Herring, *God Being My Helper,* p. 124.

67. Purkiser, *Proclaiming the Spirit,* p. 12.

68. Ryrie, *Holy Spirit,* p. 78.

69. Stott, *Baptism and Fullness,* p. 39.

70. Carter, *Wesleyan Bible Commentary,* 5:202.

71. J. Gresham Machen, *New Testament Greek for Beginners* (New York: Macmillan, 1947), pp. 48-49.

72. Williams, *Student's Commentary on the Holy Scriptures,* p. 888; Robertson, *Word Pictures in the New Testament,* 4:171; Carter, *Person and Ministry of the Holy Spirit,* p. 202; Williams, *Holy Spirit, Lord and Life-Giver,* p. 180.

73. Williams, *Holy Spirit, Lord and Life-Giver,* p. 183.

74. Robertson, *Word Pictures,* 5:59.

75. Turner and Mantey, *Gospel of John,* p. 105.

76. Harper, *Live by the Spirit,* pp. 17, 18.

77. Wiley, *Christian Theology,* 3:180.

78. Bruner, *Theology of the Holy Spirit,* p. 193.

79. Williams, *Holy Spirit, Lord and Life-Giver,* p. 198.

80. Jamieson, Fausset, and Brown, *Commentary on the Whole Bible,* p. 239.

81. Williams, *The Student's Commentary,* p. 925.

82. Mattke, "Baptism of the Holy Spirit," p. 23.

83. Ralph Earle, *Evangelical Commentary on Mark* (Grand Rapids: Zondervan, 1957), p. 30.

84. Strong, *Systematic Theology,* p. 340.

85. Williams, *Holy Spirit, Lord and Life-Giver,* p. 77.

86. Ralph Earle and Charles W. Carter, *Evangelical Commentary: The Acts of the Apostles* (Grand Rapids: Zondervan, 1959), p. 102.

87. Carter, *Wesleyan Bible Commentary,* 4:530.

88. Wiley, *Christian Theology,* 2:330.

89. Carter, *Person and Ministry of the Holy Spirit,* p. 232.

90. Chadwick, *Way to Pentecost,* p. 29.

91. Harper, *Live by the Spirit,* p. 121.

92. Wiley, *Christian Theology,* 2:317.

93. Kenneth Cain Kinghorn, *Gifts of the Spirit* (Nashville: Abingdon, 1976), p. 28.

94. Stott, *Baptism and Fullness,* p. 86.

95. Purkiser, *Proclaiming the Spirit,* p. 21.

96. Ibid., p. 30.

97. Ryrie, *Holy Spirit,* p. 85.

98. C. Peter Wagner, *Your Spiritual Gifts* (Ventura, Calif.: Regal, 1980), p. 52.

99. Kinghorn, *Gifts of the Spirit,* p. 31.

100. Ibid., p. 29.

101. Purkiser, *Proclaiming the Spirit,* p. 36.

102. Wagner, *Your Spiritual Gifts,* p. 86.

103. Oral Roberts, *My Personal Comments* (Tulsa, Okla.: Oral Roberts Evangelistic Association, 1981), pp. 105-6.

104. Taylor, *Life in the Spirit,* p. 117.

105. Ryrie, *Holy Spirit,* p. 84.

106. Carter, *Person and Ministry of the Holy Spirit,* p. 280.

107. Stott, *Baptism and Fullness,* pp. 99ff.

108. Wagner, *Your Spiritual Gifts,* pp. 86-87.

109. Stott, *Baptism and Fullness,* p. 90.

110. W. E. Vine, *An Expository Dictionary of New Testament Words* (Westwood, N.J.: Revell, 1958), p. 108.

111. Wiley, *Christian Theology,* 2:324.

112. Williams, *Holy Spirit, Lord and Life-Giver,* p. 172.

113. Turner and Mantey, *Gospel of John,* p. 296.

114. Tenney, *Gospel of Belief,* p. 228.

115. *The Salvation Army Handbook of Doctrine* (St. Albans, Herts: Campfield, 1969), p. 96.

116. Mohrman, *Let It Show,* p. 37.

117. John Wesley, *A Plain Account of Christian Perfection* (London: Epworth, 1952), p. 42.

118. Williams, *Holy Spirit, Lord and Life-Giver,* pp. 169ff.

[119]Carter, *Person and Ministry of the Holy Spirit*, pp. 293–300.

[120]Ryle, *Expository Thoughts on the Gospels*, 4:173.

[121]*Salvation Army Handbook of Doctrine*, p. 154.

[122]Thomas F. Zimmerman, "Priorities and Beliefs of Pentecostals," *Christianity Today* (September 4, 1981), p. 36.

DISCUSSION QUESTIONS

1. Enumerate reasons why it is important that the personage of the Holy Spirit be recognized and defined.
2. Why is the divinity of the Holy Spirit difficult for some to accept? What is the importance of this acceptance?
3. Discuss the fact and possible reasons why symbolic representation of the Godhead is essentially limited to the Holy Spirit.
4. There are those who see in John 3:5 the foundation for "baptismal regeneration," i.e., becoming saved by means of baptism. Discuss the theology of this.
5. Various symbols illumine various aspects of the Spirit. Which speak to the source of life? Which to the quality of life? Which mainly to the work of the Spirit? Which to the character of the Spirit?
6. What is the importance to you of all members of the Godhead being involved in human redemption? Discuss the relationship of One to the Other in this divine project. What does this say to you regarding the doctrine of the Trinity?
7. Considering Hebrews 11:39–40, compare the believer's relationship toward the Holy Spirit under the old and the new covenants.
8. Choose two of Christ's Paraclete "teachings" as being, in your estimate, the most important, and give reasons for your choice.
9. Considering the approximate dates of its appearing, what events or periods in the history of God's people was "the promise of the Father" made and then renewed during the centuries? Can you find any pattern?
10. In what ways are the "power" and the "witness," associated by Jesus with the baptism with the Holy Spirit, related one to the other?
11. In your estimation what is the importance of the fact that, while not every gift of the Spirit is available to every believer, each aspect of the fruit of the Spirit is? Discuss the results of this in the believer's spiritual life and in his service.

RECOMMENDATIONS FOR FURTHER READING

Agnew, Milton S. *The Holy Spirit: Friend and Counselor*. Kansas City, Mo.: Beacon Hill, 1980.

Blackwood, Andrew W., Jr. *The Holy Spirit in Your Life*. Grand Rapids: Baker, 1961.

Carter, Charles W. *The Person and Ministry of the Holy Spirit*. Grand Rapids: Baker, 1974.

Harper, Michael. *Live by the Spirit*. Ann Arbor, Mich.: Servant, 1979.

Kinghorn, Kenneth Cain. *Gifts of the Spirit*. Nashville: Abingdon, 1976.

Lockyer, Herbert. *The Holy Spirit of God*. Nashville: Thomas Nelson, 1981.

Purkiser, W. T. *Proclaiming the Spirit*. Kansas City, Mo.: Beacon Hill, 1975.

Stott, John R. W. *Baptism and Fullness*. Downers Grove, Ill.: InterVarsity, 1977.

Taylor, Richard S. *Life in the Spirit*. Kansas City, Mo.: Beacon Hill, 1966.

Wagner, C. Peter. *Your Spiritual Gifts*. Ventura, Calif.: Regal, 1980.

Williams, John. *The Holy Spirit, Lord and Life-Giver*. Neptune, N.J.: Loizeaux, 1980.

Wood, Laurence W. *Pentecostal Grace*. Wilmore, Ky.: Asbury, 1980.

BIBLIOGRAPHY

Abbott-Smith, G. *Manual Greek Lexicon of the New Testament*. Montreal (unlisted publisher), 1936.

Agnew, Milton S. *The Holy Spirit: Friend and Counselor*. Kansas City, Mo.: Beacon Hill, 1980.

Analytical Greek Lexicon. New York: Harper and Brothers, n.d.

Barclay, William. *The Promise of the Spirit*. Philadelphia: Westminster, 1960.

Biederwolf, William Edward. *A Help to the Study of the Holy Spirit*. Grand Rapids: Zondervan, 1936.

Blackwood, Andrew W., Jr. *The Holy Spirit in Your Life*. Grand Rapids: Baker, 1961.

Brengle, Samuel Logan. *Resurrection Life and Power*. Atlanta: The Salvation Army, 1978.

_____. *When the Holy Ghost Is Come*. Atlanta: The Salvation Army, 1978.

Brown, Dale W. *Flamed by the Spirit*. Elgin, Ill.: Brethren Press, 1978.

Bruner, Frederick Dale. *A Theology of the Holy Spirit*. Grand Rapids: Eerdmans, 1970.

Carter, Charles W. *The Person and Ministry of the Holy Spirit*. Grand Rapids: Baker, 1974.

Carter, Charles W., ed. *Wesleyan Bible Commentary*. 7 vols. Grand Rapids: Eerdmans, 1964–1969.

Carter, Charles W., and Earle, Ralph. *The Evangelical Bible Commentary, The Acts of the Apostles*. Grand Rapids: Zondervan, 1959.

Chadwick, Samuel. *The Way to Pentecost*. Fort Washington, Pa.: Christian Literature Crusade, 1975.

Conner, Walter Thomas. *The Work of the Holy Spirit*. Nashville: Broadman, 1940.

Dana, H. E., and Mantey, Julius R. *A Manual Grammar of the Greek New Testament*. New York: Macmillan, 1947.

Earle, Ralph. *Evangelical Commentary on Mark*. Grand Rapids: Zondervan, 1957.

Funk & Wagnalls Standard College Dictionary. New York: Funk & Wagnalls, 1977.

Harper, Michael. *Live by the Spirit*. Ann Arbor, Mich.: Servant, 1979.

Herring, Ralph A. *God Being My Helper*. Nashville: Broadman, 1955.

Jamieson, Fausset, and Brown. *Commentary on the Whole Bible* Grand Rapids: Zondervan, n.d.

Kinghorn, Kenneth Cain. *Gifts of the Spirit*. Nashville: Abingdon, 1976.

Lockyer, Herbert. *The Holy Spirit of God*. Nashville: Thomas Nelson, 1981.

Machen, J. Gresham. *New Testament Greek for Beginners*. New York: Macmillan, 1947.

Mattke, Robert A. "The Baptism of the Holy Spirit as Related to the Work of Entire Sanctification," *Wesleyan Theological Journal*, vol. 5, no. 1 (Spring 1970).

Mohrman, Dick. *Let It Show*. Chappaqua, N.Y.: Christian Herald, 1979.

Morgan, J. P. *The Spirit of God*. Grand Rapids: Eerdmans, 1948.

Pierson, A. T. *The Acts of the Holy Spirit*. Harrisburg, Pa.: Christian Publications, 1980.

Purkiser, W. T. *Proclaiming the Spirit*. Kansas City, Mo.: Beacon Hill, 1975.

Purkiser, W. T.; Taylor, Richard S.; Taylor, Willard H. *God, Man and Salvation: A Biblical Theology*. Kansas City, Mo.: Beacon Hill, 1977.

Roberts, Oral. *My Personal Comments*. Tulsa, Okla.: Oral Roberts Evangelistic Association, 1981.

Robertson, Archibald Thomas. *Word Pictures in the New Testament*. New York: Long and Smith, 1932.

Ryle, J. C. *Ryle's Expository Thoughts on the Gospels*. Grand Rapids: Zondervan, 1956.

Ryrie, Charles Caldwell. *The Holy Spirit*. Chicago: Moody, 1973.

Salvation Army Handbook of Doctrine, The. St. Albans, Herts: Campfield, 1969.

Stott, John R. W. *Baptism and Fullness*. Downers Grove, Ill.: InterVarsity, 1977.

Strong, Augustus Hopkins. *Systematic Theology*. Chicago: Judson, 1947.

Taylor, Richard S. *Life in the Spirit*. Kansas City, Mo.: Beacon Hill, 1966.

Tenney, Merrill C. *John: The Gospel of Belief*. Grand Rapids: Eerdmans, 1951.

Torrey, R. A. *The Holy Spirit*. Old Tappan, N.J.: Revell, 1927.

Tozer, A. W. *The Divine Conquest*. Old Tappan, N.J.: Revell, 1950.

Turner, George Allen, and Mantey, Julius R. *The Gospel of John*. Grand Rapids: Eerdmans, 1964.

Vine, W. E. *An Expository Dictionary of New Testament Words*. Westwood, N.J.: Revell, 1958.

Wagner, C. Peter. *Your Spiritual Gifts*. Ventura, Calif.: Regal, 1980.

Wesley, John. *A Plain Account of Christian Perfection*. London: Epworth, 1952.

Wiley, H. Orton. *Christian Theology*. 3 vols. Kansas City, Mo.: Beacon Hill, 1960.

Williams, George. *The Student's Commentary on the Holy Scriptures*. Grand Rapids: Kregel, 1949.

Williams, John. *The Holy Spirit, Lord and Life-Giver*. Neptune, N.J.: Loizeaux, 1980.

Wood, Laurence W. "Exegetical-Theological Reflections on the Baptism With the Holy Spirit," *Wesleyan Theological Journal*. Vol. 14, no. 2 (Fall 1979).

———. *Pentecostal Grace*. Wilmore, Ky.: Asbury, 1980.

CHAPTER 12

INITIAL SALVATION:
The Redemptive Grace of God in Christ

R. Larry Shelton

R. Larry Shelton is Director of the School of Religion and Professor of Historical Theology and Interpretation, Seattle Pacific University. From Asbury Theological Seminary he received his M.Div. and Th.M. degrees and from Fuller Theological Seminary his Th.D. degree. He served for five years as Associate Professor of Religion at Azusa Pacific College and was for two years assistant pastor of First Wesleyan Church in High Point, North Carolina. He is an elder in Pacific Northwest Conference of the Free Methodist Church.

He has coedited A Biblical Inquiry Into Soteriology, *vol. 1 of Wesleyan Perspectives, and has had numerous articles published in various journals. He is a member of the Wesleyan Theological Society, the American Society of Church History, and the Society of Biblical Literature.*

CONTENTS

INTRODUCTION / 473

I. THE RELATIONAL AND EXPERIENTIAL FOUNDATION OF SALVATION / 474
  A. The Personal Character of God / 474
    1. He is a living God / 474
    2. His names indicate His personality / 475
    3. Knowledge of Him involves intimate relationship / 475
  B. The Interpersonal Nature of the Divine-Human Relationship / 476
    1. The definition of the covenant / 476
    2. The institution of the covenant / 478
    3. The explanation of the covenant / 480

II. THE NEED FOR SALVATION / 483

III. THE PROVISION FOR SALVATION / 483
  A. The Grace of God / 483
    1. Old Testament emphases / 483
    2. New Testament emphases / 484
    3. Theological implications / 485
  B. The Atonement of Christ / 485
    1. The New Testament understanding / 486
    2. The benefits of the atonement / 491
  C. The Appropriation of Salvation / 496
    1. Faith / 496
    2. Repentance and conversion / 498
  D. A Survey of Atonement Theories / 499
    1. Ransom / 500
    2. Satisfaction / 500
    3. Moral influence / 500
    4. Penal substitution / 501
    5. Governmental / 502

IV. ALTERNATIVE MODELS OF SALVATION / 505
  A. Theological / 506
  B. Psychological / 506

V. CONCLUSION / 507

NOTES / 508

DISCUSSION QUESTIONS / 513

RECOMMENDATIONS FOR FURTHER READING / 513

BIBLIOGRAPHY / 514

INITIAL SALVATION

The Redemptive Grace of God in Christ

INTRODUCTION

The basic need of the human race is the restoration of fellowship with God. Created by a personal God and alienated by the Fall, humanity stands in need of the reconciliation provided by God through Jesus Christ. The biblical concepts that express salvation are essentially interpersonal in character and reflect the overcoming of the alienation and guilt of sin as well as the establishment of a right relationship with God. The central paradigm of this saving relationship in Scripture is the covenant in both its cultic and its interpersonal elements as understood and expressed in the life of the community. Other models of Israel's relationship with God are used, such as the images of Israel as Yahweh's son (Exod. 4:22-23) and Israel as the bride or wife of Yahweh (Jer. 2:2-3). However, the covenant analogy is the most prominent description of the relationship between God and His people, at least in the Old Testament. In spite of the impersonal concepts sometimes used by the Old Testament to convey a sense of the majesty and activity of God, the preponderance of images reflects the aspects of personality that characterize Yahweh. Although He is described as "light" (Ps. 104:2; Ezek. 1:27-28), "fire" (Exod. 19:18; Deut. 4:32, 36), and "wind" or "spirit" (Hag. 2:5; Zech. 4:6), the most consistent understanding sees Him as planning, willing, speaking, and interacting personally with humanity.[1]

The New Testament concept of salvation is focused on the Incarnation and reflects the interpersonal relationship with God through Christ in such terms as union with Christ, reconciliation, adoption, and justification. The covenant relationship between God and His people is thus central to the entire biblical message of salvation.

In approaching the biblical foundations of this concept, it is important to consider the entire canonical witness of Scripture. This requires a methodology that recognizes the unity of the Testaments and deals adequately with the theological unity of the whole canon. The biblical material will be considered in this historical setting with respect to its original message, but will also be examined with respect to its present application to and usage in the church. If we use the covenant relationship as the basic hermeneutical reference point for the doctrine of salvation, the insertion of organizing theological principles that are external to the canonical text will be minimized in the sections that examine the biblical materials.²

In the treatment of salvation from a covenant perspective, the centrality of Christ is certainly not minimized, but gains clearer focus when seen in the covenant context. Furthermore, the covenant perspective emphasizes not only the need of the individual for salvation but also makes one aware of the implications of salvation for the community and thus explicates the salvation of the individual in relationship to the community of faith. This perspective also recognizes Israel's obligations toward Yahweh and thus protects the integrity of the covenant relationship from undisciplined subjectivity by the norms of the written Law—the Torah.

I. THE RELATIONAL AND EXPERIENTIAL FOUNDATION OF SALVATION

A clear understanding of God as a personal Being who enters into a covenant relationship with those created in His image is essential to the biblical teaching on salvation. The transcendent God is actively and personally interested in His creatures and communicates and interacts with them. In the Old Testament, Yahweh initiates a continuing series of events leading to Israel's salvation. His direction of Abraham, the event of the Exodus, and the conquest of the Promised Land all focus on the dynamic and continuing interpersonal relationship between Israel and Yahweh, her covenant God.³ Likewise, in the New Testament the Incarnation—"God was reconciling the world to himself in Christ" (2 Cor. 5:19)—reveals in Jesus the personhood of the Father in historical and experiential terms. Thus the personal character of God and His interpersonal covenant relationship with humanity are the foundations for a biblical soteriology.

A. The Personal Character of God

In the Old Testament, God is seen as transcendent both qualitatively and quantitatively. However, He reveals Himself within history and interacts in the personal affairs of humanity in such a way that His transcendence in no way diminishes His personal and relational character. The transcendence of God cannot be depicted in static representations of stone or wood nor conceived of intellectually in ways that diminish His personality.⁴

1. He is a living God *('el chay)* Yahweh is differentiated from other gods by His living character. The feebleness of the gods of other nations is contrasted to the vitality of the God of Israel. It is because He is alive that He is capable of intervening decisively in history, as Elijah emphasized (1 Kings 17:1). The dependability of His threats or promises is based on His own affirmation of life: "As surely as I live, I will bring down on his head my oath" (Ezek. 17:19). Furthermore, it is because God lives that He is seen as the source of life (Jer. 38:16) and the fountain of life (Ps. 36:9).⁵ All life springs from Him. It is because He has created the world, and because all things live by His power, that He has made Himself accessible. His encounter with humanity in paradise (Gen. 2-3), His answers to prayer (Pss. 20:7; 22:21), and His communication with the prophets, as well as His works in history and nature reflect His living personality.⁶

It is also the aspect of life that forms the basis for God's eternity. The Israelites perceived the active, living aspect of God before they had any perception that He was eternal.⁷

The faith of Israel in a living God is vividly expressed in the anthropomorphic language of the Old Testament. Michaeli observes that "it is because God is living that one can speak of him as a living man, but also in speaking of him as a human being one recalls continually that he is living."⁸ Even though Israel could not make visible representations of God and recognized that there were limits to the conception of God as man, He is described as speaking (Gen. 1:3), hearing (Exod.

16:12), seeing (Gen. 6:12), smelling (1 Sam. 26:19), laughing (Pss. 2:4; 59:8). He is also said to have eyes (Amos 9:4), hands (Ps. 139:5), arms (Isa. 51:9; 52:10; Jer. 27:5), ears (Isa. 22:14), and feet (Nah. 1:3; Isa. 63:3). He is often described as having such emotions as joy (Zeph. 3:17), disgust (Lev. 20:23), and jealousy (Exod. 20:5; Deut. 5:9).[9]

Thus the Israelite understanding of God as personal is reflected by the scriptural emphasis on Him as a living God who is personally concerned with the world.

2. His names indicate His personality
In the Near East the function of a name involves the expression of the person's very being. A name is not simply a means of labeling a person but it can also become a sort of *alter ego*. The importance the Israelites gave to the names of God, particularly the names used in connection with the covenant, indicate that they perceived God to be explicitly personal in character. God's proclamation of His divine name is seen as His act of offering Himself in fellowship, and the use of His name reflects the people's assurance that God will be present with them. By the revelation of His name, He opens to the worshipers a means of access to Himself.[10] Furthermore, the meaning of the personal names of God reflects the personal character of the God they designate. They reflect the divine activity on behalf of and in communication with the worshipers.[11]

The generic name of God in the Semitic world is *El* or its plural, *Elohim*. Its essential meaning is the idea of power or the source of life and being. It is this name that Genesis uses to refer to God as Creator. The form *El,* "the Mighty One," reflects the strength of God and the One whose glory the heavens declare (Ps. 19:1). He is worthy to be worshiped and praised and is the One to whom we can turn for help in distress.[12]

The proper name of the God of Israel is Yahweh, or Jehovah. This name is connected to the verb *hāyāh* ("to be") and the use of a personal proper name indicates that Israel knew Him as a personal being and wished to recognize Him as distinct from other gods. This name literally indicates the being of God as a personal presence.[13] This name was used whenever individuals wished to be assured of God's nearness and help. By giving Israel this name, Yahweh opened to them His very person and provided them a means of access to Himself[14] as their covenant God.

Although the precise meaning of the name is obscure, it is composed of the four consonants YHWH, the "tetragrammaton," and seems to indicate "I am, was, and will be" or as Yahweh explained it to Moses: "I AM WHO I AM" (Exod. 3:14). Yahweh is God who is present with the worshiper to be what is required to meet the needs at hand.[15] This name also reflects an eternal or eschatological emphasis: "I, the LORD—with the first of them and with the last—I am he" (Isa. 41:4 NIV); "I am the first and I am the last" (Isa. 48:12 NIV). In contrast to the nothingness of the idols, Yahweh is the complete and eternal presence who knows no boundaries and no end.[16] The name also sometimes connotes existence and endurance and represents Yahweh as Creator and Father (Gen. 49:25; Deut. 32:6).[17]

Yahweh thus reveals Himself to Israel through His covenant name and, as the "Self-existent One," He pledges by His name to uphold the promises He has made that Israel will be His people and He their God. He becomes known in His personal, covenant relationship and through His name reveals His spiritual and personal activity.[18]

3. Knowledge of Him involves intimate relationship Religious faith in the Old Testament involves knowledge of God in the intimate sense of communion. This communion has similarities to the kind of intimacy found in sexual union—a profound "knowing" of another person. It also is very closely related to *ḥesed,* the solidarity and fidelity that underlies the keeping of the covenant.[19]

The "knowledge of God" does not

mean having an ontological theory about Him, but enjoying an existential relationship with Him. Porteous says, "The intimate response of man's whole being to God is what the Bible means by knowledge of God."[20] This communion is not intellectual knowledge only, but personal knowledge that inspires a response of love. It involves the reverence called for by the "fear of the Lord." In this intimate relationship there is immediate spiritual communion between God and the worshiper, and this is certainly the interpersonal faith relationship found also in the New Testament when on the basis of salvation the believer experiences this intimate interpersonal relationship with God.[21]

This spiritual knowledge of God was received by Israel in a special way through the covenant. Through God's revelation to the prophets and by His grace Israel was brought into this communion, and although the nation enjoyed the dialogue that was a part of it, Israel was to remember that God's holiness had to be reverenced and not to be presumed upon because He had chosen to reveal Himself intimately. This tension is expressed by Isaiah's encounter with Yahweh when His self-revelation is balanced by Isaiah's recognition of His holiness (Isa. 6).

Not only did Yahweh enter into the covenant relationship with Israel, but His *ḥesed* guaranteed His faithfulness to keep the relationship and obligations promised in it.[22] Thus God's mercy and lovingkindness along with Israel's obedience brought Creator and nation together in a relationship of love and communion. The transcendent holy God of Abraham, Isaac, and Jacob was also the Shepherd of Israel who revealed Himself through His grace to His people.

B. The Interpersonal Nature of the Divine-Human Relationship

The basic character of the religion of the Old Testament is interpersonal. Israel was not united to Yahweh primarily by her trust in the promises of the covenant when divorced from Yahweh Himself, nor by her faithful performance of the ritual prescribed by the Law, but she was united by the personal character of the interaction between the Creator and His elect nation as expressed in the interpersonal covenant relationship.

1. The definition of the covenant
Before proceeding to the theme of the interpersonal relationships in the covenant, it would be wise to notice the meaning of *berith*. The importance of this word is indicated by its frequency of usage in the Bible. It is used 278 times and is rendered *diatheke* in the Septuagint in all passages except two. These exceptions are in Deuteronomy 9:15, where the Greek is *martyrion,* and in 1 Kings 11:11, where *entolē* is used.[23] Davidson says that the term *berith* occurs nearly 300 times in the Old Testament.[24]

The etymology of *berith* is somewhat unclear. The verbal root behind it is *baraya,* but the meaning of this root is uncertain. Frequently, however, *baraya* has been related to the Akkadian *baru,* "to fetter."[25] Davidson concurs that the word *bind* more properly fits *berith.*[26] *Berith* is believed by some to be derived from the Hebrew *barah,* which carries the meaning "to cut," or "to cleave." In the intensive stems *barah* takes on the meaning of "to eat."[27] Brown, Driver, and Briggs translate *barah* as "eat."[28] The intensive form of *barah* also means "to choose," and this conveys the idea of cutting and separating. *Berith* may have originally meant "to cut" and may have later come to include "to choose or select."[29]

The ceremony of making a covenant is commonly called *karath berith,* or cutting a covenant. This may suggest a covenant by sacrifice as in Psalm 50:5. The Sinaitic covenant was enacted and ratified by the offering of sacrifices (Exod. 24:1-8). The covenant with Abraham in Genesis 15 reflects the covenant ceremony in which slain animals were cut in two and each half laid over against the other. A flaming torch, symbolizing the Lord as one party to the covenant, then passed between the pieces.[30] This ritual reflects the traditional pattern in the making of covenants. E. Kautzch says:

> There can be no doubt that *berith* belonged at first to secular speech and meant "dissection;" that is, the dissection of one or more sacrificial animals, so that the parties concluding the agreement passed between the pieces and invoked upon themselves the fate of these animals in case of a breach of covenant.[31]

It seems, then, that "cut," "choose," and "bind" are all involved in the concept of *berith*. The cutting may indicate the division of the victim as a symbol of the proposed bond between the parties of the covenant, and the binding may connote the obligations and trust the covenant imposed on both parties.[32]

Although the covenant relationship often involved individuals of equal status (Gen. 21, 26; 1 Sam. 20; 2 Sam. 9), the religious *berith* involved a relationship between God and another party.[33] Mendenhall shows that there is a marked resemblance in form between the Mosaic covenant and the Hittite suzerainty treaty in the second millennium B.C.[34] This type of covenant was a political agreement between a suzerain and his vassal. The purpose of the suzerainty treaty was to establish a firm relationship of mutual support between the two parties. Although the treaty established a relationship between the two kings, only the vassal took the oath of obedience. It seems that the vassal was obliged to trust in the benevolence of the sovereign and in his faithfulness to protect and deliver him. In this relationship of trust and obligation the covenant form expressed a personal relationship rather than an objective, impersonal statement of law.[35]

In the Bible there are two covenants that follow the form of the suzerainty treaty, and these are found in the Decalogue and in Joshua 24. The covenant of Moses imposed specific obligations on the tribes or clans,[36] while also binding Yahweh to specific obligations, although the covenant viewed the past acts of Yahweh in history as abundant evidence of His protection and support of Israel. The form of the prologue, stipulations, and witnesses of the covenant in Joshua 24 correspond closely with the form of the suzerainty treaty.[37]

In view of the form of the suzerainty treaty and its similarity to the pattern of the Decalogue, one sees that the *berith* at Sinai was bilateral. It was Yahweh who initiated it, and it became a mutual agreement by the people's believing response. It is important to emphasize here that the covenant was not simply Yahweh's pledging of Himself, but it required ratification by Israel's response to it. It was conditioned on obedience; it was an agreement that God had offered freely and that He could withdraw from the nation at any time it refused to be conformed to His will.[38] True, the covenant was Yahweh's agreement, but it involved the nation's response to its stipulations. When the book of the covenant was read, the people replied, "All that the LORD has spoken we will do, and we will be obedient!" (Exod. 24:7). After they had agreed to be obedient to its demands, Moses sprinkled the blood on Israel to seal the covenant and said, "Behold, the blood of the covenant, which the LORD has made with you in accordance with all these words" (Exod. 24:8). Milton realized that although it was Yahweh's covenant, its effectiveness depended on the people's response. He concluded that

> the direction of the covenant is from God to man. The covenant originates with Him; He speaks the words; He lays down the conditions; it is His covenant, which takes on the aspect of mutuality when the people respond by accepting the terms and by promising to be obedient.[39]

The covenant at Sinai, then, was a religious *berith*. Its primary meaning is "a divine constitution with signs and pledges."[40] It was a cooperative agreement initiated by Yahweh and ratified by Israel's response, with the results that

Israel became personally related to Yahweh's people and He was their personal Lord.

2. The institution of the covenant In the period of the patriarchs, there was much emphasis in the northwest-Semitic religion on the close personal tie between the clan father and his god. The god was the patron deity of the clan, and the establishing of a personal and contractual relationship between the clan chief and the clan god was a widespread phenomenon. Many northwest-Semitic names illustrate this personal relationship by forming compounds with *'ab* ("father"), *'ah* ("brother"), and *'amm* ("people" or "family"). Such names as Abiram/Ahiram ("my divine father/brother is exalted"), Eliab ("my God is a father to me"), Abimelech/Ahimelech ("my divine father/brother is my king"), and Ammiel ("the God of my people is God to me") illustrate the ancient nomad's sense of kinship between clan and deity. The god was the head of the house, and the members of the household were his family.[41]

The patriarchs expressed a deep sense of personal experience in their relationship to Yahweh. "The Genesis picture of a personal relationship between the individual and his God, supported by promise and sealed by covenant, is most authentic."[42] The patriarchal religion was a clan religion in which the clan became the family of the patron God. Israel sensed a feeling of tribal solidarity between the people and God.[43]

In the covenant at Sinai, Yahweh gave definitive expression to the binding of the people to Him in their unique knowledge of Him. Yahweh's disclosure was not grasped speculatively and was not expounded in the form of teachings about Him, but in the experience at Sinai and the historical events that this experience commemorated. He disclosed Himself as He broke in on the life of Israel in His dealings with them and molded them according to His will.[44] Thus the foundation of the normative and enduring covenant relationship was in Yahweh's gracious acts. It can scarcely be overemphasized that Yahweh's offer to covenant with Israel was an act of grace. Nothing that Abraham had ever done had merited Yahweh's promise to him, "All peoples on earth will be blessed through you" (Gen. 12:3 NIV), and it was beyond his wildest dreams to be promised innumerable offspring when he did not even have a son (Gen. 15:5; 16:1) and to be promised all the land of Canaan while he was only a nomad (Gen. 17:8). Yet, in spite of Abraham's lack of merit, Yahweh elected him and his seed, delivered them from bondage, and formalized His promises to them in the gracious covenant at Sinai. Nevertheless, both Abraham and Israel had to respond to Yahweh's offer. Abraham's obligation was to insure that circumcision would be faithfully performed on every male child of his descendants and the foreigners of his household as a sign of his covenant with Yahweh (Gen. 17:10-11) and to commit himself entirely to Yahweh's purposes. Eichrodt says:

> There is emphatic indication that the covenant cannot be actualized except by the complete self-commitment of Man to God in personal trust. Hence the obedient performance of the rite of circumcision takes on the character of an act of faith.[45]

In the covenant agreement with Israel at Sinai, Yahweh's ready assistance and faithfulness in delivering Israel from Egypt were to continue and at the same time the behavior of the people was subjected to definite standards.[46] Thus these standards of the Torah were not arbitrary, negative statutes that stifled Israel's freedom. On the contrary, the Law itself was a gift of Yahweh's grace.[47] Yahweh's central manifestation of His love for Israel was that He bestowed on her His Word, which guaranteed that His guidance would be present in all situations of Israel's history.[48] The Torah was the expression of the will of Yahweh and was the means of ordering the nation He had chosen in a manner befitting His people and in a manner suitable for the highest well-being of

Israel.[49] The Law, negatively expressed in prohibitions, forbade that which abolished the relationship that Yahweh had created in the covenant with His elect nation. Eichrodt continues:

> Thus the object of the law is to settle the relationship of the covenant-nation and of the individual to the God of the covenant and to the members of the nation who belong to the same God. Because this nation has been chosen by this God this is to be done by excluding those things which invalidate or disturb the relationship.[50]

In the word of the Law, Yahweh established a direct link with His people. Even His acts of jealousy and judgment were derived from His love, for they were attempts to prohibit the seduction of the object of His choice. Viewed from this perspective, the Law is seen as not being an oppressive element of tyrannical divine authority, but a direct proof of love, since it gave Israel tangible evidence of their elect status and their superiority over all pagan attempts to proclaim God's will (Deut. 4:6; 30:11ff.).[51]

Since the Law was the direct command of Yahweh spoken out of His love for Israel, any breach of it was an outrage against Yahweh Himself. In pagan religions the law was invested with all the authority of the national god, such as in the Code of Hammurabi; but in Israel the Law was the very Word of Yahweh. It was the divine Lawgiver who laid down the Law, and every breach of it was an offense against Him.[52] In the new legal system established by the covenant, with its markedly personal quality, transgression of the Law carried no connotation of formalistic, juristic objectivity and required no reparation by a corresponding equivalent. The transgression was not the flaunting of an impersonal, juristic norm, but it was a conflict between two wills, the divine and the human.[53] Sin was a failure to fulfill one's vows to obey God. Wright says:

> Sin is the violation of covenant and rebellion against God's personal lordship. It is more than an aberration or a failure which added knowledge can correct. It is a violation of relationship, a betrayal of trust.[54]

The basic character of sin, then, is action contrary to the norm of the Law of Yahweh. Three basic words for sin illustrate this concept: *ḥatah'* ("to miss the mark"), *'avon* ("to veer or go aside from the right way," "irregular or crooked action" with the idea implicit that the agent is aware of the culpability of his action), and *pesha'* ("rebellion, revolt").[55] Sin to the Israelite was unhealthy, for it rendered one incapable of living with others[56] or with Yahweh. When a person insisted on acting in a manner contrary to God's order, he negated the covenant purposes of fellowship with Yahweh.

The seriousness of individual sin was compounded by the belief that through ties of blood and common interest the individual was regarded as being so deeply imbedded in the community that an offense by him affected not only his own relationship with God but also that of the entire community.[57] It did, in fact, affect God's attitude toward the community and it had adverse effects on the well-being of the community.

In the face of estrangement from Yahweh by sin, the problem arises as to how sin is to be removed. The ancient religions generally conceived of sin's being removed by mechanical purification, but Israel's faith in Yahweh freed them from domination by these concepts and gave them the concept of a personally conditioned forgiveness of sins. Even though the ritual of the Law had elements that seemed to remove sin *ex opere operato* by the faithful accomplishment of external procedures using elements such as water (Lev. 14:5; Num. 8:7; 19:9), fire (Num. 31:22–23), blood (Lev. 16:14–19; Deut. 21:1ff.), or the scapegoat (Lev. 16:21–22), these elements did not involve the material removal of substantial sin, since sin was understood in interpersonal terms. They were simply means of portraying the removal of sin, and this was actually the restoration of an undisturbed relationship with the personal covenant God. The expiation of sacrificial atonement was not a mechanistic removal of sin independent of the forgiveness of the sin. The acts of atonement were part of God's free forgiveness by which He restored fellowship with the sinner.[58]

Yahweh's forgiveness, however, was conditioned on the repentance of the sinner. Repentance necessitated a deep and contrite confession of sin (Lev. 5:5).[59] The acts of external sacrifice were not effective unless they were accompanied by a penitence that resulted from true conversion.[60] Nothing was effective in restoring the relationship with Yahweh until the breach caused by unconfessed and unforgiven guilt was closed.[61] When the sinner humbly acknowledged his sin and recognized that since sin broke his relationship with God it could not remain when his relationship with God was restored, then Yahweh could forgive. But forgiveness was conditioned on confession and repentance.

It was through sacrifice that the penitent expressed his personal self-abasement and submission to God's sovereign will.[62] But it was the personal repentance of the sinner and the personal forgiveness of Yahweh, however, that restored the broken relationship. The basic element in the restoration of this relationship was love of Yahweh as it was expressed practically in a personal surrender to the Law (Deut. 6:4-5). Just as transgression threatened to disrupt the present order, love upheld it because love was the essence of fellowship with God, which was the purpose of the covenant order.[63]

In view of man's responsibility to Yahweh through the Law, it is clear not only that Yahweh pledged Himself to Israel but also that Israel was to accept her obligations for the maintenance of this bilateral relationship. As long as Israel was willing to worship no other gods and to observe the prescribed standards of cult and conduct, then Yahweh would continue to be faithful and to assist and deliver them.[64] Yahweh's promise, "You shall be my people and I will be your God," provided life with a goal and history with a meaning. Because of this definiteness, the fear of arbitrariness and caprice in the Godhead was excluded from Israel. With Yahweh, unlike pagan gods, people knew where they stood, and an atmosphere of trust and security was created in which Israel found strength to grapple with life in a hostile environment.[65]

In the covenant Yahweh united the tribes into a strong relationship of solidarity. The normative expression of the divine will in the covenant bound together the component parts and subordinated the entire nation to Yahweh's purposes.[66] In this tribal solidarity was the necessary unity and strength for the survival of the nation as well as the cooperation needed to fulfill the requirements of the standards of behavior and the cultus that were prescribed in the covenant.

The purpose, then, of the institution of the covenant was to consummate Yahweh's redemptive acts of deliverance from Egypt and to establish a pattern of behavior by which Israel could properly relate to Him.[67] The covenant provided the pattern of organization of the community around the Law, and in this sense it constituted the society that Yahweh had elected and provided for the institutions of the sacred shrine, cult, and covenant law in which Israel's religion found its expression.[68]

3. The explanation of the covenant It is clear from the preceding statements that the conception of covenant, with its resemblance to the social and political law of the day, was used to depict the relationship of Yahweh to His people. This relationship had been established in the Exodus when Yahweh had chosen Israel for His own purposes, and the "covenant was a way of making a picture out of the relationship, so that the people would understand what it meant."[69] The maintenance of the covenant depended on righteousness, the recognition of Yahweh's personal lordship.[70] Thus the covenant agreement was simply the external normative form by which Israel's personal relationship with Yahweh and Israel was maintained and described.

The most important aspect of the covenant was its basis in the interpersonal relationship between Yahweh and Israel. We have seen that in the Old Testament the covenant was more than a mere contract, for it established an artificial blood kinship between the parties involved. The word that was used to describe covenant affection and loyalty, *ḥesed,* was also used to describe the affection and loyalty of kinsmen.[71] Jonathan and David expected *ḥesed* of each other on the basis of the covenant between them (1 Sam. 20:8, 14–17). *Ḥesed* is the brotherly comradeship and loyalty that one part of a covenant must give to the other. The imagery of God as the Father-Shepherd of His people is an excellent example of the kind of behavior implied by *ḥesed.* Eichrodt says, "The father-son relationship assumes *ḥesed* as the kind of conduct binding on its members" (Gen. 47:29).[72] Thus *ḥesed* is the proper means of describing the benevolent attitudes and beneficent actions appropriate among persons bound together in a covenant relationship. The term connotes kindness and mercy, but it also involves a specific relationship whose existence implies a mutual obligation.

An excellent example of the type of relationship involved in the covenant is the ancient Semitic rite of blood-covenanting, which involved the closest possible relationship between two friends. Trumbull says the blood-covenant was "a form of mutual covenanting, by which two persons enter into the closest, the most enduring, and the most sacred of compacts, as friends and brothers, or as more than brothers, through the inter-commingling of their blood."[73] He continues by showing that the primitive mind had a belief in the possible intercommunion with God through an interunion with Him by blood. God is life and all life comes from Him. Blood is life and therefore may be a means of interunion with God. As the closest and most sacred of covenants between one human being and another is possible through an interflowing of a common blood, so the closest and most sacred of covenants between man and God, the interunion of the human nature with the divine, is possible through the offer and acceptance of a common life in a common bloodflow.[74]

This concept of sacral communion is also evident in the rite of sacrifice, which signifies personal entry into a new association. Through the sacral communion mediated by the sacrifice, Yahweh entered into a special relationship with His people and gave them a share in His own life.[75] This communion, however, is not to be confused with the pagan concept of magical power residing in the sacrificial victim in which people regarded the sacrificial meal as the most intimate possible means of contact with the power of a god. In the covenant on Sinai, the confirmation of the union with Yahweh in the covenant sacrifice led not to a physical and magical conception of the divine presence, but to a personal and moral fellowship with the Lord, whose will shaped and regulated afresh the life of His people. This communion with Yahweh through the sacrifice was concerned with the presence of God and the personal union with Him from which all life and strength derive.[76]

The rites of pagan nature religions concentrated on receiving mysterious "power" from the gods. It was an invariable mark of these rites that they had to be repeated continually, and they were effective by the *ex opere operato* method of their being correctly carried out. In the Israelite covenant the sacrifice was not repeated in order to maintain the cycle of nature or to appease Yahweh, for it created the covenant relationship for all time at its first performance. Further sacrifices simply commemorated the establishment of the covenant and expressed Israel's faithfulness to it. Correct observance of the covenant ritual was important, but the covenant relationship was maintained by Israel's moral correspondence to the will of Yahweh as expressed in His word at Sinai. The purpose of the Israelite covenant was to establish and maintain the personal communion between God and man, not simply to effect the impersonal transference of "power." In the newly established covenant relationship at Sinai, the nation submitted itself to the utterly personal lordship of Yahweh.[77] Any concept of Yahweh's involvement with His people in terms of popular nature religion was rejected. The covenant excluded the pagan idea that a continuity of nature existed between the national God and his worshipers. Israel's religion was one of election in which the grace of Yahweh established them in their personal kinship to Him through His mighty deliverance from Egypt and the enduring covenant order initiated at Sinai.[78]

This concept of a covenant based on Yahweh's grace provided an inherent defense against the danger of a legalistic distortion of the relationship into a mere agreement between two partners of equal status. The awe with which Israel viewed the sovereignty of this personal God as He acted in history stopped all thought of a mere mercenary agreement or of a relationship of parity with Him. Any attempt to substitute personal merit for the unmerited favor of Yahweh was effectively stifled by the very thought of the sovereign Lord of the universe in His lovingkindness condescending to enter into a covenant relationship with humanity. Such condescension and grace in the covenant, says Eichrodt, "lays claim to the whole man and calls him to surrender with no reservations."[79] The very peculiarity of the compact of blood-friendship demanded that he who entered it must be ready to make a complete surrender of himself in loving trust to him with whom he covenanted.[80] This trust was based on the belief that Yahweh had covenanted with Abraham and had fulfilled His promises in the Exodus and the conquest of Canaan. Israel was rescued from Egypt by Yahweh's gracious act and was now under His lordship. They were a separate people delivered by Yahweh (Num. 23:9; Deut. 33:28-29) and secure in the continuing protection of His mighty acts (Judg. 5:11; Ps. 68:19ff.). Nowhere was election attributed to any merit on the part of Israel but only to the unmerited favor of Yahweh. Israel's very existence was based on their trust of Yahweh's grace in bringing them into the covenant as His people.[81]

Although Israel had not merited the covenant and Yahweh had given it strictly by grace, the covenant was by no means amoral. As was shown above in the definition of *berith,* the covenant was morally conditioned on the response of the people; it was not simply a racial covenant. The key to entrance into the covenant was faith in Yahweh and subordination to His Law, as this was signified and sealed by circumcision (Gen. 17:11-12). Paul emphasized this contingency on faith in his letter to the Galatians. Only those who followed Abraham in his faith in Yahweh were his sons in the covenant (Gal. 3:7-9, 29). It was the spiritual descendants of Abraham who participated in the covenant by faith, not merely his physical descendants; others who were not Israelites were to be included in the blessings of Abraham, for Yahweh said that all the nations would be blessed through him (Gen. 12:3). Thus it was by faith that Israel had entered the covenant and only by faith that they could remain in it. The maintenance of the covenant by faith necessitated a proper moral response. Yahweh promised to give Canaan to Israel if they obeyed his commandments. He said:

> Behold, I set before you this day a blessing and a curse: a blessing, if ye obey the commandments of the LORD your God, which I command you this day: and a curse, if ye will not obey the commandments of the LORD your God (Deut. 11:26-28 KJV).

Yahweh initiated the covenant by grace, but Israel could maintain her obligations to it and thus remain in it only by unqualified moral obedience to the covenant stipulations. It was divinely ordained (Exod. 6:7), yet conditioned on the human obligation to accept its demands and fulfill them (Exod. 19:7, 8; 24:7, 8).[82]

II. THE NEED FOR SALVATION

While salvation is central to the biblical proclamation, the necessity for it is based on the reality of sin. It is a fallen humanity that stands in need of a Redeemer.[83] A humanity that has violated the covenant stands condemned before God. This violated relationship between God and man is seen as missing the mark, rebelling, deviating, straying from the path.[84] The one whom God has created to be His covenant-partner and to participate in the redemptive history of the covenant has denied the very purpose of his existence. The possibility of sin has become a reality,[85] and man who was created to be in fellowship with God has become alienated from Him and enslaved by evil. Deprived of the organizing and vivifying work of the Holy Spirit, he embarks on a course of self-serving pride and moral rebellion.[86] Paul declares, "All have sinned and fall short of the glory of God" (Rom. 3:23 NIV) and further explains that everyone, both Jew and Gentile, is in need of the gospel of Christ (Rom. 1:18–3:20).

Thus the covenant that brought man into a relationship with a personal God is found in disrepair because of man's disobedience. It is now necessary to survey the dynamics of the sin that makes necessary the redemptive grace of God in Christ.

The ultimate result of sin is death (Rom. 6:23), which comes because sinful man exists in a condition of alienation from God. Sin is a spiritual or religious concept, and actions can be meaningfully described as sinful only as they reflect the sinner's distorted or broken relationship to God. The assertion of self in rebellious or hostile independence from God is the primary dynamic of sin, and any act or state that results from this attitude is sin.

The results of this rebellious independence from God are the loss of the true meaning of life, the deterioration of fellowship with God, and the lowering of moral and spiritual sensitivity. Because of the interpersonal obstructions thus raised by sin, man becomes separated from covenant fellowship with God. What is needed both in the individual and the human community is the removal of these barriers and the restoration of the covenant-partner relationship.[87]

III. THE PROVISION FOR SALVATION

The need for salvation is universal (Rom. 1:16–3:20), and the primary function of the church is to proclaim the gospel of salvation through Jesus Christ (Acts 1:8). The content of this message revolves around the central affirmation "that Christ died for our sins according to the Scriptures" (1 Cor. 15:3). Although the manner in which His death is for our sins has been widely discussed, the fact of His death for us has not been contested within orthodox Christianity. It is through the cross of Jesus Christ that the will of God for the salvation of all sinners is most clearly expressed. God's love for mankind here finds historical expression in a universal offer of His grace. As Paul says, "God was in Christ reconciling the world to Himself . . . therefore, we are ambassadors for Christ . . ." (2 Cor. 5:19–20).[88]

Grace is the motivation for God's work of salvation, and He expresses it through Christ's atonement. These aspects of salvation thus require further examination.

A. The Grace of God

The biblical background for the concept of grace is found primarily, though not exclusively, in the Old Testament ideas of *hānan* and *hesed* and in the New Testament idea of *charis*, found for the most part in the writings of Paul.

1. Old Testament emphases The dominant idea of the verb *chānan* is to be gracious and have mercy on someone. It does not mean to treat someone in a condescending way so much as it denotes a particular action in which good will is somehow expressed. Being gracious presupposes a lack in the one who receives the act of grace. Schillebeeckx points out:

Grace ... is therefore a warm inclination towards another, at least as an implicit response to a crying need.... However, it emerges from this very structure that the person who gives is related to the person in need as a superior to an inferior.... The content therefore includes taking account of someone, inclining towards him and, finally granting him favour.[89]

Examples of this grace in action are God's giving Jacob the gift of his children (Gen. 33:5) and giving Israel the Torah (Ps. 119:29). Also, the pardon that follows a peace treaty involves grace as covenant love, a love that requires mutuality of commitment (see Deut. 7:2, where God forbids Israel to make such a covenant with the Canaanite nations).

The relationship between need and grace is also seen in the wisdom literature, where God answers the prayers of the pious. The concept of petitionary prayer, which depends on a responsive attitude from God, is based on the root from which *ḥānan* is derived. The person who prays for attention to his own situation relies on God's gracious response. For example, prayer for rescue from weakness (Ps. 6:2), loneliness (Ps. 25:16), distress (Ps. 31:9), and misery (Ps. 86:3) presupposes that God will act in gracious intervention. Grace consists of God's concern for His people and His faithfulness in acting consistently with His covenant commitment, or *ḥesed*.[90]

The response of Israel to God's gracious actions is praise. God's grace and faithfulness, His reliability, His care and concern for His people elicit a liturgy of joyful praise and thanksgiving (see Exod. 34:6-7).

The covenant love characteristic of the *ḥānan* of God is *ḥesed*. Etymologically *ḥesed* denoted the behavior that results in a stable community regulated by rights and duties. The basic dynamic of the concept is found in interpersonal relationships, and secondarily the word means the generous kindness and friendliness that exists between partners in a community, such as husband and wife. It is a relationship that calls for mutuality of commitment. *Ḥesed* involves generosity and "overwhelming, unexpected kindness which is forgetful of itself, completely open and ready for 'the other.'"[91]

Ḥesed also emphasizes the abundance of God's grace in forgiveness (Exod. 34:7). The proper response to this forgiveness is righteousness in relationship both to God and to the other members of the community. Thus God's grace is a summons to thanksgiving and praise as well as ethical activity in community relationships. Grace results in both liturgical and ethical expressions.[92]

2. New Testament emphases Salvation as a result of God's grace is an important New Testament emphasis (see Titus 2:11). Although the word *grace* or *charis,* is primarily a Pauline emphasis, occurring some one hundred times in this literature, Luke and Peter also use the concept frequently. Paul uses *charis* in the Corinthian letters in the sense of thanksgiving or a demonstration of favor or work of love that the Corinthians bestowed on the poor Jerusalem church (1 Cor. 16; 2 Cor. 8) and as a demonstration of God's favor (2 Cor. 9:8). He also uses *charis* as the theological foundation of salvation and thus rejects works of the Law and human righteousness as a way of salvation (Gal. 2:19-21).[93]

In Romans, Paul uses *grace* to describe the mode of God's work of salvation. Grace is God's saving generosity to mankind. It is a generosity that is unmerited and unconditional. God even loves sinners. Grace is a gift that makes possible the redemption of sinners through Christ Jesus (Rom. 3:24). God's favor to humanity is identical with the cross of Christ and is thus historically manifested as a work of God. There is no merit in striving for good, for all human preparation is void as a way of salvation. Thus the *sola gratia* foundation for salvation is maintained and the *sola fide* basis for the appropriation of God's grace by the believer is affirmed.

Paul also emphasizes another aspect of

charis in Galatians where it refers to the true doctrine that he received by revelation (Gal. 2:9). Thus "grace is the doctrine of salvation which is handed on from the Father by Jesus through the apostles, and for Paul that is the doctrine of the election of all men in Christ Jesus."[94]

Luke emphasizes the aspect of "finding favor with someone," a concept that is more closely related to the Hebrew *ḥēn*, or favor. Christians enjoy favor among all people (Acts 2:47; 7:10). Sometimes Luke uses a more theological sense of grace as proclamation of the Word, the wisdom from above (Luke 4:22; Acts 14:3). This is similar to Paul's usage in his Epistle to the Galatians and describes the joy that the divine wisdom of the gospel communicates in the gospel of Jesus Christ.[95]

3. Theological implications Grace is essentially God's love in action on behalf of sinful humanity. It is the favor of God bestowed freely and selflessly to work redemptively for all sinners. Christ's death is an act motivated solely by God's love for a sinful humanity that did not deserve it. It is unmerited love that is unrestricted in its universality and can be responded to appropriately only in faith and obedient service. Thus the gift of being made righteous by God's grace is not due to any human merit but results from God's loving response to man's infinite need.[96]

It is important to remember that God's grace is not a thing, but a personal relationship. It cannot be measured, regulated, called forth by rituals and ceremonies, or dispensed through sacraments. Grace comes from God, not the church, and testifies to the boundlessness of His "self-giving love in Christ to make it available to all, and to persuade all to accept it."[97]

Furthermore, although there is a tendency to distinguish between various kinds of grace—such as prevenient grace, enabling grace, and saving grace—it is important to understand that since it is the same God who is bestowing His love in various ways, it is also the same grace that is being expressed. Grace does function in different ways, but whenever it functions, it is God acting in loving favor for humanity. It is always His grace and is never the independent possession of the believer. It is always freely offered by God and is never earned or manipulated by works. It is always universally offered and is never selectively withheld because of some arbitrary decree in the secret counsels of God.[98] Wesleyan-Arminian theology has historically emphasized that the grace of God is universally offered but may be resisted by the perverse will of sinful humanity. H. Orton Wiley gives a summary of this theological position in his chapter on "The Preliminary States of Grace."

First, the moral inability of man, extensive total depravity, makes him unable to respond to God apart from the enabling work of grace that makes a faith response possible. Grace, however, enables fallen humanity to respond in faith. This is in contrast to the Calvinist position that views depravity as being so complete that moral response is impossible and grace must operate irresistibly to call the elect effectually to faith. Second, Wesleyan-Arminianism affirms the continuity of grace. Every aspect of salvation, from the first awareness of moral need to ultimate consummation in glorification is worked through God's grace. Third, there is a cooperation, or synergism, between divine grace and the human will. The Spirit of God does not work irresistibly, but through the concurrence of the free will of individuals. Finally, salvation is all of grace. Although the human will must respond to the offer of grace at every level of spiritual development, the will does not initiate or merit grace or salvation.[99]

B. The Atonement of Christ

The Atonement of Jesus Christ must always be seen in relationship to the Incarnation. What Christ did is inseparable from who He is. Furthermore, the Atonement, as an aspect of the Incarnation, is initiated by God as a revelation of His love and grace. It is, as Vincent Taylor states:

> a work of God upon the greatest and grandest scale; it is nothing less than the doctrine of how man, feeble in his purpose and separated from God by his sins, can be brought into a relationship of time and abiding fellowship with Him, both as an individual, and as a member of the community to which he belongs.[100]

Thus God intends through the Atonement of Christ to reconcile man and the world to Himself (John 3:16; Rom. 5:8; 8:32). The fellowship that God desires between Himself and creation has been made impossible by sin. Only "by annulling sin, destroying its roots, and removing its stain, can communion with God be attained and perfected."[101] Both the need for the reconciliation and the benefits of the Atonement are universal. Thus God through His Son has condemned sin (Rom. 8:3), tasted death for everyone (Heb. 2:9), and reconciled the world to Himself (2 Cor. 5:19). It is the purpose of God to reconcile, and He has done so through Christ.

The meaning of what Christ did on the cross developed in the understanding of the early church and throughout the historical formation of Christian thought. Essential to the earliest Christian ideas were the beliefs that Jesus, the Christ, had died and risen to deliver mankind from sin by a sacrifice of Himself in order to establish a new covenant relationship between man and God.[102] As Ladd says, "The death of Christ is . . . the supreme revelation of the love of God."[103]

1. The New Testament understanding
Although the New Testament treatment of the atonement involves numerous emphases and nuances of thought, several important issues do emerge. What Christ did on the cross was sacrificial, vicarious, universal in its effects, and triumphal in its completion.

a. Sacrificial The death of Christ was a sacrificial death. Paul and the Gospel writers connect His death with the Old Testament sacrificial ritual. For them, as Richardson notes, His death is "the sacrificial act by which a covenant was ratified between God and a New Israel, just as the old covenant was ratified in the blood of the sacrificial animals on Sinai."[104] At the making of the covenant on Sinai, Moses sprinkled the people with the blood of the sacrifice to express the completion of the agreement and the inclusion of the people in the covenant pact (Exod. 24:8). In the same way, by the cross of Christ, God made a new covenant with the New Israel to replace the neglected and broken covenant of Sinai. The frequent references to the blood of Christ (Rom. 3:25; 5:9; Eph. 1:7; 2:13; Col. 1:20) and the emphasis of Hebrews that Jesus Christ is the mediator of a "better" covenant, the covenant that Jeremiah had promised (Heb. 8:8–12), establish the connection between the death of Christ and the sacrificial renewal of the covenant.[105]

John the Baptist calls Jesus "the Lamb of God, who takes away the sin of the world!" (John 1:29). Paul also refers to Him as the Passover Lamb (1 Cor. 5:7). Christ is also seen in the Apocalypse as the sacrificial Lamb slain to purchase with His blood people of all nations for God (Rev. 5:9). The universality of Christ's atonement is stressed in Revelation 7:14, where it is said that the robes of the saints have been washed in the blood of the Lamb. Thus as Richardson shows:

> St. John is asserting that the new relationship of God and man in Christ (the new covenant) is based upon the fulfillment of the promise contained in Gen. 22:8, that God would provide the Lamb which would make atonement for universal sin. . . . Christ is the Lamb of sacrifice promised by God to Abraham . . . and thus he is the God-given universal sin bearer.[106]

Morris points out that John's use of the phrase "the Lamb of God" is intended to express the conviction that in Jesus Christ all that is foreshadowed in the sacrifices is fulfilled. Christ accomplished the perfect sacrifice for sin and embodies "all truth to which the sacrificial system pointed."

Christ is God's Lamb, for only God can produce a sacrifice that deals completely with the problem of sin.[107] In offering Himself as the perfect sacrifice, Christ gave Himself in perfect obedience and adoration to God. Only such perfect obedience is victorious over sin. Such submission in such perfect harmony with God's desire to save humanity is the ultimate righteous relationship lived out in history. It is this kind of obedience that God wishes for humanity.

The function of Christ's death as a sacrifice raises the issue of propitiation. Paul describes the work of Christ by the term *hilastērion:*

> . . . being justified as a gift by His grace through the redemption which is in Christ Jesus; whom God displayed publicly as a propitiation *(hilastērion)* in His blood through faith . . . (Rom. 3:24, 25).

Controversy surrounds the interpretation and translation of this term. The traditional rendering has been "propitiation," in which the wrath of God against sin is satisfied by the sacrifice of Christ's blood. This view sees Christ as absorbing the penalty for sin that was rightly due humanity. The penalty is exacted because God's honor has been offended by sin and must be vindicated.

A number of scholars—such as C. H. Dodd, Vincent Taylor, and Alan Richardson—have objected that this propitiatory emphasis interprets God as an irascible Deity whose anger must be appeased by revenge or the bribes of His worshipers. Dodd points out that the biblical writers rejected the idea of a vindictive and capricious Deity who had to be bribed back into a good mood by sacrificial offerings. Dodd, then, favors "expiation" as the translation of *hilastērion.* Expiation is an act directed not toward the offended party, God in this case, but toward the removal of the offense itself. It is a means of making amends, of "extinguishing" or "annulling" the sin, not toward appeasing God. The sacrifice of Christ as the representative of humanity thus makes compensatory payment for sin and makes it possible for God to forgive with integrity.[108]

Leon Morris objects that this position gives inadequate consideration to the moral nature of God whose anger is not capricious but is based on the integrity of His holy nature. Moral rebellion against a righteous God is not adequately handled by the concept of "expiation." Old Testament believers took the wrath of God very seriously. He is not thought of as being capriciously angry, but because He is a moral Being, His anger is directed against any form of wrongdoing. Also, God is merciful and provides ways for the consequences of His wrath to be averted.[109]

R. E. Fuller objects to this propitiatory interpretation because it requires that God's attitude toward the sinner be understood as changing from disfavor to forgiving love. He argues that the death of Christ is itself an act of God and that the work of Christ is not the appeasement of God by the offering of a sacrifice. He stresses that God in His mercy forgives sin by "putting forward" the Son. Through the Son, God has propitiated His own wrath. Thus Fuller reacts to the pagan bribery theory of "propitiation" but succeeds only in defining "expiation" in a propitiatory way. In fact, he cites C. K. Barrett, who prefers to use the term *expiation* but says that it has the effect of propitiation in Romans.[110] This is the tendency Dodd also seems to have in noting that Christ's "expiation" makes it possible for God to forgive! This is propitiation in that what Christ does meets God's prerequisite for forgiveness.[111]

Dodd and others have contributed significantly to the understanding of *hilastērion,* for the concept of pagan appeasement is certainly unworthy of the Bible. However, the linguistic and historical support for a propitiatory element in the *hilastērion* idea cannot be rejected because of theological presuppositions that abhor appeasement. Indeed, the total biblical context should be examined to determine in what way the propitiation idea is appropriately applied to God. In fact, Christ's death does change the attitude of God toward humanity (propitiation), not by appeasement, but because humanity also is changed (expiation) when Christ's sacrifice is accepted by faith. God's right assessment of sin as deserving of His wrath is vindicated and fellowship with Him is restored by humanity's repentance and identification with Christ's work in faith. There is no inconsistency or capriciousness in a God whose attitude toward the sinner changes from wrath to forgiveness when that sinner accepts His offer of righteousness in Christ.

b. *Vicarious* The overwhelming New Testament evidence about the death of Christ expresses the conviction that Christ died "for us," "on our behalf," or "in our stead" (Mark 10:45; Rom. 8:32; Gal. 3:13; Eph. 5:2; 1 Thess. 5:9). The idea of representative suffering is central to Paul's witness. As Taylor notes, "It is evident that St. Paul believed that in some way, and in some representative way, Christ acted for men, and that what happened to Him was of supreme moment for them."[112]

The theological term *vicarious* is derived from the Latin *vicarius,* which means "substitutionary" or "taking the place of another." Thus, to describe Christ's death as vicarious is to say that in some way He experienced or exemplified something that was due us in a way that brought the benefits of His suffering to those who were not able to gain those benefits themselves. At issue theologically is whether this vicarious work of Christ is substitutionary or only representative. Taylor much prefers the latter position. He points out that in dying, Jesus suffered in the name of mankind. He represents people in the eyes of the Father, and His suffering is a representative act of obedience. Christ's ministry is "a voluntary endurance of the consequences of human sin." Taylor rejects the interpretation that Christ's work is rendered instead of our own or that our punishment is transferred to Him. He refuses to consider a substitutionary meaning in the passages describing what Christ has done.[113]

Exegetically, what is at issue is the translation of the prepositions *anti* and *hyper.* Substitution is implied by *anti,* and representation by *hyper,* according to some scholars. While it is true that the preponderance of New Testament passages expressing this truth use *hyper,* it is problematic whether the two terms have significantly different emphases. Arndt and Gingrich point out that a substitutionary emphasis is found for *anti* in Mark 10:45, "For even the Son of Man did not come to be served, but to serve, and to give His life a ransom for [*anti*] many."[114] It is significant that the parallel "Son of Man" passage in Matthew 20:28 uses *hyper* interchangeably with the *anti* of the Marcan rendering. Two of the synoptics, at least, view the terms synonymously. Even if Mark and Matthew intend different meanings, a canonical understanding of Scripture requires that both uses be taken seriously.

David Hill also notes that the LXX use of "ransom" involves the idea of substitution. The phrase "for many" (*anti pollōn*) is a Semitic way of expressing "all" and lends a substitutionary thrust. "The death of Jesus will be the means of liberating the whole people [Israel] from captivity and slavery."[115] Thus Christ, in giving His life as a ransom, liberates those under the sentence of sin by taking their place, not merely by representing them. Ladd also notes that *hyper* is often used in place of *anti* in Hellenistic Greek. He suggests that the theological objections to a substitutionary emphasis become a problem only when the objective work of Christ is divorced from the subjective need for the appropriation of His work by faith. In the extreme penal substitutionary forms of atonement theory, the participatory involvement of the believer in the "fellowship of his sufferings" is ignored. Such positions ignore the necessity for faith response, and the substitutionary emphasis becomes an external and transactional emphasis that separates the believer from the responsibility for ethical and spiritual growth.[116] Christ's death benefits me only as I experience it in faith union, however.

Taylor has raised a valid caution in the face of these monergistic and objectivist excesses. The subjective realm of Christian experience may not be ignored, as Wesleyan-Arminian theology has rightly stressed, by viewing Christ's objective Atonement as the totality of salvation to the exclusion of willful faith response. Man has a part to play in salvation "in a response of his spirit which concerns every part of his being, his thoughts, feelings, and will; and this response is actually part of the Atonement, if by this term we mean the restoration of sinners to fellowship with God."[117] Christ's work is indeed representative, as Taylor suggests. However, the biblical material presents a balance between the extreme objectivity of the transactional substitutionary views and the subjectivity of Taylor's exclusively representational emphasis. The exegetical evidence simply will not support the weight of his attempt to polarize the meanings of *anti* and *hyper*. They function virtually synonymously.

Thus the sacrifice of Christ accomplished what we could not do for ourselves. The integrity and justice of God could not allow Him to establish a righteous relationship with a sinful humanity, although His love constrained Him to forgive. At this point, the obedience of Christ took the place of our weakness and rebellion and effected a reconciliation for us. God "made Him who knew no sin to be sin on our behalf, that we might become the righteousness of God in Him" (2 Cor. 5:21). By interposing Himself into the matrix of the consequences of our sin, Christ showed us the appropriate attitude of obedience to the Father and rejection of sin. His offering of Himself as a sacrifice of obedient worship to God prefigures the response we must make to God in faith. Because of what God did through Christ and His obedience we, therefore, are to follow Christ's example and by faith become living sacrifices who are transformed from sinful creatures to obedient servants (Rom. 12:1–2). Christ was not a sinner, but He took the place of sinners and "bore our sins in His body on the cross" (1 Peter 2:24). This was not cheap pagan appeasement. By identifying interpersonally with sinners and in conformity with God's own intentions concerning redemption, He made it possible for sinners to identify interpersonally with God through Him. He represented sinful humanity by His vicarious sacrifice of obedience to God and He accomplished in our place a reconciliation that we were unable to accomplish ourselves. As we identify by faith with Christ's life and death, we are united with God through Him. As Paul writes, "For I delivered to you as of first importance what I also received, that Christ died for our sins according to the Scriptures" (1 Cor. 15:3). The obedience that led Him to give Himself to God, even though rejection of sinful religious patterns meant the shedding of His blood, is the kind of obedience that established right relationships with God. Christ broke through the barrier of sin that had alienated a rebellious humanity from God. As the writer of Hebrews expresses it, Christ was the "pioneer of our salvation" (Heb. 2:10; 12:2). He has provided the perfect example for our relationship to God. As the perfect Son, Christ was obedient; because we are sons, we also must learn obedience. Christ is the source of our salvation, but as McCown points out, the incarnation, suffering, and obedient death of Christ "avail to us only on the basis of our obedience to him."[118]

It was thus through Christ's death that God brought judgment on sin and deliverance of sinners from its consequences. Forgiveness was made possible by the establishment of a new covenant between us and God. As Jesus said, "This is My blood of the covenant, which is to be shed on behalf of many for forgiveness of sins" (Matt. 26:28).

c. Universal The sacrificial offering of Christ's death so met the requirements of divine justice as to make salvation available to all humanity. The atonement was sufficient to deal with the whole of sinful humanity and with the whole of sin in sinful humanity. Wesleyan-Arminian theology has consistently held that the biblical teaching concerning Christ's work presents salvation as provided for all on the condition of acceptance of the Atonement by faith. The traditional Calvinist position, particularly as reflected by the canons of the Synod of Dort, has stressed a doctrine of eternal decrees by which God has elected a limited number to be included in the benefits of the Atonement.

Vernon Grounds, former president of Denver Seminary, in analyzing traditional Calvinist interpretations of a limited atonement, says:

> Despite the wide acceptance of this position, especially among contemporary evangelicals, it quite flatly contradicts the overwhelming testimony of Scripture to the universality of God's salvific grace. A mere *catena* of passages discloses the fact, for fact it is, that the divine purpose in Jesus Christ embraces not a segment of the human family but the race *in toto* . . . (John 1:29; 3:16; Rom. 5:17-21; 11:32; 1 Tim. 2:6; Heb. 2:9; 2 Pet. 3:9; 1 John 2:2). . . . It takes an exegetical ingenuity which is something other than learned virtuosity to evacuate these texts of their obvious meaning. . . .[119]

The reaction of John Wesley to the Calvinist doctrine of limited atonement was decisive. He felt that unless grace is free for all by faith there is no real gospel to proclaim. A theological determinism that consigned some to condemnation by an arbitrary decree reflects such a love, said Wesley, "as makes your blood run cold."[120] Such a doctrine has no basis in Scripture, though some heap an "abundance of texts together whereby (though none of them speak home to the point) the patrons of that opinion dazzle the eyes of the unwary. . . ." He concludes in more detail by denying that Scripture supports the doctrine:

> If this were true, we must give up all the Scriptures together; nor would the Infidels allow the Bible so honourable a title as that of a "cunningly-devised fable." But it is not true. It has no colour of truth. It is absolutely, notoriously false. . . God declares in his word these three things, and that explicitly, in so many terms: (1) "Christ died for all," (2 Cor. v. 14). . . . (2) "He is the propitiation for the sins of the whole world," (1 John 2:2). . . . And, (3) "He died for all, that they should not live unto themselves, but unto Him which died for them," (2 Cor. v. 15). . . .[121]

The victory of the Cross, then, is universal in scope, though made effectual in the believer only through faith. Christ became a "curse for us" (Gal. 3:13), and for all of us.

d. Triumphal. Not only does the atonement of Christ release humanity from the guilt and power of sin and establish a new covenant relationship with God but it also proclaims Christ's victory over the evil spiritual powers in the cosmos. Paul's world view sees humanity as being in bondage not only to the law, sin, and death but also to the evil spiritual world. Through His cross "He has abolished all rule and all authority and power. For He must reign until He has put all His enemies under His feet" (1 Cor. 15:24-25). Colossians, in particular, notes, "When He had disarmed the rulers and authorities, He made a public display of them, having triumphed over them through Him" (Col. 2:15).[122]

Aulén, in his *Christus Victor* theory of the Atonement, stresses that Christ stands as the warrior and victor over the evil powers in every form. Through Christ's victory a new age has begun. Through God's own power "Christian faith is born with a paean of victory in its heart: 'In all this we are more than conquerors,' no power whatsoever 'shall be able to separate us from the love of God, which is in Christ Jesus our Lord' (Rom. 8:37ff.)."[123] "Thanks be to God, who gives us the victory through our Lord Jesus Christ" (1 Cor. 15:57). It is no wonder that the angels around the throne, the living creatures, and the elders sang with a loud voice, "Worthy is the Lamb that was slain to receive power and riches and wisdom and might and honor and glory and blessing.... To Him who sits on the throne and to the Lamb, be blessing and honor and glory and dominion forever and ever" (Rev. 5:12-13).

2. The benefits of the atonement The New Testament utilizes various terms to describe the work of Christ. Although the term *atonement* is not a New Testament word, it is used to describe the work of Christ that deals with the problem of sin and the restoration of humanity to God. The New Testament terms deal with various aspects of what Christ's atonement accomplished for sinners.[124]

a. Redemption The Pauline literature emphasizes redemption as one objective of Christ's work. This idea is expressed by two word groups: first, *lytron* and *apolytrōsis* and, second, *agorazō* and *exagorazō*. The first set of words is used in classical and Hellenistic Greek to describe the price paid to redeem a pawned item, the money paid to ransom prisoners of war, and money to purchase a slave's freedom. An example is 1 Timothy 2:6, "who gave Himself as a ransom [*antilytron*] for all." Here the compound *anti* indicates that Christ's death was a substitute, a ransom.[125] Several times Paul uses *apolytrōsis* to indicate the price of redemption or to emphasize its cost. Examples are, "In Him we have redemption through His blood" (Eph. 1:7) and "being justified as a gift by His grace through the redemption which is in Christ Jesus" (Rom. 3:24). The eschatological aspect of the redemption of the body is also expressed by *apolytrōsis* in Romans 8:23; Ephesians 4:30; and possibly in Ephesians 1:14.[126]

The idea of "buy" or "buy back" is expressed by *(ex)agorazō*. In two references, Paul emphasizes that Christ purchases the believer. "Do you not know ... that you are not your own? For you have been bought with a price; do not become slaves of men" (1 Cor. 7:23). The believer has been purchased and is now the property of God. This analogy grew out of the social practice of the manumission of slaves, and the recipient of the ransom price is not the issue. Later theology tended to distort these passages as well as Mark 10:45 by stressing the identity of the one to whom the ransom was paid.[127]

Redemption from the curse of the law is expressed by *exagorazō* in Galatians 3:13. Those who seek righteousness in law keeping cannot perfectly obey, and so they are under a curse. God has to redeem them from that curse through Christ's death on the cross "for us." As Fuller states, "God in Christ thus absorbed into himself his own judgment upon sin, his own wrath. Here is the truth in the translation of *hilastērion* (Rom. 3:25) as propitiation rather than expiation."[128]

b. Reconciliation Paul uses the metaphor of reconciliation *(katallassō* and *katallagē)* to express the restoration of humanity to fellowship with God. The concept is derived from warfare in which two hostile parties need to be brought together. Humanity has rebelled and is alienated from God, but God initiates a means by which the estrangement can be overcome (Rom. 5:6-11). It is especially important to understand that God both initiates and accomplishes reconciliation. Christ's death is an act of God on man's behalf and is not in any way a human act of propitiatory appeasement offered to God. God propitiates Himself (Rom. 5:6-11; 1 Cor. 5:19; Eph. 2:13; Col. 1:20-22). It is also clear that there is no conflict between God the Father and Christ the Son, as if the Son appeased the Father and coerced Him to turn His wrath into love. As Ladd suggests, 2 Corinthians 5:19 should be rendered, "God, in Christ, was reconciling the world to Himself."[129]

Reconciliation is first of all objective. It is an event accomplished for man's salvation on God's initiative. Reconciliation took place while we were yet sinners (Rom. 5:8, 10), and the gospel message given to the apostles was that God had finished something for humanity. In Christ

God has removed the obstruction of sin that separated sinners from Himself and has made restoration possible, even while humanity was still His enemy. In the historical event of Christ's death and resurrection, reconciliation was completed and is to be received as a gift (Rom. 5:11). James Denney says, "The work of reconciliation, in the sense of the New Testament, is a work which is *finished,* and which we must conceive to be finished *before the gospel is preached* . . . reconciliation . . . is not something which is being done; it is something which is done."[130]

Although reconciliation is a divine act completed while humanity was in rebellion, it does not become efficacious for salvation until the believer receives it and is reconciled to God. Reconciliation thus involves both the objective act of God in Christ and the subjective acceptance of God's offer for the cessation of hostilities. Says Paul, "We beg you on behalf of Christ, be reconciled to God" (2 Cor. 5:20).[131]

The first result of being restored to fellowship is peace with God (Rom. 5:1). God's wrath is no longer a threat. A new relationship has been established with Him. Through the Cross, Christ has reconciled us to God "having put to death the enmity" (Eph. 2:16).

Since Christ has brought us the peace of God, we can be reconciled also to each other. The relationship between ourselves and God is foundational to all other relationships. As Shelton says:

> The hostility that existed between Jew and Gentile may be taken as typical of all barriers that break fellowship between men. Because of reconciliation to God in Christ, men who have been estranged from one another are to be reconciled and every dividing wall of hostility removed, because Christ is our peace.[132]

Thus reconciliation is both with God and humanity. The church is to proclaim this reconciliation in its fullness, for Christ's blood has broken both the barriers of sin between the world and God and the interpersonal hostility between all groups of people. Peace is the message of the "ministry of reconciliation" (2 Cor. 5:18; Eph. 2:16).

c. Justification Although opinions differ about the centrality of the concept of justification for Paul's theology, it is a key emphasis in his theology of salvation.[133] Paul uses the family of Greek words having the stem *dik—* to express the righteousness-justification idea. Much of the content for the words grows out of the Hebrew *tsedeq.* The *dik—* words are used frequently by Paul as follows: the adjective *dikaios* 14 times, the verb *dikaioō* 25 times, and the nouns *dikaiōma* and *dikaiosynē* 5 and 52 times, respectively.[134]

The verb *dikaioō* has a forensic basis with essentially a declaratory function. However, it is often used metaphorically in matters that have no formal legal consequence. Sanday and Headlam emphasize an exclusively forensic meaning, noting that the verb means "to pronounce righteous" one who is not really righteous. This position asserts that since the believer who is "accounted righteous" may not be actually righteous, God's declaration is an imaginary "as if" conception in which righteousness for the believer is a moral fiction.[135] However, righteousness is not a quality to be possessed, it is a relationship that is either present or absent. The person who is truly a doer of the law through faith is the one whom God acquits and pronounces righteous.

The adjective *dikaios* thus describes the person whose trust is in Christ and who is accepted by God on the basis of that faith. A personal relationship is established with God, and the person is accepted because God is pleased by the obedience of faith in Christ.[136] James Denney notes the reality of being pronounced righteous:

> When a man believes in this sense, he does the only thing which is right to do in the presence of Christ, and it puts him right with God. It really puts him right . . . God justifies the ungodly man on the basis of his

faith in Jesus, and there is nothing unreal about the justification.[137]

Thus the usage of *dikaios* has a behavioral and ethical function. The believer actually becomes righteous as behavior reflects the new life in Christ. This is not, however, the possession of an abstract virtue or quality, as in secular Greek thought, which can be imputed as an imaginary possession of the virtue that does not exist in fact. The juridical or forensic emphasis involves being "declared righteous," and the believer is put in actual right relationship with God. On the basis of God's justifying action in the death and resurrection of Christ, the sinner has been acquitted and enjoys in actuality the righteousness of a new relationship with God.[138]

In order to understand adequately Paul's doctrine of justification by faith, it is necessary to avoid the tendency to project on his use of "righteousness" the Greek idea of justice as a natural human virtue. Instead, his rendering of the *dikaiosynē theou* in Romans 1:17 and 3:21 is based on the Old Testament and rabbinic usages of righteousness. The Old Testament understanding of righteousness does include the forensic-judicial elements, but the Hebrew *tsedeq*, which the LXX translates as *dikaiosynē*, has its roots in ideas of "rightness" or conduct that conforms to expected norms. *Tsedeq* includes a relational idea that describes behavior that is faithful to the claims arising out of a relationship between two persons. The norm that determines the righteous relationship between God and Israel is the covenant relation and the responsibilities growing out of it. When both God and the people fulfill their covenant obligations to each other, righteousness prevails.[139]

The "righteousness of God" also describes the gracious divine activity leading to vindication of His people. God's righteousness is seen in His redemptive activity through which He restores His covenant nation. Isaiah sees God's righteousness working harmoniously with His lovingkindness and covenant loyalty (Isa. 42:6, 21; 45:8, 13; 46:13; 51:6). The prophets also see God's righteousness as having ethical connotations. Israel was "in the right" only when the nation, as David Hill says, was truly righteous:

> If Yahweh was to be faithful to this relationship and declare Israel "in the right". . . then Israel must *be* "in the right," she must *have* a "righteous cause," she must *possess* "righteousness" that would reflect the character of God's righteousness.[140]

The rabbinic usage of the justification-righteousness idea involved also the maintenance of the covenant. Since the temple was inoperative during this period, atonement came to involve repentance as a basis for divine forgiveness. It was necessary to repent as an act of atonement in order to receive God's mercy and maintain the covenant relationship.[141]

In the New Testament, Paul connects God's righteousness with justification and bases justification on faith in God's saving work in Christ's ministry of atonement. The Pharisaic concept of obedience to the law or repentance as a basis for being justified is completely reinterpreted. Justification is initiated by God and becomes a present reality through faith.[142]

The interpretation of Paul's use of *dikaiosynē theou*, the "righteousness of God," has involved much controversy. The Reformed tradition has tended to interpret the clause as a subjective genitive, with the righteousness describing God's activity or power. It is God's righteousness alone and is expressed through the work of Christ. Since it belongs to God, humanity cannot share it; therefore it is "imputed" to sinners who are then considered to be justified or acquitted, even though they have not actually become righteous. On the other hand, the Catholic tradition has seen the phrase as an objective genitive in which God's righteousness is a quality conferred on the subject of God's mercy. This is the basis of the idea of "impartation" in which the believer actually shares the divine quality.

Both of these interpretations suffer from

defining righteousness as a quality or virtue rather than in the covenant terms of right relationship. Cranfield notes an alternative. The "righteousness of God" is a genitive of origin by which, then, as a result of God's activity of justifying, the believer actually becomes righteous. This righteousness originates in God and is a gracious offer of relationship made effectual by faith.[143] The believer does not possess a moral quality gained by either impartation or works but is united with Christ by faith and thus actually exists in a moral relationship of noncondemnation. God pronounces believers righteous and justifies them when they fulfill by faith-obedience the requirements of the covenant relationship. This faith-obedience is based on Christ's work, because only by trust in Him can one fulfill these requirements. He is our fulfillment of the law, and when we are in union with Him, we are in covenant-union with God. This is righteousness, not a quality to be imputed or imparted, but a relationship of true covenant-union. Thus "in the act of justification, the believer also through faith begins a relationship of union with Christ that is the subjective result of the objective work of God's righteousness."[144]

Paul's use of the forensic metaphor of justification to describe release from the bondage of sin and acquittal from the condemnation of God involves more than a declaration of pardon. A faith-union with Christ, a "newness of life" that involves real moral change is also closely related (Rom. 6:1–14). In union with Christ the believer brings into subjective actuality what the objective death of Christ had accomplished in potentiality. Justification thus involved knowing Christ and being found "in Him" *(en autō)* by faith (Phil. 3:9). "Righteousness," which Paul uses synonymously with "justification," is thus not just a declaration found at the beginning of new life in Christ, but it is a state of existence. *Dikaiosynē* both acquits the sinner and breaks the bondage of sin, making righteousness a reality in the life of the believer. No imputational moral fiction adequately deals with the reality of the newness of life in Christ.[145]

This actual making righteous of the believer, which involves the impartation of the quality of "righteousness," is the beginning of sanctification (John 3:3). Justification and sanctification work together, as Wesley notes:

> [In justification] the heart is cleansed in a low degree. But yet he has not a clean heart, in the full, proper sense, till he is made perfect in love. . . .
>
> When we begin to believe, then sanctification begins and as faith increases, holiness increases, till we are created anew.[146]

Traditionally, the theology of later Wesleyanism has tended to view justification in a forensic sense while reserving participation in the actual righteousness of Christ until sanctification. As Paul teaches, however, the fullness of righteousness in justification cannot be minimized without an impoverishment of the biblical teaching on salvation. Justification and sanctification are interrelated, both are grounded on the death of Christ, and both are effected through faith as a work of the Holy Spirit.

d. Adoption Another concept in the forensic emphasis of Paul is the word *adoption (huiothesia).* Adoption describes the relationship that results from the restoration of fellowship between God and humanity when reconciliation occurs (Rom. 8:15, 23; 9:4; Gal. 4:5; Eph. 1:5). The term describes the status and position of a son *(huios).* The Holy Spirit gives evidence to believers of the sonship in which their status is no longer that of bondslaves but of sons. The status of adoption as legal declaration results in the personal experience of sonship.

Adoption finds completion in the eschatological hope. While believers now receive the Spirit of adoption, the fullness of the benefits of adoption is still in the future. Only when the redemption of our bodies is complete and we participate in the fullness of the harvest will the full meaning of adoption come to light.[147]

e. Regeneration The idea of the new birth is stressed in the Gospel of John (3:3-8). "Regeneration" *(palingenesia)* was a concept in both Jewish and Greek culture that was used to indicate a decisively new change in nature or personal life. The Old Testament prophets expected a new birth for Israel (Isa. 65:17; 66:22; Ezek. 37) that would be related to the creation of a new heaven and a new earth in a cosmic regeneration (2 Peter 3:13; Rev. 20:11; 21:1).[148]

This cosmic regeneration has been accomplished by God in Jesus Christ, although at present it is seen only through the eyes of faith. The beginning of the new creation came with the incarnation of Jesus Christ, and His death and resurrection were potentially the re-creation of all humanity. The Spirit of God gives life to this new creation (John 20:22; Ezek. 37:5-10), and the wind of Pentecost inaugurates it (Acts 2:2). As the Gospels indicate, the early Christians knew that the expected day of regeneration had arrived because of the gifts and work of the Spirit (Matt. 19:28; Mark 10:30; John 20:22). Jesus had preached that to enter the new age of the kingdom of God it was necessary to be reborn and become as little children (Matt. 18:3; Mark 10:15; John 3:3). In order to enter the new age and participate in regeneration life, one must become a new person by the Holy Spirit's work.[149]

The Pauline literature emphasizes the real, though proleptic, character of the new creation. The Christian is a new creation and walks in newness of life and spirit (Rom. 6:4; 7:6; 12:2; 2 Cor. 5:17; 4:16; Gal. 6:15; Col. 3:10). Christians are the "firstfruits" of the new age (Rom. 8:23; cf. James 1:18). While the life of the new age is now experienced, its fullness is a part of the eschatological life of the age to come. As is seen in Titus 3:5-7:

> He saved us, not on the basis of deeds which we have done in righteousness, but according to His mercy, by the washing of regeneration and renewing by the Holy Spirit, whom He poured out upon us richly through Jesus Christ our Savior, that being justified by His grace we might be made heirs according to the hope of eternal life.

Thus, through faith, one may become a new person who participates in the eschatological life of the new age through the Holy Spirit, who breathes life into the new creation as He did at the original creation (Gen. 2:7; Ezek. 37:9-14; John 5:29). The eternal life *(zoē aiōnios)* of the age to come has been brought by Christ (John 3:16; 5:26; 10:10; 20:31).[150] Christians, regenerated by the Spirit, already experience this eternal life of the Spirit (Gal. 6:8; Eph. 4:18-23; 1 Tim. 6:12, 19; 1 John 3:14), and look forward to its glorious consummation at Christ's return (1 John 3:2-3).

f. Kingdom of God The new age of messianic salvation in which the regenerated believer lives is the "kingdom of God." This phrase describes comprehensively all that salvation includes. "Kingdom" *(basileia)* is not understood so much as a place as it is the "reign" or "kingship" of God. As God's rule or sovereignty, the kingdom of God is "at hand," says Jesus (Mark 1:15). Jesus sees Himself as actually setting up the faith-community over which God reigns and in which the saints participate in reigning (Luke 22:29).[151] The kindgom is both present and future. The future eschatological kingdom will involve the final destruction of the devil and his angels (Matt. 25:41), the creation of a perfect community without evil (Matt. 13:36-43), and perfected fellowship with God at the messianic feast (Luke 13:28-29). The characteristics of the kingdom of God in its present form involve the exorcism of demons as proof of the reality of God's rule (Matt. 12:28; Mark 1:28), the binding of Satan so that believers may be delivered from his power (Matt. 12:29), present fellowship with Christ and the enjoyment of spiritual victory and righteousness (Matt. 5:6, 21-48; 18:23-35; Luke 18:14), and deliverance from physical evil through healing (Matt.

11:4–5; Mark 5:34; 10:52; John 9). Ladd summarizes the present benefits of the kingdom of God as follows:

> The mission of Jesus brought not a new teaching but a new event. It brought to men an actual foretaste of the eschatological salvation. Jesus did not promise the forgiveness of sins; he bestowed it. He did not simply assure men of the future fellowship of the Kingdom, he invited men into fellowship with himself as the bearer of the Kingdom. He did not merely promise them vindication in the day of judgment; he bestowed upon them a present righteousness. . . .[152]

g. Sanctification It is in this context of the present reality of the victorious kingdom of God that the doctrine of sanctification is most clearly seen. As a result of deliverance from the bondage of sin through being justified and united with Christ (Rom. 3:21–31; 6:1–14), the believer is enabled through faith by the power of the Holy Spirit to actualize the life of righteousness made possible by Christ's work of atonement. The Pauline usage of the indicative and the imperative is instructive here. Paul uses the indicative to describe the salvation in which the Christian participates by faith, but by his use of the imperative stresses the need for holding firm to the righteous life. For example, in Romans 6:6 he states in the aorist indicative: "Our old self was crucified," and then follows with imperatives in Romans 6:11–13, "Consider yourselves to be dead to sin . . . do not let sin reign . . . but present yourselves to God as those alive from the dead." Thus the imperative admonishes the believer to hold fast the salvation that has been received, and the content and context of these commands encourage growth in righteousness and holy living. Sanctification is the logical working out by faith of the salvation received in justification. Just as the Christian has been delivered by the Spirit from the bondage of this present evil age, so he is empowered by the Spirit to live consistent with the freedom made possible by Christ.[153]

Howard stresses that Paul uses the imperative to show that "sin must cease and the new man in Christ must live victoriously."[154] This is possible, because the indicative has shown that a new spiritual person has been created by the work of the Holy Spirit. But this new person in Christ must learn to make the Holy Spirit the new means of living and use the redeemed resources given in the new birth. "If we live by the Spirit, let us also walk by the Spirit" (Gal. 5:25). The personal relationship begun with the Holy Spirit at regeneration now moves to the deeper level of control by the Spirit, the "filling with the Spirit" that Paul describes in Ephesians 5:18–6:9.[155] Thus sanctification is intimately related to the initial justifying and regenerating work wrought by the Spirit on the basis of faith in Christ's atoning work. Sanctification is not a process of meritorious work by the believer but it is a new and deeper relationship of submission to the leadership of the Holy Spirit, also on the basis of the full victory over this age made possible by Christ. Although it is not possible to examine the dynamics of sanctification fully in this context, it must be stressed that although it does involve both a progression of growth and a crisis of faith-submission to the Holy Spirit, the life of holiness made possible by the sanctifying work of the Spirit is grounded on the Atonement and is inseparable from the totality of salvation as proclaimed in the New Testament.[156]

C. The Appropriation of Salvation

1. Faith The basic character of the covenant at Sinai was its emphasis on faith. In the covenant agreement, Yahweh said, "If you will indeed obey My voice and keep My covenant, then you shall be My own possession among all the peoples" (Exod. 19:5). Snaith explains how this stipulation was based on faith:

> But why must Israel obey the Ten Commandments? . . . The reason is given in the verse which precedes the Commandments: "I am the Lord thy God which brought thee out of the land of Egypt, out of the house of

bondage" (Ex. 20:2). The essence of the faith, therefore, is . . . that Jehovah was and is their Savior, and He has saved them, saved them now in order that they may do His Will . . . being truely *(sic)* thankful to a Husband-God who has never been anything else than faithful from the beginning.[157]

Throughout his ministry Moses placed emphasis on faith (cf. Heb. 11:24-29). Yahweh's statement of this redemption of the people from Egypt introduced the covenant, and the people responded with appropriate faith to accept it before they ever knew the detailed, external conditions (Exod. 19:8). The legal conditions that followed were only an application and demonstration of the basic requirement of faith.[158] The essence of the faith of Israel was not that they were coerced to act according to the laws of morality because Yahweh was moral; it was rather that Yahweh had been and still was their savior, and He saved them to do His will.[159] The fundamental element of faith, then, is surrender to the person of Yahweh. "Faith as interpreted by the Old Testament is always the response of man to the primary activity of God."[160]

The *niph'al* stem of *'mn* is used to denote the relationship of man to God. In passages where this usage is found, *'mn* expresses not only the correctness of external behavior toward God, but also the element of disposition, "and it is not restricted to single action performed only once, but applied to the whole of man's relationship to God."[161]

In the *hiph'il he'emin* ("to believe") the usage in relation to persons is associated with the idea of trust. This trust includes the recognition of the claim on one—the claim that is involved in the relationship of friend or servant for example—and at the same time it includes also the recognition that this claim is binding on the one who himself trusts. Thus the reciprocal interaction makes trust a two-sided relationship. In the Old Testament *he'emin* is used only for a personal relationship, for "behind the word which is trusted there stands the man who is trusted."[162]

The *hiph'il* is also used to express the relationship between God and man. The reciprocal relationship between God and man is part of the essence of faith, but this relationship is never initiated by man. Faith often involves the acknowledgment of God's demand and man's obedience to it (Deut. 9:23; Ps. 119:66).[163]

Often, *'mn* sums up all the ways by which people express their relationships to God. In Isaiah 43:10 this relationship is expressed as knowing Him. In Hosea 4:1, in addition to the acknowledgment of God, the element of emotion is included. Also in faith one's relationship to God excludes all others. It involves worshiping God, "with all your heart and with all your soul" (Deut. 6:5). Thus in the Old Testament faith means "a relationship to God which embraces the whole man in every part of his outward behavior and his inner life."[164]

On the basis of the definition of faith as interpersonal trust and surrender along with a material sharing of selves in a personal relationship, it is clear that the law was given in order to provide a means by which people could express their part in the relationship by obedient subjection to it. Neither the faith nor the obedience brings any reward as such, but "the faith relationship in itself is expounded as the righteous fulfillment of the covenant fellowship on man's part."[165] In this way justification in the covenant was based not on proper observance of the Law, but on the intimate interpersonal relationship between man and God. Faith took on the character of the attitude by which man actualized his relationship with God. Eichrodt concludes:

> Thus the Covenant which was bestowed upon the people of Israel in the fulfillment of the promise to Abraham acquires its inner vitality not from cultic event but from the conscious spiritual and physical attitude of the member of Covenant Community toward the promise of the one who established the Covenant.[166]

This interpersonal character of faith is also seen in the New Testament. In Paul's thought, faith is not simply assent to particular truths, nor is it a belief that God rewards those who seek Him, but it is the surrender of one's whole being in trust to Christ and an identification of oneself with Christ's rejection of sin and obedience to God. Faith is a turning in a new direction, an entering into a right relationship with God through personal appropriation of Christ's work. Faith is thus not directed toward a proposition, but toward a person (1 Thess. 1:8, toward God; Col 2:5, toward Christ). This interpersonal trust does not preclude intellectual belief and commitment (Rom. 10:9), nor does the work of faith merit salvation. It is the behavior of one who has been "crucified with Christ" (Gal. 2:20) and who lives as one in whom Christ dwells.[167]

In the Johannine literature, it is believing that procures salvation. Eternal life is the result of believing (John 3:16, 36; 6:40; 20:31; 1 John 5:13). Believing is also a renunciation of the world. Those who belong to Jesus no longer belong to the world and its orientation to evil (John 15:19; 17:14, 15).[168]

In Hebrews, faith is often understood as trust that God will carry out His promise and trust that He has power to work miracles (Heb. 11:11, 17-19, 29). Obedience is also seen here as resulting from faith (see Heb. 11). Paul also stresses this aspect of faith as obedience, as well as a body of doctrine to which one adheres (1 Tim. 1:19; 3:9, 16; 6:21; see also 2 Peter 1:1; Jude 3:20).

This biblical emphasis on the faith relationship to God places stress on interpersonal trust as the dynamic that unites the believer to Christ. It is through the maintenance of this faith relationship that one remains in this covenant of personal fellowship with God through the Holy Spirit. Thus the covenant model as it is initiated by God's grace and accepted and maintained on the basis of Christ's work made efficacious in the believer by his uniting with the life and death of Christ through faith is the most satisfying theological understanding of salvation.

2. Repentance and conversion

Closely related to the interpersonal trust of faith are the concepts of repentance and conversion. While the Old Testament prophets fiercely rejected cultic actions of repentance that were only mechanical formality without the involvement of the heart (Amos 5:5; Hos. 7:14; Isa. 1:10ff.; 29:13; 58:5; Jer. 14:12), the right attitude toward God's saving actions is repentance. A number of terms are used in the Old Testament to express the turning away from sin, but the idea is most fully summarized by the term *shub*. It describes the necessary behavior, "to make a turn," but it also expresses the personal aspect of turning away from a former direction and turning toward a forgiving God.[169]

Especially Hosea and Jeremiah stress conversion in their preaching. The love of God seeks alienated humanity and woos it back to Himself. Jeremiah portrays the inexhaustible possibilities of God's mercy in insisting that the heart of man should decide for God. By showing the meaning of *shub*—"turning away, turning back, inward conversion and renewal"—he exhorts every person to conversion (Jer. 23:14; 25:5; 26:3; 35:15; 36:3, 7).[170] Although the prophets see forgiveness as the free action of God, human activity is also important in conversion. Eichrodt notes that forgiveness is "a liberation for personal fellowship which reached far beyond either objective purification or legalistic remission of punishment."[171] The prophets see sin as a corrupt attitude toward Yahweh. Repentance as a personal act corresponds to this personal view of sin. Repentance is thus a turning to Yahweh with all one's being in obedience to His will. This turning requires unconditional trust in Him and the renunciation of all human idolatrous help. This conversion to Yahweh results in a new attitude of turning from evil and ungodliness. Unfortunately, this living and personal understanding of repentance and conversion tended to deteriorate into a more legal understanding in the exilic and postexilic community. The essence of conversion here becomes the turning away from cultic sins and obedience to the Law.[172]

In the New Testament, the ideas of repentance and conversion are expressed in terms derived from *strephō* and *metanoeō*. *Metanoia*, the noun form, occurs twenty-three times. It means "change of mind," "regret," "remorse" in classical Greek, but the New Testament meanings include religious and ethical connotations. Thus *metanoia* means "conversion" or "repentance." This involves changing one's mind not only in external action but also in internal intention. In the synoptic Gospels, repentance involves confessing sins with the intention of amending them (Matt. 3:6; Mark 1:5). Repentance is basic to salvation (Luke 13:1–5) and results not just in words but also in obedient action (Matt. 21:28–32). For Jesus *metanoia* is the way of salvation. God's revelation requires radical conversion and unconditional decision, a definite turning from evil and a turning toward God in total obedience (Matt. 4:17; 18:3; Mark 1:15). Jesus' proclamation of the kingdom of God is one of unconditional turning to God and unconditional turning from all that is against God. This demand for conversion is addressed to all without exception, and it is a major reason for Jesus' conflict with the Pharisees, who had come to equate repentance with legal obedience.[173]

The positive aspect of turning to God is intimately related to faith. Repentance is a break with the old walk of evil in response to the threat of divine judgment. It makes possible the establishment of a new personal relationship with God, or faith. Repentance is not faith, but the kind of faith that establishes a new relationship of interpersonal trust with God is not possible without a desire to separate oneself from the sin that has made salvation necessary. Unless there is repentance, *metanoia*, there cannot be faith, *pistis* (Matt. 21:32).[174] Jesus' hearers are "expected to commit themselves to all that Jesus himself stood for. . . . To believe in the gospel meant precisely to believe in Jesus himself," notes Guthrie. Faith and repentance are linked in Jesus' proclamation (Mark 1:15), and faith in the gospel must be complementary to repentance if forgiveness is to occur (Luke 24:47). Although forgiveness is unearned and is given by grace, the moral integrity of forgiveness requires repentance.[175]

In Acts, Peter connects repentance with forgiveness of sins (Acts 2:38; 3:19). Repentance and forgiveness are gifts of God (Acts 5:31), and repentance has been given to the Gentiles (Acts 11:18). Paul declares that God has commanded universal repentance (Acts 17:30) and that Gentiles have been called to repent and turn to God (Acts 26:20).

In his epistles Paul tends to emphasize faith rather than forgiveness. However, his understanding of faith as acceptance of God's message in response to the gospel (Rom. 10:17; 1 Cor. 1:21; Eph. 1:13) requires a decision about Jesus Christ. And although justification is realized only through a faith commitment to Jesus Christ, repentance of sins is still a prerequisite for faith and salvation (Rom. 2:4–5; 2 Cor. 7:9–10; 12:21).[176]

Therefore, repentance and conversion involve a rejection of one's former direction and a turning to God in obedience. This "turning around" must also result in the interpersonal union of faith. Neither is faith acceptable for salvation if it is merely intellectual assent to the gospel. The radical commitment indicated by *metanoia* gives integrity and foundation to faith so that forgiveness and salvation result. Thus faith, repentance, and conversion function together to appropriate the salvation made possible by Christ's atonement so that the living covenant fellowship with God may become a reality for the faithful.

D. A Survey of Atonement Theories

The reality of how salvation was made possible through the work of Christ has been variously described by means of models and metaphors in the development of Christian doctrine. Various aspects of the atonement have been stressed in the major atonement theories to develop primarily since the eleventh century. The primary theories have numerous derivative views but generally include ideas such as ransom, satisfaction, penal substitution, moral influence, representation, and governmental and classical or dramatic emphases.

1. Ransom Many of the Fathers such as Irenaeus, Origen, the Greek fathers, and Augustine emphasized the relationship of Christ's death to Satan. The ransom theory holds that Christ redeemed humanity with His blood and exchanged His soul for our souls. He thus gave His life to Satan as a ransom for those who were in bondage to Satan. Origen notes that a deceit was effected on Satan, who accepted the soul of Christ without realizing that he could not endure the presence of a sinless soul and thus could not contain Him after the captives had been released. Augustine provides a variation by noting that death was Satan's dominion, but by inflicting death on one who was sinless, he forfeited his control over it. Thus in all these approaches Satan is seen as being entitled to certain kinds of dominion and that a ransom or bartering relationship between God and Satan is entered into in order to bring about humanity's release.[177]

More recently some scholars such as Gustaf Aulén have seen this Latin, or classic, motif not so much in terms of ransom as in terms of cosmic combat. Christ, during His life and certainly in His death, struggled with the powers of darkness and emerged triumphant. For Aulén, the Atonement was not a legal transaction, as in the Latin tradition, or an inspiring example of love, as in the Greek Orthodox tradition, but it was effected in the cosmic duel in which Christ overcame the forces that held humanity in bondage.[178]

2. Satisfaction Anselm sees the need of atonement for sin as the basis of the Incarnation in his treatise, *Cur Deus Homo? (Why the God-Man?)*. Obedience is the honor humanity owes to God, and disobedience detracts from God what belongs to Him and it brings Him dishonor. The sinner owes to God a restoration of obedience as well as a satisfaction or reparation for his disobedience. Punishment of humanity would satisfy God's honor. However, disobedient humanity cannot provide adequate satisfaction, for all the contrition and obedience that can be mustered cannot even maintain the present obedience required. Furthermore the obedience of the whole world cannot offset the dishonor to God caused by one sin. The paradox is that man must satisfy God's honor but cannot. Thus the God-Man is necessary. Since Christ's life is sinless, He owes God nothing and the righteousness of His life outweighs the evil of all sin. The superogatory obedience of His life has merit to offer to God's honor to make amends for the dishonor perpetrated on His Name by humanity. There is no concept here of payment to Satan, for Anselm rejects the idea that Satan has any rights whatsoever. Neither does Anselm stress the vicarious suffering of the penalty of sin. God's honor is restored by obedience, not by suffering that is caused by a sin of ignorance.[179] Christ's obedience is thus propitiatory and meritorious.

3. Moral influence In reaction to Anselm's satisfaction emphasis, Peter Abelard advanced the view that the work of Christ's suffering and death reveals God's love for the unworthy in such a way as to inspire a response of gratitude and bring the sinner back to obedience to God. The work of Christ thus inspires moral renewal as an act of gratitude. Abelard rejected both the ransom view that Christ paid a debt to Satan and Anselm's view that He paid a debt to God.[180] He found it difficult to conceive how suffering is the only way that love is revealed. Abelard does, however, correctly perceive that Christ's work is motivated by love and the proper response to it is obedience.

Numerous variants of this moral influence theory of atonement tend to focus the atoning work to some extent on the response of the human soul to the work of Christ. Repentance becomes a work of atonement, and the objective work of God in Christ is seen to have little or no effect on God. Proponents of this theory such as Auguste Sabatier, F. D. Maurice, F. W. Robertson, Albrecht Ritschl, and Horace Bushnell have in common some form of the idea that the work of Christ proclaims God's willingness to forgive sin on the condition that it be abandoned. The death of Christ is the death of a martyr who battled against evil and at last succumbed. Christ's work breaks down our opposition to God.[181]

These theories bear a similarity to the rabbinic ideas of repentance and obedience functioning as atoning acts of justification. They rightly emphasize the moral example of Christ, but do not adequately give place to the objective aspects of God's work of transforming grace in the believer as a requisite for righteousness nor do they emphasize identification with Christ's righteousness or His objective work of atonement for us.

4. Penal substitution Having its roots in Anselm's satisfaction theory, but finding full development in the Reformation and post-Reformation eras, the idea of penal substitution sees Christ as absorbing the penalty of God's curse on sin in place of the sinner. It could be logically expected that the question would be asked as to how Christ's death satisfied God's honor.

The indulgence controversies had exposed the medieval concept of merits, and Luther was obsessed with demonstrating the sole sufficiency of Christ for salvation. For him, the inadequacy of the works of believers and his own Augustinian view of sin as depravity would not be content with Anselm's emphasis on sin as doing dishonor to God. His own discoveries of "the righteousness of God" placed salvation beyond the level even of human participation. In response to Erasmus he wrote "On the Bondage of the Will," a tract that denied every human response toward righteousness apart from God's grace alone.

The question thus arose as to how humanity could be saved in view of this radical moral corruption and helplessness.

As society and political theory had developed throughout the period of feudalism, the idea of justice came to be seen in terms of abstract law rather than the personal dignity of the age of chivalry. Justice was served when the offender was punished, not to restore personal relationships, but to satisfy the penalties required by justice. These views of retributive justice were used by Luther to describe death as the legal penalty for sin. Since the law of the age demands punishment for sin, someone must endure that punishment. Since Christ was made "to be sin for us" (2 Cor. 5:21), Luther sees Christ as the legal substitute to bear the legal penalty for sin.

Luther does see that it is God's love that moved Him to give His Son and that the benefits of Christ's work must be appropriated by faith.

Melanchthon formulated this penal theory in a more rigid way by emphasizing the objectivity of Christ's work so that it is only God who is appeased and reconciled to man. The sacrificial metaphor, as Grensted notes, is thus redefined. Sacrifice is no longer just a supreme honor of worship done to God, but an expiatory offering to turn aside the wrath of an angry Deity. Such an interpretation of sacrifice scarcely[182] does justice to the Old Testament understanding, which included several forms of offerings that did not involve the shedding of blood, and it also overlooks the fact that the most serious forms of sin had no means of sacrificial expiation. Forgiveness was based totally on God's forgiving grace in the Old Testament. The offering of sacrifices was an act of obedient and faithful worship.

John Calvin stresses that a righteous God cannot love iniquity, and so His wrath must fall on our sin. God can show His love to humanity only when His avenging justice is satisfied. Christ must therefore be the substitute and take the pain and penalties of sin on Himself. When this is done,

God transfers the righteousness of our substitute to us and, apparently by a legal fiction, imputes Christ's righteousness to the Christian. Calvin says:

> ... justified by faith is he who excluded from the righteousness of works, grasps the righteousness of Christ by faith, and clothed in it, appears in God's sight not as a sinner but as a righteous man. Therefore, we explain justification simply as the acceptance with which God receives us into his favor as righteous men. And we say that it consists in the remission of sins and the imputation of Christ's righteousness.[183]

If the individual is treated only "as if" he were righteous, how is the corruption of the soul healed? Furthermore, Calvin points out that God's wrath does not really rest on Christ, for this would be unjust. But God treats Christ as if He were angry. Christ does not actually bear God's hostility, but merely something exactly like it! Calvin says:

> Yet we do not suggest that God was ever inimical or angry toward him. How could he be angry toward his beloved Son, "in whom his heart reposed" [cf. Matt. 3:17]? How could Christ by his intercession appease the Father toward others, if he were himself hateful to God? This is what we are saying: he bore the weight of divine severity, since he was "stricken and afflicted" [cf. Isa. 53:5] by God's hand, and experienced all the signs of a wrathful and avenging God.[184]

Note the exegesis in Isaiah 53:5 that Christ was "stricken and afflicted," as Calvin adds, "by God's hand." His insistence on interpreting atonement as penal forces him to see Christ's suffering as punishment by God, but his sense of justice refuses to allow him to interpret this supposedly divine punishment on Christ as wrath. Therefore, Christ suffers not wrath, but punishment like it, and humanity does not really have righteousness but is treated as if it did. The understanding of righteousness as a moral quality rather than as a relationship requires an exclusively objective view of the atonement and an imputation of the merits of Christ to God's children in a way Grensted describes as "a mere legal fiction."[185]

Thus, along with the later Protestant Scholastics such as Quenstedt and Turretin, the Reformers interpreted the work of Christ as satisfying the demands of God's justice by receiving in Himself the penalty for our sins as the substitute for humanity. Justice is seen as exclusively retributive and transactional, with its demands being met only on penal terms.[186] While Luther saw faith as necessary for the appropriation of the benefits of Christ's work, this position tended to develop toward sacramentalism, with the result that personal faith and intimate relationship with God became secondary. Calvin, moreover, emphasized predestination and the objective Godward aspects of Christ's substitutionary work to the extent that human faith-participation in the work of Christ became overlaid by a rigid, deterministic, and juristic view of divine decrees and a virtual loss of the covenantal-interpersonal ideas of the biblical teaching on salvation.

5. Governmental The Socinians reacted against the penal substitutionary views in a manner so extreme as to abandon the idea of atonement. They did, however, make criticisms so telling that they shook the very foundations of the penal views. They pointed out that satisfaction and pardon are incompatible. If a creditor has been satisfied by a payment of a debt, there is no need then to forgive the debt. Furthermore, they questioned the justice of penal satisfaction. If, as Anselm had said, the one who makes satisfaction must be identical with the offender, then it is unjust to impose the penalty of the guilty on the innocent. Furthermore, Christ's suffering does not meet the demand of satisfaction, because sinners deserve eternal death, and Christ did not suffer eternal death, but temporal death.[187]

In defense of the Atonement, Hugo Grotius modified the substitutionary theory by viewing justice not as the need to mollify the arbitrary will of an individual ruler, but as the need for orderly government and constitutional justice in a moral universe. Grotius rejects the idea of God administering absolute, retributive justice as an offended party claiming compensation. For him, punishment is the responsibility of the State. Sin is an offense against public order and punishment involves only the restoration of order, not retributive compensation for injury. If God sees fit to modify the law that requires death as a punishment for sin, He may do so. God is free to remove punishment altogether, but punishment does serve a deterrent purpose in a moral government. Government can be maintained, then, by a substitution of Christ for sinners. The strict demands of absolute justice are relaxed. Christ voluntarily accepts the punishment deserved by all, and God's hatred of sin is vindicated by the example of Christ's suffering, with the result that individual sinners will be deterred from evil by this exhibition of God's wrath. Thus the moral influence of fear serves to maintain order.[188]

The Arminian and Wesleyan theologians adopted Grotius's governmental theory with some modifications. The Arminian Curcellaeus emphasized the idea of sacrifice rather than satisfaction through the endurance of punishment. By offering Himself as a sacrifice, Christ, according to Curcellaeus,

> did not therefore, as men often think, make satisfaction by suffering all the punishments which we had deserved for our sins. For, firstly, that does not pertain to the nature of a sacrifice, and has nothing in common with it. For sacrifices are not payments of debts, as is evident from those of the law. The beasts which were slain for sinners did not pay the penalties which they had deserved, nor was their blood a sufficient ransom for the souls of men. But they were simply offerings by which men sought to turn God to compassion, and to obtain from Him remission of sins.[189]

Thus Curcellaeus rejected the penal substitutionary and satisfaction concepts in favor of a sacrificial basis for justification. This modified the strict governmental approach and emphasized the priestly work of Christ as propitiatory but not penal.

English Arminianism was less creative in adapting the traditional governmental theory. John Wesley, while not setting forth any full theory of atonement, seemed to buy into the Anglican and Calvinistic emphasis on penal substitution. In his note on 2 Corinthians 5:21 he says, "[We] must have been consumed by the divine justice, had not this atonement been made for our sins."[190] And in commenting on 1 Peter 2:24, he says that Christ bore our sins, "that is, the punishment due them."[191] He also utilized the Anselmic idea that sin deserves infinite punishment because it is a violation of God's honor. However, he differed from the Calvinists on two important points: (1) the work of Christ is universal in its extent and (2) the work of Christ is conditional in that it becomes effective only as the individual accepts it in faith. Thus Wesley did not consistently adopt a governmental theory, though he did see the necessity of a moral government of the universe as being consistent with the character of God.[192]

Richard Watson did accept the governmental model, though he emphasized that God's government is not only based on abstract concepts of moral rectitude but is for the benefit of the human person. This opens up a more personal concept of the divine-human relationship than was seen in the strict theory of Grotius.[193]

In America the followers of Jonathan Edwards were influenced by the English Arminians, and Jonathan Edwards, Jr., with Samuel Hopkins developed modifications of the governmental theory based on a careful analysis of the ideal of justice. The result was a rejection of two of the inherent Calvinistic elements: (1) the penal view of the sufferings of Christ and (2) the doctrine of a limited atonement. They emphasized that the Atonement was not only directed objectively to God alone, but also was useful subjectively as an example and motivation for humanity to seek holiness and obedience to God.[194]

The nineteenth-century English Methodist William Burt Pope was drawn toward the governmental view, although he was unable to deal completely with the penal aspect. He says that Christ "undertook the service of man's redemption as laid upon Him, and He accomplished it through all its requirements down to the suffering of the penalty of Divine displeasure against sin." At another place, however, he virtually contradicts[195] himself by saying,

> The sufferings of Christ were those of a *Sacrifice* Divinely appointed to take the place of a penalty, and reconciled God to man as if they had been the sinner's own punishment. Christ therefore by His death did effect something in God; though strictly speaking He only carried out in act what had been already effected in purpose. . . . Arminianism holds that the Sacrifice was offered for the whole world: it must therefore for that reason also renounce the commutative theory of exact and mutual compensation; since some may perish for whom Christ died, and He would be defrauded of His reward in them.[196]

Pope thus rejects the Anselmic idea of *quid pro quo* satisfaction that led to a limited view of the Atonement in Calvin. He does not seem to see, however, that if Christ suffered the penalty that God had pronounced on sin, then God's justice is satisfied and no further condemnation can be required. Theoretically, God's justice is satisfied even for those who do not repent. This leads to universalism, a legacy from which Arminianism has not entirely escaped. Furthermore, God does not wish for some to perish for whom Christ died, because then Christ's penal work for them would be in vain. The only alternative, it seems, for the penal view is to see the penal sufferings as being substituted only for those persons who are elect, so that those who do not respond in faith are not offered the benefits of the Atonement. The result of this limited penal interpretation is predestination, and this is inconsistent with the biblical teaching of Christ's work, at least as Wesleyan-Arminians understand it.

The American Methodist John Miley sees this inconsistency and suggests a corrective. While generally following a governmental emphasis, Miley states that the divine justice must be maintained, but the personal character of God does not require penal satisfaction either for personal contentment or divine integrity. Any penal satisfaction must be found in the punishment of the actual sinner. He continues:

> To exaggerate it into a necessity for satisfaction in the punishment of Christ as substitute in penalty, is to pervert Scripture exegesis, and equally to pervert all theology and philosophy in the case. . . . God may and does wish that he may save. . . . And real as the divine displeasure is against sin and against sinners, atonement is made, not in its satisfaction, but in fulfillment of the rectoral office of justice.[197]

Miley fully accepts the atoning nature of Christ's sufferings but rejects the idea that they are penally retributive. Proper exegesis, he says, emphasizes the vicarious and redemptive suffering of Christ, but not as a penal substitute. The governmental interpretation of the atoning sufferings of Christ is not that they substitute Christ for the sinner in receiving the penalty of retributive justice, but the Atonement is provisory in that it renders people salvable but does not of necessity save them. Thus the Atonement is not the discharge of the "sinner through the merited punishment of his sin in his substitute, but an actual forgiveness, and such as can issue only in the nonexecution of penalty." The death of Christ is the declaration of God's honor and justice, not because the penalty for sin was transferred to Christ, but because the sufferings of Christ are a provisory substitute for penalty. Christ's death makes possible the remission of the penalty for sin, because the believer is actually forgiven as he is united with Christ in faith. There is no reason why sin cannot be forgiven, since forgiveness is consistent with divine justice. This, Miley says, is the only consistent soteriology for Wesleyan-Arminianism.[198] To assert that the satisfaction of God's justice by a penalty will allow forgiveness to be received on the condition of faith is inconsistent. Penal substitution is real and absolute. Miley says further:

> Sin suffers its merited punishment; absolute justice receives its full retributive claim. No further penalty can fall either upon Christ or upon the sinners replaced in his penal substitution.... Their discharge is a requirement of justice itself. Hence there cannot be a conditional penal substitution.[199]

Thus, the governmental theory, particularly as modified by the Edwardsians and such Wesleyan-Arminians as Miley and Raymond, emphasizes the idea of God as the benevolent Lord who maintains order and good government for the good of the governed. The conditionality of salvation cannot be based on a penal substitution concept that is consistent only with the juristic and predestinarian theories of the Reformers. The work of Christ is seen as sacrificial and as a revelation of God's mercy and love.

In summary, Anselm's emphasis on the importance of maintaining God's honor and on the atoning significance of Christ's obedience are important elements to be maintained in a theory of the Atonement. The emphasis on the moral influence of Christ's life and death as motivations for holiness is vital. When understood sacrificially, Christ's substitutionary atoning work on the behalf of humanity provides a way of understanding the priestly work of Christ. On our behalf, He offered Himself as a sacrifice to God, so that when we are united with Him in faith, we offer our very selves also to God. The governmental model opens up a more personal concept for understanding Christ's work than is found in the penal substitutionary judicial or transactional concepts. As modified by the Wesleyan-Arminians, the governmental idea is enhanced and the necessity for faith-union with Christ as a condition for salvation is more strongly grounded. However, all the models for these theories of the atonement are drawn from societal and political concepts that are extrabiblical. There is a need to develop an understanding of atonement and salvation that is inductively derived from a biblical model and deals with the essential elements of Christ's work.

IV. ALTERNATIVE MODELS OF SALVATION

In order to understand any concept or idea, it is helpful to find a model that is a replica or copy of certain important aspects of the idea it models. A model is an attempt to reproduce in accurate forms an accessible embodiment of the original. By emphasizing those aspects of an idea or mystery that are known to our experience, we can relate more specifically to the whole concept in question.[200] In theology, models have been widely used as concrete objectifications for abstract ideas. The biblical and theological truths relating to salvation have received this modeling treatment perhaps more intensively than any other theological concept. The models of adoption, justification, covenant, sacrifice, governmental justice, and many others are models that enable us to understand at least some aspects of the magnificent mystery of God's redemptive work. Models become misleading, however, when they begin to insert into our understanding any concepts that are not analogous to the reality of the idea they are attempting to reflect. Language itself is a form of symbolic modeling that enables us to reproduce by symbolism ideas or realities that cannot be fully expressed any other way.

In the theological models that have been developed throughout the history of doctrine to describe the atoning work of Christ, it is possible to see many correct reflections of the reality of what Christ accomplished. Conversely, the cultural and political conditioning of some of the models leads them to reflect the characteristics of specific historical periods with more accuracy than they reflect the biblical reports of the reality of Christ's work. This is the case with the penal theories of the atonement. Other theories do reflect accurate models of some aspects of Christ's work, such as the maintenance of God's honor, the morally inspiring example of Christ, the justice that characterizes a moral universe, and the vanquishing of the powers of evil. It can be seen, however, that rarely does a model represent all that the reality behind it contains. This limitation should be accepted, but care should be taken to prevent the incorporation of deficient or alien elements that render the model inaccurate as a reflection of the reality.

The use of models inductively derived from biblical material minimizes the problems of distortion and inaccuracy, provided those models themselves are not allowed to gather cultural baggage that creates theological distortions. An example is the model of propitiation that has the correct emphasis of portraying the objective effects of the Atonement on God. "Propitiation" can, however, carry pagan elements of bartering and appeasement that distort the meaning of the biblical usage of the model. When defined inductively in terms of its usage within the biblical canon, the model of the covenant is extremely useful in describing the reality of salvation and may be the most accurate and useful way of theologically analyzing the concept. A psychological model based on the biblical concept of faith-union is also instructive in arriving at an accurate, inductive definition of the reality and apppropriation of salvation. An analysis of these theological and psychological models will prove useful.

A. Theological

The covenant as a theological model for salvation is satisfying because it deals with the relationship between God and humanity in interpersonal and community terms. The tendency to see salvation as exclusively individual is corrected by the understanding of covenant as a model that involves both individual and community responsibilities and benefits. The biblical understanding of sin and righteousness in interpersonal terms is handled adequately by the covenant model, and the reality of the interrelationship between a personal God and a personal humanity is understood satisfactorily within the covenant frame of reference. Participation in the covenant is predicated on obedience, and the act of sacrifice as an expression of personal repentance, self-abasement, and obedience to God's sovereign will is accurately descriptive of the New Testament understanding of Christ's work on our behalf. The offering of the Law as an act of God's grace to instruct worshipers in appropriate behavior within the covenant relationship is consistent with God's offering of Himself through Christ as the model for appropriate faith-obedience. Thus Christ becomes the "Pioneer" who leads the New Israel, the community of faith, through a "new and living way" to God. By participation in the life and death experience of Christ by faith the believer and community are enabled to reestablish the covenant relationship that God by His grace has initiated. The maintenance of the covenant community does result in the moral consistency or order that the governmental theory stresses; however, this order must be understood not as an abstract political construct, but it should be exegeted in terms of interpersonal faith and righteousness. Thus faith is the basis of participation in the covenant relationship of salvation.

B. Psychological

The covenant understanding of the divine-human relationship through faith is enhanced by an awareness of the psychological dynamics involved in a faith relationship. Although the relationship between Christ and the believer is often described as mystical, this term has unfortunate connotations. Mystical terminology tends to minimize the identity of the human self as it is merged in the ocean of God. The psychological model of empathy is more helpful in understanding the faith-union relationship. The word *empathy* is derived from the Greek *en* ("into") and *pathos* ("passion" or "feeling"). Originally, the concept referred to the process of motor mimicry in which a person responded to a work of art or an athletic event with involuntary movements of the eyes, body, and internal organs.[201] The concept of empathy developed to include aesthetic or emotional involvement and the capacity for vicariously experiencing the feelings and volitions of another person. Psychiatrist Harry Stack Sullivan says that anxiety about anything whatsoever in the mother can induce a corresponding anxiety in her infant.[202]

Others define empathy as an emotional contagion that may be outside cognition or beyond the capacity of a person to share in the feelings of another by actually entering the other's perception of emotion and volition. One feels the same emotions as another by a vicarious sharing of experience. This is an identification with another in such a way that the perceiver vicariously experiences the same emotions and feelings as the primary feeling person.[203] Thus the union of experiences through empathy is an intensely personal relationship. It is this type of relationship that must be established between the believer and Christ, and empathy describes, at least partially, the relationship of interpersonal trust through which the life and death of Christ vicariously become the life and death of the believer through faith. Through faith the believer unites with Christ and dies with Him to sin so that Christ's resurrection also becomes the believer's life (Rom. 6:1–10). By sharing in Christ's obedient death, the believer also experiences Christ's victorious life, which overcomes death. This victory is spiritual in the present and will be actually physical in the future (1 Cor. 15).

The idea of empathy thus provides a model for understanding the vicarious faith-union through which the work of Christ becomes efficacious for the believer. It is by sharing in the obedience of Christ that the believer is reconciled to God.

V. CONCLUSION

The work of salvation is interpersonal in nature. Although some of the biblical and theological models reflect legal and governmental concepts, the foundational understanding of what occurs between God and humanity through the incarnational work of Christ is profoundly personal. Every biblical metaphor for salvation describes a transaction between a person and persons.

Also, it is clearly seen that grace is the primary motivation for the Incarnation and thus for the death of Christ as a part of the incarnational work of Christ. Justice is a characteristic of God, but an interpretation of that righteous justice as penal retribution does not adequately explain the actions of a loving God who gave His only Son. The death Christ experienced was a priestly work of sacrifice. On our behalf, Christ gives Himself in obedience as a sacrifice that establishes a new covenant with God. Just as the Sinai covenant was bilateral and required the participation of both parties, the new covenant requires that we give ourselves also in obedience to God. In union with Christ, we die. He has acted for us, and in faith His action becomes ours. As our High Priest, He sacrificially takes us to God.

Christ's death was the consequence of sin, but He was killed by sinful humanity under the guise of obedience to the Law. Reliance on the Law is seen to lead not to righteousness, but to the slaying of the Lawgiver. Christ's death expressed the lengths to which God would go, even to participating in the consequences of evil self-righteousness. Humanity, by following the rigidly legalistic forms of dealing with what was considered sin by human interpretations of the Law, revealed its own bankruptcy in restoring right fellowship with God. Christ's death reveals the consequences of sinful self-righteousness and pride. His act of submissive obedience to God in the face of the consequences of sin is the supreme example in history of the self-giving love of God, and His resurrection is the supreme example of the consequences of a righteous relationship with the Father. Righteous obedience is thus victorious over all the consequences of sin. Christ leads humanity to a new alternative as the "Pioneer" of our salvation.

Death, however, is still the consequence of sin. Christ did not absorb the penalty for sin, because sinners still face eternal death. Christ made possible a way of escape from eternal death through making union with Him possible through faith. Christ's death is propitiatory because it was a sacrificial expression of penitence on behalf of humanity. His death is expiatory because He bears sin's consequences and removes its guilt for those who are in Him. His death is vicarious because by faith-union with Him, we can experience His death and resurrection and express penitence for sin and victory over its consequences as living sacrifices (Rom. 12:1-2).

Christ's work was not just a moral example to inspire moral living, but a sacrifice of obedient worship in which we may participate vicariously through faith. Through this work, a grieved God whose faith in us has been compromised is enabled to believe in us again as He sees that we share in the grief for sin and righteous obedience that Christ expressed on our behalf. By faith, His act becomes our act. By empathy, we share Christ's love for God and His obedience to the Father's will. The love between the Father and the Son becomes the love of reconciliation between the Father and those united in will with the Son. This union removes the alienation caused by disobedience and fulfills God's purposes for salvation for all humanity —for freedom from the power of sin. The believer has no reason to remember the sinful past and has every reason to look forward to sanctification and the ultimate fulfillment of God's redemptive history in the eschatological consummation of eternity.

Finally, for Wesleyan-Arminianism, it is mandatory that the understanding of the doctrine of salvation be both biblical and synergistic. All theories of the atonement that utilize models not consistent with the biblical covenant model should be carefully examined. The subtle infusion of static and impersonal logical categories into Wesleyan thought threatens to compromise its unique interpersonal genius. The personal work of the Holy Spirit in the life of the believer and the relational character of Christ's incarnational work should not be distorted by thought forms from Reformed sources that tend to introduce rigid logical or deterministic categories into Christian doctrine. Arminius struggled valiantly against the predestinarian Calvinism of his time, and contemporary Wesleyan-Arminianism must retain these distinctives of free will and voluntary faith-response to God. The utilization of models that direct the emphasis away from biblical and Wesleyan-Arminian free will and full salvation should be resisted in contemporary Wesleyan theology. Furthermore, models that reject the objective sacrificial and vicarious nature of the work of Christ must not be allowed to diminish the commitment of Wesleyan thought to a salvation that has been completed for us only in Christ.

NOTES

[1] R. E. Clements, *Old Testament Theology* (Atlanta: John Knox, 1978), p. 58 (personality), pp. 96-97 (covenant); also Walther Eichrodt, *Theology of the Old Testament*, 2 vols. (Philadelphia: Westminster, 1961), 2:13-14. While it is open to question whether covenant is the key theme of the entire canon, it does seem to be central to the specific doctrine of salvation.

[2] For discussion of the canonical approach to biblical theology see James Sanders, *Torah and Canon* (Philadelphia: Fortress, 1972); Brevard Childs, *Biblical Theology in Crisis* (Philadelphia: Westminster, 1970); James Smart, *The Strange Silence of the Bible in the Church* (Philadelphia: Westminster, 1970).

[3] John E. Hartley, "The Message of Salvation in the Old Testament," in *An Inquiry Into Biblical*

Soteriology, ed. John E. Hartley and R. Larry Shelton (Anderson, Ind.: Warner, 1981), p. 50.

[4] Th. C. Vriezen, *An Outline of Old Testament Theology* (Newton Centre, Mass.: Branford, 1958), pp. 148, 169.

[5] Edmond Jacob, *Theology of the Old Testament* (New York: Harper and Row, 1958), p. 39.

[6] Vriezen, *Old Testament Theology*, pp. 169, 174.

[7] Jacob, *Theology of the Old Testament*, p. 38.

[8] F. Michaeli, *Dieu à l'image de l'homme*, p. 147; cited by Jacob, *Theology of the Old Testament*, p. 39.

[9] Ibid., pp. 39–40; also, see Vriezen, *Old Testament Theology*, pp. 171–73.

[10] Eichrodt, *Theology of the Old Testament*, 1:20–21.

[11] Ibid., 1:209.

[12] Herbert F. Stevenson, *Titles of the Triune God* (Westwood, N.J.: Revell, 1956), pp. 16–19; Jacob, *Theology of the Old Testament*, pp. 43–44.

[13] Vriezen, *Old Testament Theology*, pp. 194–95.

[14] Eichrodt, *Theology of the Old Testament*, pp. 1:206–7.

[15] Jacob, *Theology of the Old Testament*, pp. 48–52; Stevenson, *Titles of the Triune God*, pp. 20–21.

[16] Jacob, *Theology of the Old Testament*, p. 54.

[17] Frank M. Cross, *The Religion of Canaan and the God of Israel* (Cambridge, Mass.: Harvard University Press, 1973), pp. 68, 72. Cross presents an extensive historical critical treatment of the background of the Yahweh etymology. See also Clements, *Old Testament Theology*, pp. 62–66.

[18] Stevenson, *Titles of the Triune God*, p. 22; Eichrodt, *Theology of the Old Testament*, 1:208.

[19] Clements, *Old Testament Theology*, pp. 128–29; Jacob, *Theology of the Old Testament*, pp. 104–5.

[20] N. W. Porteous, "Old Testament Theology," in *The Old Testament and Modern Study*, ed. H. H. Rowley, p. 343; cited by Vriezen, *Old Testament Theology*, p. 129.

[21] Cited by Vriezen, *Old Testament Theology*, pp. 128–32.

[22] Jacob, *Theology of the Old Testament*, p. 104; see also the excursus on "covenant" in Frank M. Cross, *Canaanite Myth and Hebrew Epic* (Cambridge, Mass.: Harvard University Press, 1973), pp. 265–73, especially pp. 269–71.

[23] John P. Milton, *God's Covenant of Blessing* (Rock Island, Ill.: Augustana, 1961), pp. 1, 8.

[24] A. B. Davidson, "Covenant," in *A Dictionary of the Bible*, vol. 1 (Edinburgh: T. & T. Clark, 1898), p. 509.

[25] Francis Brown, S. R. Driver, and Charles A. Briggs, *Hebrew and English Lexicon of the Old Testament* (Oxford: Clarendon, 1952), p. 136.

[26] Davidson, "Covenant," p. 509.

[27] Samuel Lee, *Hebrew and English Lexicon of the Old Testament* (London: Duncant Malcolm, 1844), cited in Gesenius's *Hebrew Chaldee Lexicon*, p. clxi.

[28] Brown, Driver, and Briggs, *Hebrew and English Lexicon*, p. 136.

[29] Alan Earl Marsh, *An Inductive Study of the Nature and Purpose of the Biblical Covenant* (Asbury Theological Seminary, Th.M. thesis, 1961), p. 10.

[30] Milton, *God's Covenant of Blessing*, p. 4.

[31] E. Kautzch, *Biblische Theologie des Alten Testaments* (Tübingen: Mohr, 1911), p. 59.

[32] Marsh, *An Inductive Study*, p. 11.

[33] Milton, *God's Covenant of Blessing*, p. 4.

[34] George E. Mendenhall, *Law and Covenant in Israel and the Ancient Near East* (Pittsburgh: Biblical Colloquium, 1955), pp. 24–50.

[35] Ibid., pp. 30, 33.

[36] Ibid., p. 36.

[37] Ibid., p. 42.

[38] Eichrodt, *Theology of the Old Testament*, pp. 1:37, 44.

[39] Milton, *God's Covenant of Blessing*, p. 6.

[40] Brown, Driver, and Briggs, *Hebrew and English Lexicon*, p. 136.

[41] John Bright, *A History of Israel* (Philadelphia: Westminster, 1959), p. 90.

[42] Ibid., p. 91.

[43] Ibid., pp. 92–93.

[44] Eichrodt, *Theology of the Old Testament*, 1:37.

[45] Ibid., 2:288.

[46] Ibid., 1:38.

[47] Carl E. Braaten, *New Directions in Theology Today*, vol. 2, *History and Hermeneutics* (Philadelphia: Westminster, 1966), p. 108.

[48] Eichrodt, *Theology of the Old Testament*, 2:296.

[49] W. Gutbrod, "Law in the Old Testament," in *Bible Key Words*, ed. Gerhard Kittel, vol. 4 (New York: Harper and Row, 1962), p. 30.

[50] Ibid., p. 27.

[51] Eichrodt, *Theology of the Old Testament*, 2:296–98.

[52] Ibid., 1:75.

[53] Ibid., p. 383.

[54] G. Ernest Wright and Reginald Fuller, *The Book of the Acts of God* (Garden City, N.J.: Doubleday, 1960), p. 93.

[55] Eichrodt, *Theology of the Old Testament*, 2:381.

[56] G. Ernest Wright, *The Challenge of Israel's*

Faith (Chicago: University of Chicago Press, 1944), p. 76.

[57]Gerhard von Rad, *Old Testament Theology* (Edinburgh: Oliver and Boyd, 1962), pp. 264, 266.

[58]Eichrodt, *Theology of the Old Testament*, 2:444–45.

[59]J. Barton Payne, *The Theology of the Older Testament* (Grand Rapids: Zondervan, 1962), p. 298.

[60]H. H. Rowley, *The Meaning of Sacrifice in the Old Testament* (Manchester: John Rylands Library, 1960), p. 87.

[61]Eichrodt, *Theology of the Old Testament*, 2:309.

[62]Ibid., 2:445.

[63]Ibid., 1:256.

[64]John L. McKenzie, *Dictionary of the Bible* (Milwaukee: Bruce, 1965), p. 154.

[65]Eichrodt, *Theology of the Old Testament*, 1:38.

[66]Ibid., p. 39.

[67]Ibid., p. 37.

[68]Bright, *A History of Israel*, p. 146.

[69]Wright and Fuller, *The Book of the Acts of God*, p. 87.

[70]Ibid., pp. 87, 93.

[71]McKenzie, *Dictionary of the Bible*, p. 154.

[72]Eichrodt, *Theology of the Old Testament*, 1:233–35.

[73]Henry Clay Trumbull, *The Blood Covenant: A Primitive Rite and Its Bearing on Scripture* (Philadelphia: Wattles, 1893), p. 4.

[74]Ibid., p. 47.

[75]Eichrodt, *Theology of the Old Testament*, 1:157.

[76]Ibid., pp. 154, 157.

[77]Ibid., pp. 43–44.

[78]Ibid., p. 42.

[79]Ibid., p. 45.

[80]Trumbull, *The Blood Covenant*, p. 220.

[81]Bright, *History of Israel*, p. 133.

[82]Payne, *Theology of the Older Testament*, p. 296.

[83]Emil Brunner, *The Christian Doctrine of Creation and Redemption*, trans. Olive Wyon (Philadelphia: Westminster, 1952), pp. 89–90.

[84]Paul Ricoeur, *The Symbolism of Evil*, trans. Emerson Buchanan (Boston: Beacon, 1967), pp. 50–51, 74.

[85]Karl Barth, *Church Dogmatics*, 4 vols., ed. T. F. Torrance and G. W. Bromiley (Edinburgh: T. & T. Clark, 1960), 3(2):203–5.

[86]H. Orton Wiley, *Christian Theology*, 3 vols. (Kansas City, Mo.: Beacon Hill, 1952), 2:65.

[87]Vincent Taylor, *Forgiveness and Reconciliation* (London: Macmillan, 1952), 2:65.

[88]Clark Pinnock, "Introduction," in *Grace Unlimited*, ed. Clark Pinnock (Minneapolis: Bethany Fellowship, 1975), pp. 11ff. This is an excellent treatment of the issue of grace and the universality of the Atonement. It presents a critique of the Calvinist predestinarian soteriology; see also James D. G. Dunn, "Paul's Understanding of the Death of Jesus," in *Reconciliation and Hope: New Testament Essays on Atonement and Eschatology*, ed. Robert Banks (Grand Rapids: Eerdmans, 1974), pp. 125–41.

[89]Edward Schillebeeckx, *Christ: The Experience of Jesus as Lord*, trans. John Bowden (New York: Crossroad, 1981), p. 87; see also pp. 83–101. This is a very thorough treatment of the exegetical and theological aspects of grace.

[90]Ibid., p. 88.

[91]Ibid., p. 94.

[92]Ibid., pp. 98–101.

[93]Ibid., pp. 116–19.

[94]Ibid.; see Hans Conzelmann, *Theological Dictionary of the New Testament*, vol. IX, ed. G. Friedrich, trans. G. W. Bromiley (Grand Rapids: Eerdmans, 1974), pp. 393–95.

[95]Schillebeeckx, ibid., pp. 119–21.

[96]Philip Watson, *The Concept of Grace* (Philadelphia: Muhlenberg, 1959), pp. 12–15.

[97]Greville P. Lewis, *An Approach to Christian Doctrine* (London: Epworth, 1954), p. 67.

[98]See Pinnock, ed., *Grace Unlimited*, for a thorough refutation of the decretal theology of hyper-Calvinism.

[99]Wiley, *Christian Theology*, 2:353–55.

[100]Vincent Taylor, *The Atonement in New Testament Teaching* (London: Epworth, 1963), pp. 167, 172; W. T. Purkiser, Richard I. Taylor, Willard H. Taylor, *God, Man, and Salvation* (Kansas City, Mo.: Beacon Hill, 1977), p. 380.

[101]Taylor, *Forgiveness and Reconciliation*, p. 170.

[102]Ibid., pp. 51–52; see also pp. 50–51 for Taylor's graphic summary of the textual foundations for the various aspects of the work of Christ.

[103]George E. Ladd, *A Theology of the New Testament* (Grand Rapids: Eerdmans, 1974), p. 424.

[104]Alan Richardson, *An Introduction to the Theology of the New Testament* (New York: Harper and Row, 1958), p. 230; see Ladd, *Theology of the New Testament*, p. 425.

[105]Richardson, *Introduction*, p. 229; Ladd, *Theology of the New Testament*, p. 425.

[106]Richardson, *Introduction*, p. 229.

[107]Leon Morris, *The Apostolic Preaching of the Cross* (Grand Rapids: Eerdmans, 1965), p. 143.

108 Purkiser, Taylor, and Taylor, *God, Man, and Salvation*, p. 396; Ladd, *Theology of the New Testament*, pp. 429ff.; Morris, *Apostolic Preaching*, p. 149. Ladd cites Dodd's work in *The Bible and the Greeks* and briefly critiques his approach. See Morris pp. 144-213 for a more complete analysis.

109 Morris, *Apostolic Preaching*, p. 149; Purkiser, Taylor, and Taylor, *God, Man, and Salvation*, pp. 398-400.

110 Reginald E. Fuller, "Jesus Christ as Savior in the New Testament," *Interpretation*, vol. XXV, no. 2 (April 1981), pp. 149-50.

111 Leon Morris gives a particularly thorough treatment of the propitiation issue in *Apostolic Preaching*. He points out that those who stress only "expiation" are neglecting large segments of evidence that require a propitiatory rendering of *hilastērion* in New Testament and Septuagint usages.

112 Taylor, *Atonement*, p. 60; Ladd, *Theology of the New Testament*, pp. 426-27.

113 Taylor, *Atonement*, pp. 174-76; Purkiser, Taylor, and Taylor, *God, Man, and Salvation*, p. 385.

114 W. F. Arndt and F. W. Gingrich, *Greek-English Lexicon of the New Testament* (Chicago: University of Chicago Press, 1969), pp. 72-73; see discussion in Purkiser, Taylor, and Taylor, *God, Man, and Salvation*, pp. 385-86.

115 David Hill, *Greek Words and Hebrew Meanings: Studies in the Semantics of Soteriological Terms* (Cambridge: University Press, 1967), pp. 77-81; idem., *The Gospel of Matthew*, New Century Bible, ed. R. E. Clements and Matthew Black (Greenwood, S.C.: Attic, 1977), p. 289.

116 Ladd, *Theology of the New Testament*, p. 428.

117 Taylor, *Atonement*, pp. 93, 175-76.

118 Wayne McCown, "Such a Great Salvation," in *An Inquiry into Biblical Soteriology*, ed. Shelton and Hartley, p. 173.

119 Vernon Grounds, "God's Universal Salvific Grace," in *Grace Unlimited*, ed. Clark Pinnock, pp. 26-27. These essays are significant because they are critiques of Calvinist decretal theology, many of the authors being themselves Reformed thinkers.

120 John Wesley, "Predestination Calmly Considered," in *The Works of John Wesley*, 3rd ed., 14 vols. (Grand Rapids: Baker, 1978), 10:229.

121 Ibid., p. 225.

122 Ladd, *Theology of the New Testament*, pp. 434-35; Purkiser, Taylor, and Taylor, *God, Man, and Salvation*, p. 408.

123 Gustaf Aulén, *The Faith of the Christian Church* (Philadelphia: Muhlenberg, 1948), p. 228.

124 Ladd, *Theology of the New Testament*, p. 423; Ladd notes that while "atonement" is used by the KJV in Romans 5:11, the word is more properly translated "reconciliation."

125 Ibid., p. 433.

126 Ibid.; see also Fuller, "Jesus Christ as Savior," pp. 150-51; an extensive treatment of the concept of redemption is found in Morris, *Apostolic Preaching*, pp. 11-64.

127 Ladd, *Theology of the New Testament*, p. 434; Fuller, "Jesus Christ as Savior," p. 152.

128 Fuller, "Jesus Christ as Savior," p. 152.

129 Ladd, *Theology of the New Testament*, pp. 450-51; Richardson, *Introduction*, pp. 215-17; Fuller, "Jesus Christ as Savior," p. 153.

130 James Denney, *The Death of Christ* (Chicago: InterVarsity, 1964), pp. 85-96; Ladd, *Theology of the New Testament*, pp. 451-54.

131 Ladd, *Theology of the New Testament*, p. 456; note the prominence of "peace" in Paul (Rom. 5:1; 1 Cor. 7:15; Gal. 5:22; Eph. 4:3; Phil. 4:7; Col. 3:15; 2 Thess. 3:16).

132 R. Larry Shelton, "Justification by Faith in the Pauline Corpus," in *An Inquiry into Biblical Soteriology*, ed. R. L. Shelton and John E. Hartley (Anderson, Ind.: Warner, 1981), pp. 97-99.

133 Hill, *Greek Words and Hebrew Meanings*, p. 139; see Shelton, "Justification by Faith," pp. 99-114.

134 Norman Snaith, *The Distinctive Ideas of the Old Testament* (London: Epworth, 1960), p. 167; D.E.H. Whiteley, *The Theology of St. Paul* (Philadelphia: Fortress, 1964), p. 156; Morris, *Apostolic Preaching*, p. 284.

135 William Sanday and Arthur Headlam, *Romans*, International Critical Commentary (New York: Scribner, 1901), pp. 30-36.

136 G. Schrenk, *"Dikē,"* TDNT, 2:215; Morris, *Apostolic Preaching*, p. 271.

137 James Denney, *The Christian Doctrine of Reconciliation* (New York: Doran, 1918), p. 164.

138 Schrenk, *"Dikē,"* 2:215.

139 Hill, *Greek Words and Hebrew Meanings*, pp. 88-89; Eichrodt, *Theology of the Old Testament*, 1:240.

140 Hill, *Greek Words and Hebrew Meanings*, p. 93; Shelton, "Justification by Faith," pp. 105-7.

141 E. P. Sanders, *Paul and Palestinian Judaism* (Philadelphia: Fortress, 1977), pp. 175-80.

142 Shelton, "Justification by Faith," p. 111.

143 C.E.B. Cranfield, *The Epistle to the Romans*, vol. I, International Critical Commentary (Edinburgh: T. & T. Clark, 1977), pp. 97-98.

144 Shelton, "Justification by Faith," p. 126.

145 Ibid., pp. 114-15.

146 Wesley, *Works*, 8:403 and 8:279.

147 George E. Ladd, class notes, Theology of the New Testament, Fuller Theological Seminary, 1969.

148 Richardson, *Theology of the New Testament,* pp. 34-36.

149 Ibid.

150 Ibid.

151 Ibid., pp. 85-87.

152 Ladd, *Theology of the New Testament,* p. 80; see pp. 57-80 for Ladd's thorough discussion of the kingdom concept. Note that the "kingdom of heaven" is seen as synonymous with "kingdom of God," p. 64; see also Ladd's other books on the kingdom: *Crucial Questions About the Kingdom of God* (Grand Rapids: Eerdmans, 1952), and *Jesus and the Kingdom* (New York: Harper and Row, 1964).

153 Werner Georg Kümmel, *The Theology of the New Testament* (Nashville: Abingdon, 1973), pp. 224-28; Richard Howard, *Newness of Life* (Kansas City, Mo.: Beacon Hill, 1975), pp. 131-75.

154 Howard, *Newness of Life,* p. 156.

155 Ibid., p. 159.

156 See also Bert H. Hall, "The Pauline Doctrine of Sanctification," in *An Inquiry into Biblical Soteriology,* ed. R. Larry Shelton; R. Larry Shelton, "Sanctification in Romans Chapter Six," Th.M. thesis, Asbury Theological Seminary, Wilmore, Ky., 1968.

157 Norman Snaith, *Mercy and Sacrifice: A Study of the Book of Hosea* (London: SCM, 1957), pp. 54-55, 57.

158 Payne, *Theology of the Older Testament,* p. 308.

159 Snaith, *Mercy and Sacrifice,* p. 55.

160 Artur Weiser, "Faith," in *Bible Key Words,* 4 vols., ed. Gerhard Kittel (New York: Harper and Row, 1962), 3:1; idem, "Pisteuō," *Theological Dictionary of the New Testament,* 9 vols., ed. Gerhard Kittel and Gerhard Friedrich (Grand Rapids: Eerdmans, 1968), 6:182.

161 Weiser, "Faith," p. 8.

162 Ibid., p. 11.

163 Ibid., p. 12.

164 Ibid., pp. 13-15.

165 Eichrodt, *Theology of the Old Testament,* 2:72.

166 Ibid., p. 279.

167 Shelton, "Justification by Faith," pp. 121-22.

168 Weiser, "Faith," pp. 97-104.

169 Eichrodt, 2:465-67; see J. Behm and E. Würthwein, "Metanoia," TDNT, 4:980-86.

170 Ibid., p. 468.

171 Ibid., p. 470.

172 "Metanoia," TDNT, 4:986-89.

173 Ibid., 4:978, 999-1003.

174 Ibid., 4:1002-3; Purkiser, Taylor, and Taylor, *God, Man, and Salvation,* pp. 421-24.

175 Donald Guthrie, *New Testament Theology* (Downers Grove, Ill.: InterVarsity, 1981), pp. 574-79.

176 Ibid., pp. 587-97.

177 George Park Fisher, *History of Christian Doctrine* (New York: Scribner, 1902), pp. 86, 111, 162-63, 180.

178 David Wells, *The Search for Salvation* (Downers Grove, Ill.: InterVarsity, 1978), pp. 13, 18.

179 Fisher, *History,* pp. 219-21; Justo González, *A History of Christian Thought,* 3 vols. (Nashville: Abingdon, 1971), 2:165-66.

180 Fisher, *History,* p. 223; González, *History of Christian Thought,* 2:170-71.

181 B. B. Warfield, "Atonement," in *The New Schaff-Herzog Encyclopedia of Religious Knowledge,* 13 vols., ed. S. M. Jackson (Grand Rapids: Baker, 1949), 1:352-53.

182 L. W. Grensted, *A Short History of the Doctrine of the Atonement* (Manchester: Manchester University Press, reprint ed., 1962), pp. 191-207.

183 John Calvin, *Institutes of the Christian Religion,* 4 books, Library of Christian Classics, 26 vols. (Philadelphia: Westminster, 1967), 20:Book III, 11, 2, pp. 726ff.

184 Ibid., 20:Book II, 16, 11, p. 517.

185 Grensted, *Short History,* pp. 216-17.

186 Ibid., pp. 223, 245.

187 Ibid., pp. 284-85.

188 Ibid., pp. 291-97.

189 Ibid., p. 300; Grensted cites Curcellaeus's statement in the latter's *Institutes,* V.19.15.

190 John Wesley, *Explanatory Notes on the New Testament* (London: Epworth, 1966), p. 658; also see William R. Cannon, *The Theology of John Wesley* (Nashville: Abingdon, 1956), pp. 207-11.

191 Ibid., p. 879.

192 Cannon, *Theology of John Wesley,* pp. 209-11.

193 Grensted, *Doctrine of the Atonement,* p. 302.

194 Ibid., pp. 304-5.

195 William Burt Pope, *A Compendium of Christian Theology,* 2 vols. (London: Wesleyan Conference Office, 1880), 2:265.

196 Ibid., p. 314.

197 John Miley, *Systematic Theology,* 2 vols. (New York: Eaton and Mains, 1894), 2:186.

198 Ibid., p. 168; Miley also quotes Raymond, Whedon, and Bledsoe for support; see Miner Raymond, *Systematic Theology,* 2 vols. (New York: Phillips and Hunt, 1880), 2:257-58.

199 Miley, *Systematic Theology,* p. 123.

200 Ian T. Ramsey, *Models and Mystery* (London: Oxford University Press, 1964), pp. 1-5.

[201] Gordon Allport, *Pattern and Growth in Personality* (New York: Holt, Rinehart, and Winston, 1961), p. 533.

[202] Harry Stack Sullivan, *The Interpersonal Theory of Psychiatry* (New York: Norton, 1953), pp. 41, 74.

[203] Silvano Arieti, ed., *American Handbook of Psychiatry*, vol. 2 (New York: Basic Books, 1959), 2:1412. For a more complete analysis of empathy, particularly with reference to sanctification, see R. Larry Shelton, "Sanctification in Romans Chapter Six," Th.M. thesis, Asbury Theological Seminary, Wilmore, Ky., 1968, pp. 71-86.

DISCUSSION QUESTIONS

1. In what ways is a knowledge of the personal character of God important for a biblical understanding of salvation? Why is belief in His personality important for understanding the meaning of the covenant?
2. How is the covenant concept useful as a way of expressing the doctrine of salvation? Explain the nature of the covenant and the conditions required for Israel to enter and observe the covenant relationship.
3. Discuss the various aspects of the biblical usage of the term *grace*. In what way does grace relate to God's offer of salvation?
4. Can the death of Christ be explained adequately apart from its relationship to the Incarnation? Why or why not?
5. How is Christ's death sacrificial? What is the function of a sacrifice? What is at stake in the discussion on the propitiation-expiation issue?
6. How is the understanding of Christ's death as vicarious distorted by the penal substitutionary emphasis? How may a balance be achieved between the extreme substitutionary views and the subjective representational views of the Atonement? What is at stake here for Wesleyan-Arminian theology?
7. Enumerate and briefly discuss the various benefits of the Atonement. What interpersonal elements can be found in the metaphors for salvation?
8. Although there has been a tendency for Reformed theology to stress justification and for Wesleyan-Arminian theology to stress regeneration, why is it important for both concepts to be held in balance?
9. What is the "righteousness of God"? What problems are found in the use of the imputation-impartation distinction? In what ways is the believer actually righteous?
10. Briefly discuss the major theories of the doctrine of the Atonement. What problems are found in each? Why does the penal theory tend to result in either an emphasis on limited atonement and predestination or on universalism? If the penalty for sin is death, and Christ paid the penalty for believers, why do believers still die? How does the governmental theory modify penal substitutionary views? What are the strengths and weaknesses of the governmental view? How is it congenial to a Wesleyan-Arminian theology?
11. What strengths can be seen in these theories, and how can a covenant understanding of the atonement incorporate these strengths and avoid the weaknesses of the more transactional and impersonal theories? How does the covenant model deal with personal and community aspects of salvation? How does faith fit in?
12. How is a Wesleyan-Arminian theology consistent with the biblical evidence concerning the nature of initial salvation?

RECOMMENDATIONS FOR FURTHER READING

Cannon, William R. *The Theology of John Wesley.* Nashville: Abingdon, 1956.

Denney, James. *The Death of Christ.* Chicago: InterVarsity, 1964.

Green, E.M.B. *The Meaning of Salvation.* London: Hodder & Stoughton, 1965.

Hartley, John E., and Shelton, R. Larry, eds. *An Inquiry Into Biblical Soteriology,* Wesleyan Theological Perspectives. Vol. 1. Anderson, Ind.: Warner, 1981.

Hill, David. *Greek Words and Hebrew Meanings: Studies in the Semantics of Soteriological Terms.* Cambridge: University Press, 1967.

Ladd, George E. *A Theology of the New Testament.* Grand Rapids: Eerdmans, 1974.

Miley, John. *Systematic Theology.* 2 vols. New York: Eaton and Mains, 1894.

Outler, Albert C., ed. *John Wesley.* New York: Oxford University Press, 1964.

Pinnock, Clark, ed. *Grace Unlimited.* Minneapolis: Bethany Fellowship, 1975.

Raymond, Miner. *Systematic Theology.* 2 vols. New York: Phillips and Hunt, 1880.

Taylor, Vincent. *The Atonement in New Testament Teaching.* London: Epworth, 1963.

Wesley, John. *Explanatory Notes on the New Testament.* London: Epworth, 1966.

———. *The Works of John Wesley.* 3rd ed., 14 vols. Grand Rapids: Baker, 1978.

Wiley, H. Orton. *Christian Theology.* Vol. 2. Kansas City, Mo.: Beacon Hill, 1952.

BIBLIOGRAPHY

Allport, Gordon. *Pattern and Growth in Personality,* New York: Holt, Rinehart, and Winston, 1961.

Arieti, Silvano, ed. *American Handbook of Psychiatry.* Vol. 2. New York: Basic Books, 1959.

Arndt, W. F., and Gingrich, F. W. *Greek-English Lexicon of the New Testament.* Chicago: University of Chicago Press, 1969.

Aulén, Gustaf. *The Faith of the Christian Church.* Philadelphia: Muhlenberg, 1948.

———. *Christus Victor.* Translated by A. G. Hebert. New York: Macmillan, 1972.

Barth, Karl. *Church Dogmatics.* Vol. 3 (2). Edited by G. W. Bromiley and T. F. Torrance. Edinburgh: T. & T. Clark, 1960.

Braaten, Carl E. *New Directions in Theology Today.* Vol. 2. History and Hermeneutics. Philadelphia: Westminster, 1966.

Brown, Francis; Driver, S. R.; and Briggs, Charles A. *Hebrew and English Lexicon of the Old Testament.* Oxford: Clarendon, 1952.

Brunner, Emil. *The Christian Doctrine of Creation and Redemption,* translated by Olive Wyon. Philadelphia: Westminster, 1952.

Calvin, John. *Institutes of the Christian Religion,* 4 books. Library of Christian Classics, 26 vols. Philadelphia: Westminster, 1967.

Cannon, William R. *The Theology of John Wesley.* Nashville: Abingdon, 1956.

Childs, Brevard. *Biblical Theology in Crisis.* Philadelphia: Westminster, 1970.

Clements, R. E. *Old Testament Theology.* Atlanta: John Knox, 1978.

Conzelmann, Hans. *Theological Dictionary of the New Testament.* Vol. 9. Edited by G. Friedrich. Translated by G. W. Bromiley. Grand Rapids: Eerdmans, 1974.

Cranfield, C.E.B. *The Epistle to the Romans.* 2 vols. International Critical Commentary. Edinburgh: T. & T. Clark, 1977–1979.

Cross, Frank M. *Canaanite Myth and Hebrew Epic.* Cambridge, Mass.: Harvard University Press, 1973.

———. *The Religion of Canaan and the God of Israel.* Cambridge, Mass.: Harvard University Press, 1973.

Denney, James. *The Death of Christ.* Chicago: InterVarsity Press, 1964.

Eichrodt, Walther. *Theology of the Old Testament.* 2 vols. Philadelphia: Westminster, 1961.

Fisher, George Park. *History of Christian Doctrine.* New York: Scribner, 1902.

González, Justo. *A History of Christian Thought.* 3 vols. Nashville: Abingdon, 1971.

Green, E.M.B. *The Meaning of Salvation.* London: Hodder & Stoughton, 1965.

Grensted, L. W. *A Short History of the Doctrine of the Atonement.* Manchester: Manchester University Press, 1962.

Gutbrod, W. "Law in the Old Testament." In *Bible Key Words.* Vol. 4. Edited by Gerhard Kittel. New York: Harper and Row, 1962.

Hartley, John E., and Shelton, R. Larry, eds. *An Inquiry Into Biblical Soteriology,* Wesleyan Theological Perspectives. Vol. 1. Anderson, Ind.: Warner, 1981.

Hill, David. *Greek Words and Hebrew Meanings: Studies in the Semantics of Soteriological Terms.* Cambridge: University Press, 1967.

———. *The Gospel of Matthew,* New Century Bible. Edited by R. E. Clements and Matthew Black. Greenwood, S.C.: Attic, 1977.

Jacob, Edmond. *Theology of the Old Testament.* New York: Harper and Row, 1958.

Kautzch, E. *Biblische Theologie des Alten Testaments.* Tübingen: Mohr, 1911.

Kittel, Gerhard, and Friedrich, Gerhard, eds. *Theological Dictionary of the New Testament.* 9 vols. Grand Rapids: Eerdmans, 1968.

Kümmel, Werner Georg. *The Theology of the New Testament.* Nashville: Abingdon, 1973.

Ladd, George E. *A Theology of the New Testament.* Grand Rapids: Eerdmans, 1974.

Lewis, Greville P. *An Approach to Christian Doctrine.* London: Epworth, 1954.

Marsh, Alan Earl. "An Inductive Study of the Nature and Purpose of the Biblical Covenant." Th.M. thesis. Wilmore, Ky.: Asbury Theological Seminary, 1961.

McKenzie, John L. *Dictionary of the Bible.* Milwaukee: Bruce, 1965.

Mendenhall, George E. *Law and Covenant in Israel and the Ancient Near East.* Pittsburgh: Biblical Colloquium, 1955.

Miley, John. *Systematic Theology.* 2 vols. New York: Eaton and Mains, 1894.

Morris, Leon. *The Apostolic Preaching of the Cross.* Grand Rapids: Eerdmans, 1965.

Outler, Albert C., ed. *John Wesley.* New York: Oxford University Press, 1964.

Pannenberg, Wolfhart. *Jesus—God and Man.* Philadelphia: Westminster, 1975.

Payne, J. Barton. *The Theology of the Older Testament.* Grand Rapids: Zondervan, 1962.

Pinnock, Clark, ed. *Grace Unlimited.* Minneapolis: Bethany Fellowship, 1975.

Pope, William Burt. *A Compendium of Christian Theology.* 2 vols. London: Wesleyan Conference Office, 1880.

Purkiser, W. T.; Taylor, Willard; and Taylor, Richard S. *God, Man, and Salvation.* Kansas City, Mo.: Beacon Hill, 1977.

Ramsey, Ian T. *Models and Mystery.* London: Oxford University Press, 1964.

Rashdall, Hastings. *The Idea of Atonement in Christian Theology.* London: Macmillan, 1919.

Raymond, Miner. *Systematic Theology.* 2 vols. New York: Phillips and Hunt, 1880.

Richardson, Alan. *An Introduction to the Theology of the New Testament.* New York: Harper and Row, 1958.

Rowley, H. H. *The Meaning of Sacrifice in the Old Testament.* Manchester: John Rylands Library, 1950.

Sanders, E. P. *Paul and Palestinian Judaism.* Philadelphia: Fortress, 1977.

Sanders, James. *Torah and Canon.* Philadelphia: Fortress, 1972.

Schillebeeckx, Edward. *Christ: The Experience of Jesus as Lord.* Translated by John Bowden. New York: Crossroad, 1981.

Smart, James. *The Strange Silence of the Bible in the Church.* Philadelphia: Westminster, 1970.

Snaith, Norman. *The Distinctive Ideas of the Old Testament.* London: Epworth, 1960.

Stevenson, Hubert F. *Titles of the Triune God.* Westwood, N.J.: Revell, 1956.

Sullivan, Harry Stack. *The Interpersonal Theory of Psychiatry.* New York: Norton, 1953.

Taylor, Vincent. *The Atonement in New Testament Teaching.* London: Epworth, 1963.

———. *Jesus and His Sacrifice.* New York: St. Martin's, 1965.

———. *Forgiveness and Reconciliation.* London: Macmillan, 1952.

Thomas, Griffith. *The Principles of Theology.* London: Church Back Room Press, 1963.

Traina, Robert A. "The Atonement, History, and Kerygma: A Study in Contemporary Protestant Theology." Ph.D. dissertation, Madison, N.J.: Drew University, 1966.

Trumbull, Henry Clay. *The Blood Covenant: A Primitive Rite and Its Bearing on Scripture.* Philadelphia: Wattles, 1893.

Von Rad, Gerhard. *Old Testament Theology.* Edinburgh: Oliver and Boyd, 1965.

Vriezen, Th. C. *An Outline of Old Testament Theology.* Newton Centre, Mass.: Branford, 1958.

Warfield, B. B. "Atonement." In *The New Schaff-Herzog Encyclopedia of Religious Knowledge.* Vol. 1. Edited by S. M. Jackson. Grand Rapids: Baker, 1949.

Watson, Philip. *The Concept of Grace*. Philadelphia: Muhlenberg, 1959.
Wells, David. *The Search for Salvation*. Downers Grove, Ill.: InterVarsity Press, 1978.
Wesley, John. *Explanatory Notes on the New Testament*. London: Epworth, 1966.
_____ . *The Works of John Wesley*. 3rd ed. 14 vols. Grand Rapids: Baker, 1978.
Whiteley, D.E.H. *The Theology of St. Paul*. Philadelphia: Fortress, 1964.
Wiley, H. Orton. *Christian Theology*. Vol. 2. Kansas City, Mo.: Beacon Hill, 1952.
Wright, G. Ernest. *The Challenge of Israel's Faith*. Chicago: University of Chicago Press, 1944.
Wright, G. Ernest, and Fuller, Reginald. *The Book of the Acts of God*. Garden City, N.J.: Doubleday, 1960.

CHAPTER 13

ENTIRE SANCTIFICATION: The Divine Purification and Perfection of Man

Wilber T. Dayton

Wilber T. Dayton is Professor of Biblical Literature and Historical Theology at Wesley Biblical Seminary. He earned his B.D. degree at Houghton College, his M.A. at Butler University, and his M.R.E. and Th.D. at Northern Baptist Theological Seminary. He did postdoctoral study and research at the University of London, the British Museum, and the American Institute of Holy Land Studies. Concurrent with his teaching ministry, he has held pastorates in South Dakota, Indiana, and Ohio. He has taught at Wessington Springs College, Marion College, and Asbury Theological Seminary and was president of Houghton College from 1972 to 1976 before taking up his present position.

He has written Spirit-Filled Living, Romans A *and* Romans B *for the Aldersgate Biblical Series, and "Romans" and "Galatians" for the* Wesleyan Bible Commentary. *He has also contributed articles or essays for various other publications. He is a member of several societies, including the Society of Biblical Literature, Chicago Society of Biblical Research, Evangelical Theological Society, and Wesleyan Theological Society.*

CONTENTS

I. PRELIMINARY DEFINITION AND REMARKS / 521
    A. Elements of Definition / 521
    B. Wesley's Approach / 521
    C. Scope of the Present Study / 523

II. THE DIVINE PLAN FOR HUMAN PERFECTION / 523
    A. The Divine Requirement / 524
    B. The Divine Provision / 525
    C. The Divine Promise / 525
    D. Prayers and Exhortations / 527

III. ASPECTS OF CHRISTIAN PERFECTION / 528
    A. Entire Sanctification and Holiness / 528
    B. The Concept of Purification / 529
    C. The Concept of the Gift of the Holy Spirit / 531
    D. The Concept of Perfect Love / 532
    E. The Concept of Power / 535
    F. The Concept of Perfection / 537
    G. A Suggested Distinction / 539

IV. CHRISTIAN PERFECTION AS THE RESULT OF A CRISIS EXPERIENCE OF SANCTIFICATION / 541
    A. Implications of "Gift of the Holy Spirit" / 541
    B. An Experience Subsequent to the New Birth / 543
    C. An Experience Prior to Death / 544
    D. Implications of Greek Tenses / 546
    E. Implications of Vocabulary / 549
    F. Implications of Context and Syntax / 549

V. THE URGENCY OF THE EXPERIENCE / 552
    A. A Specific Concern of Jesus / 553
    B. Apostolic Ministry in the Book of Acts / 555
    C. Paul and the Young Churches / 557
    D. A Consistent New Testament Emphasis / 561

VI. SUMMARY OF DISTINCTIONS / 563
    A. Instantaneous and Progressive Work of God / 563
    B. Divine Grace and Human Works / 563
    C. Purity and Maturity / 563
    D. Conditions to Be Met / 564
    E. Christian Perfection Versus Absolute Perfection / 564
    F. Entire Sanctification Versus Glorification / 564
    G. The Gift and Gifts of the Spirit / 564
    H. Imputed Versus Imparted Grace / 564

VII. CONCLUSION / 565
NOTES / 565
DISCUSSION QUESTIONS / 567
RECOMMENDATIONS FOR FURTHER READING / 567
BIBLIOGRAPHY / 567

ENTIRE SANCTIFICATION

The Divine Purification and Perfection of Man

I. PRELIMINARY DEFINITION AND REMARKS

A. Elements of Definition

Entire sanctification is the act of God by which the human heart is cleansed from all sin and filled with love by the Holy Spirit who is given, through faith, to the fully consecrated believer. The resultant life of Christian holiness is known as perfect love or Christian perfection. Entire sanctification is distinct from the beginning of holiness or sanctification that comes in the new birth (or regeneration). Since it is a specific act of God, as in conversion, it is called a "second blessing" or a "second work of grace," indicating that it is distinguished also from the processes of growth in grace and the development of the skills of Christian living. Though there are human conditions and responses necessary to its reception, sanctification, as all grace, is not by works that a person does. It is a gift of God, usually understood as brought about by the baptism with the Holy Spirit.

B. Wesley's Approach

One would look in vain through Wesley's works for such a definition. Even H. Orton Wiley in his 77-page discussion of "Christian Perfection or Entire Sanctification" did not turn to the words of Wesley for theological formulations of the doctrine.[1] Although Wesley could debate long and well about what was scriptural and reasonable, he had no particular love for terms and for neatly packaged formulas. He felt that they might obscure truth more than they revealed it. In a letter to the Rev. Mr. Dodd he wrote concerning Christian perfection (which he equated with holiness):

> The opinion I have concerning it at present, I espouse merely because I think it is scriptural. If therefore I am convinced it is not scriptural, I shall willingly relinquish it. I have no particular fondness for the term. It seldom occurs either in my preaching or writings. . . . But I still think that perfection is only another term for holiness, or the image of God in man.[2]

In the preface to his published sermons, Wesley explains his aversion to systematic theology, at least insofar as it may obscure the plain meaning of the Scripture from the common person. He says:

> I design plain truth for plain people: Therefore, of set purpose, I abstain from all nice and philosophic speculations: from all

perplexed and intricate reasonings; and, as far as possible, from even the show of learning, unless in sometimes citing the original Scriptures. I labor to avoid all words which are not used in common life; and, in particular, those kinds of technical terms that so frequently occur in Bodies of Divinity; those modes of speaking which men of reading are intimately acquainted with, but which to common people are an unknown tongue.³

Holiness, sanctification, Christian perfection, perfect love, and the like were to him not creeds of systematic theology; they were simply life in the image of God as revealed in the Scriptures and as provided in redemption through Jesus Christ. There was no one orthodox and correct way of saying it, as long as one was scriptural. Simply stated, God requires and provides a purification and perfection of the heart, whereby we can have the "mind which was also in Christ Jesus" (Phil. 2:5 KJV). The proof of the doctrine is not mere reason, necessary as that is. It is the preached Word, obediently received by faith. The invitation can take the form of an appeal for the circumcision of the heart, a call to perfection, the demand for perfect love, or any other message straight from the Word of God. The only holiness in which he was interested was a scriptural holiness. His quest was more than a desire to satisfy his intellectual curiosity or to prove his orthodoxy. He must have and preach personal holiness, for "without holiness no one will see the Lord" (Heb. 12:14 NIV).

Though there is a sense in which Wesley was a superior theologian, it was no part of his purpose to build a scholasticism to preserve his own formulations. As he preached the Word to save souls, he trained his followers to do the same. Accordingly, he left behind him no systematic theology as such. Instead, his greatest works were biblical and practical. His *Explanatory Notes Upon the New Testament* consumed his greatest effort. The much larger work on the Old Testament was in the same vein. His standard *Sermons* set forth his understanding of what the Scriptures had to say to man. The *Journals, Letters,* and miscellaneous pieces are the application of the message from God to people under all sorts of circumstances. With a firm conviction that the Word of God is the revelation of the way of holiness, he answered all questions, whenever possible, by a word of Scripture.

Holiness, to both John and Charles Wesley, was not a single narrow cultic idea. It was the whole point of the gospel. John Wesley explained the rise of Methodism in terms of a personal quest for holiness. He said:

> In 1729, two young men, reading the Bible, saw they could not be saved without holiness, followed after it, and incited others so to do. In 1737 they saw holiness comes by faith. They saw likewise, that men are justified before they are sanctified; but still holiness was their point. God then thrust them out, utterly against their will, to raise a holy people.⁴

One of Wesley's favorite ways of explaining holiness was in terms of Christlikeness. He wrote:

> In the year 1729, I began not only to read, but to study, the Bible, as the one, the only standard of truth, and the only model of pure religion. Hence I saw, in a clearer and clearer light, the indispensable necessity of having "the mind which was in Christ," and of "walking as Christ also walked;" even of having, not some part only, but all the mind which was in Him, and of walking as He walked, not only in many or most respects, but in all things. And this was the light, wherein at this time I generally considered religion, as an uniform following of Christ, and entire inward and outward conformity to our Master.⁵

These observations in no sense abrogate the debt of the "theology of holiness" to Wesley. Nor do they deny the continuity between Wesley's preaching and the standard Wesleyan theologies of later times. It is simply that, for him, all revelation, as well as creation, converged on God's purpose of holiness for His people.

Wesley confined himself to exegesis and exposition of the Scriptures to this end and left to others the systematizing of the principles. To the dismay of his friends and foes, he left many questions open to the research and experience of the followers. In later times there have been both gains and losses in producing definitive theologies. It is easier to explain holiness than to lead some people into the experience. It is also difficult for others to capture the freshness of original discovery in the Word of God.

In any case, the preliminary definition with which this chapter began is a composite of elements drawn together from the Wesleyan exponents and theologians as they have attempted to systematize and harmonize the principles that Wesley rediscovered in Scripture and in experience. Admittedly, there are details and emphases in these Wesleyan interpretations that do not coincide with all of Wesley's understandings. But every effort will be made to be true first to the Scriptures, then to Wesley's understanding of the message of the Scripture, and finally to the current Wesleyan interpretation of both. In this sense, I will attempt to be both contemporary and Wesleyan, insofar as space permits.

C. Scope of the Present Study

Each statement in the preliminary definition of entire sanctification suggests a number of questions and a variety of theories and insights that affect one's understanding of the work of God and its implications. Many volumes have been written on the various facets of the topic. The scope of this chapter permits only a summary of the chief considerations, a sketch of certain evidences for the Wesleyan position, a survey of high points in the development of the doctrine, and certain implications that follow from a scriptural position concerning the divine purification and perfection of man.

Immediate attention turns to the divine plan for human perfectibility as related to Christian perfection and as distinct from absolute perfection. Then we will review various aspects of the doctrine under the terminologies of entire sanctification, holiness, purification, the gift of the Holy Spirit, perfect love, power, and perfection. This will be followed by exegetical considerations that treat Christian perfection as the result of a definite experience of sanctification. Then we will consider the priority and urgency of the matter in the words and deeds of Jesus and of the apostles. We will view certain practical considerations in terms of crisis and process, faith and works, purity and maturity, conditionality of sanctification, the gift and gifts of the Holy Spirit, and imputation versus impartation of holiness. Finally, I will present a concise statement about entire sanctification in terms of holiness and Christian perfection.

II. THE DIVINE PLAN FOR HUMAN PERFECTION

Running through the Scriptures from beginning to end is the theme that God desires the perfection of man. In the creation of man, God was the model. Man was made in God's image and after His likeness (Gen. 1:26-27). The tragedy of the Fall was, in part, man's loss of this moral likeness and of the corresponding relationship with his Maker. The rest of the Scripture is the story of God's plan and purpose to restore lost man to the divine plan for him.

Turner asserts concerning the Old Testament that

> of the more than one thousand occurrences of synonyms denoting some phase of perfection, at least eighty refer to man's character. God's ideals for man, as reflected in synonyms for perfection, are too prominent in the Old Testament to be ignored.[6]

Still stronger statements could be made of the New Testament. As the symbolism is more clearly fulfilled in personal, moral, and spiritual life, the purpose and plan of God are revealed in a perfection of love and holiness that brings to glorious conclusion the work of God, fully redeemed personalities awaiting a restored environment (Rom. 8:21).

A. The Divine Requirement

Whether the term used is *righteousness, holiness, perfection, love,* or *truth,* God's requirement is for completeness and perfection. It cannot be otherwise. Moral principles forbid exceptions, at least voluntary ones. One lie leads to another. How can one steal without being a thief, or commit adultery without becoming an adulterer? God's commandment about the particular act or attitude is "You shall not" (Exod. 20:3-17). The moral and spiritual demand is always for perfection, however impossible it is to fallen man apart from grace. The standard is beyond question. Certain implications will be discussed later.

Abraham was confronted with the standard long after he had left Ur of the Chaldees and Haran. As a pilgrim and a nomad for the sake of the kingdom of God, he had, for the most part, followed God and considered himself faithful to Him. But there were areas of his life that were not fully open to God. He had rationalized long enough. Before God would fulfill Abraham's hopes with great blessing, He made the command very explicit: "I am the Almighty God; walk before me, and be thou perfect" (Gen. 17:1 KJV). Although God had forgiven the past and was working to make Abraham the father of the faithful, an act of imperfect trust had brought the endless strife of Ishmael into the chosen family. God's standard is perfection. Abraham had disregarded this to his great loss.

Even earlier, when God thought to destroy sinful man, He delayed judgment and kept eight souls alive because of Noah, who was perfect in his generation (Gen. 6:9 KJV).

The sacrifices had to be perfect—without defect—to be accepted (Lev. 22:21; Deut. 15:21). The people were to be blameless (perfect, KJV) with the Lord their God (Deut. 18:13). They had to separate themselves completely from the abominations of the heathen. "As for God, his way is perfect" (2 Sam. 22:31) and "He sets the blameless [perfect, KJV] in His way" (v. 33). "Mark the blameless [perfect, KJV] man, and behold the upright" (Ps. 37:37). God required perfection in the Old Testament. He produced it, and He found it. He judged the lack of it with ruin and destruction.

The New Testament throbs with both anticipation and fulfillment of God's requirement. Jesus demands it: "Therefore you are to be perfect, as your heavenly Father is perfect" (Matt. 5:48). What could be more emphatic? This sentence is in the same grammatical form as the Ten Commandments when they are quoted in the New Testament. It is future indicative: "You will be." There is no escape, if you are to be spiritually alive (cf. Matt. 5:20). Again Jesus quotes Moses (Deut. 6:4-5), demanding perfect love to God and to man (Mark. 12:29-30). Paul claims one perfection (Phil. 3:15-16) and earnestly pursues another (vv. 12-13). The writer to the Hebrews issues the call to perfection (6:1, KJV) and says that without this sanctification no one will see the Lord (12:14). Sanctification and perfection are the very essence of the Christian fulfillment (12:23; 13:12).

Glory, light, life, love, blessing, faith, hope, fruit, peace, and all other terms that depict moral values and personal integrity reflect the same theme. There is a perfection required, without which the moral order collapses.

Wesley was deeply impressed by the divine requirement and its reasonableness. Though the standard was obviously beyond the reach of human works, apart from grace, he felt that he must comply. He did not dare to accommodate the doctrine to his life. He must accommodate his life to the doctrine. He said:

> I saw that "simplicity of intention, and purity of affection," one design in all we speak or do, and one desire ruling all our tempers, are indeed "the wings of the soul,"

without which she can never ascend to the mount of God. A year or two after, Mr. Law's "Christian Perfection" and "Serious Call" were put into my hands. These convinced me, more than ever, of the absolute impossibility of being half a Christian; and I determined, through His grace, (the absolute necessity of which I was deeply sensible of,) to be all-devoted to God, to give Him all my soul, my body, and my substance.[7]

It is in this context that Wesley reports his intensified study of the Bible as the "only model of pure religion" in his quest for an "entire inward and outward conformity to our Master."[8] When asked how one would avoid "setting perfection too high or too low," he replied simply: "By keeping to the Bible, and setting it just as high as the Scripture does. It is nothing higher and nothing lower than this."[9]

B. The Divine Provision

It would be mockery for God to require what He would not provide. But the God who made people can make them new creatures (2 Cor. 5:17). Perfection, righteousness, or holiness would be impossible in either the Old Testament or the New if it were not for the abundance of grace in both. Backslidden King David cried out in anguish and futility, "Create in me a clean heart, O God, and renew a steadfast spirit within me" (Ps. 51:10). A partially clean heart would not do, nor would God provide it. A sometimes right spirit would only fail. God has only one standard of requirement and of provision. An Old Testament backslider understood that and revived. Ezekiel received the same promise for the restoration of his people (11:19-20; 36:26-27). A new heart and a new spirit make a new person and a new life, whether in the Old Testament or the New. God's perfect work makes a real righteousness that conforms to God's standard.

The divine provision is all the more evident in the New Testament. The Sermon on the Mount can seem forbidding in its demands; but it is glorious in its provision and fulfillment. The blessedness of the good life is in the present tense. The salt and light are now. The inner and outer righteousness are now. The living to please God is now. The bonuses are now as well as later. The building on the rock is now, both by discipline and by grace. God never calls without providing the necessary means of fulfilling the call. All of the exhortations and even the warnings of judgment presuppose the possibility and provision of a life of holiness and perfection for those who will obey. It was with this full confidence that Wesley pressed his converts to go on to perfection and insisted that his preachers and class leaders do the same with those under their care.

C. The Divine Promise

In addition to the indications of the divine requirement and the divine provision for a perfection of righteousness and holiness, there is a promise running through the Old Testament. Sometimes it is explicit, again implicit. Sometimes it is couched in types, symbols, and ceremonies of liturgical worship. Sometimes it comes in messianic references, again it is specifically related to the Spirit of God in almost New Testament terminology. It is a promise, or an assumption of a promise, of a better day—a day of fulfillment. This is not to depreciate the effectiveness of the covenants with Adam, Noah, Abraham, Moses, and David for their day. Nor does Jacob's Peniel become less real. Nor was the taking away of Isaiah's iniquity (Isa. 6:7) only prophetic. Nor was Ezekiel's promise of a new spirit and a new heart limited to the future (11:19-20; 36:26-27). David had already claimed the promise (Ps. 51:10), and Jacob had become Israel at Peniel (Gen. 32:28). Transforming and perfecting grace was already a tradition. It was also a promise of a greater and more universal fulfillment in a day yet future. After the Christ should be glorified, then the living water of the Holy Spirit would flow not only from the Messiah but also from those who believe on Him (John 7:37-39).

The promise of spiritual health and holiness became more and more explicit in the prophets and centered more and more in the Spirit of God, or the Holy Spirit. This is especially clear in the prophecy of Joel (2:28-32), which was fulfilled at Pentecost (Acts 2). When John came baptizing with water, he affirmed plainly that Jesus' greater baptism was with the Holy Spirit (Matt. 3:11-12; Mark 1:8; Luke 13:16; John 1:26). John was only preparing the way for the One who would come and pour out the Spirit on God's people.

The promises of the prophets and of John the Baptist were taken up by Jesus in terms of the "promise of the Father." Just before His ascension, Jesus said, "I am sending forth the promise of My Father upon you" (Luke 24:49). The promise of the Father, then, becomes the promise of Jesus Himself. *He* will send the promise. As Luke ends, so Acts begins. Jesus commanded them to "wait for what the Father had promised" (Acts 1:4). This promise of the Father was fulfilled at Pentecost, as Peter said, when Jesus "received from the Father the promise of the Holy Spirit, He has poured forth this which you both see and hear" (Acts 2:33). This gift of the Holy Spirit was offered to all who would repent and be baptized (v. 38), because the promise is to "all who are far off, as many as the Lord our God shall call to Himself" (v. 39).

The fulfilled promise of the gift of the Holy Spirit—to make people holy—became a central proclamation of the apostles. In the Book of Acts the gospel message clustered around two emphases. First, Christ is risen from the dead and has completed redemption, so that all may be saved. Second, the promised gift of the Holy Spirit is now given, in all His fullness, for the perfection and enablement of believers. The life in God henceforth is life in the Spirit, for He is the Spirit of holiness (Rom. 1:4).

Wesley was very much aware of the promises of purification and perfection of the heart of the believer and he had a keen appreciation for the work of the Holy Spirit in the present dispensation. To him,

> the ministration of the New Testament was that of the "Spirit which giveth life;"—a Spirit, not only promised, but actually conferred; which should both enable Christians now to live unto God, and fulfil precepts even more spiritual than the former; and restore them hereafter to perfect life, after the ruins of sin and death.[10]

Wesley's emphasis was on "what the Holy Spirit is to every believer, for his personal sanctification and salvation."[11]

Nor did he limit the work of the Spirit to believers. Grace before salvation (prevenient grace) and even good thoughts and deeds of unsaved persons were all a part of the work of the Holy Spirit. In this sense, "there is no man that is in a state of mere nature; there is no man, unless he has quenched the Spirit, that is wholly void of the grace of God."[12]

The heart of the doctrine of entire sanctification as the purification and perfection of the believer is intact as Wesley believed and taught it. The emphasis on Pentecost has given the doctrine a handle by which many could more readily understand and preach it to the masses. If it is true and scriptural, as most Wesleyans, at least, believe, it ought to be so preached and experienced. There is no reason why entire sanctification could not come by a Pentecostal baptism of the fullness of the Spirit on those who are already born of the Spirit. But with the "clarified" understanding of the doctrine, some are concerned that there might be an increased interest in the phenomena that accompanied the gift of the Spirit at Pentecost and less insistence on full consecration and perfect love. Some indeed have emphasized signs more than the fruit of the Spirit. But the errors of people do not make void the promises and provisions of God. It is confidently believed that full salvation is provided through the Holy Spirit who is given to us. More will be said later on this subject.

D. Prayers and Exhortations

The perfection that was required, promised, provided, and fulfilled in the gift of the Holy Spirit became the constant concern of Christ and the apostles, not only in their general announcements and proclamations but also in their prayers and special exhortations. Jesus spent much of the time of the Upper Room discourse telling the disciples about the work of the Holy Spirit in strengthening, enabling, and fulfilling the life and ministry of His people (John 14-16). Then in His great high-priestly prayer (John 17), Jesus' concern culminated in the sanctification of the believers (vv. 17-19), and the consequent integration of their personalities and conduct as the true basis of the unity of the Spirit in the body of Christ. On the eve of His ascension, Jesus earnestly cautioned the disciples against leaving the city of Jerusalem without first being sure they were clothed with the power from on high (Luke 24:49), which is none other than the promised gift of the Holy Spirit (Acts 1:4).

As will be noted later, and more particularly, the very reason for Paul's writing the first Epistle to the Thessalonians was to press upon these young Christians the privilege and necessity of abounding in love and of being established in holiness before God (3:10-13). Paul was praying night and day for the perfecting of their faith. The thematic development of the book builds around the sanctification and holiness ethics of chapters 4 and 5, culminating in the great prayer for their entire sanctification and for their preservation in blamelessness until the coming of Christ (5:23-24).

The Roman Christians also received a letter from Paul when they had as yet never enjoyed the visit of an apostle. Paul's concern for them parallels that for the Thessalonians. In both instances he rejoiced in their genuine faith and their fruitful witness; but he longed to see the Romans too and had tried repeatedly to come to them with the explicit purpose of sharing with them some spiritual gift *(charisma)* to the end that they might be established (Rom. 1:11-13). As with the Thessalonians, this seems to be the main reason for writing the book. The rest of the letter is a thematic development of the importance, the privilege, and the necessity of holiness before the Lord.

In the only other exhibition of Paul's treatment of a very young church, we see the same concern. When Paul met certain disciples at Ephesus, his first question was, "Have ye received the Holy Ghost since ye believed?" (literally, as in KJV). Learning that they had not received the Holy Spirit in the New Testament fullness, Paul dropped all other business until "the Holy Spirit came on them" (Acts 19:1-6). When Paul later wrote to the Ephesians, he encouraged and strengthened them, reminding them that after they had become believers, they were sealed with the promised Holy Spirit, who is the sample and guarantee of the heavenly inheritance (Eph. 1:13-14). The great doctrinal section of the epistle ends with Paul's famous prayer (3:14-21) in which the completeness and effectiveness of the Christian life is developed in terms of the power of the Holy Spirit (v. 16), the indwelling Christ (v. 17), and the privilege of being filled with all the fullness of God (v. 19).

This perfection of believers is also the theme of the other apostles. James wrote that there has to be a cure for doublemindedness (1:8) and a victory over temptation (1:12) so that one can use the wisdom that comes from God. John declared that one must walk in the light and in love, testing the spirits (1 John 1:7; 4:1, 16). If one's life does not show forth Christ, he has no assurance of salvation (4:8). Peter reminds believers that all things are provided for holy living, but they must make their calling and election sure (2 Peter 1:3, 10). The writer to the Hebrews assures us that Christ is perfectly adequate for us to go on to perfection (6:1 KJV). Not to go on may lead to apostasy. Jude strongly warns that deviation is ungodliness and damnation (vv. 4-7). In Revelation, John records the angel's declaration that each kind knows or learns his appropriate destiny (22:11).

It is evident that God's plan from the beginning was to have a people like Himself, conformed in some vital and real sense to His own righteousness, holiness, purity, and perfection. It is not acceptable to God nor to the creature himself for a great gulf of disparity to exist between the Creator and the creature. "The wrath of God is revealed from heaven against all ungodliness and unrighteousness of men" (Rom. 1:18). But God has revealed and offered in the gospel a valid righteousness that satisfies a holy God and makes a person forever blessed (vv. 16-17). The next section will examine terms and concepts as revealed in the Scripture and as understood in theology. The object will be a better understanding of what is and what is not included in a scriptural doctrine of Christian perfection, Christian holiness, perfect love, and like terms, before attempting more technical distinctions and the practical questions of application.

III. ASPECTS OF CHRISTIAN PERFECTION

Those who object to the Wesleyan understanding of Christian perfection often center their complaints on the vocabulary or terminologies used, even though the real problem is often a theological tradition behind the choice of words. For the sake of clarity, I will not attempt to coin new words or express novel ideas but will give priority to understanding what terms have meant in the Scriptures and in the Wesleyan tradition. Understanding and communication of scriptural holiness, more than novelty and originality, are, I believe, the need. Some words and concepts are worth learning in each generation.[13]

Although there are no exact synonyms in any language, there is, for the most part, remarkable agreement in the use of a number of terms as somewhat synonymous and, at times, as almost interchangeable. This similarity, as well as the distinct connotation and symbolism, should be observed in such words as entire sanctification, Christian perfection, holiness, perfect love, gift of the Holy Spirit, purification, cleansing, and fullness of the Spirit. It is worth noting how freely and confidently these terms are used in the Wesleyan tradition and how certain other movements avoid them. One suspects that semantic differences often reflect theological cleavage that is more difficult to span.

Wesley was careful to use terms that were clearly derived from the Scripture and he was faithful to their scriptural meaning. He claims to have examined every word and construction in the Greek New Testament with care. To be biblical in this sense was more important to his purpose than to have a fine system. Wesleyans who follow his example are the most clear and convincing. There are, of course, figurative and illustrative materials in Scripture that must be handled with some degree of caution. But their contribution to one's understanding of sanctification must not be neglected. In any case, I will comment on several major scriptural and Wesleyan terms as they reflect various aspects of Christian perfection.

A. Entire Sanctification and Holiness

Since the verb *to sanctify* and the noun *holiness* are from the same Greek and Hebrew roots, the words and their correlatives may be treated together. To sanctify is to make holy. Entire sanctification refers to an act of God that renders the experience of holiness complete or perfect in some proper sense of the word. The most important word for "holy" and "holiness" in the Old Testament is *qadosh,* which occurs 830 times, always in a religious context.[14] The corresponding New Testament word, *hagios,* occurs 234 times in some form. It is used 94 times of the Holy Spirit and 64 times of persons.[15] In the Old Testament the word is often used in a figurative or symbolic context. In the New Testament the language is more explicit, and the reference is almost exclusively personal and moral.

The primary idea of holiness has to do with relationship to God. The temple was holy because it was God's house. The furnishings of the temple were holy in that they were separated from other uses and were dedicated to the service of God. The priests, likewise, were separated from relationships and activities that would pervert or mar their special calling. The primary idea of holiness was not in what they were separated from, but to whom they were dedicated. Their separation was not an end in itself, as in pagan asceticism. It found its meaning in dedication to God. The priests, the whole chosen nation, and the whole church of Jesus Christ are, primarily, to be "holy to the Lord." Consequently, entire sanctification has to do with the completeness and perfection of that relationship with God.

Inseparable from the relationship with God is the personal fitness for that relationship. Though man can never of his own works be worthy to be God's cherished possession, the Scriptures indicate that the grace of God is sufficient to restore fallen man and to keep him fit for intimate relationship with God in time and for eternity. This is Paul's prayer and word of assurance that climaxes 1 Thessalonians and might be said to be the theme of the whole Bible in one way or another: "Now may the God of peace, Himself sanctify you entirely; and may your spirit and soul and body be preserved complete, without blame at the coming of our Lord Jesus Christ. Faithful is He who calls you, and He also will bring it to pass" (5:23-24).

The means by which this likeness to God is restored is often spoken of in terms of cleansing, purification, purging, washing, renewing, baptism with the Spirit, the gift of the Spirit, and the like. Pope goes so far as to say:

> The terms which belong to this branch of Christian theology . . . constitute the largest class of homogeneous phrases in the New Testament. . . . They embrace the entire vocabulary of the Altar, its sacrifices, oblation and priesthood, Divine and human; sanctification, dedication, presentation, hallowing, consecration; sprinkling, washing, and putting away sin; purity, sanctity, love, and holiness, and with opposites of these with all their shades; sealing, anointing, and therefore the very word Christian itself.[16]

In any case, entire sanctification deals radically and fully with the moral and spiritual barriers that alienate man from God; and, from the positive side, it imparts, through the gift of the Holy Spirit, sufficient grace for a holy life, dedicated fully to God through Christ.

B. The Concept of Purification

Since sin is the great spoiler and perverter of humanity and of God's purpose for His people, purification is a dominant concept in anything that concerns restoration and the fulfillment of an adequate relationship with God. A variety of vivid symbols and figures are used to describe the work of God in relieving man of the impurities and perversions that afflict the human being as a result of sin. Sin has no meaning in the abstract. It is not a "thing" in the sense of a material object, but it is an attitude or act of persons that results in damage to the state or condition of a moral being consequent upon such alienation from God. To speak in meaningful terms to the human mind and heart, the Word of God uses concrete words for sin and its remedy as if it were speaking of material substance. Words like *wash, purge, prune,* and similar terms transcend their material sense and refer to a work of God that relieves the human heart of its impurity as earthly detergents remove material contamination. By whatever means the connection between sin and the person is broken, to that extent sin is destroyed and the moral being is free, morally well, sanctified, or holy. The emphasis of Scripture terms is on the thoroughness of the purification rather than on the choice of the figure under which it is presented.

A variety of words in both Testaments have been translated as purify, wash, purge, cleanse, and the like. Some come from ceremonial and liturgical backgrounds, but the great majority simply reflect the concrete situations of everyday life. *Katharizō* is a strong word for removing impurity in whatever way is necessary. In a vineyard, the pruning knife cuts away unproductive or dead wood, letting the sap flow (John 15:2). In the Upper Room, the baptism with the Holy Spirit (Acts 2:1-4) purified (KJV) or cleansed hearts in response to faith (Acts 15:9). Again, John uses the same Greek word to declare that the blood of Jesus cleanses us from all sin (1 John 1:7). Of the number of words translated "wash," a common one is *rachats*. It pictures one scrubbing or beating clothes to drive out imbedded dirt or treating them roughly with fuller's soap to make them white (Ps. 51:2, 7). The point seems to be that God will do what it takes to make His people pure and acceptable. Even if the stain of sin is as indelible as crimson, He will make us like pure wool (Isa. 1:18). If the impurities resist the strongest detergents, He will turn from water to the refiner's fire. Indeed, the Christ Himself "will sit as a smelter and purifier of silver," turning on the heat until the impurities are gone and only the pure metal remains (Mal. 3:2-3).

Other passages are translated by the English words *cleanse* and *clean* to cover a variety of concepts from ceremonial cleansing of altars and sanctuaries (Exod. 29:36) to curing leprosy (Matt. 8:3), to remedying conduct (James 4:8), to cleansing the heart from all sin (1 John 1:7). Again, the strength is not in the symbol used but in the effective removing of the cause of defilement or destruction. Sometimes the word *katargeō* is used; it is translated "destroyed." It is a very strong word, translated in a variety of ways, such as: destroy, bring to naught, make void, release, deliver, come to naught, cease, vanish, fail, be done away with, put away, and put down. This is the word in Romans 6:6 that denotes the destruction of the body of sin, in a context dealing with drastic concepts such as death and resurrection.

Some interpreters of Christian holiness have shown preference for the English word *eradicate,* which gathers up the meaning and context of strong words for deliverance from the carnal nature, and expresses a scriptural concept of radical cleansing and freedom from sin. Etymologically, the word means to root out, as one removes a stump of a tree. Since the English translators did not use the word even where the root occurs in the Greek (Matt. 15:13), since there was no clear precedent in early Wesleyan theology, and since some have stumbled at the figure, other Wesleyan theologians avoid the term and depend on the more common and less misunderstood words for cleansing, purifying, and purification. When the other scriptural words for purification are properly understood, this concession to the popular mind may change little of substance. Equally strong words are common in the Scripture. Whether the figure is that of a strong detergent, a consuming fire, fuller's soap, death, destruction, or digging out roots, sin is a deeper reality than a material substance, and the cure is as radical as the defilement.

Preoccupation with the negative aspect of "deliverance from" tends to obscure in many minds the fact that purification, freedom, cleansing, and the like, also have a positive thrust. Removing or cleansing from the cause of malfocus or malfunction is exactly the way to bring into focus or function. Removing the disabling pollution makes way for abundant life, and reducing the distractions and hindrances leads to personal integration. Destroying the weeds is for the purpose of letting the garden grow. It should be clear, then, that the so-called negative aspects of the gospel and especially of entire sanctification, have strong positive implications. In fact, there is no negative in the Bible except for the sake of the positive. Jesus came to destroy the works of the devil (1 John 3:8) for the specific purpose of making the work of God abound in us.

C. The Concept of the Gift of the Holy Spirit

Although the Spirit of God preceded man in the world and has been active in relation to man throughout the Old Testament, it has been already noted that the same Holy Spirit was promised by the prophets, by John the Baptist, by the Father, and by Jesus Himself. It has also been noted that the promise was fulfilled at Pentecost but that it still continued to be a central proclamation of the gospel, that all might hear and receive. Looking back to the Day of Pentecost, to their own experiences, and to later outpourings of the Spirit, the apostles changed their terminology from "promise" to "gift," "give," and "receive," with an occasional reference to "pour out."

Though the new birth means to be born of the Spirit (John 3:5), it is obvious that this is not the meaning of "the promise of the Father" nor of "the gift of the Spirit." Certainly those who received the Spirit at Pentecost had already been born of the Spirit. Indeed, Jesus seems to be chiding Nicodemus, the Old Testament scholar, for not being familiar with the only way anyone in any dispensation could enter the kingdom of God (v. 5). On another occasion, John explained clearly that none of the believers at the time had received the promised Spirit, though they were obviously born of the Spirit.[17] The Spirit is referred to as the One "whom those who believed in Him were to receive, for the Spirit was not yet given, because Jesus was not yet glorified" (John 7:39). As Wood says, "It is apparent that while the disciples possessed the presence of the Spirit before Pentecost, yet they did not 'receive [the fullness of] the Spirit' until the day of Pentecost (John 14:17).'"[18] If, then, this gift of the Spirit is distinct from the new birth or conversion, it is not strange that it is promised only to believers or to those who are invited to become believers prior to receiving the Holy Spirit (Acts 2:38). The gift of the sanctifying Spirit follows the new birth as entire sanctification follows the initial sanctification received at conversion.

The "gift" terminology appears as early as the Gospel of Luke and runs strongly through the Book of Acts. Jesus seems to have initiated it in giving this assurance: "How much more shall your heavenly Father give the Holy Spirit to those who ask Him?" (Luke 11:13). John used the same "give" and "receive" terms in explaining Jesus' words at the Feast of Tabernacles (John 7:37-39). In saying that the event had not yet happened, John referred to the future event as believers' "receiving the Spirit," and to the Holy Spirit as yet "to be given" (John 7:39). The verb and the noun of giving dominate the whole emphasis on Pentecost with its privilege for believers in the rest of the New Testament. On the day of Pentecost Peter repeated the promise that all could receive the gift of the Holy Spirit (Acts 2:38-39). Soon afterward, Peter told the high priest that the Holy Spirit was witness, "whom God has given to those who obey him" (Acts 5:32). When the Samaritan believers "received" the Holy Spirit, Simon observed how the Holy Spirit was "given" and tried to bargain for the power to produce the same results. He was condemned for trying to buy the "gift of God" (Acts 8:17-20). Again, in explaining what happened at the house of Cornelius, Peter compared it to Pentecost and called it "giving them the Holy Spirit" (Acts 15:8-9).

The same is true in the epistles. Nowhere is the Holy Spirit simply a vehicle of the gifts and enablements for performing the ministry. He is Himself the gift, dispensing grace for holy living. Paul says, "The love of God has been poured out within our hearts through the Holy Spirit who was given to us" (Rom. 5:5). Again he points out that God who called us unto holiness (KJV) also "gives His Holy Spirit" to us (1 Thess. 4:7-8). In Titus (3:6) Paul goes back to Joel's terminology as repeated at Pentecost (Joel 2:28; Acts 2:17) and says that God poured out the Holy Spirit on us richly. In a few other instances the "poured out" theme is preserved to describe the manner in which the gift is given. But the Holy Spirit Himself is always the gift that is given in this sanctifying and filling sense. There are, of course, certain "gifts" *(charismata)* that are special enablements for special ministries (Rom. 12:6–8), but they are no necessary part of the gift of the Holy Spirit. The gifts are distributed and administered as God wills. But God has called all unto holiness and has offered the Holy Spirit as the gift to all who accept His call (1 Thess. 4:7–8). The gift of the Holy Spirit is then the enablement for a life of holiness—positive and effective Christian living.

Parallel to the concept of "gift" and "giving," and quite interchangeable with it, is the concept of "receiving." As the gift of the Holy Spirit is for those who are already believers, so is the receiving. Wood lists twelve places in the New Testament where "receiving the Spirit" is descriptive of the Pentecostal fullness—of receiving the fullness of the Spirit.[19] The force of these passages is more apparent when they are viewed together. Prophetic of this giving and receiving of the Spirit are the words of Jesus (John 7:39). However, the world, or unconverted people, cannot receive the Spirit (John 14:17). But Jesus breathed on the disciples and said, prophetically, "Receive the Holy Spirit" (John 20:22). Again He promised that they would receive power when the Holy Spirit had come upon them (Acts 1:8). At Pentecost, Peter assured the multitude that the Holy Spirit could be received by all true believers (Acts 2:38). The apostles prayed that the Samaritan believers might receive the Holy Spirit (Acts 8:14–15), and they did receive Him (v. 17). Simon tried unsuccessfully to buy the power to cause others to receive the Holy Spirit (v. 19). At the house of Cornelius, "all those who were listening to the message" received the Holy Spirit (Acts 10:44, 47). Paul earnestly inquired at Ephesus if the believers had yet received the Holy Spirit (Acts 19:2). The Galatians were challenged to remember how they received the Spirit (Gal. 3:2). This is God's plan that "we might receive the promise of the Spirit through faith" (Gal. 3:14).

Wood well concludes that:

> It is apparent that "receiving the Spirit" is linked to the Pentecostal event. It is also apparent that while the disciplines possessed the presence of the Spirit before Pentecost, yet they did not "receive [the fullness of] the Spirit" until the day of Pentecost (John 14:17).[20]

Again, he correctly affirms (and elaborates in chapter 7) that the baptism with the Spirit (Acts 1:5), the Spirit "falling upon" (Acts 8:16), the Spirit "coming upon" (Acts 1:8), "filled with the Spirit" (Acts 2:4) are phrases that are more or less equivalent to "receiving the Spirit."[21]

D. The Concept of Perfect Love

"Perfect love" is a favorite synonym for "Christian perfection." Neither expression implies perfect judgment, complete wisdom, or full maturity of skills or perfection in performance. But both do imply a heart cleansed from sin and filled with the Holy Spirit. This means that "the love of God has been poured out within our hearts through the Holy Spirit who was given to us" (Rom. 5:5). It is in the context of love that Jesus demanded perfection (Matt. 5:48). To those who share His holiness (Heb. 12:10), perfect love is both possible and necessary. The "be ye perfect," in Jesus' words (Matt. 5:48 KJV), leaves no alternative if one wants to enjoy the blessedness of walking with the holy God.

God is holy (1 Peter 1:16) and God is love (1 John 4:8). Both qualities, holiness and love, belong to the essential nature of God as well as to His attributes. "Holiness must act according to love, and love must win its object to holiness."[22] Holiness and love in God are original and underived. God manifests His holiness (self-affirmation) by His love (self-communication).[23] Thus we become partakers of the divine nature (2 Peter 1:4) through the Holy Spirit. This is how we can "fervently love one another from the heart" (1 Peter 1:22).

It is in this context that Jesus could reaffirm "the first commandment of all" together with its corollary: "'And you shall love the Lord your God with all your heart, and with all your soul, and with all your mind, and with all your strength.'" This is the first commandment. "The second is this: "You shall love your neighbor as yourself'" (Mark 12:30-31). Certainly if this commandment as given by Moses (Deut. 6:4-6) had meaning enough for the ancient Jews to recite it twice daily for centuries before Pentecost, its demand for perfect love to God and man should be relevant and possible to those who have the abiding gift of the Holy Spirit.

Love is a unique requirement and privilege. Jesus called it a "commandment." The Greek word *entolē* is a compound of the word for "in" or "inner" and the word for "end" or "purpose." This principle was the inner purpose in God that governed His self-communication to us. We caught it from Him. "We love, because He first loved us" (1 John 4:19). "We have come to know and have believed the love which God has for us. God is love, and the one who abides in love abides in God, and God abides in him. By this, love is perfected with us, that we may have confidence in the day of judgment, because as He is, so also are we in this world" (vv. 16-17). This love is required, indeed, but it is more bestowed than forced. It is ours by a perfect work of God in redemption, without which we could not experience holy love.

Love, again, is a reasonable requirement. It does not require advanced maturity of performance, ripe years, or unusual brilliance of intellect. A child can love when God sheds His love abroad in the heart. Yet the most brilliant and mature person in the world cannot do more than the commandment requires. It requires his all, even in the case of the child or the handicapped person. God is utterly fair. He requires what is possible by nature and by grace. But He requires no more. Of one such person, Jesus said, "Let her alone. . . . She has done what she could" (Mark 14:6, 8).

Perfect love does not require a perfection that is inconsistent with the human as finite. Nor does it require a perfection impossible to a marred vessel or a perfection that would be inconsistent with one's natural constitution. Nor does it mean that one will never be tempted; nor does it place him beyond the need of growth and improvement. That is, nothing is required that is beyond the capacity of one who is fully cleansed, renewed, and filled with God's Spirit. If the command sounds impossible, it only seems that way. God's grace is sufficient to enable us to love perfectly according to God's standard.

Perfect love, of course, is a certain kind of love. It is not mere friendliness, or even family ties. That is, it is not *philia* or *storge*. Nor is it the longing to be near a person with whom one is "in love" *(eros)*. Nor is it the desire to "make love." It is the kind of love for which the pagan Greeks had no noun until later Christian centuries, because they knew no such love. The noun *agapē* was coined to translate the Old Testament *hesed* into the Septuagint Greek and then became very much a key word in the New Testament. It is a love that can be commanded. It is not a blind preference. It has been called "intelligent good-will." In any case, it is an expression of the whole person—intellect, moral choice, and warmth of concern. It is purer and more creative than man could invent. But by grace, *agapē* love is possible—even perfect love.

Perfect love, then, is an unmixed love. It is purposeful and intelligent concern for the will of God and the welfare of one's fellow human beings. It is concern unmixed with the carnal and the selfish. It is to "fervently love one another from the heart," which the apostle Peter admits is possible only because "you have in obedience to the truth purified your souls for a sincere love of the brethren" (1 Peter 1:22). Under those circumstances the apostle can and does command this love.

Perfect love is an impartial love. It is not based on what benefit we can receive in return. James forbids us to mix this kind of personal favoritism with faith in our Lord Jesus Christ (2:1ff.). It simply does not fit with real love at all.

It is also a practical love. Words without action are cheap and ineffective and may be positively hypocritical (James 2:14-20). We are not to love only with words or with the tongue, but "with actions and in truth" (1 John 3:16-18). That is how we can test our genuineness (v. 19).

Love must be a first and total response to God. No other love or concern can take priority over or in any way subvert the total love and dedication that is directed toward God. The primary commitment of the heart (the center of controls), the soul (the total powers of personality), the mind (the guide to all relationships and activity), and the strength (all the powers of implementing one's intentions)—the primary and total commitment of all there is of us—is to God, His will, and His concerns. That is perfect love.

But love to God is not separable from concern for the welfare of mankind, including ourselves. We cannot love God as we ought without loving our neighbor. The second commandment is like the first (Mark 12:31). Since God is love, our love for Him must include all that we can do for our fellow human beings, whom He loves. It must also include our responsibilities for ourselves and for those who depend directly on us. We are to love our neighbors as ourselves, but not to the exclusion of meeting our own needs. Strange as it may seem to some, there is more benefit from the love to one's fellows and to oneself after one has become a love-slave to God than there is in any other way. One can see this also in the Decalogue. The fact that the first four commandments are "religious"—directed toward relationship with God—only sets the stage for a workable social order as provided in the last six items. The wisdom and goodness of God in creation have tied personal and social values to a right relationship with God. In God's love for us and in our love for God a oneness is developed that meets the needs of all. Only perfect love allows God's provision to work perfectly.

Wesley did not deliberately and formally choose "perfect love" or any other term as the one central idea of which all else is only explanatory. Like the name "Methodist," the term "Christian perfection" was thrust on him by the critics to the extent that he wrote the *Plain Account of Christian Perfection*[24] to explain to friend and foe alike what was meant by the term to which most objection was made. Although Wesley avoided making a theological formula of any term, it is clear that perfect love, or at least love, was his understanding of scriptural holiness or Christian perfection. In plain terms he said:

> It were well you should be thoroughly sensible of this,—"the heaven of heavens is love." There is nothing higher in religion; there is, in effect, nothing else; if you look for anything but more love, you are looking wide of the mark, you are getting out of the royal way. And when you are asking others, "Have you received this or that blessing?" if you mean anything but more love, you mean wrong; you are leading them out of the way and putting them upon a false scent.[25]

Again, in 1771 Wesley wrote to Walter Churchey:

> Entire sanctification, or Christian perfection, is neither more nor less than pure love—love expelling sin and governing both the heart and life of a child of God. The Refiner's fire purges out all that is contrary to love, and that many times by a pleasing smart.[26]

Concerning holiness, Wesley wrote to Lawrence Coughlan:

> I told you it was love; the love of God and our neighbour; the image of God stamped on the heart; the life of God in the soul of man; the mind that was in Christ, enabling us to walk as Christ also walked.[27]

It is evident that Wesley was not setting one term against another to establish a priority of language. His one concern seemed to be to understand the Scripture in relation to the life of God in the soul. Even so, Sangster is probably correct that "his favourite term for this debated doctrine was perfect love."[28] In any case, Wesley's belief has frequently been treated in books and articles under this topic. Sangster feels that much of the neglect of Wesley's doctrine after his death could have been prevented by greater use of the positive term "perfect love" in preference to "Christian perfection," in which some see negative connotations.[29] Be that as it may, the terms all carried the same message, though emphasizing different aspects of the life of God in man.

E. The Concept of Power

In the closing days of His earthly ministry, our Lord seemed particularly concerned about the power aspect of the Pentecostal gift of the Holy Spirit. He said, "And behold, I am sending forth the promise of my Father upon you; but you are to stay in the city until you are clothed with power from on high" (Luke 24:49). Again in Acts He cautioned the disciples against wasting their energies on schedules that were beyond their control when there was work to be done and when they were about to be empowered to do that work (1:7-8). The word for power in both instances is *dynamis* from the verb *dynamai* ("to be able"). It is the word from which the terms *dynamics, dynamo, dynamite,* and the like are derived. The power can be inherent in the one exercising it, or it can, as here, be bestowed through a relationship with another, in this case with the Holy Spirit. But this power-giving relationship is not at all casual. One is *clothed* with the power. The figure implies that as the interaction between clothing and one's body constitutes warmth, so the interaction between the Holy Spirit and the indwelt believer constitutes power, but with this difference: the Holy Spirit is not dead fabric but a living and life-giving Person, the primary source of the interaction, the *dynamis* of God in man.

With man made in the image of God, this is all very reasonable. Once man is cleansed from all sin, the real barrier to union with God, the divine Spirit can freely relate Himself to the created human spirit. This relationship is so vital and dynamic that it is more than a presence with; it is an abiding in (John 14:17). Jesus, in the flesh, also could only be *with* the disciples. By the Holy Spirit He becomes "Christ *in* you, the hope of glory" (Col. 1:27). When Jesus was with His disciples in the flesh, He was a Comforter or Paraclete. The old English word *comforter* is from the Latin, which means strengthener or enabler or helper, and this is the meaning of paraclete. Whatever was needed to make the disciples able to cope with life and their ministry, they found in Jesus.

When Jesus was about to leave the disciples, He promised them another (*allos,* another of the same kind) Paraclete (John 14:16). There were a number of advantages to this Enabler. The disciples were already familiar with Him. "He abides with you"; better yet, He "will be in you" (v. 17). With redemption completed, and with the time and space categories transcended, they and we can be literally clothed with adequacy ("power from on high") by the Spirit of Pentecost (Luke 24:49). Best of all, He will "be with you forever" (John 14:16). Then Jesus adds the comforting explanation that the expected separation from the presence of Christ is only partial and temporary. "I will come to you" (v. 18). "In that day you shall know that I am in My Father, and you in Me, and I in you" (v. 20). How can this be? Again Jesus explains that both the Father and He will come and make Their abode with us (v. 23). In other words, the other "Paraclete" who comes is not only the Holy Spirit, the third person of the Trinity, but in Him and with Him is the coming of the whole Trinity. "It is to your advantage that I go away," Jesus said (John 16:7). It is a matter of exchanging the limited presence of the Son of God for the indwelling presence of the Trinity, limited only by our capacity to receive.

Paul wrote to the Ephesians in a similar vein about this indwelling fullness (3:14-20). Using two words for power, he prays that they should be "mightily strengthened by power" *(krataiōthēnai dynamei)* "through His Spirit in the inner man" (v. 16). Then this post-Pentecostal experience with the other Comforter is described in these words: "So that Christ may dwell in your hearts through faith; that you, being rooted and grounded in love, may be able to comprehend with all the saints what is the breadth and length and height and depth, and to know the love of Christ which surpasses knowledge, that you may be filled up to all the fulness of God" (vv. 17-20). The word for "be able" is the intensive *exischuō* (to "be strong enough" or to "be in a position to"). The indwelling Comforter makes the Spirit-filled believer adequate and able for that which is not possible to ordinary human ability. This is the power of Pentecost—not for a moment nor a day, but forever.

Speaking to those who were already sealed with the promised Holy Spirit, who is the sample and pledge of their eternal inheritance (Eph. 1:13-14), Paul elaborates on the power that makes for effectual Christian living. He speaks of "the exceeding greatness of God's power [*dynamis*] toward us who believe, according to the working [*energeia,* inworking or energy] of the might [*kratos*] of His strength [*ischuos*]" (v. 19), which received its supreme test in raising Christ from the dead and seating Him at the right hand of God in the heavenly places for time and eternity (vv. 20-21). His triumph made Him the "head over all things to the church, which is His body, the fulness of Him Who fills all in all" (vv. 22-23). This is the power of God available for life and service to those who receive the Holy Spirit as given.

Wesley, in his terse and almost matter-of-fact style, incorporates this concept of power into his whole doctrine of grace as manifest in Christian experience. He does not write books or sermons on it as such, but he does depend on this divine enablement or "empowerment" for the whole Christian life. In his *Explanatory Notes on the New Testament* he says simply, "Ye shall be empowered to witness my Gospel, both by your preaching and suffering" (Acts 1:8). Again, in regard to the phrase "the exceeding greatness of his power toward us who believe" (Eph. 1:19 KJV) Wesley commented, "Both in quickening our dead souls, and preserving them in spiritual life, 'according to the power which he exerted in Christ, raising him from the dead'—By the very same almighty power, whereby he raised Christ: for no less would suffice.'"[30] Whenever Wesley refers to victory, freedom from sin, perfect love, Christian perfection, or salvation in any respect, this kind of context is always expressed or implied. Power is not a separate doctrine. It is simply the grace of God at work through the Holy Spirit.

Many who are interested in Christian perfection follow Wesley's concept that power is simply the enabling operation of the Holy Spirit in the life of the believer, whatever the need may be. A. B. Simpson wrote in that vein in his two-volume work entitled *The Holy Spirit or Power from On High,*[31] which became virtually a commentary on the whole Bible as it relates to the Holy Spirit. Some who emphasize the identity of Christian perfection with the Pentecostal baptism of the Spirit tend to treat power more in the context of this special outpouring of power (Acts 1:8). Asa Mahan, for example, at the end of his book *The Baptism of the Holy Ghost* includes four chapters from C. G. Finney on "the enduement of power." Still others, not wanting to claim any sort of Christian perfection as a result of the baptism of the Holy Spirit, describe the "blessing" as an enduement of "power for service." The more "orthodox" Wesleyan interpretation would include in the concept of the work of the Spirit both moral purity (fitness to serve) and power for service (enablement to live and act as a Christian).

F. The Concept of Perfection

In spite of the repeated and almost constant insistence on perfection in the Scriptures, some still object to the concept as applied to man subsequent to the Fall. Apart from the grace of God, indeed, there could be no defense of the idea. But to deny that God can renew and restore to perfection what He once made in His own image is not only to contradict the Scriptures but to dishonor God. God is not glorified by the failure of man and certainly not by His own failure to redeem man. The contrast between sinful man and a holy God neither pleases nor honors God. "The wrath of God is revealed from heaven against all ungodliness and unrighteousness of men" (Rom. 1:18). Since the Fall, God has been working to transform man (Rom. 12:1-2) and restore him to glory and perfection. Through Him we have fruit unto holiness now, and the life we have is everlasting. However defective our performance and opinions may be, God's work in redemption is perfect. God looks on this inner perfection and remembers that the outer man is fallible and faulty.

Part of the dislike for the term *perfection* is the tendency of some to confuse Christian perfection with absolute or divine perfection. One must always remember that the two are not only different but are quite opposite. Christian perfection is a matter of the heart—of love, attitude, and relationship. It accepts human limitations and leans on the perfect Savior and Lord. Even such power and ability as one has is not by human excellence of works. It is a matter of grace. Christian perfection has none of the pride and boasting of a humanistic quest of perfection, which seeks the absolute and dreams of a goal beyond which there can be no further development or improvement. The perfection of the people of God is a growing, changing, and improving life. It moves from glory to glory by the Spirit of God (2 Cor. 3:18). Without exception, true children of God continue to improve, purifying themselves (1 John 3:1-3).

Speaking of the "perfectionist" absolutes, Mildred Wynkoop wrote:

> New Testament writers knew nothing of this kind of thinking. Biblical writers uniformly refer to man as well as nature in personal and dynamic terms. Even the perfection of God called sovereignty does not immobilize Him. He is not the victim of His own nature. His absoluteness does not rob Him of flexibility and the capacity to relate to men who have been endowed by Him with genuine, if limited, freedom.[32]

It is always dangerous, in referring to either God or man, to slip from terms of moral freedom and responsibility to deterministic and absolute ideas that paralyze thought and action. To avoid this, it is helpful to turn to the Scripture contexts and uses of the words for "perfect," observing the dynamic situations in which the words are used.

The two most common Hebrew words for perfect are *shalam* and *thamam*. *Shalam* is used of a perfect heart in fourteen passages. Its usual meaning is related to peace, according to Girdlestone, as in Isaiah 26:3, "Thou wilt keep [him] in perfect peace [*shalom shalom*]," repeating the word for peace to intensify the expression.[33] Girdlestone also says:

> The root may have originally signified oneness or wholeness, and so completeness. The KJV has rendered the verb: to be ended, to be finished, to prosper, to make amends, to pay, to perform, to recompense, to repay, to requite, to make restitution, to restore, to reward. In all these cases there is implied a bringing of some difficulty to a conclusion, a finishing off of some work, a clearing away, by payment or labor or suffering, of some charge.[34]

The word *thamam*, according to Girdlestone, is best rendered as "unblemished," "entire," and "sincere."[35] The translators have rendered it in various ways: perfect, plain, undefiled, upright, integrity, simplicity, full, without blemish, blameless, sincere, sound, without spot, whole, to be consumed, to be accomplished, to end, to fail, to be spent, to be wasted. Noah was a just man, and "perfect" in his generation (Gen. 6:9 KJV). Abraham was commanded to walk before God and to be perfect (Gen. 17:1 KJV). Sacrifices were to be free of blemish (Lev. 22:21). The Israelites were to be perfect before the Lord (Deut. 18:13). Perfection belongs to God's ways (2 Sam. 22:31 KJV). Job was perfect and upright (Job 1:1 KJV). The law of the Lord is perfect (Ps. 19:7). Even in the Old Testament the standard of perfection is high indeed, but practical, reasonable, and dynamic. With God's loving care and provision, it was possible.

In the New Testament, the various forms derived from *telos* ("goal," "end") are fairly common. About 117 instances are mentioned in *The New International Dictionary of New Testament Theology*.[36] Cremer insists that *telos* never refers merely to an end as to time or space in and for itself. It always includes the idea of an inner completion. It refers to the qualitative end, the conclusion.[37] *Teleios*, then, means "having attained the end or purpose, complete, perfect."[38] In respect to persons, it can refer to age: full-grown, mature, adult; or it can refer "to persons who are fully up to standard in a certain respect: perfect, complete, expert."[39] Likewise it can refer to one who is perfect or fully developed in a moral sense.[40] Again the emphasis is not so much on the means by which one arrives at the goal. Whether it is a maturity reached by growth or a completeness produced by an act of God, the reference is to that which is wholly in accord with God's will, especially in such passages as Romans 12:2 and 1 Corinthians 13:10.[41] Perhaps one should be reminded that God is not displeased with the relative immaturity of a babe. Nor does His pleasure with an adult or an otherwise complete and perfect person mean that there is no further progress possible in working out the implications of the will of God. The concept of perfection is practical and dynamic, reflecting a vital relationship with God.

There is another family of words that treats a more functional aspect of perfection. *Katartizō* is an intensive, compounded form that means to "put in order, restore, put to rights, put into proper condition, or complete."[42] It is sometimes used of rigging a ship for a new voyage. Paul spoke of perfecting that which was lacking in the faith of his converts (1 Thess. 3:10 KJV). It is used in Hebrews of "making . . . complete in every good thing" (13:21 KJV). Again it refers to being "made complete in the same mind and the same conviction" (1 Cor. 1:10). A "fully trained" pupil will be like his teacher (Luke 6:40). The man of God is made "perfect," fitted to perform his task (2 Tim. 3:17 KJV). It is not enough for the perfect one to be good. He must be good for something. This also is Christian perfection.

Wesley was aware of both the necessity of perfection and the limitations of human possibilities even under grace. In *A Plain Account of Christian Perfection* he summarized his view in several short propositions:

(1.) There is such a thing as perfection; for it is again and again mentioned in Scripture.
(2.) It is not so early as justification; for justified persons are to "go on unto perfection." (Heb. vi. 1)
(3.) It is not so late as death; for St. Paul speaks of living men that were perfect. (Philip. iii. 15)
(4.) It is not absolute. Absolute perfection belongs not to man, nor to angels, but to God alone.
(5.) It does not make a man infallible: None is infallible, while he remains in the body.
(6.) Is it sinless? It is not worth while to contend for a term. It is "salvation from sin."
(7.) It is "perfect love." (1 John iv. 18) This is the essence of it; its properties, or inseparable fruits, are, rejoicing evermore, praying without ceasing, and in everything giving thanks. (1 Thess. v. 16, etc.)
(8.) It is improvable. It is so far from lying in an indivisible point, from being incapable

of increase, that one perfected in love may grow in grace far swifter than he did before.⁴³

From this point, Wesley proceeds to discuss the instantaneous and gradual work of God in the heart and life of a Christian.

Elsewhere, especially in his sermons entitled "Christian Perfection"⁴⁴ and "On Perfection,"⁴⁵ Wesley explains much more fully the meaning of perfection and of the human imperfections that still cling to those who enjoy perfect love. Though the Christian is taught by divine revelation the things necessary to salvation, he is still afflicted by ignorance, error, infirmity, defects, and temptation in all other aspects of his humanity. This does not negate the grace of God that gives victory over sin and even freedom from sin, but it does affect performance in thought, word, and deed. The merits and work of the Redeemer are constantly needed, as is the powerful assistance of the Holy Spirit.

Wesley made a radical distinction between Christian perfection, which is moral and heart perfection by grace, and the absolute perfection of God, and even angelic or Adamic perfection, which is unspoiled from the creative hand of God.⁴⁶ In the sermon "On Perfection" he summarizes the matter:

> The highest perfection which man can attain, while the soul dwells in the body, does not exclude ignorance, and error and a thousand infirmities. Now, from wrong judgments, wrong words and actions will often necessarily flow: And, in some cases, wrong affections also may spring from the same source. I may judge wrong of you; I may think more or less highly of you than I ought to think; and this mistake in my judgment may not only occasion something wrong in my behaviour, but it may have a still deeper effect; it may occasion something wrong in my affection. From a wrong apprehension, I may love and esteem you either more or less than I ought. Nor can I be freed from a liableness to such a mistake, while I remain in a corruptible body. A thousand infirmities, in consequence of this, will attend my spirit, till it returns to God who gave it. And, in numberless instances, it comes short of doing the will of God, as Adam did in paradise. Hence the best of men may say from the heart,
>
> "Every moment, Lord, I need
> The merit of thy death,
>
> for innumerable violations of the Adamic as well as the angelic law." It is well therefore, for us, that we are not now under these, but under the law of love. "Love is now the fulfilling of the law," which is given to fallen man. This is now, with respect to us, "the perfect law." But even against this, through the present weakness of our understanding, we are continually liable to transgress. Therefore every man living needs the blood of atonement, or he could not stand before God.⁴⁷

For Wesley, to reject the concept of Christian perfection would be to reject holiness, because "it is only another term for holiness. They are two names for the same thing. Thus everyone that is holy is, in the Scripture sense, perfect."⁴⁸ But not only the concept of perfection is scriptural and binding, so are also the standard and limits to be derived from the Scriptures. To the question of how shall we avoid setting perfection too high or too low, Wesley said:

> By keeping to the Bible, and setting it just as high as the Scripture does. It is nothing higher and nothing lower than this,—the pure love of God and man; the loving God with all our heart and soul, and our neighbour as ourselves. It is love governing the heart and life, running through all our tempers, words, and actions.⁴⁹

G. A Suggested Distinction

Wesley and his early followers were more interested in totals than in fine philosophic distinctions. It was no problem to them that their great discovery in Scripture and in life was quite indiscriminately called entire sanctification, Christian perfection, heart purity, holiness, fullness of the Spirit, and the like. There was, of course, no lack of opponents from the outside who misunderstood and scorned the whole idea of holiness, whether in ideal, experience, or practice. But the people on the inside were more interested in seeing God work than in taking the operation apart to see why it worked. They may not have been tooled for mass production, but they were doing an excellent job of piecework in their evangelism. Many were saved and there was evidence that some, at least, were being made perfect in love.

It was inevitable that procedural questions would arise and that the proposed answers would attach to different terms crucial to understanding the doctrine and experience. One ambiguity in many minds concerned the relationship between crisis and process in sanctification. It was obvious to Wesleyans that both factors must be taken into account, but how to reconcile them was a problem. If one speaks of "entire" sanctification as an accomplished work of God, what should one call the process that follows it? Or is Christian perfection the broad term of which entire sanctification is only an aspect? The need for clarity extended beyond matters of procedure and definition. It went to the heart of the concept. Are the terms true synonyms or should a basic distinction be made at the heart of the doctrine?

W. E. Sangster spent a great deal of time, especially during the bombing of London, "thinking on perfection" and on the Methodist heritage. Although he greatly appreciated the effective evangelism of his forebears, his book *The Path to Perfection* is, in many respects, more of a critique than an exposition of Christian perfection. As compared with Wesley and the early Wesleyans, he had a tentative and hesitating grasp of the concept. In his preface he frankly admits that he "throws away parts of" the central doctrine.[50] Although not directly disparaging the Scriptures, he made considerable point of the fact that modern exegetes would often disagree with Wesley's interpretation or fail to find holiness in his thirty principal texts.[51] He was quite sure, for instance, that it was a tactical error for Wesley to use and defend the term "Christian perfection."[52] He had especially serious questions about Christian assurance.[53] Just how authentic could the wonderful testimonies be? He concludes that "no man knows what is in him."[54] Sangster may have uncovered some sensitive areas in Wesley's thinking, as judged by current critics. Many people today, for that matter, would call even Wesley's total commitment to the Scriptures simplistic; yet the Wesleyan revival went on unabated after Wesley's death. But, though Sangster was a popular preacher who claimed to have led individuals into a deeper experience of grace, his crowds are no longer at the Central Hall in London on the "path to perfection." One wonders if believers of this century are victims of a degeneration that was inherited or if the doubts and questions raised have dissipated both the ideal and the power to the point of producing that degeneration. Truth is always changing its wraps, but caution is necessary lest more be discarded than the old garment. Many suggestions have been made that have not brought us nearer to perfection.

Bishop Marston, on the other hand, calls attention to a positive suggestion made in the past century that might have some relevance to the discussion of terminology and definitions.[55] From a book of collected teachings of B. T. Roberts, the founder of the Free Methodist Church, Marston drew a distinction between entire sanctification and Christian perfection.[56] Without denying the specific act of God in entire sanctification, Roberts held that Christian perfection is a broader term not confined to a single act or its effects. He preferred a "life-process" concept that includes in Christian perfection an act of God in entire sanctification but makes room for a continuing process of which the event is a part. So conceived, Christian perfection "is not static, given once for all as a state of grace in which the Christian may rest. It is a conquest leading to further conquests by faithful service and patient endurance."[57]

Roberts started no revolution in Wesleyan doctrine and probably intended none. It may be good that he did not. But he did well to remind Wesleyans again that entire sanctification is not in isolation from life, nor is it an end to growth. Grace is not static. Rest in faith is not gaining sleep; it is strength for conquest. Whatever else is said, Christian perfection, holiness, and perfect love are bigger terms than any single act of God. They are for the whole of life. If entire sanctification is understood only in terms of an instantaneous act of God, then it is only a point in the larger "life-process" of holiness or Christian perfection. Whenever the Wesleyan message has been vital, scriptural, and effective, it has carried this double emphasis: (1) on the act of God by which His image is stamped deep on the heart and (2) on all the process of grace that precedes and follows that act. Whatever the terminology, these are the true elements.

Wesley himself emphasized both the act and the process in his explanations of the doctrine and experience. He said, "There is no perfection of degrees, none which does not admit of continual increase."[58] "State of grace" terminology, in Wesley, was not thought of in terms of the present connotation of "static." It simply referred to the moral and spiritual condition of a believer in the light of the goal and the steps taken toward that goal. Wesley was entirely clear that both instantaneous and progressive grace are essential for Christian perfection. Whether or not the process that precedes and follows the crisis of entire sanctification should be called progressive sanctification is the question. Some insist that for clarity it should. Others see a contradiction of terms in saying that the finished act is still in process. There is, of course, the option of using the scriptural terms of growth in grace, abiding in Christ, living in the Spirit, and the like for the process, saying only what the Scripture says.

IV. CHRISTIAN PERFECTION AS THE RESULT OF A CRISIS EXPERIENCE OF SANCTIFICATION

Emphasis on a crisis experience of sanctification has been evident in the matters already discussed. However, data that has been somewhat taken for granted will be examined more clearly to explore the scriptural foundation for the belief that Christian perfection is, at least in part, the direct result of a definite act of God in sanctification of the believer. As Christian righteousness begins in the new birth, it is held that Christian perfection, in some true sense, begins when "the love of God has been poured out within our hearts through the Holy Spirit who was given to us" (Rom. 5:5). Those who believe in a definite experience of entire sanctification do not deny or depreciate the progressive work of God in the human personality before conversion, between conversion and entire sanctification, and from the crisis of sanctification to eventual glorification. To avoid confusion, they may less often refer to this progressive work as sanctification. They may call it prevenient grace (before the new birth) and growth in grace (after the new birth). Well-informed Wesleyans insist on a constant dependence on the continuing work of God through the Spirit, as do other Christians. The difference is the Wesleyan insistence that a crisic event is also normal (or necessary) to "perfecting holiness" (2 Cor. 7:1), as the new birth is required for the beginning of the Christian life (John 3:3). This distinction is particularly important in view of the exclusive emphasis in some communions on sanctification as only a lifelong process. The present effort is to identify a specific event of sanctification in the life of a believer, as seen in the Scriptures and in Wesleyan theology.

A. Implications of "Gift of the Holy Spirit"

The concept of the "gift of the Holy Spirit," whether expressed in terms of baptism, purification, filling, sealing, giving, or receiving, expresses or implies an event involving an instantaneous or crisis aspect. It in no way denies a preparatory or resultant process. Indeed, it generally affirms both. In the case of Joel, the prophetic promise of the act of God and of its results was given centuries before the great fulfilling event (Joel 2:28-32; Acts 2:1-21). God was working, meanwhile, in history and in the lives of His people. But process was not enough. There had to be an identifying and transforming event. Peter recognized this fact and said, "This is what was spoken of through the prophet Joel" (Acts 2:16).

The same emphasis on event is seen in the words of Jesus and the apostles on various occasions. When Jesus offered to make His hearers fountains of living water (John 7:37-38), John hastened to explain that the fulfillment of this offer must await the event of the giving of the Spirit in the promised sense, which in turn must follow the glorification of Jesus (v. 39). Later, Jesus relates the promise of the Father (the gift of the Holy Spirit) to being "clothed with power from on high" (Luke 24:49). Not only would this come as an event; it would also come in the city of Jerusalem, where they then were. They were not to leave the area until the transforming event had occurred. In Acts, other details are added from Jesus' last visit with His disciples. Again He referred to the power *(dynamis)* as being "received" as a direct result of a newly established relationship with the Holy Spirit (Acts 1:8). This time, the Holy Spirit is described as "coming upon" the believer. The promise of the Father, from God's side, is "given" or "poured out." From man's side, He is "received" when He "comes upon" the believer. In the same vein, Jesus "breathed on them, and said to them [prophetically], 'Receive the Holy Spirit'" (John 20:22). In the mind of Jesus and the apostles, these references all find their meaning in the event of Pentecost for which Jesus was preparing the disciples.

When the event of Pentecost had taken place, it was not treated in Scripture as simply historical and dispensational. It was personal for the individuals present and it became the guarantee of Pentecostal grace to all future generations. Individuals, not groups, are "clothed with power." They receive individually the promised gift of the Holy Spirit, who "comes upon" them. Groups may be custodians of records and traditions, but individuals are the powerful witnesses (Luke 24:48). Once the initial event of Pentecostal fullness had occurred in the disciples (Acts 2:4), Peter proclaimed that they were but the first among many. The gift of the Holy Spirit at Pentecost was not to be memorialized as a great once-for-all event. It was to be repeated widely in every generation. All who present themselves as penitent believers qualify for the same "gift of the Holy Spirit." "For the promise is for you and your children, and for all who are far off, as many as the Lord our God shall call to Himself" (Acts 2:38-39). In other words, the "gift of the Holy Spirit" is promised to all believers. The meaning of Pentecost can be repeated in human experience infinitely.

This event in personal experience is seen throughout Acts and the epistles. When revival broke out in Samaria, apostles were sent from Jerusalem to assure the converts of their privilege and to pray "for them, that they might receive the Holy Spirit" (Acts 8:14-15). Their mission was successful for the true believers (v. 17) but not for Simon, whose heart was "not right before God" (v. 21). Some might think that Gentiles, especially Roman army officers, would not be included in the promise. But God overcame Peter's prejudice, sent him to the house of Cornelius in answer to Cornelius's prayer, and then made good the promise. Peter had to admit that these believing Gentiles had "received the Holy Spirit just as we did" (Acts 10:47). What could man say when "the gift of the Holy Spirit had been poured out upon the Gentiles also" (v. 45)? Still later, at Ephesus, Paul met a group of disciples who were not fully instructed. His first question was, "Have ye received the Holy Spirit since ye believed?" (Acts 19:2 KJV). Paul knew how vital it had been for him to be "filled with the Holy Spirit" soon after he became a believer (Acts 9:3-9, 17) and he was eager to share the same with all converts as early as possible. The more literal translation, placing the receiving of the Holy Spirit subsequent to their becoming believers, is preferable grammatically, as will be seen, and is more in keeping with the thematic development in the Book of Acts of the significance of the gift of the Holy Spirit. It is also more in accord with Paul's later reminder to the Ephesians that it was after they had heard the gospel and become believers that they were sealed with the Holy Spirit of promise (Eph. 1:13).

In any case, the concept of the "gift of the Holy Spirit," whatever the accompanying emphasis, involves an event as well as the processes that lead up to it and follow it. This event is sufficiently specific and recognizable to be called a crisis involving an instantaneous aspect.

B. An Experience Subsequent to the New Birth

It is worthy of note that the promises of God, whether referring specifically to the Holy Spirit or more generally to the benefits of sanctification, are addressed to those who are already believers. This, of itself, indicates that the experience under consideration is subsequent to the new birth. Again, how else could these words of John concerning the Holy Spirit be taken: "Whom the world cannot receive, because it does not behold Him or know Him, but you know Him, because He abides with you and will be in you" (John 14:17)? Wesley, in his discussion of Christian perfection, puts it simply:

(1.) There is such a thing as perfection; for it is again and again mentioned in Scripture. (2.) It is not so early as justification; for justified persons are to "go on unto perfection" (Heb. 6:1).[59]

This concept does, indeed, require a distinction between being born of the Spirit (John 3:5) and receiving the "gift" of the Spirit, as discussed in this chapter. However, any problem in the distinction is more apparent than real. It is impossible, on the basis of Scripture, to limit the work of the Holy Spirit to any one particular aspect. In creation, "the Spirit of God was moving over the surface of the waters" (Gen. 1:2). In the Old Testament, the "Spirit of the Lord came mightily upon men for otherwise impossible exploits" (e.g., Judg. 15:14). Again, concerning Bezalel it was said that the Lord "filled him with the Spirit of God, in wisdom, in understanding and in knowledge in all craftsmanship" for the work on the tabernacle (Exod. 35:31). In rebuilding the temple, Zerubbabel was reminded by God that it was "not by might nor by power, but by [God's] Spirit" (Zech. 4:6). Again, the backslidden King David prayed, "Create in me a clean heart, O God, and renew a steadfast spirit within me. Do not cast me away from Thy presence, and do not take Thy Holy Spirit from me" (Ps. 51:10-11). Such moral and spiritual transformations were, indeed, known in the Old Testament as well as in the New. God changed Saul's heart when he left Samuel (1 Sam. 10:9). The King James Version says more literally, "God gave him another heart." Jacob wrestled "until daybreak" and God gave him a new name and a new nature (Gen. 32:24-28). Abraham became a friend of God (James 2:23). Numbers of others in Old Testament times were described in terms that could be true only by the grace of God. In the light of all this, it is not surprising that Jesus chided Nicodemus, an Old Testament scholar, for not being acquainted with the new birth (John 3:10). These ancient transformations lay at the very foundation of Old Testament theology as well as of the New. Some, at least, of these changes were nothing less than being born of the Spirit. Yet we are plainly told that the Spirit was not yet given (in the Pentecostal fullness) because Jesus was not yet glorified (John 7:37-39).

In common with the Old Testament saints, then, the followers of Jesus before Pentecost could be born of the Spirit, helped by the Spirit, and enabled by the Spirit as by One who was with them (John 14:17) but was not yet the fountain of living water gushing from the inner being of a believer who had "received" the "gift of the Holy Spirit" (John 7:38).

C. An Experience Prior to Death

There is a broad and almost universal consensus in theology that some aspects of the sanctifying work of the Holy Spirit are not accomplished in the new birth. The obvious question, then, is whether sanctification is ever entire in this life or whether it is accomplished at or after death. Wesley says of this kind of perfection, "It is not so late as death; for St. Paul speaks of living men that were perfect (Phil. 3:15)."[60] Having said this, he immediately added the usual qualifying statements to avoid misunderstanding. He said, in part,

> It is not absolute.
> It does not make man infallible.
> It is "salvation from sin."
> It is "perfect love."
> It is improvable.
> It is amissible, or capable of being lost.
> It is constantly both preceded and followed by a gradual work.[61]

This view of entire sanctification in this life was, of course, in conflict with Reformed theology to the extent that the latter tended to identify sin with human frailties from which one is not delivered until death. For Calvin and many in the Reformed tradition, as Wood says, holiness, purity, and innocence were a matter of imputation.

> Purity of heart is imputed to the believer in Christ, though in practice he strives to actualize it. The Wesleyan tradition, on the other hand, stresses that the righteousness of Christ can be truly actualized in the life of the justified believer through the sanctifying Spirit.[62]

Wesley was able to come to this conclusion because of his narrower and, he believed, more scriptural view of sin. He believed that the guilt and penalty of sin were attached to disobedience and rebellion. Sin as such involves choice. It is, in some sense, a voluntary transgression of a known law.[63] Human frailty as a result of the Fall might, indeed, lead inevitably to involuntary transgressions that require the Mediator if one is to stand before God,[64] but the promises of God are sure here and now. Calvinists, then, with their definition of sin, seldom claim an entire sanctification except by imputation, while Wesleyans, with their understanding of sin, look for an actualization of Christian perfection in this life.

Roman Catholic theology also has given much attention to sanctification in this life. Confirmation in this and other liturgical communions may be traced back to an early Christian practice of the laying on of hands, "associated especially with the impartation of the Spirit."[65] Brown[66] and Lawson[67] make much of its symbolism in relation to this "gift of the Spirit" as related to a second work of grace subsequent to the new birth and baptism. Both appeal strongly to early church history for evidence. Lawson refers to Calvin's and Owen's acknowledgments of the fact in their comments on Hebrews 6:2 as well as to support by Chrysostom and other early commentators.[68]

Wood studies the parallels between the Wesleyan doctrine of Christian perfection and the Roman Catholic and Anglican rite of confirmation.[69] O'Shea is quoted as calling the rite "the sacrament in which the baptized believer receives a Spirit-filled character."[70] Again he is quoted as saying, "The Spirit we receive in confirmation is the Spirit of Pentecost. That confirmation is the individual Christian's Pentecost is shown by the prayer at the end of the rite of confirmation."[71] Wood comments that

> what is significant is that Roman Catholic theology appeals to the same biblical pas-

sages as does Wesleyan theology to support its doctrine of holiness, as well as to support its distinction between baptized believers and perfect Christians who have been filled with the Holy Spirit in the rite of confirmation.[72]

It appears, then, that the Roman Catholics and at least some Anglicans have attempted to meet the need for a doctrine of holiness, in part at least, through their sacramental system.

But has the meaning of the forms and rites come through to the full assurance of faith that has characterized some Wesleyans? That the grace of God is sufficient, none should deny. But the presence and prominence of the doctrine of purgatory in Catholic theology seems to indicate official doubt of the fullness of grace in this life. Whether or not any individuals can, under grace in this life, satisfy the demands of divine holiness, it has apparently been a growing conviction with the Catholics from early times that something more than the blood of Christ and the gift of the Holy Spirit is needed for full sanctification. Though the doctrine was slow taking "official" form and has had less than usual data in the Scripture on which to build, *A Catholic Dictionary* defines purgatory as "the place and state in which souls suffer for a while and are purged after death, before they go to Heaven, on account of their sins."[73] Charles W. Carter quotes Guardini at length on a present Roman Catholic interpretation of the doctrine:

> According to Guardini, the good and evil and the right and wrong in man are so "intertwined at every point down to the deepest roots that they cannot be clearly separated in this life." He proceeds to say that while God's judgment after death is final in its fundamental decision, the opportunity to be cleansed from the residue of sin is available to "the chaotic and fragmentary human existence." Time, as it were, will be extended into eternity long enough for justice to be satisfied. The man whose good intention God accepts, but whose life as a whole is not free from evil, will, by purging, be brought to a state that fits him for eternal life.[74]

Thus Guardini "sees justification completed in purgatorial sanctification" and supports his case by considerable psychological and ethical analysis.

Protestants fail to find biblical evidence for the concept of purgatory and so are limited in their theology to what grace can accomplish in this life or at death. Since the Bible presents death as an enemy and an imposter, it is hard for some to understand how an individual's death can do more for his sanctification than the blood of Christ and the gift of the Holy Spirit can do for him in this life. From a practical standpoint, earnest Catholics and Anglicans place a great deal of emphasis on being good "communicants," keeping in touch with the Word of God and the sacraments—through the church. Likewise, earnest Protestants of the Reformed tradition, though they do not expect sanctification to be complete in this life, nevertheless strive to actualize in their lives the holiness that they believe is imputed to them. Holiness, to a degree at least, is, then, for this life and not only after death. But the Reformed tradition does generally treat sanctification almost exclusively as a process.

Wesleyans, on the other hand, feel that they are taking the Scriptures quite seriously when they believe that entire sanctification is a crisis preceded and followed by a process in this life, all preparatory for eternity.

This is why Wesleyans are not surprised to read that the hearts of the disciples were purified by faith in the Pentecostal event (Acts 15:9) or that "they were all filled with the Holy Spirit" (Acts 2:4). That is why they have no difficulty with the statement that the Samaritans "were receiving the Holy Spirit" when the apostles laid "hands on them" (Acts 8:17) or with the fact that the "Holy Spirit fell upon" the uncircumcised believers in the house of Cornelius (Acts 10:44-45) or with the "Ephesian Pentecost" (Acts 19:1-6). It seems both scriptural and normal to Christian experience that God would so fulfill His promise of the purity and power that

He requires (Acts 1:8; 2:38-39)—and that prior to death.

D. Implications of Greek Tenses

Some are so convinced that there is no finished work of sanctification in this life that they see only a present process in the words *hagiazō* and *hagiasmos* (the verb for "sanctify" and the noun for "sanctification"). They assume that Greek grammar (etymology, tenses, and context) requires such an understanding. Though present space does not permit full exposition of the data, there is good reason to believe that the use of Greek tenses in the New Testament not only permits but seems to require the concept of a definite act or event of sanctification in this life, with effects continuing on in the process that Wesleyans generally call growth in grace.

Biblical words have indeed sometimes been handled with more heat of prejudiced interpretation than with the light of true exegesis and understanding. But it would not be wise simply to do homage to one's own prejudices or those of scholars (of whatever stripe). Rather, granting the possibility that the word *sanctify* could conceivably be used either of an act, a process, or the continuing results of an act, let us give our attention to the documents of Scripture and the general consensus of Greek scholars on the significance of tense in Greek. The approach will involve the assumption that the Greek Scriptures, as the English, were written as "plain truth for plain people," that the scholarly consensus on tenses has some relevance in understanding the plain and ordinary language of the people who first read the documents, and that the writers were assisted by the Holy Spirit in their communication so as to avoid misleading constructions that would nullify their message.

Any reasonable doubt of the ability of the Scripture writers to say what they mean has long since been erased. In a scholarly chapter, "Tense Readings of the Greek New Testament," Daniel Steele has pointed out that commentators who affirm "that the New Testament writers paid little regard to the rules of grammar" have a slovenly style of treating the tenses, and he has quoted Winer's answer, which still stands, that "strictly and properly, none of the tenses (aorist, imperfect, perfect, and pluperfect) ever stands for another, as commentators pretend."[75] The different interpretations of the verbs of the New Testament stem less from sound grammar and lexicography than from the theological biases of the interpreters. Unfortunately, no interpreter is entirely free from this risk. The present effort, then, is not to quote authorities but to examine data. What do the tenses indicate in relation to a crisis event of sanctification in this life?

The most commonly cited evidence for an event of sanctification is the frequent use of the aorist tense in the word *hagiazō*. The argument is that Greek tenses indicate not only "time" of action but also "kind" of action. In some contexts, especially in moods other than indicative, "time" is hardly considered at all; only "kind of action" is implied. It is generally agreed that the kinds of action are three, commonly called punctiliar (point of action), linear (progressive), and perfect (the combination of the two).[76] When process or continued action is expressed or implied, the present tense is generally used. In the indicative, it is also possible to express past continuous or intermittent action in the imperfect. The aorist is most like the simple past tense in English. Etymologically the word *aorist* means "not specified" as to kind of action. It is used whenever one makes simple reference to an act as occurring without specifying continuity or abiding results. Its most common use then is called "Punctiliar" from the German phrase *das Punkt* ("the point"). When the aorist is used and the verbal idea and context permit, it is normal to think in terms of an act, event, or point of action. In introducing the wide scope of uses of the aorist tense, A. T. Robertson repeats the emphasis several times "that there is at bottom only one kind of aorist (punctiliar in fact or statement).''⁷⁷ The perfect tenses (including pluperfect and future perfect) ''look at both ends of the action.''⁷⁸ They imply a process or an act ''but view it as having reached its consummation and existing in a finished state. The point of completion is always antecedent to the time implied or stated in connection with the use of the perfect.''⁷⁹

There are indeed many present tenses in the Greek New Testament concerning faith, grace, and Christian living, as one would expect. They ought not to be neglected. The disagreement is not about process in Christian experience; it is about event or crisis. The emphasis, then, in Wesleyan theology is on the fact that the key verbs concerning sanctification, holiness, and perfection are so often in the aorist tense—supposedly indicating specific action. At least as strong an argument can be made from the common use of the perfect tense with *hagiazō* (''to sanctify''), indicating a finished work of which the results abide in this present life.

One of the broadest applications of the ''tense readings'' is by Daniel Steele,⁸⁰ though others have developed the same idea in their own way.⁸¹ Steele studied a number of instances of the use of the present tense and concluded, first, that ''all exhortations to prayer and to spiritual endeavor in the resistance of temptation are usually expressed in the present tense, which strongly indicates persistence.''⁸² Examples are cited in the great prayer verses of Matthew 7:7; Mark 11:24; Luke 11:10, 13; 13:24; John 16:24; James 1:5-6. The next fact he observes

> is the absence of the aorist and the presence of the present tense whenever the conditions of final salvation are stated. Our inference is that conditions of ultimate salvation are continuous, extending through probation, and not completed in any one act. The great requirement is faith in Jesus Christ.⁸³

He shows the need of continuing faith by the uses of the present tense in John 1:13; 3:15; 5:24, 47; 6:35, 54; 11:25, 26; Rev. 22:14.

The main observation, to which he gives the greater part of his study, concerns the aorist tense. He concludes:

> But when we come to consider the work of purification in the believer's soul, by the power of the Holy Spirit, both in the new birth and in entire sanctification, we find that the aorist is almost uniformly used. This tense, according to the best New Testament grammarians, never indicates a continuous, habitual, or repeated act, but one which is momentary, and done once for all.⁸⁴

To get the full impact of the argument it is necessary to scan the Greek New Testament with special attention to the tenses in such contexts, or at least to read Daniel Steele's summary of passages and observations.⁸⁵ But a hasty look at samples does not miss the point. The leper's faith was for a definite cleansing, Jesus' touch was a point of action, and so was the cleansing (three aorists, Matt. 8:2-3). The crowd kept beseeching (imperfect) that they might touch (aorist), and as many as touched (aorist) were healed (aorist) (Matt. 14:36). The scribes and Pharisees kept polishing the outside of the cup (present), but Jesus demanded that the inside be first cleansed (aorist) (Matt. 23:25-26). While they were going (present), they were instantly healed (aorist) (Luke 17:14). Peter, though born again, had to be washed (aorist, John 13:8). Jesus' prayer for His disciples was that they be sanctified by a definite act (aorist, John 17:17-19), though Jesus Himself needed no such crisis. He constantly sanctified (dedicated) Himself (present tense) without any sin from which to be cleansed. Instantly purifying (aorist) their hearts was the result of Pentecost (Acts 15:9). Crucifixion of the old man, dying to sin, and the destruction of the body of sin are all aorist (Rom. 6:6). Even the verb in the clause ''present your bodies'' (Rom. 12:1) is aorist.

Piecemeal consecration will not lead to definite sanctification. ''Put on the Lord Jesus Christ'' is specific and definite (aorist) in Romans 13:14. Christ is the one who anointed us, sealed us, and gave the earnest of the Spirit in our hearts (all aorists, 2 Cor. 1:21-22). To be enlarged, when it is by the sudden baptism of the Holy Spirit, is crisis (aorist), not process (2 Cor. 6:13). To cleanse from all filthiness of flesh and spirit is beyond the power of daily scrubbing; the verb is in the aorist (2 Cor. 7:1). They that are Christ's have crucified (aorist) the flesh (Gal. 5:24). After the Ephesians believed (became believers, aorist), they were sealed (aorist) with the promised Holy Spirit (Eph. 1:13). To put off (aorist) the old man and to put on (aorist) the new man is God's way (Eph. 4:22, 24). Even to be filled with the full knowledge of His will is more than process; it is also aorist (Col. 1:9). "Mortify [aorist—kill at once] your members which are upon the earth" (Col. 3:5 KJV). Even the act of God in establishing the heart is definite (aorist, 1 Thess. 3:13), as is the giving of the Holy Spirit (4:8). Sanctification is specific and definite (5:23). Christ gave Himself to redeem and purify us (all three verbs in the aorist, Titus 2:14). The same Greek usage carries through Hebrews and the General Epistles as if there were no other way of reporting correctly how redemption is applied to our lives. Whenever believers are to seek a deeper experience of relationship with God, the human response to the divine call and the act of God are decisive. Without denying the importance of process before and after the event, the emphasis is on the crisic event of human choice and of abundant grace that marks a radical change in the human life and relationship.

Steele makes occasional reference to the perfect tense, with its idea of permanence—the abiding result of a completed action. Much more could have been said. At least one degree thesis has been written on the title "Perfection Tenses in the Greek New Testament."[86] It is worthy of note that most uses of the verb *hagiazō* ("to sanctify") that are not in the aorist tense are in the perfect, generally in a periphrastic construction containing that participle. The emphasis, then, is clearly on either the punctiliar act (in the aorist) or on the finished work with abiding results (in the perfect). Ignoring the ceremonial and other nonsoteriological uses of the verb in the New Testament, one finds sixteen references using the word *hagiazō* in which sanctification might be considered an act of God on human beings in need of grace. Six of these are in the aorist tense (John 17:17; 1 Cor. 6:11; Eph. 5:26; 1 Thess. 5:23; Heb. 10:29; Rev. 22:11). Seven are in the perfect tense (John 17:19; Acts 20:32; 26:18; Rom. 15:16; 1 Cor. 1:2; 2 Tim. 2:21; Heb. 10:10). Only three are in the present tense (Heb. 2:11, twice; 10:14), describing the redemptive work of Christ and the seriatim application of the benefits to the individuals. Even allowing that two of the references may apply to initial sanctification, the case is good for the concept that New Testament Greek tenses support rather than nullify the concept of human beings enjoying the benefits of a finished work of sanctification in their hearts and lives. This is what Wesleyans call a "state of grace," to refer to a life that is abundant, growing, and unfolding in this grace. No idea of a static plateau is intended.

This perfect-participle phenomenon would be much more frequent in the New Testament were it not for the common use of the adjective *hagios* (holy, saintly) which describes persons who, to some extent, participate in the ongoing benefits of an act of sanctification in their hearts. The various nouns for sanctification, perfection, and cleansing also carry the same message. To observe how these words are used by Jesus and the apostles is an edifying study.

A relevant fact may be observed about the noun *hagiasmos* (sanctification). The *-mos* ending signifies "the thing done or made or in action." In this case the "thing" is holiness. As has been observed, this sanctification may reasonably be a specific act as well as a process. But most lexicons and commentaries define it only as "the process of sanctification." In most Scripture contexts, it would be more accurate to say "the act" of sanctification or the "state" of holiness produced by that act, in keeping with the basic meaning of the verb and the tenses in which it is used.

E. Implications of Vocabulary

There is a figurative or symbolic thrust of words that becomes prominent when one reflects on the expression of any psychological or spiritual reality. For example, the English word *cleanse,* or *make clean,* in its most elementary sense suggests material objects—dirt or other foreign substance, soap, detergent, hot water, Lysol, refining fire, and the like. But in cleansing the heart, the primary reference is not to literal dirty substance and literal Lysol or scouring powder. Rather, the tangible material objects become figures, analogies, or symbols by which the less readily understood realities can be revealed. Or, to use a different figure, hell fire does not have to be the combustion of fossil fuels, but it signifies the torment and destruction of the soul as literal earthly fire assails the body. Words with material connotations are not a barrier to understanding. They are a help to one who wants to know "heavenly things."

For that matter, a case could be made for the claim that all speech is symbolic. Words are symbols by which thought is conveyed from one mind to another. Even so, there is a great deal involved in the choice of words. A look at the words used by God and His spokesmen reveals much about the particular kind of human need that exists and the particular way that God meets that need.

It would be beyond the scope of this chapter to make a detailed study of all the words that show the relative emphasis on crisis or process. But a little reflection on the key words that have been discussed should establish beyond reasonable doubt that there is a crisis or event aspect in each term and that this fact appears to have decisive influence on the choice of the word to convey the intended message. This in no sense denies the process leading up to the event nor the results that flow from it. But note the following words and see how meaningless and inappropriate they would be in the passages already studied if they had no specific reference to an event as well as to the process: baptize, promise, give, gift, receive, seal, anoint, purify, cleanse, destroy, sanctify, perfect, pour out, put off, put on, die, put to death, circumcise, purge, and fill. If God had intended to present only a process or a growth, why did He not confine His revelation to the terms that would express His thought with less confusion? Rather, the vocabulary seems to be chosen on the assumption that the saving processes are launched and culminated by decisive acts of God involving man. Entire sanctification is no exception to the general rule.

F. Implications of Context and Syntax

It is widely recognized that exegesis of any passage of Scripture involves more than identifying the Greek mood or tense in which a verb is used. Dana and Mantey correctly insist that one must investigate three matters in forming a conclusion about the particular use of a tense: "the basal function of the tense, the relation to the context, and the significance of the verbal idea."[87] No interpretation of Scripture is valid if it violates or disregards these inherently essential implications of language. Differences of opinion in applying the principles can seriously affect both the translations in the various versions and the exegesis in the commentaries. It goes without saying, then, that a mistake in the translation and exegesis level can seriously affect theology in both pulpit and pew, casting deep shadows on the life and experience of the church.

The implications of context and syntax in these respects will be illustrated briefly from two or three familiar passages. The intent is not to polish "proof texts" to "prove" a certain viewpoint. Rather, it is to show the care and consistency exercised in the production of the Scriptures. The divine author so worked on and within the human author as to avoid contradictions and confused signals—even in the grammatical constructions.

It has been noted that the aorist tense predominates in 1 Thessalonians 5:23, being used of both the act of entire sanctification and the work of God in preserving one complete and without blame. If the intended emphasis had been only on process, one would have expected *hagiazō* ("to sanctify") to be in the present tense to indicate continuous action. The problem for a beginner is that "preserve" is also an aorist, normally indicating point of action. But "point" is a relative term. Theoretically, a point has no dimension. Therefore, it cannot be literally presented on a graph as can a dimensional line (for continuity). Relatively speaking, however, a point can be presented with enough dimension to be visible, regardless of the degree of thickness of the pencil lead or the marker. In fact, one can draw a circle instead of making a dot. The question in the aorist is not how long the act or event took; it is the matter of how it is viewed. Paul is not praying about continuity—continuous or intermittent. He is looking at God's keeping act as a single unit. He wants God to put the believer under the diligent care of the Holy Spirit, who will handle the whole matter without interruption. The reference to time is not in the tense of the verb. It is in the context. The act of sanctification is immediate and decisive. The keeping takes a little longer—to "the coming of our Lord Jesus Christ." The "basal function" of the tense, then, is preserved in looking at both acts of God as punctiliar.

What about the significance of the verbal idea? If God can sanctify at all, preparatory to the preservation, He can do it as an event, as has been noted. There is, then, no contradiction between the basal function of the verb and the significance of the verbal idea in relation to "sanctify." On the other hand, in "keep" or "preserve" there is a verbal idea expressed that implies some lapse of time, or continuity. In other words, "keep" is a verb of continuity or process. But, again, there is no contradiction—only enrichment. The aorist idea of punctiliar action says nothing in itself of how long the action takes. It only views it together as an event occurring, regardless of how long it takes or whatever its result. Paul is viewing the action from God's side. The provision is for an uninterrupted "keeping" to the day of Jesus Christ.

The third element, context, will be treated more fully in the next section. Briefly, Paul is writing to believers who are rejoicing in the Lord and are an example to believers elsewhere (1 Thess. 1:6-7). There is a lack in their faith that concerns the apostle (3:10-13). The expectations of holy living are high (chaps. 4-5). Sanctification has something definite to do with the possibility of success (4:2-4). In this context, Paul prays for a specific definite event of entire sanctification soon enough to provide a solid base for being kept strong and secure to the end of this age (1 Thess. 5:23). This is not for "in the sky by and by." Paul hastens to assure them that the Faithful One will answer prayer and do exactly that. In view of the agreement of basal function of the tense, the relation to context, and the significance of the verbal idea, Wesleyans feel safe in saying with Wesley, that there is an act of God possible in this life by which believers can be entirely sanctified and prepared for a higher plane of Christian living than would be otherwise possible.

The same exegetical considerations can be applied to the Ephesus incident in Acts 19. The point that is frequently debated is in verse 2. Many have been dissatisfied with the King James translation, "Have ye received the Holy Ghost since ye believed?" There is no problem with modernizing the language to "Holy Spirit" from the older English reading of "Holy Ghost." But serious objection has been raised to the implication that the Holy Spirit was to be received subsequent to one's becoming a believer. Does not one receive the Holy Spirit *when* he becomes a believer? Is not that being "born of the

Spirit"? How, then, can one receive the Holy Spirit when he already has Him? This becomes a point where two systems clash. If the disciples (v. 1, obviously born of the Spirit) did not receive the Holy Spirit during Paul's visit (v. 6), the Wesleyan understanding of "gift," "receive," "promise," "outpouring," etc., is threatened. But if the Ephesians were first converted and then, later, received the Holy Spirit, the Reformed terminology and theology concerning sanctification is threatened. The crux of the issue is between the "since" you believed (KJV, NIV margin) and "when" you believed (NASB, NIV). Is there an answer?

Of course there are other ways of handling the problem. "Believed" need not necessarily refer to the conversion experience, when saving faith is exercised. There can be subsequent events in which one can exercise faith. As one is justified by faith, so he can be sanctified by faith (Acts 26:18). Such faith can be exercised in various times and circumstances. But Acts 19:2 is still important and should be reviewed.

If there is any validity to the Wesleyan understanding of the "promise," "gift," "outpouring," "fullness," "receive," etc. (as already reviewed), one must be open to the possibility that Paul was asking if they had received the Holy Spirit subsequent to becoming believers, as the KJV indicates. If, however, one is certain that all the above terms refer to a "new birth" that occurred only at Pentecost and at subsequent conversions, the concept of a "second work of grace" as the fulfillment of God's promise is either impossible or unrelated to Pentecost.

What does the verse say? The tense of "believe" is aorist. It is the aorist participle, normally understood as "having believed," from the Greek standpoint. English is not adapted to such free use of participles as Greek is. Normally, good English favors a temporal clause as the KJV "since ye believed." Antecedent action is "the usual idiom with the circumstantial participle. This is indeed the most common use of the aorist participle."[88] It is true that the time itself is not expressed so much in the participle as in the relationship with the main verb. But Robertson, as a good grammarian, is asserting that an aorist participle normally refers to action prior to the action of the main verb. That is, if the principle is so applied here, they became believers prior to receiving the Holy Spirit. If one stops with the normal and literal use of tense, it appears that the Wesleyans have the only right interpretation of the verse.

But Robertson hastens to say that simultaneous action is also common, even though the present participle would serve the situation better in many instances.[89] There are indeed instances of the use of the aorist participle where the focus of the thought is so much on the kind of action (point of action) that time, even relative time, hardly needs to be expressed. Where the context makes obvious any temporal aspect, the Greeks sometimes fall back on the real genius of the aorist tense—simply reference to occurring. For example, there is no obscurity in a statement like "Jesus answered and said" (John 12:30, literal translation). Nothing is gained by debating the time order of His answering and of His saying. The intent of the author is clear. Pointed reference is made to the definite action by both the aorist participle and the finite verb. But what license can be claimed to classify Acts 19:2 among these exceptions? Robertson himself admits that antecedent action is the usual idiom and that "in many examples only exegesis can determine whether antecedent or coincident action is intended," but he does list Acts 19:2 as an example of this exceptional use as coincident action.[90]

The next question is to discover why Robertson and others went out of their way to interpret the aorist participle as simultaneous action. As his pupil taught the present writer, one selects an unusual or figurative interpretation only when the literal or usual is impossible. The nature of that impossibility generally gives a clue to the direction one should look for the correct interpretation.[91] The reason for Robertson's conclusion must be found in his exegesis. It is known from his associations and his writings that he held the "Reformed view" that one "received the Holy Spirit" in the biblical sense only at conversion. Therefore he considered the usual and literal sense of the aorist participle to be impossible because it did not fit his understanding of the Bible and of the theology of Christian experience. In that case, he and the translators of NASB and NIV had no other choice but to accept the less common usage that fits his concept of the verbal idea and of the context.

Is there an acceptable alternative? From the Wesleyan understanding (on the American scene, at least), the case is quite different. For reasons already discussed, Wesleyans understand that the promise of the Holy Spirit has been given to those who are already born of the Spirit and to no others. Therefore what Robertson considered impossible, Wesleyans consider necessary—namely, one must first become a believer before he can "receive" the Holy Spirit (John 14:17; Acts 2:38). With the Wesleyan understanding, Paul's question makes sense, as does the Ephesian answer. Paul had a legitimate concern: had these believers been "clothed with power" for the Christian walk and work by receiving the Holy Spirit? They replied that they were not aware of such a privilege. Paul then led them into the experience. The basal function of the tense, the context, and the verbal idea of "receive" all unite in making a clear and intelligible statement as in the KJV, with none of the problems that worried A. T. Robertson and others. The context seems overwhelmingly evangelistic rather than simply theoretical. Paul wanted to measure their spiritual awareness and experience, not their ability to answer a more academic question of the theology of what happened in their conversion.

With a slightly different terminology, Paul seems to be rehearsing the Acts 19 event in Ephesians 1:13 with the same array of aorist participles. He reminds them that after they had heard the word of truth and had believed (become believers), they were sealed with the Holy Spirit of the promise. Now (v. 14) they who have received and been sealed find that the present fulfillment is a new sample and promise of the still greater fulfillment in their heavenly inheritance.

Wesleyan exegetes, then, find no evidence against their conviction that Christian perfection, according to the Scriptures, is the result of a definite crisis of entire sanctification, through the Holy Spirit, that is given to the individual believer. While they rely on no isolated "proof text," neither do they believe that any text from the Scripture, rightly used, negates the gospel of full salvation in this life through a divine act of entire sanctification. They feel that the concepts of Christian perfection and entire sanctification go together and they find the key to their significance in this life in the indwelling presence and power of the Holy Spirit, who achieves in us what Christ provided for us.

V. THE URGENCY OF THE EXPERIENCE

Once the concept of receiving the Holy Spirit in the sense of His indwelling fullness is grasped and accepted, we face the question of the urgency of the experience. With Wesley, this was no problem. It was holiness that he had been seeking for years before his assurance of justification. The question uppermost in his mind was how to receive this "blessing" of perfect love. Having learned, he was impelled by love to tell others. Even so, he selected his audience. When asked, "In what manner should we preach sanctification?" he replied, "Scarce at all to those who are not pressing forward: To those who are, always by way of promise; always drawing, rather than driving."[92] To Wesley it was inconceivable that one could be a healthy, growing Christian without longing for and seeking the fullness of the blessing of the gospel of Christ. Accordingly, his mission was to preach the "law and the gospel," to make plain the way of holiness, and to guide those who were earnest and growing into the bright sunlight of perfect love. To this end he compiled the *Plain Account of Christian Perfection*.[93]

Both the possibility and the urgency of the matter are made clear in Wesley's brief summary of his and his brother's settled conviction:

> (1.) That Christian perfection is that love of God and our neighbour, which implies deliverance from all sin. (2.) That this is received merely by faith. (3.) That it is given instantaneously, in one moment. (4.) That we are to expect it, not at death, but every moment; that now is the accepted time, now is the day of this salvation.[94]

The inevitable practical question was raised as to how we are to wait for this change. Wesley's answer reveals why he confined his efforts mainly to the live and growing believers:

> Not in careless indifference, or indolent inactivity; but in vigorous, universal obedience, in a zealous keeping of all the commandments, in watchfulness and painfulness, in denying ourselves, and taking up our cross daily; as well as in earnest prayer and fasting, and a close attendance on all the ordinances of God. And if any man dream of attaining it any other way, (yea, or of keeping it when attained, when he has received it even in the largest measure,) he deceiveth his own soul. It is true, we receive it by simple faith: But God does not, will not, give that faith, unless we seek it with all diligence, in the way which he hath ordained.[95]

These considerations may have something to do with the fact that the doctrine and the experience are not more popular. Most Wesleyans today would be less explicit about certain almost ascetic implications of Wesley's understanding of holiness and its quest. But Scripture compels one to agree that it is those who "walk in the light as He Himself is in the light" that know the true spiritual fellowship and receive the assurance that the "blood of Jesus His Son cleanses from all sin" (1 John 1:7).

In many years of witnessing and leading people into perfect love, Wesley learned another aspect of urgency in "going on unto perfection." It did not pay to wait for more maturity before seeking holiness. Time lag erodes readiness rather than creating it. In a letter to Thomas Rankin, July 21, 1774, Wesley said:

> I have been lately thinking a good deal on one point, wherein, perhaps we have all been wanting. We have not made it a rule, as soon as ever persons are justified, to remind them of going on unto perfection. Whereas this is the very time preferable to all others. They have then the simplicity of little children; and they are fervent in spirit, ready to cut off a right hand or pluck out the right eye. But if we once suffer this fervor to subside, we shall find it hard enough to bring them again to this point.[96]

In the same vein, a little earlier (August 9, 1772), Wesley wrote to Jane Salkeld, "Exhort all the little ones that believe to make haste and not delay the time of receiving the second blessing; and be not backward to declare what God has done for your soul to any that truly fear Him."[97] It appears that many advocates have spent their energies "proving" the possibility of such an experience prior to death instead of assuring the new converts of the immediate availability of the Pentecostal fullness and the urgency of "not leaving their Jerusalem" without it.

A. A Specific Concern of Jesus

Did Jesus and the apostles feel the same urgency in communicating the gospel of full salvation to their followers? The answer seems to be that they did and that their concern was the very source at which the Wesleyan flame was kindled.

None said more about the life of holiness and the significance of the gift of the Holy Spirit than our Lord Himself. His forerunner, John the Baptist, announced the mission of Christ as "taking away the sin of the world" (John 1:29). In the same context, he also identified Jesus as "the one who baptizes in the Holy Spirit" (v. 33). It seems that John's standard way of introducing his own mission and that of Christ was to say that he was sent to baptize with water, signifying repentance and forgiveness of sins, while Christ's mission could equally well be summarized as the promised gift of another Paraclete, the great coronation gift of the Holy Spirit, whose purging baptismal flame would burn out the dross of sin and whose abiding presence would be Christ's other self, stamping the divine image on the heart and life of the Spirit-filled believer (Luke 3:16). A reading of the Gospel accounts indicates that Jesus was deeply concerned not only that He finish the work of redemption for which He came, but that His redeemed people should receive the Holy Spirit in His fullness, for the Holy Spirit would take the things of Christ and apply them to the lives of the believers (John 16:14).

As has been noted, Jesus picked up the Old Testament prophecies and those of John the Baptist and held before the people the "promise of the Father." Even for the privileged disciples who had constant access to Jesus, it would be to their advantage to lose the physical presence of their Lord and to gain the Helper that He would send to them (John 16:7). The Helper on the inside ("Jesus' other self") could do more for their fulfillment and effectiveness than even the visible presence of the Lord Himself with them. The indwelling Spirit would, indeed, be "Christ in you, the hope of glory" (Col. 1:27). Jesus had such an appreciation for the advantages of the finished work of redemption and the application of the things of Christ through the Spirit that He kept the "promise of the Father" before His followers.

Jesus did say, "Come to me . . . and I will give you rest" (Matt. 11:28). But the fuller meaning of rest for the troubled soul was better understood after Pentecost in Hebrews (chaps. 3 and 4). At the high point of a feast day, Jesus cried out, "If any man is thirsty, let him come to Me and drink" (John 7:37). But John reminds us that the primary meaning of the invitation was prophetic. It would be the internal work of Christ through the Spirit that from our "innermost being shall flow rivers of living water" (v. 38). Jesus gave the invitation with reference to the Holy Spirit whom those who were already believing on Him would receive in the future, because there would be a new dimension of spiritual fulfillment possible after Jesus completed redemption, returned to glory, and gave the Holy Spirit at Pentecost (v. 39).

As the time of the crucifixion drew near, Jesus stepped up the emphasis on the promised gift of the Holy Spirit. Much of the Upper Room Discourse was devoted to the significance of His coming as the Sent One, who proceeds from the Father and the Son (John 14—16). On the same evening, the great high-priestly prayer of Jesus acknowledged that He had already given them life and kept them from the world (John 17:2, 12). The urgent need that remained for them was for sanctification and the integration of personality and conduct that goes with it (vv. 17, 21). The manner in which Jesus handled the discourse and prayer seems to indicate no basic change of theme—only a shift from the cause to the effect of the "coming" of the Holy Spirit in the promised sense.

If there should be any doubt about Jesus' sense of the urgency of their receiving the promised gift of the Spirit, one need only look to an appearance of Jesus after His resurrection. He breathed on them and shared His urgent concern, "Receive the Holy Spirit" (20:22). "Receive" is in the aorist tense, for "point of action." The command obviously pointed to the event at Pentecost and not solely to the continual daily appropriation of grace.

Luke adds specific details. Jesus said, "And behold, I am sending forth [present tense, as if already in process or predicted with complete and imminent certainty] the promise of My Father upon you; but you are to stay [aorist imperative, for a specific act of obedience regardless of the time required] in the city until you are clothed [aorist middle, expressing point of action] with power from on high" (Luke 24:49).

Any uncertainty of fact or time was cleared away. The event was so imminent that to leave the city would be to miss the event. And the importance of the event was so urgent that to miss it would be to face the demands of their calling quite unprepared. So ends Luke's first treatise with the disciples in Jerusalem after the Ascension. Luke's second treatise (Acts) dips back before the Ascension. Jesus is still speaking. The burden of His message is the same: Do not expect all prophetic questions to be immediately clear, but the most urgent matter for you now is spiritual (1:7-8). When the promised Holy Spirit "comes upon you," "you shall receive power" that will enable you to be bold and effective witnesses here in Jerusalem and around the world (v. 8). The urgency of receiving the gift of the Holy Spirit was such that the issue was success or failure. Jesus had no other plan but Pentecost for building His church. After a few verses of intervening events, Luke then records the receiving of the Holy Spirit (2:4). The rest of the historical Book of Acts records the effects and implications of the proclamation of the resurrection of Jesus and the gift of the Holy Spirit at Pentecost.

B. Apostolic Ministry in the Book of Acts

The urgent concern of Jesus for the sanctification of His believers seemed to have been grasped by Peter at least, as the will of God for all who would become believers. The event of Pentecost (Acts 2:1-4) attracted wide attention, especially of the religious pilgrims but also of curious spectators. When Peter had explained the event in terms of the promised outpouring of the Holy Spirit, "they were pierced to the heart" and inquired what they should do (v. 37). The response was, in effect: The promise is for you too. You may receive the gift of the Holy Spirit as soon as you qualify. God gives the gift of His Spirit only to those who know Him (cf. John 14:17). But if you repent of your sins, receive forgiveness, and affirm your faith by baptism, you will know God. Then the promise is for you and for all whom God will call to Himself (Acts 2:38-39). No waiting period is suggested. No works are required. No stage of spiritual maturity must be reached. They must only become believers. Sanctification, too, is by faith.

The urgency was already sensed in their "pierced" hearts. If they ever became believers, they wanted to be that kind—victorious and Spirit-filled. Peter was confident that God felt the same urgency. He was more ready to give than they were to receive. We are not told how many of the new converts claimed the promise that day. But there were three thousand who were converted and added to the group, attracted by the prospect of being Spirit-filled and victorious believers. It was not by works or ascetic practices that they were converted or sanctified. By faith they came into the fellowship of the divine and the miraculous (vv. 42-43). As with the Wesleys and many Wesleyans, it was the quest for holiness that led them to an assurance of salvation. God prefers to call and to lead to holiness, not to drive.

The same urgency for Pentecostal fullness is seen in the Samaritan revival. Philip found excellent response when he preached Christ (Acts 8:5-12). The baptized converts included both men and women, as at Pentecost (1:15). Philip was aware of the urgency of their receiving the gift of the Holy Spirit but may have been uncertain as to how to deal with other than Jews. When the apostles in Jerusalem heard of the unexpected revival in Samaria, they sent Peter and John (Acts 8:14). Without delay, even for extended instruction, they simply prayed for the new converts specifically that they might receive the Holy Spirit (v. 15), because none of them had received the Holy Spirit in the Pentecostal sense as yet, having been baptized only in the name of the Lord Jesus (v. 16). Perhaps as an aid to their faith and as an assurance that the promise extended beyond Judaism and Judean Jews, they started laying hands on the heads of individuals, and such individuals started receiving the Holy Spirit, as at the Jerusalem Pentecost. No "prudent delays" seem to have been considered. Now is the accepted time—as soon as possible after conversion.

When Saul, the great persecutor, was converted on the road to Damascus, his attitude toward Jesus changed immediately from blasphemy against, to obedience to, the "Lord" (Acts 9:5-6). Three days later, when Paul was still blind, God sent Ananias to meet his two urgent needs as a new believer and as an apostle-elect. Ananias said, "Brother Saul, the Lord Jesus, who appeared to you on the road by which you were coming, has sent me so that you may regain your sight, and be filled with the Holy Spirit" (v. 17). The physical miracle is recorded (v. 18) and the power of Pentecost is taken for granted. In the city where he had intended to bind the Christians, he "began immediately to proclaim Jesus in the synagogues saying, 'He is the Son of God'" (v. 20). Even his blindness was not a more urgent concern of God for Saul than his being filled with the Holy Spirit. At Pentecost and afterwards, the distinction between being born of the Spirit and being filled with the Holy Spirit seems clear. Pentecost was not the new birth. But the new birth continued to be the prerequisite of the Pentecostal gift of the fullness of the Spirit. The longstanding promise of God had become a vivid reality for all true believers who would claim the promise for their most urgent need.

The real test in the growth of the church was what to do with Gentiles who had learned something of God, with or without becoming proselytes to the Jewish faith. Caesarea had a Roman centurion in charge of a battalion of occupational troops. Though a Gentile, he was a devout person, who feared God, was generous with the Jewish people, and "prayed to God continually" (Acts 10:2). He was called righteous (v. 22). God heard and answered his prayer (v. 31). Yet to a Jew he was an unclean Gentile. It was contrary to Jewish ceremonial law to associate with him or to visit in his home (v. 28). When Peter, with certain conservative Jewish believers from Joppa, addressed Cornelius and his guests, he began to fill in the gospel data as if to convert the Gentiles. Peter may or may not have intended to discuss Pentecost. Perhaps he thought the Gentiles were not ready for it. In any case, he seemed to be trying to lead them to conversion. The fact that God had cleansed Cornelius (in some sense at least, v. 15) made a reluctant missionary of Peter but did not necessarily assure him that the Roman was a believer accepted by God. However, God ran ahead of the missionary with the gift of the Holy Spirit, poured out on the Gentiles (v. 45). Not being able to find any significant difference between this event and the Jerusalem Pentecost, Peter and the others were convinced that these people were proper candidates for the promise they had so evidently received. It came to Peter as a surprise that Gentiles were included in "as many as the Lord our God shall call to Himself" (2:39). What could Peter do but baptize these sanctified believers and "stay on for a few days" (10:48)?

In the defense of Peter's acts, it was made clear that this was a perfectly valid "Pentecost" for these Gentiles. "The Holy Spirit fell upon them" *just as* He did in the beginning at the Jerusalem Pentecost (Acts 11:15). Peter called it being "baptized with the Holy Spirit" (v. 16). It was "the same gift as He gave to us also after believing in the Lord Jesus Christ" (v. 17). God judged Cornelius to be His believing child as were the 120 in the Upper Room. Finally the critics "quieted down and glorified God, saying, 'Well then, God has granted to the Gentiles also the repentance that leads to life'" (v. 18).

Later, at the Jerusalem Conference, Peter declared that God "made no distinction between" the Jews and the Gentiles, "cleansing their hearts by faith" (Acts 15:9). "God, who knows the heart, bore witness to them, giving them the Holy Spirit" the same way He did to the believing Jews (v. 8). By this act, God removed an insurmountable barrier to world missions at the same time that He showed the urgent necessity of the gift of the Holy Spirit for normal and full citizenship in the kingdom of God.

To establish thoroughly the authenticity of the Gentile missions, to illustrate further the normalcy of the promised gift of the Holy Spirit without partiality, and to complete the thematic development of life in the Spirit in the Book of Acts, Luke included an account of the "Ephesian Pentecost." As we observed, Paul sensed the urgent need of all converts to be filled with the Spirit. When he first came to Ephesus, he met "some disciples" (Acts 19:1). They were, presumably, disciples of Christ, as *mathētēs* means elsewhere when not otherwise restricted.[98] Had they been disciples of John, the text would normally have so stated. It is not known how they received their knowledge of Jesus—whether from Apollos or from other sources.[99] Their baptism, however, was in John's tradition. The dozen or so disciples were inadequately instructed but appeared to be walking in the light they had. It was of utmost importance to Paul that they know of and receive the promised gift of the Holy Spirit that was poured out at Pentecost, in Samaria, and in Caesarea. It would be tragic and sub-Christian to try to live the Christian life without the power and indwelling presence of the Holy Spirit.

Paul's immediate question, then, was whether they had received the Holy Spirit since they had become believers (Acts 19:2). Paul made it clear that Jesus would baptize with the Holy Spirit. In the only recorded New Testament case of rebaptism, they were brought up to date in their baptism in the name of the Lord Jesus and had the symbolism of Christian baptism fulfilled when "the Holy Spirit came on them" (vv. 5-6) as He did in Jerusalem, in Samaria, in Caesarea, and (on Paul) in Damascus. The theme of the urgency of receiving the Holy Spirit in a Pentecostal fullness had now run its full cycle: the Holy Spirit came on faithful Jewish believers, on culturally and religiously "mixed" Samaritans, on Gentile immigrants (or, more precisely, occupational forces), on Gentile mission converts, and on the apostle to the Gentiles. Wesleyans do not deny the dispensational implications of Pentecost, but they do put the emphasis where the Book of Acts puts it—on personal purification and fulfillment in the lives of believers.

C. Paul and the Young Churches

Most of Paul's correspondence was addressed to well-established churches or to people with whom he had long been associated. In these cases the reader often misses Paul's understandings and techniques that contributed to the founding of churches and their strengthening.

But there are three notable exceptions to the above in the epistles of Paul besides a letter (Ephesians) that follows through on certain matters from Acts. They are: the Epistle to the Romans and the two Thessalonian epistles. In the first instance, Paul had not yet visited Rome. His only contact with these Christians had been in other parts of the empire, before they had gravitated to the capital city. Worse yet, from Paul's standpoint, they had had no formal instruction from any apostle to supply what was lacking in their faith and practice. Accordingly, Paul goes back to the fundamental principles and gives a comprehensive theology of Christian experience and practice in the Epistle to the Romans. The case of the Thessalonians was slightly different. Paul had begun a fruitful ministry in this metropolis but had been interrupted by the severe persecution of those with whom he was staying (Acts 17:1-10). Though there were remarkable conversions, Paul was not able to remain long enough to orient and instruct the young church as needed. The Thessalonian epistles fill this need. Ephesians is different still. Paul had spent considerable time in southwestern Asia (now Turkey), had led disciples to "receive" the Holy Spirit, and had challenged the people of the Lycus Valley to live with eternal values in view. In Ephesians Paul reminds them of the grace they are already familiar with and shows the strength of the Christian foundations by the superstructure they support.

In each case it is important to note the thematic development of holiness teaching, whether in terms of the announced purpose of the epistle or in elaboration of the implications of being filled with the Holy Spirit. It is clear that Paul's method with young Christians was to expose them as soon as possible to this fuller relationship to God and to hold this privilege and promise before them as the key to their survival and effectiveness. In whatever terms were available, he kept trying to express the love of Christ that passes knowledge and to challenge the believers to explore the length and breadth and height and depth of the divine fullness that belonged to them as heirs of grace and holiness.

In Romans Paul prepares his diverse readers for his message by the statement of purpose and the theme of the epistle. The first seven verses are a theological compend in and of themselves. The message is God's gospel (Rom. 1:1). He promised it long ago through His prophets in the Scriptures. It is about His Son and man's, through David (vv. 2-3). All this was confirmed to us by Christ's resurrection, proving Him to be the Messiah and Lord. This was "according to the Spirit of holiness" (v. 4). The Spirit is not only holy in Himself; He is also the source and agent of all human holiness. With this background, Paul's credentials to speak and our credentials to hear are the "grace" we share and the "apostleship" that makes Paul a special agent in communicating to us (vv. 5-7).

Paul, then, is ready to suggest, with all courtesy, that they have a profound lack that is bound to threaten their stability in the faith. They were ever in his prayers (Rom. 1:9). He wants to spend time with them, as with other churches, to give them a strong and adequate foundation for their development and effectiveness (vv. 10-11). What they need is not just more instruction and counseling. They need a spiritual gift *(pneumatikon charisma)* imparted (or shared). The "spiritual gift" that Paul received to meet his needs was "the gift of the Holy Spirit" or "fullness of the Spirit" (Acts 9:7). This established him and gave him a basis from which to solve his problems of life and ministry. So, the underlying purpose of writing the epistle was to "share" this "spiritual gift," without which it would be difficult indeed to live and to walk in the Spirit.

Out of this theme of the "Spirit of holiness" (Rom. 1:4) and the imparting of a "spiritual gift" (v. 11) comes the outline of the epistle, in which the way of holiness is set forth not only in divine provision but in personal application to the Christian life in and by the Holy Spirit. The offer of this "promise of the Father" makes him ready to preach (proclaim the good news) to them (vv. 14-15). He is perfectly confident that God's gospel is adequate, even at Rome (v. 16). It reveals (for our appropriation by faith) God's kind of righteousness (v. 17). It also clearly identifies human sin, failure, and frustration for what it is (1:18-3:20). It restores the lost righteousness through redemption in Christ Jesus (3:21-5:21). It deals effectively with our sin problem, giving freedom from sin and its bondage (6:1-7:25). All of this was impossible "in the flesh" and "by works of the law." But now that we are in Christ, the Spirit sets us "free from the law of sin and of death" (8:1-2) so that we can walk according to the Spirit with the "mind set on the Spirit" (vv. 3-9). This is real life and peace. The world does not understand this because they do not have the Spirit at all in a saving sense. But if He is not only with us (John 14:17) but "dwells" in us, the fullness we enjoy is the exact opposite of the tragic godlessness of the unbeliever (Rom. 8:9). With the indwelling Spirit, we have victory, hope, an inheritance, assistance in prayer, the work of God in our behalf, the intercession of Christ, and the security of triumphant adequacy in "the love of God which is in Christ Jesus our Lord" (vv. 10-39).

It is from this background of adequate grace in the fullness of the Spirit that there is hope for the Jews who will turn to God through faith in Christ, as for all others (Rom. 9-11). Such grace and power is the only solid basis for a sound Christian ethics. This ethics, to be successful, is first a full yielding to God, to His will, and to His transforming grace (12:1-2). Then by the power of the Holy Spirit, who lives in us, we can think and act rightly toward ourselves and the church (vv. 3-8). The principle of love will have a great number of applications in all relationships of life, but we can be overcomers through His grace (vv. 9-21). Though the human instrument has many defects, love rules in heart and life by the Spirit of God. What works in personal, religious, and social life is also the key to living under the governments and all other authority (chap. 13). Perfect love makes one sensitive to the needs of others, willing to endure inconveniences for their good, able to appreciate the good in others, and ready to cooperate unselfishly in the work of God for the good of man (chaps. 14-16).

Wesleyans feel confident that the theme of Romans is a holiness message. The more one studies the book inductively, the more evident it becomes that this is the burden of the book, thematically developed. The young Christians must at once receive the gift of the Spirit as the only key to a strong, secure, and effective life in the Spirit.

The Thessalonian epistles are no less clear in their purpose and message. If anything, Paul can speak more clearly to the people of Thessalonica because they are his own converts and those of his associates, through the Spirit. They have more memories to which to relate Paul's remarks. Moreover, they have the advantage of being zealous young converts, at the impressionable stage of spiritual development that Wesley considered preferable to all others for reminding them to "go on unto perfection."[100] They had been converted long enough to be aware of their lacks and needs but not long enough to have been hardened or discouraged by failures. It could hardly have been more than a few months after Paul's departure from Thessalonica that word came to him of their progress and he wrote the first epistle. Then, after a few more months and another report from Thessalonica, he apparently wrote 2 Thessalonians. As in the case of the Romans, Paul's disappointment resulted in the enrichment of all Christendom. When Paul was not able to visit these churches at will, he wrote inspired epistles that share with us all his sound counsel to young Christians.

Again Paul's consuming concern was that they not move past this "preferable time" without moving into the fullness of sanctification and abounding grace that would establish and keep them. With great sensitivity and delight, Paul rehearsed the many good things he knew about their sound conversion, their labor of love, their steadfast hope, and their excellent reputation and witness (1 Thess. 1). These things were more than a professional satisfaction to Paul. The daring young believers were Paul's "glory and joy" (2:20). He "really lived" when they stood "firm in the Lord" (3:8-9). Up to this point the letter is full of hope, confidence, and trust.

Finally, Paul wrote about the concern and burden of his heart. Paul earnestly prayed to see them because he felt that he could best "complete what was lacking in their faith" (1 Thess. 3:10) if he could meet them eyeball to eyeball. But, meanwhile, he used the expedient of the letter. The word for "complete" is "to perfect" or "rig up completely" (as one prepares a ship for a journey). As usual, in such cases, the tense is aorist, referring to a specific equipping. The prayer continues: "May the Lord cause you to increase and abound in love for one another" (v. 12). One would assume that such causative action of the Lord would be in the present tense for continuous action, as of growth in grace. But no, both "increase" and "abound" are in the aorist tense as of a specific and definite act. The purpose of all this completing, causing to increase, and causing to abound is not just the daily result of walking in the Spirit; it is "to establish [cause to stand] their hearts unblamable in holiness before God" so that they will still be established and growing when Jesus comes (v. 13). Again, "establish" is in the aorist tense. Paul certainly taught daily living and growth in grace, but he went out of his way in these four verbs to indicate that he was writing about a specific act or gift of God as an establishing grace (cf. Rom. 1:11).

First Thessalonians 4 gives the model of the new and abundant grace: "how you ought to walk [present tense of continuous action] and please God [same tense] just as you actually do walk [present tense]." Life in the fullness of the Spirit is not essentially different from life before. It is just "abounding yet more." This "abound" or "excel" is in the aorist tense, as directly referring to a specific enablement by the Holy Spirit's indwelling presence (4:1). The commandments are not different; only the grace and power are more abundant (v. 2). It is in this context that the word *sanctification* enters. It seems to be suggesting this new dimension of grace and love. Not that they had never loved before or known the hallowing presence, but there is a fullness of experience in sanctification that gives more sure and complete victory over the subtle temptations inherent in mortal life. Right at the center of the "will of God" is whatever act of "sanctification" will give that strength and security (v. 3). There is no etymological reason for calling sanctification a process in this context. The five aorist tenses in the six immediately preceding verses justify (or require) that sanctification here be understood as a divine transforming act, such as the passage culminates with in 5:23. Therefore, it is not necessary (or even proper) to consider "abstaining from sexual immorality" (4:3) as being in apposition with sanctification, as if they were the same thing. Sanctification (or holiness) certainly includes assistance in holy living, but it is more than any one particular detail of ethics. The KJV translation, then, which can refer to purpose or result, is better: "that ye should abstain from fornication." It was precisely in Thessalonica that some aspects of free love were expected of hospitality and sometimes thought to be a religious duty. After writing about sexual purity and marital fidelity, Paul charged the Christians to be fair in business, to love the brethren, and to have a firm hope of the Second Coming (vv. 5-18).

The final chapter sets the scene of the end times and the kind of ethical conduct that would indicate one's faithfulness to the coming One. The standard is high, perhaps impossible to one who has not had the "lack" in his faith remedied. But Paul's confident prayer is, "The God of peace Himself sanctify you entirely; and may your spirit and soul and body be preserved complete, without blame" so that you will still be found complete and blameless at the coming of our Lord Jesus Christ (1 Thess. 5:23). Both verbs, as has been observed, are also in the aorist tense, indicating a specific and definite act, as in chapters 3 and 4. Paul prayed for a definite and complete act of sanctification for the security and effectiveness of the lives of these converts. He also asked that their preservation be one uninterrupted event, free from base denials and disobedience. The confidence of Paul, however, was not only in the excellent character and stamina of the Macedonians: he was confident that God, the One calling, would do exactly what he prayed for.

When would God answer Paul's constant prayer? The prayers and the letter were for the specific purpose of bringing these young converts into the proposed experience as soon as possible. We may assume that the purpose was at least partly accomplished soon. Some supporting evidence, indeed, is found in the second epistle, which was written soon after the first—quite certainly within a year of the original visit to Thessalonica. Paul had been concerned that "the lack in their faith" be filled (1 Thess. 3:10). In the second letter Paul thanks God that their "faith is greatly enlarged" (1:3). In the first letter he had prayed that they might "increase and abound in love" (3:12). In the second he thanked God that their "love has grown ever greater" (1:3). He had prayed that they be established (1 Thess. 3:13) and excel (4:1). Afterward he spoke proudly of them for their perseverance and faith in the midst of persecution (2 Thess. 1:4). It is too much to expect that everyone made immediate ideal adjustments, but the second letter had much more confident rejoicing and much less anxious exhortation. There must, indeed, have been forward movement. Disobedience and disregard would have elicited a far different response from Paul.

We have already discussed Paul's successful concern for the disciples at Ephesus and for their receiving the Holy Spirit (Acts 19:1-6). When Paul wrote again, the theme was the same, but with a major difference. Paul was rejoicing in "every spiritual blessing" (Eph. 1:3), in God's purpose that believers be "holy and blameless" in love (v. 4), in the riches of God's grace (v. 7), in the supreme headship of Christ (v. 10), and in our heavenly inheritance (v. 12). Suddenly Paul paused to remind the Ephesians how they had become participants to such an extent. They had listened to the message of truth and had believed. After that, they "were sealed in Him with the Holy Spirit of promise" (v. 13). This stamp of sealing by the promised Holy Spirit was not their first introduction to redemption, but He was "given as a pledge [sample and guarantee] of our inheritance" (v. 14). What we experience in the fullness of the Spirit is a sample of heaven. Heaven will be the same in principle.

The rest of the doctrinal section of Ephesians (chaps. 1-3) is not so much exhortation as exultation in the unfathomable wonder of God's grace for His Spirit-filled believers. The section ends with Paul's great prayer that all might not only have "the experience" but that they should revel in God's grace and explore its dimensions with awe and wonder. The rest of the book uses God's grace as a model and basis for human relations. If God is so good to us, we can afford to be good to each other. Such is the delight of living in the Spirit.

D. A Consistent New Testament Emphasis

Once having come to the above insights and conclusions, Wesleyans see a consistent emphasis running through the whole New Testament under a variety of terms and figures.

Reference has been made in the synoptic Gospels to predictions of Pentecost and the promised gift of the Holy Spirit. Studies have been made that may indicate that it was the deliberate design of each of the first three Gospels to show the deficiencies in even the selected disciples, who later became apostles. This would be to show their need of the promised gift and to show, by contrast, the benefits to their faith and practice of their being filled with the Spirit.[101]

The fourth Gospel has already been used as the source of many quotations from Jesus, John the Baptist, and the apostle John. Acts and Romans have also furnished data for the study. The concept of Christian holiness through the Holy Spirit might be said to be developed thematically in all three books.

The First Epistle to the Corinthians has much to say about converts who are yet carnal. This seems to have much to do with the outbreaks of immorality, wrong attitudes toward marriage and sex, the use of law courts, lack of stewardship, abuses of spiritual gifts, disdain for the body and for bodily resurrection, and the like. The only cure is perfect love (chap. 13). The second epistle is, in part, a defense of Paul's apostleship against the carnal ambition of those who would split the church. Paul sets the high standard of his own dedication in the power of the Spirit over against the bickering of carnal ambition.

The theme of Galatians is similar to that of Romans—the contrast between victorious life in the Spirit and futile attempts at salvation through legalism. Ephesians has already been treated, with its theme of life in the Spirit as the foretaste of heavenly glory. Philippians elevates the model of the "mind that was in Christ Jesus" (2:5 KJV) for the believer and shows how the relative perfection of energetic Christian living is the way to the heavenly perfection toward which true believers are moving (3:8-16). Colossians shares many of the central ideas of Ephesians but more from the standpoint of the absolute supremacy of Christ in creation and in redemption. Paul, not having ministered personally to the church at Colosse, was not an eyewitness of any such "Pentecostal event" as became a strong introduction to the Ephesian letter. But exalting Christ is the work of the Holy Spirit in applying redemption to mankind. This, in its own way, is central to the Wesleyan understanding of Christian perfection.

The Thessalonian epistles have been analyzed as intentionally and thematically developed to lead young Christians into the experience and life of holiness for the relative perfection of life here and with a view to Christ's appearing.

The Pastoral Epistles are suggestions, rules, and exhortations to guide Timothy and Titus in pastoring and administering the churches under their care. They must be examples of holy living and must insist on the same attitudes, priorities, and experience on the part of those under their care. Anything else is to "fall away from the faith," paying attention to deceitful spirits and doctrines of demons (1 Tim. 4:1-2).

Philemon is a personal letter urging upon an individual the holy conduct worthy of the gospel. Philemon should forgive as he has been forgiven and should go the second mile, receiving the penitent runaway slave as a brother beloved.

Hebrews is another book that develops thematically the idea of Christian holiness. Here Christ is exalted not only as Savior but also as Sanctifier. He does what Joshua could do only in a limited and symbolic fashion. He brings true "rest" to the believer who has left the bondage to sin and yet has never entered the promised land of full participation in the blessings of the kingdom of God. What the law, history, and promises in the Old Testament symbolized, Christ, the Sanctifier, brings "to the spirits of righteous men made perfect" (12:23).

James begins with a call to perfection and completeness (1:4). Double-mindedness is the ultimate peril. It is complete instability (v. 8). Pure religion is outgoing love from an "unstained" heart (v. 27). The law and the gospel unite in perfect love (5:16-20).

In 1 Peter, the apostle rejoices in the grace of God that comes to focus in the model of and commandment for holiness of heart and life (1:15-16). The rest of the epistle is encouragement and exhortation to live and serve with this priority in view. The second epistle reminds the readers of the ample provision God has made for holy living and Christian assurance, of the danger from false teachers, and of the promise of new heavens and a new earth that will be more congenial to the heavenly kingdom.

The First Epistle of John clarifies the matter of assurance and certainty in the life of the believer (5:13). Some twelve marks are given by which one should know if he is not truly "in the faith." A corresponding number of marks certify that one is rightly reading the signals from the Spirit and the Word. Finally, certain bonuses that go with holy living are mentioned that the unsaved and even the unsanctified have not experienced. The vocabulary and imagery are reminiscent of the fourth Gospel and the words of Jesus. The theme is the absolute requirement of holiness of heart and life if one is to have assurance of eternal life. The other two epistles of John show implications of this theology in practical life in the home and in the church.

Jude is mainly concerned with warning against compromise with any contrary doctrine or wrong practice. It leads directly away from God and heaven. But God is "able to keep you from stumbling and to make you stand in the presence of His glory blameless with great joy" (v. 24).

Revelation guarantees the outcome for the "partakers of his holiness" (Heb. 12:10 KJV). Though the warfare will reach almost unbelievable proportions, the Lamb will triumph, the New Jerusalem will come, the Redeemer will dwell in the midst of His people. Death and Hades will be cast into the lake of fire. "Blessed are those who wash their robes, that they may have the right to the tree of life, and may enter by the gates into the city" (Rev. 22:14). The holy ones are confirmed in their citizenship in the everlasting kingdom of their Lord and God (v. 11).

For those who follow the Wesleyan understanding of entire sanctification and perfect love through the gift of the Holy Spirit, the whole New Testament, then, is the textbook, thematically developed to present the way to holiness and the way of holiness as the consistent Christian life.

VI. SUMMARY OF DISTINCTIONS

It is immediately evident that many things have been said about entire sanctification, Christian perfection, and the life of holiness that can be true only if they are based on a correct understanding of Scripture terms and biblical accounts. Speaking again from a Wesleyan perspective of Scripture and experience, the following distinctions are summarized.

A. Instantaneous and Progressive Work of God

Wesleyans understand that there is a specific and definite act of God in entire sanctification as revealed in the use of aorist and perfect tenses, as required by the concept of the gift of, or baptism with, the Holy Spirit and as illustrated by known events of receiving the Holy Spirit in Scripture and in history. Consistent with the instantaneous event are the benefits of grace in the life of the believer preparatory to the event of entire sanctification and the still more rapid progress that follows the event as one "grows in grace." As was noted, some call these processes sanctification. In any case, care should be taken to keep the distinction clear, to the neglect of neither the event nor the process.

B. Divine Grace and Human Works

Wesleyans know that salvation is only from God. No one can save himself by his own works. As Wesley said, "The best of men still need Christ in His priestly office, to atone for their omissions, their shortcoming (as some not improperly speak), their mistakes in judgment and practice, and their defects of various kinds."[102] God planned salvation, Christ brought it, and the Holy Spirit applies it. It is all by grace, through faith.

But works are important. The truly renewed person is saved "for good works" (Eph. 2:10). Works of obedience are part of our assurance that we are in Christ (2 Cor. 13:5) and they are a testimony to others (Matt. 5:16). Each person is finally judged in harmony with his works (Rom. 2:6). Even good works themselves are, in part, divine grace, as God works in us (Phil. 2:13).

C. Purity and Maturity

There is a distinction, indeed, between a young Spirit-filled Christian and a mature saint who has walked in the Spirit for many years. Both are pure in the sense that their hearts have been "cleansed by faith" (Acts 15:9). The mature Christian, on the other hand, has for many years, under the influence of the indwelling Holy Spirit, been sorting out values and remedying defects of attitude and performance that no longer make sense for one who is "walking in the light." This is not called sanctification *(hagiazō)* or cleansing *(katharizō),* which is God's act. The Christian "purifies [*hagnizō*] himself, just as He

[Christ] is pure" (1 John 3:3). This kind of perpetual self-improvement in the light of advancing knowledge and fresh visions of our Lord and Savior is normal and necessary to spiritual growth. It goes naturally with Christian hope. It does not deny the purification in God's act of sanctification; it only matures one in experience and life.

D. Conditions to Be Met

Since Wesleyans do not believe that unconditional election or predestination is scriptural, they have all the more reason to believe that certain responses are necessary for the appropriation of grace. Though repentance (the right and ability to repent) is given by God (Acts 11:18), we are required to repent (Acts 2:38). Though faith is enabled by God, we are required to believe (v. 38). Though only God can sanctify, we must "present [our] members as slaves to righteousness resulting in sanctification" (Rom. 6:19). Even then, we must believe, for one is "sanctified by faith" (Acts 26:18). The obedient response required for the new birth, then, is repentance and faith; and the response required for entire sanctification is consecration and faith. For growth in grace, it is walking in the light (1 John 1:7) or "walking according to the Spirit" (Rom. 8:4). This also is by faith (2 Cor. 5:7).

E. Christian Perfection Versus Absolute Perfection

Wesleyans make no claim to absolute and underived perfection. Only God has that. Nor is Christian perfection a perfection such as angels enjoy. Nor is it the original perfection of sinless Adam. Christians have all experienced results of the Fall. Christian perfection is love from "a pure heart" (1 Peter 1:22 KJV) as renewed in the image of Christ.

F. Entire Sanctification Versus Glorification

There is a confirmation in the blessings of one's inheritance that does not come until this mortal body has put on immortality. It is a part of the Christian hope (1 John 3:2). Entire sanctification simply makes us clean and energized channels of grace for living and serving in these days of probation and preparation.

G. The Gift and Gifts of the Spirit

The "gift of the Holy Spirit" should not be confused with the special enablements or the discernible phenomena that may accompany the gift. The important matter is to "receive the Holy Spirit" whom God so freely gives (John 14:16). There are varieties of gifts, ministries, effects, and manifestations. All are important in their place. But none of these is our Lord and Master. There is only one Lord Jesus Christ and one Holy Spirit. There is only one God "who works all things." If we receive the "gift of the Holy Spirit," He administers the gifts and functions as He wills (1 Cor. 12:4-11). One who has the Holy Spirit does not need a sign. It is enough to respond obediently to Him.

H. Imputed Versus Imparted Grace

"Impute" refers to how God sees us and thinks of us. "Impart" refers to what God gives us or does in us. The emphasis in Wesleyan thought is on the genuine changes wrought in the human heart by transforming grace, whether in the new birth, the crisis of entire sanctification, or the process of growth in grace and life in the Spirit. This in no way frees one from the need for mercy. God remembers that we are dust, looks to the atonement in Christ, and treats us better than we deserve. In this sense, the transformed Christian has imputed to him a righteousness and holiness that transcends his own understanding and experience. But God is also pleased to see imparted grace mirrored in His children as they demonstrate God's will in practical life (Rom. 12:1-2; 2 Cor. 3:18).

VII. CONCLUSION

Wesleyans understand that God's plan from the beginning has been for the purification and perfection of man, as seen in the divine requirement, provision, promise, and appeals. Entire sanctification is God's method of producing this holiness in man, cleansing the heart from all sin and filling it with perfect love by the Holy Spirit, who is given to the consecrated believer. This baptism with the Holy Spirit brings the relative perfection of the image of Christ in the heart of the believer and power for life and service. This experience is subsequent to the new birth but prior to death. To this the Greek syntax, vocabulary, and context agree, as do authentic biblical and historical witnesses. Wesleyans are confident that, whatever the different insights in minutiae, entire sanctification is basic to God's method of bringing His children into the "family likeness" for time and for eternity.

NOTES

[1] H. Orton Wiley, *Christian Theology,* 3 vols. (Kansas City, Mo.: Beacon Hill, 1952), 2:440-517.

[2] *The Works of John Wesley,* 14 vols. (1872; reprint ed., Grand Rapids: Zondervan, 1958), 11:450-51.

[3] Ibid., 5:2.

[4] Ibid., 8:300.

[5] Ibid., 11:367.

[6] George A. Turner, *The Vision Which Transforms* (Kansas City, Mo.: Beacon Hill, 1964), p. 51.

[7] Wesley, *Works,* 11:367.

[8] Ibid.

[9] Ibid., 11:397.

[10] Ibid., 7:508-9.

[11] Ibid., 7:514.

[12] Ibid., 6:512.

[13] J. B. Chapman, *The Terminology of Holiness* (Kansas City, Mo.: Beacon Hill, 1947), pp. 9-23.

[14] Turner, *Vision Which Transforms,* p. 16.

[15] Ibid., p. 114.

[16] W. B. Pope, *A Compendium of Christian Theology,* 3 vols. (New York: Hunt and Eaton, n.d.), 3:28.

[17] See Charles W. Carter, *The Person and Ministry of the Holy Spirit: A Wesleyan Perspective* (Grand Rapids: Baker, 1974), pp. 118-26.

[18] Laurence W. Wood, *Pentecostal Grace* (Wilmore, Ky.: Asbury, 1980), p. 17.

[19] Ibid., pp. 15-17.

[20] Ibid., p. 17.

[21] Ibid.

[22] Wiley, *Christian Theology,* 1:382.

[23] Ibid.

[24] Wesley, *Works,* 11:366-446.

[25] Ibid., p. 430.

[26] Wesley, *Letters,* 5:223.

[27] Ibid., 5:101.

[28] W. E. Sangster, *The Path to Perfection* (Nashville: Abingdon-Cokesbury, 1943), p. 77.

[29] Ibid., p. 147.

[30] John Wesley, *Explanatory Notes on the New Testament* (Naperville, Ill.: Allenson, n.d.), p. 491.

[31] A. B. Simpson, *The Holy Spirit or Power From on High,* 2 vols. (1895-1896; reprint ed., New York: Christian Alliance, 1924).

[32] Mildred Bangs Wynkoop, *A Theology of Love* (Kansas City, Mo.: Beacon Hill, 1972), p. 274.

[33] Robert B. Girdlestone, *Synonyms of the Old Testament* (Grand Rapids: Eerdmans, 1948), p. 95.

[34] Ibid., pp. 95-96.

[35] Ibid., p. 96.

[36] Colin Brown, ed., *The New International Dictionary of New Testament Theology,* 3 vols. (Grand Rapids: Zondervan, 1975-1978), 2:61.

[37] Hermann Cremer, *Biblico-Theological Lexicon of New Testament Greek* (1878; reprint ed., Edinburgh: T. & T. Clark, 1954), p. 541.

[38] Arndt and Gingrich, *A Greek-English Lexicon of the New Testament and Other Early Christian Literature,* 2nd ed. (Chicago: University of Chicago Press, 1979), p. 809.

[39] Ibid.

[40] Ibid.

[41] Brown, *New International Dictionary of New Testament Theology,* 2:62.

[42] Arndt and Gingrich, p. 417.

[43] Wesley, *Works,* 11:441-42.

[44] Ibid., 6:1-19.

[45] Ibid., 6:411-24.

[46] Ibid., 6:411-12.

47. Ibid., 6:412-13.
48. Ibid., 6:5.
49. Ibid., 11:397.
50. Sangster, *The Path to Perfection*, p. 7.
51. Ibid., pp. 37-52.
52. Ibid., pp. 146-47.
53. Ibid., pp. 160-67.
54. Ibid., p. 160.
55. Leslie R. Marston, "The Crisis-Process Issue in Wesleyan Thought," *Wesleyan Theological Journal* 4 (Spring 1969): 1.
56. Benson H. Roberts, compiler-editor, *Holiness Teachings*, compiled from the editorial writings of the late Benjamin T. Roberts (N. Chili, N.Y.: Earnest Christian, 1893).
57. Marston, "Crisis-Process Issue," p. 11.
58. Wesley, *Works*, 11:374.
59. Ibid., 11:441.
60. Ibid., 11:442.
61. Ibid.
62. Wood, *Pentecostal Grace*, pp. 252-53.
63. Wesley, *Works*, 11:396.
64. Ibid., pp. 396-97.
65. F. F. Bruce, *Commentary on the Epistle to the Hebrews* (Grand Rapids: Eerdmans, 1964), p. 116.
66. Charles Ewing Brown, *The Meaning of Sanctification* (Anderson, Ind.: Warner, 1945), pp. 37-42.
67. J. Gilchrist Lawson, *Deeper Experiences of Famous Christians* (Anderson, Ind.: Warner, 1911), pp. vii-xiii.
68. Ibid., p. xiii.
69. Wood, *Pentecostal Grace*, pp. 240-57.
70. Ibid., p. 241, quoting from William J. O'Shea, *Sacraments of Initiation* (Englewood Cliffs, N.J.: Prentice-Hall, 1965), p. 62.
71. Ibid., pp. 244-45, quoting from O'Shea, *Sacraments*, p. 63.
72. Ibid., p. 245.
73. *A Catholic Dictionary* (The Catholic Encyclopedia Dictionary), ed. Donald Attwater, 2nd ed. rev. (New York: Macmillan, 1949), p. 413.
74. Charles W. Carter, "Roman Catholic Purgatory Versus Protestant Sanctification" (an unpublished paper), p. 16, quoting from Romano Guardini, *The Last Things* (Pantheon, 1954), p. 35.
75. Daniel Steele, *Milestone Papers* (New York: Nelson and Phillips, 1878), p. 45.
76. H. E. Dana and Julius R. Mantey, *A Manual Grammar of the Greek New Testament* (New York: Macmillan, 1927), p. 179.
77. A. T. Robertson, *A Grammar of the Greek New Testament in the Light of Historical Research* (New York: Doran, 1914), p. 835.
78. Ibid., p. 200, quoting from B. L. Gildersleeve, *Syntax of Classical Greek*, p. 99.
79. Dana and Mantey, *Grammar of the Greek New Testament*, p. 200.
80. Daniel Steele, *Milestone Papers*, pp. 44-72.
81. Wiley, *Christian Theology*, 2:446-49; Brown, *The Meaning of Sanctification*, pp. 202-26.
82. Daniel Steele, *Milestone Papers*, pp. 46-47.
83. Ibid., pp. 47-52.
84. Ibid., p. 52.
85. Ibid., pp. 52-72.
86. Gordon Cary, "Perfection Tenses in the Greek New Testament" (a master's thesis), Marion College, Marion, Indiana.
87. Dana and Mantey, *Grammar of the Greek New Testament*, p. 206.
88. Robertson, *Grammar of the Greek New Testament*, p. 860.
89. Ibid.
90. Ibid., p. 861.
91. J. R. Mantey, in supervising a doctoral dissertation at Northern Baptist Theological Seminary, "The Greek Perfect Tenses in Relation to John 20:23, Matthew 16:19 and Matthew 18:18."
92. Wesley, *Works*, 11:393.
93. Ibid., 11:366-446.
94. Ibid., p. 393.
95. Ibid., pp. 402-3.
96. Wesley, *Letters*, 6:103.
97. Ibid., 5:333.
98. F. F. Bruce, *The Acts of the Apostles* (London: Tyndale, 1951), p. 353.
99. Ibid.
100. Wesley, *Letters*, 6:103.
101. Dennis F. Kinlaw, chapel address at Wesley Biblical Seminary, Jackson, Mississippi, 1980.
102. Wesley, *Works*, 11:396.

ENTIRE SANCTIFICATION

DISCUSSION QUESTIONS

1. What is the relation of the fruit of the Spirit to the witness of the Spirit (particularly in the light of 1 John)?
2. What is the relation between the gift of the Spirit and gifts of the Spirit?
3. What are the practical advantages of the emphasis on the gift of or baptism with the Holy Spirit as the means of entire sanctification—as to clarity of understanding and facility in leading believers into the experience?
4. Are there disadvantages and dangers in moving the emphasis from terms like "Christian perfection" and "perfect love" to a Pentecostal event of "receiving" or baptism?
5. What is the place of "groaning after" holiness or prolonged seeking for perfection? Is it the path to the experience or does it merely evidence a lack of appropriating faith?
6. What are the differences between holy living and asceticism? Are there values in both?
7. Is there a distinctive "holiness ethics," belonging only to the entirely sanctified?
8. To what extent is one's "level of grace" evident to observation by others? Or is it a purely private matter witnessed only by the Holy Spirit and one's own consciousness?
9. What are the advantages and disadvantages of testifying regularly in standardized theological terms as compared to acknowledging recent blessings and victories as "fruit" of the indwelling Spirit?
10. Why did Wesley so seldom base his offer of Christian perfection on his own definite claim, theologically identified?
11. What was so convincing about the witness of a number of people who believed that they were made perfect in love—so that Wesley would not preach Christian perfection without their testimony but was confident that he understood the Scriptures correctly with it?
12. What is the relation between feeling and fact in the witness of the Spirit?

RECOMMENDATIONS FOR FURTHER READING

Brown, Charles Ewing. *The Meaning of Sanctification*. Anderson, Ind.: Warner, 1945.

Cox, Leo George. *John Wesley's Concept of Perfection*. Kansas City, Mo.: Beacon Hill, 1964.

Grider, J. Kenneth. *Entire Sanctification: The Distinctive Doctrine of Wesleyanism*. Kansas City, Mo.: Beacon Hill, 1980.

Peters, John L. *Christian Perfection and American Methodism*. Nashville: Abingdon, 1956.

Rose, Delbert R. *Vital Holiness: A Theology of Christian Experience*. Minneapolis: Bethany, 1965.

Steele, Daniel. *Milestone Papers, Doctrinal, Ethical, and Experimental on Christian Progress*. New York: Nelson and Phillips, 1878.

Taylor, Richard S. *Life in the Spirit*. Kansas City, Mo: Beacon Hill, 1966.

Turner, George Allen. *Christian Holiness in Scripture, in History, and in Life*. Kansas City, Mo.: Beacon Hill, 1977.

Wesley, John. *A Plain Account of Christian Perfection*. Kansas City, Mo: Beacon Hill, 1952.

Wilcox, Leslie D. *Be Ye Holy*. Cincinnati: Revivalist, 1965.

Wood, J. A. *Wesley on Perfection*. 1885. Reprint ed. Salem, Ohio: Schmul, n.d.

Wood, Laurence W. *Pentecostal Grace*. Wilmore, Ky.: Asbury, 1980.

BIBLIOGRAPHY

Anderson, T. M. *After Sanctification*. Kansas City, Mo.: Beacon Hill, 1951.

Arndt and Gingrich. *A Greek-English Lexicon of the New Testament and Other Early Christian Literature*, 2nd ed. Chicago: University of Chicago Press, 1979.

Arthur, William. *The Tongue of Fire.* New York: Eaton and Mains, 1906.

Baker, Frank. *Representative Verse of Charles Wesley.* Nashville: Abingdon, 1962.

Boyd, Myron F., and Harris, Merne A., compilers. *Projecting Our Heritage.* Kansas City, Mo.: Beacon Hill, 1961.

Brengle, Samuel Logan. *Love-Slaves.* London: Salvationist, 1929.

——— . *The Way of Holiness.* London: Salvationist, 1960.

——— . *The Soul-Winner's Secret.* Atlanta: Supplies and Purchasing Departments, 1948.

Brockett, Henry E. *Scriptural Freedom From Sin.* Kansas City, Mo.: Kingshighway, 1941.

Brown, Charles Ewing. *The Meaning of Sanctification.* Anderson, Ind.: Warner, 1945.

Brown, Colin, ed. *The New International Dictionary of New Testament Theology.* 3 vols. Grand Rapids: Zondervan, 1975–1978.

Bruce, F. F. *The Acts of the Apostles.* London: Tyndale, 1956.

——— . *Commentary on the Epistle to the Hebrews.* Grand Rapids: Eerdmans, 1964.

Burton and Chiles. *A Compend of Wesley's Theology.* Nashville: Abingdon, 1954.

Campbell, L. M. *Witnesses to the Doctrine of Holiness.* Kansas City, Mo.: Nazarene, 1935.

Carradine, B. *The Second Blessing in Symbol.* Noblesville, Ind.: Newby Book Room, 1968.

Carter, Charles W. *The Purpose and Ministry of the Holy Spirit: A Wesleyan Perspective.* Grand Rapids: Baker, 1974.

Chadwick, Samuel. *The Call to Christian Perfection.* Kansas City, Mo.: Beacon Hill, 1950.

——— . *The Way to Pentecost.* London: Hodder and Stoughton, 1932.

Chapman, J. B. *Holiness Triumphant.* Kansas City, Mo.: Beacon Hill, 1946.

Clark, Dougan. *The Theology of Holiness.* Chicago: Christian Witness, 1884.

Cox, Leo George. *John Wesley's Concept of Perfection.* Kansas City, Mo.: Beacon Hill, 1964.

Cremer, Hermann. *Biblico-Theological Lexicon of New Testament Greek.* Reprint ed. Edinburgh: T. & T. Clark, 1954.

Dana, H. E., and Mantey, J. R. *A Manual Grammar of the Greek New Testament.* New York: Macmillan, 1927.

Dieter, Melvin Easterday. *The Holiness Revival of the Nineteenth Century.* Metuchen, N.J.: Scarecrow, 1980.

Edman, V. Raymond. *They Found the Secret.* Grand Rapids: Zondervan, 1961.

Fletcher, John. *The Works of the Rev. John Fletcher.* 4 vols. 1851. Reprint ed. Salem, Ohio: Schmul, 1974.

Foster, R. S. *Centenary Thoughts for the Pew and Pulpit of Methodism.* New York: Phillips and Hunt, 1884.

——— . *Philosophy of Christian Experience.* New York: Hunt and Eaton, 1891.

Galloway, J. B. *A Study of Holiness From the Early Church Fathers.* Kansas City, Mo.: Beacon Hill, 1950.

Geiger, Kenneth E., compiler. *Insights Into Holiness.* Kansas City, Mo.: Beacon Hill, 1962.

——— , compiler. *More Insights Into Holiness.* Kansas City, Mo.: Beacon Hill, 1963.

——— , compiler. *The Word and the Doctrine.* Kansas City, Mo.: Beacon Hill, 1965.

Girdlestone, Robert R. *Synonyms of the Old Testament.* Grand Rapids: Eerdmans, 1948 reprint.

Greathouse, William M. *From the Apostles to Wesley.* Kansas City, Mo.: Beacon Hill, 1979.

Grider, J. Kenneth. *Entire Sanctification: The Distinctive Doctrine of Wesleyanism.* Kansas City, Mo.: Beacon Hill, 1980.

Hills, A. M. *Holiness and Power for the Church and the Ministry.* 1897. Reprint ed. Jamestown, N.C.: Newby, n.d.

——— . *Holiness in the Book of Romans.* Kansas City, Mo.: Beacon Hill, 1950.

Jessop, Harry E. *Foundations of Doctrine.* Chicago: Chicago Evangelistic Institute, 1948.

——— . *The Heritage of Holiness.* Kansas City, Mo.: Beacon Hill, 1950.

Jones, Charles Edwin. *Perfectionist Persuasion.* Metuchen, N.J.: Scarecrow, 1974.

Keen, Mary P. *Memorial Papers.* Cincinnati: Revivalist, 1899.

Keen, S. A. *Pentecostal Papers*. Chicago: Christian Witness, 1895.
Lawson, J. Gilchrist. *Deeper Experiences of Famous Christians*. Anderson, Ind.: Warner, 1911.
Lowrey, Asbury. *Possibilities of Grace*. Chicago: Christian Witness, 1884.
Mahan, Asa. *The Baptism of the Holy Ghost*. 1870. Reprint ed. Jamestown, N.C.: Newby, 1972.
―――――. *Christian Perfection*. 1844. Reprint ed. Salem, Ohio: Schmul, 1975.
Metz, Donald S. *Studies in Biblical Holiness*. Kansas City, Mo.: Beacon Hill, 1971.
Nicholson, Roy S. *The Arminian Emphases*. Owosso, Mich.: Owosso College, 1962.
Peters, John L. *Christian Perfection and American Methodism*. Nashville: Abingdon, 1956.
Pope, W. B. *A Compendium of Christian Theology*. 3 vols. New York: Hunt and Eaton, n.d.
Purkiser, W. T. *Interpreting Christian Holiness*. Kansas City, Mo.: Beacon Hill, 1971.
Ralston, Thomas N. *Elements of Divinity*. Nashville: Abingdon-Cokesbury, 1924.
Robertson, A. T. *A Grammar of the Greek New Testament in the Light of Historical Research*. New York: Doran, 1914.
Rose, Delbert R. *Vital Holiness: A Theology of Christian Experience*. Minneapolis: Bethany, 1965.
Ruth, C. W. *The Second Crisis in Christian Experience*. Chicago: Christian Witness, 1912.
Sangster, W. E. *The Path to Perfection*. Nashville: Abingdon-Cokesbury, 1943.
Smith, Bernie. *Flames of Living Fire*. Kansas City, Mo.: Beacon Hill, 1950.
Steele, Daniel. *The Gospel of the Comforter*. 1897. Reprint ed. Rochester, Pa.: Schmul, 1960.
―――――. *Half Hours With St. John's Epistles*. Chicago: Christian Witness, 1901.
―――――. *Half Hours With Saint Paul*. 1894. Reprint ed. Salem, Ohio: Schmul, 1976.
―――――. *Milestone Papers, Doctrinal, Ethical, and Experimental on Christian Progress*. New York: Nelson and Phillips, 1878.
Taylor, Richard S. *Life in the Spirit*. Kansas City, Mo.: Beacon Hill, 1966.
―――――. *A Right Conception of Sin*. Kansas City, Mo.: Beacon Hill, 1951.
Turner, George A. *Christian Holiness in Scripture, in History, and in Life*. Kansas City, Mo.: Beacon Hill, 1977.
―――――. *The Vision Which Transforms*. Kansas City, Mo.: Beacon Hill, 1964.
Wesley, Charles. *Journals of Charles Wesley*. 2 vols. Reprint ed. Kansas City, Mo.: Beacon Hill, 1980.
Wesley, John. *Explanatory Notes Upon the Old Testament*. 1854. Reprint ed. Salem, Ohio: Schmul, 1975.
―――――. *John Wesley's New Testament,* used in his *Explanatory Notes Upon the New Testament*. Reprint ed. Salem, Ohio: Schmul, 1976.
―――――. *The Journal of the Rev. John Wesley*. Edited by Nehemiah Curhock. 8 vols. London: Epworth, 1938.
―――――. *The Letters of the Rev. John Wesley*. Edited by John Telford. 8 vols. London: Epworth, 1931.
―――――. *A Plain Account of Christian Perfection*. Kansas City, Mo.: Beacon Hill, 1952.
―――――. *The Works of John Wesley*. 14 vols. 1849. Reprint ed. Grand Rapids: Zondervan, 1958.
Wilcox, Leslie D. *Be Ye Holy*. Cincinnati: Revivalist, 1965.
Wiley, H. Orton. *Christian Theology*. 3 vols. Kansas City, Mo.: Beacon Hill, 1952.
Winchester, Olive M., and Price, Ross E. *Crisis Experiences in the Greek New Testament*. Kansas City, Mo.: Beacon Hill, 1953.
Williams, R. T. *Sanctification: The Experience and the Ethics*. Kansas City, Mo.: Nazarene, 1928.
Wood, A. Skevington. *Life by the Spirit*. Grand Rapids: Zondervan, 1963.
Wood, J. A. *Christian Perfection as Taught by John Wesley*. 1921. Reprint ed. Salem, Ohio: Schmul, n.d.
―――――. *Perfect Love*. 1880. Reprint ed. Marion, Ind.: Wesley, 1967.
―――――. *Purity and Maturity*. Chicago: Christian Witness, 1913.
Wood, Laurence W. *Pentecostal Grace*. Wilmore, Ky.: Asbury, 1980.
Wynkoop, Mildred Bangs. *A Theology of Love*. Kansas City, Mo.: Beacon Hill, 1972.